HOW CAN WE HELP

How much you use the Internet is primarily *up to you*. Our Internet features are designed so that you may use them on your own – even if they are not assigned by your instructor.

A good starting point is Appendix B, *Exploring the Internet*, appearing near the end of this textbook. This appendix contains both general information about the Net and chapter-by-chapter suggestions for learning more about accounting. Two features found in every chapter, *Net Connections* and an *Internet Assignment,* provide more suggestions for exploring the Net.

For convenience, all of the websites referenced in the text also are listed in the *Directory* on the inside of the back cover. To make "surfing" even easier, we maintain a home page on the Net designed specifically for students. Among the features on this page are "hot buttons" to all the sites in our *Directory*, and email links to the the authors of the text. You'll find our home page at:

www.magpie.org/cyberlab

(If you use the Net, make a bookmark for our website. You may find us helpful long after you've finished this first accounting course.)

So even if you don't plan on using the Net right away, we urge you to take a few minutes and browse though some of our "Net features." Perhaps check out our home page. Maybe we can change your mind.

FINANCIAL ACCOUNTING

FINANCIAL ACCOUNTING

Robert F. Meigs
San Diego State University

Mary A. Meigs
San Diego State University

Mark Bettner
Bucknell University

Ray Whittington
San Diego State University

edition **9**

Irwin McGraw-Hill

Boston, Massachusetts • Burr Ridge, Illinois • Dubuque, Iowa
Madison, Wisconsin • New York, New York • San Francisco, California • St. Louis, Missouri

Irwin/McGraw-Hill
A Division of The McGraw-Hill Companies

Financial Accounting

This book is printed on acid-free paper.

1 2 3 4 5 6 7 8 9 0 DOW DOW 9 0 0 9 8 7

ISBN 0-07-043436-0

Publisher: Jeff Shelstad
Associate editor: Stewart Mattson
Development editor: Kelly Lee
Marketing manager: Heather Woods, Rhonda Seelinger
Project manager: Michelle Lyon, Richard Mason
Production supervisor: Richard DeVitto
Interior and cover designer: Vargas/Williams Design
Cover illustrator: © Dick Palulian/SIS
Photo researcher: Connie Mueller
Art editor: Francis Owens, Nicole Widmyer
Compositor: York Graphic Services
Typeface: Stone Serif
Printer: R. R. Donnelley & Sons

Grateful acknowledgment is made for use of the following:
Part 1: © Tom Sandberg/The Stock Market; **Chapter 1:** © Tim Brown/Tony Stone Images; **Chapter 2:** © Eric Lessing/Art Resource; **Chapter 3:** © Valenti/Tony Stone Images; **Chapter 4:** © K.Tanaka/Woodfin Camp & Associates; **Part 2:** © Jose L. Pelaez/ The Stock Market; **Chapter 5:** Courtesy of L. L. Bean; **Chapter 6:** © Mike Yamashita/ The Stock Market; **Part 3:** © Spencer Grant/Picture Cube; **Chapter 7:** © Everett Collection; **Chapter 8:** Courtesy of LIFO; **Chapter 9:** © Robin Smith/Toby Stone Images; **Part 4:** © Myron J. Dorf/The Stock Market; **Chapter 10:** © James Marshall/The Stock Market; **Chapter 11:** © Marvin E. Newman/The Image Bank; **Chapter 12:** © The Granger Collection; **Part 5:** © Tony Stone Images; **Chapter 13:** © David W. Hamilton/The Image Bank; **Chapter 14:** © Mark Gamba/The Stock Market

Library of Congress Cataloging-in-Publication Data
Financial accounting / Robert F. Meigs. . . [et al.]. — 9th ed.
    p.   cm.
  Rev. ed. of: Financial accounting / Robert F. Meigs, Walter B.
Meigs. Mary A. Meigs. 8th ed. c1995.
  Includes index.
  ISBN 0-07-043436-0 (alk. paper)
  1. Accounting. I. Meigs, Robert F. II. Meigs, Robert F.
HF5635.M492   1997
657—dc21   97-24229
                                           CIP

http://www.mhhe.com

CONTENTS

PART TWO THE BUSINESS WORLD 211

PART THREE ACCOUNTING FOR ASSETS 305

WELCOME

We know that you may be tempted to skip over the introduction to this textbook. But you really will do better in this course if you understand the organization and features of the book, as well as the goals of its authors. So, please — take about 15 minutes and read the following Note to Students. If you don't want to read the Note to Instructors, well — that's OK.

NOTE TO STUDENTS

We hope that you will see this first accounting course as an opportunity to learn about the worlds of business and personal finance. More importantly, when you've completed the course, we hope you will view it as having been a very worthwhile experience.

Let us share with you our thoughts on this course. A first accounting course introduces you only briefly to actual accounting practices and techniques. The real focus of the course is what accounting information *means* — and how this information is *used* by decision makers.

Today, everyone needs a basic understanding of accounting information, not just those of you planning careers in business. You will work with accounting information in any career and use it in managing your personal financial activities. Using accounting information is simply a part of everyday life.

OUR APPROACH

Our goals in this text are to develop your abilities to understand accounting information and to use this information in making economic decisions.

To understand accounting information, you must also understand the economic activities that the information describes. In this book, we focus primarily upon business activities. However, most of the accounting concepts we discuss also apply to the economic activities of individuals, government, and non-profit organizations.

The purpose of accounting is to provide information useful to economic decision makers. Throughout the course, we will cast you in many decision-making roles - from "starving student" to corporate executive. Simply stated, the key to using accounting effectively is practice.

If you like, we will also show you how to use the Internet as both a learning aid and a research tool. You do not need access to the Internet to use this textbook or learn about accounting. But if you do have access to the Net, we can make your study of accounting more interesting. (Please read Exploring the Internet on the inside of our front cover.)

ELEMENTS OF THIS TEXTBOOK

This ninth edition is accompanied by a wide variety of in-text learning aids. Understanding their purpose should help you use them to greater advantage.

Chapter Introductions and Learning Objectives
Each chapter starts with a photograph and caption, which sometimes does not seem to have much to do with accounting. They are intended to illustrate a major theme of the chapter in a non-technical way, but one that you will remember.

Each chapter also includes a short set of learning objectives, which are integrated with the text discussions, chapter summaries, and assignment materials. These objectives identify the main points in each chapter and may help you study for exams. But don't limit yourself to meeting these objectives. Strive to broaden your knowledge!

Case in Point
Our Case in Point sections describe actual business events illustrating key accounting concepts. These cases have two goals. The first is to illustrate accounting concepts using "real world" examples. The second is to illustrate these concepts in a manner that you will remember.

Supplemental Topics and Appendixes
Several chapters are accompanied by *Supplemental Topic sections. We encourage you to always read these *Supplemental Topic sections - they will enhance your understanding of the Chapter. However, your instructor will decide whether these

topics are of sufficient general interest for inclusion in class discussions, homework assignments, and examinations.

In contrast to the *Supplemental Topics, our eight Appendixes provide self-contained coverage of specialized topics. Your instructor may assign specific appendixes, but we invite you to explore the others on your own.

Net Connections

Each chapter concludes with a section entitled Net Connections. These sections identify interesting sites on the Internet which may enhance your understanding of the chapter. We strongly encourage you to visit a few of these websites — even if your instructor does not make this a course requirement. (The inside of our back cover contains an Internet Directory with the addresses of all netsites referenced in the text. You can also reach these sites quickly by using the Links feature on our home page.)

End-of-Chapter Reviews

Each chapter is followed by a number of learning aids designed to help you study more efficiently. They include a Summary of Learning Objectives, a glossary of Key Terms, Self-Test Questions, a Demonstration Problem, and our Comments on the In-Text Cases.

Assignment Materials

One of the distinctive features of this ninth edition is the nature and variety of its assignment material. These assignments not only illustrate basic accounting concepts, they also provide you with opportunites to develop your analytical, communication, and interpersonal skills. We have increased our emphasis on these "success skills," because they are of such importance in today's business world.

Many of our assignments are based upon the operations of well-known companies, such as Toys "R" Us, Hershey Foods, and Microsoft. Many others are based on smaller companies which are less well-known, but just as "real." A special index at the back of the text identifies all of our references to real companies.

We have greatly increased the number of assignments well-suited to group and/or classroom discussions. We find that students can learn much from one another. This concept, often called "collaborative learning," really works!

There are six basic categories of assignments (1) Discussion Questions, (2) Exercises, (3) Problems, (4) Cases, (5) Internet Assignments, and (6) Comprehensive Problems.

Discussion Questions call for short, written answers. Merely reading over them may prove an effective way for you to evaluate your understanding of a chapter.

Exercises are short assignments, usually focusing on a single concept. They are designed to illustrate those concepts quickly and clearly. You also may find them similar to the types of exercises your instructor uses on exams.

Problems are longer than the Exercises and usually address several different concepts. Every problem also has an "analytical element," requiring you to explain or interpret the information you develop, or use that information in a business decision.

A package of partially completed Accounting Work Sheets supporting all Problems in the text is available through your bookstore. You can also download selected working papers at no charge from our home page.

Cases are intended primarily to develop your analytical and communication skills. These assignments readily lend themselves to group analysis and classroom discussions. Read a few just for fun; they present "accounting" from a different and challenging perspective.

Internet Assignments invite you to use the Net for both learning and research. (Just try not to spend too much time on the Net.) One Internet Assignment appears at the end of each chapter, and several others are available in Appendix B. As we find good new Internet Assignments, we will post them on CyberLab (our home page).

Comprehensive Problems tie together concepts presented over a span of chapters. The text includes four of these problems, ranging in length from 50-minute assignments to several hour projects. (The Accounting Work Sheets supplement supports all of our Comprehensive Problems and may save you considerable time.)

A **Checklist of Key Figures** for all Problems and Comprehensive Problems appears at the end of this text. The purpose of these figures is to let you know if your solution is "on track," and to assist you in locating errors.

Icons

Many assignments have special characteristics which are indicated by icons appearing in the left margin. For example, we have many assignments designed to show how computer software is used in accounting. A circle-and-arrow icon indicates assignments well-suited to our general ledger software (GLAS). A stack-of-paper marks those assignments best suited to our spreadsheet software (SPATS).

 Our icon of a graduating student in a cap and gown identifies assignments which relate accounting information to the daily lives of students. The group icon indicates those assignments which best lend themselves to group discussions — or a sharing of the work. A scales-of-justice logo identifies assignments raising ethical issues.

 A magnifying glass indicates the need for research beyond the chapters you have already read. Sometimes this research can be done within the textbook, or on the Internet. But on a few occasions, these assignments send you out into the business community. In short, we just back off. These assignments put the responsibility for learning directly on your shoulders.

Our world-wide-web logo identifies assignments which require access to the Internet. Because of limited computer resources, many instructors do not assign these problems. But if you have access to the Net, we urge you to visit these sites on your own. Don't limit your learning experience to the course requirements!

When assignments are based upon the operations of a real business organization, the company's name appears in **bold blue** type.

OUR USE OF COLOR

We often use color to assist you in interpreting illustrations and in conveniently locating elements of the text. For example, red is used for **emphasis** - for major chapter headings and to highlight key elements in some illustrations. We also use color to distinguish between accounting records and financial statements - accounting records are shaded or outlined in **green**, and financial statements in **blue**.

In most diagrams depicting a sequential flow of information, inputs appear in **red**, processes or actions in **green**, and output in **blue**.

These uses of color are summarized below:

SUPPLEMENTARY MATERIALS FOR YOU

We have developed several supplementary materials to make your study of accounting easier and more efficient. Some are available at no charge.

CyberLab

Our favorite supplement is CyberLab, our home page on the Internet. As we've said, you don't need the Net to use this book effectively. But for those of you with access to the Net, we invite you to visit us at:

http://www.magpie.org/cyberlab

CyberLab offers recent accounting and business news, links to netsites referenced in the text, self-test materials, new Internet Assignments, and e-mail links to the authors. And we plan to expand this site in the future. If you have any suggestions, visit CyberLab's Communications Room and let us know.

Study Guide

The Study Guide offers immediate feedback to assist you in evaluating your progress and preparing for examinations. It includes a summary of the key points in each chapter, and a wealth of self-test material, including solutions. As an additional study-aid, we explain in detail the reasoning behind the answers to each true-false and multiple choice question.

Accounting Work Sheets

This soft-cover booklet provides the appropriate type of columnar paper for each Problem and Comprehensive Problem in the textbook. In addition, problem headings and "given" data have been filled in to save you time. (Partially completed working papers are not provided for Discussion Questions, Exercises, Cases, or Internet Assignments. These assignments may be answered on ordinary notebook paper or by using a word processor.)

Problem-Solving Software

For those of you who want to see how accounting tasks are performed by computer, we offer two software packages. GLAS is our general ledger software. Its primary function is solving "accounting

How We Use Color

	Input Data	Processes	Output
In flowcharts	**Input Data**	**Processes**	**Output**
and elsewhere in the text:	**Chapter headings and for emphasis in illustrations**	**Accounting records**	**Financial statements, Internet address, and names of real companies used in assignment materials**

cycle" problems quickly, by automating the mechanical tasks. SPATS is our spreadsheet software. You can apply spreadsheet software to almost any accounting problem, but SPATS has special templates for quickly working those assignments which bear the "stack-of-paper" logo..

GLAS and SPATS are available in a Windows format. SPATS also requires Excel for Windows®.

Some Guidelines for Conducting Interviews

Several of our Cases call for you — or a member of your study group — to interview people in the business community. We ask you to appreciate that business people granting these interviews are donating their time for your benefit. For this reason, we ask that you observe a few basic guidelines:

● Please make an appointment for the interview, don't just walk in expecting to talk to someone. And be on time — recognize that time is a very valuable commodity in the business world.

● Dress appropriately and conduct yourself in a business-like manner.

● Learn the name of the person you will be interviewing, including the correct spelling and pronunciation, and his or her position within the organization.

● Write down in advance the questions you plan to ask.

● Take notes during the interview. You should never attempt to quote the person's statements from memory.

● Realize that business people may not want certain information about their business "spread around town." Tell them in advance that the general content of the interview will be discussed within your study group and, perhaps, in your classroom. Respect any requests that specific comments be kept "off-the-record."

NOTE TO INSTRUCTORS

We will now shift gears and speak primarily to instructors. Many of you may be familiar with one or more of our past editions. This ninth edition retains the same basic structure, although it has fewer chapters. But in many ways we are changing our approach to the first accounting course.

Basically, we have tried to achieve three goals in this revision. These are to make the text more (1) student-oriented, (2) contemporary, and (3) flexible. (Actually, we find these goals to be highly interrelated.)

What do we Mean by More "Student-Oriented"?

Two things: more relevant to students' needs; and more interesting, thereby motivating students to make the most of this learning opportunity.

Today, most careers do not center around the preparation of accounting information. (Even for CPAs, preparation work is limited in large part to tax returns.) But every student will be a life-long user of accounting information. In each of our last three editions, we have increased our emphasis on the interpretation and use of accounting information. We now are "where we want to be;" this is the balance we have striven for 9 years to achieve.

The new example used throughout our first four chapters now begins with a business plan. Then, as accounting information is developed, the actual results are evaluated in light of management's expectations. Our new Chapters 1 through 4 illustrate much more than the accounting cycle; they now show how accounting information is used in the processes of planning and control.

Every Problem and almost every Exercise now contain an "analytical element," asking students to interpret the information they are working with, or to use it in some form of business decision.

Now, let us address the topic of making this course more interesting. Our approach is to involve students more directly in the learning process. We challenge them to express their views, rather than merely read and remember ours. Features aimed at achieving this goal include the interactive YOUR TURN cases in every chapter, the "analytical elements" in our assignment material, and our Internet features.

Our Net features encourage students to explore interesting, accounting-related netsites on their own. And we try to make this very easy. For example, we not only provide the addresses of these sites, but our home page can transport them there with one click of a button. No instructor assistance should be required for students to use our Internet features.

We have always believed the first accounting course can be of great value to every student. But we want more - we want it to be their favorite course.

A Contemporary Course

Any course is both more relevant and more interesting if it is up-to-date. We have tried to make this text contemporary in all respects — from our examples, to our topical coverage, to our assignment material.

Our most contemporary features, of course, are provided by the Internet. Students who use our various Net features will be learning in an environment more current than any printed text - including ours.

FLEXIBLE TEXT

We cannot tell local instructors what is best for their students. Instead, we have tried to make this ninth edition as flexible as possible. That's why it's shorter - 14 chapters - with more topics left to the instructor's discretion in the form of appendixes. That's why we provide such a diversity of assignment material, and why the Internet materials are entirely optional.

Of course this textbook is supported by a wide variety of teaching aids — Solutions Manual, Test Banks (print and electronic versions), Instructor's Guide, Achievement Tests, Overhead Transparencies, a Power-Point Classroom Displays, Videos, and more. For a complete description of these items, and a chapter-by-chapter discussion of the changes in the text, please see the To the Instructor section of our Solutions Manual.

CONTRIBUTIONS BY OTHERS

We want to express our sincere thanks to the many users of preceding editions who have offered helpful suggestions for this revision. Especially helpful was the advice of:

C. Richard Aldridege, Western Kentucky University
Scott N. Cairns, Shippensburg University
Alan Cherry, Loyola Marymount University
James W. Damitio, Central Michigan University
David L. Davis, Tallahassee Community College
Roger Doerr, Hastings College
Edwin R. Etter, Syracuse University
Elizabeth Hawes, Keene State College
Julie Head, Indiana University
Charles A. Konkof, University of Wisconsin-Milwaukee
David J. Marcinko, SUNY at Albany
Jan Mardon, Green River Community College
Penny Marquette, University of Akron
Nancy L. Saltz, Lynchburg College
Nancy Schneider, Lynchburg College
W. Richard Sherman, Saint Joseph's University
Lieutenant Colonel Henry C. Smith, III, Virginia Military Institute
Teresa D. Thamer, Embry-Riddle Aeronautical University

Sterling Wetzel, Oklahoma State University
Jeffrey A. Wong, Golden Gate University

We also want to acknowledge the following individuals, each of whom has authored supplements which accompany the text: David J. Marcinko of SUNY Albany, Douglas Cloud of Pepperdine University, Jack Terry of ComSource Associates, and Leland Mansuetti and Keith Weidkamp, both of Sierra College

Our special thanks go to Professors James M. Emig of Villanova University and Nancy Schneider of Lynchburg College for assisting us with detailed reviews of our assignment material.

We appreciate the expert attention given to this project by the staff of Irwin/McGraw-Hill, especially Alan Sachs, Jeff Shelstad, Michelle Lyon, Rich DeVitto, Kelly Lee, Francis Owens, Heather Woods, and Kezia Pearlman.

The assistance of Margot Berg and Jacquie Commanday was invaluable in the preparation of the manuscript for many of the supplementary materials.

Finally, we wish to acknowledge the innumerable contributions of Walter B. Meigs, Professor Emeritus, University of Southern California. Professor Meigs is the founding author of this textbook and has participated in all of the preceding editions. Although he is now retired, his philosophy, perspective, and unique authorship skills remain apparent throughout the text.

A CLOSING COMMENT ...

We appreciate having the opportunity of addressing all of you - students and instructors alike. It is a privilege to share our views with those who will shape the future of accounting and the business world.

The writing of this text has taught us much. We have had to challenge, research, verify, and rethink much of what we thought we already knew. We also have been introduced to the wealth of useful information now emerging on the Internet. We hope the experiences of this accounting course - whether you approach it as a student or instructor - will prove as rewarding to you.

Sincerely,

Robert F. Meigs

Mary A. Meigs

Mark S. Bettner

Ray Whittington

An INTRODUCTION TO ACCOUNTING

Location:

| Search | Feedback | Help | Directory |

Document: Done

In today's business world, an understanding of accounting is much like these skydivers' equipment. It's more than useful—it's essential.

ACCOUNTING: THE LANGUAGE OF BUSINESS

CHAPTER 1

Location:

Search | Feedback | Help | Directory

Document: Done

Accounting is the language of business. It's the way business people set goals, measure results, and evaluate performance. It's difficult to participate if you don't speak the language.

1. Explain why people other than professional accountants benefit from an understanding of accounting.
2. Define *accounting*, *financial reporting*, *financial statements*, *public information*, and *generally accepted accounting principles*.
3. Prepare a balance sheet and describe its content.
4. Describe the accounting principles involved in asset valuation.
5. Indicate the effects of business transactions upon the accounting equation and the balance sheet.
6. Use a balance sheet to evaluate the solvency of an organization.
7. Identify factors contributing to the reliability of financial statements.
8. Discuss the importance of professional judgment and ethical conduct in accounting practice.
*9. Describe various career opportunities in accounting.

WHAT IS ACCOUNTING?

Many people think of accounting as a highly technical field practiced only by professional accountants. Actually, nearly everyone practices "accounting" on a daily basis. *Accounting* is simply the means by which we *measure* and *describe* economic activities. Whether you are managing a business, making investments, or deciding how to spend your money, you are working with accounting concepts and accounting information.

The purpose of accounting is to *provide decision makers with useful information about economic activities*. This includes both information about recent activities and *forecasts* of what may happen in the future. All types of decision makers—managers, investors, lenders, and consumers—use accounting information as a basis for making economic decisions. Think of *accounting* as an *information system for decision makers*.

Accounting often is called the "language of business" because it is so widely used to describe all types of business activities. Costs, prices, sales volume, profits, and return on investment—all are accounting measurements. Every investor, creditor (lender), and business manager needs a clear understanding of accounting terms and concepts if he or she is to effectively communicate and participate in the business community.

LO 1 Explain why people other than professional accountants benefit from an understanding of accounting.

But the use of accounting is not limited to the business world. Administrators of government agencies and nonprofit organizations use accounting information in the same manner as do business managers. Individuals use accounting information to manage their personal financial affairs and to file income tax returns.

The study of accounting should not be limited to students planning careers in accounting. Everyone who engages in economic activity—*which means everyone*—will benefit from an understanding of accounting information.

ACCOUNTING FROM A USER'S PERSPECTIVE

Our primary goal in this text is to develop your ability to *understand and use* accounting information in making economic decisions. To do this, you will need an understanding of:

- The *nature of the economic activities* the information describes.
- The *assumptions* and *measurement techniques* involved in developing the information.
- What information is *most relevant* to the decision at hand.

Supplemental Topic B, "Careers in Accounting."

Accounting "links" decision makers with economic activities—and with the results of their decisions

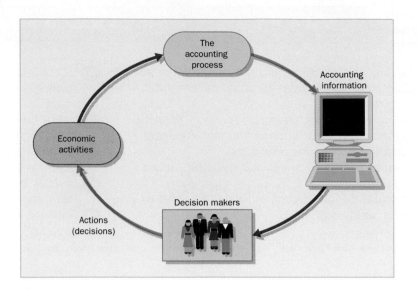

These are the topics of this first accounting course.

Accounting concepts are most highly developed and clearly defined in the business world. For this reason, we focus primarily upon the economic activities of *profit-oriented business organizations.*

FINANCIAL REPORTING

LO 2 *Define* accounting, financial reporting, financial statements, public information, *and* generally accepted accounting principles.

Many people think that financial information about large business organizations is a closely guarded secret. This is not the case.

Most "big businesses" have become large by attracting investment capital from a great many investors. Companies in which anyone may invest are said to be **publicly owned.**

With public ownership comes the responsibility to supply investors—and potential investors—with financial information about the company's operations. In the United States and most other industrialized countries, publicly owned companies are *required by law* to make certain financial information "public"—that is, *available to anyone who wants to see it.* These countries also have enacted laws to ensure that this **public information** is *reliable* and *complete.*

The process of supplying this information to decision makers outside of the business organization is called **financial reporting.**

Financial reporting provides an *overview* of a company's current financial strength, the results of its recent business operations, and its future prospects. In large part, this information is used by investors and creditors in deciding where to place their scarce investment resources. These decisions are important to society, as they determine which industries and companies receive the financial resources necessary for growth, and which do not.

Remember, however, that public information is available to *everyone.* Thus, large companies *cannot limit* the distribution of their financial information to investors and creditors. This information also is readily available to financial analysts, the news media, labor unions, environmental groups—even the companies' competitors. The flowchart on page 8 gives an indication of the many decision makers who are interested in the financial activities of large companies.

Small businesses are *not* required to provide financial information to the public. However, investors and major creditors often insist upon receiving this information before making an investment or loan.

The primary means of financial reporting is issuing a set of accounting reports called *financial statements*. These statements normally are issued every quarter, as well as at year-end. (Many companies also prepare monthly financial statements, but these normally are intended for use only by management.)

FINANCIAL STATEMENTS

Financial statements are a set of accounting reports which, taken together, describe the *financial position* of a business and the *results of its recent operations*. **Financial position** is described by identifying the company's financial resources and obligations as of a specific date.

The phrase "results of operations" refers to reports that describe the company's *financial activities* over a recent time period, such as a month, a quarter, or a year. These reports show how well, or poorly, the company has been doing. By comparing the operating results of successive years, investors often gain much insight into the company's future prospects.

A complete set of financial statements for a corporation includes four related accounting reports:

1. A **balance sheet,** which shows the financial position of the business at a specific date by describing its financial resources and obligations. *[handwritten: always tell you, assets, liability, owner's equity]*

2. An **income statement,** which reports the company's *profitability* over a recent period of time. *[handwritten: revenues, expenses in a pd. of time —]*

3. A **statement of retained earnings** (or statement of stockholders' equity), which explains changes in the amount of the owners' equity (investment in the business) over the period of time covered by the income statement. *[handwritten: sum of 2 & 3 my]*

4. A **statement of cash flows,** which summarizes the company's cash receipts and cash payments over the period of time covered by the income statement.

A complete set of financial statements also includes several pages of *notes*. These notes provide additional information that is useful in interpreting the statements.

Publicly owned companies are required by law to prepare financial statements at the end of each quarter (3-month period) and a separate set of statements covering the entire year. Small businesses are not required to prepare such statements, although many do anyway.

As a practical matter, the financial reporting requirements of large businesses have set the standards for accounting throughout the American business community. The concepts and terminology used in financial statements also are widely used by financial analysts, in loan applications, and in income tax returns. In fact, these terms and concepts have come to be known as *generally accepted accounting principles*.

AUDITS OF FINANCIAL STATEMENTS The annual financial statements of publicly owned companies are *audited* by a firm of **certified public accountants** (CPAs).[1] These auditors are experts in financial reporting and are *independent* of the company issuing the statements.

An **audit** is an investigation of the company's financial statement, designed to determine the "fairness" of the presentation. Accountants and auditors use

---

[1] The quarterly statements of these companies are *reviewed* by the CPAs, but are not audited. A review is a much shorter and less thorough investigation than an audit.

the term **fair** to describe statements that are complete, conform to generally accepted accounting principles, and are *not misleading.*

Based upon their investigation, the CPAs express their professional *opinion* as to the fairness of the annual financial statements. This opinion, called the **auditors' report,** accompanies the financial statements whenever they are distributed to persons outside of the organization.

Auditors do not guarantee the accuracy of financial statements; they express only their expert opinion as to the *fairness* of the statements. However, CPA firms stake their reputations on the thoroughness of their audits and the dependability of their audit reports. Over many years, audited financial statements have established an impressive track record of reliability.

The financial statements of small businesses often are *not* audited. This does not mean that they are unreliable, but the user does not have the same assurances of reliability as with audited statements.

INCOME TAX RETURNS Income tax returns are *not* financial statements. They are used for different purposes, and they are based upon different accounting standards.

Financial statements show the financial position of a business and the results of its operations, presented in conformity with generally accepted accounting principles. These statements are intended for use by many different decision makers, for many different purposes. For large companies, these statements often are public information.

Tax returns show the computation of *taxable income,* a legal concept defined by tax laws and regulations. In many cases, tax laws are similar to generally accepted accounting principles, but substantial differences do exist.

Tax returns are intended for use by government tax collection agencies. They are *not* public information; in fact, they are about as confidential as you can get. The government is *prohibited by law* from using tax returns for any purposes other than the collection of income taxes.

CASE IN POINT

Some drug dealers file federal income tax returns reporting the income from their illegal activities. The federal government cannot pass this information on to local law enforcement agencies. And these tax returns cannot be used in court as evidence of criminal activity (other than income tax evasion).

ANNUAL REPORTS

As part of the financial reporting process, large business organizations prepare **annual reports** of their activities. These reports are sent to all of the company's stockholders. If the company is publicly owned, the annual report is public information. There probably is a large file of these reports in your school library.

An annual report includes audited financial statements for each of the last several years. These **comparative financial statements** enable users to spot *trends* in the company's operating results and *significant changes* in its financial position.

Annual reports also include a discussion by top management of the company's operating results, current financial position, and future prospects. In addition, management may use the annual report to highlight special aspects of the company's business activities.

McDonald's Corporation devoted much of a recent annual report to a discussion of the company's concern for the environment. Included in the report was information about the company's programs for solid waste management, resource conservation, and recycling. (The annual report was printed entirely on recycled paper.)

The flowchart on the following page summarizes the process of preparing and distributing annual reports by publicly owned companies. Because these reports are public information, even the companies' competitors have access to them—and so do you.

A recent annual report of Toys "R" Us, a publicly owned corporation, appears in Appendix A at the end of this textbook.

FINANCIAL REPORTING: A MULTIMEDIA PROCESS

Financial statements and annual reports form the foundation of the financial reporting process. But the process is not limited to these printed documents. There is a wealth of information about publicly owned companies on the Internet. For example, a database called **EDGAR** (Electronic Data Gathering and Retrieval System) provides current financial information about publicly owned companies—at no charge to the user. (EDGAR's Internet address is:

www.sec.gov/cgi-bin/srch-edgar

You also can access EDGAR through hot buttons on our home page.)

Financial analysts, investment advisors, and the news media continually evaluate publicly owned companies. You can find professional analysts' evaluations in weekly publications, such as *Barrons, Business Week,* and *Forbes.* You also can find them on the Internet, hear them on "talk radio," or see them on television. (Tune in to *Wall $treet Week,* on Friday nights on PBS.)

DEVELOPING ACCOUNTING INFORMATION

Where does financial accounting information come from?

Most businesses maintain an accounting system which they use for preparing financial statements, annual reports, income tax returns, reports to management, bills to customers, and other accounting information. An **accounting system** consists of the personnel, procedures, devices, and records used to develop accounting information and to communicate this information to decision makers. Computers and other electronic devices are often used to maintain accounting systems, but handwritten forms and records may be used as well. But the heart of any accounting system is not devices, procedures, or forms—it's the people who make it work.

In every accounting system, the economic activities of the organization are *recorded* in the accounting records. The recorded data are *classified* within the system to produce useful subtotals about various types of economic activities. The information then is *summarized* in concise and readable accounting reports, designed to meet the needs of decision makers.

A FOCUS ON "TRANSACTIONS" Dollar amounts appearing in financial statements represent primarily the effects of completed transactions. A **transaction** is an exchange between one entity and another. Therefore, a transaction

THE PROCESS OF FINANCIAL REPORTING

(Audited Financial Statements and Annual Reports)

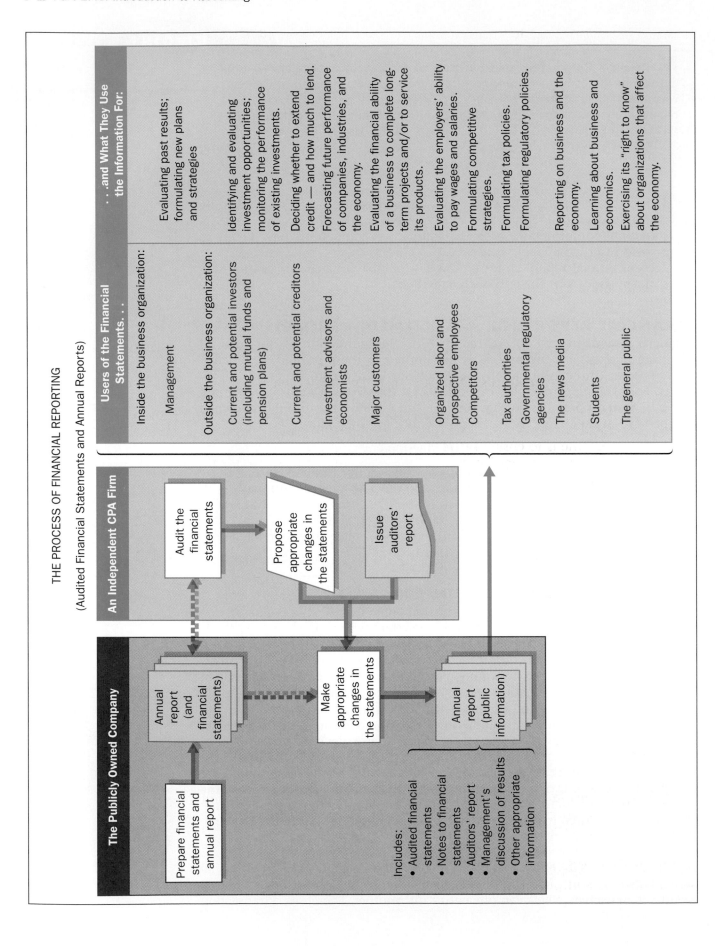

causes an *immediate change* in each entity's resources or obligations. Also, the effects of transactions usually can be measured objectively in monetary terms.[2]

Examples of transactions include purchases and sales of goods and services, and receipts and payments of cash.

There are many reasons why the dollar amounts of transactions are recorded in accounting records. First, every business *needs* a record of its past transactions. Transactions serve as the basis for billing customers, paying creditors, and keeping track of cash and other assets. But also, past transactions represent an *objective* measurement of the company's performance.

However, many important events do not qualify as *transactions*. Examples include the death or resignation of a key executive, a technological breakthrough by the company's research and development department, or the introduction of a new product by a competitor. Although these events may cause *future* changes in financial resources and obligations, they do not cause an *immediate* change. In addition, the financial effects of these events cannot be measured with much objectivity.

But accounting information includes more than just dollar amounts. Accounting reports often include *discussions* of significant nonfinancial events, even though these events have not been recorded as transactions.

THE NEED FOR INTERNAL CONTROL Many managerial decisions are based upon the information developed by the accounting system. Therefore, management needs assurance that this information is *reliable*. This assurance is provided by the company's system of **internal control.**

Internal control includes all measures designed to assure management that an organization is operating "as it should." Internal control measures serve several related purposes. One is to ensure the reliability of accounting data. Others are to prevent fraud, waste, and inefficiency; to promote compliance with management's policies; and to monitor performance at every level of the organization.

A simple example of an internal control procedure is the use of electronic cash registers to record sales transactions accurately. Other controls include hiring and training procedures, supervision of employees, performance reviews of departmental managers, and the measures taken to safeguard merchandise against theft and spoilage. The quality of internal control often determines whether a business succeeds or fails.

There is a strong relationship between accounting and internal control. A basic goal of internal control is to ensure the reliability of accounting data. At the same time, a basic goal of the accounting system is to provide management with the information necessary to achieve internal control throughout the organization. Thus, the topic of internal control goes hand-in-hand with the study of accounting.

GENERALLY ACCEPTED ACCOUNTING PRINCIPLES (GAAP)

Generally accepted accounting principles (or **GAAP**) are the ground rules for financial reporting. These principles provide the general framework to determine what information is included in financial statements, and how this

---

[2]Accountants use the term *objective* to mean neutral, free from bias, and verifiable in amount. The concept of *objectivity* is a generally accepted accounting principle and has a profound effect upon accounting practices. This concept is discussed further on page 16 and at many other points throughout this textbook.

information is to be presented. The phrase "generally accepted accounting principles" encompasses the basic objectives of financial reporting, as well as numerous broad concepts and many detailed rules. Thus, such terms as *objectives, standards, concepts, assumptions, methods,* and *rules* often are used in describing specific generally accepted accounting principles.

We already have mentioned two concepts embodied in generally accepted accounting principles: *comparability* (with different companies) and *reliability.* In this chapter we will discuss six other generally accepted accounting principles: the business entity concept, the cost principle, the going-concern assumption, the objectivity principle, the stable-dollar assumption, and the concept of adequate disclosure. These and other accounting principles will be considered further at many points throughout this book.

Let us emphasize, however, that *there is no comprehensive list of generally accepted accounting principles.* In fact, new accounting principles emerge continuously as business organizations enter into new forms of business activity.

THE NATURE OF ACCOUNTING PRINCIPLES

Accounting principles are not like physical laws; they do not exist in nature, awaiting discovery by man. Rather, they are developed by man, in light of what we consider to be the most important objectives of financial reporting. In many ways generally accepted accounting principles are similar to the rules established for an organized sport such as football or basketball. For example, accounting principles, like sports rules:

- Originate from a combination of tradition, experience, and official pronouncements.
- Require authoritative support and some means of enforcement.
- Are sometimes arbitrary.
- May change over time as shortcomings in the existing rules come to light.
- Must be clearly understood and observed by all participants in the process.

Unfortunately, accounting principles vary somewhat from country to country. The phrase "generally accepted accounting principles" refers to the accounting concepts in use in the United States. However, the principles in use in Canada, Great Britain, and a number of other countries are quite similar. Also, foreign companies that raise capital from American investors usually issue financial statements in conformity with the generally accepted accounting principles.

Several international organizations currently are attempting to establish greater uniformity among the accounting principles in use around the world.

ORGANIZATIONS INFLUENCING ACCOUNTING PRACTICE

Many organizations play an active role in developing generally accepted accounting principles and in improving the quality of financial reporting in the United States. Among the most influential of these organizations are the Financial Accounting Standards Board, Securities and Exchange Commission, American Institute of Certified Public Accountants, Institute of Management Accountants, and the American Accounting Association.

Each of these organizations maintains an educational home page on the Internet. (The addresses of these home pages appear on the inside of our back cover. Also, see our discussion of "Net Connections" on page 34.)

auth. Support + means of enforcement

FINANCIAL ACCOUNTING STANDARDS BOARD (FASB) Today, the most authoritative source of generally accepted accounting principles is the **Financial Accounting Standards Board,** known as the FASB. The FASB is a highly independent rule-making body, consisting of seven members from the accounting profession, industry, government, and accounting education. Lending support to these members are an advisory council and a large research staff.

← serve 5 yrs. + never again

The FASB is authorized to issue *Statements of Financial Accounting Standards,* which represent official expressions of generally accepted accounting principles. To date, the FASB has issued over 100 such *Statements,* along with a number of *Interpretations* and *Technical Bulletins.*

In addition to issuing authoritative *Statements,* the FASB has completed a project describing a *conceptual framework* for financial reporting. This conceptual framework sets forth the FASB's views as to the:

- Objectives of financial reporting.
- Desired characteristics of accounting information (such as relevance, reliability, and understandability).
- Elements of financial statements.
- Criteria for deciding what information to include in financial statements.
- Valuation concepts relating to financial statement amounts.

The primary purpose of the conceptual framework is to provide guidance to the FASB in developing new accounting standards.[3] By making each new standard consistent with this framework, the FASB hopes that its official *Statements* will resolve accounting problems in a logical and consistent manner. (The conceptual framework itself is not "officially binding" upon companies engaged in financial reporting, as are the FASB's *Statements.*)

The FASB is part of the private sector of the economy—*it is not a governmental agency.* The development of accounting principles in the United States traditionally has been carried out in the private sector, although the government, acting through the SEC, exercises considerable influence.

SECURITIES AND EXCHANGE COMMISSION (SEC) The **SEC** is a governmental agency with the *legal power* to establish accounting principles and financial reporting requirements for publicly owned corporations. In the past, the SEC has tended to adopt the recommendations of the FASB, rather than to develop its own set of accounting principles. Thus, accounting principles continue to be developed in the private sector, but are given the *force of law* when they are adopted by the SEC.

FASB - private sector
SEC - govt agency

To assure widespread acceptance of new accounting standards, the FASB *needs the support* of the SEC. Therefore, the two organizations work closely together in developing new accounting standards. The SEC also reviews the financial statements of publicly owned corporations to assure compliance with its reporting requirements. In the event that a publicly owned corporation fails to comply with these requirements, the SEC may initiate legal action against the company and the responsible individuals. Thus, the SEC "enforces" compliance with generally accepted accounting principles.

The SEC also maintains EDGAR, the Internet database described on page 7.

AMERICAN INSTITUTE OF CERTIFIED PUBLIC ACCOUNTANTS (AICPA) The **AICPA** is a professional association of certified public accountants. Prior to the creation of the FASB, committees of the AICPA were responsible for defining generally accepted accounting principles.

The AICPA participates actively in many aspects of accounting. For example, it has developed a *code of professional ethics* to be followed by all of its members. In addition, a committee of the AICPA establishes the professional *audit-*

---

[3]FASB, *Statement of Financial Accounting Concepts No. 1,* "Objectives of Financial Reporting by Business Enterprises," (Norwalk, CT, 1978), p. 4.

ing standards to be followed by CPAs in auditing financial statements. The AICPA also conducts research into accounting issues and works with the FASB in developing accounting principles.

INSTITUTE OF MANAGEMENT ACCOUNTANTS (IMA) The **IMA** is a professional association of management accountants. *Management accountants* develop accounting information specifically tailored to meet the needs of managers. These accountants are employed by all types of organizations— businesses, nonprofit organizations (such as the Red Cross), and government agencies.

The IMA has done much to improve the quality and reliability of accounting information. Its efforts include sponsoring educational programs, encouraging accounting research and publishing the results, and developing a code of professional ethics for its members.

AMERICAN ACCOUNTING ASSOCIATION (AAA) The **AAA** is comprised primarily of accounting educators. The Association has sponsored a number of research studies and monographs in which individual authors and Association committees have taken positions on various accounting issues. However, the AAA does not have any official authority to impose its views; its influence stems only from the prestige of its authors and the persuasiveness of their arguments.

"AUTHORITATIVE SUPPORT" FOR ACCOUNTING PRINCIPLES To qualify as "generally accepted," an accounting principle must have substantial authoritative support. Principles, standards, and rules set forth by the official rule-making bodies of the accounting profession, such as the FASB, automatically qualify as generally accepted accounting principles. However, many concepts and practices gain substantial authoritative support from *unofficial* sources, such as widespread use, or recognition in textbooks and other "unofficial" accounting literature. Thus, the phrase "generally accepted accounting principles" includes more concepts and practices than appear in the "official" literature.

FORMS OF BUSINESS ORGANIZATIONS

In the United States, a business enterprise may be organized as a *sole proprietorship,* a *partnership,* or a *corporation.* Generally accepted accounting principles apply to the financial statements of all three forms of organization.

SOLE PROPRIETORSHIPS An unincorporated business owned by one person is called a **sole proprietorship.** Often the owner also acts as manager. This form of business organization is common for small retail stores, restaurants, farms, service organizations, and professional practices in medicine, law, and public accounting.

Under the law, a sole proprietorship is *not an entity separate from its owner.* Therefore, the proprietor (owner) is *personally liable* for the debts of the business. From an accounting viewpoint, however, a sole proprietorship *is* an entity separate from its owner. Thus, the owner's *personal* resources, debts, and financial activities are *not included* in the financial statements of the business.

PARTNERSHIPS An unincorporated business owned by two or more persons voluntarily acting as partners (co-owners) is called a **partnership.** Partnerships, like sole proprietorships, are widely used for small businesses. In addition, some very large professional practices, including international CPA firms, are organized as partnerships. As in the case of the sole proprietorship, the owners of a partnership are personally responsible for all debts of the business. From an accounting standpoint, however, a partnership is a business entity *separate* from the personal affairs of its owners.[4]

CORPORATIONS A **corporation** is the only type of business organization recognized *under the law* as an entity separate from its owners. Therefore, the owners of a corporation are *not* personally liable for the debts of the business. These owners can lose no more than the amounts they have invested in the business—a concept known as *limited liability*. This concept is the principal reason why corporations are the most attractive form of business organization to many investors.

Ownership of a corporation is divided into transferrable shares of capital stock and the owners are called **stockholders.** Stock certificates are issued by the corporation to each stockholder showing the number of shares that he or she owns. The stockholders are free to sell some or all of these shares to other investors at any time. This *transferability of ownership* adds to the attractiveness of the corporate form of organization, because investors can more easily "get their money out" of the business.

There are many more sole proprietorships and partnerships than corporations, but most large businesses are organized as corporations. Thus, corporations are the dominant form of business organization in terms of the dollar volume of their business activities. In addition, it is primarily corporations that distribute their financial statements to investors and other outsiders. In this textbook we will use the *corporate form* of organization as our basic model, along with some specific references to sole proprietorships and partnerships.

YOUR TURN

You as the Owner of a Small Business

Businesses which take customers skydiving, scuba diving, mountain climbing, or white-water river rafting usually are quite small. But they almost always are organized as corporations.

Corporations are the most complicated form of business organization, and also the most expensive to establish and maintain. So why do you think these small businesses choose this structure?

*These in-text cases are intended to challenge and develop your understanding of accounting concepts and your ability to use accounting information. We ask that you answer these cases—at least in your mind—before continuing with the chapter. You may want to compare your thoughts on these matters with ours. We provide discussions of these cases following the assignment material of the chapter in which the cases appear. Our comments on this case appear on page 53.

FINANCIAL STATEMENTS: THE STARTING POINT IN THE STUDY OF ACCOUNTING

The preparation of financial statements is not the first step in the accounting process, but it is a logical point to begin the *study* of accounting. This is because most of the accounting information we see and use every day reflects the terminology and concepts used in these statements.

---

[4]Creditors of an unincorporated business often ask to see the *personal* financial statements of the business owners, as these owners ultimately are responsible for paying the debts of the business.

Financial statements convey to management and to interested outsiders a concise picture of the profitability and financial position of a business. These statements—each less than a page in length—summarize the thousands or even millions of transactions recorded during the year in the company's accounting system. Thus, financial statements are the *end product* of the accounting process. The student who acquires a clear understanding of the nature and content of these statements is in a better position to interpret and use all types of accounting information.

The three most widely used financial statements are the *balance sheet,* the *income statement,* and the *statement of cash flows.* In this introductory chapter and in Chapter 2, we shall explore the nature of the balance sheet, or *statement of financial position,* as it is often called. Once we have become familiar with the form and arrangement of the balance sheet and with the meanings of technical terms such as assets, liabilities, and owners' equity, it will be as easy for you to read and understand a report on the financial position of a business as it is for an architect to read a blueprint for a proposed building. (We shall discuss the income statement in Chapter 3, and the statement of cash flows later in the course.)

THE BALANCE SHEET

The purpose of a balance sheet is to show the financial position of a business entity at a specific date. Every business prepares a balance sheet at the end of the year, and many companies prepare one at the end of each quarter.

LO 3 *Prepare a balance sheet and describe its content.*

A balance sheet consists of a listing of the assets, the liabilities, and the owner's equity of a business. The *balance sheet date* is important, as the financial position of a business may change quickly. A balance sheet is most useful if it is relatively recent. The following balance sheet shows the financial position of Vagabond Travel Agency, Inc., at December 31, 1998.

A balance sheet shows financial position at a specific date

VAGABOND TRAVEL AGENCY, INC.					
Balance Sheet					
December 31, 1998					
Assets			**Liabilities & Stockholders' Equity**		
Cash	$ 20,500		**Liabilities:**		
Notes receivable	5,000		Notes payable		$110,000
Accounts receivable	32,500		Accounts payable		17,000
Supplies	2,000		Income taxes payable		8,000
Land	100,000		Total liabilities		$135,000
Building	80,000		**Stockholders' equity:**		
Office equipment	10,000		Capital stock	$70,000	
			Retained earnings	45,000	115,000
Total	$250,000		Total		$250,000

Let us briefly discuss several features of this balance sheet. First, the heading sets forth three things: (1) the name of the business entity, (2) the name of the financial statement, and (3) the balance sheet date. The body of the balance sheet also consists of three distinct sections: *assets, liabilities,* and *stockholders' equity.*

Notice that cash is listed first among the assets, followed by receivables, supplies, and any other assets that will *soon be converted into cash or consumed in operations.* Following these relatively "liquid" assets are the more "permanent" assets, such as land, buildings, and equipment.

Liabilities always are shown before the owners' equity. Each major type of liability (such as notes payable, accounts payable, and income taxes payable) is listed separately. Also, a figure usually is supplied showing total liabilities.

Finally, notice that the amount of total assets ($250,000) is *equal to* the total amount of liabilities and stockholders' equity (also $250,000). This relationship *always exists*—in fact, the equality of these totals is one reason that this financial statement is called the *balance sheet*.

THE CONCEPT OF THE BUSINESS ENTITY The illustrated balance sheet refers only to the financial affairs of the business entity known as Vagabond Travel Agency, Inc., and not to the personal financial affairs of its owners. Individual stockholders may have personal bank accounts, homes, automobiles, and investments in other businesses; however, these personal belongings are not part of the travel agency business, and therefore are not included in the balance sheet of this business unit.

In brief, a **business entity** is an economic unit which uses specific assets and incurs specific debts. Consequently, a separate set of financial statements may be prepared to describe the financial activities of each business entity.

ASSETS

Assets are economic resources owned by a business and expected to benefit future operations. Assets may have definite physical form such as buildings, machinery, or an inventory of merchandise. On the other hand, some assets exist not in physical or tangible form, but in the form of valuable legal claims or rights. Examples include bank accounts, amounts due from customers, and trademarks (such as the exclusive right to use the name "Coca-Cola").

One of the most basic and at the same time most controversial problems in accounting is determining the dollar values for the various assets of a business. At present, generally accepted accounting principles call for the valuation of most assets in a balance sheet at *cost,* rather than at appraised market values. The specific accounting principles supporting cost as the basis for asset valuation are discussed below.

THE COST PRINCIPLE Assets such as land, buildings, merchandise, and equipment are typical of the many economic resources that will be used in producing income for the business. The prevailing accounting view is that such assets should be recorded at their cost. When we say that an asset is shown in the balance sheet at its *historical cost,* we mean the dollar amount originally paid to acquire the asset; this amount may be very different from what the business might have to pay today to replace it.

LO 4 *Describe the accounting principles involved in asset valuation.*

For example, let us assume that a business buys a tract of land for use as a building site, paying $100,000 in cash. The amount to be entered in the accounting records as the value of the asset will be the cost of $100,000. If we assume a booming real estate market, a fair estimate of the market value of the land 10 years later might be $250,000. Although the market price or economic value of the land has risen greatly, the accounting value as shown in the accounting records and on the balance sheet would continue unchanged at the cost of $100,000. This policy of accounting for assets at their cost is often referred to as the **cost principle** of accounting.

In reading a balance sheet, it is important to bear in mind that the dollar amounts listed do not indicate the prices at which the assets could be sold, nor the price that would have to be paid to replace them. Perhaps the greatest limitation of a balance sheet is that this financial statement *does not* show "how much the business currently is worth."

THE GOING-CONCERN ASSUMPTION It is appropriate to ask *why* accountants do not change the recorded values of assets to correspond with changing market prices for these properties. One reason is that the land and building being used to house the business were acquired for *use* and not for resale; in fact, these assets cannot be sold without disrupting the business. The balance sheet of a business is prepared on the assumption that the business is a continuing enterprise, a **"going concern."** Consequently, the presently estimated prices for which the land and buildings could be sold are of less importance than if these properties were intended for sale.

THE OBJECTIVITY PRINCIPLE Another reason for using cost rather than current market values in accounting for assets is the need for a definite, factual basis for valuation. The cost of land, buildings, and many other assets purchased for cash can be rather definitely determined. Accountants use the term **objective** to describe asset valuations that are factual and can be verified by independent experts. For example, if land is shown on the balance sheet at cost, any CPA who performed an audit of the business would be able to find objective evidence that the land was actually valued at the cost incurred in acquiring it. On the other hand, estimated market values for assets such as buildings and specialized machinery are not factual and objective. Market values change constantly and estimates of the prices at which assets might be sold are largely matters of personal opinion.

Of course at the date an asset is acquired, the cost and market value are usually the same because the bargaining process which results in the sale of an asset serves to establish both the current market value of the property and the cost to the buyer. With the passage of time, however, the current market value of assets is likely to differ considerably from the cost recorded in the owners' accounting records.

THE STABLE-DOLLAR ASSUMPTION Severe inflation in several countries in recent years has raised serious doubts as to the adequacy of the conventional cost basis in accounting for assets. When inflation becomes very severe, historical cost values for assets simply lose their relevance as a basis for making business decisions. Much consideration has been given to the use of balance sheets which would show assets at current appraised values or at replacement cost rather than at historical cost.

Accountants in the United States, by adhering to the cost basis of accounting, are implying that the dollar is a stable unit of measurement, as is the gallon, the acre, or the mile. The cost principle and the **stable-dollar assumption** work very well in periods of stable prices, but are less satisfactory under conditions of rapid inflation. For example, if a company bought land 20 years ago for $100,000 and purchased a second similar tract of land today for $500,000, the total cost of land shown by the accounting records would be $600,000. This treatment ignores the fact that dollars spent 20 years ago had far greater purchasing power than today's dollar. Thus, the $600,000 total for cost of land is a mixture of two kinds of dollars with very different purchasing power.

After much research into this problem, the FASB required, on a trial basis, that large corporations annually disclose financial data adjusted for the effects of inflation. But after several years of experimentation, the FASB concluded that the costs of developing this information exceeded its usefulness. Thus, the disclosure requirement was eliminated. At the present time, the stable-dollar assumption continues in use in the United States—perhaps until challenged by more severe inflation sometime in the future.

LIABILITIES

Liabilities are debts. The person or organization to whom the debt is owed is called a **creditor.**

All businesses have liabilities; even the largest and most successful companies purchase merchandise, supplies, and services "on account." The liabilities arising from such purchases are called *accounts payable.* Many businesses borrow money to finance expansion or the purchase of high-cost assets. When taking out a loan, the borrower usually must sign a formal note payable. A *note payable* is a written promise to repay the amount owed by a particular date, and usually calls for the payment of interest as well.

Accounts payable, in contrast with notes payable, involve no written promises and generally do not call for interest payments. In essence, a note payable is a *more formal arrangement.*

When a company has both notes payable and accounts payable, the two types of liabilities are listed separately in the balance sheet. Other types of short-term liabilities, such as income taxes payable, may be either listed separately or combined with the amount shown as accounts payable.

The order in which *short-term* liabilities are listed is not important, although either notes payable or accounts payable usually appears first.[5] The liabilities section of the balance sheet should include a subtotal indicating the total amount of liabilities, as illustrated on page 14.

CREDITORS' CLAIMS HAVE PRIORITY OVER THOSE OF OWNERS Liabilities represent claims against the borrower's assets. As we shall see, the owners of a business *also* have claims to the company's assets. But in the eyes of the law, creditors' claims *take priority* over those of the owners. This means that creditors are entitled to be *paid in full,* even if such payment would exhaust the assets of the business and leave nothing for its owners.

OWNERS' EQUITY

The **owners' equity** in a corporation is called **stockholders' equity.** In the following discussion, we will use the broader term "owners' equity" because the concepts being presented are equally applicable to the ownership equity in corporations, partnerships, and sole proprietorships.

Owners' equity represents the *owners' claim* to the assets of the business. Because creditors' claims have legal priority over those of the owners, owners' equity is a *residual amount.* Owners are entitled to "what's left" after the claims of creditors have been satisfied in full. Therefore, owner's equity is always equal to *total assets minus total liabilities.* For example, using the data from the illustrated balance sheet of Vagabond Travel Agency (page 14):

Vagabond has total assets of	$250,000
And total liabilities of	135,000
Therefore, owners' equity **must be**	$115,000

Owners' equity does *not* represent a specific claim to cash or any other particular asset. Rather, it is the owners' overall financial interest in *all* of the company's assets.

---

[5]Short-term liabilities are those due within one year. Long-term liabilities are shown separately in the balance sheet, after all the short-term liabilities are listed. Long-term liabilities are addressed in Chapter 6.

INCREASES IN OWNERS' EQUITY The owners' equity in a business comes from two sources:

1. *Investment* by the owners

2. *Earnings* from profitable operation of the business

Only the first of these two sources of owners' equity is considered in this chapter. The second source, an increase in owners' equity through earnings of the business, will be discussed in Chapter 3.

DECREASES IN OWNERS' EQUITY Decreases in owners' equity also are caused in two ways:

1. *Distribution of cash or other assets* by the business to its owners (termed *dividends*)

2. *Losses* from unprofitable operation of the business

Dividends and net losses will be addressed in Chapter 3.

OWNERS' EQUITY IN CORPORATIONS AND UNINCORPORATED BUSINESSES The ownership equity of a corporation consists of two elements: capital stock and retained earnings, as shown in the following illustration:

Owners' Equity in Vagabond Travel Agency, Inc.—a Corporation

Stockholders' equity in a corporation and . . .

Stockholders' equity:

Capital stock...	$ 70,000
Retained earnings...	45,000
Total stockholders' equity	$115,000

The $70,000 shown as *capital stock* represents the amount invested in the business by its owners. The $45,000 of *retained earnings* represents the portion of owners' equity which has been accumulated through profitable operation of the business. The corporation has chosen to retain this $45,000 in the business rather than distributing these earnings to the stockholders as dividends. The total earnings of the corporation may have been considerably more than $45,000, because any earnings that were paid to stockholders as dividends would not appear on the balance sheet. The term **retained earnings** describes only the earnings which were *not* paid out in the form of dividends.

In contrast, a sole proprietorship is not required to maintain a distinction between invested capital and earned capital. Consequently, the balance sheet of a sole proprietorship will have only one item in the owners' equity section, as illustrated below:

Owner's Equity if Vagabond Were a Sole Proprietorship

. . . owner's equity in a sole proprietorship

Owner's equity:

John Smith, capital	$115,000

The equity section for a business organized as a partnership is similar to that of a sole proprietorship, except that a separate owner's capital account is shown for each partner.

WHAT IS CAPITAL STOCK?

As previously mentioned, the caption **capital stock** in the balance sheet of a corporation represents the amount invested in a business by its owners. When the owners of a corporation invest cash or other assets in the business, the corporation issues in exchange shares of capital stock as evidence of the investor's ownership equity. Thus, the owners of a corporation are termed *stockholders*.

The basic unit of capital stock is called a *share,* but a corporation may issue capital stock certificates in denominations of 1 share, 100 shares, or any other number. The total number of shares of capital stock outstanding at any given time represents 100% ownership of the corporation. Outstanding shares are those in the hands of stockholders. The number of shares owned by an individual investor determines the extent of his or her ownership of the corporation.

Assume, for example, that Draper Corporation issues a total of 5,000 shares of capital stock to investors in exchange for cash. If we assume further that Thomas Draper acquires 500 shares of the 5,000 shares outstanding, we may say that he has a 10% interest in the corporation. Suppose that Draper now sells 200 shares to Evans. The total number of shares outstanding remains unchanged at 5,000, although Draper's percentage of ownership has declined to 6% and a new stockholder, Evans, has acquired a 4% interest in the corporation. The transfer of 200 shares from Draper to Evans had *no effect* upon the corporation's assets, liabilities, or amount of stock outstanding. The only way in which this transfer of stock affects the corporation is that the list of stockholders must be revised to show the number of shares held by each owner.

THE ACCOUNTING EQUATION

A fundamental characteristic of every balance sheet is that the total figure for assets always equals the total of liabilities plus owners' equity. This agreement, or balance of total assets with the total of liabilities and owners' equity, is one reason for calling this financial statement a *"balance" sheet.* But *why* do total assets equal the total of liabilities and owners' equity? The answer can be given in one short paragraph:

The dollar totals on the two sides of the balance sheet are always equal because these two sides are *merely two views of the same business property.* The listing of assets shows us what things the business owns; the listing of liabilities and owner's equity tells us who supplied these resources to the business and how much each group supplied. Everything that a business owns has been supplied to it by the creditors or by the owners. Therefore, the total claims of the creditors plus the claims of the owners equal the total assets of the business.

The equality of assets on the one hand and of the claims of the creditors and the owners on the other hand is expressed in the following **accounting equation:**

$$\text{Assets} = \text{Liabilities} + \text{Owners' Equity}$$
$$\$250,000 = \$135,000 + \$115,000$$

The accounting equation

The amounts listed in the equation were taken from the balance sheet illustrated on page 14. The balance sheet is simply a detailed statement of this equation. To illustrate this relationship, compare the balance sheet of Vagabond Travel Agency, Inc., with the above equation.

To emphasize that the owners' equity is a *residual amount,* secondary to the claims of creditors, it is often helpful to transpose the terms of the equation, as follows:

$$\text{Assets} - \text{Liabilities} = \text{Owners' Equity}$$
$$\$250,000 - \$135,000 = \$115,000$$

Alternative form of the accounting equation

Notice that if a business has liabilities in excess of its assets, owners' equity will be a *negative* amount.

Every business transaction, no matter how simple or how complex, can be expressed in terms of its effect on the accounting equation. A thorough understanding of the equation and some practice in using it are essential to the student of accounting.

Regardless of whether a business grows or contracts, this equality between the assets and the claims against the assets is always maintained. Any increase in the amount of total assets is necessarily accompanied by an equal increase on the other side of the equation, that is, by an increase in either the liabilities or the owners' equity. Any decrease in total assets is necessarily accompanied by a corresponding decrease in liabilities or owners' equity. The continuing equality of the two sides of the balance sheet can best be illustrated by taking a brand-new business as an example and observing the effects of various transactions upon its balance sheet.

THE ACCOUNTING PROCESS: AN ILLUSTRATION

To illustrate basic accounting concepts and techniques, we will create a small auto repair business, and follow it through the first year of operations. (This example continues through several chapters.)

OVERNIGHT AUTO SERVICE: GETTING STARTED Michael McBryan is an experienced service manager at a new-car dealership. In 1998, he decides to open his own automotive repair business, to be called Overnight Auto Service.

The first step in starting any new business venture should be *careful planning.* What are the goals, and what are the strategies for achieving these goals? How much money will be needed to get the business up-and-running? Where will this money come from? What operating result does management expect to achieve? In large part, the answers to these questions are based upon accounting information.

McBryan did not have enough money to start Overnight Auto Service on his own. Therefore, he organized the business as a corporation. This allows Overnight to raise equity capital from numerous investors by issuing capital stock.

But before investing in a new business, most investors want to know much about the company's planned activities. Therefore, McBryan has developed a comprehensive *business plan,* which he shows to potential investors. We illustrate several elements of this business plan on the following page.

There are no official requirements for the content of a business plan. Basically, these plans summarize management's goals over the next several years, and the strategies for achieving them. A business plan is not a formal financial statement, but it does include financial projections and accounting terminology. As we say, accounting is the "language of business."

Business plans can serve many useful purposes. Just preparing the plans forces management to think carefully about goals, business strategies, capital requirements, and the company's profit potential. The plans also may help management raise capital from investors and creditors, especially if the business is just getting started. And in future years, these plans assist managers and investors alike in evaluating the company's progress.

Companies are not required to prepare business plans. Nonetheless, most well-managed companies do prepare such plans, and they update them as management's goals change. A business plan is not public information, but management often discusses key elements of this plan in the company's annual report.

THE EFFECTS OF BUSINESS TRANSACTIONS

McBryan was successful in issuing all 40,000 shares of Overnight's capital stock at $10 per share. Let us now see how this and other events affect the new corporation's financial position.

Overnight Auto Service

Selected Sections of the Business Plan

Description of the Company

Overnight Auto Service will provide automobile repair and maintenance services to the public. For the convenience of its customers, the company will remain open 24 hours per day, with most repair work being done at night.

Overnight Auto Service is a corporation lawfully chartered in the State of California. It currently is authorized to issue up to 50,000 shares of capital stock.

Management will provide unaudited quarterly financial statements and audited annual statements to all stockholders.

Overnight Auto Service will begin operations in a company-owned location in Santa Teresa, California. Management intends to open new service centers each coming year.

Management's Priorities

Management's top priorities are to (1) provide customers with convenient quality service at reasonable prices; (2) achieve rapid growth in sales and earnings, and (3) provide stockholders with an above-average return on investment.

Key Business Strategies

The automotive repair business is highly competitive. Management believes the following business strategies will enable Overnight Auto Service not just to compete but to prosper and grow. The company will:
1. Be open 24 hours per day, 7 days per week.
2. Complete most maintenance and repair work overnight.
3. Employ practicing mechanics to work short, part-time shifts.

Financing

Management estimates the costs of starting the business and opening the first Overnight service center at approximately $500,000. The company plans to raise $400,000 in stockholders' equity by issuing 40,000 shares of capital stock at a price of $10 per share. The additional $100,000 will be financed by long-term debt, secured by company-owned real estate.

Future service centers will be located in rented facilities and will cost approximately $80,000 per center. The cost of these centers will be financed through a combination of additional borrowing and earnings retained in the business. Management does not anticipate issuing additional shares of capital stock in the foreseeable future.

Projected Operating Results

The first Overnight Auto Service center will begin operations on or before January 2, 1999. The company plans to open 15 additional service centers within five years (see table below).

Projections of revenue and net income for the first five years of operation appear below (dollar amounts are stated in thousands):

	1999	2000	2001	2002	2003
Centers in operation	1	2	4	8	16
Revenue	$400	$675	$1,200	$2,250	$4,350
Net income	75	125	200	380	660

selling price / profit (handwritten annotation)

Management will attempt at all times to maintain cash and receivables at a combined total in excess of existing liabilities payable within the coming year.

Management believes its projections to be based upon reasonable assumptions. However, it cannot guarantee future operating results.

LO 5 *Indicate the effects of business transactions upon the accounting equation and the balance sheet.*

ISSUING STOCK: OVERNIGHT'S FIRST "TRANSACTION" On November 1, 1998, Overnight issues 40,000 shares of capital stock to McBryan and other investors in exchange for $400,000 cash.

This transaction provides the company with its first asset—$400,000 in cash—and also creates *stockholders' equity* in the business entity. A balance sheet showing the company's financial position after this first transaction appears below:

Beginning balance sheet of a new business

OVERNIGHT AUTO SERVICE Balance Sheet November 1, 1998		
Assets		**Stockholders' Equity**
Cash $400,000		Capital stock $400,000

Overnight's next two transactions involved the acquisition of a suitable site for its business operations.

PURCHASE OF AN ASSET FOR CASH As Overnight's CEO, McBryan negotiates with both the City of Santa Teresa and the Metropolitan Transit District (MTD) to purchase an empty property once used as a bus garage. (The city owns the land but the MTD owns the bus garage.)

On November 3, Overnight purchases the land (about two acres) from the City for $295,000 in cash. This transaction has two immediate effects upon the company's financial position: First, Overnight's cash is reduced by $295,000; and second, the company has acquired a new asset—Land. The company's financial position following this transaction is:

Balance sheet totals unchanged by purchase of land for cash

OVERNIGHT AUTO SERVICE Balance Sheet November 3, 1998		
Assets		**Stockholders' Equity**
Cash $105,000		Capital stock $400,000
Land 295,000		
Total $400,000		Total $400,000

PURCHASE OF AN ASSET AND FINANCING PART OF THE COST On November 5, Overnight purchases the old garage building from Metropolitan Transit Authority for $120,000. Due to the age and condition of the bus garage, Overnight was unable to immediately arrange a long-term real estate loan from a bank. However, the MTD agrees to accept a $30,000 cash down payment from Overnight, along with a short-term note payable for the $90,000 balance of the purchase price. This note requires no interest, but is due in 90 days (February 3, 1999).

As a result of this transaction, Overnight has (1) $30,000 less cash; (2) a new asset, Building, which cost $120,000; and (3) a new liability, Notes Payable, in the amount of $90,000. This transaction is reflected in the following balance sheet:

OVERNIGHT AUTO SERVICE
Balance Sheet
November 5, 1998

Assets		Liabilities & Stockholders' Equity	
Cash	$ 75,000	**Liabilities:**	
Land	295,000	Notes payable	$ 90,000
Building	120,000	**Stockholders' equity:**	
		Capital stock	400,000
Total	$490,000	Total	$490,000

There are changes on both sides of the balance sheet but the totals remain equal

The due dates of major liabilities, such as this note payable to MTD, should appear in the footnotes (called *notes*) which accompany a set of financial statements.

PURCHASE OF AN ASSET "ON ACCOUNT" On November 17, Overnight purchases tools and automotive repair equipment from Pro-Tools Corporation for $64,200. This purchase is made "on account," with the understanding that Overnight will pay one-half of the amount due by the end of November, and the balance within 60 days—that is, by January 16. After this transaction, Overnight's financial position is as follows:

OVERNIGHT AUTO SERVICE
Balance Sheet
November 17, 1998

Assets		Liabilities & Stockholders' Equity	
Cash	$ 75,000	**Liabilities:**	
Land	295,000	Notes payable	$ 90,000
Building	120,000	Accounts payable	64,200
Tools and equipment	64,200	Total liabilities	$154,200
		Stockholders' equity:	
		Capital stock	400,000
Total	$554,200	Total	$554,200

A new asset and a new liability. But the balance sheet remains "in balance"

SALE OF AN ASSET After taking delivery of the new tools and equipment, Overnight found that it had purchased more than it needed. Ace Towing, a neighboring business, offered to buy the excess items.

On November 20, Overnight sells some of its new tools to Ace for $4,200, a price equal to Overnight's cost.[6] Ace makes no down payment, but agrees to pay the amount due within 45 days. A balance sheet as of November 20 follows:

---

[6]Sales of assets at prices above or below cost result in gains or losses. Such transactions are discussed in later chapters.

OVERNIGHT AUTO SERVICE	
Balance Sheet	
November 20, 1998	

Assets		Liabilities & Stockholders' Equity	
Cash	$ 75,000	**Liabilities:**	
Accounts receivable	4,200	Notes payable	$ 90,000
Land	295,000	Accounts payable	64,200
Building	120,000	Total liabilities	$154,200
Tools and equipment	60,000	**Stockholders' equity:**	
		Capital stock	400,000
Total	$554,200	Total	$554,200

The amounts of assets change, but not the balance sheet totals

COLLECTION OF AN ACCOUNT RECEIVABLE   On November 25, Overnight receives $2,000 from Ace Towing as partial settlement of its account receivable from Ace. This transaction causes an increase in Overnight's cash, but a decrease of the same amount in accounts receivable. In essence, this transaction merely converts one asset into another of equal value; there is no change in the amount of total assets. After this transaction, Overnight's financial position is:

OVERNIGHT AUTO SERVICE	
Balance Sheet	
November 25, 1998	

Assets		Liabilities & Stockholders' Equity	
Cash	$ 77,000	**Liabilities:**	
Accounts receivable	2,200	Notes payable	$ 90,000
Land	295,000	Accounts payable	64,200
Building	120,000	Total liabilities	$154,200
Tools and equipment	60,000	**Stockholders' equity:**	
		Capital stock	400,000
Total	$554,200	Total	$554,200

Totals unchanged by collection of a receivable

PAYMENT OF A LIABILITY   On the last day of November, Overnight makes a partial payment of $32,100 on its account payable to Pro-Tools. This transaction reduces Overnight's cash and accounts payable by the same amount. Overnight's balance sheet at November 30 appears below:

OVERNIGHT AUTO SERVICE	
Balance Sheet	
November 30, 1998	

Assets		Liabilities & Stockholders' Equity	
Cash	$ 44,900	**Liabilities:**	
Accounts receivable	2,200	Notes payable	$ 90,000
Land	295,000	Accounts payable	32,100
Building	120,000	Total liabilities	$122,100
Tools and equipment	60,000	**Stockholders' equity:**	
		Capital stock	400,000
Total	$522,100	Total	$522,100

Totals reduced by payment of a liability, but by an equal amount

November was a month devoted exclusively to organizing the business and not to income-producing activities. Overnight will begin regular business operations in December (and in Chapter 3).

EFFECTS OF THESE BUSINESS TRANSACTIONS UPON THE ACCOUNTING EQUATION

The balance sheet is a detailed expression of the accounting equation:

Assets = Liabilities + Owners' Equity

In the preceding pages, we have illustrated the effects of Overnight's November transactions upon the balance sheet. Let us now illustrate the effects of these transactions upon the accounting equation.

To review, Overnight's transactions during November were as follows:

Nov. 1   Issued 40,000 shares of capital stock in exchange for $400,000 cash.

Nov. 3   Purchased land for $295,000, paying cash.

Nov. 5   Purchased a building for $120,000, paying $30,000 in cash and issuing a short-term note payable for the remaining $90,000.

Nov. 17   Purchased tools and equipment on account, $64,200.

Nov. 20   Sold some of the tools at a price equal to their cost, $4,200, collectible within 45 days.

Nov. 25   Received $2,000 in partial collection of the account receivable from the sale of tools.

Nov. 30   Paid $32,100 in partial payment of an account payable.

The table below shows the effects of these transactions upon the accounting equation. The effects of each transaction are shown in red. Notice that the "balances," shown in blue, are the amounts appearing in Overnight's balance sheets on pages 22–24. Notice also that the accounting equation *always* remains "in balance."

		Assets				=	Liabilities		+	Owners' Equity
	Cash	+ Accounts Receivable +	Land	+ Building	+ Tools and Equipment	=	Notes Payable +	Accounts Payable +		Capital Stock
Nov. 1	$400,000					=				$400,000
Balances	$400,000					=				$400,000
Nov. 3	−295,000		+295,000			=			*due Feb. 3*	
Balances	$105,000		$295,000			=				$400,000
Nov. 5	−30,000			+$120,000		=	+$90,000			
Balances	$ 75,000		$295,000	$120,000		=	$90,000			$400,000
Nov. 17					+$64,200	=		+$64,200		
Balances	$ 75,000		$295,000	$120,000	$64,200	=	$90,000	$64,200		$400,000
Nov. 20		+$4,200			−4,200	=				
Balances	$ 75,000	$4,200	$295,000	$120,000	$60,000	=	$90,000	$64,200		$400,000
Nov. 25	+2,000	−2,000				=				
Balances	$ 77,000	$2,200	$295,000	$120,000	$60,000	=	$90,000	$64,200		$400,000
Nov. 30	−32,100					=		−32,100		
Balances	$ 44,900	$2,200	$295,000	$120,000	$60,000	=	$90,000	$32,100		$400,000

THE USE OF FINANCIAL STATEMENTS BY OUTSIDERS

Most "outside" decision makers use financial statements to make *investment decisions*—that is, to select those companies in which they will invest resources, or to which they will extend credit. For this reason, financial statements are designed primarily to meet the needs of creditors and investors.[7] Two factors of concern to creditors and investors are the *solvency* and *profitability* of a business organization.

Creditors are interested in **solvency**—the ability of the business to pay its debts as they come due. Business concerns that are able to pay their debts promptly are said to be *solvent*. In contrast, a company that finds itself unable to meet its obligations as they fall due is called *insolvent*. Solvency is critical to the very survival of a business organization—a business that becomes insolvent may be forced into bankruptcy by its creditors. Once bankrupt, a business may be forced by the courts to stop its operations, sell its assets (for the purpose of paying its creditors), and end its existence.

Investors also are interested in the solvency of a business organization, but they are even more interested in its **profitability.** *Profitable operations increase the value of the owners' equity* in the business. A company that continually operates unprofitably will eventually exhaust its resources and be forced out of existence. Therefore, most users of financial statements study these statements carefully for clues to the company's solvency and future profitability.

THE SHORT RUN VERSUS THE LONG RUN   In the short run, solvency and profitability may be independent of each other. A business may be operating profitably, but nevertheless run out of cash and thereby become insolvent. On the other hand, a company may operate unprofitably during a given year yet have enough cash to pay its bills and remain solvent.

Over a longer term, however, the goals of solvency and profitability go hand in hand. If a business is to survive, it must remain solvent and, in the long run, it must operate profitably.

LO 6 *Use a balance sheet to evaluate the solvency of an organization.*

EVALUATING SHORT-TERM SOLVENCY   One key indicator of short-term solvency is the relationship between an entity's *liquid* assets and the liabilities requiring payment *in the near future*. By studying the nature of a company's assets, and the amounts and due dates of its liabilities, users of financial statements often may anticipate whether the company is likely to have difficulty in meeting its upcoming obligations. This simple type of analysis often meets the needs of many *short-term* creditors. Evaluating long-term solvency is a more difficult matter and is discussed in later chapters.

In studying financial statements, users should *always* read the accompanying notes and the auditors' report.

---

[7]In this context, *creditors* include everyone to whom the business owes money. One may become a creditor of a business either by lending it money or by providing goods and services with payment due at a later date. *Investors,* on the other hand, are those persons having or considering an *ownership* interest in the organization.

YOUR TURN

You as a Loan Officer

Assume you are a loan officer at Santa Teresa Bank. In mid-December, 1998, Overnight applies for a 120-day "working capital" loan in the amount of $50,000 to help meet cash outlays projected during the first few months of operations.

Using the company's November 30 balance sheet (page 24), evaluate Overnight's short-term solvency. Would you make this short-term loan? Also, make any constructive recommendations which you consider appropriate.

*Our comments appear on page 53. (But before you read them, what would be your decision?)

THE NEED FOR ADEQUATE DISCLOSURE

The concept of adequate **disclosure** is an important generally accepted accounting principle. Adequate disclosure means that users of financial statements are informed of any facts *necessary for the proper interpretation* of the statements. Adequate disclosure may be made either in the body of the financial statements, or in *notes* accompanying the statements.

Among the events that require disclosure are significant financial events occurring *after* the balance sheet date, but before the financial statements have been issued to outsiders. For an example, let us refer to the December 31, 1998 balance sheet of Vagabond Travel Agency, Inc., illustrated on page 14. Assume that on January 4, 1999, the building owned by Vagabond is completely destroyed by fire. As the building existed at the end of 1998, it properly is included in the balance sheet dated December 31. However, users of this balance sheet need to be informed that the building *no longer exists*. The destruction of this building should be disclosed in a note accompanying the financial statements, such as the following:

Note 7: Events occurring subsequent to the balance sheet date

On January 4, 1999, a building shown in the balance sheet at $90,000 was destroyed by fire. The Company does not insure against this type of loss. The financial effects of this loss will be reflected in the Company's 1999 financial statements. The Company is continuing operations in rented facilities.

"Notes" to the statements contain vital information

In addition to important "subsequent events," many other situations may require disclosure in notes to the financial statements. Examples include lawsuits against the company, due dates of major liabilities, assets pledged as collateral to secure loans, amounts receivable from officers or other "insiders," and contractual commitments requiring large future cash outlays.

There is no comprehensive list of the items and events that may require disclosure. As a general rule, a company should disclose any financial facts that an intelligent person would consider *necessary to the proper interpretation* of the financial statements. Events that clearly are unimportant *do not* require disclosure.

THE RELIABILITY OF FINANCIAL STATEMENTS

Why should decision makers outside an organization regard financial statements as being fair and reliable? We already have identified three factors: (1) internal control, (2) the concept of adequate disclosure, and (3) audits performed by independent accounting firms. In the United States, federal securities laws provide additional assurance as to the reliability of financial statements.

LO 7 *Identify factors contributing to the reliability of financial statements.*

FEDERAL SECURITIES LAWS The federal government has enacted laws requiring that the financial statements of publicly owned companies be prepared in conformity with generally accepted accounting principles, including the concept of adequate disclosure. Any person who *knowingly causes such financial statements to be misleading* may face criminal penalties, and may also be held financially responsible for the losses incurred by anyone relying upon the statements. These securities laws apply to the management of the company issuing the statements and also to the independent auditors.

MANAGEMENT'S INTEREST IN FINANCIAL STATEMENTS

The management of a business organization is vitally concerned with the financial position of the business, and also with its profitability. Therefore, management is anxious to receive financial statements as frequently and as quickly as possible, so that it may take action to improve areas of weak performance. Most large organizations provide managers with financial statements on at least a monthly basis.

However, managers have a special interest in the *annual* financial statements, as these are the statements most widely used by decision makers outside of the organization. For example, if creditors view the year-end balance sheet as "strong," they will be more willing to extend credit to the business than if they regard the company's financial position as weak.

A strong balance sheet is one that shows relatively little debt, and large amounts of liquid assets relative to the liabilities due in the near future. Management can—and does—take steps to make the year-end balance sheet look as strong as possible. For example, cash purchases of assets may be delayed so that large amounts of cash will be on hand at the balance sheet date. Liabilities due in the near future may be paid, or replaced with longer-term liabilities.

These actions are called **window dressing**—legitimate measures taken by management to make a business look as strong as possible at the balance sheet date. Users of year-end balance sheets should realize that while these statements are "fair" and "reliable," they do not necessarily describe the "typical" financial position of the business. In its annual financial statements, almost every company tries to put its best foot forward. Many creditors, therefore, regard monthly or quarterly balance sheets as providing a more typical picture of a company's financial position.

COMPETENCE, INTEGRITY, AND PROFESSIONAL JUDGMENT

The preparation of accounting reports is not a mechanical task that can be performed by machine or even by well-trained clerical personnel. A characteristic common to all recognized professions—such as medicine, law, and accounting—is the need for individual practitioners to resolve many problems with their own *professional judgment*. The problems encountered in the practice of a profession are often complex, and the specific circumstances unique. Consequently, no written set of rules exists to provide answers in every situation.

LO 8 Discuss the importance of professional judgment and ethical conduct in accounting practice.

In preparing the financial statements of a large business organization, the company's accountants and its independent auditors must make many "judgment calls." For example:

- What constitutes "adequate" disclosure?
- At what point should a business in financial difficulties cease to be viewed as a going-concern?
- What types of investigative procedures are necessary to assure auditors that a company's financial statements represent a fair presentation?
- Which efforts by management represent legitimate window dressing, and which are inappropriate actions that make the financial statements misleading?

Unfortunately, judgmental decisions *always involve some risk of error.* Some errors in judgment result from carelessness or inexperience on the part of the decision makers. However, others occur simply because future events did not work out as had been anticipated.

If the public is to have confidence in the judgment of professional accountants, these accountants first must demonstrate that they possess the characteristics of *competence* and *integrity.*

PROFESSIONAL COMPETENCE   Both the accounting profession and state governments have taken steps to assure the public of the technical competence of certified public accountants (CPAs). CPAs are licensed by the states, in much the same manner as states license physicians and attorneys. The licensing requirements vary somewhat from state to state, but in general, an individual must have a college education with a major in accounting, pass a rigorous examination (the *Uniform CPA Examination*), and have several years of accounting experience. In addition, most states require all CPAs to spend at least 40 hours per year in "continuing education" programs throughout their professional careers.

Beginning in the year 2000, the AICPA will require its new members to have completed 30 semester hours of college work *beyond* a bachelor's degree—that is, a fifth year of college. Many states are amending their licensing laws to include this new educational requirement.

Managerial accountants are not required to be licensed as CPAs. However, they voluntarily may earn a **Certificate in Management Accounting (CMA)** or a Certificate in Internal Auditing (CIA) as evidence of their professional competence. The requirements for becoming a CMA or CIA are similar to those for becoming a CPA.

INTEGRITY AND ETHICS

Integrity means honesty and a strong commitment to ethical conduct—doing the "right thing." For a professional accountant, integrity is just as important as competence. However, it is far more difficult to test or enforce.

Associations of professional accountants, and also the state governments, have taken steps to encourage and enforce integrity within the profession. For example, several professional associations have developed *codes of professional ethics* for their members.[8] These codes are intended to help professional accountants fulfill their professional obligations with integrity.

One concept found in all professional codes of ethics for accountants is that accountants must *never knowingly be associated with misleading accounting information.* In fact, a professional accountant should resign his or her position rather than become involved in the preparation or distribution of misleading information.

Professional accounting associations investigate the backgrounds of individuals applying to take the professional competency examinations. These examinations also include questions that test the applicant's knowledge of professional ethics. In addition, most states include the AICPA's *Code of Professional Conduct* in their licensing requirements for CPAs. Thus, violations of this code may cause a CPA to lose his or her license to practice public accounting.

Of course, the basic concepts of **ethical conduct**—acting with honor and integrity—apply to management as well as to professional accountants.

The users of financial statements should recognize that the reliability of these statements is affected by the competence, integrity, and professional judgment of the accountants and auditors involved in the financial reporting process. But as we have previously stated, audited financial statements—and the accounting profession—have established an impressive track record of reliability. More than any other factor, the competence and integrity of professional accountants ensure the fairness and reliability of financial statements.

---

[8]In accounting, codes of professional ethics have been developed by the American Institute of Certified Public Accountants (AICPA), the Institute of Management Accountants, and the Institute of Internal Auditors.

OUR APPROACH(ES) TO ETHICS In this text, we address the topic of ethical conduct on two levels. The first level involves the general concepts of honesty, fairness, and adequate disclosure. Most chapters include assignment material in which you are asked to make "judgment calls" in applying these concepts. (These assignments are identified by the scales of justice logo appearing in the left margin.)

In Chapter 14 we address ethical conduct on a more technical level—the formal codes of ethics developed within the accounting profession.

*SUPPLEMENTAL TOPIC A

ANNOTATED BALANCE SHEET OF A PUBLICLY OWNED COMPANY

Shown on the following page is the *consolidated* balance sheet of Toys "R" Us, Inc., a publicly owned corporation.[1] This balance sheet is adapted from the company's annual report, which appears in Appendix A at the end of this textbook.

The purpose of this illustration is to expose you to the balance sheet of a publicly owned corporation. At this stage of your study in accounting, you are not expected to understand every item in this financial statement. For example, we have not yet discussed such topics as deferred income taxes, foreign currency adjustments, and treasury stock.

Notice that the dollar amounts in this balance sheet are stated in *thousands* of dollars. Thus, the company's cash and cash equivalents, shown at $369,833, actually amount to *$369,833,000*. The economic activities of large corporations cannot be measured to the last dollar. Indeed, such precision would be quite unnecessary for the types of decisions made by investors and creditors.

Notice also that the Toys balance sheet contains some minor variations from our text illustrations. For example, this company combines land and buildings under the single caption "real estate." Generally accepted accounting principles provide a *reasonable degree of comparability* among the financial statements of different companies, but they *do not establish complete uniformity*.

The term "current assets" in the Toys balance sheet refers to cash and assets expected to be converted into cash or consumed in business operations within the coming year. These are the company's most "liquid" assets. Current liabilities are existing obligations payable within one year.

These balance sheet *classifications* group together assets or liabilities with similar characteristics. This assists decision makers in evaluating the company's financial position. (In our illustration, the classifications widely used in balance sheets appear in black type.)

WANT TO LEARN MORE ABOUT TOYS "R" US? Toys "R" Us is one of the companies we use most frequently in our illustrations and assignment materials. If you want to learn more about this company, a good starting point is the annual report in Appendix A. This report will tell you much about the company—its history, its financial position, the results of recent operations, and management's plans for the future.

You also can find a wealth of information on the Internet. (See "Net Connections" on pages 34–35.)

---

[1]The term "consolidated" means that this balance sheet includes the assets and liabilities of all businesses owned by Toys "R" Us. This includes Kids "R" Us, Babies "R" Us, and Toys "R" Us International.

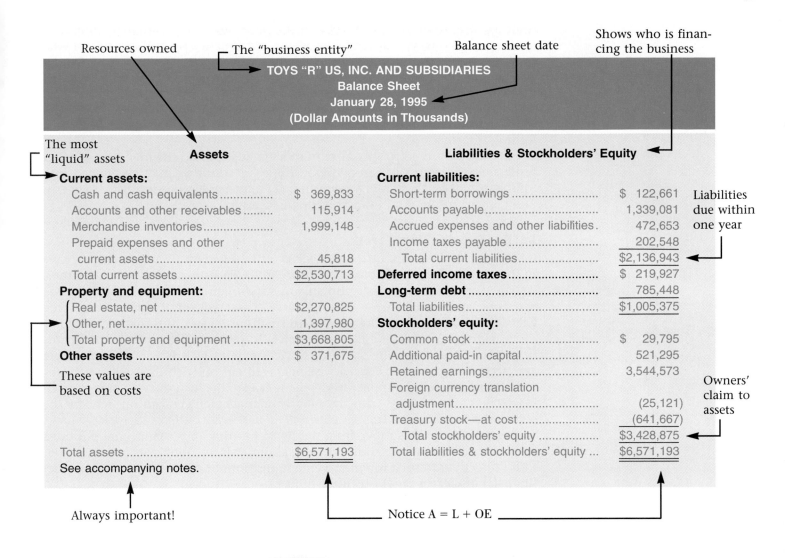

Resources owned

The "business entity"

Balance sheet date

Shows who is financing the business

TOYS "R" US, INC. AND SUBSIDIARIES
Balance Sheet
January 28, 1995
(Dollar Amounts in Thousands)

The most "liquid" assets

Assets		Liabilities & Stockholders' Equity	
Current assets:		**Current liabilities:**	
Cash and cash equivalents	$ 369,833	Short-term borrowings	$ 122,661
Accounts and other receivables	115,914	Accounts payable	1,339,081
Merchandise inventories	1,999,148	Accrued expenses and other liabilities	472,653
Prepaid expenses and other		Income taxes payable	202,548
current assets	45,818	Total current liabilities	$2,136,943
Total current assets	$2,530,713	**Deferred income taxes**	$ 219,927
Property and equipment:		**Long-term debt**	785,448
Real estate, net	$2,270,825	Total liabilities	$1,005,375
Other, net	1,397,980	**Stockholders' equity:**	
Total property and equipment	$3,668,805	Common stock	$ 29,795
Other assets	$ 371,675	Additional paid-in capital	521,295
		Retained earnings	3,544,573
		Foreign currency translation	
		adjustment	(25,121)
		Treasury stock—at cost	(641,667)
		Total stockholders' equity	$3,428,875
Total assets	$6,571,193	Total liabilities & stockholders' equity	$6,571,193

See accompanying notes.

Liabilities due within one year

These values are based on costs

Owners' claim to assets

Always important!

Notice A = L + OE

CAREERS IN ACCOUNTING

THE ACCOUNTING "PROFESSION"

Accounting—along with such fields as architecture, engineering, law, medicine, and theology—is considered a "profession." What distinguishes a profession from other disciplines? There is no widely recognized definition of a profession, but all of these fields have several characteristics in common.

LO 9 Describe various career opportunities in accounting.

First, all professions involve a complex and evolving body of knowledge. In accounting, the complexity and the ever-changing nature of the business world, financial reporting requirements, and income tax laws certainly meet this criterion.

In all professions, practitioners must use their professional judgment to resolve many problems and dilemmas. Throughout this text, we will point out situations requiring accountants to exercise professional judgment.

Of greatest importance, however, is the unique responsibility of professionals *to serve the public's best interest, even at the sacrifice of personal advantage.* This responsibility stems from the fact that the public has little technical knowledge in the professions, yet fair and competent performance by professionals is vital to the public's health, safety, or well-being. The practice of medicine, for example, directly affects public health, while engineering affects public safety. Accounting affects the public's well-being in many ways, because accounting information is used in the allocation of economic resources throughout society. Thus, accountants have a social responsibility not to be associated with misleading information.

Accountants tend to specialize in specific fields, as do the members of other professions. In terms of career opportunities, accounting may be divided into four broad areas: (1) public accounting, (2) managerial accounting, (3) governmental accounting, and (4) accounting education.

PUBLIC ACCOUNTING

Certified public accountants, called CPAs, offer a variety of accounting services to the public. These individuals may work in a CPA firm, or as sole practitioners.

The work of CPAs consists primarily of auditing financial statements, income tax work, and management advisory services (management consulting). Some CPAs also offer bookkeeping services to small businesses, but many do not.

Providing management advisory services is, perhaps, the fastest growing area in public accounting. The advisory services extend well beyond tax planning and accounting matters; CPAs advise management on such diverse issues as international mergers, manufacturing processes, and the introduction of new products. The entry of CPAs into the field of management consulting reflects the fact that *financial considerations enter into almost every business decision.*

A great many CPAs move from public accounting into managerial positions with their client organizations. These "alumni" from public accounting often move directly into such top management positions as controller, treasurer, chief financial officer, or chief executive officer.

MANAGERIAL ACCOUNTING

In contrast to the CPA who serves many clients, the managerial (or management) accountant works for one enterprise. Managerial accountants develop and interpret accounting information designed specifically to meet the various needs of management.

The chief accounting officer of an organization usually is called the **controller,** in recognition of the fact that one basic purpose of accounting data is to aid in controlling business operations. The controller is part of the top management team, which is responsible for running the business, setting its objectives, and seeing that these objectives are achieved.

In addition to developing information to assist managers, managerial accountants are responsible for operating the company's accounting system, including the recording of transactions and the preparation of financial statements, tax returns, and other accounting reports. As the responsibilities of managerial accountants are so broad, many areas of specialization have developed. Among the more important are the following.

FINANCIAL FORECASTING A financial forecast (or budget) is a plan of financial operations for some *future* period. Actually, forecasting is much like financial reporting, except that the accountant is estimating future outcomes, rather than measuring past results. A forecast provides each department of a business with financial goals. Comparison of the results actually achieved with these forecast amounts is one widely used means of evaluating departmental performance.

COST ACCOUNTING Knowing the cost of each business operation and of each manufactured product is essential to the efficient management of a business. Determining the per-unit cost of business activities and of manufactured products, and interpreting this cost data, comprise a specialized field called *cost accounting.*

INTERNAL AUDITING Large organizations usually maintain a staff of **internal auditors.** Internal auditors are charged with studying the internal control structure and evaluating the efficiency of many different aspects of the company's operations. As employees, internal auditors are not "independent" of the organization. Therefore, they *do not* perform independent audits of the company's financial statements.

Careers in managerial accounting often lead to positions in top management—just as do careers in public accounting.

GOVERNMENTAL ACCOUNTING

Governmental agencies use accounting information to allocate resources and to control their operations. Therefore, their need for management accountants is similar to that in business organizations.

In addition, the government performs several specialized audit functions.

THE GAO: WHO AUDITS THE GOVERNMENT? The General Accounting Office (GAO) audits many agencies of the federal government, and also some private organizations doing business with the government. The GAO reports its findings directly to Congress. Congress, in turn, often discloses these findings to the public.

GAO investigations may be designed either to evaluate the efficiency of an entity's operations, or to determine the fairness of accounting information reported to the government.

THE IRS: AUDITS OF INCOME TAX RETURNS Another governmental agency that performs extensive auditing work is the Internal Revenue Service (IRS). The IRS handles the millions of income tax returns filed annually by individuals and business organizations, and frequently performs auditing functions to verify data contained in these returns.

THE SEC: THE "WATCHDOG" OF FINANCIAL REPORTING The SEC works closely with the FASB in establishing generally accepted accounting principles. Each year large publicly owned corporations must file audited financial statements with the SEC. If the SEC believes that a company's financial statements are deficient in any way, it conducts an investigation. If the SEC concludes that federal securities laws have been violated, it initiates legal action against the reporting entity and responsible individuals.

Many other governmental agencies, including the FBI, the Treasury Department, and the FDIC (Federal Deposit Insurance Corporation), use accountants to audit compliance with government regulations and to investigate suspected criminal activity. People beginning their careers in governmental accounting often move into top administrative positions.

ACCOUNTING EDUCATION

Many accountants, including your instructor and the authors of this textbook, have chosen to pursue careers in accounting education. A position as an accounting faculty member offers opportunities for research and consulting, and an unusual degree of freedom in developing individual skills. Accounting educators contribute to the accounting profession in many ways. One, of course, lies in effective teaching; another, in publishing significant research findings; and a third, in influencing top students to pursue careers in accounting.

WHAT ABOUT BOOKKEEPING?

Some people think that the work of professional accountants consists primarily of bookkeeping. Actually, it doesn't. In fact, many professional accountants do *little or no* bookkeeping.

Bookkeeping is the clerical side of accounting—the recording of routine transactions and day-to-day record keeping. Such tasks are performed primarily by computers and skilled clerical personnel, not by "accountants."[1]

Professional accountants are involved more with the *interpretation and use* of accounting information than with its actual preparation. Their work includes evaluating the efficiency of operations, resolving complex financial reporting issues, forecasting the results of future operations, performing audits, engaging in tax planning, and designing efficient accounting systems. There is very little that is "routine" about the work of a professional accountant.

A person might become a proficient bookkeeper in a few weeks or months. To become a professional accountant, however, is a far greater challenge. It requires years of study, experience, and an on-going commitment to "keeping current."

We will illustrate and explain a number of bookkeeping procedures in this text, particularly in the next several chapters. But teaching bookkeeping skills is *not* our goal; the primary purpose of this text is to develop your abilities to *understand and use* accounting information in today's business world.

ACCOUNTING AS A "STEPPING STONE"

We have mentioned that many professional accountants leave their accounting careers for key positions in management or administration. An accounting background is invaluable in such positions, because top management works continuously with issues defined and described in accounting terms.

An especially useful stepping-stone is experience in public accounting. CPAs have the unusual opportunity of getting an "inside look" at many different business organizations.

NET CONNECTIONS

You may want to explore further some of the topics discussed in this chapter. The Internet is an ideal tool for such independent study.

We explain in detail how to access the Net in Appendix B of this textbook. But for those of you who already know how, here are a few interesting sites you might visit:[2]

Rutgers University maintains an excellent site that addresses a wide range of accounting issues. Reach Rutgers at:

www.rutgers.edu/accounting/raw.htm

Scroll down the Rutgers home page and see what interests you. You can use this page as a "launch pad" to reach the home pages of many professional accounting associations.

---

[1]Some CPAs do "keep books" for small businesses. But these CPAs also serve their clients in many other ways, such as preparing tax returns, doing tax planning, and acting as financial advisors.

[2]Site addresses sometimes change. If you find an address which is no longer active, please let us know.

Becker CPA Review maintains a very interesting site on careers in accounting—including information about salaries:

www.beckercpa.com

You also may want to visit EDGAR, the SEC's giant data base:

www.sec.gov/cgi-bin/srch-edgar

Once you're in EDGAR, just type in the name of a publicly owned company that you'd like to know more about.

To learn more about Toys "R" Us, either type "Toys" in the EDGAR search box, or visit one of the company's own websites. For example, try:

www.shareholder.com/toy

We'd also like you to visit our home page:

www.magpie.org/cyberlab

Among other things, we have "hot buttons," which send you directly to many of our recommended sites.

We also encourage you to surf—that is, to explore on your own. New sites open all the time. If you find something interesting, drop us a line. You'll find our e-mail addresses on our home page.

SUMMARY OF LEARNING OBJECTIVES

① Explain why people other than professional accountants benefit from an understanding of accounting.
Everyone who participates in economic activity uses accounting information. Almost everyone also generates accounting information—in income tax returns, loan applications, and often as part of a job. Accounting is the "language of business." It is difficult to participate effectively in the business world if you don't speak the language.

② Define *accounting, financial reporting, financial statements, public information,* and *generally accepted accounting principles.*
Accounting is the means by which we measure and describe economic activities. Financial reporting means supplying general-purpose financial information about a business to people *outside* the organization. This information is primarily in the form of financial statements—a set of four related accounting reports describing the financial position of the business and the results of its operations.

The financial statements of publicly owned companies are public information—meaning they are available to everyone—and are prepared in conformity with a set of "ground rules" called generally accepted accounting principles.

③ Prepare a balance sheet and describe its content.
A balance sheet is a financial statement showing the *financial position* (defined in terms of assets, liabilities, and owners' equity) of a business entity at a specific date. However, a balance sheet does *not* show how much a business is currently worth.

Assets are economic resources owned by the business; liabilities are debts or financial obligations of the business; and owners' equity is the residual claim of the owners to the assets of the business.

④ Describe the accounting principles involved in asset valuation.
Most assets are valued in accordance with the *cost principle.* This generally accepted accounting principle indicates that the valuation of assets in a balance sheet should be based upon historical cost, not upon current market value. Three other accounting principles supporting the valuation of assets at cost are the *going-concern assumption,* the *objectivity principle,* and the *stable-dollar assumption.*

⑤ Indicate the effects of business transactions upon the accounting equation and the balance sheet.
A transaction which increases total assets must also in-crease either total liabilities or owners' equity. Similarly, a transaction which decreases total assets must decrease either total liabilities or owners' equity. Some transactions increase one asset while decreasing another; such transactions do not change the total amounts of assets, liabilities, or owners' equity.

⑥ Use a balance sheet to evaluate the solvency of an organization.
One step in evaluating the short-term solvency (debt-paying ability) of a business is to compare the amount of liquid assets with the amount of liabilities coming due within the near future.

⑦ Identify factors contributing to the reliability of financial statements.
Factors contributing to the reliability of financial statements include: the objectivity principle, the concept of adequate disclosure, internal control, audits by independent CPAs, federal securities laws, and the competence and integrity of professional accountants.

⑧ Discuss the importance of professional judgment and of ethical conduct in accounting.
Accountants must rely upon their professional judgment to resolve many issues arising in accounting practice. What must be disclosed? How should transactions be recorded when no "official" accounting principles seem to apply? At what point should a business cease to be viewed as a going concern?

If the public is to have confidence in accounting information, accountants' integrity—or ethical conduct—is just as important as their technical competence. Accountants should never knowingly be associated with misleading accounting information.

⁹ Describe various career opportunities in accounting.
Career opportunities in accounting include public accounting, management accounting, governmental accounting, and accounting education. Public accountants render auditing, income tax, and management advisory services to a variety of clients. Management accountants fill the needs for accounting information within one specific organization. Governmental accounting careers include management accounting and various types of auditing. Accounting education provides career opportunities in teaching and research.

Supplemental Topic B, "Careers in Accounting."

A characteristic of an accounting textbook is that each new chapter builds upon those which have come before. For example, in the next three chapters we will expand our Overnight Auto Service example to illustrate double-entry accounting, the use of accounting records, and the measurement and reporting of business income.

Our goal in this text is to help you develop a basic understanding of accounting information. You should find this knowledge useful on an almost daily basis, whether you are a user or preparer of that information. Remember, to understand and use accounting information effectively, you also must understand:

● The *nature of the underlying economic activities.*

● The *assumptions* and *measurement techniques* involved in the accounting process.

● How to *relate accounting information* to specific business decisions.

We will focus on these topics throughout the text.

KEY TERMS INTRODUCED OR EMPHASIZED IN CHAPTER 1

Note to Students: Each chapter includes a glossary explaining the key accounting terms introduced or emphasized. You should review these glossaries carefully; an understanding of accounting terminology is an essential step in the study of accounting. These terms will appear frequently in later chapters, in problem material, and in examination questions. (Because of the broad and introductory nature of Chapter 1, this glossary is longer than those in later chapters.)

Accounting equation (p. 19)   Assets are equal to the sum of liabilities plus owners' equity (A = L + OE). This equation is reflected in the format of the balance sheet.

Accounting system (p. 7)   The personnel, procedures, records, forms, and devices used by an organization to develop and communicate accounting information.

American Accounting Association (AAA) (p. 12)   An association of accounting educators that sponsors research and takes positions on various accounting issues, but has no official authority.

American Institute of Certified Public Accountants (AICPA) (p. 11)   The national professional association of certified public accountants (CPAs). Carries on extensive research and is influential in improving accounting standards. Also develops auditing standards and administers the *Uniform CPA Examination.*

Annual report (p. 6)   A document issued annually by publicly owned corporations to their stockholders. Includes audited financial statements for several years, as well as non-financial information about the company and its operations.

Assets (p. 15)   Economic resources owned by an entity.

Auditing (p. 5)   Performing an investigation enabling the auditors to express an independent opinion (auditors' report) as to the fairness and completeness of a set of financial statements.

Auditors' report (p. 6)   The professional opinion of a CPA firm as to the fairness of the financial statements.

Balance sheet (p. 5)   The financial statement that shows the financial position of an entity by summarizing its assets, liabilities, and owners' equity at a specific date.

Business entity (p. 14)   An economic unit that controls resources, incurs obligations, and engages in business activities.

Capital stock (p. 18)   Transferable units of ownership in a corporation.

Certified Management Accountant (CMA) (p. 29)   An accountant who has demonstrated his or her professional competence by earning a Certificate in Management Accounting. These certificates are awarded by the *Institute of Management Accountants.*

Certified Public Accountant (CPA) (p. 5)   An independent professional accountant licensed by a state to offer auditing and other accounting services to clients.

Comparative financial statements (p. 6)   Financial statements for two or more years shown in side-by-side columns. Designed to assist users in identifying trends and significant changes.

Controller (p. 32)   The chief accounting officer within an organization.

Corporation (p. 13)   A business organized as a separate legal entity and chartered by a state, with ownership divided into transferable shares of capital stock.

Cost principle (p. 15)   The widely used principle of accounting for assets at their original cost to the current owner.

Creditor (p. 17)   A lender; an entity to which money is owed.

Disclosure ("adequate") (p. 27)   The accounting principle of providing any financial facts necessary for the proper *interpretation* of financial statements.

EDGAR (p. 7)   A database on the Internet, maintained by the SEC. EDGAR contains financial information about every publicly owned company in the United States, and is available at no cost to the user. Site address:

www.sec.gov/cgi-bin/srch-edgar

Ethical conduct (p. 29)   Doing "the right thing." Acting with honor and integrity, even at the sacrifice of personal advantage.

Fair (p. 6)   A term used by accountants to describe a set of financial statements that are complete, not misleading, and prepared in conformity with generally accepted accounting principles. Auditors express their opinions as to the "fairness" of financial statements.

Financial Accounting Standards Board (FASB) (p. 10)   An independent group that conducts research into accounting problems and issues authoritative pronouncements as to generally accepted accounting principles.

Financial position (p. 5)   The financial resources and obligations of an organization, as described in a balance sheet.

Financial reporting (p. 4)   The process of periodically providing "general-purpose" financial information (such as financial statements) to persons *outside* the business organization.

Financial statements (p. 5)   Four related accounting reports that concisely summarize the current financial position of an entity and the results of its operations for the preceding year (or other time period).

Generally accepted accounting principles (GAAP) (p. 9)   The accounting concepts, measurement techniques, and standards of presentation used in financial statements. Examples include the cost principle and objectivity.

Going-concern assumption (p. 16)   An assumption by accountants that a business will operate indefinitely unless specific evidence to the contrary exists, such as impending bankruptcy.

Income statement (p. 5)   A financial statement indicating the profit (or loss) of a business over a period of time, usually a year.

Institute of Management Accountants (IMA) (p. 12)   The national professional association of management accountants. Sponsors many programs which improve the usefulness of accounting information. Also establishes the criteria for becoming a certified management accountant (CMA).

Internal auditors (p. 33)   Accounting personnel who specialize in evaluating the efficiency of operations and making recommendations for improvements.

Internal control (p. 9)   All measures used within an organization to assure management that the organization is operating in accordance with management's policies and plans.

Liabilities (p. 17)   Debts or obligations of an entity that have arisen from past transactions. The claims of *creditors* against the assets of a business.

Objectivity principle (p. 16)   Accountants' tendency to base accounting measurements upon dollar amounts that are factual and subject to independent verification.

Owners' equity (p. 17)   The excess of assets over liabilities. The amount of the owners' investment in a business, including profits from successful operations which have been retained in the business.

Partnership (p. 12)   An unincorporated business owned by two or more persons voluntarily associated as partners.

Profitability (p. 26)   An increase in owners' equity resulting from successful business operations. (This concept is discussed further in Chapter 3.)

Public information (p. 4)   Information which, by law, is available to the general public. The annual financial statements of publicly owned businesses are public information.

Publicly owned corporations (p. 4)   Corporations in which members of the general public may buy or sell shares of capital stock.

Retained earnings (p. 18)   The portion of the owners' equity in a corporation that has accumulated as a result of profitable business operations.

Securities and Exchange Commission (SEC) (p. 11)   The federal agency with the legal power to establish financial reporting requirements for large, publicly owned corporations. Also enforces federal securities laws, bringing legal action against possible offenders.

Sole proprietorship (p. 12)   An unincorporated business owned by an individual.

Solvency (p. 26)   Having the financial ability to pay debts as they become due.

Stable-dollar assumption (p. 16)   An assumption by accountants that the dollar is a stable unit of measure, like the mile or the gallon. A simplifying assumption that permits adding or subtracting dollar amounts originating in different time periods. Unfortunately, the assumption technically is incorrect and may seriously distort accounting information during periods of severe inflation.

Statement of cash flows (p. 5)   A financial statement summarizing the cash receipts and cash payments in the time period covered by the income statement.

Statement of retained earnings (p. 5)   A financial statement explaining certain changes in the amount of the owners' investment in the business.

Stockholders (p. 13)   Owners of capital stock in a corporation; hence, the owners of the corporation.

Stockholders' equity (p. 17)   The *owners' equity* in an entity organized as a corporation.

Transactions (p. 7)   Events that cause an immediate change in the financial position of an entity and that can be measured objectively in monetary terms. In current practice, transactions serve as the basis for recording financial activity.

Window dressing (p. 28)   Legitimate measures taken by management to make a business look as strong as possible at the balance sheet date.

DEMONSTRATION PROBLEM

The accounting data (listed alphabetically) for Crystal Auto Wash at September 30, 19__, are shown below. The figure for Cash is not given but it can be determined when all the available information is assembled in the form of a balance sheet.

Accounts payable	$14,000	Land	$68,000
Accounts receivable	800	Machinery & equipment	65,000
Buildings	52,000	Notes payable (due in 30 days)	29,000
Capital stock	50,000	Retained earnings	99,400
Cash	?	Supplies	400
Income taxes payable	3,000		

INSTRUCTIONS

a. Prepare a balance sheet at September 30, 19__.

b. Does this balance sheet indicate that the company is in a strong financial position? Explain briefly.

SOLUTION TO DEMONSTRATION PROBLEM

a.

CRYSTAL AUTO WASH
Balance Sheet
September 30, 19__

Assets		Liabilities & Stockholders' Equity		
Cash	$ 9,200	**Liabilities:**		
Accounts receivable	800	Notes payable (due in 30 days)		$ 29,000
Supplies	400	Accounts payable		14,000
Land	68,000	Income taxes payable		3,000
Buildings	52,000	Total liabilities		$ 46,000
Machinery & equipment	65,000	**Stockholders' equity:**		
		Capital stock	$ 50,000	
		Retained earnings	99,400	149,400
Total	$195,400	Total		$195,400

b. The balance sheet indicates that Crystal Auto Wash is in a *very weak* financial position. The highly "liquid" assets—cash and receivables—total only $10,000, but the company has $46,000 in debts due in the near future. Based upon this balance sheet, the company appears to be insolvent.*

---

*Perhaps the company can generate enough cash from its daily operations to pay its debts. A balance sheet does not indicate the *rate* at which cash flows into the business. A recent statement of cash flows would be useful in making a more complete analysis of the company's financial position.

SELF-TEST QUESTIONS

The answers to these questions appear on page 53. (Note: In order to review as many chapter concepts as possible, some self-test questions include *more than one* correct answer. In these cases, indicate *all* of the correct answers.)

1. Almost *everyone* will benefit from a basic understanding of accounting terms and concepts, as this knowledge will enable them to: (Select the single *best* answer.)
   a. Become professional accountants.
   b. Act in an ethical manner.
   c. Better understand economic activities.
   d. Prepare their own income tax returns.

2. A "set" of financial statements: (Indicate all correct answers.)
   a. Is intended to assist users in evaluating the financial position, profitability, and future prospects of an entity.
   b. Is intended to assist the IRS in determining the amount of income taxes owed by a business organization.
   c. Includes "notes" disclosing items necessary for the proper interpretation of the statements.
   d. Is intended to assist investors and creditors in making decisions involving the allocation of economic resources.

3. Generally accepted accounting principles: (Indicate all correct answers.)
   a. Include only the official pronouncements of the standard-setting organizations, such as the FASB, the SEC, and the AICPA.
   b. May include customary accounting practices in widespread use even if not mentioned specifically in official pronouncements.
   c. Eliminate the need for professional judgment in the preparation of financial statements.
   d. Change and evolve as business organizations enter into new forms of business activity.

4. Which of the following statements is *not* consistent with generally accepted accounting principles relating to asset valuation?
   a. Assets are originally recorded in accounting records at their cost to the business entity.
   b. Subtracting total liabilities from total assets indicates what the owners' equity in the business is worth under current market conditions.
   c. Accountants assume that assets such as office supplies, land, and buildings will be used in business operations, rather than sold at current market prices.
   d. Accountants prefer to base the valuation of assets upon objective, verifiable evidence rather than upon appraisals or personal opinion.

5. Arrowhead Boat Shop purchased a truck for $12,000, making a down payment of $5,000 cash and signing a $7,000 note payable due in 60 days. (Indicate all correct answers.)
   a. Total assets increased by $12,000.
   b. Total liabilities increased by $7,000.
   c. From the viewpoint of a short-term creditor, this transaction makes the business less solvent.
   d. This transaction had no immediate effect upon the owners' equity in the business.

6. A transaction caused a $10,000 *decrease* in both total assets and total liabilities. This transaction could have been:
   a. Purchase of a delivery truck for $10,000 cash.
   b. An asset with a cost of $10,000 was destroyed by fire.
   c. Repayment of a $10,000 bank loan.
   d. Collection of a $10,000 account receivable.

7. Which of the following factors contribute to the *reliability* of the information contained in financial statements? (Indicate all correct answers.)
   a. The competence and integrity of professional accountants.
   b. Federal securities laws and the SEC.
   c. Internal control structures and audits by independent CPA firms.
   d. The concept of adequate disclosure.

8. Which of the following statements relating to the role of professional judgment in the financial reporting process are valid? (Indicate all correct answers.)
   a. Different accountants may evaluate similar situations differently.
   b. The determination of which items should be disclosed in notes to financial statements requires professional judgment.
   c. Once a complete list of generally accepted accounting principles is prepared, judgment need no longer enter into the financial reporting process.
   d. The possibility always exists that professional judgment later may prove to have been incorrect.

*9. Which of the following statements regarding accounting careers is the *least* valid?
   a. Management accountants, CPAs, and the SEC all participate in the process of financial reporting.
   b. The principal function of internal auditors is to issue reports on the fairness of their company's financial statements.
   c. Careers in accounting education often involve research and consulting.
   d. A background in accounting may serve as a useful stepping-stone to positions in top management.

ASSIGNMENT MATERIAL

DISCUSSION QUESTIONS

One objective of these questions is to give you an opportunity to demonstrate and develop your *communication skills*. Therefore, we ask that you answer each question in your own words.

1. In broad general terms, what is the purpose of accounting?

2. Why is a knowledge of accounting terms and concepts useful to persons other than professional accountants?

3. What is *public information?* What does this concept have to do with financial reporting?

4. In general terms, what does a set of *financial statements* describe? Identify the specific statements and other information that comprise a complete *set* of financial statements.

5. Are financial statements the *only means* by which decision makers outside of management obtain information about the financial position, profitability, and future prospects of a business?

6. What is "EDGAR"? Who is likely to use it?

7. Define the term *business transaction*. Give several examples of business transactions, and several examples of important events in the life of a business that *do not* qualify as "transactions." What is the relationship between business transactions and the information contained in financial statements?

8. Explain briefly why each of the following groups is interested in the financial statements of a business?
   a. Creditors.
   b. Potential investors.
   c. Labor unions.

---

*Supplemental Topic B, "Careers in Accounting."

9. What is the purpose of *internal control?*

10. Briefly explain the term *generally accepted accounting principles.* Where do these principles come from?

11. Which is more useful to potential investors, a company's *financial statements* for the current year or its *annual report?* Explain.

12. Identify the factors which make the corporate form of business organization attractive to investors who will not participate personally in management of the business.

13. State briefly the purpose and content of a balance sheet. Does a balance sheet show how much a business is currently "worth"? Explain.

14. Why is owners' equity considered to be a *residual claim* to the assets of a business organization? Can the owners' equity in a business be a *negative* amount? Explain.

15. The owners' equity in a business arises from what two factors? What two factors can cause decreases in owners' equity?

16. State the accounting equation in two alternative forms.

17. Why are the total assets shown in a balance sheet always equal to the total of the liabilities and the owners' equity?

18. Explain the general content and purposes of a *business plan.*

19. Can a business transaction cause one asset to increase without affecting any other asset, liability, or the owners' equity? Explain.

20. Define *solvency.* Suggest a relationship within a company's balance sheet that potential creditors might use in evaluating the company's solvency in the short term.

21. What is meant by the term "adequate disclosure"? Give several examples of items that may require "disclosure" in financial statements.

22. Describe at least four factors that contribute to the *reliability* of financial statements.

23. What is meant by the phrase "a *strong* balance sheet"?

24. Describe the term "window dressing." Why should users of financial statements be aware of this concept? Explain.

*25. Identify four broad areas of *career opportunities* in accounting. Is an accounting background of any use to an individual who does not intend to make a life-long career in accounting?

*26. What are the principal types of services rendered by CPAs? Why is experience in public accounting especially useful as a stepping-stone to a career in the top management of a business organization?

EXERCISE 1-1
You as a User of
Accounting Information

EXERCISE 1-2
Users of Accounting
Information

EXERCISES

Identify several ways in which *you* currently use accounting information in your life as a student. Also, identify several situations in which, while you are still a student, you might be required to supply financial information about yourself to others.

Boeing Company is the largest manufacturer of commercial aircraft in the United States and is a major employer in Seattle, Washington. Explain why each of the following individuals or organizations would be interested in financial information about the company.

a. **California Public Employees' Retirement System,** one of the world's largest pension funds.

b. **China Airlines,** a rapidly growing airline serving the Pacific Rim.

c. Henry James, a real estate investor considering building apartments in the Seattle area.

*Supplemental Topic B, "Careers in Accounting."

  d. Boeing's top management.

  e. **International Aerospace Machinists,** a labor union representing many Boeing employees.

EXERCISE 1-3
What Is Financial Reporting

A major focus of this course is the process of financial reporting.

a. What is meant by the term *financial reporting?*

b. What are the principal accounting reports involved in the financial reporting process? In general terms, what is the purpose of these reports?

c. Do all business entities engage in financial reporting? Explain.

d. How does society benefit from the financial reporting process?

EXERCISE 1-4
Generally Accepted Accounting Principles

Generally accepted accounting principles play an important role in financial reporting.

a. What is meant by the phrase "generally accepted accounting principles"?

b. What are the major sources of these principles?

c. Is there a comprehensive list of generally accepted accounting principles? Explain.

d. What types of accounting reports are prepared in conformity with generally accepted accounting principles?

EXERCISE 1-5
Accounting Organizations
LO 2

Describe the roles of the following organizations in establishing generally accepted accounting principles:

a. The FASB.

b. The AICPA.

c. The SEC.

d. From which of these organizations can you most easily obtain financial information about publicly owned companies?

EXERCISE 1-6
The Nature of Assets and Liabilities

a. Define assets. Give three examples of assets other than cash that might appear in the balance sheet of (1) **American Airlines** and, (2) a professional sports team such as the **Boston Celtics.**

b. Define liabilities. Give three examples of liabilities that might appear in the balance sheet of (1) American Airlines and, (2) a professional sports team such as the Boston Celtics.

EXERCISE 1-7
Preparing a Balance Sheet and an Introduction to Financial Statement Analysis

The night manager of Prestige Limousine Service, who had no accounting background, prepared the following balance sheet for the company at February 28, 1998. The dollar amounts were taken directly from the company's accounting records and are correct. However, the balance sheet contains a number of errors in its headings, format, and the classification of assets, liabilities, and owners' equity.

PRESTIGE LIMO Manager's Report 8 PM Saturday			
Assets		**Owners' Equity**	
Retained earnings	$228,000	Accounts receivable	$ 88,000
Cash	56,000	Accounts payable	60,000
Building	150,000	Capital stock	300,000
Supplies	5,000	Land	140,000
Automobiles	165,000	Income taxes payable	16,000
	$604,000		$604,000

a. Prepare a corrected balance sheet. Include a proper heading.

b. Is Prestige a corporation or an unincorporated business? How can you tell? Over the life of the company, has the business been profitable or unprofitable? Again, how can you tell?

c. Prestige does not now have enough cash to pay its accounts payable and income tax liability. Does this mean that the company is insolvent? Explain.

EXERCISE 1-8
Accounting Principles
and Asset Valuation

The following cases relate to the valuation of assets. Consider each case independently:

a. World-Wide Travel Agency has office supplies costing $1,700 on hand at the balance sheet date. These supplies were purchased from a supplier that does not give cash refunds. World-Wide's management believes that the company could sell these supplies for no more than $500 if it were to advertise them for sale. However, the company expects to use these supplies and to purchase more when they are gone. In its balance sheet, the supplies are valued at $500.

b. Zenith Corporation purchased land in 1955 for $20,000. In 1998, it purchased a similar parcel of land for $300,000. In its 1998 balance sheet, the company valued these two parcels of land at a combined value of $320,000.

c. At December 30, 1998, Lenier, Inc., purchased a computer system from a mail-order supplier for $14,000. The retail value of the system— according to the mail-order supplier—was $20,000. On January 7, however, the system was stolen during a burglary. In its December 31, 1998 balance sheet, Lenier showed this computer system at $14,000 and made no reference to its retail value or to the burglary.

In each case, indicate the appropriate balance sheet valuation of the asset under generally accepted accounting principles. If the valuation assigned by the company is incorrect, briefly explain the accounting principles that have been violated. On the other hand, if the valuation is correct, identify the accounting principles that justify this valuation.

EXERCISE 1-9
Using the Accounting
Equation

Compute the missing amount in each of the following three lines.

	Assets	= Liabilities	+ Owners' Equity
a.	$558,000	$135,000	? 423,000
b.	435,503	60,500	$375,000
c.	907,500	? 845,000	62,500

d. As a lender, which of the three companies above would you consider the least "creditworthy"?

EXERCISE 1-10
Effects of Business
Transactions

A number of business transactions carried out by Green River Farms are shown below:

a. Purchased a computer on credit.

b. Issued capital stock in exchange for cash.

c. Purchased office equipment for cash.

d. Collected an account receivable.

e. Sold land for cash at a price equal to its cost.

f. Paid a liability.

g. Returned for credit some of the office equipment previously purchased on credit but not yet paid for.

h. Sold land for cash at a price in excess of cost.

i. Borrowed money from a bank.

Indicate the effects of each of these transactions upon the total amounts of the company's assets, liabilities, and owners' equity. Organize your answer in tabular form, using the column headings shown below and the code letters **I** for increase, **D** for decrease, and **NE** for no effect. The answer for transaction **a** is provided as an example:

Transaction	Assets	Liabilities	Owners' Equity
(a)	I	I	NE

EXERCISE 1-11
Effects of Business
Transactions
 LO 5

For each of the following categories, state concisely a transaction that will have the required effect on the elements of the accounting equation.

a. Increase an asset and increase a liability.
b. Decrease an asset and decrease a liability.
c. Increase one asset and decrease another asset.
d. Increase an asset and increase owners' equity.
e. Increase one asset, decrease another asset, and increase a liability.

EXERCISE 1-12
Factors Contributing to
Solvency
 LO 6

Explain whether each of the following balance sheet items increases, reduces, or has no direct effect upon a company's short-term solvency. Explain your reasoning.

a. Cash.
b. Accounts payable.
c. Retained earnings.
d. Accounts receivable.
e. Capital stock.

EXERCISE 1-13
Audits of Financial
Statements
 LO 7

The annual financial statements of all large, publicly owned corporations are audited.

a. What is an audit of financial statements?
b. Who performs these audits?
c. What is the basic purpose of an audit?

EXERCISE 1-14
Ethics and Professional
Judgment
 LO 8

Ethical conduct and professional judgment each play important roles in the accounting process.

a. In general terms, explain why it is important to society that people who prepare accounting information act in an ethical manner.
b. Identify at least three areas in which accountants must exercise *professional judgment,* rather than merely relying upon written rules.

EXERCISE 1-15
Financial Reporting on a
Personal Basis
 LO 1,5,6,8

Assume you are applying for a car loan. The loan application asks for the current balance in your bank account—which is $320. A friend suggests the following actions to increase your chances of qualifying for this loan: Borrow $5,000 from your parents and deposit this money in your bank account. After making this deposit, include the $5,320 account balance on your loan application. Several days later, withdraw the $5,000 and repay your parents.
Evaluate these actions from the following perspectives:

a. Would they create a $5,320 balance in your bank account?
b. Would they increase your "net worth" (assets minus liabilities) and/or improve your *solvency?* Explain.
c. Is the plan ethical? Explain.

*EXERCISE 1-16
Careers in Accounting

LO 9

Four accounting majors, Maria Acosta, Kenzo Nakao, Helen Martin, and Anthony Mandella, recently graduated from Central University and began professional accounting careers. Acosta entered public accounting, Nakao became a managerial accountant with IBM, Martin joined a governmental agency, and Mandella (who had completed a graduate program) became an accounting faculty member.

Assume that each of the four graduates was successful in his or her chosen career. Identify the types of accounting *activities* in which each of these graduates might find themselves specializing several years after graduation.

EXERCISE 1-17
Toys "R" Us. Introduction
to an Annual Report

LO 2

The annual report of **Toys "R" Us** appears in Appendix A at the end of this textbook. The purpose of this exercise is to acquaint you with this report.

a. The nine major elements of this report are summarized in the report's Table of Contents. What are these nine elements?

b. For how many years does Toys "R" Us show balance sheets? For how many years does it present financial statements summarizing the company's operations?

c. What CPA firm audits the company's financial statements, and did the auditors consider these statements to be a "fair" presentation of the company's financial position and operating results?

d. Select three items from the notes accompanying these financial statements and briefly explain the importance of these items to people making decisions about investing in, or extending credit to, Toys "R" Us.

PROBLEMS

PROBLEM 1-1
Preparing a Balance Sheet
and Evaluating Solvency

LO 3,6

Listed below in random order are the items to be included in the balance sheet of Powder Bowl Lodge at December 31, 1998:

Equipment	$ 29,200	Buildings	$450,000
Land	425,000	Capital stock	-?-
Income taxes payable	14,800	Cash	16,400
Accounts receivable	10,600	Furnishings	58,700
Retained earnings	47,000	Snowmobiles	15,400
Accounts payable	53,500	Notes payable	640,000

INSTRUCTIONS

a. Prepare a balance sheet at December 31, 1998. Include a proper heading and organize your balance sheet similarly to the illustration on page 14. (After Buildings, you may list the remaining assets in any order.) You will need to compute the amount to be shown for capital stock.

b. Assume that no payment is due on the notes payable until 2002. Does this balance sheet indicate that the company is in a strong financial position as of December 31, 1998? Explain briefly.

PROBLEM 1-2
Interpreting the Effects of
Business Transactions
LO 5

Five transactions of Cyber Spiders are summarized below in equation form, with each of the five transactions identified by a letter. For each of the transactions **a** through **e** you are to write a separate sentence explaining the nature of the transaction. For example, the explanation of transaction **a** could be as follows: Purchased office equipment at a cost of $1,400; paid cash.

---

*Supplemental Topic B, "Careers in Accounting."

	Assets					=	Liabilities	+	Owners' Equity
	Cash +	Accounts Receivable +	Land +	Building +	Office Equipment =		Accounts Payable	+	Capital Stock
Balances	$ 3,200	$6,700	$31,000	$56,500	-0-		$ 9,400		$88,000
(a)	−1,400				+1,400				
Balances	$ 1,800	$6,700	$31,000	$56,500	$1,400		$ 9,400		$88,000
(b)	+10,000								+10,000
Balances	$11,800	$6,700	$31,000	$56,500	$1,400		$ 9,400		$98,000
(c)					+1,800		+$1,800		
Balances	$11,800	$6,700	$31,000	$56,500	$3,200		$11,200		$98,000
(d)	−600				+2,600		+$2,000		
Balances	$11,200	$6,700	$31,000	$56,500	$5,800		$13,200		$98,000
(e)	+500	−500							
Balances	$11,700 +	$6,200 +	$31,000 +	$56,500 +	$5,800 =		$13,200	+	$98,000

PROBLEM 1-3
Recording the Effects of Transactions
LO 5,6

Nova Communications was organized on December 1 of the current year, and had the following account balances at December 31, listed in tabular form.

	Assets				=	Liabilities		+	Owners' Equity
	Cash +	Land +	Building +	Office Equipment =		Notes Payable +	Accounts Payable	+	Capital Stock
Balances	$37,000	$95,000	$125,000	$51,250		$80,000	$28,250		$200,000

Early in January, the following transactions were carried out by Nova Communications:

1. Issued 2,500 shares of stock for $25,000 cash.
2. Purchased land and a small office building for a total price of $90,000, of which $35,000 was the value of the land and $55,000 was the value of the building. Paid $22,500 in cash and signed a note payable for the remaining $67,500.
3. Bought several computer systems on credit for $8,500 (30-day open account).
4. Obtained a loan from Capital Bank in the amount of $10,000. Signed a note payable.
5. Paid the $28,250 account payable owed as of December 31.

INSTRUCTIONS
a. List the December 31 balances of assets, liabilities, and owners' equity in tabular form as shown above. Record the effects of each of the five transactions in the manner illustrated on page 25. Show the totals for all columns after each transaction.
b. What *additional information* would you need about the notes payable before you could intelligently evaluate Nova's short-term solvency?

PROBLEM 1-4
Recording the Effects of
Transactions

LO 2,9

The items making up the balance sheet of TriState Truck Rental at December 31 are listed below in tabular form similar to the illustration of the accounting equation on page 25.

	Assets				=	Liabilities		+	Owners' Equity
Cash	+	Accounts Receivable	+	Trucks	+	Office Equipment =	Notes Payable	+	Accounts Payable +	Capital Stock
Balances $9,500		$8,900		$58,000		$3,800	$10,000		$5,200	$65,000

During a short period after December 31, TriState Truck Rental had the following transactions:

1. Bought office equipment at a cost of $2,700. Paid cash.
2. Collected $4,000 of accounts receivable.
3. Paid $3,200 of accounts payable.
4. Borrowed $10,000 from a bank. Signed a note payable for that amount.
5. Purchased two trucks for $30,500. Paid $15,000 cash and signed a note payable for the balance.
6. Issued 4,000 additional shares of capital stock for $20,000 cash.

INSTRUCTIONS
a. List the December 31 balances of assets, liabilities, and owners' equity in tabular form as shown above. Record the effects of each of the six transactions in the manner illustrated on page 25. Show the totals for all columns after each transaction.
b. Assume that TriState's notes payable require monthly payments totaling $3,000 per month. Does TriState appear solvent for the short-term (say, the next 90 days)?

PROBLEM 1-5
Preparing a Balance Sheet;
Effects of a Change
in Assets

LO 3,5

King Brothers Circus, Inc., is the name of a traveling circus. The ledger accounts of the business at June 30, 1998 are listed below in alphabetical order:

Accounts payable.........................	$ 17,400	Notes payable	$120,000
Accounts receivable....................	8,900	Notes receivable........................	2,400
Animals	-?-	Props and equipment.................	59,720
Cages...	16,420	Retained earnings......................	49,820
Capital stock	175,000	Salaries payable.........................	6,500
Cash..	21,680	Tents...	42,000
Costumes.....................................	21,000	Trucks & wagons.......................	70,560

INSTRUCTIONS
a. Prepare a balance sheet by using these items and computing the missing dollar amount for animals at June 30, 1998. Organize your balance sheet similar to the one illustrated on page 14. (After Accounts Receivable, you may list the remaining assets in any order.) Include a proper balance sheet heading.
b. Assume that late in the evening of June 30, after your balance sheet had been prepared, a fire destroyed one of the tents, which had cost $11,200. The tent was not insured. Explain what changes would be required in your June 30 balance sheet to reflect the loss of this asset.

PROBLEM 1-6
Preparing a Balance Sheet;
Effects of Business
Transactions
LO 3,5,6

The balance sheet items for The Original Malt Shop (arranged in alphabetical order) were as follows at August 1, 19__. (You are to compute the missing figure for cash.)

Accounts payable	$ 8,100	Income taxes payable	$ 4,300
Accounts receivable	5,630	Land	67,000
Buildings	84,000	Notes payable	74,900
Capital stock	55,000	Retained earnings	69,300
Cash	?	Supplies	7,000
Furniture & fixtures	44,500		

During the next two days, the following transactions occurred:

Aug. 2 Additional capital stock was issued for $25,000 cash. The accounts payable were paid in full. (No payment was made on the notes payable or income taxes payable.)

Aug. 3 Furniture was purchased at a cost of $9,800 to be paid within 10 days. Supplies were purchased for $1,250 cash from a restaurant supply center which was going out of business. These supplies would have cost $1,890 if purchased through normal channels.

INSTRUCTIONS

a. Prepare a balance sheet at August 1, 19__.

b. Prepare a balance sheet at August 3, 19__.

c. Assume the note payable does not come due for several years. Is The Original Malt Shop in a stronger financial position on August 1 or on August 3? Explain briefly.

PROBLEM 1-7
Preparing a Balance Sheet;
Discussion of Accounting
Principles
LO 3,4,5

Mary Stone is the founder and manager of Old Town Playhouse. The business, which is organized as a corporation, needs to obtain a bank loan to finance the production of its next play. As part of the loan application, Stone was asked to prepare a balance sheet for the business. She prepared the following balance sheet, which is arranged correctly, but contains several errors with respect to such concepts as the business entity and the valuation of assets, liabilities, and owners' equity.

OLD TOWN PLAYHOUSE			
Balance Sheet			
September 30, 19__			
Assets		**Liabilities & Stockholders' Equity**	
Cash	$ 7,900	**Liabilities:**	
Accounts receivable	153,100	Accounts payable	$ 4,900
Props and costumes	1,500	Salaries payable	31,600
Theater building	18,000	Income taxes payable	1,800
Lighting equipment	7,600	Total liabilities	$38,300
Automobile	13,000	Stockholders' equity	30,000
Total	$201,100	Total	$68,300

In discussions with Stone and by reviewing the accounting records of Old Town Playhouse, you discover the following facts:

1. The amount listed above as cash, $7,900, represents the amount of retained earnings at September 30, as determined by the accountant who also correctly computed the company's $1,800 income tax liability. Stone finds this confusing, because on September 30 there was $11,000 in the company's bank account, $1,900 on hand in the company's safe, and $5,000 in her personal savings account.

2. The accounts receivable, listed as $153,100, include $5,100 owed to the business by Artistic Tours. The remaining $148,000 is Stone's estimate of future ticket sales from September 30 through the end of the year (December 31).

3. Stone explains to you that the props and costumes were purchased several days ago for $16,500. The business paid $1,500 of this amount in cash and issued a note payable to Actors' Supply Co. for the remainder of the purchase price ($15,000). As this note need not be paid until January of next year, it was not included among the company's liabilities.

4. Old Town Playhouse rents the theater building from Kievits International at a rate of $2,000 a month. The $18,000 shown in the balance sheet represents the rent paid through September 30 of the current year. Kievits International acquired the building seven years ago at a cost of $135,000.

5. The lighting equipment was purchased on September 26 at a cost of $7,600, but the stage manager says that it isn't worth a dime.

6. The automobile is Stone's classic 1978 Jaguar, which she purchased two years ago for $9,000. She recently saw a similar car advertised for sale at $13,000. She does not use the car in the business, but it has a personalized license plate which reads "PLAHOUS."

7. The accounts payable include business debts of $3,800 and the $1,100 balance of Stone's personal Visa card.

8. Salaries payable includes $28,000 offered to Mario Dane to play the lead role in a new play opening next December and also $3,600 still owed to stage hands for work done through September 30.

9. When Stone founded Old Town Playhouse several years ago, she invested $10,000 in exchange for 20,000 shares of capital stock. However, Live Theatre, Inc., recently offered to buy her business for $30,000. Therefore, she listed this amount as Stockholders' Equity.

INSTRUCTIONS

a. Prepare a corrected balance sheet for Old Town Playhouse at September 30, 19__.

b. For each of the nine numbered items above, explain your reasoning in deciding whether or not to include the items in the balance sheet and in determining the proper dollar valuation.

CASES

CASE 1-1
Financial Reporting: A Multi-Media Process

In 1987, **The Procter & Gamble Company** discovered Olestra™, a product which greatly reduces the fat content and calories in potato chips and other fried foods. The product was believed to have great market potential, but could not be introduced until approval was obtained from the federal Food and Drug Administration. This approval process requires several years.

a. If the discovery of Olestra™ and its estimated market potential are examples of "transactions," how would the dollar amounts of such transactions be reflected in P&G's 1987 financial statements?

b. How could investors, creditors, and other interested people learn of this discovery and its potential benefit to P&G?

CASE 1-2
Reliability of Financial Statements
LO 7

In the early 1980s, **Chrysler Corporation** was in severe financial difficulty and desperately needed large loans if the company were to survive. What factors prevented Chrysler from simply providing potential lenders with misleading financial statements to make the company look like a risk-free investment?

CASE 1-3
Investing
LO 1

Michael McBryan has shown you the business plan for Overnight Auto Service (page 21), and wants to know if you are interested in purchasing 1,000 shares of the company's capital stock.

a. How much would this investment cost? What percentage of the corporation would you own?

b. One measure of the "return" on the stockholders' investment is net income expressed as a percentage of stockholders' equity. Using the projection in the Overnight business plan, compute the projected return on the stockholders' $400,000 equity in 1999—the first year of operations.

c. Is the net income of a corporation paid in cash to the stockholders on an annual basis? If not, how do stockholders benefit financially from owning a profitable business?

d. What are the *risks* in investing in a new business such as Overnight?

e. How does the return you computed in part **b** compare with the interest your local bank pays on savings accounts? What advantages are there to a savings account over an investment in a small business?

CASE 1-4
Using a Balance Sheet
LO 6

Sun Corporation and Terra Corporation are in the same line of business and both were recently organized, so it may be assumed that their recorded costs for assets are close to current market values. The balance sheets for the two companies are as follows at July 31, 19__.

SUN CORPORATION			
Balance Sheet			
July 31, 19__			

Assets		**Liabilities & Stockholders' Equity**		
Cash	$ 18,000	**Liabilities:**		
Accounts receivable ..	26,000	Notes payable (due in		
Land...........................	37,200	60 days)..		$ 12,400
Building......................	38,000	Accounts payable		9,600
Office equipment	1,200	Total liabilities		$ 22,000
		Stockholders' equity:		
		Capital stock	$60,000	
		Retained earnings..........	38,400	98,400
Total	$120,400	Total		$120,400

TERRA CORPORATION			
Balance Sheet			
July 31, 19__			

Assets		**Liabilities & Stockholders' Equity**		
Cash	$ 4,800	**Liabilities:**		
Accounts receivable ...	9,600	Notes payable (due in		
Land...........................	96,000	60 days)		$ 22,400
Building......................	60,000	Accounts payable		43,200
Office equipment	12,000	Total liabilities		$ 65,600
		Stockholders' equity:		
		Capital stock.................	$72,000	
		Retained earnings........	44,800	116,800
Total	$182,400	Total		$182,400

INSTRUCTIONS

a. Assume that you are a banker and that each company had applied to you for a 90-day loan of $12,000. Which would you consider to be the more favorable prospect? Explain your answer fully.

b. Assume that you are an investor considering purchasing all the capital stock of one or both of the companies. For which business would you be willing to pay the higher price? Do you see any indication of a financial crisis which you might face shortly after buying either company? Explain your answer fully. (It is recognized that for either decision, additional information would be useful, but you are to reach your decision on the basis of the information available.)

CASE 1-5
Ethics and "Window Dressing"

LO 1,4,5,6,7,8

The date is November 18, 1998. You are the chief executive officer of Flowerhill Software—a publicly owned company that is currently in financial difficulty. Flowerhill needs large new bank loans if it is to survive.

You have been negotiating with several banks, but each has asked to see your 1998 financial statements, which will be dated December 31. These statements will, of course, be audited. You are now meeting with other corporate officers to discuss the situation, and the following suggestions have been made:

a. "We are planning to buy the WordMaster Software Co. for $8 million cash in December. The owners of WordMaster are in no hurry; if we delay this acquisition until January, we'll have $8 million more cash at year-end. That should make us look a lot more solvent."

b. "At year-end, we'll owe accounts payable of about $18 million. If we were to show this liability in our balance sheet at half that amount—say, $9 million—no one would know the difference. We could report the other $9 million as stockholders' equity and our financial position would appear much stronger."

c. "We own Delta Programming $5 million, due in 90 days. I know some people at Delta. If we were to sign a note and pay them 12% interest, they'd let us postpone payment of this debt for a year or more."

d. "We own land that cost us $2 million, but today is worth at least $6 million. Let's show it at $6 million in our balance sheet, and that will increase our total assets and our stockholders' equity by $4 million."

INSTRUCTIONS

Separately evaluate each of these four proposals. Your evaluations should consider ethical and legal issues as well as accounting issues. (We recognize the overlap between ethical and legal issues, and we do not ask that you distinguish between the two.)

INTERNET 1-1

LO 2

INTERNET ASSIGNMENTS

We'd like to introduce you to EDGAR, the SEC's database of financial information about publicly owned companies. The SEC maintains EDGAR to increase the efficiency of financial reporting in the American economy and also to give the public free access to information about publicly owned companies.

INSTRUCTIONS

Access EDGAR at the following Internet address:

www.sec.gov/cgi-bin/srch-edgar

Then type MCDONALDS CORP into the search box and press the return key.

Select McDonald's *most recent* Form 10Q (a required quarterly filing which includes quarterly financial statements).

a. What is the street address of McDonald's corporate headquarters?

b. Scroll down to the balance sheet. Has the amount of the company's cash (and cash equivalents) increased or decreased since the beginning of the year?

c. Scroll down to the income statement. What was the company's net income for the most recent quarter? Is this amount up or down from the same quarter in the preceding year?

d. How much cash was provided by operations during the quarter? Where did you find this information?

e. In Form 10Q, notes to the financial statements are called "Financial Comments." Select one of McDonald's financial comments and explain why it would be of interest to investors.

f. While you're in EDGAR, pick a company that interests you and learn more about it. Be prepared to tell the class which company you selected and explain what you learned.

Note: Additional Internet assignments for this chapter appear in Appendix B and on our home page

www.magpie.org/cyberlab

ANSWERS TO SELF-TEST QUESTIONS

1. c **2.** a, c, d **3.** b, d **4.** b **5.** b, c, d **6.** c **7.** a, b, c, d
8. a, b, d **9.** b

OUR COMMENTS ON THE IN-TEXT CASES

YOU AS THE OWNER OF A SMALL BUSINESS (P. 13) The businesses described in this case all involve a risk of injury or even death for customers. Thus, the businesses might be sued for large amounts.

If these businesses were not organized as corporations, the owners would have *unlimited personal liability* for any debts of the businesses, including potential liabilities arising from business accidents. By organizing the businesses as corporations, these owners limit their potential financial loss to the amount of their equity in the business entities.

YOU AS A LOAN OFFICER (P. 27) Overnight currently does not have the financial resources to pay the $90,000 note coming due on February 3. Few lenders would make a 120-day loan to a company that does not appear able to pay existing liabilities coming due in the meantime.

Instead of looking for a 120-day loan, Overnight should try to obtain long-term financing on its real estate, such as a mortgage loan. The company then could use the proceeds from this long-term financing to pay the short-term note coming due on February 3.

Real estate mortgages typically are paid over many years through a series of relatively small monthly installments. Such financing would greatly reduce the drain on Overnight's financial resources in the months ahead. Not only would it make Overnight more solvent, it might eliminate altogether the need for a working capital loan.

The use of long-term financing to purchase real estate is a common business practice. In fact, this is the type of financing Overnight had proposed in its business plan.

CHANGES IN FINANCIAL POSITION

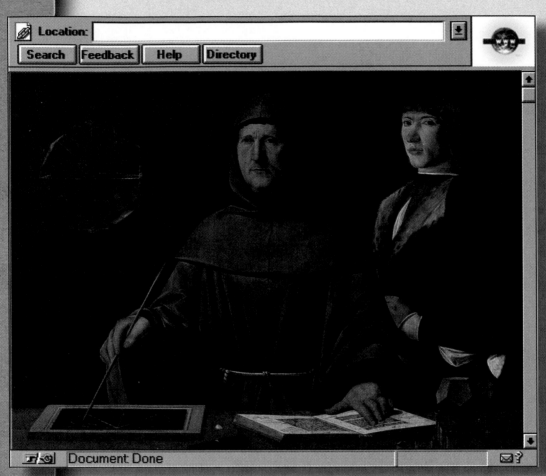

Location: [   ]

Search   Feedback   Help   Directory

Document Done

Many historians believe that writing was invented for the purpose of communicating accounting information. The principles of our "modern" system of double-entry accounting first were explained in print by Luca Pacioli (left), an Italian mathematician. Pacioli was a friend of Leonardo da Vinci; his book, *Summa de Arithmetica . . .*, was published in 1494.

Three hundred years later, Johann von Goethe, perhaps the most influential writer of the late 18th century, described Pacioli's system as a thing of timeless beauty and simplicity—one of the greatest achievements of the human intellect. Goethe was right. Even now—in a world of computers, databases, and international business activities—Pacioli's simple principles still apply.

1 Discuss the role of accounting records in an organization.

2 Describe a ledger account and a ledger.

3 State the rules of debit and credit for balance sheet accounts.

4 Explain the double-entry system of accounting.

5 Explain the purpose of a journal and its relationship to the ledger.

6 Prepare journal entries to record common business transactions.

7 Prepare a trial balance and explain its uses and limitations.

8 Describe the basic steps of the accounting cycle in both manual and computer-based accounting systems.

THE ROLE OF ACCOUNTING RECORDS

Businesses do not prepare new financial statements after every transaction. Rather, they accumulate the effects of individual business transactions in their *accounting records*. Then, at regular intervals, the data in these records are used to prepare financial statements, income tax returns, and other types of accounting reports.

LO 1 Discuss the role of accounting records in an organization.

But the need for accounting reports is not the only reason businesses maintain accounting records. Managers and employees of the business frequently use these records for such purposes as:

1. Establishing **accountability** for the assets and transactions under an individual's control.

2. Keeping track of routine business activities, such as the amounts of money in company bank accounts, amounts due from credit customers, and amounts owed to suppliers.

3. Obtaining detailed information about a particular transaction.

4. Evaluating the efficiency and performance of various departments within the organization.

5. Maintaining documentary evidence of the company's business activities. (For example, tax laws require companies to maintain accounting records supporting the amounts reported in tax returns.)

THE UPCOMING SERIES OF "ACCOUNTING SYSTEM" CHAPTERS Chapter 2 is the first of four chapters exploring various aspects of accounting systems. In this chapter, we explain the double-entry system of accounting and illustrate the "flow" of data through basic accounting records. Our examples are based upon the November transactions of Overnight Auto Service, which we described in Chapter 1. These transactions affect only the balance sheet. Business transactions that also affect the income statement are discussed in Chapters 3 and 4. In Chapter 5 we will broaden our discussion to include merchandising activities.

THE LEDGER

An accounting system includes a separate record for each item that appears in the balance sheet. For example, a separate record is kept for the asset cash, showing all increases and decreases in cash resulting from the many transactions in which cash is received or paid. A similar record is kept for every other type of

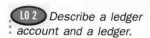
Describe a ledger
account and a ledger.

asset and liability. Separate records also are maintained for different sources of owners' equity, such as capital stock and retained earnings.

The record used to keep track of the increases and decreases in a single balance sheet item is termed a ledger account, or simply an **account.** The entire group of accounts is kept together in an accounting record called a **ledger.**[1]

In manual accounting systems, each ledger account is maintained on a separate page of columnar paper. Traditionally these pages were in a bound book; now they may be kept in a loose-leaf binder, which serves as the ledger. (This format explains why accounting records traditionally have been described as the company's "books.") In computer-based systems, of course, the ledger accounts are maintained on disc.

THE USE OF LEDGER ACCOUNTS

A ledger account is a means of accumulating in one place all the information about changes in a specific asset or liability, or in owners' equity. For example, a ledger account for the asset cash provides a record of the amounts of cash receipts, cash payments, and the current cash balance. By maintaining a Cash account, management can keep track of the amount of cash available for meeting payrolls and for making current purchases of assets or services. This record of cash is also useful in planning future operations and in advance planning of applications for bank loans.

In its simplest form, an account has only three elements: (1) a title, consisting of the name of the particular asset or liability, or type of owner's equity; (2) a left side, which is called the *debit* side; and (3) a right side, which is called the *credit* side. This form of account, illustrated below and on the following page, is called a *T account* because of its resemblance to the letter T. More complete forms of accounts will be illustrated later.

A T account—a ledger
account in its simplest form

Title of Account	
Left or Debit Side	Right or Credit Side

DEBIT AND CREDIT ENTRIES

An amount recorded on the left or debit side of an account is called a **debit,** or a *debit entry.* An amount entered on the right or credit side is called a **credit,** or a *credit entry.* Accountants also use the words debit and credit as verbs. The act of recording a debit in an account is called *debiting* the account; the recording of a credit is called *crediting* the account.

Students beginning a course in accounting often have erroneous notions about the meanings of debits and credits. For example, they may view credits as more desirable than debits. Such views have no validity in the field of accounting. Accountants use debit simply to mean an entry on the left-hand side of an account and credit to mean an entry on the right-hand side. Thus, debit and credit simply mean left and right.

To illustrate the recording of debits and credits in an account, let us go back to the five cash transactions of Overnight Auto Service, described in Chapter 1. When these cash transactions are recorded in the Cash account, the *receipts* are entered in the *debit side* of the account and the *payments* are entered in the *credit side.* The dates of the transactions also are recorded, as follows:

---

[1]The ledger also includes an account for each item appearing in the income statement. Income statement accounts are discussed in Chapter 3.

receipt   *payment*

Cash transactions entered
in ledger account

		Cash		
11/1	400,000	11/3	295,000	
11/25	2,000	11/5	30,000	
		11/30	32,100	*footings*
	402,000		*357,100*	
11/30 Balance 44,900				

Each debit and credit entry in the Cash account represents a cash receipt or a cash payment. The amount of cash owned by the business at a given date is equal to the *balance* of the account on that date.

DETERMINING THE BALANCE OF A T ACCOUNT   The balance of a ledger account is the difference between the dollar amounts of the debit and credit entries in the account. If the debit total exceeds the credit total, the account has a *debit balance;* if the credit total exceeds the debit total, the account has a *credit balance.*

In our illustrated Cash account, a line has been drawn across the account following the last cash transaction recorded in November. The total cash receipts (debits) recorded in November amount to $402,000, and the total cash payments (credits) amount to $357,100. These totals, called **footings,** are entered just above the line. (Notice that these footings are written to the left of the regular money columns so that they will not be mistaken for debit or credit entries.) By subtracting the credit total from the debit total ($402,000 − $357,100), we determine that the Cash account has a debit balance of *$44,900* on November 30.

This debit balance is entered in the debit side of the account just below the blue line. In effect, the horizontal line creates a "fresh start" in our T account, with the month-end balance representing the *net result* of all the previous debit and credit entries. The Cash account now shows the amount of cash owned by the business on November 30. In a balance sheet prepared at this date, Cash in the amount of $44,900 would be listed as an asset.

DEBIT BALANCES IN ASSET ACCOUNTS   In the preceding illustration of a cash account, increases were recorded on the left or debit side of the account and decreases were recorded on the right or credit side. The increases were greater than the decreases and the result was a debit balance in the account.

All asset accounts *normally have debit balances.* It is hard to imagine an account for an asset such as land having a credit balance, as this would indicate that the business had disposed of more land than it had ever acquired. (For other assets, such as cash, it is possible to acquire a credit balance—but such balances are only *temporary.*)

The fact that assets are located on the left side of the balance sheet is a convenient means of remembering the rule that an increase in an asset is recorded on the *left* (debit) side of the account, and also that an asset account normally has a debit *(left-hand)* balance.

LO 3 *State the rules of debit and credit for balance sheet accounts.*

Any Asset Account	
Debit	Credit
(increase)	(decrease)

Asset accounts normally have debit balances

CREDIT BALANCES IN LIABILITY AND OWNERS' EQUITY ACCOUNTS Increases in liability and owners' equity accounts are recorded by credit entries and decreases in these accounts are recorded by debits. The relationship between entries in these accounts and their position on the balance sheet may be summed up as follows: (1) liabilities and owners' equity belong on the *right* side of the balance sheet, (2) an increase in a liability or an owners' equity account is recorded on the *right* (credit) side of the account, and (3) liability and owners' equity accounts normally have credit (*right-hand*) balances.

Liability and owners' equity accounts normally have credit balances

Any Liability Account or Owners' Equity Account	
Debit (decrease)	Credit (increase)

CONCISE STATEMENT OF THE RULES OF DEBIT AND CREDIT The use of debits and credits to record changes in assets, liabilities, and owners' equity may be summarized as follows:

Rules of debit and credit

Asset Accounts	Liability & Owners' Equity Accounts
Normally have *debit balances*. Thus, increases are recorded by *debits* and decreases are recorded by *credits*.	Normally have *credit balances*. Thus, increases are recorded by *credits* and decreases are recorded by *debits*.

DOUBLE-ENTRY ACCOUNTING—THE EQUALITY OF DEBITS AND CREDITS

The rules for debits and credits are designed so that *every transaction is recorded by equal dollar amounts of debits and credits.* The reason for this equality lies in the relationship of the debit and credit rules to the accounting equation:

$$\text{Assets} = \underbrace{\text{Liabilities} + \text{Owners' Equity}}$$
$$\text{Debit balances} = \text{Credit balances}$$

If this equation is to remain in balance, any change in the left side of the equation (assets) *must be accompanied by an equal change* in the right-hand side (either liabilities or owners' equity). According to the debit and credit rules that we have just described, increases in the left side of the equation (assets) are recorded by *debits*, while increases in the right side (liabilities and owners' equity) are recorded by *credits*.

LO 4 *Explain the double-entry system of accounting.*

This system is often called **double-entry accounting.** The phrase double-entry refers to the need for both debit *and* credit entries (equal in dollar amount) to record every transaction. Virtually every business organization uses the double-entry system, regardless of whether the company's accounting records are maintained manually or by computer. In addition, the double-entry system allows us to measure net income at the same time we record the effects of transactions upon the balance sheet accounts. (The measurement of net income is discussed in Chapter 3.)

Double-entry accounting is not a new idea. The system has been in use for more than 600 years. The first systematic presentation of the double-entry system appears in a mathematics textbook written by Luca Pacioli, a friend of Leonardo da Vinci. This text was published in 1494—just two years after Columbus discovered America. Although Pacioli wrote the first textbook on this subject, surviving accounting records show that double-entry accounting had already been in use for at least 150 years.

YOUR TURN

You as a Student

You probably do not use debits and credits in accounting for your personal financial activities. Does this mean that the concept of double-entry does not apply to changes in your personal financial position? Explain and provide several examples.

*Our comments appear on page 97.

RECORDING TRANSACTIONS IN LEDGER ACCOUNTS: AN ILLUSTRATION

We now will illustrate the use of debits and credits for recording transactions in ledger accounts using the November transactions of Overnight Auto Service. Each transaction will be analyzed first in terms of increases and decreases in assets, liabilities, and owners' equity. Then we will follow the debit and credit rules to enter these increases and decreases in T accounts. We show asset accounts on the left side of our illustration; liability and owners' equity accounts on the right side. For convenience in following the transactions into the ledger accounts, both the debit and credit entries relating to the *transaction under discussion* appear in *red*. Entries relating to earlier transactions appear in *black*.

Nov. 1 Issued 40,000 shares of capital stock in exchange for $400,000 cash.

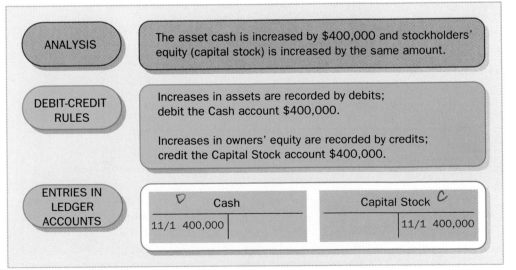

ANALYSIS — The asset cash is increased by $400,000 and stockholders' equity (capital stock) is increased by the same amount.

DEBIT-CREDIT RULES — Increases in assets are recorded by debits; debit the Cash account $400,000.

Increases in owners' equity are recorded by credits; credit the Capital Stock account $400,000.

ENTRIES IN LEDGER ACCOUNTS —

Cash		Capital Stock	
11/1 400,000			11/1 400,000

Owner invests cash in the business

Nov. 3 Purchased approximately two acres of land from the city of Santa Teresa for $295,000 cash.

Purchase of an asset for cash

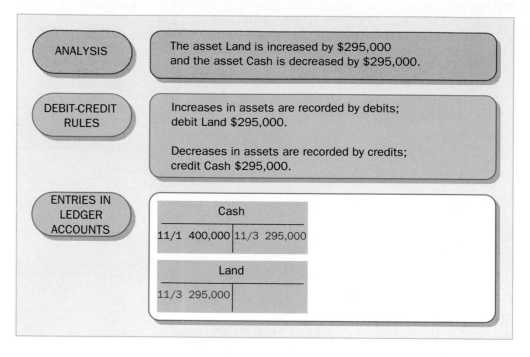

Nov. 5 Overnight completed the acquisition of its business location by purchasing the abandoned bus garage from the MTA. The purchase price was $120,000; Overnight made a $30,000 cash down payment and issued a 90-day, non-interest-bearing note payable for the remaining $90,000.

Purchase of an asset, making a small down payment

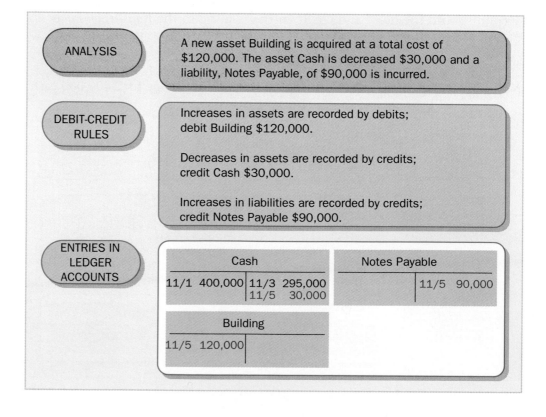

Nov. 17 Overnight purchased tools and equipment <u>on account from</u> Pro-Tools Corporation. The purchase price was $64,200.

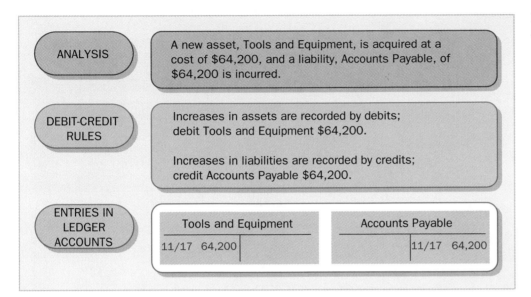

Purchase of an asset on account

Nov. 20 Overnight found that it had purchased more tools than it needed. On November 20, it sold the excess tools on account to Ace Towing at a price of $4,200. The tools were sold at a price equal to their cost, so there was no gain or loss on this transaction.

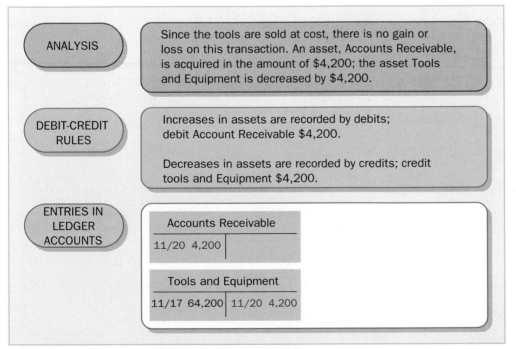

Sale of an asset on account (with no gain or loss)

Nov. 25 Overnight received $2,000 in partial collection of the account receivable from Ace Towing.

Collection of an account receivable

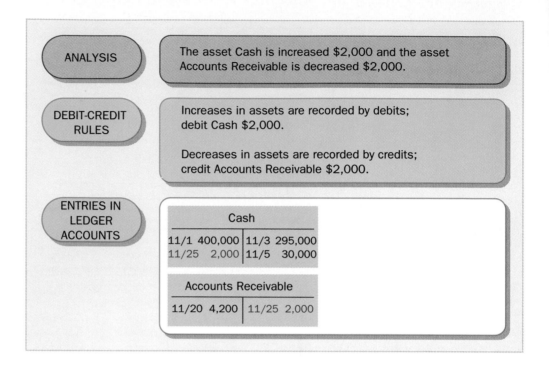

Nov. 30 Overnight made a $32,100 partial payment of its account payable to Pro-Tools Corporation.

Payment of an account payable

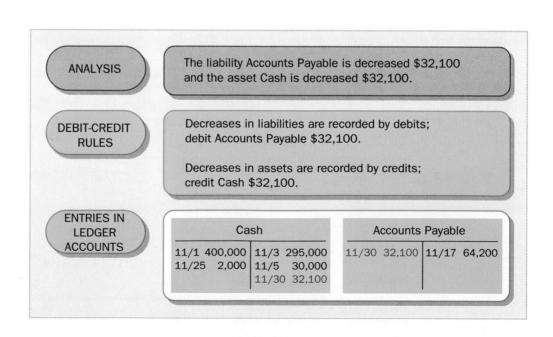

RUNNING BALANCE FORM OF ACCOUNTS

T accounts are widely used in the classroom and in accounting textbooks, because they provide a concise conceptual picture of the financial effects of a business transaction. In actual practice, however, most businesses prefer to use the *running balance* form of ledger account. This form of account has special columns for recording additional information, as illustrated below with the Cash account of Overnight:

Date		Explanation	Ref	Debit	Credit	Balance
		Cash				Account No. 1
19—						
Nov.	1			4000 00		4000 00
	3				2950 00	1050 00
	5				300 00	750 00
	25			20 00		770 00
	30				321 00	449 00

Ledger account—running balance form

The *Date* column shows the date of the transaction—which is not necessarily the same as the date on which the entry is recorded in the account. The *Explanation* column is needed only for unusual items, and in many companies it is seldom used. The *Ref* (Reference) column is used to list the page number of the journal in which the transaction is recorded, thus making it possible to trace ledger entries back to their source. (The use of a *journal* is explained later in this chapter.) In the *Balance* column of the account, the new balance is entered each time the account is debited or credited. Thus the current balance of the account is readily apparent.

THE "NORMAL" BALANCE OF AN ACCOUNT The running balance form of ledger account does not indicate specifically whether the account has a debit or credit balance. However, this causes no difficulty because we know that asset accounts normally have debit balances and that accounts for liabilities and owners' equity normally have credit balances.

Occasionally an asset account may temporarily acquire a credit balance, either as the result of an accounting error or because of an unusual transaction. For example, an account receivable may acquire a credit balance because of an overpayment by a customer. However, a credit balance in the Building account could be created only by an accounting error.

SEQUENCE AND NUMBERING OF LEDGER ACCOUNTS Accounts are usually arranged in the ledger in *financial statement order*—that is, assets first, followed by liabilities, owners' equity, revenue, and expenses. The number of accounts needed by a business will depend upon its size, the nature of its operations, and the extent to which management and regulatory agencies want detailed classification of information. An identification number is assigned to each account. A **chart of accounts** is a listing of the account titles and account numbers being used by a particular business.

In the following list of accounts, many possible account numbers have been skipped; these numbers are held in reserve so that additional accounts can be added in any section of the ledger. In this illustration, the numbers from 1 to 29 are used exclusively for asset accounts; numbers from 30 to 49 are reserved for liabilities; and numbers in the 50s signify owners' equity accounts. (Revenue and expense will be discussed in Chapter 3.) The balance sheet accounts used thus far in our Overnight Auto Service illustration are numbered as shown in the following chart of accounts:

Chart of Accounts

Account Title	Account No.
Assets:	
Cash	1
Accounts receivable	4
Land	20
Building	22
Tools and equipment	25
Liabilities:	
Notes payable	30
Accounts payable	32
Stockholders' equity:	
Capital stock	50
Retained earnings	55

In large businesses with hundreds or thousands of accounts, a more elaborate numbering system is used. Some companies use an eight- or ten-digit number for each ledger account; each of the digits carries special significance as to the classification of the account.

SEQUENCE OF ASSET ACCOUNTS   As shown in all the balance sheets we have illustrated, cash is listed first among the assets. It is followed by such assets as marketable securities, short-term notes receivable, accounts receivable, inventories of merchandise, and supplies. These are the most common examples of current assets. The term *current assets* includes cash and those assets which will shortly be converted into cash or used up in operations. Next on the balance sheet come the relatively permanent assets used in the business (often called *plant assets*). Of this group, land is listed first, followed by buildings. After these two items, any order is acceptable for other assets used in the business, such as automobiles, furniture and fixtures, computers, and other equipment.

THE JOURNAL

LO 5 *Explain the purpose of a journal and its relationship to the ledger.*

In our preceding discussion, we recorded business transactions directly in the company's ledger accounts. We did this in order to stress the effects of business transactions upon the individual asset, liability, and owners' equity accounts appearing in the company's balance sheet. In an actual accounting system, however, the information about each business transaction is initially recorded in an accounting record called the **journal.** After the transaction has been recorded in the journal, the debit and credit changes in the individual accounts are entered in the ledger. Since the journal is the accounting record in which transactions are *first recorded,* it is sometimes called the *book of original entry.*

The journal is a chronological (day-by-day) record of business transactions. The information recorded about each transaction includes the date of the transaction, the debit and credit changes in specific ledger accounts, and a brief explanation of the transaction. At convenient intervals, the debit and credit amounts recorded in the journal are transferred *(posted)* to the accounts in the ledger. The updated ledger accounts, in turn, serve as the basis for preparing the balance sheet and other financial statements.

WHY USE A JOURNAL?

Since it is technically possible to record transactions directly in the ledger, why bother to maintain a journal? The answer is that the unit of organization for the journal is the *transaction,* whereas the unit of organization for the ledger is the *account.* By having both a journal and a ledger, we achieve several advantages which would not be possible if transactions were recorded directly in ledger accounts:

1. ***The journal shows all information about a transaction in one place and also provides an explanation of the transaction.*** In a journal entry, the debits and credits for a given transaction are recorded together, but when the transaction is recorded in the ledger, the debits and credits are entered in different accounts. Since a ledger may contain hundreds of accounts, it would be very difficult to locate all the facts about a particular transaction by looking in the ledger. The journal is the record which describes all aspects of a transaction in one place.

2. ***The journal provides a chronological record of all the events in the life of a business.*** If we want to look up the facts about a transaction of some months or years back, all we need is the date of the transaction in order to locate it in the journal.

3. ***The use of a journal helps to prevent errors.*** If transactions were recorded directly in the ledger, it would be very easy to make errors, such as forgetting to enter one of the debit or credit amounts. Such errors are not likely to be made in the journal, since the offsetting debits and credits for each transaction appear together in one place.

THE GENERAL JOURNAL: ILLUSTRATION OF ENTRIES

Many businesses maintain several types of journals. The nature of operations and the volume of transactions in the particular business determine the number and type of journals needed. The simplest type of journal is called a **general journal** and is shown on the next page. A general journal has only two money columns, one for debits and the other for credits; it may be used for recording any type of transaction.

LO 6 *Prepare journal entries to record common business transactions.*

The process of recording a transaction in a journal is called *journalizing* the transaction. To illustrate the use of the general journal, we shall now journalize the November transactions of Overnight Auto Service.

Efficient use of a general journal requires two things: (1) ability to analyze the effect of a transaction upon assets, liabilities, and owners' equity and (2) familiarity with the standard form and arrangement of journal entries. Our primary interest is in the analytical phase of journalizing; the procedural steps can be learned quickly by observing the following points in the illustration on the next page:

1. The year, month, and day of the first entry on the page are written in the date column. The year and month need not be repeated for subsequent entries until a new page or a new month is begun.

2. The name of the account to be debited is written for the first line of the entry and is customarily placed at the extreme left next to the date column. The amount of the debit is entered on the same line in the *left-hand* money column.

3. The name of the account to be credited is entered on the line below the debit entry and is *indented,* that is, placed about one inch to the right of the date column. The amount credited is entered on the same line in the *right-hand* money column.

4. A brief explanation of the transaction begins on the line immediately below the last account credited. This explanation includes any data needed to identify the transaction, such as the name of the customer or supplier. The explanation is not indented.

5. A blank line should be left after each entry. This spacing causes each journal entry to stand out clearly as a separate unit and makes the journal easier to read.

6. An entry which includes more than one debit or more than one credit (such as the entry on November 5) is called a *compound journal entry*. Regardless of how many debits or credits are contained in a compound journal entry, *all the debits* are entered *before any of the credits* are listed.

7. The LP (ledger page) column just to the left of the debit money column is left blank at the time of making the journal entry. When the debits and credits are later transferred to ledger accounts, the numbers of the ledger accounts will be listed in this column to provide a convenient cross-reference with the ledger.

Journal entries for
November transactions
of Overnight Auto
Service

ledger page

Skip a line btwn journal entries

Date		Account Titles and Explanation	LP	Debit	Credit
		GENERAL JOURNAL			**Page** *1*
1998					
Nov.	1	Cash	1	400000	
		Capital Stock	50		400000
		Issued 40,000 shares of capital stock.			
	3	Land	20	295000	
		Cash	1		295000
		Purchased land for business site.			
	5	Building	22	120000	
		Cash	1		30000
		Notes Payable	30		90000
		Purchased building from MTA. Paid part			
		cash; balance payable within 90 days.			
	17	Tools and Equipment	25	64200	
		Accounts Payable	32		64200
		Purchased tools and equipment on credit			
		from *Pro-Tools Corporation*. Due in two			
		installments.			
	20	Accounts Receivable	4	4200	
		Tools and Equipment	25		4200
		Sold unused tools and equipment at cost			
		to Ace Towing. Sales price due within			
		60 days.			
	25	Cash	1	2000	
		Accounts Receivable	4		2000
		Collected part of account receivable from			
		Ace Towing.			
	30	Accounts Payable	32	32100	
		Cash	1		32100
		Made partial payment of the liability to			
		Pro-Tools Corporation.			

In journalizing transactions, remember that the *exact title* of the ledger accounts to be debited and credited should be used. For example, in recording the purchase of tools and equipment for cash, *do not* make a journal entry debiting "Tools and Equipment Purchased" and crediting "Cash Paid Out." There are no ledger accounts with such titles. The proper journal entry would consist of a debit to *Tools and Equipment* and a credit to *Cash*.

A familiarity with the general journal form of describing transactions is just as essential to the study of accounting as a familiarity with plus and minus signs is to the study of mathematics. The journal entry is a *tool* for *analyzing* and *describing* the impact of various transactions upon a business entity. The ability to describe a transaction in journal entry form requires an understanding of the nature of the transaction and its effects upon the financial position of the business.

POSTING JOURNAL ENTRIES TO THE LEDGER ACCOUNTS (AND HOW TO "READ" A JOURNAL ENTRY)

We have made the point that transactions are recorded first in the journal. Ledger accounts are updated later, through a process called **posting.** (In a computerized system, posting may occur instantaneously, rather than later.)

Posting simply means *updating the ledger accounts* for the effects of the transactions recorded in the journal. Viewed as a mechanical task, posting basically amounts to performing the steps you describe when you read a journal entry aloud.

Consider the first entry appearing in Overnight's general journal. If you were to read this entry aloud, you would say: "Debit Cash, $400,000; credit Capital Stock, $400,000." That's precisely what a person posting this entry should do: Debit the Cash account for $400,000, and credit the Capital Stock account for $400,000.

In addition, posting involves recording the date of the transaction in the ledger and creating a cross-reference between the entries in the ledger accounts and the related journal entry. In a manual accounting system, the complete posting process includes the following steps for each account title named in the journal entry:

1. Locate the corresponding account in the ledger and enter the date of the transaction.

2. Enter in the appropriate column the dollar amount being debited or credited to the ledger account.

3. In the *Ref* (posting reference) column of the ledger account, enter the *page number of the journal* from which the entry is being posted. (This creates a cross-reference between the ledger to the journal, enabling anyone using the ledger to find more information about a particular entry.)

4. Return to the journal; in the *LP* (ledger page) column, enter the *account number* of the ledger account to which the entry was posted. (The presence or absence of this account number shows at a glance which journal entries have been posted, and which have not.)

The posting of Overnight's first journal entry is illustrated on the following page.

Notice that no new information is recorded during the posting process. Posting involves copying into the ledger accounts information that *already has been recorded in the journal*. In manual accounting systems, this can be a tedious and time-consuming process; but in computer-based systems, it usually is done instantly and automatically. In addition, computerized posting greatly reduces the risk of errors.

Posting a transaction from journal to ledger accounts

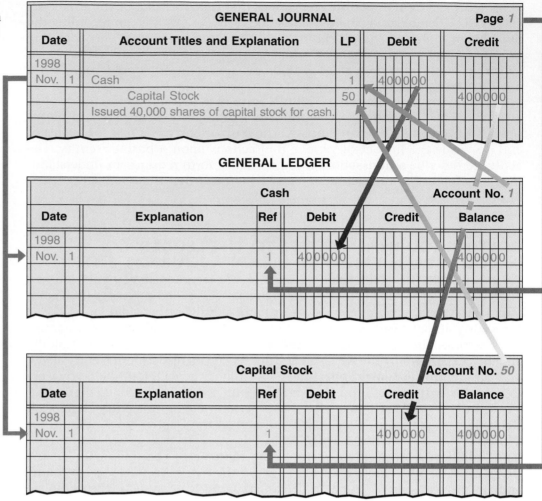

GENERAL JOURNAL					Page *1*
Date	Account Titles and Explanation	LP	Debit		Credit
1998					
Nov. 1	Cash	1	4 0 0 0 0 0		
	Capital Stock	50			4 0 0 0 0 0
	Issued 40,000 shares of capital stock for cash.				

GENERAL LEDGER

Cash					Account No. *1*
Date	Explanation	Ref	Debit	Credit	Balance
1998					
Nov. 1		1	4 0 0 0 0 0		4 0 0 0 0 0

Capital Stock					Account No. *50*
Date	Explanation	Ref	Debit	Credit	Balance
1998					
Nov. 1		1		4 0 0 0 0 0	4 0 0 0 0 0

LEDGER ACCOUNTS AFTER POSTING   After all the November transactions have been posted, Overnight's ledger appears as shown below. The accounts are arranged in the ledger in the same order as in the balance sheet—that is, assets first, followed by liabilities and owners' equity.

To conserve space in this illustration, several ledger accounts appear on a single page. In actual practice, however, each account occupies a separate page in the ledger. (In a computerized system, each account is a separate file.)

Ledger showing November transactions

Cash					Account No. *1*
Date	Explanation	Ref	Debit	Credit	Balance
1998					
Nov. 1		1	4 0 0 0 0 0		4 0 0 0 0 0
3		1		2 9 5 0 0 0	1 0 5 0 0 0
5		1		3 0 0 0 0	7 5 0 0 0
25		1	2 0 0 0		7 7 0 0 0
30		1		3 2 1 0 0	4 4 9 0 0

Accounts Receivable — Account No. 4

Date		Explanation	Ref	Debit	Credit	Balance
1998						
Nov.	20		1	4200		4200
	25		1		2000	2200

Land — Account No. 20

Date		Explanation	Ref	Debit	Credit	Balance
1998						
Nov.	3		1	295000		295000

Building — Account No. 22

Date		Explanation	Ref	Debit	Credit	Balance
1998						
Nov.	5		1	120000		120000

Tools and Equipment — Account No. 25

Date		Explanation	Ref	Debit	Credit	Balance
1998						
Nov.	17		1	64200		64200
	20		1		4200	60000

Notes Payable — Account No. 30

Date		Explanation	Ref	Debit	Credit	Balance
1998						
Nov.	5		1		90000	90000

Accounts Payable — Account No. 32

Date		Explanation	Ref	Debit	Credit	Balance
1998						
Nov.	17		1		64200	64200
	30		1	32100		32100

Capital Stock					Account No. *50*
Date	**Explanation**	**Ref**	**Debit**	**Credit**	**Balance**
1998					
Nov. 1		1		400000	400000

LO 7 *Prepare a trial balance and explain its uses and limitations.*

THE TRIAL BALANCE

Since equal dollar amounts of debits and credits are entered in the accounts for every transaction recorded, the sum of all the debits in the ledger must be equal to the sum of all the credits. If the computation of account balances has been accurate, it follows that the total of the accounts with debit balances must be equal to the total of the accounts with credit balances.

Before using the account balances to prepare a balance sheet, it is desirable to *prove* that the total of accounts with debit balances is in fact equal to the total of accounts with credit balances. This proof of the equality of debit and credit balances is called a **trial balance.** A trial balance is a two-column schedule listing the names and balances of all the accounts *in the order in which they appear in the ledger;* the debit balances are listed in the left-hand column and the credit balances in the right-hand column. The totals of the two columns should agree. A trial balance taken from Overnight's ledger follows.

OVERNIGHT AUTO SERVICE
Trial Balance
November 30, 1998

Trial balance at month-end proves ledger is in balance

	Debit	Credit
Cash	$ 44,900	
Accounts receivable	2,200	
Land	295,000	
Building	120,000	
Tools and equipment	60,000	
Notes payable		$ 90,000
Accounts payable		32,100
Capital stock		400,000
	$522,100	$522,100

USES AND LIMITATIONS OF THE TRIAL BALANCE

The trial balance provides proof that the ledger is in balance. The agreement of the debit and credit totals of the trial balance gives assurance that:

1. Equal debits and credits have been recorded for all transactions.

2. The debit or credit balance of each account has been correctly computed.

3. The addition of the account balances in the trial balance has been correctly performed.

Suppose that the debit and credit totals of the trial balance do not agree. This situation indicates that one or more errors have been made. Typical of such errors are (1) the posting of a debit as a credit, or vice versa; (2) arithmetic mistakes in determining account balances; (3) clerical errors in copying account balances into the trial balance; (4) listing a debit balance in the credit column of the trial balance, or vice versa; and (5) errors in addition of the trial balance.

The preparation of a trial balance does *not* prove that transactions have been correctly analyzed and recorded in the proper accounts. If, for example, a receipt of cash were erroneously recorded by debiting the Land account instead of the Cash account, the trial balance would still balance. Also, if a transaction were completely omitted from the ledger, the error would not be disclosed by the trial balance. In brief, *the trial balance proves only one aspect of the ledger, and that is the equality of debits and credits.*

Despite these limitations, the trial balance is a useful device. It not only provides assurance that the ledger is in balance, but it also serves as a convenient stepping-stone for the preparation of financial statements. As explained in Chapter 1, the balance sheet is a formal statement showing the financial position of the business, intended for distribution to managers, owners, bankers, and various outsiders. The trial balance, on the other hand, is merely an informal *working paper,* useful to the accountant but not intended for distribution to others. The balance sheet and other financial statements can be prepared more conveniently from the trial balance than directly from the ledger, especially if there are a great many ledger accounts.

THE ACCOUNTING CYCLE: AN INTRODUCTION

The sequence of accounting procedures used to record, classify, and summarize accounting information is often termed the **accounting cycle.** The accounting cycle begins with the initial recording of business transactions and concludes with the preparation of formal financial statements summarizing the effects of these transactions upon the assets, liabilities, and owners' equity of the business. The term *cycle* indicates that these procedures must be repeated continuously to enable the business to prepare new, up-to-date financial statements at reasonable intervals.

LO 8 *Describe the basic steps of the accounting cycle in both manual and computer-based accounting systems.*

At this point, we have illustrated a complete accounting cycle as it relates to the preparation of a balance sheet for a service-type business with a manual accounting system. The accounting procedures discussed to this point may be summarized as follows:

1. **Record transaction in the journal.** As each business transaction occurs, it is entered in the journal, thus creating a chronological record of events. This procedure completes the recording step in the accounting cycle.

2. **Post to ledger accounts.** The debit and credit changes in account balances are posted from the journal to the ledger. This procedure classifies the effects of the business transactions in terms of specific asset, liability, and owners' equity accounts.

3. **Prepare a trial balance.** A trial balance proves the equality of the debit and credit entries in the ledger. The purpose of this procedure is to verify the accuracy of the posting process and the computation of ledger account balances.

4. **Prepare financial statements.** At this point, we have discussed only one financial statement—the balance sheet. This statement shows the financial position of the business at a specific date. The preparation of financial statements summarizes the effects of business transactions occurring through the date of the statements and completes the accounting cycle.

In the next section of this chapter, and throughout the textbook, we will extend our discussion to include computer-based accounting systems. In Chapter 3, we will expand the accounting cycle to include the measurement of business income and the preparation of an income statement.

MANUAL AND COMPUTER-BASED SYSTEMS: A COMPARISON

In our preceding discussion, we have assumed the use of a manual accounting system, in which all the accounting procedures are performed manually by the company's accounting personnel. The reader may wonder about the relevance of such a discussion in an era when even many small businesses use computer-based accounting systems. However, the concepts and procedures involved in the operation of manual and computer-based accounting systems are *essentially the same*. The differences are largely a question of whether specific procedures require human attention, or whether they can be performed automatically by machine.

Computers can be programmed to perform mechanical tasks with great speed and accuracy. For example, they can be programmed to read data, to perform mathematical computations, and to rearrange data into any desired format. However, computers cannot think. Therefore, they are not able to analyze business transactions. Without human guidance, computers cannot determine which events should be recorded in the accounting records, or which accounts should be debited and credited to record an unusual event. With these abilities and limitations in mind, we will explore the effects of computer-based systems upon the basic accounting cycle.

RECORDING BUSINESS TRANSACTIONS   The recording of transactions requires two steps. First, the transaction must be *analyzed* to determine whether it should be recorded in the accounting records and, if so, which accounts should be debited and credited and for what dollar amounts. Second, the transaction must be *physically entered* (recorded) in the accounting system. As computers do not know which transactions should be recorded or how to record them properly, these decisions must be made by accounting personnel.

Differences do exist, however, in the manner in which data are physically entered into manual and computer-based systems. In manual systems, the data are entered in the form of handwritten journal entries. In a computer-based system, the data will be entered through a keyboard, an optical scanner, or other input device. Also, data entered into a computer-based system need not be arranged in the format of a journal entry. The data often are entered into a database, instead of a journal.

WHAT IS A DATABASE?   A **database** is a warehouse of information stored within a computer system. The purpose of the database is to allow information that will be used for several different purposes to be entered into the computer system *only once*. Data are originally entered into the database. Then, as data are needed, the computer refers to the database, selects the appropriate data, and arranges them in the desired format.

The information that must be entered into the database is the same as that contained in a journal entry—the date, the accounts to be debited and credited, the dollar amounts, and an explanation of the transaction. However, this information need not be arranged in the format of a journal entry. For example, in a database, accounts usually are identified by number, rather than by title. Also, short codes—such as "D" or "C"—may be used to indicate whether an account should be debited or credited. Once information has been entered in the database, the computer can arrange this information into any desired format, such as journal entries, ledger accounts, and financial statements.

POSTING TO LEDGER ACCOUNTS Posting merely copies existing information from one accounting record to another—a function which easily can be performed by a computer. In a computer-based system, data posted to the ledger accounts come directly from the database, rather than from the journal.

PREPARATION OF A TRIAL BALANCE Preparation of a trial balance involves three steps: (1) determining the balances of ledger accounts, (2) arranging the account balances in the format of a trial balance, and (3) adding up the trial balance columns and comparing the column totals. All these functions involve information already contained in the accounting system and can be performed by the computer.

PREPARATION OF FINANCIAL STATEMENTS AND RELATED DISCLO-SURES The preparation of a balance sheet and of the related disclosures are two very different tasks. The balance sheet—like the trial balance—consists of account titles and dollar amounts taken directly from the ledger. Hence, a balance sheet may be prepared automatically in a computer-based system.

Making the appropriate *disclosures* to accompany a set of financial statements, however, is a very different matter. Determining which items must be disclosed and wording the appropriate notes to the financial statements are tasks requiring *professional judgment.* Therefore, appropriate disclosures cannot be prepared automatically by a computer; they must be prepared carefully by people with *sound judgment,* as well as extensive knowledge of generally accepted accounting principles and financial reporting requirements.

At this point, our discussion of financial statements is limited to the preparation of a balance sheet. The preparation of an income statement involves additional procedures which will be discussed in the following chapter.

IN SUMMARY . . . Computers can eliminate the need for copying and rearranging information which already has been entered into the system. They also can perform mathematical computations. In short, computers eliminate most of the paper work involved in the operation of an accounting system. However, they *do not* eliminate the need for accounting personnel who can analyze business transactions and explain these events in conformity with generally accepted accounting principles.

The differences in manual and computer-based systems with respect to the accounting procedures discussed in this chapter are summarized graphically in the flowcharts on the following page. Functions which are performed by accounting personnel are printed on a white background, and tasks which can be performed automatically by the computer are printed on a gray shaded background.

JOURNALS, LEDGERS, AND ACCOUNTING EDUCATION

In this chapter, our discussion of journals and ledgers has focused upon the simplest forms of these accounting records—a manually maintained "general" journal and T accounts. While these records might be sufficient for a very small business, most organizations use more complicated and more efficient types of journals and ledgers. An increasing number of organizations use computer-based accounting systems. Even when a manual system is in use, the recording of

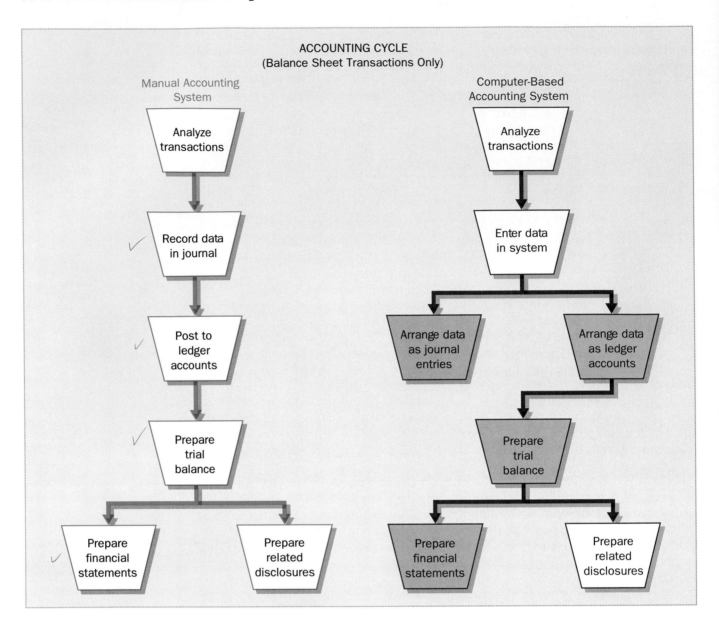

transactions can be done much more quickly in "special journals" than in the two-column general journal.[2] The formats of accounting software differ somewhat from one package to the next; also, the formats of special journals vary from one company to the next.

However, general journal entries and T accounts *illustrate the effects of transactions upon the financial position of a business* more clearly than do accounting software displays or entries in special journals. Despite their limited use in accounting practice, general journal entries and T accounts remain the preferred method of illustrating the effects of business transactions in accounting classrooms and accounting textbooks.

---

[2]Special journals are journals designed to record *one particular type* of transaction quickly and efficiently. By having several different kinds of special journals, a business may be able to record efficiently all types of transactions that occur frequently. Special journals are discussed further in Chapter 5 and Appendix C.

As a student, you should view general journal entries and T accounts as *tools for analyzing transactions and illustrating their financial effects,* not as elements of actual accounting systems. Remember, our primary goal in this course is to develop your ability to understand and use accounting information, not to train you in record-keeping procedures.[3]

THE USEFULNESS OF JOURNALS AND LEDGERS TO MANAGERS

Managers continually make use of the information contained in the accounting records. For example, to obtain information about a specific business transaction, managers may refer to the journal entry in which the transaction was recorded. To learn the current balance in such critical accounts as Cash, Accounts Receivable, and Accounts Payable, managers look to the ledger. Managers need not wait until financial statements are issued to obtain financial information about the business. They may obtain this information whenever they need it—often through desktop computers with "read only" access to the company's accounting system.[4]

In contrast, investors, creditors, and other outsiders *do not* have direct access to a company's accounting records. They obtain financial information about the business only *periodically*—when financial statements are issued.[5]

YOUR TURN

You as a Store Manager

You manage a hardware store which is part of a national chain. Every month, top management provides you with a detailed budget (forecast) of your expected sales, expenses, cash receipts, and cash outlays over each of the next three months. Your store maintains its own computer-based journals and ledgers, which are updated daily.

On April 12, the controller from the company's national headquarters calls and asks:

1. What was the purpose of the $3,000 check payable to The New York Yankees issued by your store on March 19?

2. What was the cost of your store's inventory of merchandise on hand at March 1, March 15, and March 31? (**Note:** As shown in the Toys "R" Us balance sheet on page 31, Merchandise Inventory is an asset. Usually, this asset is just called Inventory.)

Explain which accounting record—the *journal* or the *ledger*—you would find most useful in answering each of these questions.

*Our comments appear on pages 97–98.

---

[3]Although the format of accounting records varies from one business to the next, a student who understands the basic concepts of double-entry accounting should have little trouble in learning to understand and use the accounting records of any specific organization.

[4]"Read only" is an internal control that allows users of a specific computer terminal to read data, but not to alter the data or input new data into the system.

[5]Certain financial events may be disclosed to outsiders between financial statement dates, through such media as press conferences. Still, managers have far more timely access to most accounting information than do outside decision makers.

NET CONNECTIONS

Arthur Andersen & Co. is one of the world's largest public accounting firms (collectively these firms are called the "Big Six"). It also maintains an interesting home page:

www.arthurandersen.com

Visit and click on "Animated History of the Accounting Profession." Great site!

Or, you might visit one of our favorites, Rutgers Accounting Web:

www.rutgers.edu/accounting/raw.htm

Type "Double Entry" in the search box.

We also recommend Seattle University's site:

www.seattleu.edu/asbe

Then click on "PACIOLI SOCIETY." (This site might not be finished yet. But when it is, we think it will be interesting.)

*SUPPLEMENTAL TOPIC

SOME TIPS ON RECORD-KEEPING PROCEDURES

LOCATING ERRORS

In our text illustration, the trial balance is always in balance. Every accounting student soon discovers in working problems, however, that errors are easily made which prevent trial balances from balancing. The lack of balance may be the result of a single error or a combination of several errors. An error may have been made in adding the trial balance columns or in copying the balances from the ledger accounts. If the preparation of the trial balance has been accurate, then the error may lie in the accounting records, either in the journal or in the ledger accounts. What is the most efficient approach to locating the error or errors? There is no single technique which will give the best results every time, but the following procedures, done in sequence, will often save considerable time and effort in locating errors.

1. Prove the addition of the trial balance columns by adding these columns in the opposite direction from that previously followed.

2. If the error does not lie in addition, next determine the exact amount by which the schedule is out of balance. The amount of the discrepancy is often a clue to the source of the error. If the discrepancy is *divisible by 9*, this suggests either a *transposition* error or a *slide*. For example, assume that the Cash account has a balance of $2,175, but in copying the balance into the trial balance the figures are *transposed* and written as $2,157. The resulting error is $18, and like all transposition errors is *divisible by 9*. Another common error is the slide, or incorrect placement of the decimal point, as when

$2,175.00 is copied as $21.75. The resulting discrepancy in the trial balance will also be an amount divisible by 9.

To illustrate another method of using the amount of a discrepancy as a clue to locating the error, assume that the asset account Office Supplies has a *debit* balance of $420, but that it is erroneously listed on the *credit* column of the trial balance. This will cause a discrepancy of two times $420, or $840, in the trial balance totals. Errors such as recording a debit in a credit column are not uncommon. Thus, after determining the difference in the trial balance totals, you should scan the columns for an amount equal to *one-half* of the discrepancy. Also scan the journal for an amount *equal* to the discrepancy. Perhaps this amount has not been posted.

3. Compare the amounts in the trial balance with the balances in the ledger. Make sure that each ledger account balance has been included in the correct column of the trial balance.

4. Recompute the balance of each ledger account.

5. Trace all postings from the journal to the ledger accounts. As this is done, place a checkmark in the journal and in the ledger after each figure verified. When the operation is completed, look through the journal and the ledger for unchecked amounts. In tracing postings, be alert not only for errors in amount but also for debits entered as credits, or vice versa.

ODDS AND ENDS

Dollar signs are not used in journals or ledgers. Some accountants use dollar signs in trial balances; some do not. In this book, dollar signs are used in trial balances. Dollar signs should always be used in the balance sheet, the income statement, and other formal financial reports. In the balance sheet, for example, a dollar sign is placed by the first amount in each column and also by the final amount or total. Many accountants also place a dollar sign by each subtotal or other amount listed below an underlining. In the published financial statements of large corporations, the use of dollar signs is often limited to the first and last figures in a column.

When dollar amounts are being entered in the columnar paper used in journals and ledgers, commas and decimal points are not needed. On unruled paper, commas and decimal points should be used. Most of the problems and illustrations in this book are in even dollar amounts. In such cases the cents column can be left blank or, if desired, zeros or dashes may be used. A dollar amount that represents a final total within a schedule is underlined by a double rule.

SUMMARY OF LEARNING OBJECTIVES

① Discuss the role of accounting records in an organization.

Accounting records provide the information that is summarized in financial statements, income tax returns, and other accounting reports. In addition, these records are used by the company's management and employees for such purposes as:

- Establishing accountability for assets and transactions.
- Keeping track of routine business activities.
- Obtaining details about specific transactions.
- Evaluating the performance of units within the business.
- Maintaining a documentary record of the business activities. (Such a record is required by tax laws and useful for many business purposes, including audits.)

② Describe a ledger account and a ledger.

A ledger account is a device for recording the increases or decreases in one financial statement item, such as a particular asset, a type of liability, or owners' equity. The ledger is an accounting record which includes all the ledger accounts—that is, it includes a separate account for each item in the company's financial statements.

③ State the rules of debit and credit for balance sheet accounts.

Increases in assets are recorded by debits and decreases are recorded by credits. Increases in liabilities and in owners' equity are recorded by credits and decreases are recorded by debits. Notice that the debit and credit rules are related to an account's *location in the balance sheet.* If the account appears on the *left-hand side* of the balance sheet (asset accounts), increases in the account balance are recorded by *left-side entries* (debits). If the account appears on the *right-hand side* of the balance sheet (liability and owners' equity accounts), increases are recorded by *right-side entries* (credits).

④ Explain the double-entry system of accounting.

The double-entry system of accounting takes its name from the fact that every business transaction is recorded by *two types of entries:* (1) debit entries to one or more accounts and (2) credit entries to one or more accounts. In recording any transaction, the total dollar amount of the debit entries must equal the total dollar amount of the credit entries.

⑤ Explain the purpose of a journal and its relationship to the ledger.

The journal, or book of original entry, is the accounting record in which business transactions are initially recorded. The entry in the journal shows which ledger accounts have increased as a result of the transaction, and which have decreased. After the effects of the transaction have been recorded in the journal, the changes in the individual ledger accounts are then posted to the ledger.

⑥ Prepare journal entries to record common business transactions.

The effects of business transactions upon the assets, liabilities, or owners' equity of a business are recorded in the journal. Each journal entry includes the date of the transaction, the names of the ledger accounts affected, the dollar amounts of the changes in these accounts, and a brief explanation of the transaction.

⑦ Prepare a trial balance and explain its uses and limitations.

In a trial balance, separate debit and credit columns are used to list the balances of the individual ledger accounts. The two columns are then totaled to prove the equality of the debit and credit balances. This process assures that (1) the total of the debits posted to the ledger is equal to the total of the credits, and (2) the balances of the individual ledger accounts were correctly computed. While a trial balance proves the equality of debit and credit entries in the ledger, it does *not* detect errors such as failure to record a business transaction, improper analysis of the accounts affected by the transaction, or the posting of debit or credit entries to the wrong accounts.

⑧ Describe the basic steps of the accounting cycle in both manual and computer-based accounting systems.

At this stage of our study, the steps in any accounting system are: (1) record transactions in a journal, (2) post the information to the ledger accounts, (3) prepare a trial balance, and (4) prepare financial statements and the related disclosures. In a manual accounting system, all four steps are performed by accounting personnel. In a computer-based system, steps **2, 3,** and **4** (excepting *disclosures*) are performed automatically by the computer.

For the introductory student, this chapter is one of the most important in the textbook. Journal entries and T accounts will be used as instructional devices *throughout the study of accounting.* The topics of double-entry accounting and the accounting cycle serve as building blocks for much of the material presented in later chapters. We will expand our discussion of the accounting cycle in the next two chapters to include steps relating to the measurement of net income.

KEY TERMS INTRODUCED OR EMPHASIZED IN CHAPTER 2

Account (p. 56) A record used to summarize all increases and decreases in a particular asset, such as Cash, or any other type of asset, liability, owners' equity, revenue, or expense.

Accountability (p. 55) The condition of being held responsible for one's actions by the existence of an independent record of those actions. Establishing accountability is a major goal of accounting records and of internal control procedures.

Accounting cycle (p. 71) The sequence of accounting procedures applied in recording, classifying, and summarizing accounting information. The cycle begins with the occurrence of business transactions and concludes with the preparation of financial statements. This concept will be expanded in later chapters.

Chart of accounts (p. 63) This chart lists the ledger account titles and account numbers that are used by a particular business.

Credit (p. 56) An amount entered on the right-hand side of a ledger account. A credit is used to record a decrease in an asset or an increase in a liability or in owners' equity.

Database (p. 72) A storage center of information within a computer-based accounting system. The idea behind a database is that data intended for a variety of uses needs to be entered into the computer system only once, at which time the information is stored in the database. Then, as the information is needed, the computer can retrieve it from the database and arrange it in the desired format.

Debit (p. 56) An amount entered on the left-hand side of a ledger account. A debit is used to record an increase in an asset or a decrease in a liability or in owners' equity.

Double-entry accounting (p. 58) A system of recording every business transaction with equal dollar amounts of both debit and credit entries. As a result of this system, the accounting equation always remains in balance; in addition, the system makes possible the measurement of net income and also the use of error-detecting devices such as a trial balance.

Footing (p. 57) The total of amounts in a column.

General journal (p. 65) The simplest type of journal, it has only two money columns—one for credits and one for debits. This journal may be used for recording any type of transaction.

Journal (p. 64) A chronological record of transactions, showing for each transaction the debits and credits to be entered in specific ledger accounts. The simplest type of journal is called a general journal.

Ledger (p. 56) A loose-leaf book, computer files, or other record containing all the separate accounts used in financial reporting.

Posting (p. 67) The process of transferring information from the journal to accounts in the ledger.

Trial balance (p. 70) A two-column schedule listing the names and the debit or credit balances of all accounts in the ledger.

DEMONSTRATION PROBLEM

Stadium Parking, Inc., was organized on July 1 to operate a parking lot near a new sports arena. The following transactions occurred during July prior to the company beginning its regular business operations.

July 1 Issued 4,500 shares of capital stock to the owners of the corporation in exchange for their investment of $45,000 cash.

July 2 Purchased land to be used as the parking lot for a total price of $140,000. A cash down payment of $28,000 was made and a note payable was issued for the balance of the purchase price.

July 5 Purchased a small portable building for $4,000 cash. The purchase price included installation of the building on the parking lot.

July 12 Purchased office equipment on credit from Suzuki & Co. for $3,000.

July 28 Paid $2,000 of the amount owed to Suzuki & Co.

The account titles and account numbers used by Stadium Parking, Inc., to record these transactions are

Cash	1	Notes payable	30
Land	20	Accounts payable	32
Building	22	Capital stock	50
Office equipment	25		

INSTRUCTIONS

a. Prepare journal entries for the month of July.

b. Post to ledger accounts of the three-column running balance form.

c. Prepare a trial balance at July 31.

SOLUTION TO DEMONSTRATION PROBLEM

a.

GENERAL JOURNAL					Page *1*
Date	**Account Titles and Explanation**	**LP**	**Debit**	**Credit**	
19—					
July 1	Cash	1	45000		
	Capital stock	50		45000	
	Issued 4,500 shares of capital stock for cash.				
2	Land	20	140000		
	Cash	1		28000	
	Notes Payable	30		112000	
	Purchased land. Paid part cash and issued a note payable for the balance.				
5	Building	22	4000		
	Cash	1		4000	
	Purchased a small portable building for cash.				
12	Office Equipment	25	3000		
	Accounts Payable	32		3000	
	Purchased office equipment on credit from Suzuki & Co.				
28	Accounts Payable	32	2000		
	Cash	1		2000	
	Paid part of account payable to Suzuki & Co.				

b. **GENERAL LEDGER**

Cash					Account No. *1*
Date	**Explanation**	**Ref**	**Debit**	**Credit**	**Balance**
19—					
July 1		1	45000		45000
2		1		28000	17000
5		1		4000	13000
28		1		2000	11000

Land				Account No. 20	
Date	Explanation	Ref	Debit	Credit	Balance
19—					
July 2		1	140000		140000

Building				Account No. 22	
Date	Explanation	Ref	Debit	Credit	Balance
19—					
July 5		1	4000		4000

Office Equipment				Account No. 25	
Date	Explanation	Ref	Debit	Credit	Balance
19—					
July 12		1	3000		3000

Notes Payable				Account No. 30	
Date	Explanation	Ref	Debit	Credit	Balance
19—					
July 2		1		112000	112000

Accounts Payable				Account No. 32	
Date	Explanation	Ref	Debit	Credit	Balance
19—					
July 12		1		3000	3000
28		1	2000		1000

Capital Stock				Account No. 50	
Date	Explanation	Ref	Debit	Credit	Balance
19—					
July 1		1		45000	45000

c.

STADIUM PARKING, INC. Trial Balance July 31, 19___		
	Debit	**Credit**
Cash..	$ 11,000	
Land...	140,000	
Building	4,000	
Office equipment..	3,000	
Notes payable		$112,000
Accounts payable...		1,000
Capital stock..		45,000
	$158,000	$158,000

SELF-TEST QUESTIONS
Answers to these questions appear on page 97.

1. According to the rules of debit and credit for balance sheet accounts:
   a. Increases in asset, liability, and owners' equity accounts are recorded by debits.
   b. Decreases in asset and liability accounts are recorded by credits.
   c. Increases in asset and owners' equity accounts are recorded by debits.
   d. Decreases in liability and owners' equity accounts are recorded by debits.

2. Which of the following statements about accounting procedures is *not* correct?
   a. The journal shows in one place all the information about specific transactions, arranged in chronological order.
   b. A ledger account shows in one place all the information about changes in a specific asset or liability, or in owners' equity.
   c. Posting is the process of transferring debit and credit changes in account balances from the ledger to the journal.
   d. The end product of the accounting cycle consists of formal financial statements, such as the balance sheet and the income statement.

3. On March 31, the ledger for Regal Dry Cleaning consists of the following:

Cleaning equipment	$27,800	Accounts receivable..................	$21,000
Accounts payable	15,700	Cash..	6,900
Capital stock..............................	20,000	Salaries payable	9,600
Office equipment	2,000	Retained earnings......................	22,500
Automobile.................................	7,500	Cleaning supplies.......................	2,600

   In a trial balance prepared on March 31, the total of the credit column is:
   a. $67,800   b. $93,100   c. $25,300   d. $65,300

4. Sunset Tours has a $3,500 account receivable from the Del Mar Rotary. On January 20, the Rotary makes a partial payment of $2,100 to Sunset Tours. The journal entry made on January 20 by Sunset Tours to record this transaction includes:
   a. A debit to the Cash Received account of $2,100.
   b. A credit to the Accounts Receivable account of $2,100.
   c. A debit to the Cash account of $1,400.
   d. A debit to the Accounts Receivable account of $1,400.

5. The following journal entry was made in Dixie Stores' accounting records:

Cash..	12,000	
Notes receivable	48,000	
Land		60,000

This transaction:
  a. Involves the purchase of land for $60,000.
  b. Involves a $12,000 cash payment.
  c. Involves the sale of land which had cost $60,000.
  d. Causes an increase in total assets of $12,000.

ASSIGNMENT MATERIAL

DISCUSSION QUESTIONS

1. Baker Construction, Inc., is a small business owned and managed by Tom and Sheila Baker. The company has 21 employees, few creditors, and no stockholders other than the Bakers. Thus, like many small businesses, it has no obligation to issue financial statements to creditors or investors. Under these circumstances, is there any reason for this company to maintain accounting records?

2. In its simplest form, an account has only three elements or basic parts. What are these three elements?

3. At the beginning of the year, the Office Equipment account of Gulf Coast Airlines had a debit balance of $126,900. During the year, debit entries of $23,400 and credit entries of $38,200 were posted to the account. What was the balance of this account at the end of the year? (Indicate debit or credit balance.)

4. What relationship exists between the position of an account on the balance sheet and the rules for recording increases in that account?

5. State briefly the rules of debit and credit as applied to asset accounts. As applied to liability and owners' equity accounts.

6. Does the term *debit* mean increase and the term *credit* mean decrease? Explain.

7. What requirement is imposed by the double-entry system in the recording of any business transaction?

8. Explain precisely what is meant by each of the phrases listed below. Whenever appropriate, indicate whether the left or right side of an account is affected and whether an increase or decrease is indicated.
  a. A debit of $200 to the Cash account.
  b. A debit of $600 to Accounts Payable.
  c. A credit of $50 to Accounts Receivable.
  d. A debit to the Land account.
  e. Credit balance.
  f. Credit side of an account.

9. For each of the following transactions, indicate whether the account in parentheses should be debited or credited, and *give the reason* for your answer.
  a. Purchased land for cash. (Cash)
  b. Sold an old, unneeded typewriter on 30-day credit. (Office Equipment)
  c. Obtained a loan of $30,000 from a bank. (Cash)
  d. Purchased a copying machine on credit, promising to make payment in full within 30 days. (Accounts Payable)
  e. Issued capital stock to the owners of the corporation in exchange for an investment of $125,000 cash. (Capital Stock)

10. For each of the following accounts, state whether it is an asset, a liability, or owners' equity; also state whether it would normally have a debit or a credit balance: (a) Office Equipment, (b) Capital Stock, (c) Accounts Receivable, (d) Accounts Payable, (e) Cash, (f) Notes Payable, (g) Land.

11. Why is a journal sometimes called the *book of original entry?*

12. Compare and contrast a *journal* and a *ledger.*

13. What is a *compound* journal entry?

14. Since it is possible to record the effects of business transactions directly in ledger accounts, why is it desirable for a business to maintain a journal?

15. What purposes are served by a trial balance?

16. In preparing a trial balance, an accounting student listed the balance of the Office Equipment account in the credit column. This account had a balance of $2,450. What would be the amount of the discrepancy in the trial balance totals? Explain.

17. List the following five items in a logical sequence to illustrate the flow of accounting information through a manual accounting system:
    a. Debits and credits posted from journal to ledger.
    b. Preparation of a trial balance.
    c. Information entered in the journal.
    d. Preparation of financial statements.
    e. Occurrence of a business transaction.

18. Which step in the recording of transactions requires greater understanding of accounting principles: (a) the entering of transactions in the journal, or (b) the posting of entries to ledger accounts?

19. List the procedures in the *accounting cycle* as described in this chapter.

20. What is a *database?* How does a database relate to the preparation of journal entries and ledger accounts in a computer-based system?

EXERCISES

EXERCISE 2-1
Double-Entry Accounting
(and lead-in to Chapter 3)

This exercise is intended to show, on a personal level, the "duality" of double-entry accounting—that is, that a change in any asset or liability must be accompanied by an equal change elsewhere in the accounting equation.

Assume that you:

a. Purchase a bicycle from a friend, agreeing to make payment later.

b. Earn $80 working at a part-time job.

c. Lose your stereo when your apartment is burglarized.

d. Pay for the bicycle purchased in transaction **a,** above.

e. Attend a rock concert with your friends, but find that you did not bring any money. Your friends pay for your ticket and food, but you have promised to pay them back.

Briefly explain the effects of each of these transactions upon your financial position, as shown by the following equation:

Assets = Liabilities + Net Worth

(When the accounting equation is applied to an individual, the term "Net Worth" is used instead of "Owner's Equity.") Organize your answer in tabular form, using the code letters **I** for increase, **D** for decrease, **NE** for no effect.

EXERCISE 2-2
Accounting Terminology
LO 1,2,3,4,5,7,8

Listed below are nine technical accounting terms introduced in this chapter:

Ledger   Account   Database
Posting   Credit   Double-entry
Trial balance Debit   Journal

Each of the following statements may (or may not) describe one of these technical terms. For each statement, indicate the accounting term described, or answer "none" if the statement does not correctly describe any of the terms.

a. The system of accounting in which all transactions are recorded both in the journal and in the ledger. *none*

b. An entry on the left-hand side of a ledger account. *debit*

c. The process of transferring information from a journal to the ledger. *posting*

d. The accounting record in which transactions are initially recorded in a manual accounting system. *journal*

e. Information stored in a computer-based accounting system and which can be arranged into any desired format. *database*

f. A device that proves the equality of debits and credits posted to the ledger. *t.e.*

g. The accounting record from which a trial balance is prepared. *ledger*

EXERCISE 2-3
Double-Entry and the Accounting Equation
LO 3,4

A number of transactions are described below in terms of the balance sheet accounts debited and credited:

1. Debit Cash, credit Accounts Receivable

2. Debit Accounts Payable, credit Cash

3. Debit Cash, credit Capital Stock

4. Debit Equipment, credit Accounts Payable

5. Debit Land, credit Cash and Notes Payable

6. Debit Accounts Payable, credit Equipment

a. Indicate the effects of each transaction upon the elements of the accounting equation, using the code letters **I** for increase, **D** for decrease, and **NE** for no effect. Organize your answer in tabular form using the column headings shown below. The answer for transaction **1** is provided as an example.

Transaction	Assets	=	Liabilities	+	Owners' Equity
1	NE		NE		NE

b. Write a one-sentence description of each transaction.

EXERCISE 2-4
Double-Entry Accounting: Debit and Credit Rules
LO 3,4

Analyze separately each of the following transactions, using the format illustrated at the end of the exercise. In each situation, explain the debit portion of the transaction before the credit portion.

a. On April 2, Ginger Denton organized a corporation to conduct business under the name of Gulliver's Travel Services, Inc. The corporation issued 16,000 shares of capital stock to Denton in exchange for $80,000 cash.

b. On April 11, the corporation purchased an office building in an industrial park for a total price of $128,000, of which $72,000 was applicable to the land and $56,000 to the building. A cash down payment of $34,500 was made and a note payable was issued for the balance of the purchase price.

c. On April 12, office equipment was purchased on credit from ADR Company at a price of $6,400. The account payable was to be paid on May 2.

d. On April 29, a portion of the office equipment purchased on April 21 was found to be defective and was returned to ADR Company. ADR Company agreed that Gulliver's Travel Services would not be charged for the defective equipment, which had cost $950.

e. On May 21, the remaining liability to ADR Company was paid in full.

Note: the type of analysis to be made is shown by the following illustration, using transaction **(a)** as an example:

a. (1) The asset Cash was increased. Increases in assets are recorded by debits. Debit Cash, $80,000.
(2) The owners' equity was increased. Increases in owners' equity are recorded by credits. Credit Capital Stock, $80,000.

EXERCISE 2-5
T Accounts; Preparation of Trial Balance
 LO 3,4

The first five transactions of Beaumont Consulting, Inc., are described below.

1. On June 8, Beaumont Consulting, Inc., was organized and issued 95,000 shares of capital stock in exchange for $95,000 cash.

2. On June 12, land was acquired for $43,000 cash.

3. On June 14, a prefabricated building was purchased from E-Z Built Corporation at a cost of $47,900. A cash payment of $15,400 was made and a note payable was issued for the balance.

4. On June 20, office equipment was purchased at a cost of $8,600. A cash down payment of $1,600 was made, and it was agreed that the balance should be paid within 30 days.

5. On June 26, $6,500 of the amount due E-Z Built Corporation was paid. (Ignore interest expense.)

a. Enter the above transactions in T accounts drawn on ordinary notebook paper. Label each debit and credit with the number identifying the transaction.

b. Prepare a trial balance at June 30.

c. Are increases in the balance of a ledger account for a balance sheet item entered on the debit or credit side of that account? Explain.

EXERCISE 2-6
Effects of Debits and Credits on Ledger Account Balances; Trial Balance
 LO 3,4

The first six transactions of Cycle Scene Tour Agency appear in the following T accounts.

	Cash					Notes Payable	
(1)	60,000	(2)	20,000			(2)	100,000
(6)	2,300	(5)	15,000				

	Accounts Receivable					Accounts Payable	
(4)	5,000	(6)	2,300	(5)	15,000	(3)	20,000

	Land					Capital Stock	
(2)	72,000					(1)	60,000

	Building	
(2)	48,000	

	Office Equipment		
(3)	20,000	(4)	5,000

a. For each of the six transactions in turn, indicate the type of account affected (asset, liability, or owners' equity) and whether the account was increased or decreased. Arrange your answers in the form illustrated for transaction **1,** shown here as an example.

	Account(s) Debited		Account(s) Credited	
Transaction	**Type of Account(s)**	**Increase or Decrease**	**Type of Account(s)**	**Increase or Decrease**
(1)	Asset	Increase	Owners' equity	Increase

b. Write a brief description of each transaction.
c. Prepare a trial balance for Cycle Scene Tour Agency after these six transactions. Assume the date is January 10, 19__.

EXERCISE 2-7
Recording Transactions
in a Journal

Enter the following selected transactions in the two-column journal for Fraser Appliance Center. Include a brief explanation of the transaction as part of each journal entry.

Oct. 1 The corporation issued 40,000 shares of capital stock in exchange for $80,000 cash.

Oct. 5 Purchased an adjacent vacant lot for use as parking space. The price was $102,000, of which $30,600 was paid in cash; a note payable was issued for the balance.

Oct. 15 Issued a check for $976 in full payment of an account payable to Hampton Supply Co.

Oct. 18 Borrowed $30,000 cash from the bank by signing a note payable due in 90 days.

Oct. 23 Collected an account receivable of $2,900 from a customer, Jocelyn Scott.

Oct. 30 Acquired office equipment from Tower Company for $6,200. Made a cash down payment of $1,500; balance to be paid within 30 days.

Follow-up: Does the *October 5* transaction increase or reduce this company's solvency? Explain.

EXERCISE 2-8
Journal Entries to Illustrate
Effects of Transactions
LO 3,4,6

Prepare general journal entries to illustrate the effects of each of the following transactions upon the financial statements of Seacoast Airlines. You are to determine appropriate account titles.

Jan. 4 Purchased two seaplanes from Scout Aircraft at a total cost of $790,000. Paid $390,000 in cash and signed a note payable to Island Bank for the remainder.

Jan. 8 Purchased spare parts for the new planes from Breckwoldt Aviation. The parts cost $17,600, and were purchased on account.

Jan. 12 Issued 10,000 shares of Seacoast's capital stock to Earl Scoggins, the owner of Scoggins' Flight School, in exchange for a parcel of waterfront land and a floating aircraft hangar in Columbus Bay. The current value of the land is appraised at $300,000, and the floating hangar is appraised at $200,000.

Jan. 15 Returned to Breckwoldt Aviation $4,300 of the aircraft parts purchased on January 8. The return of these parts reduced by $4,300 the amount owed to Breckwoldt.

Feb. 2 Paid the remaining balance owed to Breckwoldt Aviation from the purchase on January 8.

Follow up: What was the overall effect of the *January 4* transaction upon total assets of Seacoast Airlines? Indicate type of overall effect (increase, decrease, or no effect) as well as dollar amount.

EXERCISE 2-9
Relationship Between
Journal and Ledger Accounts
 LO 3,4,5,6

Transactions are recorded *first* in a journal and *then* posted to ledger accounts. In this exercise, however, your understanding of the relationship between journal and ledger is tested by asking you to study some ledger accounts and determine what journal entries might have been made by the company's accountant to produce these ledger entries. The following accounts show the first six transactions of the Skyline Corporation. Prepare a journal entry (including written explanation) for each transaction.

Cash					Notes Payable			
Nov. 1	60,000	Nov. 8	33,600		Nov. 25	10,000	Nov. 8	100,000
		Nov. 25	10,000					

Land					Accounts Payable			
Nov. 8	70,000				Nov. 21	480	Nov. 15	3,200
Nov. 30	35,000							

Building					Capital Stock			
Nov. 8	63,600						Nov. 1	60,000
							Nov. 30	35,000

Office Equipment			
Nov. 15	3,200	Nov. 21	480

EXERCISE 2-10
Preparing a Trial Balance
 LO 7

Using the information in the ledger accounts presented in Exercise 2-9, prepare a trial balance for Skyline Corporation at November 30, 19__.

Assume the note payable is a long-term mortgage, payable in installments of $900 per month. Does Skyline appear solvent as of November 30? Explain. Does this trial balance provide a good indication of the company's *future* solvency? Again, explain.

EXERCISE 2-11
Uses and Limitations
of a Trial Balance
 LO 7

The trial balance prepared by Discount Plumbing Service at June 30 was not in balance. In searching for the error, an employee discovered that a transaction for the purchase of a calculator on credit for $380 had been recorded by a *debit* of $380 to the Office Equipment account and a *debit* of $380 to Accounts Payable. The credit column of the incorrect trial balance has a total of $129,640.

In answering each of the following five questions, explain fully the reasons underlying your answer and state the dollar amount of the error if any.

a. Was the Office Equipment account overstated, understated, or correctly stated in the trial balance?

b. Was the total of the debit column of the trial balance overstated, understated, or correctly stated?

c. Was the Accounts Payable account overstated, understated, or correctly stated in the trial balance?

d. Was the total of the credit column of the trial balance overstated, understated, or correctly stated?

e. How much was the total of the debit column of the trial balance before correction of the error?

EXERCISE 2-12
Steps in the Accounting
Cycle; Computerized
Accounting Systems
 LO 8

Various steps and decisions involved in the accounting cycle are described in the seven lettered statements below. Indicate which of these procedures are mechanical functions that can be performed by machine in a computerized accounting system, and which require the judgment of people familiar with accounting principles and concepts.

a. Decide whether or not events should be recorded in the accounting records.

b. Determine which ledger accounts should be debited and credited to describe specific business transactions.

c. Arrange recorded data in the format of journal entries.

d. Arrange recorded data in the format of ledger accounts.

e. Prepare a trial balance.

f. Prepare financial statements (except for disclosures).

g. Evaluate the debt-paying ability of one company relative to another.

EXERCISE 2-13
Manual versus Computer-based Systems

For each of the following steps in the accounting cycle, explain whether the step requires human judgment, or whether it can be performed automatically by a computer in a computer-based accounting system.

a. Record transactions as they occur.

b. Post recorded data to ledger accounts.

c. Prepare a trial balance.

d. Prepare a balance sheet and related disclosures.

EXERCISE 2-14
Different Uses for Journals and Ledgers

Briefly explain the usefulness of journal entries and of ledger accounts:

a. In the operation of an accounting system.

b. From the viewpoint of business managers who are *not* personally responsible for maintaining accounting records or preparing their company's financial statements.

c. From the viewpoint of an accounting student or an accounting instructor (assuming *general* journal entries and T accounts).

EXERCISE 2-15
Double-Entry Accounting
LO 3,4

Comparative balance sheets for **Toys "R" Us** appear on page A-8, in Appendix A at the end of this textbook.

a. Do these balance sheets suggest that Toys "R" Us uses double-entry accounting? Why?

b. The Cash account (actually called Cash and Cash Equivalents) *decreased* by $422,060 (dollar amounts in thousands) during the year.
  (1) Were the debit entries to this account greater or less than the credit entries? Explain how this is possible in a system in which debit entries and credit entries are supposed to be equal in dollar amount.
  (2) Provide an example of a transaction, involving *only balance sheet accounts,* which would cause the Cash account to (a) increase, and (b) decrease. For each of these transactions, explain whether the Cash account would be debited or credited, and also identify the *other* balance sheet account that would have been debited or credited.

PROBLEMS

PROBLEM 2-1
Journal Entries:
An Alternate Problem
LO 2,3,4,6

RTM Theater Group, Inc., is a corporation that owns and operates a chain of movie theaters. Selected business transactions of the corporation during August 1998 are listed below:

Aug. 1 Purchased cleaning supplies on account from Janitorial Supply Co., $3,000. Payment due in 30 days.

Aug. 3 Purchased projection equipment for cash from Video Concepts, $6,800.

Aug. 5   Returned to Video Concepts a projector purchased on August 3, because the lens was defective. The projector had cost RTM $2,300; Video Concepts agreed to refund within five days.

Aug. 10   Received the $2,300 refund from Video Concepts.

Aug. 12   Issued additional shares of capital stock to investors in exchange for $300,000 cash.

Aug. 15   Purchased the Village Theater for $920,000, paying $170,000 in cash and issuing a note payable for the balance of the purchase price. The assets included in the purchase price, and their values at August 15, were as follows:

Land...	$200,000
Building	525,000
Equipment...	195,000

Aug. 31   Paid in full the $3,000 account payable to Janitorial Supply Co.

INSTRUCTIONS

a. Prepare journal entries to record the above transactions. Select the appropriate account titles from the following chart of accounts:

Cash	Land	Notes payable
Accounts receivable	Buildings	Accounts payable
Cleaning supplies	Equipment	Capital stock

b. What impact did the August 15 transaction have on the financial position of RTM Theater Group, Inc.? (Indicate direction and dollar effect of this transaction on RTM's assets, liabilities, and owners' equity.)

PROBLEM 2-2
Recording Transactions in a
Journal: A Second Problem
LO 2,3,4,6

Louis Dixon, a dentist, resigned from his position with a large dental group in order to begin his own pediatric dental practice. The practice was organized as a corporation called Louis Dixon Pediatric Dentistry. The business transactions during September, while the new business was being organized, are listed below.

Sept. 1   Issued 10,000 shares of capital stock to Dixon in exchange for his equity investment of $50,000 cash.

Sept. 10   Purchased a small office building located on a large lot for a total price of $182,400, of which $106,000 was applicable to the land and $76,400 to the building. A cash payment of $26,500 was made and a note payable was issued for the balance of the purchase price.

Sept. 15   Purchased a microcomputer system from Computer Stores, Inc., for $4,680 cash.

Sept. 19   Purchased office furnishings, including dental equipment, from Turnkey Operations, Inc., at a cost of $15,760. A cash down payment of $3,760 was made, the balance to be paid in three equal installments due September 28, October 28, and November 28. The purchase was on open account and did not require signing of a promissory note.

Sept. 26   A $140 monitor in the microcomputer system purchased on September 15 stopped working. The monitor was returned to Computer Stores, Inc., which promised to refund the $140 within five days.

Sept. 28   Paid Turnkey Operations, Inc., $4,000 cash as the first installment due on the account payable for office furnishings.

Sept. 30   Received $140 cash from Computer Stores, Inc., in full settlement of the account receivable created on September 26.

INSTRUCTIONS

a. Prepare journal entries to record the above transactions. Select the appropriate account titles from the following chart of accounts:

Cash	Office furnishings
Accounts receivable	Notes payable
Land	Accounts payable
Building	Capital stock
Computer system	

b. What impact did the September 10 transaction have on the financial position of the company? (Indicate direction and dollar effect of this transaction on the corporation's assets, liabilities, and stockholders' equity.)

PROBLEM 2-3
Analyzing Transactions and
Preparing Journal Entries
LO 2,3,4,6

Yoko Toyoda is the founder and only stockholder in Perfect Portraits, Inc., a photography studio. A few of the company's business transactions that occurred during July are described below:

1. On July 2, purchased photographic equipment for $2,525, paying $750 in cash and charging the remainder on the company's 30-day account at Camera Supply Co.

2. On July 7, Perfect Portraits issued an additional 5,000 shares of its capital stock to Toyoda in exchange for $5,000 cash.

3. On July 9, returned to Camera Supply Co. $400 of photographic equipment which did not work properly. The return of this equipment reduced by $400 the amount owed to Camera Supply Co.

4. On July 25, collected cash of $900 from accounts receivable.

5. On July 31, paid the remaining $1,375 owed to Camera Supply Co.

INSTRUCTIONS

a. Prepare an analysis of each of the above transactions. Using transaction **1** as an example, the form to be used is as follows:
  1. (a) The asset Photographic Equipment was increased. Increases in assets are recorded by debits. Debit Photographic Equipment, $2,525.
  (b) The asset Cash was decreased. Decreases in assets are recorded by credits. Credit Cash, $750. A liability was incurred. Increases in liabilities are recorded by credits. Credits Accounts Payable, $1,775.

b. Prepare journal entries, including explanations, for the above transactions.

PROBLEM 2-4
Preparing a Trial Balance
and a Balance Sheet
LO 7

Environment Services, Inc., is a weather forecasting service which provides information to growers and dealers in perishable commodities. Its ledger account balances at November 30 are as shown in the following alphabetical list.

Accounts payable	$ 7,000	Land	$105,200
Accounts receivable	16,700	Notes payable	115,000
Automobiles	21,500	Notes receivable	2,400
Building	120,000	Office furniture	12,900
Capital stock	150,000	Office supplies	850
Cash	17,650	Retained earnings	49,510
Computer	18,800	Taxes payable	3,740
Computer software	5,450	Technical library	3,800

INSTRUCTIONS

a. Prepare a trial balance with the accounts arranged in financial statement order. Include a proper heading for your trial balance.

b. Prepare a balance sheet. Include a subtotal for total liabilities.

c. Explain the difference in purpose between a trial balance and a balance sheet.

PROBLEM 2-5
Short "Cycle" Problem—
Posting to Ledger Accounts;
Preparing a Trial Balance
and a Balance Sheet
LO 5,7,8

After several years of working as sous-chef at Prism, a five-star restaurant in Los Angeles, Cindy Black had saved enough money to open her own gourmet restaurant. The business will be organized as a corporation, named Onyx. During July, while organizing Onyx, Black prepared the following journal entries to record the first week's transactions. She has not posted these entries to ledger accounts. The ledger account numbers to be used are: Cash 1, Supplies 9, Land 20, Building 22, Kitchen Equipment 25, Notes Payable 30, Accounts Payable 31, and Capital Stock 50.

GENERAL JOURNAL					Page *1*
Date		**Account Titles and Explanation**	**LP**	**Debit**	**Credit**
July	1	Cash..		50,000	
		Capital Stock			50,000
		Issued capital stock in exchange for cash.			
	2	Land..		60,000	
		Building		42,850	
		Cash			25,850
		Notes Payable (Seaport Bank)....................			77,000
		Purchased the former Nobu's Cafe; the note is payable to Seaport Bank at the rate of $565 per month for 30 years.			
	3	Kitchen Equipment..		4,680	
		Accounts Payable			4,680
		Bought equipment on credit from ProChef, Inc.			
	3	Supplies		1,260	
		Accounts Payable			1,260
		Bought supplies from HB Restaurant Supply.			
	5	Accounts Payable		725	
		Kitchen Equipment			725
		Returned defective equipment to ProChef, Inc. for credit on account.			
	7	Accounts Payable		630	
		Cash			630
		Made partial payment of liability to HB Restaurant Supply.			
	7	Accounts Payable		3,955	
		Cash			3,955
		Made payment of liability to ProChef, Inc.			

INSTRUCTIONS

a. Post the journal entries to ledger accounts of the three-column running balance form.

b. Prepare a trial balance at July 8 from the ledger accounts completed in part **a.**

c. Prepare a balance sheet at July 8, 19__.

d. Describe in as much detail as you can the transaction on July 2.

PROBLEM 2-6
Preparing Journal Entries,
Posting, and Preparing
a Trial Balance

A small group of investors formed a business entity to provide bus service for a fee to public and private schools in the Walnut Creek area. The business is organized as a corporation and called Walnut Creek Transportation Services. The transactions during July, while the new business was being organized, are listed below.

July 1 The corporation issued 225,000 shares of capital stock to the owners in exchange for a total of $450,000 cash.

July 3 The new company purchased land and a building at a cost of $240,000, of which $144,000 was regarded as applicable to the land and $96,000 to the building. The transaction involved a cash payment of $60,000 and the issuance of a note payable for the balance of the purchase price.

July 5 Purchased 16 new buses at $27,000 each from Fleet Sales Company. Paid $136,000 cash, and agreed to pay $156,000 by July 31 and the remaining balance by August 15. The liability is viewed as an account payable.

July 7 Sold one of the buses at cost to YMCA Camping Services. The buyer paid $15,000 in cash and agreed to pay the balance within 30 days.

July 8 Upon inspection, one of the buses was found to be defective and was returned to Fleet Sales Company. The amount payable to this creditor was thereby reduced by 27,000.

July 20 Purchased office equipment at a cost of $4,800 cash.

July 31 Issued a check for $156,000 in partial payment of the liability to Fleet Sales Company.

The account titles and the account numbers used by the company are as follows:

Cash	10	Buses	22
Accounts receivable	11	Notes payable	31
Land	16	Accounts payable	32
Buildings	17	Capital stock	50
Office equipment	20		

INSTRUCTIONS

a. Journalize the July transactions.

b. Post to ledger accounts. Use the running balance form of ledger account.

c. Prepare a trial balance at July 31, 19__.

d. Does the corporation have sufficient cash at July 31 to pay the balance owed to Fleet Sales Company on August 15? Based upon the information provided in the problem data, will the corporation have sufficient cash by August 15 to pay the amount owed Fleet Sales Company? Explain briefly.

PROBLEM 2-7
Preparing Journal Entries,
Posting, and Preparing a
Trial Balance: An
Alternate Problem

Beach Property Management, a new corporation, was started on November 1, 1998, by Ann Chee to provide management services for the owners of apartment buildings. The organizational period extended throughout November and included the transactions listed below.

Nov. 1 The corporation issued 35,000 shares of capital stock to its owner, Ann Chee, in exchange for her investment of $35,000 cash in the business. Chee already has several clients signed up for her services. She believes that her $35,000 investment will be sufficient to acquire a business location and the office equipment necessary for her to start operations at the beginning of December.

Nov. 4 Purchased land and an office building for a price of $174,000, of which $100,000 was considered applicable to the land and $74,000 attributable to the building. A cash down payment of $34,000 was made and a note payable for $140,000 was issued for the balance of the purchase price.

Nov. 7 Purchased office equipment on credit from Eaton Office Equipment, $10,850, due in 30 days.

Nov. 9 A printer (cost $195), which was part of the November 7 purchase of office equipment, proved defective and was returned for credit to Eaton Office Equipment.

Nov. 17 Sold one-fourth of the land acquired on November 4 to Ace Parking Lots at a price of $25,000. This price is equal to the corporation's cost for this portion of the land, so there is no gain or loss on this transaction. Received a $5,000 cash down payment from Ace Parking Lots and a note receivable in the amount of $20,000, due in four monthly installments of $5,000 each, beginning on November 30. (Ignore interest.)

Nov. 30 Received cash of $5,000 as partial collection of the note receivable from Ace Parking Lots.

The account titles and account numbers to be used are

Cash	1	Office equipment	25
Notes receivable	5	Notes payable	31
Land	21	Accounts payable	32
Building	23	Capital stock	51

INSTRUCTIONS

a. Prepare journal entries for the month of November.

b. Post to ledger accounts of the three-column running balance form.

c. Prepare a trial balance at November 30, 1998.

d. The note payable is a 30-year mortgage, due in monthly installments of $1,024, beginning on December 1, 1998. Beach will collect no cash from customers until early January **1999.** From the information in this problem, does it appear that the corporation currently has enough cash to meet the obligations coming due in early December (the mortgage payment and the balanced owed to Eaton Office Products)?

e. Based on your answer to part **d,** does it appear that this company is insolvent and may be forced to close its doors before it really gets started?

f. The mortgage note payable requires monthly payments of $1,024 for 30 years. Compute the total amount expected to be paid over the life of this $140,000 note. Why does the amount you have computed exceed the amount of the note?

PROBLEM 2-8
The Accounting Cycle: A
Comprehensive Problem

The Movie Channel (TMC) was organized in June 19__, to operate as a local television station. The account titles and numbers used by the corporation are listed below:

Cash	11	Telecasting equipment	24
Accounts receivable	15	Film library	25
Supplies	19	Notes payable	31
Land	21	Accounts payable	32
Building	22	Capital stock	51
Transmitter	23		

The transactions for June 19__, were as follows:

June 1 A charter was granted to Paul and Alice Marshal for the organization of The Movie Channel. The Marshals invested $400,000 cash and received 80,000 shares of stock in exchange.

June 3 The new corporation purchased the land, buildings, and telecasting equipment previously used by a local television station which had gone bankrupt. The total purchase price was $325,000, of which $120,000 was attributable to the land, $95,000 to the building, and the remainder to the telecasting equipment. The terms of the purchase required a cash payment of $200,000 and the issuance of a note payable for the balance; the note payable is due in three years.

June 5 Purchased a transmitter at a cost of $225,000 from AC Mfg. Co., making a cash down payment of $75,000. The balance, in the form of a note payable, was to be paid in monthly installments, of $12,500, beginning June 15. (Interest expense is to be ignored.)

June 9 Purchased a film library at a cost of $150,000 from Timeless Classics, Inc., making a down payment of $50,000 cash, with the balance on account payable in 60 days.

June 12 Bought supplies costing $3,190, paying cash.

June 15 Paid $12,500 to AC Mfg. Co. as the first monthly payment on the note payable created on February 5. (Interest expense is to be ignored.)

June 25 Sold part of the film library to City College; cost was $20,000 and the selling price also was $20,000. City College agreed to pay the full amount in 30 days.

Actual business operations are expected to begin on September 1.

INSTRUCTIONS

a. Prepare journal entries for the month of June.

b. Post to ledger accounts of the three-column running balance form.

c. Prepare a trial balance at June 30, 19__.

d. Prepare a balance sheet at June 30, 19__.

e. Based upon your answers to parts **a** through **d** and information presented in the problem data, does it appear the corporation will have sufficient cash to pay existing liabilities as they come due in July? How about those that come due in August? Explain.

CASES

CASE 2-1
The Role of Accounting Records

LO 1

Interview someone familiar with the accounting system in a small local business, such as a restaurant or a retail store. (Interviews should be planned and conducted in accordance with the instructions *Note to Students* at the beginning of this textbook.)

INSTRUCTIONS

a. Does this business have any obligation to furnish financial statements to creditors or investors who are not actively involved in management? Explain briefly.

b. List specific types of accounting information that this business has either a legal or ethical obligation to develop within its accounting system. (**Note:** We recognize the overlap between legal and ethical obligations. We *do not* ask you to distinguish between these categories.)

CASE 2-2

Computer-based
Accounting Systems

LO 2,4,5

Bill Gates is planning to create a computer-based accounting system for small businesses. His system will be developed from a database program and will be suitable for use on personal computers.

The idea underlying database software is that data needed for a variety of uses is entered into the database only once. The computer is programmed to arrange this data into any number of desired formats. In the case of Gates' accounting system, it is designed so that the company's accounting personnel must enter the relevant information about each business transaction into the database. The program which Gates plans to write will then enable the computer operator to have the information arranged by the computer into the formats of (1) journal entries (with written explanations), (2) three-column running-balance-form ledger accounts, (3) a trial balance, and (4) a balance sheet.

INSTRUCTIONS

a. Identify the relevant information about each business transaction that the company's accounting personnel must enter into the database to enable Gates' program to prepare the four types of accounting records and statements described above.

b. As described in this chapter, the accounting cycle includes the steps of: (1) analyzing and recording business transactions, (2) posting the debit and credit amounts to ledger accounts, (3) preparing a trial balance, and (4) preparing financial statements (at this stage, only a balance sheet). Indicate which of these functions can be performed automatically by Gates' computer program and which must still be performed by the company's accounting personnel.

CASE 2-3

Preparing Balance Sheets
and an Introduction to
Measuring Income

Prelude to Chapter 3

Brooke Lowell, a college student with several summers' experience as a guide on bicycle camping trips, decided to go into business for herself. On June 1, Lowell organized Cape Cod Bicycle Tours, a *sole proprietorship,* by depositing $2,000 of her personal savings in a bank account in the name of the business. Also on June 1, the business borrowed an additional $3,500 cash from John Lowell (Brooke's uncle) by issuing a three-year note payable. To help the business get started, John Lowell agreed that no interest would be charged on the loan. The following transactions were also carried out by the business on June 1:

1. Bought a number of bicycles at a total cost of $6,500; paid $2,500 cash and agreed to pay the balance within 60 days.

2. Bought camping equipment at a cost of $3,200, payable in 60 days.

3. Bought supplies for cash, $650.

After the close of the season on September 10, Lowell asked another student, Tom Cummings, who had taken a course in accounting, to help determine the financial position of her business.

The only record Lowell had maintained was a checkbook with memorandum notes written on the check stubs. From this source Cummings discovered that Lowell had invested an additional $1,000 of savings in the business on July 1, and also that the accounts payable arising from the purchase of the bicycles and camping equipment had been paid in full. A bank statement received from the bank on September 10 showed a balance on deposit of $2,990.

Lowell informed Cummings that all cash received by the business had been deposited in the bank and all bills had been paid by check immediately upon receipt; consequently, as of September 10 all bills for the season had been paid. However, nothing had been paid on the note payable.

The bicycles and camping equipment were all in excellent condition at the end of the season and Lowell planned to resume operations the following summer. In fact, she had already accepted reservations from many customers who wished to return.

Cummings felt that some consideration should be given to the wear and tear on the bicycles and equipment, but he agreed with Lowell that for the present purpose the bicycles and equipment should be listed in the balance sheet at the original cost. The supplies remaining on hand had cost $75 and Lowell felt that these supplies could be used next summer.

Cummings suggested that two balance sheets be prepared, one to show the condition of the business on June 1 and the other showing the condition on September 10. He also recommended to Lowell that a complete set of accounting records be established.

INSTRUCTIONS

a. Use the information in the first paragraph (including the three numbered transactions) as a basis for preparing a balance sheet dated June 1, 19__. (Because this business is a sole proprietorship, the balance sheet will include a single owner's equity account, entitled Brooke Lowell, Capital. The owner's equity section of the balance sheet for a sole proprietorship is illustrated on page 18 in Chapter 1.)

b. Prepare a balance sheet at September 10, 19__. (Because of the incomplete information available, it is not possible to determine the amount of cash at September 10 by adding cash receipts and deducting cash payments throughout the season. The amount on deposit as reported by the bank at September 10 is to be regarded as the total cash belonging to the business at that date.)

c. By comparing the two balance sheets, compute the change in owner's equity. Explain the sources of this change in owner's equity and state whether you consider the business to be successful. Also comment on the cash position at the beginning and end of the season. Has the cash position improved significantly? Explain.

INTERNET 2-1
Accounting Software
LO 1,8

INTERNET ASSIGNMENTS

Today, much of the accounting cycle is performed by special computer accounting software. Peachtree™ was among the first companies to develop such software. You can access the Peachtree home page by opening the following Internet location:

www.peach.com

a. What accounting software programs does Peachtree offer?

b. Identify some of the "modules" (or functions) of Peachtree's accounting software.

c. Enter the keywords "accounting software" in the search engine of your browser. Are there few or many accounting software packages listed on the Internet? Why do you think this is?

Note: Additional Internet assignments for this chapter appear in Appendix B and on our home page

www.magpie.org/cyberlab

ANSWERS TO SELF-TEST QUESTIONS

1. d   **2.** c   **3.** a   **4.** b   **5.** c

OUR COMMENTS ON THE IN-TEXT CASES

YOU AS A STUDENT (P. 59)   The concept of double-entry *does* apply to your personal financial position. The financial position of an individual may be described by the equation:

Assets = Liabilities + Net Worth

Any change in the amount of any asset or liability causes an offsetting change *elsewhere* in the equation. Thus, two or more "accounts" within the accounting equation must change — this is what is meant by double-entry.

For example, your spending cash results in the acquisition of another asset, in the reduction of a liability, or in a reduction in your personal net worth (the equivalent of owners' equity in a business organization). A cash receipt implies the reduction of another asset, an increase in liabilities, or an increase in net worth.

Although individuals do not use debits and credits to record changes in their financial positions, the concept of double-entry — that is, corresponding changes in the accounting equation — still applies.

YOU AS A STORE MANAGER (P. 75) You should look to the journal to determine the purpose of the cash payment to the New York Yankees. A journal shows in one place all aspects of a particular transaction. The purpose of the payment can be determined either from the account credited, or from the written explanation of the entry.

The cost of inventory on hand at a particular date can best be determined from the ledger. This accounting record shows the balance of specific ledger accounts at specific dates. The cost of inventory on hand should appear in the Inventory account.

Little Bear Railroad, Inc.

AN INTRODUCTION TO THE ACCOUNTING PROCESS

Note to students: Accountants often find themselves confronted with situations different from anything they have encountered before. They resolve these situations by doing research and by applying their knowledge of basic accounting concepts. One objective of this problem is to demonstrate these challenging aspects of accounting.

Based upon the accounting concepts introduced in Chapters 1 and 2, you should be able to "reason out" a solution to this problem. If you prefer a more research-oriented approach, you might look up "Intangible assets," "Capital stock: issuance of," and "Unincorporated business, incorporation of" in the index of this textbook. Whichever approach you take, *be prepared to discuss your conclusions in class!*

Those of you who find this type of problem interesting may be well-suited to a career in accounting.

For many years Kim-Chung (K-C) Jones has owned and operated the Little Bear Railroad, a narrow-gauge railroad operating inside a national park. The Little Bear operates for only eight months each year — April 1 through November 30 — offering park visitors a 22-mile scenic tour of the redwood forest. The train consists of a woodburning locomotive and three passenger cars. Until March 1998, the business had been organized as a sole proprietorship.

In March, prior to opening for the 1998 season, Jones decided to reorganize the business as Little Bear Railroad, Inc., a corporation. The following events occurred as the new corporation was being organized:

Mar. 1 Jones transferred into the new corporation all of the assets and liabilities of the Little Bear Railroad. In exchange the corporation issued 100,000 shares of capital stock (assumed issuance price, $1,000,000). The business assets and liabilities, and their value at March 1, were as follows:

Cash	$ 48,000
Accounts receivable	8,600
Supplies	4,900
Spare parts	10,400
Buildings	170,000
Equipment & rolling stock	415,000
Roadbed, track, & ties	250,000
Notes payable (due in 2003)	300,000
Accounts payable	6,900

In addition to the assets and liabilities listed above, Jones also transferred into the corporation a permanent right-of-way that allowed the railroad to operate on specific portions of the national park's land. (Notice that the railroad owns no land; the land upon which it operates is part of the national park.) Jones acquired the right-of-way from the National Park Service many years ago at a cost of $100,000. However, this asset was considered to be worth $400,000 at the date that Jones transferred it into the new corporation.

Mar. 4 Jones sold 10% of her capital stock in the corporation to Adrian Wong-Boren, a relative, for $115,000 cash.

Mar. 10 The corporation borrowed $100,000 cash from Pine City Bank to provide capital for expanding its operations. A note payable was issued, due in 90 days. (Ignore interest charges.)

Mar. 12 An agreement was signed with Jay Gould Construction Co., which is to build a three-mile extension of roadbed and track within Little Bear's right-of-way through the park. Work will begin on April 1 and is to be completed by August 15, 1998. The total cost will be $240,000, payable in thirds as each mile of track is completed.

Mar. 15 The corporation purchased a replica of a 1865 steam-driven locomotive and an original 1898 dining car from The Spud, a narrow-gauge railroad in Idaho that had gone bankrupt. The purchase price was $380,000; Little Bear, Inc., paid $90,000 in cash and issued a note payable for the balance. The note, payable to Silverado Savings, is due in one year.

INSTRUCTIONS

a. Prepare all general journal entries necessary through March 15 to record these events in the accounting records of the new corporation. (Not all of these events require journal entries.)

b. Post to ledger accounts of the three-column form. (You are to create the company's ledger by assigning names and numbers to an appropriate number of ledger accounts.)

c. Prepare a trial balance at March 15, 1998.

d. Prepare a balance sheet at March 15, 1998. Also, draft a note accompanying this balance sheet to disclose the company's contractual commitment to Jay Gould Construction Co.

e. Assume that you are a loan officer at Sequoia Savings Bank. Little Bear Railroad, Inc., wants to borrow from your bank the $240,000 to pay for the three-mile extension of its track. The corporation intends to repay this loan in one year. Based solely upon the available information, does the corporation appear to be a reasonably good credit risk? Explain the reasons for your conclusion.

CHAPTER 3

MEASURING BUSINESS INCOME AND COMPLETING THE ACCOUNTING CYCLE

Location:

Search | Feedback | Help | Directory

Document: Done

Net income is not an amount of money received. Rather, it is a *measure of economic performance*. In many ways, net income serves the same purpose in the business world as do *points* in a sporting event. It tells us which companies are surging ahead, and which are falling behind.

1 Explain the nature of *net income, retained earnings, revenue,* and *expenses.*

2 Apply the *realization* and *matching* principles in recording revenue and expenses.

3 Explain *why* revenues are recorded with credits and expenses are recorded with debits.

4 Explain the nature of *adjusting entries.*

5 Define and record depreciation expense.

6 Prepare statements of income and of retained earnings. Explain how these statements relate to the balance sheet.

7 Explain the purposes of *closing entries;* prepare these entries.

8 Describe the steps in the *accounting cycle.*

9 Distinguish between the *accrual basis* and the *cash basis* of accounting.

WHAT IS NET INCOME?

L01 *Explain the nature of* net income, retained earnings, revenue, *and* expenses.

In Chapter 1, we stated that a basic objective of every business is to earn a profit, or net income. Why? The answer lies in the very definition of **net income:** *an increase in owners' equity resulting from the profitable operation of the business.* The opposite of net income, a *decrease* in owners' equity resulting from unprofitable operation of the business, is termed a **net loss.**

If you were to organize a business of your own, you would do so with the hope and expectation that the business would operate at a profit, thereby increasing your ownership equity. Individuals who invest in the capital stock of a large corporation also expect the business to earn a profit which will increase the value of their investment.

Notice that net income does not consist of cash or any other specific asset. Rather, net income is a *computation* of the overall effects of many business transactions upon *owners' equity.* The increase in owners' equity resulting from profitable operations usually is accompanied by an increase in total assets, though not necessarily an increase in cash. In some cases, however, an increase in owners' equity is accompanied by a decrease in total liabilities. The effects of earning net income upon the basic accounting equation are illustrated below:

Net income is not an asset—it's an *increase in owners' equity*

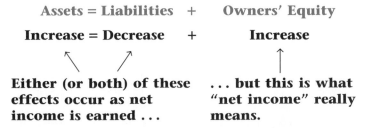

Our point is that net income represents an *increase in owners' equity* and has no direct relationship to the types or amounts of assets on hand. Even a business operating at a profit may run short of cash and become insolvent.

In the balance sheet, the changes in owners' equity resulting from profitable or unprofitable operations are reflected in the balance of the stockholders' equity account, *Retained Earnings.* The assets of the business organization appear in the *assets* section of the balance sheet.

RETAINED EARNINGS

As illustrated in Chapter 1, the Retained Earnings account appears in the stockholders' equity section of the balance sheet. Earning net income causes the balance in the Retained Earnings account to increase. However, many corporations follow a policy of distributing to their stockholders some of the resources generated by profitable operations. Distributions of this nature are termed **dividends,** and they reduce both total assets and stockholders' equity. The reduction in stockholders' equity is reflected by decreasing the balance of the Retained Earnings account.

The balance in the **Retained Earnings** account represents the total net income of the corporation over the *entire lifetime* of the business, less all amounts which have been distributed to the stockholders as dividends. In short, retained earnings represents the earnings that have been *retained* by the corporation to finance growth. Some of the largest corporations have become large by consistently retaining in the business most of the resources generated by profitable operations.

CASE IN POINT

A recent annual report of **Campbell Soup Company** shows total stockholders' equity amounting to nearly $2 billion. Stockholders originally invested only about $71 million—less than 4% of the current equity—in exchange for capital stock. By operating profitably and retaining earnings, Campbell has added more than $1¾ billion to its stockholders' equity.

THE INCOME STATEMENT: A PREVIEW

An **income statement** is a one-page financial statement which summarizes the profitability of the business entity over a specified period of time. In this statement, net income is determined by comparing for the time period: (1) the *sales price* of the goods sold and services rendered by the business with (2) the *cost* to the business of the goods and services used up in business operations. The technical accounting terms for these components of net income are *revenue* and *expenses.* Therefore, accountants say that net income is equal to *revenue minus expenses,* as shown in the following income statement.

OVERNIGHT AUTO SERVICE		
Income Statement		
For the Month Ended December 31, 1998		
Revenue:		
Repair service revenue		$20,340
Expenses:		
Advertising expense	$ 1,830	
Wages expense	12,410	
Supplies expense	600	
Depreciation expense: building	500	
Depreciation expense: tools and equipment	1,000	16,340
Income before income taxes		$ 4,000
Income taxes expense		1,600
Net income		$ 2,400

An income statement has two basic sections—revenue and expenses—which lead to the computation of net income

 money column

When we measure the net income earned by a business we are measuring its economic performance—its success or failure as a business enterprise. Investors, managers, and major creditors are anxious to see the latest available income statement and thereby judge how well the company is doing.

Later in this chapter we will show how this income statement is developed from the accounting records of Overnight Auto Service. For the moment, however, this illustration will assist us in discussing some of the basic concepts involved in measuring business income.

INCOME MUST BE RELATED TO A SPECIFIED PERIOD OF TIME Notice that our sample income statement covers a *period of time*—namely, the month of December. A balance sheet shows the financial position of a business at a *particular date*. An income statement, on the other hand, shows the results of business operations over a span of time. We cannot evaluate net income unless it is associated with a specific time period. For example, if an executive says, "My business earns a net income of $50,000," the profitability of the business is unclear. Does it earn $50,000 per month, per quarter, or per year?

CASE IN POINT

The late **J. Paul Getty,** one of the world's first billionaires, was once interviewed by a group of business students. One of the students asked Getty to estimate the amount of his income. As the student had not specified a time period, Getty decided to have some fun with his audience and responded, "I'm told that last year I made about $11,000 . . . " He paused long enough to allow the group to express surprise over this seemingly low amount, and then completed his sentence, " . . . an hour." (Incidentally, $11,000 per hour, 24 hours per day, amounts to about $100 million per year.)

ACCOUNTING PERIODS The period of time covered by an income statement is termed the company's **accounting period.** To provide the users of financial statements with timely information, net income is measured for relatively short accounting periods of equal length. This concept, called the **time period principle,** is one of the generally accepted accounting principles that guide the interpretation of financial events and the preparation of financial statements.

The length of a company's accounting period depends upon how frequently managers, investors, and other interested people require information about the company's performance. Every business prepares annual income statements, and most businesses prepare quarterly and monthly income statements as well. (Quarterly statements cover a three-month period and are prepared by all large corporations for distribution to their stockholders.)

The 12-month accounting period used by an entity is called its **fiscal year.** The fiscal year used by most companies coincides with the calendar year and ends on December 31. Some businesses, however, elect to use a fiscal year which ends on some other date. It may be convenient for a business to end its fiscal year at a time of relatively slow business activity.

CASE **IN** POINT

The Walt Disney Company ends its fiscal year on September 30. Why? For one reason, September and October are relatively slow months at Disney's theme parks. For another, September financial statements provide timely information about the preceding summer, which is the company's busiest season.

As another example, many department stores, including K Mart, Neiman-Marcus, Nordstrom, and J. C. Penney, end their fiscal years on January 31—after the rush of the holiday season.

Let us now explore the meaning of the accounting terms *revenue* and *expenses*.

REVENUE

Revenue *is the price of goods sold and services rendered during a given accounting period.* Earning revenue causes owners' equity to increase. When a business renders services or sells merchandise to its customers, it usually receives cash or acquires an account receivable from the customer. The inflow of cash and receivables from customers increases the total assets of the company; on the other side of the accounting equation, the liabilities do not change, but owners' equity increases to match the increase in total assets. Thus, revenue is the gross *increase in owners' equity* resulting from operation of the business.

Various account titles are used to describe different types of revenue. For example, Overnight records its revenue in an account entitled *Repair Services Revenue*. A business which sells merchandise rather than services, such as Wal-Mart or General Motors, uses the terms *Sales* to describe its revenue. In the professional practices of physicians, CPAs, and attorneys, revenue usually is called *Fees Earned*. A real estate office, however, might call its revenue *Commissions Earned*.

A professional sports team might have separate revenue accounts for *Ticket Sales, Concessions Revenue,* and *Revenue from Television Contracts*. Another type of revenue common to most businesses is *Interest Revenue* (or Interest Earned), stemming from the interest earned on bank deposits, notes receivable, and interest-bearing investments.

THE REALIZATION PRINCIPLE: WHEN TO RECORD REVENUE We have defined revenue as *the price of goods sold and services rendered during a given accounting period.* Thus, revenue earned by selling merchandise is recognized *when the goods are sold.* Revenue earned by rendering services to customers is recognized in the period in which the *services are rendered.*

To illustrate, assume that on July 25, KGPO Radio contracts with Rancho Ford to run two hundred 1-minute radio advertisements during August. KGPO runs these ads and receives full payment from Rancho Ford on September 6. In which month should KGPO recognize this advertising revenue—July, August, or September?

The answer is in *August*—the month in which KGPO *rendered the services* which earned the revenue.[1] In summary, revenue is recognized *when it is earned,* without regard to when payment is received. This concept is called the **realization principle.**

LO 2 *Apply the* realization *and* matching *principles in recording revenue and expenses.*

---

[1]Some readers may wonder what would happen if some of the ads were aired in August and others in September. In this case, KGPO should recognize an *appropriate portion* of the advertising revenue in August, and the remainder in September. The accounting procedures for allocating revenue between accounting periods are discussed and illustrated in the next chapter.

Because of the realization principle, revenue represents the *value of goods sold and services rendered during the accounting period,* not the amount of cash received.

EXPENSES

Expenses *are the costs of the goods and services used up in the process of earning revenue.* Examples include the cost of employees' salaries, advertising, rent, utilities, and the gradual wearing-out (depreciation) of such assets as buildings, automobiles, and office equipment. All these costs are necessary to attract and serve customers and thereby earn revenue. Expenses are often called the "costs of doing business," that is, the cost of the various activities necessary to carry on a business.

An expense always causes a *decrease in owners' equity.* The related changes in the accounting equation can be either (1) a decrease in assets, or (2) an increase in liabilities. An expense reduces assets if payment occurs at the time that the expense is incurred. If the expense will not be paid until later, as, for example, the purchase of advertising services on account, the recording of the expense will be accompanied by an increase in liabilities.

THE MATCHING PRINCIPLE: WHEN TO RECORD EXPENSES A significant relationship exists between revenue and expenses. Expenses are incurred for the *purpose of producing revenue.* In measuring net income for a period, revenue should be offset by *all the expenses incurred in producing that revenue.* This concept of offsetting expenses against revenue on a basis of cause and effect is called the **matching principle.**

Timing is an important factor in matching (offsetting) revenue with the related expenses. For example, in preparing monthly income statements, it is important to offset this month's expenses against this month's revenue. We should not offset this month's expenses against last month's revenue because there is no cause and effect relationship between the two.

To illustrate the matching principle, assume that the salaries earned by sales personnel waiting on customers during July are not paid until early August. In which month should these salaries be regarded as an expense? The answer is *July,* because this is the month in which the sales personnel's services *helped to produce revenue.*

We previously explained that revenue and cash receipts are not one and the same thing. Similarly, expenses and cash payments are not identical. The cash payment for an expense may occur before, after, or in the same period that an expense helps to produce revenue. In deciding when to record an expense, the critical question is *"In what period does this expenditure help to produce revenue?"* not "When does the cash payment occur?"

EXPENDITURES BENEFITING MORE THAN ONE ACCOUNTING PERIOD
Many expenditures made by a business benefit two or more accounting periods. Fire insurance policies, for example, usually cover a period of 12 months. If a company prepares monthly income statements, a portion of the cost of such a policy should be allocated to insurance expense for each month that the policy is in force. In this case, apportionment of the cost of the policy by months is an easy matter. If the 12-month policy costs $2,400, for example, the insurance for each month amounts to $200 ($2,400 cost ÷ 12 months).

Not all transactions can be so precisely divided by accounting periods. The purchase of a building, furniture and fixtures, machinery, a computer, or an automobile provides benefits to the business over all the years in which such an asset is used. No one can determine in advance exactly how many years of service will be received from such long-lived assets. Nevertheless, in measuring the net income of a business for a period of one year or less, the accountant must *estimate* what portion of the cost of the building and other long-lived assets is applicable to the current year. Since the allocations of these costs are estimates rather than precise measurements, it follows that income statements should be regarded as useful *approximations* of net income rather than as absolutely exact measurements.

For some expenditures, such as those for advertising or employee training programs, it is not possible to estimate objectively the number of accounting periods over which revenue is likely to be produced. In such cases, generally accepted accounting principles require that the expenditure be charged *immediately to expense*. This treatment is based upon the accounting principle of **objectivity** and the concept of **conservatism.** Accountants require *objective evidence* that an expenditure will produce revenue in future periods before they will view the expenditure as creating an asset. When this objective evidence does not exist, they follow the conservative practice of recording the expenditure as an expense. *Conservatism,* in this context, means applying the accounting treatment which results in the *lower* (more conservative) estimate of net income for the current period.

DEBIT AND CREDIT RULES FOR REVENUE AND EXPENSE

We have stressed that revenue increases owners' equity and that expenses decrease owners' equity. The debit and credit rules for recording revenue and expenses in the ledger accounts are a natural extension of the rules for recording changes in owners' equity. The rules previously stated for recording increases and decreases in owners' equity were as follows:

LO 3 *Explain* why *revenues are recorded with credits and expenses are recorded with debits.*

- *Increases* in owners' equity are recorded by *credits.*
- *Decreases* in owners' equity are recorded by *debits.*

This rule is now extended to cover revenue and expense accounts:

- *Revenue* increases owners' equity; therefore revenue is recorded by a *credit.*
- *Expenses* decrease owners' equity; therefore expenses are recorded by *debits.*

LEDGER ACCOUNTS FOR REVENUE AND EXPENSES   During the course of an accounting period, a great many revenue and expense transactions occur in the average business. To classify and summarize these numerous transactions, a separate ledger account is maintained for each major type of revenue and expense. For example, almost every business maintains accounts for Advertising Expense, Wages (or Salaries) Expense, and Depreciation Expense. At the end of the period, all the advertising expenses appear as debits in the Advertising Expense account. The debit balance of this account represents the total advertising expense of the period and is listed as one of the expense items in the income statement.

Revenue accounts are usually much less numerous than expense accounts. A small business such as Overnight Auto Service (our continuing illustration) may have only one or two types of revenue. Even a very large business may show only two or three types of revenue in its income statement.[2]

DIVIDENDS

A dividend is a distribution of assets (usually cash) by a corporation to its stockholders. In some respects, dividends are similar to expenses—they reduce both the assets and the owners' equity in the business. However, *dividends are not an expense, and they are not deducted from revenue in the income statement.* The reason why dividends are not viewed as an expense is that these payments do not serve to generate revenue. Rather, they are a *distribution of profits* to the owners of the business.

Since the declaration of a dividend reduces stockholders' equity, the dividend could be recorded by debiting the Retained Earnings account. However, a clearer

---

[2]These businesses maintain more revenue accounts than their income statements suggest. They maintain separate accounts for each type of revenue, and also for each branch or division within the company. For financial reporting purposes, however, the balances in these accounts are combined into a few very broad categories.

record is created if a separate "Dividends" account is debited for all amounts distributed as dividends to stockholders. The disposition of the Dividends account when financial statements are prepared will be illustrated later in this chapter.

The debit-credit rules for revenue, expense, and dividends are summarized below:

Debit-Credit rules related to effect on owners' equity

Owners' Equity	
Decreases recorded by Debits	Increases recorded by Credits
Expenses decrease owners' equity	Revenue increases owners' equity
Expenses are recorded by Debits	Revenue is recorded by a Credit
Dividends reduce owners' equity	
Dividends are recorded by Debits	

RECORDING REVENUE AND EXPENSE TRANSACTIONS: AN ILLUSTRATION

In Chapters 1 and 2, we discussed the transactions relating to the creation of Overnight Auto Service in November 1998. We will now continue this example into December—the first month of Overnight's regular business operations.

But first let us explain a few practical limitations on Overnight's activities. Most auto repair businesses render services to a great many customers. They sell parts as well as services. To keep our illustration short, we will assume that Overnight has only *two* customers in December: Airport Shuttle Service and Harbor Cab Co. We also assume that Overnight's customers purchased the parts used in the repair of their vehicles from an independent supplier. Thus, Overnight earns all of its revenue in December from *rendering services,* not from sales of parts or other merchandise. (Sales of merchandise will be discussed in Chapter 5.)

Overnight's transactions in December are described below, along with an analysis of each transaction and illustrations of the entries made in the company's accounting records:

Dec. 1 Paid KGPO $1,270 cash for radio advertising to be aired during December.

Incurred an expense, paying cash

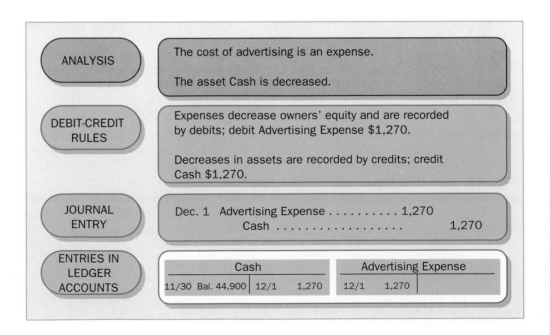

Dec. 2 Purchased newspaper advertising from *Daily Tribune* to be run in December. The cost was $560, payable within 30 days.

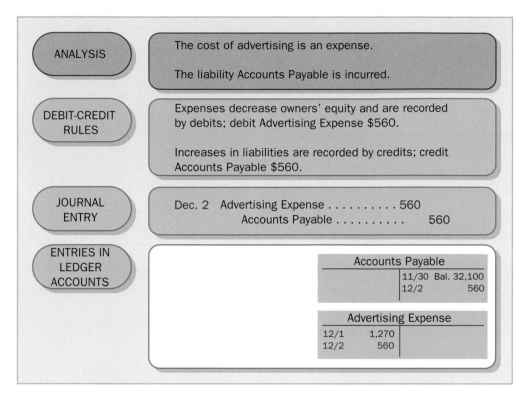

Incurred an expense to be paid later

Dec. 4 Purchased various shop supplies (such as grease, solvents, nuts, and bolts) from NAPA Auto Parts; cost $2,500, due in 30 days. These supplies are expected to meet Overnight's needs for *three or four months*.

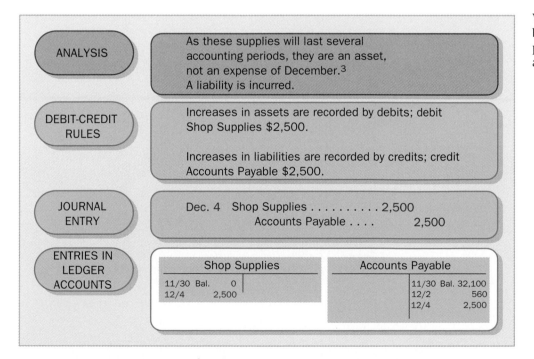

When a purchase clearly benefits future accounting periods, it's an asset, not an expense

---

[3]If the supplies are expected to be used within the *current* accounting period, their cost is debited directly to the Supplies Expense account, rather than to an asset account.

Dec. 15 Collected $9,940 cash for repairs made to vehicles of Airport Shuttle Service.

Revenue earned and collected

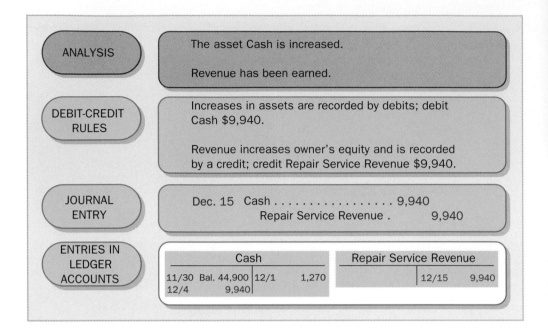

Dec. 27 Billed Harbor Cab Co. $10,400 for maintenance and repair services rendered during December. The agreement with Harbor Cab calls for payment to be received by January 10.

Revenue earned but not yet collected

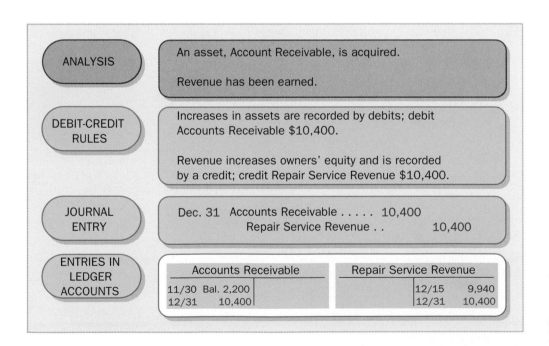

Dec. 31 Paid all employees' salaries and wages for December, $12,410.

Incurred an expense, paying cash

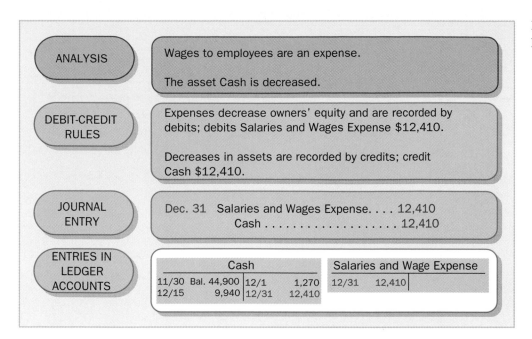

Dec. 31 Overnight declares and pays a dividend of 5 cents per share to the owners of its 40,000 shares of capital stock—a total of $2,000. (As explained earlier, dividends are *not* an expense.)

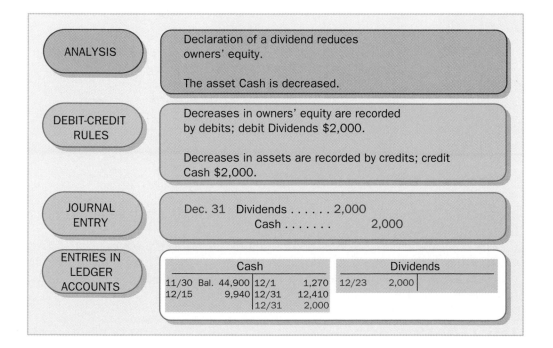

THE JOURNAL

In our illustration, journal entries were shown in a very abbreviated form. The actual entries made in Overnight's journal follow. Notice that these "formal" journal entries include short *explanations* of the transaction; the explanation

Journal entries contain more information than just dollar amounts

GENERAL JOURNAL					Page 2
Date		Account Titles and Explanation	LP	Debit	Credit
1998 Dec.	1	Advertising Expense...	70	1,270	
		Cash	1	1,270	
		Purchased radio advertising from KGPO in December.			
	2	Advertising Expense...	70	560	
		Accounts Payable	32		560
		Purchased newspaper advertising on account from *Daily Tribune;* due in 30 days.			
	4	Shop Supplies..	6		2,500
		Accounts Payable	32		2,500
		Purchased shop supplies on account from NAPA; payment due in 30 days.			
	15	Cash..	1	9,940	
		Repair Service Revenue.........................	60		9,940
		Repair services rendered to Airport Shuttle.			
	28	Accounts Receivable	4	10,400	
		Repair Service Revenue.........................	60		10,400
		Billed Harbor Cab for services rendered in December; due Jan. 10.			
	31	Salaries and Wages Expense	72	12,410	
		Cash	1		12,410
		Paid salaries and wages for December.			
	31	Dividends..	52	2,000	
		Cash	1		2,000
		Paid dividend to stockholders (5 cents per share × 40,000 shares).			

includes such details as the terms of credit transactions and the names of customers and creditors.

The column headings at the top of the illustrated journal page ("Date," "Account Titles and Explanation," "LP," "Debit," and "Credit") are seldom used in practice. They are included here as an instructional guide but will be omitted from some later illustrations of journal entries.

THE LEDGER

After the posting of these December transactions, Overnight's ledger accounts appear as shown on the following page. To conserve space, we illustrate these accounts in "T account" form, rather than the running balance form used in Chapter 2. But for convenience, we show in red the *December 31 balance* of each account. (Debit balances appear to the left of the account, credit balances appear to the right. We do not include the balances *within* the accounts, because some of them will be *adjusted* in the next step in the accounting cycle.)

THE LEDGER

Asset Accounts

Cash   1

11/1	400,000	11/3	295,000
11/25	2,000	11/5	30,000
		11/30	32,100
11/30 Bal.	44,900	12/1	1,270
12/15	9,940	12/31	12,410
		12/31	2,000

Bal. $ 39,160

Accounts Receivable   4

11/20	4,200	11/25	2,000
11/30 Bal.	2,200		
12/	10,400		

Bal. $ 12,600

Shop Supplies   6

12/4	2,500		

Bal. $ 2,500

Land   20

11/3	295,000		
11/30 Bal.	295,000		

Bal. $295,000

Building   22

11/5	120,000		
11/30 Bal.	120,000		

Bal. $120,000

Tools and Equipment   25

11/17	64,200	11/20	4,200
11/30 Bal.	60,000		

Bal. $ 60,000

Liability and Owners' Equity Accounts

Notes Payable   30

		11/5	90,000
		11/30 Bal.	90,000

Bal. $ 90,000

Accounts Payable   32

11/30	32,100	11/17	64,200
		11/30 Bal.	32,100
		12/2	560
		12/4	2,500

Bal. $ 35,160

Capital Stock   50

		11/1	400,000
		11/30 Bal.	400,000

Bal. $400,000

Dividends   52

12/31	2,000		

Bal. $ 2,000

Repair Service Revenue   60

		12/15	9,940
		12/28	10,400

Bal. $ 20,340

Advertising Expense   70

12/1	1,270		
12/2	560		

Bal. $ 1,830

Salaries and Wages Expense   72

12/31	12,410		

Bal. $12,410

The accounts in this illustration appear in *financial statement order*—that is, balance sheet accounts first (assets, liabilities, and owners' equity), followed by income statement accounts (revenue and expenses). The sequence of accounts within the balance sheet categories was explained in Chapter 2. Within the categories of revenue and expense, accounts may be listed in any order.

THE TRIAL BALANCE

A trial balance prepared from Overnight's ledger at December 31 is shown below.

OVERNIGHT AUTO SERVICE Trial Balance December 31, 1998		
Cash	$ 39,160	
Accounts receivable	12,600	
Shop supplies	2,500	
Land	295,000	
Building	120,000	
Tools and equipment	60,000	
Notes payable		$ 90,000
Accounts payable		35,160
Capital stock		400,000
Retained earnings		–0–
Dividends	2,000	
Repair service revenue		20,340
Advertising expense	1,830	
Salaries and wages expense	12,410	
	$545,500	$545,500

A trial balance proves the equality of debits and credits—but it also gives you a "feel" for how the business stands. But wait—there's more to consider

This trial balance proves the equality of the debit and credit entries in the company's ledger. Notice that the trial balance contains income statement accounts as well as balance sheet accounts. (The balance of $0 in the Retained Earnings account is a highly unusual situation. Because this is the *first month* of business operations, no entries have yet been made in this account. In the trial balance prepared for any later month, the Retained Earnings account may be expected to have a balance *other than $0*.)

ADJUSTING ENTRIES: THE NEXT STEP IN THE ACCOUNTING CYCLE

LO 4 *Explain the nature of adjusting entries.*

We will now see that there is more to the measurement of business income than merely recording transactions. Many transactions affect the revenue or expenses of *two or more* accounting periods. For example, a business may purchase equipment that will last for many years, an insurance policy that covers 12 months, or—as Overnight has done—enough supplies to last for several months.

Initially, the costs of such items are recorded as *assets,* because they will benefit the business in future accounting periods. Over time, these assets are *used up,* and their costs *become expenses* of the periods in which the goods or services are used.

How do businesses allocate the costs of such assets to expense over a span of several accounting periods? The answer is by making **adjusting entries** at the end of each accounting period. The purpose of these entries is to assign to each accounting period the appropriate amounts of revenue and expense. These entries adjust the balances of various ledger accounts—hence the name, *adjusting entries.*

There are several different types of adjusting entries, some affecting expenses and others affecting revenue. In fact, a business may make a dozen or more adjusting entries in each period. To keep our illustration short, we will assume that Overnight's accounts require only four adjusting entries at December 31, all of which involve the recognition of expenses. Other types of adjusting entries, including those affecting revenue, will be discussed and illustrated in Chapter 4.

SHOP SUPPLIES: AN ASSET THAT TURNS INTO AN EXPENSE

On December 4, Overnight purchased for $2,500 a quantity of shop supplies expected to last for three or four months. At the date of purchase, this $2,500 cost was debited to an asset account (Shop Supplies), because it was expected to *benefit future accounting periods.* But as these supplies are used, this asset gradually becomes an expense. This concept is illustrated in the following diagram:

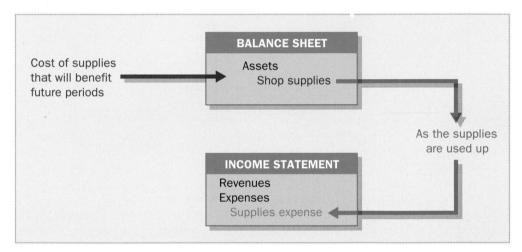

As an asset is "used up," it becomes an expense

Assume that during December, $600 worth of Overnight's shop supplies was used in business operations, and that approximately $1,900 worth remains on hand—available for use in future periods. The $600 of supplies *used* during December should be *recognized as expense* in that month; the $1,900 in supplies *still on hand* should appear in the December 31 balance sheet as an *asset.*

To transfer the cost of the supplies used during the month from the asset account to an expense account, Overnight will make the following *adjusting entry* at December 31:

GENERAL JOURNAL				Page 3
Date	**Account Titles and Explanation**	**LP**	**Debit**	**Credit**
1998 Dec. 31	Supplies Expense..	6	600	
	Shop Supplies	74		600
	To recognize as expense the cost of shop supplies used in December.			

The adjusting entry to recognize supplies used up as an expense

The idea of shop supplies being used up over several months is easy to understand. But did you know the same concept applies to assets such as buildings, automobiles, and even railroad tracks?

THE CONCEPT OF DEPRECIATION

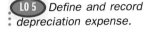 **Define and record depreciation expense.**

Depreciable assets are *physical objects* which retain their size and shape, but which eventually wear out or become obsolete. They are not physically consumed, as are assets such as supplies. But nonetheless, their economic usefulness is "used up" over time. Examples of depreciable assets include buildings and all types of equipment, fixtures, and furnishings — and even railroad tracks. Land, however, is *not* viewed as a depreciable asset, as it has an *unlimited* useful life.

Each period, a portion of a depreciable asset's usefulness *expires*. Therefore, a corresponding portion of its cost is recognized as *depreciation expense.*

WHAT IS DEPRECIATION?   In accounting, the term **depreciation** means the *systematic allocation of the cost of a depreciable asset to expense* over the asset's useful life. This process is illustrated below:

Depreciation: A process of allocating the cost of a depreciable asset to expense

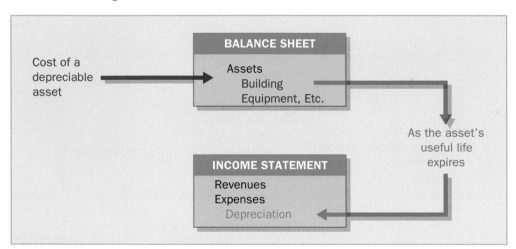

Notice the similarity of this diagram to that on the previous page.

Depreciation *is not* an attempt to record changes in the asset's market value. In the short run, the market value of some depreciable assets may even increase, but the process of depreciation continues anyway. The rationale for depreciation lies in the *matching principle.* Our goal is to offset a reasonable portion of the asset's cost against revenue in each period of the asset's **useful life.**

Depreciation expense occurs continuously over the life of the asset, but there are no daily depreciation transactions. In effect, depreciation expense is paid in advance when the asset is originally purchased. Therefore, *adjusting entries* are needed at the end of each accounting period to transfer an appropriate amount of the asset's cost to depreciation expense.

DEPRECIATION IS ONLY AN ESTIMATE   The "appropriate amount" of depreciation expense is *only an estimate.* After all, we cannot look at a building or a piece of equipment and determine precisely how much of its economic usefulness has expired during the current period.

The most widely used means of estimating periodic depreciation expense is the **straight-line method.** Under the straight-line approach, an *equal portion* of the asset's cost is allocated to depreciation expense in every period of the asset's estimated useful life. The formula for computing depreciation expense by the straight-line method is:[4]

---

[4]At this point in our discussion, we are ignoring any possible *residual value* which might be recovered upon disposal of the asset. Residual values are discussed in Chapter 9.

$$\text{Depreciation expense (per period)} = \frac{\text{Cost of the asset}}{\text{Estimated useful life}}$$

The use of an *estimated useful life* is the major reason why depreciation expense is only an estimate. In most cases, management does not know in advance exactly how long the asset will remain in use.

CASE IN POINT

How long does a building last? For purposes of computing depreciation expense, most companies estimate about 30 or 40 years. But the Empire State Building was built in 1931, and it's not likely to be torn down anytime soon. And how about Windsor Castle? While these are not "typical" examples, they illustrate the difficulty in estimating in advance just how long depreciable assets may remain in use.

In their financial statements, most companies determine depreciation expense by the straight-line method. In income tax returns, however, they often use different methods. Alternatives to the straight-line method of computing depreciation expense will be discussed in Chapter 9.

RECORDING DEPRECIATION EXPENSE: AN ILLUSTRATION

Overnight Auto Service owns two categories of depreciable assets: its building, and its tools and equipment. Because these categories of assets have different useful lives, depreciation must be computed separately for each category. Overnight elects to compute depreciation expense by the straight-line method.

DEPRECIATION ON THE BUILDING   Overnight purchased its building for $120,000. Because the building was old, management estimates that it has a remaining useful life of only 20 years. Thus, Overnight will recognize annual depreciation expense equal to ½₀ of the building's cost, or *$6,000* ($120,000 cost ÷ 20-year estimated useful life). On a monthly basis, the depreciation expense amounts to *$500* ($120,000 cost ÷ 240 months).

The adjusting entry to record depreciation on this building for the month of December appears below:

GENERAL JOURNAL				Page 3	
Date		**Account Titles and Explanation**	**LP**	**Debit**	**Credit**
1998 Dec.	31	Depreciation Expense: Building..........................	76	500	
		Accumulated Depreciation: Building...........	23		500
		To record one month's depreciation on building (cost, $120,000, divided by estimated useful life, 240 months, equals $500 per month)			

Adjusting entry to record depreciation of the building

The Depreciation Expense account will appear in Overnight's income statement for December, along with the other expenses for the month. The **Accumulated Depreciation** account will appear in the balance sheet as a deduction from the balance of the Building account, as shown below:

Showing accumulated depreciation in the balance sheet

OVERNIGHT AUTO SERVICE		
Partial Balance Sheet		
December 31, 1998		
Assets		
Cash		$ 39,160
Accounts receivable		12,600
Shop supplies		1,900
Land		295,000
Building	$120,000	
Less: Accumulated depreciation	500	119,500

The end result of crediting the Accumulated Depreciation: Building account is much the same as if the credit had been made to the Building account; that is, the net amount shown on the balance sheet for the building is reduced from $120,000 to $119,500. Although the credit side of a depreciation entry *could* be made directly to the asset account, it is customary and more efficient to record such credits in a separate account entitled Accumulated Depreciation. The original cost of the asset and the total amount of depreciation recorded over the years can more easily be determined from the ledger when separate accounts are maintained for the asset and for the accumulated depreciation.

Accumulated Depreciation: Building is an example of a **contra-asset account,** because it has a credit balance and is offset against an asset account (Building) to produce the proper balance sheet amount for the asset.

DEPRECIATION ON THE TOOLS AND EQUIPMENT Overnight also must record depreciation on its tools and equipment. These assets cost $60,000, and management estimates that they will remain in service for about 5 years. Thus, the monthly depreciation expense amounts to *$1,000* ($60,000 cost ÷ 60 months). The adjusting entry to recognize this monthly expense is:

Adjusting entry to record depreciation of tools and equipment

GENERAL JOURNAL					Page 3
Date		Account Titles and Explanation	LP	Debit	Credit
1998 Dec.	31	Depreciation Expense: Tools and Equipment.....	78	1,000	
		Accumulated Depreciation: Tools and Equipment...................................	26		1,000
		To record depreciation on tools and equipment ($30,000 ÷ 60 months).			

Similar adjusting entries to recognize depreciation expense on the building and tools and equipment will be made *each month* throughout the assets' useful lives. Once the assets have become "fully depreciated," that is, their total cost has been recognized as depreciation expense, the recognition of depreciation will stop. (We did not recognize depreciation on these assets in November, because Overnight had not yet begun its regular business operations. Depreciation begins when the assets are *placed in use* for the intended business purpose.)

DEPRECIATION IS A "NONCASH" EXPENSE   We have made the point that net income does *not* represent an inflow of cash or any other asset. Rather, it is a *computation* of the overall effect of certain business transactions upon owners' equity. The computation and recognition of depreciation expense illustrate this point.

As depreciable assets "expire," owners' equity declines; but *there is no corresponding cash outlay* in the current period. For this reason, depreciation often is called a noncash expense. Often it represents the *largest difference* between net income and the cash flows (receipts and payments) resulting from business operations.

ACCOUNTING FOR CORPORATE INCOME TAXES

Profitable businesses that are *organized as corporations* must file income tax returns and pay income taxes equal to a percentage of their taxable incomes. These taxes represent an *expense* of the business organization. Income taxes usually are paid in four quarterly installments. But if we are to properly "match" income taxes with the related revenue, **income taxes expense** should be recognized (or accrued) *in the periods in which the taxable income is earned.* This is accomplished by making an *adjusting entry* at the end of each accounting period.

COMPUTING INCOME TAXES EXPENSE   Income taxes expense is determined by applying the current *tax rate* to the taxpayer's *taxable income.* This relationship is summarized below:

$$
\begin{matrix} \text{Taxable income} \\ \text{(determined according} \\ \text{to tax regulations)} \end{matrix} \times \begin{matrix} \text{Tax rate} \\ \text{(set by law)} \end{matrix} = \begin{matrix} \text{Income taxes} \\ \text{expense} \end{matrix}
$$

Taxable income is *not* the same as "net income." Taxable income is computed in conformity with *income tax regulations,* rather than generally accepted accounting principles. The rules for computing taxable income normally change somewhat from one year to the next. In a very simple case, taxable income may be equal to revenue less all expenses *other than* income taxes expense. We will use this simplifying assumption in computing and recording Overnight's income taxes expense.[5]

The **tax rate** is the *percentage* of taxable income that must be paid as income taxes. Federal income tax rates are established by the United States Congress. These rates may change from year to year, and also vary depending upon the amount of taxable income. But for purposes of illustration, we will assume a corporate income tax rate of 40% to include the effects of both federal and state income taxes.

Under the assumptions stated above, Overnight's income taxes expense for December amounts to $1,600, determined as follows:

---

[5]The types and dollar amounts of revenue and expenses appearing in income statements often differ from those used in the determination of taxable income. Such differences will be discussed in later chapters.

Computation of income taxes expense—using several "simplifying assumptions"

Repair service revenue...		$20,340
Less: Deductible expenses:*		
Advertising..	$ 1,830	
Salaries and wages...	12,410	
Supplies used..	600	
Depreciation: building...	500	
Depreciation: tools and equipment	1,000	
Total deductible expense...		16,340
Income before income taxes (assumed to be **taxable income**)......		$ 4,000
Income taxes expense ($4,000 taxable income × 40%).............		**$ 1,600**

*Deductible expenses are those which are *legally deductible* in the determination of taxable income. These expenses may differ in nature and in amount from those appearing in an income statement. For example, income taxes expense appears in the income statement (page 103), but is not "deductible" in the determination of taxable income.

In an income statement, income taxes expense often is termed **provision for income taxes.**

RECORDING INCOME TAXES EXPENSE Income taxes expense accrues each month, but it is not payable until dates which are specified by income tax authorities. Therefore, monthly income taxes expense is recorded by an adjusting entry, such as the one shown below:

GENERAL JOURNAL					Page 2	
Date		**Account Titles and Explanation**	**LP**	**Debit**	**Credit**	
1998 Dec.	31	Income Taxes Expense..	80	1,600		
		Income Taxes Payable..............................	35		1,600	
		To record income taxes expense for the month of December ($4,000 × 40% = $1,600).				

Adjusting entry to accrue income taxes expense for November

The amount of *income taxes expense* will appear in Overnight's December income statement; *income taxes payable* is a short-term liability that will appear in the balance sheet.[6]

Income taxes expense differs from other business expenses in several ways. First, *only businesses organized as corporations incur income taxes expense.* **Unincorporated businesses,** such as sole proprietorships and partnerships, do not pay income taxes. The taxable incomes earned by unincorporated businesses are taxable directly to the *owners* of these businesses, not to the business entities themselves.

Also, paying income taxes *does not help produce revenue.* For this reason, income taxes expense usually is shown separately from other expenses in the income statement—often following a subtotal called **Income (or loss) before income taxes.** This type of presentation is illustrated on page 123.

---

[6]The Internal Revenue Service requires corporations to pay their annual income taxes in four quarterly installments, plus a final payment when the return is due.

THE ADJUSTED TRIAL BALANCE

After all the necessary adjusting entries have been journalized and posted, an **adjusted trial balance** is prepared to prove that the ledger is still in balance. It also provides a complete listing of the account balances to be used in preparing the financial statements. The following adjusted trial balance differs from the trial balance shown on page 114 because it includes several new account titles, and the balances in some existing accounts have been "adjusted." (For emphasis, the accounts affected by Overnight's four adjusting entries appear in red.)

OVERNIGHT AUTO SERVICE Adjusted Trial Balance December 31, 1998		
Cash	$ 39,160	
Accounts receivable	12,600	
Shop supplies	1,900	
Land	295,000	
Building	120,000	
Accumulated depreciation: building		$ 500
Tools and equipment	60,000	
Accumulated depreciation: tools and equipment		1,000
Notes payable		$ 90,000
Accounts payable		35,160
Income taxes payable		1,600
Capital stock		400,000
Retained earnings		–0–
Dividends	2,000	
Repair service revenue		20,340
Advertising expense	1,830	
Salaries and wages expense	12,410	
Supplies expense	600	
Depreciation expense: building	500	
Depreciation expense: tools and equipment	1,000	
Income taxes expense	1,600	
	$548,600	$548,600

Adjusted trial balance— accounts affected by end-of-period adjusting entries are shown in red

Once an adjusted trial balance has been prepared, the process of recording changes in financial position for this accounting period is complete. *Financial statements are prepared directly from the adjusted trial balance.*

Every account in the adjusted trial balance contains its end-of-the-period balance, *with the exception of the Retained Earnings account.* During the accounting period, transactions affecting retained earnings were not recorded directly in the Retained Earnings account. Rather, these transactions were recorded in the various revenue, expense, and dividends accounts. Therefore, the amount of retained earnings shown in the adjusted trial balance is the retained earnings at the *beginning* of the accounting period.[7] This will

---

[7] The amount of retained earnings at the beginning of November was $0, because November was the *first* accounting period in which Overnight engaged in business operations. The beginning amount of retained earnings for any subsequent accounting period normally will be an amount *other than $0.*

not cause a problem; as we prepare a set of financial statements, the amount of retained earnings at the *end* of the period will become apparent.

Let us now look at the process of preparing a set of financial statements directly from the amounts listed in the adjusted trial balance.

PREPARING A SET OF FINANCIAL STATEMENTS

LO 6 *Prepare statements of income and of owners' equity. Explain how these statements relate to the balance sheet.*

Now that Overnight Auto Service has been operating for a month, managers and outside parties will want to know more about the company than just its financial position. They will want to know the *results of operations*—whether the month's activities have been profitable or unprofitable. To provide this additional information, we will prepare a more complete set of financial statements, consisting of an income statement, a statement of owners' equity, and a balance sheet.[8] These statements are illustrated on the following page.

THE INCOME STATEMENT

The revenue and expenses shown in the income statement are taken directly from the company's adjusted trial balance. Overnight's income statement for December shows that revenue exceeded the expenses for the month, thus producing a net income of $2,400. Bear in mind, however, that our measurement of net income is not absolutely accurate or precise, because of the *assumptions and estimates* in the accounting process.

An income statement has certain limitations. Remember that the amounts shown for depreciation expense are based upon estimates of the useful lives of the company's building and office equipment. Also, the income statement includes only those events which have been evidenced by business transactions. Perhaps during December, Overnight's advertising has caught the attention of many potential customers. A good "customer base" is certainly an important step toward profitable operations. However, the development of a customer base is not reflected in the income statement because its value cannot be measured *objectively* until actual transactions take place. Despite these limitations, the income statement is of vital importance and indicates that the new business has been profitable during its first month of operation.

Alternative titles for the income statement include *earnings statement, statement of operations,* and *profit and loss statement.* However, *income statement* is by far the most popular term for this important financial statement. In summary, we can say that an income statement is used to summarize the *operating results* of a business by matching the revenue earned during a given time period with the expenses incurred in obtaining that revenue.

THE STATEMENT OF RETAINED EARNINGS

Retained earnings is that portion of the stockholders' equity created by earning net income and retaining the related resources in the business. The **statement of retained earnings** summarizes the increases and decreases in retained earnings resulting from the business operations of the accounting period. Increases in retained earnings result from earning net income; decreases result from net losses and from the declaration of dividends.

---

[8]A complete set of financial statements also includes a statement of cash flows, which will be illustrated and discussed in Chapter 6.

OVERNIGHT AUTO SERVICE
Income Statement
For the Month Ended December 31, 1998

Revenue:		
Repair service revenue		$20,340
Expenses:		
Advertising expense	$ 1,830	
Salaries and wages expense	12,410	
Supplies expense	600	
Depreciation expense: building	500	
Depreciation expense: tools and equipment	1,000	16,340
Income before income taxes		$ 4,000
Income taxes expense		1,600
Net income		$ 2,400

Income statement for December

Net income carries forward to the statement of retained earnings

OVERNIGHT AUTO SERVICE
Statement of Retained Earnings
For the Month Ended December 31, 1998

Retained earnings, Nov. 30, 1998	$ –0–
Net income for December	2,400
Subtotal	$2,400
Less: Dividends	2,000
Retained earnings, Dec. 31, 1998	$ 400

Statement of retained earnings for December

The ending balance of retained earnings carries forward to the balance sheet

OVERNIGHT AUTO SERVICE
Balance Sheet
December 31, 1998

Assets

Cash		$39,160
Accounts receivable		12,600
Shop supplies		1,900
Land		295,000
Building	$120,000	
Less: Accumulated depreciation	500	119,500
Office equipment _Tools + Equipment_	$ 60,000	
Less: Accumulated depreciation	1,000	59,000
Total assets		$527,160

Balance sheet at December 31 (shown in *report form*)

Liabilities & Stockholders' Equity

Liabilities:		
Notes payable		$ 90,000
Accounts payable		35,160
Income taxes payable		1,600
Total liabilities		$126,760
Stockholders' equity:		
Capital stock	$400,000	
Retained earnings	400	
Total stockholders' equity		400,400
Total liabilities & stockholders' equity		$527,160

Statement of Retained Earnings

The format of this financial statement is based upon the following relationships:

$$\text{Retained Earnings at the beginning of the period} + \text{Net Income} - \text{Dividends} = \text{Retained Earnings at the end of the period}$$

The amount of retained earnings at the *beginning* of the period is shown at the top of the statement. Next, the net income for the period is added (or net loss subtracted), and any dividends declared during the period are deducted. This short computation determines the amount of retained earnings at the *end* of the accounting period. The ending retained earnings ($400 in our example) appears at the bottom of the statement of retained earnings and also in the company's end-of-the-period balance sheet.

Our illustration of a statement of retained earnings on the preceding page is unusual in that the retained earnings at the beginning of the month is *$0*. This occurs only because December is the *first month* of Overnight's business operations. The ending retained earnings of one accounting period becomes the beginning amount for the next. Thus, the statement of retained earnings prepared for Overnight next month (January, 1999) will show beginning retained earnings of $400.

THE BALANCE SHEET

The balance sheet lists the amounts of the company's assets, liabilities, and owners' equity at the *end* of the accounting period. The balances of the asset and liability accounts are taken directly from the adjusted trial balance on page 121. The amount of retained earnings at the end of the period, $400, was determined in the *statement of retained earnings*.

Previous illustrations of balance sheets have been arranged in *account form*— that is, with assets on the left and liabilities and owners' equity on the right. The illustration on the preceding page is arranged in *report form*, with the liabilities and owners' equity sections listed *below* rather than to the right of the asset section. Both the account form and the report form of balance sheet are widely used.

RELATIONSHIP AMONG THE FINANCIAL STATEMENTS

A set of financial statements becomes easier to understand if we recognize that the income statement, statement of retained earnings, and balance sheet all are *related to one another*. These relationships are emphasized by the arrows in the right-hand margin of our illustration on page 123.

The balance sheet prepared at the end of the preceding period and the one prepared at the end of the current period both include the amount of retained earnings at the respective balance sheet dates. The statement of retained earnings summarizes the factors (net income and dividends) which have caused the amount of retained earnings to change between these two balance sheet dates. The income statement explains in greater detail the change in retained earnings resulting from profitable operation of the business. Thus, the income statement and the retained earnings statement provide informative links between successive balance sheets.

CLOSING THE TEMPORARY ACCOUNTS

LO 7 *Explain the purposes of closing entries; prepare these entries.*

As previously stated, revenue increases retained earnings, and expenses and dividends decrease retained earnings. If the only financial statement that we needed were a balance sheet, these changes in retained earnings could be recorded directly in the retained earnings account. However, owners, managers, investors, and others need to know amounts of specific revenues and expenses, and the amount of net income earned in the period. Therefore, we maintain *separate ledger accounts* to measure each type of revenue and expense, and the dividends distributed.

These revenue, expense, and dividends accounts are called *temporary,* or *nominal,* accounts, because they accumulate the transactions of *only one accounting period.* At the end of this accounting period, the changes in retained earnings accumulated in these temporary accounts are transferred into the retained earnings account. This process serves two purposes. First, it *updates the balance of the retained earnings account* for changes in retained earnings occurring during the accounting period. Second, it *returns the balances of the temporary accounts to zero,* so that they are ready for measuring the revenue, expenses, and dividends of the next accounting period.

The retained earnings account and other balance sheet accounts are called *permanent,* or *real,* accounts, because their balances continue to exist beyond the current accounting period. The process of transferring the balances of the temporary accounts into the retained earnings account is called *closing* the accounts. The journal entries made for the purpose of closing the temporary accounts are called **closing entries.**

Revenue and expense accounts are closed at the end of each accounting period by *transferring their balances* to a summary account called **Income Summary.** When the credit balances of the revenue accounts and the debit balances of the expense accounts have been transferred into one summary account, the balance of the Income Summary account will be the *net income* or *net loss* for the period. If revenue (credit balances) exceeds expenses (debit balances), the Income Summary account will have a credit balance representing net income. Conversely, if expenses exceed revenue, the Income Summary account will have a debit balance representing net loss. This is consistent with the rule that increases in owners' equity are recorded by credits and decreases are recorded by debits.

It is common practice to close the accounts only once a year, but for illustration, we will demonstrate the closing of the accounts of Overnight Auto Service at December 31, after one month's operation.

CLOSING ENTRIES FOR REVENUE ACCOUNTS

Revenue accounts have credit balances. Therefore, closing a revenue account means transferring its credit balance to the Income Summary account. This transfer is accomplished by a journal entry debiting the revenue account in an amount equal to its credit balance, with an offsetting credit to the Income Summary account. The debit portion of this closing entry returns the balance of the revenue account to zero; the credit portion transfers the former balance of the revenue account into the Income Summary account.

The only revenue account of Overnight Auto Service is Repair Service Revenue, which had a credit balance of $20,340 at December 31. The closing entry is as follows:

GENERAL JOURNAL					Page 3
Date		Account Titles and Explanation	LP	Debit	Credit
1998 Dec.	31	Repair Service Revenue..................................	60	20,340	
		Income Summary	53		20,340
		To close the Repair Service Revenue account.			

Closing a revenue account

After this closing entry has been posted, the two accounts affected will appear as follows. A few details of account structure have been omitted to simplify the illustration; a directional arrow has been added to show the transfer of the $20,340 balance of the revenue account into the Income Summary account.

Repair Service Revenue					60
Date	Expl.	Ref	Debit	Credit	Balance
Dec. 15		2		9,940	9,940
31		2		10,400	20,340
31	To close	3	20,340		– 0 –

Income Summary					53
Date	Expl.	Ref	Debit	Credit	Balance
Dec. 31	Revenue	3		20,340	20,340

CLOSING ENTRIES FOR EXPENSE ACCOUNTS

Expense accounts have debit balances. Closing an expense account means transferring its debit balance to the Income Summary account. The journal entry to close an expense account, therefore, consists of a credit to the expense account in an amount equal to its debit balance, with an offsetting debit to the Income Summary account.

There are six expense accounts in the ledger of Overnight Auto Service. Six separate journal entries could be made to close these six expense accounts, but the use of one *compound journal entry* is an easier, time-saving method of closing all six expense accounts. A compound journal entry is an entry that includes debits to more than one account or credits to more than one account.

Closing the various expense accounts by use of a compound journal entry

GENERAL JOURNAL					Page 3
Date		Account Titles and Explanation	LP	Debit	Credit
1998 Dec.	31	Income Summary....................................	53	17,940	
		Advertising Expense.......................................	70		1,830
		Salaries and Wages Expense	72		12,410
		Supplies Expense...	74		600
		Depreciation Expense: Building..................	76		500
		Depreciation Expense: Tools and			
		Equipment..	78		1,000
		Income Taxes Expense................................	80		1,600
		To close the expense accounts.			

After this closing entry has been posted, the Income Summary account has a credit balance of $2,400, and the six expense accounts have zero balances, as shown on the following page.

CLOSING THE INCOME SUMMARY ACCOUNT

The six expense accounts have now been closed and the total amount of $17,940 formerly contained in these accounts appears in the debit column of the Income Summary account. The revenue of $20,340 earned during December appears in the credit column of the Income Summary account. Since the credit entry of $20,340 representing December revenue is larger than the debit of $17,940 representing December expenses, the account has a credit balance of $2,400—the net income for December.

Advertising Expense — Account No. 70

Date		Explanation	Ref	Debit	Credit	Balance
1998 Dec.	1		2	1,270		1,270
	2		2	560		1,830
	31	To close	3		1,830	–0–

Expense accounts have zero balances after closing entries have been posted

Salaries and Wages Expense — Account No. 72

Date		Explanation	Ref	Debit	Credit	Balance
1998 Dec.	31		2	12,410		12,410
	31	To close	3		12,410	–0–

Supplies Expense — Account No. 74

Date		Explanation	Ref	Debit	Credit	Balance
1998 Dec.	31		3	600		600
	31	To close	3		600	–0–

Depreciation Expense: Building — Account No. 76

Date		Explanation	Ref	Debit	Credit	Balance
1998 Dec.	31		3	500		500
	31	To close	3		500	–0–

Depreciation Expense: Tools and Equipment — Account No. 78

Date		Explanation	Ref	Debit	Credit	Balance
1998 Dec.	31		3	1,000		1,000
	31	To close	3		1,000	–0–

Income Taxes Expense — Account No. 80

Date		Explanation	Ref	Debit	Credit	Balance
1998 Dec.	31		2	1,600		1,600
	31	To close	3		1,600	–0–

Income Summary — Account No. 53

Date		Explanation	Ref	Debit	Credit	Balance
1998 Dec.	31	Revenue	3		20,340	20,340
	31	Expenses	3	17,940		2,400

The net income of $2,400 earned during December causes an increase in owners' equity. The *credit* balance of the Income Summary account is, therefore, transferred to the Retained Earnings account by the following closing entry:

GENERAL JOURNAL					Page 3
Date		**Account Titles and Explanation**	**LP**	**Debit**	**Credit**
1998 Dec.	31	Income Summary..	53	2,400	
		Retained Earnings......................................	51		2,400
		To close the Income Summary account for			
		December by transferring the net income to the			
		Retained Earnings account.			

Net income increases the owners' equity

After this closing entry has been posted, the Income Summary account has a zero balance, and the net income for December will appear as an increase or credit entry in the Retained Earnings account, as shown below.

Income Summary account is closed to Retained Earnings

Income Summary						Account No. 53
Date		**Explanation**	**Ref**	**Debit**	**Credit**	**Balance**
1998 Dec.	31	Revenue	3		20,340	20,340
	31	Expenses	3	17,940		2,400
	31	To close	3	2,400		–0–

Retained Earnings						Account No. 51
Date		**Explanation**	**Ref**	**Debit**	**Credit**	**Balance**
1998 Dec.	31	Net Income for November	3		2,400	2,400

In our illustration the business has operated profitably with revenue in excess of expenses. Not every business is so fortunate. If the expenses of a business are larger than its revenue, the Income Summary account will have a debit balance, representing a *net loss* for the accounting period. In this case, the closing of the Income Summary account requires a debit to the Retained Earnings account and an offsetting credit to the Income Summary account. A debit balance in the Retained Earnings account is referred to as a **deficit**; it is shown as a deduction from Capital Stock in the balance sheet.

Note that the Income Summary account is used only at the end of the period, when the accounts are being closed. The Income Summary account has no entries and no balance except during the process of closing the accounts at the end of the accounting period.

CLOSING THE DIVIDENDS ACCOUNT

As explained earlier in the chapter, the payment of dividends to the stockholders is not considered an expense of the business and, therefore, is not taken into account in determining the net income for the period. Since dividends are not an expense, the Dividends account is *not* closed into the Income Summary account. Instead, it is closed directly to the Retained Earnings account, as shown by the following entry:

GENERAL JOURNAL					Page 3
Date	**Account Titles and Explanation**		**LP**	**Debit**	**Credit**
1998					
Dec. 31	Retained Earnings		51	2,000	
	Dividends		52		2,000
	To close the Dividends account.				

Dividends account is closed to Retained Earnings

After this closing entry has been posted, the Dividends account will have a zero balance, and the dividends declared during November will appear as a deduction, or debit entry, in the Retained Earnings account, as follows:

Dividends					Account No. 52
Date	**Explanation**	**Ref**	**Debit**	**Credit**	**Balance**
1998					
Dec. 31	Declaration and payment	2	2,000		2,000
31	To close	3		2,000	–0–

Retained Earnings					Account No. 51
Date	**Explanation**	**Ref**	**Debit**	**Credit**	**Balance**
1998					
Dec. 31	Net Income for December	3		2,400	2,400
31	Dividends	3	2,000		400

Retained Earnings account now reflects balance at end of period

SUMMARY OF THE CLOSING PROCESS

Let us now summarize the process of closing the accounts.

1. Close the various *revenue* accounts by transferring their balances into the Income Summary account.

2. Close the various *expense* accounts by transferring their balances into the Income Summary account.

3. Close the *Income Summary* account by transferring its balance into the Retained Earnings account.

4. Close the *Dividends* account by transferring its balance into the Retained Earnings account.

The closing of the accounts may be illustrated graphically by use of T accounts as follows:

Flowchart of the
closing process

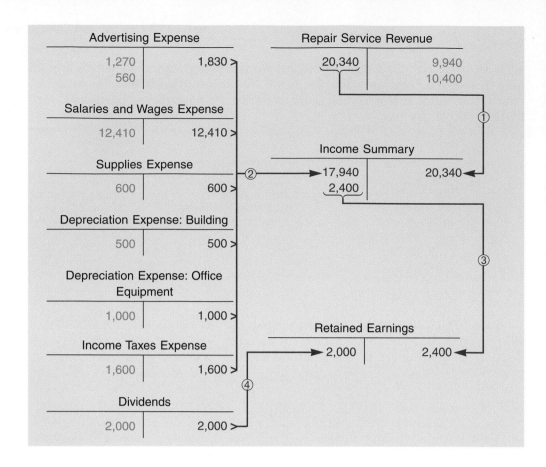

AFTER-CLOSING TRIAL BALANCE

After the revenue and expense accounts have been closed, it is desirable to prepare an **after-closing trial balance,** which of course will consist solely of balance sheet accounts. There is always the possibility that an error in posting the
closing entries may have upset the equality of debits and credits in the ledger.
The after-closing trial balance, or *post-closing trial balance* as it is often called, is
prepared from the ledger. It gives assurance that the accounts are in balance and
ready for recording transactions in the new accounting period. The after-closing
trial balance of Overnight Auto Service follows:

Only the balance sheet
accounts remain open

OVERNIGHT AUTO SERVICE After-Closing Trial Balance December 31, 1998		
Cash	$ 39,160	
Accounts receivable	12,600	
Shop supplies	1,900	
Land	295,000	
Building	120,000	
Accumulated depreciation: building		$ 500
Office equipment	60,000	
Accumulated depreciation: office equipment		1,000
Notes payable		90,000
Accounts payable		35,160
Income taxes payable		1,600
Capital stock		400,000
Retained earnings, Dec. 31		400
	$528,660	$528,660

THE COMPLETE ACCOUNTING CYCLE

In Chapter 2 we introduced the concept of the **accounting cycle.** Our illustration, however, was limited to transactions affecting the balance sheet. Now we have explained and illustrated a *complete* accounting cycle—from the initial recording of transactions to the preparation of a set of financial statements.

LO 8 *Describe the steps in the accounting cycle.*

The steps comprising this cycle are listed below, and also are illustrated in the form of a diagram:

1. ***Journalize (record) transactions.*** Enter all transactions in the journal, thus creating a chronological record of events.

2. ***Post to ledger accounts.*** Post debits and credits from the journal to the proper ledger accounts, thus creating a record classified by accounts.

3. ***Prepare a trial balance.*** Prove the equality of debits and credits in the ledger.

4. ***Make end-of-period adjustments.*** Make adjusting entries in the general journal, and post to ledger accounts.

5. ***Prepare an adjusted trial balance.*** Prove again the equality of debits and credits in the ledger. (**Note:** These are the amounts used in the preparation of financial statements.)

6. ***Prepare financial statements and appropriate disclosures.*** An income statement shows the results of operation for the period. A statement of retained earnings shows changes in retained earnings during the period. A balance sheet shows the financial position of the business at the end of the period. Financial statements should be accompanied by *notes* disclosing facts necessary for the proper interpretation of those statements.

7. ***Journalize and post the closing entries.*** The closing entries "zero" the revenue, expense, and drawing accounts, making them ready for recording the events of the next accounting period. These entries also bring the balance in the Retained Earnings account up-to-date.

8. ***Prepare an after-closing trial balance.*** This step ensures that the ledger remains in balance after posting of the closing entries.

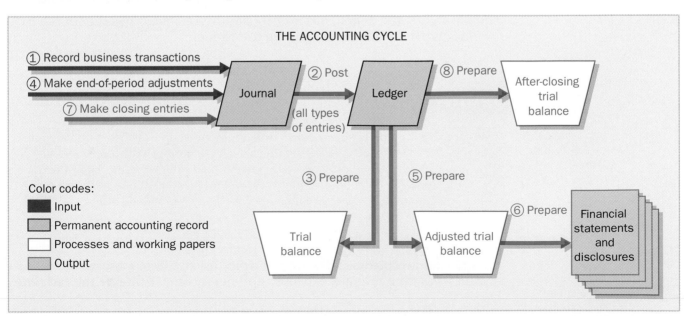

ACCOUNTING PROCEDURES IN A COMPUTER-BASED SYSTEM

The sequence of procedures performed in computer-based systems is essentially the same as in manual systems. Of course, the computer is programmed to perform a number of these steps automatically. In the preceding list, procedures 1 and 4 both involve the analysis of business transactions and judgmental decisions as to accounts to be debited and credited and the dollar amounts. These two steps in the accounting cycle require human judgment, regardless of whether the data are processed manually or by computer. As mentioned in Chapter 2, a computer-based system may call for first recording transactions in a database rather than in a journal. The computer then arranges the data into the format of journal entries, ledger accounts, trial balances, and financial statements.

Procedures such as posting and the preparation of trial balances and financial statements merely involve the *rearrangement* of recorded data and may easily be performed by computer. Of course, drafting the appropriate *disclosures* that accompany financial statements requires human judgment.

The preparation and posting of closing entries are mechanical tasks, involving the transfer of recorded data from one ledger account to another. Thus, closing entries *may be performed automatically* in a computer-based system.

THE ACCRUAL BASIS OF ACCOUNTING

LO 9 *Distinguish between the* accrual basis *and the* cash basis *of accounting.*

The policy of recognizing revenue in the accounting records when it is *earned,* and recognizing expenses when the related goods or services are *used,* is called the **accrual basis** of accounting. The purpose of accrual accounting is to measure the profitability of the *economic activities conducted* during the accounting period.

The most important concept involved in accrual accounting is the *matching principle.* Revenue is offset with all of the expenses incurred in generating that revenue, thus providing a measure of the overall profitability of the economic activity.

An alternative to accrual basis accounting is *cash basis* accounting. Under cash basis accounting, revenue is recognized when cash is collected from the customer, rather than when the company sells goods or renders services. Expenses are recognized when payment is made, rather than when the related goods or services are used in business operations.

The cash basis of accounting measures the amounts of cash received and paid out during the period, but it does *not* provide a good measure of the *profitability of activities* undertaken during the period.

CASE IN POINT

Airlines sell many tickets weeks, or even months, in advance of scheduled flights. Yet many expenses relating to a flight—such as salaries of the flight crew and the cost of fuel used—may not be paid until *after* the flight has occurred. Thus, the cash basis often would fail to "match" in one accounting period both the revenue and all expenses relating to specific flights.

Generally accepted accounting principles usually *require* use of the accrual basis in measuring revenue, expenses, and net income. However the cash basis is acceptable (and advantageous) in individuals' *income tax returns*. (Remember that income tax rules often differ from financial reporting requirements.) For this reason some small businesses—especially sole proprietorships—use the cash basis in their accounting records.

In this textbook, we will emphasize the accrual basis of accounting. Accrual basis accounting is used by virtually all businesses that distribute their financial statements to investors, stockholders, creditors, and other decision makers outside of the business organization.

DIVIDENDS—DECLARATION AND PAYMENT

Earlier in this chapter the declaration and the payment of a cash dividend were treated as a single event recorded by one journal entry. A small corporation with only a few stockholders may choose to declare and pay a dividend on the same day. In large corporations with thousands of stockholders and constant transfers of shares, an interval of a month or more will separate the date of declaration from the later date of payment.

Assume for example that on April 1 the board of directors of Universal Corporation declares the regular quarterly dividend of $1 per share on the 1 million shares of outstanding capital stock. The board's resolution specifies that the dividend will be payable on May 10 to stockholders of record on April 25. To be eligible to receive the dividend, an individual must be listed on the corporation's records as a stockholder on April 25, the date of record. Two entries are required: one on April 1 for the declaration of the dividend and one on May 10 for its payment, as shown below.

Apr. 1	Dividends...	1,000,000		Dividends declared and . . .
	Dividends payable		1,000,000	
	Declared dividend of $1 per share payable May 10 to stockholders of record Apr. 25.			
May 10	Dividends Payable	1,000,000		. . . dividends paid
	Cash...		1,000,000	
	Paid the $1 per share dividend declared on Apr. 1.			

The Dividends Payable account is a liability which comes into existence when the dividend is declared and is discharged when the dividend is paid.

The procedures of formally declaring and distributing dividends are performed only in businesses organized as corporations. In unincorporated businesses (sole proprietorships and partnerships), assets legally belong to the *owners*, not to the business entity. Thus, the owners may remove cash or other assets from the business at any time and with no formal procedures.

YOUR TURN

You as a Business Owner

You are the sole owner of a small business. The mortgage payment on your home is due, but you have very little money in your personal checking account. Therefore, you write a check for this payment from the business bank account.

Does it matter whether your business is unincorporated or organized as a corporation?

*Our comments appear on page 157.

SOME CONCLUDING REMARKS

THE ACCOUNTING CYCLE IN PERSPECTIVE

We view the accounting cycle as an efficient means of introducing basic accounting terms, concepts, processes, and reports. This is why we introduce it early in the course.

But, please, do not confuse familiarity with this sequence of procedures with a knowledge of *accounting.* The accounting cycle is but one accounting process—and a relatively simple one at that.

Computers have freed accountants today to focus upon the more *analytical* aspects of their discipline. These include, for example:

- Determining the information needs of decision makers.
- Designing systems to provide the information quickly and efficiently.
- Evaluating the efficiency of operations throughout the organization.
- Assisting decision makers in interpreting accounting information.
- Auditing (confirming the reliability of accounting information.)
- Forecasting the probable results of future operations.
- Tax planning.

We will emphasize such topics in our remaining chapters.

But let us first repeat a very basic point from Chapter 1: The need for some familiarity with accounting concepts and processes is not limited to individuals planning careers in accounting. Today, an understanding of accounting information and of the business world go hand in hand. You cannot know much about one without understanding quite a bit about the other.

A LOOK BACK AT OVERNIGHT: WAS DECEMBER A "GOOD MONTH"?

Overnight's Business plan (page 21) forecasts a net income in 1999 of $75,000. This requires an average monthly net income of $6,250. Overnight's net income for December fell well short of this level.

But let's not be short-sighted. Financial analysis involves more than comparing this month's net income with an average monthly goal. By any reasonable standard, Overnight had a *great* first month.

Most new businesses incur sizable *net losses* while they are getting started. Any business that earns a profit in its *first month of operations* is off to an impressive start.

Consider also that December traditionally is a slow month in the automotive repair business. Many people are too busy with the holidays (and perhaps too short of cash) to have much work done on their cars.

Evaluating the profitability of any business involves more than looking at the net income earned in a single month. An important consideration is the *trend* in earnings over time. Also, the analyst should consider how long the company has been in business, the characteristics of the industry, management's experience, consumer trends, competition, current and projected economic conditions—and the list goes on. Even the weather may be an important factor.

CASE IN POINT

How might a very severe winter affect the profitability (and solvency) of restaurants? Ski resorts? Construction companies? Suppliers of heating oil? New car dealers? A hotel in Buffalo, N.Y.? An airline serving "get-away" resort destinations?

Evaluating a company's profitability or solvency involves more than just looking at numbers; it requires "putting things in perspective."

NET CONNECTIONS

Each year, *Fortune* Magazine identifies the 500 largest American companies, ranked by revenue. The magazine's Internet address is:

www.fortune.com

Then click on "Fortune 500" and explore. Are there any Fortune 500 companies headquartered in your state? If so, which is the largest in terms of revenue? Is it also the most profitable?

Professor Dennis Schmidt, University of Northern Iowa, maintains a very interesting home page with an emphasis on income taxes:

www.uni.edu/schmidt

The Internal Revenue Service maintains its home page at:

www.ustreas.gov

Among other things, this site lets you download tax forms.

And you are always welcome at our home page:

www.magpie.org/cyberlab

SUMMARY OF LEARNING OBJECTIVES

1 Explain the nature of *net income, retained earnings, revenue,* and *expense.*

Net income is an increase in owners' equity that results from the profitable operation of a business during an accounting period. Net income also may be defined as revenue minus expenses. Revenue is the price of the goods sold and services rendered to customers during the period, and expenses are the costs of the goods and services used up in the process of earning revenue. Retained earnings is the element of stockholders' equity that represents the earnings of a corporation since it started business, less any losses, and less any dividends declared.

2 Apply the *realization* and *matching* principles in recording revenue and expenses.

The realization principle states that revenue should be recorded in the accounting records when it is *earned*—that is, when goods are sold or services are rendered to customers. The matching principle states that expenses should be offset against revenue on a *cause and effect* basis. Thus, an expense should be recorded in the period in which the related good or service is consumed in the process of earning revenue.

3 Explain *why* revenues are recorded with credits and expenses are recorded with debits.

The debit and credit rules for recording revenue and expenses are based upon the rules for recording *changes in owners' equity.* Earning revenue *increases* owners' equity; therefore, revenues are recorded as credit entries. Expenses *reduce* owners' equity, and are recorded as debit entries.

4 Explain the nature of *adjusting entries.*

Often a transaction affects revenues or expenses of *two or more* different periods. In these cases, adjusting entries are needed to assign to each period the appropriate amounts of revenue and expenses. These entries "adjust" the balances of various ledger accounts—hence the name, *adjusting entries.*

Adjusting entries are an essential step in the accounting cycle; they are performed at the *end* of each accounting period but prior to preparing the financial statements.

5 Define and record depreciation expense.

The term *depreciation* refers to the systematic allocation of the cost of a long-lived asset (such as equipment or a building) to expense over the asset's useful life. Depreciation is recorded at the end of each accounting period by an *adjusting entry* debiting Depreciation Expense and crediting the contra-asset account, Accumulated Depreciation.

6 Define the statements of income and of retained earnings. Explain how these statements relate to the balance sheet.

An income statement shows the revenue and expenses of a business during a specified accounting period. Expenses are offset (matched) against revenue to measure net income for the period. Net income is then listed in the statement of retained earnings as an addition to the beginning balance of retained earnings. Dividends are shown as a deduction. Thus, the statement of retained earnings shows the increases and decreases in retained earnings from one balance sheet date to the next.

7 Explain the purposes of *closing entries;* prepare these entries.

Closing entries serve two basic purposes. The first is to return the balances of the temporary owners' equity accounts (revenue, expenses, and dividends) to zero so that these accounts may be used to measure the activities of the next accounting period. The second purpose of closing entries is to update the balance of the Retained Earnings account. Four closing entries generally are needed: (1) to close the revenue accounts into the Income Summary account, (2) to close the expense accounts into the Income Summary account, (3) to close the balance of the Income Summary account (representing net income or net loss) into the Retained Earnings account, and (4) to close the Dividends account into the Retained Earnings account.

8 Describe the steps in the *accounting cycle.*

The steps in the accounting cycle may be summarized as follows: (1) journalize transactions, (2) post to ledger accounts, (3) prepare a trial balance, (4) make end-of-period adjustments, (5) prepare an adjusted trial balance, (6) prepare financial statements, (7) journalize and post closing entries, and (8) prepare an after-closing trial balance.

9 Distinguish between the *accrual basis* and the *cash basis* of accounting.

Under accrual accounting, revenue is recognized when it is earned and expenses are recognized in the period in which they contribute to the generation of revenue. Under the cash basis, on the other hand, revenue is recognized when cash is received and expenses are recognized when cash payments are made. The accrual basis gives a better measurement of profitability than does the cash basis, because the accrual basis associates the determination of income with the underlying earning process.

In Chapter 2, we introduced the double-entry system of accounting but illustrated this system using only balance sheet accounts. In this third chapter, we have seen that the double-entry system also allows us to measure revenue and expenses as we record changes in assets and liabilities. In fact, it is this double-entry system that makes possible the measurement of revenue and expenses.

We have now illustrated the complete accounting cycle for a *service-type* business. In Chapter 4, we will look more closely at one important element of this cycle — end-of-period adjusting entries — and will discuss other accounting activities performed at year-end. Accounting for *merchandising* activities will be discussed in Chapter 5.

KEY TERMS INTRODUCED OR EMPHASIZED IN CHAPTER 3

Accounting cycle (p. 131) The sequence of accounting procedures applied every period in recording transactions and preparing financial statements. These procedures begin with journalizing transactions, include adjusting and closing the accounts, and conclude with preparation of an after-closing trial balance.

Accounting period (p. 104) The span of time covered by an income statement. One year is the accounting period for much financial reporting, but financial statements are also prepared by companies for each quarter of the year and also for each month.

Accrual basis of accounting (p. 132) Calls for recording revenue in the period in which it is earned and recording expenses in the period in which they are incurred. The effect of events on the business is recognized as services are rendered or consumed rather than when cash is received or paid.

Accumulated depreciation (p. 118) A contra-asset account shown as a deduction from the related asset account in the balance sheet. Depreciation taken throughout the useful life of an asset is accumulated in this account.

Adjusted trial balance (p. 121) A listing of all ledger account balances after the amounts have been changed to include the adjusting entries made at the end of the period.

Adjusting entries (p. 115) Entries required at the end of the period to update the accounts before financial statements are prepared. Adjusting entries serve to apportion transactions properly between the accounting periods affected and to record any revenue earned or expenses incurred which have not been recorded prior to the end of the period.

After-closing trial balance (p. 130) A trial balance prepared after all closing entries have been made. Consists only of accounts for assets, liabilities, and owners' equity.

Closing entries (p. 125) Journal entries made at the end of the period for the purpose of closing temporary

accounts (revenue, expense, and dividend accounts) and transferring balances to the Retained Earnings account.

Conservatism (p. 107) The traditional accounting practice of resolving uncertainty by choosing the solution which leads to the lower (more conservative) amount of income being recognized in the current accounting period. This concept is designed to avoid overstatement of financial strength or earnings.

Contra-asset account (p. 118) An account with a credit balance which is offset against or deducted from an asset account to produce the proper balance sheet valuation for the asset.

Deficit (p. 128) A negative amount of retained earnings. Results from net losses and dividends in excess of lifetime net income.

Depreciable assets (p. 116) Physical objects with a limited life. The cost of these assets is gradually recognized as depreciation expense.

Depreciation (p. 116) The systematic allocation of the cost of an asset to expense during the periods of its useful life.

Dividend (p. 103) A distribution of cash by a corporation to its stockholders.

Expenses (p. 106) The costs of the goods and services used up in the process of obtaining revenue.

Fiscal year (p. 104) Any 12-month accounting period adopted by a business.

Income (or loss) before income taxes (p. 120) A subtotal often shown in an income statement, representing revenue less all expenses *other than* income taxes expense. Income taxes then are deducted to determine net income or loss.

Income statement (p. 103) A financial statement summarizing the results of operations of a business by matching its revenue and related expenses for a particular accounting period. Shows the net income or net loss.

Income Summary account (p. 125) The summary account in the ledger to which revenue and expense accounts are closed at the end of the period. The balance (credit balance for a net income, debit balance for a net loss) is transferred to the Retained Earnings account.

Income taxes expense (p. 119) The portion of a corporation's taxable income for the accounting period that is owed as income taxes to federal, state, and other income tax authorities. Income taxes expense differs from other expenses in that it does not help produce revenue. Thus, it usually is shown separately in the income statement, following the subtotal, income (or loss) before income taxes.

Matching principle (p. 106) The revenue earned during an accounting period is matched (offset) with the expenses incurred in generating this revenue.

Net income (p. 102)   An increase in owners' equity resulting from profitable operations. Also, the excess of revenue earned over the related expenses for a given period.

Net loss (p. 102)   A decrease in owners' equity resulting from unprofitable operations.

Objectivity principle (p. 107)   Accountants' preference for using dollar amounts that are relatively "factual"—as opposed to merely matters of personal opinion. Objective measurements can be verified.

Provision for income taxes (p. 120)   A widely used income statement caption meaning income taxes expense.

Realization principle (p. 105)   The generally accepted accounting principle that determines when revenue should be recorded in the accounting records. Revenue is realized when services are rendered to customers or when goods sold are delivered to customers.

Retained earnings (p. 103)   That portion of stockholders' equity resulting from profits earned and retained in the business.

Revenue (p. 105)   The price received for goods sold and services rendered by a business.

Statement of retained earnings (p. 122)   A financial statement showing the changes in the amount of retained earnings over the period.

Straight-line method of depreciation (p. 116)   The widely used approach of recognizing an *equal amount* of depreciation expense in each period of a depreciable asset's useful life. (Alternatives to this method are discussed in Chapter 10).

Taxable income (p. 119)   A measurement of the income subject to income taxes. Taxable income is determined in accordance with *tax regulations,* not with generally accepted accounting principles. In a simple case, taxable income is similar in amount to income before income taxes.

Tax rate (p. 119)   The percentage of taxable income owed to the government in income taxes. (Generally assumed to be 40% in our illustrations.)

Time period principle (p. 104)   To provide the users of financial statements with timely information, net income is measured for relatively short accounting periods of equal length. The period of time covered by an income statement is termed the company's accounting period.

Unincorporated business (p. 120)   A business *not* organized as a corporation. Includes sole proprietorships and partnerships.

Useful life (p. 116)   The period of time that a depreciable asset is expected to be useful to the business. This is the period over which the cost of the asset is allocated to depreciation expense.

DEMONSTRATION PROBLEM

Key Insurance Agency was organized on September 1, 19__. Assume that the accounts are closed and financial statements prepared each month. The company occupies rented office space, but owns office equipment estimated to have a useful life of 10 years from date of acquisition, September 1. The trial balance for Key Insurance Agency at November 30 is shown below.

Cash	$22,565	
Accounts receivable	7,050	
Office equipment	9,600	
Accumulated depreciation: office equipment		$ 160
Accounts payable		2,260
Income taxes payable		4,965
Capital stock		20,000
Retained earnings		7,450
Dividends	2,500	
Commissions earned		31,080
Advertising expense	2,400	
Salaries expense	18,000	
Rent expense	3,800	
	$65,915	$65,915

INSTRUCTIONS

a. Prepare the adjusting entry to record depreciation of the office equipment for the month of November.

b. Compute taxable income for November—assume this is the same as "income before income taxes." Using a corporate income tax rate of 40%, prepare the adjusting entry to accrue Key Insurance Agency's income taxes for the month of November.

c. Prepare an adjusted trial balance at November 30, 19__.

d. Prepare an income statement and a statement of retained earnings for the month ended November 30, 19__, and a balance sheet in report form at November 30, 19__.

SOLUTION TO DEMONSTRATION PROBLEM

a. Adjusting entry:

Depreciation Expense: Office Equipment	80	
Accumulated Depreciation: Office Equipment		80
To record depreciation for November ($9,600 ÷ 120 months).		

b. Taxable income (or "income before income taxes")

$$\$31,080 - \$2,400 - \$18,000 - \$3,800 - \$80 \text{ (part a)} = \$6,800$$

Adjusting entry:

Income Taxes Expense	2,720	
Income Taxes Payable		2,720
To record income taxes for November ($6,800 × 40% = $2,720).		

c.

KEY INSURANCE AGENCY
Adjusted Trial Balance
November 30, 19__

Cash	$22,565	
Accounts receivable	7,050	
Office equipment	9,600	
Accumulated depreciation: office equipment		$ 240
Accounts payable		2,260
Income taxes payable		7,685
Capital stock		20,000
Retained earnings		7,450
Dividends	2,500	
Commissions earned		31,080
Advertising expense	2,400	
Salaries expense	18,000	
Rent expense	3,800	
Depreciation expense: office equipment	80	
Income taxes expense	2,720	
	$68,715	$68,715

d.

KEY INSURANCE AGENCY
Income Statement
For the Month Ended November 30, 19__

Revenue:		
Commissions earned		$31,080
Expenses:		
Advertising expense	$ 2,400	
Salaries expense	18,000	
Rent expense	3,800	
Depreciation expense: office equipment	80	24,280
Income before income taxes		6,800
Income taxes expense		2,720
Net income		$4,080

KEY INSURANCE AGENCY
Statement of Retained Earnings
For the Month Ended November 30, 19__

Retained earnings, Oct. 31, 19__	$ 7,450
Net income for the month	4,080
Subtotal	$11,530
Dividends	2,500
Retained earnings, Nov. 30, 19__	$ 9,030

KEY INSURANCE AGENCY
Balance Sheet
November 30, 19__

Assets

Cash		$22,565
Accounts receivable		7,050
Office equipment	$ 9,600	
Less: Accumulated depreciation	240	9,360
Total assets		$38,975

contra asset → (handwritten annotation pointing to "Less: Accumulated depreciation")

Liabilities & Stockholders' Equity

Liabilities:		
Accounts payable		$ 2,260
Income taxes payable		7,685
Total liabilities		$ 9,945
Stockholders' equity:		
Capital stock	$20,000	
Retained earnings	9,030	29,030
Total liabilities & stockholders' equity		$38,975

SELF-TEST QUESTIONS

Answers to these questions appear on page 157.

1. Identify any of the following statements that correctly describe net income. (Indicate all correct answers.) Net income:
   a. Is computed in the income statement, appears in the statement of retained earnings, and increases stockholders' equity in the balance sheet.
   b. Is equal to revenue minus expenses.
   c. Is computed in the income statement, appears in the statement of retained earnings, and increases the amount of cash shown in the balance sheet.
   d. Can be determined using the account balances appearing in an adjusted trial balance.

2. Which of the following are based upon the realization principle and the matching principle? (Indicate all correct answers.)
   a. Adjusting entries.
   b. Closing entries.
   c. The accrual basis of accounting.
   d. The measurement of net income under generally accepted accounting principles.

3. Which of the following explains the debit and credit rules relating to the recording of revenue and expenses?
   a. Expenses appear on the left side of the balance sheet and are recorded by debits; revenue appears on the right side of the balance sheet and is recorded by credits.
   b. Expenses appear on the left side of the income statement and are recorded by debits; revenue appears on the right side of the income statement and is recorded by credits.
   c. The effects of revenue and expenses upon stockholders' equity.
   d. The realization principle and the matching principle.

4. The entry to recognize *depreciation expense:* (Indicate all correct answers.)
   a. Is an application of the matching principle.
   b. Is a closing entry.
   c. Usually includes an offsetting credit either to Cash or to Accounts Payable.
   d. Is an adjusting entry.

5. In the accounting cycle: (Indicate all correct answers.)
   a. Closing entries are made before adjusting entries.
   b. Financial statements may be prepared as soon as an adjusted trial balance is complete.
   c. The Retained Earnings account is not up-to-date until closing entries have been posted.
   d. Adjusting entries are made before financial statements are prepared.

6. For several years, the net income earned by Marlow Corporation has been less than the amounts distributed as dividends to the company's stockholders. Stockholders are most likely to become aware of this situation:
   a. By looking at the company's income statements.
   b. When the bank refuses to cash their dividend checks.
   c. By looking at the company's statements of retained earnings.
   d. By observing the decrease in cash from one balance sheet to the next.

7. The balance in the Retained Earnings account of Dayton Corporation at the beginning of the year was $65,000. During the year, the company earned revenue of $430,000 and incurred expenses of $360,000; dividends of $50,000 were declared and distributed, and the balance of the Cash account increased by $10,000. At year-end, the company's net income and the year-end balance in the Retained Earnings account were, respectively:
   a. $20,000 and $95,000.
   b. $70,000 and $95,000.
   c. $60,000 and $75,000.
   d. $70,000 and $85,000.

Use the following information in questions 8 and 9.

Accounts appearing in the trial balance of Westside Plumbing, Inc., at May 31 are listed below in alphabetical order:

Accounts payable	$ 2,450	Dividends	$ 1,800
Accounts receivable	3,100	Equipment	19,200
Accumulated depreciation:		Other expenses	1,300
equipment	5,100	Retained earnings	3,700
Advertising expense	150	Service revenue	4,800
Capital stock	15,000	Supplies expense	600
Cash	4,900		

No adjusting entries have yet been made to record depreciation expense of $250 and income taxes of $1,000 for May.

8. The amount of retained earnings appearing in the May 31 balance sheet should be:
   a. $5,200 **b.** $4,650 **c.** $3,400 **d.** Some other amount

9. In an *after-closing* trial balance prepared at May 31, the total of the credit column will be:
   a. $29,000 **b.** $27,200 **c.** $28,450 **d.** Some other amount

ASSIGNMENT MATERIAL

DISCUSSION QUESTIONS

1. Explain the effect of operating profitably upon the balance sheet of a business entity.
2. Does the Retained Earnings account represent a supply of cash which could be distributed to stockholders? Explain.
3. What is the meaning of the term *revenue?* Does the receipt of cash by a business indicate that revenue has been earned? Explain.
4. What is the meaning of the term *expenses?* Does the payment of cash by a business indicate that an expense has been incurred? Explain.
5. A service enterprise performs services in the amount of $500 for a customer in May and receives payment in June. In which month is the $500 of revenue recognized? What is the journal entry to be made in May and the entry to be made in June?
6. When do accountants consider revenue to be realized? What basic question about recording revenue in accounting records is answered by the *realization principle?*
7. Late in March, Classic Auto Painters purchased paint on account, with payment due in 60 days. The company used the paint to paint customers' cars during the first three weeks of April. Late in May, the company paid the paint store from which the paint had been purchased. In which month should Classic Auto Painters recognize the cost of this paint as an expense? What generally accepted accounting principle determines the answer to this question?
8. In what accounting period does the *matching principle* indicate that an expense should be recognized?
9. Explain the rules of debit and credit with respect to transactions recorded in revenue and expense accounts.
10. Supply the appropriate term (debit or credit) to complete the following statements.
    a. The Capital Stock account, Retained Earnings account, and revenue accounts are increased by _____ entries.

    b. Asset accounts and expense accounts are increased by _____ entries.

    c. Liability accounts and owners' equity accounts are decreased by _____ entries.

11. Why does any company that owns equipment or buildings need to make adjusting entries at the end of every accounting period?

12. Does a well-prepared income statement provide an exact measurement of net income for the period, or does it represent merely an approximation of net income? Explain.

13. How does depreciation expense differ from other operating expenses?

14. What is meant by the *straight-line* method of determining depreciation expense? Is the amount of depreciation expense determined under this method an estimate or an exact amount? Explain.

15. When should a business *begin* depreciating a depreciable asset? When should depreciation of a depreciable asset *cease?*

16. How is the amount of income taxes expense for a corporation determined?

17. How does income taxes expense differ from other business expenses?

18. All ledger accounts belong in one of the following five groups: asset, liability, owners' equity, revenue, and expense. For each of the following accounts, state the group in which it belongs. Also indicate whether the normal balance would be a debit or a credit.

    a. Building

    b. Depreciation Expense

    c. Accumulated Depreciation: Building

    d. Fees Earned

    e. Dividends Payable

    f. Telephone Expense

    g. Retained Earnings

    h. Income Taxes Expense

    i. Income Taxes Payable

19. For each of the following financial statements, indicate whether the statement refers to a single date or to a period of time:

    a. Balance sheet

    b. Income statement

    c. Statement of retained earnings

20. Briefly describe the content and format of an income statement and a statement of retained earnings.

21. Explain the relationships among the three financial statements discussed in this chapter—that is, the income statement, the statement of retained earnings, and the balance sheet.

22. Which of the following accounts are closed at the end of the accounting period?

Cash	Capital Stock
Fees Earned	Dividends
Income Summary	Accumulated Depreciation
Dividends Payable	Accounts Receivable
Telephone Expense	Depreciation Expense
Income Taxes Payable	Income Taxes Expense

23. Supply the appropriate term (debit or credit) to complete the following statements.

    a. When a business is operating profitably, the journal entry to close the Income Summary account will consist of a _____ to that account and a _____ to Retained Earnings.

    b. When a business is operating at a loss, the journal entry to close the Income Summary account will consist of a _____ to that account and a _____ to Retained Earnings.

c. The journal entry to close the Dividends account consists of a _____ to that account and a _____ to Retained Earnings.

24. Remington Corporation pays dividends regularly. Should these dividends be considered an expense of the business? Explain.

25. How does the accrual basis of accounting differ from the cash basis of accounting? Which gives a more accurate picture of the profitability of a business? Explain.

EXERCISE 3-1

The Matching Principle: You as a Driver

 LO 2,9

EXERCISES

The purpose of this exercise is to demonstrate the *matching principle* in a familiar setting. Assume that you own a car, which you drive about 15,000 miles each year.

a. List the various costs to you associated with owning and operating this car. Make an estimate of the total annual cost of owning and operating the car, and also the average cost-per-mile that you drive.

b. Assume also that you have a part-time job. You usually do not use your car in this job, but today your employer asks you to drive 100 miles (round trip) in order to deliver some important documents. Your employer offers to "reimburse you for your driving expenses."

You already have a full tank of gas, so you are able to drive the whole 100 miles without stopping and you don't actually spend any money during the trip. Does this mean that you have incurred no "expenses" for which you should be reimbursed? Explain.

EXERCISE 3-2

Relationship between Net Income and Owners' Equity

 LO 1,6

Total assets and total liabilities of Yato Talent Agency, Inc., as shown by its balance sheets at the beginning and end of the year were as follows:

	Beginning of Year	End of Year
Assets	$285,000	$350,000
Liabilities	90,000	125,000

Compute the net income or net loss from operations for the year in each of the following independent cases:

a. No dividends were declared or paid during the year and no additional capital stock was issued.

b. No dividends were declared or paid during the year, but additional capital stock was issued in the amount of $40,000.

c. Dividends of $30,000 were declared and paid during the year. No change occurred in capital stock.

d. Dividends of $40,000 were declared and paid during the year, and additional capital stock was issued in the amount of $15,000.

e. No dividends were declared or paid during the year, but additional capital stock was issued in the amount of $75,000.

EXERCISE 3-3

Effects of Transactions on the Accounting Equation

 LO 1,2,6,9

Tri-State Trucking Co. closes its accounts at the end of each month. Among the events occurring in *November* were the following:

a. Hauled freight for a credit customer; payment due December 10.

b. Paid Truck Service Center for repairs to trucks performed in October. (In October Tri-State Trucking had received and properly recorded the invoice for these repairs.)

c. Collected in full the amount due from a credit customer for hauling done in October.

d. Received a bill from Apex Truck Stops for fuel used in November. Payment due December 15.

e. Purchased two new trucks on November 30, paying part cash and issuing a note payable for the balance. The trucks are first scheduled for use on December 3.

f. Prepared an adjusting entry to record depreciation on trucks used for operations in November.

g. Prepared an adjusting entry to accrue income taxes expense for November.

Indicate the effects that each of these transactions will have upon the following six *total amounts* in the company's financial statements for the month of *November*. Organize your answer in tabular form, using the column headings shown below, and use the code letters **I** for increase, **D** for decrease, and **NE** for no effect. The answer to transaction (**a**) is provided as an example.

	Income Statement			Balance Sheet		
Transaction	Revenue −	Expenses =	Net Income	Assets =	Liabilities +	Owners' Equity
(a)	I	NE	I	I	NE	I

EXERCISE 3-4
Effects of Transactions on the Accounting Equation
 LO 1–6

A number of transactions of PanAm Steamship Lines are described below in terms of the accounts debited and credited:

1. Debit Wages Expense; credit Cash.
2. Debit Accounts Receivable; credit Freight Revenue.
3. Debit Dividends; credit Dividends Payable.
4. Debit Depreciation Expense: Ships; credit Accumulated Depreciation: Ships.
5. Debit Repairs Expense; credit Accounts Payable.
6. Debit Cash; credit Accounts Receivable.
7. Debit Dividends Payable; credit Cash.
8. Debit Income Taxes Expense; credit Income Taxes Payable.

a. Indicate the effects of each transaction upon the elements of the income statement and the balance sheet. Use the code letters **I** for increase, **D** for decrease, and **NE** for no effect. Organize your answer in tabular form using the column headings shown below. The answer for transaction 1 is provided as an example.

	Income Statement			Balance Sheet		
Transaction	Revenue −	Expenses =	Net Income	Assets =	Liabilities +	Owners' Equity
(1)	NE	I	D	D	NE	D

b. Write a one-sentence description of each transaction.

EXERCISE 3-5
When Is Revenue Realized?
LO 2,9

The following transactions were carried out during the month of May by M. Palmer and Company, a firm of design architects. For each of the five transactions, you are to state whether the transaction represented revenue to the firm during the month of May. Give reasons for your decision in each case.

no **a.** M. Palmer and Company received $25,000 cash by issuing additional shares of capital stock.

no **b.** Collected cash of $2,400 from an account receivable. The receivable originated in April from services rendered to a client.

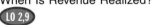

c. Borrowed $12,800 from Century Bank to be repaid in three months.

 d. Earned $83 interest on a company bank account during the month of May. No withdrawals were made from this account in May.

 e. Completed plans for guest house, pool, and spa for a client. The $5,700 fee for this project was billed to the client in May, but will not be collected until June 25.

EXERCISE 3-6
When Are Expenses Incurred?
LO 2,9

During March, the activities of Evergreen Landscaping included the following transactions and events, among others. Which of these items represented expenses in March? Explain.

a. Purchased a copying machine for $2,750 cash. (Consider only the asset purchase in your answer.)

b. Paid $192 for gasoline purchases for a delivery truck during March.

c. Paid $2,280 salary to an employee for time worked during March.

d. Paid an attorney $560 for legal services rendered in January.

e. Declared and paid an $1,800 dividend to shareholders.

f. Generated taxable income of $10,000 in March. Although no income taxes will be paid in March, the corporation is subject to an average income tax rate of 40%.

EXERCISE 3-7
Preparing Journal Entries for Revenue, Expenses, and Dividends
LO 2,3,4,9

Shown below are selected transactions of the law firm of Rodenberry & Associates, Inc.

Mar. 19 Drafted a trust agreement for Patrick Stewart. Sent Stewart an invoice for $1,200 requesting payment within 30 days. (The appropriate revenue account is entitled Legal Fees Earned.)

May 15 Declared a dividend of $60,000, payable on June 30 to stockholders of record on June 10.

May 31 Received a bill from Lawyers' Delivery Service for process service during the month of May, $2,050. Payment due by June 10. (The appropriate expense account is entitled Process Service Expense.)

June 30 Paid the dividend declared on May 15.

Dec. 31 Made a year-end adjusting entry to record depreciation expense on the firm's law library, $5,100.

Dec. 31 Made adjusting entry to accrue income taxes expense for the fourth quarter of the firm's fiscal year, $73,750. Payment to be made in the following year.

a. Prepare journal entries to record the transactions in the firm's accounting records. The firm closes its accounts at the end of each calendar year.

b. Identify any of the above transactions which *do not* cause an immediate change in total owners' equity. Explain.

EXERCISE 3-8
Adjusting Entry for Depreciation; Balance Sheet Presentation
LO 4

Aquino Pharmacy acquired a delivery truck at a cost of $21,000. Estimated life of the truck is five years. Management of Aquino Pharmacy elects to use the straight-line method of depreciation for vehicles.

a. State the amount of depreciation expense per year and per month. Give the adjusting entry to record depreciation on the truck at the end of the first month, and explain where the accounts involved would appear in the financial statements.

b. Assume the delivery truck was acquired on August 1, 1998 and that this vehicle is the only delivery truck owned by the business. Show how this truck would be reported in Aquino Pharmacy's balance sheet at December 31, 1998.

EXERCISE 3-9
Adjusting Entries
LO 4

TRC Graphics adjusts and closes its books each month. On May 31, 1998, *before* adjusting entries are recorded, the trial balance for TRC Graphics is as shown:

TRC GRAPHICS Trial Balance May 31, 1998		
	Debit	**Credit**
Cash...	$10,500	
Accounts receivable	3,000	
Equipment...	30,000	
Accumulated depreciation: equipment...............................		$ 5,500
Accounts payable..		2,500
Capital stock...		20,000
Retained earnings, May 1, 1998		4,500
Dividends..	2,500	
Fees earned..		25,000
Supplies expense...	600	
Salaries expense..	7,000	
Rent expense..	2,400	
Utilities expense...	1,500	
	$57,500	$57,500

The equipment shown above was purchased in 1997 and has an estimated useful life of five years. TRC Graphics is subject to a combined federal and state income tax rate of 40%.

a. Compute the amount of depreciation expense on the equipment for May. Give the adjusting entry to record depreciation on the equipment at the end of May.

b. Compute taxable income for TRC Graphics for May (assume taxable income is measured using the listed dollar amounts). Give the adjusting entry to accrue income taxes expense for the month of May. *13,000*

c. What is the amount of net income or loss reported in TRC Graphics' income statement for the month of May? Show computation.

d. As of the end of May, how long had TRC Graphics used the equipment in business operations? Show computation.

EXERCISE 3-10
Prepare an Income
Statement and a Statement
of Retained Earnings
LO 4,6

The following account balances, among others, appeared in the adjusted trial balance of Cortes Painting Contractors at December 31, 1998.

Salaries expense..........................	$81,800	Retained earnings, Jan. 1,	
Rent expense	9,600	1998	$57,200
Advertising expense.....................	3,200	Dividends	18,000
Depreciation expense:		Painting fees earned.....................	193,300
painting equipment	1,200	Paint & supplies expense.............	27,500
Accumulated depreciation:		Income taxes expense..................	28,000
painting equipment	3,000	Painting equipment.......................	7,200
Income taxes payable...................	4,100	Capital stock	40,000

a. From the above account balances, prepare first an income statement and then a statement of retained earnings for Cortes Painting Contractors for the year ended December 31, 1998. Include the proper headings on both financial statements. (*Hint:* You will not use all the accounts listed.)

b. In general, how is the amount of income taxes expense for a corporation determined? What was the average rate of tax used to determine the above income taxes expense for Cortes Painting Contractors? Show your computation.

EXERCISE 3-11
Preparing Closing Entries

Prepare the year-end closing entries for Cortes Painting Contractors, using the data given in Exercise 3-10. Use four separate entries, as illustrated on page 130. Indicate the balance in the Retained Earnings account that should appear in the balance sheet dated December 31, 1998.

EXERCISE 3-12
The Accounting Cycle

Listed below *in random order* are the eight steps comprising a complete accounting cycle.

   a. Prepare a trial balance.
   b. Journalize and post the closing entries.
   c. Prepare financial statements and appropriate disclosures.
   d. Post transaction data to the ledger.
   e. Prepare an adjusted trial balance.
   f. Make end-of-period adjusting entries.
   g. Journalize transactions.
   h. Prepare an after-closing trial balance.

a. List these eight steps in the logical sequence in which they would be performed.
b. Indicate which of these steps are mechanical functions that can be performed by machine in a computerized accounting system, and which require the judgment of people familiar with accounting principles and concepts.

EXERCISE 3-13
Annual Report; Fiscal Year

We have many assignments which are based on the annual report of **Toys "R" Us** (illustrated in Appendix A). Toys "R" Us uses an unusual fiscal year. If you look at the comparative income statements on page A-7, you will see that each fiscal year ends on a different date.

a. Explain this company's fiscal year policy (see the *Notes* accompanying the financial statements). Are these fiscal years—which all end on different dates—of equal length? If so, how long are they?
b. Why do you think companies such as Toys "R" Us choose to end their fiscal year a short period *after* December 31?
c. Throughout the annual report, management refers to the fiscal year ended January 28, 1995, as *1994*. In fact, they call this the 1994 annual report. Do you see any reasons for this?

PROBLEM 3-1
Revenue and Expenses

PROBLEMS

Olympia Sportfishing operates a fleet of charter fishing boats. Most customers pay in cash. However, the company allows local businesses to charter boats and pay on a monthly basis. Among the ledger accounts used by the company are the following:

Cash	Dividends	Fuel expense
Accounts payable	Income taxes payable	Repair & maintenance expense
Dividends payable	Charter revenue	Salaries expense
Accounts receivable	Advertising expense	Income taxes expense
Retained earnings	Docking Fees Expense	

Some of the company's June transactions are listed below:

June 1 Paid $3,500 to Unified Port District for June docking fees.

June 3 Placed advertising in *Fishing Magazine* for the month. The price was $900, payable in 30 days.

June 15 Cash receipts from passengers for the first half of June amounted to $29,160.

June 15 Paid a $15,000 cash dividend declared on May 14 and recorded as a liability on that date.

June 15 Paid salaries to employees for services rendered in the first half of June, $14,100.

June 21 Paid $7,980 to Nordhall Shipyards for repair work in June.

June 29 Collected $4,100 account receivable from TelCom Corp. for charter services in May.

June 30 Received a bill from Harbor Service Co. for fuel used in June, $8,755. Payable by July 10.

June 30 Billed Cyber Spyder $3,820 for private charter services rendered in June. Payment due in 30 days.

June 30 Made an adjusting entry to accrue income taxes for June, $12,800.

a. Prepare a journal entry (including explanation) for each of the above transactions.

b. You do not have all of the information concerning Olympia's revenue and expenses during June. But do you think the company operated at a profit or at a loss? Why?

PROBLEM 3-2
LO 1,2,3,9

NetCrafters provides computer consulting, system design, and set-up on both a cash and credit basis. Credit customers are required to pay within 30 days from date of billing. Among the ledger accounts used by the company are the following:

Cash	Accounts payable	Advertising expense
Accounts receivable	Dividends	Rent expense
Office equipment	Consulting fees earned	Salaries expense
Dividends payable		

Among the August transactions were the following:

Aug. 1 Provided system design and set-up for Arden Publications, a credit customer. Sent bill for $8,600, due in 30 days.

Aug. 2 Paid rent for August, $2,650.

Aug. 3 Purchased office equipment with estimated life of five years for $9,100 cash.

Aug. 10 Provided consulting for Quinn Veterinary Hospital and collected in full the charge of $5,020.

Aug. 15 Newspaper advertising to appear on August 18 was arranged at a cost of $1,610. Received bill from *Tribune* requiring payment within 30 days.

Aug. 18 Received payment in full of the $8,600 account receivable from Arden Publications for services rendered on August 1.

Aug. 20 Declared a dividend of $7,500, payable September 15.

Aug. 31 Paid salaries of $29,200 to employees for services rendered during August.

INSTRUCTIONS

a. Prepare a journal entry (including explanation) for each of the above transactions.

b. How does the transaction on August 20 (declaration of dividends in the amount of $7,500) affect net income of the corporation for August? What is the immediate impact of this transaction upon the assets, liabilities, and owners' equity of NetCrafters? (For each of these three items, state *increase, decrease,* or *no effect.*)

PROBLEM 3-3
Analyzing Transactions and
Preparing Journal Entries

LO 1,2,3,9

Garwood Marine is a boat repair yard. During August its transactions included the following:

1. On August 1, paid rent for the month of August, $4,400.

2. On August 3, at request of Kiwi Insurance, Inc., made repairs on boat of Michael Fay. Sent bill for $5,620 for services rendered to Kiwi Insurance, Inc. (Credit Repair Service Revenue.)

3. On August 9, made repairs to boat of Dennis Conner and collected in full the charge of $2,830.

4. On August 14, placed advertisement in *Yachting World* to be published in issue of August 20 at cost of $165, payment to be made within 30 days.

5. On August 25, received a check for $5,620 from Kiwi Insurance, Inc., representing collection of the receivable of August 3.

6. On August 26, made repairs on the vessel *Independent* totaling $1,890. Collected $400 cash; balance due within 30 days.

7. On August 30, sent check to *Yachting World* in payment of the liability incurred on August 14.

8. On August 31, Garwood Marine declared a $7,600 dividend.

INSTRUCTIONS

a. Write an analysis of each transaction. An example of the type of analysis desired is as follows:

    1. **(a)** Rent is an operating expense. Expenses are recorded by debits. Debit Rent Expense, $4,400.

       (b) The asset Cash was decreased. Decreases in assets are recorded by credits. Credit Cash, $4,400.

b. Prepare a journal entry (including explanation) for each of the above transactions.

PROBLEM 3-4
Preparing Journal Entries, Posting, and Preparing a Trial Balance

LO 1,2,3,4,8,9

In June 1998 Pat Campbell organized a corporation to provide crop dusting services. The company, called Campbell Crop Dusting, began operations immediately. Transactions during the month of June were as follows:

June 1 The corporation issued 60,000 shares of capital stock to Pat Campbell in exchange for $60,000 cash.

June 2 Purchased a crop-dusting aircraft from Utility Aircraft for $220,000. Made a $40,000 cash down payment and issued a note payable for $180,000.

June 4 Paid Woodrow Airport $4,500 to rent office and hangar space for the month.

June 15 Billed customers $8,320 for crop dusting services rendered during the first half of June.

June 15 Paid $5,880 salaries to employees for services rendered during the first half of June.

June 18 Paid Hannigan's Hangar $1,890 for maintenance and repair services.

June 25 Collected $4,910 of the amounts billed to customers on June 15.

June 30 Billed customers $16,450 for crop dusting services rendered during the second half of the month.

June 30 Paid $6,000 salaries to employees for services rendered during the second half of June.

June 30 Received a fuel bill from Henry's Feed & Fuel for $2,510 of aircraft fuel purchased during June. This amount is due by July 10.

June 30 Declared a $2,000 dividend payable on July 15.

The account titles and numbers used by Campbell Crop Dusting are:

Cash	1	Retained earnings	41
Accounts receivable	5	Dividends	45
Aircraft	15	Crop dusting revenue	51
Notes payable	31	Maintenance expense	61
Accounts payable	32	Fuel expense	62
Dividends payable	35	Salaries expense	63
Capital stock	40	Rent expense	64

INSTRUCTIONS

Based on the foregoing transactions:

a. Prepare journal entries. (Number journal pages to permit cross reference to ledger.)

b. Post to ledger accounts. (Number ledger accounts to permit cross reference to journal.) Enter ledger account numbers in the LP column of the journal as the posting work is done.

c. Prepare a trial balance at June 30, 1998.

d. Using the trial balance at June 30, 1998 (part **c**), compute each of the following at June 30, 1998: total assets, total liabilities, total stockholders' equity. Are these amounts the figures that would be reported for assets, liabilities, and stockholders' equity in the balance sheet at June 30, 1998? Explain your answer briefly.

PROBLEM 3-5
Adjusted Trial Balance, Part 1—Preparing Financial Statements
LO 4,6

Environmental Solutions, Inc. prepares financial statements and closes its accounts at the end of each calendar year. The following adjusted trial balance was prepared at December 31, 1998.

ENVIRONMENTAL SOLUTIONS, INC. Adjusted Trial Balance December 31, 1998		
Cash	$ 57,690	
Notes receivable	12,740	
Accounts receivable	65,090	
Land	196,000	
Building	126,000	
Accumulated depreciation: building		$ 33,600
Office equipment	33,600	
Accumulated depreciation: office equipment		13,440
Notes payable		112,000
Accounts payable		22,680
Income taxes payable		59,640
Capital stock		49,000
Retained earnings (Jan. 1, 1998)		181,300
Dividends	70,000	
Consulting fees earned		487,200
Advertising expense	31,500	
Insurance expense	38,720	
Utilities expense	15,040	
Salaries expense	245,280	
Income taxes expense	59,640	
Depreciation expense: building	4,200	
Depreciation expense: office equipment	3,360	
	$958,860	$958,860

INSTRUCTIONS

a. Prepare an income statement and a statement of retained earnings for the year ended December 31, 1998.

b. Prepare a balance sheet (in report form) as of December 31, 1998.

c. What was the average rate of income tax used to determine income taxes expense for 1998 for Environmental Solutions, Inc.? Show computation.

d. What was the estimated useful life used by Environmental Solutions in setting the depreciation rate for the building? Show computation.

PROBLEM 3-6

Adjusted Trial Balance: Part II—Preparing Closing Entries

Using the data shown in the adjusted trial balance in Problem 3-5:

a. Prepare journal entries to close the accounts. Use four entries: (1) to close the Revenue account, (2) to close the Expense accounts, (3) to close the Income Summary account, and (4) to close the Dividends account.

b. Does the amount of net income or net loss appear in the closing entries? Explain fully.

PROBLEM 3-7

Preparing Closing Entries

During the absence of the regular accountant for Kirby & Rice, a new employee, Doug Webb, prepared the closing entries from the ledger accounts for the year 19__. Webb has very little understanding of accounting and the closing entries he prepared were not satisfactory in several respects. The entries by Webb were:

Entry 1

Professional Fees Earned	273,600	
Accumulated Depreciation: Building	25,600	
Accounts Payable	86,400	
Income Taxes Payable	19,200	
Income Summary		404,800
To close accounts with credit balances.		

Entry 2

Income Summary	280,800	
Salaries Expense		206,400
Dividends		36,000
Advertising Expense		12,800
Depreciation Expense: Building		6,400
Income Taxes Expense		19,200
To close accounts with debit balances.		

Entry 3

Capital Stock	124,000	
Income Summary		124,000
To close Income Summary account.		

INSTRUCTIONS

a. For each entry, identify any errors which Webb made.

b. Prepare four correct closing entries, following the pattern illustrated on page 130.

c. Using the information presented above (and considering your answers to parts **a** and **b**), compute net income or net loss of Kirby & Rice for the year 19__. Show computation.

PROBLEM 3-8

End-of-period Adjusting and Closing Procedures; Preparing Financial Statements

Pat and Lee Mason own all the stock of Computer Graphics, Inc. In addition to being the only stockholders, they are salaried employees of the corporation. There are two other employees, who earn combined salaries totaling $3,000 per month. The building and office equipment used in the business were acquired on January 1 of the current year and were immediately placed in use. Useful life of the building was estimated to be 30 years and that of the office equipment five years. The company closes its accounts monthly; on March 31 of the current year, the trial balance is as follows:

COMPUTER GRAPHICS, INC. Trial Balance March 31, 19—		
Cash..	$ 22,250	
Accounts receivable..	7,500	
Land...	30,000	
Building..	90,000	
Accumulated depreciation: building......................................		$ 500
Office equipment..	21,000	
Accumulated depreciation: office equipment.......................		700
Accounts payable...		14,750
Income taxes payable..		29,100
Capital stock...		60,000
Retained earnings		43,700
Dividends	10,000	
Fees earned..		50,000
Advertising expense	900	
Automobile rental expense	500	
Salaries expense	16,000	
Telephone expense..	600	
	$198,750	$198,750

INSTRUCTIONS

From the trial balance and supplementary data given, prepare the following as of March 31, 19__.

a. Adjusting entries for depreciation during March of building and of office equipment.

b. Adjusting entry to accrue income taxes expense for March. Assume Computer Graphics is subject to a combined federal and state income tax rate of 40%.

c. Adjusted trial balance.

d. Income statement and a statement of retained earnings for the month of March, and a balance sheet at March 31 in report form.

e. Closing entries.

f. After-closing trial balance.

g. What was the total "compensation" paid by Computer Graphics, Inc., to the Masons in March?

PROBLEM 3-9
Complete Accounting Cycle
LO 1–9

After completing her medical education, April Stein established her own medical practice. The practice was organized as a corporation, named April Stein, M.D., APC (A Professional Corporation). The following transactions occurred during the corporation's first month of operations:

May 1 Issued 25,000 shares of capital stock to April Stein, M.D., in exchange for $25,000 cash.

May 1 Paid office rent for May, $1,700.

May 2 Purchased office equipment for cash, $16,200

May 3 Purchased medical instruments from Niles Instrument, Inc., at a cost of $9,000. A cash down payment of $1,000 was made and a note payable was issued for the remaining $8,000. The note is due in 60 days and does not bear interest.

May 4 Retained by Brandon Construction to be on call for emergency service at a monthly fee of $1,200. The fee for May was collected in cash.

May 15 Excluding the retainer of May 4, fees earned during the first 15 days of the month amounted to $4,800, of which $1,800 was in cash and $3,000 was in accounts receivable.

May 15 Paid Mary Hester, R.N., her salary for the first half of May, $1,200.

May 16 Dr. Stein wanted to establish a policy of paying dividends at the end of every calendar quarter. Therefore, the corporation declared a $1,000 dividend payable on June 30.

May 19 Treated Michael Tracy for minor injuries received in an accident during employment at Brandon Construction. No charge was made as these services were covered by Brandon's payment on May 4.

May 27 Treated Cynthia Knight, who paid $75 cash for an office visit and who agreed to pay $105 on June 1 for laboratory medical tests completed May 27.

May 31 Excluding the treatment of Cynthia Knight on May 27, fees earned during the last half of month amounted to $15,000, of which $6,300 was in cash and $8,700 was in accounts receivable.

May 31 Paid salaries totaling $6,200: $1,200 to Mary Hesler, R.N., for the second half of the month, and $5,000 to Avery Sloan, M.D., for the month of May.

May 31 Received a bill from McGraw Medical Supplies in the amount of $640 representing the amount of medical supplies used during May.

May 31 Paid utilities for the month, $320.

OTHER INFORMATION

Dr. Stein estimated the useful life of medical instruments at three years and of office equipment at five years. The account titles to be used and the account numbers are as follows:

Cash	10	Retained earnings	45
Accounts receivable	13	Dividends	47
Medical instruments	20	Income summary	49
Accumulated depreciation: medical		Fees earned	50
instruments	21	Medical supplies expense	60
Office equipment	22	Rent expense	61
Accumulated depreciation: office		Salaries expense	62
equipment	23	Utilities expense	63
Notes payable	30	Depreciation expense: medical	
Accounts payable	31	instruments	64
Dividends payable	32	Depreciation expense: office	
Income taxes payable	33	equipment	65
Capital stock	40	Income taxes expense	66

INSTRUCTIONS

a. Journalize the above transactions. (Number journal pages to permit cross-reference to ledger.)

b. Post to ledger accounts. (Use running balance form of ledger account. Number ledger accounts to permit cross reference to journal.)

c. Prepare a trial balance at May 31, 19__.

d. Prepare adjusting entries to record depreciation for the month of May and post to ledger accounts. (For medical instruments, cost $9,000 ÷ 3 years × $\frac{1}{12}$. For office equipment, cost $16,200 ÷ 5 × $\frac{1}{12}$.)

e. Prepare the adjusting entry to accrue income taxes expense for May and post to ledger accounts. The corporation is subject to a combined federal and state income tax rate of 40%. (*Hint:* First determine the corporation's taxable income; that is, revenue less all expenses *other than* income taxes expense.)

f. Prepare an adjusted trial balance.

g. Prepare an income statement and a statement of retained earnings for May, and a balance sheet as of May 31, 19__, in report form.

h. Prepare closing entries and post to ledger accounts.

i. Prepare an after-closing trial balance.

j. Dr. Stein is disappointed in her first month's earnings, as she had expected to earn at least $100,000 from her practice during the first year. Based upon the transactions you have recorded in May, assess her prospects of achieving that goal. Explain your reasoning.

CASES

CASE 3-1
Revenue Recognition
LO 2,9

The realization principle determines when a business should recognize revenue. Listed below are three common business situations involving revenue. After each situation, we give two alternatives as to the accounting period (or periods) in which the business might recognize this revenue. Select the appropriate alternative by applying the realization principle, and explain your reasoning.

a. Airline ticket revenue: Most airlines sell tickets well before the scheduled date of the flight. (Period ticket sold; period of flight)

b. Sales on account: In June 1998, a San Diego-based furniture store had a big sale, featuring "No payments until 1999." (Period furniture sold; periods that payments are received from customers)

c. Magazine subscriptions revenue: Most magazine publishers sell subscriptions for future delivery of the magazine. (Period subscription sold; periods that magazines are mailed to customers)

CASE 3-2
Expense Recognition
LO 2,9

As a basis for deciding when to recognize expense, we have discussed the *matching principle,* the need for *objective evidence* to recognize the existence of an asset, and the concept of *conservatism.* Shown below are three costs that ultimately become expenses. Each situation is followed by two alternatives as to when the business might record this expense. Select the appropriate alternative based upon the principles described above, and explain your answer.

a. Computers: Most businesses own them, and they are expensive. Due to the rapid advances in technology, it is very difficult to estimate in advance how long the business will keep them. (Period computers purchased; periods of an estimated useful life)

b. Advertising: In 1995, **Microsoft** launched its *Windows 95* operating system with a very expensive advertising campaign. Windows 95 has been a major source of revenue for Microsoft ever since. (1995, when the product was launched; estimated number of years over which Windows 95 will be sold.)

c. Interest expense: On some loans, the borrower does not pay any interest until the end of the loan. This practice is very common on short-term loans, such as 60 or 90 days, but may also occur in some special types of long-term borrowing. (Periods comprising the life of the loan; period in which interest is paid)

CASE 3-3
Measuring Income "Fairly"
LO 1,2,5

Kim Morris purchased Print Shop, Inc., a printing business, from Chris Stanley. Morris made a cash down payment and also agreed to make annual payments equal to 40% of the company's net income in each of the next three years. (Such "earn-outs" are a common means of financing the purchase of a small business.) Stanley was disappointed, however, when Morris reported a first year's net income far below Stanley's expectations.

The agreement between Morris and Stanley did not state precisely how "net income" was to be measured. Neither Morris nor Stanley were familiar with accounting concepts. Their agreement stated only that the net income of the corporation should be measured in a "fair and reasonable manner."

In measuring net income, Morris applied the following policies:

1. Revenue was recognized as cash when received from customers. Most customers paid in cash, but a few were allowed 30-day credit terms.

2. Expenditures for ink and paper, which are purchased weekly, were charged directly to Supplies Expense, as were the Morris family's weekly grocery and dry cleaning bills.

3. Morris set her annual salary at $60,000, which Stanley had agreed was reasonable. She also paid salaries of $30,000 per year to her husband and to each of her two teenage children. These family members did not work in the business on a regular basis, but they did help out when things got busy.

4. Income taxes expense included the amount paid by the corporation, as well as the Morris family's taxes on their salaries. (Assume the amounts of these income taxes were computed correctly.)

5. Depreciation was computed by the straight-line basis, using the following useful lives:

Printing equipment and Morris's car	3 years
Building	10 years
Land	20 years

(This business owns a great deal of equipment, so depreciation is one of its largest expenses.)

INSTRUCTIONS

a. Discuss the "fairness and reasonableness" of these income-measurement policies. (Remember, these policies do *not* have to conform to generally accepted accounting principles. But they should be *fair and reasonable.*)

b. Do you think that the net *cash flow* generated by this business (cash receipts less cash outlays) is higher or lower than the company's net income? Why?

c. How might Morgan and Stanley have created an "earn-out" agreement that would be less subject to disputes? (*Hint:* After dealing with the "measurement" issues, look up "Reviews of financial statements" in the index.)

INTERNET ASSIGNMENTS

INTERNET 3-1
Big Companies
in Your State
(General
Information)

Each year, *Fortune* magazine ranks the leading 500 American-based corporations in terms of total revenue earned. Visit the *Fortune* home page at:

www.fortune.com

Then click on "Fortune 500."

a. Scroll down to "The Fortune 500 Ranked by Performance." List the criteria by which this page will allow you to rank these 500 companies. (Visit a few of these listings to see how they work.)

b. Scroll back up to "Ranking within States." Identify the three largest Fortune 500 companies headquartered in your state. (If less than three companies are headquartered in your state, select a neighboring state.) For each of these companies, indicate the total revenue and net income (profits) earned last year (dollar amounts are in millions).

c. Select one of the companies listed in part **b.** Locate this company in the EDGAR database:

www.sec.gov/cgi-bin/srch-edgar

Select the company's "Form 10K" and locate comparative income statements for the past three years. Comment on the pattern of changes in total revenue and net income over the past three years.

Note: Additional Internet assignments for this chapter appear in Appendix B and on our home page:

www.magpie.org/cyberlab

ANSWERS TO SELF-TEST QUESTIONS

1. a, b, and d   **2.** a, c, and d   **3.** c   **4.** a and d   **5.** b, c, and d
6. c   **7.** d   **8.** c   **9.** b

OUR COMMENTS ON THE IN-TEXT CASE

YOU AS A BUSINESS OWNER (P. 133)   Indeed it does. If the business is *unincorporated,* its assets belong to you. Thus, you may withdraw these assets from the business at any time and use them for any purpose. But if the business is a corporation, these assets belong to *the corporate entity.* Even though you are the sole owner of the company, you may *not* withdraw assets from the business without *proper authorization.* Thus, your personal use of corporate assets must be viewed as compensation to you (i.e., salary), a loan, or a dividend.

Note: For income tax purposes, treating this expenditure as a loan probably is the best alternative. If you treat it as either salary or a dividend, you are receiving taxable income. Tax planning often plays a major role in transactions between a corporation and its owners.

Location:

Search   Feedback   Help   Directory

Document: Done

Closing out the old year and ringing in the new! It's a tradition everywhere—but for accountants, it takes much longer than one night. Year-end is our "busy season." There is much to be done—adjusting and closing the accounts, financial statements, audits, annual reports, income tax returns, next year's budget—and everyone wants the work "done yesterday."

(1) Identify annual accounting activities that make year-end the "busy season."

(2) Explain the purpose of adjusting entries.

(3) Describe and prepare the four basic types of adjusting entries.

(4) Explain how income taxes affect pretax profits and losses.

(5) Explain the concept of *materiality*.

(6) Explain the concept of *adequate disclosure*.

(7) Explain how *interim* financial statements are prepared in a business that closes its accounts only at year-end.

(*8) Prepare a worksheet and explain its usefulness.

THE "BUSY SEASON"

LO 1 *Identify annual accounting activities that make year-end the "busy season."*

Accounting is an on-going, year-round activity. Decision makers need—and accountants provide—up-to-date accounting information on a daily basis. But the end of a company's fiscal year is an especially busy time. Most companies close their accounts only once each year—at their fiscal year-end. And there is much to be done—taking inventory,[1] making adjusting entries, preparing financial statements, drafting the *notes* that accompany the statements, preparing income tax returns, developing budgets for the coming year, and, perhaps, undergoing an audit.

Publicly owned companies—those with shares listed on a stock exchange—have obligations to release annual and quarterly information to their stockholders and also to the public. These companies don't just "prepare financial statements"; they publish *annual reports*.

An annual report includes comparative financial statements for several years and a wealth of other information about the company's financial position, business operations, and future prospects. But before these reports are issued, the financial statements must be *audited* by a firm of certified public accountants (CPAs). Thus, both the company's accountants and the CPAs are under great time pressure to get their work done and the annual report issued. A copy of the annual report is sent to each stockholder; copies also are available to the general public upon request.

Publicly owned companies also must file their audited financial statements and detailed supporting schedules with the Securities and Exchange Commission (SEC). And then there are the income tax returns—maybe lots of income tax returns.

CASE IN POINT

Coca-Cola does business in more than 195 countries—and in all 50 of the United States. Shortly after its December 31 year-end, the Company must file more than 200 separate income tax returns, each measuring the taxable income earned in a different geographic region. Many of these returns run hundreds of pages in length—and each must be prepared according to the local tax regulations. (Even within the United States, income tax regulations vary from one state to the next.)

Supplemental Topic, "The Worksheet."
[1]Many companies that sell merchandise take a complete physical inventory at year-end. The phrase "taking inventory" means counting all of the merchandise on hand and determining its cost. This accounting procedure will be discussed further in Chapter 5.

Many businesses expect their accounting departments to develop comprehensive *budgets* for the coming fiscal year. These budgets show in detail the planned financial operations of every department within the organization, usually on a month-by-month basis. They are used throughout the year—both to coordinate the activities of different departments and as a basis for evaluating departmental performance. Much of the planning involved in the budgeting process is done well before year-end. Nonetheless, the work generally becomes much more intense as the new year approaches.

As explained in Chapter 3, a company's fiscal year *need not* coincide with the calendar year. Some companies elect to end their fiscal year during a seasonal low point in business activity. However most companies *do* end their fiscal year on December 31—or, as accountants say, at *12/31*. Thus, many accountants refer to the months of December through March as the "busy season."

Our goal in these few paragraphs is only to *identify* the annual accounting activities that often take place around year-end. We cannot adequately discuss all of these activities in a single chapter. In this chapter, we will focus primarily upon *end-of-period adjusting entries* and the *preparation of financial statements.* Taking inventory, annual reports, audits, and income taxes are addressed in greater depth elsewhere in this text.

ADJUSTING ENTRIES: A CLOSER LOOK

We introduced adjusting entries in Chapter 3, using as examples the entries to record supplies expense, depreciation, and income taxes expense. We will now see that other types of expenses—and also revenue—may require "adjustment" at the end of the accounting period. But first, let us review the role of adjusting entries in the accounting cycle.

THE NEED FOR ADJUSTING ENTRIES

For purposes of measuring income and preparing financial statements, the life of a business is divided into a series of *accounting periods*. This practice enables decision makers to compare the financial statements of successive periods and to identify significant trends.

LO 2 *Explain the purpose of adjusting entries.*

But measuring the net income of relatively short accounting periods poses a problem: Some transactions affect the revenue or expenses of *more than one period*. Therefore, **adjusting entries** are needed at the end of each period. The purpose of these entries is to assign to each period the appropriate amounts of revenue and expense.

For example, magazine publishers often sell two- or three-year subscriptions to their publications. At the end of each accounting period, these publishers make *adjusting entries* recognizing the portion of their advance receipts earned during the current period. Most companies own depreciable assets. At the end of each period, these companies make *adjusting entries* to allocate part of the cost of these assets to depreciation expense.

In summary, adjusting entries are needed whenever transactions affect the revenue or expenses of *more than one accounting period*. These entries assign revenues to the periods in which they are *earned,* and expenses to the periods in which the related goods or services are *used.*

In theory, a business could make adjusting entries on a daily basis. But as a practical matter, these entries are made *only at the end of each accounting period.* Thus, "adjusting the accounts" is an end-of-the-period procedure associated with the preparation of financial statements.

TYPES OF ADJUSTING ENTRIES

The exact number of adjustments needed at the end of each accounting period depends upon the nature of the company's business activities. However, most adjusting entries fall into one of four general categories:[2]

1. ***Entries to apportion recorded costs.*** A cost that will benefit more than one accounting period usually is recorded by debiting an asset account. In each period that benefits from the use of this asset, an adjusting entry is made to allocate a portion of the asset's cost to expense.

2. ***Entries to apportion unearned revenue.*** A business may collect in advance for services to be rendered to customers in future accounting periods. In the period in which these services are actually rendered, an adjusting entry is made to record the portion of the revenue earned during the period.

3. ***Entries to record unrecorded expenses.*** An expense may be incurred in the current accounting period even though no bill has yet been received and payment will not occur until a future period. Such unrecorded expenses are recorded by an adjusting entry made at the end of the accounting period.

4. ***Entries to record unrecorded revenue.*** Revenue may be earned during the current period, but not yet billed to customers or recorded in the accounting records. Such unrecorded revenue is recorded by making an adjusting entry at the end of the period.

LO 3 *Describe and prepare the four basic types of adjusting entries.*

un. ex ,until you record it

Adjusting entries bridge the gap between the dates upon which transactions occur, and the periods in which revenue is *earned* and expenses are *incurred.* Each type of adjusting entry is directly related either to *past or future transactions.* These relationships are summarized in the time-line diagram on the following page.

CHARACTERISTICS OF ADJUSTING ENTRIES

It will be helpful to keep in mind two important characteristics of all adjusting entries. First, every adjusting entry *involves the recognition of either revenue or expense.* Revenue and expenses represent changes in owners' equity. However, owners' equity cannot change by itself; *there also must be a corresponding change in either assets or liabilities.* Thus, every adjusting entry affects both an income statement account (revenue or expense) and a balance sheet account (asset or liability).

Second, adjusting entries are based upon the concepts of accrual accounting, *not upon monthly bills or month-end transactions.* No one sends a bill saying, "Depreciation expense on your building amounts to $500 this month." Yet, we must be aware of the need to estimate and record depreciation expense if we are to measure net income properly for the period. Making adjusting entries requires a greater understanding of accrual accounting concepts than does the recording of routine business transactions. In many businesses, the adjusting entries are made by the company's controller or by a professional accountant, rather than by the regular accounting staff.

YEAR-END AT OVERNIGHT AUTO SERVICE

To illustrate the various types of adjusting entries, we will again use our example involving Overnight Auto Service. We will skip ahead to December 31, 1999—the end of the company's first complete year of operations. This will enable us to illustrate the preparation of *annual* financial statements, rather than statements which cover only a single month.

---

[2]A fifth category of adjusting entries consists of adjustments to the balance sheet valuation of certain assets, such as marketable securities and accounts receivable. Valuation adjustments are explained and illustrated in Chapter 7.

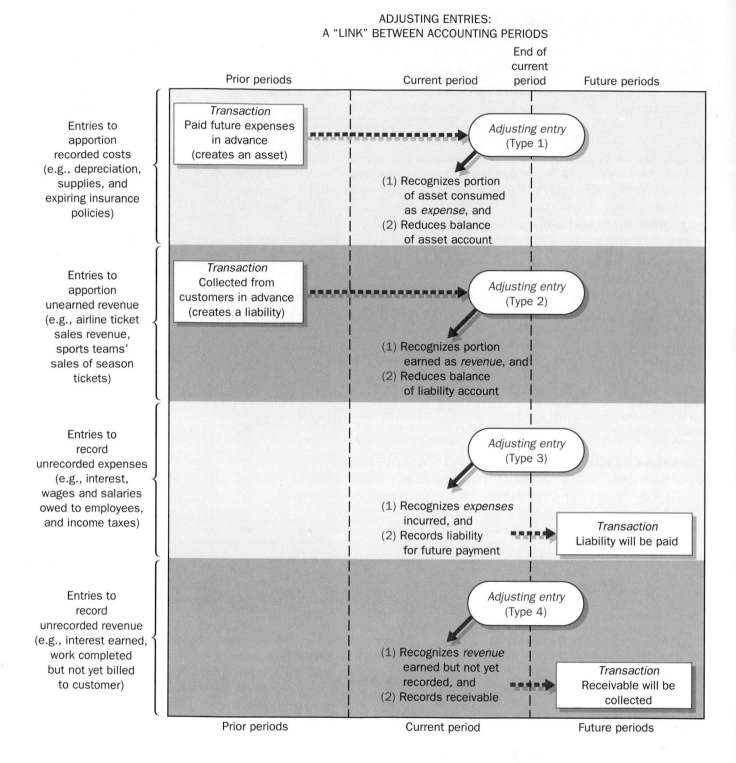

ADJUSTING ENTRIES:
A "LINK" BETWEEN ACCOUNTING PERIODS

In Chapter 3, we assumed that Overnight adjusted and closed its accounts at the *end of each month.* This allowed us to keep our first illustration short, but closing the accounts every month is not a common business practice. Most companies *adjust* their accounts every month, but make closing entries *only at year-end.* We will assume that Overnight has been following this approach throughout 1999.

The company's *unadjusted* trial balance as of December 31, 1999 follows:

OVERNIGHT AUTO SERVICE Trial Balance December 31, 1999		
Cash	$ 68,920	
Accounts receivable	13,530	
Shop supplies	1,700	
Unexpired insurance	4,500	
Land	295,000	
Building	120,000	
Accumulated depreciation: building		$ 6,000
Tools and equipment	63,000	
Accumulated depreciation: tools and equipment		12,250
Notes payable		80,000
Accounts payable		1,660
Income taxes payable		8,500
Interest payable		600
Unearned rent revenue		6,000
Capital stock		400,000
Retained earnings		400
Dividends	30,000	
Repair service revenue		400,450
Advertising expense	5,950	
Salaries and wages expense	205,310	
Supplies expense	9,900	
Depreciation expense: building	5,500	
Depreciation expense: tools and equipment	11,250	
Utilities expense	16,800	
Insurance expense	13,500	
Interest expense	6,000	
Income taxes expense	45,000	
	$915,860	$915,860

When temporary accounts are closed only at year-end, their balances represent the year-to-date

Because Overnight now closes its accounts only at year-end, the balances in the revenue, expense, and dividends accounts represent the activities of the *entire year*, rather than those of a single month. But Overnight last *adjusted* its accounts on November 30; therefore, it is still necessary to make adjusting entries for the month of December.

In the next few pages we illustrate several transactions, as well as the related adjusting entries. Both are shown in the format of general journal entries. To help distinguish between transactions and adjusting entries, transactions will be shown in **blue.** For emphasis, adjusting entries will be printed in **red.**

APPORTIONING RECORDED COSTS

When a business makes an expenditure that will benefit more than one accounting period, the amount usually is debited to an asset account. At the end of each period benefiting from this expenditure, an adjusting entry is made to transfer an appropriate portion of the cost from the asset account to an expense account. This adjusting entry reflects the fact that part of the asset has been used up—or become expense—during the current accounting period.

An adjusting entry to apportion a recorded cost consists of a debit to an expense account and a credit to an asset account (or a contra-asset account). Examples of these adjustments include the entries to record depreciation expense and to apportion the costs of **prepaid expenses.**

PREPAID EXPENSES Payments in advance are often made for such items as insurance, rent, and office supplies. If the advance payment (or prepayment) will benefit more than just the current accounting period, the cost *represents an asset* rather than an expense. The cost of this asset will be allocated to expense in the accounting periods in which the services or the supplies are used. In summary, *prepaid expenses are assets;* they become expenses only as the goods or services are used up.

SHOP SUPPLIES To illustrate, consider Overnight's accounting policies for shop supplies. As supplies are purchased, their cost is debited to the asset account, Shop Supplies. It is not practical to make journal entries every few minutes as supplies are used. Instead, an estimate is made of the supplies remaining on hand at the end of each month; the supplies which are "missing" are assumed to have been used.

Prior to making adjusting entries at December 31, the balance in Overnight's Shop Supplies account is $1,700. Assume that at December 31, McBryan estimates there are about $1,000 worth of shop supplies remaining on hand. This suggests supplies costing about $700 have been *used* in December; thus, the following *adjusting entry* is made:

Transferring the cost of supplies used from the asset account to expense	Dec. 31	Supplies Expense 700	
		Shop Supplies...	700
		Estimate of shop supplies used in December.	

This adjusting entry serves two purposes: (1) it charges to expense the cost of supplies used in December, and (2) it reduces the balance of the Shop Supplies account to $1,000—the estimated amount of supplies on hand at December 31.

INSURANCE POLICIES Insurance policies also are a prepaid expense. These policies provide a service, insurance protection, over a specific period of time. As the time passes, the insurance policy *expires*—that is, it is "used up" in business operations.

To illustrate, assume that on March 1, Overnight purchased for $18,000 a one-year insurance policy providing comprehensive liability insurance and insurance against fire and damage to customers' vehicles while in Overnight's facilities. This expenditure (a *transaction*) was debited to an asset account, as shown below:

Purchase 12 months of insurance coverage	Mar. 1	Unexpired Insurance 18,000	
		Cash...	18,000
		Purchased an insurance policy providing coverage for the next 12 months.	

This $18,000 expenditure provides insurance coverage for a period of one year. Therefore, $\frac{1}{12}$ of this cost, or $1,500, is recognized as insurance expense every month. The insurance expense for the month of December is recorded by the following *adjusting entry* at month-end:

Cost of insurance coverage expiring in December	Dec. 31	Insurance Expense 1,500	
		Unexpired Insurance......................................	1,500
		Insurance expense for December.	

Notice the similarities between the *effects* of this adjusting entry and the one that we previously made for shop supplies. In both cases, the entries transfer to expense that portion of an asset which was used up during the period.

RECORDING PREPAYMENTS DIRECTLY IN THE EXPENSE ACCOUNTS In our illustration, payments for shop supplies and for insurance covering more than one period were debited to asset accounts. However, some companies follow an alternative policy of debiting such prepayments directly to an expense account, such as Supplies Expense. At the end of the period, the adjusting entry then would be to debit Shop Supplies and credit Supplies Expense for the cost of supplies which had *not* been used.

This alternative method leads to the *same results* as does the procedure used by Overnight. Under either approach, the cost of supplies used during the current period is treated as an *expense,* and the cost of supplies still on hand is carried forward in the balance sheet as an *asset.*

In this text, we will follow Overnight's practice of recording prepayments in asset accounts and then making adjustments to transfer these costs to expense accounts as the assets expire. This approach correctly describes the *conceptual flow of costs* through the elements of financial statements. That is, a prepayment *is* an asset that later becomes an expense. The alternative approach is used widely in practice only because it is an efficient "shortcut," which standardizes the recording of transactions and may reduce the number of adjusting entries needed at the end of the period. Remember, our goal in this course is to develop your ability to *understand and use* accounting information, not to train you in bookkeeping procedures.

DEPRECIATION OF BUILDINGS The recording of depreciation expense at the end of an accounting period provides another example of an adjusting entry which *apportions a recorded cost.* The adjusting entry to record depreciation on Overnight's building is the same every month throughout the building's estimated useful life (20 years). This entry, essentially the same as illustrated in Chapter 3, is:

Dec. 31	Depreciation Expense: Building.. 500	
	Accumulated Depreciation: Building..	500
	Monthly depreciation on building ($120,000 ÷ 240 mo.).	

The adjusting entry for monthly depreciation on the building

The monthly depreciation expense is based upon the following facts: the building cost $120,000, and has an estimated useful life of 20 years (240 months). Under the *straight-line* method of depreciation, the cost assumed to expire each month is $1/240$ of $120,000, or $500.[3]

Accountants often use the term **book value** (or **carrying value**) to describe the net valuation of an asset in a company's accounting records. For depreciable assets, such as buildings and equipment, book value is equal to the cost of the asset, less the related amount of accumulated depreciation. After Overnight has posted its December adjusting entries, the accumulated depreciation on the building will total $6,500 (the unadjusted balance of $6,000 plus the $500 recognized in December). Thus, the book value of the building is $113,500 ($120,000 − $6,500).

Book value is significant primarily for accounting purposes. It represents costs that will be offset against the revenue of future periods. Also, it gives users of financial statements an indication of the age of a company's depreciable assets. But

---

[3]The straight-line method of depreciation was introduced in Chapter 3; alternative methods are discussed in Chapter 9. Once a business selects a depreciation method, it should apply that method *consistently* throughout the asset's useful life.

book value is *not* intended to represent the asset's *current market value.* Remember, balance sheets are based primarily upon *costs,* rather than estimated market values.

DEPRECIATION ON TOOLS AND EQUIPMENT Overnight depreciates its tools and equipment over a period of five years (60 months), using the straight-line method. The December 31 trial balance shows that the company owns tools and equipment which cost $63,000. Therefore, the adjusting entry to record December's depreciation expense is:

Monthly depreciation on tools and equipment—why is it higher than last year?

Dec. 31 Depreciation Expense: Tools and Equipment 1,050
           Accumulated Depreciation: Tools and
              Equipment 1,050
       Monthly depreciation on tools and equipment
       ($63,000 ÷ 60 months = $1,050/mo.).

Some readers may remember that Overnight recognized only $1,000 in depreciation expense on tools and equipment in December of 1998. If the company is using the straight-line method, why might the amount of monthly depreciation expense have *increased?* The answer is quite basic—Overnight now owns more tools and equipment than it did in 1998.

What is the book value of Overnight's tools and equipment at December 31, 1999? If you said *$49,700* you're right.[4]

APPORTIONING UNEARNED REVENUE

In some instances, customers may *pay in advance* for services to be rendered in later accounting periods. For example, a football team collects much of its revenue in advance through the sale of season tickets. Health clubs collect in advance by selling long-term membership contracts. Airlines sell many of their tickets well in advance of a scheduled flight.

For accounting purposes, amounts collected in advance *do not represent revenue,* because these amounts have *not yet been earned.* Amounts collected from customers in advance are recorded by debiting the Cash account and crediting an *unearned revenue* account. **Unearned revenue** also may be called *deferred revenue.*

When a company collects money in advance from its customers, it has an *obligation* to render services in the future. Therefore, the balance of an unearned revenue account is considered to be a liability; *it appears in the liability section of the balance sheet, not in the income statement.* Unearned revenue differs from other liabilities because it usually will be settled by rendering services, rather than by making payment in cash. In short, it will be *worked off* rather than *paid off.* Of course if the business is unable to render the service, it must discharge this liability by refunding money to its customers.

CASE IN POINT

The largest liability in the balance sheet of **UAL Corporation (United Airlines)** is "Advance ticket sales." This account, with a balance of more than $1 billion, represents unearned revenue resulting from the sale of tickets for future flights. Most of this unearned revenue will be earned as the future flights occur. Some customers, however, will change their plans and will return their tickets to United Airlines for a cash refund.

---

[4]Cost, $63,000, less accumulated depreciation which, after the December 31 adjusting entry, amounts to $13,300.

When the company renders the services for which customers have paid in advance, it is working off its liability to these customers and is earning the revenue. At the end of the accounting period, an adjusting entry is made to transfer an appropriate amount from the unearned revenue account to a revenue account. This adjusting entry consists of a debit to a liability account (unearned revenue) and a credit to a revenue account.

To illustrate these concepts, assume that on December 1, Harbor Cab Co. agreed to rent outdoor parking space on Overnight's property to park taxicabs when they are not in service. The agreed-upon rent is $2,000 per month, and Harbor paid for the first three months in advance. The journal entry to record this *transaction* on December 1 was:

Dec. 1	Cash..	6,000	
	Unearned Rent Revenue..		6,000
	Collected in advance from Harbor Cab for rental of		
	outdoor parking space for 3 months		

An "advance"—it's not revenue, it's a liability

Remember that Unearned Rent Revenue is a *liability* account, *not a revenue account.* Overnight will earn rental revenue *gradually* over a three-month period as it provides parking space to Harbor Cab. At the end of each of these three months, Overnight will make an *adjusting entry* transferring $2,000 from the Unearned Revenue account to an "Earned" Revenue account, which will appear in Overnight's income statement. The first in this series of monthly transfers will be made at December 31 with the following adjusting entry:

Dec. 31	Unearned Rent Revenue..	2,000	
	Rent Revenue Earned..		2,000
	Portion of rent received in advance from Harbor		
	Cab that was earned in December ($6,000 ÷ 3 mo.).		

An adjusting entry showing that some unearned revenue has now been earned

After this adjusting entry has been posted, the Unearned Rent Revenue account will have a $4,000 credit balance. This balance represents Overnight's obligation to render $4,000 worth of services over the next two months and will appear in the liability section of the company's balance sheet. The Rent Revenue Earned account will appear in Overnight's income statement.

RECORDING ADVANCE COLLECTIONS DIRECTLY IN THE REVENUE ACCOUNTS We have stressed that amounts collected from customers in advance represent *liabilities,* not revenue. However, some companies follow an accounting policy of crediting these advance collections directly to revenue accounts. The adjusting entry then should consist of a debit to the revenue account and a credit to the unearned revenue account for the portion of the advance payments *not yet earned.* This alternative accounting practice leads to the same results as does the method used in our illustration.

In this text, we will follow the originally described practice of crediting advance payments from customers to an unearned revenue account.

RECORDING UNRECORDED EXPENSES

This type of adjusting entry recognizes expenses that will be paid in *future* transactions; therefore, no cost has yet been recorded in the accounting records. Salaries of employees and interest on borrowed money are common examples of expenses which accumulate from day to day, but which usually are not recorded until they are paid. These expenses are said to **accrue** over time, that is, to grow or to accumulate. At the end of the accounting period, an adjusting entry should be made to record any expenses which have accrued, but which have not yet been recorded. Since these expenses will be paid at a future date, the adjusting entry consists of a debit to an expense account and a credit to a liability account. We shall now use the example of Overnight Auto Service to illustrate this type of adjusting entry.

ACCRUAL OF SALARIES AND WAGES EXPENSE Overnight, like many businesses, pays its employees every *other* Friday. This month, however, ends on the Friday falling *between* two payroll dates. Thus, Overnight's employees have worked for a week in December *for which they have not yet been paid.*

Time cards and salary rates indicate that since the last payroll date, Overnight's employees are owed $3,650 for services rendered between the last payroll date and December 31. The following adjusting entry should be made to record this amount as both an expense of the current period and as a liability:

Wages owed as of month-end

Dec. 31	Salaries and Wages Expense	3,650	
	Salaries and Wages Payable		3,650
	To accrue salaries and wages owed to employees, but unpaid as of month-end.		

This adjusting entry increases Overnight's salaries and wages expense for 1999 and also creates a liability—salaries and wages payable—that will appear in the December 31 balance sheet (page 176).

On Friday, January 7, Overnight will pay its regular biweekly payroll. Let us assume that this payroll amounts to $7,500. In this case, the entry to record payment will be as follows:[5]

Payment of wages earned in two accounting periods

2000			
Jan. 7	Salaries and Wages Expense (for January)	3,850	
	Salaries and Wages Payable (accrued in December)	3,650	
	Cash		7,500
	Biweekly payroll, $3,650 of which had been accrued at December 31.		

ACCRUAL OF INTEREST EXPENSE In November, *1998,* Overnight purchased its building, an old bus garage, from Metropolitan Transit District. Overnight issued a $90,000 short-term note payable for much of the purchase price.

Unfortunately, Overnight has never been able to arrange long-term financing on the old bus garage. Instead, it paid $10,000 of the original liability, and the remaining $80,000 is being financed through short-term bank loans which must be renewed every three months. The proceeds of each new loan are used to repay the "old" loan as it comes due.

The facts surrounding the most recent of these short-term loans are as follows: On October 31, Overtime borrowed $80,000 from American National Bank. This loan is to be repaid in three months (on January 31, 2000), along with interest computed at the annual rate of 9%. The entry made on October 31 to record this borrowing transaction appears below:

Oct. 31	Cash..	80,000	
	Notes Payable..		80,000
	Borrowed cash from American National Bank, issuing a 9%, $80,000 note payable, due in three months.		

---

[5]In this illustration, we do not address the details associated with payroll taxes and amounts withheld. These topics are discussed in the *Supplemental Topic* at the end of Chapter 10.

On January 31, Overnight must pay the bank $81,800. This represents the $80,000 amount borrowed, *plus $1,800 interest* ($80,000 × .09 × $\frac{3}{12}$). The $1,800 interest charge covers a period of *three months*. Although no payment will be made until January 31, interest expense is *incurred* at the rate of $600 per month,[6] as shown below:

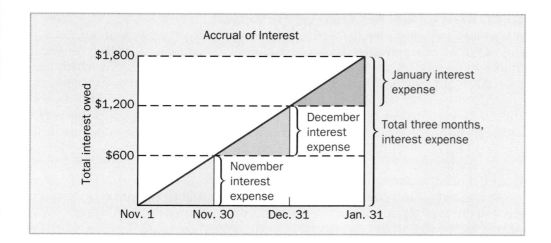

At the end of November and of December, Overnight makes an adjusting entry recognizing the interest expense which has accrued during that month. The adjusting entry at December 31 appears below:

Dec. 31	Interest Expense...	600	
	Interest Payable		600
	Interest expense accrued during December on		
	3-month note payable ($80,000 × .09 × $\frac{1}{12}$).		

Adjusting entry for interest accrued during December

(A similar entry was made on November 30.)

This entry increases the amount of interest expense recognized during the year from $6,000 (unadjusted trial balance on page 163) to *$6,600*, the amount which will appear in Overnight's 1999 income statement. Both the $80,000 note payable to American National Bank and the $1,200 in interest payable will appear as *liabilities* in December 31 balance sheet (page 176).

The entry at January 31 to record repayment of this loan, including $1,800 in interest charges, will be:

2000			
Jan. 31	Notes Payable...	80,000	
	Interest Payable (from November and December)	1,200	
	Interest Expense (for January).................................	600	
	Cash		81,800
	Repaid $80,000 note payable to American National		
	Bank, including $1,800 in interest charges.		

Payment of interest expense incurred over several months

Notice that only *$600* of the total interest charge is recognized as expense in January. Through the process of adjusting entries, we have spread the total $1,800 interest charge over the three months in which this expense was incurred.

---

[6]To simplify this illustration we are assuming no compounding of interest. The concepts of compound interest are addressed in Appendix D.

ACCRUAL OF INCOME TAXES EXPENSE Income taxes expense accrues as taxable income is earned. But the amount of income taxes expense depends upon the amounts of revenue earned during the period, and all other expenses incurred. Therefore, we will defer further discussion of Overnight's income taxes expense until we have finished adjusting other accounts.

RECORDING UNRECORDED REVENUE

A business may earn revenue during the current accounting period but not bill the customer until a future accounting period. This situation is likely to occur if additional services are being performed for the same customer, in which case the bill might not be prepared until all services are completed. Any revenue which has been *earned but not recorded* during the current accounting period should be recorded at the end of the period by means of an adjusting entry. This adjusting entry consists of a debit to an account receivable and a credit to the appropriate revenue account. The term *accrued revenue* often is used to describe revenue which has been earned during the period but which has not been recorded prior to the closing date.

To illustrate this type of adjusting entry, assume that in December, Overnight entered into an agreement to perform routine maintenance on several vans owned by Airport Shuttle Service. Overnight agreed to maintain these vans for a flat fee of $1,500 per month, payable on the fifteenth of each month.

No entry was made to record the signing of this agreement, because no services had yet been rendered. Overnight began rendering services on *December 15,* but the first monthly payment will not be received until January 15. Therefore, Overnight should make the following adjusting entry at December 31 to record the revenue *earned* from Airport Shuttle during the month:

Adjusting entry recognizing revenue earned, but not yet billed or collected	Dec. 31 Accounts Receivable... 750	
	Repair Service Revenue..	750
	To recognize revenue from services rendered on Airport Shuttle maintenance contract during December. Account is settled on the 15th of each month.	

The collection of the first monthly fee from Airport Shuttle will occur in the next accounting period (January 15, to be exact). Of this $1,500 cash receipt, half represents collection of the receivable recorded on December 31; the other half represents revenue earned in January. Thus, the entry to record the receipt of $1,500 from Airport Shuttle on January 15 will be:

Entry to record collection of accrued revenue	2000	
	Jan. 15 Cash 1,500	
	Accounts Receivable..	750
	Repair Service Revenue	750
	Collected from Airport Shuttle for van maintenance, Dec. 15 thru Jan. 15.	

The net result of the December 31 adjusting entry has been to divide the revenue from maintenance of Airport Shuttle's vans between December and January in proportion to the services rendered during each month.

ACCRUAL OF INCOME TAXES EXPENSE: THE FINAL ADJUSTING ENTRY

The accrual of income taxes expense was illustrated in Chapter 3. As a corporation earns taxable income, it incurs income taxes expense, and also a liability to governmental tax authorities. This liability normally is paid in four installments, called *estimated quarterly payments.* The first three payments normally are made on April 15, June 15, and September 15. The final installment actually is due on *December 15;* but for purposes of our illustration and assignment materials, we will assume the final estimated payment is not due until *January 15.*[7]

LO 4 *Explain how income taxes affect pretax profits and losses.*

In its unadjusted trial balance, Overnight shows income taxes expense of $45,000. This is the income taxes expense recognized from *January 1, 1999 through November 30, 1999.* Income taxes accrued through September 30 have already been paid. Thus, the $8,500 liability for income taxes payable represents only the income taxes accrued in *October and November.*

The amount of income taxes expense accrued for any given month is only an *estimate.* The actual amount of income taxes cannot be determined until the company prepares its annual income tax return. In our illustrations and assignment materials, we estimate income taxes expense at *40% of taxable income.* We also assume that taxable income is equal to *Income before income taxes,* a subtotal often shown in an income statement. This subtotal is total revenue less all expenses *other than* income taxes.[8]

In 1999, Overnight earned income before income taxes of $121,000 (see the income statement on page 176). Therefore, income taxes expense *for the year* is estimated at *$48,400* ($121,000 × 40%). Income taxes expense recognized through November 30 amounts to $ 5,000 (see the unadjusted trial balance on page 175). Therefore, an additional *$3,400* in income taxes expense has accrued during December ($48,400 − $45,000). The adjusting entry to record this expense is:

Dec. 31	Income Taxes Expense...	3,400	
	Income Taxes Payable..		3,400
	Estimated income taxes applicable to taxable income		
	earned during December.		

Adjusting entry to record income taxes for December

This entry increases the balance in the Income Taxes Expense account to $48,400, and the liability for income taxes payable to $11,900 ($8,500 + $3,400). The entry to record payment of this liability on January 15 will be:

2000			
Jan. 15	Income Taxes Payable...	11,900	
	Cash		11,900
	Paid final installment on 1999 income tax liability.		

(The payment of income taxes is a *transaction,* not an adjusting entry.)

INCOME TAXES IN UNPROFITABLE PERIODS What happens to income taxes expense when *losses* are incurred? In these situations, the company recognizes a "negative amount" of income taxes expense. The adjusting entry to record income taxes at the end of an *unprofitable* accounting period consists of a *debit* to Income Taxes Payable, and a *credit* to Income Taxes Expense.

"Negative" income taxes expense means that the company may be able to recover from the government some of the income taxes recognized as expense

---

[7]This assumption enables us to accrue income taxes in December in the same manner as in other months. Otherwise, income taxes for this month would be recorded as a mid-month transaction, rather than in an end-of-month adjusting entry.

[8]As explained in Chapter 3, the amounts of some revenue and expenses may differ between income tax returns and income statements. Such differences are discussed in later chapters.

in prior periods.[9] If the Income Taxes Payable account has a *debit* balance at year-end, it is reclassified as an *asset,* called "Income Tax Refund Receivable." A credit balance in the Income Taxes Expense account is offset against the amount of the before-tax loss, as shown below:

Partial Income Statement—for an *Unprofitable* Period

Income tax benefit can reduce a pretax loss

Income (loss) before income taxes	$(20,000)
Income tax benefit (recovery of previously recorded taxes)	8,000
Net loss	$(12,000)

We have already seen that income taxes *expense* reduces the amount of before-tax *profits.* Notice now that income tax *benefits*—in the form of tax refunds—can reduce the amount of a pretax *loss.* Thus, income taxes reduce the size of *both* profits and losses.

ADJUSTING ENTRIES AND ACCOUNTING PRINCIPLES

Adjusting entries are *tools* by which accountants apply the **realization** and **matching** principles. Through these entries, revenues are recognized as they are *earned,* and expenses are recognized as the related goods and services are *used.*

Another generally accepted accounting principle also plays a major role in the making of adjusting entries—the concept of *materiality.*

THE CONCEPT OF MATERIALITY

LO 5 *Explain the concept of materiality.*

The term **materiality** refers to the *relative importance* of an item or an event. An item is "material" if knowledge of the item might reasonably *influence the decisions* of users of financial statements. Accountants must be sure that all material items are properly reported in financial statements.

However, the financial reporting process should be *cost effective*—that is, the value of the information should exceed the cost of its preparation. By definition, the accounting treatment accorded to **immaterial** items is of *little or no consequence to decision makers.* Therefore, accountants do not waste time accounting for immaterial items; these items may be handled in the *easiest and most convenient manner.*

In summary, the concept of materiality allows accountants to use estimated amounts and even to ignore other accounting principles if the results of these actions *do not have a "material effect"* upon the financial statements. Materiality is one of the most important generally accepted accounting principles; you will encounter applications of this concept throughout the study of accounting.

MATERIALITY AND ADJUSTING ENTRIES The concept of materiality enables accountants to shorten and simplify the process of making adjusting entries in several ways. For example:

1. Businesses purchase many assets which have a very low cost, or which will be consumed quickly in business operations. Examples include wastebaskets, lightbulbs, and janitorial supplies. The materiality concept permits charging such purchases *directly to expense accounts,* rather than to asset accounts. This treatment conveniently eliminates the need for an adjusting entry at the end of the period to transfer a portion of these costs from an asset account to

---

[9]Tax refunds may be limited to tax payments in recent years. In this introductory discussion, we assume the company has paid sufficient taxes in prior years to permit a full recovery of any "negative tax expense" relating to the loss in the current period.

expense. This accounting short-cut is acceptable as long as the cost of the *unused* items on hand at the end of the period is "immaterial."

2. Some expenses, such as telephone bills and utility bills, may be charged to expense as the bills are *paid,* rather than as the services are used. Technically this treatment violates the *matching principle.* However, accounting for utility bills on a cash basis is very convenient, as the monthly cost of utility service is not even known until the utility bill is received. Under this "cash basis" approach, one month's utility bill is charged to expense each month. Although the bill charged to expense is actually the *prior* month's bill, the resulting "error" in the financial statements is not likely to be material.

3. Adjusting entries to accrue unrecorded expenses or unrecorded revenue may be ignored if the dollar amounts are immaterial.

4. If the amount of error is not likely to be material, adjusting entries may be based on *estimates.* For example, on page 164 we illustrate an adjusting entry allocating part of the $1,700 balance in the Supplies account to expense. The amount of supplies used during the period ($700) was based upon an *estimate* of the supplies still on hand ($1,000). This $1,000 estimate is an "educated guess"; no one actually counts all of the shop supplies on hand and looks up their cost.

MATERIALITY IS A MATTER OF PROFESSIONAL JUDGMENT Whether or not a specific item or event is material is a matter of *professional judgment.* In making these judgments, accountants consider several factors.

First, what constitutes a material amount varies with the size of the organization. For example, a $1,000 expenditure may be material in relation to the financial statements of a small business, but not to the statements of a large corporation such as General Electric.[10] There are no official rules as to what constitutes a material amount, but most accountants would consider amounts of less than 2 or 3% of net income to be *immaterial,* unless there were other factors to consider.

One such "other factor" is the *cumulative effect* of numerous "immaterial" events. Each of a dozen items may be immaterial when considered by itself. When viewed together, however, the *combined effect* of all twelve items may be material.

Finally, materiality depends upon the *nature* of the item, as well as its dollar amount. Assume, for example, that several managers systematically have been stealing money from the company that they manage. Stockholders probably would consider this fact important, even if the dollar amounts were small in relation to the company's annual earnings.

Note to students: In the assignment material accompanying this textbook, you are to consider all dollar amounts to be material, unless the problem raises the question of materiality.

EFFECTS OF THE ADJUSTING ENTRIES
We now have discussed nine separate adjusting entries that Overnight will make at December 31. These entries appear below in the format of journal entries. (Overnight also recorded many transactions throughout the month of December. The company's December transactions are not illustrated, but were accounted for in the manner described in Chapters 2 and 3.)

---

[10]This point is emphasized by the fact that GE rounds the dollar amounts shown in its financial statements to the *nearest $1 million.* This rounding of financial statement amounts is, in itself, an application of the materiality concept.

Adjusting entries are recorded only at the end of the period

GENERAL JOURNAL					Page 46
Date		Account Titles and Explanation	LP	Debit	Credit
1999 Dec.	31	Supplies Expense		700	
		Shop Supplies....................................			700
		Shop supplies used in December.			
	31	Insurance Expense		1,500	
		Unexpired Insurance........................			1,500
		Insurance expense for December.			
	31	Depreciation Expense: Building....................		500	
		Accumulated Depreciation: Building............			500
		Monthly depreciation on building = ($120,000 ÷ 240 mo.).			
	31	Depreciation Expense: Tools and Equipment		1,050	
		Accumulated Depreciation:Tools and Equipment.............................			1,050
		Monthly depreciation on tools and equipment ($63,000 ÷ 60 mo.).			
	31	Unearned Rent Revenue		2,000	
		Rent Revenue Earned			2,000
		Portion of rent received in advance from Harbor Cab that was earned in December ($6,000 ÷ 3 mo.).			
	31	Salaries and Wages Expense............................		3,640	
		Salaries and Wages Payable......................			3,640
		To accrue salaries and wages owed to employees, but unpaid as of month-end.			
	31	Interest Expense...		600	
		Interest Payable			600
		Interest expense accrued during December on 3-month note payable ($80,000 × .09 × $\frac{1}{12}$).			
	31	Accounts Receivable...		750	
		Repair Service Revenue............................			750
		To recognize revenue from services rendered on Airport Shuttle maintenance contract during December.			
	31	Income Taxes Expense......................................		3,400	
		Income Taxes Payable			3,400
		Estimated income taxes applicable to taxable income earned in December.			

After these adjustments are posted to the ledger, Overnight's ledger accounts will be up-to-date (except for the balance in the Retained Earnings account).

The company's **adjusted trial balance** at December 31, 1999, appears as follows. (For emphasis, those accounts affected by the month-end adjusting entries are shown in *red*.)

OVERNIGHT AUTO SERVICE Adjusted Trial Balance December 31, 1999		
Cash	$ 68,920	
Accounts receivable	14,280	
Shop supplies	1,000	
Unexpired insurance	3,000	
Land	295,000	
Building	120,000	
Accumulated depreciation: building		$ 6,500
Tools and equipment	63,000	
Accumulated depreciation: tools and equipment		13,300
Notes payable		80,000
Accounts payable		1,660
Salaries and wages payable		3,680
Income taxes payable		11,900
Interest payable		1,200
Unearned rent revenue		4,000
Capital stock		400,000
Retained earnings (*Note:* still must be updated for transactions recorded in the accounts listed below. Closing entries serve this purpose.)		400
Dividends	30,000	
Repair service revenue		401,200
Rent revenue earned		2,000
Advertising expense	5,950	
Salaries and wages expense	208,950	
Supplies expense	10,600	
Depreciation expense: building	6,000	
Depreciation expense: tools and equipment	12,300	
Utilities expense	16,800	
Insurance expense	15,000	
Interest expense	6,600	
Income taxes expense	48,400	
	$925,800	$925,800

Balance sheet accounts

Statement of retained earnings accounts

← temporary accounts start off year at 0 balances

Income statement accounts

PREPARING THE STATEMENTS

As explained in Chapter 3, the income statement, statement of retained earnings and balance sheet can be prepared *directly from the amounts listed in the adjusted trial balance*. (For illustrative purposes, we have made marginal notes beside the adjusted trial balance indicating which accounts appear in which financial statements.) Overnight's financial statements for the year-ended December 31, 1999 are illustrated on the following page.

The income statement is prepared first, because the amount of net income appears in the statement of retained earnings. The statement of retained earnings, in turn, determines the amount of retained earnings appearing in the balance sheet.

OVERNIGHT AUTO SERVICE
Income Statement
For the Year Ended December 31, 1999

Amounts are taken directly from the adjusted trial balance

Revenue:		
Repair service revenue		$401,200
Rent revenue earned		2,000
Total revenue		$403,200
Expenses:		
Advertising	$ 5,950	
Salaries and wages	208,950	
Supplies	10,600	
Depreciation: building	6,000	
Depreciation: tools and equipment	12,300	
Utilities	16,800	
Insurance	15,000	
Interest	6,600	282,200
Income before income taxes		$121,000
Income taxes		48,400
Net income		$ 72,600

Net income also appears in the statement of retained earnings

OVERNIGHT AUTO SERVICE
Statement of Retained Earnings
For the Year Ended December 31, 1999

Analysis of what happened to that account

Retained earnings, Dec. 31, 1998	$ 400
Add: Net income	72,600
Subtotal	$ 73,000
Less: Dividends	30,000
Retained earnings, Dec. 31, 1999	$ 43,000

The ending balance in the Retained Earnings account also appears in the balance sheet

OVERNIGHT AUTO SERVICE
Balance Sheet
December 31, 1999

Assets

Cash		$ 68,920
Accounts receivable		14,280
Shop supplies		1,000
Unexpired insurance		3,000
Land		295,000
Building	$120,000	
Less: Accumulated depreciation	6,500	113,500
Tools and equipment	$ 63,000	
Less: Accumulated depreciation	13,300	49,700
Total assets		$545,400

Liabilities & Stockholders' Equity

Liabilities:	
Notes payable	$ 80,000
Accounts payable	1,660
Salaries and wages payable	3,640
Income taxes payable	11,900
Interest payable	1,200
Unearned rent revenue	4,000
Total liabilities	$102,400
Stockholders' equity:	
Capital stock	400,000
Retained earnings	43,000
Total liabilities and stockholders' equity	$545,400

DRAFTING THE "NOTES" THAT ACCOMPANY FINANCIAL STATEMENTS

To the users of financial statements, **adequate disclosure** is perhaps the most important accounting principle. This principle simply means that financial statements should be accompanied by any information necessary for the statements to be *interpreted properly.*

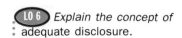

LO 6 *Explain the concept of* adequate disclosure.

Most disclosures appear within the several pages of **notes** (or *footnotes*) that accompany the financial statements. Drafting these notes can be one of the most challenging tasks confronting accountants at the end of the period. The content of these notes often cannot be drawn directly from the accounting records. Rather, drafting these notes requires an *in-depth understanding* of the company and its operations, of accounting principles, and of how decision makers interpret and use accounting information.

Two items always disclosed in the notes to financial statements are the accounting methods in use and the due dates of major liabilities. Thus, Overnight's 1999 financial statements should include the following notes:

Note 1: Depreciation policies

Depreciation expense in the financial statements is computed by the straight-line method. Estimated useful lives are 20 years for the building and 5 years for tools and equipment.

Note 2: Maturity dates of liabilities

The Company's notes payable consist of a single obligation which matures on January 31 of the coming year. The maturity value of this note, including interest charges, will amount to $81,800.

The second note should be of great importance to users of Overnight's financial statements. Where is the company going to get the money to pay this note in only one month? It certainly doesn't have enough liquid resources on hand at December 31. Therefore, Overnight must either refinance this loan, or come up with lots of cash—fast.

WHAT TYPES OF INFORMATION MUST BE DISCLOSED?

There is no comprehensive list of the information that should be disclosed in financial statements. The "adequacy" of disclosure is based upon a combination of official rules, tradition, and accountants' *professional judgment.*

As a general rule, a company should disclose any facts that an intelligent person would consider necessary for the statements to be *interpreted properly.* In addition to accounting methods in use and the due dates of major liabilities, businesses may need to disclose such matters as:

- Lawsuits pending against the business.
- Scheduled plant closings.
- Governmental investigations into the safety of the company's products or the legality of its pricing policies.
- Significant events occurring *after* the balance sheet date, but before the financial statements are actually issued.
- Specific customers that account for a large portion of the company's business.
- Unusual transactions or conflicts of interest between the company and its key officers.

Let us stress again that *there is no comprehensive list of items that must be disclosed.* Throughout this course, we will identify and discuss many items that may require disclosure in financial statements.

In some cases, companies must even disclose information that could have a *damaging effect* upon the business. For example, a manufacturer may need to disclose that it is being sued by customers who have been injured by its products. The fact that a disclosure might prove embarrassing—or even damaging to the business—is *not* a valid reason for keeping the information "secret." The concept of adequate disclosure demands a *good faith effort* by management to keep the users of financial statements informed about the company's operations.

Companies are *not* required to disclose information that is immaterial, or which does not have a direct *financial* impact upon the business. For example, a company is not required by generally accepted accounting principles to disclose the resignation, firing, or death of a key executive. Of course, companies often *do* disclose such nonfinancial events on a voluntary basis.

Disclosures that accompany financial statements should be limited to *facts* and *reasonable estimates.* They should not include *optimistic speculation* that cannot be substantiated.

For a realistic look at the types of disclosure made by a publicly owned corporation, we refer readers to pages A-11–A-15 of Appendix A.

CLOSING THE ACCOUNTS

Accountants sometimes use the phrase "closing the accounts" to describe *all* of the year-end procedures. But technically, closing the accounts refers only to one

Closing entries derived from the adjusted trial balance

	GENERAL JOURNAL				Page 27
Date	**Account Titles and Explanation**		**LP**	**Debit**	**Credit**
1999 Dec. 31	Repair Service Revenue			401,200	
	Rent Revenue Earned			2,000	
	Income Summary				403,200
	To close the revenue accounts.				
31	Income Summary			330,600	
	Advertising Expense				5,950
	Salaries and Wages Expense				208,950
	Supplies Expense				10,600
	Depreciation Expense: Building				6,000
	Depreciation Expense: Tools and				
	Equipment				12,300
	Utilities Expense				16,800
	Insurance Expense				15,000
	Interest Expense				6,600
	Income Taxes Expense				48,400
	To close the expense accounts.				
31	Income Summary			72,600	
	Retained Earnings				72,600
	To close the Income Summary account.				
31	Retained Earnings			30,000	
	Dividends				30,000
	To close the Dividends account.				

specific step in the accounting cycle. This step consists of closing (or transferring) the balances of all revenue, expense, and dividends accounts into the Retained Earnings account.

Closing accounts is not at all difficult—balances are simply transferred from one account to another. In a computer-based system, this is done with the touch of a button. Overnight, however, has a manual accounting system. The entries to close its revenue and expense accounts, as well as the dividends account, at December 31, 1999, are illustrated on the previous page.

After these entries are posted, the revenue, expense, and dividends accounts will have zero balances and be ready for use in measuring the activities of the coming year.

As the final step in its accounting cycle, Overnight will prepare an after-closing trial balance:

OVERNIGHT AUTO SERVICE After-Closing Trial Balance December 31, 1999		
Cash	$ 68,920	
Accounts receivable	14,280	
Shop supplies	1,000	
Unexpired insurance	3,000	
Land	295,000	
Building	120,000	
Accumulated depreciation: building		$ 6,500
Tools and equipment	63,000	
Accumulated depreciation: tools and equipment		13,300
Notes payable		80,000
Accounts payable		1,660
Salaries and wages payable		3,640
Income taxes payable		11,900
Interest payable		1,200
Unearned rent revenue		4,000
Capital stock		400,000
Retained earnings, December 31, 1999		43,000
	$565,200	$565,200

The balances in the "temporary" equity accounts have been closed into the Retained Earnings account

In comparison with the adjusted trial balance (page 175), an after-closing trial balance contains only *balance sheet* accounts. Also, the Retained Earnings account has a new date and a new balance. Through the closing of the revenue, expense, and dividends accounts, the Retained Earnings account has been brought up-to-date.

A LAST LOOK AT OVERNIGHT: WAS 1999 A "GOOD YEAR"?
In Chapter 3, we briefly evaluated Overnight after its first month of operations. Let us now consider the financial results of its first fiscal year.

EVALUATING PROFITABILITY In its business plan, Overnight set first-year targets of $400,000 for total revenue and $75,000 for net income. With revenue of $403,200 and net income of $72,600, the company is pretty much on target.

The net income for this first year of operations amounts to 18.15% of the stockholders' $400,000 investment. This is a very impressive rate of return for the first year of operations.

But in evaluating profitability, the real question is not how the business *did,* but how it *is likely to do in the future.* To earn a substantial profit in the first year indicates good potential. The company's customer base probably is growing. Also, the Harbor Cab contract should contribute $22,000 more to revenue next year than it did in 1999. And if Harbor stores its cabs at Overnight's location, Overnight becomes a likely candidate for performing maintenance and repairs on these vehicles.

All-in-all, it appears that Overnight is off to an impressive start.

EVALUATING SOLVENCY   Solvency, at least in the short-term, may be independent of profitability. And in short-term, Overnight has potential cash flow problems.

In the very near future, Overnight may be confronted with several major cash expenditures. The company must meet its biweekly payroll on January 7, and its $11,900 liability for income taxes is payable on January 15. Of greater importance, the company's $80,000 note to American National Bank comes due on January 31—just one month away. Together, these scheduled cash outlays substantially exceed the combined total of Overnight's cash and accounts receivable.

In addition, the company needs to renew its insurance policies in about two months, and plans to open a new location in the coming year. Where will the cash come from?

Overnight probably can handle the payroll, income taxes, insurance, and even opening a new location—but not the repayment of its $80,000 bank loan. If the bank will not renew this loan, Overnight will have serious problems. Thus, the company is "at the mercy of the bank."

Overnight can solve this problem by replacing the short-term note payable with a long-term mortgage loan. In our opinion, this should be among the company's top financial priorities.

FOCUSING MANAGEMENT'S ATTENTION   One of the primary uses of accounting information is to *direct management's attention* to problems and opportunities. We have mentioned the opportunity inherent in the new rental agreement with Harbor Cab. Management also should review the income statement to determine whether any expenses appear to be excessive.

Our attention immediately is drawn to the amounts of *insurance expense* and *utilities expense.* We do not know that either expense is excessive, but both appear to offer at least a *potential* for significant cost savings.

Before renewing its insurance policies, Overnight should obtain competitive quotes from several insurance companies. Perhaps comparable insurance is available for substantially less than $18,000 per year. With respect to the utilities expense (which averages $1,400 per month), management should consider such factors as:

● Is the lighting system efficient? (Especially important as the lights are on all night.)

● Is the heating system efficient and is the building adequately insulated?

● Are employees using company phones for personal calls?

At first glance, these items may seem small and unimportant. But if Overnight could have saved 25% on its utility bills ($4,200), its net income for 1999 would have *exceeded* the $75,000 projected in the business plan.

PREPARING FINANCIAL STATEMENTS COVERING DIFFERENT PERIODS OF TIME

Many businesses prepare financial statements every quarter, as well as at year-end. In addition, they may prepare financial statements covering other time periods, such as one month or the year-to-date.

When a business closes its accounts *only at year-end,* the revenue, expense, and dividends accounts have balances representing the activities of the *year to date.* Thus at, say, June 30, these account balances represent the activities recorded over the past six months. The year-to-date (YTD) financial statements can be prepared directly from the adjusted trial balance. But how might this business prepare financial statements covering only the month of June? Or the quarter (three months) ended June 30?

The answer is by doing a little *subtraction.* As an example, let us assume that the balance in Overnight's Repair Service Revenue account was as shown below at the following dates in 1999:

March 31 (end of the first quarter)	$ 80,000
May 31	150,000
June 30	195,000

L0 7 *Explain how interim financial statements are prepared in a business that closes its accounts only at year-end.*

At each date the account balances represent the revenue earned since the beginning of the year. Thus, the March 31 balance represents three-months' revenue, the May 31 balance, five-months' revenue, and the June 30 balance, the revenue earned over a period of six months.

To prepare an income statement for the *six months* ended June 30, we simply use the June 30 balance in the revenue account—*$195,000.* But to prepare an income statement for the *month* ended June 30, we would have to subtract from the June 30 balance of this account, its balance as of May 31. The remainder, *$45,000,* represents the amount of revenue recorded in the account during June ($195,000 − $150,000 = $45,000).

To prepare an income statement for the *quarter* ended June 30, we would subtract from the June 30 balance in this revenue account, its balance as of March 31. Thus, the revenue earned during the second quarter (ended June 30) amounts to *$115,000* ($195,000 − $80,000).

This process of subtracting prior balances from the current balance is repeated for each revenue and expense account, and also for dividends.

This sounds like a bigger job than it really is. There are only about ten or fifteen accounts involved, and in a computerized system, the entire process is done automatically. Even in a manual system, a person using a 10-key adding machine can complete this process in a few minutes.

No such computations are required for the balance sheet accounts. A balance sheet always is based upon the account balances *at the balance sheet date.* Therefore, a June 30 balance sheet looks exactly the same, *regardless* of the time period covered by the other financial statements.

YOUR TURN

You as Overnight's Accountant

Shown below are amounts taken from Overnight's December 31 income statement (page 176). We also have supplied amounts from the year-to-date income statement Overnight prepared at *November 30* (not previously illustrated). Using this information, we have determined most of the income statement amounts for the *month* ended December 31, 1999.

You are to determine the six missing amounts, and explain your reasoning. Then comment upon whether December was an above- or below-average month for Overnight. Explain the basis for your conclusion and probable reasons for these December results.

	Year-to-Date as of		Month Ended
	Dec. 31	Nov. 30	Dec. 31
Revenue:			
Repair service revenue	$401,200	$372,400	$28,800
Rent revenue earned	2,000	0	2,000
Total revenue	$403,200	$372,400	$30,800
Expenses:			
Advertising expense	$ 5,950	$ 5,600	$ 350
Salaries and wages expense	208,950	193,050	15,900
Supplies expense	10,600	9,900	700
Depreciation: building	6,000	5,500	500
Depreciation: tools and equipment	12,300	?	?
Utilities	16,800	15,100	1,700
Insurance	15,000	13,500	1,500
Interest	6,600	6,000	600
Total expenses (other than taxes)	$282,200	$259,900	$22,300
Income before income taxes:	$121,000	$112,500	$ 8,500
Income taxes	48,400	?	?
Net income	$ 72,600	$?	$?

*Our comments appear on page 206.

NET CONNECTIONS

The Fischer College of Business at Ohio State University maintains a very useful site called Business Job Finder:

www.cob.ohio-state.edu/~fin/osujobs.htm

If you explore the Accounting section of this site, you can learn much about key accounting functions, such as financial reporting, budgeting, auditing, and tax work. The site also discusses skill requirements, salaries, and working conditions. While you're there, check out Internet Resources, and visit the Accounting Hall of Fame.

Notice under Work Hours, there is a range of 40, up to (gulp) *70,* hours per week.* This illustrates the intense time-pressure arising from deadlines in auditing, financial reporting, and tax work.

*Some accountants do indeed work 70-hour weeks during the busy season, but this is not typical. Employers generally do not require 70-hour workweeks; in fact, many *prohibit* them. We think 50 to 60 would be a more representative estimate of busy-season hours.

Some firms allow accounting personnel to exchange the long hours of the busy season for additional vacation time later in the year. Others pay various forms of overtime compensation.

*SUPPLEMENTAL TOPIC

THE WORKSHEET

A **worksheet** illustrates in one place the relationships between the unadjusted trial balance, proposed adjusting entries, and the financial statements. A worksheet is prepared at the end of the period, but *before* the adjusting entries are formally recorded in the accounting records. It is not a formal step in the accounting cycle. Rather, it is the "scratch pad" upon which accountants work out the details of the proposed end-of-period adjustments. It also provides them with a preview of how the financial statements will look.

LO 8 *Prepare a worksheet and explain its usefulness.*

A worksheet for Overnight Auto Service at December 31, 1999 is illustrated on the following page.

ISN'T THIS REALLY A "SPREADSHEET"?
Yes. The term "worksheet" is a holdover from the days when these schedules were prepared manually on large sheets of columnar paper. Today, most worksheets are prepared on a computer using spreadsheet software, such as Lotus 1-2-3™ or Excel™, or with **general ledger software** such as Peachtree™ or DacEasy™.

Since the worksheet is just the accountant's scratch pad, it often isn't printed out in "hard copy"—it may exist only on a computer screen. But the concept remains the same; the worksheet displays *in one place* the unadjusted account balances, proposed adjusting entries, and financial statements as they will appear if the proposed adjustments are made.

WHAT'S IT USED FOR?
A worksheet serves several purposes. It allows accountants to *see the effects* of adjusting entries without actually entering these adjustments in the accounting records. This makes it relatively easy for them to correct errors or make changes in estimated amounts. It also enables accountants and management to preview the financial statements before the final drafts are developed. Once the worksheet is complete, it serves as the source for recording adjusting and closing entries in the accounting records and also for preparing financial statements.

Another important use of the worksheet is in the preparation of **interim financial statements.** Interim statements are financial statements developed at various points *during* the fiscal year. Most companies close their accounts only once each year. Yet they often need to develop quarterly or monthly financial statements. Through the use of a worksheet, they can develop these interim statements *without* having to formally adjust and close their accounts.

THE MECHANICS: HOW IT'S DONE
Whether done manually or on a computer, the preparation of a worksheet involves five basic steps. We first will describe these steps as if the worksheet were

---

™Registered trademarks of the respective manufacturers.

OVERNIGHT AUTO SERVICE
Worksheet
For the Year Ended December 31, 1999

	Trial Balance Dr	Trial Balance Cr	Adjustments* Dr	Adjustments* Cr	Adjusted Trial Balance Dr	Adjusted Trial Balance Cr	Income Statement Dr	Income Statement Cr	Balance Sheet Dr	Balance Sheet Cr
Balance sheet accounts:										
Cash	68,920				68,920				68,920	
Accounts receivable	13,530		(h) 750		14,280				14,280	
Shop supplies	1,700			(a) 700	1,000				1,000	
Unexpired insurance	4,500			(b) 1,500	3,000				3,000	
Land	295,000				295,000				295,000	
Building	120,000				120,000				120,000	
Accumulated depreciation: building		6,000		(c) 500		6,500				6,500
Tools and equipment	63,000				63,000				63,000	
Accumulated depreciation: tools & equipment		12,250		(d) 1,050		13,300				13,300
Notes payable		80,000				80,000				80,000
Accounts payable		1,660				1,660				1,660
Income taxes payable		8,500		(i) 3,400		11,900				11,900
Interest payable		600		(g) 600		1,200				1,200
Unearned rent revenue		6,000	(e) 2,000			4,000				4,000
Capital stock		400,000				400,000				400,000
Retained earnings		400				400				400
Dividends	30,000				30,000				30,000	
Salaries and wages payable				(f) 3,640		3,640				3,640
Income statement accounts:										
Repair service revenue		400,450		(h) 750		401,200		401,200		
Advertising expense	5,950				5,950		5,950			
Salaries and wages expense	205,310		(f) 3,640		208,950		208,950			
Supplies expense	9,900		(a) 700		10,600		10,600			
Depreciation expense: building	5,500		(c) 500		6,000		6,000			
Depreciation expense: tools and equipment	11,250		(d) 1,050		12,300		12,300			
Utilities expense	16,800				16,800		16,800			
Insurance expense	13,500		(b) 1,500		15,000		15,000			
Interest expense	6,000		(g) 600		6,600		6,600			
Income taxes expense	45,000		(i) 3,400		48,400		48,400			
	915,860	915,860								
Rent revenue earned				(e) 2,000		2,000		2,000		
			14,140	14,140	925,800	925,800	330,600	403,200	595,200	522,600
Net income							72,600			72,600
Totals							403,200	403,200	595,200	595,200

*Adjustments:
(a) Shop supplies used in December.
(b) Portion of insurance cost expiring in December.
(c) Depreciation on building for December.
(d) Depreciation of tools and equipment for December.
(e) Earned one-third of rent revenue collected in advance from Harbor Cab.
(f) Unpaid wages owed to employees at December 31.
(g) Interest payable accrued during December.
(h) Repair service revenue earned in December but not yet billed.
(i) Income taxes expense for December.

being prepared manually. Afterward, we will explain how virtually all of the mechanical steps can be performed automatically by a computer.

1. ***Enter the ledger account balances in the Trial Balance columns.*** The worksheet begins with an unadjusted trial balance—that is, a listing of the ledger account balances at the end of the period *prior* to making any adjusting entries. In our illustration, the unadjusted trail balance appears in *blue*.

   Notice our inclusion of the captions "Balance Sheet accounts" and "Income Statement accounts." These captions are optional, but they help clarify the relationships between the ledger accounts and the financial statements. (***Hint:*** A few lines should be left blank immediately below the last balance sheet account. It is often necessary to add a few more accounts during the adjusting process. Additional income statement accounts can be added on the lines below the trial balance totals.)

2. ***Enter the adjustments in the Adjustments columns.*** The next step is the most important: Enter the appropriate end-of-period adjustments in the Adjustments columns. In our illustration, these adjustments appear in *red*.

   Notice that each adjustment includes both debit and credit entries, which are linked together by the small "key letters" appearing to the left of the dollar amount. Thus, adjusting entry **a** consists of a $700 debit to Supplies Expense and a $700 credit to Shop Supplies. Just as individual adjusting entries involve equal debit and credit amounts, so the totals of the debit and credit Adjustment columns should be equal.

   Sometimes the adjustments require adding accounts to the original trial balance. (The two ledger account titles printed in *red* were added during the adjusting process.)

3. ***Prepare an adjusted trial balance.*** Next, an adjusted trial balance is prepared. The balances in the original trial balance *(blue)* are adjusted for the debit or credit amounts in the adjustments columns *(red)*. This process of horizontal addition or subtraction is called *cross-footing*. The adjusted trial balance is totaled to determine that the accounts remain in balance.

   At this point, the entire worksheet is virtually complete. We have emphasized that financial statements are prepared *directly from the adjusted trial balance.* Thus, we have only to arrange these accounts into the format of financial statements. For this reason, we show the adjusted trial balance amounts in *blue*—both in the Adjusted Trial Balance columns and when these amounts are *extended* (carried forward) into the financial statement columns.

4. ***Extend the adjusted trial balance amounts into the appropriate "financial statement" columns.*** The balance sheet accounts—assets, liabilities, and owners' equity—are extended into the Balance Sheet columns; income statement amounts, into the Income Statement columns. (The "Balance Sheet" and "Income Statement" captions in the original trial balance should simplify this procedure. Notice that each amount is extended to one and only one column. Also, the account retains the same debit or credit balance as shown in the adjusted trial balance.)

5. ***Total the financial statement columns; determine and record net income or net loss.*** The final step in preparing the worksheet consists of totaling the income statement and balance sheet columns and then bringing each set of columns "into balance." These tasks are performed on the bottom three lines of the worksheet. In our illustration, the amounts involved in this final step are shown in *black*.

When the Income Statement and Balance Sheet columns are first totaled, the debit and credit columns will not agree. But each set of columns should be out-of-balance by the *same amount*—and that amount should be the amount of net income or net loss for the period.

Let us briefly explain *why* both sets of columns initially are out-of-balance by this amount. First consider the Income Statement columns. The credit column contains the revenue accounts, and the debit column, the expense accounts. The difference, therefore, represents the net income (net loss) for the period.

Now consider the Balance Sheet columns. All of the balance sheet accounts have up-to-date amounts *except* for the Retained Earnings account, which still contains the balance from the *beginning* of the period. To bring the Retained Earnings account up-to-date, we must add net income and subtract any dividends. The dividends already appear in the Balance Sheet debit column. So what's the only thing missing? The net income (or net loss) for the period.

To bring both sets of columns into balance, we enter the net income (or net loss) on the next line. The same amount will appear in both the Income Statement columns and the Balance Sheet columns. But in one set of columns it appears as a debit, and in the other, it appears as a credit.[1] After this amount is entered, each set of columns should balance.

COMPUTERS DO THE "PENCIL-PUSHING" When a worksheet is prepared by computer, accountants perform only *one* of the steps listed above—*entering the adjustments.* The computer automatically lists the ledger accounts in the form of a trial balance. After the accountant has entered the adjustments, the software automatically computes the adjusted account balances and completes the worksheet. (Once the adjusted balances are determined, completing the worksheet involves nothing more than putting these amounts in the appropriate column and determining the column totals.)

"WHAT IF . . . :" A SPECIAL APPLICATION OF WORKSHEET SOFTWARE

We have discussed a relatively simple application of the worksheet concept—illustrating the effects of proposed *adjusting entries* upon account balances. But the same concept can be applied to proposed *future transactions*. The effects of the proposed transactions simply are entered in the Adjustments columns. Thus, without disrupting the accounting records, accountants can prepare schedules showing how the company's financial statements might be affected by such events as a merger with another company, a 15% increase in sales volume, or the opening of a new location.

There is a tendency to view worksheets as mechanical and old fashioned. This is not at all the case. Today, the mechanical aspects are handled entirely by computer. The real purpose of a worksheet is to show quickly and efficiently how specific events or transactions will affect the financial statements. This isn't just bookkeeping—in many cases, it's *planning.*

---

[1]To bring the Income Statement columns into balance, net *income* is entered in the *debit column.* This is because the credit column (revenue) exceeds the debit column (expenses). But in the balance sheet, net income is an element of owners' equity, which is represented by a credit. In event of a net *loss,* this situation reverses.

SUMMARY OF LEARNING OBJECTIVES

1 Identify annual accounting activities that make year-end the "busy season."

Accounting activities performed shortly before or after year-end may include taking inventory, adjusting and closing the accounts, preparing financial statements and the related notes, preparing income tax returns, and—if the company is publicly owned—undergoing an audit and publishing an annual report.

2 Explain the purpose of adjusting entries.

The purpose of adjusting entries is to allocate revenue and expenses among accounting periods in accordance with the *realization* and *matching* principles. These end-of-period entries are necessary because revenue may be earned and expenses incurred in periods *other than* the one in which the related transactions are recorded.

3 Describe and prepare the four basic types of adjusting entries.

The four basic types of adjusting entries are entries to: (1) apportion recorded costs (debit expense, credit either an asset or contra-asset account); (2) apportion unearned revenue (debit unearned revenue, which is a liability account, and credit revenue); (3) record unrecorded expenses (debit expense, credit a liability); and (4) record unrecorded revenue (debit a receivable, credit revenue).

4 Explain how income taxes affect pretax profits and losses.

Income taxes *reduce* the amount of either before-tax income or a before-tax loss. If a company earns taxable income, it must *pay* income taxes, thus reducing the amount of income left "in the business." But if a company sustains a before-tax *loss,* it may *recover* some of the income taxes paid in prior years. Thus, the income taxes expense for the current year becomes an *inflow,* which lessens the amount of loss.

5 Explain the concept of *materiality.*

The concept of materiality allows accountants to use estimated amounts and even to ignore other accounting principles if these actions will not have a "material" effect upon financial statements. A material effect is one that might reasonably be expected to influence the decisions made by users of financial statements. Thus, accountants may account for *immaterial* items and events in the easiest and most convenient manner.

6 Explain the concept of *adequate disclosure.*

Adequate disclosure is a generally accepted accounting principle, meaning that financial statements should include any information that an intelligent person needs to *interpret the statements* properly. The appropriate disclosures usually are contained in several pages of *notes* which accompany the statements.

7 Explain how *interim* financial statements are prepared in a business that closes its accounts only at year-end.

When a business closes its accounts only at year-end, the revenue, expense, and dividends accounts have balances representing the activities of the *year to date.* To prepare an income statement for any period shorter than the year to date, we *subtract* from the current balance in the revenue or expense account the balance in the account as of the beginning of the desired period. This process of subtracting prior balances from the current balance is repeated for each revenue and expense account, and also for the dividends account. No such computations are required for the balance sheet accounts, as a balance sheet is based upon the account balances at the balance sheet date.

8 Prepare a worksheet and explain its usefulness.

A worksheet is a "testing ground" on which the ledger accounts are adjusted, balanced, and arranged in the format of financial statements. A worksheet consists of a trial balance, the end-of-period adjusting entries, an adjusted trial balance, and columns showing the ledger accounts arranged as an income statement and as a balance sheet. The completed worksheet is used as the basis for preparing financial statements and for recording adjusting and closing entries in the formal accounting records.

In Chapter 4 we have completed our study of the accounting cycle for a service-type business and have completed our continuing illustrated example of Overnight Auto Service. In Chapter 5 we will extend these concepts by focusing on some additional steps needed to account for the *inventories* which fill the sales counters and storerooms of a wholesale or retail merchandising business.

Supplemental Topic, "The Worksheet."

KEY TERMS INTRODUCED OR EMPHASIZED IN CHAPTER 4

Accrue (p. 167)   To grow or accumulate over time, for example, interest expense.

Adequate disclosure (p. 177)   The generally accepted accounting principle of providing in the financial statements any information that users need to properly interpret those statements.

Adjusted trial balance (p. 175)   A schedule indicating the balances in ledger accounts *after* end-of-period adjusting entries have been posted. The amounts shown in the adjusted trial balance are carried directly into financial statements.

Adjusting entries (p. 160)   Entries made at the end of the accounting period for the purpose of recognizing revenue and expenses which are not properly measured when the transactions are originally journalized.

Book value (p. 165)   The net amount at which an asset appears in financial statements. For depreciable assets, book value represents cost minus accumulated depreciation. Also called **carrying value.**

Carrying value   See **book value.**

General ledger software (p. 183)   Computer software used to record transactions, maintain journals and ledgers, and prepare financial statements. Also includes spreadsheet capabilities for showing the effects of proposed adjusting entries or transactions upon the financial statements without actually recording these entries in the accounting records.

Immaterial (p. 172)   Something of little or no consequence. Immaterial items may be accounted for in the most *convenient* manner, without regard to other theoretical concepts.

Interim financial statements (p. 183)   Financial statements prepared for periods of less than one year (includes monthly and quarterly statements).

Matching (principle) (p. 172)   The accounting principle of offsetting revenue with the expenses incurred in producing that revenue. Requires recognition of expenses in the periods that the related goods and services are *used* in the effort to produce revenue.

Materiality (p. 172)   The relative importance of an item or amount. Items significant enough to influence decisions are said to be *material*. Items lacking this importance are considered **immaterial.** The accounting treatment accorded to immaterial items may be guided by convenience, rather than by theoretical principles.

Notes (accompanying financial statements) (p. 177)   Supplemental disclosures which accompany financial statements. These notes provide users with various types of information considered necessary for the proper interpretation of the statements.

Prepaid expenses (p. 164)   Assets representing advance payment of the expenses of future accounting periods. As time passes, adjusting entries are made to transfer the related costs from the asset account into an expense account.

Realization (principle) (p. 172)   The accounting principle that governs the timing of revenue recognition. Basically, the principle indicates that revenue should be recognized in the period in which it is *earned*.

Unearned revenue (p. 166)   An obligation to deliver goods or render services in the future, stemming from the receipt of advance payment.

Worksheet (p. 183)   A multicolumn schedule showing the relationships among the current account balances (a trial balance), proposed adjusting entries or transactions, and the financial statements that would result if these adjusting entries or transactions were recorded. Used both at the end of the accounting period as an aid to preparing financial statements, and for planning purposes.

DEMONSTRATION PROBLEM*

Internet Consulting Service, Inc., adjusts its accounts every month, but closes them only at December 31. At December 31, 1999, the unadjusted balances in the ledger accounts were as follows. (Bear in mind, month-end adjusting entries for December have not yet been made.)

---

*Supplemental Topic, "The Worksheet."

INTERNET CONSULTING SERVICE, INC. Trial Balance December 31, 1999		
Cash	$ 49,100	
Consulting fees receivable	23,400	
Prepaid office rent	6,300	
Prepaid dues and subscriptions	300	
Supplies	600	
Equipment	36,000	
Accumulated depreciation: equipment		$ 10,200
Notes payable		5,000
Income taxes payable		12,000
Unearned consulting fees		5,950
Capital stock		30,000
Retained earnings		32,700
Dividends	60,000	
Consulting fees earned		257,180
Salaries expense	88,820	
Telephone expense	2,550	
Rent expense	22,000	
Income taxes expense	51,000	
Dues and subscriptions expense	560	
Supplies expense	1,600	
Depreciation expense: equipment	6,600	
Miscellaneous expenses	4,200	
	$353,030	$353,030

OTHER DATA

a. On December 1, the company signed a new rental agreement and paid three months' rent in advance at a rate of $2,100 per month. This advance payment was debited to the Prepaid Office Rent account.

b. Dues and subscriptions expired during December amounted to $50.

c. An estimate of supplies on hand was made at December 31; the estimated cost of the unused supplies was $450.

d. The useful life of the equipment has been estimated at five years (60 months) from date of acquisition.

e. Accrued interest on notes payable amounted to $100 at year-end. (Set up accounts for Interest Expense and for Interest Payable.)

f. Consulting services valued at $2,850 were rendered during December to clients who had made payment in advance.

g. It is the custom of the firm to bill clients only when consulting work is completed or, in the case of prolonged engagements, at monthly intervals. At December 31, engineering services valued at $11,000 had been rendered to clients but not yet billed. No advance payments had been received from these clients.

h. Salaries earned by employees but not paid as of December 31 amount to $1,700.

i. Income taxes expense for the year is estimated at $56,000. Of this amount, $51,000 has been recognized as expense in prior months, and $39,000 has been paid to tax authorities. The company plans to pay the $17,000 remainder of its income tax liability on January 15.

INSTRUCTIONS

Prepare a 10-column worksheet for the year ended December 31, 1999. (Solution appears on the following page.)

SELF-TEST QUESTIONS

The answers to these questions appear on page 207.

1. For a publicly owned company, indicate which of the following accounting activities are likely to occur at or shortly after year-end. (More than one answer may be correct.)
   a. Preparing of income tax returns.
   b. Adjusting and closing the accounts.
   c. Drafting disclosures that accompany the financial statements.
   d. An audit of the financial statements by a firm of CPAs.

2. The purpose of adjusting entries is to:
   a. Adjust the Retained Earnings account for the revenue, expense, and dividends recorded during the accounting period.
   b. Adjust daily the balances in asset, liability, revenue, and expense accounts for the effects of business transactions.
   c. Apply the realization principle and the matching principle to transactions affecting two or more accounting periods.
   d. Prepare revenue and expense accounts for recording the transactions of the next accounting period.

3. Before month-end adjustments are made, the January 31 trial balance of Rover Excursions contains revenue of $27,900 and expenses of $17,340. Adjustments are necessary for the following items:

   Portion of prepaid rent applicable to January, $2,700
   Depreciation for January, $1,440
   Portion of fees collected in advance earned in January, $3,300
   Fees earned in January, not yet billed to customers, $1,950

   Net income in Rover Excursions' January income statement is:
   a. $10,560   **b.** $17,070   **c.** $7,770   **d.** Some other amount

4. The CPA firm auditing Mason Street Recording Studios found that retained earnings were understated and liabilities were overstated. Which of the following errors could have been the cause?
   a. Making the adjustment entry for depreciation expense twice.
   b. Failure to record interest accrued on a note payable.
   c. Failure to make the adjusting entry to record revenue which had been earned but not yet billed to clients.
   d. Failure to record the earned portion of fees received in advance.

5. Assume Fisher Corporation usually earns taxable income, but sustains a *loss* in the current period. The entry to record income taxes expense in the current period will most likely: (Indicate all correct answers.)
   a. Increase the amount of that loss.
   b. Include a credit to the Income Taxes Expense account.
   c. Be an adjusting entry, rather than an entry to record a transaction completed during the period.
   d. Include a credit to Income Taxes Payable.

SOLUTION TO DEMONSTRATION PROBLEM

INTERNET CONSULTING SERVICE, INC.
Worksheet
For the Year Ended December 31, 1999

	Trial Balance Dr	Trial Balance Cr	Adjustments* Dr	Adjustments* Cr	Adjusted Trial Balance Dr	Adjusted Trial Balance Cr	Income Statement Dr	Income Statement Cr	Balance Sheet Dr	Balance Sheet Cr
Balance sheet accounts:										
Cash	49,100				49,100				49,100	
Consulting fees receivable	23,400		(g)11,000		34,400				34,400	
Prepaid office rent	6,300			(a) 2,100	4,200				4,200	
Prepaid dues and subscriptions	300			(b) 50	250				250	
Supplies	600			(c) 150	450				450	
Equipment	36,000				36,000				36,000	
Accumulated depreciation: equipment		10,200		(d) 600		10,800				10,800
Notes payable		5,000				5,000				5,000
Income taxes payable		12,000		(i) 5000		17,000				17,000
Unearned consulting fees		5,950	(f) 2,850			3,100				3,100
Capital stock		30,000				30,000				30,000
Retained earnings		32,700				32,700				32,700
Dividends	60,000				60,000				60,000	
Salaries payable				(h) 1,700		1,700				1,700
Interest payable				(e) 100		100				100
Income statement accounts:										
Consulting fees earned		257,180		(f) 2,850 (g)11,000		271,030		271,030		
Salaries expense	88,820		(h) 1,700		90,520		90,520			
Telephone expense	2,550				2,550		2,550			
Rent expense	22,000		(a) 2,100		24,100		24,100			
Income taxes expense	51,000		(i) 5,000		56,000		56,000			
Dues and subscriptions expense	560		(b) 50		610		610			
Supplies expense	1,600		(c) 150		1,750		1,750			
Depreciation expense: equipment	6,600		(d) 600		7,200		7,200			
Miscellaneous expense	4,200				4,200		4,200			
	353,030	353,030								
Interest expense			(e) 100		100		100			
			23,550	23,550	371,430	371,430	187,030	271,030	184,400	14,400
Net income							84,000			84,000
Totals							271,030	271,030	184,400	184,400

*Adjustments:
(a) Rent expense for December.
(b) Dues and subscriptions expense for December.
(c) Supplies used in December ($600–$450).
(d) Depreciation expense ($36,000 ÷ 60 mos.)
(e) Accrued interest on notes payable.
(f) Consulting services performed for clients who paid in advance.
(g) Services rendered but not billed.
(h) Salaries earned but not paid.
(i) Estimated income taxes expense.

6. The concept of *materiality:* (Indicate all correct answers.)
   a. Requires that financial statements be accurate to the nearest dollar, but need not show cents.
   b. Is based upon what users of financial statements are thought to consider important.
   c. Permits accountants to ignore other generally accepted accounting principles in certain situations.
   d. Permits accountants to use the easiest and most convenient means of accounting for events that are *immaterial.*

7. Indicate those items for which generally accepted accounting principles *require* disclosure in notes accompanying the financial statements. (More than one answer may be correct.)
   a. A large lawsuit was filed against the company two days *after* the balance sheet date.
   b. The depreciation method in use, given that several different methods are acceptable under generally accepted accounting principles.
   c. Whether small but long-lived items — such as electric pencil sharpeners and hand-held calculators — are charged to asset accounts or to expense accounts.
   d. As of year-end, the chief executive officer had been hospitalized because of chest pains.

8. Ski West adjusts its accounts at the end of each month, but closes them only at the end of the calendar year (December 31). The ending balances in the Equipment Rental Revenue account and the Cash account in February and March appear below.

	Feb. 28	Mar. 31
Cash	$14,200	$26,500
Equipment rental revenue	12,100	18,400

Ski West prepares financial statements showing separately the operating results of each month. In the financial statements prepared for the *month* ended March 31, Equipment Rental Revenue and Cash should appear as follows:
   a. Equipment Rental Revenue, $18,400; Cash, $26,500
   b. Equipment Rental Revenue, $18,400; Cash, $12,300
   c. Equipment Rental Revenue, $6,300; Cash, $26,500
   d. Equipment Rental Revenue, $6,300; Cash, $12,300

*9. A worksheet can be used for all of the following purposes *except:*
   a. Showing accountants and management how proposed adjusting entries and transactions will affect the financial statements.
   b. Developing end-of-period adjusting entries prior to actually recording these adjustments in the accounting records.
   c. Reducing to a single page the presentation of financial information within the company's annual report.
   d. Preparing interim financial statements without actually adjusting or closing the accounts.

ASSIGNMENT MATERIAL

DISCUSSION QUESTIONS

1. Identify three or more accounting activities that take place primarily at year-end, as opposed to uniformly throughout the year.
2. What is the purpose of making adjusting entries? Your answer should relate adjusting entries to the goals of accrual accounting.

Supplemental Topic, "The Worksheet."

3. Do all transactions involving revenue or expenses require adjusting entries at the end of the accounting period? If not, what is the distinguishing characteristic of those transactions which do require adjusting entries?

4. Do adjusting entries affect income statement accounts, balance sheet accounts, or both? Explain.

5. Why does the recording of adjusting entries require a better understanding of the concepts of accrual accounting than does the recording of routine revenue and expense transactions occurring throughout the period?

6. Why does the purchase of a one-year insurance policy four months ago give rise to insurance expense in the current month?

7. If services have been rendered to customers during the current accounting period but no revenue has been recorded and no bill has been sent to the customers, why is an adjusting entry needed? What types of accounts should be debited and credited by this entry?

8. What is meant by the term *unearned revenue?* Where should an unearned revenue account appear in the financial statements? As the work is done, what happens to the balance of an unearned revenue account?

9. The weekly payroll for employees of Ryan Company, who work a five-day week, amounts to $20,000. All employees are paid up-to-date at the close of business each Friday. If December 31 falls on Thursday, what year-end adjusting entry is needed?

10. Explain how income taxes affect the amounts of pretax profits and pretax losses.

11. Briefly explain the concept of *materiality.* If an item is not material, how is the item treated for financial reporting purposes?

12. In Chapter 1, assets were defined as economic resources owned by a business and expected to benefit future business operations. By this definition, the gasoline in the tank of a business automobile, unused typewriter ribbons, and even ballpoint pens are actually "assets." Why, then, are purchases of such items routinely charged directly to expense?

13. Explain the accounting principle of *adequate disclosure.*

14. Briefly describe the content of the *notes* that accompany financial statements.

*15. Explain several purposes that may be served by preparing a worksheet (or using computer software that achieves the goals of a worksheet).

EXERCISES

EXERCISE 4-1
Estimated Fax Payments for Individuals

We have made the point that corporations must make *estimated* income tax payments during the year. So must many individuals.

You can find out about the estimated tax payments required of individuals by looking at federal tax Form 1040-ES and the related instructions. Most copy centers have a book of state and federal income tax forms and instructions from which you may make copies. This information also is available on the Internet at:

www.irs.ustreas.gov

Click on "Open Mailbox" and select "Forms and Publications."

Investigate. Who must make estimated income tax payments? When are these payments due? What are the penalties for failure to make these estimated tax payments?

EXERCISE 4-2
Effects of Adjusting Entries

Security Service Company adjusts its accounts at the end of the month. On November 30, adjusting entries are prepared to record:

---

*Supplemental Topic, "The Worksheet."

a. Depreciation expense for November.

b. Interest expense that has accrued during November.

c. Revenue earned during November which has not yet been billed to customers.

d. Salaries payable to company employees, which have accrued since the last payday in November.

e. The portion of the company's prepaid insurance which has expired during November.

f. Earning a portion of the amount collected in advance from a customer, Harbor Restaurant.

Indicate the effect of each of these adjusting entries upon the major elements of the company's financial statements—that is, upon revenue, expenses, net income, assets, liabilities, and owners' equity. Organize your answer in tabular form, using the column headings shown below and the symbols **I** for increase, **D** for decrease, and **NE** for no effect. The answer for adjusting entry **a** is provided as an example.

	Income Statement			Balance Sheet		
Adjusting Entry	**Revenue −**	**Expenses =**	**Net Income**	**Assets =**	**Liabilities +**	**Owners' Equity**
a	NE	I	D	D	NE	D

EXERCISE 4-3
Preparing Adjusting Entries for Recorded Costs and Recorded Revenue

 LO 2,3

The Outlaws, a professional football team, prepare financial statements on a monthly basis. Football season begins in August, but in July the team engaged in the following transactions:

a. Paid $1,500,000 to Dodge City as advance rent for use of Dodge City Stadium for the five-month period from August 1 through December 31. This payment was debited to the asset account, Prepaid Rent.

b. Collected $2,560,000 cash from sales of season tickets for the team's eight home games. This amount was credited to Unearned Ticket Revenue.

During the month of August, The Outlaws played one home game and two games on the road. Their record was two wins, one loss.

Prepare the two adjusting entries required at August 31 to apportion this recorded cost and recorded revenue.

EXERCISE 4-4
Preparing Adjusting Entries for Unrecorded Revenue and Expenses

LO 2,3

The law firm of Dale & Clark prepares its financial statements on a monthly basis. Among the items requiring adjustment at December 31 are the following:

1. Salaries to staff attorneys are paid on the fifteenth day of each month. Salaries accrued since December 15 amount to $17,800 and have not yet been recorded.

2. The firm is defending J. R. Stone in a civil lawsuit. The agreed-upon legal fees are $2,100 per day while the trial is in progress. The trial has been in progress for nine days during December and is not expected to end until late January. No legal fees have yet been billed to Stone. (Legal fees are recorded in an account entitled Legal Fees Earned.)

a. Prepare the two adjusting entries required at December 31 to record the accrued salaries expense and the accrued legal fees revenue.

b. Assume that salaries paid to staff attorneys on January 15 amount to $35,000 for the period December 15 through January 15. How much of this amount is considered salaries expense of *January?* (Although not required, you may wish to prepare the journal entry at January 15 to record payment of staff attorneys.)

c. Assume that on January 29, Dale & Clark receives $60,900 from J. R. Stone in full settlement of legal fees for services in the civil lawsuit. What portion of this amount constitutes revenue earned in *January?* (Although not required, you may wish to prepare the journal entry at January 29 to record receipt of the $60,900.)

EXERCISE 4-5
Distinction Between Adjusting and Closing Process

When Torretti Company began business on August 1, it purchased a one-year fire insurance policy and debited the entire cost of $7,200 to Unexpired Insurance. Torretti *adjusts* its accounts at the end of each month, and *closes* its books at the end of the year.

a. Give the *adjusting entry* required at December 31 with respect to this insurance policy.

b. Give the *closing entry* required at December 31 with respect to insurance expense. Assume that this policy is the only insurance policy Torretti had during the year.

c. Compare the dollar amount appearing in the December 31 adjusting entry (part **a**) with that in the closing entry (part **b**). Are the dollar amounts the same? Why or why not? Explain.

EXERCISE 4-6
Get Your Tickets Early
LO 3

When **TransWorld Airlines (TWA)** sells tickets for future flights, it debits cash and credits an account entitled Advance Ticket Sales. With respect to this Advance Ticket Sales account:

a. What does the balance of the account represent? Where should the account appear in TWA's financial statements?

b. Explain the activity that normally *reduces* the balance of this account. Can you think of any *other* transaction that would reduce this account?

EXERCISE 4-7
Preparing Various Adjusting Entries

Hill Company adjusts its accounts at the end of each month. Prepare the adjusting entries required at December 31 based on the following information. (Not all of these items may require adjusting entries.)

a. A bank loan had been obtained on December 1. Accrued interest on the loan at December 31 amounts to $1,050. No interest expense has yet been recorded.

b. Depreciation of office equipment is based on an estimated life of five years. The balance in the Office Equipment account is $24,000; no change has occurred in the account during the year.

c. Interest revenue earned on United States government bonds during December amounts to $750. This accrued interest revenue has not been recorded or received as of December 31.

d. On December 31, an agreement was signed to lease a truck for 12 months beginning January 1 at a rate of 35 cents a mile. Usage is expected to be 2,000 miles per month and the contract specifies a minimum payment equivalent to 18,000 miles a year.

e. The company's policy is to pay all employees up-to-date each Friday. Since December 31 fell on Monday, there was a liability to employees at December 31 for one day's pay amounting to $2,800.

WHAT'S THE EFFECT? Assume that *prior* to making December 31 adjusting entries, Hill Company's net income was $129,350. Compute net income *after* December adjustments have been recorded. Show you work.

EXERCISE 4-8
Notes Payable and Interest
LO 2,3

Ventura Company adjusts its accounts *monthly* and closes its accounts on December 31. On October 31, 1998, Ventura Company signed a note payable and borrowed $120,000 from a bank for a period of six months at an annual interest rate of 9%.

a. How much is the total interest expense over the life of the note? How much is the monthly interest expense? (Assume equal amounts of interest expense each month.)

b. In the company's annual balance sheet at December 31, 1998, what is the amount of the liability to the bank?

c. Prepare the journal entry to record issuance of the note payable on October 31, 1998.

d. Prepare the adjusting entry to accrue interest on the note at December 31, 1998.

e. Assume the company prepared a balance sheet at March 31, 1999. State the amount of the liability to the bank at this date.

EXERCISE 4-9
Income Taxes

During the first 10 months of 1998, RedCar Transit Co. earned income before taxes (taxable income) of $900,000. The company prepares monthly financial statements and estimates income taxes expense as *40%* of the income (or loss) before income taxes. In November, RedCar earned income before taxes of $150,000. In December, however, employees went on strike and the company sustained a $220,000 *loss* before income taxes.

a. Prepare the adjusting entries necessary at November 30 and December 31 to recognize the estimated monthly income taxes expense.

b. Illustrate the last three lines of the company's income statement—income (or loss) before income taxes, income taxes, and net income (or loss)—for (1) the *month* ended November 30, 1998, (2) the *month* ended December 31, 1998 and (3) the *year* ended December 31, 1998.

EXERCISE 4-10
Relationship of Adjusting
Entries to Business
Transactions
LO 2,3

Among the ledger accounts used by Glenwood Speedway are the following: Prepaid Rent, Rent Expense, Unearned Admissions Revenue, Admissions Revenue, Prepaid Printing, Printing Expense, Concessions Receivable, and Concessions Revenue. For each of the following items, write first the journal entry (if one is needed) to record the external transaction and second the adjusting entry, if any, required on May 31, the end of the fiscal year.

a. On May 1, borrowed $300,000 cash from National Bank by issuing a 12% note payable due in three months.

b. On May 1, paid rent for six months beginning May 1 at $30,000 per month.

c. On May 2, sold season tickets for a total of $910,000 cash. The season includes 70 racing days: 20 in May, 25 in June, and 25 in July.

d. On May 4, an agreement was reached with Snack-Bars, Inc., allowing that company to sell refreshments at the track in return for 10% of the gross receipts from refreshment sales.

e. On May 6, schedules for the 20 racing days in May and the first 10 racing days in June were printed and paid for at a cost of $12,000.

f. On May 31, Snack-Bars, Inc., reported that the gross receipts from refreshment sales in May had been $165,000 and that the 10% owed to Glenwood Speedway would be remitted on June 10.

SOMETHING TO CONSIDER Assume that the May 1 payment of $180,000 rent was properly recorded as Prepaid Rent, but that the May 31 adjusting entry for this item was inadvertently omitted. What is the effect, if any, of this omission on Glenwood's financial statements at May 31? (Specifically consider the financial statement elements Revenue, Expense, Net Income, Assets, Liabilities, and Owners' Equity at May 31; indicate whether each would be overstated, understated, or not affected by the omission.)

EXERCISE 4-11
Concept of Materiality

The concept of materiality is a generally accepted accounting principle.

a. Briefly explain the concept of materiality.

b. Is $2,500 a "material" dollar amount? Explain.

c. Describe two ways in which the concept of materiality may save accountants time and effort in making adjusting entries.

EXERCISE 4-12
Adjusting Entries and
Materiality

LO 3,5

Overnight makes no adjusting entry for utility services used each month (electricity, gas, telephone, water). Instead, it charges the cost of these services to expense when the bills are received, usually about 10 days after month-end.

a. Does this policy result in a correct "matching" of revenue and the expenses incurred in generating that revenue? What is the justification for Overnight's accounting policy for utility bills?

b. Might this "cash basis" accounting policy appropriately be extended to any revenue or expenses for which Overnight *did* make adjusting entries at December 31, 1999? If so, identify these revenues or expenses and explain your reasoning.

EXERCISE 4-13
Accounting Principles

LO 2,5,6, & Review

For each of the situations described below, indicate the generally accepted accounting principle that is being *violated*. Choose from the following principles:

Matching	Materiality
Cost	Realization
Objectivity	Adequate disclosure

If you do not believe that the practice violates any of these principles, answer "None," and explain.

a. The financial statements include no mention of a large lawsuit filed against the company, because the suit has not been settled as of year-end. *a.d.*

b. The bookkeeper of a large metropolitan auto dealership depreciates the $7.20 cost of metal wastebaskets over a period of 10 years. *none*

c. A small commuter airline recognizes no depreciation expense on its aircraft because the planes are maintained in "as good as new" condition. *matching*

d. Palm Beach Hotel recognizes room rental revenue on the date that a reservation is received. For the winter season, many guests make reservations as much as a year in advance. *obj.*

EXERCISE 4-14
Interim Results

LO 7

Paradise Inn ends its fiscal year on April 30. The business adjusts its accounts monthly, but closes them only at year-end (April 30). The busy season in Paradise—in terms of tourist trade—is from November 1 through March 31.

Sam Morse, owner of the Paradise Inn, has learned to keep a "close eye" on two accounts in his accounting systems—Guest Revenue and Cash. The balances of these accounts at the ends of each of the last five months appear below:

	Feb. 28	Jan. 31	Dec. 31	Nov. 30	Oct. 31
Guest revenue	$460,000	$384,000	$304,000	$229,000	$175,000
Cash	142,000	105,000	65,000	31,500	4,500

On February 28, Morse prepares an income statement and balance sheet for his inn. You are to indicate the amounts that should be shown in these statements for (1) guest revenue, and (2) cash, assuming that these statements are prepared for:

a. The *month* ended February 28.

b. The "busy season to date"—that is, November 1 through February 28.

In terms of guest revenue and net increase in cash, which has been Paradise Inn's best month? (Indicate the dollar amounts.)

*EXERCISE 4-15
What were the Adjustments?

LO 3,8

Shown below are the Trial Balance and Adjusted Trial Balance columns of the worksheet prepared for Fisher Insurance Agency for the month ended January 31, 1999. The company last closed its accounts on December 31, 1998.

	Trial Balance		Adjusted Trial Balance	
	Dr	Cr	Dr	Cr
Balance sheet accounts:				
Cash	$ 9,080		$ 9,080	
Commissions receivable	5,000		5,850	
Office supplies	600		350	
Office equipment	6,600		6,600	
Accumulated depreciation: office equipment		$2,420		$ 2,530
Accounts payable		1,660		1,660
Unearned commissions		400		190
Salaries payable				550
Income taxes payable				2,220
Capital stock		10,000		10,000
Retained earnings		2,400		2,400
Dividends	1,000		1,000	
Income statement accounts:				
Commissions earned		12,900		13,960
Salaries expense	6,000		6,550	
Rent expense	1,500		1,500	
Office supplies expense			250	
Depreciation expense: office equipment			110	
Income taxes expense			2,220	
	$29,780	$29,780	$33,510	$33,510

By comparing the two trial balances shown above, it is possible to determine which accounts have been adjusted. You are to prepare the adjusting journal entries which must have been made to cause these changes in account balances. Include an explanation as part of each adjusting entry.

*EXERCISE 4-16
Preparing Financial Statements from an Adjusted Trial Balance

LO 8

From the adjusted trial balance columns of the worksheet shown in Exercise 4-15, prepare an income statement and a statement of retained earnings for Fisher Insurance Agency for the month ended January 31, 1999, and also a balance sheet (in report form) at January 31.

EXERCISE 4-17
Disclosures in an Annual Report
LO 6

The annual report of **Toys "R" Us** appears in Appendix A at the end of this textbook.

a. Review the notes accompanying the consolidated financial statements (pages A-11–A-14). Identify the topical headings of the 10 notes (shown in *blue*).

b. Explain in some detail the content of the note entitled "Quarterly Financial Data."

c. Which three months comprise this company's *fourth* quarter? (Don't worry about a couple of days on either end.)

Supplemental Topic, "The Worksheet."

d. Does the annual performance of this company appear to be highly dependent upon the results of any single quarter? Discuss.

PROBLEMS

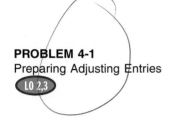

PROBLEM 4-1
Preparing Adjusting Entries
LO 2,3

Inn at the Falls adjusts its accounts *monthly* and closes them only at year-end. Most guests of the resort pay at the time they check out, and the amounts collected are credited to Guest Revenue. A few guests pay in advance for rooms, and these amounts are credited to Unearned Guest Revenue at the time of receipt. The following information is available as a source for preparing adjusting entries at December 31.

1. On November 1, a suite of rooms was rented to ADM Corp. for six months at a monthly rental of $3,200. The entire six-months' rent of $19,200 was collected in advance and credited to Unearned Guest Revenue.

2. A limousine to carry guests to and from the airport was rented beginning December 18 from Transport Rentals, Inc., at a daily rate of $120. No rental payment has yet been made. (The limousine has been rented for 14 days in December.)

3. A six-month loan in the amount of $30,000 was obtained on December 1. Interest is to be computed at a rate of 10% per year and is payable when the loan is due. No interest has been paid and no interest expense has been recorded.

4. Depreciation on the resort's buildings is based upon an estimated useful life of 30 years. The original cost of the buildings was $1,755,000. Inn at the Falls uses the straight-line method.

5. In December, Inn at the Falls entered into an agreement to host the annual symposium of ACE (Americans for a Clean Environment) in April of next year. The resort expects to earn rental revenue of at least $45,000.

6. A one-year fire insurance policy was purchased on September 1. The premium of $7,200 for the entire life of the policy had been paid on September 1 and recorded as Unexpired Insurance.

7. Salaries earned by employees but not yet recorded or paid amount to $7,900.

8. As of December 31, the Inn has earned $11,075 rental revenue from current guests who will not be billed until they are ready to check out. (Debit Accounts Receivable.)

9. The Inn's accountant estimates income taxes for the current year will amount to $104,000. Of this amount, $75,000 has already been paid and recognized as expense. The remaining $29,000 will be paid before January 15.

INSTRUCTIONS

a. For each of the above numbered items, draft a separate adjusting journal entry (including explanation) if the information indicates that an adjusting entry is needed. One or more of the above items may not require any adjusting entry.

b. Explain how accountants can estimate corporate income taxes expense before the corporation's income tax return has been prepared. Explain also why Inn at the Falls has paid $75,000 in corporate income taxes even before the accountant estimated the amount due for the year.

PROBLEM 4-2
Analysis of Adjusted Data;
Preparing Adjusting Entries
LO 2,3

Windsong, Inc., operates a large catamaran which takes tourists at several island resorts on diving and sailing excursions. The company adjusts its accounts at the end of each month. Selected account balances appearing on the June 30 *adjusted* trial balance are as follows:

Prepaid rent	$ 6,000	
Unexpired insurance	2,800	
Catamaran	46,200	
Accumulated depreciation: catamaran		$27,500
Unearned passenger revenue		2,400

OTHER DATA

1. The catamaran is being depreciated over a 7-year (or 84-month) estimated useful life, with no residual value.

2. The unearned passenger revenue represents tickets good for future rides sold to a resort hotel for $15 per ticket on June 1. During June, 140 of the tickets were used.

3. Six-months' dock rent had been prepaid on June 1.

4. The unexpired insurance is a 12-month fire insurance policy purchased on March 1.

INSTRUCTIONS

a. Determine
1. The age of the catamaran in months.
2. How many $15 tickets for future rides were sold to the resort hotel on June 1.
3. The monthly rent expense.
4. The original cost of the 12-month fire insurance policy.

b. Prepare the adjusting entries to be made on June 30.

PROBLEM 4-3
Preparing Adjusting Entries from a Trial Balance
LO 2,3,4

Note: No worksheet is required in Problem 4-3. Problem 4-4 uses the same information and requires preparation of a worksheet.

Jim Rockford operates a private investigating business called Rockford Investigations, Inc. Some clients are required to pay in advance for the company's services, while others are billed after the services have been rendered. Advance payments are credited to an account entitled Unearned Retainer Fees, which represents unearned revenue. The business adjusts its accounts each month and closes its accounts at the end of each quarter. At March 31, the end of the first quarter, the trial balance appeared as follows:

ROCKFORD INVESTIGATIONS, INC. Trial Balance March 31, 19___		
Cash	$ 39,450	
Fees receivable	37,800	
Unexpired insurance	1,600	
Prepaid rent	5,400	
Office supplies	1,050	
Office equipment	17,100	
Accumulated depreciation: office equipment		$ 5,700
Accounts payable		3,900
Income taxes payable		19,000
Unearned retainer fees		24,000
Capital stock		10,000
Retained earnings		19,600
Dividends	20,000	
Fees earned		103,120
Depreciation expense	570	
Rent expense	3,000	
Office supplies expense	450	
Insurance expense	800	
Telephone expense	1,200	
Travel expense	8,400	
Salaries expense	29,500	
Income taxes expense	19,000	
	$185,320	$185,320

unearned retainer fees – services performed, but not billed

OTHER DATA

a. The useful life of the office equipment was estimated at five years. *depreciation*

b. Fees of $13,400 were earned during the month by performing services for clients who had paid in advance. *fees*

c. Salaries earned by employees during the month but not yet recorded or paid amounted to $1,665. *salary expense*

d. On March 1, the business moved into a new office and paid the first three months' rent in advance. *rent – 9000*

e. Investigative services rendered during the month but not yet collected or billed to clients amounted to $3,900. *services*

f. Office supplies on hand March 31 are estimated at $700.

g. On January 1, $2,400 was paid as the premium for six months' liability insurance.

h. The amount of income taxes accruing in March is not yet known, but will be determined in part **c** of this problem. Taxes for the quarter ending March 31 are payable on April 15.

INSTRUCTIONS

a. Prepare the eight adjusting entries required at March 31. (You must work parts **b** and **c** of this problem before you can complete the income taxes adjusting entry.)

b. Prepare a schedule for the quarter ended March 31 determining (after adjusting entries): (1) total revenue, (2) total expenses *other than* income taxes, (3) income before income taxes, (4) income taxes expense (assume a tax rate of 40%), and (5) net income.

c. Determine the amount of income taxes expense to be recognized in the adjusting entry at March 31. Using this amount, complete the final adjusting entry in part **a.**

d. Does the company appear to have sufficient financial resources to pay its income tax liability on April 15, as well as paying other liabilities coming due in the near future? Explain.

*PROBLEM 4-4
Adjusting Entries In
Worksheet Format
LO 2,3,8

This problem is based upon the trial balance provided in Problem 4-3 plus the other data in the eight numbered items. In this problem, however, we do not ask you to compute the amount of income taxes expense to be recognized in the eighth adjusting entry. Simply assume income taxes expense for March to be $9,500. (**Note:** This amount *differs slightly* from the amount of income taxes expense we use in Problem 4-3.)

a. Prepare a 10-column worksheet for the quarter ended March 31. Use the format illustrated in the **Supplemental Topic* following this chapter.

b. Do your adjusting entries increase revenue by *more* or *less* than they increase expense? Do month-end adjustments always have this overall effect? Explain.

PROBLEM 4-5
Interim Financial Statements
LO 6

Guardian Insurance Agency adjusts its accounts monthly, but closes them only at the end of the calendar year. Shown below are the adjusted balances of the revenue and expense accounts at September 30 of the current year, and at the ends of two earlier months:

	Sept. 30	Aug. 31	June 30
Commissions earned	$144,000	$128,000	$90,000
Advertising expense	28,000	23,000	15,000
Salaries expense	36,000	32,000	24,000
Rent expense	22,500	20,000	15,000
Depreciation expense	2,700	2,400	1,800

*Supplemental Topic, "The Worksheet."

Guardian is organized as a *sole proprietorship,* therefore, this business entity does not recognize income taxes expense.

INSTRUCTIONS

a. Prepare a three-column income statement, showing net income for three separate time periods, all of which end on September 30. Use the format illustrated below. Show supporting computations for the amounts of revenue reported in the first two columns.

GUARDIAN INSURANCE AGENCY Income Statement For the Following Time Periods in 19___			
	Month Ended Sept. 30	Quarter Ended Sept. 30	9 Months Ended Sept. 30
Revenue:			
Commissions earned	$____(1)	$____(2)	$____
Expenses:			

b. Briefly explain how you determined the dollar amounts for each of the three time periods. Would you apply the same process to the balances in Guardian's balance sheet accounts? Explain.

c. Assume that Guardian adjusts *and closes* its accounts at the end of *each month.* Briefly explain how you then would determine the revenue and expenses that would appear in each of the three columns of the income statement prepared in part **a.**

*PROBLEM 4-6
Making Use of a
Completed Worksheet

A 10-column worksheet for Internet Consulting Service, Inc. is illustrated on page 191. Using the information contained in that worksheet, prepare in journal entry form the adjusting and closing entries at December 31, 1999. Did you have to make any computations, or was all of the information available from the worksheet? Could these entries have been made automatically by computer? Explain.

*PROBLEM 4-7
Preparing a Worksheet

Pickwood Theater adjusts its accounts *each month* and closes them only at year-end (December 31). At *August 31,* the trial balance and other information below were available for adjusting the accounts:

Supplemental Topic, "The Worksheet."

PICKWOOD THEATER Trial Balance August 31, 19__		
Cash	$ 20,000	
Prepaid film rental	31,200	
Land	120,000	
Building	168,000	
Accumulated depreciation: building		$ 14,000
Fixtures and equipment	36,000	
Accumulated depreciation: fixtures and equipment		12,000
Notes payable		180,000
Accounts payable		4,400
Unearned admissions revenue (YMCA)		1,000
Income taxes payable		4,740
Capital stock		40,000
Retained earnings		46,610
Dividends	15,000	
Admissions revenue		305,200
Concessions revenue		14,350
Salaries expense	68,500	
Film rental expense	94,500	
Utilities expense	9,500	
Depreciation expense: building	4,900	
Depreciation expense: fixtures and equipment	4,200	
Interest expense	10,500	
Income taxes expense	40,000	
	$622,300	$622,300

OTHER DATA

a. Film rental expense for the month is $15,200. However, the film rental expense for several months has been paid in advance.

b. The building is being depreciated over a period of 20 years (240 months).

c. The fixtures and equipment are being depreciated over a period of 5 years (60 months).

d. On the first of each month, Pickwood pays the interest which accrued in the prior month on its note payable. At August 31, accrued interest payable on this note amounts to $1,500.

e. Pickwood allows the local YMCA to bring children attending summer camp to the movies on any weekday afternoon for a fixed fee of $500 per month. On June 28, the YMCA made a $1,500 advance payment covering the months of July, August, and September.

f. Pickwood receives a percentage of the revenue earned by Tastie Corporation, the concessionaire operating the snack bar. For snack bar sales in August, Tastie owes Pickwood $2,250, payable on September 10. No entry has yet been made to record this revenue. (Credit Concessions Revenue.)

g. Salaries earned by employees, but not recorded or paid as of August 31, amount to $1,700. No entry has yet been made to record this liability and expense.

h. Income taxes expense for August is estimated at $4,200. This amount will be paid in the September 15 installment payment.

i. Utilities expense is recorded as monthly bills are received. No adjusting entries for utilities expense are made at month-end.

INSTRUCTIONS

a. Prepare a 10-column worksheet utilizing the trial balance and adjusting data provided above. At the bottom of your worksheet, include a brief explanation keyed to each adjusting entry.

b. Refer to the balances shown in the *unadjusted* trial balance at August 31. How many *months'* worth of expense are included in each of the following account balances? (Remember, Pickwood Theater adjusts its accounts *monthly* and closes them *annually.*)
1. Utilities expense
2. Depreciation expense
3. Accumulated depreciation: building

c. Assume Pickwood has been operating profitably all year. Although the August 31 trial balance shows substantial income taxes *expense,* income taxes *payable* is a much smaller amount. This relationship is quite "normal" throughout much of the year. Explain.

CASES

CASE 4-1
Working for the Competition

This problem focuses upon the following question: *Is it ethical for a CPA (or a CPA firm) to provide similar accounting services to companies that compete directly with one another?*

INSTRUCTIONS

a. *Before* doing any research, discuss this question as a group. Identify potential arguments on *each side* of the issue.

b. Arrange an interview with a practicing (or retired) public accountant. Learn the accounting profession's position on this issue, and discuss the various arguments developed in part **a.** (**Note:** All interviews are to be conducted in accordance with the guidelines in the *Note to Students* section of the introduction to this textbook.)

c. Develop your group's position on this issue and be prepared to explain it in class. Explain why you have chosen to overlook the conflicting arguments developed in part **a.** (If your group is not in agreement, dissenting members may draft a "dissenting opinion.")

CASE 4-2
Accrual Accounting—
An Application

Southwest Airlines Co. credits the proceeds from advance ticket sales to an account entitled Air Traffic Liability. The company's 1995 annual report showed the following trend in the balance of this account over a three-year period:

	1995	1994	1993
Air traffic liability (in millions)	$131	$106	$96

The first note accompanying Southwest's financial statements, entitled "Summary of Significant Accounting Policies," includes the following disclosure:

> Revenue recognition: Passenger revenue is recognized when the transportation is provided. Tickets sold but not yet used are included in "Air traffic liability."

INSTRUCTIONS

a. Why does Southwest recognize ticket sales revenue when transportation is provided, rather than when tickets are sold?

b. Should Southwest recognize flight expenses, such as aircraft fuel and flight crew's salaries, in the period that flights occur or in the period in which tickets are sold? Explain.

c. What does the balance in the Air Traffic Liability account represent?

d. How does Southwest normally discharge this liability?

e. Explain the most probable reason for the increase in the amount of this liability from year to year.

f. Based solely upon the trend in the amount of this liability, would you expect the annual amounts of passenger revenue earned by Southwest to be increasing or decreasing over this three-year period? Explain.

CASE 4-3
Adjusting Entries: An
Unstructured Problem
LO 2,3

The purpose of this problem is to help you understand the need for adjusting entries in a specific business situation. You are to prepare examples of "typical" adjusting entries which might be made at the end of an accounting period by a company that owns and operates a large hotel. You are to decide upon the types of assets, liabilities, revenue, and expenses that might be involved in these entries. Prepare two examples of *each of the four basic types of adjusting entries.* Thus, you will prepare a total of eight adjusting entries.

You need not include dollar amounts — simply enter "xxx" in the debit and credit columns. However, your written explanations of each entry should describe specific facts that make the adjustment necessary. For example, one adjusting entry that a hotel might make to apportion unearned revenue is shown below:

a. Examples of adjusting entries to apportion recorded revenue:

(1) Unearned Banquet Revenue... xxx
         Banquet Revenue xxx
    To recognize revenue earned this period from catering
    the National Football League awards banquet in the
    hotel. The League had paid for this banquet in an
    earlier accounting period.

CASE 4-4
The Concept of Materiality
LO 5

The concept of materiality is one of the most basic generally accepted accounting principles.

a. Answer the following questions:
   1. Why is the materiality of a transaction or an event a matter of professional judgment?
   2. What criteria should accountants consider in determining whether a transaction or an event is "material"?
   3. Does the concept of materiality mean that financial statements are not precise, down to the last dollar? Does this concept make financial statements less useful to most users?

b. **Avis Rent-a-Car** purchases a large number of cars each year for its rental fleet. The cost of any individual automobile is immaterial to Avis, which is a very large corporation. Would it be acceptable for Avis to charge the purchase of automobiles for its rental fleet directly to expense, rather than to an asset account? Explain.

CASE 4-5
Adequate Disclosure
LO 6

Listed below are five items which may — or may not — require disclosure in the notes that accompany financial statements.

a. Mandella Construction Co. uses the "percentage-of-completion" method to recognize revenue on long-term construction contracts. This is one of two acceptable methods of accounting for such projects. Over the life of the project, both methods produce the same results; but the annual results may differ substantially.

b. One of the most popular artists at Spectacular Comics is leaving the company and going to work for a competitor.

c. Shortly after the balance sheet date, but before the financial statements are issued, one of Coast Foods' two processing plants was damaged by a tornado. The plant will be out of service for at least three months.

d. The management of Soft Systems believes that the company has developed systems software that will make Windows virtually obsolete. If management is correct, the company's profits could increase tenfold or more.

e. College Property Management (CPM) withheld a $500 security deposit from students who, in violation of their lease, kept a dog in their apartment. The students have sued CPM for this amount in small claims court.

For each case, explain what, if any, disclosure is required under generally accepted accounting principles. Explain your reasoning.

INTERNET ASSIGNMENTS

INTERNET 4-1
Toys "R" Us:
An Update
(General)

Turn to the 1994 annual report of **Toys "R" Us** in Appendix A.

a. Read the top paragraph in both the left- and right-hand columns of the letter addressed "To Our Stockholders." As of January 1995, had this company established a "pattern" in its reported earnings and sales? Does management appear confident that this pattern will continue? Explain fully.

b. Obtain financial information about Toys' sales or earnings in 1996 and later years. Try www.shareholder.com/toy and then click on "SEC Documents Search." Alternatively, go right into EDGAR, or launch your search from our home page.

yes Has Toys continued to report record sales and earnings? What was the primary cause of the "setback" in fiscal 1995? (The 1995 fiscal year ended February 3, 1996; Form 10K was filed on April 23 of that year.) Has the company since "recovered"?

2⁄8

Note: Additional Internet assignments for this chapter appear in Appendix B and on our home page:

www.magpie.org/cyberlab

OUR COMMENTS ON THE IN-TEXT CASE

YOU AS OVERNIGHT'S ACCOUNTANT (P. 182) The missing amounts can be determined as follows:

● Depreciation expense on tools and equipment through November 30. This amount appears in the December 31 *unadjusted* trial balance on page 163. It is $12,250.

● Depreciation expense on tools and equipment for December is $1,050 (the cost of this asset, $63,000, divided by 60 months).

● Overnight estimates income taxes expense at 40% of income before income taxes, or $45,000 year to date through November 30, and $3,400 for the month of December.

● Net income is equal to income before income taxes less the amounts of those taxes. This is $67,500 year to date as of November 30, and $5,100 for the month of December.

December was a *below-average* month for Overnight. Through November 30, monthly revenue had averaged $33,855 ($372,400 ÷ 11 months) and average monthly net income was $6,136 ($67,500 ÷ 11 months). In both cases, the December amounts were below these monthly averages.

The probable reasons for the below-average monthly results relate primarily to the holiday season. People generally do not have their cars serviced during this period unless it becomes absolutely necessary. Also, the mechanics who generate Overnight's revenue may be taking more days off and working fewer hours than usual. (Notice that December salaries and wages are below the average of the preceding 11 months. This suggests that less work is being performed.) Also, utilities expense during December is somewhat *higher* than average, probably due to higher heating and lighting costs.

ANSWERS TO SELF-TEST QUESTIONS

1. a, b, c, d **2.** c **3.** d $11,670 ($27,900 − $17,340 − $2,700 − $1,440 + $3,300 + $1,950) **4.** d **5.** b, c **6.** b, c, d **7.** a, b **8.** c ***9.** c

---

**Supplemental Topic*, "The Worksheet."

COMPREHENSIVE PROBLEM

Friend with a Truck, Inc.

A COMPREHENSIVE ACCOUNTING CYCLE PROBLEM

On September 1, Anthony and Christine Ferrara formed a corporation called Friend With A Truck, Inc., for the purpose of operating an equipment rental yard. The new corporation was able to begin operations immediately by purchasing the assets and taking over the location of Rent-It, an equipment rental company that was going out of business.

Friend With A Truck, Inc., uses the following chart of accounts:

Cash	1		Capital Stock	30
Accounts Receivable	4		Retained Earnings	35
Prepaid Rent	6		Dividends	38
Unexpired Insurance	7		Income Summary	40
Office Supplies	8		Rental Fees Earned	50
Rental Equipment	10		Salaries Expense	60
Accumulated Depreciation:			Maintenance Expense	61
Rental Equipment	12		Utilities Expense	62
Notes Payable	20		Rent Expense	63
Accounts Payable	22		Office Supplies Expense	64
Interest Payable	25		Depreciation Expense	65
Salaries Payable	26		Interest Expense	66
Dividends Payable	27		Income Taxes Expense	67
Unearned Rental Fees	28			
Income Taxes Payable	29			

The corporation closes its accounts and prepares financial statements at the end of each month. During September, the corporation entered into the following transactions:

Sept. **1**   Issued to Anthony and Christine Ferrara 20,000 shares of capital stock in exchange for a total of $80,000 cash.

Sept. **1**   Purchased for $180,000 all of the equipment formerly owned by Rent-It. Paid $70,000 cash and issued a one-year note payable for $110,000, plus interest at the annual rate of 9%.

Sept. **1**   Paid $9,000 to Shapiro Realty as three months' advance rent on the rental yard and office formerly occupied by Rent-It.

Sept. 4   Purchased office supplies on account from Modern Office Co., $1,630. Payment due in 30 days. (These supplies are expected to last for several months; debit the Office Supplies asset account.)

Sept. 8   Received $10,000 cash as advance payment on equipment rental from McBryan Construction Company. (Credit Unearned Rental Fees.)

Sept. 12   Paid salaries for the first two weeks in September, $3,600.

Sept. 15   Excluding the McBryan advance, equipment rental fees earned during the first 15 days of September amounted to $8,100, of which $6,800 was received in cash.

Sept. 17   Purchased on account from Earth Movers, Inc., $340 in parts needed to repair a rental tractor. (Debit an expense account.) Payment is due in 10 days.

Sept. 23   Collected $210 of the accounts receivable recorded on September 15.

Sept. 25   Rented a backhoe to Mission Landscaping at a price of $100 per day, to be paid when the backhoe is returned. Mission Landscaping expects to keep the backhoe for about two or three weeks.

Sept. 26   Paid biweekly salaries, $3,600.

Sept. 27   Paid the account payable to Earth Movers, Inc., $340.

Sept. 28   Declared a dividend of 10 cents per share, payable on October 15.

Sept. 29   Friend With A Truck was named, along with Mission Landscaping and Collier Construction, as a co-defendant in a $25,000 lawsuit filed on behalf of Kevin Davenport. Mission Landscaping had left the rented backhoe in a fenced construction site owned by Collier Construction. After working hours on September 26, Davenport had climbed the fence to play on parked construction equipment. While playing on the backhoe, he fell and broke his arm. The extent of Friend With A Truck's legal and financial responsibility for this accident, if any, cannot be determined at this time. (**Note:** This event does not require a journal entry at this time, but may require disclosure in notes accompanying the statements.)

Sept. 29   Purchased a 12-month public-liability insurance policy for $2,700. This policy protects the company against liability for injuries and property damage caused by its equipment. However, the policy goes into effect on October 1, and affords no coverage for the injuries sustained by Kevin Davenport on September 26.

Sept. 30   Received a bill from Universal Utilities for the month of September, $270. Payment is due in 30 days.

Sept. 30   Equipment rental fees earned during second half of September and received in cash amounted to $8,450.

DATA FOR ADJUSTING ENTRIES

a. The advance payment of rent on September 1 covered a period of three months.

b. Interest accrued on the note payable to Rent-It amounted to $825 at September 30.

c. The rental equipment is being depreciated by the straight-line method over a period of 10 years.

d. Office supplies on hand at September 30 are estimated at $1,100.

e. During September, the company earned $4,840 of the rental fees paid in advance by McBryan Construction Co. on September 8.

f. As of September 30, Friend With A Truck has earned five days' rent on the backhoe rented to Mission Landscaping on September 25.

g. Salaries earned by employees since the last payroll date (September 26) amounted to $900 at month-end.

h. It is estimated that Friend With A Truck, Inc., is subject to a combined federal and state income tax rate of 40% of income before income taxes (total revenue minus all expenses *other than* income taxes). These taxes will be payable on December 15.

INSTRUCTIONS

a. Journalize the above transactions.

b. Post to ledger accounts. (Use a running balance form of ledger accounts. Enter numbers of journal pages and ledger accounts to complete the cross-referencing between the journal and ledger.)

c. Prepare a 10-column worksheet for the month ended September 30, 19__.

d. Prepare an income statement and a statement of retained earnings for the month of September, and a balance sheet (in report form) as of September 30.

e. Prepare required disclosures to accompany the September 30 financial statements of Friend With a Truck, Inc. Your solution should include a separate note addressing each of the following areas: (1) depreciation policy, (2) maturity dates of major liabilities, and (3) potential liability due to pending litigation.

f. Prepare adjusting and closing entries and post to ledger accounts.

g. Prepare an after-closing trial balance as of September 30.

h. During September, this company's cash balance has fallen from $80,000 to less than $20,000. Does it appear headed for insolvency in the near future? Explain your reasoning.

i. Would it be ethical for Christine Ferrara to maintain the accounting records for this company, or must they be maintained by someone who is *independent* of the organization?

THE BUSINESS WORLD

Location:

Search Feedback Help Directory

Document: Done

An understanding of accounting information and of the business world go hand in hand. You can't know much about one without understanding the other.

ACCOUNTING FOR MERCHANDISING ACTIVITIES

L.L.Bean®
Freeport, Maine, USA
Sporting gear and apparel since 1912
for people who love the outdoors

PRODUCT GUIDE
FREE CATALOGS
PARK SEARCH
WHAT'S NEW

SHOP L.L. BEAN
EXPLORE THE OUTDOORS
DISCOVER L.L. BEAN
CONNECT WITH L.L. BEAN
FIND YOUR WAY

• FREE Catalogs
• Customer Service
• Product Guide
• Home
• How to Order
• Your Shopping List
• Address Book

Location:
Search Feedback Help Directory

Document: Done

America is the land of creative merchandising. It is the birth-place of electronic malls, television shopping channels, mail-order catalogs, and membership warehouse clubs. Merchandising businesses range in size from sidewalk vendors to corporate giants.

Every successful merchandising business makes extensive use of accounting information. It keeps track of inventory—what's in stock, which products are the best sellers, and when to buy more merchandise. It also keeps track of the amounts owed to each supplier and due from each credit customer. And it keeps a sharp eye on the trends in net sales and gross profit.

Because accounting is the "language of business," it is also the language of buying and selling.

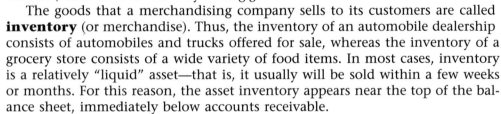

1. Describe the *operating cycle* of a merchandising company.
2. Define *subsidiary ledgers* and explain their usefulness.
3. Account for purchases and sales of merchandise in a *perpetual* inventory system.
4. Explain how a *periodic* inventory system operates.

5. Discuss the factors to be considered in selecting an inventory system.
6. Define *special journals* and explain their usefulness.
7. Compute *gross profit margin* and explain its usefulness.
*8. Account for cash discounts, merchandise returns, transportation costs, and sales taxes.

MERCHANDISING COMPANIES

In the preceding chapters we have illustrated the accounting cycle for organizations that render *services* to their customers. Merchandising companies, in contrast, earn their revenue by selling *goods*.

The goods that a merchandising company sells to its customers are called **inventory** (or merchandise). Thus, the inventory of an automobile dealership consists of automobiles and trucks offered for sale, whereas the inventory of a grocery store consists of a wide variety of food items. In most cases, inventory is a relatively "liquid" asset—that is, it usually will be sold within a few weeks or months. For this reason, the asset inventory appears near the top of the balance sheet, immediately below accounts receivable.

THE OPERATING CYCLE OF A MERCHANDISING COMPANY

The series of transactions through which a business generates its revenue and its cash receipts from customers is called the **operating cycle.** The operating cycle of a merchandising company consists of the following basic transactions: (1) purchases of merchandise; (2) sales of the merchandise, often on account; and (3) collection of the accounts receivable from customers. As the world *cycle* suggests, this sequence of transactions repeats continuously. Some of the cash collected from the customer is used to purchase more merchandise, and the cycle begins anew.

This continuous sequence of merchandising transactions is illustrated on the following page.

LO 1 *Describe the operating cycle of a merchandising company.*

COMPARING MERCHANDISING ACTIVITIES WITH MANUFACTURING

ACTIVITIES Most merchandising companies purchase their inventories from other business organizations in a *ready-to-sell* condition. Companies that manufacture their inventories, such as General Motors, Apple Computer, and Boeing Aircraft, are called *manufacturers,* rather than merchandisers. The operating cycle of a manufacturing company is longer and more complex than that of a merchandising company, because the first transaction—purchasing merchandise—is replaced by the many activities involved in manufacturing the merchandise.

Supplemental Topic, "Additional Merchandising Transactions."

The operating cycle repeats
continuously

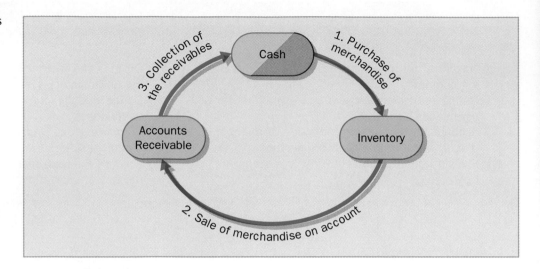

Our examples and illustrations in this chapter are limited to companies that purchase their inventory in a ready-to-sell condition. The basic concepts, however, also apply to manufacturers.

RETAILERS AND WHOLESALERS   Merchandising companies include both retailers and wholesalers. A *retailer* is a business that sells merchandise directly to the public. Retailers may be large or small; they vary in size from giant department store chains, such as Sears and Wal-Mart, to small neighborhood businesses, such as gas stations and convenience stores. In fact, more businesses engage in retail sales than in any other types of business activity.

The other major type of merchandising company is the *wholesaler*. Wholesalers buy large quantities of merchandise from several different manufacturers and then resell this merchandise to many different retailers. As wholesalers do not sell directly to the public, even the largest wholesalers are not well known to most consumers. Nonetheless, wholesaling is a major type of merchandising activity.

CASE IN POINT

The nation's largest wholesale distributor of food products is **Fleming Companies, Inc.,** which sells to approximately 10,000 grocery and convenience stores in 43 states. Fleming's annual sales amount to more than $17 billion—and that's measured in "wholesale" prices.

The concepts discussed in the remainder of this chapter apply equally to retailers and to wholesalers.

INCOME STATEMENT OF A MERCHANDISING COMPANY

Selling merchandise introduces a new and major cost of doing business: the *cost* to the merchandising company of the goods which it resells to its customers. This cost is termed the **cost of goods sold.** In essence, the cost of goods sold is an *expense;* however, this item is of such importance to a merchandising company that it is shown separately from other expenses in the income statement.

A highly condensed income statement for a merchandising business appears on the following page. In comparison with the income statement of a service-type business, the new features of this statement are the inclusion of *cost of goods sold* and a subtotal called **gross profit.**

COMPUTER BARN Condensed Income Statement For the Year Ended December 31, 1998	
Revenue from sales..	$900,000
Less: Cost of goods sold...	540,000
Gross profit...	$360,000
Less: Expenses	270,000
Net income	$ 90,000

Condensed income
statement for a
merchandising company

Revenue from sales represents the *sales price* of merchandise sold to customers during the period. The cost of goods sold, on the other hand, represents the *cost* incurred by the merchandising company for purchasing these goods from the company's suppliers. The difference between revenue from sales and the cost of goods sold is called *gross profit* (or gross margin).

Gross profit is a useful means of measuring the profitability of sales transactions, but it does *not* represent the overall profitability of the business. A merchandising company has many expenses other than the cost of goods sold. Examples include salaries, rent, advertising, and depreciation. The company earns a net income only if its gross profit exceeds the sum of its other expenses.

WHAT ACCOUNTING INFORMATION DOES A MERCHANDISING COMPANY NEED?

Before we illustrate how a merchandising company accounts for the transactions in its operating cycle, let us consider the basic types of information which the company's accounting system should develop. The company needs accounting information that will (1) meet its financial reporting requirements, (2) serve the needs of company personnel in conducting daily business operations, and (3) meet any special reporting requirements, such as information required by income tax authorities.

To meet its financial reporting requirements, a merchandising company must measure and record its revenue from sales transactions, and also the cost of goods sold. (Other types of revenue and expenses must also be recorded, but this is done in the same manner as in service-type business.) In addition, the accounting system must provide a complete record of the company's assets and liabilities.

The information appearing in financial statements is very condensed. For example, the amount shown as accounts receivable in a balance sheet represents the *total* accounts receivable at the balance sheet date. Managers and other company employees need much more detailed accounting information than that provided in financial statements. In billing customers, for example, the company's billing clerks need to know the amount receivable from each credit customer. In addition, the accounting system must provide the billing clerks with the dates and amounts of all charges and payments affecting each customer's account.

In most respects, the information needed for income tax purposes parallels that used in the financial statements. Differences between income tax rules and financial reporting requirements will be discussed in later chapters.

Let us now see how the accounting system of a merchandising company meets the company's needs for financial information.

GENERAL LEDGER ACCOUNTS

Up to now, we have been recording transactions only in *general ledger* accounts. These general ledger accounts are used to prepare financial statements and other accounting reports which *summarize* the financial position of a business and the results of its operations.

Although general ledger accounts provide a useful *overview* of a company's financial activities, they do not provide much of the *detailed information* needed by managers and other company employees in daily business operations. This detailed information is found in accounting records called subsidiary ledgers.

SUBSIDIARY LEDGERS: A SOURCE OF NEEDED DETAILS

LO 2 *Define subsidiary ledgers and explain their usefulness.*

A **subsidiary ledger** contains a separate account for each of the *items* included in the balance of a general ledger account. For example, an *accounts receivable subsidiary ledger* contains a separate account for *each credit customer.* If the company has 500 credit customer, there are 500 accounts in the accounts receivable subsidiary ledger. The balances of these 500 subsidiary ledger accounts add up to the balance in the general ledger account.

An accounts receivable subsidiary ledger provides the information used in billing credit customers, and in reviewing their creditworthiness. The ledger includes information on the dates and amounts of past charges and payments, the current balance owed, and the customer's billing address. In fact, this ledger provides a *complete history* of the credit transactions between the company and the individual customer.

When you call the phone company, electric company, or other businesses to inquire about your bill, they always ask you for your account number. This is the number assigned to your account in their accounts receivable subsidiary ledger. The company representative then calls this account up on a computer screen and is ready to discuss the details of your past transactions.

Most businesses maintain a number of different subsidiary ledgers, each providing detailed information about a different general ledger account. A general ledger account which summarizes the content of a subsidiary ledger is called a **controlling account** (or control account.)

For convenience, the word "subsidiary" can be omitted in describing a specific subsidiary ledger. Thus, the accounts receivable subsidiary ledger might simply be called the accounts receivable ledger (or customer ledger).

SUBSIDIARY LEDGERS NEEDED FOR MERCHANDISING TRANSACTIONS
In addition to a subsidiary ledger for accounts receivable, every merchandising company also maintains an *accounts payable subsidiary ledger,* showing the amount owed to each creditor. Many merchandising companies also maintain an *inventory subsidiary ledger,* with a separate account for each type of merchandise that the company sells. Thus, the inventory ledger of a large department store contains thousands of accounts. Each of these accounts shows, for *one type of product,* the quantities, per-unit costs, and total costs of all units purchased, sold, and currently in inventory.

The following diagram shows the relationship between several subsidiary ledgers and the related controlling accounts in the general ledger.

OTHER TYPES OF SUBSIDIARY LEDGERS
In this chapter we discuss the subsidiary ledgers for inventory, accounts payable, and accounts receivable. How-

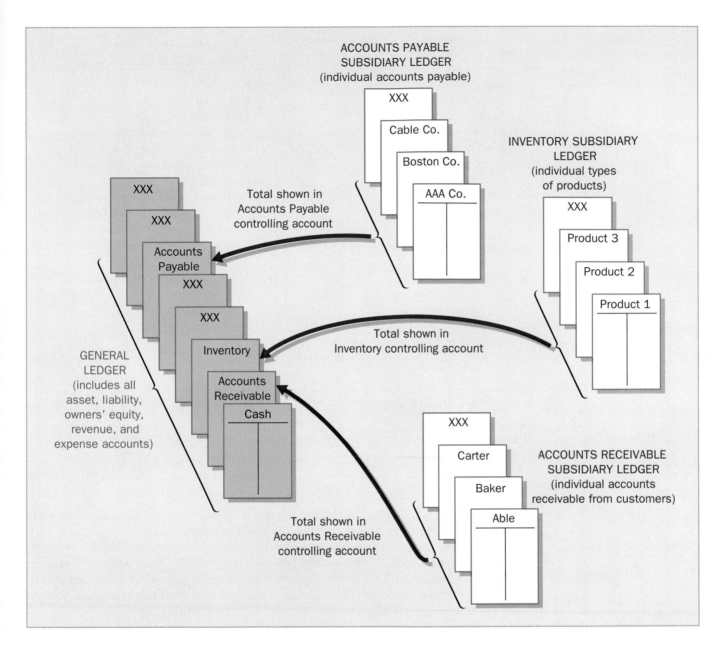

ACCOUNTS PAYABLE
SUBSIDIARY LEDGER
(individual accounts payable)

XXX
Cable Co.
Boston Co.
AAA Co.

INVENTORY SUBSIDIARY
LEDGER
(individual types
of products)

XXX
Product 3
Product 2
Product 1

Total shown in
Accounts Payable
controlling account

XXX
XXX
Accounts
Payable
XXX
XXX
Inventory
Accounts
Receivable
Cash

Total shown in
Inventory controlling account

GENERAL
LEDGER
(includes all
asset, liability,
owners' equity,
revenue, and
expense accounts)

XXX
Carter
Baker
Able

ACCOUNTS RECEIVABLE
SUBSIDIARY LEDGER
(individual accounts
receivable from customers)

Total shown in
Accounts Receivable
controlling account

ever, subsidiary ledgers also are maintained for many other general ledger accounts. The schedule on the next page lists some of the general ledger accounts usually supported by a subsidiary ledger.

Subsidiary ledgers are intended to meet the information needs of the company's *managers and employees.* These accounting records are *not* used in the preparation of financial statements, nor are they usually made available to persons outside of the business organization.

POSTING TO SUBSIDIARY LEDGER ACCOUNTS Any transaction which affects the balance of a subsidiary ledger account *also* affects the balance of the related controlling account. Thus, entries affecting subsidiary ledger accounts must be *posted twice*—once to the subsidiary ledger account and once to the controlling account in the general ledger.

To illustrate, assume that on July 12 Hillside Company collects a $1,000 account receivable from L. Brown, a credit customer. This transaction is illustrated below in the form of a general journal entry:

Controlling Account in the General Ledger	Unit of Organization Within the Subsidiary Ledger
Cash	Each bank account
Notes receivable	Each note receivable
Accounts receivable	Each credit customer
Inventory	Each type of product offered for sale
Plant assets	Each asset (or group of similar assets)
Notes payable	Each note payable
Accounts payable	Each creditor
Capital stock (only in a business organized as a corporation)	Each stockholder (this ledger shows each stockholder's name, address, and the number of shares owned)
Sales (or any revenue account)	Each department, branch location, or product line
Cost of goods sold	Same organization as the sales ledger
Many expense accounts	Each department incurring these types of expense
Payroll expenses (including payroll taxes)	Each employee

Date		Account Titles and Explanation	LP	Debit	Credit
July	12	Cash...		1,000	
		Accounts Receivable (L. Brown)			1,000
		Collected an account receivable.			

Assume that in the general ledger the account number for the Cash account is 101 and the account number of the Accounts Receivable controlling account is 120. Hillside also maintains an accounts receivable subsidiary ledger, in which customers' accounts are arranged alphabetically. (We will assume that the company has only one bank account and, therefore, does not maintain a subsidiary ledger for cash.)

Our original journal entry is repeated below, along with the appropriate posting references included in the LP (Ledger Page) column.

Date		Account Titles and Explanation	LP	Debit	Credit
July	12	Cash...	101	1,000	
		Accounts Receivable (L. Brown)	120/✓		1,000
		Collected an account receivable.........................			

Notice the "double posting" of the credit entry

The account numbers 101 and 120 entered in this column indicate that the entry has been posted to both the Cash account and the Accounts Receivable controlling account in the general ledger. The check mark (✓) indicates that the credit portion of the entry also has been posted to the account for L. Brown in the accounts receivable subsidiary ledger.

(In homework assignments in this text, you often are asked to describe the effects of business transactions in the form of general journal entries. You should *not* include posting references in these entries unless you actually have posted the data to ledger accounts.)

RECONCILING SUBSIDIARY LEDGERS WITH THE CONTROLLING AC-COUNT Periodically, accountants *reconcile* a subsidiary ledger with the controlling account—that is, they determine that the sum of the subsidiary ledger account balances *does,* in fact, equal that of the controlling account.

Reconciling a subsidiary ledger is an *internal control activity* that may bring to light certain types of errors. For example, this activity should detect a failure to post a transaction to the subsidiary ledger or a mechanical error in computing an account balance. Unfortunately, it does *not* provide assurance that all transactions were posted to the *correct account* within the subsidiary ledger. If a debit or credit entry is posted to the wrong account in the subsidiary ledger, the subsidiary ledger and controlling account will remain "in balance." These types of posting errors are difficult to detect and are one reason why individuals and businesses that purchase merchandise on account should review carefully the monthly bill they receive from their suppliers.

SUBSIDIARY LEDGERS IN COMPUTER-BASED SYSTEMS At first, it may seem that maintaining subsidiary ledgers with hundreds or thousands of separate accounts would involve a great deal of work. However, business organizations big enough to require large subsidiary ledgers use computer-based accounting systems. In a computer-based accounting system, subsidiary ledger accounts and general ledger accounts are posted *automatically* as transactions are recorded. In addition, the computer automatically reconciles the subsidiary ledgers with the controlling accounts. Thus, no significant effort is required of accounting personnel to maintain subsidiary ledgers in a computer-based system.[1]

YOUR TURN

You as a Credit Manager

Assume you are the credit manager for Wilson, Inc., a small manufacturer of toys. You have just received a request from Dave's Toy Store asking that the store's credit limit be increased from $30,000 to $50,000. Dave has been a customer of Wilson for the past five years.

Describe the information that you can obtain from the accounts receivable ledger that will assist you in making the decision about whether to increase Dave's credit limit. What *other information* would assist you in making this decision?

*Our comments appear on page 254.

TWO APPROACHES USED IN ACCOUNTING FOR MERCHANDISING TRANSACTIONS

Either of two approaches may be used in accounting for merchandising transactions: (1) a *perpetual inventory system* or (2) a *periodic inventory system*. In past decades, both systems were in widespread use. Today, however, most large businesses (and many smaller ones) use perpetual systems. Periodic systems are used primarily in small businesses with manual accounting systems.

---

[1]The maintenance of subsidiary ledgers was one of the earliest applications of computers in the business world. For a large organization, the time savings in this area alone justified the cost of a computer-based accounting system. Prior to the use of computers, large business organizations employed many clerical workers solely for the purpose of posting transactions to subsidiary ledger accounts.

PERPETUAL INVENTORY SYSTEMS

LO 3 *Account for purchases and sales of merchandise in a perpetual inventory system.*

In a **perpetual inventory system,** merchandising transactions are recorded *as they occur.* The system draws its name from the fact that the accounting records are kept perpetually up-to-date. Purchases of merchandise are recorded by debiting an asset account entitled Inventory. When merchandise is sold, two entries are necessary: one to recognize the *revenue earned* and the second to recognize the related *cost of goods sold.*[2] This second entry also reduces the balance of the Inventory account to reflect the sale of some of the company's inventory.

A perpetual inventory system uses an *inventory subsidiary ledger.* This ledger provides company personnel with up-to-date information about each type of product that the company sells, including the per-unit cost and the number of units purchased, sold, and currently on hand.

To illustrate the perpetual inventory system, we will follow specific items of merchandise through the operating cycle of Computer Barn, a retail store. The transactions comprising this illustration are as follows:

Sept. 1 Purchased 10 Regent CX-21 computer monitors on account from Okawa Wholesale Co. The monitors cost $600 each, for a total of $6,000; payment is due in 30 days.

Sept. 7 Sold 2 monitors on account to RJ Travel Agency at a retail sales price of $1,000 each, for a total of $2,000. Payment is due in 30 days.

Oct. 1 Paid the $6,000 account payable to Okawa Wholesale Co.

Oct. 7 Collected the $2,000 account receivable from RJ Travel Agency.

In addition to a general ledger, Computer Barn maintains separate subsidiary ledgers for accounts receivable, inventory, and accounts payable.

PURCHASES OF MERCHANDISE Purchases of inventory are recorded at cost. Thus, Computer Barn records its purchase of the 10 computer monitors on September 1 as follows:

Purchase of merchandise: the start of the cycle

Inventory..	6,000	
Accounts Payable (Okawa Wholesale Co.)		6,000
Purchased 10 Regent CX-21 computer monitors for $600 each;		
payment due in 30 days.		

The data contained in this entry are posted to the general ledger *and also to the subsidiary ledgers.* First, the entry is posted to the Inventory and Accounts Payable controlling accounts in the general ledger. The debit to Inventory also is posted to the Regent CX-21 Monitors account in the inventory subsidiary ledger.[3] The quantity of monitors purchased (10) and the per-unit cost ($600)

---

[2] In some perpetual systems, only the number of *units* sold is recorded at the time of sale, and the dollar costs are entered at a later date—perhaps monthly. Such variations in perpetual systems are discussed in Chapter 8.

[3] In journal entries, it is common practice to indicate specific suppliers and customers using a parenthetic note following the account title Accounts Payable or Accounts Receivable. Similar notations usually are *not* used with the Inventory account, because *many different types of products* may be purchased or sold in a single transaction. The detailed product information used in posting to the inventory ledger is found in the *invoice* (bill) which the seller sends to the buyer.

also are recorded in this subsidiary ledger account. (This subsidiary ledger account is illustrated on the following page.)

The credit to Accounts Payable also is posted to the account for Okawa Wholesale Co. in Computer Barn's accounts payable subsidiary ledger.

SALES OF MERCHANDISE   The revenue earned in a sales transaction is equal to the *sales price* of the merchandise and is credited to a revenue account entitled Sales. Except in rare circumstances, sales revenue is considered "realized" when the merchandise is *delivered to the customer,* even if the sale is made on account. Therefore, Computer Barn will recognize the revenue from the sale to RJ Travel Agency on September 7, as shown below:

Accounts Receivable (RJ Travel Agency)	2,000	
Sales		2,000
Sold 2 Regent CX-21 monitors for $1,000 each; payment due in 30 days.		

Entries to record a sale . . .

[handwritten: ← revenue recognition entry]

The *matching principle* requires that revenue be matched (offset) with all of the costs and expenses incurred in producing that revenue. Therefore, a *second journal entry* is required at the date of sale to record the cost of goods sold.

[handwritten: ← cost recognition entry]

Cost of Goods Sold	1,200	
Inventory		1,200
To transfer the cost of 2 Regent CX-21 monitors ($600 apiece) from Inventory to the Cost of Goods Sold account.		

. . . and the related cost of goods sold

[handwritten: — wherever you have a sale in a merchandizing co.]

Notice that this second entry is based upon the *cost* of the merchandise to Computer Barn, not upon its retail sales price. The per-unit cost of the Regent monitors ($600) was determined from the inventory subsidiary ledger (see page 222).

Both of the journal entries relating to this sales transaction are posted to Computer Barn's general ledger. In addition, the $2,000 debit to Accounts Receivable (first entry) is posted to the account for RJ Travel Agency in the accounts receivable ledger. The credit to Inventory (second entry) also is posted to the Regent CX-21 Monitors account in the inventory subsidiary ledger.

PAYMENT OF ACCOUNTS PAYABLE TO SUPPLIERS   The payment to Okawa Wholesale Co. on October 1 is recorded as follows:

Accounts Payable (Okawa Wholesale Co.)	6,000	
Cash		6,000
Paid account payable.		

Payment of an account payable

Both portions of this entry are posted to the general ledger. In addition, payment of the account payable is entered in the Okawa Wholesale Co. account in the Computer Barn's accounts payable subsidiary ledger.

COLLECTION OF ACCOUNTS RECEIVABLE FROM CUSTOMERS   On October 7, collection of the account receivable from RJ Travel Agency is recorded as follows:

Cash	2,000	
Accounts Receivable (RJ Travel Agency)		2,000
Collected an account receivable from a credit customer.		

Collection of an account receivable

Both portions of this entry are posted to the general ledger; the credit to Accounts Receivable also is posted to the RJ Travel Agency account in the accounts receivable ledger.

Collection of the cash from RJ Travel Agency completes Computer Barn's operating cycle with respect to these two units of merchandise.

THE INVENTORY SUBSIDIARY LEDGER An inventory subsidiary ledger includes a separate account for each type of product in the company's inventory. Computer Barn's subsidiary inventory record for Regent monitors is illustrated below:

Inventory subsidiary
ledger account

Item	Regent CX-21					Primary supplier	Okawa Wholesale Co.		
Description	Computer monitor					Secondary supplier	Forbes Importers, Inc.		
Location	Storeroom 2					Inventory level: Min: 2	Max: 10		

	Purchased			Sold			Balance		
Date	Units	Unit Cost	Total	Units	Unit Cost	Cost of Goods Sold	Units	Unit Cost	Total
Sept. 1	10	$600	$6,000				10	$600	$6,000
7				2	$600	$1,200	8	$600	$4,800

When Regent CX-21 monitors are purchased, the quantity, unit cost, and total cost are entered in this subsidiary ledger account. When any of these monitors are sold, the number of units, unit cost, and total cost of the units sold also are recorded in this subsidiary ledger account. After each purchase or sales transaction, the Balance columns are updated to show the quantity, unit cost, and total cost of the monitors still on hand.[4]

An inventory ledger provides useful information to a variety of company personnel. A few examples of the company personnel who utilize this information on a daily basis are listed below:

● *Sales managers* use the inventory ledger to see at a glance which products are selling quickly and which are not.

● *Accounting personnel* use these records to determine the unit costs of merchandise sold.

● *Sales personnel* use this subsidiary ledger to determine the quantities of specific products currently on hand and the physical location of this merchandise.

● *Employees responsible for ordering merchandise* refer to the inventory ledger to determine when specific products should be reordered, the quantities to order, and the names of major suppliers.

When a *physical inventory* is taken, management uses the inventory ledger to determine on a product-by-product basis whether *inventory shrinkage* has been reasonable or excessive.

---

[4]In our illustration, all of the Regent monitors were purchased on the same date and have the same unit cost. Often a company's inventory of a given product includes units acquired at several *different* per-unit costs. This situation is addressed in Chapter 8.

TAKING A PHYSICAL INVENTORY

The basic characteristic of the perpetual inventory system is that the Inventory account is *continuously updated* for all purchases and sales of merchandise. Over time, however, normal inventory shrinkage usually causes some discrepancies between the quantities of merchandise shown in the inventory records and the quantities actually on hand. **Inventory shrinkage** refers to unrecorded decreases in inventory resulting from such factors as breakage, spoilage, employee theft, and shoplifting.

In order to ensure the accuracy of their perpetual inventory records, most businesses take a *complete physical count* of the merchandise on hand at least once a year. This procedure is called **taking a physical inventory,** and it usually is performed near year-end.

Once the quantity of merchandise on hand has been determined by a physical count, the per-unit costs in the inventory ledger accounts are used to determine the total cost of the inventory. The Inventory controlling account and also the accounts in the inventory subsidiary ledger then are *adjusted* to the quantities and dollar amounts indicated by the physical inventory.

To illustrate, assume that at year-end the Inventory controlling account and inventory subsidiary ledger of Computer Barn both show an inventory with a cost of $72,200. A physical count, however, reveals that some of the merchandise listed in the accounting records is missing; the items actually on hand have a total cost of $70,000. Computer Barn would make the following adjusting entry to correct its Inventory controlling account:

Cost of Goods Sold	2,200	Adjusting for inventory
Inventory	2,200	shrinkage

To adjust the perpetual inventory records to reflect the results
of the year-end physical count.

Computer Barn also will adjust the appropriate accounts in its inventory subsidiary ledger to reflect the quantities indicated by the physical count.

Reasonable amounts of inventory shrinkage are viewed as a normal cost of doing business and simply are debited to the Cost of Goods Sold account, as illustrated above.[5]

CLOSING ENTRIES IN A PERPETUAL INVENTORY SYSTEM

As explained and illustrated in Chapter 3, revenue and expense accounts are *closed* at the end of each accounting period. A merchandising business with a perpetual inventory system makes closing entries which parallel those of a service-type business. The Sales account is a revenue account and is closed into the Income Summary account along with other revenue accounts. The Cost of Goods Sold account is closed into the Income Summary account in the same manner as the other expense accounts.

PERIODIC INVENTORY SYSTEMS

A periodic inventory system is an *alternative* to a perpetual inventory system. In a periodic inventory system, no effort is made to keep up-to-date records of either the inventory or the cost of goods sold. Instead, these amounts are only determined "periodically"—usually at the end of each year.

---

[5]If a large inventory shortage is caused by an event such as a fire or theft, the cost of the missing or damaged merchandise may be debited to a special loss account, such as Fire Loss. In the income statement, a loss is deducted from revenue in the same manner as an expense.

OPERATION OF A PERIODIC INVENTORY SYSTEM

LO 4 Explain the operation of a periodic inventory system.

A traditional periodic inventory system operates as follows. When merchandise is purchased, its cost is debited to an account entitled *Purchases,* rather than to the Inventory account. When merchandise is sold, an entry is made to recognize the sales revenue, but *no entry* is made to record the cost of goods sold or to reduce the balance of the Inventory account. As the inventory records are not updated as transactions occur, there is no inventory subsidiary ledger.

The foundation of the periodic inventory system is the taking of a *complete physical inventory* at year-end. This physical count determines the amount of inventory appearing in the balance sheet. The cost of goods sold for the entire year then is determined by a short computation.

DATA FOR AN ILLUSTRATION To illustrate, assume that Special Occasions, a party supply store, has a periodic inventory system. At December 31, 1998, the following information is available:

1. The inventory on hand at the end of *1997* cost $14,000.

2. During 1998, purchases of merchandise for resale to customers totaled $130,000.

3. Inventory on hand at the end of *1998* cost $12,000.

The inventories at the end of 1997 and at the end of 1998 were determined by taking a complete physical inventory at (or very near) each year-end. (Because the Inventory account was not updated as transactions occurred during 1998, it still shows a balance of $14,000—the inventory on hand at the *beginning* of the year.)

The $130,000 cost of merchandise purchased during 1998 was recorded in the Purchases account.

RECORDING PURCHASES OF MERCHANDISE Special Occasions made many purchases of merchandise during 1998. The entry to record the first of these purchases is illustrated below:

Jan. 6	Purchases...	2,000	
	Accounts Payable (Paper Products Co.)..................................		2,000
	Purchased inventory on account; payment		
	due in 30 days.		

This entry was posted to the Purchases and Accounts Payable accounts in the general ledger. The credit portion also was posted to the account for Paper Products Co. in Special Occasions' accounts payable subsidiary ledger. The debit to Purchases was *not* "double-posted," as there is *no inventory subsidiary ledger* in a periodic system.

COMPUTING THE COST OF GOODS SOLD The year-end inventory is determined by taking a complete physical count of the merchandise on hand. Once the ending inventory is known, the cost of goods sold for the entire year can be determined by a short computation. This computation is shown below, using the 1998 data for Special Occasions:

Computation of the cost of goods sold

Inventory (beginning of the year) (1)...	$ 14,000
Add: Purchases (2)	130,000
Cost of goods available for sale	$144,000
Less: Inventory (end of the year) (3)..	12,000
Cost of goods sold..	$132,000

RECORDING INVENTORY AND THE COST OF GOODS SOLD Special Occasions has now determined its inventory at the end of 1998 and its cost of goods sold for the year. But neither of these amounts has yet been recorded in the company's accounting records.

In a periodic system, the ending inventory and the cost of goods sold are recorded during the company's year-end *closing procedures.* (The term "closing procedures" refers to the end-of-period adjusting and closing entries.)

CLOSING PROCESS IN A PERIODIC INVENTORY SYSTEM

There are several different ways of recording the ending inventory and cost of goods sold in a periodic system, but they all produce the same results. One approach is to *create* a Cost of Goods Sold account with the proper balance as part of the closing process. Once this account has been created, the company can complete its closing procedures in the same manner as if a perpetual inventory system had been in use.

CREATING A COST OF GOODS SOLD ACCOUNT A Cost of Goods Sold account is created with two special closing entries. The first entry creates the new account by bringing together the costs contributing toward the cost of goods sold. The second entry adjusts the Cost of Goods Sold account to its proper balance, and also records the ending inventory in the Inventory account.

The costs contributing to the cost of goods sold include (1) beginning inventory, and (2) purchases made during the year. These costs are brought together by closing both the Inventory account (which contains its beginning-of-the-year balance) and the Purchases account into a new account entitled Cost of Goods Sold. This year-end closing entry is:

Dec. 31	Cost of Goods Sold...	144,000	Creating a Cost of Goods
	Inventory (beginning balance)............................	14,000	Sold account . . .
	Purchases..	130,000	
	To close the temporary accounts contributing to the cost		
	of goods sold for the year.		

Special Occasions' Cost of Goods Sold account now includes the cost of all goods *available for sale* during the year. Of course, not all of these goods were sold; the physical inventory taken at the end of 1997 shows that merchandise costing $14,000 is still on hand. Therefore, a second closing entry is made transferring the cost of merchandise still on hand *out* of the Cost of Goods Sold account and *into* the Inventory account. For Special Occasions, this second closing entry is:

Dec. 31	Inventory (year-end balance)	12,000	. . . and adjusting its
	Cost of Goods Sold...	12,000	balance
	To reduce the balance of the Cost of Goods Sold account		
	by the cost of merchandise still on hand at year-end.		

With these two entries, Special Occasions has created a Cost of Goods Sold account with a balance of $132,000 ($144,000 – 12,000), and also brought its Inventory account up-to-date.

COMPLETING THE CLOSING PROCESS Special Occasions may now complete its closing process in the same manner as a company using a perpetual inventory system. The company will make the "usual" four closing entries, closing the (1) revenue accounts, (2) expense accounts (including Cost of Goods Sold), (3) Income Summary account, and (4) Dividends account.

COMPARISON OF PERPETUAL AND PERIODIC INVENTORY SYSTEMS

Perpetual systems are used when management needs information throughout the year about inventory levels and gross profit. Periodic systems are used when the primary goals are to develop annual data and to minimize record-keeping requirements. A single business may use *different inventory systems* to account for *different types of merchandise.*

WHO USES PERPETUAL SYSTEMS? When management or employees *need up-to-date information about inventory levels,* there is no substitute for a perpetual inventory system. Almost all manufacturing companies use perpetual systems. These businesses need current information to coordinate their inventories of raw materials with their production schedules. Most large merchandising companies—and many small ones—also use perpetual systems.

In the days when all accounting records were maintained by hand, businesses that sold many types of low-cost products had no choice but to use periodic inventory systems. A Wal-Mart store, for example, may sell several thousand items *per hour.* Imagine the difficulty of keeping a perpetual inventory system up-to-date if the records were maintained by hand. But with today's *point-of-sale terminals* and *bar-coded merchandise,* many high-volume retailers now use perpetual inventory systems. In fact, Wal-Mart has been a leader in developing perpetual inventory systems for retailers.

Perpetual inventory systems are not limited to businesses with point-of-sale terminals. Many small businesses with manual accounting systems also use perpetual inventory systems. However, these businesses may update their inventory records on a weekly or a monthly basis, rather than at the time of each sales transaction.

Whether accounting records are maintained manually or by computer, most businesses use perpetual inventory systems in accounting for products with a *high per-unit cost.* Examples include automobiles, heavy machinery, electronic equipment, home appliances, and jewelry. Management has a greater interest in keeping track of inventory when the merchandise is expensive. Also, sales volume usually is low enough that a perpetual system can be used, even if accounting records are maintained by hand.

WHO USES PERIODIC SYSTEMS? Periodic systems are used when the need for current information about inventories and sales *does not justify the cost* of maintaining a perpetual system. In a small retail store, for example, the owner may be so familiar with the inventory that formal perpetual inventory records are unnecessary. Most businesses—large and small—use periodic systems for inventories that are *immaterial* in dollar amount, or when management has little interest in the quantities on hand.

As stated previously, businesses that sell many low-cost items and have manual accounting systems sometimes have no choice but to use the periodic method.

CASE IN POINT

Dale's Market is a small grocery store in San Diego, California. Sales are recorded on a mechanical cash register at the checkout stand. The daily register tapes show only the sales prices of the items sold. Even if Dale were willing to spend all night updating his inventory records, he has no place to start. His accounting system does not indicate the types or costs of products sold during the day.

SELECTING AN INVENTORY SYSTEM

Accountants—and business managers—often must select an inventory system appropriate for a particular situation. Some of the factors usually considered in these decisions are listed below:

LO 5 *Discuss factors to be considered in selecting an inventory system.*

Factors Suggesting a Perpetual Inventory System	Factors Suggesting a Periodic Inventory System
Large company with professional management.	Small company, run by owner.
Management and employees want information about items in inventory and the quantities of specific products that are selling.	Accounting records of inventories and specific product sales are not needed in daily operations. Such information is developed primarily for use in annual income tax returns.
Items in inventory have a high per-unit cost.	Inventory consists of many different kinds of low-cost items.
Low volume of sales transactions or a computerized accounting system, (e.g., point-of-sale terminals).	High volume of sales transactions and a manual accounting system.
Merchandise stored in multiple locations or in warehouses separate from the sales sites.	Lack of full-time accounting personnel.
	All merchandise stored at the sales site (e.g., in the store).

THE TREND IN TODAY'S BUSINESS WORLD   Advances in technology are quickly extending the use of perpetual inventory systems to more businesses and more types of inventory. This trend is certain to continue. Throughout this textbook, you may assume that a *perpetual inventory system* is in use unless we specifically state otherwise.

YOUR TURN

You as a Buyer for a Retail Business

Assume you are in charge of purchasing merchandise for Acme Hardware Stores. You are currently making a decision about the purchase of barbecues for sale during the upcoming summer season. You must decide how many of each brand and type of barbecue to order. Describe the types of accounting information that would be useful in making this decision, and where this information might be found.

*Our comments appear on page 254.

MODIFYING AN ACCOUNTING SYSTEM

Throughout this textbook we illustrate the effects of many transactions using the format of a two-column *general journal*. This format is ideal for textbook illustrations, as it allows us to concisely show the effects of *any type* of business transactions.

LO 6 *Define special journals and explain their usefulness.*

But while general journal entries are useful for our purposes, they are *not* the most efficient way for a business to record routine transactions. A supermarket, for example, may sell 10,000 to 15,000 items *per hour.* Clearly, it would not be practical to make a general journal entry to record each of these sales transactions.

Therefore, most businesses use *special journals,* rather than a general journal, to record *routine transactions which occur frequently.*

SPECIAL JOURNALS PROVIDE SPEED AND EFFICIENCY

A **special journal** is an accounting record or device designed to record *a specific type of routine transaction quickly and efficiently.*

Some special journals are maintained by hand. An example is the *check register* in your personal checkbook. If properly maintained, this special journal provides an efficient record of all cash disbursements made by check.

But many special journals are highly automated. Consider the **point-of-sale terminals** that you see in supermarkets and large retail stores. These devices record sales transactions and the related cost of goods sold as quickly as the barcoded merchandise can be passed over the scanner.

Relative to the general journal, the special journals offer the following advantages:

- Transactions are recorded faster and more efficiently.
- Many special journals may be in operation at one time, further increasing the company's ability to handle a large volume of transactions.
- Automation may reduce the risk of errors.
- Employees maintaining special journals generally do not need expertise in accounting.
- The recording of transactions may be an automatic "side effect" of other basic business activities, such as collecting cash from customers.

Most businesses use separate special journals to record transactions such as sales of merchandise, cash receipts, cash payments, purchases of merchandise on account, and payrolls. There are no "rules" for the design or content of special journals. Rather they are tailored to suit the needs, activities, and resources of the particular business organization.

Let us stress that the *accounting principles* used in special journals are the *same* as those used for transactions recorded in a general journal. The differences lie in the *recording techniques,* not in information that is recorded.

Remember also that special journals are *highly specialized* in terms of the transactions they can record. Thus, every business still needs a general journal to record transactions that do not fit into any of its special journals, including, for example, adjusting entries, closing entries, and unusual events such as a loss sustained from a fire.

EVALUATING THE PERFORMANCE OF A MERCHANDISING COMPANY

In evaluating the performance of a merchandising business, managers and investors look at more than just net income. Two key measures of past performance and future prospects are trends in the company's *net sales* and *gross profit.*

NET SALES

Net sales is the most widely used measure of *dollar sales volume.* In the income statement of almost every merchandising or manufacturing business, revenue from merchandise sales is termed net sales.

"Net sales" is smaller than "gross sales." It is equal to the balance of the Sales revenue account, less some minor adjustments for transactions such as refunds to customers. (We illustrate and explain these transactions in the *Supplemental Topic* section at the end of this chapter.)

Most investors and business managers consider the *trend* in net sales to be a key indicator of both past performance and future prospects. Increasing sales suggest the probability of larger profits in future periods. Declining sales, on the other hand, may provide advance warning of financial difficulties.

As a measure of performance, the trend in net sales has some limitations, especially when the company is adding new stores. For these companies, an increase in overall net sales in comparison to the prior year may have resulted *solely* from sales at the new stores. Sales at *existing* stores may even be declining. As a result, business managers and investors also focus on measures that adjust for changes in the number of stores from period to period, including:

1. **Comparable store sales.** Net sales at established stores, excluding new stores opened during the period. Indicates whether customer demand is rising or falling at established locations. (Also called *same-store sales.*)

2. **Sales per square foot of selling space.** A measure of how effectively the company is using its physical facilities (such as floor space, or, in supermarkets, shelf space).

GROSS PROFIT MARGINS

Increasing net sales is *not enough* to ensure increasing profitability. Some products are more profitable than others. In evaluating the profitability of sales transactions, managers and investors keep a close eye on the company's **gross profit margin** (also called *gross profit rate*).

LO 7 *Compute* gross profit margin *and explain its usefulness.*

Gross profit margin is the dollar amount of gross profit, expressed as a *percentage* of net sales revenue. Gross profit margins can be computed for the business as a whole, for specific sales departments, and also for individual products.

To illustrate the computation of gross profit margin, assume that Computer Barn has two separate sales departments. One of these departments sells computer hardware, and the other sells software. The sales, cost of goods sold, and gross profit of these departments in 1998 are as follows:

	Hardware Department	Software Department	The Entire Company
Sales	$400,000	$500,000	$900,000
Cost of goods sold	300,000	240,000	540,000
Gross profit	$100,000	$260,000	$360,000

We also will include in this illustration two products sold in the Software Department: Report Writer (a word processing program) and Dragon Slayer (a computer game). *Per-unit* information about these products appears below:

	Report Writer	Dragon Slayer
Sales price	$100	$50
Cost of goods sold	65	20
Gross profit	$ 35	$30

THE "OVERALL" GROSS PROFIT MARGIN   The average gross profit margin (gross profit rate) earned by Computer Barn in 1998 is 40% (gross profit, $360,000, divided by net sales, $900,000 = 40%). But each sales department may have a gross profit margin that differs from that of the business viewed as a whole.

DEPARTMENTAL PROFIT MARGINS   Departmental profit margins are computed using *departmental* gross profit and net sales information, as illustrated below:

Hardware Department ($100,000 ÷ $400,000) 25%
Software Department ($260,000 ÷ $500,000)... 52%

PROFIT MARGINS FOR INDIVIDUAL PRODUCTS   Finally, profit margins can be computed for specific products using *per-unit* amounts:

Report Writer ($35 ÷ $100) 35%
Dragon Slayer ($30 ÷ $50) 60%

Notice that Dragon Slayer has a higher profit margin, even though Report Writer is the more expensive product. This higher profit margin means that *at a given dollar of sales volume* (say, $10,000 in sales) Dragon Slayer is the more profitable product.

USING INFORMATION ABOUT PROFIT MARGINS

Investors usually compute companies' overall gross profit rates from one period to the next. High—or increasing—margins generally indicate popular products and successful marketing strategies. A substandard or declining profit margin, on the other hand, often indicates weak customer demand or intense price competition.[6]

Management uses information about departments and products for many purposes. These include setting prices, deciding which products to carry and to advertise, and evaluating the performance of departmental managers. By concentrating sales efforts on the products and departments with the *highest margins,* management usually can increase the company's overall gross profit rate.

A CLOSING COMMENT   Remember that only a perpetual inventory system provides management with current information about departmental gross profit and profit margins. This is the primary reason why many large companies use perpetual systems.

NET CONNECTIONS

The Gap is one of the largest retailers of casual apparel. Review some of the sales information that may be accessed from the company's interactive home page.

www.gap.com

Visit the home page of the National Association of College Bookstores to look up the average gross margins (profits) for some of the products sold at your college bookstore.

www.nacs.org

---

[6]We discuss the interpretation of gross profit rates in greater depth in Chapter 6.

Amazon.com is the world's largest electronic book seller. The company sells all types of books at discounted prices over the Internet from the following home page site:

www.amazon.com

Browse the company's book titles, noting the estimated shipping dates. Without a good perpetual information system, it would be impossible for Amazon.com to provide its customers with this shipping information.

*SUPPLEMENTAL TOPIC

ADDITIONAL MERCHANDISING TRANSACTIONS

In addition to the basic transactions illustrated and explained in this chapter, merchandising companies must account for a variety of additional transactions relating to purchases and sales of merchandise. Examples include discounts offered to credit customers for prompt payment, merchandise returns and refunds, transportation costs, and collecting and remitting sales taxes.

LO 8 *Account for cash discounts, merchandise returns, transportation costs, and sales taxes.*

In our discussion of these transactions, we assume the use of a *perpetual* inventory system.

TRANSACTIONS RELATING TO PURCHASES

Purchases of merchandise are recorded at cost. However, this cost may be affected by such factors as cash discounts and transportation charges.

CREDIT TERMS AND CASH DISCOUNTS

Manufacturers and wholesalers normally sell merchandise *on account*. The credit terms are stated in the seller's bill, or *invoice*. One common example of credit terms is "net 30 days," or "n/30," meaning full payment is due in 30 days. Another common form of credit terms is "10 eom," meaning payment is due 10 days after the end of the month in which the purchase occurred.

Manufacturers and wholesalers usually allow their customers 30 or 60 days in which to pay for credit purchases. Frequently, however, sellers offer their customers a small discount to encourage earlier payment.

Perhaps the most common credit terms offered by manufacturers and wholesalers are *2/10, n/30*. This expression is read "2, 10, net 30," and means that full payment is due in 30 days, but that the buyer may take a *2% discount* if payment is made within 10 days. The period during which the discount is available is termed the *discount period*. Because the discount provides an incentive for the customer to make an early cash payment, it is called a *cash discount*. Buyers, however, often refer to these discounts as *purchase discounts*, while sellers frequently call them *sales discounts*.

Most well-managed companies have a policy of taking advantage of all cash discounts available on purchases of merchandise.[1] These companies initially record

---

[1]The terms 2/10, n/30 offer the buyer a 2% discount for sending payment 20 days before it is otherwise due. Saving 2% over only 20 days is equivalent to earning an annual rate of return of more than 36% ($2\% \times 365/20 = 36.5\%$). Thus, taking cash discounts represents an excellent investment opportunity. Most companies take advantage of all cash discounts, even if they must borrow the necessary cash from a bank to make payment within the discount period.

purchases of merchandise at the *net cost*—that is, the invoice price *minus* any available discount. After all, this is the amount that the company expects to pay.

To illustrate, assume that on November 3 Computer Barn purchases 100 spreadsheet programs from PC Products. The cost of these programs is $100 each, for a total of $10,000. However, PC Products offers credit terms of 2/10, n/30. If Computer Barn pays for this purchase within the discount period, it will have to pay only *$9,800,* or 98% of the full invoice price. Therefore, Computer Barn will record this purchase as follows:

Purchase recorded at net cost

Inventory	9,800	
Accounts Payable (PC Products)		9,800

To record purchase of 100 spreadsheet programs at net cost
($100 × 98% × 100 units).

If the invoice is paid within the discount period, Computer Barn simply records payment of a $9,800 account payable.

Through oversight or carelessness, Computer Barn might fail to make payment within the discount period. In this event, Computer Barn must pay PC Products the entire invoice price of *$10,000,* rather than the recorded liability of $9,800. The journal entry to record payment *after the discount period*—on, say, December 3—is:

Recording the loss of a cash discount

Accounts Payable (PC Products)	9,800	
Purchase Discounts Lost	200	
Cash		10,000

To record payment of invoice after expiration of discount period.

Notice that the additional $200 paid because the discount period has expired is debited to an account entitled Purchase Discounts Lost. Purchase Discounts Lost is an *expense account.* The only benefit to Computer Barn from this $200 expenditure was a *20-day delay* in paying an account payable. Thus, the lost purchase discount is basically a *finance charge,* similar to interest expense. In an income statement, finance charges usually are classified as nonoperating expenses.

The fact that purchase discounts *not taken* are recorded in a separate expense account is the primary reason why a company should record purchases of merchandise at *net cost.* The use of a Purchase Discounts Lost account immediately brings to management's attention any failure to take advantage of the cash discounts offered by suppliers.

RECORDING PURCHASES AT GROSS INVOICE PRICE As an alternative to recording purchases at net cost, some companies record merchandise purchases at the gross (total) invoice price. If payment is made within the discount period, these companies must record the amount of the purchase discount *taken.*

To illustrate, assume that Computer Barn followed a policy of recording purchases at gross invoice price. The entry on November 3 to record the purchase from PC Products would have been:

Purchase recorded at gross price

Inventory	10,000	
Accounts Payable (PC Products)		10,000

To record purchase of 100 spreadsheet programs at gross invoice price ($100 × 100 units).

If payment is made within the discount period, Computer Barn will discharge this $10,000 account payable by paying only $9,800. The entry will be:

Accounts Payable (PC Products)	10,000	
Cash		9,800
Purchase Discounts Taken		200

Paid a $10,000 invoice within the discount period; taking a
2% purchase discount.

Buyer records discounts taken

Purchase Discounts Taken is treated as a reduction in the cost of goods sold.

Both the net cost and gross price methods are widely used and produce substantially the same results in financial statements.[2] A shortcoming in the gross price method, however, is that it does *not* direct management's attention to discounts lost. Instead, these lost discounts are "buried" in the costs assigned to inventory. For this reason, we recommend the net cost method and use it throughout this textbook.

RETURNS OF UNSATISFACTORY MERCHANDISE

On occasion, a purchaser may find the purchased merchandise unsatisfactory and want to return it to the seller for a refund. Most sellers permit such returns.

To illustrate, assume that on November 9 Computer Barn returns to PC Products five of the spreadsheet programs purchased on November 3, because these programs were not properly labeled. As Computer Barn has not yet paid for this merchandise, the return will reduce the amount that Computer Barn owes PC Products. The gross invoice price of the returned merchandise was $500 ($100 per program). Remember, however, that Computer Barn records purchases at *net cost*. Therefore, these spreadsheet programs are carried in Computer Barn's inventory subsidiary ledger at a per-unit cost of *$98*, or $490 for the five programs being returned. The entry to record this purchase return is:

Accounts Payable (PC Products)	490	
Inventory		490

Returned 5 defective spreadsheet programs to supplier. Net
cost of the returned items, $490 ($100 × 98% × 5 units).

Return is based upon recorded acquisition cost

The reduction in inventory must also be recorded in the subsidiary ledger accounts.

TRANSPORTATION COSTS ON PURCHASES

The purchaser sometimes may pay the costs of having the purchased merchandise delivered to its premises. Transportation costs relating to the *acquisition* of inventory, or any other asset, are *not expenses* of the current period; rather, these charges are *part of the cost of the asset* being acquired.[3] If the purchaser is able to associate transportation costs with specific products, these costs should be debited directly to the Inventory account as part of the "cost" of the merchandise.

Often, many different products arrive in a single shipment. In such cases, it may be impractical for the purchaser to determine the amount of the total transportation cost applicable to each product. For this reason, many companies follow the convenient policy of debiting all transportation costs on inbound shipments of merchandise to an account entitled *"Transportation-in."* The dollar amount of transportation-in usually is too small to show separately in the financial statements. Therefore, this amount is merely included in the amount reported in the income statement as cost of goods sold. At the end of

---

[2]The net cost method values the ending inventory at net cost, whereas the gross cost method shows this inventory at gross invoice price. This difference, however, is *immaterial*.
[3]The "cost" of an asset includes all reasonable and necessary costs of getting the asset to an appropriate location and putting it into usable condition.

the period, the Transportation-in account is closed into the Income Summary account in the same manner as the Cost of Goods Sold account.

This treatment of transportation costs is not entirely consistent with the *matching principle*. Some of the transportation costs may apply to merchandise still in inventory rather than to goods sold during the current period. We have mentioned, however, that transportation costs are relatively small in dollar amount. The accounting principle of *materiality,* therefore, usually justifies accounting for these costs in the most convenient manner.

TRANSACTIONS RELATING TO SALES

Credit terms and merchandise returns also affect the amount of sales revenue earned by the seller. To the extent that credit customers take advantage of cash discounts or return merchandise for a refund, the seller's revenue is reduced. Thus, revenue shown in the income statement of a merchandising concern is often called net sales.

The term *net sales* means total sales revenue *minus* sales returns and allowances and *minus* sales discounts. The following partial income statement illustrates this relationship:

What are "net sales"?

COMPUTER BARN		
Partial Income Statement		
For the Year Ended December 31, 1998		
Revenue:		
Sales...		$912,000
Less: Sales returns and allowances	$8,000	
Sales discounts	$4,000	12,000
Net sales..		$900,000

The details of this computation seldom are shown in an actual income statement. The normal practice is to begin the income statement with the amount of net sales.

SALES RETURNS AND ALLOWANCES

Most merchandising companies allow customers to obtain a refund by returning any merchandise considered to be unsatisfactory. If the merchandise has only minor defects, customers sometimes agree to keep the merchandise if an *allowance* (reduction) is made in the sales price.

Under the perpetual inventory system, two entries are needed to record the sale of merchandise: one to recognize the revenue earned and the other to transfer the cost of the merchandise from the Inventory account to Cost of Goods Sold. If some of the merchandise is returned, both of these entries are partially reversed.

First, let us consider the effects upon revenue of granting either a refund or an allowance. Both refunds and allowances have the effect of nullifying previously recorded sales and reducing the amount of revenue earned by the business. The journal entry to reduce sales revenue as the result of a sales return (or allowance) is shown below:

Sales Returns and Allowances...	200	
Accounts Receivable (or Cash)..		200

Customer returned merchandise purchased on account for
$200. Allowed customer full credit for returned merchandise.

A sales return reverses recorded revenue . . .

Sales Returns and Allowances is a **contra-revenue account**—that is, it is deducted from gross sales revenue as a step in determining net sales.

Why use a separate Sales Returns and Allowances account rather than merely debiting the Sales account? The answer is that using a separate contra-revenue account enables management to see both the total amount of sales *and also* the amount of sales returns. The relationship between these amounts gives management an indication of *customer satisfaction* with the merchandise.

If merchandise is returned by the customer, a second entry is made to remove the cost of this merchandise from the Cost of Goods Sold account and restore it to the inventory records. This entry is:

Inventory	160	
Cost of Goods Sold..		160

To restore in the Inventory account the cost of merchandise
returned by a customer.

. . . and the recorded cost of goods sold

Notice that this entry is based upon the *cost* of the returned merchandise to the seller, *not upon its sales price*. (This entry is not necessary when a sales *allowance* is granted to a customer who keeps the merchandise.)

Special accounts are maintained in the inventory subsidiary ledger for returned merchandise. Often this merchandise will be returned to the supplier or sold to a damaged-goods liquidator rather than being offered again for sale to the company's regular customers.[4]

SALES DISCOUNTS

We have explained that sellers frequently offer cash discounts, such as 2/10, n/30, to encourage customers to make early payments for purchases on account.

Sellers and buyers account for cash discounts quite differently. To the seller, the "cost" associated with cash discounts is not the discounts *lost* when payments are delayed, but rather the discounts *taken* by customers that do pay within the discount period. Therefore, sellers design their accounting systems to measure the sales discounts *taken* by their customers. To achieve this goal, the seller records the sale and the related account receivable at the *gross* (full) invoice price.

To illustrate, assume that Computer Barn sells merchandise to Susan Hall for $1,000, offering terms of 2/10, n/30. The sales revenue is recorded at the full invoice price, as shown below:

Accounts Receivable (Susan Hall)	1,000	
Sales..		1,000

Sold merchandise on account. Invoice price, $1,000; terms,
2/10, n/30.

Sales are recorded at the gross sales price

[4]An inventory of returned merchandise should not be valued in the accounting records at a cost which exceeds its *net realizable value*. The possible need to write down the carrying value of inventory is discussed in Chapter 8.

If Hall makes payment after the discount period has expired, Computer Barn merely records the receipt of $1,000 cash in full payment of this account receivable. If Hall pays *within* the discount period, however, she will pay only *$980* to settle her account. In this case, Computer Barn will record the receipt of Hall's payment as follows:

<table>
<tr><td>Cash ....</td><td>980</td><td></td></tr>
<tr><td>Sales Discounts..</td><td>20</td><td></td></tr>
<tr><td>   Accounts Receivable (Susan Hall)..</td><td></td><td>1,000</td></tr>
<tr><td colspan="3">Collected a $1,000 account receivable from a customer who
took a 2% discount for early payment.</td></tr>
</table>

Seller records discounts taken by customers (margin note)

Sales Discounts is another contra-revenue account. In computing net sales, sales discounts are deducted from gross sales along with any sales returns and allowances. (If the customer has returned part of the merchandise, a discount may be taken only on the gross amount owed *after* the return.)

Contra-revenue accounts have much in common with expense accounts; both are deducted from gross revenue in determining net income, and both have debit balances. Thus, contra-revenue accounts (Sales Returns and Allowances and Sales Discounts) are closed into the Income Summary account *in the same manner as expense accounts.*

DELIVERY EXPENSES

If the seller incurs any costs in delivering merchandise to the customer, these costs are debited to an expense account entitled Delivery Expense. In an income statement, delivery expense is classified as a regular operating expense, not as part of the cost of goods sold.

ACCOUNTING FOR SALES TAXES

Sales taxes are levied by many states and cities on retail sales.[5] Sales taxes actually are imposed upon the consumer, not upon the seller. However, the seller must collect the tax, file tax returns at times specified by law, and remit to governmental agencies the taxes collected.

For cash sales, sales tax is collected from the customer at the time of the sales transaction. For credit sales, the sales tax is included in the amount charged to the customer's account. The liability to the governmental unit for sales taxes may be recorded at the time the sale is made, as shown in the following journal entry:

Sales tax recorded at time of sale (margin note)

<table>
<tr><td>Cash (or Accounts Receivable)..</td><td>1,070</td><td></td></tr>
<tr><td>   Sales Tax Payable...</td><td></td><td>70</td></tr>
<tr><td>   Sales ....</td><td></td><td>1,000</td></tr>
<tr><td colspan="3">To record sales of $1,000, subject to 7% sales tax.</td></tr>
</table>

This approach requires a separate credit entry to the Sales Tax Payable account for each sale. At first glance, this may seem to require an excessive amount of bookkeeping. However, today's electronic cash registers automatically record the sales tax liability at the time of each sale.

---

[5]Sales taxes are applicable only when merchandise is sold to the *final consumer;* thus, no sales taxes are levied when manufacturers or wholesalers sell merchandise to retailers.

SUMMARY OF LEARNING OBJECTIVES

① Describe the *operating cycle* of a merchandising company.

The operating cycle is the repeating sequence of transactions by which a company generates revenue and cash receipts from customers. In a merchandising company, the operating cycle consists of the following transactions: (1) purchases of merchandise, (2) sale of the merchandise—often on account, and (3) collection of accounts receivable from customers.

② Define *subsidiary ledgers* and explain their usefulness.

Subsidiary ledgers provide a detailed record of the individual items comprising the balance of a general ledger controlling account. With respect to merchandising transactions, subsidiary ledgers are needed to keep track of the amounts receivable from individual customers, the amounts owed to specific suppliers, and the quantities of specific products in inventory.

③ Account for purchases and sales of merchandise in a *perpetual* inventory system.

In a perpetual inventory system, purchases of merchandise are recorded by debiting the asset Inventory account. Two entries are required to record each sale; one to recognize sales revenue and the second to record the cost of goods sold. This second entry consists of a debit to the expense account Cost of Goods Sold, and a credit to Inventory.

④ Explain how a *periodic* inventory system operates.

In a periodic system, up-to-date records are *not* maintained for inventory or the cost of goods sold. Thus, less record keeping is required than in a perpetual system.

The beginning and ending inventories are determined by taking a complete physical count at each year-end. Purchases are recorded in a Purchases account, and no entries are made to record the cost of individual sales transactions. Instead, the cost of goods sold is determined at year-end by a computation such as the one shown below (dollar amounts are provided only for purposes of example):

Beginning inventory	$ 30,000
Add: Purchases	180,000
Cost of goods available for sale	$210,000
Less: Ending inventory	40,000
Cost of Goods Sold	$170,000

The amounts of inventory and the cost of goods sold are recorded in the accounting records during the year-end closing procedures.

⑤ Discuss factors to be considered in selecting an inventory system.

In general terms, a perpetual system should be used when (1) management and employees need timely information about inventory levels and product sales, and (2) the company has the resources to develop this information at a reasonable cost. A periodic system should be used when the usefulness of current information about inventories does *not justify the cost* of maintaining a perpetual system.

Perpetual systems are most widely used in large companies with computerized accounting systems, and in businesses that sell high-cost merchandise. Periodic systems are most often used in small businesses with manual accounting systems and which sell many types of low-cost merchandise.

⑥ Define *special journals* and explain their usefulness.

Special journals are accounting records or devices designed to record a specific type of transaction in a highly efficient manner. Because a special journal is used only to record a specific type of transaction, the journal may be located at the transaction site and maintained by employees other than accounting personnel. Thus, special journals reduce the time, effort, and cost of recording routine business transactions.

⑦ Compute gross profit margin and explain its usefulness.

Gross profit margin (or gross profit rate) is computed by dividing the dollar amount of gross profit by the related (net) sales revenue. Profit margins can be computed for the business as a whole, and also for individual sales departments, products, and sales transactions.

Investors evaluate a company's overall gross profit rate to gain insight into the strength of the company's products in the marketplace. Management uses departmental and product-line profit margins in setting prices, deciding which products to sell, evaluating departmental performance, and formulating marketing strategies.

⑧ Account for cash discounts, merchandise returns, transportation costs, and sales taxes.

Buyers should record purchases at the *net* cost and record any cash discounts lost in an expense account. Sellers record sales at the gross sales price and record in a contra-revenue account all cash discounts *taken* by customers.

The buyer records a purchase return by crediting the Inventory account for the net cost of the returned merchandise. In recording a sales return, the seller makes two entries: one debiting Sales Returns and Allowances (a contra-revenue account) for the amount of the refund, and the other transferring the cost of the returned merchan-

---

*Supplemental Topic, "Additional Merchandising Transactions."

dise from the Cost of Goods Sold account back into the Inventory account.

Buyers record transportation charges on purchased merchandise either as part of the cost of the merchandise, or as part of the cost of goods sold. Sellers view the cost of delivering merchandise to customers as an operating expense.

Sales taxes are collected by retailers from their customers and paid to state and city governments. Thus, collecting sales taxes increases the retailer's assets and liabilities. Paying the sales tax to the government is payment of the liability, not an expense.

You now have seen how both service-type businesses and merchandising companies measure and report the results of their operations. Many of the illustrations, examples, and assignments throughout the remainder of this textbook will involve merchandising companies.

KEY TERMS INTRODUCED OR EMPHASIZED IN CHAPTER 5

Comparable store sales (p. 229)   Sales at stores with an existing sales "track record." (Also called **same-store sales.**)

Contra-revenue account (p. 235)   A debit balance account which is offset against revenue in the revenue section of the income statement. Examples include Sales Discounts, and Sales Returns and Allowances.

Controlling account (p. 216)   A general ledger account which summarizes the content of a specific subsidiary ledger.

Cost of goods sold (p. 214)   The cost to a merchandising company of the goods it has sold to its customers during the period.

Gross profit (p. 214)   Net sales revenue minus the cost of goods sold.

Gross profit margin (p. 229)   Gross profit expressed as a percentage of net sales. Also called **gross profit rate.**

Inventory (p. 213)   Any type of merchandise intended for resale to customers.

Inventory shrinkage (p. 223)   The loss of merchandise through such causes as shoplifting, breakage, and spoilage.

Net sales (p. 229)   Gross sales revenue less sales returns and allowances and minus sales discounts. The most widely used measure of dollar sales volume; usually the first figure shown in an income statement.

Operating cycle (p. 213)   The repeating sequence of transactions by which a business generates its revenue and cash receipts from customers.

Periodic inventory system (p. 223)   An alternative to the perpetual inventory system. It eliminates the need for recording the cost of goods sold as sales occur. However, the amounts of inventory and the cost of goods sold are not known until a complete physical inventory is taken at year-end.

Perpetual inventory system (p. 220)   A system of accounting for merchandising transactions in which the Inventory and Cost of Goods Sold accounts are kept perpetually up-to-date.

Point-of-sale (POS) terminals (p. 228)   Electronic cash registers used for computer-based processing of sales transactions. The POS terminal identifies each item of merchandise from its *bar code* and then automatically records the sale and updates the computer-based inventory records. These terminals permit the use of perpetual inventory systems in many businesses that sell a high volume of low-cost merchandise.

Sales per-square-foot of selling space (p. 229)   A measure of efficient use of available space.

Special journal (p. 228)   An accounting record or device designed for recording a particular type of transaction quickly and efficiently. A business may use many different kinds of special journals.

Subsidiary ledger (p. 216)   A ledger containing separate accounts for each of the items making up the balance of a controlling account in the general ledger. The total of the account balances in a subsidiary ledger are equal to the balance in the general ledger controlling account.

Taking a physical inventory (p. 223)   The procedure of counting all merchandise on hand and determining its cost.

DEMONSTRATION PROBLEM

STAR-TRACK sells satellite tracking systems for receiving television broadcasts from communications satellites in space. At December 31, 1998, the company's inventory amounted to $44,000. During the first week in January 1999, STAR-TRACK made only one purchase and one sale. These transactions were as follows:

Jan. 3   Sold a tracking system to Mystery Mountain Resort for $20,000 cash. The system consisted of seven different devices, which had a total cost to STAR-TRACK of $11,200.

Jan. 7   Purchased two Model 400 and four Model 800 satellite dishes from Yamaha Corp. The total cost of this purchase amounted to $10,000; terms 2/10, n/30.

STAR-TRACK records purchases of merchandise at net cost. The company has full-time accounting personnel and uses a manual accounting system.

INSTRUCTIONS

a. Briefly describe the operating cycle of a merchandising company.

b. Prepare journal entries to record these transactions, assuming that STAR-TRACK uses a perpetual inventory system.

c. Explain what information in part **b** should be posted to subsidiary ledgers accounts.

d. Compute the balance in the Inventory controlling account at January 7.

e. Prepare journal entries to record the two transactions, assuming that STAR-TRACK uses a *periodic* inventory system.

f. Compute the cost of goods sold for the first week of January, assuming use of the periodic system. As the amount of ending inventory, use your answer to part **d.**

g. Which type of inventory system do you think STAR-TRACK should use? Explain your reasoning.

h. Determine the gross profit margin on the January 3 sales transaction.

SOLUTION TO THE DEMONSTRATION PROBLEM

a. The operating cycle of a merchandising company consists of purchasing merchandise, selling that merchandise to customers (often on account), and collecting the sales proceeds from these customers. In the process, the business converts cash into inventory, the inventory into accounts receivable, and the accounts receivable into cash.

b. Journal entries assuming use of a *perpetual* inventory system:

GENERAL JOURNAL					
Date		**Account Titles and Explanation**	**LP**	**Debit**	**Credit**
1999 Jan.	3	Cash..		20,000	
		Sales..			20,000
		Sold tracking system to Mystery Mountain Resort.			
	3	Cost of Goods Sold		11,200	
		Inventory...			11,200
		To record cost of merchandise sold.			
	7	Inventory		9,800	
		Accounts Payable (Yamaha Corp.).............			9,800
		Purchased merchandise. Terms, 2/10, n/30; net cost, $9,800 ($10,000, less 2%).			

c. The debits and credits to the Inventory account should be posted to the appropriate accounts in the inventory subsidiary ledger. The information posted would be the costs and quantities of the types of merchandise purchased or sold. The account payable to Yamaha also should be posted to the Yamaha account in STAR-TRACK's accounts payable ledger.

No postings are required to the accounts receivable ledger, as this was a cash sale. If STAR-TRACK maintains more than one bank account, however, the debit to cash should be posted to the proper account in the cash subsidiary ledger.

d. <u>$42,600</u> ($44,000 beginning balance, less $11,200, plus $9,800).

e. Journal entries assuming use of a *periodic* inventory system:

GENERAL JOURNAL					
1999 Jan.	3	Cash...		20,000	
		Sales..			20,000
		Sold tracking system to Mystery Mountain Resort.			
	7	Purchases		9,800	
		Accounts Payable (Yamaha Corp.).............			9,800
		Purchased merchandise. Terms, 2/10, n/30; net cost, $9,800 ($10,000, less 2%).			

f. Computation of the cost of goods sold:

Inventory, January 1...	$44,000
Add: Purchases	9,800
Cost of goods available for sale	$53,800
Less: Inventory, January 7 (per part d)	42,600
Cost of goods sold...	$11,200

g. STAR-TRACK should use a *perpetual* inventory system. The items in its inventory have a high per-unit cost. Therefore, management will want to know the costs of the individual products included in specific sales transactions, and also will want to keep track of the items in stock. Although the company has a manual accounting system, its volume of sales transactions is low enough that maintaining a perpetual inventory record will not be difficult.

h. Gross profit = Sales revenue − Cost of goods sold

$$= \$20,000 - \$11,200$$

$$= \$8,800$$

Gross profit margin = Gross profit ÷ Sales revenue

$$= \$8,800 \div \$20,000$$

$$= 44\%$$

SELF-TEST QUESTIONS

Answers to these questions appear on page 254.

1. Mark and Amanda Carter own an appliance store and a restaurant. The appliance store sells merchandise on a 12-month installment plan; the restaurant sells only for cash. Which of the following statements are true? (More than one answer may be correct.)

    a. The appliance store has a longer operating cycle than the restaurant.

    b. The appliance store probably uses a perpetual inventory system, whereas the restaurant probably uses a periodic system.

    c. Both businesses require subsidiary ledgers for accounts receivable and inventory.

    d. Both businesses probably have subsidiary ledgers for accounts payable.

2. Which of the following types of information are found in subsidiary ledgers, but *not* in the general ledger? (More than one answer may be correct.)

    a. Total cost of goods sold for the period.

    b. The quantity of a particular product sold during the period.

    c. The dollar amount owed to a particular creditor.

    d. The portion of total current assets that consists of cash.

3. Marietta Corporation uses a *perpetual* inventory system. The company sells merchandise costing $3,000 at a sales price of $4,300. In recording this transaction, Marietta will make all of the following entries *except:*

    a. Credit Sales, $4,300.

    b. Credit Inventory, $4,300.

    c. Debit Cost of Goods Sold, $3,000.

    d. Credit one or more accounts in the inventory subsidiary ledger for amounts totaling $3,000.

4. Fashion House uses a *perpetual* inventory system. At the beginning of the year, inventory amounted to $50,000. During the year, the company purchased merchandise for $230,000, and sold merchandise costing $245,000. A physical inventory taken at year-end indicated shrinkage losses of $4,000. *Prior to recording these shrinkage losses,* the year-end balance in the company's Inventory account was:

    a. $31,000   **b.** $35,000   **c.** $50,000   **d.** Some other amount.

5. Best Hardware uses a *periodic* inventory system. Its inventory was $38,000 at the beginning of the year and $40,000 at the end. During the year, Best made purchases of merchandise totaling $107,000. Identify all of the correct answers:

    a. To use this system, Best must take a complete physical inventory twice each year.

    b. Prior to making adjusting and closing entries at year-end, the balance in Best's Inventory account is $38,000.

    c. The cost of goods sold for the year is $109,000.

    d. As sales transactions occur, Best makes no entries to update its inventory records or record the cost of goods sold.

6. The two basic approaches to accounting for inventory and the cost of goods sold are the *perpetual* inventory system and the *periodic* inventory system. Indicate which of the following statements are correct. (More than one answer may be correct.)

    a. Most large merchandising companies and manufacturing businesses use periodic inventory systems.

    b. As a practical matter, a grocery store or a large department store could not maintain a perpetual inventory system without the use of point-of-sale terminals.

    c. In a periodic inventory system the cost of goods sold is not determined until a complete physical inventory is taken.

    d. In a perpetual inventory system, the Cost of Goods Sold account is debited promptly for the cost of merchandise sold.

7. Two of the lawnmowers sold by Garden Products Co. are the LawnMaster and the Mark 5. LawnMasters sell for $250 apiece, which results in a 35% profit margin. Each Mark 5 costs Garden Products $300 and sells for $400. Indicate all correct answers.

    a. The dollar amount of gross profit is greater on the sale of a Mark 5 than a LawnMaster.

    b. The profit margin is higher on Mark 5s than on LawnMasters.

    c. Garden profits more by selling one Mark 5 than by selling one LawnMaster.

    d. Garden profits more by selling $2,000 worth of Mark 5s than $2,000 worth of LawnMasters.

*8. Big Brother, a retail store, purchased 100 television sets from Krueger Electronics on account at a cost of $200 each. Krueger offers credit terms of 2/10, n/30. Big Brother uses a perpetual inventory system and records purchases at *net cost*. Big Brother determines that 10 of these television sets are defective and returns them to Krueger for full credit. In recording this return, Big Brother will:
   a. Debit Sales Returns and Allowances.
   b. Debit Accounts Payable, $1,960.
   c. Debit Cost of Goods Sold, $1,960.
   d. Credit Inventory, $2,000.

ASSIGNMENT MATERIAL

DISCUSSION QUESTIONS

1. Describe the operating cycle of a merchandising company.

2. Compare and contrast the merchandising activities of a wholesaler and a retailer.

3. The income statement of a merchandising company includes a major type of cost which does not appear in the income statement of a service-type business. Identify this cost and explain what it represents.

4. During the current year, Green Bay Company earned a gross profit of $350,000, whereas New England Company earned a gross profit of only $280,000. Does this mean that Green Bay is more profitable than New England? Explain.

5. Thornhill Company's income statement shows gross profit of $432,000, cost of goods sold of $638,000, and other expenses totaling $390,000. Compute the amounts of (a) revenue from sales (net sales) and (b) net income.

6. Explain the need for subsidiary ledgers in accounting for merchandising activities.

7. All Night Auto Parts, Inc., maintains subsidiary ledgers for accounts receivable, inventory, and accounts payable. Explain in detail what information from the following journal entry should be posted, and to which subsidiary and general ledger accounts.

Inventory	420	
Accounts Payable (Boss Automotive)...		420
Purchased 12 Boss LoadMaster II shock absorbers. Cost,		
$35 per unit.		

8. What is meant by the phrase "reconciling a subsidiary ledger"? In general terms, what is the purpose of this procedure?

9. Define the term *inventory shrinkage*. How is the amount of inventory shrinkage determined in a business using a perpetual inventory system, and how is this shrinkage recorded in the accounting records?

10. Briefly contrast the accounting procedures in *perpetual* and *periodic* inventory systems.

11. Miracle Home Cleanser uses a *periodic* inventory system. During the current year the company purchased merchandise with a cost of $55,000. State the cost of goods sold for the year under each of the following alternative assumptions:
   a. No beginning inventory; ending inventory $3,500.
   b. Beginning inventory $10,000; no ending inventory.

---

*Supplemental Topic, "Additional Merchandising Transactions."

    c. Beginning inventory $2,000; ending inventory $7,200.

    d. Beginning inventory $8,000; ending inventory $1,400.

12. Evaluate the following statement: "Without electronic point-of-sale terminals, it simply would not be possible to use perpetual inventory systems in businesses which sell large quantities of many different products."

13. Explain the distinguishing characteristics of (a) a general journal, and (b) a special journal.

14. Western Stores, a chain of hardware stores, had an increase in net sales of 8% for this year in relation to the prior year. Does this mean that the company's marketing strategies, such as advertising, pricing, and product mix, are succeeding?

15. Define the term *gross profit margin*. Explain several ways in which management might improve a company's overall profit margin.

*16. How does a balance arise in the Purchase Discounts Lost account? Why does management pay careful attention to the balance (if any) in this account?

*17. European Imports pays substantial freight charges to obtain inbound shipments of purchased merchandise. Should these freight charges be debited to the company's Delivery Expense account? Explain.

*18. Outback Sporting Goods purchases merchandise on terms of 4/10, n/60. The company has a "line of credit" which enables it to borrow money as needed from Northern Bank at an annual interest rate of 13%. Should Outback pay its suppliers within the 10-day discount period if it must draw on its line of credit (borrow from Northern Bank) to make these early payments? Explain.

*19. TireCo is a retail store in a state that imposes a 6% sales tax. Would you expect to find sales tax expense and sales tax payable in TireCo's financial statements? Explain.

*20. A seller generally records sales at the full invoice price, but the buyer often records purchases at *net cost*. Explain the logic of the buyer and seller recording the transaction at different amounts.

EXERCISES

EXERCISE 5-1
Determining the
Information Needs
for Ordering Merchandise

LO 3

Assume that you have been given the responsibility of ordering tee shirts to be sold at a series of 10 summer rock concerts that will be sponsored by your student organization. The tee shirts, which will be specifically designed for each concert, will come in two styles, short and long sleeve. You must decide on the optimal number of tee shirts to order for each concert. The following information about last year's activities is all that is available to help you make your decisions:

1. Last year, the short sleeve and long sleeve tee shirts were sold on the night of the concert at $15 and $20, respectively. On the following day, any unsold tee shirts were put on sale on campus at a reduced price of $7.50. Any shirts not sold on that day were donated to a local orphanage.

2. For each concert, you have (a) the total cost of the shirts for that concert, (b) the amount of cash receipts from the combined sales on the night of the concert and on the next day, and (c) the total attendance figures.

    a. Describe the *additional information* about last year's shirt sales that would be useful in making your ordering decisions.

    b. Explain how you would make the ordering decisions for this year, assuming that you had *both* the information described above and the additional information identified in part **a.**

    c. Describe the types of information from this year's shirt sales that you would record and pass on to the person performing this task next year.

---

*Supplemental Topic, "Additional Merchandising Transactions."

EXERCISE 5-2
Effects of Basic
Merchandising
Transactions

Shown below are selected transactions of Kiger's, a retail store which uses a perpetual inventory system:

a. Purchased merchandise on account.

b. Recognized the revenue from a sale of merchandise on account. (Ignore the related cost of goods sold.)

c. Recognized the cost of goods sold relating to the sale in transaction **b.**

d. Collected in cash the account receivable from the customer in transaction **b.**

e. Following the taking of a physical inventory at year-end, made an adjusting entry to record a normal amount of inventory shrinkage.

Indicate the effects of each of these transactions upon the elements of the company's financial statements shown below. Organize your answer in tabular form, using the column headings shown below. (Notice that the cost of goods sold is shown separately from all other expenses.) Use the code letters **I** for increase, **D** for decrease, and **NE** for no effect.

	Income Statement				Balance Sheet		
Transaction	Net Sales	− Cost of Goods Sold	− All Other Expenses	= Net Income	Assets	= Liabilities	+ Owners' Equity
a	_____	_____	_____	_____	_____	_____	_____

EXERCISE 5-3
Subsidiary Ledgers
LO 2,8

Listed below are eight typical merchandising transactions of Everyday Auto Parts, a retail auto supply store.

a. Purchased merchandise from Acme Wholesale on account.

b. Paid an account payable to a supplier.

c. Sold merchandise for cash.

d. Sold merchandise on account.

e. Collected an account receivable from a customer.

*f. Returned merchandise to a supplier, receiving credit against the amount owed.

*g. Gave a cash refund to a customer who returned merchandise.

*h. Reduced the account receivable from a credit customer who returned merchandise.

Among the accounting records of Everyday Auto Parts are subsidiary ledgers for inventory, accounts receivable, and accounts payable. For each of the eight transactions, you are to indicate any subsidiary ledger (or ledgers) to which the transaction would be posted. Use the codes below:

Inv = Inventory subsidiary ledger
AR = Accounts receivable subsidiary ledger
AP = Accounts payable subsidiary ledger

Also indicate whether each posting causes the balance in the subsidiary ledger account to *increase* or *decrease*. Organize your answer in tabular form as illustrated below. The answer for transaction **a** is provided as an example.

Transaction	Subsidiary Ledger	Effect upon Subsidiary Account Balance
a	Inv	Increase
	AP	Increase

*Supplemental Topic, "Additional Merchandising Transactions."

EXERCISE 5-4
Posting to Subsidiary
Ledgers

In addition to a general ledger, LeatherWorks maintains subsidiary ledgers for accounts receivable, inventory, and accounts payable (the company does not maintain a subsidiary ledger for cash). Two entries appearing in the company's journal are illustrated, along with the posting references, which have been entered in the LP column:

GENERAL JOURNAL			
Account Titles and Explanation	**LP**	**Debit**	**Credit**
Inventory...	130/✓	2,500	
Accounts Payable (Pucci, Inc.)...........................	✓		2,500
Purchased 50 shoulder bags from Pucci, Inc., @ $50; payment due in 30 days.			
Cash	101	6,000	
Accounts Recievable (The Bag Man).............................	105		6,000
Collected an account receivable.			

a. Based upon the posting references shown, explain in detail the accounts to which the debit and credit portions of each journal entry apparently have been posted.

b. Does it appear that the posting of each entry has been completed properly? Explain. (Assume that illustrated account numbers are correct.)

EXERCISE 5-5
Perpetual Inventory System
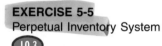

Concord Products uses a perpetual inventory system. On January 1 the Inventory account had a balance of $84,500. During the first few days of January the following transactions occurred:

Jan. 2 Purchased merchandise on credit from Smith Company for $9,200.

Jan. 3 Sold merchandise for cash, $22,000. The cost of this merchandise was $14,300.

a. Prepare entries in general journal form to record the above transactions.

b. What was the balance of the Inventory account at the close of business January 3?

EXERCISE 5-6
Evaluating Performance

Shown below are selected statistics from the recent annual reports of two well-known retailers.

	Sears, Roebuck and Co.	Broadway Stores, Inc.
Percentage increase (decrease) in net sales	7.2%	(0.3%)
Percentage increase in comparable store net sales	4.7%	3.1%

a. Explain the meaning and significance of each of the two measures.

b. Evaluate the performance of the two companies based on the two measures.

EXERCISE 5-7
Taking a Physical Inventory
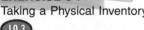

Electronics Warehouse uses a perpetual inventory system. At year-end, the Inventory account has a balance of $314,000, but a physical count shows that the merchandise on hand has a cost of only $309,100.

a. Explain the probable reason(s) for this discrepancy.

b. Prepare the journal entry required in this situation.

c. Indicate all the accounting records to which your journal entry in part **b** should be posted.

EXERCISE 5-8
Periodic Inventory Systems
 LO 4

Warren's Gift Shop uses a periodic inventory system. At the end of 1998, the accounting records include the following information:

Inventory (as of December 31, 1998)	$ 10,400
Net sales	198,500
Purchases	105,000

A complete physical inventory taken at December 31, 1999 indicates merchandise costing *$9,600* remains in stock.

a. How were the amounts of beginning and ending inventory determined?

b. Compute the amount of the cost of goods sold in 1999.

c. Prepare two closing entries at December 31, 1999 which will have the effects of creating a Cost of Goods Sold account with the appropriate balance, and bringing the Inventory account up-to-date.

d. Prepare a partial income statement showing the shop's gross profit for the year.

e. Describe why a company such as Warren's Gift Shop would use a periodic inventory system rather than a perpetual inventory system.

EXERCISE 5-9
Relationships within Periodic
Inventory Systems
 LO 4

This exercise stresses the relationships between the information recorded in a periodic inventory system and the basic elements of an income statement. Each of the five lines represents a separate set of information. You are to copy the table and fill in the missing amounts. A net loss in the right-hand column is to be indicated by placing brackets around the amount, as for example, in line **e** (25,000).

	Net Sales	Beginning Inventory	Net Purchases	Ending Inventory	Cost of Goods Sold	Gross Profit	Expenses	Net Income or (Loss)
a.	300,000	95,000	130,000	44,000	?	119,000	90,000	?
b.	600,000	90,000	340,000	?	330,000	?	?	25,000
c.	700,000	230,000	?	185,000	490,000	210,000	165,000	?
d.	900,000	?	500,000	150,000	?	260,000	300,000	?
e.	?	260,000	?	255,000	660,000	225,000	?	(25,000)

EXERCISE 5-10
Selecting an Appropriate
Inventory System
 LO 5

Select a specific merchandising business in your area. Briefly describe the nature of the business, and indicate whether you think a perpetual or a periodic inventory system is more appropriate. *Explain your reasoning and be prepared to discuss your answer in class.* (Notice that you are not asked to determine the type of inventory system actually in use.)

EXERCISE 5-11
Gross Profit Margins
 LO 7

Shown below is selected information from the recent annual reports of three well-known retailers. (Dollar amounts are stated in millions.)

	Kmart	Nordstrom	Toys "R" Us
Net sales	$34,389	$? *4114*	$7,169
Cost of goods sold	26,996	2,806	?
Gross profit *26996*	?	1,308	?
Gross profit rate	*7393*?%	*1308* ?%	30.7%
		21.5 *31.8*	

gross margin

a. Copy this table, filling in the missing amounts and percentages. (Round dollar amounts to the nearest million, and percentages to the nearest tenth of one percent.)

b. Based upon this data, comment upon the relative sales volume and gross profit margins of Kmart and Toys "R" Us. Is this data consistent with your knowledge (or impression) of these two retailers?

---

*EXERCISE 5-12
Cash Discounts

LO 8

Key Imports sold merchandise to Marine Systems for $8,000, offering terms of 2/10, n/30. Marine Systems paid for the merchandise within the discount period. Both companies use perpetual inventory systems.

a. Prepare journal entries in the accounting records of Key Imports to account for this sale and the subsequent collection. Assume the original cost of the merchandise to Key Imports had been $4,800.

b. Prepare journal entries in the accounting records of Marine Systems to account for the purchase and subsequent payment. Marine Systems records purchases of merchandise at *net cost.*

c. Assume that because of a change in personnel, Marine Systems failed to pay for this merchandise within the discount period. Prepare the journal entry in the accounting records of Marine Systems to record payment *after* the discount period.

EXERCISE 5-13
Evaluating Performance
of a Merchandising
Company
LO 7

The annual report of **Toys "R" Us, Inc.,** appears in Appendix A. The report includes *"Management's Discussion—Results of Operations and Financial Condition."*

a. Calculate the gross profit percentage for Toys "R" Us for the three years shown in the income statements on page A-7 (fiscal 1994, 1993, and 1992).

b. Read the first paragraph of *"Management's Discussion—Results of Operations and Financial Condition"* (page A-6) and extract any measures of sales effectiveness that are contained therein.

c. Evaluate the company's trend in sales and gross profit to date.

d. Read the top paragraph in the right-hand column of the letter addressed "To Our Stockholders" (page A-2). Does it appear that management is confident these trends will continue into the coming year?

PROBLEMS

PROBLEM 5-1
The Only Lumberyard
in Snow Valley

LO 1,3,7

Tyler Lumber Co. is the only lumberyard in Snow Valley, a remote mountain town and popular ski resort. Some of Tyler's transactions during 1999 are as follows:

Nov. 5 Sold lumber on account to Snow Valley Construction, $66,950. The inventory subsidiary ledger shows the cost of this merchandise to Tyler was $45,525.

---

*Supplemental Topic, "Additional Merchandising Transactions."

Nov.   **9**   Purchased lumber on account from Lonesome Pine Mill, $190,000.

Dec.   **5**   Collected in cash the $66,950 account receivable from Snow Valley Construction.

Dec.   **9**   Paid the $190,000 owed to Lonesome Pine Mill.

Dec. 31   Company personnel counted the inventory on hand and determined its cost to be $910,400. The accounting records, however, indicate inventory of $918,950 and a cost of goods sold of $3,476,110. The physical count of the inventory was observed by the company's auditors and is considered correct.

INSTRUCTIONS

a. Prepare journal entries to record these transactions and events in the accounting records of Tyler Lumber Co. (The company uses a perpetual inventory system.)

b. Prepare a partial income statement showing the company's gross profit for the year. (Net sales for the year amount to $5,124,500.)

c. Tyler purchases lumber at the same wholesale prices as other lumber companies. Due to its remote mountain location, however, the company must pay between $90,000 and $100,000 per year in extra transportation charges to receive delivery of its purchased lumber. (These additional charges are included in the amount shown as cost of goods sold.)

Assume that an index of key business ratios in your library shows retail lumberyards of Tyler's approximate size (in total assets) average net sales of $5,000,000 per year and a gross profit rate of *26%*.

Is Tyler Lumber Co. able to pass its extra transportation costs on to its customers? Does the company appear to suffer or benefit financially from its remote location? Explain your reasoning and support your conclusions with specific accounting data comparing the operations of Tyler Lumber Co. with the industry averages.

PROBLEM 5-2
Perpetual Inventory
System and an Inventory
Subsidiary Ledger

LO 1,2,3

Facts-by-FAX sells facsimile machines, copiers, and other types of office equipment. On May 10, the company purchased for the first time a new plain-paper fax machine manufactured by Mitsui Corporation. Transactions relating to this product during May and June were as follows:

May 10   Purchased five P-500 facsimile machines on account from Mitsui Corporation, at a cost of $560 each. Payment due in 30 days.

May 23   Sold four P-500 facsimile machines on account to Foster & Cole, stockbrokers; sales price, $900 per machine. Payment due in 30 days.

May 24   Purchased an additional seven P-500 facsimile machines on account from Mitsui. Cost, $560 per machine; payment due in 30 days.

June 9   Paid $2,800 cash to Mitsui Corporation for the facsimile machines purchased on May 10.

June 19   Sold two P-500 facsimile machines to Tri-State Realty for cash. Sales price, $950 per machine.

June 22   Collected $3,600 from Foster & Cole in full settlement of the credit sale on May 23.

INSTRUCTIONS

a. Prepare journal entries to record these transactions in the accounting records of Facts-by-FAX. (The company uses a perpetual inventory system.)

b. Post the appropriate information from these journal entries to an inventory subsidiary ledger account like the one illustrated on page 217.)

c. How many Mitsui P-500 facsimile machines were in inventory on May 31? From what accounting record did you obtain the answer to this question?

d. Describe the types of information contained in any inventory subsidiary ledger account and explain how this information may be useful to various company personnel in conducting daily business operations.

PROBLEM 5-3
Evaluating the Sales
Performance of a
Merchandising
Company

Shown below is information from the financial reports of Ultra Department Stores for the last few years.

	1999	1998	1997
Net sales (in millions)...	$13,454	$12,987	$12,224
Number of stores	1,180	1,172	1,130
Square feet of selling space (in millions)	61.5	59.0	54.8
Average net sales of comparable stores (in millions)............	$ 10.9	$ 11.2	$ 11.5

INSTRUCTIONS

a. Calculate the following statistics for Ultra Department Stores:

1. The percentage change in net sales from 1997 to 1998 and 1998 to 1999. *Hint:* The percentage change is computed by dividing the dollar amount of the change between years by the amount of the base year. For example, the percentage change in net sales from 1997 to 1998 is computed by dividing the difference between 1998 and 1997 net sales by the amount of 1997 net sales, or ($12,987 − $12,224) ÷ $12,224 = 3.6% increase.

2. The percentage change in net sales per square foot of selling space from 1997 to 1998 and 1998 to 1999.

3. The percentage change in comparable store sales from 1997 to 1998 and 1998 to 1999.

b. Evaluate the sales performance of Ultra Department Stores.

PROBLEM 5-4
The Periodic Inventory
System

Mountain Mabel's is a small general store located just outside of Yellowstone National Park. The store uses a periodic inventory system. Every January 1, Mabel and her husband close the store and take a complete physical inventory while watching the Rose Parade on television. Last year, the inventory amounted to $5,200; this year it totaled $3,800. During the current year, the business recorded sales of $125,000 and purchases of $62,000.

INSTRUCTIONS

a. Compute the cost of goods sold for the current year.

b. Explain why a small business such as this might use the periodic inventory system.

c. Explain some of the *disadvantages* of the periodic system to a larger business, such as a Sears store.

PROBLEM 5-5
Comparison of Inventory
Systems

Explorer Scopes sells state-of-the-art telescopes to individuals and organizations interested in studying the solar system. At December 31 last year, the company's inventory amounted to $120,000. During the first week of January this year, the company made only one purchase and one sale. These transactions were as follows:

Jan. 2 Sold one telescope costing $37,200 to Central State University for cash, $62,000.

Jan. 5 Purchased merchandise on account from Lunar Optics, $80,000. Terms, net 30 days.

INSTRUCTIONS

a. Prepare journal entries to record these transactions assuming that Explorer Scopes uses the perpetual inventory system. Use separate entries to record the sales revenue and the cost of goods sold for the sale on January 2.

b. Compute the balance of the Inventory account on January 7.

c. Prepare journal entries to record the two transactions, assuming that Explorer Scopes uses the periodic inventory system.

d. Compute the cost of goods sold for the first week of January assuming use of a periodic inventory system. Use your answer to part **b** as the ending inventory.

e. Which inventory system do you believe that a company such as Explorer Scopes would probably use? Explain your reasoning.

*PROBLEM 5-6
Comparison of Net Cost and Gross Price Methods

Fedders TV uses a perpetual inventory system. Shown below are three recent merchandising transactions:

June 10 Purchased 10 televisions from Shogun Electronics on account. Invoice price, $250 per unit, for a total of $2,500. The terms of purchase were 2/10, n/30.

June 15 Sold one of these televisions for $400 cash.

June 20 Paid the account payable to Shogun within the discount period.

INSTRUCTIONS

a. Prepare journal entries to record these transactions assuming that Fedders records purchases of merchandise at:
  1. Net cost
  2. Gross invoice price

b. Assume that Fedders did *not* pay Shogun within the discount period, but instead paid the full invoice price on July 10. Prepare journal entries to record this payment assuming that the original liability had been recorded at:
  1. Net cost
  2. Gross invoice price

c. Assume that you are evaluating the efficiency of Fedder's bill-paying procedures. Which accounting method—net cost or gross invoice price—provides you with the most *useful* information? Explain.

*PROBLEM 5-7
Merchandising Transactions

Shown below is a series of related transactions between Texas Wholesale Corp. and Boot Hill, a chain of retail stores:

Feb. 9 Texas Wholesale Corp. sold Boot Hill 100 pairs of boots on account, terms 1/10, n/30. The cost of these boots to Texas Wholesale was $32 per pair, and the sales price was $50 per pair.

Feb. 12 United Express charged $162 for delivering this merchandise to Boot Hill. These charges were split evenly between the buyer and seller, and were paid immediately in cash.

Feb. 13 Boot Hill returned 10 pairs of boots to Texas Wholesale because they were the wrong style. Texas Wholesale allowed Boot Hill full credit for this return.

Feb. 19 Boot Hill paid the remaining balance due to Texas Wholesale within the discount period.

Both companies use a perpetual inventory system.

---

*Supplemental Topic, "Additional Merchandising Transactions."

INSTRUCTIONS

a. Record this series of transactions in the general journal of Texas Wholesale Corp. (The company records sales at gross sales price.)

b. Record this series of transactions in the general journal of Boot Hill. (The company records purchases of merchandise at *net cost* and uses a Transportation-in account to record transportation charges on inbound shipments.)

c. Boot Hill does not always have enough cash on hand to pay for purchases within the discount period. However, it has a line of credit with its bank, which enables Boot Hill to easily borrow money for short periods of time at an annual interest rate of 9%. (The bank charges interest only for the number of days until Boot Hill repays the loan.) As a matter of general policy, should Boot Hill take advantage of 1/10, n/30 cash discounts even if it must borrow the money to do so at an annual rate of 9%? Explain fully—and illustrate any supporting computations.

*PROBLEM 5-8
A Comprehensive Problem

LO 1–8

Best Business Products (BBP) sells business machines. At December 31, 1998, BBP's inventory amounted to $240,000. During the first week in January 1999, the company made only one purchase and one sale. These transactions were as follows:

Jan. 2 Purchased 10 copiers and 20 fax machines from Sharp. The total cost of these machines was $90,000, terms 3/10, n/60.

Jan. 6 Sold five different types of machines on account to Pace Corporation. The total sales price was $60,000, terms 5/10, n/90. The total cost of these five machines to BBP was $37,200.

BBP has a full-time accountant and a computer-based accounting system. It records sales at the gross sales price and purchases at net cost, and maintains subsidiary ledgers for accounts receivable, inventory, and accounts payable.

INSTRUCTIONS

a. Briefly describe the operating cycle of a merchandising company. Identify the assets and liabilities directly affected by this cycle.

b. Prepare journal entries to record these transactions, assuming that BBP uses a perpetual inventory system.

c. Explain the information in part **b** that should be posted to subsidiary ledgers accounts.

d. Compute the balance in the Inventory controlling account at the close of business on Jan. 6.

e. Prepare journal entries to record the two transactions assuming that BBP uses a *periodic* inventory system.

f. Compute the cost of goods sold for the first week of January assuming use of the periodic system. (Use your answer to part **d** as the ending inventory.)

g. Which type of inventory system do you think BBP would most likely use? Explain your reasoning.

h. Compute the gross profit margin on the January 6 sales transaction.

CASES AND UNSTRUCTURED PROBLEMS

CASE 5-1
What Would You Expect?

LO 5

In each of the following situations, indicate whether you would expect the business to use a periodic inventory system or a perpetual inventory system. Explain the reasons for your answer.

**Supplemental Topic,* "Additional Merchandising Transactions."

a. The Frontier Shop is a small retail store that sells boots and western clothing. The store is operated by the owner, who works full time in the business, and by one part-time salesclerk. Sales transactions are recorded on an antique cash register. The business uses a manual accounting system, which is maintained by ACE Bookkeeping Service. At the end of each month, an employee of ACE visits The Frontier Shop to update its accounting records, prepare sales tax returns, and perform other necessary accounting services.

b. Allister's Corner is an art gallery in the Soho district of New York. All accounting records are maintained manually by the owner, who works in the store on a full-time basis. The store sells three or four paintings each week, at sales prices ranging from about $5,000 to $50,000 per painting.

c. A publicly owned corporation publishes about 200 titles of college-level textbooks. The books are sold to college bookstores throughout the country. Books are distributed to these bookstores from four central warehouses, located in California, Texas, Ohio, and Virginia.

d. Toys-4-You operates a national chain of 86 retail toy stores. The company has a state-of-the-art computerized accounting system. All sales transactions are recorded on electronic point-of-sale terminals. These terminals are tied into a central computer system which provides the national headquarters with information about the profitability of each store on a weekly basis.

e. Mr. Jingles is an independently owned and operated ice cream truck.

f. TransComm is a small company that sells very large quantities of a single product. The product is a low-cost, 3.5 inch, double-sided, double-density floppy computer disc, manufactured by a large Japanese company. Sales are made only in large quantities, primarily to chains of computer stores and large discount stores. This year, the average sales transaction has amounted to $14,206 worth of merchandise. All accounting records are maintained by a full-time employee using commercial accounting software and a personal computer.

CASE 5-2
Hey, You! Put That Back!
LO 4,7

Village Hardware is a retail store selling hardware, small appliances, and sporting goods. The business follows a policy of selling all merchandise at exactly twice the amount of its cost to the store and uses a *periodic* inventory system.

At year-end, the following information is taken from the accounting records:

Net sales	$400,000
Inventory, January 1	40,000
Purchases	205,000

A physical count indicates merchandise costing $34,000 is on hand at December 31.

INSTRUCTIONS

a. Prepare a partial income statement showing computation of the gross profit for the year.

b. Upon seeing your income statement, the owner of the store makes the following comment: "Inventory shrinkage losses are really costing me. If it weren't for shrinkage losses, the store's gross profit would be 50% of net sales. I'm going to hire a security guard and put an end to shoplifting once and for all."

   Determine the amount of loss from inventory "shrinkage" stated (1) at cost, and (2) at retail sales value. (*Hint:* Without any shrinkage losses, the cost of goods sold and the amount of gross profit would each amount to 50% of net sales.)

c. Assume that Village Hardware could virtually eliminate shoplifting by hiring a security guard at a cost of $1,500 per month. Would this strategy be profitable? Explain your reasoning.

CASE 5-3
Out of Balance
LO 2

Marcus Dean works in the accounts payable department of Artistic Furniture, a large retail furniture store. At month-end, Dean's supervisor assigned him the task of reconciling the accounts payable subsidiary ledger with the controlling account.

Dean found that the balance of the controlling account was $4,500 higher than the sum of the subsidiary ledger accounts. He traced this error to a transaction occurring early in the month. Artistic had purchased $9,400 in merchandise on account from Appalachian Woods, a regular supplier. The transaction had been recorded correctly in Artistic's journal, and posted correctly to the Inventory and Accounts Payable accounts in the general ledger. The $9,400 credit to Accounts Payable, however, had erroneously been posted as *$4,900* to the Appalachian Woods account in Artistic's accounts payable subsidiary ledger.

Artistic uses its subsidiary ledger as the basis for making payment to its suppliers. In the middle of the month, Artistic had sent a check to Appalachian in the amount of $4,900. This $4,900 payment was recorded and posted correctly to both the general and subsidiary ledger accounts. Thus, at the end of the month the subsidiary ledger account for Appalachian Woods had a zero balance.

Dean learned that Appalachian had failed to detect Artistic's error. The month-end statement from Appalachian simply said "Account paid in full." Therefore, Dean proposed the following "correcting entry" to bring Artistic's controlling account into balance with the subsidiary ledger and the supplier's month-end statement:

Accounts Payable	4,500	
Miscellaneous Revenue		4,500

To reduce Accounts Payable controlling account for unpaid amount that was not rebilled by the supplier.

This entry is to be posted to the general ledger accounts, but not to the accounts payable subsidiary ledger.

INSTRUCTIONS

a. Will the proposed correcting entry bring the Accounts Payable controlling account into agreement with the accounts in the subsidiary ledger?

b. Identify and discuss any ethical considerations that you see in this situation, and suggest an appropriate course of action.

CASE 5-4
Group Assignment
with Business
Community
Involvement
LO 3,4,5,6

Identify one local business that uses a perpetual inventory system, and another that uses a periodic system. Interview an individual in each organization who is familiar with the inventory system and the recording of sales transactions. (Interviews are to be planned and conducted in accordance with the instructions in the Preface of this textbook.)

INSTRUCTIONS

Separately for each business organization:

a. Describe the procedures used in accounting for sales transactions, keeping track of inventory levels, and determining the cost of goods sold. (Ignore the types of "additional transactions" addressed in the *Supplemental Topic* section of this chapter.)

b. Explain the reasons offered by the person interviewed as to *why* the business uses this type of system.

c. Indicate whether your group considers the system in use appropriate under the circumstances. If not, recommend specific changes. *Explain your reasoning.*

Supplemental Topic, "Additional Merchandising Transactions."

INTERNET ASSIGNMENTS

You can find a large amount of information on the Internet to evaluate the performance of companies. Many companies provide links to this information on their home pages. Access the home page of **Gap, Inc.,** at the following Internet location:

www.gap.com

Click on "Financial Information" under the category "Company" to view a listing of the information that is available about the company.

INSTRUCTIONS

a. Click on one of the "Monthly Sales Reports" and evaluate the company's sales performance for the month and year-to-date.

b. Under the category "SEC filings," click on "Gap's page" to get to the SEC's EDGAR database of financial information about publicly owned companies. Select the Gap's most recent 10-Q, which is a required quarterly filing that includes quarterly financial statements. Use the financial statements and "Management's Discussion and Analysis of Operations" to answer the following questions:

1. Did sales increase or decrease in the current quarter in relation to the same quarter in the preceding year?

2. Did inventory increase or decrease in the current quarter in relation to the same quarter in the preceding year?

3. How many new stores did the company open this quarter? How many did it close?

4. What was the amount of sales per average square foot of selling space in this quarter? Was this an improvement over the same quarter for the preceding year?

Note: Additional Internet Assignments for this chapter appear in Appendix B and on our home page (www.mcgrawhill.com/financial-mbw).

OUR COMMENTS ON THE IN-TEXT CASES

YOU AS A CREDIT MANAGER (P. 219)   The accounts receivable subsidiary ledger provides a historical record of sales to Dave's Toy Store. You, as the credit manager, can readily see how much Dave has purchased from your company for the last week, month, year, or any longer period of time. The ledger also provides you with information about Dave's payment history. You can determine definitely whether Dave's Toy Store has paid its bills from your company on a timely basis.

Other information that would be useful for your decision would be recent financial statements of Dave's Toy Stores, and current credit reports from agencies such as Dun & Bradstreet.

YOU AS A BUYER FOR A RETAIL BUSINESS (P. 227)   If Acme maintains perpetual inventory records, these records would provide a host of information that would be useful to your purchasing decision. From the perpetual inventory records, you can determine the number, brand, and type of barbecues currently on hand, and the number of each sold in prior summer seasons. This information will be very useful in estimating the merchandise needs for the current season.

If Acme does not have perpetual inventory records, you would be forced to make your decision without this information about inventory on hand and prior sales, or to spend a significant amount of time developing the information.

ANSWERS TO SELF-TEST QUESTIONS

1. a, b, d   **2.** b, c   **3.** b   **4.** b   **5.** b, d   **6.** b. c, d   **7.** a, c   ***8.** b

---

Supplemental Topic, "Additional Merchandising Transactions."

INTRODUCTION TO FINANCIAL STATEMENT ANALYSIS AND THE STATEMENT OF CASH FLOWS

Location:

| Search | Feedback | Help | Directory |

Document: Done

In today's global economy, investment capital is always "on the move." Through organized capital markets such as the *New York Stock Exchange,* investors each day shift billions of investment dollars among different companies, industries, and nations. Capital flows to those areas in which investors expect to earn the greatest returns with the least risk. How do investors forecast risk and potential returns? Primarily by analyzing accounting information.

1 Explain the nature and purpose of *classifications* in financial statements.

2 Prepare a classified balance sheet. Compute widely used measures of liquidity and credit risk.

3 Interpret and evaluate financial ratios and measurements.

4 Explain owners' *personal* liability for the debts of a business.

5 Prepare a multiple-step and a single-step income statement.

6 Compute widely used measures of profitability.

7 Describe the purpose, content, and format of a statement of cash flows.

The goal of accounting is to provide economic decision makers with useful information. Let us now see how decision makers may use the information contained in financial statements to gain insight into a company's financial position, profitability, and future prospects. As our primary example, we will use the 1998 financial statements of Computer Barn—the merchandising company introduced in Chapter 5.

FINANCIAL STATEMENTS ARE DESIGNED FOR ANALYSIS

Financial statements are designed to assist users in identifying key relationships and trends. The financial statements of most publicly owned companies are "classified," and are presented in "comparative form." Often, the word "consolidated" appears in the headings of the statements. Users of financial statements should have a clear understanding of these terms.

LO 1 *Explain the nature and purpose of* classifications *in financial statements.*

Most business organizations prepare **classified financial statements,** meaning that items with certain characteristics are placed together in a group, or "classification." The purpose of these classifications is to *develop useful subtotals* which will assist users of the statements in their analyses. These classifications and subtotals are standardized throughout most of American business, a practice which assists decision makers in comparing the financial statements of different companies.

In **comparative financial statements,** the financial statement amounts *for several years* appear side by side in vertical columns. This assists investors in identifying and evaluating significant changes and trends.

Most large corporations own other companies through which they conduct some of their business activities. A corporation which owns other businesses is the **parent company,** and the owned companies are called **subsidiaries.** For example, PepsiCo., which makes Pepsi Cola, also owns and operates Pizza Hut, Taco Bell, and Frito-Lay. In essence, these subsidiaries are "parts" of the organization generally known as PepsiCo. **Consolidated financial statements** present the financial position and operating results of the parent company and its subsidiaries *as if they were a single business organization.*

FOR EXAMPLE . . . At this point, take a brief look at the financial statements of Toys "R" Us, which appear in Appendix A at the end of the text. These financial statements illustrate all of the concepts discussed above; they are classified, presented in comparative form, and describe a consolidated business entity. These financial statements also have been *audited* by Ernst & Young, an international public accounting firm.

MEASURES OF LIQUIDITY AND CREDIT RISK

In the following sections of this chapter, we introduce a number of ratios and other computations used in financial statement analysis. Most of these computations are used in evaluating liquidity and credit risk, or profitability.

Measures of liquidity and credit risk are of interest primarily to *creditors* of the organization. However, equity investors too have an interest in a company's liquidity. If a company becomes *insolvent,* it may be forced into bankruptcy. Eventually, the company may have to cease operations and sell its assets to satisfy the claims of creditors. Such a sequence of events may greatly reduce—or perhaps eliminate—the owners' equity in the company.

The most common measures of liquidity (or solvency) and credit risk are developed from a *classified balance sheet.* Before introducing these measures, let us discuss the format and content of a classified balance sheet.

A CLASSIFIED BALANCE SHEET

In a classified balance sheet, assets usually are presented in three groups: (1) current assets, (2) plant and equipment, and (3) other assets. Liabilities are classified into two categories: (1) current liabilities and (2) long-term debt. A classified balance sheet for Computer Barn appears on the following page.

The classifications **current assets** and **current liabilities** are especially useful in evaluating the short-term liquidity—or solvency—of the business entity.

CURRENT ASSETS   Current assets are relatively "liquid" resources. This category includes cash, investments in marketable securities, receivables, inventories, and prepaid expenses. To qualify as a current asset, an asset must be capable of *being converted into cash* within a relatively short period of time, without interfering with normal business operations. *1 year*

The time period in which current assets are expected to be converted into cash usually is one year. If a company requires more than a year to complete its normal operating cycle, however, the *length of the operating cycle* defines current assets.[1] Thus, inventory and accounts receivable normally qualify as current assets, even if these assets require more than one year to convert into cash.

In a balance sheet, current assets are listed in order of liquidity. (The closer an asset is to becoming cash, the greater its liquidity.) Thus, cash always is listed first among the current assets, followed by investments in marketable securities, receivables, inventory, and prepaid expenses.[2]

CURRENT LIABILITIES   Current liabilities are *existing debts* which must be paid within the same time period used in defining current assets. Among the most common current liabilities are notes payable (due within one year), accounts payable, unearned revenue, and accrued expenses, such as income taxes

LO 2 *Prepare a classified balance sheet. Compute widely used measures of liquidity and credit risk.*

---

[1]The time period used in defining current assets is one year or the length of the operating cycle, whichever is *longer.* Most businesses have an operating cycle far shorter than one year. However, companies that sell merchandise on long-term installment contracts, or that manufacture products such as ships, may have an operating cycle of several years. The user of financial statements should recognize that certain current assets are less liquid as the length of the operating cycle increases.

[2]Prepaid expenses do not actually "convert" into cash, but they *substitute* for cash by eliminating the need to make certain future cash outlays.

A classified balance sheet

(handwritten margin notes)
converted into cash w/in 1 year
Cash w/in 1 year
Expected to operating cycle,
to be used Unexpired Insurance
in business

2

3

4 pay in 1 yr.

5

6

COMPUTER BARN			
Balance Sheet			
December 31, 1998			

Assets

Current assets:

Cash			$ 30,000
Marketable securities			11,000
Notes receivable			5,000
Accounts receivable			60,000
Inventory			70,000
Prepaid expenses			4,000
Total current assets			$180,000

Plant and equipment:

Land		$151,000	
Building	$120,000		
Less: Accumulated depreciation	9,000	111,000	
Sales fixtures & equipment	$ 45,000		
Less: Accumulated depreciation	27,000	18,000	
Total plant and equipment			280,000

Other assets:

Land held as a future building site			170,000
Total assets			$630,000

Liabilities & Stockholders' Equity

Current liabilities:

Notes payable (due in 6 months)		$ 10,000
Accounts payable		62,000
Income taxes payable		13,000
Sales taxes payable		3,000
Accrued expenses payable		8,000
Unearned revenue and customer deposits		4,000
Total current liabilities		$100,000

Long-term liabilities:

Mortgage payable (due in 10 years)		110,000
Total liabilities		$210,000

Stockholders' equity:

Capital stock (15,000 shares issued and outstanding)	$150,000	
Retained earnings	270,000	
Total stockholders' equity		420,000
Total liabilities & stockholders' equity		$630,000

payable, salaries payable, or interest payable. In the balance sheet, notes payable usually are listed first, followed by accounts payable; other types of current liabilities may be listed in any sequence.

The *relationship* between current assets and current liabilities is more important than the total dollar amount in either category. Current liabilities must be paid in the near future, and the cash to pay these liabilities normally comes from current assets. Thus, decision makers evaluating the *short-term* liquidity of a business often compare the relative amounts of current assets and current liabilities, whereas an evaluation of *long-term* credit risk requires a comparison of total assets to total liabilities.

We will now use the classified balance sheet to examine some widely applied measures of short-term liquidity and long-term credit risk.

WORKING CAPITAL

Working capital is a measurement often used to express the relationship between current assets and current liabilities. **Working capital** is the *excess* of current assets over current liabilities. Computer Barn's working capital amounts to *$80,000*, computed as follows:

Current assets	$180,000	Working capital varies by
Less: Current liabilities	$100,000	industry and company size
Working capital	$ 80,000	

Recall that current assets are expected to convert into cash within a relatively short period of time, and that current liabilities usually require a prompt cash payment. Thus, working capital measures a company's potential excess *sources* of cash over its upcoming *uses* of cash.

The amount of working capital that a company needs to remain solvent varies with the size of the organization and the nature of its business activities.[3] An analyst familiar with the nature of a company's operations usually can determine from the amount of working capital whether the company is in a sound financial position or is heading for financial difficulties.

CURRENT RATIO

The most widely used measure of short-term debt-paying ability is the **current ratio.** This ratio is computed by *dividing* total current assets by total current liabilities.

In the illustrated balance sheet of Computer Barn, current assets amount to $180,000 and current liabilities total $100,000. Therefore, Computer Barn's current ratio is *1.8 to 1*, computed as follows:

Current assets	$180,000	The most widely used
Current liabilities	$100,000	measure of liquidity
Current ratio ($180,000 ÷ $100,000)	1.8 to 1	

A current ratio of 1.8 to 1 means that the company's current assets are 1.8 times as large as its current liabilities.

The *higher* the current ratio, the more solvent the company appears to be. Many bankers and other short-term creditors traditionally have believed that a retailer should have a current ratio of at least 2 to 1 to qualify as a good credit risk. By this standard, Computer Barn comes up a little short; the company might *not* receive a top credit rating from a bank or other short-term creditor.

QUICK RATIO

Inventory and prepaid expenses are the *least liquid* of the current assets. In a business with a long operating cycle, it may take many months to convert inventory into cash. Therefore, some short-term creditors prefer the **quick ratio** to the current ratio as a measure of short-term solvency.

The quick ratio compares only the *most liquid* current assets—called **quick assets**—with current liabilities. Quick assets include cash, marketable securities, and receivables—the current assets which can be converted most quickly into cash. Computer Barn's quick ratio at the end of 1998 is *1.06 to 1*, computed as follows:

---

[3]A company with current liabilities in excess of its current assets has a *negative* amount of working capital. Negative working capital does not necessarily mean that a company is insolvent. Any company with a current ratio of less than 1 to 1 has a negative amount of working capital. As explained in the "Case in Point" on the next page, many major telephone companies fall into this category.

Quick assets (cash, marketable securities, and receivables)	$106,000
Current liabilities	$100,000
Quick ratio ($106,000 ÷ $100,000)	1.06 to 1

Traditionally, a quick ratio of 1 to 1 is considered satisfactory. Quick ratios are especially useful in evaluating the solvency of companies that have inventories of slow-moving merchandise (such as real estate), or inventories which have become excessive in size.

A "more demanding" measure of liquidity

DEBT RATIO

If a business fails and must be liquidated, the claims of creditors take priority over those of the owners. But if the business has accumulated a great deal of debt, there may not be enough assets even to make full payment to all creditors.

A basic measure of the safety of creditors' claims is the **debt ratio,** which states total liabilities as a *percentage* of total assets. A company's debt ratio is computed by dividing total liabilities by total assets, as shown below for Computer Barn:

Total liabilities	$210,000
Total assets	$630,000
Debt ratio ($210,000 ÷ $630,000)	33$1/3$%

The debt ratio is not a measure of short-term liquidity. Rather, it is a measure of creditors' *long-term* risk. The smaller the portion of total assets financed by creditors, the smaller the risk that the business may become unable to pay its debts. From the creditors' point of view, the *lower* the debt ratio, the *safer* their position.

Most financially sound American companies traditionally have maintained debt ratios under 50%. But again, the financial analyst must be familiar with industry characteristics. Banks, for example, have very high debt ratios—usually over 90%.

EVALUATING FINANCIAL RATIOS

We caution users of financial statements *against* placing much confidence in rules of thumb, such as *a current ratio should be at least 2 to 1, a quick ratio should be at least 1 to 1,* or that *a debt ratio should be under 50%.* To interpret any financial ratio properly, the decision maker must first understand the characteristics of the company and the industry in which it operates.

Retailers, for example, tend to have higher current ratios than do wholesalers or manufacturing companies. Service-type businesses—which have no inventory—generally have lower current ratios than merchandising or manufacturing companies. Large businesses with good credit ratings and reliable sources of cash receipts are able to operate with lower current ratios than are small companies.

LO 3 *Interpret and evaluate financial ratios and measurements.*

CASE IN POINT

Large telephone companies are regarded within the business community as pillars of financial strength. Yet these companies do not have high current ratios. Such financially sound companies as Bell Atlantic, BellSouth, NYNEX, and Pacific Telesis often operate with current ratios of less than 1 to 1.

Although a high current ratio is one indication of strong debt-paying ability, an extremely high ratio—say 4 or 5 to 1—may indicate that *too much* of the company's resources are tied up in current assets. In maintaining such a highly liquid position, the company may be using its financial resources inefficiently. (In later chapters we will examine how financial statement data can be used to evaluate how *efficiently* businesses manage their most liquid assets.)

STANDARDS FOR COMPARISON   Financial analysts generally use two criteria in evaluating the reasonableness of a financial ratio. One criterion is the *trend* in the ratio over a period of years. By reviewing this trend, analysts are able to determine whether a company's performance or financial position is improving or deteriorating. Second, analysts often compare a company's financial ratios with those of *similar companies,* and also with *industry-wide averages.* These comparisons assist analysts in evaluating a particular ratio in light of the company's current business environment.

ANNUAL REPORTS   Publicly owned corporations issue **annual reports** that provide a great deal of information about the company. For example, annual reports include comparative financial statements that have been audited by a firm of independent public accountants. They also include five- or ten-year *summaries* of key financial data, and **management's discussion and analysis** of the company's operating results, liquidity, and financial position. It is in this section of the report that management identifies and discusses favorable and unfavorable trends, and events that may affect the company in the future. (For an example, see page A-6 in Appendix A.)

Annual reports are mailed directly to all stockholders of the corporation. They are also available to the public either through the Internet, in libraries, or by writing or calling the Stockholder Relations Department of the corporation.

INDUSTRY INFORMATION   Financial information about *entire industries* is available through financial publications (such as Dun & Bradstreet, Inc.), and through on-line databases (such as Media General Financial Services). Such information allows investors and creditors to compare the financial health of an individual company with the industry "viewed as a whole."

CASE IN POINT

Media General Financial Services continuously updates financial ratios for individual companies and provides norms for entire industries. As an example of industry norm data, the average current ratios of several industry groupings are shown below for a recent year:

Industry Group	Average Current Ratio
Air transportation (major carriers)	.9 to 1
Retail (general merchandise)	1.9 to 1
Retail (apparel)	2.3 to 1
Wholesale (grocery)	1.2 to 1
Manufacturing (computers)	1.6 to 1
Telephone (regional)	.8 to 1

USEFULNESS AND LIMITATIONS OF FINANCIAL RATIOS A financial ratio expresses the relationship of one amount to another. Most users of financial statements find that certain ratios assist them in quickly evaluating the financial position, profitability, and future prospects of a business. A comparison of key ratios for several successive years usually indicates whether the business is becoming stronger or weaker. Ratios also provide a way to compare quickly the financial strength and profitability of different companies.

Users of financial statements should recognize, however, that ratios have several limitations. For example, management may enter into year-end transactions which temporarily improve key ratios—a process called **window dressing.**

To illustrate, the balance sheet of Computer Barn (page 258) includes current assets of $180,000 and current liabilities of $100,000, indicating a current ratio of *1.8 to 1.* What would happen if shortly before year-end, management used $20,000 of the company's cash to pay accounts payable? This transaction would reduce current assets to $160,000 and current liabilities to $80,000. However, it would also *increase* the company's year-end current ratio to a more impressive *2 to 1* ($160,000 ÷ $80,000).

Financial statement ratios contain the same limitations as do the dollar amounts used in financial statements. For example, most assets are valued at historical cost rather than current market value. Also, financial statement ratios express only *financial* relationships. They give no indication of a company's progress in achieving nonfinancial goals, such as improving customer satisfaction or worker productivity. A thorough analysis of investment opportunities involves more than merely computing and comparing financial ratios.

NO RATIO EVER TELLS THE WHOLE STORY Each financial ratio focuses upon only *one aspect* of a company's total financial picture. A high current ratio, for example, does not guarantee solvency, nor does a low current ratio signal that bankruptcy is near. There are numerous factors of greater importance to a company's future performance than one or more financial ratios.

In summary, ratios are useful tools, but they can be interpreted properly only by individuals who understand the characteristics of the company and its environment.

YOUR TURN

You as a Potential Investor

Assume that you have several thousand dollars to invest in the stock market. Given that "people will always have to eat," you have decided to explore the possibility of investing in Wendy's and McDonalds. Your analysis of each company's financial statements reveals that both have negative working capital and both have current and quick ratios of less than 1 to 1.

Based upon your findings, should you be concerned about the short-term liquidity (solvency) of these two companies? Explain.

*Our comments appear on page 301.

CONCLUDING COMMENT—SOLVENCY, CREDIT RISK, AND THE LAW

Accountants view a business entity as separate from the other economic activities of its owners, regardless of how the business is organized. The law, however, draws an important distinction between *corporations* and *unincorporated* business organizations. Users of financial statements should understand this legal distinction, as it may affect both creditors and owners.

Under the law, the owners of unincorporated businesses (sole proprietorships and partnerships) are *personally liable* for any and all debts of the business organization. Therefore, creditors of unincorporated businesses often base their lending decisions upon the solvency of the *owners,* rather than the financial strength of the business entity.[4]

If a business is organized as a corporation, however, the owners (stockholders) are *not* personally responsible for the debts of the business. Creditors may look *only to the business entity* in seeking payment of their claims. Therefore, the solvency of the business entity becomes much more important if the business is organized as a corporation.

SMALL CORPORATIONS AND LOAN "GUARANTEES" Small corporations often do not have sufficient financial resources to qualify for the credit they need. In such cases, creditors may require that one or more of the company's stockholders personally guarantee (or "co-sign") specific debts of the business entity. By co-signing debts of the corporation, the individual stockholders *do* become personally liable for the debt if the corporation fails to make payment.

LO 4 *Explain owners' personal liability for the debts of a business.*

CASE IN POINT

A small family-owned restaurant supply business was organized as a corporation. To operate efficiently, the business needed to purchase merchandise on account. However, the corporation had so few current assets that suppliers were unwilling to extend credit. To obtain credit for the business, a major stockholder pledged his vacation home—a condominium on the Hawaiian Island of Maui—to secure the company's debt to a particular supplier. With this additional security, the supplier allowed the business to purchase large quantities of merchandise on account.

Unfortunately, the small business became insolvent and was forced into bankruptcy. Not only did the owners' equity in this corporation become worthless, but one stockholder also lost his vacation home to the company's creditors.

MEASURES OF PROFITABILITY

Measures of a company's *profitability* are of interest primarily to equity investors and management, and are drawn from the income statement. The measures that we discuss in this chapter include percentage changes in key measurements, gross profit rates, operating income, net income as a percentage of sales, earnings per share, return on assets, and return on equity.

CLASSIFICATIONS IN THE INCOME STATEMENT
An income statement may be prepared in either the *multiple-step* or the *single-step* format. The multiple-step income statement is more useful in illustrating accounting concepts, and has been used in all of our illustrations thus far. A multiple-step income statement for Computer Barn is shown on the following page.

---

[4]In a *limited* partnership, only the *general partners* are personally responsible for the debts of the business. Every limited partnership must have one or more general partners.

This income statement also is *classified,* meaning that revenue and expenses have been classified into several categories. (For comparative purposes, this income statement is illustrated in single-step form on page 269.)

MULTIPLE-STEP INCOME STATEMENTS

LO 5 *Prepare a multiple-step and a single-step income statement.*

A multiple-step income statement draws its name from the *series of steps* in which costs and expenses are deducted from revenue. As a first step, the cost of goods sold is deducted from net sales to determine the subtotal *gross profit.* As a second step, operating expenses are deducted to obtain a subtotal called **operating income** (or income from operations). As a final step, income taxes expense and other "nonoperating" items are taken into consideration to arrive at *net income.*

Notice that the income statement is divided into four major sections: (1) revenue, (2) cost of goods sold, (3) operating expenses, and (4) nonoperating items. Multiple-step income statements are noted for their numerous sections and the development of significant subtotals.

THE REVENUE SECTION In a merchandising company, the revenue section of the income statement usually contains only one line, entitled *net sales.* (Other types of revenue, if any, appear in the final section of the statement.)

Income statement in multiple-step format

COMPUTER BARN Income Statement For the Year Ended December 31, 1998			
Net sales			$900,000
Less: Cost of goods sold (including transportation-in)			540,000
Gross profit			$360,000
Less: Operating expenses:			
Selling expenses:			
Sales salaries and commissions	$64,800		
Advertising	42,000		
Delivery service	14,200		
Depreciation: store equipment	9,000		
Other selling expenses	6,000		
Total selling expenses		$136,000	
General & administrative expenses:			
Administrative & office salaries	$93,000		
Utilities	3,100		
Depreciation: building	3,000		
Other general & administrative expenses	4,900		
Total general & administrative expenses		104,000	
Total operating expenses			240,000
Operating income			$120,000
Less (add): Nonoperating items:			
Interest expense	$12,000		
Purchase discounts lost	1,200		
Interest revenue	(3,200)		10,000
Income before income taxes			$110,000
Income taxes expense			38,000
Net income			$ 72,000
Earnings per share			$4.80

(handwritten note: Choice of management / Finance Chgs)

Investors and managers are vitally interested in the *trend* in net sales. As one means of evaluating this trend, they often compute the percentage change in net sales from year to year. A **percentage change** is the dollar amount of the *change* in a financial measurement, expressed as a percentage. It is computed by dividing the dollar amount of increase or decrease by the dollar amount of the measurement *before* the change occurred. (Dollar changes *cannot* be expressed as percentages if the financial statement amount in the earlier period is zero, or has changed from a negative amount to a positive amount.)

In our economy, most prices increase over time. The average increase in prices during the year is called the *rate of inflation.* Because of inflation, a company's net sales may increase slightly from year to year even if the company is not selling greater amounts of merchandise. If a company's physical sales volume is increasing, net sales usually will grow faster than the rate of inflation.

If a company's sales grow faster than the *industry average,* the company increases its **market share**—that is, its share of total industry sales.

Publicly owned corporations include in their annual reports schedules summarizing operating data—such as net sales—for a period of five or ten years. This data is also readily available through several on-line databases.

CASE IN POINT

Within his lifetime, Sam Walton built **Wal-Mart** from a single retail store into one of the world's largest merchandising companies. And—as of 1996—Wal-Mart was still growing fast. An excerpt from five-year summary data obtained using the Internet appears below (dollar amounts are in millions):

Operating Results	1996	1995	1994	1993	1992
Net sales	$92,627	$82,494	$67,344	$55,484	$43,887
Percentage increase	14%	22%	21%	26%	35%

To emphasize the company's rate of growth, the percentage change in each year's sales is shown relative to that of the prior year. During this five-year period, the rate of inflation ranged between 3% and 6%, and industry sales grew at a compound annual rate of less than 10% (Wal-Mart's percentage increases reflect an annual compound growth rate of over 20% for the five-year period). By anyone's standards, Wal-Mart's net sales have increased at an impressive rate. But notice that the rate of sales growth appears to be slowing.

THE COST OF GOODS SOLD SECTION The second section of a merchandising company's income statement shows cost of goods sold for the period. Cost of goods sold usually appears as a single dollar amount, which includes such incidental items as transportation-in and normal shrinkage losses.

GROSS PROFIT: A KEY SUBTOTAL In a multiple-step income statement, gross profit appears as a subtotal. This makes it easy for users of the income statement to compute the company's *gross profit rate* (or profit margin).

As explained in Chapter 5, the gross profit rate is gross profit expressed as a *percentage of net sales.* In 1996, Computer Barn earned an average gross profit rate of *40%,* computed as follows:

LO 6 *Compute widely used measures of profitability.*

Dollar amount of gross profit		$360,000
Net sales		$900,000
Gross profit rate ($360,000 ÷ $900,000)		**40%**

In evaluating the gross profit rate of a particular company, the analyst should consider the rates earned in prior periods, and also the rates earned by *other companies* in the same industry. For most merchandising companies, gross profit rates usually lie between 20% and 50%, depending upon the types of products they sell. These rates usually are lowest on fast-moving merchandise, such as groceries, and highest on specialty and novelty products.

Under normal circumstances, a company's gross profit rate tends to remain *reasonably stable* from one period to the next. Significant changes in this rate may provide investors with an early indication of changing consumer demand for the company's products.

CASE IN POINT

The gross profit rates earned by several well-known corporations are shown below for a three-year period. With the exception of **Apple Computer,** note the stability of each company's gross profit rate from one year to the next:

Company	1995	1994	1993
Mattel (toys)	48%	50%	50%
Sony (electronics)	27%	26%	27%
Safeway (groceries)	27%	27%	27%
Microsoft (software)*	85%	83%	83%
Apple Computer	25%	25%	34%

Throughout the 1980's, Apple Computer consistently averaged a gross profit rate *in excess of 55%*—the highest of any computer manufacturer. The reason was that the company did not license other companies to make clones of its Macintosh computer. If you wanted a "Mac," you had to buy it from Apple. The advent of Microsoft Windows in 1990 enabled less-expensive computers to imitate the Mac. The subsequent release of Windows 95, coupled with Apple's decision to license Mac clones, has continued to erode the company's gross profit rate throughout the 1990's.

*The profit margins of software companies are unusually *high* because the cost of manufacturing software is very low in relation to its sales price. The costs of *developing* software products may be quite substantial, but all development costs appear on the income statement as an operating expense, and are therefore *not included* in the cost of goods sold. Although Microsoft is a very successful company, the *characteristics of the software industry* explain why its profit margins are so much higher than those of the other companies listed.

THE OPERATING EXPENSE SECTION   Operating expenses are incurred for the purpose of *producing revenue*. These expenses often are subdivided into the classifications of *selling expenses* and *general and administrative expenses*. Subdividing operating expenses into functional classifications aids management and other users of the statements in separately evaluating different aspects of the company's operations. For example, selling expenses often rise and fall in concert with changes in net sales. Administrative expenses, on the other hand, usually remain more constant from one period to the next.

OPERATING INCOME: ANOTHER KEY SUBTOTAL Some of the revenue and expenses of a business stem from activities other than the company's basic business operations. Common examples include interest earned on investments and income taxes expense.

Operating income (or income from operations) shows the relationship between revenue earned form customers and expenses incurred in producing this revenue. In effect, operating income measures the profitability of a company's *basic business operations* and leaves out other types of revenue and expenses.

NONOPERATING ITEMS Revenue and expenses which are not directly related to the company's primary business activities are listed in a final section of the income statement following the determination of operating income.

Two significant nonoperating items are interest expense and income taxes expense. Interest expense stems from the manner in which assets are *financed,* not the manner in which these assets are used in business operations. Income taxes expense is not included among the operating expenses because paying income taxes *does not help to produce revenue.* Nonoperating revenues, such as interest and dividends earned on investments, also are listed in this final section of the income statement.

NET INCOME Most equity investors consider net income (or net loss) to be the most important figure in the income statement. This amount represents the overall increase (or decrease) in owners' equity resulting from all business activities during the period.

Financial analysts often compute net income as a *percentage of net sales* (net income divided by net sales). This measurement provides an indication of management's *ability to control expenses,* and to retain a reasonable portion of its revenue as profit.

The "normal" ratio of net income to net sales varies greatly by industry. In some industries, companies may be successful by earning a net income equal to only 2 or 3% of net sales. In other industries, net income may amount to as much as 20 or 25% of net sales revenue. In 1998, Computer Barn's net income in 1998 amounts to *8%* of net sales, which is very good for a computer retailer.

Net income	$72,000
Net sales	$900,000
Net income as a percentage of net sales ($72,000 ÷ $900,000)	8%

EARNINGS PER SHARE

Ownership of a corporation is evidenced by *shares* of capital stock. What does the net income of a corporation mean to someone who owns, say, 100 shares of a corporation's capital stock? To assist individual stockholders in relating the corporation's net income to *their ownership shares,* large corporations compute **earnings per share,** and show these amounts at the bottom of their income statements.[5]

In the simplest case, earnings per share is net income, expressed on a per share basis. For example, the balance sheet on page 258 indicates that Com-

---

[5]Only large corporations are *required* to report earnings on a per share basis. For small businesses such as Computer Barn, the reporting of earnings per share is optional.

puter Barn has 15,000 shares of capital stock outstanding.[6] Assuming these shares had been outstanding all year, earnings per share amounts to *$4.80:*

Net income	$72,000
Shares of capital stock outstanding	15,000
Earnings per share ($72,000 ÷ 15,000 shares)	$4.80

Earnings per share is perhaps the most widely used of all accounting ratios. The *trend* in earnings per share—and the expected earnings in future periods—are *major factors* affecting the market value of a company's shares.

PRICE-EARNINGS RATIO

Financial analysts express the relationship between the market price of a company's stock and the underlying earnings per share as a **price-earnings ratio** (or p/e ratio). This ratio is computed by dividing the current market price per share of the company's stock by annual earnings per share. (A p/e ratio cannot be computed for a period in which the company incurs a net loss).

To illustrate, assume that at the end of 1998, Computer Barn's capital stock is trading among investors at a market price of *$96* per share. The p/e ratio of the company's stock is computed below:

Current market price per share of stock	$96
Earnings per share (for the last 12 months)	$4.80
Price-earnings ratio ($96 ÷ $4.80)	20

Technically, this ratio is "20 to 1." But it is common practice to omit the "to 1," and merely to describe a p/e ratio by the first number. The p/e ratios of many publicly owned corporations are quoted daily in the financial pages of many newspapers.

The p/e ratio reflects *investor's expectations* concerning the company's *future performance*. The more optimistic these expectations, the higher the p/e ratio is likely to be. Traditionally, stocks of financially sound companies with stable earnings usually sell at between 12 and 15 times earnings. If investors anticipate rapid earnings growth, p/e ratios rise into the twenties, thirties, or even higher.

A p/e ratio of 10 or less often indicates that investors expect earnings to *decline* from the current level. It may also mean, however, that the stock is *undervalued.* Likewise, a stock with a p/e ratio of 30 or more usually means that investors expect earnings to *increase* from the current level. However, it may also signal that the stock is *overvalued.*

One word of caution. If earnings decline to *very low levels,* the price of the stock usually does not follow the earnings "all the way down." Therefore, a company with *very low earnings* is likely to have a *high p/e ratio* even if investors are not optimistic about future earnings.

SINGLE-STEP INCOME STATEMENTS

In their annual reports, many publicly owned corporations present their financial statements in a highly condensed format. For this reason, the *single-step* income statement is widely used in annual reports.

The single-step form of income statement takes its name from the fact that all costs and expenses are deducted from total revenue in a single step. No subtotals are shown for gross profit or for operating income, although the statement provides investors with enough information to compute these subtotals on their

---

[6]Assume that all 15,000 shares have been outstanding throughout the year. Computation of earnings per share in more complex situations will be addressed in Chapter 12.

own. The 1998 income statement of Computer Barn appears below in a single-step format:

COMPUTER BARN Income Statement For the Year Ended December 31, 1998		
Revenue:		
Net sales		$900,000
Interest earned		3,200
Total revenue		$903,200
Less: Cost and expenses:		
Cost of goods sold	$540,000	
Selling expenses	136,000	
General & administrative expenses	104,000	
Interest expense	12,000	
Purchase discounts lost	1,200	
Income taxes expense	38,000	
Total costs and expenses		831,200
Net income		$ 72,000
Earnings per share		$4.80

Income statement in the single-step format

EVALUATING THE ADEQUACY OF NET INCOME

How much net income must a business earn to be considered successful? Obviously, the dollar amount of net income that investors consider adequate depends upon the *size of the business.* An annual net income of $1 million might seem impressive for an automobile dealership, but would represent very poor performance for a company the size of General Motors.

Investors usually consider two factors in evaluating a company's profitability: (1) the trend in earnings, and (2) the amount of current earnings in relation to the amount of the resources needed to produce the earnings.

Most investors regard the *trend* in earnings from year to year as more important than the amount of net income in the current period. Equity investors stand to benefit from the company's performance over the long-run. Years of steadily increasing earnings may increase the value of the stockholders' investment manyfold.

In evaluating the current level of earnings, many investors use *return on investment* analysis.

RETURN ON INVESTMENT (ROI)

In Chapter 1 we explained that a basic purpose of accounting is to assist decision makers in efficiently allocating and using economic resources. In deciding where to invest their money, equity investors want to know how efficiently companies utilize resources. The most common method of evaluating the efficiency with which financial resources are employed is to compute the *rate of return* earned on these resources. This rate of return is called the *return on investment,* or *ROI.*

Mathematically, computing the return on investment is a simple concept: the annual return (or profit) generated by the investment is stated as a *percentage* of the average amount invested throughout the year. The basic idea is illustrated by the following formula:

$$\textbf{Return on investment (ROI)} = \frac{\textbf{Return}}{\textbf{Average amount invested}}$$

ROI general formula

The return is earned *throughout* the period. Therefore, it is logical to express this return as a percentage of the *average* amount invested during the period, rather than the investment at year-end. The average amount invested usually is computed by adding the amounts invested as of the beginning and end of the year, and dividing this total by 2.

The concept of ROI is applied in many different situations, such as evaluating the profitability of a business, a branch location, or a specific investment opportunity. As a result, a number of variations in the basic ROI ratio have been developed, each suited to a particular type of analysis. These ratios differ in the manner in which "return" and "average amount invested" are defined. We will discuss two common applications of the ROI concept: **return on assets** and **return on equity.**

RETURN ON ASSETS (ROA)

This ratio is used in evaluating whether management has earned a reasonable return with the assets under its control. In this computation, "return" usually is defined as *operating income,* since interest expense and income taxes are determined by factors other than the manner in which assets are used. The *return on assets* is computed as follows:

The "return" on total assets is operating income

$$\textbf{Return on assets (ROA)} = \frac{\textbf{Operating income}}{\textbf{Average total assets}}$$

Let us now determine the return on assets earned by the management of Computer Barn in 1998. Operating income, as shown in the income statement on page 264, amounts to *$120,000*. Assume that Computer Barn's assets at the beginning of 1998 totaled $570,000. The illustrated balance sheet on page 258 shows total assets of $630,000 at year-end. Therefore, the company's *average* total assets during the year amounted to *$600,000* [($570,000 + $630,000) ÷ 2]. The return on assets in 1998 is *20%*, determined as follows:

$$\frac{\textbf{Operating income}}{\textbf{Average total assets}} = \frac{\textbf{\$120,000}}{\textbf{\$600,000}} = \textbf{20\%}$$

Most successful businesses earn a return on average total assets of, perhaps, 15% or more. At this writing, businesses must pay interest rates of between 6% and 12% in order to borrow money. If a business is well-managed and has good future prospects, management certainly should be able to earn a return on assets that is higher than the company's cost of borrowing.

RETURN ON EQUITY (ROE)

The return on assets measures the efficiency with which management has utilized the assets under its control, regardless of whether these assets were financed with debt or equity capital. The *return on equity* ratio, in contrast, looks only at the return earned by management on the stockholders' investment—that is, upon *owners' equity.*

The "return" to stockholders is the *net income* of the business. Thus, return on equity is computed as follows:

The "return" on equity is net income

$$\textbf{Return on equity (ROE)} = \frac{\textbf{Net income}}{\textbf{Average total stockholders' equity}}$$

To illustrate, let us again turn to the 1998 financial statements of Computer Barn. In 1998, the company earned net income of *$72,000*. The year-end balance sheet (page 258) shows total stockholders' equity of $420,000. To enable us to complete our computation, we will assume that the stockholders' equity at the *beginning* of the year amounted to $380,000. Therefore, the *average* stockholders' equity for the year amounts to *$400,000* [($380,000 + $420,000) ÷ 2]. The return on stockholders' equity in 1998 is *18%*, computed as follows:

$$\frac{\textbf{Net income}}{\textbf{Average total stockholders' equity}} = \frac{\$72,000}{\$400,000} = 18\%$$

Traditionally, stockholders have expected to earn an average annual return of perhaps 12% or more from equity investments in large, financially strong companies. Annual returns on equity of 30% or more are not uncommon, especially in rapidly growing companies with new or highly successful products.

The return on equity may be higher or lower than the overall return on assets, depending upon how the company has financed its assets, and upon the amounts of its nonoperating revenue and expenses. A company that suffers a net loss provides its stockholders with a *negative* return on stockholders' equity.

CASE IN POINT

The returns on assets and on equity earned by a few well-known corporations in recent years are shown below:

	Return on assets	Return on equity
Coca-Cola	23%	55%
Hershey Foods	17%	17%
Fuji Film	10%	7%
Exxon	7%	16%
Toyota	2%	5%
Ames Department Stores	(3%)	(20%)

Many companies earn approximately the same rates of return year after year. In others, the annual rates of return fluctuate greatly.

INTRODUCTION TO THE STATEMENT OF CASH FLOWS

In addition to an income statement, statement of retained earnings, and balance sheet, a complete set of financial statements includes a **statement of cash flows.** The basic purpose of this fourth financial statement is to provide information about a company's *cash receipts* and *cash payments* during the accounting period.[7] An example of a statement of cash flows follows:

LO 7 *Describe the purpose, content, and format of a statement of cash flows.*

---

[7]In a statement of cash flows, "cash" includes certain short-term investments called *cash equivalents.* Cash equivalents are discussed in Chapter 7.

Cash flows are classified
into three basic categories

COMPUTER BARN Statement of Cash Flows For the Year Ended December 31, 1998		
Cash flows from operating activities:		
Cash collected from customers	$ 890,500	
Interest received	500	
Cash receipts from operating activities		$ 891,000
Payments to suppliers and employees	$(772,500)	
Interest paid	(12,500)	
Income taxes paid	(25,000)	
Cash payments for operating activities		(810,000)
Net cash provided by operating activities		$ 81,000
Cash flows from investing activities:		
Payments to purchase marketable securities	$ (8,000)	
Receipts from sales of marketable securities	4,000	
Payments to acquire plant assets	(17,000)	
Receipts from disposals of plant assets	3,000	
Net cash used in investing activities		(18,000)
Cash flows from financing activities:		
Proceeds from borrowing	$ 10,000	
Repayments of amounts borrowed	(29,000)	
Proceeds from issuance of capital stock	8,000	
Dividends paid to stockholders	(32,000)	
Net cash used in financing activities		(43,000)
Net increase in cash during the year		$20,000
Cash, December 31, 1997 (per balance sheet)		10,000
Cash, December 31, 1998 (per balance sheet)		$ 30,000

[handwritten margin notes: "For test: Choose where accounts go. 3 choices", "in income statement", "purchase: market sec. land, building, equip.", "activity to acquire $"]

The term **cash flows** describes both cash receipts (inflows) and cash payments (outflows). In our illustration, the specific types of cash flows appear in *blue*. Cash *outflows* are designated by brackets around the dollar amount.

CASH FLOWS ARE NOT "ACCOUNT BALANCES" Notice that the cash flows in our statement are identified by *descriptive captions,* rather than by ledger account titles. Most businesses design their chart of ledger accounts to measure revenue and expenses, rather than cash flows. Although the different types of cash flows are not recorded in separate ledger accounts, they can be computed easily at the end of the accounting period.

At present, our goal is only to explain the general *content* and *format* of the cash flow statement; the techniques of *computing* specific cash flows are illustrated and explained in Chapter 13.

CLASSIFICATIONS OF CASH FLOWS

In the financial statement illustrated above, cash flows are classified according to the *nature of the underlying business activity.* The three basic classifications are: **operating activities, investing activities,** and **financing activities.** (In our illustration, these three classifications are printed in *black.*)

OPERATING ACTIVITIES The operating activities section shows the *cash effects* of revenue and expense transactions. To illustrate the difference between "revenue and expenses" and the "cash effects" of the underlying transactions, let us consider a sale on account. In the income statement, a credit sale is recognized as revenue when the sale occurs. The *cash effect* of a credit sale occurs at a later date—when cash is collected from the customer. Similar timing differences often exist between the recognition of an expense and the related cash payment.

In summary, an income statement measures the "profitability" of business operations *without regard to when cash is received or paid.* The operating activities section of a cash flow statement provides additional information about the company's operations by showing the related cash receipts and cash payments.[8]

The concept of "operating activities" in the statement of cash flows differs from that of "operating income" in an income statement. In the income statement, operating income includes only the revenue and expenses relating to the company's *primary business activities.* In the statement of cash flows, operating activities include the cash effects of *all types* of revenue and expense transactions, including interest and income taxes.

INVESTING ACTIVITIES   Investing activities are the cash flows stemming from purchases and disposals of plant assets and/or investments.

FINANCING ACTIVITIES   Financing activities include most of the cash flows between an organization and (1) its owners (stockholders), and (2) creditors who *lend money* to the business.[9] Typical sources of cash from investing activities include the proceeds from borrowing or from the issuance of stock. Common cash outlays include repayment of amounts borrowed (but not including interest payments) and dividends paid to stockholders.

NET CASH FLOWS

The term **net cash flow** refers to a category of cash receipts *less any related cash outlays.* A statement of cash flows includes *subtotals* showing the net cash flow of each category of business activity. (In our illustration, these subtotals are shown in *red,* as are the last three lines in the statement.)

RELATIONSHIP BETWEEN CASH FLOWS AND THE BALANCE SHEET   The last three lines of the cash flow statement reconcile the net cash flow for the period with the amounts of cash appearing in the company's balance sheets. This reconciliation "proves" that the cash flow statement *explains fully* the change in the amount of cash owned from one balance sheet date to the next. Notice that the "bottom line" of Computer Barn's cash flow statement (page 272) is the amount of cash appearing in the year-end balance sheet (page 258).

THE CRITICAL IMPORTANCE OF CASH FLOW FROM OPERATING ACTIVITIES   In the long run, a business *must* generate a positive net cash flow from its operating activities if it is to survive. A business with negative cash flows from operating activities will not be able to raise cash indefinitely from other sources. Creditors and stockholders quickly tire of investing in companies that do not generate positive cash flows from their business operations.

As the net cash flow from operating activity remains *after* payment of ordinary expenses and operating liabilities, it is considered a key measure of liquidity.

---

[8]In our illustration, cash flows from operating activities are presented in a format called the *direct method.* An alternative format, termed the *indirect method* is explained and illustrated in Chapter 13.

[9]Payments to creditors who provide *goods or services* to the business usually are viewed as the "cash effects of expense transactions" and, therefore, are classified as *operating activities.* This reasoning also applies to *interest payments,* which are classified as operating activities, rather than financing activities.

CASH FLOWS FROM INVESTING AND FINANCING ACTIVITIES It is *not* important for the net cash flows from investing or financing activities to be positive in any given year. In fact, many successful businesses usually report negative net cash flows for these activities.

Purchases of plant assets require cash outlays. Therefore, growing businesses usually report *negative* net cash flows from investing activities.

Major financing transactions—borrowing, the issuance of capital stock, or the repayment of a large loan—occur infrequently. In any given year, many companies engage in none of these transactions. When they do, a single transaction is likely to determine whether the financing activities' cash flow for the entire year is positive or negative.

However many successful corporations pay *dividends* on a regular basis. In the absence of other financing transactions, dividend payments cause many successful companies to report negative net cash flows from their financing activities.

YOUR TURN

You as an Industry Analyst

Assume that you are an industry analyst for a large investment firm. Your area of specialization is the general merchandise retail sector. You have been tracking closely the performance of the K-Mart Corporation, trying to determine whether the company can remain solvent.

A recent statement of cash flows reported the company's net cash inflow at $742 million dollars for the year. This amount was broken down as follows (dollar amounts shown are in millions):

Cash flow from operating activities	$(104)
Cash flow from investing activities	321
Cash flow from financing activities	525
Increase in cash for the year	$ 742

Given that K-Mart increased its cash by $742 million dollars during the year, can you conclude that the company is solvent? Explain.

*Our comments appear on page 301.

WHO USES INFORMATION ABOUT CASH FLOWS?

Outsiders—investors and creditors—use the statement of cash flows primarily for evaluating the *solvency* of a business. By studying the cash flow statements for a series of years, they gain insight into such questions as:

- Is the company becoming more or less solvent?
- Do operating activities consistently generate enough cash to assure prompt payment of operating expenses, maturing liabilities, interest obligations, and dividends?
- Do operating activities also generate enough cash to finance growth and/or create a likelihood of increases in the dividends paid to stockholders?

● Is the company's ability to generate cash from operating activities improving or deteriorating?

In the short run, solvency and profitability may be *independent* of one another. That is, even a profitable business may run out of cash and become insolvent. On the other hand, an unprofitable business may remain solvent for years if it has vast resources or borrowing ability. In assessing the future prospects of any business organization, equity investors should evaluate both the company's profitability *and* its solvency. Creditors—especially short-term creditors—often attach greater importance to solvency than to profitability.

MANAGEMENT'S INTEREST IN CASH FLOWS

No group of decision makers is more interested in a company's cash flows than management. Management is responsible for keeping the business solvent and for using resources efficiently. **Cash budgets** are accounting reports specifically designed to assist management in meeting these responsibilities.

CASH BUDGETS Cash budgets are *forecasts of the cash flows expected to occur in future periods*. In developing these budgets, accountants work closely with departmental managers throughout the business organization. Forecasting future cash flows involves forecasting the future levels of all types of operating, investing, and financing activities.

Cash budgets are similar to statements of cash flows in that both reports reflect cash receipts and payments. However, these reports differ in several important ways. The basic differences are summarized in the following table:

Statement of Cash Flows	Cash Budget
A *formal financial statement*, distributed to decision makers outside of the organization.	*Not* a financial statement; used primarily by decision makers *within* the organization.
Reflects the *actual* results of *past* cash transactions.	Shows the *expected* results of *future* cash transactions.
Summarize the *overall* cash flows of the entire business entity for a period of one year.	Shows in *detail* the cash flows expected from each department within the business, usually on a monthly basis.

Management uses cash budgets both in planning future operations and in evaluating past performance. The process of preparing the budget makes management aware of the cash flows likely to occur in future periods. If cash shortages appear likely, management is forewarned and has an opportunity to take preventive actions.

As each period progresses, the accounting department gathers information about the *actual* cash flows taking place. Detailed comparisons are made between the actual cash flows and the previously budgeted amounts. Management uses these comparisons as one means of evaluating departmental performance and the effectiveness of business strategies.

SOME CONCLUDING COMMENTS

SOURCES OF FINANCIAL INFORMATION

For the most part, our discussion in this chapter has been limited to the kinds of analysis that can be performed by "outsiders" who do not have access to the company's accounting records. Investors and creditors must rely to a considerable extent upon the financial statements published in annual and quarterly reports. In the case of publicly owned corporations, additional information is filed with the Securities and Exchange Commission (SEC) and is available to the public in "hard copy," as well as on the Internet. In fact, the Internet is by far the fastest growing source of *free* information available to decision makers in this information age. (See Appendix B for a variety of Internet exercise and problem materials).

Many financial analysts who evaluate the financial statements and future prospects of publicly owned companies sell their conclusions and investment recommendations for a fee. For example, detailed financial analyses of most large companies are available from Standard & Poor's, Moody's Investors Service, and The Value Line Investment Survey. Anyone may subscribe to these investment services.

Bankers and major creditors usually are able to obtain detailed financial information from borrowers simply by requesting it as a condition for granting a loan. Suppliers and other trade creditors may obtain some financial information about almost any business from credit-rating agencies, such as Dun & Bradstreet.

FINANCIAL ANALYSIS AND STOCK PRICE

Assume that a company has rapidly increasing net sales and earnings, and also earns high returns on assets and stockholders' equity. Is its stock a "good buy" at the present price? Maybe; but maybe not.

Stock prices, like p/e ratios, are a *measure of investors' expectations.* A company may be highly profitable and growing fast. But if investors had expected even better performance, the market price of its stock may decline. Similarly, if a troubled company's losses are smaller than expected, the price of its stock may rise.

In financial circles, evaluating stock price by looking at the underlying profitability of the company is termed **fundamental analysis.** This approach to investing works better in the long run than in the short run. In the short run, stock prices can be significantly affected by many factors, including short-term interest rates, current events, fads, and rumors. But in the long run, good companies increase in value.

In summary, successful investing requires more than an understanding of accounting concepts. It requires experience, judgment, patience, and the ability to absorb some losses. And good luck helps a lot. But a knowledge of accounting concepts is invaluable to the long-term investor—and it reduces the risk of "getting burned."

SUMMARY OF ANALYTICAL MEASUREMENTS

The financial ratios and other measurements introduced in this chapter—and their significance—are summarized in the following table:

Ratio or Other Measurement	Method of Computation	Sign
Liquidity measures:		
Current ratio	$\dfrac{\text{Current assets}}{\text{Current liabilities}}$	A measure o paying ability
Quick ratio	$\dfrac{\text{Quick assets}}{\text{Current liabilities}}$	A measure of short-term paying ability.
Working capital	Current assets − Current liabilities	A measure of short-term debt-paying ability.
Net cash provided by operating activities	Appears in the statement of cash flows	Indicates the cash generated by operations *after* allowing for cash payment of expenses and operating liabilities.
Measure of long-term credit risk:		
Debt ratio	$\dfrac{\text{Total liabilities}}{\text{Total assets}}$	A measure of creditors' long-term risk.
Profitability measures:		
Percentage change	$\dfrac{\text{Dollar amount of change}}{\substack{\text{Financial statement amount} \\ \text{in the earlier year}}}$	The *rate* at which an amount is increasing or decreasing.
Gross profit rate	$\dfrac{\text{Dollar gross profit}}{\text{Net sales}}$	A measure of the profitability of the company's products.
Operating income	Gross profit − Operating expenses	The profitability of a company's "basic" business activities.
Net income as a percentage of net sales	$\dfrac{\text{Net income}}{\text{Net sales}}$	An indicator of management's ability to control costs.
Earnings per share*	$\dfrac{\text{Net income}}{\substack{\text{Average number of shares} \\ \text{outstanding}}}$	Net income applicable to each share of capital stock.
Return on assets	$\dfrac{\text{Operating income}}{\text{Average total assets}}$	A measure of the productivity of assets, regardless of how the assets are financed.
Return on equity	$\dfrac{\text{Net income}}{\text{Average total equity}}$	The rate of return earned on the stockholders' equity in the business.
Measure of investors' expectations:		
Price-earnings ratio	$\dfrac{\text{Per-share market stock price}}{\text{Earnings per share}}$	A measure of investors' enthusiasm about the company's future prospects.

*In many situations, this "simple case" formula must be modified. The computation of earnings per share in such situations is discussed in Chapter 12.

NET CONNECTIONS

This chapter has provided you with an introduction to financial statement analysis. However, before deciding to sink your entire life savings in the stock market, we suggest that you learn as much as possible about the complex *world of Wall Street.*

The Internet provides a wealth of resources to get you started. Shown below is a list of interesting investment sites. These resources provide valuable tools and information for novices and professionals alike. Check them out!

Site Name	Site Address
Wall Street Research Network	www.wsrn.com
CNN Financial Network	www.cnnfn.com
Stockmaster	www.stockmaster.com
The Finance Virtual Library	www.cob.ohio-state.edu/dept/fin/overvw.htm
Business Research Starting Point	www.stpt.com
Bloomberg Personal	www.bloomberg.com
NETworth	www.networth.galt.com
Corporate Finance Network	www.corpfinet.com
Investor Guide	www.investorguide.com

SUMMARY OF LEARNING OBJECTIVES

① Explain the nature and purpose of *classifications* in financial statements.

In classified financial statements, items with certain common characteristics are placed together in a group, or "classification." The purpose of these classifications is to develop subtotals which will assist users in analyzing the financial statements.

② Prepare a classified balance sheet. Compute widely used measures of liquidity and credit risk.

In a classified balance sheet, assets are subdivided into the categories of *current assets, plant and equipment,* and *other assets.* Liabilities are classified either as *current* or *long-term.* A classified balance sheet is illustrated on page 258.

The liquidity measures derived from the balance sheet are:

Working capital. Current assets minus current liabilities.

Current ratio. Current assets divided by current liabilities.

Quick ratio. Quick assets divided by current liabilities.

A measure of long-term credit risk is the *debt ratio,* which is total liabilities expressed as a percentage of (divided by) total assets.

③ Interpret and evaluate financial ratios and measurements.

The interpretation of any ratio requires an understanding of the business and the environment in which it operates. Users of financial statements often compare a company's financial ratios in the current year with (1) those ratios in prior years, and (2) the ratios of similar companies or the industry viewed as a whole. The first comparison indicates whether the company's condition is improving or deteriorating. The second assists the user in interpreting the ratio within the company's business environment.

④ Explain owners' *personal* liability for the debts of a business.

In unincorporated businesses (sole proprietorships and partnerships), the owners are personally liable for all debts of the business. If the business is organized as a corporation, however, the owners generally are *not* personally liable for the debts of the business. Thus, creditors of the business may look only to the assets of the business entity for payment of their claims. However, creditors may require that one or more stockholders personally guarantee a particular liability as a condition for extending credit to a corporation.

⑤ Prepare a multiple-step and a single-step income statement.

In a multiple-step income statement, the cost of goods sold is deducted from net sales to provide the subtotal, gross profit. Operating expenses then are deducted to arrive at income from operations. As a final step, nonoperating items are added together and subtracted from income to arrive at net income. In a single-step income statement, all revenue items are listed first, and then all expenses are combined and deducted from total revenue. The multiple-step format is illustrated on page 264, and the single-step format on page 269.

⑥ Compute widely used measures of profitability.

The profitability measures discussed in this chapter are:

Percentage change. The dollar amount of change in a financial statement item from one period to the next, expressed as a percentage of (divided by) the item value in the earlier of the two periods being compared.

Gross profit rate. Dollar amount of gross profit divided by net sales. A measure of the profitability of a company's products.

Net income as a percent of sales. Net income divided by net sales. A measure of management's ability to control expenses.

Earnings per share. In the simplest case, net income divided by shares of capital stock outstanding. Indicates the earnings applicable to each share of stock.

Price-earnings ratio. Market price of the stock, divided by earnings per share. A measure of investors' optimism regarding future profitability.

Return on assets. Operating income divided by average total assets. Measures the return generated by assets, regardless of how the assets are financed.

Return on equity. Net income divided by average total equity. Indicates the rate of return earned on owners' equity.

⑦ Describe the purpose, content, and format of a statement of cash flows.

The purpose of a statement of cash flows is to provide information about cash receipts and cash payments during the period. The statement describes the nature of the company's cash flows, and classifies these cash flows as operating activities, investing activities, or financing activities. All of the cash flows then are combined to show the overall change in the balance of the Cash account during the period.

One of the basic goals in this text is to develop your ability to interpret and use accounting information. Throughout the remainder of this course — and in the business world — you often will be asked to apply the background information and analytical techniques introduced in this chapter.

KEY TERMS INTRODUCED OR EMPHASIZED IN CHAPTER 6

Annual report (p. 261) A document issued annually by publicly owned companies to their stockholders. Includes audited comparative financial statements, management's discussion and analysis of performance and liquidity, and other information about the company.

Cash budget (p. 275) A forecast of future cash flows. Cash budgets are not financial statements; they are intended only for use by management in planning and controlling business operations.

Cash flows (p. 272) A term describing cash receipts (inflows) and cash payments (outflows).

Classified financial statements (p. 256) Financial statements in which similar items are arranged in groups, and subtotals are shown to assist users in analyzing the statements.

Consolidated financial statements (p. 256) Financial statements that show the combined activities of a *parent company* and its *subsidiaries*.

Comparative financial statements (p. 256) Financial statements of one company for two or more years presented in a side-by-side format to facilitate comparison.

Current assets (p. 257) Cash and other assets which can be converted into cash within one year or the operating cycle (whichever is longer) without interfering with normal business operations.

Current liabilities (p. 257) Existing liabilities which must be paid within one year or the operating cycle (whichever is longer).

Current ratio (p. 259) Current assets divided by current liabilities. A measure of short-term debt-paying ability.

Debt ratio (p. 260) Total liabilities divided by total assets. Represents the portion of total assets financed by debt, rather than by equity capital.

Earnings per share (p. 267) Net income expressed on a per-share basis.

Financing activities (p. 272) A classification within a statement of cash flows. Includes such transactions as borrowing, repaying borrowed amounts, raising equity capital, and making cash payments to owners.

Fundamental analysis (p. 276) Evaluating the reasonableness of a company's stock price by evaluating the performance and financial strength of the company.

Investing activities (p. 272) A classification within a statement of cash flows. Includes cash receipts and cash payments stemming from acquisitions or disposals of plant assets or investments.

Management's discussion and analysis (p. 261) A discussion by management of the company's perfor-mance during the current year, and its financial position at year-end. These discussions are included in the annual reports of publicly owned companies.

Market share (p. 265) A company's percentage share of total dollar sales within its industry.

Net cash flow (p. 273) Cash receipts minus directly related cash outlays.

Operating activities (p. 272) A classification within a statement of cash flows. Represents the cash effects of revenue and expense transactions.

Operating income (p. 264) A subtotal in a multiple-step income statement representing the income stemming from the company's principal business activities.

Parent company (p. 256) A corporation that does portions of its business through other companies that it owns (termed *subsidiaries*).

Percentage change (p. 265) The change in a dollar amount between two accounting periods, expressed as a percentage of the amount in an earlier period. Used in evaluating rates of growth (or decline).

Price-earnings (p/e) ratio (p. 268) The current market price of a company's capital stock, expressed as a multiple of earnings per share. Reflects investors' expectations regarding future earnings.

Quick assets (p. 259) The most liquid current assets. Includes only cash, marketable securities, and receivables.

Quick ratio (p. 259) Quick assets (cash, marketable securities, and receivables) divided by current liabilities. A measure of short-term debt-paying ability.

Return on assets (p. 270) Operating income expressed as a percentage of average total assets. A measure of the efficiency with which management utilizes the assets of a business.

Return on equity (p. 270) Net income expressed as a percentage of average total stockholders' equity. A measure of the rate of return earned on the stockholders' equity in the business.

Statement of cash flows (p. 271) A financial statement that provides information about the cash receipts and cash payments of an organization during the accounting period.

Subsidiary (p. 256) A company that is owned and operated by a *parent company*. In essence, the subsidiary is a part of the parent organization.

Window dressing (p. 262) Legitimate measures taken by management to make a business look as strong as possible at the balance sheet date.

Working capital (p. 259) Current assets less current liabilities. A measure of short-term debt-paying ability.

DEMONSTRATION PROBLEM

The following data is adapted from a recent annual report of **Gateway 2000,** a desktop computer manufacturer and mail order company (dollar amounts are stated in millions):

	1996	1995
Balance sheet data:		
Quick assets	$ 574	$ 497
Current assets	866	649
Current liabilities	525	349
Average stockholders' equity	466	350
Average total assets	950	760
Income statement data:		
Net sales	$3,676	$2,701
Gross profit	616	358
Operating income	249	141
Net income	173	96

During 1996, the company used a significant amount of its cash reserves to finance the expansion of property, plant, and equipment.

INSTRUCTIONS

a. Compute the following for 1996 and 1995. (Round to one decimal place.)
1. Working capital
2. Current ratio
3. Quick ratio

b. Comment upon the trends in the liquidity measures and state whether Gateway 2000 appears to be solvent at the end of 1996.

c. Compute the percentage changes for 1996 in the amounts of net sales and net income. (Round to one-tenth of one percent.)

d. Compute the following for 1996 and 1995. (Round to one-tenth of one percent.)
1. Gross profit rate
2. Net income as a percentage of sales
3. Return on average assets
4. Return on average stockholders' equity

e. Comment upon the trends in the profitability measures computed in parts **c** and **d.**

SOLUTION TO DEMONSTRATION PROBLEM

a.

	1996	1995
1. Working capital:		
($866 − $525)	$341	
($649 − $349)		$300
2. Current ratio:		
($866 ÷ $525)	1.6 to 1	
($649 ÷ $349)		1.9 to 1
3. Quick ratio:		
($574 ÷ $525)	1.1 to 1	
($497 ÷ $349)		1.4 to 1

b. Working capital at the end of 1996 has increased relative to 1995, whereas the current and quick ratios have both decreased slightly (due in large part to cash expenditures for the purchase of property, plant, and equipment). The decline in these ratios appears to be of little significance, as Gateway remains close to industry norms (page 261).

c. Percentage change from 1995:   **1996**

Net sales: [($3,676 − $2,701)] ÷ $2,701]... + 36.1%
Net income: [($173 − $96)] ÷ $96] .... + 80.2%

d.	**1996**	**1995**
1. Gross profit rate:		
($616 ÷ $3,676)	16.8%	
($358 ÷ $2,701)		13.3%
2. Net income as a percentage of sales:		
($173 ÷ $3,676)	4.7%	
($96 ÷ $2,701)		3.6%
3. Return on average assets:		
($249 ÷ $950)	26.2%	
($141 ÷ $760)		18.6%
4. Return on average equity:		
($173 ÷ $466)	37.1%	
($96 ÷ $350)		27.4%

e. The trends in all of the profitability measures are positive. Net sales are increasing faster than the rate of inflation (which was about 4% in 1995 and 1996). At first glance it may appear that both the gross profit rate and net income as a percentage of sales are rather low. However, the desktop computer industry is extremely competitive, which places a "squeeze" on profit margins throughout the industry. Note the rise in both the gross profit rate and net income as a percentage of sales. These trends indicate that costs and expenses are not increasing as quickly as revenue (signs of efficient management).

It is also apparent that management is using resources more efficiently to generate higher returns to shareholders, as both ROI measures in 1996 have increased significantly over 1995 levels. Finally, the return on equity is higher than the overall return on assets. This suggests that management has financed assets in a manner advantageous to stockholders.

SELF-TEST QUESTIONS
Answers to these questions appear on page 301.

1. Which of the following usually is *least* important as a measure of short-term liquidity?
 a. Quick ratio
 b. Current ratio
 c. Debt ratio
 d. Cash flow from operating activities.
2. In each of the last five years, the net sales of Delta Co. have increased at about half the rate of inflation, but net income has increased at approximately *twice* the rate of inflation. During this period, the company's total assets, liabilities, and equity have remained almost unchanged; dividends are approximately equal to net income. These relationships suggest (indicate all correct answers):
 a. Management is successfully controlling costs and expenses.
 b. The company is selling more merchandise every year.
 c. The annual return on assets has been increasing.
 d. Financing activities are likely to result in a net use of cash.

3. From the viewpoint of a stockholder, which of the following relationships do you consider of the *least* significance?
   a. The return on assets consistently is higher than the industry average.
   b. The return on equity has increased in each of the last five years.
   c. Net income is greater than the amount of working capital.
   d. The return on assets is greater than the rate of interest being paid to creditors.

4. The following data are available from the annual report of Newport Marine:

Current assets	$ 480,000		Current liabilities	$300,000
Average total assets	2,000,000		Operating income	240,000
Average total equity	800,000		Net income	80,000

   Which of the following statements are correct? (More than one statement may be correct.)
   a. The return on equity exceeds the return on assets.
   b. The current ratio is .625 to 1.
   c. Working capital is $1,200,000.
   d. None of the above answers are correct.

5. Hunter Corporation's net income was $400,000 in 1997 and $160,000 in 1998. What percentage increase in net income must Hunter achieve in 1999 to offset the decline in profits in 1998?
   a. 60%   b. 150%   c. 600%   d. 67%

6. The cash flows shown in the statement of cash flows are grouped into which of the following major categories?
   a. Operating activities, investing activities, and financing activities.
   b. Cash receipts, cash disbursements, and noncash activities.
   c. Direct cash flows and indirect cash flows.
   d. Operating activities, investing activities, and collecting activities.

7. In financial statement analysis, the most difficult of the following items to predict is whether:
   a. The company's market share is increasing or declining.
   b. The company will be solvent in six months.
   c. Profits will increase in the coming year.
   d. The market price of capital stock will rise or fall over the next two months.

ASSIGNMENT MATERIAL

DISCUSSION QUESTIONS

1. What is the basic purpose of *classifications* in financial statements? Identify the classifications widely used in a balance sheet, a multiple-step income statement, and a statement of cash flows.

2. Distinguish between the terms *classified, comparative,* and *consolidated* as they apply to financial statements. May a given set of financial statements have more than one of these characteristics?

3. Identify three liquidity measures. Explain briefly how each is computed.

4. What is the characteristic common to all *current assets?* Many retail stores regularly sell merchandise on installment plans, calling for payments over a period of 24 or 36 months. Do such receivables qualify as current assets? Explain.

5. What is the *quick ratio?* Under what circumstances are short-term creditors most likely to regard a company's quick ratio as more meaningful than its current ratio?

6. The current assets of Madison Corporation are cash, $80,000; accounts receivable, $340,000; and inventory, $120,000. Current liabilities amount to $300,000. Compute the current ratio, quick ratio, and the amount of working capital.

7. How is the debt ratio computed? Is this ratio a measure of short-term solvency, or something else?

8. We have introduced a number of ratios often computed by users of financial statements. In general terms, with what standards are the results of these computations compared? Explain the purpose of these comparisons.

9. Are the owners of a business personally liable for the debts of the business entity? Explain.

10. Distinguish between a multiple-step and a single-step income statement. Which format results in the higher amount of net income?

11. Identify four ratios or other analytical tools used to evaluate profitability. Explain briefly how each is computed.

12. Assume that the net sales of a large department store have grown annually at a rate of 5% over each of the last several years. Do you think that the store is selling 5% more merchandise each year? Explain.

13. How does income taxes expense differ from normal operating expenses such as advertising and salaries? How is income taxes expense presented in a multiple-step income statement?

14. Distinguish between *operating income* and *net income.*

15. Net sales of the Springfield General Store have been increasing at a reasonable rate, but net income has been declining steadily as a percentage of these sales. What appears to be the problem?

16. Why might earnings per share be more significant to a stockholder in a large corporation than the total amount of net income?

17. Assume that the President of the United States announced an intention to limit the prices and profits of pharmaceutical companies as part of an effort to control health care costs. What effect would you expect the President's statements to have on the p/e ratios and stock prices of pharmaceutical companies such as **Merck** and **Bristol-Myers/Squibb?** Explain.

18. Under what circumstances might a company have a high p/e ratio even when investors are *not* optimistic about the company's future prospects?

19. Is the rate of return on investment (ROI) intended to measure solvency or some other aspect of business operations? Explain.

20. Briefly describe the purpose of a statement of cash flows.

21. Give two examples of cash receipts and two examples of cash payments that fall into each of the following classifications:
    a. Operating activities
    b. Investing activities
    c. Financing activities

22. In the long run, is it more important for a business to have positive cash flows from its operating activities, investing activities, or financing activities?

23. Explain the nature and usefulness of *cash budgets.* Contrast a cash budget with a statement of cash flows.

24. Describe several sources of financial information about publicly owned corporations which are readily available to investors and creditors.

25. If all profitability measures for a particular company show positive trends, is the company's stock price sure to rise? Explain.

EXERCISES

EXERCISE 6-1
Evaluating
Employment
Opportunities

LO 3,6

Assume that you will soon graduate from college and that you have job offers with two pharmaceutical firms. The first offer is with Alpha Research, a relatively new and aggressive company. The second is with Omega Scientific, a very well established and conservative company.

Financial information pertaining to each firm, and to the pharmaceutical industry as a whole, is shown below:

Financial Measure	Alpha	Omega	Industry Average
Current ratio	2.2 to 1	4.5 to 1	2.5 to 1
Quick ratio	1.2 to 1	2.8 to 1	1.5 to 1
Return on assets	17%	8%	10%
Return on equity	28%	14%	16%
P/e ratio	20 to 1	10 to 1	12 to 1

The Omega offer is for $36,000 per year. The Alpha offer is for $32,000. However, unlike Omega, Alpha awards its employees a stock option bonus based upon profitability for the year. Each option enables the employee to purchase shares of Alpha's common stock at a significantly reduced price. The more profitable this company is, the more stock each employee can buy at a discount.

Show how the above information may help you justify accepting the Alpha Research offer, even though the starting salary is $4,000 lower than the Omega Scientific offer.

EXERCISE 6-2
Accounting Terminology

LO 1-7

Listed below are twelve technical accounting terms introduced or emphasized in this chapter.

P/e ratio ~~Market share~~ Current ratio
Debt ratio Earnings per share Operating income
Quick ratio Operating activities Return on equity
~~Subsidiary~~ Comparative financial statements Parent company

Each of the following statements may (or may not) describe one of these technical terms. For each statement, indicate the term described, or answer "None" if the statement does not correctly describe any of the terms.

a. A ratio that relates the total net income of a corporation to the holdings of individual stockholders.

b. The classification in a statement of cash flows from which it is most important to generate positive cash flows.

c. A measure of the long-term safety of creditors' positions.

d. A measure of investors' expectations of the future profitability of a business.

e. An ROI measure of the effectiveness with which management utilizes a company's resources, regardless of how those resources are financed.

f. A company that does business through other companies that it owns.

g. A measure of the profitability of a company's *primary* business activities.

h. The most widely used measure of short-term debt-paying ability.

i. A form of business organization in which the owners are *personally* liable for the debts of the business organization.

j. Financial statements in which similar items are grouped in a manner that develops useful subtotals.

EXERCISE 6-3
Recognition of
Industry
Characteristics

 LO 1,3

EXERCISE 6-4
Measures of
Liquidity

 LO 1,2,3

Reebok is a manufacturer of popular athletic footwear. **Bell Atlantic** is the largest telephone company in the northeastern United States. Both companies are solvent and profitable. Which company would you expect to have the higher current ratio? Which company do you believe has the greater debt-paying ability? Explain fully the reasons for your answers.

Tyco Toys is a manufacturer of toys and children's products. Shown below are selected items appearing in a recent balance sheet (dollar amounts are in millions.)

Cash and short-term investments	$ 47.3
Receivables	159.7
Inventories	72.3
Prepaid expenses and other current assets	32.0
Total current liabilities	130.1
Total liabilities	279.4
Total stockholders' equity	344.0

a. Using the information above, compute the amounts of Tyco's (1) quick assets, and (2) total current assets.

b. Compute the company's (1) quick ratio, (2) current ratio, and (3) working capital (Round ratios to one decimal place.)

c. Discuss whether the company appears solvent from the viewpoint of a short-term creditor.

EXERCISE 6-5
Multiple-Step
Income Statements

 LO 5,6

Net sales
− CGS
gross profit
− operating exp
operating income

THE GAP, INC. Statement of Earnings For the Year Ended February 3, 1996	
Net sales	$4,395,253
Costs and expenses:	
Cost of goods sold	(2,821,455)
Operating expenses	(1,004,396)
Interest revenue	15,797
Earnings before income taxes	$ 585,199
Income taxes	(231,160)
Net earnings = *net income*	$ 354,039
Earnings per share	$1.58

Comparative balance sheets report average total assets for the year of *$2,343,068* and average total equity of *$1,640,437* (dollar amounts in thousands, except earnings per share).

a. Prepare an income statement for the year in a multiple-step format.

b. Compute the (1) gross profit rate, (2) net income as a percentage of net sales, (3) return on assets, and (4) return on equity for the year. (Round computations to the nearest one-tenth of one percent.)

c. Explain why interest revenue is not included in the company's gross profit computation.

EXERCISE 6-6
Logical Gross
Profit
Relationships
 LO 3

Several factors must be considered in interpreting a company's gross profit rate.

a. Companies such as **Lotus Development** and **Microsoft** usually enjoy a higher gross profit rate on sales of a particular software product when it is first introduced than they do in later years. Why?

b. For each of the following pairs of businesses, indicate which you would expect to have the higher gross profit rate. Briefly explain the reasons for your answer.
1. A grocery store or a retail furniture store.
2. **Neiman-Marcus** (a chain of high-fashion department stores) or **Wal-Mart** (a rapidly growing chain of discount stores).

EXERCISE 6-7
P/e Ratios
 LO 3,6

In the late 1980's, **Ford Motor Company** was growing fast. Its earnings per share for the three-year period ended December 31, 1988, were as follows:

	1988	1987	1986
Earnings per share	$5.48	$4.53	$3.08

At the end of 1988, the company's common stock was trading at approximately $27.50 per share. Earnings per share for the five-year period that followed 1988 are shown below:

	1993	1992	1991	1990	1989
Earnings per share	$2.27	($0.77)	($2.40)	$0.93	$4.11

a. Compute the percentage increase in Ford's earnings per share in 1987 and in 1988. (Round to one-tenth of one percent).

b. Compute the p/e ratio of Ford's stock at the end of 1988. (Round to the nearest whole number.)

c. What does the p/e ratio indicate about investors' expectations? Were these expectations substantiated in the five years subsequent to 1988? Explain.

EXERCISE 6-8
Relationships
Within an
Income Statement
 LO 3,5

Coast Hardware and Fashion Center have similar amounts of assets, net sales, operating expenses, and net income. However, Coast has a higher cost of goods sold, whereas Fashion Center has higher interest expense.

Indicate which of these companies has the higher **(a)** gross profit rate, and **(b)** return on assets. In each case, explain the reasoning behind your answer.

EXERCISE 6-9
Ethics of Disclosure
 LO 3,6

For over a decade, Comtex Corporation has experienced rapid growth in net sales and gross profit rates. To emphasize this trend, each year the company's annual report includes separate full-color graphs of net sales and gross profit rates for a five-year period.

For the current year, Comtex once again experienced record sales levels. However, due to factors beyond management's control, its gross profit rate dropped substantially in comparison to prior years. As a result of this decline, management decided to eliminate the gross profit rate graph from the annual report and show *only* the five-year graph of increasing net sales.

Is it ethical for management to "hide" from investors the fact that the company's gross profit rate has declined? Explain.

EXERCISE 6-10
ROI
LO 3,6

Shown below are selected data from a recent annual report of **Sprint Corporation**, a large telecommunications provider. (Dollar amounts are in millions.)

	Beginning of the Year	End of the Year
Total assets	$14,548	$15,196
Total stockholders' equity	4,562	4,674
Operating income		2,422
Net income		349

a. Compute for the year Sprint's return on average total assets. (Round computations to the nearest one-tenth of one percent.)

b. Compute for the year Sprint's return on average total stockholders' equity. (Round computations to the nearest one-tenth of one percent.)

c. Could the increase in Sprint's total stockholders' equity for the year be the result of an increase in *market value* of the company's stock? Explain.

EXERCISE 6-11
Computing and Interpreting Rates of Change
LO 3,6

Selected information from the financial statements of Golden Harvest appears below:

	1998	1997
Net sales	$2,200,000	$2,000,000
Total expenses	1,998,000	1,800,000

a. Compute the percentage change in 1998 for the amounts of (1) net sales and (2) total expenses.

b. Using the information developed in part **a**, express your opinion as to whether the company's *net income* for 1998:
  1. Increased at a greater or lower percentage rate than did net sales.
  2. Represented a larger or smaller percentage of net sales revenue than in 1997. For each answer, explain your reasoning *without* making any computations or references to dollar amounts.

EXERCISE 6-12
Format of a Statement of Cash Flows
LO 3,7

The accounting staff of Cajun Chef has assembled the following information for the year ended December 31, 1998.

Cash, beginning of year	$ 38,600
Cash, end of year	57,600
Cash paid to acquire plant assets	19,000
Proceeds from short-term borrowing	10,000
Loans made to borrowers	5,000
Collections on loans (excluding interest)	4,000
Interest and dividends received	12,000
Cash received from customers	815,000
Proceeds from sales of plant assets	7,000
Dividends paid	80,000
Cash paid to suppliers and employees	635,000
Interest paid	19,000
Income taxes paid	71,000

a. Using this information, prepare a formal statement of cash flows. Include a proper heading for the statement, and classify all figures into the following three categories: operating activities, investing activities, and financing activities. Place brackets around the dollar amounts of all cash disbursements.

b. Based upon the statement of cash flows prepared in part **a,** did Cajun Chef generate adequate cash flows from operating activities to finance the purchase of plant assets during the year? Do you think that the $10,000 proceeds from short-term borrowing were used to acquire plant assets? Defend your answer.

EXERCISE 6-13
Research Problem

Obtain from your library (or other source) the most recent annual report of a publicly owned company.

a. Using the annual report data, compute the basic measures of liquidity, long-term credit risk, and profitability summarized in the table on page 277. Compare these measures to the appropriate industry norms available in your library. Briefly comment on your findings.

b. Using the financial pages of a daily newspaper (such as *The Wall Street Journal*), determine (1) the current market price of your company's common stock, (2) its 52-week high and low market prices, and (3) its p/e ratio. Briefly comment on your findings.

c. Based upon your analysis in parts **a** and **b,** make a recommendation as to whether investors should buy shares of the stock, hold the shares they currently own, or sell the shares they currently own. Defend your position.

EXERCISE 6-14
Quality of
Cash Flows

Weis Markets is a rapidly expanding East Coast supermarket chain that recently reported sales exceeding $2 billion, net profit of over $80 million, and dividends to stockholders of nearly $35 million. Summary data from the company's statement of cash flows is shown below. (Dollar amounts are stated in thousands.)

Net cash flows from operating activities	$ 96,835
Net cash flows from investing activities	(37,508)
Net cash flows from financing activities	(60,053)
Net decrease in cash during the year	(726)
Beginning cash (per balance sheet)	$ 4,011
Ending cash (per balance sheet)	$ 3,285

Is the net decrease in cash reported in the company's statement of cash flows likely to be of serious concern? Defend your answer.

EXERCISE 6-15
Toys "R" Us
Management
Discussion and
Analysis

The annual report of a publicly owned corporation includes *management's discussion and analysis* of the company's operations, financial condition, and liquidity. The annual report of **Toys "R" Us, Inc.,** including the discussion and analysis by management, appears in Appendix A at the end of this textbook.

Read management's discussion and analysis. Identify at least five items that should be of interest to investors, but which investors would *not* be able to determine for themselves from the financial statements. Briefly discuss the *usefulness* of each disclosure to investors. Be prepared to explain your findings in class, including references to the appropriate pages and paragraphs in the illustrated discussion.

PROBLEMS

PROBLEM 6-1
Solvency of
Safeway

L0 1–3

Safeway, Inc., is one of the world's largest supermarket chains. Shown below are selected items adapted from a recent Safeway balance sheet. (Dollar amounts are in millions.)

Cash	$ 74.8
Receivables	152.7
Merchandise inventories..	1,191.8
Prepaid expenses..	95.5
Fixtures and equipment..	2,592.9
Retained earnings	284.4
Total current liabilities...	1,939.0

INSTRUCTIONS

a. Using the information above, compute the amounts of Safeway's total current assets and total quick assets.

b. Compute the company's (1) current ratio, (2) quick ratio, and (3) working capital. (Round to one decimal place.)

c. From these computations, are you able to conclude whether Safeway is a good credit risk for short-term creditors, or on the brink of bankruptcy? Explain.

d. Is there anything unusual about the operating cycle of supermarkets that would make you think that they normally would have lower current ratios than, say, large department stores?

e. What *other types of information* could you utilize in performing a more complete analysis of Safeway's solvency?

PROBLEM 6-2
Balance Sheet
Measures of Liquidity
and Credit Risk

L0 1–3

A recent balance sheet of **Tootsie Roll Industries** included the following items, among others. (Dollar amounts are stated in thousands.)

C QA Cash	$ 47,524
C QA Marketable securities (short-term)	55,926
C QA Accounts receivable	23,553
C Inventories	32,210
C Prepaid expenses...	5,736
C Retained earnings	121,477
Notes payable to banks (due within one year)..	20,000
Accounts payable	5,912
Dividends payable	1,424
Accrued liabilities (short-term)	21,532
Income taxes payable..	6,438

The company also reported total assets of $353,816 thousand, total liabilities of $81,630 thousand, and a return on total assets of *18.1%.*

INSTRUCTIONS

a. Compute Tootsie Roll's (1) quick assets, (2) current assets, and (3) current liabilities.

b. Compute Tootsie Roll's (1) quick ratio, (2) current ratio, (3) working capital, and (4) debt ratio. (Round to one decimal place.)

c. Discuss the company's liquidity from the viewpoints of (1) short-term creditors, (2) long-term creditors, and (3) stockholders.

PROBLEM 6-3
Measures of
Liquidity
LO 1–3

Some of the accounts appearing in the year-end financial statements of Diet Frozen Dinners appear below. This list includes all of the company's current assets and current liabilities.

Sales	$1,980,000
Accumulated depreciation: equipment	370,000
Notes payable (due in 90 days)	70,000
Retained earnings	221,320
Cash	47,600
Capital stock	150,000
Marketable securities	175,040
Accounts payable	125,430
Mortgage payable (due in 15 years)	320,000
Salaries payable	7,570
Dividends	25,000
Income taxes payable	14,600
Accounts receivable	230,540
Inventory	179,600
Unearned revenue	10,000
Unexpired insurance	4,500

INSTRUCTIONS

a. Prepare a schedule of the company's current assets and current liabilities. Select the appropriate items from the above list.

b. Compute the current ratio and the amount of working capital. Explain how each of these measurements is computed. State, with reasons, whether you consider the company to be in a strong or weak current position.

PROBLEM 6-4
Classified Financial
Statements; Ratio
Analysis
LO 1,2,5,6

Westport Department Store has advertised for an accounting student to work in its accounting department during the summer, and you have applied for the job. To determine whether you are familiar with the content of classified financial statements, the controller of Westport has developed the following problem based upon the store's operations in the year ended December 31, 1998:

Available information (dollar amounts in thousands):

Net sales	$10,000
Net income	? *800*
Current liabilities	2,000
Selling expenses	1,000
Long-term liabilities	1,600
Total assets (and total liabilities & stockholders' equity)	6,800
Stockholders' equity	?
Gross profit	? *3,000*
Cost of goods sold	7,000
Current assets	4,000
Income taxes expense and other nonoperating items	220
Operating income	? *980*
General and administrative expenses	980
Plant and equipment	2,600
Other assets	?

8 IS
7 BS

INSTRUCTIONS

a. Using the captions given above, prepare for Westport Department Store a condensed:

    1. Classified balance sheet at December 31, 1998.

    2. Multiple-step income statement for the year ended December 31, 1998.

Show supporting computations used in determining any missing amounts. (***Note:*** Your financial statements should include only as much detail as these captions permit. For example, the first asset listed in your balance sheet will be "Current assets . . . $4,000.")

b. Compute at year-end the company's:

    1. Current ratio.

    2. Working capital.

c. Compute the company's 1998:

    1. Gross profit rate.

    2. Return on total assets. (Round to the nearest percent.)

    3. Return on total stockholders' equity.

(***Note:*** In the last two computations, use the amounts of total assets and stockholders' equity from your classified balance sheet as a substitute for the average amounts during the year.)

d. Assume that you get the summer job with Westport Department Store. Your first project is to compute the store's working capital and current ratio as of June 1, 1999. You notice that both measures differ significantly from the December 31, 1998, amounts computed in part **b.** Explain why these measures may have changed so dramatically in just five months.

PROBLEM 6-5
Researching
AST Research

The personal computer industry has undergone many pressures throughout the 1990s. Competition among a growing number of manufacturers has resulted in lower selling prices and reduced gross profit rates industry-wide. In addition to pricing constraints, rapidly changing technology has shortened product life-cycles significantly.

Perhaps no firm in the industry has suffered more from these pressures than **AST Research.** AST designs and manufactures a broad line of personal computers and network server systems. The company's gross profit rate has been drastically eroded in recent years by (1) price competition throughout the industry, and (2) an increased demand for those AST products with the lowest gross profit rates.

Locate a copy of AST's annual report for 1995 or a more recent year. (Your library may have these reports on file in either hard copy or electronically. If you are unable to locate an annual report, your instructor may be willing to provide you with the data needed to complete part **a.**)

a. Rounding dollar amounts to the nearest million and computations to the nearest one-tenth of one percent, determine:

    1. The annual percentage change in AST's net sales in each of the *four* years from 1992 through 1995.

    2. AST's gross profit rate in each of the *three* years, 1993 through 1995.

b. Comment upon how price competition and "sales mix" appear to have affected the sales growth and margins of AST from 1993 through 1995.

c. Locate and summarize at least one article from a *recent* business publication discussing how AST has been responding to the challenges created by market pressures.

PROBLEM 6-6
Basic Ratio
Analysis

Blockbuster Entertainment Corporation operates under the name **Blockbuster Video** and is engaged primarily in the business of renting video tapes. Shown below are selected data from a recent annual report. (Dollar amounts are stated in thousands.)

	Beginning of the Year	End of the Year
Total current assets	$ 54,130	$ 92,592
Total current liabilities	63,481	83,357
Total assets	234,698	417,413
Total stockholders' equity	124,058	208,189
Operating income		76,141
Net income		44,152

The company has long-term liabilities which bear interest at annual rates ranging from 11% to 16%.

INSTRUCTIONS

a. Compute the company's current ratio at (1) the *beginning* of the year and (2) the *end* of the year. (Carry to two decimal places.)

b. Compute the company's working capital at (1) the beginning of the year, and (2) the end of the year. (Express dollar amounts in thousands.)

c. Is the company's short-term debt-paying ability improving or deteriorating? As a short-term creditor, would you consider the company to be as good a credit risk as, say, **BellSouth**—a regional telephone company with a current ratio of *.9 to 1?* Explain.

d. Compute the company's (1) return on average total assets, and (2) return on average stockholders' equity. (Round average assets and average equity to the nearest dollar, and final computations to the nearest 1 percent.)

e. As an equity investor, do you think that Blockbuster's management is utilizing the company's resources in a reasonably efficient manner? Explain.

PROBLEM 6-7
Ratios; Goodyear
vs. BF Goodrich

Goodyear Tire and Rubber and **B.F. Goodrich** are two of the world's largest publicly owned manufacturers of tire products. Shown below are data from the companies' recent annual reports. Dollar amounts are stated in thousands.

	Goodyear	Goodrich
Total current assets	$3,841,600	$ 950,000
Total current liabilities	2,736,300	600,700
Total quick assets	1,883,300	459,300
Average total assets	9,789,600	2,489,600
Average stockholders' equity	3,281,700	1,000,800
Operating income	1,135,400	242,900
Net income	611,000	118,000

INSTRUCTIONS

a. Compute the following for each company (round computations to one decimal place.)
  1. Current ratio.
  2. Quick ratio.
  3. Working capital.
  4. Return on average total assets.
  5. Return on average total stockholders' equity.

b. From the viewpoint of a short-term creditor, which of these companies appears to have the greater short-term debt-paying ability? Explain.

c. In which company does management appear to be using the resources under its control most efficiently? Explain the reasons for your answer.

PROBLEM 6-8
A Shorter Version of Comprehensive Problem **3** Using Prior Year's Data

LO 2,3,6

The following data is adapted from a recent annual report of Toys "R" Us (dollar amounts in millions):

	For Years Ended	
	1/28/95	1/29/94
Balance sheet data:		
Quick assets	$ 486	$ 890
Current assets	2,531	2,708
Current liabilities	2,137	2,075
Average stockholders' equity	3,289	3,019
Average total assets	6,360	5,736
Income statement data:		
Net sales	$8,746	$7,946
Gross profit	2,738	2,451
Operating income	912	821
Net income	532	483
Cash flow data:		
Net cash provided by operating activities	$ 589	$ 657

INSTRUCTIONS

a. Compute the following for each of the above years (round to the nearest decimal place):
 1. Quick ratio.
 2. Current ratio.
 3. Working capital.

b. Comment upon the trends in the liquidity measures and state whether the company appears solvent at January 28, 1995.

c. Compute the percentage changes in the amounts of net sales and net income for the year ending January 28, 1995.

d. Compute the following for each of the above years (round to one-tenth of one percent):
 1. Gross profit rate.
 2. Net income as a percentage of net sales.
 3. Return on average assets.
 4. Return on average stockholders' equity.

e. Comment upon the trends in the profitability measures computed in parts c and d.

PROBLEM 6-9
Statement of Cash Flows

LO 3,7

For the last five years, ShowTime Video has successfully operated two video rental stores in Baltimore. The company's cash flows for 1998 appear below:

Interest paid	$ (20,000)
Dividends paid to stockholders	(50,000)
Cash receipts from customers	550,000
Payments to suppliers and employees	(370,000)
Purchases of plant assets	(420,000)
Proceeds from long-term borrowing	300,000
Repayment of short-term debt	(25,000)
Interest received from investments	10,000
Income taxes paid	(45,000)

At December 31, **1997,** the company's balance sheet showed cash of $96,000.

INSTRUCTIONS

a. Arrange this information into the format of a statement of cash flows.

b. Is the company more or less solvent at the end of 1998 than it was at the beginning of the year? Explain.

c. ShowTime Video has a policy of paying dividends equal to approximately 40% of its net cash flow from operating activities. As operating cash flows have been very stable over the past five years, the company has paid dividends of approximately $50,000 per year. In coming years, would you expect the amount of ShowTime's dividend payments to increase, decrease, or remain about the same? Explain your reasoning.

PROBLEM 6-10
Statement of
Cash Flows

The Boston Celtics Limited Partnership is a publicly owned company that owns the professional basketball team known as the **Boston Celtics.** (The Celtics are the only professional sports team that is publicly owned.) The following items are adapted from the statement of cash flows sent to its partners at the end of a past fiscal year (dollar amounts are stated in thousands):

Cash receipts:

Regular season receipts:

Ticket sales	$14,355
Television and radio	10,214
Other, principally advertising	1,346
Playoff receipts	5,020
Interest received	723
Proceeds from league expansion	2,955
Proceeds from sales of marketable securities	2,816

Cash payments:

Regular season expenditures:

Team expenses (including players' salaries)	(10,683)
Game expenses	(2,363)
Playoff expenses paid	(84)
General and administrative expenses paid	(3,153)
Selling and promotion expenses paid	(599)
Ticket refunds paid	(3,813)
Payment of deferred player compensation	(1,019)
Payments to acquire marketable securities	(5,996)
Loans made to players	(496)
Other expenditures for investing activities	(2)
Distributions to partners	(10,400)

Cash balances:

Beginning of the year	2,577
End of the year	1,398

Approximately half of the teams in the National Basketball Association (NBA) participate annually in a five-round series of playoffs that determine the national champion. The Celtics often participate in these playoffs, but in this year, they were eliminated in the first round.

INSTRUCTIONS

a. Rearrange this information into a statement of cash flows. (Proceeds from league expansion were received as a result of the National Basketball Association selling franchises to new "expansion teams." The Celtics classify these proceeds as an operating activity.)

b. For the year to which this data pertains, the Celtics were profitable. Why, then, are there no income taxes payments included among the Celtics' operating activities?

c. Identify special "industry characteristics" that one should consider in forecasting the Celtics' future cash flows from operating activities.

d. Assume that you expect no significant changes in ticket sales, television revenues, investing activities, and financing activities (other than distributions to partners). Is there any reason to think that distributions to partners might change significantly in the near future?

PROBLEM 6-11
Financial Statement
Analysis

Shown below are selected data from the financial statements of Carriage Trade, a retail furniture store.

From the balance sheet:

Cash	$ 30,000
Accounts receivable	150,000
Inventory	200,000
Plant assets (net of accumulated depreciation)	500,000
Current liabilities	150,000
Total stockholders' equity	300,000
Total assets	1,000,000

From the income statement:

Net sales	$1,500,000
Cost of goods sold	1,080,000
Operating expenses	315,000
Interest expense	84,000
Income taxes expense	6,000
Net income	15,000

From the statement of cash flows:

Net cash provided by operating activities (including interest paid of $79,000)		$ 40,000
Net cash used in investing activities		(46,000)
Financing activities:		
Amounts borrowed	$ 50,000	
Repayment of amounts borrowed	(14,000)	
Dividends paid	(20,000)	
Net cash provided by financing activities		16,000
Net increase in cash during the year		$ 10,000

INSTRUCTIONS

a. Explain how the interest expense shown in the income statement could be $84,000, when the interest payment appearing in the statement of cash flows is only $79,000.

b. Compute the following (round to one decimal place):
   1. Current ratio.
   2. Quick ratio.
   3. Working capital.
   4. Debt ratio.

c. Comment upon these measurements and evaluate Carriage Trade's short-term debt-paying ability.

   d. Compute the following ratios (assume that the year-end amounts of total assets and total stockholders' equity also represent the average amounts throughout the year):
   1. Return on assets.
   2. Return on equity.

   e. Comment upon the company's performance under these measurements. Explain *why* the return on assets and return on equity are so different.

   f. Discuss (1) the apparent safety of long-term creditors' claims, and (2) the prospects for Carriage Trade continuing its dividend payments at the present level.

CASES

CASE 6-1
Evaluating
Debt-Paying
Ability

LO 1–4

You are a loan officer with First Kansas Bank. Dan Scott owns two successful restaurants, each of which has applied to your bank for a $250,000 one-year loan for the purpose of opening a second location. Condensed balance sheets for the two business entities are shown below:

KANSAS STEAK RANCH				
Balance Sheet				
December 31, 1998				
Assets			**Liabilities & Stockholders' Equity**	
Current assets...............	$ 75,000		Current liabilities...........................	$ 30,000
Plant and equipment......	300,000		Long-term liabilities	200,000
			Capital stock.................................	100,000
			Retained earnings	45,000
			Total liabilities &	
Total assets..................	$375,000		stockholders' equity..................	$375,000

THE STOCKYARDS				
Balance Sheet				
December 31, 1998				
Assets			**Liabilities & Owners' Equity**	
Current assets...............	$ 24,000		Current liabilities...........................	$ 30,000
Plant and equipment......	301,000		Long-term liabilities	200,000
			Capital, Dan Scott........................	95,000
			Total liabilities &	
Total assets..................	$325,000		owners' equity	$325,000

   Both restaurants are popular and have been successful over the last several years. Kansas Steak Ranch has been slightly more profitable, but the operating results for the two businesses have been quite similar. You think that either restaurant's second location should be successful. On the other hand, you know that restaurants are a very "faddish" type of business, and that their popularity and profitability can change very quickly.

Dan Scott is one of the wealthiest people in Kansas. He made a fortune—estimated at more than $2 billion—as the founder of Micro Time, a highly successful manufacturer of computer software. Scott now is retired and spends most of his time at Second Life, his 50,000 acre cattle ranch. Both of his restaurants are run by experienced professional managers.

INSTRUCTIONS

a. Compute the current ratio and working capital of each business entity.

b. Based upon the information provided in this case, which of these businesses do you consider to be the better credit risk? Explain fully.

c. What simple measure might you insist upon which would make the other business as good a credit risk as the one you identified in part **b?** Explain.

CASE 6-2
Strategies to
Improve the
Current Ratio

LO 3

Home Improvement Centers owns a chain of nine retail stores which sell building materials, hardware, and garden supplies. In early October, the company's current ratio is 1.7 to 1. This is about normal for the company, but is lower than the current ratios of several large competitors. Management feels that to qualify for the best credit terms from its suppliers, the company's year-end balance sheet should indicate a current ratio of at least 2 to 1.

INSTRUCTIONS

a. Indicate whether taking each of the following actions would increase or decrease the company's current ratio. Explain your reasoning.
   1. Pay some of the company's current liabilities.
   2. Purchase large amounts of inventory on account.
   3. Offer credit customers a special discount if they pay their account balance prior to year-end.

b. Propose several other ethical steps which management might take to increase the company's current ratio prior to year-end.

CASE 6-3
Statement of
Cash Flows

LO 3,7

The Emerald City and Humpty's are retail stores that sell computer software. A summary of each store's net cash flows for the last three years appears below. (Dollar amounts are stated in thousands.)

The Emerald City	1998	1997	1996
Net cash provided by (used in) operating activities	$ (10)	$ 40	$ 85
Net cash provided by (used in) investing activities	50	20	(10)
Net cash provided by (used in) financing activities	80	50	20
Increase (decrease) in cash during the year	$120	$110	$ 95
Cash balance at year-end (per balance sheet)	$335	$215	$105
Humpty's			
Net cash provided by operating activities	$320	$260	$210
Net cash provided by (used in) investing activities	(200)	(100)	(50)
Net cash provided by (used in) financing activities	(150)	(100)	(70)
Increase (decrease) in cash during the year	$(30)	$ 60	$ 90
Cash balance at year-end (per balance sheet)	$260	$290	$230

INSTRUCTIONS

a. Explain briefly the nature of (1) *operating activities,* (2) *investing activities,* and (3) *financing activities* as these terms are used in a statement of cash flows.

b. Explain the meaning of the phrase, "Net cash provided by (used in) . . . activities." As part of your answer, explain the use of brackets ( ) as indicated by this caption.

c. For each of the three cash flow classifications discussed in part **a,** describe two types of transactions that involve (1) cash receipts, and (2) cash payments.

d. Which of these stores appears "healthier" in terms of its cash flows? Explain your reasoning and include a brief discussion of any **trends** relevant to your conclusion.

CASE 6-4
Effects of
Business
Strategies

 LO 3,7

Computer World is a retail computer store that sells both to business organizations and individuals. Creditworthy businesses are allowed to purchase merchandise on 30-day credit terms; individuals normally are required to pay cash. Merchandise on the sales floor is displayed on racks and counter tops, but is not hooked up for actual operation. There are two demonstration rooms in the back of the store where salespeople can demonstrate the operation of various products.

Computer World's management is considering the probable future effects of the following three business strategies:

1. Allow creditworthy individuals to purchase merchandise on 6- and 12-month installment plans.

2. Change to a new supplier for purchases of certain high-cost merchandise. The new supplier charges slightly higher prices than the current supplier, but will allow Computer World 90 days to pay for credit purchases, instead of only 30 days.

3. Remodel the interior of the store around six functional "workstations" that will permit immediate demonstration of various products. (The remodeling would involve some construction work. This work would be inconvenient but would not require any suspension of business operations.)

INSTRUCTIONS

a. Indicate the effects that you would expect implementation of each strategy to have upon net income and upon net cash flow from operating activities in (1) the immediate future—say, the next two months—and (2) the "long run"—say, after the strategy has been in effect for one year. Organize your answer in the columnar format illustrated below; use the code letters **I** for increase, **D** for decrease, and **NE** for no effect.

	Short-term effects		Long-term effects	
Strategy	Net Income	Operating Cash Flow	Net Income	Operating Cash Flow
1				

b. Explain the reasoning behind your answers.

CASE 6-5
Cash Budgets

 LO 3,7

Red Onion operates a chain of 38 retail produce markets. The stores purchase produce from local suppliers; all merchandise is sold for cash.

A summary of the current year's budgeted and actual operating cash flows of the downtown Seattle store appears below:

	Actual Cash Flows	Budgeted Cash Flows	Over or (Under) Budget
Cash sales	$1,250,000	$1,500,000	$(250,000)
Payments to produce suppliers	$ 500,000	$ 600,000	$(100,000)
Expenses other than payroll and bonuses	350,000	320,000	30,000
Payroll to store personnel	295,000	300,000	(5,000)
Bonuses to store personnel	75,000	50,000	25,000
Total cash expenditures	$1,220,000	$1,270,000	$ (50,000)
Net cash flow from operating activities	$ 30,000	$ 230,000	$(200,000)

INSTRUCTIONS

Assume that you are the regional sales manager and are responsible for 15 Red Onion stores operating in Washington, Oregon, and Idaho. Comment upon the overall performance of the downtown Seattle store. Discuss each of the listed cash flows, indicating whether you view the actual cash flow as a satisfactory level of performance.

INTERNET 6-1
Evaluating
Solvency and
Stock Price
LO 2,3,6

INTERNET ASSIGNMENTS

PART I

Visit the home page of Ben & Jerry's Ice Cream by opening the following Internet connection:

www.benjerry.com

From the menu, select "Site Index." From the index, choose "Visit our Library." Spend some time learning about the company by reading about new products, press releases, and comments from the CEO. Next, select the company's most recent annual report from the library "shelves."

INSTRUCTIONS

a. Compute the following measures of short-term solvency at the end of the most recent year: (1) working capital, (2) current ratio, and (3) quick ratio

b. Compute the following measures of profitability for the most recent year-end: (1) return on assets, and (2) return on equity.

c. Using the five-year summary data from the company's annual report, compute the following percentages:
   1. Sales growth percentage for the past *four* years.
   2. Gross profit percentage for the past *five* years.
   3. Net income as a percentage of sales for the past *five* years.

d. Using the measures computed in parts **a, b,** and **c** discuss briefly the company's prospects for short-term solvency and profitability.

PART II

Visit the Stockmaster home page by opening the following Internet connection:

www.stockmaster.com

In the space provided next to "Stocks," enter the following stock symbol for Ben & Jerry's Ice Cream: **BJICA.**

INSTRUCTIONS

a. Based upon the company's p/e ratio reported by Stockmaster, do investor expectations of future earnings seem positive or negative?

b. Examine the graph of the company's stock price over time. Discuss any trends you may observe.

c. Based upon all of the data you have gathered, register your vote with Stockmaster (at the bottom of the screen) regarding how positive or negative you are about the company's stock for the next three months. How does your vote compare to votes cast by other "expert" investors?

Additional Internet assignments for this chapter are found in Appendix B at the end of this textbook.

OUR COMMENTS ON THE IN-TEXT CASES

YOU AS A POTENTIAL INVESTOR (P. 262) It is common for fast food restaurants (such as **Wendy's** and **McDonald's**) to report seemingly low measures of short-term liquidity. This does not mean, however, that these companies will have difficulty paying their current liabilities as they become due. In fact, both Wendy's and McDonald's are extremely *liquid* companies. The reason why the financial measures of their liquidity appear insufficient is that (1) all their sales are cash sales and, therefore, they have no accounts receivable, and (2) their inventory converts into cash at a faster rate than their current liabilities come due.

YOU AS AN INDUSTRY ANALYST (P. 274) There simply isn't enough information provided in **K-Mart's** statement of cash flows to form a conclusion regarding the company's ability to remain solvent. The fact that K-Mart reported an increase in cash of $742 million dollars for the year does *not* necessarily mean that the company is becoming increasingly solvent.

It is important to note that cash flows from operations were actually *negative* for the year. In the long run, all companies must be able to generate positive operating cash flows to survive. K-Mart's total cash flow for the year was positive only because cash flows from investing and financing activities were positive. Interestingly, cash flows from investing activities were positive due to the liquidation of numerous K-Mart stores nationwide, whereas cash flows from financing were positive due to significant borrowing activity throughout the year.

ANSWERS TO SELF-TEST QUESTIONS

1. c   **2.** a, c, d   **3.** c   **4.** d (see below)   **5.** b   **6.** a   **7.** d

Why answers a, b, and c in question **4** are incorrect:

a. The return on assets, 12% ($240,000 ÷ $2,000,000), exceeds the return on equity, which is 10% ($80,000 ÷ $800,000).

b. The current ratio is 1.6 to 1 ($480,000 ÷ $300,000).

c. Working capital amounts to $180,000 ($480,000 − $300,000).

Toys "R" Us, Inc.*

ANALYSIS OF THE FINANCIAL STATEMENTS OF A PUBLICLY OWNED CORPORATION

The purpose of this Comprehensive Problem is to acquaint you with the content of an annual report. It is based upon the January 28, 1995 annual report of **Toys "R" Us, Inc.** (fiscal year 1994), reproduced in Appendix A of this textbook. The problem contains three major parts, which are independent of one another. *Part I* is designed to familiarize you with the content of an annual report; *part II* involves analysis of the company's liquidity; and *part III* analyzes the trend in its profitability.

If you work this problem as a group assignment, each group member should be prepared to discuss the group's findings and conclusions in class.

A word of caution: Toys "R" Us ends its fiscal years on unusual dates. Before answering questions about this company's financial statements, read the note entitled "Fiscal Year" on page A-11 of the annual report.

PART I
Annual reports include not only comparative financial statements, but also the following sources of information:

- *Financial Highlights,* a summary of key statistics for the past five or ten years.
- A letter from management addressed *To Our Stockholders.*
- A discussion by management of the results of operations and the company's financial condition.
- Several pages of *Notes* that accompany the financial statements.
- Reports by management and by the independent auditors in which they express their respective responsibilities for the financial statements.

INSTRUCTIONS
Answer each of the following questions and briefly explain *where* in the statements, notes, or other sections of the annual report you located the information used in your answer.

a. Who is primarily responsible for the content of the financial statements—the independent auditors, management, or the company's Board of Directors? In general

---

*Logo and data courtesy, of Toys "R" Us, Inc.

terms, what measures have been undertaken by *management* to ensure reliability of the statements?

b. How many years are covered in each of the four types of comparative financial statements? Were all of these statements audited? Name the auditors. What were the auditors' conclusions concerning these statements?

c. Toys "R" Us combines its statement of retained earnings with another financial statement. Were are details about changes in the amount of retained earnings found?

d. Over the past three years, have the company's annual net cash flows been positive or negative from (1) operating activities, (2) investing activities, and (3) financing activities? Has the company's cash balance increased or decreased during each of these three years?

e. Why do the company's fiscal years end on different dates (that is, January 28, January 29, and January 30)? Are these fiscal years of equal length? Upon what date will the company's *next* fiscal year end?

f. What was the amount of net sales during the *fourth quarter* of the fiscal year ended January 28, 1995? What was the percentage change in this fourth quarter's net sales relative to sales in the fourth quarter of the prior year? Comment upon the pattern of quarterly sales *within* the year, and offer your own explanation for this pattern.

g. What does management point out as evidence of the company's strong financial position (liquidity)?

h. How many stores did the company operate at the end of the fiscal year ended January 28, 1995? How many stores does it plan to open during 1995 (the *next* fiscal year)?

i. In how many foreign countries did the company's International Division operate during 1994? In what specific countries did the company begin operations in 1994?

PART II

Assume that you are the credit manager of a medium-size toy manufacturer. (Your company's annual sales are about $2 billion per year.) Toys "R" Us wants to make credit purchases from your company of approximately $15 million per month, with payment due in 60 days.

INSTRUCTIONS

a. As general background, read the letter addressed *To Our Stockholders* and *Management's Discussion—Results of Operations and Financial Condition.* Next, compute the following for the fiscal years ending January 28, 1995 and January 29, 1994 (round dollar amounts to the nearest million, percentages to the nearest tenth of one percent, and other computations to one decimal place):
  1. Current ratio.
  2. Quick ratio.
  3. Amount of working capital.
  4. Percentage change in working capital from the prior year.
  5. Percentage change in cash (and cash equivalents) from the prior year.

b. Based upon the most recent year, compute the approximate percentage of the annual merchandise purchases of Toys "R" Us that your company would be supplying.

c. Based upon your analysis in part **a,** does the company's liquidity appear to have *increased* or *decreased* during the most recent fiscal year? Explain.

d. Comment upon the company's current ratio and quick ratio in relation to any rules of thumb mentioned in Chapter 6.

e. Other than the ability of Toys "R" Us to pay for its purchases, do you see any major considerations which should enter into your company's decision? Explain.

f. Your company assigns each customer one of the four credit ratings listed below. Assign a credit rating to Toys "R" Us and write a memorandum explaining your decision. (In your memorandum, you may refer to any of your computations or observations in parts **a** through **d,** and to any information contained in the annual report.)

POSSIBLE CREDIT RATINGS

A Outstanding Little or no risk of inability to pay. For customers in this category, we fill any reasonable order without imposing a credit limit. The customer's credit is reevaluated annually.

B Good Customer has good debt-paying ability, but is assigned a credit limit which is reviewed every 90 days. Orders above the credit limit are accepted only on a cash basis.

C Marginal Customer appears sound, but credit should be extended only on a 30-day basis and with a relatively low credit limit. Creditworthiness and credit limit are reevaluated every 90 days.

D Unacceptable Customer does not qualify for credit.

PART III

As general background, read the *Financial Highlights,* the letter addressed *To Our Stockholders,* and *Management's Discussion—Results of Operations and Financial Condition.*

INSTRUCTIONS

a. Compute the following for the fiscal years ending January 28, 1995 and January 29, 1994 (round dollar amounts to millions, and percentages to the nearest tenth of one percent):

1. Percentage change in net sales (relative to the prior year).
2. Percentage change in net income.
3. Percentage change in the number of stores operating at year-end.
4. Gross profit rate.
5. Net income as a percentage of sales.
6. Return on average total assets. (***Note:*** The Toys "R" Us income statement does not include a subtotal for operating income, but it provides the information you need to compute this amount. Show your computations.)
7. Return on average total equity.

b. Explain the significance of net sales increasing faster than the number of stores.

c. At the end of 1994, the market price of the company's capital stock was approximately $29 per share. *Assume* that you project a 10% increase in both net sales and net income for 1995. Does this mean that you should also project the price of the company's capital stock to increase by 10% during 1995? Explain.

Accounting for Assets

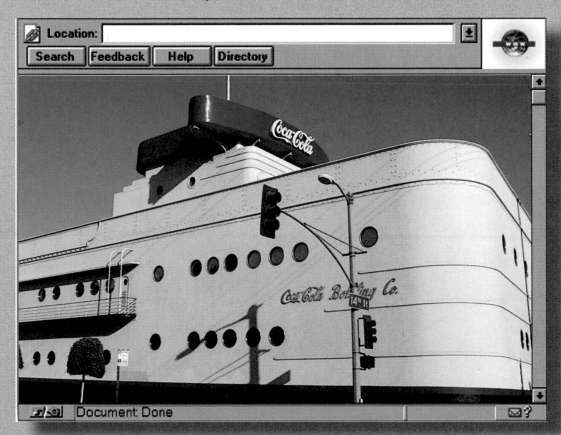

Location:

Search   Feedback   Help   Directory

Coca-Cola Bottling Co.

Document: Done

What's the most valuable asset in this picture? It
isn't the factory, it's the name in the fancy print. But
the factory is listed in Coca-Cola's balance sheet, and
the famous trademark isn't. If you want to understand
accounting information, you must understand the assumptions and measurement techniques involved in
the accounting process.

FINANCIAL ASSETS

Location:

Search | Feedback | Help | Directory

Document: Done

Willie Sutton said he robbed banks because "that's where the money is."

But times have changed. Today, most "money" exists only as entries in accounting records—balances in bank accounts, investments in stocks and bonds, and amounts due from customers. It isn't moved around in money bags as much as by phone, by check, and with little plastic cards. Not even banks keep much of the "green stuff" on hand anymore.

1 Define financial assets and explain their valuation in the balance sheet.

2 Describe the objectives of cash management.

3 Explain means of achieving internal control over cash transactions.

4 Prepare a bank reconciliation and explain its purpose.

5 Account for uncollectible receivables using the allowance and direct write-off methods.

6 Evaluate the liquidity of various financial assets.

7 Explain how transactions discussed in this chapter affect net income and cash flows.

*8 Account for transactions involving marketable securities.

**9 Explain, compute, and account for the accrual of interest revenue.

HOW MUCH CASH SHOULD A BUSINESS HAVE?

Most business people would say, "As little as necessary."

Every business needs enough cash to pay its bills. A business that runs out of cash will be forced to close its doors. But cash is not a very productive asset—that is, it generates little or no revenue. In fact, banks are prohibited by law from paying interest on corporate checking accounts. Therefore, many financially sound companies store their financial resources in forms other than cash.

The term **financial assets** describes not just cash, but also those assets easily and directly *convertible into known amounts of cash.* These assets include cash, short-term investments (also called **marketable securities**), and receivables. We address these three types of financial assets in a single chapter because they are so closely related. All of these assets represent *forms of money;* financial resources flow quickly among these asset categories.

L0 1 *Define financial assets and explain their valuation in the balance sheet.*

In a well-managed company, daily cash receipts are deposited promptly in the bank. Often, a principal source of these daily receipts is the collection of accounts receivable. If the daily receipts exceed routine cash outlays, the company can meet its obligations while maintaining relatively low balances in its bank accounts.

Cash that will not be needed in the immediate future often is invested in marketable securities. These short-term investments are more productive than cash, because they earn revenue—in the forms of interest and dividends. If the business should need more cash than it has in its bank accounts, it can easily convert some of its marketable securities back into cash.

In summary, businesses "store" money in three basic forms: cash, short-term investments, and receivables. The flow of cash among these types of financial assets is summarized in the illustration at the top of the following page.

THE VALUATION OF FINANCIAL ASSETS

In the balance sheet, financial assets are shown at their *current values,* meaning the amounts of cash that these assets represent. Interestingly, current value is measured differently for each type of financial asset.

---

*Supplemental Topic A, "Accounting for Marketable Securities."
**Supplemental Topic B, "Notes Receivable and Interest Revenue."

Money "flows" among the
financial assets

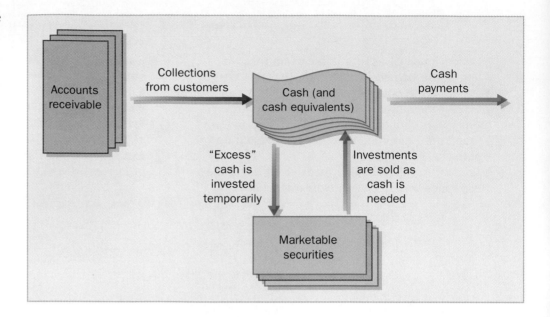

The current value of cash is simply its face amount. But the current value of marketable securities may change daily, based upon fluctuations in stock prices, interest rates, and other factors. Therefore, short-term investments appear in the balance sheet at their current *market values*. (Notice that the valuation of these investments represents an exception to the cost principle.)

Accounts receivable, like cash, have stated face amounts. But large companies usually do not expect to collect every dollar of their accounts receivable. Some customers simply will be unable to make full payment. Therefore, receivables appear in the balance sheet at the estimated *collectible* amount—called **net realizable value.**

These three methods of determining the current value of financial assets are summarized below:

Type of Financial Asset	Basis for Valuation in the Balance Sheet
Cash (and cash equivalents)	Face amount
Short-term investments (marketable securities)	Current market value
Receivables	Net realizable value

CASH

Accountants define *cash* as money on deposit in banks and any items that banks will accept for deposit. These items include not only coins and paper money, but also checks, money orders, and travelers' checks. Banks also accept drafts signed by customers using bank credit cards, such as Visa and Master-Card. Thus, sales to customers using bank cards are *cash sales,* not credit sales.

Most companies maintain several bank accounts and also keep a small amount of cash on hand. Therefore, the Cash account in the general ledger is a *controlling account*. A cash subsidiary ledger includes separate accounts corresponding to each bank account and each supply of cash on hand within the organization.

REPORTING CASH IN THE BALANCE SHEET

Cash is listed first in the balance sheet, because it is the most liquid of all current assets. For purposes of balance sheet presentation, the balance in the Cash controlling account is combined with that of the controlling account for **cash equivalents.**

CASH EQUIVALENTS Some short-term investments are so liquid that they are termed cash equivalents. Examples include money market funds, U.S. Treasury bills, and high-grade commercial paper (very short-term notes payable issued by large, creditworthy corporations). These assets are considered so similar to cash that they are combined with the amount of cash in the balance sheet. Therefore, the first asset listed in the balance sheet usually is called Cash and Cash Equivalents.

stable market value.

To qualify as a cash equivalent, an investment must be very safe, have a very stable market value, and mature within 90 days of the date of acquisition. Investments in even the highest quality stocks and bonds of large corporations are *not* viewed as meeting these criteria. Short-term investments which do not qualify as cash equivalents are listed in the balance sheet as Marketable Securities, which appears second among the current assets.

"RESTRICTED" CASH Some bank accounts are restricted as to their use, so that they are not available to meet the normal operating needs of the company. For example, a bank account may contain cash specifically earmarked for the acquisition of plant assets. Bank accounts in some foreign countries are restricted by laws that prohibit transferring the money to another country. Cash that is not available for paying current liabilities should not be viewed as a current asset. Therefore, restricted cash should be listed just below the current asset section of the balance sheet in the section entitled Investments and Funds.

As a condition for granting a loan, banks often required the borrower to maintain a **compensating balance** (minimum average balance) on deposit in a non-interest-bearing checking account. This agreement does not actually prevent the borrower from using the cash, but does mean the company must quickly replenish this bank account. Compensating balances are included in the amount of cash listed in the balance sheet, but these balances should be disclosed in the notes accompanying the financial statements.

LINES OF CREDIT Many businesses arrange **lines of credit** with their banks. A line of credit means that the bank has agreed *in advance* to lend the company any amount of money up to a specified limit. The company can borrow this money at any time simply by drawing checks upon a special bank account. A liability to the bank arises as soon as any money is borrowed—that is, as soon as a portion of the credit line is "used."

The *unused* portion of a line of credit is neither an asset nor a liability; it represents only the *ability* to borrow money quickly and easily. Although an unused line of credit does not appear as an asset or a liability in the balance sheet, it increases the company's solvency. Thus, unused lines of credit usually are *disclosed* in notes accompanying the financial statements.

A recent annual report of **J.C. Penney,** the giant retailer, included the following note to the financial statements:

Confirmed lines of credit available to J.C. Penney amounted to $1.2 billion. None was in use at [the balance sheet date].

THE STATEMENT OF CASH FLOWS

A balance sheet shows the cash owned at the end of the accounting period. Cash *transactions* of the accounting period are summarized in a different financial statement—the statement of cash flows.

In both the balance sheet and the statement of cash flows, the term "cash" includes cash equivalents. Transfers of money between bank accounts and cash equivalents do *not* appear in a statement of cash flows, because these transactions do not change the amount of cash owned. However, any *interest* received from owning cash equivalents is included in the statement of cash flows as cash receipts from operating activities.

CASH MANAGEMENT

The term **cash management** refers to planning, controlling, and accounting for cash transactions and cash balances. Because cash moves so readily between bank accounts and other financial assets, "cash management" really means the management of *all financial resources.* Efficient management of these resources is essential to the success—even to the survival—of every business organization. The basic objectives of cash management are:

LO 2 *Describe the objectives of cash management.*

● **Provide accurate accounting for cash receipts, cash disbursements, and cash balances.** A large portion of the total transactions of a business involve the receipt or disbursement of cash. Also, cash transactions affect every classification within the financial statements—assets, liabilities, owners' equity, revenue, and expenses. If financial statements are to be reliable, it is *absolutely essential* that cash transactions be recorded correctly.

● **Prevent or minimize losses from theft or fraud.** Cash is more susceptible to theft than any other asset and, therefore, requires physical protection.

● **Anticipate the need for borrowing and assure the availability of adequate amounts of cash for conducting business operations.** Every business organization must have sufficient cash to meet its financial obligations as they come due. Otherwise, its creditors may force the business into bankruptcy.

● **Prevent unnecessarily large amounts of cash from sitting idle in bank accounts which produce no revenue.** Well-managed companies frequently review their bank balances for the purpose of transferring any excess cash into cash equivalents or other investments that generate revenue.

USING EXCESS CASH BALANCES EFFICIENTLY Cash equivalents are safe and liquid investments, but they generate only a modest rate of return. These investments are useful for investing *temporary* surpluses of cash, which soon will be needed for other purposes. If a business has large amounts of cash that can be invested on a long-term basis, however, it should expect to earn a higher rate of return than is available from cash equivalents. Cash which is available for long-term investment may be used to finance growth and expansion of the business, or to repay debt. If the cash is not needed for business purposes, it should be distributed to the company's stockholders.

YOUR TURN

You as a Financial Advisor

Assume that you were hired by Whitlock Corporation to help manage its financial assets. The company has historically kept an average cash balance of $5 million in a corporate checking account. Whitlock's chief financial officer is very conservative and risk averse. On numerous occasions he has openly refused to "play the stock market" with company funds.

As a financial advisor, propose several low-risk investment alternatives for the company's $5 million cash surplus.

*Our comments appear on page 362.

INTERNAL CONTROL OVER CASH

Internal control over cash is sometimes regarded merely as a means of preventing fraud and theft. A good system of internal control, however, will also aid in achieving the other objectives of efficient cash management, including accurate accounting for cash transactions, anticipating the need for borrowing, and the maintenance of adequate but not excessive cash balances.

The major steps in achieving internal control over cash transactions and cash balances include:

LO 3 *Explain means of achieving internal control over cash transactions.*

- Separate the function of handling cash from the maintenance of accounting records. Employees who handle cash *should not have access to the accounting records,* and accounting personnel should not have access to cash.

- For each department within the organization prepare a *cash budget* (or forecast) of planned cash receipts, cash payments, and cash balances, scheduled month-by-month for the coming year.

- Prepare a *control listing* of cash receipts at the time and place the money is received. For cash sales, this listing may be a cash register tape, created by ringing up each sale on a cash register. For checks received through the mail, a control listing of incoming checks should be prepared by the employee assigned to open the mail.

- Require that all cash receipts be *deposited daily* in the bank.

- Make all payments *by check.* The only exception should be for small payments to be made in cash from a *petty cash fund.* (Petty cash funds are discussed later in this chapter.)

- Require that the validity and amount of every expenditure be verified *before* a check is issued in payment. Separate the function of approving expenditures from the function of signing checks.

- Promptly reconcile bank statements with the accounting records.

A company may supplement its system of internal control by obtaining a fidelity bond from an insurance company. Under a fidelity bond, the insurance company agrees to reimburse an employer for *proven* losses resulting from fraud or embezzlement by bonded employees.

CASH OVER AND SHORT In handling over-the-counter cash receipts, a few errors in making change inevitably will occur. These errors may cause a cash shortage or overage at the end of the day when the cash is counted and compared with the reading on the cash register.

For example, assume that total cash sales recorded on the point-of-sale terminals during the day amount to $4,500.00. However, the cash receipts in the register drawers total only $4,487.30. The following entry would be made to adjust the accounting records for this $12.70 shortage in the cash receipts:

Cash Over and Short.. 12.70
    Cash.. 12.70
To record a $12.70 shortage in cash receipts for the day
($4,500.00 − $4,487.30).

The account entitled Cash Over and Short is debited with shortages and credited with overages. If the account has a debit balance, it appears in the income statement as miscellaneous expense; if it has a credit balance, it is shown as miscellaneous revenue.

CASH DISBURSEMENTS

To achieve adequate internal control over cash disbursements, all payments—except those from petty cash—should be *made by check*. The use of checks automatically provides a written record of each cash payment. In addition, adequate internal control requires that every transaction requiring a cash payment be *verified, approved,* and *recorded* before a check is issued. Responsibility for approving cash disbursements should be *clearly separated* from the responsibility for signing checks.

THE VOUCHER SYSTEM One widely used method of establishing internal control over cash disbursements is a voucher system. In a typical **voucher system,** the accounting department is responsible for approving cash payments and for recording the transactions. In approving an expenditure, the accounting department will examine such supporting documents as the supplier's invoice, the purchase order, and the receiving report. Once payment has been approved, the accounting department signs a **voucher** authorizing payment and records the transaction in the accounting records. (Other names for a "voucher" include *invoice approval form* and *check authorization.*)

The voucher and supporting documents then are sent to the treasurer or other official in the finance department. This official reviews the voucher and supporting documents before issuing a check. When the check is signed, the voucher and supporting documents are perforated or stamped "PAID" to eliminate any possibility of their being presented later in support of another check.

Notice that neither the personnel in the accounting department nor in the finance department are in a position to make unapproved cash disbursements. Accounting personnel, who approve and record disbursements, are not authorized to sign checks. Finance department personnel, who issue and sign checks, are not authorized to issue a check unless they have first received an authorization voucher from the accounting department.

BANK STATEMENTS

Each month the bank provides the depositor with a statement of the depositor's account, accompanied by the checks paid and charged to the account during the month.[1] As illustrated on the following page, a bank statement shows the balance on deposit at the beginning of the month, the deposits, the

---

[1]Large businesses usually receive bank statements on a weekly basis.

checks paid, any other debits and credits during the month, and the new balance at the end of the month. (To keep the illustration short, we have shown a limited number of deposits rather than one for each business day in the month.)

A bank statement provides an independent record of cash transactions.

WESTERN NATIONAL BANK
100 OLYMPIC BOULEVARD
LOS ANGELES, CALIFORNIA

CUSTOMER ACCOUNT NO. 501390
PARKVIEW COMPANY
109 PARKVIEW ROAD
LOS ANGELES, CALIFORNIA

Bank Statement
For the Month Ended July 31, 1998

Date	Deposits and Credits	Checks and Debits		Balance
June 30				5,029.30
July 1	300.00			5,329.30
July 2	1,250.00	1,100.00		5,479.30
July 3		415.20	10.00	5,054.10
July 8	993.60			6,047.70
July 10		96.00	400.00	5,551.70
July 12	1,023.77	1,376.57		5,198.90
July 15		425.00		4,773.90
July 18	1,300.00	2,095.75		3,978.15
July 22	500.00 CM	85.00	5.00 DM	4,388.15
July 24	1,083.25	1,145.27		4,326.13
July 30	711.55	50.25 NSF		4,987.43
July 31	24.74 INT	12.00 SC		5,000.17

EXPLANATION OF SYMBOLS

CM Credit Memoranda   INT Interest on average balance
DM Debit Memoranda   NSF Not Sufficient Funds
E Error correction   SC Service Charge

Summary of activity:
Previous statement balance, June 30, 1998 .... $5,029.30
Deposits and credit memoranda (9 items) 7,186.91
Checks and debit memoranda (13 items) .... (7,216.04)
Current statement balance, July 31, 1998 .... $5,000.17

RECONCILING THE BANK STATEMENT

A **bank reconciliation** is a schedule *explaining any differences* between the balance shown in the bank statement and the balance shown in the depositor's accounting records. Remember that both the bank and the depositor are maintaining independent records of the deposits, the checks, and the current balance of the bank account. Each month, the depositor should prepare a bank reconciliation to verify that these independent sets of records are in agreement. This reconciliation may disclose internal control failures, such as unauthorized cash disbursements or failures to deposit cash receipts, as well as errors in either the bank statement or the depositor's accounting records. In addition, the reconciliation identifies certain transactions which must be

LO 4 *Prepare a bank reconciliation and explain its purpose.*

recorded in the depositor's accounting records, and helps to determine the "actual" amount of cash on deposit.

For strong internal control, the employee who reconciles the bank statement should not have any other responsibilities for cash.

NORMAL DIFFERENCES BETWEEN BANK RECORDS AND ACCOUNTING RECORDS The balance shown in a monthly bank statement seldom equals the balance appearing in the depositor's accounting records. Certain transactions recorded by the depositor may not have been recorded by the bank. The most common examples are:

- **Outstanding checks.** Checks issued and recorded by the company, but not yet presented to the bank for payment.
- **Deposits in transit.** Cash receipts recorded by the depositor, but which reached the bank too late to be included in the bank statement for the current month.

In addition, certain transactions appearing in the bank statement may not have been recorded by the depositor. For example:

- **Service charges.** Banks often charge a fee for handling small accounts. The amount of this charge usually depends upon both the average balance of the account and the number of checks paid during the month.
- **Charges for depositing NSF checks.** NSF stands for "Not Sufficient Funds." When checks are deposited in an account, the bank generally gives the depositor immediate credit. On occasion, one of these checks may prove to be uncollectible, because the maker of the check does not have sufficient funds in his or her account. In such cases, the bank will reduce the depositor's account by the amount of this uncollectible item and return the check to the depositor marked "NSF."

  The depositor should view an NSF check as an account receivable from the maker of the check, not as cash.
- **Credits for interest earned.** The checking accounts of *unincorporated* businesses often earn interest. At month-end, this interest is credited to the depositor's account and reported in the bank statement. (As previously mentioned, current law prohibits interest on corporate checking accounts.)
- **Miscellaneous bank charges and credits.** Banks charge for services—such as printing checks, handling collections of notes receivable, and processing NSF checks. The bank *deducts* these charges from the depositor's account and notifies the depositor by including a debit memorandum in the monthly bank statement. If the bank collects a note receivable on behalf of the depositor, it credits the depositor's account and issues a credit memorandum.[2]

In a bank reconciliation, the balances shown in the bank statement and in the accounting records both are *adjusted for any unrecorded transactions*. Additional adjustment may be required to correct any errors discovered in the bank statement or in the accounting records.

STEPS IN PREPARING A BANK RECONCILIATION The specific steps in preparing a bank reconciliation are:

---

[2]Banks view each depositor's account as a *liability*. Debit memoranda are issued for transactions that reduce this liability, such as bank service charges. Credit memoranda are issued to recognize an increase in this liability, as results, for example, from interest earned by the depositor.

1. Compare deposits listed on the bank statement with the deposits shown in the accounting records. Any deposits not yet recorded by the bank are deposits in transit and should be added to the balance shown in the bank statement.

2. Arrange paid checks in sequence by serial numbers and compare each check with the corresponding entry in the accounting records. Any checks issued but not yet paid by the bank should be listed as outstanding checks to be deducted from the balance reported in the bank statement.

3. Add to the balance per the depositor's accounting records any credit memoranda issued by the bank which have not been recorded by the depositor.

4. Deduct from the balance per the depositor's records any debit memoranda issued by the bank which have not been recorded by the depositor.

5. Make appropriate adjustments to correct any errors in either the bank statement or the depositor's accounting records.

6. Determine that the adjusted balance of the bank statement is equal to the adjusted balance in the depositor's records.

7. Prepare journal entries to record any items in the bank reconciliation listed as adjustments to the balance per depositor's records.

ILLUSTRATION OF A BANK RECONCILIATION   The July bank statement sent by the bank to Parkview Company was illustrated on page 313. This statement shows a balance of cash on deposit at July 31 of *$5,000.17*. Assume that on July 31, Parkview's ledger shows a bank balance of *$4,262.83*. The employee preparing the bank reconciliation has identified the following reconciling items:

1. A deposit of $410.90 made after banking hours on July 31 does not appear in the bank statement.

2. Four checks issued in July have not yet been paid by the bank. These checks are:

Check No.	Date	Amount
801	June 15	$100.00
888	July 24	10.25
890	July 27	402.50
891	July 30	205.00

3. Two credit memoranda were included in the bank statement:

Date	Amount	Explanation
July 22	$500.00	Proceeds from collection of a non-interest-bearing note receivable from J. David. Parkview Company had left this note with the bank's collection department.
July 31	24.74	Interest earned on average account balance during July.

4. Three debit memoranda accompanied the bank statement:

Date	Amount	Explanation
July 22	$ 5.00	Fee charged by bank for handling collection of note receivable.
July 30	50.25	Check from customer J. B. Ball deposited by Parkview Company charged back as NSF.
July 31	12.00	Service charge by bank for the month of July.

5. Check no. 875 was issued July 20 in the amount of $85 but was erroneously recorded in the cash payments journal as $58. The check, in payment of telephone expense, was paid by the bank and correctly listed at $85 in the bank statement. In Parkview's ledger, the Cash account is *overstated* by $27 because of this error ($85 − $58 = $27.)

The July 31 bank reconciliation for Parkview Company is shown below. (The numbered arrows coincide both with the steps in preparing a bank reconciliation listed on page 315 and with the reconciling items listed above.)

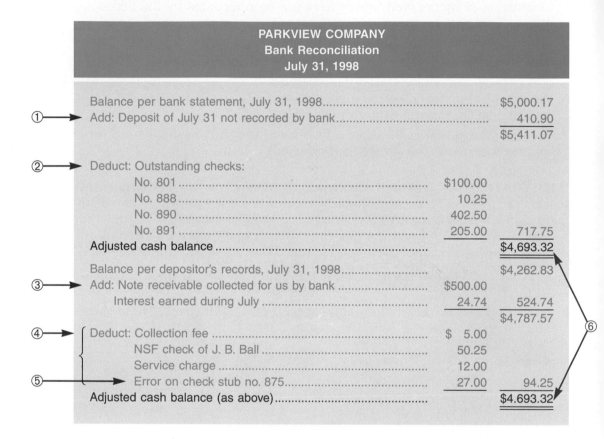

PARKVIEW COMPANY
Bank Reconciliation
July 31, 1998

Balance per bank statement, July 31, 1998			$5,000.17
① Add: Deposit of July 31 not recorded by bank			410.90
			$5,411.07
② Deduct: Outstanding checks:			
No. 801		$100.00	
No. 888		10.25	
No. 890		402.50	
No. 891		205.00	717.75
Adjusted cash balance			$4,693.32
Balance per depositor's records, July 31, 1998			$4,262.83
③ Add: Note receivable collected for us by bank		$500.00	
Interest earned during July		24.74	524.74
			$4,787.57
④ Deduct: Collection fee		$ 5.00	
NSF check of J. B. Ball		50.25	
Service charge		12.00	
⑤ Error on check stub no. 875		27.00	94.25
Adjusted cash balance (as above)			$4,693.32

⑥

UPDATING THE ACCOUNTING RECORDS The last step in reconciling a bank statement is to update the depositor's accounting records for any unrecorded cash transactions brought to light. In the bank reconciliation, every adjustment to the *balance per depositor's records* is a cash receipt or a cash payment that has not been recorded in the depositor's accounts. Therefore, *each of these items should be recorded.*

In this illustration and in our assignment material, we will follow a policy of making one journal entry to record the unrecorded cash receipts, and another to record the unrecorded cash reductions. (Acceptable alternatives would be to make separate journal entries for each item or to make one compound entry for all items.) Based on our recording policy, the entries to update the accounting records of Parkview Company are:

Per bank credit
memoranda . . .

Cash	524.74	
Notes Receivable		500.00
Interest Revenue		24.74

To record collection of note receivable from J. David collected by
bank and interest earned on bank account in July.

Bank Service Charges .... *exp*	17.00	
Accounts Receivable (J. B. Ball)	50.25	
Telephone Expense	27.00	
Cash		94.25

... per bank debit
memoranda (and
correction of an error)

To record bank charges (service charge, $12; collection fee, $5);
to reclassify NSF check from customer J. B. Ball as an account
receivable; and to correct understatement of cash payment for
telephone expense.

PETTY CASH FUNDS

We have emphasized the importance of making all significant cash disbursements by check. However, every business finds it convenient to have a small amount of cash on hand with which to make some minor expenditures. Examples of these expenditures include such things as small purchases of office supplies, taxi fares, and doughnuts for an office meeting.

To create a petty cash fund, a check is drawn payable to "Petty Cash" for a round amount, such as $200, which will cover these small expenditures for a period of two or three weeks. This check is cashed and the money is kept on hand in a petty cash box. One employee is designated as the *custodian* of the fund.

The custodian makes all payments from this fund and obtains a receipt or prepares a "petty cash voucher" explaining the nature and amount of each expenditure. At the end of the period (or when the fund runs low), a check is drawn payable to Petty Cash reimbursing the fund for the expenditures made during the period. The issuance of this check is recorded by debiting the appropriate expense accounts and crediting Cash. As a practical matter, the entire debit portion of this entry often is charged to the Miscellaneous Expense account.

THE CASH BUDGET AS A CONTROL DEVICE

Many businesses prepare detailed *cash budgets* which include forecasts of the monthly cash receipts and expenditures of each department within the organization. Management (or the internal auditors) will investigate any cash flows that differ significantly from the budgeted amounts. Thus, each department manager is held accountable for the monthly cash transactions occurring within his or her department.

SHORT-TERM INVESTMENTS

Companies with large amounts of liquid resources usually hold most of these resources in the form of marketable securities, rather than cash.

CASE IN POINT

The first and most liquid asset listed in the 1996 balance sheet of **Microsoft Corporation** was "Cash and short-term investments . . . $6.94 billion." But who wants nearly $7 billion sitting in a corporate checking account and not earning any interest? Certainly not Microsoft. A footnote indicates that less than 10% of this asset was held in the form of cash. More than 90% was invested in short-term interest-bearing securities. If we assume Microsoft earns interest on these investments at an annual rate of, say, 5%, that's more than $345 million in interest revenue per year.

Marketable securities consist primarily of investments in bonds and in the capital stocks of publicly owned corporations. These marketable securities are "traded" (bought and sold) daily on organized securities exchanges, such as the New York Stock Exchange, the Tokyo Stock Exchange, and Mexico's Bolsa. A basic characteristic of all marketable securities is that they are *readily marketable*— meaning that they can be purchased or sold quickly and easily *at quoted market prices.*

Investments in marketable securities earn a return for the investor in the form of interest, dividends, and—if all goes well—an increase in market value. Meanwhile, these investments are *almost as liquid as cash itself.* They can be sold immediately over the telephone, simply by placing a "sell order" with a brokerage firm such as Merrill Lynch, or Smith Barney Shearson.

Because of their liquidity, investments in marketable securities usually are listed second among the current assets, immediately after cash.[3]

[handwritten margin note: Set value of marketable securities to market value]

MARK-TO-MARKET: A NEW PRINCIPLE OF ASSET VALUATION

Accounting principles are not "carved in stone." Rather, they evolve and change as the accounting profession seeks to increase the usefulness of accounting information. A recent change in the way companies account for short-term investments provides an excellent case in point.

Until recently, short-term investments were shown in the balance sheet at the lower of their cost or current market value. This valuation method reflected the *cost principle,* tempered by *conservatism.* But in 1993, the FASB changed the rules. Short-term investments in marketable securities now appear in the balance sheet at their *current market value* as of the balance sheet date.[4]

To achieve this goal, the balance sheet valuation of these investments is *adjusted to market value* at the balance sheet date. Hence, this valuation principle often is called **mark-to-market.** When the value of marketable securities is adjusted to current market value, an offsetting entry is made to an account entitled, **Unrealized Holding Gain (or Loss) on Investments.** This account may appear either as a special stockholders' equity account in the balance sheet, or in the income statement, depending upon how the securities are *classified.*

The new principle requires that marketable securities be classified as one of three types: (1) available-for-sale securities, (2) trading securities, or (3) held-to-maturity securities. These classifications are based, in large part, upon management's *intent* regarding the length of time the securities will be held.

The following table describes the intent of each classification, and the corresponding treatment of unrealized holding gains and losses.

Classification	Management's Intent	Treatment of Unrealized Holding Gains and Losses
Available for sale securities	Held for short-term resale (often 6 to 18 months)	Reported in stockholders' equity section of the balance sheet
Trading securities	Held for immediate resale (often within hours or days)	Reported in "other" revenue (expense) section of the income statement
Held to maturity securities	Debt securities intended to be held until they mature	Reported in stockholders' equity section of the balance sheet

---

[3]Investments which are *not* readily marketable, or which management intends to hold on a long-term basis, are *not* classified as current assets. Such investments will be discussed in later accounting courses.

[4]FASB, *Statement of Financial Accounting Standards No. 115,* "Accounting for Certain Investments in Debt and Equity Securities," (Norwalk, Conn., 1993).

Most corporations classify their marketable securities as *available for sale*. In view of this fact, the remainder of our discussion focuses exclusively upon this particular classification. As noted in the above table, holding gains and losses that arise when available-for-sale securities are adjusted to market value affect *only the balance sheet;* they have *no effect* upon the income statement.

To illustrate, assume that Foster Corporation classifies all of its short-term investments as available for sale. The company currently owns marketable securities which had cost *$200,000,* but now have a market value of *$230,000.* A condensed balance sheet appears below:

FOSTER CORPORATION Balance Sheet December 31, 19 ___			
Assets		**Liabilities & Stockholders' Equity**	
Current assets:		**Liabilities:**	
Cash	$ 50,000	(Detail not shown)	$350,000
Marketable securities (cost,		**Stockholders' equity:**	
$200,000; market value,		Capital stock	100,000
$230,000)	230,000	Retained earnings	420,000
Accounts receivable	300,000	Unrealized holding	
Total current assets	$580,000	gain on investments ..	30,000
Other assets:			
(Detail not shown)	320,000		
Total	$900,000	Total	$900,000

Although the $200,000 cost of the marketable securities is *disclosed* in the balance sheet, the basis for the valuation in the "money columns" is *$230,000,—* the securities' *current market value.*

The difference between cost and current market value also appears as an *element of stockholders' equity,* labeled Unrealized Holding Gain (or Loss) on Investments. When the market value of the investments is *above* cost, this special equity account represents a holding *gain.* But if the market value is below cost, the equity account represents a holding *loss,* and is shown as a *reduction* in total stockholders' equity.

Unrealized holding gains and losses are *not* subject to income taxes. Income taxes are levied upon gains and losses only when the investments are sold. Nonetheless, unrealized gains and losses are shown in the balance sheet net of the expected *future* income tax effects. These expected future tax effects are included in the company's tax liability, rather than in the amount shown as unrealized holding gain or loss. Such "deferred tax adjustments" are beyond the scope of our introductory discussion and will be addressed in later accounting courses. In the discussions and assignment materials of this chapter, holding gains and losses simply represent the difference between the cost and the current market value of the securities owned.

Accounting for marketable securities, including the mark-to-market adjustments, is discussed further in *Supplemental Topic A,* at the end of this chapter.

OUR ASSESSMENT OF MARK-TO-MARKET The authors of this text commend the FASB on this recent change in accounting principles. Reporting short-term investments at market value substantially enhances the usefulness of the balance sheet in evaluating the solvency of a business.

ACCOUNTS RECEIVABLE

One of the key factors underlying the growth of the American economy is the trend toward selling goods and services on account. Accounts receivable comprise the largest financial asset of many merchandising companies.

Accounts receivable are relatively liquid assets, usually converting into cash within a period of 30 to 60 days. Therefore, accounts receivable from customers are classified as current assets, appearing in the balance sheet immediately after cash and short-term investments in marketable securities.

Sometimes companies sell merchandise on longer-term installment plans, requiring 12, 24, or even 48 months to collect the entire amount receivable from the customer. By definition, the normal period of time required to collect accounts receivable is part of a company's *operating cycle*. Therefore, accounts receivable arising from "normal" sales transactions usually are classified as current assets, even if the credit terms extend beyond one year.[5]

ACCOUNTS RECEIVABLE AND CASH FLOWS In a statement of cash flows, the cash receipts from collecting receivables are included in the subtotal, net cash flow from operating activities. Collections of accounts receivable often represent a company's largest and most consistent source of cash receipts. Thus, monitoring the collection of receivables is an important part of efficient cash management.

In summary, a company's ability to generate the cash needed for routine business operations often depends upon the amount, collectibility, and **maturity dates** of its receivables.

UNCOLLECTIBLE ACCOUNTS

We have stated that accounts receivable are shown in the balance sheet at the estimated collectible amount—called *net realizable value*. No business wants to sell merchandise on account to customers who will be unable to pay. Many companies even maintain their own credit departments that investigate the creditworthiness of each prospective customer. Nonetheless, if a company makes credit sales to hundreds—perhaps thousands—of customers, some accounts inevitably will turn out to be uncollectible.

A limited amount of uncollectible accounts is not only expected—it is evidence of a sound credit policy. If the credit department is overly cautious, the business may lose many sales opportunities by rejecting customers who should have been considered acceptable credit risks.

REFLECTING UNCOLLECTIBLE ACCOUNTS IN THE FINANCIAL STATEMENTS An account receivable that has been determined to be uncollectible is no longer an asset. The loss of this asset represents an *expense*, termed Uncollectible Accounts Expense.

In measuring business income, one of the most fundamental principles of accounting is that revenue should be *matched* with (offset by) the expenses incurred in generating that revenue. Uncollectible accounts expense is *caused by selling goods* on credit to customers who fail to pay their bills. Therefore, this

LO 5 *Account for uncollectible receivables using the allowance and direct write-off methods.*

---

[5]As explained in Chapter 5, the period used to define current assets and current liabilities is one year or the company's operating cycle, whichever is longer. The *operating cycle* is the period of time needed to convert cash into inventory, the inventory into accounts receivable, and the accounts receivable back into cash.

expense is incurred in the month in which the *related sales* are made, even though specific accounts receivable may not be determined to be uncollectible until a later accounting period. Thus, an account receivable that originates from a credit sale in January and is determined to be uncollectible in August represents an expense in *January.*

To illustrate, assume that World Famous Toy Co. begins business on January 1, 1998, and makes most of its sales on account. At January 31, accounts receivable amount to $250,000. On this date, the credit manager reviews the accounts receivable and estimates that approximately $10,000 of these accounts will prove to be uncollectible. The following adjusting entry should be made at January 31:

Uncollectible Accounts Expense..	10,000	
Allowance for Doubtful Accounts...		10,000

Provision for uncollectible accounts

To record the portion of total accounts receivable estimated to be uncollectible.

The Uncollectible Accounts Expense account created by the debit part of this entry is closed into the Income Summary account in the same manner as any other expense account. The Allowance for Doubtful Accounts which was credited in the above journal entry will appear in the balance sheet as a deduction from the face amount of the accounts receivable. It serves to reduce the accounts receivable to their *net realizable value* in the balance sheet, as shown by the following illustration:

WORLD FAMOUS TOY CO. Partial Balance Sheet January 31, 1998		
Current assets:		
Cash and cash equivalents		$ 75,000
Marketable securities...		25,000
Accounts receivable..	$250,000	
Less: Allowance for doubtful accounts	10,000	240,000
Inventory..		300,000
Total current assets...		$640,000

How much is the estimated net realizable value of the accounts receivable?

THE ALLOWANCE FOR DOUBTFUL ACCOUNTS

There is no way of telling in advance *which* accounts receivable will prove to be uncollectible. It is therefore not possible to credit the accounts of specific customers for our estimate of probable uncollectible accounts. Neither should we credit the Accounts Receivable controlling account in the general ledger. If the Accounts Receivable controlling account were to be credited with the estimated amount of doubtful accounts, this controlling account would no longer be in balance with the total of the numerous customers' accounts in the subsidiary ledger. The only practical alternative, therefore, is to credit a separate account called **Allowance for Doubtful Accounts** with the amount estimated to be uncollectible.

The Allowance for Doubtful Accounts often is described as a *contra-asset* account or a *valuation* account. Both of these terms indicate that the Allowance for Doubtful Accounts has a credit balance, which is offset against the asset Accounts Receivable to produce a more useful and reliable measure of a company's liquidity.

ESTIMATING THE AMOUNT OF UNCOLLECTIBLE ACCOUNTS Before financial statements are prepared at the end of the accounting period, an estimate of the expected amount of uncollectible accounts receivables should be made. This estimate is based upon past experience and modified in accordance with current business conditions. Losses from uncollectible receivables tend to be greater during periods of recession than in periods of growth and prosperity. Because the allowance for doubtful accounts is necessarily an estimate and not a precise calculation, *professional judgment* plays a considerable part in determining the size of this valuation account.

MONTHLY ADJUSTMENTS OF THE ALLOWANCE ACCOUNT In the adjusting entry made by World Famous Toy Co. at January 31, the amount of the adjustment ($10,000) was equal to the estimated amount of uncollectible accounts. This is true only because January was the first month of operations and this was the company's first estimate of its uncollectible accounts. In future months, the amount of the adjusting entry will depend upon two factors: (1) the *estimate* of uncollectible accounts, and (2) the *current balance* in the Allowance for Doubtful Accounts. Before we illustrate the adjusting entry for a future month, let us first see why the balance in the allowance account may change during the accounting period.

WRITING OFF AN UNCOLLECTIBLE ACCOUNT RECEIVABLE

Whenever an account receivable from a specific customer is determined to be uncollectible, it no longer qualifies as an asset and should be written off. To *write off* an account receivable is to reduce the balance of the customer's account to zero. The journal entry to accomplish this consists of a credit to the Accounts Receivable controlling account in the general ledger (and to the customer's account in the subsidiary ledger), and an offsetting debit to the Allowance for Doubtful Accounts.

To illustrate, assume that early in February, World Famous Toy Co. learns that Discount Stores has gone out of business and that the $4,000 account receivable from this customer is now worthless. The entry to write off this uncollectible account receivable is:

Writing off a receivable "against the allowance"

Allowance for Doubtful Accounts.. 4,000
    Accounts Receivable (Discount Stores)... 4,000
To write off the receivable from Discount Stores as uncollectible.

The important thing to note in this entry is that the debit is made to the Allowance for Doubtful Accounts and *not* to the Uncollectible Accounts Expense account. The estimated expense of credit losses is charged to the Uncollectible Accounts Expense account at the end of each accounting period. When a particular account receivable is later determined to be worthless and is written off, this action does not represent an additional expense but merely confirms our previous estimate of the expense. If the Uncollectible Accounts Expense account were first charged with *estimated* credit losses and then later charged with *proven* credit losses, we would be double-counting the actual uncollectible accounts expense.

Notice also that the entry to write off an uncollectible account receivable reduces both the asset account and the contra-asset account by the same amount. Thus, writing off an uncollectible account *does not change* the net realizable value of accounts receivable in the balance sheet. The following illustration shows the net realizable value of World Famous Toy Co.'s accounts receivable before and after the write-off of the account receivable from Discount Stores:

Before the Write-Off		**After the Write-Off**	
Accounts receivable	$250,000	Accounts receivable	$246,000
Less: Allowance for doubtful		Less: Allowance for doubtful	
accounts.................................	10,000	accounts.................................	6,000
Net realizable value...................	$240,000	Net realizable value...................	$240,000

What happens to net realizable value?

Let us repeat the point that underlies the whole "allowance approach." Credit losses should be recognized in the period in which the *sale occurs,* not the period in which the account is determined to be uncollectible. The reasoning for this position is based upon the *matching principle.*

WRITE-OFFS SELDOM AGREE WITH PREVIOUS ESTIMATES The total amount of accounts receivable actually written off will seldom, if ever, be exactly equal to the estimated amount previously credited to the Allowance for Doubtful Accounts.

If the amounts written off as uncollectible turn out to be less than the estimated amount, the Allowance for Doubtful Accounts will continue to show a credit balance. If the amounts written off as uncollectible are greater than the estimated amount, the Allowance for Doubtful Accounts will acquire a *temporary debit balance,* which will be eliminated by the adjustment at the end of the period.

RECOVERY OF AN ACCOUNT RECEIVABLE PREVIOUSLY WRITTEN OFF

Occasionally a receivable which has been written off as worthless will later be collected in full or in part. Such collections are often referred to as *recoveries* of bad debts. Collection of an account receivable previously written off is evidence that the write-off was an error; the receivable should therefore be reinstated as an asset.

Let us assume, for example, that a past-due account receivable in the amount of $200 from J. B. Barker was written off on February 16 by the following entry:

Allowance for Doubtful Accounts	200	
Accounts Receivable (J. B. Barker)		200
To write off the receivable from J. B. Barker as uncollectible.		

Barker account considered uncollectible

On February 27, the customer, J. B. Barker, pays the account in full. The entry to restore Barker's account will be:

Accounts Receivable (J. B. Barker)..	200	
Allowance for Doubtful Accounts		200
To reinstate as an asset an account receivable previously written off.		

Barker account reinstated

Notice that this entry is *exactly the opposite* of the entry made when the account was written off as uncollectible. A separate entry will be made in the cash receipts journal to record the collection from Barker. This entry will debit Cash and credit Accounts Receivable (J. B. Barker).

MONTHLY ESTIMATES OF CREDIT LOSSES

At the end of each month, management should again estimate the probable amount of uncollectible accounts and adjust the Allowance for Doubtful Accounts to this new estimate.

To illustrate, assume that at the end of February the credit manager of World Famous Toy Co. analyzes the accounts receivable and estimates that approximately *$11,000* of these accounts will prove uncollectible. Currently, the Allowance for Doubtful Accounts has a credit balance of only *$6,000*, determined as follows:

<table>
<tr><td>Current balance in the
allowance account</td><td>Balance at January 31 (credit)</td><td></td><td>$10,000</td></tr>
<tr><td></td><td>Less: Write-offs of accounts considered worthless:</td><td></td><td></td></tr>
<tr><td></td><td> Discount Stores</td><td>$4,000</td><td></td></tr>
<tr><td></td><td> J. B. Barker</td><td>200</td><td>4,200</td></tr>
<tr><td></td><td>Subtotal</td><td></td><td>$ 5,800</td></tr>
<tr><td></td><td>Add: Recoveries of accounts previously written off: J. B. Barker</td><td></td><td>200</td></tr>
<tr><td></td><td>Balance at end of February (prior to adjusting entry)</td><td></td><td>$ 6,000</td></tr>
</table>

To increase the balance in the allowance account to $11,000 at February 28, the month-end adjusting entry must add $5,000 to the allowance. The entry will be:

<table>
<tr><td>Increasing the allowance
for doubtful accounts</td><td>Uncollectible Accounts Expense</td><td>5,000</td><td></td></tr>
<tr><td></td><td> Allowance for Doubtful Accounts</td><td></td><td>5,000</td></tr>
<tr><td></td><td colspan="3">To increase the Allowance for Doubtful Accounts to $11,000,
computed as follows:</td></tr>
<tr><td></td><td> Required allowance at Feb. 28</td><td>$11,000</td><td></td></tr>
<tr><td></td><td> Credit balance prior to adjustment</td><td>6,000</td><td></td></tr>
<tr><td></td><td> Required adjustment</td><td>$ 5,000</td><td></td></tr>
</table>

ESTIMATING CREDIT LOSSES—THE "BALANCE SHEET" APPROACH The most widely used method of estimating the probable amount of uncollectible accounts is based upon an **aging of the accounts receivable.** This method is sometimes called the *balance sheet* approach, because the method emphasizes the proper balance sheet valuation of accounts receivable.

"Aging" accounts receivable means classifying each receivable according to its age. An aging schedule for the accounts receivable of Valley Ranch Supply is illustrated below:

Analysis of Accounts Receivable by Age December 31, 1998						
	Total	**Not Yet Due**	**1–30 Days Past Due**	**31–60 Days Past Due**	**61–90 Days Past Due**	**Over 90 Days Past Due**
Animal Care Center	$ 9,000	$ 9,000				
Butterfield, John D..	2,400			$ 2,400		
Citrus Groves, Inc...	4,000	3,000	$ 1,000			
Dairy Fresh Farms..	1,600				$ 600	$1,000
Eastlake Stables.....	13,000	7,000	6,000			
(Other customers)...	70,000	32,000	22,000	9,600	2,400	4,000
Totals	$100,000	$51,000	$29,000	$12,000	$3,000	$5,000

An aging schedule is useful to management in reviewing the status of individual accounts receivable and in evaluating the overall effectiveness of credit and collection policies. In addition, the schedule is used as the basis for estimating the amount of uncollectible accounts.

The longer an account is past due, the greater the likelihood that it will not be collected in full. Based upon past experience, the credit manager estimates the percentage of credit losses likely to occur in each age group of accounts receivable. This percentage, when applied to the total dollar amount in the age group, gives the estimated uncollectible portion for that group. By adding together the estimated uncollectible portions for all age groups, the *required balance* in the Allowance for Doubtful Accounts is determined. The following schedule lists the group totals from the aging schedule and shows how the estimated total amount of uncollectible accounts is computed:

Estimated Uncollectible Accounts Receivable December 31, 1998			
	Age Group Total	Percentage Considered Uncollectible*	Estimated Uncollectible Accounts
Not yet due	$ 51,000	1	$ 510
1–30 days past due	29,000	3	870
31–60 days past due	12,000	10	1,200
61–90 days past due	3,000	20	600
Over 90 days past due	5,000	50	2,500
Totals	$100,000		$5,680

*These percentages are estimated each month by the credit manager, based upon recent experience and current economic conditions.

At December 31, Valley Ranch Supply has total accounts receivable of $100,000, of which $5,680 are estimated to be uncollectible. Thus, an adjusting entry is needed to increase the Allowance for Doubtful Accounts from its present level to $5,680. If the allowance account currently has a credit balance of, say, $4,000, the month-end adjusting entry should be in the amount of *$1,680.*[6]

AN ALTERNATIVE APPROACH TO ESTIMATING CREDIT LOSSES The procedures above describe the *balance sheet* approach to estimating and recording credit losses. This approach is based upon an aging schedule, and the Allowance for Doubtful Accounts is *adjusted to a required balance.* An alternative method, called the *income statement* approach, focuses upon estimating the uncollectible accounts *expense* for the period. Based upon past experience, the un-

[6]If accounts receivable written off during the period *exceed* the Allowance for Doubtful Accounts at the last adjustment date, the allowance account temporarily acquires a *debit balance.* This situation seldom occurs if the allowance is adjusted each month, but often occurs if adjusting entries are made only at year-end.

If Valley Ranch Supply makes only an annual adjustment for uncollectible accounts, the allowance account might have a debit balance of, say, $10,000. In this case, the year-end adjusting entry should be for *$15,680* in order to bring the allowance to the required credit balance of $5,680.

Regardless of how often adjusting entries are made, the balance in the allowance account of Valley Ranch Supply should be *$5,680 at year-end.* Uncollectible accounts expense will be the same for the year, regardless of whether adjusting entries are made annually or monthly. The only difference is in whether this expense is recognized in one annual adjusting entry or in 12 monthly adjusting entries, each for a smaller amount.

collectible accounts expense is estimated at some percentage of net credit sales. The adjusting entry is made in the *full amount of the estimated expense,* without regard for the current balance in the Allowance for Doubtful Accounts.

To illustrate, assume that a company's past experience indicates that about 2% of its credit sales will prove to be uncollectible. If credit sales for September amount to $150,000, the month-end adjusting entry to record uncollectible accounts expense is:

The "income
statement" approach

Uncollectible Accounts Expense	3,000	
Allowance for Doubtful Accounts		3,000

To record uncollectible accounts expense, estimated at 2% of
credit sales ($150,000 × 2% = $3,000).

This approach is fast and simple—no aging schedule is required and no consideration is given to the existing balance in the Allowance for Doubtful Accounts. The aging of accounts receivable, however, provides a more reliable estimate of uncollectible accounts because of the consideration given to the age and collectibility of specific accounts receivable at the balance sheet date.

In past years, many small companies used the income statement approach in preparing monthly financial statements, but used the balance sheet method in annual financial statements. Today, however, most businesses have computer software that quickly and easily prepares monthly aging schedules of accounts receivable. Thus, most businesses today use the *balance sheet approach* in their monthly as well as annual financial statements.

CONSERVATISM IN THE VALUATION OF ACCOUNTS RECEIVABLE We previously have made reference to the accounting concept of **conservatism.** In accounting, "conservatism" means resolving uncertainty in a manner that minimizes the risk of overstating the company's current financial position. With respect to the valuation of accounts receivable, conservatism suggests that the allowance for doubtful accounts should be *at least adequate.* That is, it is better to err on the side of the allowance being a little too large, rather than a little too small.

Notice that conservatism in the valuation of assets also leads to a conservative measurement of net income in the current period. The larger the valuation allowance, the larger the current charge to uncollectible accounts expense.

DIRECT WRITE-OFF METHOD

Some companies do not use any valuation allowance for accounts receivable. Instead of making end-of-period adjusting entries to record uncollectible accounts expense on the basis of estimates, these companies recognize no uncollectible accounts expense until specific receivables are determined to be worthless. This method makes no attempt to match revenue with the expense of uncollectible accounts. Uncollectible accounts expense is recorded in the period in which individual accounts receivable are determined to be worthless, rather than in the period in which the sales were made.

When a particular customer's account is determined to be uncollectible, it is written off directly to Uncollectible Accounts Expense, as follows:

Uncollectible Accounts Expense	250	
Accounts Receivable (Bell Products)		250

To write off the receivable from Bell Products as uncollectible.

When the **direct write-off method** is used, the accounts receivable will be listed in the balance sheet at their gross amount, and *no valuation allowance* will be used. The receivables, therefore, are not stated at estimated net realizable value.

In some situations, use of the direct write-off method is acceptable. If a company makes most of its sales for cash, the amount of its accounts receivable will be small in relation to other assets. The expense from uncollectible accounts should also be small. Consequently, the direct write-off method is acceptable because its use does not have a *material* effect on the reported net income. Another situation in which the direct write-off method works satisfactorily is in a company which sells all or most of its output to a few large companies which are financially strong. In this setting there may be no basis for making advance estimates of any credit losses.

INCOME TAX REGULATIONS AND FINANCIAL REPORTING

In Chapter 1 we made the point that companies often use different accounting methods in preparing their income tax returns and their financial statements. The accounting treatments accorded to uncollectible accounts receivable provide an excellent example of this concept.

Current income tax regulations *require* taxpayers to use the direct write-off method in determining the uncollectible accounts expense used in computing *taxable income*. From the standpoint of accounting theory, the allowance method is better, because it enables expenses to be *matched* with the related revenue and thus provides a more logical measurement of net income. Therefore, most companies use the allowance method in their financial statements.[7]

INTERNAL CONTROLS FOR RECEIVABLES

One of the most important principles of internal control is that employees who have custody of cash or other negotiable assets must not maintain accounting records. In a small business, one employee often is responsible for handling cash receipts, maintaining accounts receivable records, issuing credit memoranda, and writing off uncollectible accounts. Such a combination of duties is an invitation to fraud. The employee in this situation is able to remove the cash collected from a customer without making any record of the collection. The next step is to dispose of the balance in the customer's account. This can be done by issuing a credit memo indicating that the customer has returned merchandise, or by writing off the customer's account as uncollectible. Thus, the employee has the cash, the customer's account shows a zero balance due, and the books are in balance.

In summary, employees who maintain the accounts receivable subsidiary ledger should *not have access* to cash receipts. The employees who maintain accounts receivable or handle cash receipts should *not* have authority to issue credit memoranda or to authorize the write-off of receivables as uncollectible. These are classic examples of incompatible duties.

MANAGEMENT OF ACCOUNTS RECEIVABLE

Management has two conflicting objectives with respect to the accounts receivable. On the one hand, management wants to generate as much sales revenue as possible. Offering customers lengthy credit terms, with little or no interest, has proven to be an effective means of generating sales revenue.

Every business, however, would rather sell for cash than on account. Unless receivables earn interest, they are nonproductive assets which produce no rev-

---

[7]An annual survey of accounting practices of 600 publicly owned corporations consistently shows more than 500 of these companies using the allowance method in their financial statements. All of these companies, however, use the direct write-off method in their income tax returns.

enue as they await collection. Therefore, another objective of cash management is to minimize the amount of money tied up in the form of accounts receivable.

Several tools are available to a management which must offer credit terms to its customers yet wants to minimize the company's investment in accounts receivable. We have already discussed offering credit customers cash discounts (such as 2/10, n/30) to encourage early payment. Other tools include *factoring* accounts receivable and selling to customers who use national credit cards.

FACTORING ACCOUNTS RECEIVABLE

The term **factoring** describes transactions in which a business either sells its accounts receivable to a financial institution (often called a *factor*) or borrows money by pledging its accounts receivable as collateral (security) for the loan. In either case, the business obtains cash immediately instead of having to wait until the receivables can be collected.

Factoring accounts receivable is a practice limited primarily to small business organizations which do not have well-established credit. Large and solvent organizations usually are able to borrow money using unsecured lines of credit, so they need not factor their accounts receivable.

CREDIT CARD SALES

Many retailing businesses minimize their investment in receivables by encouraging customers to use credit cards such as American Express, Visa, and Master-Card. A customer who makes a purchase using one of these cards signs a multiple-copy form, which includes a *credit card draft*. A credit card draft is similar to a check which is drawn upon the funds of the credit card company rather than upon the personal bank account of the customer. The credit card company promptly pays cash to the merchant to redeem these drafts. At the end of each month, the credit card company bills the credit card holder for all the drafts it has redeemed during the month. If the credit card holder fails to pay the amount owed, it is the credit card company which sustains the loss.

By making sales through credit card companies, merchants receive cash more quickly from credit sales and avoid uncollectible accounts expense. Also, the merchant avoids the expenses of investigating customers' credit, maintaining an accounts receivable subsidiary ledger, and making collections from customers.

BANK CREDIT CARDS Some widely used credit cards (such as Visa and MasterCard) are issued by banks. When the credit card company is a bank, the retailing business may deposit the signed credit card drafts directly in its bank account. Because banks accept these credit card drafts for immediate deposit, sales to customers using bank credit cards are recorded as *cash sales*.

In exchange for handling the credit card drafts, the bank makes a monthly service charge which usually runs between 1¼ and 3½% of the amount of the drafts. This monthly service charge is deducted from the merchant's bank account and appears with other bank service charges in the merchant's monthly bank statement.

OTHER CREDIT CARDS When customers use nonbank credit cards (such as American Express and Carte Blanche), the retailing business cannot deposit the credit card drafts directly in its bank account. Instead of debiting Cash, the merchant records an account receivable from the credit card company. Periodically, the credit card drafts are mailed (or transmitted electronically) to the credit card company, which then sends a check to the merchant. Credit card companies, however, do not redeem the drafts at the full sales price. The agreement between the credit card company and the merchant usually allows the credit card company to take a discount of between 3½% and 5% when redeeming the drafts.

To illustrate, assume that Bradshaw Camera Shop sells a camera for $200 to a customer who uses a Quick Charge credit card. The entry would be:

Accounts Receivable (Quick Charge Co.)	200	
Sales		200
To record sale to customer using Quick Charge credit card.		

This receivable is from the credit card company

At the end of the week, Bradshaw Camera Shop mails credit card drafts totaling $1,200 to Quick Charge Company, which redeems the drafts after deducting a 5% discount. When payment is received by Bradshaw, the entry is

Cash	1,140	
Credit Card Discount Expense..	60	
Accounts Receivable (Quick Charge Co.)		1,200
To record collection of account receivable from Quick Charge Co., less 5% discount.		

The expense account, Credit Card Discount Expense, is included among the selling expenses in the income statement of Bradshaw Camera Shop.

EVALUATING THE QUALITY OF ACCOUNTS RECEIVABLE

Collecting accounts receivable *on time* is important; it spells the success or failure of a company's credit and collection policies. A past-due receivable is a candidate for write-off as a credit loss. To help us judge how good a job a company is doing in granting credit and collecting its receivables, we compute the ratio of net sales to average receivables. This **accounts receivable turnover rate** tells us how many times the company's average investment in receivables was converted into cash during the year. The ratio is computed by dividing annual net sales by average accounts receivable.[8]

LO 6 *Evaluate the liquidity of various financial assets.*

For example, recent financial statements of 3M (Minnesota Mining and Manufacturing Company) show net sales of $9.4 billion. Receivables were $1.6 billion at the beginning of the year and $1.4 billion at the end of the year. Adding these two amounts and dividing the total by 2 gives us average receivables of $1.5 billion. Now we divide the year's net sales by the average receivables ($9.4 ÷ $1.5 = 6.3); the result indicates an accounts receivable turnover rate of *6.3 times* per year for 3M. The higher the turnover rate the more liquid the company's receivables.

Another step that will help us judge the liquidity of a company's accounts receivable is to convert the accounts receivable turnover rate to the *number of days* (on average) required for the company to collect its accounts receivable. This is a simple calculation: divide the number of days in the year by the turnover rate. Continuing our 3M example, divide 365 days by turnover rate of 6.3 (365 ÷ 6.3 = 57.9 days). This calculation tells us that on average, 3M waited approximately *58 days* to make collection of a sale on credit.

The data described above for computing the accounts receivable turnover rate and the average number of days to collect accounts receivable can be concisely stated as shown in the following equations:

---

[8]From a conceptual point of view, net *credit* sales should be used in computing the accounts receivable turnover rate. It is common practice, however, to use the net sales figure, as the portion of net sales made on account usually is not disclosed in financial statements.

Accounts Receivable Turnover

$$\frac{\text{Net Sales}}{\text{Average Accounts Receivable}} = \frac{\$9.4}{(\$1.6 + \$1.4) \div 2} = \frac{\$9.4}{\$1.5} = 6.3 \text{ times}$$

Average Number of Days to Collect Accounts Receivable

$$\frac{\text{Days in Year}}{\text{Accounts Receivable Turnover}} = \frac{365}{6.3} = 58 \text{ days}$$

Management closely monitors these ratios in evaluating the company's policies for extending credit to customers and the effectiveness of its collection procedures. Short-term creditors, such as factors, banks, and merchandise suppliers, also use these ratios to evaluate a company's ability to generate the cash necessary to pay it short-term liabilities.

In the annual audit of a company by a CPA firm, the independent auditors will verify receivables by communicating directly with the people who owe the money. This *confirmation* process is designed to provide evidence that the customers and other debtors actually exist, and that they acknowledge their indebtedness. The CPA firm also may verify the credit rating of major debtors.

YOUR TURN

You as Credit Manager

Assume that you were hired by Regis Department Stores in 1995 to develop and implement a new credit policy. At the time of your hire, the average collection period for an outstanding receivable was in excess of 90 days (far greater than the industry average). Thus, the primary purpose of the new policy was to better screen credit applicants in an attempt to improve the quality of the company's accounts receivable.

Shown below are sales and accounts receivable data for the past four years (in thousands):

	1998	1997	1996	1995
Sales	$17,000	$14,580	$9,600	$9,000
Average Accounts Receivable	$ 1,700	$ 1,620	$1,600	$1,800

Based upon the above data was the credit policy you developed successful? Explain.

*Our comments appear on page 362.

CONCENTRATIONS OF CREDIT RISK Assume that a business operates a single retail store in a town in which the major employer is a steel mill. What would happen to the collectibility of the store's accounts receivable if the steel mill were to close, leaving most of the store's customers unemployed? This situation illustrates what accountants call a *concentration of credit risk,* because many of the store's credit customers can be affected *in a similar manner* by certain changes in economic conditions. Concentrations of credit risk occur if a significant portion of a company's receivables are due from a few major customers, or from customers operating in the same industry or geographic region.

The FASB requires companies to disclose all significant concentrations of credit risk in the notes accompanying their financial statements. The basic purpose of these disclosures is to assist users of the financial statements in evaluating the extent of the company's vulnerability to credit losses stemming from changes in specific economic conditions.

NOTES RECEIVABLE AND INTEREST CHARGES

Accounts receivable usually do not bear interest. When interest will be charged, creditors usually require the debtor to sign a formal promissory note. Accounting for notes receivable and interest charges is discussed in *Supplemental Topic B* at the end of this chapter.

FINANCIAL ASSETS: REPORTING THE EFFECTS OF TRANSACTIONS

Early in this chapter, we summarized the valuation of financial assets in the balance sheet (page 308). The following table summarizes the reporting of transactions involving these assets in the *income statement* and *statement of cash flows*. Transactions preceded by an asterisk (*) are illustrated and explained in one of the two *Supplemental Topic* sections accompanying this chapter.

LO 7 *Explain how transactions discussed in this chapter affect net income and cash flows.*

	Presentation in the:	
Transactions	**Income Statement**	**Statement of Cash Flows**
Cash sales	Included in net sales	Cash receipts from operating activities
Investments in cash equivalents	No effect	Omitted—not a cash transaction
Conversion of cash equivalents back into cash	No effect	Omitted—not a cash transaction
Interest received from cash equivalents	*Nonoperating revenue	Cash receipts from operating activities
Investments in marketable securities	No effect	Cash used in investing activities
Conversion of marketable securities into cash	Nonoperating item (only the amount of gain or loss)	Cash receipts from investing activities (total proceeds)
*Interest and dividends from investments	*Nonoperating revenue (recognized *as received*)	Cash receipts from operating activities
*Year-end mark-to-market adjustment of available-for-sale marketable securities	No effect	Omitted—not a cash transaction
Sales on account	Included in net sales	Omitted—not a cash transaction
Collections of accounts receivable	No effect	Cash receipts from operating activities
Addition to an allowance for doubtful accounts	Operating expense	Omitted—not a cash transaction
Write-off of an uncollectible account against the allowance	No effect	Omitted—not a cash transaction
Write off of an account using the direct write-off method	Operating expense	Omitted—not a cash transaction
*Interest revenue on notes receivable	Nonoperating revenue (recognized *as earned*)	Cash receipts from operating activities (recognized *as received*)

NET CONNECTIONS

Many businesses invest idle cash in marketable securities rather than letting it accumulate in a non-interest-bearing checking account. These investments can provide very high returns. Unfortunately, due to their potential volatility, they can also subject a business to very high risks.

Many businesses rely upon the investment advice of full-service brokers to assist them in managing their marketable securities portfolios. Others believe that they do not need the ongoing consultation offered by full-service brokers, and elect to buy and sell their marketable securities using discount brokers or the Internet.

There is much to learn before selecting a full-service broker, a discount broker, or an on-line service. To find out more about the risks, costs, and range of services that each of these alternatives offer, visit the following Internet address for investors:

www.investorguide.com/brokerages.htm

To learn about specific brokerage firms, including complaints filed against them by investors, visit the home pages of the National Association of Securities Dealers, Inc., and the Securities and Exchange Commission at the following addresses:

www.nasdr.com
www.sec.gov

*SUPPLEMENTAL TOPIC A

ACCOUNTING FOR MARKETABLE SECURITIES

LO 8 *Account for transactions involving marketable securities.*

There are four basic "accountable events" relating to investments in marketable securities: (1) purchase of the investments, (2) receipt of dividend revenue and interest revenue, (3) sales of securities owned, and (4) end-of-period mark-to-market adjustment.

PURCHASES OF MARKETABLE SECURITIES

Investments in marketable securities originally are recorded at cost, which includes any brokerage commissions.[1] To illustrate, assume that MedCo purchases as a short-term investment 4,000 shares of the capital stock of AT&T. The purchase price is *$50 per share,* plus a brokerage commission of *$800.* The entry to record the purchase of these shares is:

Marketable Securities (AT&T capital stock)	200,800	
Cash		200,800
Purchased 4,000 shares of AT&T capital stock. Total cost, $200,800 ($50 × 4,000 shares + $800); cost per share, $50.20 ($200,800 ÷ 4,000 shares).		

---

[1]In purchasing some types of interest-bearing securities, the investor also must purchase any accrued interest. The amount of accrued interest should be debited to a separate account, entitled Accrued Interest Receivable. Accounting for accrued interest is explained in *Supplemental Topic B,* beginning on page 336.

Marketable Securities is a controlling account, representing the balance sheet value of *all* of MedCo's short-term investments. MedCo—like most investors— also maintains a *marketable securities subsidiary ledger,* with a separate account for each type of security owned. (Notice the computation in the explanation of our journal entry of the $50.20 *cost per share.* This amount will be used in computing any gains or losses when MedCo sells some of these investment shares.)

RECOGNITION OF INVESTMENT REVENUE

Most investors recognize interest and dividend revenue *as it is received.* Thus, the entries involve a debit to Cash and a credit either to Interest Revenue or Dividend Revenue.

To illustrate, assume that MedCo receives an $0.80 per share dividend on its 4,000 shares of AT&T. The entry to record this cash receipt is:

Cash	3,200	
Dividend Revenue		3,200
Received a quarterly cash dividend of 80 cents per share on 4,000 shares of AT&T capital stock.		

The policy of recognizing revenue as it is received eliminates the need for adjusting entries to accrue any investment revenue receivable at year-end.[2]

SALES OF INVESTMENTS

When an investment is sold, a gain or a loss often results. A sales price in excess of cost produces a **gain,** whereas a sales price below cost results in a **loss.**

SALE AT A PRICE RESULTING IN A GAIN To illustrate, assume that MedCo sells 1,000 shares of its AT&T stock for $55 per share, less a brokerage commission of $200. The entry would be:

Cash		54,800	
Marketable Securities (AT&T capital stock)			50,200
Gain on Sale of Investments			4,600
Sold 1,000 shares of AT&T capital stock at a gain:			
Sales price ($55 × 1,000 shares − $200)	$54,800		
Cost ($50.20 per share × 1,000 shares)	50,200		
Gain on sale	$ 4,600		

This transaction results in a gain because MedCo sold the shares at a price above cost. The gain—representing the profit on the sale—increases MedCo's net income for the period. At the end of the period, the credit balances in any gain accounts are closed into the Income Summary account, along with the credit balances of the revenue accounts.

SALE AT A PRICE RESULTING IN A LOSS Assume that several months later, MedCo sells another 1,000 shares of its AT&T stock, this time at a price *below*

---

[2]Dividend revenue does not accrue from day to day, but interest revenue does. There is nothing wrong with accruing interest revenue receivable at the end of each accounting period, but this usually is unnecessary. Accountants seldom make adjusting entries for immaterial amounts. In most cases, recognizing interest revenue as it is *received* produces essentially the same annual results as recording this revenue as it accrues. Thus, the convenient practice of recognizing interest revenue as it is received often is justified by the principle of *materiality.*

cost. The sales price is $48 per share, again less a brokerage commission of $200. The entry would be:

Cash..	47,800	
Loss on Sales of Investments	2,400	
Marketable Securities (AT&T capital stock)		50,200
Sold 1,000 shares of AT&T capital stock at a loss:		
Sales price ($48 × 1,000 shares − $200)............................	$47,800	
Cost ($50.20 per share × 1,000 shares).............................	50,200	
Gain (loss) on sale...	$ (2,400)	

This loss decreases MedCo's net income for the period. At the end of the period, the debit balances in any loss accounts are closed into the Income Summary account, along with the debit balances of expense accounts.

ADJUSTING MARKETABLE SECURITIES TO MARKET VALUE

At the end of each accounting period, the balance in the Marketable Securities account is adjusted to its *current market value*. Hence, this adjustment is described by the phrase, "mark-to-market." Mark-to-market is an interesting concept, because it represents a *departure from the cost principle*. At present, marketable securities are the only assets likely to appear in the balance sheet at an amount *above cost*.

The mark-to-market adjustment is easy to make, and involves only two accounts: (1) the Marketable Securities controlling account, and (2) a special owners' equity account, entitled Unrealized Holding Gain (or Loss) on Investments. The adjustment to the Marketable Securities account may be either a debit or a credit—whichever is necessary to adjust the account's balance to current market value.[3] (The market values of securities owned can be determined easily from the morning newspaper—remember, marketable securities trade daily at *quoted market prices*.)

When we change the valuation of an asset, there is a corresponding change in either total liabilities or total owners' equity. In the case of the mark-to-market adjustment, the corresponding change is recorded in the owners' equity account, Unrealized Holding Gain (or Loss) on Investments.

THE MARK-TO-MARKET ADJUSTMENT: AN ILLUSTRATION Assume that prior to making any adjusting entry, MedCo's Marketable Securities account has a balance of *$250,000* at year-end. If the current market value of the securities owned is, say, *$265,000*, MedCo will make the following adjustment at year-end:

Marketable Securities	15,000	
Unrealized Holding Gain (or Loss) on Investments............................		15,000
To adjust the balance sheet valuation of marketable securities to their current market value of $265,000.		

---

[3]The adjustment to the Marketable Securities account does *not* change the carrying value of individual securities. This adjustment is based upon the total value of *all* securities owned. Thus, mark-to-market adjustments *do not affect* the amounts of realized gains or losses recognized when specific securities are sold. Realized gains and losses are determined by comparing the *cost* of the securities sold with the proceeds from the sale.

But if the market value of the securities were only *$240,000—$10,000 less* than the balance in the Marketable Securities account—the adjusting entry would be:

Unrealized Holding Gain (or Loss) on Investments.................................... 10,000
    Marketable Securities...   10,000
To adjust the balance sheet valuation of marketable securities owned
to a market value of $240,000.

Notice that the Unrealized Holding Gain (or Loss) account may have either a debit or credit balance. A debit balance represents an unrealized holding *loss,* meaning that the current market value of the securities owned is *below* the investor's cost. A credit balance represents an unrealized holding *gain,* indicating that market value of the securities *exceeds* the investor's cost.

MARK-TO-MARKET AFFECTS ONLY THE BALANCE SHEET In Chapter 4 we made the point that adjusting entries usually affect both the balance sheet and the income statement. The mark-to-market adjustment of marketable securities is an exception to this rule—it affects *only the balance sheet.*[4]

The gains and losses recorded in the mark-to-market adjusting entries are *unrealized*—that is, they have not been "finalized" through sales of the securities. These unrealized gains and losses are *not* included in the investor's income statement. Rather, the Unrealized Holding Gain (or Loss) account appears in the *stockholders' equity section of the balance sheet,* just below the Retained Earnings account.

Because the Unrealized Holding Gain (or Loss) account does not enter into the determination of net income, it is not closed at the end of the accounting period. Instead, its balance is adjusted from one period to the next. At any balance sheet date, the Unrealized Holding Gain (or Loss) account represents the *difference between* the cost of the marketable securities owned and their current market value.

REPORTING INVESTMENT TRANSACTIONS IN THE FINANCIAL STATEMENTS

In a multiple-step income statement, interest revenue, dividend revenue, and gains and losses from sales of investments usually appear as *nonoperating items,* after the determination of income from operations.

In a statement of *cash flows,* receipts of dividends and interest are classified as *operating activities.* Purchases and sales of marketable securities are classified as *investing activities,* regardless of whether sales transactions result in a gain or a loss. (In the statement of cash flows, the *total sales proceeds* are listed as cash receipts from investing activities, regardless of whether the investment is sold at a gain or at a loss.)

MARK-TO-MARKET AND INCOME TAXES In income tax returns, the gains and losses on sales of investments are called *capital gains* and *capital losses.* Capital gains and losses are included in income tax returns only when the securities are *sold.* Thus, mark-to-market adjustments *do not* enter into the computation of income taxable.

---

[4]This exception applies only to those short-term investments classified as available-for-sale and held-to-maturity securities. It does not apply to short-term investments classified as trading securities. Held-to-maturity securities and trading securities are addressed in an intermediate financial accounting course.

NOTES RECEIVABLE AND INTEREST REVENUE

A promissory note is an unconditional promise in writing to pay on demand or at a future date a definite sum of money.

The person who signs the note and thereby promises to pay is called the *maker* of the note. The person to whom payment is to be made is called the *payee* of the note. In the illustration below, Pacific Rim Corp. is the maker of the note and First National Bank is the payee.

Simplified form of promissory note

$100,000	Los Angeles, California	July 10, 19__
One year	AFTER DATE Pacific Rim Corp.	PROMISES TO PAY
TO THE ORDER OF	First National Bank	
---One hundred thousand and no/100---		DOLLARS
PLUS INTEREST COMPUTED AT THE RATE OF	12% per annum	
	SIGNED	*G. L. Smith*
	TITLE	Treasurer

From the viewpoint of the maker, Pacific Rim, the illustrated note is a liability and is recorded by crediting the Notes Payable account. However, from the viewpoint of the payee, First National Bank, this same note is an asset and is recorded by debiting the Notes Receivable account. The maker of a note expects to pay cash at the *maturity date* (or due date); the payee expects to receive cash at that date.

NATURE OF INTEREST

LO 9 *Explain, compute, and account for the accrual of interest revenue.*

Interest is a charge made for the use of money. A borrower incurs interest expense. A lender earns interest revenue. When you encounter notes payable in a company's financial statements, you know that the company is borrowing and you should expect to find interest expense. When you encounter notes receivable, you should expect interest revenue.

COMPUTING INTEREST   A formula used in computing interest is as follows:

$$\textbf{Interest} = \textbf{Principal} \times \textbf{Rate of Interest} \times \textbf{Time}$$

(Often expressed as $I = P \times R \times T$)

Interest rates usually are stated on an *annual basis*. For example, the total interest charge on a $100,000, one-year, 12% note receivable is computed as follows:

$$\textbf{P} \times \textbf{R} \times \textbf{T} = \textbf{\$100,000} \times \textbf{.12} \times \textbf{1} = \textbf{\$12,000}$$

If the term of the note were only *four months* instead of one year, the total interest revenue earned in the life of the note would be $4,000, computed as shown below:

$$P \times R \times T = \$100{,}000 \times .12 \times \tfrac{4}{12} = \$4{,}000$$

In making interest computations, it is convenient to assume that each month has *30* days. Thus, a year has *360* days and each month represents $\tfrac{1}{12}$ of the year. As these assumptions greatly simplify the computation of interest and assist students in focusing upon the underlying concepts, we will use them in our illustrations and assignment material.[1]

If the term of a note is expressed in days, the exact number of days in each month must be considered in determining the maturity date of the note. The day on which a note is dated is not counted, but the date upon which it matures is. Thus, a two-day note dated today matures the day *after* tomorrow.

To illustrate these concepts, assume that a 60-day, 12% note for $100,000 is drawn on June 10. The *total* interest charge on this note will be $2,000, computed as follows:

$$P \times R \times T = \$100{,}000 \times .12 \times \tfrac{60}{360} = \$2{,}000$$

The $102,000 **maturity value** of the note ($100,000 principal, plus $2,000 interest) will be payable on *August 9*. The maturity date is determined as follows:

Days remaining in June (30 − 10)	20
Days in July	31
Subtotal	51
Days in August needed to complete the term of the note (including maturity date)	9
Specified term of note (in days)	60

ACCOUNTING FOR NOTES RECEIVABLE

In most fields of business, notes receivable are seldom encountered; in some fields they occur frequently and may constitute an important part of total assets. In banks and financial institutions, for example, notes receivable often represent the company's largest asset category and generate most of the company's revenue. Some retailers that sell on installment plans, such as Sears, Roebuck & Co., also own large amounts of notes receivable from customers.

All notes receivable are usually posted to a single account in the general ledger. A subsidiary ledger is not essential because the notes themselves, when filed by due dates, are the equivalent of a subsidiary ledger and provide any necessary information as to maturity, interest rates, collateral pledged, and other details. The amount debited to Notes Receivable is always the *face amount* of the note, regardless of whether or not the note bears interest. When an interest-bearing note is collected, the amount of cash received may be larger than the face amount of the note. The interest collected is credited to an Interest Revenue account, and only the face amount of the note is credited to the Notes Receivable account.

---

[1]Prior to the widespread use of computers, these assumptions were widely used in the business community. Today, however, most financial institutions compute interest using a 365-day year and the actual number of days in each month. The differences between these assumptions are *not material* in dollar amount.

ILLUSTRATIVE ENTRIES   Assume that on December 1 a 90-day, 12% note receivable is acquired from a customer, Marvin White, in settlement of an existing account receivable of $30,000. The entry for acquisition of the note is as follows:

Note received to replace
account receivable

Notes Receivable	30,000	
Accounts Receivable (Marvin White)		30,000
Accepted 90-day, 12% note in settlement of account receivable.		

At December 31, the end of the company's fiscal year, the interest earned to date on notes receivable should be accrued by an adjusting entry as follows:

Adjusting entry for interest
revenue earned in
December

Interest Receivable..	300	
Interest Revenue		300
To accrue interest for the month of December on Marvin White		
note ($30,000 × 12% × ¹⁄₁₂ = $300).		

To simplify this illustration, we will assume our company makes adjusting entries *only at year-end*. Therefore, no entries are made to recognize the interest revenue accruing during January and February.

On March 1 (90 days after the date of the note) the note matures. The entry to record collection of the note will be:

Collection of principal
and interest

Cash	30,900	
Notes Receivable		30,000
Interest Receivable...		300
Interest Revenue		600
Collected 90-day, 12% note from Marvin White ($30,000 × 12% × ³⁄₁₂ =		
$900 interest of which $600 was earned in current year).		

The preceding three entries show that interest is being earned throughout the life of the note and that the interest should be apportioned between years on a time basis. The revenue of each year will then include the interest actually earned in that year.

IF THE MAKER OF A NOTE DEFAULTS   A note receivable which cannot be collected at maturity is said to have been **defaulted** by the maker. Immediately after the default of a note, an entry should be made by the holder to transfer the amount due from the Notes Receivable account to an account receivable from the debtor.

To illustrate, assume that on March 1, our customer, Marvin White, had defaulted on the note used in the preceding example. In this case, the entry on March 1 would have been:

Accounts Receivable (Marvin White)	30,900	
Notes Receivable		30,000
Interest Receivable...		300
Interest Revenue		600
To record default by Marvin White on 90-day, 12% note.		

Notice that the interest earned on the note is recorded through the maturity date and is included in the account receivable from the maker. The interest receivable on a defaulted note is just as valid a claim against the maker as is the principal amount of the note.

If the account receivable from White cannot be collected, it ultimately will be written off against the Allowance for Doubtful Accounts. Therefore, the balance in the Allowance for Doubtful Accounts should provide for estimated uncollectible *notes* receivable as well as uncollectible *accounts* receivable.

For many companies, the provision for doubtful accounts is small and does not have a material effect upon net income for the period. Notes receivable, however, are the largest and most important asset for nearly every bank. Interest on these notes is a bank's largest and most important type of revenue. Thus, the collectibility of notes owned by a bank is a key factor in determining the success or failure of that bank.

Citicorp, the nation's largest bank, recently added a staggering $3 billion to its allowance for doubtful loans to developing countries. The related debit to expense caused Citicorp to report one of the largest net losses for a single quarter (three-month period) in the history of American business. Citicorp is not alone in having problems with uncollectible loans. In recent years, uncollectible loans have been the largest expense in the income statements of many American banks and savings and loan associations.

DISCOUNTING NOTES RECEIVABLE In past years some companies sold their notes receivable to banks in order to obtain cash prior to the maturity dates of these notes. As the banks purchased these notes at a "discount" from their maturity values, this practice became known as *discounting* notes receivable.

Discounting notes receivable is not a widespread practice today because most banks no longer purchase notes receivable from their customers. Interestingly, the practice of discounting notes receivable is most widespread among banks themselves. Many banks sell large "packages" of their notes receivable (loans) to agencies of the federal government or to other financial institutions. From a conceptual point of view, discounting notes receivable is essentially the same as selling accounts receivable to a factor.

THE DECISION OF WHETHER TO ACCRUE INTEREST

The concept of interest accruing from day to day applies not only to notes receivable, but to all interest-bearing investments (such as cash equivalents and bonds), and to interest-bearing debt. But in our discussions of cash equivalents and marketable securities, we stated that investors generally recognize interest revenue as it is received. In accounting for notes receivable, why did we accrue the interest earned, instead of recognizing revenue as cash was received?

The answer lies in the concept of *materiality*. Interest does, in fact, accrue from day to day. But the interest revenue earned from cash equivalents and investments in marketable securities usually represents only a small part of the investor's total revenue. In short, it usually is *not material* in relation to other financial statement amounts. Thus, the principle of materiality often justifies investor's accounting for this revenue in the most convenient manner.

Most notes receivable, however, are owned by *financial institutions*. For these businesses, interest revenue *is* material. In fact, it generally is the company's primary source of revenue. In these circumstances, greater care must be taken to assign interest revenue to the period in which it actually is *earned*.

SUMMARY OF LEARNING OBJECTIVES

1 Define financial assets and explain their valuation in the balance sheet.

Financial assets are cash and other assets that convert directly into *known amounts* of cash. The three basic categories are cash, marketable securities, and receivables. In the balance sheet, financial assets are listed at the *current value*. For cash, this means the face amount; for marketable securities, current market value; and for receivables, net realizable value.

2 Describe the objectives of cash management.

The objectives of cash management are accurate accounting for cash transactions, the prevention of losses through theft or fraud, and maintaining adequate—but not excessive—cash balances.

3 Explain means of achieving internal control over cash transactions.

The major steps in achieving internal control over cash transactions are as follows: (1) separate cash handling from the accounting function, (2) prepare departmental cash budgets, (3) prepare a control listing of all cash received through the mail and from over-the-counter cash sales, (4) deposit all cash receipts in the bank daily, (5) make all payments by check, (6) verify every expenditure before issuing a check in payment, and (7) promptly reconcile bank statements.

4 Prepare a bank reconciliation and explain its purpose.

The cash balance shown on the month-end bank statement usually will differ from the amount of cash shown in the depositor's ledger. The difference is caused by items which have been recorded by either the depositor or the bank, but not recorded by both. Examples are outstanding checks and deposits in transit. The bank reconciliation adjusts the cash balance per the books and the cash balance per the bank statement for any unrecorded items, and thus produces the correct amount of cash to be included in the balance sheet at the end of the month.

The purpose of a bank reconciliation is to achieve the control inherent in the maintenance of two independent records of cash transactions; one record maintained by the depositor and the other by the bank. When these two records are reconciled (brought into agreement), we gain assurance of a correct accounting for cash transactions.

5 Account for uncollectible receivables using the allowance and direct write-off methods.

Under the allowance method, the portion of each period's credit sales expected to prove uncollectible is *estimated*. This estimated amount is recorded by a debit to Uncol-

lectible Accounts Expense and a credit to the contra-asset account, Allowance for Doubtful Accounts. When specific accounts are determined to be uncollectible, they are written off by debiting Allowance for Doubtful Accounts and crediting Accounts Receivable.

Under the direct write-off method, uncollectible accounts are charged to expense in the period that they are determined to be worthless.

The allowance method is theoretically preferable because it is based upon the matching principle. However, only the direct write-off method may be used in income tax returns.

6 Evaluate the liquidity of various financial assets.

The most liquid financial asset is cash, followed by cash equivalents, marketable securities, and receivables. The liquidity of receivables varies depending upon their collectibility and maturity dates.

The allowance for doubtful accounts should provide for those receivables which may prove to be uncollectible. However, users of financial statements may also want to evaluate the concentrations-of-credit-risk disclosure and, perhaps, the credit ratings of major debtors. The accounts receivable turnover rate provides insight as to how quickly receivables are collected.

7 Explain how transactions discussed in this chapter affect net income and cash flows.

These effects are summarized in the table on page 331.

*8 Account for transactions involving marketable securities.

When securities are purchased, they are recorded at cost. Interest and dividends generally are recognized as revenue when they are received. When securities are sold, the cost is compared to the sales price, and the difference is recorded as a gain or a loss. At the end of each accounting period, the balance of the controlling account is adjusted to reflect the *current market value* of the securities owned.

**9 Explain, compute, and account for the accrual of interest revenue.

Interest is a contractual amount that accumulates (accrues) day by day. The amount of interest accruing over a time period may be computed by the formula: *Principal × Rate × Time.*

Whether interest revenue is recognized as it *accrues* or as it *is received* depends upon the *materiality* of the amounts involved.

---

*Supplemental Topic A, "Accounting for Marketable Securities."
**Supplemental Topic B, "Notes Receivable and Interest Revenue."

This is the first of three chapters in which we explore the issues involved in accounting for assets. The central theme in these chapters is the *valuation* of assets.

The valuation of assets affects not only the balance sheet, but also the measurement of net income. With respect to cash, there is little question as to the appropriate valuation. The savings and loan crisis in the late 1980s, however, showed that the valuation of notes receivable requires professional judgment and can be a measurement of critical importance.

In the next two chapters, we explore the valuation of inventories and of plant assets. For each of these assets, you will see that several *alternative* valuation methods are acceptable. These different methods, however, may produce *significantly different results*. An understanding of these alternative accounting methods is essential to the proper use and interpretation of financial statements and also in the preparation of income tax returns.

KEY TERMS INTRODUCED OR EMPHASIZED IN CHAPTER 7

Accounts receivable turnover rate (p. 329)   A ratio used to measure the liquidity of accounts receivable and the reasonableness of the accounts receivable balance. Computed by dividing net sales by average receivables.

Aging the accounts receivable (p. 324)   The process of classifying accounts receivable by age groups such as current, 1–30 days past due, 31–60 days past due, etc. A step in estimating the uncollectible portion of the accounts receivable.

Allowance for Doubtful Accounts (p. 321)   A valuation account or contra-account relating to accounts receivable and showing the portion of the receivables estimated to be uncollectible.

Bank reconciliation (p. 313)   An analysis that explains the difference between the balance of cash shown in the bank statement and the balance of cash shown in the depositor's records.

Cash equivalents (p. 309)   Very short-term investments which are so liquid that they are considered equivalent to cash. Examples include money market funds, U.S. Treasury bills, certificates of deposit, and commercial paper. These investments must mature within 90 days of acquisition.

Cash management (p. 310)   Planning, controlling, and accounting for cash transactions and cash balances.

Compensating balance (p. 309)   A minimum average balance that a bank may require a borrower to leave on deposit in a non-interest-bearing account.

Conservatism (p. 326)   A traditional practice of resolving uncertainties by choosing an asset valuation at the lower end of the range of reasonableness. Also refers to the policy of postponing recognition of revenue to a later date when a range of reasonable choice exists. Designed to avoid overstatement of financial strength and earnings.

Default (p. 338)   Failure to pay interest or principal of a promissory note at the due date.

Direct write-off method (p. 326)   A method of accounting for uncollectible receivables in which no expense is recognized until individual accounts are determined to be worthless. At that point the account receivable is written off, with an offsetting debit to uncollectible accounts expense. Fails to match revenue and related expenses.

Factoring (p. 328)   Transactions in which a business either sells its accounts receivable to a financial institution (often called a *factor*) or borrows money by pledging its accounts receivable as collateral.

Financial assets (p. 307)   Cash and assets convertible directly into known amounts of cash (such as marketable securities and receivables).

Gain (p. 333)   An increase in owners' equity resulting from a transaction *other than* earning revenue or investment by the owners. The most common example is the sale of an asset at a price *above* book value.

Line of credit (p. 309)   A prearranged borrowing agreement in which a bank stands ready to advance the borrower without delay any amount up to a specified credit limit. Once "used," a line of credit becomes a liability. The unused portion of the line represents the *ability* to borrow cash without delay.

Loss (p. 333)   A decrease in owner's equity resulting from any transaction other than an expense or a distribution to the owners. The most common example is sale of an asset at a price *below* book value.

Marketable securities (p. 307)   Highly liquid investments, primarily in stocks and bonds, that can be sold at quoted market prices in organized securities exchanges.

Mark-to-market (p. 318)   The balance sheet valuation standard now applied to investments in marketable securities. Involves adjusting the controlling account for all securities owned to its total market value at each balance sheet date. (Represents an exception to the cost principle.)

Maturity date (p. 320)   The date on which a note becomes due and payable.

Maturity value (p. 337)   The value of a note at its maturity date, consisting of principle plus interest.

Net realizable value (p. 308)   The balance sheet valuation standard applied to receivables. Equal to the gross amount of accounts and notes receivable, less an estimate of the portion that may prove to be uncollectible.

NSF check (p. 314)   A customer's check which was deposited but returned because of a lack of funds (Not Sufficient Funds) in the account on which the check was drawn.

Unrealized Holding Gain (or Loss) on Investments (p. 318) A special owners' equity account representing the difference between the cost of investments owned and their market value at the balance sheet date. In short, gains or losses on these investments which have not been "realized" through sale of the securities.

Voucher (p. 312) A written authorization used to approve a transaction for recording and payment.

Voucher system (p. 312) An accounting system designed to provide strong internal control over cash disbursements. Requires that every transaction which will result in a cash payment be verified, approved, and recorded before a check is prepared.

DEMONSTRATION PROBLEM

Shown below are selected transactions of Gulf Corp. during the month of December.

Dec. 5 Sold 2,000 shares of AT&T capital stock at $53 per share, less a brokerage commission of $200. These marketable securities had been acquired nine months earlier at a total cost of $112,000.

Dec. 8 An account receivable from S. Willis in the amount of $700 is determined to be uncollectible and is written off against the Allowance for Doubtful Accounts.

Dec. 15 Unexpectedly received $200 from F. Hill in full payment of her account. The $200 account receivable from Hill had previously been written off as uncollectible.

Dec. 20 Sold 1,000 shares of IBM capital stock at a price of $60 per share, less a brokerage commission of $150. These investment shares had been acquired at a total cost of $52,000.

Dec. 31 Replenished the petty cash fund. Petty cash vouchers indicated office supplies expense, $44; miscellaneous expense, $32.

Dec. 31 The month-end bank reconciliation includes the following items: outstanding checks, $12,320; deposit in transit, $3,150; check from customer T. Jones returned "NSF," $358; bank service charges, $10; bank collected $20,000 in maturing U.S. Treasury bills (a cash equivalent) on the company's behalf. (These Treasury bills had cost $19,670, so the amount collected includes $330 interest revenue.)

DATA FOR ADJUSTING ENTRIES

1. An aging of accounts receivable indicates probable uncollectible accounts totaling $9,000. Prior to the month-end adjustment, the Allowance for Doubtful Accounts has a credit balance of $5,210.

2. Prior to any year-end adjustment, the balance in the Marketable Securities account was $213,800. At year-end, marketable securities owned had a cost of $198,000 and a market value of $210,000.

INSTRUCTIONS

a. Prepare entries in general journal entry form for the December transactions. In adjusting the accounting records from the bank reconciliation, make one entry to record any increases in the Cash account and a separate entry to record any decreases.

b. Prepare the month-end adjustments indicated by the two numbered paragraphs.

c. What is the adjusted balance in the Unrealized Gain (or Loss) on Investments account at December 31? Where in the financial statements does this account appear?

SOLUTION TO DEMONSTRATION PROBLEM

a.

GENERAL JOURNAL

Dec. 5	Cash	105,800	
	Loss on Sale of Investments	6,200	
	Marketable Securities		112,000
	Sold 2,000 shares of AT&T capital stock at a price below cost.		
8	Allowance for Doubtful Accounts	700	
	Accounts Receivable (S. Willis)		700
	To write off receivable from S. Willis as uncollectible.		
15	Accounts Receivable (F. Hill)	200	
	Allowance for Doubtful Accounts		200
	To reinstate account receivable previously written off as uncollectible.		
15	Cash	200	
	Accounts Receivable (F. Hill)		200
	To record collection of account receivable.		
20	Cash	59,850	
	Marketable Securities		52,000
	Gain on Sale of Investments		7,850
	Sold 1,000 shares of IBM at a price above cost.		
31	Office Supplies Expense	44	
	Miscellaneous Expense	32	
	Cash		76
	To replenish petty cash fund.		
31	Cash	20,000	
	Cash Equivalents		19,670
	Interest Revenue		330
	To record collection of maturing T-bills by bank.		
31	Accounts Receivable (T. Jones)	358	
	Bank Service Charges	10	
	Cash		368
	To record bank service charge and to reclassify NSF check from T. Jones as an account receivable.		

b. **Adjusting Entries**

Dec. 31	Uncollectible Accounts Expense	3,790	
	Allowance for Doubtful Accounts		3,790
	To increase Allowance for Doubtful Accounts to $9,000 ($9,000 − $5,210 = $3,790).		
31	Unrealized Gain (or Loss) on Investments	3,800	
	Marketable Securities		3,800
	To reduce the balance in the Marketable Securities account to a market value of $210,000.		

c. The Unrealized Gain (or Loss) on Investments account will have a *$12,000 credit balance,* representing the unrealized gain on securities owned as of December 31. (The unrealized gain is equal to the $210,000 market value of these securities, less their $198,000 cost.) The account appears in the stockholders' equity section of Gulf Corp.'s balance sheet.

SELF-TEST QUESTIONS
The answers to these questions appear on page 363.

1. In general terms, financial assets appear in the balance sheet at:
  a. Face value.
  b. Current cash value.
  c. Cost
  d. Estimated future sales value.

2. Which of the following practices contributes to efficient cash management?
  a. Never borrow money—maintain a cash balance sufficient to make all necessary payments.
  b. Record all cash receipts and cash payments at the end of the month when reconciling the bank statements.
  c. Prepare monthly forecasts of planned cash receipts, payments, and anticipated cash balances up to a year in advance.
  d. Pay each bill as soon as the invoice arrives.

3. Each of the following measures strengthens internal control over cash receipts *except:*
  a. The use of a voucher system.
  b. Preparation of a daily listing of all checks received through the mail.
  c. The deposit of cash receipts intact in the bank on a daily basis.
  d. The use of cash registers.

USE THE FOLLOWING DATA FOR QUESTIONS 4 AND 5:
Quinn Company's bank statement at January 31 shows a balance of $13,360, while the ledger account for Cash in Quinn's ledger shows a balance of $12,890 at the same date. The only reconciling items are the following:

● Deposit in transit, $890.
● Bank service charge, $24.
● NSF check from customer Greg Denton in the amount of $426.
● Error in recording check No. 389 for rent: check was written in the amount of $1,320, but was recorded improperly in the accounting records as $1,230.
● Outstanding checks, $?????

4. What is the total amount of outstanding checks at January 31?
  a. $1,048   **b.** $868   **c.** $1,900   **d.** $1,720

5. Assuming a single journal entry is made to adjust Quinn Company's accounting records at January 31, the journal entry includes:
  a. A debit to Rent Expense for $90.
  b. A credit to Accounts Receivable, G. Denton, for $426.
  c. A credit to Cash for $450.
  d. A credit to Cash for $1,720.

6. Which of the following best describes the application of generally accepted accounting principles to the valuation of accounts receivable?
  a. Realization principle—Accounts receivable are shown at their net realizable value in the balance sheet.
  b. Matching principle—The loss due to an uncollectible account is recognized in the period in which the sale is made, not in the period in which the account receivable is determined to be worthless.

    c. Cost principle—Accounts receivable are shown at the initial cost of the merchandise to customers, less the cost the seller must pay to cover uncollectible accounts.

    d. Principle of conservatism—Accountants favor using the lowest reasonable estimate for the amount of uncollectible accounts.

7. On January 1, Dillon Company had a $3,100 credit balance in the Allowance for Doubtful Accounts. During the year, sales totaled $780,000 and $6,900 of accounts receivable were written off as uncollectible. A December 31 aging of accounts receivable indicated the amount probably uncollectible to be $5,300. (No recoveries of accounts previously written off were made during the year.) Dillion's financial statements for the current year should include:

    a. Uncollectible accounts expense of $9,100.

    b. Uncollectible accounts expense of $5,300.

    c. Allowance for Doubtful Accounts with a credit balance of $1,500.

    d. Allowance for Doubtful Accounts with a credit balance of $8,400.

8. Under the *direct write-off* method of accounting for uncollectible accounts:

    a. The current year uncollectible accounts expense is less than the expense would be under the income statement approach.

    b. The relationship between the current period net sales and current period uncollectible accounts expense illustrates the matching principle.

    c. The Allowance for Doubtful Accounts is debited when specific accounts receivable are determined to be worthless.

    d. Accounts receivable are not stated in the balance sheet at net realizable value, but at the balance of the Accounts Receivable controlling account.

9. Which of the following actions is *least* likely to increase a company's accounts receivable turnover?

    a. Encouraging customers to use bank credit cards, such as Visa and MasterCard, rather than other national credit cards, such as American Express and Diners' Club.

    b. Offer customers larger cash discounts for making early payments.

    c. Reduce the interest rate charged to credit customers.

    d. Sell accounts receivable to a factor.

*10. Puget Sound Co. sold marketable securities costing $80,000 for $92,000 cash. In the company's income statement and statement of cash flows, respectively, this will appear as:

    a. A $12,000 gain, and a $92,000 cash receipt.

    b. A $92,000 gain, and an $8,000 cash receipt.

    c. A $12,000 gain, and an $80,000 cash receipt.

    d. A $92,000 sale, and a $92,000 cash receipt.

**11. On October 1, 1997 Coast Financial lent Barr Corporation $300,000, receiving in exchange a nine-month, 12% note receivable. Coast ends its fiscal year on December 31, and makes adjusting entries to accrue interest earned on all notes receivable. The interest earned on the note receivable from Barr Corporation during *1998* will amount to:

    a. $9,000   **b.** $18,000   **c.** $27,000   **d.** $36,000

ASSIGNMENT MATERIAL

DISCUSSION QUESTIONS

1. Briefly describe the flow of cash among receivables, cash, and marketable securities.

---

*Supplemental Topic A, "Accounting for Marketable Securities."
**Supplemental Topic B, "Notes Receivable and Interest Revenue"

2. Different categories of financial assets are valued differently in the balance sheet. These different valuation methods have one common goal. Explain.

3. What are *cash equivalents?* Provide two examples. Why are these items often combined with cash for the purpose of balance sheet presentation?

4. What are lines of credit? From the viewpoint of a short-term creditor, why do lines of credit increase a company's solvency? How are the unused portions of these lines presented in financial statements?

5. Does the expression "efficient management of cash" mean anything more than procedures to prevent losses from fraud or theft? Explain.

6. Why are cash balances in *excess* of those needed to finance business operations viewed as relatively nonproductive assets? Suggest several ways in which these excess cash balances may be utilized effectively.

7. Mention some principles to be observed by a business in establishing strong internal control over cash receipts.

8. What is the basic control feature in a *voucher system?*

9. List two items often encountered in reconciling a bank statement which may cause cash per the bank statement to be *larger* than the balance of cash shown in the depositor's accounting records.

10. Describe the nature and usefulness of a *cash budget.*

11. Why are investments in marketable securities usually regarded as current assets?

12. Why must an investor who owns numerous marketable securities maintain a marketable securities subsidiary ledger?

13. Explain the valuation procedure termed *mark-to-market* for short-term investments classified as available-for-sale securities.

14. What does the account Unrealized Holding Gain (or Loss) on Investment represent? How is this account presented in the financial statements for short-term investments classified as available-for-sale securities?

15. Explain the relationship between the *matching principle* and the need to estimate uncollectible accounts receivable.

16. In making the annual adjusting entry for uncollectible accounts, a company may utilize a *balance sheet approach* to make the estimate, or it may use an *income statement approach.* Explain these two alternative approaches.

17. What is the direct write-off method of handling credit losses as opposed to the allowance method? What is its principal shortcoming?

18. Must companies use the same method of accounting for uncollectible accounts receivable in their financial statements and in their income tax returns? Explain.

19. What are the advantages to a retailer of making credit sales only to customers who use nationally recognized credit cards?

20. Alta Mine Company, a restaurant that had always made cash sales only, adopted a new policy of honoring several nationally known credit cards. Sales did not increase, but many of Alta Mine's regular customers began charging dinner bills on the credit cards. Has the new policy been beneficial to Alta Mine Company? Explain.

21. How is the accounts receivable turnover rate computed? Why is this rate significant to short-term creditors?

22. How does an annual audit by a CPA firm provide assurance that a company's accounts receivable and notes receivable are fairly presented in the company's financial statements?

23. Explain how each of the following are presented in (1) a multiple-step income statement, and (2) a statement of cash flows.
    a. Sale of marketable securities at a loss.

b. Adjusting entry to create (or increase) the allowance for doubtful accounts.

c. Entry to write off an uncollectible account against the allowance.

d. Adjusting entry to increase the balance in the Marketable Securities account to a higher market value (assume these investments are classified as available-for-sale securities).

*24. The market values of some marketable securities may change from day to day. How do these changes in market value affect the investor's *taxable income?*

**25. Determine the maturity date and maturity value of each of the following notes. (Assume a 360-day year in computing interest and maturity values, but count actual days to the maturity dates.)

a. A $10,000, 7% one-year note dated July 1, 1998.

b. A $20,000, 8%, 90-day note dated March 1.

EXERCISES

EXERCISE 7-1
You as a Student
LO 4

Assume that the following information relates to your most recent bank statement dated September 30:

Balance per bank statement at September 30 .... $3,468.52

Checks written that had not cleared bank as of September 30:

#203	University tuition	2,200.00
#205	University bookstore	181.14
#208	Rocco's pizza	12.87
#210	Stereo purchase	525.99
#211	October apartment rent	350.00

Interest amounting to $3.75 was credited to your account by the bank in September. The bank's service charge for the month was $5.00. In addition to your bank statement, you also received a letter from your parents informing you that they had made a $1,400.00 electronic funds transfer directly into your account on October 2. After reading your parent's letter, you looked in your checkbook and discovered its balance was $199.77. Adding your parent's deposit brought that total up to $1,599.77.

Prepare a bank reconciliation to determine your correct checking account balance. Explain why neither your bank statement nor your checkbook show this amount.

EXERCISE 7-2
Financial Assets
LO 1,2

The following financial assets appeared in the balance sheet of Fantasy Comics:

Current assets:

Cash	$250,000
Marketable securities	850,000
Accounts receivable	600,000

a. Define financial assets.

b. A different approach is used in determining the balance sheet value for each category of financial assets although these three approaches all serve a common goal. Explain.

c. Why do companies hold much of their financial assets in the form of marketable securities and receivables instead of cash?

---

*Supplemental Topic A, "Accounting for Marketable Securities."
**Supplemental Topic B, "Notes Receivable and Interest Revenue."

d. Define the following items and explain how they would be presented in Fantasy Comics' financial statements.
   1. Cash equivalents.
   2. A large compensating balance in the company's checking account.
   3. Unused lines of credit.

EXERCISE 7-3
Grandmother's
Secret

LO 3

The former bookkeeper of White Electric Supply is currently serving four to eight years in prison for embezzling nearly $416,000 in less than five years. She describes herself as "an ordinary mother of three kids and a proud grandmother of four." Like so many other "ordinary" employees, she started out by taking only small amounts. By the time she was caught, she was stealing lump sums of $5,000 and $10,000.

Her method was crude and simple. She would write a check for the correct amount payable to a supplier for, say, $15,000. However, she would record in the company's check register an amount significantly greater, say, $20,000. She would then write a check payable to herself for the $5,000 difference. In the check register, next to the number of each check she had deposited in her personal bank account, she would write the word "void," making it appear as though the check had been destroyed. This process went undetected for nearly five years.

a. What controls must have been lacking at White Electric Supply to enable the bookkeeper to steal nearly $416,000 before being caught?

b. What the bookkeeper did was definitely unethical. But *what if* one of her grandchildren had been ill and needed an expensive operation? If this had been the case, would it have been ethical for her to take company funds to pay for the operation if she intended to pay the company back in full? Defend your answer.

EXERCISE 7-4
Embezzlement, She
Wrote

LO 3

D. J. Fletcher, a trusted employee of Bluestem Products, found herself in personal financial difficulties and decided to "borrow" (steal) $3,000 from the company and to conceal her theft.

As a first step, Fletcher removed $3,000 in currency from the cash register. This amount represented the bulk of the cash received in over-the-counter sales during the three business days since the last bank deposit. Fletcher then removed a $3,000 check from the day's incoming mail; this check had been mailed in by a customer, Michael Adams, in full payment of his account. Fletcher made no journal entry to record the $3,000 collection from Adams, but deposited the check in Bluestem Products' bank account in place of the $3,000 over-the-counter cash receipts she had stolen.

In order to keep Adams from protesting when his month-end statement reached him, Fletcher made a journal entry debiting Sales Returns and Allowances and crediting Accounts Receivable—Michael Adams. Fletcher posted this entry to the two general ledger accounts affected and also to Adams's account in the subsidiary ledger for accounts receivable.

a. Did these actions by Fletcher cause the general ledger to be out of balance or the subsidiary ledger to disagree with the controlling account? Explain.

b. Assume that Bluestem Products prepares financial statements at the end of the month without discovering the theft. Would any items in the balance sheet or the income statement be in error? Explain.

c. Several weaknesses in internal control apparently exist in Bluestem Products. Indicate three specific changes needed to strengthen internal control over cash receipts.

EXERCISE 7-5
Bank Reconciliation

LO 4

Shown below is the information needed to prepare a bank reconciliation for Data Flow, Inc., at December 31.

1. At December 31, cash per the bank statement was $15,981; cash per the company's records was $17,445.

2. Two debit memoranda accompanied the bank statement: service charges for December of $24, and a $600 check drawn by Jane Jones marked "NSF."

3. Cash receipts of $4,353 on December 31 were not deposited until January.

4. The following checks had been issued in December but were not included among the paid checks returned by the bank: no. 620 for $978, no. 630 for $2,052, and no. 641 for $483.

    a. Prepare a bank reconciliation at December 31.

    b. Prepare the necessary journal entry or entries to update the accounting records.

    c. Assume that the company is normally *not* required to pay a bank service charge if it maintains a minimum average daily balance of $1,000 throughout the month. If the company's average daily balance for December had been $4,500, why did it have to pay a $24 service charge?

EXERCISE 7-6
Cash and Cash Equivalents

The following footnote appeared in a recent financial statement of **Westinghouse Electric:**

> The Corporation considers all investment securities with a maturity of three months or less when acquired to be cash equivalents. All cash and temporary investments are placed with high-credit quality financial institutions, and the amount of credit exposure to any one financial institution is limited. At December 31, cash and cash equivalents include restricted funds of $42 million.

a. Are the company's cash equivalents debt or equity securities? How do you know?

b. Explain what is meant by the statement that "the credit exposure to any one financial institution is limited."

c. Explain what is meant by the term "restricted funds" used in the footnote.

EXERCISE 7-7
Interest Rate Shopping

Well managed companies frequently transfer excess cash into revenue-generating cash equivalents, such as bank money market accounts. These accounts differ with respect to the minimum balances they require and the interest rates that they pay. Shown below, for example, is recent information about money market accounts offered by several large banks:

Bank	Minimum Balance	Annual Percentage Rate
First Federal	$ 2,500	3.50%
Chase Manhattan	25,000	5.55%
Republic Bank	5,000	5.02%
Bank of America	25,000	3.20%
Citibank	25,000	5.11%

Contact several banks in your area that offer money market accounts. Be certain to find out: (1) the minimum balances they require, (2) their respective interest rates, (3) whether they are insured against losses, and (4) the type of securities in which each money market account is invested, such as commercial paper, U.S. Treasury bills, etc. (**Note:** All interviews are to be conducted in accordance with the guidelines in the *Note to Students* section of the introduction to this textbook).

    If you were a manager with $500,000 of excess cash to invest for 90 days or less, to which of these money market accounts would you transfer funds? Defend your answer.

EXERCISE 7-8
The Nature of Marketable Securities
LO 8

Many companies hold much of their total financial assets in the form of marketable securities.

a. Define marketable securities. Why are these securities considered to be financial assets?

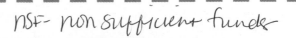
NSF- non sufficient funds

b. What is the basic advantage of keeping financial assets in the form of marketable securities instead of in cash?

c. Explain how investments in marketable securities are valued in the investor's balance sheet.

d. Discuss whether the valuation of marketable securities represents a departure from (1) the cost principle, and (2) the objectivity principle.

e. Do you think that mark-to-market benefits the *users* of financial statements? Explain.

EXERCISE 7-9
Estimating
Uncollectible
Accounts
LO 5

The credit manager of Olympic Sporting Goods has gathered the following information about the company's accounts receivable and credit losses during the current year:

Net credit sales for the year		$3,000,000
Accounts receivable at year-end		360,000
Uncollectible accounts receivable:		
Actually written off during the year	$43,650	
Estimated portion of year-end receivables expected to prove		
uncollectible (per aging schedule)	18,000	61,650

Prepare one journal entry summarizing the recognition of uncollectible accounts expense for the entire year under each of the following independent assumptions:

direct write off method

a. Uncollectible accounts expense is estimated at an amount equal to 1½% of net credit sales.

allowance method

b. Uncollectible accounts expense is recognized by adjusting the balance in the Allowance for Doubtful Accounts to the amount indicated in the year-end aging schedule. The balance in the allowance account at the *beginning* of the current year was $15,000. (Consider the effect of the write-offs during the year upon the balance in the Allowance for Doubtful Accounts.)

dir. writeoff

c. The company uses the direct write-off method of accounting for uncollectible accounts.

d. Which of the three methods gives investors and creditors the most accurate assessment of a company's liquidity? Defend your answer.

EXERCISE 7-10
Industry
Characteristics
and Collection
Performance
LO 6

The following information was taken from recent annual reports of **Huffy Corporation** and **Pennsylvania Power & Light** (Huffy is a manufacturer of bicycles and Pennsylvania Power & Light is a public utility—dollar amounts are stated in thousands):

	Huffy	PP & L
Net sales	$685,000	$2,800,000
Average accounts receivable	114,000	200,000

a. Compute for each company the accounts receivable turnover rate for the year.

b. Compute for each company the number of days (on average) required to collect an outstanding receivable (round answer to the nearest whole day).

c. Explain why the figures computed for Huffy in parts **a** and **b** are so different from those computed for Pennsylvania Power & Light.

EXERCISE 7-11
Analyzing the Effects
of Transactions
LO 7

Six events pertaining to financial assets are described below.

a. Invested idle cash in marketable securities and classified them as available-for-sale.

b. Collected an account receivable.

c. Sold marketable securities at a loss (proceeds from the sale were equal to the current market value reflected in the last balance sheet).

d. Determined a particular account receivable to be uncollectible and wrote it off against the allowance for doubtful accounts.

e. Received interest earned on an investment in marketable securities (company policy is to recognize interest as revenue *when received*).

f. Made a mark-to-market adjustment increasing the balance in the Marketable Securities account to reflect a rise in the market value of securities owned.

Indicate the effects of each transaction or adjusting entry upon the financial measurements in the four column headings listed below. Use the code letters, **I** for increase, **D** for decrease, and **NE** for no effect.

Transaction	Current Assets	Net Income	Net Cash Flow from Operating Activities	Net Cash Flow (from Any Source)
a				

---

*EXERCISE 7-12
Mark-to-Market
LO 8

Giant Foods accumulates large amounts of excess cash throughout the year. It typically invests these funds in marketable securities until they are needed. The company's most recent financial statements reported a $594,000 unrealized loss on short-term investments. Footnotes to these financial statements disclose that Giant classifies its short-term investments as available-for-sale securities.

a. Explain the meaning of Giant's unrealized loss on short-term investments.

b. How is the unrealized loss reported in Giant's financial statements?

c. Is the unrealized loss included in the computation of Giant's taxable income? Explain.

d. Evaluate the mark-to-market concept from the perspective of Giant's short-term creditors.

---

*EXERCISE 7-13
Accounting for Marketable Securities
LO 8

Clean Air Management pays income taxes at a rate of 30% on capital gains. At December 31, *1998*, the company owns marketable securities that had cost $50,000, but have a current market value of $180,000.

a. How will the users of Clean Air's financial statements be made aware of this substantial increase in the market value of the company's investments?

b. As of December 31, 1998, how much income taxes has Clean Air paid on the increase in the value of these investments? Explain.

c. Prepare a journal entry at January 4, 1999 to record the sale of these investments for $180,000 in cash.

d. What effect will this transaction have upon Clean Air's income tax obligation for 1999?

**EXERCISE 7-14
Notes and Interest
LO 9

On September 1, a six-month, 9% note receivable is acquired from Shaun Young, a customer, in settlement of his $22,000 account receivable.

Prepare journal entries to record:

---

*Supplemental Topic A, "Accounting for Marketable Securities."
**Supplemental Topic B, "Notes Receivable and Interest Revenue."

a. The receipt of the note on September 1.

b. The adjustment to record accrued interest revenue on December 31.

c. Collection of the principal and interest on March 1.

EXERCISE 7-15
Toys "R" Us
Lines of
Credit

The annual report of **Toys "R" Us** appears in Appendix A at the end of this textbook. Read management's discussion and analysis of liquidity, capital resources, and short-term financing requirements.

a. During what time of year does the company rely most upon its available line of credit? Explain why.

b. Was the interest rate associated with outstanding lines of bank credit higher or lower at January 28, 1995, than it was at January 29, 1994? By how much?

c. Does the unused portion of the company's lines of credit represent a liability? Explain your answer.

PROBLEMS

PROBLEM 7-1
Cash Management

St. Jude Medical, Inc., is a publicly owned corporation engaged in the manufacture of heart valves and other medical products. In recent years, the company has accumulated large amounts of cash and cash equivalents as a result of profitable operations. A recent annual report showed cash and cash equivalents amounting to more than 50% of the company's total assets. During the period that these large holdings of cash and cash equivalents have been accumulated, the company has paid no cash dividends.

Some financial analysts thought St. Jude was holding too much cash.

a. Why would anyone think that a company was holding "too much cash"?

b. What can a corporation do to efficiently utilize cash balances in excess of the amounts needed for current operations?

c. Evaluate St. Jude's policies of accumulating liquid resources instead of paying dividends from the perspectives of:
    1. The company's creditors.
    2. The company's stockholders.

PROBLEM 7-2
Reporting
Financial
Assets
LO 1

Explain how each of the following items is reported in a complete set of financial statements, including the accompanying notes. (In one or more cases, the item may not appear in the financial statements.) The answer to the first item is provided below as an example.

a. Cash equivalents.

b. Cash in a special fund being accumulated for the purpose of retiring a specific long-term liability.

c. Compensating balances.

d. The amount by which the current market value of securities classified as available-for-sale exceeds their cost.

e. The allowance for doubtful accounts receivable.

f. The accounts receivable turnover rate.

g. Realized gains and losses on investments sold during the period.

h. Proceeds from converting cash equivalents into cash.

i. Proceeds from converting investments in marketable securities into cash.

Example: a. Cash equivalents normally are *not* shown separately in financial statements. Rather, they are combined with other types of cash and reported under the caption, "Cash and Cash Equivalents." A note to the statements often shows the "breakdown" of this asset category.

PROBLEM 7-3
Bank Reconciliation
LO 4

The cash transactions and cash balances of Norfleet Farm for July were as follows:

1. The ledger account for Cash showed a balance at July 31 of $16,766.95.

2. The July bank statement showed a closing balance of $18,928.12.

3. The cash received on July 31 amounted to $4,017.15. It was left at the bank in the night depository chute after banking hours on July 31 and therefore was not recorded by the bank on the July statement. *4017.15*

4. Also included with the July bank statement was a debit memorandum from the bank for $7.65 representing service charges for July.

5. A credit memorandum enclosed with the July bank statement indicated that a non-interest-bearing note receivable for $4,545 from Rene Manes, left with the bank for collection, had been collected and the proceeds credited to the account of Norfleet Farm.

6. Comparison of the paid checks returned by the bank with the entries in the accounting records revealed that check no. 821 for *$835.02*, issued July 15 in payment for office equipment, had been erroneously entered in Norfleet's records as *$853.02*.

7. Examination of the paid checks also revealed that three checks, all issued in July, had not yet been paid by the bank: no. 811 for $861.12; no. 814 for $640.80; no. 823 for $301.05.

8. Included with the July bank statement was a $180 check drawn by Howard Williams, a customer of Norfleet Farm. This check was marked "NSF." It had been included in the deposit of July 27 but had been charged back against the company's account on July 31.

INSTRUCTIONS

a. Prepare a bank reconciliation for Norfleet Farm at July 31.

b. Prepare journal entries (in general journal form) to adjust the accounts at July 31. Assume that the accounts have not been closed.

c. State the amount of cash which should be included in the balance sheet at July 31..

d. Explain why the balance per the company's bank statement is often larger than the balance shown in its accounting records.

PROBLEM 7-4
"Charmed..."
LO 3,4

Equipment Rental Company had poor internal control over its cash transactions. Facts about the company's cash position at November 30, 1998 are described below.

The accounting records showed a cash balance of $29,959.00, which included a deposit in transit of $3,420.60. The balance indicated in the bank statement was $18,299.40. Included in the bank statement were the following debit and credit memoranda:

Debit Memoranda:

Check from customer G. Davis, deposited by Equipment Rental Co., but charged back as NSF	$1,500.00
Bank service charges for November	25.00

Credit Memorandum:

Proceeds from collection of a note receivable from Regal Farms which Equipment Rental Co. had left with the bank's collection department	3,000.00

Outstanding checks as of November 30 were as follows:

Check No.	Amount
8231	$ 340.30
8263	800.50
8288	145.20
8294	2,100.00

Melanie Charm, the company's cashier, has been abstracting portions of the company's cash receipts for several months. Each month, Charm prepares the company's bank reconciliation in a manner that conceals her thefts. Her bank reconciliation for November is illustrated as follows:

Balance per bank statement, Nov. 30		$18,299.40
Add: Deposits in transit	$4,320.60	
Collection of note from Regal Farms	3,000.00	7,320.60
Subtotal		$26,620.00
Less: Outstanding checks:		
No. 8231	$ 340.30	
8263	800.50	
8288	145.20	1,186.00
Adjusted cash balance per bank statement		$25,434.00

Balance per accounting records, Nov. 30		$29,959.00
Add: Credit memorandum from bank		3,000.00
Subtotal		$26,959.00
Less: Debit memoranda from bank:		
NSF check of G. Davis	$1,500.00	
Bank service charges	25.00	1,525.00
Adjusted cash balance per accounting records		$25,434.00

INSTRUCTIONS

a. Determine the amount of the cash shortage which has been concealed by Charm in her bank reconciliation. (As a format, we suggest that you prepare the bank reconciliation correctly. The amount of the shortage then will be the difference between the adjusted balances per the bank statement and per the accounting records. You can then list this unrecorded cash shortage as the final adjustment necessary to complete your reconciliation.)

b. Carefully review Charm's bank reconciliation and explain in detail how she concealed the amount of the shortage. Include a listing of the dollar amounts that were concealed in various ways. This listing should total the amount of the shortage determined in part **a.**

c. Suggest some specific internal control measures which appear to be necessary for Equipment Rental Company.

PROBLEM 7-5
Aging Accounts Receivable; Write-Offs

LO 5

Public Image, a firm specializing in marketing and publicity services, uses the balance sheet approach to estimate uncollectible accounts expense. At year-end an aging of the accounts receivable produced the following classification:

Not yet due	$333,000
1–30 days past due	135,000
31–60 days past due	58,500
61–90 days past due	13,500
Over 90 days past due	22,500
Total	$562,500

On the basis of past experience, the company estimated the percentages probably uncollectible for the above five age groups to be as follows: Group 1, 1%; Group 2, 3%; Group 3, 10%; Group 4, 20%; and Group 5, 50%.

The Allowance for Doubtful Accounts before adjustment at December 31 showed a credit balance of $8,100.

INSTRUCTIONS

a. Compute the estimated amount of uncollectible accounts based on the above classification by age groups.

b. Prepare the adjusting entry needed to bring the Allowance for Doubtful Accounts to the proper amount.

c. Assume that on January 10 of the following year, Public Image learned that an account receivable which had originated on September 1 in the amount of $8,550 was worthless because of the bankruptcy of the customer, Cranston Manufacturing. Prepare the journal entry required on January 10 to write off this account.

d. The company is considering the adoption of a policy whereby customers whose outstanding accounts become more than 60 days past due will be required to sign an interest-bearing note for the full amount of their outstanding balance. What advantages would such a policy offer?

PROBLEM 7-6
Accounting for
Uncollectible
Accounts

LO 5

Maps & Globes, Inc., is a manufacturer that makes all sales on 30-day credit terms. Annual sales are approximately $25 million. At the end of 1997, accounts receivable were presented in the company's balance sheet as shown below:

Accounts receivable from customers	$2,350,000
Less: Allowance for doubtful accounts	70,000

During 1998, $740,000 in accounts receivable were written off as uncollectible. Of these accounts written off, receivables totaling $24,000 were unexpectedly collected. At the end of 1998, an aging of accounts receivable indicated a need for an $80,000 allowance to cover possible failure to collect the accounts currently outstanding.

Maps & Globes makes adjusting entries in its accounting records *only at year-end.* Monthly and quarterly financial statements are prepared from work sheets, without any adjusting or closing entries actually being entered in the accounting records. (In short, you may assume the company adjusts its accounts only at year-end.)

INSTRUCTIONS

a. Prepare the following in the form of general journal entries:
    1. One entry to summarize all accounts written off against the allowance for doubtful accounts during 1998.
    2. Entries to record the $24,000 in accounts receivable which were unexpectedly collected.

3. The adjusting entry required at December 31, 1998 to increase the allowance for doubtful accounts to $80,000.

b. Notice that the allowance for doubtful accounts was only $70,000 at the end of 1997, but uncollectible accounts during 1998 totaled $716,000 ($740,000 less the $24,000 reinstated). Do these relationships appear reasonable, or was the allowance for doubtful accounts greatly understated at the end of 1997? Explain.

PROBLEM 7-7
Accounts Receivable:
A Comprehensive
Problem

LO 5

Nagano International has 420 accounts receivable in its subsidiary ledger. All accounts are due in 30 days. On December 31, an aging schedule was prepared. The results are summarized below:

Customer	Total	Not Yet Due	1–30 Days Past Due	31–60 Days Past Due	61–90 Days Past Due	Over 90 Days Past Due
(418 names) Subtotals	$863,125	$458,975	$236,700	$108,350	$22,500	$36,600

Two accounts receivable were accidentally omitted from this schedule. The following data is available regarding these accounts:

1. J. Ardis owes $10,625 from two invoices: invoice no. 218, dated Sept. 14, in the amount of $7,450; and invoice no. 568, dated Nov. 9, in the amount of $3,175.

2. N. Selstad owes $9,400 from two invoices: invoice no. 574, dated Nov. 19, in the amount of $3,375; and invoice no. 641, dated Dec. 5, in the amount of $6,025.

INSTRUCTIONS

a. Complete the aging schedule as of December 31 by adding to the column subtotals an aging of the accounts of Ardis and Selstad.

b. Prepare a schedule to compute the estimated portion of each age group that will prove uncollectible and the required balance in the Allowance for Doubtful Accounts. Arrange your schedule in the format illustrated on page 324. The following percentages of each age group are estimated to be uncollectible: Not yet due, 1%; 1–30 days, 4%; 31–60 days, 10%; 61–90 days, 30%; over 90 days, 50%.

c. Prepare the journal entry to bring the Allowance for Doubtful Accounts up to its required balance at December 31. Prior to making this adjustment, the account has a credit balance of $34,500.

d. Show how accounts receivable would appear in the company's balance sheet at December 31.

e. On January 7 of the following year, the credit manager of Nagano International learns that the $10,625 account receivable from J. Ardis is uncollectible because Ardis has declared bankruptcy. Prepare the journal entry to write off this account.

f. Suggest two policies that the company could adopt that may decrease the average time receivables remain outstanding before they are collected.

PROBLEM 7-8
Hey, Pal . . .
When You Gonna
Pay for This Beer?

LO 6

Shown below are the net sales and the average amounts of accounts receivable of two beverage companies in a recent year:

	(Dollars in Millions)	
	Average Accounts Receivable	Net Sales
Adolph Coors Company	$147	$ 1,764
Anheuser-Busch Companies, Inc.	652	11,394

INSTRUCTIONS

a. For each of these companies, compute:

1. The number of times that the average balance of accounts receivable turned over during this fiscal year. (Round to the nearest tenth.)
2. The number of days (on average) that each company must wait to collect its accounts receivable. (Round to the nearest day.)

b. Based upon your computations in part **a,** which company's accounts receivable appear to be the more "liquid" asset? Explain briefly.

*PROBLEM 7-9
Accounting for
Marketable
Securities

LO 1,8

At December 31, 1997, Colton Manufacturing Co. owned the following investments in the capital stock of publicly owned companies (all classified as available-for-sale securities):

	Cost	Current Market Value
Wolfe Computer, Inc. (5,000 shares: cost, $50 per share; market value, $65)	$250,000	$325,000
Quality Foods (4,000 shares: cost, $80 per share; market value, $75)	320,000	300,000
Totals	$570,000	$625,000

In *1998,* Colton engaged in the following two transactions:

Apr. 10 Sold 1,000 shares of its investment in Wolfe Computer at a price of $66 per share, less a brokerage commission of $200.

Aug. 7 Sold 2,000 shares of its Quality Foods stock at a price of $72 per share, less a brokerage commission of $300.

At December 31, 1998, the market values of these stocks were: Wolfe Computer, $60 per share; Quality Foods, $70.

INSTRUCTIONS

a. Illustrate the presentation of marketable securities and the unrealized holding gain or loss in Colton's balance sheet at December 31, *1997.* Include a caption indicating the section of the balance sheet in which each of these accounts appears.

b. Prepare journal entries to record the transactions on April 10 and August 7.

c. Prior to making a mark-to-market adjustment at the end of 1998, determine the unadjusted balance in the Marketable Securities controlling account and the Unrealized Holding Gain (or Loss) on Investments. (Assume that no unrealized gains or losses have been recognized since last year.)

d. Prepare a schedule showing the cost and market values of securities owned at the end of 1998. (Use the same format as the schedule illustrated above.)

e. Prepare the "mark-to-market" adjusting entry required at December 31, 1998.

f. Illustrate the presentation of the marketable securities and unrealized holding gain (or loss) in the balance sheet at December 31, *1998.* (Follow the same format as in part **a.**)

g. Illustrate the presentation of the net *realized* gains (or losses) in the 1998 income statement. Assume a multiple-step income statement and show the caption identifying the section in which this amount would appear.

---

*Supplemental Topic A, "Accounting for Marketable Securities."

h. Explain how both the realized and unrealized gains and losses will affect the company's 1998 income tax return.

*PROBLEM 7-10
Gains, Losses, Risk, and Return

LO 1,2,8

Early in 1996, Cross Industries invested $400,000 in cash that was not needed in current operations in the capital stocks of two publicly owned companies: **Apple Computer** and **Zebra Technologies.** During 1996, Apple paid dividends of 48 cents per share, and Zebra paid no dividends. At year-end, the marketable securities subsidiary ledger shows the following values for these investments:

	Cost	Current Market Value
Apple Computer (5,000 shares: cost, $40 per share; market value, $30)	$200,000	$150,000
Zebra Technologies (10,000 shares: cost, $20 per share; market value, $25)	200,000	250,000

Early in 1997, Cross told its broker to sell 2,000 shares of Apple and 1,000 shares of Zebra "at the market." Ten minutes later, the broker reported that both transactions had been executed. Total sale proceeds were $62,000 for the Apple shares, and $24,000 for the Zebra.

INSTRUCTIONS

a. Separately compute Cross's unrealized holding gain (or loss) in each of these investments as of December 31, 1996. Indicate the total unrealized holding gain or loss that will appear in the company's 1996 financial statements, and explain where in the statements this amount will appear. (Assume that the company classified these investments as available-for-sale marketable securities.)

b. Explain how the cost and market values shown in the subsidiary ledger are used in determining (1) balance sheet presentation of the investments, and (2) the *realized* gains or losses reported in the income statement for the period in which the investments are sold.

c. Prepare two separate journal entries to record the sales in 1997 of (1) 2,000 shares of Apple, and (2) 1,000 shares of Zebra.

d. Briefly comment about the *liquidity, risks,* and *potential return* of investments in capital stocks relative to, say, cash equivalents that are very safe and yield a "sure" return of, say, 4%. Cite data from this problem in support of your comments.

**PROBLEM 7-11
Notes Receivable

LO 9

Far Corners Imports sells a variety of merchandise to retail stores on open account, but it insists that any customer who fails to pay an invoice when due must replace it with an interest-bearing note. The company adjusts and closes its accounts at December 31. Among the transactions relating to notes receivable were the following:

Sept. 1 Received from a customer (Party Plus) a nine-month, 9% note for $42,000 in settlement of an account receivable due today.

June 1 Collected in full the nine-month, 9% note receivable from Party Plus, including interest.

a. Prepare journal entries (in general journal form) to record: (1) the receipt of the note on September 1; (2) the adjustment for interest on December 31; and (3) collection

---

*Supplemental Topic A, "Accounting for Marketable Securities."
**Supplemental Topic B, "Notes Receivable and Interest Revenue."

of principal and interest on June 1. (To better illustrate the allocation of interest revenue between accounting periods, we will assume Far Corners makes adjusting entries *only at year-end*.)

b. Assume that instead of paying the note on June 1, the customer (Party Plus) had defaulted. Give the journal entry by Far Corners Imports to record the default. Assume that Party Plus has sufficient resources that the note eventually will be collected.

c. Explain why the company insists that any customer who fails to pay an invoice when due must replace it with an interest-bearing note.

CASES

CASE 7-1
Cash
Management
LO 2

Most banks offer a variety of "cash management" options to individuals and small business. These include, for example, T-bills, money market funds, daily "sweeps" of checking accounts, and CDs.

INSTRUCTIONS

a. Arrange an interview with a representative of a local bank. Inquire as to the options which the bank provides for temporarily investing cash balances not needed in the near future. Gain an understanding of the various cash management options available to individuals and to small businesses, including the expected yields. (***Note:*** All interviews are to be conducted in accordance with the guidelines in the *Note to Students* section of the introduction to this textbook.)

b. Briefly explain each of the options discussed in this interview, along with the expected yields (if determinable). Identify the option you consider best suited to:
   1. An individual whose checking account often has as much as $10,000 that will not be needed within the next 30 days.
   2. A small business which has about $400,000 in liquid resources that will not be needed for the next nine months.
Explain the reasons for your choices and be prepared to explain these reasons in class.

CASE 7-2
"Improving"
the Balance
Sheet
LO 1,2,4,5,6,8

Affections manufactures candy and sells only to retailers. It is not a publicly owned company and its financial statements are not audited. But the company frequently must borrow money. Its creditors insist that the company provide them with unaudited financial statements at the end of each quarter.

In October 1998, management met to discuss the fiscal year ending next December 31. Due to a soft economy, Affections was having difficulty collecting its accounts receivable, and its cash position was unusually low. Management knew that if the December 31 balance sheet did not look good, the company would have difficulty borrowing the money it would need to boost production for Valentines Day.

Thus, the purpose of the meeting was to explore ways in which Affections might "improve" its December 31 balance sheet. Some of the ideas discussed appear below:

1. Offer customers purchasing Christmas candy a 10% discount if they make payment within 30 days.

2. Allow a 30-day grace period on all accounts receivable overdue at the end of the year. As these accounts will no longer be overdue, the company will not need an allowance for overdue accounts.

3. For purposes of balance sheet presentation, combine all forms of cash, including cash equivalents, compensating balances, and unused lines of credit.

4. Require officers who have borrowed money from the company to repay the amounts owed at December 31. This would convert into cash the "notes receivable from officers," which now appear in the balance sheet as noncurrent assets. The loans could be renewed immediately after year-end.

5. Show investments in marketable securities at their market value, rather than at cost.

6. Treat inventory as a financial asset and show it at current sales value. As Affections is not a publicly owned company, it is not legally required to prepare its financial statements in conformity with generally accepted accounting principles.

7. On December 31, draw a large check against the company's bank account and deposit it in another bank. The check won't clear the first bank until after year-end. This will substantially increase the amount of cash in bank accounts at year-end.

INSTRUCTIONS

a. Separately evaluate each of these proposals. Consider ethical issues as well as accounting issues.

b. Do you consider it ethical for management to hold this meeting in the first place? That is, should management plan in advance how to "improve" financial statements that will be distributed to creditors and investors?

CASE 7-3
Accounting
Principles
LO 1,5,9

In each of the situations described below, indicate the accounting principles or concepts, if any, that have been violated and explain briefly the nature of the violation. If you believe the practice is *in accord* with generally accepted accounting principles, state this as your position and defend it.

a. A small business in which credit sales fluctuate greatly from year to year uses the direct write-off method both for income tax purposes and in its financial statements.

b. A manufacturing company charges all of its petty cash expenditures to Miscellaneous Expense, rather than to the various expense accounts which reflect the nature of each expenditure.

c. Computer Systems often sells merchandise in exchange for interest-bearing notes receivable, maturing in 6, 12, or 24 months. The company records these sales transactions by debiting Notes Receivable for the maturity value of the notes, crediting Sales for the sales price of the merchandise, and crediting Interest Revenue for the balance of the maturity value of the note. The cost of goods sold also is recorded.

d. A company has $400,000 in unrestricted cash, $1 million in a bank account specifically earmarked for the construction of a new factory, and $2 million in cash equivalents. In the balance sheet, these amounts are combined and shown as "Cash and cash equivalents . . . $3.4 million."

e. The credit manager of Audio Products estimates that between $1 million and $1.6 million of the company's accounts receivable will prove uncollectible. In its financial statements, Audio Products establishes an allowance for doubtful accounts of $1 million.

CASE 7-4
If Things Get
Any Better,
We'll Be Broke
LO 6,7

Loud Max, Inc., sells stereo equipment. Traditionally, the company's sales have fallen into the following categories: cash sales, 25%; customers using national credit cards, 35%; sales on account (due in 30 days), 40%. With these policies, the company earned a modest profit, and monthly cash receipts exceeded monthly cash payments by a comfortable margin. Uncollectible accounts expense was approximately 1% of net sales. (The company uses the direct write-off method in accounting for uncollectible accounts receivable.)

Two months ago, the company initiated a new credit policy which it calls "Double Zero." Customers may purchase merchandise on account, with no down payment and no interest charges. The accounts are collected in 12 monthly installments of equal amounts.

The plan has proven quite popular with customers, and monthly sales have increased dramatically. Despite the increase in sales, however, Loud Max is experiencing cash flow problems—it hasn't been generating enough cash to pay its suppliers, most of which require payment within 30 days.

The company's bookkeeper has prepared the following analysis of monthly operating results:

	Before Double Zero	Last Month
Sales:		
Cash	$12,500	$ 5,000
National credit card	17,500	10,000
30-day accounts	20,000	–0–
Double Zero accounts	–0–	75,000
Total monthly sales	$50,000	$ 90,000
Cost of goods sold and expenses	40,000	65,000
Net income	$10,000	$ 25,000
Cash receipts:		
Cash sales	$12,500	$ 5,000
National credit card companies	17,500	10,000
30-day accounts	19,500	–0–
Double Zero accounts	–0–	11,250
Total monthly cash receipts	$49,500	$ 26,250
Accounts written off as uncollectible	$ 500	$–0–
Accounts receivable at month-end	$20,000	$135,000

The bookkeeper offers the following assessment: "Double Zero is killing us. Since we started that plan, our accounts receivable have increased nearly sevenfold, and they're still growing. We can't afford to carry such a large nonproductive asset on our books. Our cash receipts are down to nearly half of what they used to be. If we don't go back to more cash sales and receivables which can be collected more quickly, we'll become insolvent."

Maxwell "Loud Max" Swartz, founder and chief executive officer, shouts back: "Why do you say that our accounts receivable are nonproductive? They're the most productive asset we have! Since we started Double Zero, our sales have nearly doubled, our profits have more than doubled, and our bad debt expense has dropped to nothing!"

INSTRUCTIONS

a. Is it logical that the Double Zero plan is causing sales and profits to increase while also causing a decline in cash receipts? Explain.

b. Why has the uncollectible accounts expense dropped to zero? What would you expect to happen to the company's uncollectible accounts expense in the future—say, next year? Why?

c. Do you think that the reduction in monthly cash receipts is permanent or temporary? Explain.

d. In what sense are the company's accounts receivable a "nonproductive" asset?

e. Suggest several ways that Loud Max (the company) may be able to generate the cash it needs to pay its bills without terminating the Double Zero plan.

f. Would you recommend that the company continue offering Double Zero financing, or should it return to the use of 30-day accounts? Explain the reasons for your answer and identify any unresolved factors which might cause you to change this opinion in the future.

INTERNET 7-1
Learning
About "CDs"
LO 1,2,6

INTERNET ASSIGNMENTS

Prudent cash management is an important function in any business. Large amounts of excess cash sitting idle in non-interest-bearing checking accounts can cost a firm thousands—even millions—of dollars annually in foregone revenue. Thus, many businesses invest large amounts of idle cash in jumbo money market accounts and/or jumbo certificates of deposit (CDs). Managers learn quickly that returns of cash equivalents can vary significantly by state, by financial institution, and by investment type.

Visit the Bloomberg home page by opening the following Internet connection:

www.Bloomberg.com

From the menu, select "Financial Analysis." Next, choose "Money and Credit Markets." Spend some time learning about the interest rates paid on jumbo money market accounts and jumbo CDs in various states.

INSTRUCTIONS

a. Which states currently pay the highest rates of interest on these accounts? Which large banks in these states offer such investments?

b. Which states currently pay the lowest rates of interest on these accounts? Which large banks in these states offer such investments?

c. How do the interest rates in your state compare to national and regional averages?

d. Return to the Bloomberg home page and select, "World Markets." Describe how the interest rates of U.S. Treasury securities compare to those of jumbo money market accounts and CDs.

Additional Internet assignments for this chapter are found in Appendix B at the end of this textbook.

OUR COMMENTS ON THE IN-TEXT CASES

AS A FINANCIAL ADVISOR (P. 311) Alternative uses for the company's cash surplus may include investments in: (1) certificates of deposit—CDs—with staggered maturity dates, (2) short-term notes issued by the United States Treasury Department, or (3) money market accounts. If these alternatives are deemed unacceptable, management may wish to distribute a cash dividend to the company's shareholders. As a financial advisor, you should alert management to the fact that the $5 million checking account balance may not be as safe as they think. Should the bank run into financial problems, the FDIC would insure only a fraction of the $5 million total.

AS A CREDIT MANAGER (P. 330) Shown below are accounts receivable turnover rates and average-days-outstanding figures for the past four years (**Note:** Days outstanding were computed by dividing 365 days by the turnover rate):

	1998	1997	1996	1995
Sales	$17,000	$14,580	$9,600	$9,000
Divided by				
Average accounts receivable	1,700	1,620	1,600	1,800
Turnover rate	10 times	9 times	6 times	5 times
Days outstanding	37 days	41 days	61 days	73 days

Based upon this data, it appears that the new credit policy was successful in two ways. First, over the four-year period, it resulted in the doubling of the company's accounts receivable turnover rate (and thereby reduced its average collection period from 72 days to 36 days). Furthermore, the new policy successfully improved the quality of accounts receivable without adversely affecting sales growth.

ANSWERS TO SELF-TEST QUESTIONS
1. b   **2.** c   **3.** a   **4.** c   **5.** a   **6.** b   **7.** a   **8.** d   **9.** c
10. a   **11.** b ($300,000 × 12% × 6/12)

INVENTORIES AND THE COST OF GOODS SOLD

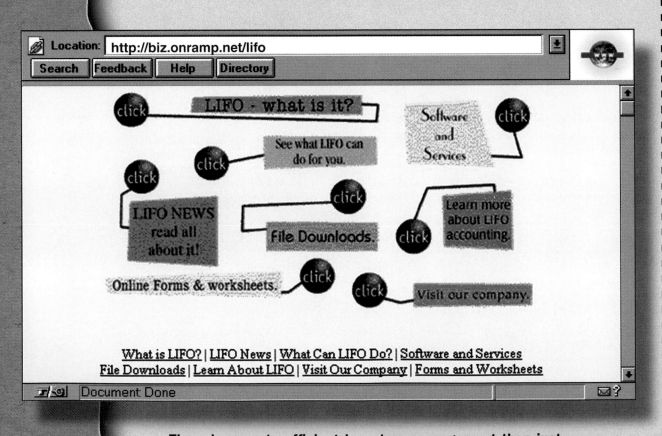

Location: http://biz.onramp.net/lifo

Search | Feedback | Help | Directory

click — LIFO - what is it?

Software and Services — click

click — See what LIFO can do for you.

click

LIFO NEWS read all about it!

click — File Downloads.

Learn more about LIFO accounting. — click

Online Forms & worksheets. — click

click — Visit our company.

What is LIFO? | LIFO News | What Can LIFO Do? | Software and Services
File Downloads | Learn About LIFO | Visit Our Company | Forms and Worksheets

Document: Done

There is more to efficient inventory management than just keeping goods on the shelves. What's selling well and what isn't? What "flow assumption" should a company use? LIFO, FIFO, gross profit method—what does it all mean? Let's find out.

1 In a perpetual inventory system, determine the cost of goods sold using (a) specific identification, (b) average cost, (c) FIFO, and (d) LIFO. Discuss the advantages and shortcomings of each method.

2 Explain the need for taking a physical inventory.

3 Record shrinkage losses and other year-end adjustments to inventory.

4 In a periodic inventory system, determine the ending inventory and cost of goods sold using (a) average cost, (b) FIFO, and (c) LIFO.

5 Explain the effects of errors in inventory valuation upon the income statement.

6 Estimate the cost of goods sold and ending inventory by the gross profit method and by the retail method.

7 Compute the inventory turnover rate and explain its uses.

*8 Define a "LIFO reserve" and explain its implications to users of financial statements.

INVENTORY DEFINED

One of the largest current assets of a retail store or of a wholesale business is the *inventory* of merchandise. The sale of this merchandise is the major source of revenue. In a merchandising company, the inventory consists of all goods owned and held for sale to customers. Inventory is converted into cash within the company's *operating cycle* and, therefore, is regarded as a current asset.[1] In the balance sheet, inventory is listed immediately after accounts receivable, because it is just one step further removed from conversion into cash than are the accounts receivable.

In a merchandising company, all of the inventory is purchased in a ready-to-sell condition. A manufacturing company, however, has three types of inventory: (1) *finished goods,* which are ready to sell; (2) *work in process,* which are goods in the process of being manufactured; and (3) *materials,* which are the raw materials and component parts used in the manufacture of finished products. All three classes of inventory are included in the current asset section of the balance sheet.[2]

THE FLOW OF INVENTORY COSTS

Inventory is an asset and—like most other assets—usually is shown in the balance sheet at its cost.[3] As items are sold from this inventory, their costs are removed from the balance sheet and transferred into the cost of goods sold, which is offset against sales revenue in the income statement. This "flow of costs" is illustrated in the following diagram:

**Supplemental Topic,* "LIFO Reserves."

[1]As explained in Chapter 5, the *operating cycle* of a merchandising business is the period of time required to convert cash into inventory, inventory into accounts receivable, and these accounts receivable into cash. Assets expected to be converted into cash within one year or the operating cycle, whichever is longer, are regarded as current assets.

[2]In a manufacturing company, the manufacturing process is part of the operating cycle. Therefore, raw materials and work in process are considered current assets even if completion of the manufacturing process requires more than one year.

[3]Some companies deal in inventories which can be sold in a worldwide market at quoted market prices. Examples include mutual funds, stock brokerages, and companies that deal in commodities such as agricultural crops or precious metals. Often these companies value their inventories at market price rather than at cost. Our discussions in this chapter are directed to the far more common situation in which inventories are valued at cost.

"Flow" of costs through
financial statements

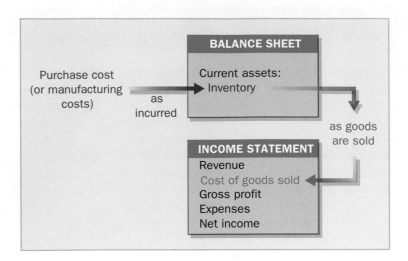

In a perpetual inventory system, entries in the accounting records parallel this flow of costs. When merchandise is purchased, its cost (net of allowable cash discounts) is debited to the asset account Inventory. As the merchandise is sold, its cost is removed from the Inventory account and debited to the Cost of Goods Sold account.

The valuation of inventory and of the cost of goods sold are of critical importance to managers and to users of financial statements. In most cases, inventory is a company's largest current asset, and the cost of goods sold is its largest expense. These two accounts have a significant effect upon the financial statement subtotals and ratios used in evaluating the solvency and profitability of the business.

Several different methods of "pricing" inventory and of measuring the cost of goods sold are acceptable under generally accepted accounting principles. These different methods may produce significantly different results, both in a company's financial statements and in its income tax returns. Therefore, managers and investors alike should understand the usual effects of the different inventory valuation methods.

WHICH UNIT DID WE SELL? DOES IT REALLY MATTER?

Purchases of merchandise are recorded in the same manner under all of the inventory valuation methods. The differences in these methods lie in determining *which costs* should be removed from the Inventory account when merchandise is sold.

We illustrated the basic entries relating to purchases and sales of merchandise in Chapter 5. In that introductory discussion, however, we made a simplifying assumption: all of the units in inventory had been acquired at the same unit costs. In practice, a company often has in its inventory units of a given product which were acquired at *different costs*. Acquisition costs may vary because the units were purchased at different dates, or from different suppliers.

When identical units of inventory have different unit costs, a question naturally arises as to *which of these costs* should be used in recording sales transactions.

DATA FOR AN ILLUSTRATION

To illustrate the alternative methods of measuring the cost of goods sold, assume that Lake Mead Electric Company sells electrical equipment and supplies. Included in the company's inventory are five Elco AC-40 generators. These generators are identical; however, two were purchased on January 5 at a per-unit cost of *$1,000*, and the other three were purchased a month later, shortly after Elco had announced a price increase, at a per unit cost of *$1,200*. These purchases are reflected in Mead's inventory subsidiary ledger as follows:

Inventory subsidiary
ledger record

Item	Elco AC-40					Primary supplier	Elco Manufacturing		
Description	Portable generator					Secondary supplier	Vegas Wholesale Co.		
Location	Daily St. warehouse					Inventory level: Min:	2	Max:	5

	Purchased			Sold			Balance		
Date	Units	Unit Cost	Total	Units	Unit Cost	Cost of Goods Sold	Units	Unit Cost	Total
Jan. 5	2	$1,000	$2,000				2	$1,000	$2,000
Feb. 5	3	1,200	3,600				⌠2	1,000⌡	
							⌡3	1,200⌡	5,600

Notice that on February 5, the balance columns contain two "layers" of unit cost information, representing the units purchased at the two different unit costs. A new **cost layer** is created whenever units are acquired at a different per-unit cost. (As the units comprising a cost layer are sold, the layer is eliminated from the inventory. Therefore, a business is unlikely to have more than three or four cost layers in its inventory at any given time.)

Now assume that on March 1, Mead sells one of these Elco generators to Boulder Construction Company for $1,800, cash. What cost should be removed from the Inventory account and recognized as the cost of goods sold—$1,000 or $1,200?

In answering such questions, accountants may use an approach called **specific identification,** or they may adopt a **cost flow assumption.** Either of these approaches is acceptable. Once an approach has been selected, however, it should be *applied consistently* in accounting for all sales of this particular type of merchandise.

SPECIFIC IDENTIFICATION

The specific identification method can be used only when the actual costs of individual units of merchandise can be determined from the accounting records. For example, each of the generators in Mead's inventory may have an identification number, and these numbers may appear on the purchase invoices. With this identification number, Mead's accounting department can determine whether the generator sold to Boulder Construction had cost $1,000 or $1,200. The *actual cost* of this particular unit then is used in recording the cost of goods sold.

COST FLOW ASSUMPTIONS

If the items in inventory are *homogeneous* in nature (identical, except for insignificant differences), it is *not necessary* for the seller to use the specific identification method. Rather, the seller may follow the more convenient practice of using a *cost flow assumption.* (In practice, the phrase "cost flow assumption" often is shortened to "flow assumption.")

When a flow assumption is in use, the seller simply makes an *assumption* as to the sequence in which units are withdrawn from inventory. For example, the seller might assume that the oldest merchandise always is sold first, or that the most recently purchased items are the first to be sold.

Three flow assumptions are in widespread use:

1. *Average cost.* This assumption values all merchandise—units sold and units remaining in inventory—at the *average* per-unit cost. (In effect, the average-

LO 1 *In a perpetual inventory system, determine the cost of goods sold using (a) specific identification, (b) average cost, (c) FIFO, and (d) LIFO. Discuss the advantages and shortcomings of each method.*

cost method assumes that units are withdrawn from the inventory in random order.)

2. ***First-in, first-out (FIFO).*** As the names implies, FIFO involves the assumption that goods sold are the *first* units that were purchased—that is, the *oldest* goods on hand. Thus, the remaining inventory is comprised of the most recent purchases.

3. ***Last-in, first-out (LIFO).*** Under LIFO, the units sold are assumed to be those *most recently* acquired. The remaining inventory, therefore, is assumed to consist of the earliest purchases.

The cost flow assumption selected by a company *need not* correspond to the actual physical movement of the company's merchandise. When the units of merchandise are identical (or nearly identical), it *does not matter* which units are delivered to the customer in a particular sales transaction. Therefore, in measuring the income of a business that sells units of identical merchandise, accountants consider the flow of *costs* to be more important than the physical flow of the merchandise.

The use of a flow assumption *eliminates the need for separately identifying each unit sold and looking up its actual cost.* Experience has shown that these flow assumptions provide useful and reliable measurements of the cost of goods sold, as long as they are applied consistently to all sales of the particular type of merchandise.

AVERAGE-COST METHOD

When the **average-cost method** is in use, the *average cost* of all units in the inventory is computed after every purchase. This average cost is computed by dividing the total cost of goods available for sale by the number of units in inventory. As the average cost may change following each purchase, this method also is called *moving average*.

As of January 5, Mead has only two Elco generators in its inventory, each acquired at a purchase cost of $1,000. Therefore, the average cost is $1,000 per unit. After the purchase on February 5, Mead has five Elco generators in inventory, acquired at a total cost of $5,600 (2 units @ $1,000, plus 3 units @ $1,200 = $5,600). Therefore, the *average* per-unit cost now is *$1,120* ($5,600 ÷ 5 units = $1,120).

On March 1, two entries are made to record the sale of one of these generators to Boulder Construction Company. The first recognizes the revenue from this sale, and the second recognizes the cost of the goods sold. These entries follow, with the cost of goods sold measured by the average-cost method:

Cash	1,800	
Sales		1,800
To record the sale of one Elco AC-40 generator		

Cost of Goods Sold	1,120	
Inventory		1,120
To record the cost of one Elco AC-40 generator sold to Boulder Construction Co. Cost determined by the average-cost method.		

(The entry to recognize the $1,800 in sales revenue remains the same, regardless of the inventory method in use. Therefore, we will not repeat this entry in our illustrations of the other cost flow assumptions.)

When the average-cost method is in use, the inventory subsidiary ledger is modified slightly from the format illustrated on the preceding page. Following the sale on March 1, Mead's subsidiary ledger card for Elco generators will appear as follows, modified to show the average unit cost.

Inventory subsidiary
record—average cost basis

	Purchased			Sold			Balance		
Date	Units	Unit Cost	Total	Units	Average Unit Cost	Cost of Goods Sold	Units	Average Unit Cost	Total
Jan. 5	2	$1,000	$2,000				2	$1,000	$2,000
Feb. 5	3	1,200	3,600				5	1,120*	5,600
Mar. 1				1	$1,120	$1,120	4	1,120	4,480

*$5,600 total cost ÷ 5 units = $1,120.

Notice that the unit cost column for purchases still shows actual unit costs— $1,000 and $1,200. The unit cost columns relating to sales and to the remaining inventory, however, show the *average unit cost* ($5,600 total ÷ 5 units = $1,120). As all units are valued at this same average cost, the inventory has only one cost layer.

Under the average-cost assumption, all items in inventory are assigned the *same* per-unit cost (the average cost). Hence, it does not matter which units are sold; the cost of goods sold always is based upon the current average unit cost. When one generator is sold on March 1, the cost of goods sold is $1,120; if four generators were sold on this date, the cost of goods sold would be $4,480 (4 units × $1,120 per unit).

FIRST-IN, FIRST-OUT METHOD

The **first-in, first-out method,** often called *FIFO,* is based upon the assumption that the *first merchandise purchased is the first merchandise sold.* Thus, the accountant for Mead Electric would assume that the generator sold on March 1 was one of those purchased on *January 5.* The entry to record the cost of goods sold would be:

Cost of Goods Sold 1,000
    Inventory 1,000
To record the cost of one Elco AC-40 generator sold to Boulder
Construction Co. Cost determined by the FIFO flow assumption.

Following this sale, Mead's inventory ledger would appear as follows:

Inventory subsidiary
record—FIFO basis

	Purchased			Sold			Balance		
Date	Units	Unit Cost	Total	Units	Unit Cost	Cost of Goods Sold	Units	Unit Cost	Total
Jan. 5	2	$1,000	$2,000				2	$1,000	$2,000
Feb. 5	3	1,200	3,600				2	1,000	
							3	1,200	5,600
Mar. 1				1	$1,000	$1,000	1	1,000	
							3	1,200	4,600

Notice that FIFO uses actual purchase costs, rather than an average cost. Thus, if merchandise has been purchased at several different costs, the inventory will include several different cost layers. The cost of goods sold for a given sales transaction also may involve several different cost layers. To illustrate, assume that Mead had sold *four* generators to Boulder Construction, instead of only one. Under the FIFO flow assumption, Mead would assume that it first sold the two generators purchased on January 5, and then two of those purchased on February 5. Thus, the total cost of goods sold ($4,400) would include items at *two different unit costs,* as shown below:

2 generators from January 5 purchase @ $1,000	$2,000
2 generators from February 5 purchase @ $1,200	2,400
Total cost of goods sold (4 units)	$4,400

As the cost of goods sold always is recorded at the oldest available purchase costs, the units remaining in inventory are valued at the more recent acquisition costs.

LAST-IN, FIRST-OUT METHOD

The **last-in, first-out method,** commonly known as *LIFO,* is among the most widely used methods of determining the cost of goods sold and valuing inventory. As the name suggests, the *most recently* purchased merchandise (the last in) is assumed to be sold first. If Mead were using the LIFO method, it would assume that the generator sold on March 1 was one of those acquired on *February 5,* the most recent purchase date. Thus, the cost transferred from inventory to the cost of goods sold would be *$1,200.*

The journal entry to record the cost of goods sold is illustrated below, along with the inventory subsidiary ledger record after this entry has been posted:

Cost of Goods Sold	1,200	
Inventory		1,200

To record the cost of one Elco AC-40 generator sold to Boulder Construction Co. Cost determined by the LIFO flow assumption.

Inventory subsidiary record—LIFO basis

	Purchased			Sold			Balance		
Date	Units	Unit Cost	Total	Units	Unit Cost	Cost of Goods Sold	Units	Unit Cost	Total
Jan. 5	2	$1,000	$2,000				2	$1,000	$2,000
Feb. 5	3	1,200	3,600				{2	1,000	
							{3	1,200	5,600
Mar. 1				1	$1,200	$1,200	{2	1,000	
							{2	1,200	4,400

The LIFO method uses actual purchase costs, rather than an average cost. Thus, the inventory may have several different cost layers. If a sale includes more units than are included in the most recent cost layer, some of the goods sold are assumed to come from the next most recent layer. For example, if Mead had sold four generators (instead of one) on March 1, the cost of goods sold determined under the LIFO assumption would be $4,600, as shown below:

3 generators from February 5 purchase @ $1,200	$3,600
1 generator from January 5 purchase @ $1,000	1,000
Total cost of goods sold (4 units)	$4,600

As LIFO transfers the most recent purchase costs to the cost of goods sold, the goods remaining in inventory are valued at the oldest acquisition costs.

EVALUATION OF THE METHODS

All three of the cost flow assumptions described above are acceptable for use in financial statements and in income tax returns. As we have explained, it is not necessary that the physical flow of merchandise correspond to the cost flow assumption. Different flow assumptions may be used for different types of inventory, or for inventories in different geographical locations.

The only requirement for using a flow assumption is that the units to which the assumption is applied should be *homogeneous* in nature—that is, nearly identical to one another. If each unit is unique, the specific identification method is needed in order to achieve a proper matching of sales revenue with the cost of goods sold.

As discussed below, each inventory valuation method has certain advantages and shortcomings. In the final analysis, the selection of inventory valuation methods is a managerial decision. However, the method (or methods) used in financial statements always should be disclosed in notes accompanying the statements.

SPECIFIC IDENTIFICATION   The specific identification method is best suited to inventories of high-priced, low-volume items. This is the only method which exactly parallels the physical flow of the merchandise. If each item in the inventory is unique, as in the case of valuable paintings, custom jewelry, and most real estate, specific identification is clearly the logical choice.

The specific identification method has an intuitive appeal, because it assigns actual purchase costs to the specific units of merchandise sold or in inventory. However, when the units in inventory are identical (or nearly identical), the specific identification method may produce *misleading results* by implying differences in value which—under current market conditions—do not exist.

As an example, assume that a coal dealer has purchased 100 tons of coal at a cost of $60 per ton. A short time later, the company purchases another 100 tons of the *same grade* of coal—but this time, the cost is $80 per ton. The two purchases are in separate piles; thus, it would be possible for the company to use the specific identification method in accounting for sales.

Assume now that the company has an opportunity to sell 10 tons of coal at a retail price of $120 per ton. Does it really matter from which pile this coal is removed? The answer is *no;* the coal is a homogeneous product. Under current market conditions, the coal in each pile is equally valuable. To imply that it is more profitable to sell coal from one pile rather than the other is an argument of questionable logic.

Let us try to make this point in a more personal way: Would you be willing to shovel the more recently purchased coal out of the way so that the customer can get its truck back to the lower-cost coal pile?

AVERAGE COST   Identical items will have the same accounting values only under the average-cost method. Assume for example that a hardware store sells a given size nail for 65 cents per pound. The hardware store buys the nails in

100-pound quantities at different times at prices ranging from 40 to 50 cents per pound. Several hundred pounds of nails are always on hand, stored in a large bin. The average-cost method properly recognizes that when a customer buys a pound of nails it is not necessary to know exactly which nails the customer selected from the bin in order to measure the cost of goods sold. Therefore, the average-cost method avoids the shortcomings of the specific identification method. It is not necessary to keep track of the specific items sold and of those still in inventory. Also, it is not possible to manipulate income merely by selecting the specific items to be delivered to customers.

A shortcoming in the average-cost method is that changes in current replacement costs of inventory are concealed because these costs are averaged with older costs. Thus, neither the valuation of ending inventory nor the cost of goods sold will quickly reflect changes in the current replacement cost of merchandise.

FIRST-IN, FIRST-OUT The distinguishing characteristic of the FIFO method is that the oldest purchase costs are transferred to the cost of goods sold, while the most recent costs remain in inventory.

Over the last 50 years, we have lived in an inflationary economy, which means that most prices tend to rise over time. When purchase costs are rising, the FIFO method assigns *lower* (older) costs to the cost of goods sold and the higher (more recent) costs to the goods remaining in inventory.

By assigning lower costs to the cost of goods sold, FIFO usually causes a business to report somewhat *higher profits* than would be reported under the other inventory valuation methods. Some companies favor the FIFO method for financial reporting purposes, because their goal is to report the highest net income possible. For income tax purposes, however, reporting more income than necessary results in paying more income taxes than necessary.

Some accountants and decision makers believe that FIFO tends to *overstate* a company's profitability. Revenue is based upon current market conditions. By offsetting this revenue with a cost of goods sold based upon older (and lower) prices, gross profits may be overstated consistently.

A conceptual advantage of the FIFO method is that inventory is valued at recent purchase costs. Therefore, this asset appears in the balance sheet at an amount closely approximating its current replacement cost.

LAST-IN, FIRST-OUT The LIFO method is one of the most interesting and controversial flow assumptions. The basic assumption in the LIFO method is that the most recently purchased units are sold first and that the older units remain in inventory. This assumption is *not* in accord with the physical flow of merchandise in most businesses. Yet, there are strong logical arguments in support of the LIFO method, in addition to income tax considerations.

For the purpose of measuring income, most accountants consider the *flow of costs* more important than the physical flow of merchandise. Supporters of the LIFO method contend that the measurement of income should be based upon *current market conditions*. Therefore, current sales revenue should be offset by the *current* cost of the merchandise sold. Under the LIFO method, the costs assigned to the cost of goods sold are relatively current, because they stem from the most recent purchases.Under the FIFO method, on the other hand, the cost of goods sold is based upon "older" costs.

Income tax considerations, however, provide the principal reason for the popularity of the LIFO method. Remember that the LIFO method assigns the most recent inventory purchase costs to the cost of goods sold. In the common situation of rising prices, these "most recent" costs are also the highest costs. By reporting a higher cost of goods sold than results from other inventory valuation methods, the LIFO method usually results in *lower taxable income.* In short, if inventory costs are rising, a company can reduce the amount of its income tax obligation by using the LIFO method in its income tax return.

It may seem reasonable that a company would use the LIFO method in its tax return to reduce taxable income, and use the FIFO method in its financial statements to increase the amount of net income reported to investors and creditors. However, income tax regulations allow a corporation to use LIFO in its income tax return *only* if the company also uses LIFO in its financial statements. Thus, income tax considerations often provide the overriding reason for selecting the LIFO method.

There is one significant shortcoming to the LIFO method. The valuation of the asset inventory is based upon the company's "oldest" inventory acquisition costs. After the company has been in business for many years, these "oldest" costs may greatly understate the current replacement cost of the inventory. Thus, when an inventory is valued by the LIFO method, the company also should disclose the current replacement cost of the inventory in a note to the financial statements.

During periods of rising inventory replacement costs, the LIFO method results in the lowest valuation of inventory and measurement of net income. Therefore, LIFO is regarded as the most *conservative* of the inventory pricing methods. FIFO, on the other hand, is the least conservative method.[4]

DO INVENTORY METHODS REALLY AFFECT PERFORMANCE?

Except for their effects upon income taxes, the answer to this question is *no.*

During a period of rising prices, a company might *report* higher profits by using FIFO instead of LIFO. But the company would not really *be* any more profitable. An inventory valuation method affects only the *allocation of costs* between the Inventory account and the Cost of Goods Sold account. It has *no effect* upon the total costs actually *incurred* in purchasing or manufacturing inventory. Except for income taxes, differences in the profitability reported under different inventory methods exist "only on paper."

The inventory method in use *does* affect the amount of income taxes owed. To the extent that an inventory method reduces these taxes, it *does* increase profitability.

INVENTORY METHODS AND CASH FLOWS The cash payments relating to inventory occur when suppliers are *paid.* In a statement of cash flows, these outlays are included among the cash payments for operating activities. For merchandising and manufacturing businesses, these payments represent the companies' largest use of cash. Inventory valuation methods have *no effect* upon the cash paid to purchase or manufacture inventory. They do, however, affect cash payments for income taxes.

The table on the following page summarizes characteristics of the basic inventory valuation methods.

THE PRINCIPLE OF CONSISTENCY

The principle of **consistency** is one of the basic concepts underlying reliable financial statements. This principle means that once a company has adopted a particular accounting method, it should *follow that method consistently,* rather than switch methods from one year to the next. Thus, once a company has adopted a particular inventory flow assumption (or the specific identification

---

[4]During a prolonged period of *declining* inventory replacement costs, this situation reverses: FIFO becomes the most conservative method, and LIFO the least conservative.

Inventory Valuation Methods: A Summary

Valuation Method	Costs Allocated to:		Comments
	Cost of Goods Sold	Inventory	
Specific identification	Actual costs of the units sold	Actual cost of units remaining	• Parallels physical flow • Logical method when units are unique • May be misleading when the units are identical
Flow assumptions (acceptable only for an inventory of *homogeneous units*):			
Average cost	Number of units sold, times the *average unit cost*	Number of units on hand, times the *average unit cost*	• Assigns all units the same *average unit cost* • Current costs are averaged in with older costs
First-in, first-out (FIFO)	Costs of *earliest purchases* on hand immediately prior to the sale (first-in, first-out)	Costs of *most recently* purchased units	• Cost of goods sold is based on older costs • Inventory valued at current costs • May overstate income during periods of rising prices; may increase income taxes due
Last-in, first-out (LIFO)	Cost of *most recently purchased* units (last-in, first-out)	Costs of *earliest purchases* (assumed *still* to be in inventory)	• Cost of goods sold shown at recent prices • Inventory shown at old (and perhaps out of date) costs • Most conservative method during periods of rising prices; often results in lower income taxes

method), it should continue to apply that assumption to all sales of that type of merchandise.

The principle of consistency does *not* prohibit a company from *ever* changing its accounting methods. If a change is made, however, the reasons for the change must be explained, and the effects of the change upon the company's net income must be fully disclosed.[5]

JUST-IN-TIME (JIT) INVENTORY SYSTEMS

In recent years, much attention has been paid to the **just-in-time** inventory concept in manufacturing operations. The phrase "just-in-time" usually means that purchases of raw materials and component parts arrive just in time for use in the manufacturing process—often within a few hours of the time they are scheduled for use. A second application of the just-in-time concept is completing the manufacturing process just in time to ship the finished goods to customers.

One advantage of a just-in-time system lies in reducing the amount of money tied-up in inventories of raw materials and finished goods. Also, the manufacturing company does not need to maintain large inventory storage facilities. A disadvantage of a just-in-time system is that a delay in the arrival of essential materials may bring manufacturing operations to a halt. Therefore, just-in-time scheduling of incoming materials is feasible only when the suppliers—and the transportation systems—are highly reliable.

CASE IN POINT

One of the pioneers of just-in-time manufacturing is **Toyota,** the Japanese automaker. Toyota's main plant is located in an area of Japan called "Toyota City." Many of the company's suppliers of direct materials also are located in Toyota City and produce materials primarily for Toyota. Thus, the suppliers' economic survival depends upon meeting their delivery schedules at the Toyota plant.

Although a just-in-time system reduces the size of a company's inventories, it does not eliminate them entirely. A recent annual report of Toyota, for example, shows inventories in excess of *$3 billion.* (Toyota values some of these inventories by the specific identification method, and others by LIFO.)

The concept of minimizing inventories applies more to manufacturing operations than to retailers. Ideally, manufacturers have buyers "lined up" for their merchandise even before the goods are produced. Many retailers, in contrast, want to offer their customers a large selection of in-stock merchandise—which means a big inventory.

The just-in-time concept actually involves much more than minimizing the size of inventories. It has been described as the "philosophy" of constantly working to increase efficiency throughout the organization. One basic goal of an accounting system is to provide management with useful information about the efficiency—or inefficiency—of operations.

---

[5]Disclosure of the effects of such "accounting changes" is discussed in Chapter 12. A change in the method of pricing inventory requires the approval of the Internal Revenue Service.

LO 2 *Explain the need for taking a physical inventory.*

TAKING A PHYSICAL INVENTORY

In Chapter 5 we explained the need for businesses to make a complete physical count of the merchandise on hand at least once a year. The primary reason for this procedure of "taking inventory" is to adjust the perpetual inventory records for unrecorded **shrinkage losses,** such as theft, spoilage, or breakage.

The **physical inventory** usually is taken at (or near) the end of the company's fiscal year.[6] Often a business selects a fiscal year ending in a season of low activity. For example, most large retailers use a fiscal year ending in January.

LO 3 *Record shrinkage losses and other year-end adjustments to inventory.*

RECORDING SHRINKAGE LOSSES

In most cases, the year-end physical count of the inventory reveals some shortages or damaged merchandise. The costs of missing or damaged units are removed from the inventory records using the same flow assumption as is used in recording the costs of goods sold.

To illustrate, assume that a company's inventory subsidiary ledger shows the following 158 units of a particular product in inventory at year-end:

8 units purchased November 2 @ $100	$ 800
150 units purchased December 10 @ $115	17,250
Total (158 units)	$18,050

A year-end physical count, however, discloses that only *148* of these units actually are on hand. Based upon this physical count, the company should adjust its inventory records to reflect the loss of 10 units.

The inventory flow assumption in use affects the measurement of shrinkage losses in the same way it affects the cost of goods sold. If the company uses *FIFO,* for example, the missing units will be valued at the oldest purchase costs shown in the inventory records. Thus, 8 of the missing units will be assumed to have cost $100 per-unit and the other 2, $115 per-unit. Under FIFO, the shrinkage loss amounts to *$1,030* (8 units @ $100 + 2 units @ $115). But if this company uses *LIFO,* the missing units all will be assumed to have come from the most recent purchase (on December 10). Therefore, the shrinkage loss amounts to *$1,150* (10 units @ $115).

If shrinkage losses are small, the costs removed from inventory may be charged (debited) directly to the Cost of Goods Sold account. If these losses are *material* in amount, the offsetting debit should be entered in a special loss account, such as Inventory Shrinkage Losses. In the income statement, a loss account is deducted from revenue in the same manner as an expense account.

LCM AND OTHER WRITE-DOWNS OF INVENTORY

In addition to shrinkage losses, the value of inventory may decline because the merchandise has become obsolete or is unsalable for other reasons.

---

[6]The reason for taking a physical inventory near year-end is to ensure that any shrinkage losses are reflected in the annual financial statements. The stronger the company's system of internal control over inventories, the further this procedure may be moved away from the balance sheet date. Obviously, no one wants to spend New Year's Eve counting inventory.

CASE IN POINT

Several years ago, a deranged individual inserted a deadly poison into a few packages of Tylenol, a widely used medication. This criminal act of "product tampering" resulted in several tragic deaths. In response, **Johnson & Johnson,** the maker of Tylenol, promptly recalled all packages of this product and destroyed the entire inventory. The company later reintroduced Tylenol—this time in tablet form (rather than capsules) and in a tamperproof container. Other drug manufacturers quickly followed Johnson & Johnson's lead and changed the form and the packaging of their over-the-counter products.

The Tylenol tragedy often is studied by business managers and business students alike. The company's response is considered a classic example of fast, responsible, and effective action in a time of crisis.

If inventory has become obsolete or is otherwise unsalable, its carrying value in the accounting records should be *written down* to zero (or to its "scrap value," if any). A **write down** of inventory reduces both the carrying value of the inventory and also the net income of the current period. The reduction in income is handled in the same manner as a shrinkage loss. If the write-down is relatively small, the loss is debited directly to the Cost of Goods Sold account. If the write-down is *material in amount,* however, it is charged to a special loss account, perhaps entitled Loss from Write-down of Inventory.

THE LOWER-OF-COST-OR-MARKET (LCM) RULE An asset is an economic resource. It may be argued that no economic resource is worth more than it would cost to *replace* that resource in the open market. For this reason, accountants traditionally have valued inventory in the balance sheet at the lower of its (1) cost or (2) market value. In this context, "market value" means *current replacement cost.* Thus, the inventory is valued at the lower of its historical cost or its current replacement cost.

The **lower-of-cost-or-market** rule may be applied in conjunction with any flow assumption and also with the specific identification method. If the current replacement cost of the ending inventory is substantially *below* the cost shown in the accounting records, the inventory is written down to this replacement cost. The offsetting debit is charged to either the Cost of Goods Sold account or the Loss from Write-down of Inventory account, depending upon the materiality of the dollar amount.

In their financial statements, most companies state that inventory is valued at the lower-of-cost-or-market. In our inflationary economy, however, the lower of these two amounts usually is cost, especially for companies using LIFO.[7]

THE YEAR-END CUTOFF OF TRANSACTIONS
Making a proper *cutoff* of transactions is an essential step in the preparation of reliable financial statements. A proper cutoff simply means that the transactions occurring near year-end are *recorded in the right accounting period.*

One aspect of a proper cutoff is determining that all purchases of merchandise through the end of the period are recorded in the inventory records and

---

[7]A notable exception is the petroleum industry, in which the replacement cost of inventory can fluctuate very quickly and in either direction. Large oil companies occasionally report LCM adjustments of several hundred million dollars in a single year.

included in the physical count of merchandise on hand at year-end. Of equal importance is determining that the cost of all merchandise sold through the end of the period has been removed from the inventory accounts and charged to the Cost of Goods Sold. This merchandise should *not* be included in the year-end physical count.

If some sales transactions have not been recorded as of year-end, the quantities of merchandise shown in the inventory records will exceed the quantities actually on hand. When the results of the physical count are compared with the inventory records, these unrecorded sales easily could be mistaken for inventory shortages.

Making a proper cutoff may be difficult if sales transactions are occurring while the merchandise is being counted. For this reason, most businesses count their physical inventory during nonbusiness hours, even if they must shut down their sales operations for a day.

MATCHING REVENUE AND THE COST OF GOODS SOLD Accountants must determine that both the sales revenue and the cost of goods sold relating to sales transactions occurring near year-end are recorded in the *same* accounting period. Otherwise, the revenue and expense from these transactions will not be properly matched in the company's income statements.

GOODS IN TRANSIT A sale should be recorded *when title to the merchandise passes to the buyer.* In making a year-end cutoff of transactions, questions may arise when goods are in transit between the seller and the buyer as to which company owns the merchandise. The answer to such questions lies in the terms of shipment. If these terms are **F.O.B.** (free on board) **shipping point,** title passes at the point of shipment and the goods are the property of the buyer while in transit. If the terms of the shipment are **F.O.B. destination,** title does not pass until the shipment reaches its destination and the goods belong to the seller while in transit.

Many companies ignore these distinctions, because goods in transit always arrive within a day or two. In such cases, the amount of merchandise in transit usually is *not material* in dollar amount, and the company may follow the *most convenient* accounting procedures. It usually is most convenient to record all purchases when the inbound shipments arrive and all sales when the merchandise is shipped to the customer.

In some industries, however, goods in transit may be very material. Oil companies, for example, often have millions of dollars of inventory in transit in pipelines and supertankers. In these situations, the company must consider the terms of each shipment in recording its purchases and sales.

PERIODIC INVENTORY SYSTEMS

In our preceding discussions, we have emphasized the perpetual inventory system—that is, inventory records which are kept continuously up-to-date. Virtually all large business organizations use perpetual inventory systems.

LO 4 *In a periodic inventory system, determine the ending inventory and the cost of goods sold using (a) average cost, (b) FIFO, and (c) LIFO.*

Some small businesses, however, use *periodic* inventory systems. In a periodic inventory system, the cost of merchandise purchased during the year is debited to a *Purchases* account, rather than to the Inventory account. When merchandise is sold to a customer, an entry is made recognizing the sales revenue, but no entry is made to reduce the inventory account or to recognize the cost of goods sold.

The inventory on hand and the cost of goods sold for the year are not determined until year-end. At the end of the year, all goods on hand are counted and priced at cost. The cost assigned to this ending inventory is then used to compute the cost of goods sold, as shown below. (The dollar amounts are assumed for the purpose of completing the illustration.)

Inventory at the beginning of the year	$10,000
Add: Purchases during the year	80,000
Cost of goods available for sale during the year	$90,000
Less: Inventory at the end of the year	7,000
Cost of goods sold	$83,000

The only item in this computation that is kept continuously up-to-date in the accounting records is the Purchases account. The amount of inventory at the beginning and end of the year are determined by annual physical counts.

Determining the cost of the year-end inventory involves two distinct steps: counting the merchandise and pricing the inventory, that is, determining the cost of the units on hand. Together, these procedures determine the proper valuation of inventory and also the cost of goods sold.

APPLYING FLOW ASSUMPTIONS IN A PERIODIC SYSTEM   In our discussion of perpetual inventory systems, we have emphasized the costs which are transferred from inventory *to the cost of goods sold*. In a periodic system, the emphasis shifts to determining the costs which should be assigned *to inventory* at the end of the period.

To illustrate, assume that The Kitchen Counter, a retail store, uses a periodic inventory system. The year-end physical inventory indicates that 12 units of a particular model food processor are on hand. Purchases of these food processors during the year are as follows:

	Number of Units	Cost Per Unit	Total Cost
Beginning inventory	10	$ 80	$ 800
First purchase (Mar. 1)	5	90	450
Second purchase (July 1)	5	100	500
Third purchase (Oct. 1)	5	120	600
Fourth purchase (Dec. 1)	5	130	650
Available for sale	30		$3,000
Units in ending inventory	12		
Units sold	18		

This schedule shows that 30 food processors were available for sale in the course of the year, of which 12 are still on hand. Thus, 18 of these food processors apparently were sold.[8] We will now use this data to determine the cost of the year-end inventory and the cost of goods sold using the specific identification method, and the average-cost, FIFO, and LIFO flow assumptions.

SPECIFIC IDENTIFICATION   If specific identification is used, the company must identify the 12 food processors on hand at year-end and determine their actual costs from purchase invoices. Assume that these 12 units have an actual

---

[8]The periodic inventory method does not distinguish between merchandise sold and shrinkage losses. Shrinkage losses are included automatically within the cost of goods sold.

total cost of $1,240. The cost of goods sold then is determined by subtracting this ending inventory from the cost of goods available for sale:

Cost of goods available for sale	$3,000
Less: Ending inventory (specific identification)	1,240
Cost of goods sold	$1,760

AVERAGE COST   The average cost is determined by dividing the total cost of goods available for sale during the year by the total number of units available for sale. Thus, the average per-unit cost is *$100* ($3,000 ÷ 30 units). Under the average-cost method, the ending inventory would be priced at $1,200 (12 units × $100 per unit), and the cost of goods sold would be *$1,800* ($3,000 cost of goods available for sale, less $1,200 in costs assigned to the ending inventory).

FIFO   Under the FIFO flow assumption, the oldest units are assumed to be the first sold. The ending inventory therefore is assumed to consist of the *most recently* acquired goods. (Remember, we are now talking about the goods *remaining in inventory,* not the goods sold.) Thus, the inventory of 12 food processors would be valued at the following costs:

5 units from the December 1 purchase @ $130	$ 650
5 units from the October 1 purchase @ $120	600
2 units from the July 1 purchase @ $100	200
Ending inventory, 12 units at FIFO cost	$1,450

The cost of goods sold would be *$1,550* ($3,000 − $1,450).

Notice that the FIFO method results in an inventory valued at relatively recent purchase costs. The cost of goods sold, however, is based upon the older acquisition costs.

LIFO   Under LIFO, the last units purchased are considered to be the first goods sold. Therefore, the ending inventory is assumed to contain the *earliest* purchases. The 12 food processors in inventory would be priced as follows:

10 units from the beginning inventory @ $80	$800
2 units from the March 1 purchase @ $90	180
Ending inventory, 12 units at LIFO cost	$980

The cost of goods sold under the LIFO method is *$2,020* ($3,000 − $980).

Notice that the cost of goods sold under LIFO is *higher* than that determined by the FIFO method ($2,020 under LIFO, as compared with $1,550 under FIFO). LIFO always results in a higher cost of goods sold when purchase costs are rising. Thus, LIFO tends to minimize both reported net income and income taxes during periods of rising prices.

Notice also that the LIFO method may result in an ending inventory that is priced *well below* its current replacement cost.

RECEIVING THE MAXIMUM TAX BENEFIT FROM THE LIFO METHOD   Many companies that use LIFO in a perpetual inventory system *restate* their year-end inventory at the costs indicated by the *periodic* LIFO costing procedures illustrated above. This "restatement" is accomplished by either debiting or crediting the Inventory account and making an offsetting entry to the Cost of Goods Sold account.

Often, restating ending inventory using periodic costing procedures results in older (and lower) unit costs than those shown in the periodic inventory records. By assigning less cost to the ending inventory, it follows that more of these costs will be assigned to the cost of goods sold. A higher cost of goods sold, in turn, means less taxable income.

Let us briefly explain why applying LIFO at year-end may result in a lower valuation of inventory than does applying LIFO on a perpetual basis. Consider the last purchase in our example. This purchase of 5 food processors was made on December 31, at the relatively high unit cost of $130. Assuming these units were not sold prior to year-end, they would be included in the year-end inventory in perpetual inventory records, even if these records were maintained on a LIFO basis. When the ending inventory is priced using "periodic LIFO," however, this last-minute purchase is *not* included in inventory, but rather in the cost of goods sold.

Both the LIFO and average-cost methods produce somewhat different valuations of inventory under perpetual and periodic costing procedures. Only companies using LIFO, however, usually adjust their perpetual records to indicate the unit costs determined by periodic costing procedures. When FIFO is in use, the perpetual and periodic costing procedures result in exactly the same valuation of inventory.

PRICING THE YEAR-END INVENTORY BY COMPUTER If purchase records are maintained by computer, the computer can compute the value of the ending inventory automatically using any of the flow assumptions discussed above. The computer operator must only enter the number of units on hand at year-end. A computer also can apply the specific identification method, but the computer operator then must enter an identification number for each unit in the ending inventory. This is one reason why the specific identification method usually is not used for inventories consisting of a large number of low-cost items.

IMPORTANCE OF AN ACCURATE VALUATION OF INVENTORY

The most important current assets in the balance sheets of most companies are cash, accounts receivable, and inventory. Of these assets, inventory often is the largest. It also is the only current asset for which alternative valuation methods are considered acceptable.

Because of the relatively large size of inventory, and the fact that products may be stored in many different locations, an error in inventory valuation may not be readily apparent. But in many cases, even a small error in the valuation of inventory may have a material effect upon net income. Therefore, care should be taken in counting and pricing the inventory at year-end.

An error in the valuation of inventory will affect several balance sheet measurements, including current assets, the current ratio, and total owners' equity. It also will affect key figures in the *income statement,* including the cost of goods sold, gross profit, and net income. And remember that the ending inventory of one year is the beginning inventory of the next. Thus, an error in inventory valuation will *"carry over"* into the income statement of the following year.

EFFECTS OF AN ERROR IN VALUING ENDING INVENTORY To illustrate, assume that some items of merchandise in a company's inventory are overlooked during the year-end physical count. As a result of this error, the ending inventory will be *understated.* The costs of the uncounted merchandise erroneously will be transferred out of the Inventory account and included in the cost of goods sold. This overstatement of the cost of goods sold, in turn, results in an understatement of gross profit and net income.[9]

INVENTORY ERRORS AFFECT TWO YEARS An error in the valuation of ending inventory affects not only the financial statements of the current year, but also the income statement for the *following* year.

Assume that the ending inventory in 1998 is *understated* by $10,000. As we have described above, the cost of goods sold in 1998 will be overstated by this amount, and both gross profit and net income will be *understated*.

The ending inventory in 1998, however, becomes the *beginning inventory* in 1999. An understatement of the beginning inventory results in an understatement of the cost of goods sold and, therefore, an *overstatement* of gross profit and net income in 1999.

Notice that the original error has exactly the *opposite effects* upon the net incomes of the two successive years. Net income was *understated* by the amount of the error in 1998, and *overstated* by the same amount in 1999. For this reason inventory errors are said to be "counterbalancing" or "self-correcting" over a two-year period.

The fact that offsetting errors occur in the financial statements of two successive years does not lessen the consequences of errors in inventory valuation. Rather, this *exaggerates* the misleading effects of the error upon *trends* in the company's performance from one year to the next.

LO 5 *Explain the effects of errors in inventory valuation upon the income statement.*

CASE IN POINT

Some small businesses purposely have understated ending inventory in their income tax returns as an easy—though fraudulent—means of understating taxable income. In the following year, however, the effects of this error will reverse, and taxable income will be overstated. To avoid paying income taxes on this overstated income, the business may again understate its ending inventory, this time by an even greater amount. If this type of tax fraud continues for very long, the inventory becomes so understated that the situation becomes obvious.

When the **Internal Revenue Service** audits the income tax return of a small business, the IRS agents invariably try to determine whether inventory has been understated. If such an understatement exists, they will try to determine the taxpayer's intent. If the understatement has been allowed to reverse itself in the following year, the auditors probably will view the incident as an honest mistake. If they find a consistent pattern of understated inventories, however, they may decide to prosecute the taxpayer for income tax evasion—a criminal offense.

EFFECTS OF ERRORS IN INVENTORY VALUATION: A SUMMARY The following table summarizes the effects of an error in the valuation of ending inventory over two successive years. In this table we indicate the effects of the error on various financial statement measurements using the code letters **U** (Understated), **O** (Overstated), and **NE** (No Effect). The effects of errors in the valuation of inventory are the same regardless of whether the company uses a perpetual or a periodic inventory system.

---

[9]If income tax effects are ignored, the amount of the error is exactly the same in inventory, gross profit, and net income. If tax effects are considered, the amount of the error may be lessened in the net income figure.

Original Error: Ending Inventory Understated

	Year of the Error	Following Year
Beginning inventory	NE	U
Cost of goods available for sale	NE	U
Ending inventory	U	NE
Cost of goods sold	O	U
Gross profit	U	O
Net income	U	O
Owners' equity at year-end	U	NE

Original Error: Ending Inventory Overstated

	Year of the Error	Following Year
Beginning inventory	NE	O
Cost of goods available for sale	NE	O
Ending inventory	O	NE
Cost of goods sold	U	O
Gross profit	O	U
Net income	O	U
Owners' equity at year-end	O	NE

TECHNIQUES FOR ESTIMATING THE COST OF GOODS SOLD AND THE ENDING INVENTORY

Taking a physical inventory every month would be very expensive and time-consuming. Therefore, if a business using a periodic inventory system is to prepare monthly or quarterly financial statements, it usually *estimates* the amounts of its inventory and cost of goods sold. One approach to making these estimates is called the gross profit method; another—used primarily by retail stores—is the retail method.

THE GROSS PROFIT METHOD

The **gross profit method** is a quick, simple technique for estimating the cost of goods sold and the amount of inventory on hand. In using this method, it is assumed that the rate of gross profit earned in the preceding year will remain the same for the current year. When we know the rate of gross profit, we can divide the dollar amount of net sales into two elements: (1) the gross profit and (2) the cost of goods sold. We view net sales as 100%. If the gross profit rate, for example, is 40% of net sales, the cost of goods sold must be 60%. In other words, the cost of goods sold percentage (or **cost ratio**) is determined by deducting the gross profit rate from 100%.

LO 6 *Estimate the cost of goods sold and the ending inventory by the gross profit method and by the retail method.*

When the gross profit rate is known, the ending inventory can be estimated by the following procedures:

1. Determine the *cost of goods available for sale* from the general ledger records of beginning inventory and net purchases.

2. Estimate the *cost of goods sold* by multiplying the net sales by the cost ratio.

3. Deduct the *cost of goods sold* from the *cost of goods available for sale* to find the estimated ending inventory.

To illustrate, assume that Metro Hardware has a beginning inventory of $50,000 on January 1. During the month of January, net purchases amount to $20,000 and net sales total $30,000. Assume that the company's normal gross profit rate is 40% of net sales; it follows that the cost ratio is *60%*. Using these facts, the inventory on January 31 may be estimated as follows:

Goods available for sale:		
Beginning inventory, Jan. 1		$50,000
Purchases..		20,000
Cost of goods available for sale..		$70,000
Deduct: Estimated cost of goods sold:		
Net sales..	$30,000	
Cost ratio (100% − 40%)..	60%	
Estimated cost of goods sold ($30,000 × 60%)...........................		18,000
Estimated ending inventory, Jan. 31..		$52,000

Step 1 . . . (aligned with "Cost of goods available for sale")

Step 2 . . . (aligned with "Estimated cost of goods sold")
Step 3 . . . (aligned with "Estimated ending inventory")

The gross profit method of estimating inventory has several uses apart from the preparation of monthly financial statements. For example, if an inventory is destroyed by fire, the company must determine the amount of the inventory on hand at the date of the fire in order to file an insurance claim. The most convenient way to determine this inventory amount is often the gross profit method.

The gross profit method is also used at year-end after the taking of a physical inventory to confirm the overall reasonableness of the amount determined by the counting and pricing process.

THE RETAIL METHOD

The **retail method** of estimating inventory and the cost of goods sold is quite similar to the gross profit method. The basic difference is that the retail method is based upon the cost ratio of the *current period,* rather than that of the prior year.

To determine the cost ratio of the current period, the business must keep track of both the cost of all goods available for sale during the period and also the *retail sales prices* assigned to these goods. To illustrate, assume that during June the cost of goods available for sale in Tennis Gallery totaled $45,000. The store had offered this merchandise for sale to its customers at retail prices totaling $100,000. The cost ratio in June was *45%* ($45,000 ÷ $100,000). This cost ratio is used to estimate the monthly cost of goods sold and the month-end inventory by the same procedures as are applied under the gross profit method.

Many retail stores also use their current cost ratio as a quick method of pricing the inventory counted at year-end. In a retail store, the retail sales price is clearly marked on the merchandise. Therefore, employees quickly can determine the retail price of the ending inventory. This retail price may be reduced to a close approximation of cost simply by multiplying by the cost ratio.

Assume, for example, that the annual physical inventory at Tennis Gallery indicates the merchandise on hand at year-end has a retail sales price of $120,000. If the cost ratio for the year has been 44%, the cost of this inventory is approximately $52,800 ($120,000 × 44%). This version of the retail method approximates valuation of the inventory at average cost. A variation of this method approximates a LIFO valuation of the ending inventory.

"TEXTBOOK" INVENTORY SYSTEMS CAN BE MODIFIED . . . AND THEY OFTEN ARE

In this chapter we have described the basic characteristics of the most common inventory systems. In practice, businesses often modify these systems to suit their particular needs. Some businesses also use *different inventory systems for different purposes.*

We described one modification in Chapter 5—a company that maintains very little inventory may simply charge (debit) all purchases directly to the cost of goods sold. Another common modification is to maintain perpetual inventory records showing only the *quantities* of merchandise bought and sold, with no dollar amounts. Such systems require less record keeping than a full-blown perpetual system, and they still provide management with useful information about sales and inventories. To generate the dollar amounts needed in financial statements and tax returns, these companies might use the gross profit method, the retail method, or a periodic inventory system.

Businesses such as restaurants often update their inventory records by physically counting products on a daily or weekly basis. In effect, they use frequent periodic counts as the basis for maintaining a perpetual inventory system.

In summary, "real-world" inventory systems often differ from the illustrations in a textbook. But the underlying principles remain much the same.

CASE IN POINT

Apple Computer maintains a perpetual inventory system. The daily entries reflect only the *quantities* of units produced and sold—not the dollar costs. Dollar amounts are computed and recorded in the inventory records at the end of the month. In transferring costs from inventory accounts to the cost of goods sold, Apple uses a FIFO flow assumption. But the inventory "cost layers" don't represent units purchased at different prices—they represent units manufactured in different months.

Sears and Wal-Mart maintain perpetual inventory records showing both quantities and dollar amounts. But the dollar amounts are recorded at *retail prices*. When cost data are needed, these companies apply cost ratios to the retail amounts.

Fleming Cos. is the world's largest food wholesaler. To assist management in monitoring sales, profit margins, and inventory, Fleming maintains a perpetual inventory system. In its interim financial statements, however, it uses the *gross profit method.* Why? Some of Fleming's inventories are subject to significant spoilage losses. The gross profit method automatically provides for normal amounts of shrinkage. Adjusting the perpetual records to reflect these losses would require a complete physical inventory.

EVALUATING THE LIQUIDITY OF INVENTORY

Inventory often is the largest of a company's current assets. But how liquid is this asset? How quickly will it be converted into cash? As a step toward answering these questions, short-term creditors often compute the **inventory turnover rate.**

INVENTORY TURNOVER RATE

The inventory turnover rate is equal to the cost of goods sold divided by the average amount of inventory (beginning inventory plus ending inventory, divided by 2). This ratio indicates how many *times* in the course of a year the company is able to sell the amount of its average inventory. The higher this rate, the more quickly the company sells its inventory.

LO 7 *Compute the inventory turnover rate and explain its uses.*

To illustrate, a recent annual report of J.C. Penney shows a cost of goods sold of $10,492 million and average inventory of $2,407 million. The inventory turnover rate for Penney's, therefore, is *4.36 to 1* ($10,492 million ÷ $2,407 million). We may compute the number of *days* required for the company to sell its inventory by dividing 365 days by the turnover rate. Thus, J.C. Penney requires *84 days* to turn over (sell) the amount of its average inventory (365 days ÷ 4.36).

Users of financial statements find the inventory turnover rate useful in evaluating the liquidity of the company's inventory. In addition, managers and independent auditors use this computation to help identify inventory which is not selling well and which may have become obsolete. A declining turnover rate indicates that merchandise is not selling as quickly as it used to.

CONVERTING THE INVENTORY INTO CASH Most businesses sell merchandise on account. Therefore, inventory often is not converted into cash as soon as it is sold. To determine how quickly inventory is converted into cash, we must combine the number of days required to *sell the inventory* with the number of days required to *collect the accounts receivable.*

Computation of the number of days required to collect accounts receivable was illustrated and explained in the preceding chapter. To review, the *accounts receivable turnover rate* is computed by dividing net sales by the average accounts receivable. The number of days required to collect these receivables then is determined by dividing 365 days by this turnover rate. Data for the J.C. Penney annual report indicate that the company needed *97 days* (on average) to collect its accounts receivable.

LENGTH OF THE OPERATING CYCLE The *operating cycle* of a merchandising company is the average time period between the purchase of merchandise and the conversion of this merchandise back into cash. In other words, the merchandise acquired as inventory gradually is converted into accounts receivable by selling the goods on account, and these receivables are converted into cash through the process of collection.

The operating cycle of J.C. Penney was approximately *181 days,* computed by adding the average 84 days required to sell its inventory and the 97 days required to collect its accounts receivable from customers. From the viewpoint of short-term creditors, the shorter the operating cycle, the higher the quality of the company's current assets.

YOUR TURN

You as a Banker

Assume that you are a commercial loan officer at a large bank. One of your clients recently submitted an application for a $300,000 five-year loan. You have worked with this business before on numerous occasions, and have periodically been forced to deal with late and missed payments attributed to cash flow problems. Thus, you are surprised to see in the business plan accompanying the application that management expects to reduce the company's operating cycle from 190 days to 90 days. A footnote to the business plan indicates that the reduction in the operating cycle will result from (1) a tighter credit policy, and (2) the implementation of a just-in-time inventory system.

As a banker, are you comfortable that these changes are related to the company's operating cycle?

*Our comments appear on page 410.

ACCOUNTING METHODS CAN AFFECT ANALYTICAL RATIOS

The accounting methods selected by a company may affect the ratios and financial statement subtotals used in evaluating the company's financial position and the results of its operations. To illustrate, let us consider the effects of inventory valuation methods upon inventory turnover rates.

Assume that during a period of rising prices Alpha Company uses LIFO, whereas Beta Company uses FIFO. In all other respects, the two companies *are identical;* they have the same size inventories, and they purchase and sell the same quantities of merchandise at the same prices and on the same dates. Thus, each company *physically* turns over its inventory at *exactly the same rate.*

Because Alpha uses the LIFO method, however, its inventory is valued at older (and lower) costs than is the inventory of Beta Company. Also, Alpha's cost of goods sold includes more recent (and higher) costs than does Beta's. When these amounts are used in computing the inventory turnover rate (cost of goods sold divided by average inventory), Alpha *appears* to have the higher turnover rate.

We already have stated that the inventories of these two companies are turning over at exactly the same rate. Therefore, the differences in the turnover rates computed from the companies' financial statements are caused *solely by the different accounting methods used in the valuation of the companies' inventories.*

Inventory turnover is not the only ratio which will be affected. Alpha will report lower current assets than Beta and, therefore, a lower current ratio and less working capital. In addition, using LIFO will cause Alpha to report less gross profit and lower net income than Beta.

Users of financial statements must understand the typical effects of different accounting methods. Also, a financial analyst should be able to restate on a *comparable basis* the financial statements of companies that use different accounting methods. Notes accompanying the financial statements usually provide the information necessary for comparing the operating results of companies using LIFO with those of companies using the FIFO method.

CASE IN POINT

Oshkosh B'Gosh, Inc. (a publicly owned maker of children's clothing) uses LIFO. However, a note accompanying the financial statements reads in part:

Although the LIFO method results in a better matching of costs and revenue, information relating to the first-in, first-out (FIFO) method may be useful in comparing operating results to those companies not on LIFO. Had earnings been reported on a FIFO basis the results would have been: . . . .

In the remainder of the note, the company discloses the ending inventory, cost of goods sold, and net income that would have resulted from use of the FIFO method.

NET CONNECTIONS

There is so much more to managing inventory than simply keeping goods on the shelves. But how does one learn more about inventory handbooks, consulting services, and seminars? One quick way is through the Internet. To find out more about managing inventories, visit the Inventory Management home page at:

www.inventorymanagement.com

To learn more about "cutting edge" technological breakthroughs and management innovations—including computerized inventory controls and just-in-time systems—visit the home page of the American Production and Inventory Control Society at:

www.industry.net/apics

*SUPPLEMENTAL TOPIC

LIFO RESERVES

LO 8 *Define a "LIFO reserve" and explain its implications to users of financial statements.*

We have stated that the significant shortcoming in the LIFO method is that the asset inventory is valued at the company's "oldest" inventory acquisition costs. After a period of years, these outdated costs may significantly understate the current replacement cost of the inventory. The difference between the LIFO cost of an inventory and its current replacement cost often is called a **LIFO reserve.**[1]

CASE IN POINT

In a recent balance sheet, **General Motors** reported inventories of approximately $8 billion, valued by the LIFO method. A note accompanying the balance sheet, however, explained that the current replacement cost of these inventories exceeded $10.4 billion. Therefore, GM had a "LIFO reserve'' of more than $2.4 billion.

THE SIGNIFICANCE OF A LIFO RESERVE

Users of financial statements should understand the implications of a large LIFO reserve.

COMPARING LIFO AND FIFO INVENTORIES   A LIFO reserve indicates that the company's inventory is *undervalued* in terms of its current replacement cost and in terms of the valuation that would have resulted from use of the FIFO method. Thus, the inventories of companies using LIFO are not directly comparable to those of companies using FIFO. Fortunately, this problem is solved in the notes to the financial statements: Companies using LIFO disclose the current replacement cost (or FIFO cost) of their inventories.

LIQUIDATION OF A LIFO RESERVE   The existence of a LIFO reserve may cause a company's profits to rise dramatically if inventory falls to an abnormally low level at year-end. As the company reduces its inventories, the costs transferred to the cost of goods sold will come from older—and lower—cost layers. The inclusion of these old and low costs in the cost of goods sold can cause the

---

[1]The phrase "LIFO reserve" is used by accountants, investors, and business managers in conversation and many types of financial literature. The FASB, however, discourages use of the word "reserve" in formal financial statements, as this word has several different meanings. Therefore, in financial statements a LIFO reserve is likely to be described as "the difference between the LIFO cost and current (replacement) cost of inventory."

company's gross profit rate to soar. This situation is called a **"liquidation" of the LIFO reserve.**

Many factors may cause the liquidation of a LIFO reserve. For example, the company may be unable to make the purchases necessary to replenish its inventory because of shortages or strikes. Often a company discontinues a particular product line and sells its entire inventory of this merchandise. Also, management deliberately may delay making normal year-end purchases in order to liquidate a portion of the company's LIFO reserve.

The user of financial statements should recognize that the abnormal profits which result from the liquidation of a LIFO reserve *do not* represent an improvement in financial performance. Rather, these profits are a one-time occurrence, resulting from old and relatively low unit costs temporarily being used in measuring the cost of goods sold. Users of financial statements easily can determine whether a company's reported earnings are affected by the liquidation of a LIFO reserve. This liquidation occurs whenever a company using LIFO ends its fiscal year with its inventory at a substantially lower level than at the beginning of the year. If material in dollar amount, the financial impact of this liquidation should be disclosed in notes accompanying the financial statements.

ASSESSING THE INCOME TAX BENEFITS OF USING LIFO A LIFO reserve represents the amount by which a company has reduced its taxable income over the years through use of the LIFO method. Referring to our Case in Point, General Motors has reduced its taxable income (over a long span of years) by more than $2.4 billion. If we assume that GM pays income taxes at a rate of, say, 33%, using LIFO has saved the company about $800 million in income taxes.

YOUR TURN

You as a Business Owner

Assume that you have been using the LIFO inventory method in your building supply business for the past ten years. Each year, your accountant brings to your attention the significant tax savings that have resulted from your decision to use LIFO instead of FIFO.

During December, a major supplier was unable to make deliveries due to a strike by the truck drivers' union. As a consequence, inventory levels at year-end were nearly depleted. You have just received a call from your accountant informing you that taxable income for the year ended December 31 was unexpectedly high, and that the estimated tax payments made throughout the year fell far short of the company's actual tax liability.

The news from your accountant made you angry and confused, as you were certain that LIFO always results in the lowest possible taxable income during periods of rising prices. While the past year was inflationary, income taxes were much higher than expected. What happened?

*Our comments appear on page 410.

SUMMARY OF LEARNING OBJECTIVES

① **In a perpetual inventory system, determine the cost of goods sold using (a) specific identification, (b) average cost, (c) FIFO, and (d) LIFO. Discuss the advantages and shortcomings of each method.**

Under the *specific identification method,* the actual costs of the specific units sold are transferred from inventory to the cost of goods sold. (Debit Cost of Goods Sold, credit Inventory.) This method achieves the proper matching of sales revenue and cost of goods sold when the individual units in the inventory are unique. However, the method becomes cumbersome and may produce misleading results if the inventory consists of homogeneous items.

The remaining three methods are *flow assumptions,* which should be applied only to an inventory of homogeneous items.

Under the *average-cost method,* the average cost of all units in the inventory is computed and used in recording the cost of goods sold. This is the only method in which all units are assigned the same (average) per-unit cost.

FIFO (first-in, first-out) is the assumption that the first units purchased are the first units sold. Thus, inventory is assumed to consist of the most recently purchased units. FIFO assigns current costs to inventory, but older (and often lower) costs to the cost of goods sold.

LIFO (last-in, first-out) is the assumption that the most recently acquired goods are sold first. This method matches sales revenue with relatively current costs. In a period of inflation, LIFO usually results in lower reported profits and lower income taxes than the other methods. However, the "oldest" purchase costs are assigned to inventory, which may result in inventory becoming grossly understated in terms of current replacement costs.

② **Explain the need for taking a physical inventory.**

In a perpetual inventory system, a physical inventory is taken to adjust the inventory records for shrinkage losses. In a periodic inventory system, the physical inventory is the basis for determining the cost of the ending inventory and for computing cost of goods sold.

③ **Record shrinkage losses and other year-end adjustments to inventory.**

Shrinkage losses are recorded by removing from the Inventory account the cost of the missing or damaged units. The offsetting debit may be to Cost of Goods Sold, if the shrinkage is normal in amount, or to a special loss account. If inventory is found to be obsolete or unsalable, it is written down to zero (or its scrap value, if any). If inventory is valued at the lower-of-cost-or-market, it is written down to its current replacement cost, if at year-end this amount is substantially below the cost shown in the inventory records.

④ **In a periodic inventory system, determine the ending inventory and the cost of goods sold using (a) average cost, (b) FIFO, and (c) LIFO.**

The cost of goods sold is determined by combining the beginning inventory with the purchases during the period, and subtracting the cost of the ending inventory. Thus, the cost assigned to ending inventory also determines the cost of goods sold.

Under the average-cost method, the ending inventory is determined by multiplying the number of units on hand by the average cost of the units available for sale during the year. Under FIFO, the units in inventory are priced using the unit costs from the *most recent* cost layers. Under the LIFO method, inventory is priced using the unit costs in the oldest cost layers.

⑤ **Explain the effects of errors in inventory valuation upon the income statement.**

In the current year, an error in the costs assigned to *ending* inventory will cause an opposite error in the cost of goods sold and, therefore, a repetition of the original error in the amount of gross profit. For example, understating ending inventory results in an overstatement of the cost of goods sold, and an understatement of gross profit.

The error has exactly the opposite effects upon the cost of goods sold and the gross profit of the following year, because the error is now in the cost assigned to *beginning* inventory.

⑥ **Estimate the costs of goods sold and ending inventory by the gross profit method and by the retail method.**

Both the gross profit and retail methods use a *cost ratio* to estimate the cost of goods sold and ending inventory. The cost of goods sold is estimated by multiplying net sales by this cost ratio; ending inventory then is estimated by subtracting this cost of goods sold from the cost of goods available for sale.

In the gross profit method, the cost ratio is 100% minus the company's historical gross profit rate. In the retail method, the cost ratio for the current period is computed by keeping track of both the cost and the retail prices of merchandise available for sale.

⑦ **Compute the inventory turnover rate and explain its uses.**

The inventory turnover rate is equal to the cost of goods sold divided by the average inventory. Users of financial statements find the inventory turnover rate useful in evaluating the liquidity of the company's inventory. In addition, managers and independent auditors use this computation to help identify inventory which is not selling well and which may have become obsolete.

⑧ **Define a "LIFO reserve" and explain its implications to users of financial statements.**

A LIFO reserve is the amount by which the current replacement cost of inventory exceeds the LIFO cost shown in the accounting records.

If a company has a large LIFO reserve, neither its inventory nor its cost of goods sold are comparable to those of a company using FIFO. Also, a LIFO reserve may cause earnings to increase dramatically if inventory falls below normal levels. Notes accompanying the financial statements provide the statement users with information useful in evaluating the implications of a LIFO reserve.

In this chapter we have seen that different inventory valuation methods can have significant effects on net income as reported in financial statements, and on income tax returns as well. In the following chapter, we will see that a similar situation exists with respect to the alternative methods used in depreciating plant and equipment.

KEY TERMS INTRODUCED OR EMPHASIZED IN CHAPTER 8

Average-cost method (p. 368)   A method of valuing all units in the inventory at the same average per-unit cost, which is recomputed after every purchase.

Consistency (in inventory valuation) (p. 373)   An accounting standard that calls for the use of the same method of inventory pricing from year to year, with full disclosure of the effects of any change in method. Intended to make financial statements comparable.

Cost flow assumptions (p. 367)   Assumptions as to the sequence in which units are removed from inventory for the purpose of sale. Need not parallel the physical movement of merchandise if the units are homogeneous.

Cost layer (p. 367)   Units of merchandise acquired at the same unit cost. An inventory comprised of several cost layers is characteristic of all inventory valuation methods except *average cost*.

Cost ratio (p. 383)   The cost of merchandise expressed as a percentage of its retail selling price. Used in inventory estimating techniques, such as the *gross profit method* and the *retail method*.

First-in, first-out (FIFO) method (p. 369)   A method of computing the cost of inventory and the cost of goods sold based on the assumption that the first merchandise acquired is the first merchandise sold, and that the ending inventory consists of the most recently acquired goods.

F.O.B. destination (p. 378)   A term meaning the seller bears the cost of shipping goods to the buyer's location. Title to the goods remains with the seller while the goods are in transit.

F.O.B. shipping point (p. 378)   The buyer of goods bears the cost of transportation from the seller's location to the buyer's location. Title to the goods passes at the point of shipment and the goods are the property of the buyer while in transit.

Gross profit method (p. 383)   A method of estimating the cost of the ending inventory based upon the assumption that the rate of gross profit remains approximately the same from year to year.

Inventory turnover rate (p. 385)   The cost of goods sold divided by the average amount of inventory. Indicates how many times the average inventory is sold during the course of the year.

Just-in-time (JIT) inventory system (p. 375)   A technique designed to minimize a company's investment in inventory. In a manufacturing company, this means receiving purchases of raw materials just in time for use in the manufacturing process, and completing the manufacture of finished goods just in time to fill sales orders. Just-in-time also may be described as the philosophy of constantly striving to become more efficient.

Last-in, first-out (LIFO) method (p. 370)   A method of computing the cost of goods sold by use of the prices paid for the most recently acquired units. Ending inventory is valued on the basis of prices paid for the units first acquired.

LIFO reserve (p. 388)   The difference between the current replacement cost of a company's inventory and the LIFO cost shown in the accounting records. The fact that a LIFO reserve can become very large is the principal shortcoming of the LIFO method.

Liquidation of a LIFO reserve (p. 389)   Selling merchandise from a LIFO inventory to the point at which old and relatively low costs are transferred from Inventory into the cost of goods sold. Tends to inflate reported profits.

Lower-of-cost-or-market (LCM) rule (p. 377)   A method of inventory pricing in which goods are valued at original cost or replacement cost (market), whichever is lower.

Physical inventory (p. 376)   A systematic count of all goods on hand, followed by the application of unit prices to the quantities counted and development of a dollar valuation of the ending inventory.

Retail method (p. 384)   A method of estimating the cost of goods sold and ending inventory. Similar to the gross profit method, except that the cost ratio is based upon current cost-to-retail price relationships rather than upon those of the prior year.

---

*Supplemental Topic, "LIFO Reserves."

Shrinkage losses (p. 376)   Losses of inventory resulting from theft, spoilage, or breakage.

Specific identification (p. 367)   Recording as the cost of goods sold the actual costs of the specific units sold. Necessary if each unit in inventory is unique, but not if the inventory consists of homogeneous products.

Write-down (of an asset) (p. 377)   A reduction in the carrying value of an asset because it has become obsolete or its usefulness has otherwise been impaired. Involves a credit to the asset account, with an offsetting debit to a loss account.

DEMONSTRATION PROBLEM

The Audiophile sells high-performance stereo equipment. Massachusetts Acoustic recently introduced the Carnegie-440, a state-of-the-art speaker system. During the current year, The Audiophile purchased nine of these speaker systems at the following dates and acquisition costs:

Date	Units Purchased	Unit Cost	Total Cost
Oct. 1	2	$3,000	$ 6,000
Nov. 17..	3	3,200	9,600
Dec. 1..	4	3,250	13,000
Available for sale during the year.......................................	9		$28,600

On *November 21,* The Audiophile sold four of these speaker systems to the Boston Symphony. The other five Carnegie-440s remained in inventory at December 31.

INSTRUCTIONS

Assume that The Audiophile uses a *perpetual inventory system.* Compute (1) the cost of goods sold relating to the sale of Carnegie-440 speakers to the Boston Symphony, and (2) the ending inventory of these speakers at December 31, using each of the following flow assumptions:

a. Average cost

b. First-in, first-out (FIFO)

c. Last-in, first-out (LIFO)

Show the number of units and the unit costs of the cost layers comprising the cost of goods sold and the ending inventory.

SOLUTION TO DEMONSTRATION PROBLEM

a. (1) Cost of goods sold (at average cost):

Average unit cost at Nov. 21 [($6,000 + $9,600) ÷ 5 units]...... $ 3,120

Cost of goods sold (4 units × $3,120 per unit) $12,480

(2) Inventory at Dec. 31 (at average cost):

Units remaining after sale of November 21 (1 unit @ $3,120) $ 3,120

Units purchased on Dec. 1 (4 units @ $3,250) 13,000

Total cost of 5 units in inventory $16,120

Average unit cost at Dec. 31.. $ 3,224

Inventory at Dec. 31 (5 units × $3,224 per unit) $16,120

b. (1) Cost of goods sold (FIFO basis):

(2 units @ $3,000 + 2 units @ $3,200)......................... $12,400

(2) Inventory at Dec. 31 (4 units @ $3,250 + 1 unit @ $3,200) $16,200

c. (1) Cost of goods sold (LIFO basis):

(3 units @ $3,200 1 + unit @ $3,000).................................. $12,600

(2) Inventory at Dec. 31 (4 units @ $3,250 + 1 unit @ $3,000) $16,000

SELF-TEST QUESTIONS

The answers to these questions appear on page 410.

1. The primary purpose for using an inventory flow *assumption* is to:
  a. Parallel the physical flow of units of merchandise.
  b. Offset against revenue an appropriate cost of goods sold.
  c. Minimize income taxes.
  d. Maximize the reported amount of net income.

2. Ace Auto Supply uses a perpetual inventory record. On March 10, the company sells two Shelby four-barrel carburetors. Immediately prior to this sale, the perpetual inventory records indicate three of these carburetors on hand, as shown below:

Date	Quantity Purchased	Unit Cost	Units on Hand	Total Cost
Feb. 4	1	$220	1	$220
Mar. 2	2	235	3	690

With respect to this sale on March 10: (More than one of the following answers may be correct.)
  a. If the average-cost method is used, the cost of goods sold is $460.
  b. If these carburetors have identification numbers, Ace must use the specific identification method to determine the cost of goods sold.
  c. If the company uses LIFO, the cost of goods sold will be $15 higher than if it were using FIFO.
  d. If the company uses LIFO, the carburetor *remaining* in inventory after the sales will be assumed to have cost $220.

3. T-Shirt City uses a *periodic* inventory system. During the first year of operations, the company made four purchases of a particular product. Each purchase was for 500 units and the prices paid were: $9 per unit in the first purchase, $10 per unit in the second purchase, $12 per unit in the third purchase, and $13 per unit in the fourth purchase. At year-end, 650 of these units remained unsold. Compute the cost of goods sold under the FIFO method and LIFO method, respectively.
  a. $13,700 (FIFO) and $16,000 (LIFO)
  b. $8,300 (FIFO) and $6,000 (LIFO)
  c. $16,000 (FIFO) and $13,700 (LIFO)
  d. $6,000 (FIFO) and $8,300 (LIFO)

4. Trent Department Store uses a perpetual inventory system but adjusts its inventory records at year-end to reflect the results of a complete physical inventory. In the physical inventory taken at the ends of 1998 and 1999, Trent's employees failed to count the merchandise in the store's window displays. The cost of this merchandise amounted to $13,000 at the end of 1998 and $19,000 at the end of 1999. As a result of these errors, the cost of goods sold for 1999 will be:
  a. Understated by $19,000.
  b. Overstated by $6,000.
  c. Understated by $6,000.
  d. None of the above.

5. In July 1998, the accountant for LBJ Imports is in the process of preparing financial statements for the quarter ended June 30, 1998. The physical inventory, however, was last taken on June 5 and the accountant must establish the approximate cost at June 30 from the following data:

Physical inventory, June 5, 1998	$900,000
Transactions for the period June 5–June 30:	
Sales	700,000
Purchases	400,000

The gross profit on sales has consistently averaged 40% of sales. Using the gross profit method, compute the approximate inventory cost at June 30, 1998.

a. $420,000   **b.** $880,000   **c.** $480,000   **d.** $1,360,000

6. Allied Products maintains a large inventory. The company has used the LIFO inventory method for many years, during which the purchase costs of its products have risen substantially. (More than one of the following answers may be correct.)

   a. Allied would have reported a *higher* net income in past years if it had been using the average-cost method.

   b. Allied's financial statements imply a *higher* inventory turnover rate than they would if the company were using FIFO.

   c. If Allied were to let its inventory fall far below normal levels, the company's gross profit rate would *rise.*

   d. Allied's current ratio is *lower* than it would be if the company were using FIFO.

ASSIGNMENT MATERIAL

DISCUSSION QUESTIONS

1. Is the cost of merchandise acquired during the period classified as an asset or an expense? Explain.

2. Briefly describe the advantages of using a cost flow assumption, rather than the specific identification method, to value an inventory.

3. Under what circumstances do generally accepted accounting principles permit the use of an inventory cost flow assumption? Must a flow assumption closely parallel the physical movement of the company's merchandise?

4. Assume that a company has in its inventory units of a particular product which were purchased at several different per-unit costs. When some of these units are sold, explain how the cost of goods sold is measured under each of the following flow assumptions:

   a. Average cost
   b. FIFO
   c. LIFO

5. A large art gallery has in inventory more than one hundred paintings. No two are alike. The least expensive is priced at more than $1,000 and the higher-priced items carry prices of $100,000 or more. Which of the four methods of inventory valuation discussed in this chapter would you consider to be most appropriate for this business? Give reasons for your answer.

6. During a period of steadily increasing purchase costs, which inventory flow assumption results in the highest reported profits? The lowest taxable income? The valuation of inventory which is closest to current replacement cost? Briefly explain your answers.

7. Assume that during the first year of Hatton Corporation's operation, there were numerous purchases of identical items of merchandise. However, there was no change during the year in the prices paid for this merchandise. Under these special circumstances how would the financial statements be affected by the choice between the FIFO and LIFO methods of inventory valuation?

8. Apex Corporation operates in two locations: New York and Oregon. The LIFO method is used in accounting for inventories at the New York facility and the specific identification method for inventories at the Oregon location. Does this concurrent use of two inventory methods indicate that Apex is violating the accounting principle of consistency? Explain.

9. What are the characteristics of a *just-in-time* inventory system? Briefly explain some advantages and risks of this type of system.

10. Why do most companies that use perpetual inventory systems also take an annual *physical inventory?* When is this physical inventory usually taken? Why?

11. Under what circumstances might a company write down its inventory to carrying value below cost?

12. What is meant by the year-end *cutoff* of transactions? If merchandise in transit at year-end is material in dollar amount, what determines whether these goods should be included in the inventory of the buyer or the seller? Explain.

13. Briefly explain the operation of a *periodic* inventory system. Include an explanation of how the cost of goods sold is determined.

14. Assume that a *periodic* inventory system is in use. Explain which per-unit acquisition costs are assigned to the year-end inventory under each of the following inventory costing procedures:
    a. The average-cost method
    b. FIFO
    c. LIFO

15. Why do companies using LIFO in a perpetual inventory system often restate their ending inventory at the per-unit costs that result from applying *periodic* LIFO costing procedures?

16. Explain why errors in the valuation of inventory at the end of the year are sometimes called "counterbalancing" or "self-correcting."

17. Briefly explain the *gross profit method* of estimating inventories. In what types of situations is this technique likely to be useful?

18. Estimate the ending inventory by the gross profit method, given the following data: beginning inventory $40,000, net purchases $100,000, net sales $112,000, average gross profit rate of 25% of net sales.

19. A store using the *retail inventory method* takes its physical inventory by applying current retail prices as marked on the merchandise to the quantities counted. Does this procedure indicate that the inventory will appear in the financial statements at retail selling price? Explain.

20. How is the *inventory turnover rate* computed? Why is this measurement of interest to short-term creditors?

21. Baxter Corporation has been using FIFO during a period of rising costs. Explain whether you would expect each of the following measurements to be higher or lower if the company had been using LIFO.
    a. Net income
    b. Inventory turnover rate
    c. Current ratio
    d. Income taxes expense

22. In anticipation of *declining* inventory replacement costs, the management of Computer Products Co. elects to use the *FIFO* inventory method rather than LIFO. Explain how this decision should affect the company's future:
    a. Rate of gross profit.
    b. Net cash flow from operating activities.

*23. What is a *LIFO reserve?* What is likely to happen to the gross profit rate of a company with a large LIFO reserve if it sells most of its inventory?

Supplemental Topic, "LIFO Reserves."

EXERCISE 8-1
Accounting Terminology

LO 1–8

EXERCISES

Listed below are nine technical accounting terms introduced in this chapter.

Retail method	FIFO method	Average-cost method
Gross profit method	LIFO method	Lower-of-cost-or-market
Flow assumption	*LIFO reserve	Specific identification

Each of the following statements may (or may not) describe one of these technical terms. For each statement, indicate the term described, or answer "None" if the statement does not correctly describe any of the terms.

a. A pattern of transferring unit costs from the Inventory account to the cost of goods sold which may (or may not) parallel the physical flow of merchandise.

b. The excess of the current replacement cost of any inventory of merchandise over the cost of the inventory determined by the LIFO assumption.

c. The only flow assumption in which all units of merchandise are assigned the same per-unit cost.

d. The method used to record the cost of goods sold when each unit in the inventory is unique.

e. The most conservative of the flow assumptions during a period of sustained inflation.

f. The flow assumption which provides the most current valuation of inventory in the balance sheet.

g. A technique for estimating the cost of goods sold and the ending inventory which is based upon the relationship between cost and sales price during the *current* accounting period.

EXERCISE 8-2
Cost Flow Assumptions

LO 1

On May 10, Merlin Computers sold 80 Portex lap-top computers to College Text Publishers. At the date of this sale, Merlin's perpetual inventory records included the following cost layers for the Portex lap-tops:

Purchase Date	Quantity	Unit Cost	Total Cost
April 9	60	$800	$48,000
May 1	40	850	34,000
Total on Hand	100		$82,000

Prepare journal entries to record the cost of the 80 Portex lap-tops sold on May 10, assuming that Merlin Computers uses the:

a. Specific identification method (50 of the units sold were purchased on April 9, and the remaining units were purchased on May 1).

b. Average-cost method.

c. FIFO method.

d. LIFO method.

e. Discuss briefly the financial reporting differences that may arise from choosing the FIFO method over the LIFO method.

EXERCISE 8-3
Evaluating Alternative
Inventory Methods

LO 1

Notes to the financial statements of two well-known clothing manufacturers follow:

Supplemental Topic, "LIFO Reserves."

J. P. Stevens & Co., Inc.

Inventories: The inventories are stated at the lower of cost, determined principally by the LIFO method, or market.

Bobbie Brooks, Incorporated

Inventories: Inventories are stated at the lower of cost (first-in, first-out method) or market value.

Assuming a period of rising prices:

a. Which company is using the more "conservative" method of pricing its inventories? Explain.

b. Based upon the inventory methods in use in their financial statements, which company is in the better position to minimize the amount of income taxes that it must pay? Explain.

c. Could either company increase its cash collections from customers or reduce its cash payments to suppliers of merchandise by switching from FIFO to LIFO, or from LIFO to FIFO? Explain.

EXERCISE 8-4
Physical Flow Versus
Cost Flow

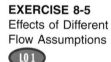

The Warm-Up Shop sells heating oil, coal, and kerosene fuel to residential customers. Heating oil is kept in large storage tanks which supply the company's fleet of delivery trucks. Coal is kept in huge bins which are loaded and emptied from the top by giant scooping machines. Kerosene is sold "off the shelf" in 5-gallon containers at the company's retail outlet. Separate inventory records are maintained for each fuel type.

a. Which of the cost flow assumptions (average-cost, FIFO, or LIFO) best describes the *physical flow* of:
1. The heating oil inventory? Explain.
2. The coal inventory? Explain.
3. The kerosene inventory? Explain.

b. Which of these cost flow assumptions is likely to result in the *lowest* income tax liability for the company? Explain.

c. Explain why management keeps separate inventory records for its heating oil, coal, and kerosene inventories.

EXERCISE 8-5
Effects of Different
Flow Assumptions

LO 1

Forbidden Beach, a chain of retail stores, uses FIFO. Shown below are selected data from the company's most recent financial statements (dollar amounts are in thousands):

Cost of goods sold	$48,000
Income before income taxes	10,000
Income taxes expense (and payments)	3,500
Net income	6,500
Net cash provided by operating activities	7,200

A footnote to the statements disclosed that had Forbidden Beach been using *LIFO,* the cost of goods sold would have been $51,200.

(The company's income taxes expenses amounts to 35% of income before taxes; assume income taxes are paid in cash in the same year they are recognized as expense.)

a. Explain how LIFO can result in a higher cost of goods sold. Would you expect the LIFO method to result in the company's inventory being shown at a greater amount?

b. Assuming that Forbidden Beach had been using *LIFO,* compute the following amounts for the current year. Show supporting computations, with dollar amounts in thousands.
1. Income before income taxes.
2. Income taxes expense (which are equal to cash payments).
3. Net income.
4. Net cash provided by operating activities.

EXERCISE 8-6
Dealing with the Bank

Avery Frozen Foods owes the bank $50,000 on a line of credit. Terms of the agreement specify that the Avery must maintain a minimum current ratio of 1.2 to 1, or the entire outstanding balance becomes immediately due in full. To date, the company has complied with the minimum requirement. However, management has just learned that a failed warehouse freezer has ruined thousands of dollars worth of frozen foods inventory. If the company records this loss, its current ratio will drop to approximately 0.8 to 1.

Whether any or all of this loss may be covered by insurance currently is in dispute, and will not be known for at least 90 days—perhaps much longer. There are several reasons why the insurance company may have no liability.

In trying to decide how to deal with the bank, management is considering the following options: (1) postpone recording the inventory loss until the dispute with the insurance company is resolved, (2) increase the current ratio to 1.2 to 1 by making a large purchase of inventory on account, (3) explain to the bank what has happened, and request that it be flexible until things get back to normal.

a. Given that the company hopes for at least partial reimbursement from the insurance company, is it really unethical for management to postpone recording the inventory loss in the financial statements it submits to the bank?

b. Is it possible to increase the company's current ratio from 0.8 to 1 to 1.2 to 1 by purchasing more inventory on account? Explain.

c. What approach do you think the company should follow in dealing with the bank?

EXERCISE 8-7
Transfer of Title

Fraser Company had two large shipments in transit at December 31. One was a $90,000 inbound shipment of merchandise (shipped December 28, F.O.B. shipping point) which arrived at the Fraser receiving dock on January 2. The other shipment was a $55,000 outbound shipment of merchandise to a customer, which was shipped and billed by Fraser on December 30 (terms F.O.B. shipping point) and reached the customer on January 3.

In taking a physical inventory on December 31, Fraser counted all goods on hand and priced the inventory on the basis of average cost. The total amount was $480,000. No goods in transit were included in this figure.

What amount should appear as inventory on the company's balance sheet at December 31? Explain. If you indicate an amount other than $480,000, state which asset or liability other than inventory also would be changed in amount.

EXERCISE 8-8
Inventory Write-Downs

Late in 1998, Software City began carrying WordCrafter, a new word processing software program. At December 31, Software City's perpetual inventory records included the following cost layers in its inventory of WordCrafter programs:

Purchase Date	Quantity	Unit Cost	Total Cost
November 14	6	$400	$2,400
December 12	20	310	6,200
Total available for sale at Dec. 31	26		$8,600

a. At December 31, Software City takes a physical inventory and finds that all 26 units of WordCrafter are on hand. However, the current replacement cost (wholesale price) of this product is only $250 per unit. Prepare the entries to record:

1. This write-down of the inventory to the lower-of-cost-or-market at December 31.
2. The cash sale of 10 WordCrafter programs on January 9, at a retail price of $350 each. Assume that Software City uses the FIFO flow assumption. (Company policy is to charge LCM adjustments of less than $2,000 to Cost of Goods Sold and larger amounts to a separate loss account.)

b. Now assume that the current replacement cost of the WordCrafter programs is $405 each. A physical inventory finds only 23 of these programs on hand at December 31.

1. Prepare the journal entry to record the shrinkage loss assuming that Software City uses the FIFO flow assumption.
2. Prepare the journal entry to record the shrinkage loss assuming that Software City uses the LIFO flow assumption.
3. Which cost flow assumption (FIFO or LIFO) results in the lowest net income for the period? Would using this assumption really mean that the company's operations are less efficient? Explain.

EXERCISE 8-9
It Comes With the Territory

Inventory write-downs are more common in some industries than in others. For instance, in the pharmaceutical, food processing, and certain "high tech" industries, large inventory adjustments are commonplace.

Find a recent article about a company that reported an inventory write-down. Do such write-downs occur frequently throughout this industry? What caused the need for the adjustment? In your opinion, was there anything management could have done to avoid the write-down? Did the adjustment have a significant impact on the company's financial statements? Be prepared to discuss your findings in class.

EXERCISE 8-10
Costing Inventory in a
Periodic System

Herbor Company uses a *periodic* inventory system. The company's records show the beginning inventory of product no. T12 on January 1 and the purchases of this item during the current year to be as follows:

Jan. 1 Beginning inventory	900 units @ $10.00	$ 9,000
Feb. 23 Purchase	1,200 units @ $11.00	13,200
Apr. 20 Purchase	3,000 units @ $11.20	33,600
May 4 Purchase	4,000 units @ $11.60	46,400
Nov. 30 Purchase	900 units @ $13.00	11,700
Totals	10,000 units	$113,900

A physical count indicates 1,600 units in inventory at year-end.

Determine the cost of the ending inventory, based upon each of the following methods of inventory valuation. (Remember to use *periodic* inventory costing procedures.)

a. Average cost

b. FIFO

c. LIFO

d. Which of the above methods (if any) result in the same ending inventory valuation under *both* periodic and perpetual costing procedures? Explain.

EXERCISE 8-11
Effects of Errors in
Inventory Valuation

Norfleet Company prepared the following condensed income statements for two successive years:

	1999	1998
Sales	$1,500,000	$1,440,000
Cost of goods sold	879,600	914,400
Gross profit on sales	$ 620,400	$ 525,600
Operating expenses	460,500	447,000
Net income	$ 159,900	$ 78,600

At the end of 1998 (right-hand column above) the inventory was understated by $50,400, but the error was not discovered until after the accounts had been closed and financial statements prepared at the end of 1999. The balance sheets for the two years showed owner's equity of $414,200 at the end of 1998 and $460,400 at the end of 1999. (Norfleet is organized as a sole proprietorship and does not incur income taxes expense.)

a. Compute the corrected net income figures for 1998 and 1999.

b. Compute the gross profit amounts and the gross profit percentages for each year based upon corrected data.

c. What correction, if any, should be made in the amounts of the company's owner's equity at the end of 1998 and at the end of 1999?

EXERCISE 8-12
Estimating Inventory by
the Gross Profit Method

LO 6

When Anne Blair arrived at her store on the morning of January 29, she found empty shelves and display racks; thieves had broken in during the night and stolen the entire inventory. Blair's accounting records showed that she had had $55,800 inventory on January 1 (cost value). From January 1 to January 29, she had made net sales of $200,000 and net purchases of $142,800. The gross profit during the last several years had consistently averaged 30% of net sales. Blair wishes to file an insurance claim for the theft loss. You are to use the *gross profit method* to estimate the cost of her inventory at the time of the theft. Show computations.

EXERCISE 8-13
Estimating Inventory by
the Retail Method –

LO 6 *used by
sophisticated
retail stores*

Westlake Accessories uses a periodic inventory system, but needs to determine the approximate amount of inventory at the end of each month without taking a physical inventory. From the following information, you are to estimate the cost of goods sold and the cost of the July 31 inventory by the *retail method* of inventory valuation.

	Cost Price	Retail Selling Price
Inventory of merchandise, June 30	$264,800	$400,000
Purchases during July	170,400	240,000
Goods available for sale during July	$435,200	$640,000
Net sales during July		$275,200

EXERCISE 8-14
Inventory Turnover Rate

LO 7

A recent annual report of **General Electric Company** (GE) shows: cost of goods sold, $22,107; inventory at the beginning of the year, $5,321; and inventory at the end of the year, $4,574. (These dollar amounts are in millions.)

a. Compute the inventory turnover rate for the year (round to the nearest tenth).

b. Using the assumption of 365 days in a year, compute the number of days required for the company to sell the amount of its average inventory (round to the nearest day).

c. Assume that an average of 68 days are required for GE to collect its accounts receivable. What is the length of GE's *operating cycle*?

EXERCISE 8-15*
Cost Flows, Cash Flows,
and LIFO Reserves

LO 8

A recent balance sheet of **Wal-Mart** contains the following presentation of inventories (dollar amounts are in thousands):

Inventories:

At replacement cost	$9,779,981	
Less LIFO reserve	511,672	
LIFO		$9,268,309

The income statement indicates that the company pays income taxes equal to approximately 37% of income before taxes.

a. Assume that if Wal-Mart had used *FIFO*, inventory would appear at the amount shown as replacement cost. Over the life of the company, determine the *cumulative amounts* by which the use of LIFO has *reduced* the following financial statement amounts. (Include a brief explanation of each answer.)

---

*Supplemental Topic, "LIFO Reserves."

1. Taxable income
2. Income taxes expense
3. Net income

b. Would Wal-Mart's net income over the years have been higher or lower had the company been using *FIFO?* How about the net cash flows provided by operating activities? Explain fully.

c. Assume that in the coming year, Wal-Mart liquidates some of its LIFO reserve. What effect would you expect this action to have upon the company's *gross profit rate?* Explain.

EXERCISE 8-16
Toys "R" Us
Operating Cycle

The annual report of **Toys "R" Us** appears in Appendix A at the end of this textbook. Using figures from the income statement and balance sheet, answer the following questions:

a. What was the company's inventory turnover rate for the year ending January 28, 1995?

b. Using your answer from part **a,** what was the average number of days that merchandise remained in stock before it was sold?

c. Are the figures computed in parts **a** and **b** subject to seasonal fluctuations? Explain your answer.

d. Would you expect the company's operating cycle to be influenced significantly by its accounts receivable turnover rate? Explain your answer.

PROBLEMS

PROBLEM 8-1
Evaluating Different
Inventory Methods

A note to the recent financial statements of **The Quaker Oats Company** includes the following information:

Inventories: Inventories are valued at the lower-of-cost-or-market, using various cost methods. The percentage of year-end inventories valued using each of the methods is as follows:

June 30 (fiscal year-end)

Average cost	54%
Last-in, first-out (LIFO)	29%
First-in, first-out (FIFO)	17%

INSTRUCTIONS

a. Does the company's use of three different inventory methods violate the accounting principle of consistency?

b. Assuming that the replacement cost of inventories has been steadily rising, would the company's reported net income be higher or lower if all inventories were valued by the FIFO method?

c. Assume that management's primary objective is to minimize income taxes. Which inventory valuation method would you recommend using in the income tax returns? Would this recommendation influence your choice of inventory valuation methods used in the financial statements? Explain your answers.

PROBLEM 8-2
Perpetual Inventory
Records; FIFO

A perpetual inventory system is used by Black Hawk, Inc., and separate inventory records are maintained for each type of product in stock. The following transactions show beginning inventory, purchases, and sales of CT-300, a cellular telephone, for the month of May:

May 1	Balance on hand, 20 units, cost $40 each		$800
May 5	Sale, 8 units, sales price $60 each		480
May 6	Purchase, 20 units, cost $45 each		900
May 21	Sale, 10 units, sales price $60 each		600
May 31	Sale, 15 units, sales price $65 each		975

INSTRUCTIONS

a. Record the beginning inventory, the purchases, the cost of goods sold, and the running balance on an inventory subsidiary record like the one illustrated on page 369. Use the *first-in, first-out* (FIFO) method.

b. Prepare general journal entries to record the purchases and sales in May. Assume that all transactions were on account.

c. Explain why the company's choice of the FIFO method may result in a more "accurate" presentation of its balance sheet than its income statement.

PROBLEM 8-3
Perpetual Inventory Records in a Small Business; LIFO

Executive Suites, Inc., uses a perpetual inventory system. This system includes a perpetual inventory record for each of the 60 types of products the company keeps in stock. The following transactions show the purchases and sales of a particular desk chair (product code DC-7) during September:

Sept. 1	Balance on hand, 50 units, cost $60 each	$3,000
Sept. 4	Purchase, 20 units, cost $65 each	1,300
Sept. 8	Sale, 35 units, sales price $100 each	3,500
Sept. 9	Purchase, 40 units, cost $65 each	2,600
Sept. 20	Sale, 60 units, sales price $100 each	6,000
Sept. 25	Purchase, 40 units, cost $70 each	2,800
Sept. 30	Sale, 5 units, sales price $110 each	550

INSTRUCTIONS

a. Record the beginning inventory, the purchases, the cost of goods sold, and the running balance on an inventory subsidiary record like the one illustrated on page 370). Use the *last-in, first out* (LIFO) method.

b. Prepare general journal entries to record these purchases and sales in September. Assume that all transactions were on account.

c. Explain why the company's choice of the LIFO method may result in a more "accurate" presentation of its income statement than its balance sheet.

PROBLEM 8-4
Four Methods of Inventory Valuation

On January 15, 1998, California Irrigation sold 1,000 RainMaster-30 oscillating sprinkler heads to Rancho Landscaping. Immediately prior to this sale, California's perpetual inventory records for this sprinkler head included the following cost layers:

Purchase Date	Quantity	Unit Cost	Total Cost
December 12, 1997	600	$9.25	$ 5,550
January 9, 1998	900	9.50	8,550
Total on hand	1,500		$14,100

INSTRUCTIONS

(*Note:* We present this problem in the normal sequence of the accounting cycle—that is, journal entries before ledger entries. However, you may find it helpful to work part **b** first.)

a. Prepare a separate journal entry to record the cost of goods sold relating to the January 15 sale of 1,000 RainMaster-30 sprinkler heads, assuming that California Irrigation uses:
   1. Specific identification (500 of the units sold were purchased on December 12, and the remaining 500 were purchased on January 9).
   2. Average cost.
   3. FIFO.
   4. LIFO.

b. Complete a subsidiary ledger record for RainMaster-30 sprinkler heads using each of the four inventory valuation methods listed above. Your inventory records should show both purchases of this product, the sale on January 15, and the balance on hand at December 12, January 9, and January 15. Use the formats for inventory subsidiary records illustrated on pages 367–370 of this chapter.

c. Refer to the cost of goods sold figures computed in part **a.** For financial reporting purposes, can the company use the valuation method that resulted in the *lowest* cost of goods sold if, for tax purposes, it used the method that resulted in the *highest* cost of goods sold? Explain.

Problems 8-5 and 8-6 are based upon the following data: SK Marine sells high-performance marine equipment to power boat owners. Apollo Outboard recently introduced the world's first 400 horsepower outboard motor—the Apollo 400. During the current year, SK purchased eight of these motors—all intended for resale to customers—at the following dates and acquisition costs:

Purchase Date	Units Purchased	Unit Cost	Total Cost
July 1	2	$4,450	$ 8,900
July 22	3	4,600	13,800
Aug. 3	3	4,700	14,100
Available for sale during the year	8		$36,800

On *July 28*, SK sold four of these motors to Mr. G Racing Associates. The other four motors remained in inventory at September 30, the end of SK's fiscal year.

PROBLEM 8-5
Alternative Flow
Assumptions

Assume that SK uses a *perpetual inventory system*. (See data above.)

INSTRUCTIONS

a. Compute (a) the cost of goods sold relating to the sale on July 28, and (b) the ending inventory of Apollo outboard motors at September 30, using each of the following flow assumptions:
  1. Average cost
  2. FIFO
  3. LIFO
Show the number of units and the unit costs of each cost layer comprising the cost of goods sold and the ending inventory.

b. In part **a**, you have determined SK's cost of Apollo motors sold using three different inventory flow assumptions.
  1. Which of these methods will result in SK Marine reporting the *highest net income* for the current year? Would this always be the case? Explain.
  2. Which of these methods will *minimize the income taxes owed* by SK for the year? Would you expect this usually to be the case? Explain.
  3. May SK use the method resulting in the highest net income in its financial statements, and one which minimizes taxable income in its income tax returns? Explain.

PROBLEM 8-6
Periodic Costing
Procedures

Assume that SK Marine uses a *periodic inventory system*. (See data preceding Problem 8-5.)

INSTRUCTIONS
Compute the ending inventory of Apollo motors at September 30 and the cost of goods sold through this date under each of the following periodic costing procedures. Show the number of units and the unit costs in each cost layer of the *ending inventory*. (You may determine the cost of goods sold by deducting ending inventory from the cost of goods available for sale.)

a. Average cost

b. FIFO

c. LIFO

d. If Apollo uses the LIFO method for financial reporting purposes can it use the FIFO method for income tax purposes? Explain.

PROBLEM 8-7
Year-End Adjustments;
Shrinkage Losses and LCM

Bunyon's Trees & Shrubs uses a perpetual inventory system. At December 31, the perpetual inventory records indicate the following quantities of a particular 5-gallon tree:

	Quantity	Unit Cost	Total Cost
First purchase (oldest)	230	$18	$ 4,140
Second purchase	200	19	3,800
Third purchase	170	20	3,400
Total	600		$11,340

A year-end physical inventory, however, shows only 560 of these trees on hand.

In its financial statements, Bunyon's values its inventories at the lower-of-cost-or-market. At year-end, the per-unit replacement cost of this tree is $21. (Use $2,000 as the "level of materiality" in deciding whether to debit losses to Cost of Goods Sold or to a separate loss account.)

INSTRUCTIONS

Prepare the journal entries required to adjust the inventory records at year-end, assuming that:

a. Bunyon's uses:
   1. Average cost
   2. Last-in, first-out

b. Bunyon's uses the first-in, first-out method. However, the replacement cost of the trees at year-end is $15 apiece, rather than the $21 stated originally. [Make separate journal entries to record (1) the shrinkage losses, and (2) the restatement of the inventory at a "market" value lower than cost. Record the shrinkage losses first.]

c. Assume that the company had been experiencing monthly inventory shrinkage of 20 to 50 trees for several months. In response, management placed several hidden security cameras throughout the premises. Within days, an employee was caught "on film" loading potted trees into his pickup truck. The employee's attorney asked that the case be dropped because the company had "unethically used a hidden camera to entrap his client." Do you agree with the attorney? Defend your answer.

PROBLEM 8-8
Periodic Inventory Costing
Procedures

Audio Shop uses a periodic inventory system. One of the most popular items carried in stock by Audio Shop is an 8-inch speaker unit. The inventory quantities, purchases, and sales of this unit for the most recent year are shown below.

	Number of Units	Cost Per Unit	Total Cost
Inventory, Jan. 1	2,700	$30.00	$ 81,000
First purchase (May 12)	3,540	30.60	108,324
Second purchase (July 9)	2,400	31.05	74,520
Third purchase (Oct. 4)	1,860	32.10	59,706
Fourth purchase (Dec. 18)	3,000	32.55	97,650
Goods available for sale	13,500		$421,200
Units sold during the year	10,400		
Inventory, Dec. 31	3,100		

INSTRUCTIONS

a. Using *periodic* costing procedures, compute the cost of the December 31 inventory and the cost of goods sold for the 8-inch speaker units during the year under each of the following cost flow assumptions:

1. First-in, first-out

2. Last-in, first-out

3. Average cost

b. Which of the three inventory pricing methods provides the most realistic balance sheet valuation of inventory in light of the current replacement cost of the speaker units? Does this same method also produce the most realistic measure of income in light of the costs being incurred by Audio Shop to replace the speakers when they are sold? Explain.

PROBLEM 8-9

Comparison of Periodic and Perpetual Inventory Systems

During 1998, Playground Specialists purchased six BigGym redwood playground sets at the following dates and acquisition costs:

Date	Units Purchased	Unit Cost	Total Cost
Aug. 4...	2	$2,100	$ 4,200
Sep. 23...	2	2,300	4,600
Oct. 2	2	2,560	5,120
Available for sale during the year............................	6		$13,920

On *September 25,* the company sold three of these BigGym sets to the Department of Parks and Recreation. The other three sets remained in inventory at December 31.

INSTRUCTIONS

a. Assume that Playground Specialists uses a *perpetual inventory system.* Using each of the flow assumptions listed below, compute (a) the cost of goods sold relating to the sale of BigGym playground sets on September 25, and (b) the cost of the BigGym sets in inventory at December 31.

1. Average cost

2. FIFO

3. LIFO

Show the number of units and the unit costs of each cost layer comprising the cost of goods sold and the ending inventory.

b. Assume that Playground Specialists uses a *periodic inventory system.* Compute the ending inventory of BigGym playground sets at December 31, and the related cost of goods sold under each of the following year-end costing procedures:

1. Average cost

2. FIFO

3. LIFO

Show the number of units and the unit costs in each cost layer of the ending inventory. (You may determine the cost of goods sold by deducting ending inventory from the cost of goods available for sale.)

c. Now assume that Playground Specialists maintains perpetual inventory records and uses the LIFO flow assumption. At year-end, however, the company *adjusts its inventory records* to reflect the costs indicated by applying *periodic* LIFO costing procedures (as in part **b**). Prepare a journal entry to adjust the Inventory account for the revaluation of the BigGym playground sets in the year-end inventory.

d. Explain why a company using a perpetual inventory system would restate its year-end inventory to the unit costs indicated by periodic LIFO costing procedures.

PROBLEM 8-10
Effects of Inventory
Errors on Earnings

LO 5

The owners of Night & Day Window Coverings are offering the business for sale as a go-ing concern. The income statements of the business for the three years of its existence are summarized below:

	1999	1998	1997
Net sales	$860,000	$850,000	$800,000
Cost of goods sold	481,600	486,000	480,000
Gross profit on sales	$378,400	$364,000	$320,000
Gross profit percentage	44%	43%*	40%

*Rounded to nearest full percentage point.

In negotiations with prospective buyers of the business, the owners of Night & Day are calling attention to the rising trends of the gross profit and of the gross profit percent-age as very favorable elements.

Assume that you are retained by a prospective purchaser of the business to make an investigation of the fairness and reliability of Night & Day's accounting records and fi-nancial statements. You find everything in order except for the following: (1) An arith-metic error in the computation of inventory at the end of 1997 had caused a $24,000 understatement in that inventory, and (2) a duplication of figures in the computation of inventory at the end of 1999 had caused an overstatement of $43,000 in that inven-tory. The company uses the periodic inventory system and these errors had not been brought to light prior to your investigation.

INSTRUCTIONS

a. Prepare a revised three-year schedule similar to the one illustrated above.

b. Comment on the trend of gross profit and gross profit percentage before and after the revision.

PROBLEM 8-11
Retail Method

LO 6

Cherry Vanilla is called a "record" store, but its sales consist almost entirely of tapes and CDs. The company uses a periodic inventory system but also uses the retail method to estimate its monthly, quarterly, and annual cost of goods sold and ending inventory.

During the current year, Cherry Vanilla offered for sale merchandise which had cost a total of *$385,000*. As required by the retail method, the company also kept track of the retail sales value of this merchandise, which amounted to *$700,000*. The store's net sales for the year were *$620,000*.

INSTRUCTIONS

a. Using the retail method, estimate (1) the cost of goods sold during the year, and (2) the inventory at the end of the year.

b. At year-end, Cherry Vanilla takes a physical inventory. The manager walks through the store counting each type of product and reading its retail price into a tape recorder. From this tape recording, an employee prepares a schedule listing the entire ending inventory at retail sales prices. The inventory on hand at year-end had a retail sales value of *$70,400*.

  1. Use the cost ratio determined in part **a** to reduce the inventory counted by the manager from its retail value to an estimate of its cost.

  2. Determine the estimated shrinkage losses (measured at cost) incurred by Cherry Vanilla during the year.

  3. Compute the store's gross profit for the year. (Include shrinkage losses in the cost of goods sold.)

c. What controls might the company implement to reduce inventory shrinkage?

PROBLEM 8-12
What if They'd Used FIFO?

LO 1,7

Oshkosh B'Gosh, Inc., uses LIFO. Recent financial statements included the following data (dollars in thousands):

Average inventory (throughout the year)	$ 81,554
Current assets (at year-end)	115,852
Current liabilities (at year-end)	27,175
Net sales	315,076
Cost of goods sold	209,006
Gross profit	106,070

A note accompanying these statements indicated that had the company used the *FIFO* inventory method (dollars in thousands):

1. Average inventory would have been $88,474 ($6,920 *higher* than the LIFO amount).
2. Ending inventory would have been valued at a cost of $96,115 ($6,781 *higher* than the LIFO cost).
3. The cost of goods sold would have been $209,284 ($278 *higher* than that reported in the company's income statement).

INSTRUCTIONS

a. Using the data contained in the company's financial statements (based upon the LIFO method), compute the following analytical measurements. (Round to the nearest tenth.)
   1. Inventory turnover rate
   2. Current ratio
   3. Gross profit rate

b. *Recompute* the three ratios required in part **a** in a manner that will be *directly comparable* to those of a company using the FIFO method in its financial statements. (Round to the nearest tenth.)

c. Notice that the cost of goods sold is *higher* under FIFO than LIFO. What circumstances must the company have encountered to cause this somewhat unusual situation?

CASES

CASE 8-1
Say What?

LO 7

Lewis Galoob Toys, Inc., manufactures toys, including the popular Micro-Machines. A recent annual report indicates (dollar amounts in thousands): sales, $134,334; cost of goods sold, $82,875; average inventories, $13,325. Galoob's accounts receivable turnover rate was 3.9.

Toys "R" Us is the world's largest chain of retail toy stores. It offers customers an extremely large selection of merchandise; in fact, it might be described as a giant "toys warehouse." Toys "R" Us sells only for cash (including bank credit cards).[11] The company's annual report appears in Appendix A of this textbook, following Chapter 14.

INSTRUCTIONS

a. Compute the following for each of these companies:
   1. Inventory turnover rate. (Round to the nearest tenth; for Toys "R" Us, use statistics for the year ended January 28, 1995.)
   2. Number of days required to sell a quantity of goods equal to the average inventory. (Round to the nearest day.)
   3. Number of days (on average) required to collect accounts receivable. [Round to the nearest day. For Galoob, compute this number using the accounts receivable

---

[11]The small amounts of accounts receivable listed in the Toys "R" Us balance sheet are refunds due from *suppliers,* not receivable from credit sales.

turnover rate as described in Chapter 7 (page 330). For Toys "R" Us, assume *zero* days, as the company makes only cash sales.]

   4. The operating cycle (to the nearest full day).

b. Based upon the nature of these companies, why do you think that Toys "R" Us has the lower inventory turnover rate?

c. From the viewpoint of a short-term creditor, explain whether you consider the inventory of one of these companies significantly more liquid than that of the other.

d. Assume you have heard the following rumor: "Galoob currently supplies about 40% of the merchandise sold by Toys "R" Us. But the two companies are about to sign a contract that will make Galoob the *sole supplier* for Toys "R" Us' worldwide operations. This should more than double Galoob's annual sales."

   Using the data available in this assignment, comment upon the potential validity of this statement.

CASE 8-2
It's Not Right, but at Least
It's Consistent

(***Note to students:*** This case requires some research beyond the content of this chapter. We ask that you read the section of Chapter 14 dealing with "Ethical Conduct in the Accounting Profession." Notice especially the discussions relating to *confidentiality*.) Our Little Secret is a small manufacturer of swimsuits and other beach apparel. The company is closely held and has no external reporting obligations, other than payroll reports and income tax returns. The company's accounting system is grossly inadequate. Accounting records are maintained by clerical employees with little knowledge of accounting and with many other job responsibilities. Management has decided that the company must hire a competent controller, who can establish and oversee an adequate accounting system.

Amy Lee, CPA, has applied for this position. During a recent interview, Dean Frost, the company's director of personnel, said "Amy, the job is yours. But you should know that we have a big inventory problem here.

"For some time now, it appears that we have been understating our ending inventory in income tax returns. No one knows when this all got started, or who was responsible. We never even counted our inventory until a few months ago. But the problem is pretty big. In our latest tax return—that's for 1998—we listed inventory at only about half its actual cost. That's an understatement of, maybe, $400,000.

"We don't know what to do. We sure don't want a big scandal—tax evasion, and all that. Maybe the best thing is continue understating inventory by the same amount as we did in 1998. That way, taxable income will be correctly stated in future years. Anyway, this is just something I thought you should know about."

INSTRUCTIONS

a. Briefly identify the ethical issues raised for Lee by Frost's disclosure.

b. From Lee's perspective, evaluate the possible solution proposed by Frost.

c. Identify and discuss the alternative ethical courses of action which are open to Lee.

CASE 8-3
FIFO vs. LIFO: A
Challenging Analysis

WhiteOut, a successful manufacturer of ski apparel, has been using LIFO during a period of rising prices.

INSTRUCTIONS

a. Indicate whether each of the following financial measurements would have been *higher, lower,* or *unaffected* had the company been using FIFO. Explain the reasoning behind your answers.

   1. Gross profit rate
   2. Reported net income
   3. Current ratio (assume greater than 1 to 1)
   4. Inventory turnover rate

5. Accounts receivable turnover rate
6. Cash payments to merchandise suppliers
7. Net cash flow from operating activities (assume positive)

b. Provide *your own* assessment of whether using LIFO has made WhiteOut more or less (1) solvent, (2) "well-off." Explain fully.

*CASE 8-4

Call Up the (LIFO) Reserves!

Steel Specialties has been in business for 52 years. The company maintains a perpetual inventory system, uses a LIFO flow assumption, and ends its fiscal year at December 31. At year-end, the cost of goods sold and inventory are adjusted to reflect periodic LIFO costing procedures.

A railroad strike has delayed the arrival of purchases ordered during the last several months of 1998, and Steel Specialties has not been able to replenish its inventories as merchandise is sold. At December 22, one product appears in the company's perpetual inventory records at the following unit costs:

Purchase Date	Quantity	Unit Cost	Total Cost
Nov. 14, 1954	3,000	$6	$18,000
Apr. 12, 1955	2,000	8	16,000
Available for sale at Dec. 22, 1998	5,000		$34,000

Steel Specialties has another 8,000 units of this product on order at the current wholesale cost of $30 per unit. Because of the railroad strike, however, these units have not yet arrived (the terms of purchase are F.O.B. destination). Steel Specialties also has an order from a customer who wants to purchase 4,000 units of this product at the retail sales price of $45 per unit. Steel Specialties intends to make this sale on December 30, regardless of whether or not the 8,000 units on order arrive by this date. (The 4,000-unit sale will be shipped by truck, F.O.B. shipping point.)

INSTRUCTIONS

a. Are the units in inventory really almost 40 years old? Explain.

b. Prepare a schedule showing the sales revenue, cost of goods sold, and gross profit that will result from this sale on December 30, assuming that the 8,000 units currently on order (1) arrive before year-end, and (2) do not arrive until sometime in the following year. (In each computation, show the number of units comprising the cost of goods sold and their related per-unit costs.)

c. Comment upon these results.

d. Might management be wise to delay this sale by a few days? Explain.

INTERNET ASSIGNMENTS

INTERNET 8-1

Forensic Accounting

The management of Precious Metals, Inc., has been encountering inventory shrinkage for several months. They fear that someone has been tampering with the company's computerized inventory records. A suspect has been identified, and the company's attorney has been contacted for advice. The attorney suggests that the company engage the services of a "forensic accountant" to gather evidence for use in a court of law.

Visit the Forensic Accounting home page at the following Internet address:

www.forensicaccounting.com

---

*Supplemental Topic, "LIFO Reserves."

INSTRUCTIONS

Describe how a forensic accountant might help management determine whether the suspect they have identified has been tampering with the company's computerized inventory records.

Additional Internet assignments for this chapter are found in Appendix B at the end of this textbook.

OUR COMMENTS ON THE IN-TEXT CASES

YOU AS A BANKER (P. 386)   Over time, a tighter credit policy is likely to improve the quality of the company's credit accounts, and should decrease the average time that its accounts receivable remain outstanding. Likewise, the adoption of a just-in-time inventory system will increase inventory turnover, and will have the potential to greatly reduce the length of time that cash remains tied-up in inventory. In short, if the changes suggested by management are successful, they should result in a reduced operating cycle. Whether they will reduce the cycle by 100 days remains to be seen, however. It is the banker's professional responsibility to view these projections with cautious optimism.

YOU AS A BUSINESS OWNER (P. 389)   The LIFO method normally does result in a lower taxable income during periods of rising prices, as long as the old, low-cost inventory "layers" are not depleted. In our example, the truck drivers' strike forced the business to sell almost all of its inventory — including the old, low-cost layers. When these items were sold, their relatively low and outdated acquisition costs were matched against the revenues of the current period. As a consequence, the unusually high gross profit on these sales drove taxable income up unexpectedly. This risk associated with the LIFO method is sometimes referred to as the *liquidation of the LIFO reserve.*

ANSWERS TO SELF-TEST QUESTIONS
1. b   **2.** a, c, d   **3.** a   **4.** b   **5.** b   **6.** a, b, c, d

CHAPTER 9

PLANT ASSETS AND DEPRECIATION

Just as different flow assumptions may be used in accounting for inventories, different depreciation methods may be used in accounting for plant assets. These methods affect the measurement of net income, but they have no effect upon cash flows—except for income taxes. If this is beginning to sound familiar, you're developing a "feel" for accounting information.

1. Determine the cost of plant assets.
2. Distinguish between capital expenditures and revenue expenditures.
3. Compute depreciation by the straight-line and declining-balance methods.
4. Compute depreciation for income tax purposes using *MACRS*.

5. Account for disposals of plant assets.
6. Explain the nature of intangible assets, including goodwill.
7. Account for the depletion of natural resources.
8. Explain the cash effects of transactions involving plant assets.

The term **plant assets** (or *plant and equipment*) describes long-lived assets acquired for use in business operations rather than for resale to customers. Plant assets comprise the largest category of assets in most balance sheets. A recent balance sheet of Exxon Corporation, for example, shows "Property, plant, and equipment" of more than *$65 billion*. This amounts to more than *70%* of Exxon's total assets.

PLANT ASSETS AS A "STREAM OF FUTURE SERVICES"

Plant assets are similar to long-term prepaid expenses. Ownership of a delivery truck, for example, may provide about 100,000 miles of transportation. The cost of the truck is entered in an asset account, which in essence represents the *advance purchase* of these transportation services. Similarly, a building represents the advance purchase of many years of housing services. As the years go by, these services are utilized by the business, and the cost of the plant asset gradually is transferred to depreciation expense.

MAJOR CATEGORIES OF PLANT ASSETS

Plant and equipment items are often classified into the following groups:

1. ***Tangible plant assets.*** The term "tangible" denotes physical substance, as exemplified by land, a building, or a machine. This category may be subdivided into two distinct classifications:
   a. Plant property subject to depreciation; included are plant assets of limited useful life such as buildings and office equipment.
   b. Land. The only plant asset not subject to depreciation is land, which has an unlimited term of existence.

2. ***Intangible assets.*** The term "intangible assets" is used to describe assets which are used in the operation of the business but have no physical substance and are noncurrent. Examples include patents, copyrights, trademarks, franchises, and goodwill. Current assets such as accounts receivable or prepaid rent are not included in the intangible classification, even though they are lacking in physical substance.

3. ***Natural resources.*** A site acquired for the purpose of extracting or removing some valuable resource such as oil, minerals, or timber is classified as a *natural resource,* not as land. This type of plant asset is gradually converted into *inventory* as the natural resource is extracted from the site.

ACCOUNTABLE EVENTS IN THE LIVES OF PLANT ASSETS

For all categories of plant assets, there are three basic *accountable events:* (1) acquisition, (2) allocation of the acquisition cost to expense over the asset's useful life (depreciation), and (3) sale or disposal.

ACQUISITIONS OF PLANT ASSETS

The cost of a plant asset includes all expenditures that are *reasonable* and *necessary* for getting the asset to the desired location and *ready for use*. Thus, many incidental costs may be included in the cost assigned to a plant asset. These include, for example, sales taxes on the purchase price, delivery costs, and installation costs.

LO 1 *Determine the cost of plant assets.*

But only reasonable and necessary costs should be included. Assume, for example, that a machine is dropped and damaged while it is being unloaded. The cost of repairing this damage should be recognized as expense of the current period, *not* added to the cost of the machine. Although it is necessary to repair the machine, it was not necessary to drop it—and that's what brought about the need for the repairs.

Companies often purchase plant assets on an installment plan, or by issuing a note payable. Interest charges after the asset is ready for use are recorded as interest expense, not as part of the cost of the asset. But if a company constructs a plant asset for its own use, the interest charges *during the construction period* are viewed as part of the asset's cost.[1]

DETERMINING COST: AN EXAMPLE

The concept of including in the cost of a plant asset all of the incidental charges necessary to put the asset in use is illustrated by the following example. A factory in Minneapolis orders a machine from a San Francisco tool manufacturer at a list price of $10,000. Payment will be made in 48 monthly installments of $250, which include $2,000 in interest charges. Sales taxes of $600 must be paid, as well as freight charges of $1,250. Installation and other "start-up" costs amount to $400. The cost of this machine to be debited to the Machinery account is computed below:

List price*	$10,000
Sales taxes	600
Transportation charges	1,250
Cost of installation and set-up	400
Total	$12,250

All reasonable and necessary costs are capitalized

*The $2,000 in interest charges on the installment purchase will be recognized as interest expense over the next 48 months. (Accounting for installment notes payable is discussed in the next chapter.)

SOME SPECIAL CONSIDERATIONS

LAND When land is purchased, various incidental costs are generally incurred, in addition to the purchase price. These additional costs may include commissions to real estate brokers, escrow fees, legal fees for examining and insuring the title, delinquent taxes paid by the purchaser, and fees for surveying, draining, clearing, and grading the property. All these expenditures become part of the cost of the land.

Sometimes land purchased as a building site has on it an old building which is not suitable for the buyer's use. In this case, the only useful "asset" being acquired is the land. Therefore, the entire purchase price is charged to the Land account, along with the costs of tearing down and removing the unusable building.

---

[1]*FASB Statement No. 34*, "Capitalization of Interest Costs," (Norwalk, Conn.: 1979).

LAND IMPROVEMENTS Improvements to real estate such as driveways, fences, parking lots, landscaping, and sprinkler systems have a limited life and are therefore subject to depreciation. For this reason they should be recorded in a separate account entitled Land Improvements.

BUILDINGS Old buildings are sometimes purchased with the intention of repairing them prior to placing them in use. Repairs made under these circumstances are charged to the Buildings account. After the building has been placed in use, ordinary repairs are considered to be maintenance expense when incurred.

EQUIPMENT When equipment is purchased, all of the sales taxes, delivery costs, and costs of getting the equipment "in good running order" are treated as part of the cost of the asset. Once the equipment has been placed in operation, maintenance costs—including interest, insurance, and property taxes—are treated as expenses of the current period.

ALLOCATION OF A LUMP-SUM PURCHASE Several different types of plant assets often are purchased at one time. Separate controlling accounts are maintained for each type of plant asset, such as land, buildings, and equipment.[2]

When land and buildings (and perhaps other assets) are purchased for a lump sum, the purchase price must be *allocated* among the types of assets acquired. An appraisal may be needed for this purpose. Assume, for example, that Holiday Workout purchases a complete fitness center from Golden Health Spas. Holiday purchases the entire facility at a bargain price of $800,000. The allocation of this cost on the basis of an appraisal is illustrated below:

	Value per Appraisal	Percentage of Appraised Value	Allocation of $800,000 Cost
Land	$ 250,000	25%	$200,000
Land improvements	50,000	5%	40,000
Building	300,000	30%	240,000
Equipment	400,000	40%	320,000
Total	$1,000,000	100%	$800,000

Total cost is allocated in proportion to appraised values

Assuming that Holiday purchased this facility for cash, the journal entry to record this acquisition would be:

The journal entry allocating the total cost

Land	200,000	
Land improvements	40,000	
Building	240,000	
Equipment	320,000	
Cash		800,000
To record purchase of fitness center from Golden Health Spas for cash.		

CAPITAL EXPENDITURES AND REVENUE EXPENDITURES

Expenditures for the purchase or expansion of plant assets are called **capital expenditures** and are recorded in asset accounts. Accountants often use the verb **capitalize** to mean charging an expenditure to an asset account rather than to an expense account. Expenditures for ordinary repairs, maintenance,

---

[2]Each controlling account is supported by a subsidiary ledger providing information about the cost, annual depreciation, and book value of each asset (or group of similar assets).

fuel, and other items necessary to the ownership and use of plant and equipment are called **revenue expenditures** and are recorded by debiting expense accounts. The charge to an expense account is based on the assumption that the benefits from the expenditure will be used up in the current period, and the cost should therefore be deducted from the revenue of the period in determining the net income. Charging an expenditure directly to an expense account is often called "expensing" the item.

A business may purchase many small items which will benefit several accounting periods but which have a relatively low cost. Examples of such items include auto batteries, wastebaskets, and pencil sharpeners. Such items are theoretically capital expenditures, but if they are recorded as assets in the accounting records it will be necessary to compute and record the related depreciation expense in future periods. We have previously mentioned the idea that the extra work involved in developing more precise accounting information should be weighed against the benefits that result. Thus, for reasons of convenience and economy, expenditures which are *not material* in dollar amount are treated in the accounting records as expenses of the current period.

In brief, any material expenditure that will benefit several accounting periods is considered a *capital expenditure.* Any expenditure that will benefit only the current period or that is not material in amount is treated as a *revenue expenditure.*

Many companies develop formal policy statements defining capital and revenue expenditures as a guide toward consistent accounting practice from year to year. These policy statements often set a minimum dollar amount (such as $500) for expenditures that are to be capitalized.

LO 2 *Distinguish between capital expenditures and revenue expenditures.*

DEPRECIATION

We first introduced the concept of depreciation in Chapter 3. We will now expand that discussion to address such topics as residual values, alternative depreciation methods, and depreciation (or cost recovery) for income tax purposes.

ALLOCATING THE COST OF PLANT AND EQUIPMENT OVER THE YEARS OF USE

Tangible plant assets, with the exception of land, are of use to a company for only a limited number of years. **Depreciation,** as the term is used in accounting, is the *allocation of the cost of a tangible plant asset to expense in the periods in which services are received from the asset.* In short, the basic purpose of depreciation is to achieve the *matching principle*—that is, to offset the revenue of an accounting period with the costs of the goods and services being consumed in the effort to generate that revenue.

Earlier in this chapter, we described a delivery truck as a stream of "transportation services" to be received over the years that the truck is owned and used. The cost of the truck initially is debited to an asset account, because this purchase of these transportation services will benefit many future accounting periods. As these services are received, however, the cost of the truck gradually is removed from the balance sheet and allocated to expense, through the process called depreciation.

The journal entry to record depreciation expense consists of a debit to Depreciation Expense and a credit to Accumulated Depreciation. The credit portion of the entry removes from the balance sheet that portion of the asset's cost estimated to have been used up during the current period. The debit portion of the entry allocates this expired cost to expense.

Depreciation: a process of allocating the cost of an asset to expense

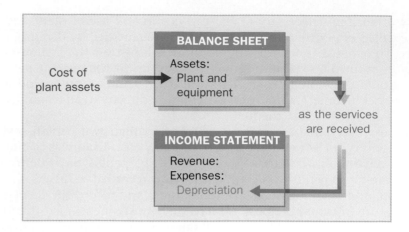

Separate Depreciation Expense and Accumulated Depreciation accounts are maintained for different types of depreciable assets, such as factory buildings, delivery equipment, and office equipment. These separate accounts help accountants to measure separately the costs of different business activities, such as manufacturing, sales, and administration.

DEPRECIATION IS NOT A PROCESS OF VALUATION Depreciation is a process of *cost allocation,* not a process of valuation. Accounting records do not attempt to show the current market values of plant assets. The market value of a building, for example, may increase during some accounting periods within the building's useful life. The recognition of depreciation expense continues, however, without regard to such temporary increases in market value. Accountants recognize that the building will render useful services only for a limited number of years, and that the full cost of the building should be *systematically allocated to expense* during these years.

Depreciation differs from most other expenses in that it does not depend upon cash payments at or near the time the expense is recorded. For this reason, depreciation often is called a "noncash" expense. Bear in mind, however, that large cash payments may be required at the time depreciable assets are purchased.

BOOK VALUE Plant assets are shown in the balance sheet at their book values (or *carrying values*). The **book value** of a plant asset is its *cost minus the related accumulated depreciation.* Accumulated depreciation is a contra-asset account, representing that portion of the asset's cost that has *already* been allocated to expense. Thus, book value represents the portion of the asset's cost that remains to be allocated to expense in future periods.

CAUSES OF DEPRECIATION

The need to systematically allocate plant asset costs over multiple accounting periods arises from two major causes: (1) deterioration, and (2) obsolescence.

PHYSICAL DETERIORATION Physical deterioration of a plant asset results from use, as well as from exposure to sun, wind, and other climatic factors. When a plant asset has been carefully maintained, it is not uncommon for the owner to claim that the asset is as "good as new." Such statements are not literally true. Although a good repair policy may greatly lengthen the useful life of a machine, every machine eventually reaches the point at which it must be discarded. In brief, the making of repairs does not eliminate the need for recognition of depreciation.

OBSOLESCENCE The term *obsolescence* means the process of becoming out of date or obsolete. An airplane, for example, may become obsolete even though it is in excellent physical condition; it becomes obsolete because better planes of superior design and performance have become available.

CASE IN POINT

Chrysler Corporation recently opened the Jefferson North Assembly Plant in the heart of Detroit. Did Chrysler build this plant because existing facilities had become physically deteriorated beyond use? The answer is no. While existing facilities could still be used to produce automobiles, their production methods had become obsolete.

The Jefferson North Assembly Plant employs the most innovative technologies in the automotive industry. As a result, Chrysler can produce vehicles of higher quality, at a lower cost, and with less pollution, than ever before.

METHODS OF COMPUTING DEPRECIATION

In preceding chapters, we have computed depreciation only by the **straight-line depreciation** method. Companies actually may use any of several different depreciation methods. Generally accepted accounting principles require only that a depreciation method result in a *rational and systematic* allocation of cost over the asset's useful life.

LO 3 *Compute depreciation by the straight-line and declining-balance methods.*

The straight-line method allocates an *equal portion* of depreciation expense to each period of the asset's useful life. Most of the other depreciation methods are various forms of accelerated depreciation. The term **accelerated depreciation** means that larger amounts of depreciation are recognized in the early years of the asset's life, and smaller amounts are recognized in the later years. Over the entire life of the asset, however, both the straight-line method and accelerated methods recognize the same *total* amount of depreciation.

The differences between the straight-line methods and accelerated methods are illustrated in the following graphs:

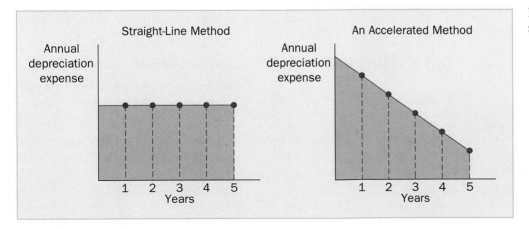

Both methods recognize the same *total* depreciation

There is only one straight-line method. But there are several accelerated methods, each producing slightly different results. Different depreciation methods may be used for different assets. Of course, the depreciation methods in use should be disclosed in notes accompanying the financial statements.

In this chapter, we illustrate and explain straight-line depreciation and several variations of the most widely used accelerated method, which is called *fixed-percentage-of-declining-balance.* Two other depreciation methods are discussed briefly in the *Supplemental Topic* at the end of the chapter.

DATA FOR OUR ILLUSTRATIONS   Our illustrations of depreciation methods are based upon the following data: On January 2, S&G Wholesale Grocery acquires a new delivery truck. The data and estimates needed for the computation of the annual depreciation expense are:

Cost	$17,000
Estimated residual value	$ 2,000
Estimated useful life	5 years

THE STRAIGHT-LINE METHOD

The straight-line method was introduced in Chapter 3. Under this method an *equal portion* of the asset's cost is recognized as depreciation expense in each period of the asset's useful life.

Annual depreciation expense is computed by deducting the estimated **residual value** (or salvage value) from the cost of the asset and dividing the remaining *depreciable cost* by the years of estimated useful life. Using the data in our example, the annual straight-line depreciation is computed as follows:

$$\frac{\textbf{Cost} - \textbf{Residual Value}}{\textbf{Years of Useful Life}} = \frac{\$17,000 - \$2,000}{5 \textbf{ years}} = \$3,000 \textbf{ per year}$$

This same depreciation computation is shown below in tabular form.

Computing depreciation by straight-line method

Cost of the depreciable asset	$17,000
Less: Estimated residual value (amount to be realized by sale of asset when it is retired from use)	2,000
Total amount to be depreciated (depreciable cost)	$15,000
Estimated useful life	5 years
Depreciation expense each year ($15,000 ÷ 5)	$ 3,000

The following schedule summarizes the effects of straight-line depreciation over the entire life of the asset:

Depreciation Schedule: Straight-Line Method

Year	Computation	Depreciation Expense	Accumulated Depreciation	Book Value
				$17,000
First	$15,000 × ⅕	$ 3,000	$ 3,000	14,000
Second	$15,000 × ⅕	3,000	6,000	11,000
Third	$15,000 × ⅕	3,000	9,000	8,000
Fourth	$15,000 × ⅕	3,000	12,000	5,000
Fifth	$15,000 × ⅕	3,000	15,000	2,000
Total		$15,000		

Constant annual depreciation expense

(We present several depreciation schedules in this chapter. In each schedule we highlight in red those features that we want to emphasize.)

Notice that the depreciation expense over the life of the truck totals *$15,000*—the cost of the truck *minus the estimated residual value.* The residual value is *not* part of the cost "used up" in business operations. Instead, the residual value is expected to be recovered in cash upon disposal of the asset.

In practice, residual values are ignored if they are not expected to be *material* in amount. Traditionally, buildings, office equipment, furniture, fixtures, and special-purpose equipment seldom are considered to have significant residual values. Assets such as vehicles, aircraft, and computer systems, in contrast, often do have residual values which are material in amount.

It often is convenient to state the portion of an asset's depreciable cost which will be written off during the year as a percentage, called the *depreciation rate.* When straight-line depreciation is in use, the depreciation rate is simply **1** divided by the *life* (in years) of the asset. The delivery truck in our example has an estimated life of 5 years, so the depreciation expense each year is ⅕, or **20%,** of the depreciable amount. Similarly, an asset with a 10-year life has a depreciation rate of ¹⁄₁₀, or **10%;** and an asset with an 8-year life, a depreciation rate of ⅛, or **12½%.**

DEPRECIATION FOR FRACTIONAL PERIODS When an asset is acquired in the middle of an accounting period, it is not necessary to compute depreciation expense to the nearest day or week. In fact, such a computation would give a misleading impression of great precision. Since depreciation is based upon an estimated useful life of many years, the depreciation applicable to any one year is *only an approximation.*

One widely used method of computing depreciation for part of a year is to round the calculation to the nearest whole month. In our example, S&G acquired the delivery truck on January 2. Therefore, we computed a "full year's" depreciation for the year of acquisition. Assume, however, that the truck had been acquired later in the year, say, on *October 1.* Thus, the truck would have been in use for only 3 months (or ³⁄₁₂) of the first year. In this case, depreciation expense for the first year would be limited to only *$750,* or ³⁄₁₂ of a full year's depreciation ($3,000 × ³⁄₁₂ = $750).

An even more widely used approach, called the **half-year convention,** is to record six months' depreciation on all assets acquired during the year. This approach is based upon the assumption that the actual purchase dates will average out to approximately midyear. The half-year convention is widely used for assets such as office equipment, automobiles, and machinery. For buildings, however, income tax rules require that depreciation be computed for the actual number of months that the building is owned.

Assume that S&G Wholesale Grocery uses straight-line depreciation with the half-year convention. Depreciation on the $17,000 delivery truck with the 5-year life is summarized below:

Depreciation Schedule
Straight-line Method with Half-Year Convention

Year	Computation	Depreciation Expense	Accumulated Depreciation	Book Value
				$17,000
First.......................	$15,000 × ⅕ × ½	$ 1,500	$ 1,500	15,500
Second	$15,000 × ⅕	3,000	4,500	12,500
Third	$15,000 × ⅕	3,000	7,500	9,500
Fourth	$15,000 × ⅕	3,000	10,500	6,500
Fifth........................	$15,000 × ⅕	3,000	13,500	3,500
Sixth.......................	$15,000 × ⅕ × ½	1,500	15,000	2,000
Total...........................		$15,000		

Straight-line with the half-year convention

When the half-year convention is in use, we ignore the date upon which the asset was actually purchased. We simply recognize *one-half year's depreciation* in both the first year and last year of the depreciation schedule. Notice that our depreciation schedule now includes depreciation expense in 6 years, instead of 5. Taking only a partial year's depreciation in the first year always extends the depreciation program into one additional year.

The half-year convention enables us to treat similar assets acquired at different dates during the year as a single group. For example, assume that an insurance company purchases hundreds of desk-top computers throughout the current year at a total cost of $600,000. The company depreciates these computers by the straight-line method, assuming a 5-year life and no residual value. Using the half-year convention, the depreciation expense on all of the computers purchased during the year may be computed as follows: $600,000 ÷ 5 years × $\frac{6}{12}$ = $60,000. If we did not use the half-year convention, depreciation would have to be computed separately for computers purchased in different months.

THE DECLINING-BALANCE METHOD

By far the most widely used accelerated depreciation method is called **fixed-percentage-of-declining-balance.** However the method is used primarily in *income tax returns,* rather than financial statements.

Under the declining-balance method, an accelerated *depreciation rate* is computed as a specified percentage of the straight-line depreciation rate. Annual depreciation expense then is computed by applying this accelerated depreciation rate to the undepreciated cost (current book value) of the asset. This computation may be summarized as follows:

$$\frac{\text{Depreciation}}{\text{Expense}} = \frac{\text{Remaining}}{\text{Book Value}} \times \frac{\text{Accelerated}}{\text{Depreciation Rate}}$$

The accelerated depreciation rate *remains constant* throughout the life of the asset. Hence, this rate represents the "fixed-percentage" described in the name of this depreciation method. The book value (cost minus accumulated depreciation) *decreases every year,* and represents the "declining-balance."

Thus far, we have described the accelerated depreciation rate as a "specified percentage" of the straight-line rate. Most often, this specified percentage is 200%, meaning that the accelerated rate is exactly twice the straight-line rate. As a result, the declining-balance method of depreciation often is called *double-declining-balance* (or 200%-declining-balance). Tax rules, however, often specify a *lower* percentage, such as 150% of the straight-line rate. This version of the declining-balance method may be described as "150%-declining-balance."[3]

DOUBLE-DECLINING-BALANCE   To illustrate the double-declining-balance method, consider our example of the $17,000 delivery truck. The estimated useful life is 5 years; therefore, the straight-line depreciation rate is 20% (1 ÷ 5 years). Doubling this straight-line rate indicates an accelerated depreciation rate of 40%. Each year, we will recognize as depreciation expense 40% of the truck's current book value, as shown below:

Depreciation Schedule: 200% Declining-Balance Method

Year	Computation	Depreciation Expense	Accumulated Depreciation	Book Value	
				$17,000	
First	$17,000 × 40%	$ 6,800	$ 6,800	10,200	Declining-balance at twice
Second	$10,200 × 40%	4,080	10,880	6,120	the straight-line rate
Third	$6,120 × 40%	2,448	13,328	3,672	
Fourth	$3,672 × 40%	1,469	14,797	2,203	
Fifth	$2,203 × 40% = ~~881~~	203	15,000	2,000	
Total		$15,000			

Notice that the estimated residual value of the delivery truck *does not* enter into the computation of depreciation expense until the very end. This is because the declining-balance method provides an *"automatic"* residual value. As long as each year's depreciation expense is equal to only a portion of the undepreciated cost of the asset, the asset *will never be entirely written off.* However, if the asset has a significant residual value, depreciation should *stop at this point.* Since our delivery truck has an estimated residual value of *$2,000,* the depreciation expense for the fifth year should be *limited to $203,* rather than the $881 indicated by taking 40% of the remaining book value. By limiting the last year's depreciation expense in this manner, the book value of the truck at the end of the fifth year will be equal to its $2,000 estimated residual value.

In the schedule illustrated above, we computed a full year's depreciation in the first year, because the asset was acquired on January 2. But if the half-year convention were in use, depreciation in the first year would be *reduced by half,* to $3,400. The depreciation in the second year would be ($17,000 − $3,400) × 40%, or *$5,440.*

150%-DECLINING-BALANCE   Now assume that we wanted to depreciate this truck using 150% of the straight-line rate. In this case, the depreciation rate will be 30%, instead of 40% (a 20% straight-line rate × 150% = 30%). The depreciation schedule appears as follows:

---

[3]The higher the specified percentage of the straight-line rate, the "more accelerated" this depreciation method becomes. Experience and tradition have established 200% of the straight-line rate as the maximum level. Tax rules often specify lower percentages in order to "slow down" the rates at which taxpayers may depreciate specific types of assets in their income tax returns.

Depreciation Schedule: 150% Declining-Balance Method

Year	Computation	Depreciation Expense	Accumulated Depreciation	Book Value
				$17,000
First..............................	$17,000 × 30%	$ 5,100	$5,100	11,900
Second.........................	$11,900 × 30%	3,570	8,670	8,330
Third............................	$8,330 × 30%	2,499	11,169	5,831
Fourth	($5,831 − $2,000) ÷ 2	1,916*	13,085	3,915
Fifth.............................	$3,915 − $2,000	1,915*	15,000	2,000
Total..........................		$15,000		

Declining-balance at 150% of the straight-line rate

*Switched to the straight-line method for years 4 and 5.

Notice that we switched to straight-line depreciation in the last 2 years. The undepreciated cost of the truck at the end of Year 3 was *$5,831*. To depreciate the truck to an estimated residual value of $2,000 at the end of Year 5, $3,831 in depreciation expense must be recognized over the next 2 years. At this point, *larger depreciation charges* can be recognized if we simply allocate this $3,831 by the straight-line method, rather than continuing to compute 30% of the remaining book value. (In our table, we round the allocation of this amount to the nearest dollar.)

Allocating the remaining book value over the remaining life by the straight-line method does *not* represent a change in depreciation methods. Rather, a "switch to straight-line" when this will result in larger depreciation is *part of the declining-balance method*. This is the way in which we arrive at the desired residual value.

MACRS: THE "TAX METHOD"

In 1986, Congress adopted the *Modified Accelerated Cost Recovery System*, called **MACRS** (pronounced "*makers*").[4] Companies may use straight-line depreciation for income tax purposes, but most prefer to use an accelerated method. MACRS is the *only* accelerated depreciation method that may be used in federal income tax returns (for assets placed in service after 1986).

Under MACRS, all plant assets are assigned one of eight recovery periods: 3, 5, 7, 10, 15, 20, 27½, or 39 years. For example, some special-purpose manufacturing tools are classified as "3-year property," meaning that they are depreciated over a three-year life. Automobiles, light trucks, and computers are "5-year property." Any depreciable asset which is not assigned a specific class life is treated as "7-year property."

MACRS depreciation is based upon the fixed-percentage-of-declining-balance method, with one modification—there is *no provision for residual value*. Thus, 100% of the asset's cost is allocated to expense over the specific recovery period. Assets with recovery periods of 10 years or less are depreciated by the 200%-declining-balance method; assets with recovery periods of 15 or 20 years are depreciated by the 150%-declining-balance method. The half-year convention normally is applied in all recovery periods of 20 years or less.[5]

Actually, taxpayers need not compute MACRS depreciation using the declining-balance methods. The Internal Revenue Service publishes *depreciation rate tables* which show the percentage of cost that many be deducted in each year of the recovery period. These tables automatically apply the half-year convention, and also switch to straight-line in the appropriate year to maximize the taxpayer's deduction for depreciation.

LO 4 Compute depreciation for income tax purposes using MACRS.

---

[4]Tax laws use the phrase "cost recovery," instead of the term "depreciation." In this text, we use these terms interchangeably.

[5]The 27½- and 39-year recovery periods apply to residential and nonresidential real property, respectively. Depreciation over these periods is based upon the straight-line method, with amounts in partial years rounded to the nearest month.

A MACRS depreciation rate table for all recovery periods up to 20 years appears below:

MACRS Depreciation Rates*
Recovery Periods

Year	3 Years	5 Years	7 Years	10 Years	15 Years	20 Years	
1	33.33%	20.00%	14.29%	10.00%	5.00%	3.750%	These tables simplify the computation of depreciation for income tax purposes
2	44.45	32.00	24.49	18.00	9.50	7.219	
3	14.81	19.20	17.49	14.40	8.55	6.677	
4	7.41	11.52	12.49	11.52	7.70	6.177	
5		11.52	8.93	9.22	6.93	5.713	
6		5.76	8.92	7.37	6.23	5.285	
7			8.93	6.55	5.90	4.888	
8			4.46	6.55	5.90	4.522	
9				6.56	5.91	4.462	
10				6.55	5.90	4.461	
11				3.28	5.91	4.462	
12					5.90	4.461	
13					5.91	4.462	
14					5.90	4.461	
15					5.91	4.462	
16					2.95	4.461	
17						4.462	
18						4.461	
19						4.462	
20						4.461	
21						2.231	
Total	100.00%	100.00%	100.00%	100.00%	100.00%	100.000%	

*****Caution:** This table is intended for demonstration purposes only. Congress may change the depreciation rates permitted for income tax purposes at any time. Therefore, this table should not be used in the preparation of actual income tax returns. Complete and up-to-date depreciation tables are available without charge from the Internal Revenue Service.

The percentage of the asset's cost that can be deducted in the first year is relatively small, reflecting the half-year convention. After the first year, the percentages start out relatively high and then decline—the basic characteristic of an accelerated depreciation method. Near the end of the recovery period, the percentages stop changing. This represents the switch to the straight-line method in order to depreciate the asset fully.

Notice that the depreciation rates in each recovery period add up to 100%. This demonstrates that the MACRS method fully depreciates all assets, with no provision for salvage value.

COMPUTING DEPRECIATION FOR INCOME TAX PURPOSES: AN ILLUSTRATION   To illustrate the use of the rate table, let us consider our example of S&G Grocery's delivery truck, which cost $17,000. (For tax purposes, we will disregard the $2,000 residual value.) Under current tax rules, light-duty trucks are considered 5-year property.[6] The depreciation expense that may be deducted in the federal income tax return each year is determined as follows:

---

[6]The fact that the estimated useful life of this asset also is 5 years is a mere coincidence. In some cases, recovery periods differ substantially from the estimated useful life. Depreciation for tax purposes is based upon the recovery periods designated by Congress, *without regard* to the useful lives estimated by the company's management.

Depreciation Schedule: MACRS Income Tax Method

Year	Computation (Cost × Rate from IRS Table)	Depreciation Expense	Accumulated Depreciation	Basis (Book Value)
1	$17,000 × 20%	$ 3,400	$ 3,400	$13,600
2	$17,000 × 32%	5,440	8,840	8,160
3	$17,000 × 19.20%	3,264	12,104	4,896
4	$17,000 × 11.52%	1,958	14,062	2,938
5	$17,000 × 11.52%	1,958	16,020	980
6	$17,000 × 5.76%	980	17,000	–0–
Total		$17,000		

Depreciation (or cost recovery) using the MACRS table

Notice that "5-year property" actually is depreciated over 6 years. The extra year results from application of the half-year convention. Also, notice that in tax schedules the term **basis** replaces *book value*. The concepts of basis and book value are quite similar. Both terms represent the *undepreciated cost* of the asset; that is, cost less accumulated depreciation. *Book value* represents the cost of the asset less the accumulated depreciation *recognized in financial statements. Basis,* in contrast, represents the cost of the asset less the accumulated depreciation *claimed in income tax returns.* Stated another way, basis means "book value for tax purposes."

WHICH DEPRECIATION METHODS DO MOST BUSINESSES USE?

Most businesses use the straight-line method of depreciation in their financial statements and accelerated methods in their income tax returns. The reasons for these choices are easy to understand.

Accelerated depreciation methods result in higher charges to depreciation expense and, therefore, lower reported net income than straight-line depreciation. Most publicly owned companies want to appear as profitable as possible—certainly as profitable as their competitors. Therefore, the overwhelming majority of publicly owned companies use straight-line depreciation in their financial statements (see the graph on page 441).

For income tax purposes, it's a different story. Management usually wants to report the *lowest* possible taxable income in the company's income tax returns. Accelerated depreciation methods can substantially reduce both taxable income and tax payments for a period of years.[7]

Accounting principles and income tax laws both permit companies to use *different depreciation methods* in financial statements and their income tax returns. Therefore, most companies use straight-line depreciation in their financial statements and accelerated methods (MACRS or other variations of the declining-balance method) in their income tax returns.

THE DIFFERENCES IN DEPRECIATION METHODS: ARE THEY "REAL"? Using the straight-line depreciation method will cause a company to *report* higher profits than would be reported if an accelerated method were in use. But *is* the company more profitable than if it had used an accelerated method? The answer is *no!* Depreciation—no matter how it is computed—*is only an estimate.* The amount of this estimate has *no effect* upon the actual financial position of the business.

---

[7]For a *growing* business, the use of accelerated depreciation in income tax returns may reduce taxable income *every* year. This is because a growing business may always have more assets in the early years of their recovery periods than in the later years.

Thus, a business that uses an accelerated depreciation method in its financial statements is simply measuring its net income *more conservatively* than a business that uses straight-line.

However, the benefits of using an accelerated method for income tax purposes *are* real, because the amount of depreciation claimed affects the amount of taxes owed. In the preceding chapter, we made the point that if a company wants to use LIFO in its income tax return, it *must* use LIFO in its financial statements. *No such requirement exists for depreciation methods.* A company may use an accelerated method in its income tax returns and the straight-line method in its financial statements—and most companies do.

YOUR TURN

You as a Business Consultant

Assume you are consultant to a promising new service company. The company is owned privately by a pool of 100 investors. However, its goal is to "go public" after just five years of operations. The company's current investment in buildings and office equipment is expected to be adequate until its stock is traded publicly.

Management has recently given you a business plan to review. In it, you note that an accelerated method of depreciation was used in making all income projections. Using this information, you have recomputed depreciation expense under the straight-line method. A comparison of your depreciation expense figures for the next 5 years with those of management is shown below (based on average useful life of 20 years):

	Annual Depreciation Expense (in 000's)	
	Accelerated	Straight-line
Year 1	$2,000	$1,000
Year 2	1,800	1,000
Year 3	1,620	1,000
Year 4	1,450	1,000
Year 5	1,305	1,000

Explain to management why the company should consider using straight-line depreciation for financial reporting purposes instead of the accelerated method.

*Our comments appear on page 460.

FINANCIAL STATEMENT DISCLOSURES

A company should *disclose* in notes to its financial statements the methods used to depreciate plant assets. Readers of these statements should recognize that accelerated depreciation methods transfer the costs of plant assets to expense more quickly than does the straight-line method. Thus, accelerated methods result in more *conservative* (lower) balance sheet valuations of plant assets and measurements of net income.

ESTIMATES OF USEFUL LIFE AND RESIDUAL VALUE Estimating the useful lives and residual values of plant assets is a *responsibility of management*. These estimates usually are based upon the company's past experience with similar assets, but they also reflect the company's current circumstances and management's future plans. Thus, the estimated lives of similar assets may vary from one company to another.

The estimated lives of plant assets affect the amount of net income reported each period. The longer the estimated useful life, the smaller the amount of cost transferred each period to depreciation expense, and the larger the amount of reported net income. Bear in mind, however, that all large corporations are *audited* annually by a firm of independent public accountants. One of the responsibilities of these auditors is to determine that management's estimates of the useful lives of plant assets are reasonable under the circumstances.

Automobiles typically are depreciated over relatively short estimated lives—say, from 3 to 5 years. Most other types of equipment are depreciated over a period of from 5 to 15 years. Buildings are depreciated over much longer lives—perhaps 30 to 50 years for a new building, and 15 years or more for a building acquired used.

THE PRINCIPLE OF CONSISTENCY   The *consistent* application of accounting methods is a generally accepted accounting principle. With respect to depreciation methods, this principle means that a company should *not change* from year to year the method used in computing the depreciation expense for a given plant asset. However, management *may* use different methods in computing depreciation for different assets. Also, as we have stressed repeatedly, a company may—and often *must*—use different depreciation methods in its financial statements and income tax returns.

REVISION OF ESTIMATED USEFUL LIVES   What should be done if, after a few years of using a plant asset, management decides that the asset actually is going to last for a considerably longer or shorter period than was originally estimated? When this situation arises, a *revised estimate* of useful life should be made and the periodic depreciation expense decreased or increased accordingly.

The procedure for correcting the depreciation program is to spread the remaining undepreciated cost of the asset *over the years of remaining useful life.* This correction affects only the amount of depreciation expense that will be recorded in the current and future periods. The financial statements of past periods are *not* revised to reflect changes in the estimated useful lives of depreciable assets.

To illustrate, assume that a company acquires a $10,000 asset which is estimated to have a 5-year useful life and no residual value. Under the straight-line method, the annual depreciation expense is $2,000. At the end of the third year, accumulated depreciation amounts to $6,000, and the asset has an undepreciated cost (or book value) of $4,000.

At the beginning of the fourth year, it is decided that the asset will last for 5 *more* years. The revised estimate of useful life is, therefore, a total of 9 years. The depreciation expense to be recognized for the fourth year and for each of the remaining years is $800, computed as follows:

Revision of depreciation program

Undepreciated cost at end of third year ($10,000 − $6,000)	$4,000
Revised estimate of **remaining years** of useful life	5 years
Revised amount of annual depreciation expense ($4,000 ÷ 5)	$ 800

DISPOSAL OF PLANT AND EQUIPMENT

When depreciable assets are disposed of at any date other than the end of the year, an entry should be made to record depreciation for the *fraction of the year* ending with the date of disposal. If the half-year convention is in use, six months' depreciation should be recorded on all assets disposed of during the year. In the following illustrations of the disposal of items of plant and equipment, it is assumed that any necessary entries for fractional-period depreciation already have been recorded.

LO 5 *Account for disposals of plant assets.*

As units of plant and equipment wear out or become obsolete, they must be scrapped, sold, or traded in on new equipment. Upon the disposal or retirement of a depreciable asset, the cost of the property is removed from the asset account, and the accumulated depreciation is removed from the related contra-asset account. Assume, for example, that office equipment purchased 10 years ago at a cost of $20,000 has been fully depreciated and is no longer useful. The entry to record the scrapping of the worthless equipment is as follows:

Accumulated Depreciation: Office Equipment..	20,000	
Office Equipment..		20,000

To remove from the accounts the cost and the accumulated depreciation on fully depreciated office equipment now being scrapped. No salvage value.

Scrapping fully depreciated asset

Once an asset has been fully depreciated, no more depreciation should be recorded on it, even though the property may be in good condition and is still in use. The objective of depreciation is to spread the *cost* of an asset over the periods of its usefulness; in no case can depreciation expense be greater than the amount paid for the asset. When a fully depreciated asset remains in use beyond the original estimate of useful life, the asset account and the Accumulated Depreciation account should remain in the accounting records without further entries until the asset is retired.

GAINS AND LOSSES ON DISPOSALS OF PLANT AND EQUIPMENT

Since the residual values and useful lives of plant assets are only estimates, it is not uncommon for plant assets to be sold at prices which differ from their book value at the date of disposal. When plant assets are sold, any gain or loss on the disposal is computed by comparing the *book value with the amount received from the sale*. A sales price in excess of the book value produces a gain; a sales price below the book value produces a loss. These gains or losses, if material in amount, should be shown separately in the income statement in computing the income from operations.

CASE IN POINT

Asset dispositions occur frequently in many businesses, and the gains and losses that result often are material in amount. For instance, recent financial statements of U.S. Steel and Dow Chemical reported gains on asset dispositions of $40 million and $24 million, respectively. The income statements of Consolidated Freightlines and Ford Motor Company, on the other hand, reported losses on asset dispositions of $4 million and $235 million, respectively.

DISPOSAL AT A PRICE ABOVE BOOK VALUE Assume that a machine which cost $10,000 and currently has a book value of $2,000 is sold for $3,000 cash. The journal entry to record this disposal is as follows:

Gain on disposal of
plant asset

Cash..	3,000	
Accumulated Depreciation: Machinery	8,000	
Machinery		10,000
Gain on Disposal of Plant Assets		1,000
To record sale of machinery at a price above book value.		

DISPOSAL AT A PRICE BELOW BOOK VALUE Now assume that the same machine is sold for $500. The journal entry in this case would be as follows:

Loss on disposal of
plant asset

Cash	500	
Accumulated Depreciation: Machinery......................................	8,000	
Loss on Disposal of Plant Assets..	1,500	
Machinery..		10,000
To record sale of machinery at a price below book value.		

The disposal of a depreciable asset at a price *equal to* book value would result in neither a gain nor a loss. The entry for such a transaction would consist of a debit to Cash for the amount received, a debit to Accumulated Depreciation for the balance accumulated, and a credit to the asset account for the original cost.

GAINS AND LOSSES FOR INCOME TAX PURPOSES

As a result of using different depreciation methods, an asset's basis for tax purposes may *differ* significantly from its book value in the accounting records. When an asset is retired, any gain or loss is determined by comparing its disposal price with its undepreciated cost. The "undepreciated cost," however, is *book value* for purposes of financial reporting, and *basis* for income tax purposes. If the asset's basis differs from its book value, it follows that the gain or loss computed for income tax purposes will *differ* from that reported in the company's financial statements.

To illustrate, let us again refer to the example of S&G's delivery truck. Assume that this truck is depreciated by the *straight-line method* in S&G's financial statements and is depreciated by *MACRS* in the company's income tax returns. In both cases, the company applies the half-year convention. The depreciation to be recognized for both purposes over the life of the asset is summarized below:

Summary of Depreciation for
Financial Statements and Income Tax Purposes
(Half-Year Convention)

End of Year	In Financial Statements			In Federal Income Tax Returns		
	Depreciation	Accumulated Depreciation	Book Value	Depreciation	Accumulated Depreciation	Basis
1	$ 1,500	$ 1,500	$15,500	$ 3,400	$ 3,400	$13,600
2	3,000	4,500	12,500	5,440	8,840	8,160
3	3,000	7,500	9,500	3,264	12,104	4,896
4	3,000	10,500	6,500	1,958	14,062	2,938
5	3,000	13,500	3,500	1,958	16,020	980
6	1,500	15,000	2,000	980	17,000	–0–
Totals	$15,000			$17,000		

(handwritten: 17,600 above Book Value column header; 17,000 above Basis column header)

Notice that the basis of this truck for tax purposes is always *lower* than its book value in the financial statements. This is because the truck is being depreciated by an *accelerated* method for tax purposes, but by the straight-line method in S&G's financial statements. Also, the depreciation method used in federal income tax returns makes no provision for salvage value.

Now assume that on April 10, Year 4, S&G sells this delivery truck for *$7,000* cash. The gain or loss for financial statement purposes is determined by comparing this $7,000 disposal price with the *book value* at the date of disposal. The gain or loss for tax purposes, on the other hand, is determined by comparing the $7,000 disposal price with the *tax basis* of the truck at the disposal date.

DEPRECIATION IN THE YEAR OF DISPOSAL Prior to computing the gain or loss on disposal, we must recognize depreciation for the fraction of Year 4 during which the truck was owned and determine both the book value and the tax basis of the asset at the disposal date. As the half-year convention is in use, it does not matter when during Year 4 the asset is sold; in Year 4, we will recognize *one-half* of the depreciation which had been scheduled for the full year.

The following schedule indicates the book value and the tax basis of this delivery truck at any disposal date in Year 4:

	In Financial Statements	For Tax Purposes	
Undepreciated cost at the end of Year 3:			Book value and basis: the same idea, but different dollar amounts
Book value in financial statements...	$9,500		
Basis in income tax returns..		$4,896	
Less: Depreciation in year of disposal:			
For financial statements ($3,000 × ½)	1,500		
For tax purposes ($1,958 × ½)..		979	
Book value at date of disposal	$8,000		
Tax basis at date of disposal		$3,917	

COMPUTING THE GAIN OR LOSS The gain or loss to be recognized in the company's financial statements and income tax returns now may be determined as follows:

	In Financial Statements	For Tax Purposes	
Disposal price	$7,000	$7,000	Different depreciation methods result in different amounts of gain or loss upon disposal
Less: Undepreciated cost:			
Book value at date of disposal	8,000		
Tax basis at date of disposal..		3,917	
Loss on disposal (in financial statements)	$1,000		
Gain on disposal (for tax purposes)...		$3,083	

WHICH AMOUNTS ARE RECORDED IN THE ACCOUNTING RECORDS?

A primary purpose of the general ledger is to enable a company to prepare financial statements. Therefore, only those transactions which affect *financial statements* are recorded in the general ledger. Data regarding plant assets which are used exclusively in income tax returns may be accumulated in special work sheets or computer files, or in the company's plant and equipment *subsidiary* ledger.

At April 10, Year 4, S&G will make two journal entries to record the sale of its delivery truck. The first entry will update the Accumulated Depreciation account for the depreciation recognized *for financial statement purposes* in Year 4.

This entry is:

Depreciation Expense: Delivery Truck..	1,500	
Accumulated Depreciation: Delivery Truck...............................		1,500

To record a half year's depreciation on delivery truck in the year of disposal ($3,000 × ½).

The $979 in depreciation which will be claimed in the company's Year 4 income tax return is *not* recorded in the journals or general ledger.

The second entry required at April 10, Year 4, records the sale of the truck for $7,000 and the loss to be recognized *for financial statement purposes:*

Cash...	7,000	
Loss on Disposal of Plant Assets..	1,000	
Accumulated Depreciation	9,000	
Delivery Truck...		17,000

To record sale of delivery truck for $7,000 cash and loss on disposal.
(Accumulated depreciation: $7,500 at the end of Year 3 + $1,500
recorded in Year 4 = $9,000.)

The $3,083 gain which will be reported in the company's Year 4 income tax return may be recorded in special income tax records, but *not* in the company's general ledger accounts.

TRADING IN USED ASSETS ON NEW

Certain types of depreciable assets, such as automobiles and trucks, sometimes are traded in on new assets of the same kind. In most instances, a trade-in is viewed as both a *sale* of the old asset and a purchase of a new one.

To illustrate, assume that Rancho Landscape has an old pickup truck which originally cost $10,000, but which now has a book value (and tax basis) of $2,000. Rancho trades in this old truck on a new one with a fair market value of $15,000. The truck dealership grants Rancho a trade-in allowance of $3,500 for the old truck, and Rancho pays the remaining $11,500 cost of the new truck in cash. Rancho Landscape should record this transaction as follows:

Vehicles (new truck)...	15,000	
Accumulated Depreciation: Trucks (old truck)	8,000	
Vehicles (old truck)		10,000
Gain on Disposal of Plant Assets..		1,500
Cash...		11,500

Traded-in old truck on a new one costing $15,000. Received $3,500
trade-in allowance on the old truck, which had a book value of $2,000.

Notice that Rancho views the $3,500 trade-in allowance granted by the truck dealership as the *sales price* of the old truck. Thus, Rancho recognizes a *$1,500 gain* on the disposal (trade-in) of this asset ($3,500 trade-in allowance − $2,000 book value = $1,500 gain).

For financial reporting purposes, gains and losses on routine trade-ins are recorded in the accounting records whenever the transaction also involves the payment of a significant amount of cash (or the creation of debt).[8]

---

[8]The FASB Emerging Issues Task Force takes the position that when 25% or more of the transaction value is comprised of cash or monetary obligations, the transaction should be viewed as *monetary,* rather than nonmonetary. Thus, gains on most routine trade-ins should be *recognized in full,* rather than "deferred" as they are for income tax purposes. See *EITF Abstract Nos. 84-29, 86-29,* and *87-29.*

INCOME TAX RULES REQUIRE SPECIAL TREATMENT OF "LIKE-KIND" EXCHANGES   Income tax rules do *not* permit recognition of gains or losses on exchanges of "like-kind" assets—that is, assets which are used for similar purposes. Thus, the $1,500 gain recorded in our example is not regarded as taxable income.[9] Also, the tax basis of the new truck is only *$13,500,* not the $15,000 recorded in the accounting records. For income tax purposes, the basis of a "like-kind" asset acquired in an exchange is equal to the *tax basis* of the asset traded in, plus any "boot" (additional amount paid or owed).

Small businesses, which have no financial reporting requirements other than income tax returns, *usually use this "tax method"* in accounting for trade-ins. If Rancho had used the tax method, the cost debited to the Vehicles account would have been $13,500, and no gain on disposal of plant assets would have been recorded. Some large businesses also record trade-ins by the tax method as a matter of convenience, as gains or losses on trade-ins usually are immaterial in amount.

A CONCLUDING COMMENT . . .   The accounting rules applicable to trade-ins are more complex for the entity receiving boot than for the entity which pays it. Also, special rules may apply whenever the amount of boot included in a like-kind exchange is unusually small (less than 25% of the transaction amount). As these special accounting rules do not affect normal trade-ins of used equipment for new, we will defer the discussion of such transactions to the intermediate accounting course.

OTHER INCOME TAX REPORTING OBLIGATIONS

In the preceding discussions of depreciation for income tax purposes, we have focused primarily upon the current MACRS rules. MACRS applies to all assets acquired since December 31, 1986. But assets acquired in earlier years are subject to different tax rules.

Also, MACRS is used in *federal* income tax returns. Most *states* also levy income taxes. A company that operates in several states may have to file a state income tax return in every state in which it does business. Multinational corporations often file income tax returns in several different countries. The tax rules of individual states and of foreign countries frequently differ from those of our own federal government. Thus, a business may have to compute depreciation, basis, and gains and losses in several different ways.

Large businesses usually have an income tax department within their accounting departments. Smaller businesses often delegate most of their tax accounting to a firm of certified public accountants.

INTANGIBLE ASSETS

CHARACTERISTICS

As the word *intangible* suggests, assets in this classification have no physical substance. Leading examples are goodwill, patents, and trademarks. Intangible assets are classified in the balance sheet as a subgroup of plant assets. However, not all assets which lack physical substance are regarded as intangible assets. An account receivable, for example, or a short-term prepayment is of nonphysical nature but is classified as a current asset and is not regarded as an intangible.

LO 6 *Explain the nature of intangible assets, including goodwill.*

---

[9]Had the trade-in allowance been less than book value, the resulting loss would *not be deductible* in the determination of taxable income.

In brief, *intangible assets are assets which are used in the operation of the business but which have no physical substance and are noncurrent.*

The basis of valuation for intangible assets is cost. In some companies, certain intangible assets such as trademarks may be of great importance but may have been acquired without incurring any significant cost. Intangible assets appear in the balance sheet at their *cost.* Therefore, the assets are listed only if significant costs are incurred in their acquisition or development. If these costs are *insignificant,* they are treated as revenue expenditures (ordinary expenses).

OPERATING EXPENSES VERSUS INTANGIBLE ASSETS

For an expenditure to qualify as an intangible asset, there must be reasonable evidence of future benefits. Many expenditures offer some prospects of yielding benefits in subsequent years, but the existence and life span of these benefits is so uncertain that most companies treat these expenditures as operating expenses. Examples are the expenditures for intensive advertising campaigns to introduce new products and the expense of training employees to work with new types of machinery or office equipment. There is little doubt that some benefits from these outlays continue beyond the current period, but because of the uncertain duration of the benefits, it is almost universal practice to treat expenditures of this nature as expense of the current period.

AMORTIZATION

The term **amortization** is used to describe the systematic write-off to expense of the cost of an intangible asset over its useful life. The usual accounting entry for amortization consists of a debit to Amortization Expense and a credit to the intangible asset account. There is no theoretical objection to crediting an accumulated amortization account rather than the intangible asset account, but this method is seldom encountered in practice.

Although it is difficult to estimate the useful life of an intangible such as a trademark, it is highly probable that such an asset will not contribute to future earnings on a permanent basis. The cost of the intangible asset should, therefore, be deducted from revenue during the years in which it may be expected to aid in producing revenue. Under the current rules of the Financial Accounting Standards Board, the maximum period for amortization of an intangible asset cannot exceed *40 years.*[10] The straight-line method normally is used for amortizing intangible assets.

GOODWILL

Business executives used the term **goodwill** in a variety of ways before it became part of accounting terminology. One of the most common meanings of goodwill in a nonaccounting sense concerns the benefits derived from a favorable reputation among customers. To accountants, however, goodwill has a very specific meaning not necessarily limited to customer relations. It means the *present value of future earnings in excess of the normal return on net identifiable assets.* Above-average earnings may arise not only from favorable customer relations but also from such factors as superior management, manufacturing efficiency, and weak competition.

The **present value** of future cash flows is the amount that a knowledgeable investor would pay today for the right to receive those future cash flows. (The present value concept is discussed further in later chapters and in Appendix D.)

The phrase *normal return on net identifiable assets* also requires explanation. *Net assets* means the owners' equity in a business, or assets minus liabilities.

---

[10]*APB Opinion No. 17,* "Intangible Assets," AICPA (New York: 1970), par. 29.

Goodwill, however, is not an *identifiable* asset. The existence of goodwill is implied by the ability of a business to earn an above-average return; however, the cause and precise dollar value of goodwill are largely matters of personal opinion. Therefore, **net identifiable assets** mean all assets *except goodwill,* minus liabilities.

A *normal return* on net identifiable assets is the rate of return which investors demand in a particular industry to justify their buying a business at the fair market value of its net identifiable assets. A business has goodwill when investors will pay a *higher* price because the business earns *more* than the normal rate of return.

Assume that two similar restaurants are offered for sale and that the normal return on the fair market value of the net identifiable assets of restaurants of this type is 15% a year. The relative earning power of the two restaurants during the past five years is shown below:

	Mandarin Coast	Golden Dragon	
Fair market value of net identifiable assets.....................................	$1,000,000	$1,000,000	Which business is "worth more"?
Normal rate of return on net assets...	15%	15%	
Normal earnings, computed as 15% of net identifiable assets	150,000	150,000	
Average actual net income for past five years.............................	$ 150,000	$ 200,000	
Earnings in excess of normal...	$ –0–	$ 50,000	

An investor presumably would be willing to pay $1,000,000 to buy Mandarin Coast, because this restaurant earns the normal 15% return which justifies the fair market value of its net identifiable assets. Although Golden Dragon has the same amount of net identifiable assets, an investor probably would be willing to pay *more* for Golden Dragon than for Mandarin Coast, because Golden Dragon has a long record of superior earnings. The *extra amount* that a buyer would pay to purchase Golden Dragon represents the value of this business's *goodwill.*

CASE **IN** POINT

Boston Scientific is a rapidly growing company that has expanded its operations, in large part, by purchasing existing companies. The company's recent acquisitions include Symbiosis Corporation, Endotech, Ltd., and MinTec, Inc. Boston Scientific must be betting that these companies will generate earnings in excess of normal returns, as the amount it paid exceeds the fair market value of the net identifiable assets by *$160 million.* This premium is shown in the company's balance sheet as goodwill.

ESTIMATING GOODWILL How much will an investor pay for goodwill? Above-average earnings in past years are of significance to prospective purchasers only if they believe that these earnings *will continue* after they acquire the business. Investors' appraisals of goodwill, therefore, will vary with their estimates of the *future earning power* of the business. Very few businesses, however, are able to maintain above-average earnings for more than a few years. Consequently, the purchaser of a business will usually limit any amount paid for goodwill to not more than four or five times the amount by which annual earnings exceed normal earnings.

Arriving at a fair value for the goodwill of an ongoing business is a difficult and subjective process. Any estimate of goodwill is in large part a matter of personal opinion. The following are two methods which a prospective purchaser might use in estimating a value for goodwill:

1. Value the business as a whole, and then subtract the current market value of the net identifiable assets.

The value of a business often is expressed through the *price-earnings ratio* (p/e ratio) of the company's stock. As discussed in Chapter 6, a p/e ratio shows the current relationship between the market price of a company's stock and the company's earnings.

Assume that highly successful restaurants in this area currently sell at about 6½ times annual earnings.[11] This p/e ratio suggests that Golden Dragon is worth about $1,300,000 ($200,000 average net income × 6½). As the net identifiable assets have a market value of $1,000,000, this implies the existence of *$300,000* in goodwill.

2. Capitalize the amount by which earnings exceed normal amounts.

"Capitalizing" an earnings stream means dividing those earnings by the investor's required rate of return. The result is the maximum amount which the investor could pay for the excess earnings in order to achieve the required rate of return on the investment. To illustrate, assume that the prospective buyer decides to capitalize the $50,000 annual excess earnings of Golden Dragon at a rate of 25%. This approach results in a *$200,000* estimate ($50,000 ÷ .25 = $200,000) for the value of goodwill. (Note that $50,000 per year represents a 25% return on a $200,000 investment.)

A weakness in the capitalization method is that *no provision is made for the recovery* of the investment. If the prospective buyer is to earn a 25% return on the $200,000 investment in goodwill, either the excess earnings must continue *forever* (an unlikely assumption) or the buyer must be able to recover the $200,000 investment at a later date by selling the business at a price above the fair market value of net identifiable assets.

Notice that our two approaches resulted in very different estimates of Golden Dragon's goodwill—$300,000 and $200,000. Such differences occur often in practice. The value of goodwill depends upon *future performance*. Therefore, there is *no* "surefire way" of determining its real value. At best, the value of a company's goodwill is only an educated guess.

RECORDING GOODWILL IN THE ACCOUNTS Because of the difficulties in objectively estimating the value of goodwill, this asset is recorded only when it is *purchased*. Goodwill is "purchased" when one company buys another. The purchaser records the identifiable assets it has purchased at their fair market values, and then debits any additional amount paid to an asset account entitled Goodwill.

Generally accepted accounting principles require that recorded goodwill be amortized to expense over a period that does not *exceed* 40 years. However, the accounting concept of *conservatism* suggests that goodwill usually should be amortized over a much shorter period. For this reason, many companies amortize purchased goodwill over periods of 10 or 20 years.

BUT MOST GOODWILL NEVER GETS RECORDED! Many businesses never purchase goodwill but *generate it internally* by developing good customer relations, superior management, or other factors that result in above-average earnings. Because there is no objective way of determining the value of goodwill un-

---

[11]Investments in small business involve more risk and less liquidity than investments in publicly owned companies. For these reasons, the p/e ratios of small businesses tend to be substantially lower than those of publicly owned corporations.

less the business is sold, internally generated goodwill is *not recorded* in the accounting records. Thus, goodwill may be an important asset of a successful business, but *may not even appear* in the company's balance sheet.

The absence of internally generated goodwill is, perhaps, the principal reason why a balance sheet does not indicate a company's current market value.

GOODWILL OR BAD JUDGMENT?   Some companies have paid huge amounts for "goodwill," only to discover that the businesses they have purchased do *not* continue to earn above-normal rates of return. In these cases, the goodwill is not an asset with future economic value. Rather, it indicates that the company paid too high a price to acquire the other business. If it becomes apparent that purchased goodwill does *not* have real economic value, it should be written off immediately. (See the Case in Point on page 438.)

In summary, the best evidence of a company's goodwill is not the amount listed in the balance sheet. Rather, it is a long and on-going track record of *above-average earnings*.

PATENTS

A patent is an exclusive right granted by the federal government for manufacture, use, and sale of a particular product. The purpose of this exclusive grant is to encourage the invention of new products and processes. When a company acquires a patent by purchase from the inventor or other holder, the purchase price should be recorded by debiting the intangible asset account, Patents.

Patents are granted for a period of 17 years, and the period of amortization should not exceed that period. However, if the patent is likely to lose its usefulness in less than 17 years, amortization should be based on the shorter estimated useful life. Assume that a patent is purchased from the inventor at a cost of $100,000, after 5 years of the legal life have expired. The remaining *legal* life is, therefore, 12 years. But if the estimated *useful* life is only 4 years, amortization should be based on this shorter period. The entry to be made to record the annual amortization expense would be:

Amortization Expense: Patents	25,000	
Patents...		25,000

Entry for amortization of patent

To amortize cost of patent on a straight-line basis over an estimated life of 4 years.

TRADEMARKS AND TRADE NAMES

Coca-Cola's famous name, usually written in a distinctive typeface, is a classic example of a trademark known around the world. A trademark is a name, symbol, or design that identifies a product or group of products. A permanent exclusive right to the use of a trademark, brand name, or commercial symbol may be obtained by registering it with the federal government.

The costs of developing a trademark or brand name often consist of advertising campaigns, which should be treated as expense when incurred. If a trademark or brand name is *purchased,* however, the cost may be substantial. Such cost should be capitalized and amortized to expense over a period of not more than 40 years. If the use of the trademark is discontinued or its contribution to earnings becomes doubtful, any unamortized cost should be written off immediately.

FRANCHISES

A franchise is a right granted by a company or a governmental unit to conduct a certain type of business in a specific geographical area. An example of a franchise is the right to operate a McDonald's restaurant in a specific neighborhood. The cost of franchises varies greatly and often may be quite substantial. When the cost of a franchise is small, it may be charged immediately to expense or amortized over a short period such as 5 years. When the cost is material, amortization should be based upon the life of the franchise (if limited); the amortization period, however, may not exceed 40 years.

COPYRIGHTS

A copyright is an exclusive right granted by the federal government to protect the production and sale of literary or artistic materials for the life of the creator plus 50 years. The cost of obtaining a copyright in some cases is minor and therefore is chargeable to expense when paid. Only when a copyright is *purchased* will the expenditure be *material enough* to warrant its being capitalized and spread over the useful life. The revenue from copyrights is usually limited to only a few years, and the purchase cost should, of course, be amortized over the years in which the revenue is expected.

OTHER INTANGIBLES AND DEFERRED CHARGES

Among the other intangibles found in the published balance sheets of large corporations are moving costs, plant rearrangement costs, organization costs, formulas, processes, name lists, and film rights. Some companies group items of this type under the title of Deferred Charges, meaning expenditures that will provide benefits beyond the current year and will be written off to expense over their useful economic lives. It is also common practice to combine these items under the heading of Other Assets, which is listed at the bottom of the balance sheet.

RESEARCH AND DEVELOPMENT (R&D) COSTS

The spending of billions of dollars each year on research and development of new products is a striking characteristic of U.S. industry. The annual research and development expenditures of some companies often exceed $1 billion, and account for a substantial percentage of their total costs and expenses.

CASE IN POINT

Research and development outlays are higher in some lines of business than in others. Shown below are recent R&D figures of several well-known companies from four different industries:

	Recent annual R&D Cost (in millions)	Percentage of total expenses and costs
Chemical Products		
Dupont...........................	$1,000	3%
Dow Chemical...............	808	5%
Computer Hardware		
Sun Microsystems.........	$ 660	10%
Silicon Graphics............	335	13%
Pharmaceuticals		
Eli Lilly & Co..................	$1,100	20%
Pfizer............................	1,100	19%
Computer Software		
NetScape.......................	$ 25	28%
Microsoft........................	610	25%

In the past, some companies treated all research and development costs as expenses in the year incurred; other companies in the same industry recorded these costs as intangible assets to be amortized over future years. This diversity of practice prevented financial statements of different companies from being comparable.

The lack of uniformity in accounting for R&D was ended when the Financial Accounting Standards Board ruled that all research and development expenditures should be charged to expense *when incurred.*[12] This action by the FASB had the beneficial effect of reducing the number of alternative accounting practices and helping to make financial statements of different companies more comparable.

NATURAL RESOURCES

ACCOUNTING FOR NATURAL RESOURCES

LO 7 *Account for the depletion of natural resources.*

Mining properties, oil and gas reserves, and tracts of standing timber are leading examples of natural resources. The distinguishing characteristics of these assets are that they are physically removed from their natural environment and are converted into inventory. Theoretically, a coal mine might be regarded as an underground "inventory" of coal; however, such an inventory is certainly not a current asset. In the balance sheet, mining property and other natural resources are classified as property, plant, and equipment. Once the coal is removed from the ground, however, this coal *does* represent inventory.

We have explained that plant assets such as buildings and equipment depreciate because of physical deterioration or obsolescence. A mine or an oil reserve does not depreciate for these reasons, but it is gradually *depleted* as the natural resource is removed from the ground. Once all of the coal has been removed from a coal mine, for example, the mine is "fully depleted" and will be abandoned or sold for its residual value.

To illustrate the **depletion** of a natural resource, assume that Rainbow Minerals pays $45 million to acquire the Red Valley Mine, which is believed to contain 10 million tons of coal. The residual value of the mine after all of the coal is removed is estimated to be $5 million. The depletion that will occur over the life of the mine is the original cost minus the residual value, or $40 million. This depletion will occur at the rate of *$4 per ton* ($40 million ÷ 10 million tons) as the coal is removed from the mine. If we assume that 2 million tons are mined during the first year of operations, the entry to record the depletion of the mine would be as follows:

Inventory	8,000,000	
Accumulated Depletion: Red Valley Mine		8,000,000
To record depletion of the Red Valley Mine for the year;		
2,000,000 tons mined @ $4 per ton.		

Recording depletion

Once removed from the mine, coal becomes merchandise available for sale. Therefore, the estimated cost of this coal is debited to the Inventory account. As the coal is sold, this cost is transferred from the Inventory account to the Cost of Goods Sold account.

Accumulated Depletion is a *contra-asset account* similar to the Accumulated Depreciation account; it represents the portion of the mine which has been used

[12]FASB, *Statement No. 2,* "Accounting for Research and Development Costs" (Norwalk, Conn.: 1974), par. 12.

up (depleted) to date. In Rainbow Mineral's balance sheet, the Red Valley Mine now appears as follows:

The mine gradually is turned into inventory

Property, Plant & Equipment:
Mining properties: Red Valley Mine................................. $45,000,000
Less: Accumulated depletion... 8,000,000 $37,000,000

DEPRECIATION OF BUILDINGS AND EQUIPMENT CLOSELY RELATED TO NATURAL RESOURCES Buildings and equipment installed at a mine or drilling site may be useful only at that particular location. Consequently, such assets should be depreciated over their normal useful lives, or over the life of the natural resource, *whichever is shorter.* Often depreciation on such assets is computed using the units-of-output method, which is discussed in the *Supplemental Topic* at the end of this chapter.

DEPRECIATION, AMORTIZATION, AND DEPLETION— A COMMON GOAL

The processes of depreciation, amortization, and depletion discussed in this chapter all have a common goal. That goal is to *allocate the acquisition cost of a long-lived asset to expense over the years in which the asset contributes to revenue.* By allocating the acquisition cost of long-lived assets over the years which benefit from the use of these assets, we stress again the importance of the *matching principle.* The determination of income requires the matching of revenue with the expenses incurred to produce that revenue.

THE IMPAIRMENT OF PLANT ASSETS

On occasion, it may become apparent that a company cannot reasonably expect to recover the cost of certain plant assets, either through use or through sale. For example, an oil company may pay a high price for land that it hopes contains large deposits of oil. If the company finds no oil, however, it may become apparent that the land is worth far less than its cost.

If the cost of an asset cannot be recovered through future use or sale, the asset should be *written down* to its net realizable value. The offsetting debit is to a loss account. These write-downs generally do *not* enter into the determination of taxable income.

CASE IN POINT

In 1989, Coniston Partners bought a controlling interest in **Flagstar,** which owns Denny's and four other restaurant chains. The price paid by Coniston resulted in the recording of more than $1.7 billion in goodwill, to be amortized over 40 years.

But the above-average earnings expected from Flagstar did not materialize. In each of the next four years, Flagstar *lost* money (after allowing for amortization of the goodwill). In 1993, the company wrote off the unamortized goodwill—which still amounted to about $1.5 billion. This resulted in a huge loss in 1993. But some analysts said that this write-off would help "straighten out" the company's balance sheet and make it easier to report profits in future years.

PLANT TRANSACTIONS: THE CASH EFFECTS

LO 8 *Explain the cash effects of transactions involving plant assets.*

The cash effects of plant and equipment transactions are *very different* from the effects reported in the income statement. Cash payments for plant assets occur when those assets are *purchased*—or, more precisely, when payment is made. Cash receipts often occur when assets are sold. (These receipts are equal to the *total proceeds* received from the sale, not just the amount of any gain.) Cash flows relating to acquisitions and disposals of plant assets appear in the statement of cash flows, classified as *investing activities*.

NONCASH CHARGES   Depreciation and amortization appear in the income statement. But these both are **noncash charges** (or noncash expenses), meaning that they do not require cash payment at or near the time that the expense is recorded. The adjusting entries to record these expenses *reduce net income,* but have *no effect upon cash flows.* As a result, the recording of depreciation and amortization tend to make net income *less* than the net cash flow from operating activities.

Entries to write down plant assets that have become impaired also are noncash charges. Such write-downs reduce net income, but have no immediate effects upon cash flows. Hence, they are another example of "noncash" charges against earnings.

NONCASH INVESTING ACTIVITIES   Not all purchases and sales of plant assets result in cash payments or cash receipts during the current accounting period. For example, a company may finance the purchase of plant assets by issuing notes payable, or it may sell plant assets in exchange for notes receivable. The noncash aspects of investing and financing activities are summarized in a special schedule that accompanies a statement of cash flows. This schedule will be illustrated and explained in Chapter 13.

＊SUPPLEMENTAL   TOPIC

OTHER DEPRECIATION METHODS

Most companies that prepare financial statements in conformity with generally accepted accounting principles use the straight-line method of depreciation. However, any "rational and systematic" method is acceptable, as long as costs are allocated to expense in a reasonable manner. Several such methods are discussed below.

THE UNITS-OF-OUTPUT METHOD
Under the **units-of-output** method, depreciation is based upon some measure of output, *other than* the passage of time. When depreciation is based upon units of output, more depreciation is recognized in the periods in which the assets are most heavily used.

To illustrate this method, consider S&G's delivery truck, which cost $17,000 and has an estimated salvage value of $2,000. Assume that S&G plans to retire this truck after it has been driven 100,000 miles. The depreciation rate *per mile of operation* amounts to *15 cents,* computed as follows:

$$\frac{\text{Cost} - \text{Residual Value}}{\text{Estimated Units of Output (Miles)}} = \frac{\text{Cost per}}{\text{Unit of Output (Mile)}}$$

$$\frac{\$17,000 - \$2,000}{100,000 \text{ miles}} = \$0.15 \text{ Depreciation per Mile}$$

At the end of each year, the amount of depreciation to be recorded would be determined by multiplying the 15-cent rate by the number of miles the truck had been driven during the year. After the truck has gone 100,000 miles, it is fully depreciated, and the depreciation program is stopped.

This method provides an excellent matching of expense with revenue. However, the method should be used only when the total units of output can be estimated with reasonable accuracy. Also, this method is used only for assets such as vehicles and certain types of machinery. Assets such as buildings, computers, and furniture do not have well-defined "units of output."

In many cases, units-of-output is an *accelerated method*. Often assets are used more extensively in the earlier years of their useful lives than in the later years.

MACRS

We have explained that most businesses use MACRS in their federal income tax returns. Some small businesses also use this method in their financial statements, simply so that they do not have to compute depreciation in several different ways. MACRS is based upon the declining-balance method, which, in itself, is acceptable for use in financial statements. MACRS should be used in financial statements only if the *designated "recovery periods"* and the *assumption of no salvage value* are reasonable. Otherwise, MACRS will fail to properly match depreciation expense with revenue over the asset's estimated useful life.

SUM-OF-THE-YEARS' DIGITS

Sum-of-the-years' digits, or **SYD,** is a form of accelerated depreciation. It generally produces results which lie in between the double-declining-balance and 150%-declining-balance methods.

SYD is something of a "traditional" topic in accounting textbooks. But it is the most complex of the accelerated methods—especially when partial years are involved. And SYD is rarely used in today's business world. As shown in the table on the following page, only 11 of the 600 corporations surveyed—less than 2%—make any use of this method. Because of its complexity, it is even less frequently used in small businesses. SYD is seldom used for income tax purposes, because tax laws usually define allowable depreciation rates in terms of the declining-balance method. For these reasons, we will defer coverage of the mechanics of this method to later accounting courses.

DECELERATED DEPRECIATION METHODS

Depreciation methods do exist which recognize *less* depreciation expense in the early years of an asset's useful life, and *more in the later years.* Such methods may achieve a reasonable matching of depreciation expense and revenue when the plant asset is expected to become *increasingly productive* over time. Utility companies, for example, may use these methods for new power plants which will be more fully utilized as the population of the area increases.

These depreciation methods are rarely used; thus, we will again defer coverage to later accounting courses.

DEPRECIATION METHODS IN USE: A SURVEY

Every year, the American Institute of Certified Public Accountants conducts a survey of 600 publicly owned companies to determine the accounting methods most widely used in financial statements.

The various depreciation methods in use during a recent year are summarized below:

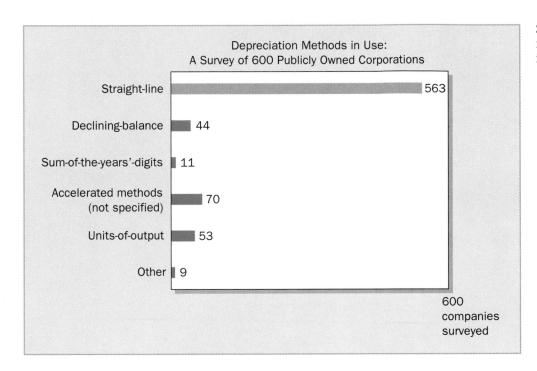

Depreciation Methods in Use:
A Survey of 600 Publicly Owned Corporations

Method	Count
Straight-line	563
Declining-balance	44
Sum-of-the-years'-digits	11
Accelerated methods (not specified)	70
Units-of-output	53
Other	9

600 companies surveyed

Straight-line is clearly the method most widely used in financial statements.

Notice that the number of methods in use exceeds 600. This is because some companies use different depreciation methods for different types of assets.

Bear in mind this survey indicates only the depreciation methods used in financial statements. In income tax returns, most companies use accelerated depreciation methods such as MACRS.

NET CONNECTIONS

Have you ever had an exciting idea for a new invention and wondered if someone has thought of it before? Now you can use the Internet to access the U.S. Patent Office and research whether you have been "beaten to the punch." Simply visit the following address:

www.uspto.gov

At this location you can search existing patents, tour the Patent Museum, learn how to apply for a patent, order copies of existing patents, access links to patent attorneys, find out about job opportunities, and more!

Perhaps you would rather capitalize on other people's ideas and inventions by investing in a business franchise. What franchise opportunities are available? How can you investigate a franchise opportunity? How much of an investment is required to purchase a particular franchise? How are annual franchise fees determined? Find out about hundreds of franchise opportunities by visiting the Franchise Annual: On-Line at the following address:

www.vaxxine.com/franchise

442 ■ Part 3: Accounting for Assets

If you go into business for yourself, you will begin to acquire depreciable assets. Depreciation expense is deductible for income tax purposes. Access the home page of the Internal Revenue Service at the following Internet address:

www.irs.ustreas.gov

A keyword search on the term Depreciation will enable you to: (1) download tax forms used to depreciate fixed assets, (2) obtain official IRS publications pertaining to depreciation, and (3) learn how depreciation for income tax purposes has evolved over the past 20 years.

SUMMARY OF LEARNING OBJECTIVES

1 Determine the cost of plant assets.

Plant assets are long-lived assets acquired for use in the business and not for resale to customers. The matching principle of accounting requires that we include in the plant and equipment accounts those costs which will provide services over a period of years. During these years, the use of the plant assets contributes to the earning of revenue. The cost of a plant asset includes all expenditures reasonable and necessary in acquiring the asset and placing it in a position and condition for use in the operations of the business.

2 Distinguish between capital expenditures and revenue expenditures.

Capital expenditures include any material expenditure that will benefit several accounting periods. Therefore, these expenditures are charged to asset accounts (capitalized), and will be recognized as expense in future periods.

Revenue expenditures are charged directly to expense accounts because either (1) there is no objective evidence of future benefits, or (2) the amounts are *immaterial*.

3 Compute depreciation by the straight-line and declining-balance methods.

Straight-line depreciation assigns an equal portion of an asset's cost to expense in each period of the asset's life. Declining-balance is an accelerated method. Each year, a fixed (and relatively high) depreciation rate is applied to the remaining book value of the asset. There are several variations of declining-balance depreciation, including MACRS.

4 Compute depreciation for income tax purposes using *MACRS.*

Under MACRS, a specific recovery period is designated for every type of depreciable asset, and the allowable depreciation method is specified for each recovery period. The IRS publishes tables showing the percentage of an asset's cost which may be recognized as expense during each year of the recovery period. In general, the depreciation rates used in MACRS are based either upon 200%- or 150%-declining balance, with the half-year convention applied in the year of acquisition and in the year of retirement.

5 Account for disposals of plant assets.

When plant assets are disposed of, depreciation should be recorded to the date of disposal. The cost is then removed from the asset account and the total recorded depreciation is removed from the accumulated depreciation account. The sale of a plant asset at a price above or below book value results in a gain or loss to be reported in the income statement.

Because different depreciation methods are used for income tax purposes, the gain or loss reported in income tax returns may differ from that shown in the income statement. It is the gain or loss shown in the financial statement which is recorded in the company's general ledger accounts.

6 Explain the nature of intangible assets, including goodwill.

Intangible assets are assets owned by the business which have no physical substance and are noncurrent, but are used in business operations. Examples include trademarks and patents.

Among the most interesting intangible assets is goodwill. Goodwill is the present value of future earnings in excess of a normal return on net identifiable assets. It stems from such factors as a good reputation, loyal customers, and superior management. Any business that earns significantly more than a normal rate of return actually "has" goodwill. But goodwill is recorded in the accounts only if it is *purchased* by acquiring another business at a price higher than the fair market value of its net identifiable assets.

All intangible assets, including goodwill, should be amortized to expense over their useful economic lives. This period may not exceed 40 years, but usually is much shorter.

7 Account for the depletion of natural resources.

Natural resources (or wasting assets) include mines, oil fields, and standing timber. Their cost is converted into inventory as the resource is mined, pumped, or cut. This allocation of the cost of a natural resource to inventories is called depletion. The depletion rate per unit extracted equals the cost of the resource (less residual value) divided by the estimated number of units it contains.

8 Explain the cash effects of transactions involving plant assets.

Depreciation is a "noncash" expense; cash expenditures for the acquisition of plant assets are *independent* of the amount of depreciation for the period. Cash payments to acquire plant assets (and cash receipts from disposals) appear in the statement of cash flows, classified as investing activities.

Write-downs of plant assets also are "noncash charges," which do not involve cash payments.

This chapter completes our discussion of the valuation of the major types of business assets. To review, we have seen that cash is reported in the financial statements at face value, marketable securities at market value, accounts receivable at their net realizable value, inventories at the lower-of-cost-or-market, and plant assets at cost less accumulated depreciation. Two ideas that are consistently reflected in each of these valuation bases are the *matching principle* and the concept of *conservatism*. In the next chapter, we will turn our attention to the measurement of liabilities.

KEY TERMS INTRODUCED OR EMPHASIZED IN CHAPTER 9

Accelerated depreciation (p. 417) Methods of depreciation that call for recognition of relatively large amounts of depreciation in the early years of an asset's useful life and relatively small amounts in the later years.

Amortization (p. 432) The systematic write-off to expense of the cost of an intangible asset over the periods of its economic usefulness.

Basis (p. 424) The book value or undepreciated cost of an asset for income tax purposes. Cost less the accumulated depreciation claimed in prior years' income tax returns.

Book value (p. 416) The cost of a plant asset minus the total recorded depreciation, as shown by the Accumulated Depreciation account. The remaining undepreciated cost is also known as *carrying value.*

Capital expenditure (p. 414) A cost incurred to acquire a long-lived asset. An expenditure that will benefit several accounting periods.

Capitalize (p. 414) A verb with two different meanings in accounting. The first is to debit an expenditure to an asset account, rather than directly to expense. The second is to determine the amount of an investment by dividing the annual return by the investor's required rate of return.

Depletion (p. 437) Allocating the cost of a natural resource to the units removed as the resource is mined, pumped, cut, or otherwise consumed.

Depreciation (p. 415) The systematic allocation of the cost of an asset to expense over the years of its estimated useful life.

Fixed-percentage-of-declining-balance depreciation (p. 420) An accelerated method of depreciation in which the rate is a multiple of the straight-line rate, and is applied each year to the *undepreciated cost* of the asset. Most commonly used is double the straight-line rate.

Goodwill (p. 432) The present value of expected future earnings of a business in excess of the earnings normally realized in the industry. Recorded when a business entity is purchased at a price in excess of the fair value of its net identifiable assets (excluding goodwill) less liabilities.

Half-year convention (p. 419) The practice of taking six months' depreciation in the year of acquisition and in the year of disposition, rather than computing depreciation for partial periods to the nearest month. This method is widely used and is acceptable for both income tax reporting and financial reports, as long as it is applied to *all* assets of a particular type acquired during the year. The half-year convention generally is *not* used for buildings.

Intangible assets (p. 412) Those assets which are used in the operation of a business but which have no physical substance and are noncurrent.

MACRS (p. 422) The Modified Accelerated Cost Recovery System. The only accelerated depreciation method permitted in federal income tax returns for assets acquired after December 31, 1986. Depreciation is based upon prescribed recovery periods and depreciation rates.

Natural resources (p. 412) Mines, oil fields, standing timber, and similar assets which are physically consumed and converted into inventory.

Net identifiable assets (p. 433) Total of all assets, *except goodwill,* minus liabilities.

Noncash charge or expense (p. 439) A charge against earnings—either an expense or a loss—which does *not* require a cash expenditure at or near the time of recognition. Thus, the charge reduces net income, but does not affect cash flows (except, perhaps, for income tax payments). Examples are depreciation and the write-off of asset values because an asset has become impaired.

Plant assets (p. 412) Long-lived assets that are acquired for use in business operations rather than for resale to customers.

Present value (p. 432) The amount that a knowledgeable investor would pay today for the right to receive future cash flows. The present value is always less than the sum of the future cash flows because the investor requires a return on the investment.

Residual (salvage) value (p. 418) The portion of an asset's cost expected to be recovered through sale or trade-in of the asset at the end of its useful life.

Revenue expenditure (p. 415) Any expenditure that will benefit only the current accounting period.

Straight-line depreciation (p. 417) A method of depreciation which allocates the cost of an asset (minus any residual value) equally to each year of its useful life.

Sum-of-the-years' digits depreciation (p. 440) A long-established but seldom-used method of accelerated depreciation. Usually produces results that lie in-between 200%- and 150%-declining balance.

Tangible plant assets (p. 412) Plant assets which have physical substance, but which are not natural resources. Include land, buildings, and all types of equipment.

Units-of-output (p. 439) A depreciation method in which cost (minus residual value) is divided by the estimated units of lifetime output. The unit depreciation cost is multiplied by the actual units of output each year to compute the annual depreciation expense.

DEMONSTRATION PROBLEM

On April 1, 1998, Argo Industries purchased new equipment at a cost of $325,000. Useful life of this equipment was estimated at 5 years, with a residual value of $25,000. For income tax purposes, however, this equipment is classified as "3-year property."

INSTRUCTIONS

Compute the annual depreciation expense for each year until this equipment becomes fully depreciated under each depreciation method listed below. (Because you will record depreciation for only a fraction of a year in 1998, depreciation will extend through 2003 in all methods except MACRS.) Show supporting computations.

a. Straight-line, with depreciation for fractional years rounded to the nearest whole month.

b. 200%-declining-balance, with the half-year convention. Limit depreciation in 2003 to an amount which reduces the undepreciated cost to the estimated residual value.

c. MACRS accelerated rates for "3-year property."

SOLUTION TO DEMONSTRATION PROBLEM

	Method of Depreciation		
	a	b	c
Year	Straight-Line	200%-Declining-Balance	MACRS
1998	$ 45,000	$ 65,000	$108,322.50
1999	60,000	104,000	144,462.50
2000	60,000	62,400	48,132.50
2001	60,000	37,440	24,082.50
2002	60,000	22,464	–0–
2003	15,000	8,696	–0–
Totals	$300,000	$300,000	$325,000.00

Supporting computations:

a.

1998: ($325,000 − $25,000) × ⅕ × 9/12 = $45,000
1999–2002: $300,000 × ⅕ = $60,000
2003: $300,000 × ⅕ × 3/12 = $15,000

c.

1998: $325,000 × 33.33% = $108,322.50
1999: 325,000 × 44.45% = 144,462.50
2000: 325,000 × 14.81% = 48,132.50
2001: 325,000 × 7.41% = 24,082.50

b.

	Undepreciated Cost	Rate	Depreciation Expense
1998:	$325,000 ×	40% × ½ =	$ 65,000
1999:	260,000 ×	40% =	104,000
2000:	156,000 ×	40% =	62,400
2001:	93,600 ×	40% =	37,440
2002:	56,160 ×	40% =	22,464
2003:	33,696 −	$25,000 =	8,696

SELF-TEST QUESTIONS

The answers to these questions appear on page 460.

1. In which of the following situations should the named company *not* record any depreciation expense on the asset described?
   a. Commuter Airline is required by law to maintain its aircraft in "as good as new" condition.
   b. Metro Advertising owns an office building that has been increasing in value each year since it was purchased.
   c. Computer Sales Company has in inventory a new type of computer, designed "never to become obsolete."
   d. None of the above answers is correct—in each case, the named company should record depreciation on the asset described.

2. Which of the following statements is (are) correct?
   a. Accumulated depreciation represents a fund being accumulated for the replacement of plant assets.
   b. The cost of a machine includes the cost of repairing damage to the machine during the installation process.
   c. A company may use different depreciation methods in its financial statements and its income tax return.
   d. The use of an accelerated depreciation method causes an asset to wear out more quickly than does use of the straight-line method.

3. On April 1, 1998, Sanders Construction paid $10,000 for equipment with an estimated useful life of 10 years and a residual value of $2,000. The company uses the double-declining-balance method of depreciation and applies the half-year convention to fractional periods. In 1999, the amount of depreciation expense to be recognized on this equipment is:
   a. $1,600   b. $1,440   c. $1,280   d. Some other amount

4. Evergreen Mfg. is a rapidly growing company that acquires more equipment every year. Evergreen uses straight-line depreciation in its financial statements and MACRS in its tax returns. Identify all correct statements:
   a. Using straight-line depreciation in the financial statements instead of an accelerated method increases Evergreen's reported net income.
   b. Using straight-line depreciation in the financial statements instead of an accelerated method increases Evergreen's annual net cash flow.
   c. Using MACRS instead of straight-line in income tax returns increases Evergreen's net cash flow.
   d. As long as Evergreen keeps growing, it will report more depreciation in its income tax returns *each year* than it does in its financial statements.

5. Delta Company sold a plant asset that originally had cost $50,000 for $22,000 cash. If Delta correctly reports a $5,000 gain on this sale, the *accumulated depreciation* on the asset at the date of sale must have been:
   a. $33,000   b. $28,000   c. $23,000   d. Some other amount

6. In which of the following situations would Burton Industries include goodwill in its balance sheet?
   a. The fair market value of Burton's net identifiable assets amounts to $2,000,000. Normal earnings for this industry is 15% of net identifiable assets. Burton's net income for the past five years has averaged $390,000.
   b. Burton spent $800,000 during the current year for research and development for a new product which promises to generate substantial revenue for at least 10 years.
   c. Burton acquired Baxter Electronics at a price in excess of the fair market value of Baxter's net identifiable assets.
   d. A buyer wishing to purchase Burton's entire operation has offered a price in excess of the fair market value of Burton's net identifiable assets.

ASSIGNMENT MATERIAL

DISCUSSION QUESTIONS

1. **Coca-Cola's** distinctive trademark is more valuable to the company than are its bottling plants. But the company's bottling plants are listed in the balance sheet, and the famous trademark isn't. Explain.

2. Identify the basic "accountable events" in the life of a depreciable plant asset. Which of these events directly affect the net income of the current period? Which directly affect cash flows (other than income tax payments)?

3. Which of the following characteristics would prevent an item from being included in the classification of plant and equipment? (a) Intangible, (b) limited life, (c) unlimited life, (d) held for sale in the regular course of business, (e) not capable of rendering benefits to the business in the future. Explain.

4. The following expenditures were incurred in connection with a large new machine acquired by a metals manufacturing company. Identify those which should be included in the cost of the asset. (a) Freight charges, (b) sales tax on the machine, (c) payment to a passing motorist whose car was damaged by the equipment used in unloading the machine, (d) wages of employees for time spent in installing and testing the machine before it was placed in service, (e) wages of employees assigned to lubrication and minor adjustments of machine one year after it was placed in service.

5. What is the distinction between a *capital expenditure* and a *revenue expenditure?*

6. If a capital expenditure is erroneously treated as a revenue expenditure, will the net income of the current year be overstated or understated? Will this error have any effect upon the net income reported in future years? Explain.

7. Shoppers' Market purchased for $220,000 a site upon which it planned to build a new store. The site consisted of three acres of land, and included an old house and two barns. County property tax records showed the following appraised values for this property: land, $160,000; buildings, $40,000. Indicate what Shoppers' should do with this $220,000 cost in its financial statements, and explain your reasoning.

8. Which of the following statements best describes the nature of depreciation?
   a. Regular reduction of asset value to correspond to the decline in market value as the asset ages.
   b. A process of correlating the book value of an asset with its gradual decline in physical efficiency.
   c. Allocation of cost in a manner that will ensure that plant and equipment items are not carried on the balance sheet at amounts in excess of net realizable value.
   d. Allocation of the cost of a plant asset to the periods in which benefits are received.

9. Should depreciation continue to be recorded on a building when ample evidence exists that the current market value is greater than original cost and that the rising trend of market values is continuing? Explain.

10. Explain what is meant by an *accelerated* depreciation method. Are accelerated methods more widely used in financial statements or in income tax returns? Explain.

11. One accelerated depreciation method is called *fixed-percentage-of-declining-balance.* Explain what is meant by the terms "fixed-percentage" and "declining-balance." For what purpose is this method most widely used?

12. An accountant for a large corporation said the company computes depreciation on its plant assets by using several different methods. But a note to the company's financial statements says all depreciation is computed by the straight-line method. Explain.

13. What criteria determine the depreciation methods that a company may use in (a) its financial statements, and (b) its income tax returns? Which methods are most widely used for each purpose?

14. Puget Sound Co. wants to simplify its accounting system by using only one depreciation method for all purposes. Would it be acceptable for the company to use MACRS in its financial statements? Explain.

15. Criticize the following quotation:
"We shall have no difficulty in paying for new plant assets needed during the coming year because our estimated outlays for new equipment amount to only $80,000, and we have more than twice that amount in our accumulated depreciation account at present."

16. Explain two approaches to computing depreciation for a fractional period in the year in which an asset is purchased. (Neither of your approaches should require the computation of depreciation to the nearest day or week.)

17. Assume that a company acquires an asset at a cost of $10,000. Compute under MACRS the depreciation (cost recovery) allowed to a taxpayer in the year of acquisition, assuming this asset is classified as:
   a. 3-year property.
   b. 7-year property.
   c. 20-year property.

18. a. Does the accounting principle of consistency require a company to use the same method of depreciation for all of its plant assets?
   b. Is it acceptable for a corporation to use different depreciation methods in its financial statements and its income tax returns?

19. After 4 years of using a machine acquired at a cost of $15,000, Ohio Construction Company determined that the original estimated life of 10 years had been too short and that a total useful life of 12 years was a more reasonable estimate. Explain briefly the method that should be used to revise the depreciation program, assuming that straight-line depreciation has been used. Assume that the revision is made after recording depreciation and closing the accounts at the end of 4 years of use of the machine.

20. Upon disposal of a plant asset, the gain or loss shown in financial statements often differs from that reported in income tax returns. Explain why. Also explain in which reports you would expect to see larger gains (or smaller losses), and why.

21. Define *intangible assets*. Would an account receivable arising from a sale of merchandise under terms of 2/10, n/30 qualify as an intangible asset under your definition?

22. Over what period of time should the cost of various types of intangible assets be amortized by regular charges against revenue? (Your answer should be in the form of a principle or guideline rather than a specific number of years.) What method of amortization is generally used?

23. Under what circumstances should *goodwill* be recorded in the accounts?

24. In reviewing the financial statements of Digital Products Company with a view to investing in the company's stock, you notice that net tangible assets total $1 million, that goodwill is listed at $400,000, and that average earnings for the past five years have been $50,000 a year. How would these relationships influence your thinking about the company?

25. Mineral King recognizes $20 depletion for each ton of ore mined. During the current year the company mined 600,000 tons but sold only 500,000 tons, as it was attempting to build up inventories in anticipation of a possible strike by employees. How much depletion should be deducted from revenue of the current year?

26. Explain the meaning of an *impairment* of an asset. Provide several examples. What accounting event should occur when an asset has become substantially impaired?

27. Several years ago March Metals purchased for $120,000 a well-known trademark for padlocks and other security products. After using the trademark for three years, March Metals discontinued it altogether when the company withdrew from the lock business and concentrated on the manufacture of aircraft parts. Amortization of the trademark at the rate of $3,000 a year is being continued on the basis of a 40-year-life, which the owner of March Metals says is required by accounting standards. Do you agree? Explain.

EXERCISES

EXERCISE 9-1
You As a Student
LO 3,4

Assume that you recently applied for a student loan in order to go to graduate school. As part of the application process, your bank requested a list of your assets. Aside from an extensive CD collection, your only other asset is a pick-up truck. You purchased the truck six years ago for $15,000. Its current fair market value is approximately $5,000.

a. What factors caused your pick-up truck to depreciate $10,000 in value?

b. Assume that the bank is willing to lend you money for graduate school. However, even with the loan, you still need to raise an additional $5,000. Do you think that the bank will lend you $5,000 more for graduate school if you agree to use your truck as collateral? Explain.

c. Assume that the truck has been used solely in a delivery service business that you operated while in college.
  1. Would your balance sheet necessarily show $10,000 in accumulated depreciation related to the truck? Explain.
  2. For tax purposes, how much has the truck been depreciated over the past six years? (Assume MACRS was used).

EXERCISE 9-2
Distinguishing Capital
Expenditures from
Revenue Expenditures
LO 1,2

Identify the following expenditures as capital expenditures or revenue expenditures:

a. Immediately after acquiring a new delivery truck, paid $225 to have the name of the store and other advertising material painted on the vehicle.

b. Painted delivery truck at a cost of $250 after two years of use.

c. Purchased new battery at a cost of $40 for 2-year-old delivery truck.

d. Installed an escalator at a cost of $12,500 in a three-story building which had previously been used for some years without elevators or escalators.

e. Purchased a pencil sharpener at a cost of $8.50.

f. Original life of the delivery truck had been estimated at 4 years and straight-line depreciation of 25% yearly had been recognized. After 3 years' use, however, it was decided to recondition the truck thoroughly, including a new engine.

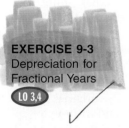

EXERCISE 9-3
Depreciation for
Fractional Years
LO 3,4

On November 2, Glass Recycling Company purchased special-purpose equipment at a cost of $600,000. The useful life of the equipment was estimated to be 5 years, with a residual value of $90,000. The company uses straight-line depreciation (half-year convention) for financial reporting purposes and the Modified Accelerated Cost Recovery System (MACRS) for tax purposes.

a. Compute the depreciation expense to be recognized in each calendar year for financial reporting purposes.

b. Compute the depreciation expense to be recognized each calendar year for tax reporting purposes. Use the table on page 423. Assume that the equipment qualifies as *3-year property.*

c. Explain why the equipment qualifies as *3-year property* for tax purposes, even though its estimated useful life is 5 years.

EXERCISE 9-4
Depreciation
Methods

LO 3,4

On April 15, 1997, Delta Company acquired a new machine with an estimated useful life of 5 years. Cost of the equipment was $55,000, with a residual value of $5,000. For tax purposes, this machinery is classified as "5-year property."

a. Compute the amounts of depreciation recognized in each of the first 3 years (1997, 1998, and 1999) under each of the three depreciation methods listed below. In each case, assume the half-year convention is applied in 1997. (Remember, the MACRS tables *automatically* apply the half-year convention.)
  1. Straight-line.
  2. Double-declining-balance.
  3. MACRS.

b. Comment upon significant differences or similarities that you observe among the patterns of depreciation expense recognized under these methods.

EXERCISE 9-5
Evaluation of
Disclosures in
Annual Reports

LO 3,4

A recent annual report of **H. J. Heinz Company** includes the following note:

Depreciation: For financial reporting purposes, depreciation is provided on the straight-line method over the estimated useful lives of the assets. Accelerated depreciation methods generally are used for income tax purposes.

a. Is the company violating the accounting principle of consistency by using different depreciation methods in its financial statements and in its income tax returns? Explain.

b. *Why* do you think that the company uses accelerated depreciation methods in its income tax returns?

c. Would the use of accelerated depreciation in the financial statements be more "conservative," or less "conservative," than the current practice of using the straight-line method? Explain.

EXERCISE 9-6
Revision of
Depreciation
Estimates

LO 3

Grain Products uses straight-line depreciation on all its depreciable assets. The accounts are adjusted and closed at the end of each calendar year. On January 4, 1997, the corporation purchased machinery for cash at a cost of $80,000. Useful life was estimated to be 10 years and residual value $12,000. Depreciation for partial years is recorded to the nearest full month.

In 1999, after almost 3 years of experience with the equipment, management decided that the estimated life of the equipment should be revised from 10 years to 6 years. No change was made in the estimate of residual value. The revised estimate of useful life was decided upon *prior* to recording depreciation for the period ended December 31, 1999.

a. Prepare journal entries in chronological order for the above events, beginning with the purchase of the machinery on January 4, 1997. Show separately the depreciation for 1997, 1998, and 1999.

b. What factors may have caused the company to revise its estimate of the equipment's useful life?

EXERCISE 9-7
Accounting for
Trade-Ins

LO 5

Ogilvie Construction traded in a used crane on a similar new one. The original cost of the old crane was $60,000, and in both Ogilvie's accounting records and income tax returns the accumulated depreciation amounted to $48,000. The new crane cost $75,000, but Ogilvie was given a trade-in allowance of $15,000.

a. What amount of cash must Ogilvie pay? *new − trade in*

b. Compute the gain or loss that would be reported on disposal of the old crane under generally accepted accounting principles. *trade in − book value old*

c. Compute the cost basis of the new crane for *income tax* purposes. *book value old + cash paid*

d. Assume that the trade-in allowance was only *$7,000*, which implies a $5,000 loss on disposal. From an income tax standpoint, would it be more advantageous for Ogilvie to sell the old crane for $7,000, or trade it in for the $7,000 allowance? Explain.

EXERCISE 9-8
Unrecorded
vs. Recorded
Goodwill

Food Lion, Inc., and **Safeway, Inc.,** are two profitable grocery chains. At the end of 1995, Food Lion's balance sheet showed total assets of $2.8 billion, and no goodwill. Safeway's balance sheet showed total assets of $5.2 billion, including $324 million in goodwill.

Throughout the late 1980s and early 1990s, Food Lion's rates of return were among the strongest in the industry. Safeway's profitability during this period was strong, but not as outstanding as Food Lion's. By the end of 1992, however, a growing number of Food Lion stores had begun to lose money. Thus, in 1993, the company decided to close 88 of its most unprofitable stores. A $170.5 million loss related to the closing of these properties was reported in the company's 1993 income statement. By the end of 1993, Food Lion had barely generated a profit, earning only $0.01 per share of common stock. Food Lion's profitability measures have improved during the past several years, but not to the outstanding levels it once had achieved.

a. Explain why Safeway includes goodwill in its balance sheet and why Food Lion, which is profitable, does not.

b. In writing about Food Lion prior to 1993, one analyst said that the company possessed unrecorded goodwill. What do you think the analyst meant by the phrase, "unrecorded goodwill"? Based on the information provided in this exercise, do you agree with the analyst's statement? Explain.

c. The $170.5 million loss reported in Food Lion's 1993 income statement was a non-cash charge against earnings. Explain what is meant by the phrase, "a noncash charge against earnings."

EXERCISE 9-9
Estimating
Goodwill

During the past several years the annual net income of Goldtone Appliance Company has averaged $540,000. At the present time the company is being offered for sale. Its accounting records show the book value of net assets (total assets minus all liabilities) to be $2,800,000. The fair market value of Goldtone's net identifiable assets, however, is $3,000,000.

An investor negotiating to buy the company offers to pay an amount equal to the fair market value for the net identifiable assets and to assume all liabilities. In addition, the investor is willing to pay for goodwill an amount equal to net earnings in excess of 15% on the fair market value of net identifiable assets, capitalized at a rate of 25%.

On the basis of this agreement, what price should the investor offer for Goldtone Appliance?

EXERCISE 9-10
Ethics: "Let the
Buyer Beware"

Bill Gladstone has owned and operated Gladstone's Service Station for over 30 years. The business, which is currently the town's only service station, has always been extremely profitable. In 1998, Gladstone decided that he wanted to sell the business and retire. His asking price exceeds the fair market value of its net identifiable assets by nearly $50,000. Gladstone attributes this premium to the above-normal returns that the service station has always generated.

Gladstone recently found out about two issues that could have a profound effect upon the future of the business: (1) A well-known service station franchise will be built across the street from his station in approximately 18 months, and (2) one of his underground fuel tanks *may* have developed a very slow leak.

a. How might these issues affect the $50,000 in goodwill that Gladstone included in his selling price?

b. Assume that Gladstone is *not* disclosing this information to potential buyers. Does he have an ethical obligation to do so? Defend your answer.

EXERCISE 9-11
Depletion of
Natural Resources

LO 7

King Mining Company purchased the Lost Creek Mine for $15,000,000 cash. The mine was estimated to contain 2 million tons of ore and to have a residual value of $3,000,000.

During the first year of mining operations at the Lost Creek Mine, 400,000 tons of ore were mined, of which 300,000 tons were sold.

a. Prepare a journal entry to record depletion of the Lost Creek Mine during the year.

b. Show how the mine and the accumulated depletion would appear in King Mining Company's balance sheet after the first year of operations.

c. Will the entire amount of depletion computed in part **a** be deducted from revenue in determining the income for the year? Explain.

d. Indicate how the journal entry in part **a** affects the company's current ratio. Do you believe that the activities summarized in this entry do, in fact, make the company any more or less liquid?

EXERCISE 9-12
Researching a
Real Company
LO 5

Locate an annual report in your library (or some other source) that includes a large gain or loss on the disposal of fixed assets. Report to the class the amount of the gain or loss and where in the company's income statement it is reported. Describe how the gain or loss is reported in the company's statement of cash flows. Summarize any discussion in the footnotes concerning the cause of the disposal.

EXERCISE 9-13
Effects of
Transactions on
Various Financial
Measurements
LO 5,7,8

Six events pertaining to plant assets are described below.

a. Purchased plant assets for cash.

b. Recognized depreciation expense for financial statement purposes (different methods are used for income tax purposes).

c. Recognized depreciation for income tax purposes.

d. Sold old equipment for cash at a price *below* both its book value and tax basis.

e. Due to the poor performance of several units of the business, unamortized goodwill is written off all at one time. This write-off does *not* reduce taxable income.

f. The cost of coal removed from a mine is recorded by debiting Inventory and crediting Accumulated Depletion. (The coal has not yet been sold.)

Indicate the immediate effects of each transaction or adjusting entry upon the financial measurements in the four column headings listed below. Use the code letters **I** for increase, **D** for decrease, and **NE** for no effect. (*Note:* Indicate only the immediate effects of these transactions. Do not attempt to anticipate how a change in taxable income will affect future tax payments or the current ratio.)

Transaction	Current Assets	Net Income	Taxable Income	Net Cash Flow (from All Sources)
a				

EXERCISE 9-14*
Units-of-Output
Method

LO 9

During the current year, Airport Auto Rentals purchased 60 new automobiles at a cost of $13,000 per car. The cars will be sold to a wholesaler at an estimated $4,000 each as soon as they have been driven 50,000 miles. Airport Auto Rentals computes depreciation expense on its automobiles by the units-of-output method, based upon mileage.

a. Compute the amount of depreciation to be recognized for each mile that a rental automobile is driven.

b. Assuming that the 60 rental cars are driven a total of 1,650,000 miles during the current year, compute the total amount of depreciation expense that Airport Auto Rentals should recognize on this fleet of cars for the year.

*Supplemental Topic, "Other Depreciation Methods."

c. In this particular situation, do you believe the units-of-output depreciation method achieves a better matching of expenses with revenue than would the straight-line method? Explain.

EXERCISE 9-15
Toys "R" Us
Choice of
Depreciation
Method

 LO 1,3

The annual report of **Toys "R" Us** appears in Appendix A at the end of this textbook. Use the report to answer the following questions:

a. What method of computing depreciation expense does the company use?

b. Why do you think that the company uses the method of computing depreciation identified in part **a?**

c. The company's income statement reports depreciation and amortization expense. What types of intangible assets would you guess require amortization?

PROBLEMS

PROBLEM 9-1
Determining the Cost
of Plant Assets

LO 1,2

Early this summer, Crystal Car Wash purchased new "brushless" car washing equipment for all 10 of its car washes. The following information refers to the purchase and installation of this equipment.

1. The list price of the brushless equipment was $7,200 for the equipment needed at each car wash. Because Crystal Car Wash purchased 10 sets of equipment at one time, it was given a special "package price" of $63,000 for all of the equipment. Crystal paid $23,000 of this amount in cash (no cash discount was allowed) and issued a 90-day, 8% note payable for the remaining $40,000. Crystal paid this note promptly at its maturity date, along with $800 in accrued interest charges.

2. In addition to the amounts described above, Crystal paid sales taxes of $3,780 at the date of purchase.

3. Freight charges for delivery of the equipment totaled $3,320.

4. Crystal paid a contractor $2,250 per location to install the equipment at six of Crystal's car washes. Management was able to find a less expensive contractor who installed the equipment in the remaining four car washes at a cost of $1,900 per location.

5. During installation, one of the new machines was accidentally damaged by an employee of Crystal Car Wash. The cost to repair this damage, $914, was paid by Crystal.

6. As soon as the machines were installed, Crystal Car Wash paid $5,700 for a series of radio commercials advertising the fact that it now uses brushless equipment in all of its car washes.

INSTRUCTIONS

a. In one sentence, make a general statement summarizing the nature of the expenditures properly included in the cost of plant and equipment.

b. For each of the six numbered paragraphs, indicate which items should be included by Crystal Car Wash in the cost debited to the Equipment account. Also briefly indicate the accounting treatment that should be accorded to any items that you *do not* regard as part of the cost of the equipment.

c. Prepare a list of the expenditures that should be included in the cost of the equipment. (Determine the total cost of the equipment at all 10 locations; do not attempt to separate costs by location.)

d. Prepare a journal entry at the end of the current year to record depreciation on this equipment. Crystal depreciates this equipment by the straight-line method over an estimated useful life of 10 years, assumes zero salvage value, and applies the half-year convention.

PROBLEM 9-2
Comparison of
Straight-line and
MACRS

LO 3,4

On October 26, 1998, Atlantic Iron Works acquired new machinery at a cost of $50,000. The machinery has an estimated useful life of 5 years, with a residual value of $20,000. For income tax purposes, this machinery qualifies as 3-year property.

a. Compute the annual depreciation expense for each year using each of the two depreciation methods listed below. Because you will record depreciation for only a fraction of a year in 1998, the straight-line depreciation schedule will extend to the year 2003.
   1. Straight-line, using the half-year convention.
   2. MACRS, the method Atlantic uses in its income tax returns.

b. In this situation, would it be appropriate for Atlantic Iron to use MACRS in its financial statements as well as in its income tax returns? Explain the reasoning behind your answer.

PROBLEM 9-3
Comparison of
Straight-Line and
MACRS

LO 3,4

Micro Circuit Co. purchased new equipment on October 4, 1998 at a cost of $80,000. The useful life of this equipment was estimated at 5 years, with no salvage value.

INSTRUCTIONS
a. Beginning with calendar 1998, compute the annual depreciation expense for each year using each of the two methods listed below.
   1. Straight-line, with depreciation in fractional years rounded to the nearest month.
   2. MACRS. (Under MACRS guidelines, this equipment is classified as 5-year property.

b. In this situation, would it be appropriate for Micro Circuit to use MACRS in both its financial statements and its federal income tax returns? Explain the reasoning behind your answer.

PROBLEM 9-4
Alternative
Depreciation
Methods—Including
Fractional Periods
and MACRS

LO 3,4

On March 29, 1998, Global Manufacturing purchased new equipment with a cost of $100,000, an estimated useful life of 5 years, and an estimated residual value of $10,000. For income tax purposes, this equipment is classified as 5-year property.

INSTRUCTIONS
a. Compute the annual depreciation expense for each year until this equipment becomes fully depreciated under each of the depreciation methods listed below. (Because you will record depreciation for only a fraction of a year in 1998, depreciation will extend through 2003.) Show supporting computations.
   1. Straight-line, with depreciation for fractional years rounded to the nearest whole month.
   2. 200%-declining-balance, with the half-year convention. (Limit depreciation in 2003 to an amount which reduces the undepreciated cost to the estimated residual value.)
   3. MACRS accelerated rates for 5-year property.

b. Global has two conflicting objectives. Management wants to report the highest possible earnings to stockholders in the near future, yet also wants to minimize the taxable income reported to the IRS. Indicate the depreciation method which the company will probably use in (1) its financial statements and (2) its federal income tax return. Explain the reasons for your answers.

c. Explain the similarities and differences between the 200%-declining-balance method and the depreciation allowed under MACRS.

PROBLEM 9-5
Disposal of
Plant Assets

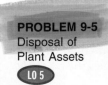

LO 5

During 19__, Crown Developers disposed of plant assets in the following transactions:

Feb. 10   Office equipment costing $14,000 was given to a scrap dealer. No proceeds were received from the scrap dealer. At the date of disposal, accumulated depreciation on the office equipment amounted to $11,900.

Apr. 1 Crown sold land and a building to Villa Associates for $630,000, receiving $200,000 in cash and a 5-year, 10% note receivable for $430,000. Crown's accounting records showed the following amounts: Land, $120,000; Building, $350,000; Accumulated Depreciation: Building (as of April 1), $115,000. 5&5

Aug. 15 Crown traded in an old truck for a new one. The old truck had cost $11,000, and accumulated depreciation amounted to $7,000. The list price of the new truck was $17,000; Crown received a $5,000 trade-in allowance for the old truck and paid the $12,000 balance in cash. (Trucks are included in the Vehicles account.)

Oct. 1 Crown traded in its old computer system as part of the purchase of a new system. The old computer had cost $150,000 and, as of October 1, accumulated depreciation amounted to $110,000. The new computer had a list price of $90,000. Crown was granted a $10,000 trade-in allowance for the old computer system, paid $30,000 in cash, and issued a $50,000, 2-year, 9% note payable to Action Computers for the balance. (Computers are included in the Office Equipment account.)

INSTRUCTIONS

a. Prepare journal entries to record each of these transactions. Assume that depreciation expense on each asset already has been recorded up to the date of disposal. Thus, you need not update the accumulated depreciation figures stated in the problem.

b. Several of the asset disposals made during the year involved the payment of boot. Explain what is meant by the term, "boot."

PROBLEM 9-6
Depreciation and
Taxable Gains and
Losses
LO 3,4,5

On March 2, 1998, Gourmet Market purchased a delivery truck for $10,000. For financial statement purposes, this asset was depreciated by the straight-line method, using an estimated useful life of 5 years, a residual value of $2,000, and the half-year convention. For income tax purposes, the truck was depreciated by the MACRS accelerated rates (in the table on page 423) as 5-year property. On September 4, 2000, Gourmet Market sells the truck for $5,200 cash.

a. Prepare a schedule showing side-by-side the annual amounts of depreciation expense that management will recognize in (1) the company's financial statements and (2) its income tax returns. Continue this schedule until the asset is fully depreciated for both purposes.

b. For *financial statement purposes,* compute (1) the book value of the truck at the date of disposal and (2) the amount of gain or loss on the sale.

c. For *income tax purposes,* compute (1) the *basis* of this asset at the date of disposal and (2) the amount of gain or loss on the sale.

d. Prepare journal entries (in general journal form) to record in Gourmet Market's accounting records (1) depreciation on the truck for the year of disposal and (2) the sale of the truck. Date both entries September 4, 2000.

e. Was the truck considered 5-year property for income tax purposes because its estimated useful life for financial reporting purposes was also 5 years? In other words, had its estimated useful life for financial reporting purposes been 7 years, would it have been considered 7-year property for tax purposes? Explain.

PROBLEM 9-7
A Comprehensive
Disposal Problem
LO 3,4,5

On October 12, 1998, Speedy Print purchased a color photocopy machine at a cost of $20,000. Management estimated that the machine would have a useful life of 8 years and a residual value of $4,000. Speedy Print uses straight-line depreciation in its financial statements, rounding depreciation for partial periods to the nearest full month. In income tax returns, the company uses the MACRS accelerated rates (from the table on page 423). Copiers are classified as 5-year property.

Speedy Print found that not many of its customers used the color copier. Therefore, on March 19, 2000, Speedy Print sold this machine to Commercial Graphics Company for $10,000 cash.

INSTRUCTIONS

a. Prepare a schedule showing side-by-side the annual amounts of depreciation expense that management originally expects to recognize over the 8-year life of this asset in (1) the company's financial statements and (2) its income tax returns.

b. For *financial statement purposes,* compute (1) the book value of the copier at the date of disposal and (2) the gain or loss on the sale.

c. For *income tax purposes,* compute (1) the *basis* of the copier at the date of disposal and (2) the taxable gain or loss on the sale.

d. Prepare journal entries to record in Speedy Print's accounting records (1) depreciation on the copier for 2000 (through the date of disposal) and (2) the sale of the color copier. (Prepare both entries in general journal form and date them March 19, 2000.)

e. For income tax purposes, did the gain or loss computed in part **c** have any cash flow consequences? Explain.

PROBLEM 9-8
Accounting for
Intangible Assets
Under GAAP

LO 6

During the current year, Homes Sales Corporation incurred the following expenditures which should be recorded either as operating expenses of the current year or as intangible assets:

a. Expenditures for the training of new employees. The average employee remains with the company for 7 years, but is retrained for a new position every 3 years.

b. Purchased from another company the trademark to a household product. The trademark has an unlimited legal life, and the product is expected to contribute to revenue indefinitely.

c. Incurred significant research and development costs to develop a dirt-resistant fiber. The company expects that the fiber will be patented and that sales of the resulting products will contribute to revenue for at least 50 years. The legal life of the patent, however, will be 17 years.

d. An expenditure to acquire the patent on a popular video game. The patent has a remaining legal life of 14 years, but Home Sales expects to produce and sell the game for only 3 years.

e. Spent a large amount to sponsor a television mini-series about the French Revolution. The purpose in sponsoring the program was to make television viewers more aware of the company's name and its product lines.

INSTRUCTIONS
Explain whether each of the above expenditures should be recorded as an operating expense or an intangible asset. If you view the expenditure as an intangible asset, indicate the number of years over which the asset should be amortized. Explain your reasoning.

PROBLEM 9-9
Depletion of an Oilfield;
Units of Output
Depreciation

LO 7 and 'Supp. Topic

On March 17, 1998, Texas Oil Company began operations at its Southfork Oil Field. The oil field had been acquired several years earlier at a cost of $14.4 million. The field is estimated to contain 4 million barrels of oil and to have a residual value of $2 million after all of the oil has been pumped out. Equipment costing $560,000 was purchased for use at the Southfork Field. This equipment will have no economic usefulness once Southfork is depleted; therefore, it is depreciated on a units-of-output basis.

Supplemental Topic, "Other Depreciation Methods."

Texas Oil also built a pipeline at a cost of $3,400,000 to serve the Southfork Field. Although this pipeline is physically capable of being used for many years, its economic usefulness is limited to the productive life of the Southfork Field and there is no residual value. Therefore, depreciation of the pipeline also is based upon the estimated number of barrels of oil to be produced.

Production at the Southfork Field amounted to 460,000 barrels in 1998 and 530,000 barrels in 1999.

$12.4 mil

INSTRUCTIONS

a. Compute the per-barrel depletion rate of the oil field and the per-barrel depreciation rates of the equipment and the pipeline. *3.13 ; 4*

b. Make the year-end adjusting entries required at December 31, 1998, and December 31, 1999, to record depletion of the oil field and the related depreciation. (Make separate entries to record depletion of the oil field, depreciation of the equipment, and depreciation of the pipeline.)

c. Show how the Southfork Field should appear in Texas Oil's balance sheet at the end of 1999. (Use "Oil Reserves: Southfork Field" as the title of the asset account; show accumulated depletion, but do not include the equipment or pipeline.)

d. Explain why the entire $14.4 million cost of the Southfork Oil Field is not subject to depletion. In other words, after all of the oil reserves are depleted, what of any salvage value remains?

PROBLEM 9-10
Effects of
Transactions upon
Financial Measurements
LO 5,7,8

Listed below are eight events affecting the operations of Midwest Mining & Manufacturing Co. during the current year:

1. Purchased plant assets for cash.

2. For financial statement purposes, the company decides to use an accelerated depreciation method for assets acquired in the current year. In the past, the company had used the straight-line method. (Different depreciation methods are used for income tax purposes.)

3. Depreciation is recorded for tax purposes by a method different from that used in the financial statements.

4. Sold old equipment for cash at a price *below* book value, but *above* tax basis.

5. Traded in an old automobile for a new one. Received a trade-in allowance that exceeded the old car's book value and its income tax basis. Most of the purchase price of the new car was paid in cash.

6. Due to a change in production methods, many pieces of equipment became idle. Decided this equipment had become impaired, and wrote it down to scrap value. (No deduction may be taken for income tax purposes until this equipment actually is sold or scrapped.)

7. Recorded amortization of intangible assets (assume deductible for income tax purposes).

8. Recorded depletion of a natural resource by debiting Inventory. (The products have not yet been sold.)

INSTRUCTIONS

a. Indicate the immediate effects of each transaction or adjusting entry upon the financial measurements in the four column headings listed below. Use the code letters, **I** for increase, **D** for decrease, and **NE** for no effect. (***Note:*** Indicate only the *immediate* effects of these transactions. Do not attempt to anticipate how a change in taxable income will affect future tax payments or the current ratio.)

Transaction 1	Current Ratio	Net Income	Taxable Income	Net Cash Flow (From All Sources)

b. For each of these eight events, *explain fully* the reasoning behind your answers. Also, be prepared to explain this reasoning in class.

CASES

CASE 9-1

Flagstar "Bites the Bullet"

LO 6

This assignment is based upon the Case in Point on page 438. **Flagstar** is the company that owns and operates **Denny's Restaurants.** In 1989, **Coniston Partners** purchased a controlling interest in Flagstar. Based upon the acquisition price, new and current values were assigned to Flagstar's assets.

a. How did the $1.7 billion in goodwill come to be recorded in the company's balance sheet?

b. Why was remaining unamortized goodwill written-off in 1993? Illustrate this write-off in the form of a general journal entry. What were the effects of this write-off upon net income and net cash flows for 1993?

c. What did analysts mean when they said that this write-off would help "straighten-out" the company's balance sheet? Explain fully.

d. How will this write-off make it easier for the company to report profits in future years?

CASE 9-2

Are Useful Lives "Flexible"?

LO 3

Robert Lynch is the controller of Print Technologies, a publicly owned company. The company is experiencing financial difficulties and is aggressively looking for ways to cut costs.

Suzanne Bedell, the CEO, instructs Lynch to lengthen from 5 to 10 years the useful life used in computing depreciation on certain special-purpose machinery. Bedell believes that this change represents a substantial cost savings, as it will reduce the depreciation expense on these assets by nearly one-half.

(*Note:* The proposed change affects only the depreciation expense recognized in financial statements. Depreciation deductions in income tax returns will not be affected.)

INSTRUCTIONS

a. Discuss the extent to which Bedell's idea will, in fact, achieve a "cost savings." Consider the effects upon both net income and cash flows.

b. Who is responsible for estimating the useful lives of plant assets?

c. Discuss any ethical issues that Lynch should consider with respect to Bedell's instructions.

CASE 9-3

Departures from GAAP—Are They Ethical?

LO 1

Martin Cole owns Delta Construction Co. The company maintains accounting records for the purposes of exercising control over its construction activities, and meeting its reporting obligations regarding payrolls and income tax returns. As it has no other financial reporting obligations, Delta does not prepare formal financial statements.

The company owns land and several other assets with current market values well in excess of their historical costs. Cole directs the company's accountant, Maureen O'Shaughnessey, to prepare a balance sheet in which assets are shown at estimated market values. Cole says this type of balance sheet will give him a better understanding of "where the business stands." He also thinks it will be useful in obtaining bank loans, as loan applications always ask for the estimated market values of real estate owned.

INSTRUCTIONS

a. Would the financial statements requested by Cole be in conformity with generally accepted accounting principles?

b. Is Delta Construction under any legal or ethical obligation to prepare financial statements that *do* conform to generally accepted accounting principles?

c. Discuss any ethical issues that O'Shaughnessey should consider with respect to Cole's request.

CASE 9-4
Depreciation Policies in
Annual Reports
LO 3,4

Shown below is a note accompanying a recent financial statement of **International Paper Company:**

Plant, Properties, and Equipment

Plant, properties, and equipment are stated at cost less accumulated depreciation.

For financial reporting purposes, the company uses the units-of-production method of depreciating its major pulp and paper mills and certain wood products facilities, and the straight-line method for other plants and equipment.

Annual straight-line depreciation rates for financial reporting purposes are as follows: buildings 2½% to 8%; machinery and equipment 5% to 33%; woods equipment 10% to 16%. For tax purposes, depreciation is computed utilizing accelerated methods.

INSTRUCTIONS

a. Are the depreciation methods used in the company's financial statements determined by current income tax laws? If not, who is responsible for selecting these methods? Explain.

b. Does the company violate the consistency principle by using different depreciation methods for its paper mills and wood products facilities than it uses for its other plant and equipment? If not, what does the principle of consistency mean? Explain.

c. What is the estimated useful life of the machinery and equipment being depreciated with a straight-line depreciation rate of:
1. 5%.
2. 33% (round to the nearest year).
Who determines the useful lives over which specific assets are to be depreciated?

d. Why do you think the company uses accelerated depreciation methods for income tax purposes, rather than using the straight-line method? Explain.

INTERNET ASSIGNMENT

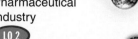

INTERNET 9-1
R&D in the
Pharmaceutical
Industry
LO 2

The pharmaceutical industry spends billions of dollars each year on research and development. Rather than capitalize these R&D expenditures as intangible assets, companies are required to charge them to expense in the year incurred.

Perform a keyword search of Pharmaceutical Companies using the following search engine:

www.yahoo.com

Your search will result in a list of companies that research and develop pharmaceutical products. Select five of these companies and obtain their 10-K reports (using EDGAR) at the following Internet address:

www.sec.gov/cgi-bin/srch-edgar

INSTRUCTIONS

a. For each of the companies you selected, determine:
1. Total R&D expense for the most current year.
2. Total R&D expense as a percentage of total costs and expenses.

3. Total R&D expense as a percentage of net sales.
4. The percentage by which operating income would have been increased had the entire R&D expenditure been recorded as an intangible asset instead of being charged to expense.

b. Using information from the 10-K reports, summarize briefly the kinds of drugs being researched and developed by each of these companies. As a potential investor, which company appears to be the most innovative and promising? Explain.

Additional Internet assignments for this chapter are found in Appendix B at the end of this textbook.

OUR COMMENTS ON THE IN-TEXT CASES

YOU AS A BUSINESS OWNER (P. 419) Many factors may influence the useful life and residual value of a truck. These factors may include: (1) The miles the truck will be driven each year, (2) the amount of maintenance it receives, (3) road conditions, (4) the climate in which it is driven, and (5) new technologies that make new trucks more fuel efficient and or powerful.

To the extent that the company can prevent excessive physical deterioration and obsolescence from occurring, estimates of the truck's useful life and residual value will increase. A prolonged life and high residual value will reduce depreciation expense reported by the company each year. If, on the other hand, the truck is expected to undergo excessive abuse, or become obsolete, estimates of its useful life and residual value will decrease. This, in turn, will increase the amount of depreciation expense reported by the company each year.

YOU AS A BUSINESS CONSULTANT (P. 425) As shown, using the accelerated method requires higher charges to depreciation expense and, therefore, results in a lower reported net income than the straight-line method. Of course, the manner in which depreciation is computed has no *real effect* upon a company's profitability or financial position. However, because this business intends to go public within five years, management may want the company to appear as profitable as generally accepted accounting principles will allow.

ANSWERS TO SELF-TEST QUESTIONS

1. c (Depreciation is not recorded on inventory.)   **2.** c   **3.** d $1,800, computed 20% [$10,000 − ($10,000 × 20% × ½)]   **4.** a, c, d   **5.** a [Cost, $50,000, less book value, $17,000 (sales price, less gain)]   **6.** c

Alpine Village and Nordic Sports

CONCEPTS OF ASSET VALUATION AND EFFECTS UPON NET INCOME

Chris Scott, a former Olympic skier, wants to purchase an established ski equipment and clothing shop in Aspen, Colorado. Two such businesses currently are available for sale: Alpine Village and Nordic Sports. Both businesses are organized as corporations and have been in business for three years. Summaries of the current balance sheet data of both shops are shown below:

Assets	Alpine Village	Nordic Sports
Cash	$ 29,200	$ 35,800
Accounts receivable	171,600	190,800
Inventory	141,700	150,400
Plant and equipment:		
Land	32,000	41,000
Building (net of accumulated depreciation)	87,480	104,900
Equipment (net of accumulated depreciation)	8,900	8,300
Goodwill		22,200
Total assets	$470,880	$553,400

Liabilities & Stockholders' Equity		
Total liabilities	$194,400	$176,200
Stockholders' equity	276,480	377,200
Total liabilities & stockholders' equity	$470,880	$553,400

Income statements for the last three years show that Alpine Village has reported total net income of $210,480 since the business was started. The income statements of Nordic Sports show total net income of $262,200 for the same 3-year period.

With the permission of the owners of the two businesses, Scott arranges for a certified public accountant to review the accounting records of both companies. This investigation discloses the following differences in accounting policies at the two businesses:

ACCOUNTS RECEIVABLE Nordic Sports uses the direct write-off method of recording uncollectible accounts expense. The accountant believes that the $190,800 of accounts receivable appearing in the company's balance sheet includes about $18,000 in uncollectible accounts. Alpine Village makes monthly estimates of its uncollectible accounts and shows accounts receivable in its balance sheet at estimated net realizable value.

INVENTORIES   Nordic Sports uses the first-in, first-out **(FIFO)** method of pricing its inventory. Had the company used the last-in, first-out **(LIFO)** method, the balance sheet valuation of inventory would be about $12,000 lower. Alpine Village uses the LIFO method to value inventory; if it had used FIFO, the balance sheet valuation of inventory would be about $10,000 greater.

BUILDINGS   In its financial statements, Nordic Sports depreciates its building over an estimated life of 40 years, using the straight-line method. Alpine Village depreciates its building over 20 years, using the double-declining balance method. Alpine has owned its building for 3 years, and the accumulated depreciation on the building now amounts to $32,520. (Both companies use MACRS depreciation in their income tax returns.)

GOODWILL   Three years ago, each business provided $24,000 in prize money for ski races held in the area. Nordic Sports charged this expenditure to goodwill, which it is amortizing over a period of 40 years. Alpine Village charged its $24,000 prize money expenditure directly to advertising expense.

INSTRUCTIONS

a. Prepare a revised summary of the balance sheet data in a manner that makes the information about the two companies more comparable. You will adjust the asset values of one company or the other so that the balance sheet data for both companies meet the following standards:

  1. Accounts receivable are valued at estimated net realizable value.
  2. Inventories are valued by the method that will minimize income taxes during a period of rising prices.
  3. Depreciation on the buildings is based upon the straight-line method and an estimated useful life of 40 years.
  4. The cost of the $24,000 payment of prize money is treated in the manner required by generally accepted accounting principles.

  After making the indicated adjustments to the valuation of certain assets, show "stockholders' equity" at the residual amount needed to bring total liabilities and stockholders' equity into agreement with total assets.

  When you revalue an asset of either company, show supporting computations.

b. Revise the cumulative amount of net income reported by each company during the last three years, taking into consideration the changes in accounting methods and policies called for in part **a.**

c. Assume that after revision of asset values as described in part **a,** the revised book value of net identifiable assets is not materially different from aggregate fair market value of net identifiable assets. Therefore, Scott is willing to buy either company at a price equal to the revised amount of stockholders' equity as determined in part **a,** plus an amount for goodwill. For goodwill, Scott is willing to pay four times the amount by which average annual net income exceeds a 20% return on this revised stockholders' equity.

  Determine the price that Scott is willing to pay for each of the two companies. Base your computations on the revised data about stockholders' equity and net income that you developed in parts **a** and **b.** (***Hint:*** Remember that the cumulative net income in part **b** was earned over a 3-year period. To find average *annual* net income, divide this amount by 3.)

ACCOUNTING FOR LIABILITIES AND OWNERS' EQUITY

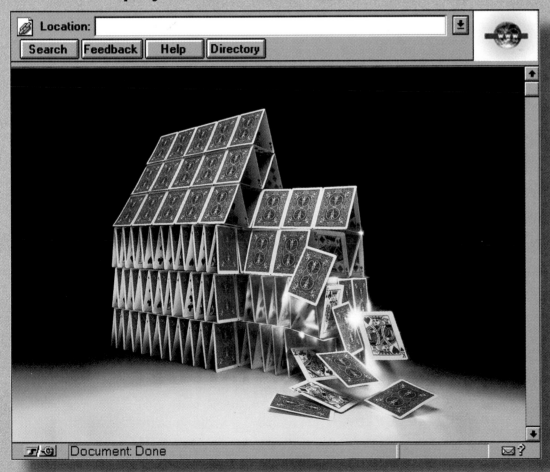

Location:

| Search | Feedback | Help | Directory |

Document: Done

The left side of a balance sheet tells us what a business owns. The right side tells about the capital structure—that is, how the company is financed. Some businesses have a capital structure that is "rock solid," but many do not. More businesses fail because of a shaky or inadequate capital structure than for any other reason.

When we read a balance sheet, we look at the right side first. We don't want to invest in a "house of cards."

LIABILITIES

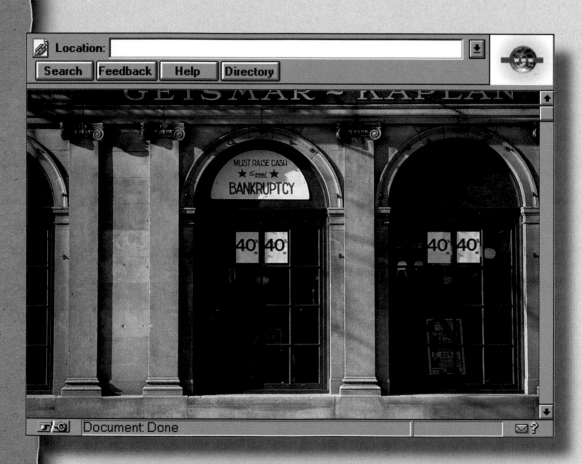

Businesses—like individuals—have debts. They owe money to suppliers, lenders, employees, the government—and sometimes to the plaintiffs in a lawsuit. Some businesses have very little debt. Others have substantial debt, but use it to their advantage. In some companies, however, debt becomes an overwhelming problem.

1. Define liabilities and distinguish between current and long-term liabilities.
2. Account for notes payable and interest expense.
3. Describe the costs relating to payrolls.
4. Prepare an amortization table allocating payments between interest and principal.
5. Describe corporate bonds and explain the tax advantage of debt financing.

6. Explain the concept of present value.
7. Account for postretirement costs.
8. Describe and account for deferred income taxes.
9. Evaluate the safety of creditors' claims.
*10. Define *loss contingencies* and explain their presentation in financial statements.
**11. Account for bonds issued at a *discount* or *premium.*

In the preceding three chapters, we have discussed the major groups of business assets. We will now shift our attention to the *right* side of the balance sheet, which shows how the company's assets have been financed.

There are two basic ways of financing assets: with liabilities or with owners' equity. The mix of liabilities and owners' equity in a particular business is termed the company's **capital structure.**

In this chapter, we emphasize liabilities; in the next two chapters, we focus upon owners' equity.

THE NATURE OF LIABILITIES

Liabilities may be defined as *debts or obligations arising from past transactions or events,* and requiring settlement at a future date. All liabilities have certain characteristics in common; however, the specific terms of different liabilities, and the rights of the creditors, vary greatly.

LO1 *Define liabilities. Distinguish between current and long-term liabilities.*

DISTINCTION BETWEEN DEBT AND EQUITY Businesses have two basic sources of financing: liabilities and owners' equity. Liabilities differ from owners' equity in several respects. The feature which most clearly distinguishes the claims of creditors from owners' equity is that all liabilities eventually *mature*— that is, they come due. Owners' equity does not mature. The date upon which a liability comes due is called the **maturity date.**[1]

Although all liabilities mature, their maturity dates vary. Some liabilities are so short in term that they are paid before the financial statements reach the users' desk. Long-term liabilities, in contrast, may not mature for many years. The maturity dates of key liabilities may be a critical factor in the solvency of a business.

The providers of borrowed capital are *creditors* of the business, not owners. As creditors, they have financial claims against the business, but usually do *not* have the right to control business operations. The traditional roles of owners, managers, and creditors may be modified, however, in an *indenture contract.* Creditors sometimes insist upon being granted some control over business operations as a condition of making a loan, particularly if the business is in poor

---

*Supplemental Topic A, "Estimated Liabilities, Loss Contingencies, and Commitments."
**Supplemental Topic B, "Bonds Issued at a Discount or Premium"
[1]Some liabilities are *due on demand,* which means that the liability is payable upon the creditor's request. From a bank's point of view, customers' checking accounts are "demand liabilities." Liabilities due on demand may come due at any time, and are classified as current liabilities.

financial condition. Indenture contracts may impose such restrictions as limits upon management salaries and upon dividends, and may require the creditor's approval for additional borrowing or for large capital expenditures.

The claims of creditors have *legal priority* over the claims of owners. If a business ceases operations and liquidates, creditors must be *paid in full* before any distributions are made to the owners. The relative security of creditors' claims, however, can vary among the creditors. Sometimes the borrower pledges title to specific assets as **collateral** for a loan. If the borrower defaults on a secured loan, the creditor may foreclose upon the pledged assets. Assets which have been pledged as security for loans should be identified in notes accompanying the borrower's financial statements.

Liabilities which are not secured by specific assets are termed *general credit obligations.* The priorities of general credit obligations vary with the nature of the liability, and the terms of indenture contracts.

MANY LIABILITIES BEAR INTEREST   Most long-term liabilities, and some short-term ones, require the borrower to pay interest. Only interest accrued *as of the balance sheet date* appears as a liability in the borrower's balance sheet. The borrower's obligation to pay interest in *future* periods sometimes is disclosed in the notes to the financial statements, but it is not shown as an existing liability.

ESTIMATED LIABILITIES   Most liabilities are for a definite dollar amount, clearly stated by contract. Examples include notes payable, accounts payable, and accrued expenses, such as interest payable and salaries payable. In some cases, however, the dollar amount of a liability must be *estimated* at the balance sheet date.

Estimated liabilities have two basic characteristics: The liability is *known to exist,* but the precise dollar amount cannot be determined until a later date. For instance, the automobiles sold by most auto makers are accompanied by a warranty obligating the auto maker to replace defective parts for a period of several years. As each car is sold, the auto maker *incurs a liability* to perform any work which may be required under the warranty. The dollar amount of this liability, however, can only be estimated.

CURRENT LIABILITIES

Current liabilities are obligations that must be paid within one year or within the operating cycle, whichever is longer. Another requirement for classification as a current liability is the expectation that the debt will be paid from current assets (or through the rendering of services). Liabilities that do not meet these conditions are classified as long-term liabilities.

The time period used in defining current liabilities parallels that used in defining current assets. As explained in Chapter 6, the amount of *working capital* (current assets less current liabilities) and the *current ratio* (current assets divided by current liabilities) are valuable indicators of a company's ability to pay its debts in the near future.

Among the most common examples of current liabilities are accounts payable, short-term notes payable, the current portion of long-term debt, accrued liabilities (such as interest payable, income taxes payable, and payroll liabilities), and unearned revenue.

ACCOUNTS PAYABLE

Accounts payable often are subdivided into the categories of *trade* accounts payable and *other* accounts payable. Trade accounts payable are short-term obligations to suppliers for purchases of merchandise. Other accounts payable include liabilities for any goods and services other than merchandise.

Technically, the date at which a trade account payable comes into existence depends upon whether goods are purchased F.O.B. shipping point, or F.O.B. destination. Under F.O.B. shipping point, a liability arises, and title to the goods transfers, when the merchandise is *shipped* by the supplier. Under F.O.B. destination, a liability does not arise, and title of ownership does not transfer, until the goods are actually *received* by the buyer. However, unless *material* amounts of merchandise are purchased on terms F.O.B. shipping point, most companies follow the convenient practice of recording trade accounts payable when merchandise is received.

NOTES PAYABLE

Notes payable are issued whenever bank loans are obtained. Other transactions which may give rise to notes payable include the purchase of real estate or costly equipment, the purchase of merchandise, and the substitution of a note for a past-due account payable.

LO 2 *Account for notes payable and interest expense.*

Notes payable usually require the borrower to pay an interest charge. Normally, the interest rate is stated separately from the **principal amount** of the note.[2]

To illustrate, assume that on November 1 Porter Company borrows $10,000 from its bank for a period of six months at an annual interest rate of 12%. Six months later on May 1, Porter Company will have to pay the bank the principal amount of $10,000, plus $600 interest ($10,000 $\times$ .12 $\times$ $\frac{6}{12}$). As evidence of this loan, the bank will require Porter Company to issue a note payable similar to the one illustrated below:

Note payable written in the principal amount with the interest rate stated separately

---

Miami, Florida	November 1, 19__

Six months	**AFTER THIS DATE**	Porter Company

PROMISES TO PAY TO SECURITY NATIONAL BANK THE SUM OF $ ___$10,000___

WITH INTEREST AT THE RATE OF ___12%___ **PER ANNUM.**

SIGNED ___John Caldwell___

TITLE ___Treasurer___

The journal entry in Porter Company's accounting records for this November 1 borrowing is:

Cash...	10,000	
Notes Payable...		10,000
Borrowed $10,000 for six months at 12% interest per year.		

Face amount of note

Notice that no liability is recorded for the interest charges when the note is issued. At the date that money is borrowed, the borrower has a liability *only for*

---

[2]Accounting textbooks traditionally have illustrated an alternative form of note in which the interest charges are included in the face amount. This form of note is seldom used today, largely because of the disclosure requirements under "truth-in-lending" laws.

the principal amount of the loan; the liability for interest accrues day by day over the life of the loan. At December 31, two months' interest expense has been incurred, and the following year-end adjusting entry is made:

A liability for interest accrues day by day

Interest Expense	200	
Interest Payable		200

To record interest expense incurred through year-end on 12%,
6-month note dated Nov. 1 ($10,000 × 12% × ²⁄₁₂ = $200).

For simplicity, we will assume that Porter Company makes adjusting entries *only at year end.* Thus, the entry on May 1 to record payment of the note will be:

Payment of principal and interest

Notes Payable	10,000	
Interest Payable	200	
Interest Expense	400	
Cash		10,600

To record payment of 12%, 6-month note on maturity
date and to recognize interest expense incurred since
January 1 ($10,000 × .12% × ⁴⁄₁₂ = $400)

If Porter Company paid this note *prior* to May 1, interest charges usually would be computed only through the date of early payment.[3]

THE CURRENT PORTION OF LONG-TERM DEBT

Some long-term debts, such as mortgage loans, are payable in a series of monthly or quarterly installments. In these cases, the *principal* amount due within one year (or the operating cycle) is regarded as a current liability, and the remainder of the obligation is classified as a long-term liability.

As the maturity date of a long-term liability approaches, the obligation eventually becomes due within the current period. Long-term liabilities which become payable within the coming year are *reclassified* in the balance sheet as current liabilities.[4] Changing the classification of a liability does not require a journal entry; the obligation merely is shown in a different section of the balance sheet.

ACCRUED LIABILITIES

Accrued liabilities arise from the recognition of expenses for which payment will be made in a future period. Thus, accrued liabilities also are called *accrued expenses.* Examples of accrued liabilities include interest payable, income taxes payable, and a number of liabilities relating to payrolls. As accrued liabilities stem from the recording of expenses, the *matching* principle governs the timing of their recognition.

All companies incur accrued liabilities. In most cases, however, these liabilities are paid at frequent intervals. Therefore, they usually do not accumulate to large amounts. In a balance sheet, accrued liabilities frequently are included in the amount shown as "accounts payable."

PAYROLL LIABILITIES

The preparation of a payroll is a specialized accounting function beyond the scope of this course. But we believe that every business student should have

---

[3]Computing interest charges only through the date of payment is the normal business practice. However, some notes are written in a manner requiring the borrower to pay interest for the full term of the note even if payment is made early. Borrowers should look carefully at these terms.
[4]Exceptions are made to this rule if the liability will be *refinanced* (that is, extended or renewed) on a long-term basis, or if a special *sinking fund* has been accumulated for the purpose of repaying this obligation. In these cases, the debt remains classified as a long-term liability, even though it will mature within the current period.

some understanding of the various costs associated with payrolls. Every employer must compute, record, and pay a number of costs in addition to the wages and salaries owed to employees. In fact, one might say that the total wages and salaries expense (or gross pay) represents only the "starting point" of payroll computations.

To illustrate, assume that a manufacturing company employs 50 highly skilled factory employees. If monthly wages for this workforce average $100,000, the costs incurred by this employer in a "typical" monthly payroll might be as follows:

LO 3 *Describe the costs relating to payrolls.*

Gross pay (wages expense)	$100,000
Social Security and Medicare taxes	7,650
Federal and state unemployment taxes	6,200
Workers' compensation insurance premiums	4,000
Group health insurance premiums	10,500
Contributions to employee pension plan and other postretirement costs	5,000
Total factory payroll costs for January	$133,350

Notice the costs in addition to employees' wages

The amounts shown in red are **payroll taxes** and insurance premiums required by law. Costs shown in green currently are not required by law, but often are included in the total "compensation package" provided to employees.

In our example total payroll-related costs exceed wages expense *by more than 30%*. This relationship will vary from one employer to the next, but our illustration is typical of many payrolls.

PAYROLL TAXES AND MANDATED COSTS All employers must pay Social Security and Medicare taxes on the wages or salary paid to each employee. These taxes typically amount to about 7⅔% of the employee's earnings.[5] Unemployment taxes apply only to the *first $7,000* earned by each employee during the year. Thus, these taxes tend to drop off dramatically as the year progresses.

Workers' compensation is a state-mandated program that provides insurance to employees against job-related injury. The premiums vary greatly by state and by occupational classification. In some high-risk industries (e.g., roofers), workers' compensation premiums may exceed 50% of the employees' wages.

OTHER PAYROLL-RELATED COSTS Many employers pay some or all of the costs of health insurance for their employees and also make contributions to employee pension plans. Annual health insurance premiums usually cost between $1,800 and $3,600 per employee (including family members). Contributions to employees' pension plans, if any, vary greatly among employers.

AMOUNTS WITHHELD FROM EMPLOYEES' PAY Our illustration specifies only those taxes levied upon the employer. Employees, too, incur taxes upon their earnings. These include federal and state income taxes, and the employees' shares of Social Security and Medicare taxes. Employers must withhold these amounts from the employees' pay and forward them directly to the appropriate tax authorities. (The net amount of cash actually paid to employees—that is, total wages and salaries expense less the amounts withheld—often is called the employees' *take-home pay.*

Amounts withheld from employees' pay do *not* represent taxes upon the employer. These amounts are simply portions of the original wages and salaries ex-

---

[5]Social Security and Medicare taxes of the *same amount* are also levied upon the employees, and are withheld from their paychecks. Thus, total Social Security and Medicare amounts to more than 15% of gross wages and salaries. There is a limit on the portion of an employee's earnings subject to Social Security taxes. However, this limit, now just over $65,000 (and increasing annually) exceeds most employee's annual earnings. There is no cap on employee wages or salaries subject to Medicare taxes.

pense that must be sent directly to tax authorities, rather than paid to the employees. With respect to these taxes, the employer is required by law to act as the tax *collector*. In the employer's balance sheet, these withholdings represent current liabilities until they are deposited with the proper tax authorities.

UNEARNED REVENUE

A liability for unearned revenue arises when a customer pays in advance. Upon receipt of an advance payment from a customer, the company debits Cash and credits a liability account such as Unearned Revenue, or Customers' Deposits. As the services are rendered to the customer, an entry is made debiting the liability account and crediting a revenue account. Notice that the liability for unearned revenue normally is "paid" by rendering services to the creditor, rather than by making cash payments.

Unearned revenue ordinarily is classified as a current liability, as the activities involved in earning revenue are part of the business's normal operating cycle.

LONG-TERM LIABILITIES

Long-term obligations usually arise from major expenditures, such as acquisitions of plant assets, the purchase of another company, or refinancing an existing long-term obligation which is about to mature. Thus, transactions involving long-term liabilities are relatively few in number, but often involve large dollar amounts. In contrast, current liabilities usually arise from routine operating transactions.

Many businesses regard long-term liabilities as an alternative to owners' equity as a source of "permanent" financing. Although long-term liabilities eventually mature, they often are *refinanced*—that is, the maturing obligation simply is replaced with a new long-term liability.

MATURING OBLIGATIONS INTENDED TO BE REFINANCED

One special type of long-term liability is an obligation which will mature in the current period, but which is expected to be refinanced on a long-term basis. For example, a company may have a bank loan which comes due each year, but is routinely extended for the following year. Both the company and the bank may intend for this arrangement to continue on a long-term basis.

If management has both the *intent* and the *ability* to refinance soon-to-mature obligations on a long-term basis, these obligations are classified as long-term liabilities. In this situation, the accountant looks to the *economic substance* of the situation, rather than to its legal form.

When the economic substance of a transaction differs from its legal form or its outward appearance, financial statements should reflect the *economic substance*. Accountants summarize this concept with the phrase, *"Substance takes precedence over form."* Today's business world is characterized by transactions of ever-increasing complexity. Recognizing those situations in which the substance of a transaction differs from its form is one of the greatest challenges confronting the accounting profession.

INSTALLMENT NOTES PAYABLE

Purchases of real estate and certain types of equipment often are financed by the issuance of long-term notes which call for a series of installment payments. These payments (often called **debt service**) may be due monthly, quarterly, semiannually, or at any other interval. If these installments continue until the debt is completely repaid, the loan is said to be "fully amortizing." Often, however, installment notes contain a "due date" at which the remaining unpaid balance is to be repaid in a single "balloon" payment.

Some installment notes call for installment payments equal to the periodic interest charges (an "interest only" note). Under these terms, the principal amount of the loan is payable at a specified maturity date. More often, however, the installment payments are *greater* than the amount of interest accruing during the period. Thus, only a portion of each installment payment represents interest expense, and the remainder of the payment reduces the principal amount of the liability. As the amount owed is reduced by each payment, the portion of each successive payment representing interest expense will *decrease,* and the portion going toward repayment of principal will *increase.*

ALLOCATING INSTALLMENT PAYMENTS BETWEEN INTEREST AND PRINCIPAL In accounting for an installment note, the accountant must determine the portion of each payment that represents interest expense, and the portion that reduces the principal amount of the liability. This distinction is made in advance by preparing an **amortization table.**

LO 4 *Prepare an amortization table allocating payments between interest and principal.*

To illustrate, assume that on October 15, 1998, King's Inn purchases furnishings at a total cost of $16,398. In payment, the company issues an installment note payable for this amount, plus interest at 12% per annum (or 1% per month). This note will be paid in 18 monthly installments of $1,000 each, beginning on November 15. An amortization table for this installment note payable follows (amounts of interest expense are *rounded to the nearest dollar*):

AMORTIZATION TABLE
(12% Note Payable for $16,398; Payable in 18 Monthly Installments of $1,000)

Interest Period	Payment Date	(A) Monthly Payment	(B) Interest Expense (1% of the Last Unpaid Balance)	(C) Reduction in Unpaid Balance (A) – (B)	(D) Unpaid Balance
Issue date	Oct. 15, 1998	—	—	—	$16,398
1	Nov. 15	$1,000	$164	$836	15,562
2	Dec. 15	1,000	156	844	14,718
3	Jan. 15, 1999	1,000	147	853	13,865
4	Feb. 15	1,000	139	861	13,004
5	Mar. 15	1,000	130	870	12,134
6	Apr. 15	1,000	121	879	11,255
7	May 15	1,000	113	887	10,368
8	June 15	1,000	104	896	9,472
9	July 15	1,000	95	905	8,567
10	Aug. 15	1,000	86	914	7,653
11	Sept. 15	1,000	77	923	6,730
12	Oct. 15	1,000	67	933	5,797
13	Nov. 15	1,000	58	942	4,855
14	Dec. 15	1,000	49	951	3,904
15	Jan. 15, 2000	1,000	39	961	2,943
16	Feb. 15	1,000	29	971	1,972
17	Mar. 15	1,000	20	980	992
18	Apr. 15	1,000	8*	992	–0–

*In the last period, interest expense is equal to the amount of the final payment minus the remaining unpaid balance. This compensates for the cumulative effect of rounding interest amounts to the nearest dollar.

PREPARING AN AMORTIZATION TABLE   Let us explore the content of this table. First, notice that the payments are made on a *monthly* basis. Therefore, the amounts of the payments (column A), interest expense (column B), and reduction in the unpaid balance (column C) are all *monthly amounts.*

The interest rate used in the table is of special importance; this rate must coincide with the period of time *between payment dates*—in this case, one month. Thus, if payments are made monthly, column B must be based upon the *monthly* rate of interest. If payments were made quarterly, this column would use the quarterly rate of interest.

An amortization table begins with the original amount of the liability ($16,398) listed at the top of the unpaid balance column. The amounts of the monthly payments, shown in column A, are specified by the installment contract. The monthly interest expense, shown in column B, is computed for each month by applying the monthly interest rate to the unpaid balance at the *beginning of that month.* The portion of each payment that reduces the amount of the liability (column C) is simply the remainder of the payment (column A minus column B). Finally, the unpaid balance of the liability (column D) is reduced each month by the amount indicated in column C.

Rather than continuing to make monthly payments, King's Inn could settle this liability at any time by paying the amount currently shown as the unpaid balance.

Notice that the amount of interest expense listed in column B *changes every month.* In our illustration, the interest expense is *decreasing* each month, because the unpaid balance is continually decreasing.[6]

Preparing each horizontal line in an amortization table involves making the same computations, based upon a new unpaid balance. Thus, an amortization table of any length can be easily and quickly prepared by computer. (Most "money management" software includes a program for preparing amortization tables.) Only three items of data need to be entered into the computer: (1) the original amount of the liability, (2) the amount of periodic payments, and (3) the interest rate (per payment period).

USING AN AMORTIZATION TABLE   Once an amortization table has been prepared, the entries to record each payment are taken directly from the amounts shown in the table. For example, the entry to record the first monthly payment (November 15, 1998) is:

Interest Expense	164	
Installment Note Payable	836	
Cash		1,000
Made November payment on installment note payable.		

Similarly, the entry to record the *second* payment, made on *December 15, 1998* is:

Interest Expense	156	
Installment Note Payable	844	
Cash		1,000
Made December payment on installment note payable.		

Payment is allocated between interest and principal

Notice that interest expense is less in December

---

[6]If the monthly payments were *less* than the amount of the monthly interest expense, the unpaid balance of the note would *increase* each month. This, in turn, would cause the interest expense to increase each month. This pattern, termed *negative amortization,* occurs temporarily in some "adjustable-rate" home mortgages.

At December 31, 1998, King's Inn should make an adjusting entry to record one-half month's accrued interest on this liability. The amount of this adjusting entry is based upon the unpaid balance shown in the amortization table as of the last payment (December 15). This entry is:

Interest Expense	74	
Interest Payable		74

Adjusting entry to record interest expense on installment note
for the last half of December: $14,718 \times 1\% \times \frac{1}{2} = \$74$.

Year-end adjusting entry

THE CURRENT PORTION OF LONG-TERM DEBT Notice that as of December 31, 1998, the unpaid balance of this note is $14,718. As of December 31, *1999,* however, the unpaid balance will be only $3,904. Thus, the principal amount of this note will be reduced by *$10,814* during 1999 ($14,718 − $3,904 = $10,814). In the balance sheet prepared at December 31, 1998, the $10,814 portion of this debt which is scheduled for repayment within the *next 12 months* should be classified as a *current liability.* The remaining $3,904 should be classified as a long-term liability.

SPECIAL TYPES OF LIABILITIES

The types of liabilities discussed up to this point are encountered in all types of business organizations—large and small. We will now address some special types of liabilities which are found primarily in the financial statements of large, publicly owned corporations.

BONDS PAYABLE

Financially sound corporations may arrange limited amounts of long-term financing by issuing notes payable to banks or to insurance companies. But to finance a large project, such as developing an oil field or purchasing a controlling interest in the capital stock of another company, a corporation may need more capital than any single lender can supply. When a corporation needs to raise large amounts of long-term capital—perhaps 50, 100, or 500 million dollars (or more)—it generally sells additional shares of capital stock or issues **bonds payable.**

LO 5 *Describe corporate bonds and explain the tax advantage of debt financing.*

WHAT ARE BONDS?

The issuance of bonds payable is a technique for splitting a very large loan into a great many transferable units, called bonds. Each bond represents a *long-term, interest-bearing note payable,* usually in the face amount (or par value) of $1,000, or some multiple of $1,000. The bonds are sold to the investing public, enabling many different investors (bondholders) to participate in the loan.

Bonds usually are very long-term notes, maturing in perhaps 30 or 40 years. The bonds are transferable, however, so individual bondholders may sell their bonds to other investors at any time. Most bonds call for semiannual interest payments to the bondholders, with interest computed at a specified *contract rate* throughout the life of the bond. Thus, investors often describe bonds as "fixed income" investments.

An example of a corporate bond issue is the 8½% bonds of Pacific Bell (a Pacific Telesis company, known as PacBell), due August 15, 2031. Interest on these bonds is payable semiannually on February 15 and August 15. With this bond issue, PacBell borrowed $225 million by issuing 225,000 bonds of $1,000 each.

PacBell did not actually print and issue 225,000 separate notes payable. Each bondholder is issued a single *bond certificate* indicating the number of bonds purchased. An illustration of a bond certificate appears below. This specimen certificate is in the face amount of $25,000 and, therefore, represents ownership of 25 bonds. Investors such as mutual funds, banks, and insurance companies often buy thousands of bonds at one time.

THE ISSUANCE OF BONDS PAYABLE When bonds are issued, the corporation usually utilizes the services of an investment banking firm, called an **underwriter.** The underwriter guarantees the issuing corporation a specific price for the entire bond issue and makes a profit by selling the bonds to the investing public at a higher price. The corporation records the issuance of the bonds at the net amount received from the underwriter. The use of an underwriter assures the corporation that the entire bond issue will be sold without delay, and the entire amount of the proceeds will be available at a specific date.

TRANSFERABILITY OF BONDS Corporate bonds, like capital stocks, are traded daily on organized securities exchanges, such as the *New York Bond Exchange.* The holders of a 25-year bond issue need not wait 25 years to convert their investments into cash. By placing a telephone call to a broker, an investor may sell bonds within a matter of minutes at the going market price. This quality of *liquidity* is one of the most attractive features of an investment in corporate bonds.

QUOTED MARKET PRICES Bond prices are quoted as a *percentage* of their face value or *maturity* value, which is usually $1,000. The maturity value is the amount the issuing company must pay to redeem the bond at the date it matures (becomes due). A $1,000 bond quoted at *102* would therefore have a market price of $1,020 (102% of $1,000). Bond prices are quoted at the nearest one-

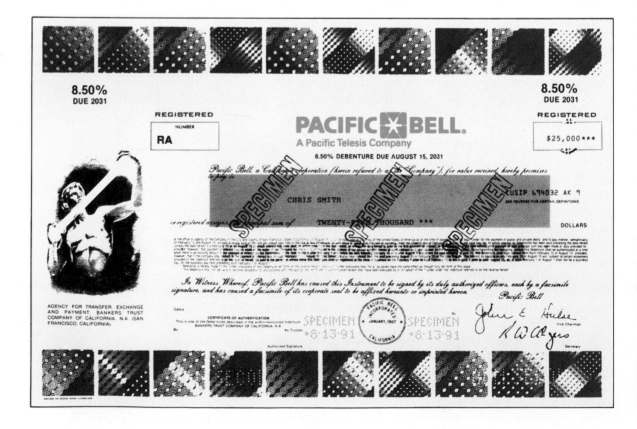

eighth of a percentage point. The following line from the financial page of a daily newspaper summarizes the previous day's trading in bonds of Sears, Roebuck and Company.

Bonds	Sales	High	Low	Close	Net Change
Sears R 7⅞'07	245	97½	95½	97	+1

What is the market value of this bond?

This line of condensed information indicates that 245 of Sears, Roebuck and Company's 7⅞%, $1,000 bonds maturing in 2007 were traded during the day. The highest price is reported as 97½, or $975 for a bond of $1,000 face value. The lowest price was 95½, or $955 for a $1,000 bond. The closing price (last sale of the day) was 97, or $970. This was one point above the closing price of the previous day, an increase of $10 in the price of a $1,000 bond.

TYPES OF BONDS Bonds secured by the pledge of specific assets are called *mortgage bonds*. An unsecured bond is called a *debenture bond;* its value rests upon the general credit of the corporation. A debenture bond issued by a very large and strong corporation may have a higher investment rating than a secured bond issued by a corporation in less satisfactory financial condition.

Bond interest is paid semiannually by mailing to each bondholder a check for six months' interest on the bonds he or she owns.[7] Almost all bonds are *callable,* which means that the corporation has the right to redeem the bonds *in advance* of the maturity date by paying a specified *call price.* To compensate bondholders for being forced to give up their investments, the call price usually is somewhat higher than the face value of the bonds.

Traditionally, bonds have appealed to conservative investors, interested primarily in a reliable income stream and in the safety of the principal which they have invested. To make a bond issue more attractive to these investors, some corporations create a bond **sinking fund,** designated for repaying the bonds at maturity. At regular intervals, the corporation deposits cash into this sinking fund. A bond sinking fund is not classified as a current asset, because it is not available for the payment of current liabilities. Such funds are shown in the balance sheet under the caption "Long-term Investments," which appears just below the current asset section.

As an additional attraction to investors, corporations sometimes include a conversion privilege in the bond indenture. A **convertible bond** is one which may be exchanged at the option of the bondholder for a specified number of shares of common stock. Thus, the market value of a convertible bond tends to fluctuate with the market value of an equivalent number of shares of common stock.

"JUNK BONDS" In recent years, some corporations have issued securities which have come to be known as **junk bonds.** This term describes a bond issue which involves a substantially greater risk of default than normal. A company issuing junk bonds usually has so much long-term debt that its ability to meet interest and principal repayment obligations has become questionable. To compensate bondholders for this unusual level of risk, junk bonds promise a substantially higher rate of interest than do "investment quality" bonds.

---

[7]In recent years, corporations have issued only *registered* bonds, for which interest is paid by mailing a check to the registered owners of the bonds. In past decades, some companies issued *coupon bonds* or *bearer bonds,* which had a series of redeemable coupons attached. At each interest date, the bondholder had to "clip" the coupon and present it to a bank to collect the interest. These bonds posed a considerable hazard to investors—if the investor lost the coupon, or forgot about an interest date, he or she received no interest. In many states, issuing coupon bonds now is illegal.

CASE **IN** POINT

The risk associated with junk bonds can make them a real gamble for investors in more ways than one. Donald Trump recently sold $1.2 billion in junk bonds, secured primarily by the Trump Taj Mahal and the Trump Plaza—the largest casino junk bond issue in history. The risk did not scare away high-rolling investors, however, who eagerly placed bets on the chance of receiving an 11.25% contract rate of interest.

TAX ADVANTAGE OF BOND FINANCING

A principal advantage of raising money by issuing bonds instead of stock is that interest payments are *deductible* in determining income subject to corporate income taxes. Dividends paid to stockholders, however, are *not deductible* in computing taxable income.

To illustrate, assume that a corporation pays income taxes at a rate of *30%* on its taxable income. If this corporation issues $10 million of 10% bonds payable, it will incur interest expense of $1 million per year. This interest expense, however, will reduce taxable income by $1 million, thus reducing the corporation's annual income taxes by $300,000. As a result, the *after-tax* cost of borrowing the $10 million is only *$700,000,* as shown below:

Interest expense ($10,000,000 × 10%)	$1,000,000
Less: Income tax savings ($1,000,000 deduction × 30%)	300,000
After-tax cost of borrowing	$700,000

A short-cut approach to computing the after-tax cost of borrowing is simply multiplying the interest expense by *1 minus the company's tax rate,* as follows: $1,000,000 × (1 − .30) = $700,000.

ACCOUNTING FOR BONDS PAYABLE

Accounting for bonds payable closely parallels accounting for notes payable. The "accountable events" in the life of a bond issue usually are (1) issuance of the bonds, (2) semiannual interest payments, (3) accrual of interest payable at the end of each accounting period,[8] and (4) retirement of the bonds at maturity.

To illustrate these events, assume that on March 1, 1998, Wells Corporation issues $1 million of 12%, 20-year bonds payable.[9] These bonds are dated March 1, 1998, and interest is computed from this date. Interest on the bonds is payable semiannually, each September 1 and March 1. If all of the bonds are sold at par value (face amount), the issuance of the bonds on March 1 will be recorded by the following entry:

Entry at the issuance date

Cash	1,000,000	
Bonds Payable		1,000,000
Issued 12% 20-year bonds payable at a price of 100.		

---

[8]To simplify our illustrations, we assume in all of our examples and assignment material that adjusting entries for accrued bond interest payable are made *only at year-end.* In practice, these adjustments usually are made on a monthly basis.
[9]The amount of $1 million is used only for purposes of illustration. As explained earlier, actual bond issues are for many millions of dollars.

Every September 1 during the life of the bond issue, Wells Corporation must pay $60,000 to the bondholders ($1,000,000 × .12 × ½ = $60,000). This semi-annual interest payment will be recorded as shown below:

Bond Interest Expense	60,000	
Cash		60,000

Semiannual payment of bond interest.

Entry to record semiannual interest payments

Every December 31, Wells Corporation must make an adjusting entry to record the four months' interest which has accrued since September 1:

Bond Interest Expense	40,000	
Bond Interest Payable		40,000

To accrue bond interest payable for four months ended Dec. 31 ($1,000,000 × .12 × ⁴⁄₁₂ = $40,000).

Adjusting entry at year-end—if necessary

The accrued liability for bond interest payable will be paid within a few months and, therefore, is classified as a current liability.

Two months later, on March 1, a semiannual interest payment is made to bondholders. This transaction represents payment of the four months' interest accrued at December 31, and of two months' interest which has accrued since year-end. Thus, the entry to record the semiannual interest payments every March 1 will be:

Bond Interest Expense	20,000	
Bond Interest Payable	40,000	
Cash		60,000

To record semiannual interest payment to bondholders, and to recognize two months' interest expense accrued since year-end ($1,000,000 × .12 × ²⁄₁₂ = $20,000).

Interest payment following the year-end adjusting entry

When the bonds mature 20 years later on March 1, 2018, two entries are required: One to record the regular semiannual interest payment, and a second to record the retirement of the bonds. The entry to record the retirement of the bond issue is:

Bonds Payable	1,000,000	
Cash		1,000,000

Paid face amount of bonds at maturity.

Redeeming the bonds at the maturity date

BONDS ISSUED BETWEEN INTEREST DATES The semiannual interest dates (such as January 1 and July 1, or April 1 and October 1) are printed on the bond certificates. However, bonds are often issued between the specified interest dates. The *investor* is then required to pay the interest accrued to the date of issuance *in addition* to the stated price of the bond. This practice enables the corporation to pay a full six months' interest on all bonds outstanding at the semiannual interest payment date. The accrued interest collected from investors who purchase bonds between interest payment dates is thus returned to them on the next interest payment date.

To illustrate, let us modify our illustration to assume that Wells Corporation issues $1 million of 12% bonds at a price of 100 on *May 1*—two months *after* the date printed on the bonds. The amount received from the bond purchasers now will include two months' accrued interest, as follows:

Bonds issued between
interest dates

Cash..	1,020,000	
Bonds Payable...		1,000,000
Bond Interest Payable..		20,000
Issued $1,000,000 face value of 12%, 20-year bonds at 100 plus		
accrued interest for two months ($1,000,000 × 12% × ²⁄₁₂ = $20,000).		

Four months later on the regular semiannual interest payment date, a full
six months' interest ($60 per $1,000 bond) will be paid to all bondholders,
regardless of when they purchased their bonds. The entry for the semiannual
interest payment is illustrated below:

Notice only part of the
interest payment is charged
to expense

Bond Interest Payable...	20,000	
Bond Interest Expense..	40,000	
Cash..		60,000
Paid semiannual interest on $1,000,000 face value of 12% bonds.		

Now consider these interest transactions from the standpoint of the *investors*.
They paid for two months' accrued interest at the time of purchasing the bonds,
and then received checks for six months' interest after holding the bonds for
only four months. They have, therefore, been reimbursed properly for the use
of their money for four months.

When bonds are subsequently sold by one investor to another, they sell at
the quoted market price *plus accrued interest* since the last interest payment date.
This practice enables the issuing corporation to pay all the interest for an interest period to the investor owning the bond at the interest date. Otherwise,
the corporation would have to make partial payments to every investor who
bought or sold the bond during the interest period.

The amount which investors will pay for bonds is the *present value* of the
principal and interest payments they will receive. Before going further in our
discussion of bonds payable, it will be helpful to review the concepts of present
value and effective interest rate.

THE CONCEPT OF PRESENT VALUE

LO 6 *Explain the concept of present value.*

The concept of present value is based upon the "time value" of money—the
idea that receiving money today is preferable to receiving money at some later
date. Assume, for example, that a bond will have a maturity value of $1,000
five years from today but will pay no interest in the meantime. Investors would
not pay $1,000 for this bond today, because they would receive no return on
their investment over the next five years. There are prices less than $1,000, how-
ever, at which investors would buy the bond. For example, if the bond could
be purchased for $600, the investor could expect a return (interest) of $400 from
the investment over the five-year period.

The **present value** of a future cash receipt is the amount that a knowledgeable investor will pay *today* for the right to receive that future payment.
The exact amount of the present value depends upon (1) the amount of the future payment, (2) the length of time until the payment will be received, and
(3) the rate of return required by the investor. However, the present value will
always be *less* than the future amount. This is because money received today
can be invested to earn interest and grow to a larger amount in the future.

The rate of interest which will cause a given present value to grow to a given
future amount is called the *discount rate* or *effective rate.* The effective interest
rate required by investors at any given time is regarded as the going *market rate*
of interest. (The procedures for computing the present value of a future amount
are illustrated in Appendix D at the end of this textbook. The concept of present value is very useful in managing your personal financial affairs. We suggest
that you read Appendix D—even if it has not been assigned.)

THE PRESENT VALUE CONCEPT AND BOND PRICES The price at which bonds will sell is the present value to investors of the future principal and interest payments. If the bonds sell at par, the market rate is equal to the *contract interest rate* (or nominal rate) printed on the bonds. The *higher* the effective interest rate that investors require, the *less* they will pay for bonds with a given contract rate of interest. For example, if investors insist upon a 10% return, they will pay less than $1,000 for a 9%, $1,000 bond. Thus, if investors require an effective interest rate *greater* than the contract rate of interest, the bonds will sell at a *discount* (a price less than their face value). On the other hand, if market conditions support an effective interest rate of *less* than the contract rate, the bonds will sell at a *premium* (a price above their face value).

A corporation wishing to borrow money by issuing bonds must pay the going market rate of interest. Since market rates of interest fluctuate constantly, it must be expected that the contract rate of interest may vary somewhat from the market rate at the date the bonds are issued. Thus, bonds may be issued at a slight discount or premium. (The issuance of bonds at a discount or premium is discussed in *Supplemental Topic B* at the end of this chapter.)

BOND PRICES AFTER ISSUANCE

As stated earlier, many corporate bonds are traded daily on organized securities exchanges at quoted market prices. After bonds are issued, their market prices vary *inversely* with changes in market interest rates. As interest rates rise, investors will be willing to pay less money to own a bond that pays a given contract rate of interest. Conversely, as interest rates decline, the market prices of bonds rise.

CASE IN POINT

IBM sold to underwriters $500 million of 9⅜%, 25-year debenture bonds. The underwriters planned to sell the bonds to the public at a price of 99⅝. Just as the bonds were offered for sale, however, a change in Federal Reserve credit policy started an upward surge in interest rates. The underwriters encountered great difficulty selling the bonds. Within one week, the market price of the bonds had fallen to 94½. The underwriters dumped their unsold inventory at this price and sustained one of the largest underwriting losses in Wall Street history.

During the months ahead, interest rates soared to record levels. Within five months, the price of the bonds had fallen to 76⅜. Thus, nearly one-fourth of the market value of these bonds evaporated in less than half a year. At this time, the financial strength of IBM was never in question; this dramatic loss in market value was caused entirely by rising interest rates.

Changes in the current level of interest rates are not the only factors influencing the market prices of bonds. The length of time remaining until the bonds mature is another major force. As a bond nears its maturity date, its market price normally moves closer and closer to the maturity value. This trend is dependable because the bonds are redeemed at par value on the maturity date.

VOLATILITY OF SHORT-TERM AND LONG-TERM BOND PRICES When interest rates fluctuate, the market prices of long-term bonds are affected to a far greater extent than are the market prices of bonds due to mature in the near future. To illustrate, assume that market interest rates suddenly soar from 9% to 12%. A 9% bond scheduled to mature in but a few days will still have a market value of approximately $1,000—the amount to be collected in a few days from the issuing corporation. However, the market price of a 9% bond maturing in 10 years will drop significantly. Investors who must accept these "below market" interest payments for many years will buy the bonds only at a discounted price.

In summary, fluctuations in interest rates have a far greater effect upon the market prices of long-term bonds than upon the prices of short-term bonds.

Remember that after bonds have been issued, they belong to the bondholder, *not to the issuing corporation*. Therefore, changes in the market price of bonds subsequent to their issuance *do not* affect the amounts shown in the financial statements of the issuing corporation, and these changes are not recorded in the company's accounting records.

YOUR TURN

You as a Financial Advisor

Assume that you are the financial advisor for a recently retired couple. Your clients want to invest their savings in such a way as to receive a stable stream of cash flow every year throughout their retirement. They have expressed their concerns to you regarding the volatility of long-term bond prices when interest rates fluctuate.

If your clients invest their savings in a variety of long-term bonds and hold these bonds until maturity, will interest rate fluctuations affect their annual cash flow during their retirement years?

*Our comments appear on page 515.

EARLY RETIREMENT OF BONDS PAYABLE

Bonds are sometimes retired before the maturity date. The principal reason for retiring bonds early is to relieve the issuing corporation of the obligation to make future interest payments. If interest rates decline to the point that a corporation can borrow at an interest rate below that being paid on a particular bond issue, the corporation may benefit from retiring those bonds and issuing new bonds at a lower interest rate.

Most bond issues contain a call provision, permitting the corporation to redeem the bonds by paying a specified price, usually a few points above par. Even without a call provision, the corporation may retire its bonds before maturity by purchasing them in the open market. If the bonds can be purchased by the issuing corporation at less than their carrying value, a *gain* is realized on the retirement of the debt. If the bonds are reacquired by the issuing corporation at a price in excess of their carrying value, a *loss* must be recognized.[10]

For example, assume that Briggs Corporation has outstanding a 13%, $10 million bond issue, callable on any interest date at a price of 104. Assume also that the bonds were issued at par and will not mature for nine years. Recently,

---

[10]The FASB has ruled that the gains and losses from early retirements of debt be classified in a special section of the income statement and identified as *extraordinary items*. The presentation of extraordinary items is explained and illustrated in Chapter 12.

however, market interest rates have declined to less than 10%, and the market price of Briggs' bonds has increased to 106.[11]

Regardless of the market price, Briggs can call these bonds at 104. If the company exercises this call provision for 10% of the bonds ($1,000,000 face value), the entry will be:

Bonds Payable	1,000,000		Bonds called at a price above carrying value
Loss on Early Retirement of Bonds	40,000		
Cash		1,040,000	

To record the call of $1 million in bonds payable at a call price of 104.

Notice that Briggs *called* these bonds, rather than repurchasing them at market prices. Therefore, Briggs is able to retire these bonds at their call price of 104. (Had the market price of the bonds been *below* 104, Briggs might have been able to retire the bonds at less cost by purchasing them in the open market.)

LEASE PAYMENT OBLIGATIONS

A company may purchase the assets needed in its business operations or, as an alternative, it may lease them. A *lease* is a contract in which the lessor gives the lessee the right to use an asset for a specified period of time in exchange for periodic rental payments. The **lessor** is the owner of the property; the **lessee** is a tenant or renter. Examples of assets frequently acquired by lease include automobiles, building space, computers, and equipment.

OPERATING LEASES

When the lessor gives the lessee the right to use leased property for a limited period of time but retains the usual risks and rewards of ownership, the contract is known as an **operating lease.** An example of an operating lease is a contract leasing office space in an office building. If the building increases in value, the *lessor* can receive the benefits of this increase by either selling the building or increasing the rental rate once the lease term has expired. On the other hand, if the building declines in value, it is the lessor who bears the loss.

In accounting for an operating lease, the lessor views the monthly lease payments received as rental revenue, and the lessee regards these payments as rental expense. No asset or liability (other than a short-term liability for accrued rent payable) relating to the lease appears in the lessee's balance sheet. Thus, operating leases are sometimes termed **off-balance-sheet financing.**

CAPITAL LEASES

Some lease contracts are intended to provide financing to the lessee for the eventual purchase of the property or to provide the lessee with use of the property over most of its useful life. These lease contracts are called **capital leases** (or financing leases). In contrast to an operating lease, a capital lease transfers most of the risks and rewards of ownership from the lessor to the *lessee.* Assume, for example, that City Realty leases a new automobile for a period of three years. Also assume that at the end of the lease, title to the automobile transfers to City Realty at no additional cost. Clearly, City Realty is not merely "renting"

---

[11]Falling interest rates cause bond prices to rise. On the other hand, falling interest rates also provide the issuing company with an incentive to call the bonds and, perhaps, replace them with bonds bearing a lower rate of interest. For this reason, call prices often serve as an approximate "ceiling" on market prices.

the use of the automobile; rather, it is using the lease agreement as a means of *financing the purchase* of the car.

From an accounting viewpoint, capital leases are regarded as *essentially equivalent to a sale* of the property by the lessor to the lessee, even though title to the leased property has not been transferred. Thus, a capital lease should be recorded by the *lessor as a sale* of property and by the *lessee as a purchase.* In such lease agreements, an appropriate interest charge usually is added to the regular sales price of the property in determining the amount of the lease payments.

Some companies use capital lease agreements as a means of financing the sale of their products to customers. In accounting for merchandise "sold" through a capital lease, the lessor debits *Lease Payments Receivable* and credits *Sales* for an amount equal to the *present value* of the future lease payments. In most cases, the present value of these future payments is equal to the regular sales price of the merchandise. In addition, the lessor transfers the cost of the leased merchandise from the Inventory account to the Cost of Goods Sold account. When lease payments are received, the lessor should recognize an appropriate portion of the payment as representing interest revenue and the remainder as a reduction in Lease Payments Receivable.

When equipment is acquired through a capital lease, the lessee should *debit an asset account,* Leased Equipment, and *credit a liability account,* Lease Payment Obligation, for the present value of the future lease payments. Lease payments made by the lessee are allocated between Interest Expense and a reduction in the liability, Lease Payment Obligation. The portion of the lease payment obligation that will be repaid within the next year is classified as a current liability, and the remainder is classified as long-term.

No rent expense is involved in a capital lease. The asset account, Leased Equipment, is depreciated over the life of the equipment rather than the life of the lease. Accounting for capital leases is illustrated in Appendix D at the end of this textbook.

DISTINGUISHING BETWEEN CAPITAL LEASES AND OPERATING LEASES
The FASB has taken the position that the "risks and returns of ownership" transfer to the lessee under any of the following circumstances:

● The lease transfers ownership of the property to the lessee at the end of the lease term.

● The lease contains a "bargain purchase option."

● The lease term is equal to 75% or more of the estimated economic life of the leased property.

● The present value of the minimum lease payments amounts to 90% or more of the fair value of the lease property.

Thus, if a lease contains any of the provisions, it is viewed as a capital lease. Otherwise, it is accounted for as an operating lease.

LIABILITIES FOR PENSIONS AND OTHER POSTRETIREMENT BENEFITS

PENSIONS   Many employers agree to pay their employees a pension; that is, monthly cash payments for life, beginning upon retirement. Pensions are not an expense of the years in which cash payments are made to retired workers. Employees earn the right to receive the pension *while they are working for their employer.* Therefore, the employer's cost of future pension payments *accrues* over the years that each employee is on the payroll.

LO 7 *Account for postretirement costs.*

Of course, the amounts of the retirement benefits that will be paid to to-day's workers after they retire is not known with certainty. Among other things, these amounts depend upon how long retired employees live. Therefore, the employer's obligation for future pension payments arising during the current year *can only be estimated.*

Employers do not usually pay retirement pensions directly to retired employees. Most employers meet their pension obligations by making periodic deposits in a **pension fund** (or pension plan) throughout the years of each worker's employment.

A pension fund is *not an asset* of the employer. Rather, it is an *independent entity* managed by a trustee (usually a bank or an insurance company). As the employer makes deposits in the pension fund, the trustee invests the money in securities such as stocks and bonds. Over time, the pension fund earns investment income and normally accumulates to a balance far in excess of the employer's deposits. It is the *pension fund*—not the employer—that disburses monthly pension benefits to retired workers.

If the employer meets *all* of its estimated pension obligations by promptly depositing cash in a pension fund, the pension fund is said to be *fully funded.* The operation of a fully funded pension plan is summarized in the illustration below.

If a pension plan is fully funded, *no liability* for pension payments appears in the employer's balance sheet. The employer's obligation is discharged in the *current period* through the payments made to the pension fund. The employer records each payment to this fund by debiting Pension Expense and crediting Cash.

Most pension plans are fully funded; therefore, most corporations do *not* report any pension liability. However, an employer must credit a liability account, Unfunded Pension Liability, for any portion of its periodic pension expense which *is not* paid immediately to the pension fund.

DETERMINING PENSION EXPENSE From a conceptual point of view, the pension expense of a given period is the *present value* of the future pension rights granted to employees as a result of their services during the period. The computation of annual pension expense is complex and involves many assumptions. The amount of this expense is not computed by accountants, but rather by an **actuary.** Among the factors considered by the actuary are:

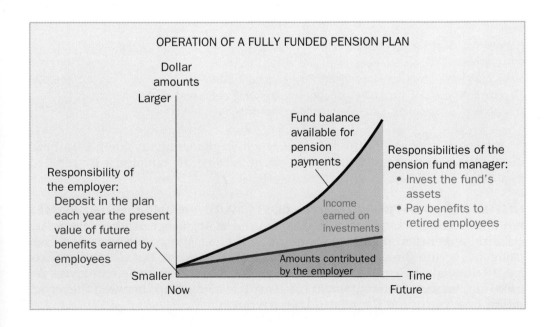

OPERATION OF A FULLY FUNDED PENSION PLAN

- Average age, retirement age, and life expectancy of employees.
- Employee turnover rates.
- Compensation levels and estimated rate of pay increases.
- Expected rate of return to be earned on pension fund assets.

As a step in determining the pension expense for the year, the actuary estimates the employer's total pension liability as of year-end. Thus, the estimates are updated annually, and estimating errors in prior years are "corrected" in the current year.

For example, assume that the actuarial firm of Gibson & Holt computes a pension expense for Cramer Cable Company of $400,000 for 1998. This amount represents the present value of pension rights granted to Cramer's employees for the work they performed during the year. To fully fund this obligation, Cramer transfers $400,000 to National Trust Co., the trustee of the company's pension plan.

An entry summarizing Cramer's fully funded pension expense for 1998 is shown below:

Pension Expense	400,000	
Cash		400,000

Pension expense for the year as determined by actuarial firm of
Gibson & Holt. Fully funded by payments to National Trust Co.

POSTRETIREMENT BENEFITS OTHER THAN PENSIONS In addition to pension plans, many companies have promised their employees other types of **postretirement benefits,** such as continuing health insurance. In most respects, these "nonpension" postretirement benefits are accounted for in the same manner as are pension benefits. Most companies, however, do not fully fund their obligations for nonpension postretirement benefits. Thus, recognition of the annual expense often includes a credit to an unfunded liability for part of the cost.

Continuing with our illustration of Cramer Cable Company, assume that Gibson & Holt computes for the company a $250,000 "nonpension" postretirement benefits expense for 1998. However, unlike its pension expense, Cramer does *not* fully fund its nonpension obligations.

For 1998, only $140,000 of the total amount was paid in cash. The entry to summarize this expense for the year is:

Nonpension Postretirement Benefits Expense	250,000	
Cash		140,000
Unfunded Liability for Nonpension Postretirement Benefits		110,000

To record nonpension postretirement benefits expense per report of
Gibson & Holt, actuaries. Expense funded to the extent of $140,000.

Any portion of the unfunded liability which the company intends to fund during the next year is classified as a *current liability;* the remainder is classified as a *long-term liability*.

UNFUNDED POSTRETIREMENT COSTS ARE "NONCASH" EXPENSES Postretirement costs are recognized as expense as workers earn the right to receive these benefits. If these costs are fully funded, the company makes cash payments within the current period equal to this expense. But if these benefits are *not* funded, the cash payments are not made until after the employees retire. Thus, an unfunded retirement plan involves a long "lag" between the recognition of expense and the related cash payments.

Unfunded retirement benefits often are called a "noncash" expense. That is, the expense is charged against current earnings, but there are no corresponding cash payments in the period. In the journal entry above, notice that expense exceeds the cash outlays by $110,000 ($250,000 − $140,000 = $110,000). This corresponds to the growth in the unfunded liability.

UNFUNDED LIABILITIES FOR POSTRETIREMENT COSTS: CAN THEY REALLY BE PAID? Many of America's largest and best-known corporations have obligations for unfunded postretirement benefits that can only be described as enormous. For many companies, this liability is equal to, or *greater than,* the total amount of stockholders' equity.

CASE IN POINT

General Motors reports an unfunded liability for postretirement costs of more than *$35 billion.* That compares with total stockholders' equity of a little more than $6 billion. One might say that GM's employees have a far greater "financial stake" in the company's long-term prospects than do its stockholders.

Until recently, companies were not required to show their unfunded liability for postretirement costs in their balance sheets. Instead, they charged benefit payments for retired workers directly to expense. This "pay-as-you-go" treatment, however, fails to achieve the *matching principle.* It is the cost of benefits earned by *today's* workers that are helping the company produce revenue, not the cost of benefits paid to workers who have already retired.

The FASB recently changed the rules for measuring postretirement costs. Companies now must estimate the present value of the retirement benefits earned each year by their employees. This estimated amount is recognized as expense, and any unfunded portion is recorded as a liability.

Now that these liabilities are "on the books," many people are stunned by their size. They wonder—with just cause—whether General Motors and other large corporations can really pay liabilities this large. Interesting question.

Let us suggest some things to consider in evaluating a company's ability to pay its unfunded liability for postretirement costs. First, remember that this liability represents only the *present value* of the estimated future payments. Thus, the future payments are expected to be *substantially more* than the amount shown in the balance sheet. Next, this liability may *continue to grow,* especially if the company has more employees today than in the past. On the other hand, this liability does *not* have to be paid all at once. It will be paid over a *great many years*—the life span of today's workforce.

In evaluating a company's ability to meet its postretirement obligations, we suggest looking to the *statement of cash flows,* rather than the balance sheet. In the cash flow statement, payments of postretirement costs are classified as operating activities. Thus, if a company has a steadily increasing net cash flow from operating activities, it apparently is able to handle these costs—at least at present.

But if the net cash flow from operating activities starts to decline, the company may have no choice but to reduce the benefits it provides to retired employees. Often these benefits are *not* contractual and can be reduced at management's discretion.

DEFERRED INCOME TAXES

LO 8 *Describe and account for deferred income taxes.*

We have seen in earlier chapters that differences sometimes exist between the dates that certain revenue or expense are recognized in financial statements and the dates these items are reported in income tax returns. For example, a company may use the straight-line method of depreciation in its financial reports, but use an accelerated method in its income tax returns.

Another example—installment sales—will be discussed in Chapter 14. When a company sells merchandise on an "installment plan," it usually recognizes the sales revenue immediately for financial reporting purposes. But in its income tax returns, the company may use the *installment method,* which *postpones* recognition of this sales revenue until payments are received from the customer.

Because of such *timing differences* between accounting principles and tax rules, income reported in the income statement of one year may appear in the income tax return of a *different* year. Most timing differences result in *postponing* (deferring) the recognition of income for tax purposes. The recognition of income in income tax returns may be postponed by those tax rules allowing the taxpayer either to (1) accelerate the recognition of expenses (such as accelerated depreciation methods), or (2) delay the recognition of revenue (such as the installment method).

In summary, income appearing in the income statement today may not be subject to income taxes until future years. However, the *matching principle* requires that the income shown in an income statement be offset by all related income taxes expense, regardless of when these taxes will be paid. Thus, the entry to record a corporation's income taxes expense might appear as follows:

Payment of some taxes expense often can be deferred

Income Taxes Expense	1,000,000	
Income Taxes Payable		800,000
Deferred Income Taxes		200,000

To record corporate income taxes applicable to the income of the current year.

Income Taxes Payable is a current liability representing the portion of the income taxes expense that must be paid when the company files its income tax return for the current year. That portion of the income taxes expense which is deferred to future tax returns is credited to a liability account entitled **Deferred Income Taxes.**[12]

DEFERRED INCOME TAXES IN FINANCIAL STATEMENTS Whether deferred income taxes are classified as current or long-term liabilities depends upon the classification of the assets and liabilities that *caused* the tax deferrals. For example, installment receivables are classified as current assets. Therefore, if the methods used in accounting for installment receivables result in deferred taxes, the deferred taxes are classified as a current liability. Depreciable assets, however, are not viewed as current assets. Therefore, if deferred taxes result from the use of accelerated depreciation methods in income tax returns, the deferred tax liability is classified as long-term.

The amount of income taxes deferred during the current period is recognized as expense, but does *not* require an immediate cash outlay. To the extent that a company is able to defer income taxes, its net cash flow from operating ac-

---

[12]Some timing differences, such as those associated with postretirement costs, may require that companies report deferred income taxes as an *asset account* instead of a liability. In this chapter, we limit our examples to the more common situations in which deferred income taxes are classified as liabilities.

tivities will *exceed* its net income. Bear in mind, however, that deferred income taxes are tax obligations that have been *postponed* to future periods. The company has *not eliminated* its obligation to pay these taxes.

Growing businesses often are able to defer part of their income taxes expense every year. Of course, some of the income taxes deferred in prior years constantly are coming due. Nonetheless, the liability for deferred taxes usually continues to grow as the company grows—just as does the overall liability for accounts payable.

Accounting for deferred taxes involves a number of complex issues which will be addressed in the intermediate accounting course.

LIABILITIES AND CASH FLOWS

How the payment of liabilities is classified in a statement of cash flows depends upon the type of transaction creating that liability. If the liability stems from the *recognition of an expense* or the purchase of inventory, payment is viewed as an *operating activity*. Thus, payments of trade accounts payable, accrued expenses, pension obligations, and income taxes are all classified as operating activities. Most interest payments also are classified as operating activities.[13]

Bear in mind that some expenses entering into the determination of net income *do not require immediate cash payments*. Examples include deferred income taxes and unfunded postretirement costs. The recognition of such "noncash expenses" reduces net income to an amount *less than* the net cash flow resulting from operating activities during the period.

If a liability is incurred for the purpose of borrowing cash or financing the purchase of a plant asset, repayment of the principal amount is classified as a *financing activity*.

LIABILITIES AND FINANCIAL STATEMENT DISCLOSURES

A company should disclose the *maturity dates* of its major liabilities. These disclosures assist users of the financial statements in evaluating the company's ability to meet obligations maturing in the near future.

The FASB also requires companies to disclose the *current value* of most long-term liabilities.[14] This information helps users of the statements evaluate the likelihood of the company's attempting to retire these liabilities *prior* to the scheduled maturity dates.

EVALUATING THE SAFETY OF CREDITOR'S CLAIMS

Creditors, of course, want to be sure that their claims are safe—that is, that they will be paid on time. Actually, *everyone* associated with a business—management, owners, employees—should be concerned with the company's ability

LO 9 *Evaluate the safety of creditors' claims.*

---

[13]As explained in Chapter 9, interest incurred while a plant asset is *under construction* is "capitalized" as part of the cost of that asset. Interest payments that are capitalized are classified as investing activities, rather than operating activities.

[14]*Current value* means either market value (as in the case of bonds payable) or the *present value* of the expected future payments (as with unfunded postretirement obligations). The current value disclosure requirement does *not* apply to a company's obligation for deferred income taxes.

to pay its debts. If a business becomes *insolvent* (unable to pay its obligations), it may be forced into **bankruptcy.**[15]

Not only does management want the business to remain solvent, it wants the company to maintain a high *credit rating* with agencies such as Dun & Bradstreet and Standard & Poor's. A high credit rating helps a company borrow money more easily and at lower interest rates.

In evaluating debt-paying ability, short-term creditors and long-term creditors look at different relationships. Short-term creditors are interested in the company's *immediate* solvency. Long-term creditors, in contrast, are interested in the company's ability to meet its interest obligations over a *period of years,* and also its ability to repay or refinance large obligations as they come due.

We have already introduced several measures of short-term solvency and of long-term credit risk. These measures are summarized in the table on page 490—along with the *interest coverage ratio,* which is discussed below.

INTEREST COVERAGE RATIO Creditors, investors, and managers all feel more comfortable when a company has enough income to cover its interest payments by a wide margin. One widely used measure of the relationship between earnings and interest expense is the **interest coverage ratio.**

The interest coverage ratio is computed by dividing *operating income* by the annual interest expense. From a creditor's point of view, the higher this ratio, the better. In past years, most companies with good credit ratings had interest coverage ratios of, perhaps, 4 to 1 or more. With the spree of junk bond financing in the 1980s, many large corporations have let their interest coverage ratios decline below 2 to 1. In most cases, their credit ratings have dropped accordingly.

YOUR TURN

You as a Loan Officer

Assume that you are a loan officer for First Federal National Bank. A local business wishes to obtain a 5-year loan in the amount of $150,000 to purchase a new piece of equipment. All of the company's solvency ratios look promising except for its interest coverage ratio, which is 3 to 1.

The company's CEO contends that this ratio is acceptable, considering that the company's $375,000 in operating income for the year included depreciation expense of $200,000 and a nonpension postretirement benefits expense of $50,000 (all of which was unfunded). Interest expense was, of course, $125,000 ($375,000 ÷ $125,000 = 3 times coverage).

What point was the CEO trying to make? Do you agree?

*Our comments appear on page 515.

LESS FORMAL MEANS OF DETERMINING CREDITWORTHINESS Not all decisions to extend credit involve formal analysis of the borrower's financial statements. Most suppliers of goods or services, for example, will sell "on ac-

---

[15]Bankruptcy is a legal status under which the company's fate is determined largely by the U.S. Bankruptcy Court. Sometimes the company is "reorganized" and allowed to continue its operations. In other cases, the business is closed and its assets are sold. Often managers and employees lose their jobs. In almost all bankruptcies, the company's creditors and owners incur legal costs and sustain financial losses.

count" to almost any long-established business—unless they know the customer to be in severe financial difficulty. If the customer is not a well-established business, these suppliers may investigate the customer's "credit history" by contacting a credit-rating agency.

In lending to small businesses organized as corporations, lenders usually require key stockholders to *personally guarantee* repayment of the loan.

HOW MUCH DEBT SHOULD A BUSINESS HAVE?

All businesses incur some debts as a result of normal business operations. These include, for example, accounts payable and accrued liabilities. But many businesses aggressively use long-term debt, such as mortgages and bonds payable, to finance growth and expansion. Is this wise? Does it benefit the stockholders? The answer hinges on another question: *Can the borrowed funds be invested to earn a return higher than the rate of interest paid to creditors?*

Using borrowed money to finance business operations is called applying **leverage.** Extensive use of leverage—that is, a great deal of debt—sometimes benefits a business dramatically. But if things don't work out, it can "wipe out" the borrower.

If borrowed money can be invested to earn a rate of return *higher* than the interest rates paid to the lenders, net income and the return on stockholders' equity will *increase*.[16] For example, if you borrow money at an interest rate of 9% and invest it to earn 15%, you will benefit from "the spread."

But leverage is a double-edged sword—the effects may be favorable *or unfavorable*. If the rate of return earned on the borrowed money falls *below* the rate of interest being paid, the use of borrowed money *reduces* net income and the return on equity. Companies with large amounts of debt sometimes become victims of their own debt-service requirements.

The effects of leverage may be summarized below:

Relationship of Return on Assets to Interest Rate on Borrowed Funds	Effect Upon Net Income and Return on Equity
Return on Assets > Interest Rates being Paid	Increase
Return on Assets < Interest Rates being Paid	Decrease

Bear in mind that over time, both the return on assets and the interest rates that the company must pay may *change*.

The more leverage a company applies, the greater become the effects upon net income and the return on equity. Using more leverage simply means having more debt. Therefore, the *debt ratio* is a basic measure of the amount of leverage being applied.

The following table provides a summary of common measures used by creditors and investors to evaluate a company's short-term and long-term debt paying ability.

---

[16]The rate of return earned on invested capital usually is viewed as the overall *return on assets*—that is, operating income divided by average total assets. *Return on equity* is net income expressed as a percentage of average stockholders' equity. Both of these "return on investment" measures were discussed in Chapter 6 (pages 269–271).

Measures of Debt-Paying Ability

Short-Term	Long-Term
Quick ratio—Quick assets divided by current liabilities; a stringent measure of solvency.	Debt ratio—Total liabilities divided by total assets. Measures percentage of capital structure financed by creditors.
Current ratio—Current assets divided by current liabilities; the most common measure of solvency, but less stringent than the quick ratio.	Interest coverage ratio—Operating income divided by interest expense. Shows how many times the company "earns" its annual interest obligations.
Working capital—Current assets less current liabilities; the "uncommitted" liquid resources.	Trend in net cash flow from operating activities—Indicates trend in "cash generating ability." Determined from comparative statements of cash flow.
Turnover rates—Measures of how quickly receivables are collected or inventory is sold. (Computed separately for receivables and inventory.)	Trend in net income—Less related to debt-paying ability than cash flow, but still an excellent measure of long-term financial health.
Operating cycle—The period of time required to convert inventory into cash.	
Net cash flow from operating activities—Measures company's ability to generate cash. (Shown in the statement of cash flows.)	
Lines of credit—Indicates ready access to additional cash should the need arise.	

NET CONNECTIONS

Would you lend a large sum of money to a complete stranger? Probably not. Most likely, you would want to learn as much as possible about the borrower's "creditworthiness" before handing over your hard-earned cash. The same concept applies to making an investment in corporate bonds. Before purchasing a bond, smart investors obtain a wide range of important information about the issuing company—including its *credit rating*.

What exactly are credit ratings? Who provides them? What rating criteria are used? To find out more, access the Internet and visit three of the world's largest credit rating services: Moody's Investors Service, Standard & Poor's Ratings Services, and Fitch Investors Service, L.P.

Using Moody's, you can view highlights of recent rating decisions, read credit research summaries, and learn about current economic events and conditions which effect credit ratings. The Moody's address is:

www.moodys.com

From the Standard and Poor's home page you can download the entire handbook of criteria used to evaluate corporate bonds, find out about upcoming credit rating seminars and teleconferences, and order educational materials related to various investment activities. The Standard and Poor's address is:

www.ratings.standardpoor.com

Fitch Investors Service, L.P., provides recent credit market press releases, company research announcements, and summaries of new ratings and rating changes. The Fitch address is:

www.fitchinv.com

ESTIMATED LIABILITIES, LOSS CONTINGENCIES, AND COMMITMENTS

ESTIMATED LIABILITIES

The term estimated liabilities refers to *liabilities which appear in financial statements at estimated dollar amounts.* Let us again consider the example of the auto maker's liability to honor its new car warranties. A manufacturer's liability for warranty work is recorded by an entry debiting Warranty Expense and crediting Liability for Warranty Claims. The *matching principle* requires that the expense of performing warranty work be recognized in the period in which the products are *sold,* in order to offset this expense against the related sales revenue. As the warranty may extend several years into the future, the dollar amount of this liability (and expense) must be estimated. Rather than estimate when warranty work will be performed, accountants traditionally have classified the liability for warranty claims as a current liability.

By definition, estimated liabilities involve some degree of uncertainty. However, the liabilities are (1) known to exist, and (2) the uncertainty as to dollar amount is *not so great* as to prevent the company from making a reasonable estimate and recording the liability.

LOSS CONTINGENCIES

Loss contingencies are similar to estimated liabilities, but may involve much more uncertainty. A loss contingency is a *possible loss* (or expense), stemming from *past events,* that will be resolved as to existence and amount by some future event.

Central to the definition of a loss contingency is the element of *uncertainty*— uncertainty as to the amount of loss and, in some cases, uncertainty as to *whether or not any loss actually has been incurred.* A common example of a loss contingency is a lawsuit pending against a company. The lawsuit is based upon past events, but until the suit is resolved, uncertainty exists as to the amount (if any) of the company's liability.

LO 10 *Define* loss contingencies *and explain their presentation in financial statements.*

Loss contingencies differ from estimated liabilities in two ways. First, a loss contingency may involve a *greater degree of uncertainty.* Often the uncertainty extends to whether or not any loss or expense actually has been incurred. In contrast, the loss or expense relating to an estimated liability is *known to exist.*

Second, the concept of a loss contingency extends not only to possible liabilities, but also to possible *impairments of assets.* Assume, for example, that a bank has made large loans to a foreign country now experiencing political instability. Uncertainty exists as to the amount of loss, if any, associated with this loan. From the bank's point of view, this loan is an asset that may be impaired, not a liability.

LOSS CONTINGENCIES IN FINANCIAL STATEMENTS The manner in which loss contingencies are presented in financial statements depends upon the *degree of uncertainty involved.*

Loss contingencies are *recorded* in the accounting records only when both of the following criteria are met: (1) it is *probable* that a loss has been incurred, and (2) the amount of loss can be *reasonably estimated.* An example of a loss contingency that usually meets these criteria and is recorded in the accounts is the estimated loss from doubtful accounts receivable.

When these criteria are *not* met, loss contingencies still are *disclosed* in financial statements if there is a *reasonable possibility* that a material loss has been incurred. Pending lawsuits, for example, usually are disclosed in notes accompanying the financial statements, but the loss, if any, is not recorded in the accounting records until the lawsuit is settled.

Companies need *not* disclose loss contingencies if the risk of a material loss having occurred is considered *remote*.

Notice the *judgmental nature* of the criteria used in accounting for loss contingencies. These criteria involve assessments as to whether the risk of material loss is "probable," "reasonably possible," or "remote." Thus, the *professional judgments* of the company's management, accountants, legal counsel, and auditors are the deciding factor in accounting for loss contingencies.

When loss contingencies are disclosed in footnotes to the financial statements, the footnote should describe the nature of the contingency and, if possible, provide an estimate of the amount of possible loss. If a reasonable estimate of the amount of possible loss cannot be made, the footnote should include the range of possible loss or a statement that an estimate cannot be made. The following footnote is typical of the disclosure of the loss contingency arising from pending litigation:

Footnote disclosure of a loss contingency

Note 8: Contingencies

In October of the current year, the Company was named as defendant in a lawsuit alleging patent infringement and claiming damages of $408 million. The Company denies all charges in this case and is preparing its defenses against them. The Company is advised by legal counsel that it is not possible at this time to determine the ultimate legal or financial responsibility with respect to this litigation.

Sometimes a *portion* of a loss contingency qualifies for immediate recognition, whereas the remainder only meets the criteria for disclosure. Assume, for example, that a company is required by the "Superfund Act" to clean-up an environmental hazard over a 10-year period. The company cannot predict the total cost of the project, but considers it "probable" that it will lose at least $1 million. The company should recognize a $1 million expected loss and record it as a liability. In addition, it should disclose in the footnotes to the financial statements that the actual cost ultimately may exceed the recorded amount.

CASE IN POINT

DuPont accrues a liability for environmental remediation activities when it is probable that a liability has been incurred and reasonable estimates of the liability can be made. Much of this accrual relates to the Superfund Act which mandates that the company clean up its waste sites over the next two decades.

Remediation activities tend to occur over relatively long periods of time and vary substantially in cost from site to site. The company's assessment of remediation costs is a continuous process that takes into account the relevant factors affecting each specific site. DuPont has accrued over $600 million related to future environmental clean-up activities. Although the company cannot estimate with precision the actual amount it will eventually incur, it apparently believes that costs of at least $600 million appear "probable."

Notice that loss contingencies relate only to possible losses from *past events.* For DuPont, these "past events" were related to the improper disposal of hazardous wastes. The risk that losses may result from *future* events is *not* a loss contingency. The risk of future losses generally is *not* disclosed in financial statements for several reasons.[17] For one, any disclosure of future losses would be sheer speculation. For another, no one can foresee all of the events which might give rise to future losses.

COMMITMENTS

Contracts for future transactions are called **commitments.** They are not liabilities, but, if material, they are disclosed in footnotes to the financial statements. For example, a professional baseball club may issue a 3-year contract to a player at an annual salary of, say, $5 million. This is a commitment to pay for services to be rendered in the future. There is no obligation to make payment until the services are received. As liabilities stem only from *past transactions,* this commitment has not yet created a liability.

Other examples of commitments include a corporation's long-term employment contract with a key officer, a contract for construction of a new plant, and a contract to buy or sell inventory at future dates. The common quality of all these commitments is an intent to enter into transactions *in the future.* Commitments that are material in amount should be disclosed in notes to the financial statements.

**SUPPLEMENTAL TOPIC B

BONDS ISSUED AT A DISCOUNT OR A PREMIUM

Underwriters normally sell corporate bonds to investors either at par or at a price very close to par. Therefore, the underwriter usually purchases these bonds from the issuing corporation at a discount—that is, at a price below par. The discount generally is quite small—perhaps 1 or 2% of the face amount of the bonds.

When bonds are issued, the borrower records a liability equal to the *amount received.* If the bonds are issued at a small discount—which is the normal case—this liability is slightly smaller than the face value of the bond issue. At the maturity date, of course, the issuing corporation must redeem the bonds at full face value. Thus, over the life of the bond issue, the borrower' liability gradually *increases* from the original issue price to the maturity value.

BOND DISCOUNT: PART OF THE COST OF BORROWING   When bonds are issued at a discount, the borrower must repay more than the amount originally borrowed. Thus, any discount in the issuance price becomes an "extra cost" in the overall borrowing transaction.

In terms of cash outlays, the "extra cost" represented by the discount is not paid until the bonds mature. But the *matching principle* may require the bor-

---

[17]The risk of future losses *is* disclosed if this risk stems from *existing contracts,* such as a written guarantee of another company's indebtedness (called a loan guarantee, or an accommodation endorsement).

rower to recognize this cost gradually over the life of the bond issue.[1] After all, the borrower does benefit from the use of the borrowed funds throughout this entire period.

ACCOUNTING FOR BOND DISCOUNT: AN ILLUSTRATION

LO 11 *Account for bonds issued at a discount or premium.*

To illustrate, assume that on January 1, 1998 SCUBA TECH sells $1 million of 9%, 40-year bonds to an underwriter at a price of *98* ($980 for each bond). On January 1, 1998, it receives $980,000 cash from the underwriter and records a liability in this amount. But when these bonds mature in 40 years, SCUBA TECH will owe its bondholders $1,000,000. Thus, the company's liability to bondholders will *increase by $20,000* over the life of the bond issue. The gradual "growth" in this liability is illustrated below:

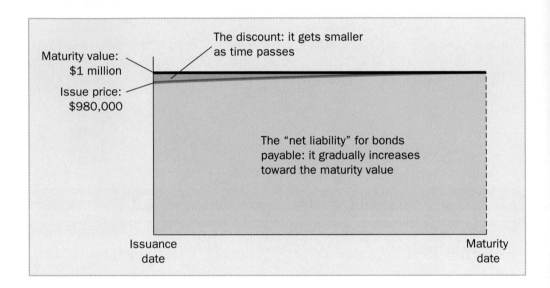

Notice that the long-term liability is increasing very *gradually*—at an average rate of $500 per year ($20,000 increase ÷ 40-year life of the bond issue).

When bonds are issued, the amount of any discount is debited to an account entitled *Discount on Bonds Payable*. Thus, SCUBA TECH will record the issuance of these bonds as follows:

Cash...	980,000	
Discount on Bonds Payable...	20,000	
Bonds Payable		1,000,000
Issued $1,000,000 face value 40-year bonds to an underwriter		
at a price of 98.		

SCUBA TECH's liability at the date of issuance will appear as follows:

The "net" liability for bonds payable

Long-term liabilities:

Bonds Payable...	$1,000,000	
Less: Discount on Bonds Payable	20,000	$980,000

---

[1]If the amount of the discount is immaterial, it may be charged directly to expense as a matter of convenience.

The debit balance account, Discount on Bonds Payable, is a *contra-liability account*. In the balance sheet, it is shown as a *reduction* in the amount of the long-term liability. Thus, the net liability originally is equal to the *amount borrowed*.

AMORTIZATION OF THE DISCOUNT   Over the 40-year life of the bond issue, adjusting entries are made to gradually transfer the balance in the Discount account into interest expense. Thus, the balance in the Discount account gradually declines, and the carrying value of the bonds—face value *less* the unamortized discount—rises toward the bonds' maturity value.

At the end of each year, SCUBA TECH will make the following *adjusting entry* to amortize the bond discount:

Interest Expense..	500	
Discount on Bonds Payable		500
Recognized one year's amortization of discount on 40-year bonds payable ($20,000 original discount × ¹⁄₄₀).		

Notice that amortization of the discount *increases* SCUBA TECH's annual interest expense. It does not, however, require any immediate cash outlay. The interest expense represented by the discount will not be paid until the bonds mature.

ACCOUNTING FOR BOND PREMIUM

If bonds are issued at a *premium* (a price above par), the borrower would again record the liability at the amount borrowed. The amount in excess of par value would be credited to a special account entitled Premium on Bonds Payable. In the balance sheet, bond premium is *added* to the face value of the bonds to determine the net liability. As this premium is amortized, the carrying value of the liability gradually *declines* toward the maturity value.

Amortization of bond premium is recorded by debiting Premium on Bonds Payable and *crediting* Interest Expense. Therefore, amortization of a premium *reduces* the annual interest expense to an amount *less* than the annual cash payments made to bondholders.

BOND DISCOUNT AND PREMIUM IN PERSPECTIVE

From a conceptual point of view, investors might pay a premium price to purchase bonds that pay an *above-market* rate of interest. If the bonds pay a *below-market* rate, investors will buy them only at a discount.

But these concepts seldom come into play when bonds are issued. Most bonds are issued *at* the market rate of interest. Corporate bonds *almost never* are issued at a premium. Bonds often are issued at a small discount, but this discount represents only the underwriter's profit margin, not investors' response to a below-market interest rate.[2] The annual effects of amortizing bond discount or premium are diluted further because these amounts are amortized over the entire life of the bond issue—usually 20 years or more.

In summary, bond discounts and premiums *seldom have a material effect* upon a company's annual interest expense or its financial position.[3] For this reason, we defer further discussion of this topic to the intermediate accounting course.

---

[2]Professor Bill Schwartz of Virginia Commonwealth University conducted a study of 685 bond issues in a given year. *None* of these bonds was issued at a premium, and *over* 95% were issued either at par or at a discount of less than 2% of face value.

[3]Some companies issue *zero-coupon* bonds which pay *no* interest, but are issued at huge discounts. In these situations, amortization of the discount *is* material and may comprise much of the company's total interest expense. Zero-coupon bonds are a specialized form of financing that will be discussed in later accounting courses and courses in corporate finance.

SUMMARY OF LEARNING OBJECTIVES

① Define liabilities and distinguish between current and long-term liabilities.
Liabilities are debts arising from past transactions or events, and which require payment (or the rendering of services) at some future date. Current liabilities are those maturing within one year or the company's operating cycle (whichever is longer) *and* which are expected to be paid from current assets. Liabilities classified as long-term include obligations maturing more than one year in the future, and also shorter-term obligations that will be refinanced or paid from noncurrent assets.

② Account for notes payable and interest expense.
Initially, a liability is recorded only for the *principal* amount of a note—that is, the amount owed *before* including any interest charges. Interest expense accrues over time. Any accrued interest expense is recognized at the end of an accounting period in an adjusting entry that records both the expense and a short-term liability for accrued interest payable.

③ Describe the costs relating to payrolls.
The basic cost of payrolls is, of course, the salaries and wages earned by employees. However, all employers also incur costs for various payroll taxes, such as the employer's share of Social Security and Medicare, workers' compensation premiums, and unemployment insurance. Many employers also incur costs for various "fringe" benefits, such as providing employees with health insurance and postretirement benefits. (These additional "payroll-related" costs often amount to 30 to 40% of the basic wages and salaries expense.)

④ Prepare an amortization table allocating payments between interest and principal.
An amortization table includes four "money" columns, showing (1) the amount of each payment, (2) the portion of the payment representing interest expense, (3) the portion of the payment that reduces the principal amount of the loan, and (4) the remaining unpaid balance (or principal amount). The table begins with the original amount of the loan listed in the unpaid balance column. A separate line then is completed showing the allocation of each payment between interest and principal reduction, and indicating the new unpaid balance subsequent to the payment.

⑤ Describe corporate bonds and explain the tax advantage of debt financing.
Corporate bonds are transferable long-term notes payable. Each bond usually has a face value of $1,000 (or a multiple of $1,000), calls for semiannual interest payments at a contractual rate, and has a stated maturity date. By issuing thousands of bonds to the investing public at one time, the corporation divides a very large and long-term loan into a great many transferable units.

The principal advantage of issuing bonds instead of capital stock is that interest payments to bondholders *are deductible in determining taxable income,* whereas dividend payments to stockholders are not.

⑥ Explain the concept of present value.
The basic concept of present value is that an amount of money that will not be paid or received until some future date is equivalent to a *smaller amount* of money today. This is because the smaller amount available today could be invested to earn interest and thereby accumulate over time to the larger future amount. The amount which, if available today, is considered equivalent to the future amount is termed the **present value** of that future amount.

The concept of present value is used in the valuation of all long-term liabilities except deferred taxes. It also determines the current values of financial instruments and is widely used in investment decisions. Readers who are not familiar with this concept are encouraged to now read Appendix C at the end of this textbook.

⑦ Account for postretirement costs.
The annual expense for postretirement costs is the *present value* of the future benefits earned by employees as a result of their services during the current year. This amount is estimated by an actuary. To the extent that the employer "funds" this expense each year—that is, contributes cash to a pension plan—no liability arises. However, the employer must report a liability for any *unfunded* postretirement obligations. (Pension plans usually are fully funded, meaning that the employer reports no liability for pension payments. But other postretirement benefits, such as health insurance for retired workers, normally are *not* fully funded.)

⑧ Describe and account for deferred income taxes.
Timing differences sometimes exist between the dates that certain revenue or expense items are recognized in financial statements and the dates these items are reported in tax returns. Most of these timing differences result in postponing (deferring) the recognition of income for tax purposes. That portion of the income taxes expense which is deferred to future tax returns is credited to a liability account entitled Deferred Income Taxes.

⑨ Evaluate the safety of creditors' claims.
Short-term creditors may evaluate the safety of their claims using such measures of solvency as the current ratio, quick ratio, the available lines of credit, and the debtor's credit rating. Long-term creditors look more to signs of stability and long-term financial health, including the debt ratio, interest coverage ratio, and the

trends in net income and net cash flow from operating activities.

🔟 Define *loss contingencies* and explain their presentation in financial statements.

A loss contingency is a possible loss (or expense) stemming from past events that will be resolved as to existence and amount by some future event. Loss contingencies are accrued (recorded) if it is both (1) *probable* that a loss has been incurred, and (2) the amount of loss can be estimated reasonably. Even if these conditions are not met, loss contingencies should be disclosed if it is *reasonably possible* that a material loss has been incurred.

⑪ Account for bonds issued at a *discount* or *premium*.

When bonds are issued at a discount, the borrower must repay more than the amount originally borrowed. Thus, any discount in the issuance price becomes additional cost in the overall borrowing transaction. The matching principle requires that the borrower recognize this cost gradually over the life of the bond issue as interest expense.

If bonds are issued at a premium, the borrower will repay an amount less than the amount originally borrowed. Thus, the premium serves to reduce the overall cost of the borrowing transaction. Again, the matching principle requires that this reduction in interest expense be recognized gradually over the life of the bond issue.

Businesses have two basic means of financing their assets and business operations: with liabilities, or with owners' equity. In the next two chapters, we turn our attention to the owners' equity in various types of business organizations.

KEY TERMS INTRODUCED OR EMPHASIZED IN CHAPTER 10

Accrued liabilities (p. 468)   The liability to pay an expense which has accrued during the period. Also called *accrued expenses*.

Actuary (p. 483)   A statistician who performs computations involving assumptions as to human life spans. One function is computing companies' liabilities for pensions and postretirement benefits.

Amortization table (p. 471)   A schedule that indicates how installment payments are allocated between interest expense and repayments of principal.

Bankruptcy (p. 488)   A legal status in which the financial affairs of an insolvent business (or individual) are managed, in large part, by the U.S. Bankruptcy Court.

Bonds payable (p. 473)   Long-term debt securities which subdivide a very large and long-term corporate debt into transferable increments of $1,000 or multiples thereof.

Capital lease (p. 481)   A lease contract which finances the eventual purchase by the lessee of leased property. The lessor accounts for a capital lease as a sale of property; the lessee records an asset and a liability equal to the present value of the future lease payments. Also called a *financing lease*.

Capital structure (p. 465)   The combination of liabilities and owners' equity used in financing total assets. Capital structure is described by the "right-hand" side of the balance sheet.

Collateral (p. 466)   Assets which have been pledged to secure specific liabilities. Creditors with secured claims can foreclose upon (seize title to) these assets if the borrower defaults.

Commitments (p. 493)   Agreements to carry out future transactions. Not a liability because the transaction has not yet been performed, but may be disclosed in footnotes to the financial statements.

Convertible bond (p. 475)   A bond which may be exchanged (at the bondholders' option) for a specified number of shares of the company's capital stock.

Debt service (p. 470)   The combined cash outlays required for repayment of principal amounts borrowed and for payments of interest expense during the period.

Deferred income taxes (p. 486)   A liability to pay income taxes expense which has been postponed into the income tax returns of future years.

Estimated liabilities (p. 466)   Liabilities known to exist, but which must be recorded in the accounting records at estimated dollar amounts.

Interest coverage ratio (p. 488)   Operating income divided by interest expense. Indicates the number of times that the company was able to earn the amount of its interest charges.

Junk bonds (p. 475)   Bonds payable that involve a greater than normal risk of default and, therefore, must pay higher than normal rates of interest in order to be attractive to investors.

Lessee (p. 481)   The tenant, user, or renter of leased property.

Lessor (p. 481)   The owner of property leased to a lessee.

Leverage (p. 489)   The use of borrowed money to finance business operations.

---

*Supplemental Topic A, "Estimated Liabilities, Loss Contingencies, and Commitments."

**Supplemental Topic B, "Bonds Issued at a Discount or a Premium."

Loss contingency (p. 491) A situation involving uncertainty as to whether or not a loss has occurred. The uncertainty will be resolved by a future event. An example of a loss contingency is the possible loss relating to a law suit pending against a company. Although loss contingencies are sometimes recorded in the accounts, they are more frequently disclosed only in footnotes to the financial statements.

Maturity date (p. 465) The date upon which a liability becomes due.

Off-balance-sheet financing (p. 481) An arrangement in which the use of resources is financed without the obligation for future payments appearing as a liability in the balance sheet. An operating lease is a common example of off-balance-sheet financing.

Operating lease (p. 481) A lease contract which is in essence a rental agreement. The lessee has the use of the leased property, but the lessor retains the usual risks and rewards of ownership. The periodic lease payments are accounted for as rent expense by the lessee and as rental revenue by the lessor.

Payroll taxes (p. 469) Taxes levied upon an employer based upon the amount of wages and salaries being paid to employees during the period. Include the employers' share of Social Security and Medicare taxes, unemployment taxes, and (though not called a "tax") **workers' compensation** premiums.

Pension fund (p. 483) A fund managed by an independent trustee into which an employer company makes periodic payments. The fund is used to make pension payments to retired employees.

Postretirement benefits (p. 484) Benefits that will be paid to retired workers. The **present value** of the future benefits earned by workers during the current period is an expense of the period. If not fully funded, this expense results in a liability for unfunded postretirement benefits. (For many companies, these liabilities have become very large.)

Present value (of a future amount) (p. 478) The amount of money that an informed investor would pay today for the right to receive the future amount, based upon a specific rate of return required by the investor.

Principal amount (p. 467) The unpaid balance of an obligation, exclusive of any interest charges for the current period.

Sinking fund (p. 475) Cash set aside by a corporation at regular intervals (usually with a trustee) for the purpose of repaying a bond issue at its maturity date.

Underwriter (p. 474) An investment banking firm which handles the sale of a corporation's stocks or bonds to the public.

Workers' compensation (p. 469) A state-mandated insurance program insuring workers against job-related injuries. Premiums are charged to employers as a percentage of the employees' wages and salaries. The amounts vary by state and by the employees' occupations but, in some cases, can be very substantial.

DEMONSTRATION PROBLEM

Listed below are selected items from the financial statements of G & H Pump Mfg. Co. for the year ended December 31, 1998.

Deferred income taxes	$ 140,000
Note payable to Porterville Bank	99,000
Income taxes payable	63,000
Loss contingency relating to lawsuit	200,000
Accounts payable and accrued expenses	163,230
Mortgage note payable	240,864
Bonds payable	2,200,000
Unamortized premium on bonds payable	1,406
Accrued bond interest payable	110,000
Pension expense	61,400
Unfunded liability for nonpension postretirement benefits	807,000
Unearned revenue	25,300

OTHER INFORMATION

1. $26,000 of the deferred taxes arose from assets or liabilities classified as current.

2. The note payable owed to Porterville Bank is due in 30 days. G & H has arranged with this bank to renew the note for an additional two years.

3. G & H has been sued for $200,000 by someone claiming the company's pumps are excessively noisy. It is reasonably possible, but not probable, that a loss has been sustained.

4. The mortgage note is payable at $8,000 per month over the next three years. During the next 12 months, the principal amount of this note will be reduced to $169,994.

5. The bonds payable mature in seven months. A sinking fund has been accumulated to repay the full maturity of this bond issue.

6. The company's pension plan is fully funded. During *1999*, the company intends to fund $100,000 of its unfunded liability for *nonpension* postretirement benefits.

INSTRUCTIONS

a. Using this information, prepare the current liabilities and long-term liabilities sections of a classified balance sheet at December 31, 1998.

b. Explain briefly how the information in each of the six numbered paragraphs affected your presentation of the company's liabilities.

SOLUTION TO DEMONSTRATION PROBLEM
a.

G & H PUMP MFG. CO. Partial Balance Sheet December 31, 1998		
Liabilities:		
Current liabilities:		
Accounts payable and accrued expenses.....................		$ 163,230
Income taxes payable..		63,000
Accrued bond interest payable.....................................		110,000
Unearned revenue		25,300
Current portions of long-term debt:		
Deferred income taxes..	$ 26,000	
Mortgage note payable	70,870	
Unfunded liability for nonpension postretirement		
benefits...	100,000	196,870
Total current liabilities...		$ 558,400
Long-term liabilities:		
Note payable to Porterville Bank...................................		$ 99,000
Deferred income taxes..		114,000
Mortgage note payable..		169,994
Bonds payable	$2,200,000	
Add: Premium on bonds payable	1,406	2,201,406
Unfunded liability for nonpension postretirement		
benefits...		707,000
Total long-term liabilities..		$3,291,400
Total liabilities...		$3,849,800

b. **1.** The $26,000 in deferred income taxes arising from current items is classified as a current liability, and the remaining $114,000 ($140,000 − $26,000) as long term.

2. Although the note payable to Porterville Bank is due in 30 days, it is classified as a long-term liability as it will be refinanced on a long-term basis.

3. The pending lawsuit is a loss contingency requiring disclosure, but is not listed in the liability section of the balance sheet.

4. The $70,870 of the mortgage note which will be repaid within the next 12 months ($240,864 − $169,994) is a current liability; the remaining balance, due after Dec. 31, 1999, is long-term debt.

5. Although the bonds payable mature in seven months, they will be repaid from a sinking fund, rather than from current assets. Therefore, these bonds retain their long-term classification.

6. As the pension fund is fully funded, the employer has no pension liability. The portion of the unfunded nonpension postretirement benefits that will be funded next year is a current liability, and the remainder is classified as long-term.

SELF-TEST QUESTIONS

Answers to these questions appear on page 516.

1. Which of the following is characteristic of liabilities, rather than of equity? (More than one answer may be correct.)
   a. The obligation matures.
   b. Compensation paid to the provider of the capital is deductible in the determination of taxable income.
   c. The capital providers' claims are *residual* in the event of liquidation of the business.
   d. The capital providers normally have the right to exercise control over business operations.

2. On October 1, Dalton Corp. borrows $100,000 from National Bank, signing a 6-month note payable for that amount, plus interest to be computed at a rate of 9% per annum. Indicate all correct answers.
   a. Dalton's liability at October 1 is only $100,000.
   b. The maturity value of this note is $104,500.
   c. At December 31, Dalton will have a liability for accrued interest payable in the amount of $4,500.
   d. Dalton's total liability for this loan at November 30 is $101,500.

3. Identify all correct statements concerning payrolls and related payroll costs:
   a. Both employers and employees pay Social Security taxes and Medicare.
   b. Workers' compensation premiums are withheld from employees' wages.
   c. An employer's total payroll costs usually exceed total wages expense by about 7½%.
   d. Under current law, employers are required to pay Social Security taxes on employees' earnings, but are not required to pay for health insurance.

4. Identify those types of information which can readily be determined from an amortization table for an installment loan. (More than one answer may be correct.)
   a. Interest expense on this liability for the current year.
   b. The present value of the future payments under current market conditions.
   c. The unpaid balance remaining after each payment.
   d. The portion of the unpaid balance that is a current liability.

5. Which of the following statements are correct? (More than one statement may be correct.)
   a. A bond issue is a technique for subdividing a very large loan into a great many small, transferable units.
   b. Bond interest payments are contractual obligations, whereas the board of directors determines whether or not dividends will be paid.
   c. As interest rates rise, the market prices of bonds fall; as interest rates fall, bond prices tend to rise.

d. Bond interest payments are deductible in determining income subject to income taxes, whereas dividends paid to stockholders are not deductible.

6. Identify all statements which are *consistent* with the concept of present value. (More than one answer may be correct.)

a. The present value of a future amount always is *less* than that future amount.

b. An amount of money available today is considered *more* valuable than the *same sum* which will not become available until a future date.

c. The amount of an unfunded liability for postretirement benefits is substantially *less* than the actual amounts expected to be paid to retired workers.

d. The liability for an installment note payable is recorded at only the *principal* amount, rather than the sum of the scheduled future payments.

7. Silverado maintains a fully funded pension plan. During 1998, $1 million was paid to retired workers, and workers currently employed by the company earned the right to receive pension payments expected to total $6 million *over their lifetimes*. Silverado's pension *expense* for 1998 amounts to:

a. $1

b. $6 million

c. $7 million

d. Some other amount

8. Deferred income taxes result from:

a. The fact that bond interest is deductible in the computation of taxable income.

b. Depositing income taxes due in future years in a special fund managed by an independent trustee.

c. Timing differences between when income is recognized in financial statements and in income tax returns.

d. The inability of a bankrupt company to pay its income tax liability on schedule.

9. Identify those trends which are *unfavorable* from the viewpoint of a bondholder. (More than one answer may be correct.)

a. Market interest rates are steadily rising.

b. The issuing company's interest coverage ratio is steadily rising.

c. The issuing company's net cash flow from operating activities is steadily declining.

d. The issuing company's debt ratio is steadily declining.

*10. A basic difference between *loss contingencies* and "real" liabilities is:

a. Liabilities stem from past transactions; loss contingencies stem from future events.

b. Liabilities always are recorded in the accounting records, whereas loss contingencies never are.

c. The extent of uncertainty involved.

d. Liabilities can be large in amount, whereas loss contingencies are immaterial.

*11. Which of the following situations require recording a liability in 1998? (More than one answer may be correct.)

a. In 1998, a company manufactures and sells stereo equipment which carries a three-year warranty.

b. In 1998, a theater group receives payments in advance from season ticket holders for productions to be performed in 1999.

c. A company is a defendant in a legal action. At the end of 1998, the company's attorney feels it is possible the company will lose, and that the amount of the loss might be material.

d. During 1998, a midwest agricultural cooperative is concerned about the risk of loss if inclement weather destroys the crops.

---

*Supplemental Topic A, "Estimated Liabilities, Loss Contingencies, and Commitments."

ASSIGNMENT MATERIAL

DISCUSSION QUESTIONS

1. Define liabilities. Identify several characteristics that distinguish liabilities from owners' equity.

2. Explain the relative priority of the claims of owners and of creditors to the assets of a business. Do all creditors have equal priority? Explain.

3. Define current liabilities and long-term liabilities. Under what circumstances might a 10-year bond issue be classified as a current liability? Under what circumstances might a note payable maturing 30 days after the balance sheet date be classified as a long-term liability?

4. Jonas Company issues a 90-day, 12% note payable to replace an account payable to Smith Supply Company in the amount of $8,000. Draft the journal entries (in general journal form) to record the issuance of the note payable and the payment of the note at the maturity date.

5. Explain why an employer's "total cost" of a payroll may exceed by a substantial amount the total wages and salaries earned by employees.

6. What are workers' compensation premiums? Who pays them? Who pays Social Security and Medicare taxes?

7. Ace Garage has an unpaid mortgage loan of $63,210, payable at $1,200 per month. An amortization table indicates that $527 of the current monthly payment represents interest expense. What will be the amount of this mortgage obligation immediately *after* Ace makes this current payment?

8. A friend of yours has just purchased a house and has incurred a $50,000, 11% mortgage, payable at $476.17 per month. After making the first monthly payment, he received a receipt from the bank stating that only $17.84 of the $476.17 had been applied to reducing the principal amount of the loan. Your friend computes that at the rate of $17.84 per month, it will take over 233 years to pay off the $50,000 mortgage. Do you agree with your friend's analysis? Explain.

9. Briefly explain the income tax advantage of raising capital by issuing bonds rather than by selling capital stock.

10. Tampa Boat Company pays federal income taxes at a rate of 30% on taxable income. Compute the company's annual *after-tax* cost of borrowing on a 10%, $5 million bond issue. Express this after-tax cost as a percentage of the borrowed $5 million.

11. Why is a *present value* of a future amount always *less* than the future amount?

12. Why do bond prices vary inversely with interest rates?

13. Some bonds now being bought and sold by investors on organized securities exchanges were issued when interest rates were much higher than they are today. Would you expect these bonds to be trading at prices above or below their face values? Explain.

14. *The Wall Street Journal* recently quoted a market price of *102* for an issue of **8% Nabisco** bonds. What would be the market price for $25,000 face value of these bonds (ignoring accrued interest)? Is the market rate of interest for bonds of this quality higher or lower than 8%? Explain.

15. The 6% bonds of Central Gas & Electric are selling at a market price of 72, whereas the 6% bonds of Interstate Power are selling at a price of 97. Does this mean that Interstate Power has a better credit rating than Central Gas & Electric? Explain. (Assume current long-term interest rates are in the 11 to 13% range.)

16. Explain how the lessee accounts for an operating lease and a capital lease. Why is an operating lease sometimes called *off-balance-sheet financing?*

17. Ortega Industries has a fully funded pension plan. Each year, pension expense runs in excess of $10 million. At the present time, employees are entitled to receive pension benefits with a present value of $125 million. Explain what liability, if any, Ortega Industries should include in its balance sheet as a result of this pension plan.

18. Why do large corporations often show no liability for pensions owed to retired employees, but huge liabilities for "nonpension postretirement benefits"?

19. When are the costs of postretirement benefits recognized as expense? When are the related cash payments made?

20. What is meant by the term *deferred income taxes?* How is this item presented in financial statements?

21. A $200 million bond issue of NDP Corp. (a solvent company) recently matured. The entire maturity value was paid from a bond sinking fund. What effect did this transaction have upon the company's current ratio? Upon its debt ratio? Explain.

22. As a result of issuing 20-year bonds payable, Low-Cal Foods now has an interest coverage ratio of .75 to 1. Should this ratio be of greater concern to short-term creditors or to stockholders? Explain.

23. There is an old business saying that "You shouldn't *be* in business if your company doesn't earn higher than bank rates." This means that if a company is to succeed, its return on assets should be *significantly higher* than its cost of borrowing. Why is this so important?

*24. Define *estimated liabilities* and provide two examples. Are estimated liabilities recorded in accounting records?

*25. What is the meaning of the term *loss contingency?* Give several examples. How are loss contingencies presented in financial statements? Explain.

*26. What is the meaning of the term *commitment?* Give several examples. How are commitments usually presented in financial statements? Explain.

**27. Does issuing bonds at a discount increase or decrease the issuing company's cost of borrowing? Explain.

EXERCISES

Assume that you will have a 10-year, $5,000 loan to repay to your parents when you graduate from college next month. The loan, plus 8% annual interest on the unpaid balance, is to be repaid in ten annual installments of $745 each, beginning one year after you graduate. You have accepted a well-paying job and are considering an early settlement of the entire unpaid balance in just three years (immediately after making the third annual payment of $745).

Prepare an amortization schedule showing how much money you will need to save in order to pay your parents the entire unpaid balance of your loan three years after your graduation. (Round amounts to the nearest dollar.)

Listed below are eight events or transactions of GemStar Corporation.

a. Made an adjusting entry to record interest on a short-term note payable.

b. Made a monthly installment payment of a fully amortizing, 6-month, interest-bearing installment note payable.

c. Recorded a regular bi-weekly payroll, including the amounts withheld from employees, the issuance of paychecks, and payroll taxes upon the employer.

---

*Supplemental Topic A, "Estimated Liabilities, Loss Contingencies, and Commitments."
**Supplemental Topic B, "Bonds Issued at a Discount or a Premium."

d. Came within 12 months of the maturity date of a note payable originally issued for a period of 18 months.

e. Made an adjusting entry to accrue interest payable on a long-term bond issue.

f. Leased equipment, signing a long-term capital lease.

g. Recognized pension expense for the year and made the annual payment to a fully funded pension plan.

h. Made an adjusting entry to record income taxes expense, part of which will be deferred to future income tax returns (assume deferred taxes are a long-term liability).

Indicate the effects of each of these transactions u.pon the following financial statement categories. Organize your answer in tabular form, using the illustrated column headings. Use the following code letters to indicate the effects of each transaction upon the accounting element listed in the column heading:

I = Increase   **D** = Decrease   **NE** = No Effect

	Income Statement			Balance Sheet			
Transaction	Revenue − Expenses =		Net Income	Assets =	Current Liab. +	Long-Term Liab. +	Owners' Equity
a.							

EXERCISE 10-3
Effects of Transactions upon Various Financial Measurements
LO 1,4,5,7

Eight events relating to liabilities are described below.

a. Paid the liability for interest payable accrued at the end of the last accounting period.

b. Made the current monthly payment on a 12-month installment note payable, including interest and a partial repayment of principal.

c. Recorded a 5-year capital lease payment obligation.

d. Made a monthly payment of the lease payment obligation described in **c,** above. (Ignore any effects on the long-term portion of this obligation.)

e. Recorded the cost of *fully funded* postretirement benefits earned by employees (assume payment is made immediately).

f. Recorded the cost of *unfunded* postretirement benefits earned by employees (a portion of these unfunded benefits are due next year).

g. Recorded income taxes expense for the period, part of which is deferred. (The deferred taxes are classified as a long-term liability.)

h. Made the year-end adjusting entry to amortize a small discount on bonds payable.

Indicate the effects of each transaction or adjusting entry upon the financial measurements in the five column headings listed below. Use the code letters, **I** for increase, **D** for decrease, and **NE** for no effect.

Transaction	Current Liabilities	Long-Term Liabilities	Net Income	Net Cash Flow from Operating Activities	Net Cash Flow (from All Sources)
a.					

EXERCISE 10-4
Financial Statement Presentation of Liabilities
LO 1,5,10

Using the following information, prepare a listing of Sorrento Company's (a) current liabilities and (b) long-term liabilities. If you do not list a particular item in either schedule, briefly explain your reasoning.

---

*Supplemental Topic A, "Estimated Liabilities, Loss Contingencies, and Commitments."

b *a*

not owed now, leave out

Lease payment obligation (of which $18,400 will be repaid within the next
12 months).. $ 67,200

Interest expense that will arise from existing liabilities over the next 12 months. 134,000

Lawsuit pending against the company claiming $500,000 in damages. Legal
counsel can make no reasonable estimate of the company's potential liability
at this time... 500,000

b 20-year bond issue which matures in 10 months. (The issue will be repaid
from a sinking fund)... 1,000,000

a Accrued interest payable on the 20-year bond issue as of the balance
sheet date.. 22,000

3-year commitment to Charlene Doyle as chief financial officer at a salary
of $140,000 per year... 420,000

b Note payable due in 60 days, but which will be extended for an additional
18 months.. 75,000

EXERCISE 10-5
Employees—What
Do They Really Cost?

LO 3

WHAP!, Inc., manufactures golf clubs. Shown below is a summary of the company's annual payroll-related costs.

Wages and salaries expense (of which $580,000 was withheld from
employees' pay and forwarded directly to tax authorities)............................ $2,000,000

Payroll taxes... 160,000

Workers' compensation premiums... 70,000

Group health insurance premiums 200,000

Contributions to employees' pension plan (fully funded)............................. 120,000

Other postretirement benefits:

Funded... $35,000

Unfunded 60,000 95,000

a. Compute WHAP!'s total payroll-related costs for the year.

b. Compute the net amount of cash actually paid to employees (their "take-home pay").

c. Express total payroll-related costs as a percentage of (1) total wages and salaries expense and (2) employees' "take-home pay." (Round both computations to the nearest 1 percent.)

d. How were the costs of postretirement benefits determined? Which of these amounts
results in a liability? Will the amount of the payments be more or less than the
amount now shown as a liability? Explain.

EXERCISE 10-6
Use of an Amortization
Table

LO 4

Blue Cays Marina has a $200,000 mortgage liability. This mortgage is payable in monthly
installments of $2,057, which include interest computed at the rate of 12% per year (1%
per month).

a. Prepare a partial amortization table showing the original balance of this loan, and
the allocation of the *first two* monthly payments between interest expense and reduction in the unpaid balance. (Round amounts to the nearest dollar.)

b. Prepare the journal entry to record the *second* monthly payment.

c. Will monthly interest increase, decrease, or stay the same over the life of the loan?
Explain your answer.

EXERCISE 10-7
After-Tax Cost of
Borrowing

NY Central, Inc., issued $20 million of 12% bonds payable at face value. The company
pays income taxes at an average rate of 35% of its taxable income.

Compute the company's annual *after-tax* cost of borrowing on this bond issue, stated
as (a) a total dollar amount and (b) a percentage of the amount borrowed.

no Collateral

EXERCISE 10-8
Bond Interest (Bonds
Issued at Par)
LO 5

On March 31, Bancor Corporation received authorization to issue $30 million of 12%, 30-year debenture bonds. Interest payment dates were March 31 and September 30. The bonds were all issued at par on April 30, one month after the interest date printed on the bonds.

a. Prepare the journal entry at April 30, to record the sale of the bonds.

b. Prepare the journal entry at September 30, to record the semiannual bond interest payment.

c. Prepare the adjusting entry at December 31, to record bond interest accrued since September 30.

d. Explain *why* the issuing corporation charges the initial purchasers of the bonds for interest accrued prior to the issuance date.

EXERCISE 10-9
Bond Price Volatility
LO 5,11*

Select a bond issue from the financial pages of a daily newspaper (such as *The Wall Street Journal*). Track the activity of the bond issue over a 3-day period.

a. What volume of bonds was traded each day?

b. What was the closing price of the bonds at the end of each day?

c. What factors may have influenced the price volatility of these bonds?

EXERCISE 10-10
Basic Entries for a Bond
Issue: Issuance, Interest
Payment, and Retirement
LO 5,11*

La Paloma Corporation issued $10 million of 15-year, 10½% bonds on July 1, 1998, at 98½. Interest is due on June 30 and December 31 of each year, and the bonds mature on June 30, 2013. The fiscal year ends on December 31; bond discount is amortized by the straight-line method. Prepare the following journal entries:

a. July 1, 1998, to record the issuance of the bonds.

b. December 31, 1998, to pay interest and amortize the bond discount (make two entries).

c. June 30, 2013, to pay interest, amortize the bond discount, and retire the bonds at maturity (make three entries).

d. Briefly explain the effect of amortizing the bond discount upon (1) annual net income and (2) annual net cash flow from operating activities. (Ignore possible income tax effects.)

EXERCISE 10-11
Accounting for Leases
LO 6

On July 1, City Hospital leased equipment from MedTech Instruments for a period of five years. The lease calls for monthly payments of $2,000 payable in advance on the first day of each month, beginning July 1.

Prepare the journal entry needed to record this lease in the accounting records of City Hospital on July 1 under each of the following independent assumptions:

a. The lease represents a simple rental arrangement.

b. At the end of five years, title to this equipment will be transferred to City Hospital at no additional cost. The present value of the 60 monthly lease payments is $90,809, of which $2,000 is paid in cash on July 1.

c. Why is situation **a,** the operating lease, sometimes called *off-balance-sheet financing?*

d. Would it be acceptable for a company to account for a capital lease as an operating lease in order to report rent expense rather than a long-term liability?

**Supplemental Topic B, "Bonds Issued at a Discount or a Premium."

EXERCISE 10-12
Pension Plans

LO 6,7

At the end of the current year, Krepshaw Power Tools, Inc., received the following information from its actuary:

Pension expense	$1,790,000
Nonpension postretirement benefits expense....................................	316,000

The pension plan is fully funded. Krepshaw has funded only $23,000 of the nonpension postretirement benefits this year.

a. Prepare the journal entry to summarize pension expense for the entire year.

b. Prepare the journal entry to summarize the nonpension postretirement benefits expense for the entire year.

c. If the company becomes insolvent in future years, what prospects, if any, do today's employees have of receiving the pension benefits which they have earned to date?

d. Does the company have an ethical responsibility to fully fund its nonpension postretirement benefits?

Prepare a separate journal entry to summarize for the entire year (a) the pension expense and (b) the nonpension postretirement benefits expense.

EXERCISE 10-13
Deferred Income Taxes

LO 8

The following journal entry summarizes for the current year the income taxes expense of American Coachworks:

Income Taxes Expense	14,000,000	
Cash..		9,000,000
Income Taxes Payable		2,900,000
Deferred Income Taxes....................................		2,100,000
To record income taxes expense for the current year.		

Of the deferred income taxes, only $240,000 is classified as a current liability.

a. Define *deferred income taxes payable.*

b. What is the amount of income taxes which the company has paid or expects to pay in conjunction with its income tax return for the current year?

c. Illustrate the allocation of the liabilities shown in the above journal entry between the classifications of *current liabilities* and *long-term liabilities.*

EXERCISE 10-14
Safety of Creditors'
Investments

LO 9

Shown below are data from recent reports of two publicly owned toy makers. Dollar amounts are stated in thousands.

	Tyco Toys, Inc.	Hasbro, Inc.
Total assets..	$615,132	$2,616,388
Total liabilities	349,792	1,090,776
Interest expense...	28,026	37,588
Operating income	13,028	304,672

a. Compute for each company (1) the debt ratio and (2) the interest coverage ratio. (Round the debt ratio to the nearest percent and the interest coverage ratio to two decimal places.)

b. In your opinion, which of these companies would a long-term creditor probably view as the safer investment? Explain.

EXERCISE 10-15
Toys "R" Us
Examining Long-Term
and Short-Term Debt
LO 1

Use the annual report of **Toys "R" Us** to answer the following questions (see Appendix A at the end of the textbook).

a. Identify two long-term bond issues which are payable in a currency other than U.S. dollars.

b. The company's statement of cash flows reports a net decrease in cash of $117,201 related to short-term borrowings. Verify this amount using figures from the accompanying balance sheet.

c. Are the company's future lease commitments primarily operating lease commitments or capital lease commitments?

PROBLEMS

PROBLEM 10-1
Liabilities: Recognition
and Disclosure
LO 1,7,10*

The events described below occurred at Redford Grain Corporation on December 31, the last day of the company's fiscal year.

a. The company was named as defendant in a $30 million lawsuit. Redford's legal counsel stated that the lawsuit was without merit and that Redford would defend itself vigorously in court. However, the legal counsel also stated that it was impossible at this time to predict the outcome of the litigation, or the liability, if any, which might ultimately be determined.

b. Signed a note payable to obtain a bank loan. The note was in the principal amount of $300,000, to mature in nine months, plus interest of $22,500 (computed at 10% per year).

c. Recorded income taxes expense for the year at an estimated amount of $220,000, which included $30,000 in deferred taxes resulting from the use of accelerated depreciation methods in income tax returns. The actual amount of tax expense will not be known until March, when the company files its income tax return for the year ended December 31.

d. The general ledger included an account entitled Income Taxes Withheld with a balance at December 31 of $16,500.

e. Recognized $2,700,000 in pension expense for the year. The pension plan is fully funded.

f. Recognized $650,000 in postretirement expense *other* than pensions. Of this amount $270,000 was paid this year and $300,000 will be funded next year.

g. On December 31 signed a contract with another grain dealer calling for the purchase by Redford of 50,000 bushels of wheat per month for six months at a price of $4 per bushel, a price slightly below market value.

h. Signed a contract with a labor union on December 31 specifying annual increases in wage rates of 5% for the next three years. The increase in labor costs for the first year of the agreement was estimated to be $1,200,000.

INSTRUCTIONS

For each of the above eight events, you are to state the dollar amount (if any) which would appear in the current liability section of Redford Corporation's balance sheet at December 31. For any event which does not affect current liabilities, you are to indicate whether it should appear in the financial statements and the proper location and amount.

PROBLEM 10-2
Effects of Transactions
on Financial Statements
LO 1,2,3,4,7,10*

Fifteen transactions or events affecting Laptop Computer, Inc., are listed below:

a. Made a year-end adjusting entry to accrue interest on a note payable which has the interest rate stated separately from the principal amount.

b. A liability classified for several years as long-term becomes due within the next 12 months.

---

*Supplemental Topic A, "Estimated Liabilities, Loss Contingencies, and Commitments."

c. Recorded the regular bi-weekly payroll, including payroll taxes, amounts withheld from employees, and the issuance of paychecks.

d. Earned an amount previously recorded as unearned revenue.

e. Made arrangements to extend a bank loan due in 60 days for another 18 months.

f. Made a monthly payment on a fully amortizing installment note payable. (Assume this note is classified as a current liability.)

g. Called bonds payable due in seven years at a price above the carrying value of the liability in the accounting records.

h. Made a monthly payment on an operating lease.

i. Made a monthly payment on a capital lease. (Assume only eight months remain in the lease term.)

j. Recorded pension expense on a fully funded pension plan.

k. Recorded nonpension postretirement expense; the liability is unfunded, but 20% of the amount of expense will be funded within 12 months.

l. Recorded income taxes expense for the year, including a considerable amount of deferred taxes (assume deferred taxes are long-term liabilities).

*m. Recorded an estimated liability for warranty claims.

*n. Entered into a two-year commitment to buy all hard drives from a particular supplier at a price 10% below market.

*o. Received notice that a lawsuit has been filed against the company for $7 million. The amount of the company's liability, if any, cannot be reasonably estimated at this time.

INSTRUCTIONS

Indicate the effects of each of these transactions upon the following elements of the company's financial statements. Organize your answer in tabular form, using the column headings shown below. Use the following code letters to indicate the effects of each transaction upon the accounting element listed in the column heading:

I = Increase   **D** = Decrease   **NE** = No Effect

	Income Statement			Balance Sheet			
Transaction	Revenue	− Expenses	= Net Income	Assets =	Current Liab. +	Long-Term Liab. +	Owners' Equity

a.

PROBLEM 10-3
Balance Sheet Presentation of Liabilities
10.1,2,4,10

Listed below are selected items from the accounting records of GOOD 'N' LITE Candy Co. for the year ended December 31, 1998:

Note payable to Northwest Bank	$200,000
Income taxes payable	43,000
Accrued expenses and payroll taxes	59,800
Mortgage note payable	301,080
Accrued interest on mortgage note payable	2,508
Trade accounts payable	129,345
Unearned revenue	52,100
Potential liability in pending lawsuit	750,000

*Supplemental Topic A, "Estimated Liabilities, Loss Contingencies, and Commitments."

OTHER INFORMATION

1. The note payable to Northwest Bank is due in 60 days. Arrangements have been made to renew this note for an additional 12 months.

2. The mortgage note payable requires payments of $10,000 per month for the next 36 months. An amortization table shows that as of December 31, 1999, this note will be paid down to $212,430.

3. Accrued interest on the mortgage note payable is paid monthly.

4. GOOD 'N' LITE has been sued for $750,000 in a contract dispute. It is not possible at this time to make a reasonable estimate of the possible loss, if any, which the company may have sustained.

INSTRUCTIONS

a. Using this information, prepare the current liabilities section and long-term liabilities section of a classified balance sheet at December 31, 1998. (Within each classification, items may be listed in any order.)

b. Explain briefly how the information in each of the four numbered paragraphs affected your presentation of the company's liabilities.

PROBLEM 10-4
Notes Payable;
Accruing Interest

LO 2

During the fiscal year ended December 31, Dunleer Corporation carried out the following transactions involving notes payable.

Aug.   6   Borrowed $11,200 from Tom Hutchins, issuing to him a 45-day, 12% note payable.

Sept. 16   Purchased office equipment from Harper Company. The invoice amount was $16,800 and Harper Company agreed to accept as full payment a 12%, 3-month note for the invoice amount.

Sept. 20   Paid the Hutchins note plus accrued interest.

Nov.   1   Borrowed $235,000 from Sun National Bank at an interest rate of 12% per annum; signed a 90-day note payable.

Dec.   1   Purchased merchandise in the amount of $3,000 from Kramer Co. Gave in settlement a 90-day note bearing interest at 14%. (A perpetual inventory system is in use.

Dec. 16   The $16,800 note payable to Harper Company matured today. Paid the interest accrued and issued a new 30-day, 16% note to replace the maturing note.

INSTRUCTIONS

a. Prepare journal entries (in general journal form) to record the above transactions. Use a 360-day year in making the interest calculations.

b. Prepare the adjusting entry needed at December 31, prior to closing the accounts. Use one entry for all three notes.

c. Provide a possible explanation why the new 30-day note payable to Harper Company pays 16% interest instead of the 12% rate charged on the September 16 note.

PROBLEM 10-5
Preparation and Use of
an Amortization Table

LO 4

On September 1, 1998, Kansas Steak House signed a 30-year, $540,000 mortgage note payable to Dodge City Savings and Loan in conjunction with the purchase of a restaurant. This mortgage note calls for interest at the rate of 12% per year (1% per month), and monthly payments of $5,555. The note is fully amortizing over a period of 360 months (30 years).

Dodge City Savings sent Kansas Steak House an amortization table showing the allocation of the monthly payments between interest and principal over the life of the loan. A small part of this amortization table is illustrated below. (For convenience, amounts have been rounded to the nearest dollar.)

Amortization Table
(12%, 30-Year Mortgage Note Payable for $540,000; Payable in 360 Monthly Installments of $5,555)

Interest Period	Payment Date	Monthly Payment	Interest Expense	Reduction in Unpaid Balance	Unpaid Balance
Issue date	Sept. 1, 1998	—	—	—	$540,000
1	Oct. 1	$5,555	$5,400	$155	539,845
2	Nov. 1	$5,555	5,398	157	539,688

INSTRUCTIONS

a. Explain whether the amounts of interest expense and the reductions in the unpaid balance are likely to change in any predictable pattern from month to month.

b. Prepare journal entries to record the first two monthly payments on this mortgage.

c. Complete this amortization table for two more monthly installments—those due on December 1, 1998 and January 1, 1999. (Round amounts to the nearest dollar.)

d. Will any amounts relating to this 30-year mortgage be classified as *current* liabilities in the December 31, 1998, balance sheet of Kansas Steak House? Explain, but you need not compute any additional dollar amounts.

PROBLEM 10-6
Amortization Table and
Installment Debt

LO 4

On December 31, 1997, Kay Architectural Services purchased equipment at a cost of $20,215, paying $5,000 cash and issuing a 2-year installment note payable for $15,215. This note calls for four semiannual installments of $4,800, which include interest computed at the annual rate of 20% per year (10% per semiannual period). Payments are due on June 30 and December 31. The first payment is due June 30, 1998, and the note will be fully amortized at December 31, 1999.

Kay can retire this note at any interest payment date by paying the unpaid balance plus any accrued interest.

INSTRUCTIONS

a. Prepare an amortization table showing the allocation of each of the four semiannual payments between interest expense and reductions in the principal amount of the note.

b. Prepare journal entries to record the issuance of this note and each of the four semiannual payments in 1998 and 1999.

c. Assume that on December 31, 1998, Kay decided to pay the entire unpaid balance of this note. Prepare a journal entry to record the early retirement of this note. (Assume that the semiannual payment due on this date already has been paid.)

d. Illustrate the presentation of this note in the company's balance sheet at December 31, 1997. (Show separately the current and long-term portions of this debt.)

PROBLEM 10-7
Bond Interest (Bonds
Issued at Par)

LO 5

Bar Harbor Gas & Electric obtained authorization to issue $90 million face value of 10%, 20-year bonds, dated May 1, 1998. Interest payment dates were November 1 and May 1. Issuance of the bonds did not take place until August 1, 1998. On this date all the bonds were sold at a price of 100 plus three months' accrued interest.

INSTRUCTIONS

Prepare the necessary entries in general journal form on:

a. August 1, 1998, to record the issuance of the bonds.

b. November 1, 1998, to record the first semiannual interest payment on the bond issue.

c. December 31, 1998, to accrue bond interest expense through year-end.

d. May 1, 1999, to record the second semiannual interest payment.

e. What was the prevailing market rate of interest on the date the bonds were issued? How do you know?

PROBLEM 10-8
Amortization of a
Bond Discount

On May 1, 1998, Festival Cruise Ships, Inc., sold a $60 million face value, 11%, 10-year bond issue to an underwriter at a price of 98. Interest is payable semiannually on May 1 and November 1. Company policy is to amortize bond discount by the straight-line method at each interest payment date and at year-end. The company's fiscal year ends at December 31.

INSTRUCTIONS

a. Prepare journal entries to record the issuance of these bonds, the payment of interest at November 1, 1998, and bond interest expense through year-end.

b. Show the proper balance sheet presentation of all liabilities relating to this bond issue at December 31, 1998. Include captions indicating whether the liabilities are classified as current or long-term.

c. Why do you think that Festival was able to receive a price of only 98 for these bonds, rather than being able to issue them at par? What will issuing these bonds at a discount mean about the relationship between Festival's annual bond interest expense and the amount of cash paid annually to bondholders? Explain.

PROBLEM 10-9
Amortization of a
Bond Discount and
a Premium

On September 1, 1998, American Farm Equipment issued $60 million in 10% debenture bonds. Interest is payable semiannually on March 1 and September 1, and the bonds mature in 20 years. Company policy is to amortize bond discount or premium by the straight-line method at each interest payment date and at year-end. The company's fiscal year ends at December 31.

INSTRUCTIONS

a. Make the necessary adjusting entries at December 31, 1998, and the journal entry to record the payment of bond interest on March 1, 1999, under each of the following assumptions:
  1. The bonds were issued at 98.
  2. The bonds were issued at 101.

b. Compute the net bond liability at December 31, 1999, under assumptions **1** and **2** above.

c. Under which of the above assumptions, **1** or **2,** would the investor's effective rate of interest be the higher? Explain.

PROBLEM 10-10
Factors Affecting
Bond Prices

Occidental Petroleum has two bond issues outstanding with the following characteristics:

Issue	Interest rate	Maturity	Current price
A	10⅛%	2001	112
B	10⅛%	2009	118

**Supplemental Topic B, "Bonds Issued at a Discount or a Premium."

INSTRUCTIONS

Answer the following questions regarding these bond issues:

a. Which issue, A or B, has the higher effective rate of interest? How can you tell?

b. Assume that the bonds of both issues have face values of $1,000 each. How much total interest does each bond from *issue A* provide investors in *twelve months?* How much total interest does each bond from *issue B* provide investors in *twelve months?*

c. Note that both issues are by the same company, have the same contract rate of interest, and have identical credit ratings. In view of these facts, explain the current price difference of each issue.

PROBLEM 10-11
Reporting Liabilities
in a Balance Sheet
LO 1,5,7,8

Listed below are selected items from the accounting records of Gulf Coast Telephone Company (GulfTel) for the year ended December 31, 1998 (dollar amounts in thousands):

Accounts payable	$ 65,600
Accrued expenses payable (other than interest)	11,347
6¾% Bonds payable, due Feb. 1, 1999	100,000
8½% Bonds payable, due June 1, 1999	250,000
Unamortized bond discount (8½% bonds of '99)	260
11% Bonds payable, due June 1, 2008	300,000
Unamortized bond premium (11% bonds of '08)	1,700
Accrued interest payable	7,333
Bond interest expense	61,000
Other interest expense	17,000
Notes payable (short-term)	110,000
Lease payment obligations—capital leases	23,600
Pension obligation	410,000
Unfunded obligations for postretirement benefits other than pensions	72,000
Deferred income taxes	130,000
Income taxes expense	66,900
Income taxes payable	17,300
Operating income	280,800
Net income	134,700
Total assets	2,093,500

OTHER INFORMATION

1. The 6¾% bonds due in February 1999 will be refinanced in January 1999 through the issuance of $150,000 in 9%, 20-year general debentures.

2. The 8½% bonds due June 1, 1999, will be repaid entirely from a bond sinking fund.

3. GulfTel is committed to total lease payments of $14,400 in 1999. Of this amount, $7,479 is applicable to operating leases, and $6,921 to capital leases. Payments on capital leases will be applied as follows: $2,300 to interest expense and $4,621 to reduction in the capitalized lease payment obligation.

4. GulfTel's pension plan is fully funded with an independent trustee.

5. The obligation for postretirement benefits other than pensions consists of a commitment to maintain health insurance for retired workers. During 1999, GulfTel will fund $18,000 of this obligation.

6. The $17,300 in income taxes payable relates to income taxes levied in 1998 and must be paid on or before March 15, 1999. No portion of the deferred tax liability is regarded as a current liability.

INSTRUCTIONS

a. Using this information, prepare the current liabilities and long-term liabilities sections of a classified balance sheet as of December 31, 1998. (Within each classification, items may be listed in any order.)

b. Explain briefly how the information in each of the six numbered paragraphs affected your presentation of the company's liabilities.

c. Compute as of December 31, 1998, the company's (1) debt ratio and (2) interest coverage ratio.

d. Based solely upon information stated in this problem, indicate whether this company appears to be an outstanding, medium, or poor long-term credit risk. State specific reasons for your conclusion.

CASES

CASE 10-1
The Nature of Liabilities
LO 1,3,10*

Listed below are eight publicly owned corporations and a liability which regularly appears in each corporation's balance sheet:

a. **Wells Fargo & Company** (banking): Deposits: interest bearing

b. **The New York Times Company:** Unexpired subscriptions

c. **The Hollywood Park Companies** (horse racing): Outstanding mutuel tickets

d. **American Greetings** (greeting cards and gift wrap products manufacturer): Sales returns

e. **Wausau Paper Mills Company:** Current maturities of long-term debt

f. **Club Med., Inc.** (resorts): Amounts received for future vacations

g. **Apple Computer, Inc.:** Accrued marketing and distribution

h. **General Motors Corporation:** Postretirement costs other than pensions

INSTRUCTIONS

Briefly explain what you believe to be the nature of each of these liabilities, including how the liability arose and the manner in which it is likely to be discharged.

CASE 10-2
Payrolls
LO 3

Interview the owner of a small business, or an employee responsible for payrolls. (You may find this more interesting if you select a business in which the employees are exposed to some job-related risk of injury, such as construction.) Determine the items that cause differences between the gross wages and salaries earned by employees during a pay period and both:

1. The employees' take-home pay.

2. The employer's total related payroll costs.

Also inquire as to whether any of these amounts tend to increase or decrease in later pay periods.

Be prepared to explain in class the relative size of each item as a percentage of gross wages and salaries expense. Also be prepared to explain the *absence* of any of the payroll costs discussed in this text.

(**Note:** All interviews are to be conducted in accordance with the guidelines discussed in the *Note to Students* at the beginning of this textbook.)

CASE 10-3
Loss Contingencies
LO 10*

Discuss each of the following situations, indicating whether the situation is a loss contingency which should be recorded or disclosed in the financial statements of Aztec Airlines. If the situation is not a loss contingency, explain how (if at all) it should be reported in the company's financial statements. (Assume that all dollar amounts are material.)

*Supplemental Topic A, "Estimated Liabilities, Loss Contingencies, and Commitments."

a. Aztec estimates that $700,000 of its accounts receivable will prove to be uncollectible.

b. The company's president is in poor health and has previously suffered two heart attacks.

c. As with any airline, Aztec faces the risk that a future airplane crash could cause considerable loss.

d. Aztec is being sued for $10 million for failing to adequately provide for passengers whose reservations were cancelled as a result of the airline overbooking certain flights. This suit will not be resolved for a year or more.

INTERNET ASSIGNMENTS

INTERNET 10-1
Credit Ratings
on Bonds
LO 9

The Internet provides a wealth of information concerning long-term liabilities, bond rating agencies, and credit markets. Visit the home page of Bonds Online at the following Internet address:

www.bonds-online.com

INSTRUCTIONS

a. From the home page menu, select Research. From the research menu select, Bond Basics. Identify four basic bond principles that the authors of the home page feel every investor should know.

b. Return to the main Research page.
   1. Identify four major bond rating services.
   2. Using "cut & paste" commands, create a table that illustrates the rating symbols and definitions used by each of these services.

c. Select Corporate from the Bonds Online home page (or, go to the home page of one of the investment services identified in part **1**). Either approach should enable you to locate one company with a relatively high credit rating, and one with a relatively low credit rating. Then, using EDGAR, examine the most recent 10-K reports filed by these companies. The EDGAR address is:

www.sec.gov/edaux/searches.htm

   1. Summarize briefly any credit-rating issues discussed in each company's 10-K report.
   2. For each company, compute some of the basic measures of solvency and profitability identified in Chapter 6 (refer to the financial measurements in the table on page 277). Discuss how the two companies differ with respect to these financial measures.

OUR COMMENTS ON THE IN-TEXT CASES

YOU AS A FINANCIAL ADVISOR (P. 480)   The interest payments generated by a bond remain constant, regardless of fluctuations in market interest rates that occur over the bond's life. Thus, if bond issuers consistently fulfill their responsibility to make timely interest payments, the couple's annual cash flow from their investment will remain relatively stable throughout their retirement.

Fluctuations in market interest rates could adversely affect the couple should they decide to sell any of their bonds *before* the bonds mature. If interest rates are relatively high at the time the bonds are sold, their selling price may be substantially less than their redemption value at maturity.

YOU AS A LOAN OFFICER (P. 488)   The point that the CEO was trying to make is that $250,000 of the company's total expenses for the year were "noncash" expenses. As such, these expenses reduced operating income without reducing cash flow from operations. While impossible to determine from the limited information provided, the company's ability to service its debt *may be* better than the low interest coverage ratio suggests.

It is interesting to note that some credit analysts *add back* significant noncash expenses to income from operations when computing the interest coverage ratio. In this case, the addition of these two noncash items would increase the company's interest coverage ratio to 5 to 1 [($375,000 + $200,000 + $50,000) ÷ 125,000 = 5 times coverage].

ANSWERS TO SELF-TEST QUESTIONS

1. a, b   **2.** a, b, d   **3.** a, d   **4.** a, c, d   **5.** a, b, c, d   **6.** a, b, c, d
7. d   **8.** c   **9.** a, c   ***10.** c   ***11.** a, b

Supplemental Topic A, "Estimated Liabilities, Loss Contingencies, and Commitments."

FORMS OF BUSINESS ORGANIZATION

Location:

Search | Feedback | Help | Directory

Document: Done

Businesses range in size from sidewalk vendors to multinational organizations. They vary greatly in the nature of their operations, their need for capital, the number of owners, and the legal form of the business organization. In the dollar volume of business activity, large corporations dominate our economy. But did you know that more than four times as many businesses are organized as sole proprietorships or partnerships than as corporations?

1 Explain how the accounts and the financial statements of a *sole proprietorship* differ from those of a corporation.

2 Describe the basic characteristics of a *partnership*.

3 Discuss the advantages and disadvantages of organizing a business as a corporation.

4 Explain the rights of stockholders and the roles of corporate directors and officers.

5 Account for the issuance of capital stock.

6 Contrast the features of *common stock* with those of *preferred stock*.

7 Discuss the factors affecting the market price of preferred stock and of common stock.

8 Explain the meaning and significance of book value, market value, and par value of capital stock.

*9 Account for the incorporation of an existing business.

Assume that you are planning to start a new business. How would you choose the form of business organization? Most people choose a sole proprietorship—these simple business units are far more numerous than partnerships or corporations. In a recent year the federal Bureau of the Census reported the existence of more than 12 million sole proprietorships, compared with fewer than 3 million corporations, and something over 1 million partnerships. The popularity of the sole proprietorship is explained in large part by the ease and relatively low cost of its formation.

On the other hand, almost every *large* business is organized as a corporation. In recent years the annual revenue of General Motors has exceeded *$160 billion*. Exxon has reported revenue in excess of $110 billion, and IBM over $75 billion. The revenue of the 10 largest corporations exceeds the combined revenue of all of this country's 12 million sole proprietorships. In the dollar volume of business activities, the corporation is clearly the dominant form of organization.

SOLE PROPRIETORSHIPS

LO1 *Explain how the accounts and the financial statements of a* sole proprietorship *differ from those of a corporation.*

Any unincorporated business owned by one person is called a **sole proprietorship.** This form of organization is common among small retail stores, farms, service businesses, and professional practices. Most of these businesses, however, tend to be small, needing relatively little capital.

An important characteristic of the sole proprietorship is that, from a *legal* viewpoint, the business and its owner are *not* regarded as separate entities. Thus, the owner is *personally liable* for the debts of the business. If the business becomes insolvent, creditors can force the owner to sell his or her personal assets to pay the business debts.

From an accounting viewpoint, however, a sole proprietorship *is* regarded as an entity *separate from the other affairs of its owner*. For example, assume that Jill Green owns two sole proprietorships—a gas station and a shoe store. The assets, liabilities, revenue, and expenses relating to the gas station would not appear in the financial statements of the shoe store. Also, Green's personal assets, such as her house, furniture, and savings account, would not appear in the financial statements of either business entity.

*Supplemental Topic, "Incorporating a Going Concern."

ACCOUNTING FOR THE OWNER'S EQUITY IN A SOLE PROPRIETORSHIP

A balance sheet for a sole proprietorship shows the entire ownership equity as a single dollar amount. No effort is made to distinguish between the amount originally invested by the owner and the later increase or decrease in owner's equity as a result of profitable or unprofitable operations. A corporation must maintain separate accounts for capital stock and retained earnings, because distributions to owners in the form of dividends cannot legally exceed the earnings of the corporation. In an unincorporated business, however, the owner is free to withdraw assets from the business at any time and in any amount.

The accounting records for a sole proprietorship do not include accounts for capital stock, retained earnings, or dividends. Instead of these accounts, a **capital account** and a **drawing account** are maintained for the owner.

THE OWNER'S CAPITAL ACCOUNT In a sole proprietorship, the title of the capital account includes the name of the owner, as, for example, *John Jones, Capital*. The capital account is credited with the amount of the proprietor's original investment in the business and also with any subsequent investments. When the accounts are closed at the end of each accounting period, the Income Summary account is closed into the owner's capital account. Thus the capital account is credited with the net income earned (or debited with the net loss incurred). Withdrawals by the proprietor during the period are debited to a drawing account, which later is closed into the capital account.

THE OWNER'S DRAWING ACCOUNT A withdrawal of cash or other assets by the owner reduces the owner's equity in the business and could be recorded by debiting the owner's capital account. However, a clearer record is created if a separate Drawing account is maintained. This drawing account (entitled, for example, *John Jones, Drawing*) replaces the Dividends account used by a corporation.

The drawing account is debited for any of the following transactions:

1. Withdrawals of cash or other assets. If the proprietor of a clothing store, for example, withdraws merchandise for personal use, the Drawing account is debited for the cost of the goods withdrawn. The offsetting credit is to the Inventory account (or to the Purchases account if a periodic inventory system is in use).

2. Payment of the proprietor's personal bills out of the business bank account.

3. Collection of an account receivable of the business, with the cash collected being retained personally by the proprietor.

Withdrawals by the proprietor (like dividends to stockholders) are not an expense of the business. Expenses are incurred for the purpose of generating revenue, and a withdrawal of cash or other assets by the proprietor does not have this purpose.

CLOSING THE ACCOUNTS

The revenue and expense accounts of a sole proprietorship are closed into the Income Summary account in the same way as for a corporation. The Income Summary account then is closed to the proprietor's Capital account, rather than to a Retained Earnings account. To complete the closing of the accounts, the balance of the Drawing account is transferred into the proprietor's Capital account.

FINANCIAL STATEMENTS FOR A SOLE PROPRIETORSHIP

The balance sheet of a sole proprietorship differs from that of a corporation principally in the owner's equity section. To see how ownership equity appears in the balance sheet of a sole proprietorship and also in the balance sheet of a corporation, you may wish to review the illustration in Chapter 1 (page 18).

A *statement of owner's equity* may be prepared in a form similar to the statement of retained earnings used by a corporation. The statement of owner's equity, however, shows additional investments made by the owner as well as the earnings retained in the business. An illustration follows:

JONES INSURANCE AGENCY Statement of Owner's Equity For the Year Ended December 31, 19__	
John Jones, capital, Jan. 1, 19__	$ 80,400
Add: Additional investments	10,000
Net income for year	30,500
Subtotal	$120,900
Less: Withdrawals	34,000
John Jones, capital, Dec. 31, 19__	$ 86,900

Note that withdrawals may exceed net income

The *income statement* of a proprietorship differs from that of a corporation in two significant respects. First, the income statement for a sole proprietorship does not include any salary expense representing managerial services rendered by the owner. One reason for not including a salary to the owner-manager is that such individuals are able to set their salaries at any amount they choose. The use of an unrealistic salary to the proprietor would lessen the significance of the income statement as a device for measuring the earning power of the business. It is more logical to regard the owner-manager as earning the *entire* net income of the business rather than working for a salary.

A second distinctive feature of the income statement of a sole proprietorship is the absence of any income taxes expense. Unlike a corporation, a sole proprietorship is *not subject to income taxes.* This is because the law does not view a sole proprietorship as an entity separate from its owner. Thus, the owner of an unincorporated business includes the net income of the business on his or her *personal income tax return,* along with any taxable income from other sources. The owner of an unincorporated business must pay income taxes upon the *net income* of the business, regardless of the amount of assets withdrawn during the year.

EVALUATING THE FINANCIAL STATEMENTS OF A PROPRIETORSHIP

THE ADEQUACY OF NET INCOME Sole proprietorships do not recognize any salary expense relating to the owner, nor any interest expense on the capital that the owner has invested in the business. Thus, if the business is to be considered successful, its net income should *at least* provide the owner with reasonable compensation for any personal services and equity capital which the owner has provided to the business.

In addition, the net income of a sole proprietorship should be adequate to compensate the owner for taking significant *risks.* Many small businesses fail. The owner of a sole proprietorship has *unlimited personal liability* for the debts of the business. Therefore, if a sole proprietorship sustains large losses, the owner can lose *much more* than the amount of his or her equity investment.

In summary, the net income of sole proprietorship should be sufficient to compensate the owner for three factors: (1) personal services rendered to the business, (2) capital invested, and (3) the degree of financial risk which the owner is taking.

EVALUATING SOLVENCY   For a business organized as a *corporation,* creditors often base their lending decisions upon the relationships between assets and liabilities in the corporation's balance sheet. But if the business is organized as a sole proprietorship, the balance sheet is less useful to creditors.

Remember, the assets listed in the balance sheet are owned by the *proprietor,* not by the business. The owner can transfer assets in and out of the business at will. Also, it is the *owner* who is financially responsible for the company's debts. Therefore, the ability of a sole proprietorship to pay its debts depends upon *solvency of the owner,* not upon the relationships among the assets and liabilities appearing in the company's balance sheet.

The solvency of a sole proprietor may be affected by many things which *do not appear* in the financial statements of the business. For example, the owner may have great personal wealth—or overwhelming personal debts.

In summary, creditors of a sole proprietorship should look past the balance sheet of the business. The real issue is the debt-paying ability of the *owner.* Thus, creditors of the business may ask the owner to supply *personal* financial information. They also may investigate the owner's credit history, using such credit-rating agencies as TRW.

A WORD OF CAUTION   In Chapter 1 we discussed several factors which *promote the reliability* of the financial statements of publicly owned companies. Among these safeguards were the structure of internal control, audits by independent accountants, federal securities laws, and the competence and integrity of the professional accountants.

Let us stress that these safeguards apply to the **public information** distributed by publicly owned companies. However, they often *do not* apply to financial information provided by small businesses.

Small businesses may not have the resources—or the need—to establish strong internal control. The financial information that they develop usually is *not* audited. Federal securities laws apply only to companies that are publicly owned. And the accounting records of a sole proprietorship often are maintained by the owner, who may have little experience in accounting.

PARTNERSHIPS

LO 2 *Describe the basic characteristics of a partnership.*

A **partnership** is an unincorporated business having two or more owners. From an accounting point of view, a partnership is much like a sole proprietorship. Separate capital accounts and drawings accounts are maintained for each owner. A new feature of partnership accounting, however, is that the net income of the business must be *allocated among the various owners.* If disputes are to be avoided, every partnership should have a *partnership contract* which clearly explains how profits and losses are to be allocated among the owners.

Like a sole proprietorship, a partnership does not pay income taxes. Rather, the partners include in their personal income tax returns their *respective shares* of the partnership's net income. Each partner pays income taxes upon his or her share of the *partnership's net income,* not upon the amount of assets withdrawn during the year.

Two factors are of special importance to any person considering forming or entering a partnership. First, unless special legal arrangements are made, each partner has *unlimited personal liability* for the debts of the business. Next, each partner has the right to bind the partnership to business-related contracts—a concept called **mutual agency.**

Unlimited personal liability and mutual agency can be a very dangerous combination. In short, each partner is personally responsible for the other partner's business actions. There is an old proverb in the business community: One should be as cautious in entering a partnership as in entering a marriage.

UNINCORPORATED BUSINESSES AND THE GOING-CONCERN ASSUMPTION Most unincorporated businesses have *limited lives.* Even though an unincorporated business may operate indefinitely under a series of different owners, each change in ownership represents the creation of a *new business entity.*[1]

Accountants, however, apply the *going-concern assumption* to unincorporated business entities, as well as to corporations. The going-concern assumption is abandoned only if it becomes evident that the business soon will *cease operations* and liquidate its assets. A probable change in ownership at some future date is *not* cause for abandoning this assumption.

When *complete* changes in ownership actually take place, the new owners usually revalue the assets of the business to reflect their acquisition costs.

CORPORATIONS

The corporate form is the "organization of choice" for many businesses—large and small. The owners of a corporation are called *stockholders.* In many small corporations, there are only one or two stockholders. But in large corporations, such as IBM and AT&T, there are literally millions.

A **corporation** is the only form of business organization recognized under the law as a *legal entity,* with rights and responsibilities *separate from those of its owners.* The assets of a corporation belong to the corporation *itself,* not to the stockholders. The corporation is responsible for its own debts, and must pay income taxes on its earnings. As a "separate legal entity," a corporation has status in court; it may enter into contracts, and it may sue and be sued as if it were a person.

The major advantages and disadvantages of this form of business organization are summarized on the following page.

WHY BUSINESSES INCORPORATE

There are many reasons why businesses incorporate, but the two of greatest importance are (1) limited shareholder liability and (2) transferability of ownership.

We have previously discussed the concept of **limited personal liability.** This simply means that shareholders have no *personal* liability for the debts of the corporation. Thus, if the corporation becomes insolvent, the most that a stockholder usually can lose is the amount of his or her equity investment. In this era of multimillion dollar lawsuits, limited personal liability appeals to the owners of large and small businesses alike.

Another special feature of the corporation is the *transferability of ownership*— the idea that ownership is represented by transferable shares of capital stock. For a small, family-owned business, this provides a convenient means of gradually transferring ownership and control of the business from one generation to the next. For a large company, it makes ownership of the business a *highly liquid investment,* which can be purchased and sold in organized securities ex-

---

[1]A few partnerships, such as large CPA firms and law firms, have taken specific legal steps to ensure continuity of the business entity despite routine changes in partner personnel. In the more normal situation, any change in the number or identities of the partners creates a new partnership entity.

changes.[2] This liquidity is essential to a large corporation's being able to raise equity capital from thousands—perhaps millions—of individual investors.

Advantages of the Corporate Form	Disadvantages of the Corporate Form
1. Stockholders have no personal liability for the debts of the business Stockholders are not *personally* liable for the debts of a corporation. Thus, the most that a stockholder can lose by investing in a corporation is the amount of his or her investment. This concept is called *limited personal liability,* and often is cited as the greatest advantage of the corporate form of organization.	**1. Heavy taxation** Corporate earnings are subject to double taxation. First, the corporation must pay *corporate income taxes* on its earnings. Second, stockholders must pay *personal income taxes* on any portion of these earnings which they receive as *dividends.* Together, these two levels of taxation may consume from 60% to 70% of a corporation's pretax earnings.
2. Transferability of ownership Ownership of a corporation is evidenced by *transferrable shares of stock,* which may be sold by one investor to another. Investment in these shares have the advantage of *liquidity,* because investors easily may convert their corporate ownership into cash by selling their shares.	**2. Greater regulation** Corporations are affected by state and federal laws to a far greater extent than are unincorporated businesses. For example, the owners' ability to *remove business assets* from a corporation is restricted by law. A corporation must obtain authorization from government agencies to issue capital stock. Also, federal laws require publicly owned corporations to make extensive public disclosure of their financial activities.
3. Professional management The stockholders own a corporation, but they do not manage it on a daily basis. To administer the affairs of the corporation, the stockholders elect a *board of directors.* The directors, in turn, hire professional managers to run the business. An individual stockholder has *no right* to participate in management *unless he or she has been hired by the directors as a corporate manager.*	**3. Cost of formation** An *unincorporated business* can be formed at little or no cost. Forming a corporation, however, normally requires the services of an attorney.
4. Continuity of existence Changes in the names and identities of stockholders do not directly affect the corporation. Therefore, the corporation may continue its operations *without disruption,* despite the retirement or death of individual stockholders. This characteristic is essential in the undertaking of most large-scale business ventures.	**4. Separation of ownership and management** The separation of ownership and management is an advantage in many cases, but may be a disadvantage in others. If stockholders do not approve of the manner in which management runs the business, they may find it difficult to take the united action necessary to remove that management group.

LO 3 *Discuss the advantages and disadvantages of organizing a business as a corporation.*

---

[2]These securities exchanges include, among others, the New York Stock Exchange, the National Association of Securities Dealers' Automated Quotations (NASDAQ), the Tokyo Stock Exchange, and Mexico's Bolsa. Collectively, stock exchanges often are described simply as *"the stock market."*

There are many other reasons why specific businesses may be organized as corporations—we cannot possibly discuss them all. For example, some states allow an individual or a corporation to own *only one liquor license.* A business which needs to serve liquor at several different sites, such as a chain of hotels or restaurants, must organize *each location* as a separate corporation.

PUBLICLY OWNED CORPORATIONS

The capital stock of most large corporations can be bought and sold (traded) through organized securities exchanges. As these shares are available for purchase by the general public, these large corporations are said to be **publicly owned.**

Far more people have a financial interest in the shares of publicly owned companies than one might expect. If you purchase the stock of such a corporation, you become a stockholder with a *direct* ownership interest—that is, *you* are a stockholder. But mutual funds and pension funds invest heavily in the stocks of many publicly owned corporations. Thus, if you invest in a mutual fund, or you are covered by a pension plan, you probably have an *indirect* financial interest in the stocks of many publicly owned corporations.

CASE IN POINT

The stockholders in **General Motors** include more than one million men and women, and many pension funds, mutual investment funds, labor unions, universities, and other organizations. Almost every person covered by an employee pension plan has an indirect ownership interest in GM.

Corporations whose shares are *not* traded on any organized stock exchanges are said to be **closely held.** Because there is no organized market for buying and selling their shares, these corporations usually have relatively few stockholders. Often, a closely held corporation is owned by one individual or by the members of one family.

PUBLICLY OWNED CORPORATIONS FACE DIFFERENT RULES Government seeks to protect the interests of the public. Therefore, publicly owned corporations are subject to far more regulation than those which are closely held. For example, publicly owned corporations are *required by law* to:

● Disclose much of their financial information to the public. (These disclosures are termed **public information.**)

● Prepare and issue quarterly and annual financial statements in conformity with generally accepted accounting principles. (These statements are public information.)

● Have their annual financial statements audited by an independent firm of Certified Public Accountants.

● Comply with federal securities laws, which include both criminal penalties and civil liability for deliberately or carelessly distributing misleading information to the public.

● Submit much of their financial information to the Securities Exchange Commission for review.

Closely held corporations normally are exempt from these requirements. But our discussions will focus upon the accounting and reporting issues confronting *publicly owned companies.* After all, these are the companies whose financial statements you are most likely to see—and the companies in which you are likely to invest.

FORMATION OF A CORPORATION

In the United States, a corporation is brought into existence under the laws of a particular state. The state in which the corporation is formed is called the *state of incorporation.*

The state of incorporation is not necessarily where the corporation does business. Rather, this state often is selected because of the leniency of its laws regulating corporate activities. Indeed, many corporations conduct most—sometimes all—of their business activities *outside* the state in which they are incorporated.

The first step in forming a corporation is to obtain a *corporate charter* from the state of incorporation. To obtain this charter, the organizers of the corporation submit an application called the *articles of incorporation.* Once the charter is obtained, the stockholders in the new corporation hold a meeting to elect a *board of directors* and to pass *bylaws* which will govern the corporation's activities. The directors in turn hold a meeting at which the top corporate officers and managers are appointed.

ORGANIZATION COSTS Forming a corporation is more costly than starting a sole proprietorship. The costs may include, for example, attorneys' fees, incorporation fees paid to the state, and other outlays necessary to bring the corporation into existence. These costs are charged to an asset account entitled Organization Costs. In the balance sheet, organization costs appear under the Other Assets caption.

Conceptually, organization costs are an *intangible asset* that will benefit the corporation over its entire life. But as a practical matter, most corporations amortize this asset to expense over a period of only five years, as allowed under income tax regulations. Because the amortization of organization costs usually is *immaterial* in dollar amount, this convenient treatment is justified by the accounting principle of *materiality.*

Thus, you will seldom see organization costs in the balance sheet of a publicly owned corporation. They have long since been amortized to expense.

RIGHTS OF STOCKHOLDERS A corporation is owned collectively by its stockholders. Each stockholder's ownership interest is determined by the number of *shares* that he or she owns.

LO 4 *Explain the rights of stockholders and the roles of corporate directors and officers.*

Assume that a corporation issues 10,000 shares of capital stock. If you own 1,000 of these shares, you own *10%* of the corporation. If you acquire another 500 shares from another stockholder, you will own *15%.*

Each stockholder receives from the corporation a **stock certificate** indicating the number of shares he or she owns. (An illustration of a stock certificate appears on the following page.)

The ownership of capital stock in a corporation usually carries the following basic rights:

1. To vote for directors and on certain other key issues. A stockholder has one vote for each share owned. The issues upon which stockholders may vote are specified in the corporation's bylaws.

   Any stockholder—or group of stockholders—that owns *more than 50%* of the capital stock has the power to elect the board of directors and to set

basic corporate policies. Therefore, these stockholders "control" the corporation. Beyond their voting rights, stockholders have *no managerial authority* unless they have been appointed by the board to a management role.

2. To participate in any *dividends* declared by the board of directors. Stockholders in a corporation *may not* make withdrawals of company assets, as may the owners of unincorporated businesses. However, the directors may elect to distribute some or all of the earnings of a profitable corporation to its stockholders in the form of cash *dividends*.

   Dividends can be distributed only after they have been formally *declared* (authorized) by the board of directors. Also, the dividends are paid to all shareholders in proportion to the number of shares owned.

3. To share in the distribution of assets if the corporation is liquidated. When a corporation ends its existence, the creditors must first be paid in full. Any remaining assets are divided among the shareholders—again, in proportion to the number of shares owned.

Stockholders' meetings usually are held once each year. At these meetings, stockholders may ask questions of management and also vote upon certain issues. In large corporations, these meetings usually are attended by relatively few people—often less than 1% of the company's stockholders. Prior to these meetings, however, the management group requests that stockholders who do not plan to attend send in *proxy statements,* granting management the voting rights associated with their shares.

Through this proxy system, management usually can secure the voting rights from enough shares to ensure its control of the corporation. In a publicly owned corporation, dissatisfied stockholders seldom are able to muster the voting power to overrule management. Therefore, dissatisfied stockholders normally sell their shares and invest in a company more to their liking.

FUNCTIONS OF THE BOARD OF DIRECTORS   The primary functions of the **board of directors** are to set corporate policies and to protect the interests of the stockholders. Specific duties of the directors include hiring corporate officers and setting these officers' salaries, declaring dividends, and reviewing the findings of both internal auditors and independent auditors.

A closely held corporation might have only one active director—who is also the principal stockholder. But publicly owned corporations have larger boards—usually a dozen people or more.

The board of a large corporation always includes several members of top management. In recent years, increasing importance has been attached to the inclusion of "outside" directors. The term *outside directors* refers to individuals who are *not* officers of the corporation and, therefore, bring an *independent perspective* to the board.

CASE **IN** POINT

A recent annual report of **General Mills** includes a report from the *audit committee* of the company's board of directors. The first paragraph of this report describes the committee's responsibilities:

The Audit Committee of the Board of Directors is composed of six outside directors. Its primary function is to oversee the Company's system of internal controls, financial reporting practices and audits to ensure their quality, integrity and objectivity are sufficient to protect stockholders' assets.

FUNCTIONS OF THE CORPORATE OFFICERS The top management of a corporation is appointed (hired) by the board of directors. These individuals are called the *corporate officers,* or, more simply, "top management." Individual stockholders *do not* have the right to transact corporate business *unless they have been properly appointed to a managerial post.*

The top level of management usually includes a president or chief executive officer (CEO), a controller, a treasurer, and a secretary. In addition, a vice-president usually oversees each functional area, such as sales, personnel, and production.

The responsibilities of the controller, treasurer, and secretary are most directly related to the accounting phase of business operation. The *controller,* or chief accounting officer, is responsible for the maintenance of adequate internal control and for the preparation of accounting records and financial statements. Such specialized activities as budgeting, tax planning, and preparation of tax returns are usually placed under the controller's jurisdiction. The *treasurer* has custody of the company's funds and is generally responsible for planning and controlling the company's cash position. The treasurer's department also has responsibility for relations with the company's financial institutions and major creditors.

The *secretary* represents the corporation in many contractual and legal matters and maintains minutes of the meetings of directors and stockholders. Other responsibilities of the secretary are to coordinate the preparation of the annual report and to manage the investor relations department. In small corporations, one officer frequently acts as both secretary and treasurer.

The organization chart below indicates lines of authority extending from stockholders to the directors to the president and other officers.

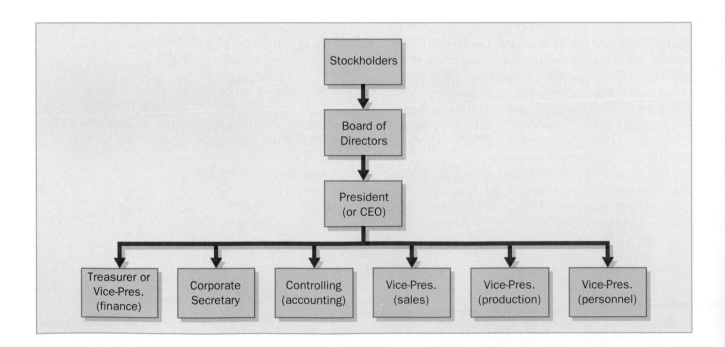

AUTHORIZATION AND ISSUANCE OF CAPITAL STOCK

The articles of incorporation specify the number of shares that a corporation has been authorized to issue by the state of incorporation. Issues of capital stock that will be sold to the general public must be approved by the federal Securities and Exchange Commission, as well as by state officials.

Corporations normally obtain authorization for more shares than they initially plan to issue. This way, if more capital is needed later, the corporation already has the authorization to issue additional shares.

The number of shares which have been *issued* and are in the hands of stockholders are called the *outstanding* shares. At any time, these outstanding shares represent 100% of the stockholders' equity in the corporation.

STATE LAWS AFFECT THE BALANCE SHEET PRESENTATION OF STOCK-HOLDERS' EQUITY The number of ledger accounts that a corporation must use in the stockholders' equity section of its balance sheet is determined largely by state laws. We have seen that corporations use separate owners' equity accounts (Capital Stock and Retained Earnings) to represent (1) paid-in capital and (2) earned capital. Up to this point we have assumed that all paid-in capital is presented in a single ledger account entitled Capital Stock. But this often is not the case.

Some corporations issue several *different types* (or classes) or capital stock. In these situations, a separate ledger account is used to indicate each type of stock outstanding. A legal concept called *par value* also affects the balance sheet presentation of paid-in capital.

PAR VALUE **Par value** (or stated value) represents the *legal capital* per share—the amount below which stockholders' equity cannot be reduced, except by losses from business operations (or by special legal action). The directors cannot declare a dividend that would cause total stockholders' equity to fall below the par value of the outstanding shares. Par value, therefore, may be regarded as a minimum cushion of equity capital existing for the protection of creditors.

Because of the legal restrictions associated with par value, state laws require corporations to show separately in the stockholders' equity section of the balance sheet the par value of shares issued. The special balance sheet presentation has led some people to believe that par value has some special significance. In most corporations, the par value of the shares issued is such a small portion of total stockholders' equity that it is *insignificant.*

A corporation may set the par value of its stock at $1 per share, $5 per share, or any other amount that it chooses. Most large corporations set the par value of their common stocks at nominal amounts, such as 1 cent per share or $1 per share. The par value of the stock is *no indication of its market value;* the par value merely indicates the amount per share to be entered in the Capital Stock account. The common stocks of Ford and AT&T have par values of $1; COMPAQ Computer's stock has a par value of 1 cent, and Microsoft stock has a par value of one-tenth of a cent. The market value of all these securities is far above their par value. Microsoft's stock, for example, has recently traded at a market value in excess of $100 per share, or more than *100,000 times* its par value.

ISSUANCE OF PAR VALUE STOCK Mere authorization of a stock issue does not bring an asset into existence, nor does it give the corporation any capital. The obtaining of authorization from the state for a stock issue merely affords a legal opportunity to obtain assets through the sale of stock.

LO 5 *Account for the issuance of capital stock.*

When par value stock is *issued,* the Capital Stock account is credited with the par value of the shares issued, regardless of whether the issuance price is more or less than par. Assuming that 50,000 shares of $2 par value stock have been authorized and that 10,000 of these authorized shares are issued at a price of $2 each, cash would be debited and Capital Stock would be credited for $20,000. When stock is sold for more than par value, the Capital Stock account is credited with the par value of the shares issued, and a separate account, **Additional Paid-in Capital,** is credited for the excess of selling price over par.

If, for example, our 10,000 shares were issued at a price of $10 per share, the entry would be:

Stockholders' investment in excess of par value

Cash	100,000	
Capital Stock		20,000
Additional Paid-in Capital		80,000
Issued 10,000 shares of $2 par value stock at a price of $10 a share.		

The additional paid-in capital does not represent a profit to the corporation. It is part of the *invested capital* and it will be added to the capital stock in the balance sheet to show the total paid-in capital. The stockholders' equity section of the balance sheet is illustrated on the following page. (The $150,000 in retained earnings is assumed in order to have a complete illustration.)

Corporation's capital classified by source

Stockholders' equity:

Capital stock, $2 par value; authorized, 50,000 shares; issued and outstanding, 10,000 shares	$ 20,000
Additional paid-in capital	80,000
Total paid-in capital	$100,000
Retained earnings	150,000
Total stockholders' equity	$250,000

If stock is issued by a corporation for *less* than par, the account Discount on Capital Stock should be debited for the difference between the issuance price and the par value. The issuance of stock at a discount is seldom encountered; it is illegal in many states.

NO-PAR STOCK   Some states allow corporations to issue stock without designating a par or stated value. When this "no-par" stock is issued, the *entire issue price* is credited to the Capital Stock account and is viewed as legal capital not subject to withdrawal.

COMMON STOCKS AND PREFERRED STOCKS

The account title Capital Stock is widely used when a corporation has issued only *one type* of stock. In order to appeal to as many investors as possible, however, many corporations issue several types (or classes) of capital stock, each providing investors with different rights and opportunities.

LO 6 *Contrast the features of common stock with those of preferred stock.*

The basic type of capital stock issued by every corporation often is called **common stock.** Common stock possesses the traditional rights of ownership—voting rights, participation in dividends, and a residual claim to assets in the event of liquidation. When any of these rights is modified, the term **preferred stock** (or sometimes Class B Common) is used to describe the resulting type of capital stock. A few corporations issue two or more classes of preferred stock, with each class having distinctive features designed to appeal to a particular type of investor. In summary, we may say that *every* corporation has common stock, and that some corporations also have one or more types of preferred stock.

The following stockholders' equity section illustrates the balance sheet presentation for a corporation having both preferred and common stock:

Stockholders' equity:

9% cumulative preferred stock, $100 par value, authorized 100,000 shares, issued 50,000 shares.............................	$ 5,000,000
Common stock, $5 par value, authorized 3 million shares, issued 2 million shares	10,000,000
Additional paid-in capital:	
Preferred	200,000
Common...	20,000,000
Total paid-in capital	$35,200,000
Retained earnings...	13,500,000
Total stockholders' equity	$48,700,000

Balance sheet presentation of common stock and of preferred stock

CHARACTERISTICS OF PREFERRED STOCK

Most preferred stocks have the following distinctive features:

1. Preferred as to dividends
2. Cumulative dividend rights
3. Preferred as to assets in event of the liquidation of the company
4. Callable at the option of the corporation
5. No voting power

Another very important but less common feature is a clause permitting the *conversion* of preferred stock into common at the option of the holder. Preferred stocks vary widely with respect to the special rights and privileges granted. Careful study of the terms of the individual preferred stock contract is a necessary step in the evaluation of any preferred stock.

STOCK PREFERRED AS TO DIVIDENDS Stock preferred as to dividends is entitled to receive each year a dividend of specified amount before any dividend is paid on the common stock. The dividend usually is stated as a dollar amount per share. Some preferred stocks state the dividend preference as a *percentage of par value.* For example, a *9%* preferred stock with a par value of $100 per share would mean that $9 must be paid yearly on each share of preferred stock before any dividends are paid on the common. (Preferred stocks often have par values substantially higher than do common stocks. This is largely a matter of tradition, and has little significance.)

CASE **IN** POINT

Consolidated Edison has three issues of preferred stock which are publicly traded on the New York Stock Exchange. The first issue is a $5 preferred stock, which pays annual dividends of $5 per share. The other two issues include a 4.65% preferred and a 6% preferred. As both of these issues have $100 par values, they pay annual dividends of $4.65 and $6.00 per share, respectively.

Dividends on all three issues of preferred stock must be paid in full before Consolidated Edison pays any dividend on its common stock.

The holders of preferred stock have no assurance that they will always receive the indicated dividend. A corporation is obligated to pay dividends to stockholders only when the board of directors declares a dividend. Dividends must be paid on preferred stock before anything is paid to the common stockholders, but if the corporation is not prospering, it may decide not to pay any dividends at all. For a corporation to pay dividends, profits must be earned and cash must be available. However, preferred stocks generally offer investors *more assurance* of regular dividend payments than do common stocks.

CUMULATIVE PREFERRED STOCK   The dividend preference carried by most preferred stocks is a *cumulative* one. If all or any part of the regular dividend on the preferred stock is omitted in a given year, the amount omitted is said to be *in arrears* and must be paid in a subsequent year before any dividend can be paid on the common stock.

Assume that a corporation was organized January 1, 1996, with 10,000 shares of $8 cumulative preferred stock and 50,000 shares of common stock. Dividends paid in 1996 were at the rate of $8 per share of preferred stock and $2 per share of common. In 1997, earnings declined sharply and the only dividend paid was $2 per share on the preferred stock. No dividends were paid in 1998. What is the status of the preferred stock at December 31, 1998?

Dividends are *in arrears* in the amount of *$14* per share ($6 omitted during 1997 and $8 omitted in 1998). On the entire issue of 10,000 shares of preferred stock, the dividends in arrears amount to *$140,000*.

Dividends in arrears are not listed among the liabilities of a corporation, because no liability exists until a dividend is declared by the board of directors. Nevertheless, the amount of any dividends in arrears on preferred stock is an important factor to investors and should always be *disclosed*. This disclosure is usually made by a note accompanying the balance sheet such as the following:

Footnote disclosure of dividends in arrears

> **Note 6: Dividends in arrears**
>
> As of December 31, 1998, dividends on the $8 cumulative preferred stock were in arrears to the extent of $14 per share and amounted in total to $140,000.

In 1999, we shall assume that the company earned large profits and wished to pay dividends on both the preferred and common stocks. Before paying a dividend on the common, the corporation must pay the $140,000 in arrears on the cumulative preferred stock *plus* the regular $8 per share applicable to the current year. The preferred stockholders would, therefore, receive a total of $220,000 in dividends in 1999 ($22 per share); the board of directors would then be free to declare dividends on the common stock.

For a *noncumulative* preferred stock, any unpaid or omitted dividend is lost forever. However, very few preferred stocks are noncumulative.

STOCK PREFERRED AS TO ASSETS   Most preferred stocks carry a preference as to assets in the event of liquidation of the corporation. If the business is terminated, the preferred stock is entitled to payment in full of its par value or a higher stated liquidation value before any payment is made on the common stock. This priority also includes any dividends in arrears.

CALLABLE PREFERRED STOCK   Most preferred stocks include a *call provision*. This provision grants the issuing corporation the right to repurchase the stock from the stockholders at a stipulated *call price*. The call price is usually slightly higher than the par value of the stock. For example, $100 par value preferred stock may be callable at $105 or $110 per share. In addition to paying the call price, a corporation which redeems its preferred stock must pay any dividends in arrears. A call provision gives a corporation flexibility in adjusting its capital structure.

CONVERTIBLE PREFERRED STOCK In order to add to the attractiveness of preferred stock as an investment, corporations sometimes offer a *conversion privilege* which entitles the preferred stockholders to exchange their shares for common stock in a stipulated ratio. If the corporation prospers, its common stock will probably rise in market value, and dividends on the common stock will probably increase. The investor who buys a convertible preferred stock rather than common stock has greater assurance of regular dividends. In addition, through the conversion privilege, the investor is assured of sharing in any substantial increase in value of the company's common stock.

As an example, assume that Remington Corporation issued a 9%, $100 par, convertible preferred stock on January 1, at a price of $100 per share. Each share was convertible into four shares of the company's $10 par value common stock at any time. The common stock had a market price of $20 per share on January 1, and an annual dividend of $1 per share was being paid. During the next few years, Remington Corporation's earnings increased, the dividend on the common stock was raised to an annual rate of $3, and the market price of the common stock rose to $40 per share. At this point the preferred stock would have a market value of *at least $160,* since it could be converted at any time into four shares of common stock with a market value of $40 each. In other words, the market value of a convertible preferred stock will tend to move in accordance with the price of the common.

When the dividend rate is increased on the common stock, some holders of the preferred stock may convert their holdings into common stock in order to obtain a higher cash return on their investments. If the holder of 100 shares of the preferred stock presented these shares for conversion, Remington Corporation would make the following journal entry:

9% Convertible Preferred Stock	10,000		Conversion of preferred
Common Stock		4,000	stock into common
Additional Paid-in Capital: Common Stock		6,000	
To record the conversion of 100 shares of preferred stock,			
par $100, into 400 shares of $10 par value common stock.			

Note that the issue price recorded for the 400 shares of common stock is based upon the *carrying value of the preferred stock* in the accounting records, not upon market prices at the date of conversion. (If the preferred stock originally had been issued at a price greater than par value, its carrying value would include a proportionate share of the related additional paid-in capital, as well as the par value.)

OTHER FEATURES OF PREFERRED STOCK Occasionally you may encounter preferred stock with some very unusual characteristics. For example, there are "participating preferreds," allowing preferred stockholders to participate in increases in the *common* stock dividend. There also are "super preferreds," granting enormous voting rights—perhaps the controlling interest—to the preferred stockholders. And there are "redeemable preferreds," allowing preferred shareholders to sell their shares back to the corporation at an agreed-upon price. We will leave further discussion of such unusual features of preferred stock to more advanced courses in accounting and corporate finance.

THE ROLE OF AN UNDERWRITER

When a large amount of stock is to be issued, most corporations use the services of an investment banking firm, frequently referred to as an **underwriter.** The underwriter guarantees the issuing corporation a specific price for the stock and makes a profit by selling the shares to the investing public at a slightly higher price. The corporation records the issuance of the stock at the net amount received from the underwriter. The use of an underwriter assures the corporation that the entire stock issue will be sold without delay and that the entire amount of funds to be raised will be available on a specific date.

The price that a corporation will ask for a new issue of stock is based upon such factors as (1) expected future earnings and dividends, (2) the financial strength of the company, and (3) the current state of the investment markets. However, if the corporation asks too much, it simply will not find an underwriter or other buyers willing to purchase the shares.

STOCK ISSUED FOR ASSETS OTHER THAN CASH

Corporations generally sell their capital stock for cash and use the cash to buy the various types of assets needed in the business. Sometimes, however, a corporation may issue shares of its capital stock in a direct exchange for land, buildings, or other assets. Stock may also be issued in payment for services rendered by attorneys and promoters in the formation of the corporation.

When a corporation issues capital stock in exchange for services or for assets other than cash, the transaction should be recorded at the current *market value* of the goods or services received. For some types of assets such as land or buildings, the services of a firm of professional appraisers may be useful in establishing current market value.

Often, the best evidence as to the market value of these goods or services is the *market value of the shares* issued in exchange. For example, assume that a company issues 10,000 shares of its $1 par value common stock in exchange for land. Competent appraisers may have differing opinions as to the market value of the land. But let us assume that the company's stock is currently selling on a stock exchange for $90 per share. It is logical to say that the cost of the land to the company is $900,000, the market value of the shares issued in exchange.

In summary, these transactions should be recorded either at the current market value of (1) the assets received or (2) the shares issued in exchange—*whichever can be determined more objectively*.

Once the valuation has been decided, the entry to record the issuance of the stock in exchange for the land is as follows:

Notice the use of current market values

Land	900,000	
Common Stock		10,000
Additional Paid-in Capital: Common Stock......................................		890,000

To record the issuance of 10,000 shares of $1 par value common stock in exchange for land. Current market value of stock ($90 per share) used as basis for valuing the land.

(For a more comprehensive illustration of issuing stock for assets other than cash, see the *Supplemental Topic* "Incorporating a Going Concern" at the end of this chapter.)

SUBSCRIPTIONS TO CAPITAL STOCK

Small, newly formed corporations sometimes offer investors an opportunity to "subscribe" to shares of the company's capital stock. Under a subscription plan, the investors agree to purchase specified numbers of shares at a stated price *at a future date,* often by making a series of installment payments. The stock is issued after the entire subscription price has been collected.

Selling stock through subscriptions is similar to selling merchandise on a "layaway" plan. One reason for this procedure is to attract small investors. Another reason is to appeal to investors who prefer not to invest cash until the corporation is ready to start business operations. Accounting for subscriptions to capital stock is explained and illustrated in the intermediate accounting course.

DONATED CAPITAL

On occasion, a corporation may receive assets as a gift. To increase local employment, for example, some cities have given corporations the land upon which to build factories. When a corporation receives such a gift, both total assets and total stockholders' equity increase by the market value of the assets received. *No profit is recognized when a gift is received;* the increase in stockholders' equity is regarded as *paid-in capital.* The receipt of a gift is recorded by debiting the appropriate asset accounts and crediting an account entitled **Donated Capital.**

The Donated Capital account appears in the stockholders' equity section of the balance sheet, along with any Additional Paid-In Capital accounts (as illustrated on page 546). In addition, the *notes* accompanying the financial statements normally explain the nature of the donation.

CASE IN POINT

The annual report of **Lands' End, Inc.** includes the following footnote that describes the $8.4 million of donated capital on the company's balance sheet:

Donated capital: In 1988 and 1989, a corporation owned by the principal shareholder of the company contributed $7.0 million and $1.4 million in cash, respectively, to the company in order to fund the cost of constructing an activity center in Dodgeville for use by company employees. These transactions were recorded as donated capital.

ISSUANCE OF CAPITAL STOCK: THE CASH EFFECTS

In a statement of cash flows, transactions with owners of a business are classified as *financing activities.* The issuance of capital stock for cash represents a cash *receipt* from financing activities. Distributions of cash to the owners, such as the payment of cash dividends, represent cash *outlay* classified as financing activities.

NONCASH FINANCING ACTIVITIES   Transactions with owners do not always have an immediate effect on cash flows. Consider an exchange of the corporation's capital stock for a noncash asset, such as land. Cash is not increased or decreased by this transaction. These types of noncash transactions are described in a special schedule that accompanies the statement of cash flows. This schedule is presented and explained in Chapter 13.

RETAINED EARNINGS OR DEFICIT

Capital provided to a corporation by stockholders in exchange for shares of either preferred or common stock is called **paid-in capital,** or *contributed capital.* The second major type of stockholders' equity is retained earnings. The amount of the Retained Earnings account at any balance sheet date represents the accumulated earnings of the company since the date of incorporation, minus any losses and minus all dividends distributed to stockholders.

For example, assume a corporation has $1,000,000 in paid-in capital and has retained $600,000 from profitable operations. The stockholders' equity section of the balance sheet might appear as follows:

Paid-in capital and
earned capital

Stockholders' equity:

Capital stock, $10 par value, 100,000 shares authorized, 20,000 shares issued	$ 200,000
Additional paid-in capital	800,000
Total paid-in capital	$1,000,000
Retained earnings	600,000
Total stockholders' equity	$1,600,000

But if this same company had been *unprofitable* and incurred *losses* of $300,000 since its organization, the stockholders' equity section of the balance sheet would be as follows:

Paid-in capital reduced by
losses incurred

Stockholders' equity:

Capital stock, $10 par value, 100,000 shares authorized, 20,000 shares issued	$ 200,000
Additional paid-in capital	800,000
Total paid-in capital	$1,000,000
Less: Deficit	300,000
Total stockholders' equity	$ 700,000

This second illustration tells us that $300,000 of the original $1,000,000 invested by stockholders has been consumed in unprofitable business operations. The term **deficit** indicates a *negative* amount of retained earnings. (Notice the amount of *paid-in* capital ($1,000,000) is the *same* in both illustrations.)

STOCKHOLDER RECORDS IN A CORPORATION

A large corporation with shares listed on the New York Stock Exchange usually has millions of shares outstanding and hundreds of thousands of stockholders. Each day many stockholders sell their shares; the buyers of these shares become new members of the company's family of stockholders.

A corporation must have an up-to-date record of the names and addresses of this constantly changing army of stockholders so that it can send dividend checks, financial statements, and voting forms to the right people.

STOCKHOLDERS SUBSIDIARY LEDGER When there are numerous stockholders, it is not practical to include a separate account for each stockholder in the general ledger. Instead, a single controlling account entitled Capital Stock appears in the general ledger, and a **stockholders subsidiary ledger** is maintained. This ledger contains an account for each individual stockholder. Entries in the stockholders subsidiary ledger are made in *number of shares,* rather than in dollars. Thus, each stockholder's account shows the number of shares owned and the dates of acquisitions and sales. This record enables the corporation to send each stockholder a single dividend check, even though the stockholder may have acquired shares on different dates.

A corporation which has more than one type of capital stock will maintain a separate set of stockholders subsidiary records for each issue.

STOCK TRANSFER AGENT AND STOCK REGISTRAR   Large, publicly owned corporations use an independent **stock transfer agent** and a **stock registrar** to maintain their stockholder records and to establish strong internal control over the issuance of stock certificates. These transfer agents and registrars are usually large banks or trust companies. When stock certificates are to be transferred from one owner to another, the old certificates are sent to the transfer agent, who cancels them, makes the necessary entries in the stockholders subsidiary ledger, and prepares a new certificate for the new owner of the shares. This new certificate then must be registered with the stock registrar before it represents valid and transferable ownership of stock in the corporation.

Small, closely held corporations generally do not use the services of independent registrars and transfer agents. In these companies, the stockholder records usually are maintained by a corporate officer. To prevent the accidental or fraudulent issuance of an excessive number of stock certificates, the corporation should require that each certificate be signed by at least two designated corporate officers.

BOOK VALUE PER SHARE OF COMMON STOCK

Because the equity of each stockholder in a corporation is determined by the number of shares he or she owns, an accounting measurement of interest to many stockholders is book value per share of common stock. **Book value per share** is equal to the net assets represented by one share of stock. The term *net assets* means total assets minus total liabilities; in other words, net assets are equal to *total stockholders' equity*. Thus, in a corporation which has issued common stock only, the book value per share is computed by dividing total stockholders' equity by the number of shares outstanding (or subscribed).

For example, assume that a corporation has 4,000 shares of capital stock outstanding and the stockholders' equity section of the balance sheet is as follows:

Stockholders' Equity:	
Capital stock, $1 par value (4,000 shares outstanding)	$ 4,000
Additional paid-in capital	40,000
Retained earnings	76,000
Total stockholders' equity	$120,000

How much is book value per share?

The book value per share is *$30;* it is computed by dividing the stockholders' equity of $120,000 by the 4,000 shares of outstanding stock. In computing book value, we are not concerned with the number of authorized shares but merely with the *outstanding* shares, because the total of the outstanding shares represents 100% of the stockholders' equity.

BOOK VALUE WHEN A COMPANY HAS BOTH PREFERRED AND COMMON STOCK   Book value is usually computed only for common stock. If a company has both preferred and common stock outstanding, the computation of book value per share of common stock requires two steps. First, the redemption value or *call price* of the entire preferred stock issue and any *dividends in arrears* are deducted from total stockholders' equity. Second, the remaining amount of stockholders' equity is divided by the number of common shares outstanding to determine book value per common share. This procedure reflects the fact that the common stockholders are the *residual owners* of the corporate entity.

To illustrate, assume that the stockholders' equity of Video Company at December 31 is as follows:

Two classes of stock

Stockholders' Equity

8% preferred stock, $100 par, callable at $110;	
10,000 shares authorized and outstanding	$1,000,000
Common stock, $10 stated value; authorized 100,000	
shares, issued and outstanding 50,000 shares....................................	500,000
Additional paid-in capital: common stock...	750,000
Retained earnings	130,000

Because of a weak cash position, Video Company has paid no dividends during the current year. As of December 31, dividends in arrears on the cumulative preferred stock total *$80,000.*

All the equity belongs to the common stockholders, except the $1.1 million call price ($110 × 10,000 shares) applicable to the preferred stock and the $80,000 of dividends in arrears on preferred stock. The calculation of book value per share of common stock is shown below:

Total stockholders' equity		$2,380,000
Less: Equity of preferred stockholders:		
Call price of preferred stock	$1,100,000	
Dividends in arrears..	80,000	1,180,000
Equity of common stockholders		$1,200,000
Number of common shares outstanding.......................................		50,000
Book value per share of common stock ($1,200,000 ÷ 50,000 shares)		$24

MARKET VALUE

After shares of stock have been issued, they are sold by one investor to another. The prices at which these shares change hands represents the *current market price* of the stock. This market price may differ *substantially* from such amounts as par value, the original issue prices, and the current book value. Which is the *most relevant* amount? That depends upon your point of view.

After shares are issued, *they belong to the stockholder,* not to the issuing corporation. Thus, changes in the market price of these shares affect the financial position *of the stockholder,* but *not that of the issuing company.* This concept explains why the issuing company and stockholders apply very different accounting principles to the same outstanding shares.

ACCOUNTING BY THE ISSUER   From the viewpoint of the issuing company, outstanding stock represents *an amount invested in the company by its owners at a particular date.* While the market value of the stockholders' investment may change, the amount of resources which they originally invested *does not.*

Thus, the company issuing stock records *the issue price*—that is, the proceeds received from issuing the stock—in its paid-in capital accounts. The balances in these accounts remain *unchanged* unless (1) more shares are issued or (2) outstanding shares are permanently retired (i.e., preferred stock is called).

In a single day, the market price of **IBM's** capital dropped over $31 per share, falling from $135 to $103.25. Of course, this was not a "typical" day. The date, October 19, 1987, will long be remembered as "Black Monday." On this day, stock prices around the world suffered the greatest one-day decline in history.

Stocks listed on the New York Stock Exchange lost about 20% of their value in less than six hours. Given that the annual dividends on these stocks averaged about 2% of their market value, this one-day "market loss" was approximately equal to the loss by investors of all dividend revenue for about 10 years.

How did this disastrous decline in IBM's stock price affect the balance sheet of IBM? Actually, it didn't.

IBM's stock isn't owned by IBM—it's owned by the company's stockholders.

ACCOUNTING BY THE INVESTOR From the *investor's* point of view, shares in a publicly owned company are an *asset,* usually termed Marketable Securities.

To the investor, the *current market value* of securities owned is far more relevant than the original issue price—or than the securities' par values or book values. The *market value* indicates what the securities are "worth" today. Changes in market value *directly affect* the investor's solvency, financial position, and net worth. For these reasons, investors show investments in marketable securities at current market value in their balance sheets.[3]

Because market prices are of such importance to investors, we will briefly discuss the factors which most affect the market prices of preferred and common stocks.

MARKET PRICE OF PREFERRED STOCK

Investors buy preferred stocks primarily to receive the dividends that these shares pay. Thus dividend rate is one important factor in determining the market price of a preferred stock. Another important factor is *risk*. In the long run, a company must be profitable enough to pay dividends. If there is a distinct possibility that the company will *not* operate profitably and pay dividends, the price of its preferred stock will decline.

LO 7 *Discuss the factors affecting the market price of preferred stock and of common stock.*

A third factor greatly affecting the value of preferred stocks is the level of *interest rates*. What happens to the market price of an 8% preferred stock, originally issued at a par value of $100, if government policies and other factors cause long-term interest rates to rise to, say, 15 or 16%? If investments offering a return of 16% with the same level of risk are readily available, investors will no longer pay $100 for a share of preferred stock which provides a dividend of only $8 per year. Thus, the market price of the preferred stock will fall to about half of its original issue price, or about $50 per share. At this market price, the stock offers a 16% return (called the **dividend yield**) to an investor purchasing the stock.

However, if the prevailing long-term interest rates should again decline to the 8% range, the market price of an 8% preferred stock should quickly rise to approximately par value. In summary, the market price of preferred stock *varies inversely with interest rates*. As interest rates rise, preferred stock prices decline; as interest rates fall, preferred stock prices rise.

---

[3]The valuation of marketable securities at market value, rather than at the investor's historical cost, is a relatively new accounting principle, termed *mark-to-market*. This concept is discussed in Chapter 7, including *Supplemental Topic A.*

CASE IN POINT

The preceding point is illustrated by the performance of **Philadelphia Electric's** 9½%, $100 par value, preferred stock as interest rates have fluctuated over the years:

	Long-Term Interest Rates*	Stock Price
August 1981	15¼%	$60
April 1985	13½%	68
August 1989	9¼%	99
February 1994	7¼%	106

*The long-term interest rates cited in this example are the market yields of federally insured 30-year fixed-rate mortgages.

MARKET PRICE OF COMMON STOCK

Prevaling interest rates also affect the market price of common stock. However, dividends paid to common stockholders are not fixed in amount. Both the amount of the dividend and the market price of the stock may increase dramatically if the corporation is successful. Alternatively, if the company is unsuccessful, the common stockholders may not even recover their original investment. Therefore, the most important factors in the market price of common stock are *investors' expectations* as to the future profitability of the business, and the *risk* that this level of profitability may not be achieved.

CASE IN POINT

In early 1982, things looked bad for **Ford Motor Company.** The country was in the midst of a recession and auto sales were down. In each of the two preceding years, Ford had lost over $1 billion, and the company recently had stopped paying dividends. Investors were pessimistic about the company's future, and Ford's common stock traded for less than $4 per share.*

Over the next five years, an improving economy, a weak dollar, and such popular new models as the Taurus helped to turn Ford around. Earnings and dividends increased steadily. By 1987, Ford was among the most profitable corporations in the world, earning net income of more than $4½ billion and paying a substantial dividend. In mid-1987, the company's common stock was trading for more than $50 per share.*

*Per share prices have been adjusted for stock splits. Stock splits are discussed in Chapter 12.

Bear in mind that after shares have been issued they belong to the *stockholders,* not to the issuing corporation. Therefore, changes in the market price of the shares *do not affect the financial statements of the corporation,* and these changes are not recorded in the corporation's accounting records. The paid-in capital shown in a corporate balance sheet represents the amount received *when the stock was issued,* not the current market value of shares.

"FOLLOWING" THE MARKET

As we have stated, the balance sheet of a corporation *does not* indicate the current market value of the shares outstanding. In the notes accompanying their financial statements, however, companies *do* disclose the *range* of their stock's price—the high price and low—for each quarter within their fiscal year.

There are much easier ways to follow market prices. For example, the current market prices of publicly owned corporations appear daily in the financial pages of many newspapers.[4]

Shown below is a typical newspaper summary of the daily trading in two issues of Ford Motor Company. The date was early in January of 1995.

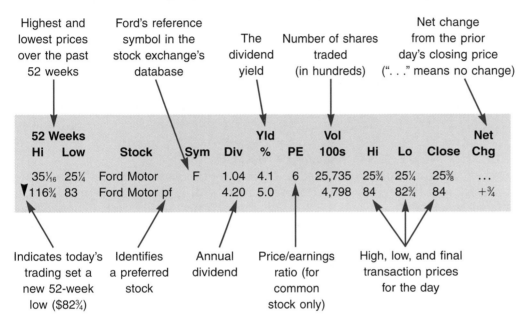

Current stock prices appear in the daily newspaper

Ford's stocks are listed on the New York Stock Exchange. Similar summaries are published daily for every stock listed on this exchange.

On this date, Ford's stocks were trading near their 52-week lows. As indicated by the p/e ratio of *6,* the common stock is trading at only six times Ford's earnings per share.[5] This is a relatively low p/e ratio—not one that investors would apply to a company whose earnings were expected to increase. But then, Ford had an excellent year in 1994, with record sales and profits. Ford's common stock "normally" sells at about 8 times analysts' estimates of *next* year's earnings. Apparently, investors did not think the company would do as well in 1995 as it did in 1994. (Ford's earnings per share declined from $4.97 in 1994 to $3.58 in 1995—so investors had things "pretty well figured out."

The preferred stock also was trading near its 52-week low. In fact, the little downward arrow to the left of the 52-week prices indicates that on this day, the preferred stock set a *new* 52-week low ($82¾).

But in January 1995 the Federal Reserve had just raised interest rates in the United States for the *seventh time* in less than 12 months. As we have said, pre-

---

[4]For some investors, following market prices becomes virtually an obsession. Home computers can access up-to-the-minute stock prices through database services. You can even carry a beeper which will signal you the moment that specific stocks trade above or below designated prices.

[5]The concepts of *price/earnings* (p/e) *ratios* and earnings per share were introduced in Chapter 6 and will be discussed again in Chapter 12. The p/e ratio is based on the earnings for the last four quarters, but it indicates investors' *expectations* as to future earnings levels. A high p/e ratio, say 15 or above, indicates that investors expect earnings to *increase.* A lower ratio, say 8 or below, usually indicates they are expecting future earnings to *decline.*

ferred stock prices *vary inversely* with interest rates. Thus, in January 1995, *most* preferred stocks were trading at (or near) their 52-week lows. (And increases in the interest rate affect much more than the prices of preferred stocks. For example, they also depress auto sales.)

YOUR TURN

You as an Investor

Assume that you are considering making a short-term investment in one of two stocks, a common stock or a preferred stock. You expect that the return on the two investments will be similar, and they have similar amounts of risk. In addition, you believe that interest rates will be increasing significantly in the next six months. Make a decision as to which stock is the better investment and support your choice.

*Our comments appear on page 563.

BOOK VALUE AND MARKET PRICE

To some extent, *book value* is used in evaluating the reasonableness of the market price of a stock. However, it must be used with great caution; the fact that a stock is selling at less than book value does not necessarily indicate a bargain.

LO 8 *Explain the significance of par value, book value, and market value of capital stock.*

Book value is a historical concept, representing the amounts invested by stockholders plus the amounts earned and retained by the corporation. If a stock is selling at a price well *above* book value, investors believe that management has created a business worth substantially more than the historical cost of the resources entrusted to its care. This, in essence, is the sign of a successful corporation. If the excess of market price over book value becomes very great, however, investors should consider whether the company's prospects really justify a market price so much above the underlying book value of the company's resources.

On the other hand, if the market price of a stock is *less than* book value, investors believe that the company's resources are worth less than their cost while under the control of current management. Thus, the relationship between book value and market price is one measure of investors' *confidence in a company's management.*

CASE IN POINT

Shortly after the introduction of its Windows software, the common stock of **Microsoft Corp.** rose to a market value of more than $100 per share, although its book value per share was only about $6.50. Investors believed that Microsoft's products—and its management—made the business worth far more than the historical amounts of capital that had been invested.

In contrast, the common stock of Tucson Electric Power recently sold at a market price of $5 per share, although its book value was more than $20 per share. This utility company had invested heavily in plant assets intended to generate more electrical power. Unfortunately, demand for this power did not develop, and the company found itself unable to sell its additional output. These new facilities produced very little revenue but increased operating expenses substantially. Although these new facilities had a high book value, investors did not consider them to be worth the amounts that management had invested.

SELECTING AN APPROPRIATE FORM OF BUSINESS ORGANIZATION

Anyone planning to start a business should give careful thought to the form of organization. Among the factors most often considered are:

● The personal liability of the owner(s) for business debts.

● Income tax considerations

● The amount of equity capital that must be raised.

● The owners' need for flexibility in withdrawing assets from the business.

● Whether all owners are to have managerial authority.

● The need for continuity in business operations, despite future changes in ownership.

● The ease and cost of forming the business.

The following table contrasts the corporate form of business with a sole proprietorship and a partnership.

Characteristics of Forms of Business Organizations

	Sole Proprietorship	Partnership*	Corporation
1. Legal status	Not a separate legal entity	Not a separate legal entity	Separate legal entity
2. Liability of owners for business debts	Personal liability for business debts	Personal liability for partnership debts	No personal liability for corporate debts
3. Accounting status	Separate entity	Separate entity	Separate entity
4. Tax status	Income taxable to owner	Income taxable to partners	Files a corporate tax return and pays income taxes on its earnings
5. Persons with managerial authority	Owner	Every partner	Hired professional managers
6. Continuity of the business	Entity ceases with retirement or death of owner	New partnership is formed with a change in partners	Indefinite existence

*The characteristics described above relate to an organization termed a "general partnership." These characteristics may be modified in organizations structured as "limited partnerships" or "limited liability partnerships." For comprehensive coverage of the characteristics of various forms of partnerships, we recommend a course in Business Law.

WHAT TYPES OF BUSINESSES CHOOSE THE CORPORATE FORM OF ORGANIZATION?

The answer, basically, is *all kinds*.

When we think of "corporations," we often think of large, well-known companies such as IBM, General Motors, and AT&T. Indeed, almost all large businesses are organized as corporations. Limited shareholder liability, transferability of ownership, professional management, and continuity of existence make the corporation the best form of organization for pooling the resources of a great many equity investors.

Not all corporations, however, are large and publicly owned. A great many small businesses are organized as corporations. In fact, many corporations have *only one stockholder*.

CASE IN POINT

All avid sports fans have seen **"The Chicken"**—the colorful, comic, and acrobatic entertainer who frequently appears at major sporting events. This big feathered bird is also a successful business venture, known as *The Famous San Diego Chicken*. Ted Giannoulas wears many hats in this closely held corporation: He's the president, board of directors, sole stockholder, and—most importantly—the man in the chicken suit.

YOUR TURN

You as a Loan Officer

GOTCHA! is a small business that manufactures board games. It is one of the many business ventures of Gayle Woods, who is very wealthy and one of your bank's most valued customers. He has done business with your bank for more than 20 years, and the balance in his personal checking account normally exceeds $500,000. GOTCHA! is organized as a corporation, and Woods is the only stockholder.

GOTCHA! has applied for a $200,000 line of credit which it intends to use to purchase copyrights to additional board games. Although the company is profitable, its most recent balance sheet shows total assets of only $52,000, including $47,000 in copyrights. The corporation has just under $3,000 in liabilities and over $49,000 in stockholders' equity.

Do you consider GOTCHA! a good credit risk? Would you make the loan? Under what conditions?

*Our comments appear on page 564.

NET CONNECTIONS

A large amount of information exists on the Internet about incorporating a business. Resident Agents of Nevada, Inc. has a home page that describes the basics of incorporation and the advantages and disadvantages. You can find it at:

www.nevada.org

There are a number of places on the Net where you can get the current market prices of stocks. Two we particularly like are StockMaster and PCQUOTE, which can be accessed at:

www.stockmaster.com

www.pcquote.com

*SUPPLEMENTAL TOPIC

INCORPORATING A GOING CONCERN

Many businesses begin life as a sole proprietorship or partnership. As they grow, they may reorganize as a closely held corporation—that is, a corporation owned by a small group of people. Eventually the business may "go public," meaning that it issues stock to the general public, and its shares are traded on an organized stock exchange.

CASE IN POINT

Microsoft today is among the world's largest corporations. But it started small—and not that long ago. Some key dates in the company's history are summarized below:

1975 William Gates and Paul Allen (both college students) formed a partnership and called it "Microsoft."

1981 Microsoft was reorganized as a closely held corporation.

1986 The corporation made its first "public offering" of capital stock. This converted Microsoft into a publicly owned corporation.

1993 The market capitalization of Microsoft—that is, the total market value of its capital stock—temporarily surpassed that of IBM.

When an existing business is reorganized as a corporation, the corporation is a *new business entity*. The valuation of the corporation's assets and liabilities is based upon their *current market value* when the new entity is established, not upon their values in the accounting records of the "old" business entity.

LO 9 *Account for the incorporation of an existing business.*

Assume, for example, that Devin Ryan has long owned and operated a sole proprietorship called Ryan Engineering. In January, 1998, Ryan decides to *incorporate* his business. He obtains a corporate charter and transfers to the new corporation all of the assets used in his sole proprietorship. The new corporation also assumes responsibility for all of the proprietorship's business debts. In exchange for these "net assets" (assets less liabilities), Ryan receives 20,000 shares of no-par capital stock in the new corporation.

The following table lists the assets, liabilities, and owner's equity of the sole proprietorship at the date the new business is formed. The left-hand column indicates the values of these items in the proprietorship's accounting records. The right-hand column indicates the *current market value* of these items on this date. (In each column, owner's equity is equal to total assets, less total liabilities.)

	Values in Proprietorship's Accounting Records	Current Market Values
Cash	$ 30,000	$ 30,000
Accounts receivable	75,000	60,000
Inventory	10,000	15,000
Land	40,000	100,000
Building	60,000	50,000
Equipment	70,000	80,000
Notes payable	55,000	55,000
Accounts payable	20,000	20,000
Owner's equity	210,000	260,000

The entry to record the incorporation of this business is:

The new business records the assets acquired at current market value

Cash	30,000	
Accounts Receivable	60,000	
Inventory	15,000	
Land	100,000	
Building	50,000	
Equipment	80,000	
Notes Payable		55,000
Accounts Payable		20,000
Capital Stock		260,000

Acquired assets and assumed liabilities of Ryan Engineering; issued 20,000 shares of capital stock in exchange.

Notice that this entry is based upon the *current market values* of the assets received (and of the liabilities assumed). After all, these are the "values" that the new business entity receives in exchange for its shares of capital stock.

SUMMARY OF LEARNING OBJECTIVES

① Explain how the accounts and the financial statements of a *sole proprietorship* differ from those of a corporation.

The balance sheet of a sole proprietorship shows the entire ownership equity as a single dollar amount, whereas a corporation balance sheet shows separately the amount of paid-in capital and the amount of retained earnings. The income statement of a sole proprietorship does not include salary paid to the owner or income taxes among the expenses. These differences arise from the fact that a corporation is a legal entity separate from its owner.

The ledger accounts of a sole proprietorship do not include accounts for capital stock, retained earnings, or dividends. Instead, a capital account and a drawing account are maintained for the owner.

② Describe the basic characteristics of a *partnership*.

Among the most important characteristics of a partnership are (1) every partner has *unlimited personal liability* for the debts of the business and (2) the concept of *mutual agency*—the right of each partner to bind the firm to business-related contracts. In addition, the net income of the partnership is allocated among the partners, and each partner may withdraw assets from the partnership at will. (Note: some of these rights may be restricted by an agreement among the partners.)

Partnerships do not pay income taxes; rather, the partners include their respective shares of the partnership's net income in their personal income tax returns. Also, most partnerships have limited lives, as any change in partners usually creates a new partnership entity.

③ Discuss the advantages and disadvantages of organizing a business as a corporation.

The primary advantages are: no personal liability of stockholders for the debts of the business, the transferability of ownership shares, continuity of existence, ability to hire professional management, and the relative ease of accumulating large amounts of capital. The primary disadvantages are: "double taxation" of earnings and greater governmental regulation.

④ Explain the rights of stockholders and the roles of corporate directors and officers.

Stockholders in a corporation normally have the right to elect the board of directors, to share in dividends declared by the directors, to share in the distribution of assets if the corporation is liquidated, and to subscribe to additional shares if the corporation decides to increase the number of shares outstanding.

The directors formulate company policies, review the actions of the corporate officers, and protect the interests of the company's stockholders. Corporate officers are professional managers appointed by the board of directors to manage the business on a daily basis.

⑤ Account for the issuance of capital stock.

When capital stock is issued, appropriate asset accounts are debited for the *market value* of the goods or services received in exchange for the stock. A capital stock account (which indicates the type of stock issued) is credited for the *par value* of the issued shares. *Any excess* of the market value received over the par value of the issued shares is credited to an additional paid-in capital account.

⑥ Contrast the features of *common stock* with those of *preferred stock*.

Common stock represents the true "residual ownership" of a corporation. These shares have voting rights and cannot be called. Also, the common stock dividend is not fixed in dollar amount—thus, it may increase or decrease based upon the company's performance.

Preferred stock has preference over common stock with respect to dividends and to distributions in the event of liquidation. This "preference" means that preferred stockholders must be paid in full before any payments are made to holders of common stock. The dividends on preferred stock usually are fixed in amount. In addition, the stock usually is callable at the option of the issuing corporation and often has no voting rights. Preferred stocks sometimes have special features, such as being convertible into shares of common stock.

⑦ Discuss the factors affecting the market price of preferred stock and of common stock.

The market price of preferred stock varies *inversely* with interest rates. As interest rates rise, preferred stock prices decline; as interest rates fall, preferred stock prices rise. If a company's ability to continue the preferred dividend is in doubt, the solvency of the company also affects preferred stock prices.

Interest rates also affect the market price of common stock. However, common stock dividends are not fixed in amount. Both the amount of the dividend and the market value of the stock may fluctuate, based upon the prosperity of the company. Therefore, the principal factor in the market price of common stock is *investors' expectations* as to the future profitability of the company.

⑧ Explain the meaning and significance of book value, market value, and par value of capital stock.

Book value is the amount of net assets represented by each share of common stock. Book value may be either higher or lower than the current market value; however, it may give an indication of the reasonableness of the current market price.

Market value is the current price at which shares of stock may be bought or sold. When a stock is traded on an organized stock exchange, the market price is quoted daily in the financial press. Market price is based upon a combination of factors, including investors' expectations of future earnings, dividend yield, interest rates, and alternative investment opportunities.

Par value is the amount of legal capital per share—that is, the amount below which stockholders' equity cannot be reduced except by losses or special legal action. Thus, par value is a minimum cushion of equity capital existing for the protection of creditors. Par value is not directly related either to market value or to book value.

⑨ Account for the incorporation of an existing business.

The incorporation of an existing business normally involves the new corporation issuing capital stock in exchange for the assets of the unincorporated business. In addition, the corporation may assume responsibility for the liabilities of the former organization. The dollar amounts used in recording this transaction should reflect the *current market value* of the assets being acquired. This represents the "cost" to the new business entity.

In this chapter, we have described the three common forms of business entity—sole proprietorships, partnerships, and corporations. From an accounting view, these entities are quite similar. All three forms of organization prepare similar financial statements, based upon the same accounting principles. We have also illustrated the transactions involved in issuing capital stock. The next chapter continues this discussion of transactions that affect stockholders' equity. In addition, it also describes how a corporation reports the results of operations.

KEY TERMS INTRODUCED OR EMPHASIZED IN CHAPTER 11

Additional paid-in capital (p. 529) Amounts invested in a corporation by stockholders (or as donated capital) in excess of the par value or stated value of any shares issued in exchange. In short, *paid-in capital* in excess of *legal capital.*

Board of directors (p. 527) Persons elected by common stockholders to direct the affairs of a corporation.

Book value per share (p. 537) The stockholders' equity represented by each share of common stock, computed by dividing common stockholders' equity by the number of common shares outstanding.

Capital account (p. 519) An account indicating the amount of an owner's equity in an unincorporated business.

Closely held corporation (p. 524) A corporation owned by a small group of stockholders. Not publicly owned.

Common stock (p. 530) A type of capital stock which possesses the basic rights of ownership including the right to vote. Represents the residual element of ownership in a corporation.

Corporation (p. 522) A business organized as a legal entity separate from its owners. Chartered by the state with ownership divided into shares of transferable stock. Stockholders are not liable for debts of the corporation.

Deficit (p. 536) Accumulated losses incurred by a corporation. A negative amount of retained earnings.

Dividend yield (p. 539) The annual dividend paid to a share of stock, expressed as a percentage of the stock's market value. Indicates the "rate of return" represented by the dividend.

Donated capital (p. 535) Capital given to a corporation, with no payment being made or capital stock being issued in exchange. Shown in the balance sheet as an element of paid-in capital.

Double taxation (p. 523) The fact that corporate income is taxed to the corporation when earned and then again taxed to the stockholders when distributed as dividends.

Drawing account (p. 519) The account used to record the withdrawals of cash or other assets by the owner (or owners) of an unincorporated business. Closed at the end of the period by transferring its balance to the owner's capital account.

Limited personal liability (p. 522) The concept that the owners of a corporation are not personally liable for the debts of the business. Thus, stockholders' potential financial losses are limited to the amount of their equity investment.

Mutual agency (p. 522) Authority of each partner to act as agent for the partnership within its normal scope of operations and to enter into contracts which bind the partnership.

Paid-in capital (p. 535) The amounts invested in a corporation by its stockholders (also includes donated capital).

Partnership (p. 521) An unincorporated business owned by two or more persons voluntarily associated as partners.

Par value (or stated value) (p. 529) The legal capital of a corporation. Represents the minimum amount per share invested in the corporation by its owners and cannot be withdrawn except by special legal action.

Supplemental Topic, "Incorporating a Going Concern."

Preferred stock (p. 530)   A class of capital stock usually having preferences as to dividends and in the distribution of assets in event of liquidation.

Public information (p. 521)   Information which, by law, must be made available to the general public. Includes the quarterly and annual financial statements—and other financial information—about *publicly owned corporations*.

Publicly owned corporation (p. 524)   Any corporation whose shares are offered for sale to the general public.

Sole proprietorship (p. 518)   An unincorporated business owned by one person.

Stock certificate (p. 525)   A document issued by a cor-

poration (or its transfer agent) as evidence of the ownership of the number of shares stated on the certificate.

Stock registrar (p. 537)   An independent fiscal agent, usually a large bank, retained by a corporation to provide assurance against overissuance of stock certificates.

Stock transfer agent (p. 537)   A bank or trust company retained by a corporation to maintain its records of capital stock ownership and make transfers from one investor to another.

Stockholders subsidiary ledger (p. 536)   A record showing the number of shares owned by each stockholder.

Underwriter (p. 533)   An investment banking firm which handles the sale of a corporation's stock to the public.

DEMONSTRATION PROBLEM

The stockholders' equity section of Rockhurst Corporation's balance sheet appears below:

Stockholders' equity:

$6 preferred stock, $100 par value, callable at		
$102 per share, 200,000 shares authorized		$12,000,000
Common stock, $5 par value, 5,000,000 shares authorized		14,000,000
Additional paid-in capital:		
Preferred	$ 360,000	
Common	30,800,000	31,160,000
Retained earnings		2,680,000
Total stockholders' equity		$59,840,000

INSTRUCTIONS

On the basis of this information, answer the following questions and show any necessary supporting computations.

a. How many shares of preferred stock have been issued?

b. What is the total annual dividend requirement on the outstanding preferred stock?

c. How many shares of common stock have been issued?

d. What was the average price per share received by the corporation for its common stock?

e. What is the total amount of legal capital?

f. What is the total paid-in capital?

g. What is the book value per share of common stock? (Assume no dividends in arrears.)

SOLUTION TO DEMONSTRATION PROBLEM

a. 120,000 shares ($12,000,000 total par value, divided by $100 par value per share)

b. $720,000 (120,000 shares × $6 per share)

c. <u>2,800,000</u> shares ($14,000,000 total par value, divided by $5 par value per share)

d. Par value of common shares issued and subscribed $14,000,000
Additional paid-in capital on common shares... <u>30,800,000</u>
   Total issue price of common shares $44,800,000
Number of common shares issued (part **c**)... 2,800,000
Average issue price per share ($44,800,000 ÷ 2,800,000 shares).............. <u>$16</u>

e. <u>$26,000,000</u> ($12,000,000 preferred, $14,000,000 common)

f. <u>$57,160,000</u> ($26,000,000 legal capital, plus $31,160,000 additional paid-in capital)

g. Total stockholders' equity $59,840,000
Less: Claims of preferred stockholders (120,000 shares ×
   $102 call price) .... <u>12,240,000</u>
Equity of common stockholders... $47,600,000
Number of common shares outstanding (part c)...................................... 2,800,000
Book value per share ($47,600,000 ÷ 2,800,000 shares) .... <u>$17</u>

SELF-TEST QUESTIONS

The answers to these questions appear on page 564.

1. Which of the following statements are characteristic of most unincorporated businesses, such as sole proprietorships and partnerships? (Indicate all correct answers.)
  a. Although the owners have limited lives, the business entity is assumed to be a going concern.
  b. The business entity does not pay income taxes on its earnings.
  c. If the business fails, the owners' potential losses are limited to the amounts of their equity.
  d. Owners do not receive dividends, but may withdraw assets from the business at will.

2. When a business is organized as a corporation:
  a. Stockholders are liable for the debts of the business only in proportion to their percentage ownership of capital stock.
  b. Stockholders do *not* have to pay personal income taxes on dividends received, because the corporation is subject to income taxes on its earnings.
  c. Fluctuations in the market value of outstanding shares of capital stock do *not* affect the amount of stockholders' equity shown in the balance sheet.
  d. Each stockholder has the right to bind the corporation to contracts and to make other managerial decisions.

3. Great Plains Corporation was organized with authorization to issue 100,000 shares of $1 par value common stock. Forty thousand shares were issued to Tom Morgan, the company's founder, at a price of $5 per share. No other shares have yet been issued.
  a. Morgan owns *40%* of the stockholders' equity of the corporation.
  b. The corporation should recognize a $160,000 gain on the issuance of these shares.
  c. If the balance sheet includes retained earnings of $50,000, total *paid-in* capital amounts to $250,000.
  d. In the balance sheet, the Additional Paid-in Capital account will have a $160,000 balance, regardless of the profits earned or losses incurred since the corporation was organized.

4. Which of the following is *not* a characteristic of the *common stock* of a large, publicly owned corporation?
  a. The shares may be transferred from one investor to another without disrupting the continuity of business operations.
  b. Voting rights in the election of the board of directors.
  c. A cumulative right to receive dividends.
  d. After issuance, the market value of the stock is unrelated to its par value.

5. Tri-State Electric is a profitable utility company that has increased its dividend to *common* stockholders every year for 42 consecutive years. Which of the following is least likely to affect the market price of the company's *preferred* stock by a significant amount?
   a. The company's earnings are expected to increase significantly over the next several years.
   b. An increase in long-term interest rates.
   c. The board of directors announces its intention to increase common stock dividends in the current year.
   d. Whether or not the preferred stock carries a conversion privilege.

6. The following information is taken from the balance sheet and related disclosures of Blue Oyster Corporation:

Total paid-in capital	$5,400,000
Outstanding shares:	
Common stock, $5 par value	100,000 shares
6% preferred stock, $100 par value, callable at $108 per share.........	10,000 shares
Preferred dividends in arrears...	2 years
Total stockholders' equity	$4,700,000

For this question, more than one answer may be correct.
   a. The preferred dividends in arrears amount to $120,000 and should appear as a liability in the corporate balance sheet.
   b. The book value per share of common stock is $35.
   c. The stockholders' equity section of the balance sheet should indicate a deficit of $700,000.
   d. The company has paid no dividend on its *common* stock during the past two years.

ASSIGNMENT MATERIAL

DISCUSSION QUESTIONS

1. Terry Hanson owns Hanson Sporting Goods, a retail store organized as a sole proprietorship. He also owns a home which he purchased for $200,000, but which is worth $250,000 today. (Hanson has a $140,000 mortgage against this house.) Explain how this house and mortgage should be classified in the financial statements of Hanson Sporting Goods.

2. Jane Miller is the proprietor of a small manufacturing business. She is considering the possibility of joining in partnership with Tom Bracken, whom she considers to be thoroughly competent and congenial. Prepare a brief statement outlining the advantages and disadvantages of the potential partnership to Miller.

3. Compare the right of partners to withdraw assets from a partnership with the right of stockholders to receive dividends from a corporation. Explain any significant differences in these rights.

4. Susan Reed is a partner in Computer Works, a retail store. During the current year, she withdraws $45,000 in cash from this business, and also takes for her personal use inventory costing $3,200. Her share of the partnership net income for the year amounts to $39,000. What amount must Reed report on her personal income tax return?

5. Olin Cole owns Cole Engineering, a highly successful business which is organized as a sole proprietorship. Cole is planning on retiring within the next several years, and there is no one in his family qualified to take over the business. Should Cole's accountant continue to prepare financial statements on the assumption that Cole Engineering is a going concern? Explain.

6. Distinguish between corporations and partnerships in terms of the following characteristics:
   a. Owners' liability for debts of the business
   b. Transferability of ownership interest
   c. Continuity of existence
   d. Federal taxation on income

7. What are the basic rights of the owner of a share of corporate stock? In what way are these basic rights commonly modified with respect to the owner of a share of preferred stock?

8. Explain the meaning of the term *double taxation* as it applies to corporate profits.

9. Explain the significance of *par value*. Does par value indicate the reasonable market price for a share of stock? Explain.

10. Describe the usual nature of the following features as they apply to a share of preferred stock: (a) cumulative, (b) convertible, and (c) callable.

11. When stock is issued by a corporation in exchange for assets other than cash, accountants face the problem of determining the dollar amount at which to record the transaction. Discuss the factors to be considered and explain their significance.

12. State the classification (asset, liability, stockholders' equity, revenue, or expense) of each of the following accounts:
    a. Subscriptions Receivable
    b. Organization Costs
    c. Preferred Stock
    d. Retained Earnings
    e. Capital Stock Subscribed
    f. Paid-in Capital in Excess of Par Value
    g. Income Taxes Payable

13. If the Retained Earnings account has a debit balance, how is it presented in the balance sheet and what is it called?

14. A professional baseball team received as a gift from the city the land upon which to build a stadium. What effect, if any, will the receipt of this gift have upon the baseball team's balance sheet and income statement? Explain.

15. Explain the following terms:
    a. Stock transfer agent
    b. Stockholders ledger
    c. Underwriter
    d. Stock registrar

16. What does *book value per share* of common stock represent? Does it represent the amount common stockholders would receive in the event of liquidation of the corporation? Explain briefly.

17. How is book value per share of common stock computed when a company has both preferred and common stock outstanding?

18. What would be the effect, if any, on book value per share of common stock as a result of each of the following independent events: (a) a corporation obtains a bank loan; (b) a dividend is declared (to be paid in the next accounting period).

19. In the great stock market crash of October 19, 1987, the market price of **IBM's** capital stock fell by over $31 per share. Explain the effects, if any, of this decline in share price on IBM's balance sheet.

EXERCISES

EXERCISE 11-1
Form of Organization

Assume that you have recently obtained your scuba instructor's certification, and have decided to start a scuba diving school.

a. Describe the advantages and disadvantages of organizing your scuba diving school as a:
  1. Sole proprietorship
  2. Corporation

b. State your opinion about which form of organization would be best and explain the basis for your opinion.

EXERCISE 11-2
Evaluation of Financial Statements of a Sole Proprietorship

First National Bank is considering making a $25,000 loan to The Coffee Brake, a gourmet drive-through coffee stand. The Coffee Brake is a sole proprietorship that is owned by Sam Ballew. First National has obtained current financial statements of the business, including the balance sheet that shows total owner's equity of more than $400,000.

a. Explain why the balance sheet of a sole proprietorship is of limited value to a creditor such as First National.

b. What additional information would be critical to First National in deciding whether or not to make the loan?

EXERCISE 11-3
Accounting Terminology
LO 1,2,5,6,8

Listed below are eleven technical accounting terms introduced or emphasized in this chapter:

Par value	Retained earnings	Preferred stock	Unlimited personal
Book value	Deficit	Common stock	liability for debts
Market value	Dividend in arrears	Paid-in capital	Double taxation

Each of the following statements may (or may not) describe one of these technical terms. For each statement, indicate the term described, or answer "None" if the statement does not correctly describe any of the terms.

a. A major *disadvantage* of an unincorporated form of business organization, such as a sole proprietorship or a partnership.

b. The type of capital stock for which the dividend usually is fixed in amount.

c. Cash provided by profitable operations that is available for distribution to stockholders as dividends.

d. The per-share value of common stock that reflects investors' expectations of future profitability.

e. A dividend paid to common stockholders that is smaller than the dividend paid in the prior year.

f. That portion of stockholders' equity arising from the issuance of capital stock.

g. The type of capital stock most likely to increase in value as a corporation becomes increasingly profitable.

h. The net assets represented by one share of common stock.

i. A distribution of cash by a corporation to its owners.

EXERCISE 11-4
Capital and Drawing Accounts of Sole Proprietorship

John Stewart owns Steamers & Beer, a seafood restaurant organized as a sole proprietorship. Explain what effect, if any, recording the following transactions will have upon the balance of Stewart's capital account and drawing account.

a. Stewart brings his personal computer from home to use full time in the business.

b. Stewart pays a number of his personal bills from the business bank account.

c. Stewart hires his daughter to work in the restaurant while she is home from college during semester break. Her salary, paid from the business account, is $800.

d. Stewart writes a check from his personal bank account to pay a liability of the business.

e. At the end of the accounting period, the balance of Stewart's drawing account is closed into his capital account.

EXERCISE 11-5
Preparing an Income
Statement and State-
ment of Owner's Equity
 LO 1

From the following account balances, prepare first an income statement and then a statement of owner's equity for Harris Painting Contractors, a sole proprietorship, for the year ended December 31, 1998. Include the proper headings on both financial statements.

C. Harris, Capital, Dec. 31, 1997....	$ 27,200	Rent Expense	$9,600
C. Harris, Drawing...........................	18,000	Advertising Expense....................	3,200
Painting Fees Earned	140,000	Depreciation Expense: Painting	
Paint & Supplies Expense	27,500	Equipment	1,200
Salaries Expense...........................	66,800		

EXERCISE 11-6
Preparing Closing Entries
 LO 1

Prepare the year-end closing entries for Harris Painting Contractors, using the data given in Exercise 11-5. Indicate the balance in the owner's capital account that should appear in the balance sheet dated December 31, 1998.

EXERCISE 11-7
Stockholders'
Equity Section of a
Balance Sheet
 LO 5

When Enviro Systems, Inc., was formed, the company was authorized to issue 5,000 shares of $100 par value, 8% cumulative preferred stock, and 100,000 shares of $2 stated value common stock. The preferred stock is callable at $106.

Half of the preferred stock was issued at a price of $103 per share, and 70,000 shares of the common stock were sold for $13 per share. At the end of the current year, Enviro Systems, Inc., has retained earnings of $297,000.

a. Prepare the stockholders' equity section of the company's balance sheet at the end of the current year.

b. Assume Enviro Systems' common stock is trading at $22 per share and its preferred stock is trading at $105 per share at the end of the current year. Would the stockholders' equity section prepared in part **a** be affected by this additional information?

EXERCISE 11-8
Dividends: Preferred and
Common
 LO 6

A portion of the stockholders' equity section from the balance sheet of Pippin Corporation appears below:

Stockholders' equity:	
Preferred stock, 9% cumulative, $50 par, 60,000 shares authorized and issued	$3,000,000
Preferred stock, 10% noncumulative, $100 par, 8,000 shares authorized and issued	800,000
Common stock, $5 par, 500,000 shares authorized and issued	2,500,000
Total paid-in capital	$6,300,000

Assume that all the stock was issued on January 1, 19__, and that no dividends were paid during the first two years of operations. During the third year, Pippin Corporation paid total cash dividends of $1,000,000.

a. Compute the amount of cash dividends paid during the third year to each of the three classes of stock.

b. Compute the dividends paid *per share* during the third year for each of the three classes of stock.

c. What was the average issue price of each type of preferred stock? Why would an investor buy noncumulative preferred stock, when cumulative stock is available from the same company at half the price per share?

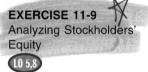

EXERCISE 11-9
Analyzing Stockholders'
Equity
LO 5,8

The year-end balance sheet of Maui Corporation includes the following stockholders' equity section (with certain details omitted):

Stockholders' equity:

par value *
#shares issued

Capital stock:	
7% cumulative preferred stock, $100 par value,	
callable at $105..	$ 15,000,000
Common stock, $5 par value, 5,000,000 shares	
authorized, 4,000,000 shares issued...	20,000,000
Additional paid-in capital:	
Preferred...	300,000
Common...	44,000,000
Retained earnings	64,450,000
Total stockholders' equity	$143,750,000

From this information, compute answers to the following questions:

a. How many shares of preferred stock have been issued? *150,000*

b. What is the total amount of the annual dividends paid to preferred stockholders?

c. What was the average issuance price per share of common stock?

d. What is the amount of legal capital and the amount of total paid-in capital?

e. What is the book value per share of common stock?

f. It is possible to determine the fair market value per share of common stock from the stockholders' equity section above? Explain.

EXERCISE 11-10
Reporting the Effects of
Transactions
LO 5,7

Five events pertaining to Lowlands Manufacturing Co. are described below.

a. Issued common stock for cash.

b. Issued common stock for equipment.

c. The market value of the corporation's stock increased. *NO effect*

d. Declared and paid a cash dividend to stockholders.

e. Received a building site as a donation from the city.

Indicate the immediate effects of the events on the financial measurements in the four columnar headings listed below. Use the code letters, **I** for increase, **D** for decrease, and **NE** for no effect.

revenue   *cash*

Stockholders'   *p.p.*

Event	Current Assets	Owners' Equity	Net Income	Net Cash Flow (from Any Source)
a				

EXERCISE 11-11
Computing Book Value
LO 5,8

Presented below is the information necessary to compute the net assets (stockholders' equity) and book value per share of common stock for Ringside Corporation:

8% cumulative preferred stock, $100 par (callable at $110)	$200,000
Common stock, $5 par, authorized 100,000 shares, issued 60,000 shares	300,000
Additional paid-in capital	452,800
Deficit	146,800
Dividends in arrears on preferred stock, 1 full year	16,000

a. Compute the amount of net assets (stockholders' equity).

b. Compute the book value per share of common stock.

c. Is book value per share (answer to part **b**) the amount common stockholders should expect to receive if Ringside Corporation were to cease operations and liquidate? Explain.

EXERCISE 11-12
Reading the Financial Pages
LO 7

Presented below is an excerpt from a newspaper listing of stock transactions for a particular day. It presents the information about **Delta Airlines** stock for the day.

Stock	Div	Vol 100s	Hi	Lo	Close	Net Chg
Delta Air	.20	1,705	50⅞	50½	50¾	+¼
Delta Air pf	3.50	236	46⅝	46⅛	46½	+¼

From this information, answer the following questions:

a. How many shares of Delta Airlines preferred stock were sold on this day?

b. If you had purchased 100 shares of Delta Airlines common at the lowest price of the day, what would be the total purchase price of the stock?

c. What was the closing price of a share of Delta Airlines preferred stock on the *previous* day?

d. Assume that you are assured of obtaining the $3.50 per share annual dividend on the preferred stock of Delta Airlines, and you can buy and resell the stock at any time for $46.50 per share. Would it be better to invest in the stock, or to deposit your available funds in a savings account that pays interest at an annual rate of 6%? Explain your answer.

*EXERCISE 11-13
Incorporation of an
Existing Business
LO 5,9

Tucker Enterprises is a sole proprietorship owned by William Tucker. Because Tucker hopes to attract other equity investors, he has decided to incorporate the business. The following items appear as follows on the balance sheet of the sole proprietorship: cash, $10,000; accounts receivable, $65,000; inventory, $105,000; store equipment, $80,000; accounts payable, $40,000.

Tucker determines that the assets on the balance sheet are recorded at amounts that approximate their fair market values, except for accounts receivable, which have a value of $55,000, and store equipment, which is worth $95,000. You are to incorporate Tucker Enterprises by making a general journal entry to record the investment by Tucker. Assume that Tucker Enterprises issued 25,000 shares of no-par capital stock to Tucker for the assets and liabilities of the business.

Supplemental Topic, "Incorporating a Going Concern."

EXERCISE 11-14
Annual Reports;
Finding Information
 LO 5,8

On page A-13 of Appendix A is a note to the financial statements of **Toys "R" Us** that describes the details of the stockholders' equity of the company.

a. What is the par value of the company's common stock?

b. How many shares of stock are authorized and explain the meaning of authorized shares?

c. How many shares of stock are issued and explain the meaning of issued shares?

d. Total stockholders' equity for Toys "R" Us at January 28, 1995 was $3,428,875,000. Does this mean that the total stock outstanding is worth this amount? Explain your answer.

PROBLEMS

 PROBLEM 11-1
Sole Proprietorship: Use
of Capital and Drawing
Account
LO 1

Dean Engineering is a sole proprietorship owned by Sharon Dean. During the month of April, Dean's ownership equity was affected by the following events:

Apr. 7 Dean invested an additional $20,000 cash in the business.

Apr. 15 Dean withdrew $6,500 in cash and used the money to pay her personal income taxes.

Apr. 22 Dean collected from J. Barker an $1,800 account receivable of the business and deposited the money in her personal checking account.

Apr. 30 Dean drew a check payable to herself on the business bank account in the amount of $4,000. She had stipulated this amount as her monthly salary as owner-manager of the business.

Apr. 30 The Income Summary account showed a credit balance of $7,200; the accounts of Dean Engineering are closed monthly.

INSTRUCTIONS

a. Prepare journal entries for each of the above events in the accounts of Dean Engineering. Include the entries necessary to close the Income Summary account and Dean's drawing account at April 30.

b. Prepare a statement of owner's equity for the month ended April 30. Assume that the balance of Dean's capital account on April 1 was $57,800.

c. How much taxable income did Dean earn from her business in April? In general terms, explain how income taxes are levied upon the earnings of a sole proprietorship.

d. What would Dean Engineering's net income have been in April if Dean had set her monthly salary at $12,000 instead of $4,000? Explain. Also, what effect would this change have upon Dean's taxable income?

 PROBLEM 11-2
Comparison of
Proprietorship
with Corporation
 LO 1,3

California Eyeshades is a retail store owned solely by Paul Turner. During the month of November, the equity accounts were affected by the following events:

Nov. 9 Turner invested an additional $15,000 in the business.

Nov. 15 Turner withdrew $1,500 for his salary for the first two weeks of the month.

Nov. 30 Turner withdrew $1,500 for his salary for the second two weeks of the month.

Nov. 30 California Eyeshades distributed $1,000 of earnings to Turner.

INSTRUCTIONS

a. Assuming that the business is organized as a sole proprietorship:
  1. Prepare the journal entries to record the above events in the accounts of California Eyeshades.
  2. Prepare the closing entries for the month of November. Assume that after closing all of the revenue and expense accounts, the Income Summary account has a credit balance of $5,000.

b. Assuming that the business is organized as a corporation:

   1. Prepare the journal entries to record the above events in the accounts of California Eyeshades. Assume that the distribution of earnings on November 30 was payment of a dividend that was declared on November 20.

   2. Prepare the closing entries for the month of November. Assume that after closing all of the revenue and expense accounts (except Income Taxes Expense), the Income Summary account has a credit balance of $2,000. Before preparing the closing entries, prepare the entries to accrue income taxes expense for the month and to close the Income Taxes Expense account to the Income Summary account. Assume that the corporate income tax rate is *30%*.

c. Explain the causes of the differences in net income between California Eyeshades as a sole proprietorship and California Eyeshades as a corporation.

d. Describe the effects of the business operations on Turner's individual income tax return, assuming that the business is organized as (1) a sole proprietorship and (2) a corporation.

PROBLEM 11-3
Stockholders' Equity Section

LO 5

Kevin Smith organized EZ Moving Company in January 1996. The corporation immediately issued at $9 per share one-half of its 200,000 authorized shares of $1 par common stock. On January 2, 1997, the corporation sold at par the entire 10,000 authorized shares of 8%, $100 par value, cumulative preferred stock. On January 2, *1998*, the company again needed money and issued 5,000 shares of an authorized 10,000 shares of $9, no-par, cumulative preferred stock for a total of $508,000.

The company suffered losses in its first two years, reporting a deficit of $170,000 at the end of 1997. During 1998 and 1999 combined, the company earned a total of $750,000. Dividends of 50 cents per share were paid on common stock in 1998 and $1.60 per share in 1999.

INSTRUCTIONS

a. Prepare the stockholders' equity section of the balance sheet at December 31, 1999. Include a supporting schedule showing your computation of retained earnings or deficit at the balance sheet date.

b. Assume that on January 2, 1997, the corporation could have borrowed $1,000,000 at 8% interest on a long-term basis instead of issuing the 10,000 shares of the $100 par value cumulative preferred stock at par value. Identify two reasons why a corporation would issue cumulative preferred stock rather than finance operations with long-term debt.

PROBLEM 11-4
Reporting Stockholders' Equity: Two Short Cases

LO 5

The two cases described below are independent of each other. Each case provides the information necessary to prepare the stockholders' equity section of a corporate balance sheet.

1. Early in 1996, Bell Corporation was formed with authorization to issue 50,000 shares of $1 par value common stock. All shares were issued at a price of $8 per share. The corporation reported a net loss of $82,000 for 1996 and a net loss of $25,000 in 1997. In 1998, net income was $70,000. No dividends were declared in any of the three years.

2. Parker Industries was organized early in 1994 and authorized to issue 200,000 shares of $10 par value common and 30,000 shares of $100 par value cumulative preferred stock. All the preferred stock was issued at par and 120,000 shares of common stock were sold for $16 per share.

   The preferred stock was callable at 105% of its $100 par value and was entitled to dividends of 10% before any dividends were paid to common. During the first five years of its existence, the corporation earned a total of $3,200,000 and paid dividends of 50 cents per share each year on the common stock.

INSTRUCTIONS

a. For each of the independent situations described, prepare in good form the stockholders' equity section of the balance sheet as of December 31, 1998. Include a supporting schedule for each case showing your determination of the balance of retained earnings that should appear in the balance sheet.

b. As of December 31, compute for each company the book value per share of common stock.

c. For each company, briefly explain why the book value is either higher or lower than the price at which the stock was originally issued.

PROBLEM 11-5
Stockholders' Equity: a Short, Comprehensive Problem
LO 5

Early in the year Roger Gordon and several friends organized a corporation called Mobile Communications, Inc. The corporation was authorized to issue 50,000 shares of $100 par value, 10% cumulative preferred stock and 400,000 shares of $2 par value common stock. The following transactions (among others) occurred during the year:

Jan. 6 Issued for cash 20,000 shares of common stock at $14 per share. The shares were issued to Gordon and 10 other investors.

Jan. 7 Issued an additional 500 shares of common stock to Gordon in exchange for his services in organizing the corporation. The stockholders agreed that these services were worth $7,000.

Jan. 12 Issued 2,500 shares of preferred stock for cash of $250,000.

June 4 Acquired land as a building site in exchange for 15,000 shares of common stock. In view of the appraised value of the land and the progress of the company, the directors agreed that the common stock was to be valued for purposes of this transaction at $15 per share.

Nov. 15 The first annual dividend of $10 per share was declared on the preferred stock to be paid December 20.

Dec. 20 Paid the cash dividend declared on November 15.

Dec. 31 After the revenue and expenses were closed into the Income Summary account, that account indicated a net income of $106,500.

INSTRUCTIONS

a. Prepare journal entries in general journal form to record the above transactions. Include entries at December 31 to close the Income Summary account and the Dividends account.

b. Prepare the stockholders' equity section of the Mobile Communications, Inc., balance sheet at December 31.

c. What factors should the board of directors have considered in deciding that the stock issued on June 4 should be valued at $15 per share?

PROBLEM 11-6
Analysis of an Equity Section
LO 5,6,7,8

Quanex Corporation is a publicly owned company. The following information is excerpted from a recent balance sheet. Dollar amounts (except for per share amounts) are stated in thousands.

Stockholders' equity:

Convertible $17.20 preferred stock, no par value, 1,000,000 shares authorized; 345,000 shares issued and outstanding; $250 per share liquidation preference (call price)	$ 86,250
Common stock, par value $0.50; 25,000,000 shares authorized	6,819
Additional paid-in capital	87,260
Retained earnings	57,263
Total stockholders' equity	$237,592

INSTRUCTIONS

From this information, answer the following questions:

a. How many shares of common stock have been issued?

b. What is the total amount of the annual dividends paid to preferred stockholders?

c. What is the total amount of paid-in capital?

d. What is the book value per share of common stock?

e. Briefly explain the advantages and disadvantages to Quanex of being publicly owned rather than operating as a closely held corporation.

f. What is meant by the term "convertible" used in the caption of the preferred stock? Is there any more information that investors need to know in order to evaluate this conversion feature?

g. Assume that the preferred stock currently is selling at *$248* per share. Does this provide a higher or lower dividend yield than an 8%, $50 par value preferred with a market price of $57 per share? Show computations (round to the nearest tenth of one percent). Explain why one preferred stock might yield less than another.

---

*PROBLEM 11-7
Incorporation of a
Proprietorship
LO 5,9

PEANUTS is a retail store that sells baby products. The business is organized as a sole proprietorship. At March 31, 1999, the assets, liabilities, and owner's equity are as shown below. On this date, the owner plans to incorporate the business.

	Values in the Proprietorship's Records	Current Market Values
Cash	$ 20,000	$ 20,000
Accounts receivable	35,000	30,000
Inventory	110,000	125,000
Store equipment	95,000	100,000
Notes payable	50,000	50,000
Accounts payable	10,000	10,000
Owner's equity	200,000	215,000

a. Explain which values should be entered in the accounting records of the new corporation—and why.

b. Prepare the general journal entry to record the formation of the new corporation. Assume that the corporation issued 10,000 shares of stock in exchange for acquisition of assets and liabilities of the proprietorship.

c. Explain *why* the owner of PEANUTS might want to incorporate the business.

---

*PROBLEM 11-8
Incorporating a
Going-concern
LO 1,3,9

Pancho's Cantina is the best Mexican restaurant in town—some customers say the best anywhere. For years, the restaurant was a sole proprietorship owned by Wayne Label. Many of Label's friends and customers had offered to invest in the business if he ever decided to open new locations. So, early this year, Label decided to expand the business. He formed a new corporation, called Pancho's Cantinas, Inc., which planned to issue stock and use the money received to open new Pancho's restaurants in various locations.

The new corporation is authorized to issue 100,000 shares of $1 par value capital stock. In April the corporation entered into the following transactions:

---

*Supplemental Topic, "Incorporating a Going Concern."

Apr. 1 Issued 25,000 shares of capital stock to Label in exchange for the assets of the original Pancho's Cantina. These assets and their current market values on this date are listed below.

Inventory	$ 20,000
Land	305,000
Building	280,000
Equipment and fixtures	145,000

Apr. 15 Issued for cash 25,000 shares of capital stock at a price of $30 per share. These shares were issued to Label's family, friends, several employees of the original Pancho's, and fourteen regular customers.

Apr. 20 Received an invoice from an attorney for $6,200 for services relating to the formation of the new corporation. This invoice is due in 30 days.

Apr. 30 Issued 100 shares of capital stock to Label in exchange for $3,000 cash, thus assuring Label voting control of the corporation.

The new corporation will begin operation of the original Pancho's Cantina on May 1. Therefore, the corporation had no revenue or expenses relating to restaurant operations during April. No depreciation of plant assets or amortization of organization costs will be recognized until May, when operations get under way.

INSTRUCTIONS

a. Prepare journal entries to record the April transactions in the accounting records of the new corporation.

b. Prepare a classified balance sheet for the corporation as of April 30, 19__.

c. Explain how the incorporation of Pancho's will affect Label's:
   1. Ability to withdraw assets from the business
   2. Role in day-to-day operations
   3. Liability for business debts
   4. Personal income tax obligations

d. Does Pancho's appear to be a closely held corporation, or publicly owned?

e. Did Label really need to increase his stockholdings on April 30 to have effective "voting control" of the corporation? Explain.

CASES

CASE 11-1
Here's How I Want
This Recorded

L0 1

Mark Tutwyler, owner of Tutwyler Farms, recently was named Farmer of the Year in Clinton County. Joanne Williams, an introductory accounting student, works for Tutwyler as a part-time bookkeeper. She maintains the accounting records for Tutwyler Farms, and also helps Tutwyler keep track of his personal affairs.

Tutwyler Farms is a sole proprietorship with no financial reporting responsibilities to creditors or investors. In fact, the business does not prepare formal financial statements. Tutwyler uses the information in the accounting records in managing the business and in his personal income tax return.

Two recent events are troubling Williams. Today, Tutwyler told her that he was "a little short of cash this month," and asked her to prepare a check on the business bank account to pay his personal VISA bill.

Also, he instructed her to debit the entire $1,800 cost of his family's annual vacation at Walt Disney World to the Travel Expense account in the company's ledger. Nothing has yet been recorded, but Williams knows that only the airfare, $700, has been paid from the business bank account. The remaining costs, consisting of hotel bills, meals, and admission tickets to Walt Disney World, were paid from Tutwyler's personal bank account.

Evaluate these situations separately, explaining whether you believe that Williams has cause for concern. Make your personal recommendations as to Williams' appropriate course of action.

CASE 11-2
Par, Book, and Market Values. An Open-Ended Discussion

Microsoft Corp. is the producer of such software products as *Windows*™, *Excel*™, and *Word*™. In mid-1990, an investment service published the following per-share amounts relating to Microsoft's only class of capital stock:

Par value	$ 0.001
Book value (estimated)	6.50
Market value	73.00

INSTRUCTIONS

a. Without reference to dollar amounts, explain the nature and significance of *par value, book value,* and *market value.*

b. Comment upon the *interrelationships,* if any, among the per-share amounts shown for Microsoft Corp. What do these amounts imply about the company and its operations? Also comment upon what these amounts imply about the security of *creditors'* claims against the company.

CASE 11-3
Factors Affecting the Market Prices of Preferred and Common Stocks

ADM Labs is a publicly owned company with several issues of capital stock outstanding. Over the past decade, the company has consistently earned modest profits and has increased its common stock dividend annually by 5 or 10 cents per share. Recently the company introduced several new products which you believe will cause future sales and profits to increase dramatically. You also expect a gradual increase in long-term interest rates from their present level of about 11% to, perhaps, 12 to 12½%. Based upon these forecasts, explain whether you would expect to see the market prices of the following issues of ADM capital stock increase or decrease. Explain your reasoning in each answer.

a. 10%, $100 par value, preferred stock (currently selling at $90 per share).

b. $5 par value common stock (currently paying an annual dividend of $2.50 and selling at $40 per share).

c. 7%, $100 par value, convertible preferred stock (currently selling at $125 per share).

CASE 11-4
Factors Affecting the Market Prices of Common Stocks

Each of the following situations describes a recent event that affected the stock market price of a particular company.

a. The price of a common share of **McDonnell Douglas, Inc.** increased by 5⅛ dollars per share in the several days after it was announced that Saudia Airlines would order $6 billion of commercial airliners from Boeing and McDonnell Douglas.

b. **Citicorp's** common stock price fell 3⅜ per share shortly after the Federal Reserve Board increased the discount rate by ¼%. The discount rate is the rate charged to banks for short-term loans they need to meet their reserve requirements.

c. The price of a common share of **Ventitex, Inc.,** a manufacturer of medical devices, fell 10¼ (27.7%) after it was announced that representatives of the Federal Drug Administration paid a visit to the company.

INSTRUCTIONS

For each of the independent situations described, explain the likely underlying rationale for the change in market price of the stock.

CASE 11-5
Using the
"Financial Pages"
LO 7

On page 541 we illustrated market information about **Ford Motor Company's** $4.20 preferred stock in late January 1995.

a. Using the financial pages of a daily newspaper, indicate the *current* market price of this preferred stock and its dividend yield. Show the *computation* of the dividend yield appearing in your paper.

b. In January 1995, investors could earn about 6% on bank deposits. Did investors who instead purchased Ford's preferred stock at a price of $84 per share expect interest rates to rise or fall? Explain.

c. In January 1995, the Federal Reserve's discount rate was 5¼%. In a newspaper such as *The Wall Street Journal,* locate today's Federal Reserve discount rate. (In the *Journal,* this rate appears in the Money Rates column in Section C.) Is the change in the price of Ford's preferred stock since January of 1995 what you might expect?

CASE 11-6
Selecting a
Form of Business
Organization
LO 2,3

Interview the owners of two local small businesses. One business should be organized as a corporation and the other as either a sole proprietorship or a partnership. Inquire as to:

● *Why* this form of entity was selected.

● Have there been any unforeseen complications with this form of entity?

● Is the form of entity likely to be changed in the foreseeable future? And if so, why?

(**Note:** All interviews are to be conducted in accordance with the guidelines discussed in the *Notes to Student* in the beginning of this textbook.)

INTERNET ASSIGNMENT

INTERNET 11-1
Incorporating
in Delaware
LO 3,4

Over one-half of the Fortune 500 companies, and nearly one-half of all companies traded on the major stock exchanges, are incorporated in Delaware. T.L.M. Corporate Agents, Inc., offers a wide range of services to companies that choose to incorporate in Delaware.

Visit the T.L.M. home page at the following Internet address:

www.delcorp.com

Select FAQ's from the main menu (**Note:** FAQ's stands for "frequently asked questions.")

INSTRUCTIONS

Using information from T.L.M.'s home page, answer the following questions:

a. Why do so many companies incorporate in Delaware?

b. Approximately how long does it take for a proprietorship or a partnership to incorporate?

c. Under what circumstances can a shareholder be held responsible for the debts of a Delaware corporation?

d. What is a limited liability company (an L.L.P.)? How is it similar to a partnership?

OUR COMMENTS ON THE IN-TEXT CASES

YOU AS AN INVESTOR (P. 542) While rising interest rates are not favorable for the market price on any type of stock, the market value of preferred stock is affected more so than is common stock. If interest rates increase, the value of the preferred stock will fall. Since you are investing for the short term, you probably should invest in the common stock rather than the preferred stock.

YOU AS A LOAN OFFICER (P. 544)   GOTCHA! does *not* appear to be a good credit risk for a $200,000 loan. The company has few liquid assets which can be used to repay a loan. Also, the proposed loan is very large in relation to the small corporation's assets and owners' equity. Because GOTCHA! is organized as a corporation, Woods is not personally responsible for the company's debts—unless he agrees to be.

Most loan officers would want to find a way to make this loan. They certainly would not want to refuse a 20-year customer of the bank a loan that amounts to less than half of the normal balance he maintains in his checking account. But they would ask that Woods *personally guarantee* the loan, rather than depending solely upon GOTCHA! for repayment. (Woods will not be offended by this requirement; in situations such as this, it is standard business practice.)

ANSWERS TO SELF-TEST QUESTIONS

1. a, b, d   **2.** c   **3.** d   **4.** c   **5.** c   **6.** b, c, d

REPORTING UNUSUAL EVENTS AND SPECIAL EQUITY TRANSACTIONS

Location:

Search | Feedback | Help | Directory

Document: Done

The unexpected can happen—and the impact can be of great consequence. Such events deserve special consideration—by investors, management, and, in many cases, by government and the public. That's why these events are reported *separately* from the results of routine business operations.

1. Describe how *discontinued operations*, *extraordinary items*, and *accounting changes* are presented in the income statement.
2. Compute *earnings per share*.
3. Distinguish between basic and diluted earnings per share.
4. Account for *stock dividends* and *stock splits*, and explain the probable effect of these transactions upon market price.
5. Describe and prepare a statement of retained earnings.
6. Define prior *period adjustments* and explain how they are presented in financial statements.
7. Account for treasury stock transactions.
8. Explain the cash effects of equity transactions.
9. Describe and prepare a statement of stockholders' equity.
*10. Describe *stock options* as a form of compensation to managers.

In this chapter we explore special topics relating primarily to the financial statements of large corporations. The chapter is divided into two major parts. In the first part, we show how an income statement is organized to present certain "unusual" items separately from the income or loss from normal business activities. Also, we illustrate and explain the presentation of earnings per share, with emphasis upon the interpretation of the different per-share amounts. In the second part, we look at various stockholders' equity transactions, including cash dividends, stock dividends, stock splits, prior period adjustments, and treasury stock transactions.

REPORTING THE RESULTS OF OPERATIONS

The most important aspect of corporate financial reporting, in the view of most investors, is the determination of periodic income. Both the market price of common stock and the amount of cash dividends per share depend on the current and future earnings of the corporation.

DEVELOPING PREDICTIVE INFORMATION

An income statement tells us a great deal about the performance of a company over the past year. For example, study of the income statement makes clear the types and amounts of revenue earned and expenses incurred, as well as the amounts of gross profit and net income. But what can the current income statement tell us about the probable *future* earnings of the corporation? By analyzing the *trend* of earnings over time, we can often develop a reasonable estimate of future earnings, especially if we take into account significant changes in the corporation's business, its industry, and economic conditions.

If the transactions summarized in the income statement for the year just completed were of a normal recurring nature, such as selling merchandise, paying employees, and incurring other normal expenses, we can reasonably assume that the operating results were typical and that somewhat similar results can be expected in the following year. However, in any business, unusual and nonrecurring events may occur which cause the current year's net income to be quite different from the income we would expect the company to earn in the future. For example,

Supplemental Topic, "Employee Stock Plans."

the company may have sustained large losses in the current year from an earthquake or some other event which is not likely to recur in the near future.

Ideally, the results of unusual and nonrecurring transactions should be shown in a separate section of the income statement *after* the income or loss from normal business activities has been determined. Income from *normal and recurring* activities presumably should be a more useful figure for *predicting future earnings* than is a net income figure which includes the results of nonrecurring events. The problem in creating such an income statement, however, is in determining which events are so unlikely to recur that they should be excluded from the results of "normal" operations. Three categories of events that require special treatment in the income statement are (1) the results of *discontinued operations*, (2) *extraordinary items*, and (3) the cumulative effects of *changes in accounting principles*.

REPORTING UNUSUAL ITEMS—AN ILLUSTRATION

To illustrate the presentation of these items, assume that Ross Corporation operates both a small chain of retail stores and two motels. Near the end of the current year, the company sells both motels to a national hotel chain. In addition, Ross Corporation reports two "extraordinary items" and also changes the method it uses in computing depreciation expense. An income statement illustrating the correct format for reporting these events appears below.

ROSS CORPORATION
Income Statement
For the Year Ended December 31, 1999

Net sales..		$8,000,000
Cost and expenses:		
Cost of goods sold..	$4,500,000	
Selling expenses..	1,500,000	
General and administrative expenses	920,000	
Loss on settlement of lawsuit	80,000	
Income taxes (on continuing operations)	300,000	7,300,000
Income from continuing operations		$ 700,000
Discontinued operations:		
Operating loss on motels (net of $90,000 income tax benefit).................................	$ (210,000)	
Gain on sale of motels (net of $195,000 income taxes)	455,000	245,000
Income before extraordinary items and cumulative effect of accounting change.....................		$ 945,000
Extraordinary items:		
Gain on condemnation of land by State Highway Department (net of $45,000 income taxes)	$ 105,000	
Loss from earthquake damage to Los Angeles store (net of $75,000 income tax benefit)..	(175,000)	(70,000)
Cumulative effect of change in accounting principle:		
Effect on prior years' income of change in method of computing depreciation (net of $60,000 income taxes)		140,000
Net income		$1,015,000

Notice the order in which the "special items" are reported

(handwritten annotation) must have before extra. items

Note: This income statement is designed to illustrate the presentation of various "unusual events." Rarely, if ever, will all these types of events appear in the income statement of one company within a single year.

CONTINUING OPERATIONS

The first section of the income statement contains only the results of *continuing business activities*—that is, the retail stores. Notice that the income taxes expense shown in this section relates *only to continuing operations*. The income taxes relating to the "special items" are shown separately in the income statement as adjustments to the amounts of these items.

INCOME FROM CONTINUING OPERATIONS The subtotal *income from continuing operations* measures the profitability of the ongoing operations. This subtotal should be helpful in making predictions of the company's future earnings. For example, if we predict no significant change in the profitability of its retail stores, we would expect Ross Corporation to earn a net income of approximately $700,000 next year.

DISCONTINUED OPERATIONS

If management enters into a formal plan to sell or discontinue a **segment of the business,** the results of that segment's operations are shown separately in the income statement. This enables users of the financial statements to better evaluate the performance of the company's ongoing (continuing) operations.

Two items are included in the **discontinued operations** section of the income statement: (1) the income or loss from *operating* the segment prior to its disposal and (2) the gain or loss on *disposal* of the segment. Notice also that the income taxes relating to the discontinued operations are *shown separately* from the income taxes expense relating to continuing business operations.

DISCONTINUED OPERATIONS MUST BE A "SEGMENT" OF THE BUSINESS To qualify for separate presentation in the income statement, the discontinued operations must represent an *entire segment* of the business. A "segment" of a business is a separate line of business activity or an operation that services a distinct category of customers.

For example, Pizza Hut once was a segment of PepsiCo. From time to time, PepsiCo closed individual Pizza Hut stores. Such store closures did *not* qualify as "discontinued operations," because PepsiCo remained in the pizza parlor business. But when PepsiCo disposed of the entire Pizza Hut chain, these restaurant activities were shown in PepsiCo's income statement as discontinued operations.

DISCONTINUED OPERATIONS ARE NOT REALLY "UNUSUAL" In recent years, a characteristic of the American economy has been the "restructuring" of many large corporations. As part of this restructuring, corporations often sell

L0 1 *Describe how* discontinued operations, extraordinary items, *and* accounting changes *are presented in the income statement.*

CASE IN POINT

In one recent year, **TWA** sold Hilton International, a hotel chain, to Allegis (parent company of United Airlines). Later that year, Allegis disposed of several segments of its business, including Hilton hotels and Hertz rental cars. In the same year, Sears sold its savings bank segment, RJR Nabisco sold its Heublein (wine and spirits) segment, Owens-Illinois sold its forest products division, and Metromedia sold its cellular telephone operations. All in all, several hundred large corporations reported discontinued operations.

one or more segments of the business. Thus, the presence of "discontinued operations" is not uncommon in the income statements of large corporations.

EXTRAORDINARY ITEMS

The second category of events requiring disclosure in a separate section of the income statement is extraordinary items. An **extraordinary item** is a gain or loss that is (1) *material in amount,* (2) *unusual in nature,* and (3) *not expected to recur in the foreseeable future.* By definition, extraordinary items are extremely rare; hence, they seldom appear in financial statements. An example of an extraordinary item is the loss of a company's plant due to an earthquake.

When a gain or loss qualifies as an extraordinary item, it appears after the section on discontinued operations (if any), following the subtotal Income before Extraordinary Items. Since the extraordinary item is so unusual, this subtotal is considered necessary to show investors what the net income *would have been* if the unusual event *had not occurred.* Extraordinary items are shown net of any related income tax effects.

OTHER "UNUSUAL" GAINS AND LOSSES   Some transactions are not typical of normal operations but also do not meet the criteria for separate presentation as extraordinary items. Among such events are losses incurred because of strikes and the gains or losses resulting from sales of plant assets. Such items, if material, should be individually listed as items of revenue or expense, rather than being combined with other items in broad categories such as sales revenue or general and administrative expenses.

In the illustrated income statement of Ross Corporation (page 567), the $80,000 loss resulting from the settlement of a lawsuit was disclosed separately in the income statement but was *not* listed as an extraordinary item. This loss was important enough to bring to the attention of readers of the financial statements, but most lawsuits are not so unusual or infrequent as to be considered extraordinary items.

DISTINGUISHING BETWEEN THE UNUSUAL AND THE "EXTRAORDINARY"   In the past, some corporate managements had a tendency to classify many *losses* as extraordinary, while classifying most *gains* as "ordinary." This resulted in reporting higher Income Before Extraordinary Items, although this subtotal was often adjusted downward at the bottom of the income statement. To counter this potentially misleading practice, the accounting profession now defines extraordinary items very carefully, and intends for them to be quite rare.

A key question is whether the event is *likely to happen again,* considering the company's environment. A farm located along the banks of the Mississippi River may, from time to time, incur flood damage. Even if these floods are, say, 10 years apart, the resulting losses would *not* be considered extraordinary. Such losses *are* expected to happen again.

Now consider a business located in San Francisco which sustains damage from an earthquake. Earthquakes do reoccur in this region, but the likelihood of one particular business sustaining material damage in multiple incidents is remote. Therefore, material damage caused by earthquakes generally *is* considered extraordinary. The same reasoning applies to tornadoes and lightning— such events are not expected to "strike twice in the same place."

There is no comprehensive list of extraordinary items. Thus, the classification of a specific event is a matter of *judgment.* The following table is intended to provide you with a "feel" for how these judgments are made.

Event	Analysis
Losses from a natural disaster which affects the company only at *infrequent* intervals.	Not extraordinary—likely to happen again.
Losses from a natural disaster *not* likely to affect the company again.	Extraordinary—not expected to happen again.
Gains or losses from seizures of assets by a government—either through expropriation or condemnation.	Specifically called extraordinary by the FASB. For a multinational company, such losses may happen again. But for political reasons, it is better to assume that they won't.
Material loss from theft.	Extraordinary. Small theft losses, like shoplifting, are routine. But *material* theft losses are not.
Losses from inventories that have become obsolete.	Not extraordinary—happens all the time.
Losses from an inventory made unsalable by a *newly enacted law.*	The FASB specifically identifies as extraordinary the immediate financial impact of newly enacted laws.
Receipt by a company of a large gift.	Does not appear in the income statement. Assets received as a gift are accounted for as *donated capital*—see Chapter 11.
Losses incurred from *acts of terrorism,* such as the bombing of the World Trade Center in New York.	Extraordinary—not likely to affect the same business twice. (The judgmental element of financial reporting involves *social responsibility.* Most accountants would be reluctant to dignify acts of terrorism as being anything other than isolated events.)

RESTRUCTURING CHARGES One important type of "unusual" loss relates to restructuring of operations. As indicated previously, restructuring of operations has become a common aspect of the American economy. In fact, the 1990s have been labeled the decade of corporate downsizing. As companies struggle to meet the competitive challenges of a global economy, they are incurring significant costs to close plants, reduce workforce, and consolidate operating facilities.

Restructuring charges consist of items such as losses on write-downs or sales of plant assets, severance pay for terminated workers, and expenses related to the relocation of operations and remaining personnel. They are presented in the company's income statement as a single item in determining operating income. If the restructuring involves discontinuing a segment of the business, the expenses related to that aspect of the restructuring are presented as discontinued operations.

A recent income statement of **Digital Equipment Corporation** included the following expense in determining net income from operations:

Restructuring charges.. $1,500,000,000

As stated in the notes to the financial statements, the charges were for the costs of employee separations, facility consolidations, asset retirements, relocations, and related costs. Approximately 10,000 employees were separated from the company, and several plants were closed in the United States and Europe. Other operations were moved from leased to owned facilities, and consolidated where appropriate.

CHANGES IN ACCOUNTING PRINCIPLES

The accounting principle of *consistency* means that a business should continue to use the same accounting principles and methods from one period to the next. However, this principle does not mean that a business can *never* make a change in its accounting methods. A change may be made if the need for the change can be justified and the effects of the change are *properly disclosed* in the financial statements.

THE "CUMULATIVE EFFECT" OF AN ACCOUNTING CHANGE
In reporting most changes in accounting principle, the *cumulative effect* of the change upon the income of *prior* years is shown in the income statement of the year in which the change is made. To compute this one-time "catch-up adjustment," we recompute the income of prior years *as if the new accounting method had always been in use.* The difference between this recomputed net income and the net income actually reported in those periods is the "cumulative effect" of the accounting change.

To illustrate, assume that Ross Corporation has been using the double-declining-balance method of depreciation but decides in the current year to change to the straight-line method. The company determines that if the straight-line method had always been in use, the total net income of prior years would have been $140,000 higher than was actually reported. This $140,000 is the *cumulative effect* of the change in accounting principle and is shown as a separate item in the current year's income statement (following discontinued operations and extraordinary items, if any). Depreciation expense in the current and future years' income statements is computed by the straight-line method, just as if this method had always been in use.

The importance of segregating the financial statement effects of accounting changes was dramatically illustrated by the 1992 financial statements of **General Motors Corporation.** In that year, the company began accruing the costs of postretirement benefits other than pensions over the working life of its employees. Prior to the adoption of this policy the company had been expensing the costs as they were paid. This change in accounting principles resulted in a charge for the cumulative effect of the accounting change in the 1992 income statement of over *$20 billion.*

The effects of this accounting change on GM's financial statements were enormous. The company reported a $21 billion net loss for the year—the largest corporate loss in history. GM's retained earnings, accumulated over more than *80 years*, were erased from the balance sheet and replaced by a *deficit* of more than $3 billion. But what were the effects on GM's cash position and its obligations to retirees? There weren't any. The only change was in the way GM *accounts* for these obligations.

CHANGES IN PRINCIPLE VERSUS CHANGES IN ESTIMATE A change in accounting principle refers to a change in the *method* used to compute financial statement amounts, not to a change in the underlying estimates. For example, a switch from straight-line to another method of computing depreciation is regarded as a change in accounting principle. However, a change in the estimated useful life used in computing depreciation expense is a *change in estimate*. This distinction is an important one. When we change an accounting *principle* (method), the cumulative effect of the change upon the income of prior years usually is reported as a one-time adjustment to income in the year of the change. Changes in *estimate*, however, affect only the current year and future years; no effort is made to recompute the income of prior years.

YOUR TURN

You as an Investor

One of the most important determinants of a company's stock price is expected future earnings. Assume that you are considering investing in Unison Corporation, and are evaluating the company's profitability in the current year. The net income of the corporation, which amounted to $2,000,000, includes the following items:

Loss on a discontinued segment of the business (net of income tax benefit)	$750,000
Extraordinary loss (net of income tax benefit)	300,000
Cumulative effect of change in accounting principle (increase in net income, net of related income taxes)	500,000

Adjust net income to develop a number that represents a good starting point for predicting the future net income of Unison Corporation. Explain the reason for each of the adjustments. Explain how this adjusted number may help you predict future earnings for the company.

*Our comments appear on page 610.

EARNINGS PER SHARE (EPS)

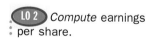

LO 2 *Compute* earnings per share.

Perhaps the most widely used of all accounting statistics is **earnings per share** of common stock. Everyone who buys or sells stock in a corporation needs to know the annual earnings per share. Stock market prices are quoted on a per-share basis. If you are considering investing in IBM stock at a price of, say, $120 per share, you need to know the earnings per share and the annual dividend per share in order to decide whether this price is reasonable. In other words, how much earning power and how much dividend income would you be getting for each share you buy?

The relationship between earnings per share and stock price is expressed by the **price-earnings ratio** (p/e ratio). This ratio is simply the current stock price divided by the earnings per share for the year (last four quarters). (A p/e ratio is *not* computed if the company has sustained a net *loss* for this period.) P/e ratios are of such interest to investors that they are published daily in the financial pages of major newspapers (an example appears in Chapter 11 on page 541).

Stock prices actually reflect investors' expectations of *future* earnings. The p/e ratio, however, is based upon the earnings over the *past* year. Thus, if investors expect earnings to *increase* substantially from current levels, the p/e ratio will be quite high—perhaps 20, 30, or even more. But if investors expect earnings to *decline* from current levels, the p/e ratio will be quite low, say, 8 or less. A mature company with very stable earnings usually sells between 10 and 12 times earnings. Thus, the p/e ratio reflects *investors' expectations* of the company's future prospects.[1]

Let us now look more closely at the measurement which *underlies* the p/e ratio—*earnings per share.*

COMPUTING EARNINGS PER SHARE To compute earnings per share, the common stockholders' share of the company's net income is divided by the average number of common shares outstanding. Notice that the concept of earnings per share applies only to *common stock;* preferred stockholders have no claim to earnings beyond the stipulated preferred stock dividends.

Computing earnings per share is easiest when the corporation has issued only common stock, and the number of outstanding shares has not changed during the year. In this case, earnings per share is equal to net income divided by the number of shares outstanding.

WHAT HAPPENS IF MORE SHARES ARE ISSUED? In many companies, however, the number of shares of stock outstanding changes one or more times during the year. If additional shares are sold during the year, or if shares of common stock are retired (repurchased from the shareholders), the computation of earnings per share is based upon the *weighted-average* number of shares outstanding.[2]

The weighted-average number of shares for the year is determined by multiplying the number of shares outstanding by the fraction of the year that number of shares outstanding remained unchanged. For example, assume that 100,000 shares of common stock were outstanding during the first nine months of 1998 and 140,000 shares during the last three months. Assume also that the increase in shares outstanding resulted from the sale of 40,000 shares for cash. The weighted-average number of shares outstanding during 1998 would be *110,000* determined as follows:

100,000 shares × $\frac{9}{12}$ of a year	75,000
140,000 shares × $\frac{3}{12}$ of a year	35,000
Weighted-average number of common shares outstanding	110,000

This procedure gives more meaningful earnings per share data than if the total number of shares outstanding at the end of the year were used in the calculations. By using the weighted-average number of shares, we recognize that the proceeds from the sale of the 40,000 shares were available to generate earnings only during the last three months of the year. Although the weighted-average number of shares outstanding must be used in earnings-per-share com-

---

[1]A word of caution—if current earnings are *very low,* the p/e ratio tends to be quite high *regardless* of whether future earnings are expected to rise or fall. In such situations, the p/e ratio is not a meaningful measurement.

[2]When the number of shares outstanding changes as a result of a stock split or a stock dividend (discussed later in this chapter), the computation of the weighted-average number of shares outstanding should be adjusted *retroactively* rather than weighted for the period the new shares were outstanding. Earnings per share data for prior years thus will be consistently stated in terms of the current capital structure.

putations, this figure does not appear in the stockholders' equity section of the balance sheet. A balance sheet prepared at year-end reports the *actual* number of shares outstanding at that date, regardless of when these shares were issued.

PREFERRED DIVIDENDS AND EARNINGS PER SHARE   When a company has preferred stock outstanding, the preferred stockholders participate in net income to the extent of the preferred stock dividends. To determine the earnings *applicable to the common stock,* we first deduct from net income the amount of current year preferred dividends. The annual dividend on *cumulative* preferred stock is *always* deducted, even if not declared by the board of directors for the current year. Noncumulative preferred dividends are deducted only if declared.

To illustrate, let us assume that Tanner Corporation has 200,000 shares of common stock and 10,000 shares of $6 cumulative preferred stock outstanding throughout the year. Net income for the year totals $560,000. Earnings per share of common stock would be computed as follows:

Net income	$560,000
Less: Dividends on preferred stock (10,000 shares × $6)	60,000
Earnings applicable to common stock	$500,000
Weighted-average number of common shares outstanding	200,000
Earnings per share of common stock ($500,000 ÷ 200,000 shares)	$2.50

Even when there are dividends in arrears, only the *current year's* cumulative preferred stock dividend is deducted in the earnings per share computation. Dividends in arrears from previous years have already been deducted in the prior years' earnings per share computations.

PRESENTATION OF EARNINGS PER SHARE IN THE INCOME STATEMENT   All publicly owned corporations are *required* to present earnings per share data in their income statements.[3] If an income statement includes subtotals for Income from Continuing Operations, or for Income before Extraordinary Items, per-share figures are shown for these amounts as well as for net income. These additional per-share amounts are computed by substituting the amount of the appropriate subtotal for the net income figure in the preceding calculation.

To illustrate all of the potential per-share computations, we will expand our Tanner Corporation example to include income from continuing operations and income before extraordinary items. We should point out, however, that all of these figures seldom appear in the same income statement. Very few companies have discontinued operations, an extraordinary item, and an accounting change to report in the same year. The condensed income statement shown below is intended to illustrate the proper format for presenting earnings per share figures and to provide a review of the calculations.

---

[3]The FASB has exempted closely held corporations (those not publicly owned) from the requirement of computing and reporting earnings per share. See *FASB Statement No. 23,* "Suspension of the Reporting of Earnings per Share and Segment Information by Nonpublic Enterprises (Norwalk, Conn.: 1978).

TANNER CORPORATION Condensed Income Statement For the Year Ended December 31, 1999		
Net sales		$9,000,000
Costs and expenses (including taxes on continuing operations)		8,310,000
Income from continuing operations		$ 690,000
Loss from discontinued operations (net of income tax benefits)		(90,000)
Income before extraordinary items and cumulative effect of accounting change		$ 600,000
Extraordinary loss (net of income tax benefit)	$(120,000)	
Cumulative effect of accounting change (net of related income taxes)	80,000	(40,000)
Net income		$ 560,000
Earnings per share of common stock:		
Earnings from continuing operations		$3.15[a]
Loss from discontinued operations		(.45)
Earnings before extraordinary items and cumulative effect of accounting change		$2.70[b]
Extraordinary loss		(.60)
Cumulative effect of accounting change		.40
Net earnings		$2.50[c]

[a]($690,000 − $60,000 preferred dividends) ÷ 200,000 shares
[b]($600,000 − $60,000) ÷ 200,000 shares
[c]($560,000 − $60,000) ÷ 200,000 shares

Earnings per share figures are required in the income statements of publicly owed companies

INTERPRETING THE DIFFERENT PER-SHARE AMOUNTS To informed users of financial statements, each of these figures has a different significance. Earnings per share from continuing operations represents the results of continuing and ordinary business activity. This figure is the most useful one for predicting future operating results. *Net earnings* per share, on the other hand, shows the overall operating results of the current year, including any discontinued operations or extraordinary items.

Unfortunately, the term *earnings per share* often is used without qualification in referring to various types of per-share data. When using per-share information, it is important to know exactly *which* per-share statistic is being presented. For example, the price-earnings ratios (market price divided by earnings per share) for common stocks listed on major stock exchanges are reported daily in *The Wall Street Journal* and many other newspapers. Which earnings per share figures are used in computing these ratios? If a company reports an extraordinary gain or loss, the price-earnings ratio is computed using the per-share *earnings before the extraordinary item*. Otherwise, the ratio is based upon *net earnings* per share.

BASIC AND DILUTED EARNINGS PER SHARE
Let us assume that a company has an outstanding issue of preferred stock that is convertible into shares of common stock at a rate of, say, two shares of common for each share of preferred. The conversion of this preferred stock would

LO 3 *Distinguish between basic and diluted earnings per share.*

increase the number of common shares outstanding and might *dilute* (reduce) earnings per share. Any common stockholder interested in the trend of earnings per share will want to know what effect the conversion of the preferred stock would have upon this statistic.

To inform investors of the potential dilution which might occur, two figures are presented for each earnings per share statistic. The first figure, called **basic earnings per share,** is based upon the weighted-average number of common shares *actually outstanding* during the year. Thus, this figure ignores the potential dilution represented by the convertible preferred stock. The second figure, called **diluted earnings per share,** shows the *impact that conversion* of the preferred stock would have upon basic earnings per share.

Basic earnings per share are computed in the same manner as illustrated in our preceding example of Tanner Corporation. Diluted earnings per share, on the other hand, are computed on the assumption that all the preferred stock *had been converted into common stock at the beginning of the current year.*[4] (The mechanics of computing diluted earnings per share are covered in the intermediate accounting course.)

It is important to remember that diluted earnings per share represent a *hypothetical case.* This statistic is computed even though the preferred stock actually was *not* converted during the year. The purpose of showing diluted earnings per share is to warn common stockholders what *could* have happened. When the difference between basic and diluted earnings per share becomes significant, investors should recognize the *risk* that future earnings per share may be reduced by conversions of other securities into additional shares of common stock.

When a company reports both basic and diluted earnings per share, the price-earnings ratio shown in newspapers is based upon the *primary figure.*

OTHER STOCKHOLDERS' EQUITY TRANSACTIONS

CASH DIVIDENDS

Investors buy stock in a corporation in the hope of getting their original investment back with a reasonable return on that investment. The return on a stock investment is a combination of two forms: (a) the increase in value of the stock (stock appreciation), and (b) cash dividends.

Many profitable corporations do not pay dividends. Generally, these corporations are in an early stage of development, and must conserve cash for the purchase of plant and equipment or for other needs of the company. These "growth companies" cannot obtain sufficient financing at reasonable interest rates to finance their operations, so they must rely on their earnings. It is usually only after a significant number of years of profitable operations that the board of directors will decide that paying a cash dividend is appropriate.

---

[4]If the preferred stock had been issued during the current year, we would assume that it was converted into common stock on the date it was issued.

The preceding discussion suggests three requirements for the payment of a cash dividend. These are:

1. *Retained earnings.* Since dividends represent a distribution of earnings to stockholders, the theoretical maximum for dividends is the total undistributed net income of the company, represented by the credit balance of the Retained Earnings account. As a practical matter, many corporations limit dividends to somewhere near 40% of annual net income, in the belief that a major portion of the net income must be retained in the business if the company is to grow and to keep pace with its competitors.

2. *An adequate cash position.* The fact that the company reports large earnings does not mean that it has a large amount of cash on hand. Cash generated from earnings may have been invested in new plant and equipment, or in paying off debts, or in acquiring a larger inventory. There is no necessary relationship between the balance in the Retained Earnings account and the balance in the Cash account. The traditional expression of "paying dividends out of retained earnings" is misleading. Cash dividends can be paid only "out of" cash.

3. *Dividend action by the board of directors.* Even though a company's net income is substantial and its cash position seemingly satisfactory, dividends are not paid automatically. A formal action by the board of directors is necessary to declare a dividend.

DIVIDEND DATES

Four significant dates are involved in the distribution of a dividend. These are:

1. *Date of declaration.* On the day on which the dividend is declared by the board of directors, a liability to make the payment comes into existence.

2. *Date of record.* The **date of record** always follows the date of declaration, usually by a period of two or three weeks, and is always stated in the dividend declaration. In order to be eligible to receive the dividend, a person must be listed in the corporation's records as the owner of the stock on this date.

3. *Ex-dividend date.* The **ex-dividend date** is significant for investors in companies whose stocks trade on stock exchanges. To permit the compilation of the list of stockholders as of the record date, it is customary for the stock to go *ex-dividend* three business days before the date of record. A stock is said to be selling ex-dividend on the day that it *loses* the right to receive the latest declared dividend. A person who buys the stock before the ex-dividend date is entitled to receive the dividend; conversely, a stockholder who sells shares before the ex-dividend date does not receive the dividend.

4. *Date of payment.* The declaration of a dividend always includes announcement of the date of payment as well as the date of record. Usually the date of payment comes two to four weeks after the date of record.

Journal entries are required only on the dates of declaration and of payment, as these are the only "transactions" affecting the corporation declaring the dividend. These entries were illustrated in the preceding chapter. For your convenience, similar entries are illustrated on the following page, this time indicating the official date of record.

Entries made on declaration date and . . .	Dec. 15	Dividends	100,000	
		Dividends Payable		100,000
		To record declaration of a cash dividend of $1 per share on the 100,000 shares of common stock outstanding. Payable Jan. 25 to stockholders of record on Jan. 10		
. . . on payment date	Jan. 25	Dividends Payable	100,000	
		Cash		100,000
		To record payment of $1 per share dividend declared Dec. 15 to stockholders of record on Jan. 10.		

Notice that no entries are made either on the date of record (January 10), or on the ex-dividend date. These dates are of importance only in determining *to whom* the dividend checks should be sent. From the stockholders' point of view, it is the *ex-dividend date* which determines who receives the dividend. The date of record is of significance primarily to the stock transfer agent and the stock registrar.

Just when is the ex-dividend date in our example? It falls three *business days* before the date of record. Weekends and holidays are not counted as "business days." Thus, if January 10 is a Friday, the ex-dividend date is *January 7*. But if January 10 falls on a Monday, the ex-dividend date would be *January 5*. In this case, investors would need to purchase their shares on or before *January 4* if they are to receive this dividend.

At the end of the accounting period, a closing entry is required to transfer the debit balance of the Dividends account into the Retained Earnings account. (Some companies follow the alternative practice of debiting Retained Earnings when the dividend is declared instead of using a Dividends account. Under either method, the balance of the Retained Earnings account ultimately is reduced by all dividends declared during the period.)

Most dividends are paid in cash, but occasionally a dividend declaration calls for payment in assets *other than* cash. A large distillery once paid a dividend consisting of a bottle of whiskey for each share of stock. (This must have posed quite a storage problem to an investor owning several thousand shares.) When a corporation goes out of existence (particularly a small corporation with only a few stockholders), it may choose to distribute noncash assets to its owners rather than first converting these assets into cash.

LIQUIDATING DIVIDENDS

A *liquidating dividend* occurs when a corporation pays a dividend that *exceeds the balance in the Retained Earnings account.* Thus, the dividend returns to stockholders all or part of their paid-in capital investment. Liquidating dividends usually are paid only when a corporation is going out of existence or is making a permanent reduction in the size of its operations. Normally dividends are paid as a result of profitable operations; stockholders may assume that a dividend represents a distribution of profits unless they are notified by the corporation that the dividend is a return of invested capital.

STOCK DIVIDENDS

Stock dividend is a term used to describe a distribution of *additional shares of stock* to a company's stockholders in proportion to their present holdings. In brief, the dividend is payable in *additional shares of stock* rather than in cash. Most stock dividends consist of additional shares of common stock distributed to holders of common stock, and our discussion will be limited to this type of stock dividend.

An important distinction must be drawn between a cash dividend and a stock dividend. In a *cash dividend,* assets are distributed by the corporation to the stockholders. Thus, a cash dividend reduces both assets and stockholders' eq-

LO 4 *Account for stock dividends and stock splits, and explain the probable effect of these transactions upon market price.*

uity. In a *stock dividend,* however, *no assets are distributed.* Thus, a stock dividend causes *no change* in assets or in total stockholders' equity. Each stockholder receives additional shares, but his or her percentage ownership in the corporation is *no larger than before.*

To illustrate this point, assume that a corporation with 2,000 shares of stock is owned equally by James Davis and Susan Miller, each owning 1,000 shares of stock. The corporation declares a stock dividend of 10% and distributes 200 additional shares (10% of 2,000 shares), with 100 shares going to each of the two stockholders. Davis and Miller now hold 1,100 shares apiece, but each *still owns one-half of the business.* Furthermore, the corporation has not changed in size; its assets and liabilities and its total stockholders' equity are exactly the same as before the dividend.

Now let us consider the logical effect of this stock dividend upon the *market price* of the company's stock. Assume that before the stock dividend, the outstanding 2,000 shares in our example had a market price of $110 per share. This price indicates a total market value for the corporation of $220,000 (2,000 shares × $110 per share). As the stock dividend does not change total assets or total stockholders' equity, the total market value of the corporation *should remain $220,000* after the stock dividend. As 2,200 shares are now outstanding, the market price of each share *should fall* to $100 ($220,000 ÷ 2,200 shares). In short, the market value of the stock *should fall in proportion* to the number of new shares issued. Whether the market price per share *will* fall in proportion to a small increase in number of outstanding shares is another matter. (In fact, market price often *rises* after the declaration of a stock dividend. Puzzling, but true.)

ENTRIES TO RECORD A STOCK DIVIDEND In accounting for *small* stock dividends (say, less than 20%), the *market value* of the new shares is transferred from the Retained Earnings accounts to the paid-in capital accounts. This process sometimes is called *capitalizing* retained earnings. The overall effect is the same as if the dividend had been paid in cash, and the stockholders had immediately reinvested the cash in the business in exchange for additional shares of stock. Of course, no cash actually changes hands—the new shares of stock are sent directly to the stockholders.

To illustrate, assume that on June 1, Aspen Corporation has outstanding 100,000 shares of $5 par value common stock with a market value of $25 per share. On this date, the company declares a 10% stock dividend, distributable on July 15 to stockholders of record on June 20. The entry at June 1 to record the *declaration* of this dividend is:

Retained Earnings	250,000		Stock dividend declared;
Stock Dividend to Be Distributed		50,000	note use of market price
Additional Paid-in Capital: Stock Dividends		200,000	of stock

Declared a 10% stock dividend consisting of 10,000 shares (100,000 shares × 10%) of $5 par value common stock, market price $25 per share. Distributable July 15 to stockholders of record on June 20.

The Stock Dividend to Be Distributed account is *not a liability,* because there is no obligation to distribute cash or any other asset. If a balance sheet is prepared between the date of declaration of a stock dividend and the date of distribution of the shares, this account, as well as Additional Paid-in Capital: Stock Dividends, should be presented in the stockholders' equity section of the balance sheet.

Notice that the Retained Earnings account was debited for the *market value* of the shares to be issued (10,000 shares × $25 per share = $250,000). Notice also that *no change* occurs in the total amount of stockholders' equity. The amount removed from the Retained Earnings account was simply transferred into two other stockholders' equity accounts.

On July 15, the entry to record the *distribution* of the dividend shares is:

Stock dividend distributed

Stock Dividend to Be Distributed	50,000	
Common Stock		50,000
Distributed 10,000 share stock dividend declared June 1.		

Large stock dividends (for example, those in excess of 20 to 25%) should be recorded by transferring *only the par or stated value* of the dividend shares from the Retained Earnings account to the Common Stock account. Large stock dividends generally have the effect of proportionately reducing the market price of the stock. For example, a 100% stock dividend would reduce the market price by about 50%, because twice as many shares would be outstanding. A 100% stock dividend is very similar to the 2-for-1 *stock split* discussed in the following section of this chapter.

REASONS FOR STOCK DIVIDENDS Although stock dividends cause *no change* in total assets, liabilities, or stockholders' equity, they are popular both with management and with stockholders. Management likes stock dividends because they do not cost anything (other than administrative costs)—the corporation does not distribute any assets.

Stockholders like stock dividends because they receive more shares, often the stock price does *not* fall proportionately, and the dividend is not subject to income taxes (until the shares received are sold). Also, *large* stock dividends tend to keep the stock price down in a "trading range" that appeals to most investors.

CASE IN POINT

An investor who purchased 100 shares of **Home Depot, Inc.,** early in 1985 would have paid about $1,700. By 1995, ten years later, that stock was worth over *$44,000.*

Does this mean that each share increased in value from $17 to more than $440? No—in fact, this probably couldn't happen. Investors like to buy stock in "lots" of 100 shares. At $440 per share, who could afford 100 shares? Certainly not the average "small investor."

Home Depot's board of directors *wanted* to attract small investors. These investors help create more demand for the company's stock—and in many cases, they also become loyal customers.

So as the price of Home Depot's stock rose, the board declared numerous large stock dividends. By 1994, an investor who had purchased 100 shares in 1985 owned over *1,000* shares. But, most importantly, each of these shares was trading in the "low forties," a price quite affordable to the average investor.

As Home Depot's board knows well, investors don't buy stocks at prices they can't afford.

STOCK SPLITS

A corporation may *split* its stock by increasing the number of outstanding shares of common stock and reducing the par or stated value per share in proportion. As with a large stock dividend, the purpose of a **stock split** is to reduce substantially the market price of the common stock, with the intent of making the stock more affordable to investors.

For example, assume that Pelican Corporation has outstanding 1 million shares of $10 par value stock. The market price is $90 per share. The corporation now reduces the par value from $10 to $5 per share and increases the number of shares from 1 million to 2 million. This action would be called a 2-for-1 stock split. A stockholder who owned 100 shares of the stock before the split would own 200 shares after the split. Since the number of outstanding shares has been doubled without any change in total assets or total stockholders' equity, the market price of the stock should drop from $90 to approximately $45 a share.

A stock split does not change the balance of any ledger account; consequently, the transaction may be recorded merely by *a memorandum entry* in the general journal and in the Common Stock account. For Pelican Corporation, this memorandum entry might read:

Sept. 30	Memorandum: Issued additional 1 million shares of common stock in a 2-for-1 stock split. Par value reduced from $10 per share to $5 per share.

Memorandum entry to record a stock split

The description of common stock also is changed in the balance sheet to reflect the lower par value and the greater number of shares outstanding.

Stock may be split in any desired ratio. Among the more common ratios are 2 for 1, 3 for 2, and 3 for 1. The determining factor is the number of shares needed to bring the price of the stock into the desired trading range. For example, assume that a $5 par value stock is selling at a price of $150 per share and that management wants to reduce the price to approximately $30 per share. This objective may be accomplished with a *5-for-1* stock split ($150 ÷ 5 = $30). Par value *after* the 5-for-1 stock split is $1 per share ($5 par value × ⅕).

DISTINCTION BETWEEN STOCK SPLITS AND LARGE STOCK DIVIDENDS What is the difference between a 2-for-1 stock split and a 100% stock dividend? There is very little difference; both will double the number of outstanding shares without changing total stockholders' equity, and both should serve to cut the market price of the stock approximately in half. The stock dividend, however, will cause a transfer from the Retained Earnings account to the Common Stock account equal to the par or stated value of the dividend shares. A 2-for-1 stock split will reduce the par value per share by one-half, but it will not change the dollar balance of any account.

After an increase in the number of shares as a result of a stock split or stock dividend, earnings per share are computed in terms of the increased number of shares. In presenting 5- or 10-year summaries, the earnings per share for earlier years are *retroactively restated* to reflect the increased number of shares currently outstanding and thus make the year to year trend of earnings per share a more valid comparison.

YOUR TURN

You as a Board Member

Assume that you are a member of the board of directors of Petstuff, Inc. a chain of pet supply stores. The corporation has been in existence for about eight years, and has grown significantly in terms of number of stores, sales, and net income.

At a recent stockholders meeting, several stockholders complained that the board of directors had not declared any cash dividends. They noted that the corporation had a large amount of retained earnings, and the board was just keeping the earnings in the business. Respond to the concerns of these stockholders.

*Our comments appear on page 610.

STATEMENT OF RETAINED EARNINGS

LO 5 *Describe and prepare a statement of retained earnings.*

The term *retained earnings* refers to the portion of stockholders' equity derived from profitable operations. Retained earnings is increased by earning net income and is reduced by incurring net losses and by the declaration of dividends.

In addition to a balance sheet, an income statement, and a statement of cash flows, a complete set of financial statements includes a **statement of retained earnings,** as illustrated below:

SHORE LINE CORPORATION Statement of Retained Earnings For the Year Ended December 31, 1999		
Retained earnings, December 31, 1998		$600,000
Net income for 1999		180,000
Subtotal		$780,000
Less: Cash dividends:		
Preferred stock ($5 per share)	$ 17,500	
Common stock ($2 per share)	55,300	
10% stock dividend	140,000	212,800
Retained earnings, December 31, 1999		$567,200

PRIOR PERIOD ADJUSTMENTS

LO 6 *Define* prior period adjustments *and explain how they are presented in financial statements.*

On occasion, a company may discover that a *material error* was made in the measurement of net income in a prior year. Since net income is closed into the Retained Earnings account, an error in reported net income will cause an error in the amount of retained earnings shown in all subsequent balance sheets. When such errors come to light, they should be corrected. The correction, called a **prior period adjustment,** is shown in the *statement of retained earnings* as an adjustment to the balance of retained earnings at the beginning of the current year. The amount of the adjustment is shown net of any related income tax effects.

To illustrate, assume that late in 1999 Shore Line Corporation discovers that it failed to record depreciation on certain assets in 1998. After considering the income tax effects of this error, the company finds that the net income reported in 1998 was overstated by $35,000. Thus, the current balance of the Retained Earnings account ($600,000 at December 31, 1998) also is *overstated by $35,000*. The statement of retained earnings in *1999* will include a *correction* of the retained earnings at the beginning of the year.

Notice the adjustment to beginning retained earnings

SHORE LINE CORPORATION Statement of Retained Earnings For the Year Ended December 31, 1999		
Retained earnings, December 31, 1998		
As originally reported		$600,000
Less: Prior period adjustment for error in recording 1998 depreciation expense (net of $15,000 income taxes)		35,000
As restated		$565,000
Net income for 1999		180,000
Subtotal		$745,000
Less: Cash dividends:		
Preferred stock ($5 per share)	$ 17,500	
Common stock ($2 per share)	55,300	
10% stock dividend	140,000	212,800
Retained earnings, December 31, 1999		$532,200

Prior period adjustments rarely appear in the financial statements of large, publicly owned corporations. The financial statements of these corporations are audited annually by certified public accountants and are not likely to contain material errors which subsequently will require correction by prior period adjustments. Such adjustments are much more likely to appear in the financial statements of closely held corporations that are not audited on an annual basis.

RESTRICTIONS OF RETAINED EARNINGS   Some portion of retained earnings may be restricted because of various contractual agreements. A "restriction" of retained earnings prevents a company from declaring a dividend that would cause retained earnings to fall below a designated level. Most companies disclose restrictions of retained earnings in notes accompanying the financial statements. For example, a company with retained earnings of $10 million might include the following note in its financial statements:

Note 7: Restriction of retained earnings
As of December 31, 1998, certain long-term debt agreements prohibited the declaration of cash dividends that would reduce the amount of retained earnings below $5,200,000. Retained earnings in excess of this restriction total $4,800,000.

Footnote disclosure of restrictions placed on retained earnings

TREASURY STOCK

Corporations frequently reacquire shares of their own capital stock by purchase in the open market. Paying out cash to reacquire shares will reduce the assets of the corporation and reduce the stockholders' equity by the same amount. One reason for such purchases is to have stock available to reissue to officers and employees under stock option or bonus plans. Other reasons may include a desire to increase the reported earnings per share or to support the current market price of the stock.

Treasury stock may be defined as shares of a corporation's own capital stock that have been issued and later *reacquired by the issuing company,* but that have not been canceled or permanently retired. Treasury shares may be held indefinitely or may be issued again at any time. Shares of capital stock held in the treasury are not entitled to receive dividends, to vote, or to share in assets upon dissolution of the company. In the computation of earnings per share, shares held in the treasury are not regarded as outstanding shares.

RECORDING PURCHASES OF TREASURY STOCK

Purchases of treasury stock should be recorded by debiting the Treasury Stock account with the cost of the stock.[5] For example, if Torrey Corporation reacquires 1,500 shares of its own $5 par stock at a price of $100 per share, the entry is as follows:

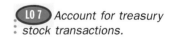 *Account for treasury stock transactions.*

Treasury Stock	150,000	
Cash		150,000
Purchased 1,500 shares of $5 par treasury stock at $100 per share.		

Note that the Treasury Stock account is debited for the *cost* of the shares purchased, not their par value.

---

[5]State laws may prescribe different methods of accounting for treasury stock transactions. In this text, we illustrate only the widely used "cost method."

TREASURY STOCK IS NOT AN ASSET   When treasury stock is purchased, the corporation is eliminating part of its stockholders' equity by a payment to one or more stockholders. The purchase of treasury stock should be regarded as a *reduction of stockholders' equity,* not as the acquisition of an asset. For this reason, the Treasury Stock account should appear in the balance sheet *as a deduction in the stockholders' equity section.*[6] The presentation of treasury stock in a corporate balance sheet is illustrated on page 587.

REISSUANCE OF TREASURY STOCK

When treasury shares are reissued, the Treasury Stock account is credited for the cost of the shares reissued and Additional Paid-in Capital from Treasury Stock Transactions is debited or credited for any *difference* between cost and the reissue price. To illustrate, assume that 1,000 of the treasury shares acquired by Torrey Corporation at a cost of $100 per share are now reissued at a price of $115 per share. The entry to record the reissuance of these shares at a price above cost would be:

Treasury stock reissued at a price above cost

Cash	115,000	
Treasury Stock...		100,000
Additional Paid-in Capital: Treasury Stock Transactions.................		15,000
Sold 1,000 shares of treasury stock, which cost $100,000, at a price of $115 per share.		

If treasury stock is reissued at a price below cost, additional paid-in capital from previous treasury stock transactions is reduced (debited) by the excess of cost over the reissue price. To illustrate, assume that Torrey Corporation reissues its remaining 500 shares of treasury stock (cost $100 per share) at a price of $90 per share. The entry would be:

Reissued at a price of below cost

Cash	45,000	
Additional Paid-in Capital: Treasury Stock Transactions...........................	5,000	
Treasury Stock		50,000
Sold 500 shares of treasury stock, which cost $50,000, at a price of $90 each.		

If there is no additional paid-in capital from previous treasury stock transactions, the excess of the cost of the treasury shares over the reissue price may be recorded as a debit to Retained Earnings.

NO PROFIT OR LOSS ON TREASURY STOCK TRANSACTIONS   Notice that *no gain or loss is recognized on treasury stock transactions,* even when the shares are reissued at a price above or below cost. A corporation earns profits by selling goods and services to outsiders, not by issuing or reissuing shares of its own capital stock. When treasury shares are reissued at a price above cost, the corporation receives from the new stockholder an amount of paid-in capital that is larger than the reduction in stockholders' equity that occurs when the corporation acquired the treasury shares. Conversely, if treasury shares are reissued at a price below cost, the corporation ends up with less paid-in capital as a result of the purchase and reissuance of the shares. Thus, any changes in stock-

---

[6]Despite a lack of theoretical support, a few corporations do classify treasury stock as an asset, on the grounds that the shares could be sold for cash just as readily as shares owned in another corporation. The same argument could be made for treating unissued shares as assets. Treasury shares are basically the same as unissued shares, and an unissued share of stock is definitely not an asset.

holders' equity resulting from treasury stock transactions are regarded as changes in *paid-in capital* and are *not* included in the measurement of net income.

RESTRICTION OF RETAINED EARNINGS FOR TREASURY STOCK OWNED
Purchases of treasury stock, like cash dividends, are distributions of assets to the stockholders in the corporation. Many states have a legal requirement that distributions to stockholders (including purchases of treasury stock) cannot exceed the balance in the Retained Earnings account. Therefore, retained earnings usually are restricted by an amount equal to the *cost* of any shares held in the treasury.

STOCK "BUYBACK" PROGRAMS
In past years, most treasury stock transactions involved relatively small dollar amounts. Hence, the topic was not of much importance to investors or other users of financial statements. Late in 1987, however, many corporations initiated large "buyback" programs, in which they repurchased huge amounts of their own common stock.[7] As a result of these programs, treasury stock has become a very material item in the balance sheets of many corporations.

CASE IN POINT

Shown below is the cost of the treasury stock listed in the balance sheets of several publicly owned corporations at the end of a recent year.

Company	At Cost (in thousands)	Treasury Stock As a % of Other Elements of Stockholders' Equity*
Coca-Cola	$ 5,201,194	57
Exxon	16,887,000	33
Lotus	287,655	41
King World	162,054	32

*To place these holdings in perspective, we have shown the cost of the treasury stock as a percentage of total stockholders' equity before *deducting the cost of the repurchased shares.*

These large buyback programs serve several purposes. First, by creating demand for the company's stock in the marketplace, these programs tend to increase the market value of the shares. Also, reducing the number of shares outstanding usually increases earnings per share. When stock prices are low, some companies find that they can increase earnings per share by a greater amount through repurchasing shares than through expanding business operations.

---

[7]On October 19, 1987, a date known as *Black Monday,* stocks around the world suffered the largest one-day decline in history. Within hours of the market's close on Black Monday, many large corporations announced their intention to enter the market and spend hundreds of millions of dollars repurchasing their own shares. In the opinion of the authors, these announcements helped stabilize the investment markets and avoid a possible stock market "collapse."

EQUITY TRANSACTIONS: THE CASH EFFECTS

L0 8 *Explain the cash effects of equity transactions.*

Transactions between the corporation and its owners are classified in the statement of cash flows as *financing activities*. Accordingly, cash dividends are presented as a cash outflow from financing activities. Property dividends have no effect on cash flows and are shown in a special schedule accompanying the statement of cash flows.

STOCK DIVIDENDS AND STOCK SPLITS Stock dividends and stock splits have no effect on cash flow. In fact, these transactions have very little effect on the corporation's financial statements. A stock dividend simply results in a reclassification of amounts from the Retained Earnings account to the Capital Stock and Additional Paid-In Capital accounts. A memorandum entry changing the number of shares of stock outstanding and its par value is the only entry necessary to record a stock split.

TREASURY STOCK TRANSACTIONS Since treasury stock transactions do not give rise to gains or losses, they have no effect on the corporation's net income. Any difference between the purchase price of the treasury stock and the reissue price is recorded as an increase or decrease in the Additional Paid-In Capital account.

However, purchases and sales of treasury stock *do* affect cash flows. When treasury stock is purchased by a corporation, cash flow from financing activities is decreased by the amount paid for the stock. Cash flow from financing activities is increased by the proceeds from the reissuance of the stock.

STATEMENT OF STOCKHOLDERS' EQUITY

L0 9 *Describe and prepare a statement of stockholders' equity.*

Many corporations expand their statement of retained earnings to show the changes during the year in *all* of the stockholders' equity accounts. This expanded statement, called a **statement of stockholders' equity,** is illustrated below for Shore Line Corporation.

	5% Convertible Preferred Stock ($100 par value)	Common Stock ($10 par value)	Additional Paid-in Capital	Retained Earnings	Treasury Stock	Total Stockholders' Equity
SHORE LINE CORPORATION — Statement of Stockholders' Equity — For the Year Ended December 31, 1998						
Balances, Dec. 31, 1997	$400,000	$200,000	$300,000	$600,000	$ –0–	$1,500,000
Prior period adjustment (net of $15,000 taxes)				(35,000)		(35,000)
Issued 5,000 common shares @ $52		50,000	210,000			260,000
Conversion of 1,000 preferred into 3,000 common shares	(100,000)	30,000	70,000			
Distributed 10% stock dividend (2,800 shares at $50; market price)		28,000	112,000	(140,000)		
Purchased 1,000 shares of common stock for the treasury at $47 a share					(47,000)	(47,000)
Net income				180,000		180,000
Cash dividends:						
Preferred ($5 a share)				(17,500)		(17,500)
Common ($2 a share)				(55,300)		(55,300)
Balances, Dec. 31, 1998	$300,000	$308,000	$692,000	$532,200	$(47,000)	$1,785,200

The top line of this statement shows the beginning balance in each stockholders' equity account. All of the transactions affecting these accounts during the year then are listed in summary form, along with the related changes in the balances of specific stockholders' equity accounts. The bottom line of the statement shows the ending balance in each stockholders' equity account and should agree with the amounts shown in the year-end balance sheet.

A statement of stockholders' equity is not a required financial statement. However, it is widely used as a substitute for the statement of retained earnings because it presents a more complete description of the transactions affecting stockholders' equity. Notice that the Retained Earnings column of this statement contains the same items as those shown in the statement of retained earnings illustrated on page 582.

ILLUSTRATION OF A STOCKHOLDERS' EQUITY SECTION

The stockholders' equity section of a balance sheet illustrated below includes some of the items discussed in this chapter. For illustrative purposes, we also show the computation of book value per share. (This computation is not shown in an actual balance sheet.) You should be able to explain the nature and origin of each account and disclosure printed in red.

The published financial statements of leading corporations indicate that there is no one standard arrangement for the various items making up the stockholders' equity section. Variations occur in the selection of titles, in the sequence of items, and in the extent of detailed classification. Many companies, in an effort to avoid excessive detail in the balance sheet, will combine several related ledger accounts into a single balance sheet item.

Stockholders' Equity		
Capital stock:		
8% Preferred stock, $100 par value, call price $110 per share, authorized and issued 2,000 shares		$200,000
Common stock, $5 par value, authorized 100,000 shares, issued 33,000 shares (of which 3,000 are held in the treasury)		165,000
Additional paid-in capital:		
From issuance of common stock	$250,000	
From stock dividends	50,000	
From treasury stock transactions	10,000	310,000
Total paid-in capital		$675,000
Retained earnings (of which $87,000, an amount equal to the cost of treasury stock owned, is not available for dividends)		232,000
Subtotal		$907,000
Less: Treasury stock (3,000 shares of common, at cost)		87,000
Total stockholders' equity		$820,000

Book value per share: $820,000 − (2,000 preferred shares × $110) = $600,000 equity of common stockholders; $600,000 ÷ 30,000 outstanding common shares = $20 per share.

NET CONNECTIONS

Stock trading is an interesting and challenging activity. A number of Internet sites that provide information about buying and selling stock are available. As a starting point, you might want to visit the New York Stock Exchange at:

www.nyse.com

While you are there visit the trading floor.

Next, try the Internet site of the American Association of Individual Investors at:

www.aaii.org

This site contains a glossary of investment terms. You might want to look at that organization's definition of the price/earnings ratio.

Finally, Silicon Investors has a very interesting site that provides a large amount of information about all types of high-tech stocks. It can be found at:

www.techstocks.com

---

*SUPPLEMENTAL TOPIC

EMPLOYEE STOCK PLANS

Many corporations issue stock through employee stock plans. The simplest is a *stock purchase plan,* which allows employees to purchase a limited number of shares at a small discount from the current market price. The purpose of these plans is to encourage employees to invest in the company—and to accumulate financial resources.

Companies account for these transactions in the same manner as if the shares were sold to outsiders.

Such plans are called *noncompensatory* stock purchase plans, a term derived from income tax regulations. A key element of these plans is that employees can only buy the stock *when it is offered.* They *do not* have an option to buy it at the stated price at some later date.

STOCK OPTION PLANS

Stock option plans are quite different. These plans are available only to *management personnel* and often represent a major part of the manager's total "compensation package." Hence, they are termed *compensatory* stock option plans.

Under a stock option plan, managers are given an *option* to purchase many shares of the company's stock at a specified *option price.* The option price generally is the market price on the date the option is granted to the manager. This option normally extends over a period of several years. Thus, if the stock price later increases, the manager will be able to purchase the shares at a below-market value.

To illustrate, assume Printex Corp. makes you an offer to become the company's chief financial officer (CFO). The company offers you a salary of $100,000 per year, with options to purchase up to 100,000 shares of the company's stock at today's market price of $10 per share. To be eligible to *exercise* these options (buy the shares), you must stay with Printex for three years. After that, you may purchase any number of these shares at $10 each at any time during the next three years.

If Printex' stock price soars to $50 per share, these options allow you to purchase *$5,000,000* worth of stock ($50 × 100,000 shares) for only *$1,000,000* ($10 × 100,000 shares). But now assume that during the three years you are el-

LO 10 *Describe* stock options *as a form of compensation to managers.*

igible to exercise your options, the stock *never trades for more than $10 per share*. In this case, you will not exercise your options; they will expire and become worthless. As you can see, these options provide you with a strong "vested interest" in seeing the price of Printex' stock increase.

Let us look at stock options from several different perspectives.

THE COMPANY'S PERSPECTIVE Stock options are an attractive form of compensation from the company's point of view for several reasons. They encourage managers to work toward the goal of increasing the company's stock price, which benefits all stockholders. This form of compensation requires no cash outlays by the company. Also, it encourages managers to *stay with the company*— at least until they become eligible to exercise their options.

THE MANAGER'S PERSPECTIVE Managers like stock options. They offer at least the *potential* of larger financial rewards than the company would pay as a salary. Also, managers pay *no income taxes* on options granted to them, or upon purchases of shares at the option price. The income taxes on this form of compensation are deferred until the manager *sells* the shares.

THE STOCKHOLDERS' PERSPECTIVE Many stockholders, however, *dislike* stock option plans. They argue that issuing substantial numbers of shares at a below-market price *dilutes* the value of the outstanding shares and future earnings per share. Critics view stock options as managers "giving away" equity in the company—*to themselves.*

ACCOUNTING FOR STOCK OPTIONS

At the date of issuance, the value of stock options lies only in the prospect of *future increases* in the stock price. Thus, it is difficult to estimate the value (if any) of these options. However, it is reasonable to assume that options *do have some value*. This is evidenced by the tendency of the stock prices of most successful companies to increase over the long term—and also by the popularity of stock options with managers.

The FASB recommends that companies *estimate* the value of stock options when they are issued and record the transaction using this estimated amount. Under this *fair value method*, the company debits an asset account called Deferred Compensation, and credits an additional paid-in capital account. The balance in the Deferred Compensation account then is *amortized to salaries expense* over the period the executive must wait to become eligible to exercise the options.

However, the FASB does not *require* companies to use this fair value method. It also allows an alternative method, under which the granting of stock options is *not recorded at all*. The rationale behind this approach is that no assets have changed hands, no liabilities have been incurred, and no new shares have yet been issued.

When this alternative approach is used, terms of the options must be *disclosed* in a note to the financial statements. (This note must include disclosure of what net income *would have been* had the fair value method been used.)

Virtually all publicly owned companies elect to use the disclosure approach rather than the fair value method, because recording and amortizing deferred compensation expense might substantially reduce the company's reported earnings. And this, in turn, might reduce the stock price—which runs counter to the reason for issuing stock options in the first place.

SUMMARY OF LEARNING OBJECTIVES

① Describe how *discontinued operations*, *extraordinary items*, and *accounting changes* are presented in the income statement.

Each of these "unusual" items is shown in a separate section of the income statement, after determination of the income or loss from ordinary and continuing operations. Each special item is shown net of any related income tax effects.

② Compute *earnings per share*.

Net earnings per share is computed by dividing the income applicable to the common stock by the weighted average number of common shares outstanding. If the income statement includes subtotals for Income from Continuing Operations, or for Income before Extraordinary Items, per-share figures are shown for these amounts, as well as for net income.

③ Distinguish between basic and diluted earnings per share.

Diluted earnings per share must be computed only for companies that have outstanding securities convertible into shares of common stock. In such situations, the computation of basic earnings per share is based upon the number of common shares actually outstanding during the year. The computation of diluted earnings, however, is based upon the potential number of common shares outstanding if the various securities were converted into common shares. The purpose of showing diluted earnings is to warn investors of the extent to which conversions of securities could dilute basic earnings per share.

④ Account for *stock dividends* and *stock splits*, and explain the probable effect of these transactions upon market price.

Small stock dividends are recorded by transferring the market value of the additional shares to be issued from retained earnings to the appropriate paid-in capital accounts. (Large stock dividends—over 20 or 25%—are recorded at par value, rather than market value.) A stock split, on the other hand, is recorded only by a memorandum entry indicating that the number of outstanding shares has been increased and that the par value per share has been reduced proportionately. Both stock dividends and stock splits increase the number of shares outstanding, but neither transaction changes total stockholders' equity. Therefore, both stock dividends and stock splits should reduce the market price per share in proportion to the number of additional shares issued.

⑤ Describe and prepare a statement of retained earnings.

A statement of retained earnings shows the changes in the balance of the Retained Earnings account during the period. In its simplest form, this financial statement shows the beginning balance of retained earnings, adds the net income for the period, subtracts any dividends declared, and thus computes the ending balance of retained earnings. Any **prior period adjustments** also are shown in this financial statement.

⑥ Define *prior period adjustments* and explain how they are presented in financial statements.

A prior period adjustment is an entry to correct any error in the amount of net income reported in a *prior* year. As the income of the prior year has already been closed into retained earnings, the error is corrected by debiting or crediting the Retained Earnings account. Prior period adjustments appear in the statement of retained earnings as adjustments to beginning retained earnings. They are *not* reported in the income statement for the current period.

⑦ Account for treasury stock transactions.

Purchases of treasury stock are recorded by debiting a contra-equity account entitled Treasury Stock. No profit or loss is recorded when the treasury shares are reissued at a price above or below cost. Rather, any difference between the reissuance price and the cost of the shares is debited or credited to a paid-in capital account.

⑧ Explain the cash effects of equity transactions.

While stockholders' equity transactions may affect cash flow, they have no effect upon the net income of the corporation. Equity transactions that affect cash flow from financing activities include cash dividends and treasury stock transactions. Stock dividends and stock splits have no effect on cash flow.

⑨ Describe and prepare a statement of stockholders' equity.

This expanded version of the statement of retained earnings explains the changes during the year in each stockholders' equity account. It is not a required financial statement, but is often prepared instead of a statement of retained earnings. The statement lists the beginning balance in each stockholders' equity account, explains the nature and the amount of each change, and thus computes the ending balance in each equity account.

⑩ Describe *stock options* as a form of compensation to managers.

A stock option is the right to purchase stock at a stated price over an extended period of time. Thus, offering stock options as a form of compensation motivates managers to take those actions most likely to increase stock price.

This chapter completes our discussion of capital stock and stockholders' equity. In our remaining chapters, we will continue our use of the corporate entity as the basis for discussions and illustrations.

In the next chapter, we turn our attention to the statement of cash flows. We introduced this statement in Chapter 6 and since have explained the "cash effects" of many transactions. Now we will see how a cash flow statement is prepared from accounting records maintained on the accrual basis.

KEY TERMS INTRODUCED OR EMPHASIZED IN CHAPTER 12

Basic earnings per share (p. 576) Net income applicable to the common stock divided by weighted-average number of common shares outstanding during the year.

Date of record (p. 577) The date on which a person must be listed as a shareholder in order to be eligible to receive a dividend. Follows the date of declaration of a dividend by two or three weeks.

Diluted earnings per share (p. 576) Earnings per share computed under the assumption that all convertible securities had been converted into additional common shares at the beginning of the current year. The purpose of this hypothetical computation is to warn common stockholders of the risk that future earnings per share might be diluted by the conversion of other securities into common stock.

Discontinued operations (p. 568) The net operating results (revenue and expenses) of a segment of a company which has been or is being sold, as well as the gain or loss on disposal.

Earnings per share (p. 572) Net income applicable to the common stock divided by the weighted-average number of common shares outstanding during the year.

Ex-dividend date (p. 577) A date three days prior to the date of record specified in a dividend declaration. A person buying a stock prior to the ex-dividend date also acquires the right to receive the dividend. The three-day interval permits the compilation of a list of stockholders as of the date of record.

Extraordinary items (p. 569) Transactions and events that are material in dollar amount, unusual in nature, and occur infrequently—for example, a large earthquake loss. Such items are shown separately in the income statement after the determination of Income before Extraordinary Items.

Price-earnings (p/e) ratio (p. 572) Market price of a share of common stock divided by annual earnings per share.

Prior period adjustment (p. 582) A correction of a material error in the earnings reported in the financial statements of a prior year. Prior period adjustments are recorded directly in the Retained Earnings account and are not included in the income statement of the current period.

Restructuring charges (p. 570) Costs related to reorganizing and downsizing the company to make the company more efficient. These costs are presented in the income statement as a single line item in determining operating income.

Segment of a business (p. 568) Those elements of a business that represent a separate and distinct line of business activity or that service a distinct category of customers.

Statement of retained earnings (p. 582) A basic financial statement explaining the change during the year in the amount of retained earnings. May be expanded into a statement of stockholders' equity.

Statement of stockholders' equity (p. 586) An expanded version of a statement of retained earnings. Summarizes the changes during the year in all stockholders' equity accounts. Not a required financial statement, but widely used as a substitute for the statement of retained earnings.

Stock dividend (p. 578) A distribution of additional shares to common stockholders in proportion to their holdings.

Stock options (p. 588) The right to purchase stock at a stated price over an extended period of time.

Stock split (p. 580) An increase in the number of shares outstanding with a corresponding decrease in par value per share. The additional shares are distributed proportionately to all common shareholders. The purpose is to reduce market price per share and encourage wider public ownership of the company's stock. A 2-for-1 stock split will give each stockholder twice as many shares as previously owned.

Treasury stock (p. 583) Shares of a corporation's stock which have been issued and then reacquired, but not canceled.

DEMONSTRATION PROBLEM

The stockholders' equity of Sutton Corporation at December 31, 1998, is shown below:

Stockholders' equity:	
Common stock, $10 par, 100,000 shares authorized, 40,000 shares issued	$ 400,000
Additional paid-in capital: common stock	200,000
Total paid-in capital	$ 600,000
Retained earnings..	1,500,000
Total stockholders' equity	$2,100,000

Transactions affecting stockholders' equity during 1998 are as follows:

Mar. 31 A 5-for-4 stock split proposed by the board of directors was approved by vote of the stockholders. The 10,000 new shares were distributed to stockholders.

Apr. 1 The company purchased 2,000 shares of its common stock on the open market at $37 per share.

July 1 The company reissued 1,000 shares of treasury stock at $45 per share.

July 1 Issued for cash 20,000 shares of previously unissued $8 par value common stock at a price of $45 per share.

Dec. 1 A cash dividend of $1 per share was declared, payable on December 30, to stockholders of record at December 14.

Dec. 22 A 10% stock dividend was declared; the dividend shares are to be distributed on January 15 of the following year. The market price of the stock on December 22 was $48 per share.

The net income for the year ended December 31, 1998, amounted to $177,000, after an extraordinary loss of $35,400 (net of related income tax benefits).

INSTRUCTIONS

a. Prepare journal entries (in general journal form) to record the transactions relating to stockholders' equity that took place during the year.

b. Prepare the lower section of the income statement for 1998, beginning with the *income before extraordinary items* and showing the extraordinary loss and the net income. Also illustrate the presentation of earnings per share in the income statement, assuming that earnings per share is determined on the basis of the *weighted-average* number of shares outstanding during the year.

c. Prepare a statement of retained earnings for the year ending December 31, 1998.

SOLUTION TO DEMONSTRATION PROBLEM

a.

		GENERAL JOURNAL		Page 1
Date		Account Titles and Explanations	Debit	Credit
Mar.	31	Memorandum: A 5-for-4 stock split increased the number of shares of common stock outstanding from 40,000 to 50,000 and reduced the par value from $10 to $8 per share. The 10,000 new shares were distributed.		
Apr.	1	Treasury Stock	74,000	
		Cash..		74,000
		Acquired 2,000 shares of treasury stock at $37.		
July	1	Cash..	45,000	
		Treasury Stock		37,000
		Additional Paid-in Capital: Treasury		
		Stock Transactions		8,000
		Sold 1,000 shares of treasury stock at $45 per share.		
	1	Cash..	900,000	
		Common Stock, $8 par...............................		160,000
		Additional Paid-in Capital: Common Stock............		740,000
		Issued 20,000 shares.		
Dec.	1	Dividends...	69,000	
		Dividends Payable		69,000
		To record declaration of cash dividend of $1 per share on 69,000 shares of common stock outstanding (1,000 shares in treasury are not entitled to receive dividends).		
		Note: Entry to record the payment of the cash dividend is not shown here since the action does not affect the stockholders' equity.		
	22	Retained Earnings	331,200	
		Stock Dividends to Be Distributed........................		55,200
		Additional Paid-in Capital: Stock Dividends...........		276,000
		To record declaration of 10% stock dividend consisting of 6,900 shares of $8 par value common stock to be distributed on Jan. 15 of next year.		
	31	Income Summary...	177,000	
		Retained Earnings		177,000
		To close Income Summary account.		
	31	Retained Earnings	69,000	
		Dividends		69,000
		To close Dividends account.		

b.

SUTTON CORPORATION Partial Income Statement For the Year Ended December 31, 1998	
Income before extraordinary items	$212,400
Extraordinary loss (net of income tax benefits).....................................	(35,400)
Net income	$177,000
Earnings per share:*	
Income before extraordinary items...	$3.60
Extraordinary loss...	(0.60)
Net income...	$3.00

*On 59,000 weighted-average number of shares of common stock outstanding during 1998 determined as follows:

Jan. 1–Mar. 31: (40,000 + 10,000 shares issued pursuant to a 5 for 4 split) × ¼ of year	12,500
Apr. 1–June 30: (50,000 − 2,000 shares of treasury stock) × ¼ of year	12,000
July 1–Dec. 31: (50,000 + 20,000 shares of new stock − 1,000 shares of treasury stock) × ½ of year	34,500
Weighted-average number of shares outstanding	59,000

c.

SUTTON CORPORATION Statement of Retained Earnings For the Year Ended December 31, 1998		
Retained earnings, December 31, 1997.................................		$1,500,000
Net income for 1998		177,000
Subtotal...		$1,677,000
Less: Cash dividends ($1 per share)...................................	$ 69,000	
10% stock dividend.......................................	331,200	400,200
Retained earnings, December 31, 1998.................................		$1,276,800

SELF-TEST QUESTIONS

The answers to these questions appear on page 610.

1. The primary purpose of showing special types of events separately in the income statement is to:
  a. Increase earnings per share.
  b. Assist users of the income statement in evaluating the profitability of normal, ongoing operations.
  c. Minimize the income taxes paid on the results of ongoing operations.
  d. Prevent unusual losses from recurring.

2. Which of the following situations would *not* be presented in a separate section of the current year's income statement of Marlow Corporation? During the current year:
  a. Marlow's St. Louis headquarters are destroyed by a tornado.

    b. Marlow sells its entire juvenile furniture operations and concentrates upon its remaining children's clothing segment.

    c. Marlow changes from the straight-line method of depreciation to the double-declining-balance method.

    d. Marlow's accountant discovers that the entire price paid several years ago to purchase company offices in Texas had been charged to a Land account; consequently, no depreciation has ever been taken on these buildings.

3. When a corporation has outstanding both common and preferred stock:

    a. Basic and diluted earnings per share are reported only if the preferred stock is cumulative.

    b. Earnings per share are reported for each type of stock outstanding.

    c. Earnings per share may be computed without regard to the amount of dividends declared on common stock.

    d. Earnings per share may be computed without regard to the amount of the annual preferred dividends.

4. The statement of retained earnings:

    a. Need not be prepared if a separate statement of stockholders' equity accompanies the financial statements.

    b. Indicates the amount of cash available for the payment of dividends.

    c. Includes prior period adjustments and cash dividends, but not stock dividends.

    d. Shows revenue, expenses, and dividends for the accounting period.

5. On December 10, 1997, Totem Corporation reacquired 2,000 shares of its own $5 par stock at a price of $60 per share. In 1998, 500 of the treasury shares are reissued at a price of $70 per share. Which of the following statements is correct?

    a. The treasury stock purchased is recorded at cost and is shown in Totem's December 31, 1997, balance sheet as an asset.

    b. The two treasury stock transactions result in an overall reduction in Totem's stockholders' equity of $85,000.

    c. Totem recognizes a gain of $10 per share on the reissuance of the 500 treasury shares in 1998.

    d. Totem's stockholders' equity was increased by $110,000 when the treasury stock was acquired.

ASSIGNMENT MATERIAL

DISCUSSION QUESTIONS

1. What is the purpose of arranging an income statement to show subtotals for *Income from Continuing Operations* and for *Income before Extraordinary Items?*

2. Pappa Joe's owns 30 pizza parlors and a minor league baseball team. During the current year, the company sold three of its pizza parlors and closed another when the lease on the building expired. Should any of these events be classified as "discontinued operations" in the company's income statement? Explain.

3. Define *extraordinary items*. Give three examples of losses which qualify as extraordinary items and three examples of losses which would *not* be classified as extraordinary.

4. In an effort to make the company more competitive, Rytech, Inc. has incurred significant expenses related to reduction in the number of employees, consolidation of offices and facilities, and disposition of assets that are no longer productive. Explain how these costs would be presented in the financial statements of the company, and describe how an investor should view these costs in predicting future earnings of the company.

5. Both the *cumulative effect of a change in accounting principle* and *a prior period adjustment* affect the income of past accounting periods. Distinguish between these two items and explain how each is shown in the financial statements.

6. In the current year, Garden Products decided to switch from use of an accelerated method of depreciation to the straight-line method. Will the cumulative effect of this change in accounting principle increase or decrease the amount of net income reported in the current year? Explain.

7. *Earnings per share* and *book value per share* are statistics that relate to common stock. When both preferred and common stock are outstanding, explain the computation involved in determining the following:
   a. Earnings allocable to the common stockholders
   b. Aggregate book value allocable to the common stockholders

8. Assume a corporation has only common stock outstanding. Is the number of common shares used in the computation of earnings per share *always* the same as the number of common shares used in computing book value per share for this corporation? Is the number of common shares used in computing these two statistics *ever* the same? Explain.

9. Explain how each of the following is computed:
   a. Price-earnings ratio
   b. Basic earnings per share
   c. Diluted earnings per share

10. Throughout the year, Gold Seal Company had 4 million shares of common stock and 120,000 shares of convertible preferred stock outstanding. Each share of preferred is convertible into four shares of common. What number of shares should be used in the computation of (a) basic earnings per share and (b) diluted earnings per share?

11. A financial analyst notes that Baxter Corporation's earnings per share have been rising steadily for the last five years. The analyst expects the company's net income to continue to increase at the same rate as in the past. In forecasting future basic earnings per share, what special risk should the analyst consider if Baxter's primary earnings are significantly larger than its diluted earnings?

12. Explain the significance of the following dates relating to dividends: date of declaration, date of record, date of payment, ex-dividend date.

13. What is the purpose of a *stock split?*

14. Distinguish between a *stock split* and a *stock dividend*. Is there any reason for the difference in accounting treatment of these two events?

15. What are *prior period adjustments?* How are they presented in financial statements?

16. Identify three items that may appear in a statement of retained earnings as changes in the amount of retained earnings.

17. What is *treasury stock?* Why do corporations purchase their own shares? Is treasury stock an asset? How should it be reported in the balance sheet?

18. In many states, the corporation law requires that retained earnings be restricted for dividend purposes to the extent of the cost of treasury shares. What is the reason for this legal rule?

19. A *statement of stockholders' equity* sometimes is described as an "expanded" statement of retained earnings. Why?

*20. Describe stock options as a form of compensation to managers.

---

*Supplemental Topic, "Employee Stock Plans."

EXERCISES

EXERCISE 12-1
Stock Dividends
and Stock
Splits

LO 4

Assume that when you were in high school you saved $1,000 to invest for your college education. You purchased 200 shares of Tidal Wave Incorporated, a small but profitable company. Over the three years that you have owned the stock, the corporation's board of directors took the following actions:

1. Declared a 2-for-1 stock split.
2. Declared a 20% stock dividend.
3. Declared a 3-for-1 stock split.

The current price of the stock is $10 per share.

a. Calculate the current number of shares and the market value of your investment.

b. Explain the likely reason why the board of directors of the company has not declared a cash dividend.

c. State your opinion as to whether or not you would have been better off if the board of directors had declared a cash dividend instead of the stock dividend and stock splits.

EXERCISE 12-2
Accounting Terminology

LO 1,2,3,4,6,7,10

Listed below are nine technical accounting terms introduced or emphasized in this chapter:

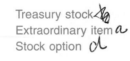

P/e ratio f	Treasury stock b	Discontinued operations g
Stock dividend c	Extraordinary item a	Prior period adjustment e
Basic earnings per share $\mathfrak{g}$	Stock option d	Diluted earnings per share h

Each of the following statements may (or may not) describe one of these technical terms. For each statement, indicate the term described, or answer "None" if the statement does not correctly describe any of the terms.

a. A gain or loss that is material in amount, unusual in nature, and not expected to recur in the foreseeable future.

b. The asset represented by shares of capital stock that have not yet been issued.

c. A distribution of additional shares of stock that reduces retained earnings but causes no change in total stockholders' equity.

d. The right to buy shares of stock at a specified price over an extended period of time.

e. An adjustment to the beginning balance of retained earnings to correct an error previously made in the measurement of net income.

f. A statistic expressing a relationship between the current market value of a share of common stock and the underlying earnings per share.

g. A separate section sometimes included in an income statement as a way to help investors evaluate the profitability of ongoing business activities.

h. A hypothetical figure indicating what earnings per share would have been if all securities convertible into common stock had been converted at the beginning of the current year.

EXERCISE 12-3
Discontinued
Operations

LO 1,2

During the current year, SunSports, Inc., operated two business segments: a chain of surf and dive shops and a small chain of tennis shops. The tennis shops were not profitable and were sold near year-end to another corporation. SunSports' operations for the current year are summarized on the following page. The first two captions, "Net sales" and "Costs and expenses," relate only to the company's continuing operations.

Net sales..	$9,800,000
Costs and expenses (including applicable income taxes).....................................	8,600,000
Operating loss from tennis shops (net of income tax benefit)	192,000
Loss on sale of tennis shops (net of income tax benefit)	348,000

The company had 150,000 shares of a single class of capital stock outstanding throughout the year.

a. Prepare a condensed income statement for the year. At the bottom of the statement, show any appropriate earnings-per-share figures. (A condensed income statement is illustrated on page 575.)

b. Which earnings-per-share figure in part **a** do you consider most useful in predicting future operating results for SunSports, Inc.? Why?

EXERCISE 12-4
Reporting an
Extraordinary Item

For the year ended December 31, Global Exports had net sales of $9,000,000, costs and other expenses (including income taxes) of $6,200,000, and an extraordinary gain (net of income tax) of $700,000.

a. Prepare a condensed income statement (including earnings per share), assuming that 1,000,000 shares of common stock were outstanding throughout the year.

b. Which earnings-per-share figure is used in computing the price-earnings ratio for Global Exports reported in financial publications such as *The Wall Street Journal?* Explain briefly.

EXERCISE 12-5
Computing Earnings per
Share: Effect of Preferred
Stock
LO 2

The net income of Tiny Tot Furniture, Inc., amounted to $1,850,000 for the current year.

a. Compute the amount of earnings per share assuming that the shares of capital stock outstanding throughout the year consisted of:
  1. 200,000 shares of $1 par value common stock and no preferred stock.
  2. 100,000 shares of 8%, $100 par value preferred stock and 300,000 shares of $5 par value common stock. The preferred stock has a call price of $105 per share.

b. Is the earnings-per-share figure computed in part **a(2)** considered to be basic or diluted? Explain.

EXERCISE 12-6
Restating Earnings per
Share After a Stock Dividend

The 1993 annual report of **Microsoft Corp.** included the following comparative summary of earnings per share over the last three years:

	1994	1993	1992	1991
Earnings per share	1.88	$3.15	$2.41	$1.64
		1.575	1.205	

In 1994, Microsoft Corp. declared and distributed a 100% stock dividend. Following this stock dividend, the company reported earnings per share of $1.88 for 1994.

a. Prepare a three-year schedule similar to the one above, but compare earnings per share during the years 1994, 1993, and 1992. (**Hint:** All per-share amounts in your schedule should be based on the number of shares outstanding after the stock dividend.)

b. In preparing your schedule, which figure (or figures) did you have to restate? Why? Explain the logic behind your computation.

EXERCISE 12-7
Cash Dividends, Stock
Dividends, and Stock Splits

Universal Cable Corporation has 1,000,000 shares of $1 par value capital stock outstanding on January 1. The following equity transactions occurred during the current year:

Apr. 30 Distributed additional shares of capital stock in a 2-for-1 stock split. Market price of stock was $35 per share.

June 1 Declared a cash dividend of 60 cents per share.

July 1 Paid the 60-cent cash dividend to stockholders.

Aug. 1 Declared a 5% stock dividend. Market price of stock was $19 per share.

Sept. 10 Issued shares pursuant to the 5% stock dividend declared on August 1.

Dec. 1 Declared a 50% stock dividend. Market price of stock was $23 per share.

a. Prepare journal entries to record the above transactions.

b. Compute the number of shares of capital stock outstanding at year-end.

c. What is the par value per share of Universal Cable stock at the end of the year?

d. Determine the effect of each of the following on *total* stockholders' equity: stock split, declaration and payment of a cash dividend, declaration and distribution of a small stock dividend, declaration and distribution of a large stock dividend. (Your answers should be *increase, decrease,* or *no effect.*)

EXERCISE 12-8
Effect of Stock Dividends
on Stock Price

Tarreytown Corporation has a total of 80,000 shares of common stock outstanding and no preferred stock. Total stockholders' equity at the end of the current year amounts to $5 million and the market value of the stock is $66 per share. At year-end, the company declares a 10% stock dividend—one share for each ten shares held. If all parties concerned clearly recognize the nature of the stock dividend, what should you expect the market price per share of the common stock to be on the ex-dividend date?

EXERCISE 12-9
Reporting the Effects of
Transactions

Five events pertaining to Lowlands Manufacturing Co. are described below.

a. Declared and paid a cash dividend.

b. Issued a 10% stock dividend.

c. Issued a 2-for-1 stock split.

d. Purchased treasury stock.

e. Reissued the treasury stock at a price greater than the purchase price.

Indicate the immediate effects of the events on the financial measurements in the four columnar headings listed below. Use the code letters, **I** for increase, **D** for decrease, and **NE** for no effect.

Event	Current Assets	Owners' Equity	Net Income	Net Cash Flow (from Any Source)

EXERCISE 12-10
Effects of Various
Transactions upon Earnings
per Share

Explain the immediate effects, if any, of each of the following transactions upon a company's net earnings per share:

a. Split the common stock 3-for-1.

b. Realized a gain from the sale of a discontinued operation.

c. Switched from an accelerated method of depreciation to the straight-line method, resulting in a large debit to the Accumulated Depreciation account.

d. Declared and paid a cash dividend on common stock.

e. Declared and distributed a stock dividend on common stock.

f. Acquired several thousand shares of treasury stock.

EXERCISE 12-11
Where to Find Financial
Information

 LO 1,5,9

You have now been exposed to the following financial statements issued by corporations: balance sheet, income statement, statement of retained earnings, statement of stockholders' equity, and the statement of cash flows. Listed below are various items frequently of interest to a corporation's owners, potential investors, and creditors, among others. You are to specify which of the above corporate financial statements, if any, reports the desired information. If the listed item is not reported in any formal financial statement issued by a corporation, indicate an appropriate source for the desired information.

a. Number of shares of stock outstanding as of year-end.

b. Total dollar amount of cash dividends declared during the current year.

c. Market value per share at balance sheet date.

d. Cumulative dollar effect of an accounting error made in a previous year.

e. Cumulative dollar effect of switching from one generally accepted accounting principle to another acceptable accounting method during the current year.

f. Explanation of why the number of shares of stock outstanding at the end of the current year is greater than the number outstanding at the end of the prior year.

g. Earnings per share of common stock.

h. Book value per share.

i. Price/earnings (p/e) ratio.

j. The total amount the corporation paid to buy back shares of its own stock which it now holds.

*EXERCISE 12-12
Stock Options

 LO 10

Assume that you are a manager who has been with Cyber Spider for two years. You have just become eligible to exercise stock options on up to 10,000 shares at an option price of $30 per share. You can exercise these options at any time over the next four years (providing that you are still with the company). Currently, Cyber Spider's stock price is $52 per share.

a. What "economic gain" would you realize if you exercised all of your options today and immediately sold the shares? (Ignore brokerage commissions and income taxes.)

b. Why might you choose *not* to exercise the options today, but instead, just "sit tight"?

c. Why might you exercise *some* of the options today, and sell the shares acquired, while holding on to the remaining options?

EXERCISE 12-13
Price/Earnings Ratio
and Stock
Transactions

 LO 2,7,9

The financial statements of **Toys "R" Us** begin on page A-7 of Appendix A.

a. Assuming that the market price per share of the company's stock was $33.50 on January 28, 1995, calculate the price-earnings ratio of the company's stock on that date.

b. Calculate the book value per share of the company's stock at January 28, 1995. (**Hint:** The number of shares outstanding can be obtained from the Consolidated Statement of Stockholders' Equity.)

c. After examining the Consolidated Statement of Stockholders' Equity on page A-10, calculate the average price per share of the shares of stock repurchased for the year ended January 28, 1995.

d. State the cost of the treasury stock of the company at January 28, 1995.

e. Explain *why* a company like Toys "R" Us might decide to buy treasury stock.

*Supplemental Topic, "Employee Stock Plans."

PROBLEMS

PROBLEM 12-1
Reporting Unusual
Events; Using
Predictive Subtotals

LO 1,2

Gulf Coast Airlines operated both an airline and several motels located near airports. During the year just ended, all motel operations were discontinued and the following operating results were reported:

Continuing operations (airlines):

Net sales...	$51,120,000
Costs and expenses (including income taxes on	
continuing operations)...	43,320,000

Other data:

Operating income from motels (net of income taxes)	864,000
Gain on sale of motels (net of income taxes)..	4,956,000
Extraordinary loss (net of income tax benefit)	3,360,000

The extraordinary loss resulted from the destruction of an airliner by terrorists.

Gulf Coast Airlines had 1,200,000 shares of capital stock outstanding throughout the year.

INSTRUCTIONS

a. Prepare a condensed income statement, including proper presentation of the discontinued motel operations and the extraordinary loss. Include all appropriate earnings per share figures.

b. Assume that you expect the profitability of Gulf Coast's airlines operations to *decline by 6%* next year, and the profitability of the motels to decline by 10%. What is your estimate of the company's net earnings per share next year?

PROBLEM 12-2
Format of an
Income Statement
and a Statement of
Retained Earnings

LO 1,2,5,6

Shown below are data relating to the operations of Ashton Software, Inc., during 1998:

Continuing operations:

Net sales...	$19,850,000
Costs and expenses (including applicable income taxes)	16,900,000

Other data:

Operating income during 1998 on segment of the business	
discontinued near year-end (net of income taxes).....................................	140,000
Loss on disposal of discontinued segment (net of income	
tax benefit)	550,000
Extraordinary loss (net of income tax benefit)...	900,000
Cumulative effect of change in accounting principle	
(increase in net income, net of related income taxes)...............................	100,000
Prior period adjustment (increase in 1995 depreciation	
expense, net of income tax benefit)	250,000
Cash dividends declared...	950,000

INSTRUCTIONS

a. Prepare a condensed income statement for 1998, including earnings per share statistics. Ashton Software, Inc., had 200,000 shares of $1 par value common stock and 80,000 shares of $6.25, $100 par value preferred stock outstanding throughout the year.

b. Prepare a statement of retained earnings for the year ended December 31, 1998. As originally reported, retained earnings at December 31, 1997 amounted to $6,450,000.

c. Compute the amount of cash dividend *per share of common stock* declared by the board of directors for 1998. Assume no dividends in arrears on the preferred stock.

d. Assume that 1999 earnings per share is a single figure and amounts to $8.00. Assume also that there are no changes in outstanding common or preferred stock in 1999. Do you consider the $8.00 earnings-per-share figure in 1999 to be a favorable or unfavorable statistic in comparison with 1998 performance? Explain.

PROBLEM 12-3
Reporting Unusual
Events: A
Comprehensive
Problem
 LO 1,2,5,6,7

The following income statement was prepared by a new and inexperienced employee in the accounting department of Keller Interiors, a business organized as a corporation.

KELLER INTERIORS
Income Statement
For the Year Ended December 31, 1998

Net sales...		$10,800,000
Gain on sale of treasury stock...		54,000
Excess of issuance price over par value of		
capital stock		510,000
Prior period adjustment (net of income taxes)...................		60,000
Extraordinary gain (net of income taxes)...........................		36,000
Total revenue...		$11,460,000
Less:		
Cost of goods sold..	$6,000,000	
Selling expenses...	1,104,000	
General and administrative expenses	1,896,000	
Loss from settlement of litigation..................................	24,000	
Income taxes on continuing operations.........................	720,000	
Operating loss on discontinued operations		
(net of income tax benefit)	252,000	
Loss on disposal of discontinued operations		
(net of income tax benefit)	420,000	
Cumulative effect of change in accounting		
principle (net of income tax benefit)	84,000	
Dividends declared on capital stock..............................	350,000	
Total costs and expenses...		10,850,000
Net income...		$ 610,000

INSTRUCTIONS

a. Prepare a corrected income statement for the year ended December 31, 1998, using the format illustrated on page 567. Include at the bottom of your income statement all appropriate earnings-per-share figures. Assume that throughout the year, the company had outstanding a weighted average of 200,000 shares of a single class of capital stock.

b. Prepare a statement of retained earnings for 1998. (As originally reported, retained earnings at December 31, 1997 amounted to $1,400,000.)

c. What does the $54,000 "gain on sale of treasury stock" represent? How would you report this "gain" in Keller's financial statements at December 31, 1998?

PROBLEM 12-4
Effects of Stock Dividends,
Stock Splits, and Treasury
Stock Transactions

 LO 4,7

At the beginning of the year, Exotic Adventures, Inc., has total stockholders' equity of $840,000 and 40,000 outstanding shares of a single class of capital stock. During the year, the corporation completes the following transactions affecting its stockholders' equity accounts:

Jan. 10 A 5% stock dividend is declared and distributed. (Market price, $20 per share.)

Mar. 15 The corporation acquires 2,000 shares of its own capital stock at a cost of $21.00 per share.

May 30 All 2,000 shares of the treasury stock are reissued at a price of $31.50 per share.

July 31 The capital stock is split 2-for-1.

Dec. 15 The board of directors declares a cash dividend of $1.10 per share, payable on January 15.

Dec. 31 Net income of $260,400 (equal to $3.10 per share) is reported for the year ended December 31.

INSTRUCTIONS

Compute the amount of total stockholders' equity, the number of shares of capital stock outstanding, and the book value per share following each successive transaction. Organize your solution as a three-column schedule with these separate column headings: (1) Total Stockholders' Equity, (2) Number of Shares Outstanding, and (3) Book Value per Share.

PROBLEM 12-5
Preparing a State-
ment of Stockholders'
Equity

 LO 4,7,9

Shown below is a summary of the transactions affecting the stockholders' equity of Marble Oasis Corporation during the current year:

Prior period adjustment (net of income tax benefit)	$ (80,000)
Issuance of common stock: 10,000 shares of $10 par value capital stock at $34 per share	340,000
Declaration and distribution of 5% stock dividend (6,000 shares, market price $36 per share)	(216,000)
Purchased 1,000 shares of treasury stock at $35	(35,000)
Reissued 500 shares of treasury stock at a price of $36 per share	18,000
Net income	720,000
Cash dividends declared ($1 per share)	(125,500)

Parentheses ( ) indicate a debit change—a reduction—in stockholders' equity.

INSTRUCTIONS

a. Prepare a statement of stockholders' equity for the year. Use the column headings and beginning balances shown below. (Notice that all additional paid-in capital accounts are combined into a single column.)

	Capital Stock ($10 par value)	Additional Paid-in Capital	Retained Earnings	Treasury Stock	Total Stock- holders' Equity
Balances, January 1, 19__	$1,100,000	$1,800,000	$900,000	$ –0–	$3,800,000

b. What was the overall effect on total stockholders' equity of the 5% stock dividend of 6,000 shares? What was the overall effect on total stockholders' equity of the cash dividend declared? Do these two events have the same impact upon stockholders' equity? Why or why not?

PROBLEM 12-6
Recording Stock
Dividends and
Treasury Stock
Transactions

LO 4,7

At the beginning of 1998, OverNight Letter showed the following amounts in the stockholders' equity section of its balance sheet:

Stockholders' equity:	
Capital stock, $1 par value, 500,000 shares authorized,	
382,000 issued	$ 382,000
Additional paid-in capital: capital stock	4,202,000
Total paid-in capital	$4,584,000
Retained earnings	2,704,600
Total stockholders' equity	$7,288,600

The transactions relating to stockholders' equity during the year are as follows:

Jan. 3 Declared a dividend of $1 per share to stockholders of record on January 31, payable on February 15.

Feb. 15 Paid the cash dividend declared on January 3.

Apr. 12 The corporation purchased 6,000 shares of its own capital stock at a price of $40 per share.

May 9 Reissued 4,000 shares of the treasury stock at a price of $44 per share.

June 1 Declared a 5% stock dividend to stockholders of record at June 15, to be distributed on June 30. The market price of the stock at June 1 was $42 per share. (The 2,000 shares remaining in the treasury do not participate in the stock dividend.)

June 30 Distributed the stock dividend declared on June 1.

Aug. 4 Reissued 600 of the 2,000 remaining shares of treasury stock at a price of $37 per share.

Dec. 31 The Income Summary account, showing net income for the year of $1,928,000 was closed into the Retained Earnings account.

Dec. 31 The $382,000 balance in the Dividends account was closed into the Retained Earnings account.

INSTRUCTIONS

a. Prepare in general journal form the entries to record the above transactions.

b. Prepare the stockholders' equity section of the balance sheet at December 31, 1998. Use the format illustrated on page 587. Include a supporting schedule showing your computation of retained earnings at that date.

c. Compute the maximum cash dividend per share which legally could be declared at December 31, 1998 without impairing the paid-in capital of OverNight Letter. (**Hint:** The availability of retained earnings for dividends is restricted by the cost of treasury stock owned.)

PROBLEM 12-7
Effects of
Transactions

LO 8

Cipher, Inc., manufactures a variety of computer peripherals, such as tape drives and printers. Listed below are five events which occurred during the current year.

1. Declared a $1.00 per share cash dividend.

2. Paid the cash dividend.

3. Purchased 1,000 shares of treasury stock for $20.00 per share.

4. Reissued 500 shares of the treasury stock at a price of $18.00 per share.

5. Declared a 15 percent stock dividend.

INSTRUCTIONS

a. Indicate the effects of each of these events upon the financial measurements in the four columnar headings listed on the next page. Use the following code letters: **I** for increase, **D** for decrease, and **NE** for no effect.

Event	Current Assets	Owners' Equity	Net Income	Net Cash Flow (from Any Source)

b. For each event, *explain fully* the reasoning behind your answers. Also be prepared to explain this reasoning in class.

PROBLEM 12-8
Preparing the Stockholders' Equity Section: A Challenging Case

LO 4,7

The Mandella family decided early in 1997 to incorporate their family-owned vineyards under the name Mandella Corporation. The corporation was authorized to issue 500,000 shares of a single class of $10 par value capital stock. Presented below is the information necessary to prepare the stockholders' equity section of the company's balance sheet at the end of 1997 and at the end of 1998.

1997. In January the corporation issued to members of the Mandella family 150,000 shares of capital stock in exchange for cash and other assets used in the operation of the vineyards. The fair market value of these assets indicated an issue price of $30 per share. In December, Joe Mandella died, and the corporation purchased 10,000 shares of its own capital stock from his estate at $34 per share. Because of the large cash outlay to acquire this treasury stock, the directors decided not to declare cash dividends in 1997 and instead declared a 10% stock dividend to be distributed in January of 1998. The stock price at the declaration date was $35 per share. (The treasury shares do not participate in the stock dividend.) Net income for 1997 was $940,000.

1998. In January the corporation distributed the stock dividend declared in 1997, and in February, the 10,000 treasury shares were sold to Maria Mandella at $39 per share. In June, the capital stock was split 2 for 1. (Approval was obtained to increase the authorized number of shares to 1 million.) On December 15, the directors declared a cash dividend of $2 per share, payable in January of 1999. Net income for 1998 was $1,080,000.

INSTRUCTIONS
Using the format illustrated on page 587, prepare the stockholders' equity section of the balance sheet at:

a. December 31, 1997

b. December 31, 1998

Show any necessary computations in supporting schedules.

PROBLEM 12-9
Format of an Income Statement; EPS

LO 1,2

The following information is excerpted from the financial statements in a recent annual report of **Bally Manufacturing Corporation.** (Dollar figures and shares of stock are in thousands.)

Extraordinary loss on extinguishment of debt	$ (8,490)
Loss from continuing operations	$(16,026)
Cumulative effect of change in accounting for income taxes	$(28,197)
Income from discontinued operations	$ 6,215
Preferred stock dividend requirements	$ (2,778)
Weighted-average number of shares of common stock outstanding	46,559

INSTRUCTIONS
a. Rearrange the items to present in good form the last portion of the income statement for Bally Manufacturing Corporation, beginning with "Loss from continuing operations."

b. Calculate the amount of *net loss* per share for the period. (Do *not* calculate per-share amounts for subtotals, such as income from continuing operations, or loss before extraordinary items, etc. You are required only to compute a single earnings-per-share amount.)

CASES

CASE 12-1
What's This?
LO 1

The following events have been reported in the financial statements of large, publicly owned corporations.

a. Atlantic Richfield Company (ARCO) sold or abandoned the entire "noncoal minerals" segment of its operations. In the year of disposal, this segment had an operating loss. ARCO also incurred a loss of $514 million on disposal of its noncoal minerals segment of the business.

b. American Airlines increased the estimated useful life used in computing depreciation on its aircraft. If the new estimated life had always been in use, the net income reported in prior years would have been substantially higher.

c. Union Carbide Corp. sustained a large loss as a result of the explosion of a chemical plant.

d. AT&T changed the method used to depreciate certain assets. Had the new method always been in use, the net income of prior years would have been $175 million lower than was actually reported.

e. Georgia Pacific Corporation realized a $10 million gain as a result of condemnation proceedings in which a governmental agency purchased assets from the company in a "forced sale."

INSTRUCTIONS

Indicate whether each event should be classified as a discontinued operation, an extraordinary item, the cumulative effect of an accounting change, or included among the revenue and expenses of normal and recurring business operations. Briefly explain your reasons for each answer.

CASE 12-2
Is There Life
Without Baseball?
LO 1

Midwestern Publishing, Inc., publishes two newspapers and, until recently, owned a professional baseball team. The baseball team had been losing money for several years and was sold at the end of 1997 to a group of investors who plan to move it to a larger city. Also in 1997, Midwestern suffered an extraordinary loss when its Raytown printing plant was damaged by a tornado. The damage has since been repaired. A condensed income statement follows:

MIDWESTERN PUBLISHING, INC.		
Income Statement		
For the Year Ended December 31, 1997		
Net revenue		$41,000,000
Costs and expenses		36,500,000
Income from continuing operations		$ 4,500,000
Discontinued operations:		
Operating loss on baseball team	$(1,300,000)	
Gain on sale of baseball team	4,700,000	3,400,000
Income before extraordinary items		$ 7,900,000
Extraordinary loss:		
Tornado damage to Raytown printing plant		(600,000)
Net income		$ 7,300,000

INSTRUCTIONS

On the basis of this information, answer the following questions. Show any necessary computations and explain your reasoning.

a. What would Midwestern's net income have been for 1997 if it *had not* sold the baseball team?

b. Assume that for 1998, you expect a 7% increase in the profitability of Midwestern's newspaper business but had projected a $2,000,000 operating loss for the baseball team if Midwestern had continued to operate the team in 1998. What amount would you forecast as Midwestern's 1998 net income *if the company had continued to own and operate the baseball team?*

c. Given your assumptions in part **b,** but given that Midwestern *did* sell the baseball team in 1997, what would you forecast as the company's estimated net income for 1998?

d. Assume that the expenses of operating the baseball team in 1997 amounted to $32,200,000, net of any related income tax effects. What was the team's *net revenue* for the year?

CASE 12-3
Using Earnings per Share Statistics
LO 1,2,3

For many years American Studios has produced television shows and operated several FM radio stations. Late in the current year, the radio stations were sold to Times Publishing, Inc. Also during the current year, American Studios sustained an extraordinary loss when one of its camera trucks caused an accident in an international grand prix auto race. Throughout the current year, the company had 3 million shares of common stock and a large quantity of convertible preferred stock outstanding. Earnings per share reported for the current year were as follows:

	Basic	Diluted
Earnings from continuing operations	$8.20	$6.80
Earnings before extraordinary items	$6.90	$5.50
Net earnings	$3.80	$2.40

INSTRUCTIONS

a. Briefly explain why American Studios reports diluted earnings per share amounts as well as basic earnings per share. What is the purpose of showing investors the diluted figures?

b. What was the total dollar amount of the extraordinary loss sustained by American Studios during the current year?

c. Assume that the price-earnings ratio shown in the morning newspaper for American Studios' common stock indicates that the stock is selling at a price equal to 10 times the reported earnings per share. What is the approximate market price of the stock?

d. Assume that you expect both the revenue and expenses involved in producing television shows to increase by 10% during the coming year. What would you forecast as the company's basic earnings per share for the coming year under each of the following independent assumptions? (Show your computations and explain your reasoning.)

   1. *None* of the convertible preferred stock is converted into common stock during the coming year.

   2. *All* of the convertible preferred stock is converted into common stock at the beginning of the coming year.

CASE 12-4
Interpreting a
Statement of
Stockholders'
Equity

LO 9

The following information is excerpted from the Statement of Common Stockholders' Equity included in a recent annual report of **The Quaker Oats Company and Subsidiaries.** (Dollar figures are in millions.)

	Common Stock		Additional Paid-in Capital	Retained Earnings	Treasury Stock	
	Shares	Amount			Shares	Amount
Balances, beginning of year	83,989,396	$420.0	$19.5	$ 998.4	4,593,664	$(132.9)
Net income				203.0		
Cash dividends declared on common stock				(95.2)		
Common stock issued for stock option plans			(1.4)		(601,383)	16.7
Repurchases of common stock					1,229,700	(68.6)
Balances, year-end	83,989,396	$420.0	$18.1	$1,106.2	5,221,981	$(184.8)

INSTRUCTIONS

Use the information presented above to answer the following questions.

a. How many shares of common stock are outstanding at the *beginning* of the year? At the *end* of the year?

b. What was the total common stock dividend declared during the above year? Quaker's annual report disclosed that the common stock dividend during the above year was $1.20 per share (30 cents per quarter). Approximately how many shares of common stock were entitled to the $1.20 per share dividend during the year? Is this answer compatible with your answers to part **a?**

c. The above statement indicates that common stock was both issued during the year and repurchased during the year, yet the number of common shares shown and the common stock amount (first and second columns) did not change from beginning to end of the year. Explain.

d. What was the average price per share Quaker paid to acquire the treasury shares held at the *beginning* of the year?

e. Was the aggregate issue price of the 601,383 treasury shares issued during the year for stock option plans higher or lower than the cost Quaker paid to acquire those treasury shares? (**Hint:** Analyze the impact upon Additional Paid-in Capital.)

f. What was the average purchase price per share paid by Quaker to acquire treasury shares *during the current year?*

g. In its annual report, Quaker disclosed that the (weighted) average number of common shares outstanding during the year was 79,307,000. In part **a,** above, you determined the number of common shares outstanding as of the end of the year. Which figure is used in computing *earnings per share?* Which is used in computing *book value per share?*

*CASE 12-5
Classification of
Unusual Items—
and the Potential
Financial Impact

LO 1,2,8,10

Elliot-Cole is a publicly owned international corporation, with operations in over 90 countries. Net income has been growing at approximately 15% per year, and the stock consistently trades at about 20 times earnings.

As part of their compensation packages, members of the corporation's top management have been granted *stock options,* entitling them to buy large quantities of the company's stock at a stipulated price. At the time these options were granted, this stipulated price was equal to the stock's market price. Due to the company's success, however, today's market price is well above the stipulated "option price." Thus, managers can realize substantial gains by exercising their options and reselling the shares at the market price.

During the current year, political unrest and economic upheaval threatened Elliot-Cole's business operations in three foreign countries. At year-end, the company's auditors insisted that management write off the company's assets in these countries, stating that these assets were "severely impaired." Said one corporate official, "We can't argue with that. Each of these countries is a real trouble spot. We might be pulling out of these places at any time, and any assets probably would just be left behind."

Management agreed that the carrying value of Elliot-Cole's assets in these three countries should be reduced to "scrap value"—which was nothing. These write-downs amounted to approximately 18% of the company's income *prior* to recognition of these losses. (These write-offs are for financial reporting purposes only; they have *no effect* upon the company's income tax obligations.)

At the meeting with the auditors, one of Elliot-Cole's officers states, "There's no doubt we should write these assets off. But of course, this is an extraordinary loss. A loss of this size can't be considered a routine matter."

INSTRUCTIONS

a. Explain the logic behind writing down the book values of assets which are still in operation.

b. Evaluate the officer's statement concerning the classification of these losses. Do you agree that they should be classified as an extraordinary item? Explain.

c. Explain the effect that the classification of these losses—that is, as ordinary or extraordinary—will have in the current period upon Elliot-Cole's:
   1. Net income.
   2. Income before extraordinary items.
   3. Income from continuing operations.
   4. Net cash flow from operating activities.

d. Explain how the classification of these losses will affect the p/e ratio reported in newspapers such as *The Wall Street Journal.*

e. Does management appear to have any "self-interest" in the classification of these losses? Explain.

f. Explain how (if at all) these write-offs are likely to affect the earnings of *future* periods.

g. What "ethical dilemma" confronts management in this case?

INTERNET ASSIGNMENTS

INTERNET 12-1
Comparing
Price/earnings
Ratios

LO 2

The normal price-earnings ratio of a company varies depending on expected future earnings of the company and the general price level of the stock market. On average, mature companies have lower price-earnings ratios, usually less than 20, than do emerging companies, which may be over 100. This is because of the steep growth in earnings that is characteristic of an emerging company.

---

*Supplemental Topic, "Employee Stock Plans."

a. Visit *Fortune* magazine's Internet site and select a Fortune 500 corporation. The site's address is

www.fortune.com

b. Visit NASDAQ's home page at

www.nasdaq.com

and select a small corporation.

c. Get a Detailed Quote for the company from PCQUOTE's Internet site at

www.pcquote.com

Indicate the current price of each corporation's stock, including its high and low price for the day. (**Note:** If either of the companies has a net loss for the most recent period, go back and replace it with a profitable company.)

d. Compare the price-earnings ratios (as shown on the Detailed Quote screen) of the two companies. Speculate as to why one company has a higher price-earnings ratio than the other.

Note: Additional Internet assignments are available in Appendix B and on our home page.

OUR COMMENTS ON THE IN-TEXT CASES

YOU AS AN INVESTOR (P. 572) The best starting point for estimating future net income would be net income from *continuing operations*. It is calculated as $2,550,000 ($2,000,000 + $750,000 + $300,000 − $500,000). Discontinued operations, extraordinary items, and accounting changes generally would not be expected to be experienced in future years.

YOU AS A BOARD MEMBER (P. 581) Just because the corporation has earnings does not mean that there is cash available for dividends. The earnings may be invested in new stores, inventories, or any other types of assets. Since the corporation is small and growing, it is likely in need of all of the capital it can get. Profitable operations are one of the most important sources of financing for a small business.

To appease the stockholders, the board of directors might consider declaring a stock dividend or a stock split. This would provide the stockholders with additional shares of stock, while retaining the company's liquid resources in the business.

ANSWERS TO SELF-TEST QUESTIONS

1. b   **2.** d   **3.** c   **4.** a   **5.** b

A LOOK BACK— AND AHEAD

For the most part, we have completed our technical discussions of how financial accounting information is developed and used. Our primary goal in these final chapters is to review key concepts to ensure that you have a "general understanding" that will serve you well.

As we said at the beginning of this text, an understanding of accounting is not just useful—in today's business world, it's essential.

PART FIVE

MEASURING CASH FLOWS

Every business measures its cash flows. Why? Management needs this information to keep the business solvent, maintain internal control, evaluate departmental performance, plan future business activities, and meet financial reporting requirements. Investors and creditors, too, look closely at a company's cash flows. A business which does not generate enough cash to meet its obligations just isn't going to "make it."

1. Explain the purpose and usefulness of a statement of cash flows.
2. Describe how cash transactions are classified within a statement of cash flows.
3. Compute the major cash flows relating to operating activities.
4. Explain why net income differs from net cash flow from operating activities.
5. Distinguish between the direct and indirect methods of reporting operating cash flow.

6. Compute the cash flows relating to investing and financing activities.
7. Discuss the likely effects of various business strategies upon cash flows.
*8. Compute net cash flow from operating activities using the *indirect* method.
**9. Explain the role of a worksheet in preparing a statement of cash flows.

In Chapter 1, we introduced two key financial objectives of every business organization: *operating profitably* and *staying solvent.* Operating profitably means increasing the amount of the owners' equity through the activities of the business; staying solvent means being able to pay the debts and obligations of the business as they come due.

An income statement is designed to measure the success or failure of the business in achieving its objective of profitable operations. To some extent, a balance sheet shows whether or not the business is solvent. It shows, for example, the nature and amounts of current assets and current liabilities. From this information, users of the financial statements may compute such measures of solvency as the current ratio and the amount of working capital.

However, assessing the ability of a business to remain solvent involves more than just evaluating the liquid resources on hand at the balance sheet date. How much cash does the company receive during a year? What are the sources of these cash receipts? What expenditures are made each year for operating activities and for investing and financing activities? To answer these questions, companies prepare a third major financial statement, called the *statement of cash flows.*

We introduced the statement of cash flows in Chapter 6. In many subsequent chapters, we have explained the cash effects of various transactions. In this chapter we summarize our previous discussions and expand upon them. Next, we illustrate how a statement of cash flows can be prepared from accrual-basis accounting records and, more importantly, explain the *differences* between accrual-based measurements and cash flows. In the final section of the chapter, we discuss strategies for *improving* the net cash flow from operating activities.

STATEMENT OF CASH FLOWS

PURPOSE OF THE STATEMENT

The basic purpose of a statement of cash flows is to provide information about the *cash receipts* and *cash payments* of a business entity during the accounting period. (The term **cash flows** includes both cash receipts and cash payments.) In addition, the statement is intended to provide information about all the *investing* and *financing* activities of the company during the period. Thus, a statement of cash flows should assist investors, creditors, and others in assessing such factors as:

LO 1 *Explain the purpose and usefulness of a statement of cash flows.*

---

*Supplemental Topic A, "The Indirect Method."
**Supplemental Topic B, "A Worksheet for Preparing a Statement of Cash Flows."

- The company's ability to generate positive cash flows in future periods.
- The company's ability to meet its obligations and to pay dividends.
- The company's need for external financing.
- Reasons for differences between the amount of net income and the related net cash flow from operating activities.
- Both the cash and noncash aspects of the company's investment and financing transactions for the period.
- Causes of the change in the amount of cash and cash equivalents between the beginning and the end of the accounting period.

In summary, a statement of cash flows helps users of financial statements evaluate a company's ability to "come up with the cash"—both on a short-run and on a long-run basis. For this reason, the statement of cash flows is useful to virtually everyone interested in the company's financial health: short- and long-term creditors, investors, management—and both current and prospective competitors.

EXAMPLE OF A STATEMENT OF CASH FLOWS

An example of a statement of cash flows appears below. Cash outflows are shown in parentheses.[1]

ALLISON CORPORATION Statement of Cash Flows For the Year Ended December 31, 19__		
Cash flows from operating activities:		
Cash received from customers..	$ 870,000	
Interest and dividends received..	10,000	
Cash provided by operating activities............................		$880,000
Cash paid to suppliers and employees.............................	$(764,000)	
Interest paid..	(28,000)	
Income taxes paid	(38,000)	
Cash disbursed for operating activities..........................		(830,000)
Net cash provided by operating activities.............................		$ 50,000
Cash flows from investing activities:		
Purchases of marketable securities	$ (65,000)	
Proceeds from sales of marketable securities....................	40,000	
Loans made to borrowers..	(17,000)	
Collections on loans	12,000	
Purchases of plant assets	(160,000)	
Proceeds from sales of plant assets................................	75,000	
Net cash used in investing activities.....................................		(115,000)
Cash flows from financing activities:		
Proceeds from short-term borrowing................................	$ 45,000	
Payments to settle short-term debts	(55,000)	
Proceeds from issuing bonds payable	100,000	
Proceeds from issuing capital stock.................................	50,000	
Dividends paid	(40,000)	
Net cash provided by financing activities.............................		100,000
Net increase (decrease) in cash...		$ 35,000
Cash and cash equivalents, beginning of year.....................		20,000
Cash and cash equivalents, end of year		$ 55,000

---

[1]In this illustration, net cash flow from operating activities is determined by the *direct method.* An alternative approach, called the *indirect method,* is illustrated later in this chapter.

CLASSIFICATION OF CASH FLOWS

The cash flows shown in the statement are grouped into three major categories: (1) **operating activities,** (2) **investing activities,** and (3) **financing activities.**[2] We will now look briefly at the way cash flows are classified among these three categories.

LO 2 *Describe how cash transactions are classified within a statement of cash flows.*

OPERATING ACTIVITIES   The operating activities section shows the *cash effects* of revenue and expense transactions. To illustrate this concept, consider the effects of credit sales. Credit sales are reported in the income statement in the period when the sales occur. But the cash effects occur later—when the receivables are collected in cash. Similar differences may exist between the recognition of an expense and the related cash payment. Consider, for example, the expense of postretirement benefits earned by employees during the current period. If this expense is not funded with a trustee, the cash payments may not occur for many years—after today's employees have retired.

In summary, cash flows from operating activities include:

Cash Receipts	Cash Payments
Collections from customers for sales of goods and services	Payments to suppliers of merchandise and services, including payments to employees
Interest and dividends received	Payments of interest
Other receipts from operations, as, for example, proceeds from settlement of litigation	Payments of income taxes
	Other expenditures relating to operations, as, for example, payments in settlement of litigation

Notice that receipts and payments of *interest* are classified as operating activities, not as investing or financing activities.

INVESTING ACTIVITIES   Cash flows relating to investing activities include:

Cash Receipts	Cash Payments
Cash proceeds from selling investments or plant assets	Payments to acquire investments or plant assets
Cash proceeds from collecting principal amounts on loans	Amounts advanced to borrowers

FINANCING ACTIVITIES   Cash flows classified as financing activities include the following:

Cash Receipts	Cash Payments
Proceeds from both short-term and long-term borrowing	Repayments of amounts borrowed (excluding interest payments)
Cash received from owners (as, for example, from issuing stock)	Payments to owners, such as cash dividends

Repayment of amounts borrowed refers to repayment of *loans,* not to payments made on accounts payable or accrued liabilities. Payments of accounts payable and of accrued liabilities are considered "payments to suppliers of merchandise and

---

[2]A fourth classification, "effects of changes in exchange rates on cash," is used in the cash flow statements of companies with foreign currency holdings. This fourth classification will be discussed in the intermediate accounting course.

services" and are classified as a cash outflow from operating activities. Also, remember that all interest payments are classified as operating activities.

WHY ARE RECEIPTS AND PAYMENTS OF INTEREST "OPERATING ACTIVITIES"?   One might argue that interest receipts from investing activities, and that interest payments are related to financing activities. The FASB considered this point of view but decided instead to classify interest receipts and payments as operating activities. The FASB wanted net cash flow from operating activities to reflect the cash effects of the revenue and expense transactions entering into the determination of net income. As interest revenue and interest expense enter into the determination of net income, the FASB decided to classify the related cash flows as operating activities. Payments of dividends, however, *do not* enter into the determination of net income. Therefore, dividend payments are viewed as financing activities.

CASH AND "CASH EQUIVALENTS"   For purposes of preparing a statement of cash flows, the FASB has defined "cash" as including *both cash and cash equivalents*. **Cash equivalents** are short-term, highly liquid investments, such as money market funds, commercial paper, and Treasury bills. Transfers of money between a company's bank accounts and these cash equivalents are *not viewed as cash receipts or cash payments*. Money is considered "cash" regardless of whether it is held in currency, in a bank account, or in the form of cash equivalents. However, any interest received from owning cash equivalents is included in cash receipts from operating activities.

Cash equivalents are limited to short-term, highly liquid investments such as those specified above. Marketable securities, such as investments in the stocks and bonds of other companies, *do not qualify as cash equivalents*. Therefore, purchases and sales of marketable securities *do* result in cash flows that are reported in the statement of cash flows.

CRITICAL IMPORTANCE OF CASH FLOW FROM OPERATING ACTIVITIES

In the long run, a business must generate a positive net cash flow from its operating activities if the business is to survive. A business with negative cash flows from operations will not be able to raise cash from other sources indefinitely. In fact, the ability of a business to raise cash through financing activities is highly dependent upon its ability to generate cash from its normal business operations. Creditors and stockholders are reluctant to invest in a company that does not generate enough cash from operating activities to ensure prompt payment of maturing liabilities, interest, and dividends.

THE APPROACH TO PREPARING A STATEMENT OF CASH FLOWS

The items listed in an income statement or a balance sheet represent the balances of specific general ledger accounts. Notice, however, that the captions used in the statement of cash flows *do not* correspond to specific ledger accounts. A statement of cash flows summarizes *cash transactions* during the accounting period. The general ledger, however, is maintained on the *accrual basis* of accounting, not the cash basis. Thus, an amount such as "Cash received from customers . . . $870,000" does not appear as the balance in a specific ledger account.

In a very small business, it may be practical to prepare a statement of cash flows directly from the special journals for cash receipts and cash payments. For most businesses, however, it is easier to prepare the statement of cash flows by examining the income statement and the *changes* during the period in all of the balance sheet accounts *except for* Cash. This approach is based upon the double-entry system of accounting; any transaction affecting cash must also affect some other asset, liability, or owners' equity account.[3] The change in these *other accounts* makes clear the nature of the cash transaction.

To illustrate this approach, assume that the Marketable Securities controlling account of Allison Corporation shows the following activity during the year:

Balance, January 1, 19__	$ 70,000
Debit entries during the year	65,000
Credit entries during the year	(44,000)
Balance, December 31, 19__	$ 91,000

Also assume that the company's income statement for the year includes a *$4,000 loss* on sales of marketable securities.

The *debit entries* in the Marketable Securities account represent the cost of securities *purchased* during the year. These debit entries provide the basis for the item *"Purchases of marketable securities . . . $(65,000)"* appearing in the investing activities section of the statement of cash flows (page 614). Thus, increases in the asset marketable securities correspond to an outflow of cash.

The credit entries of $44,000 represent the *cost* of securities sold during the year. Remember, however, that the income statement shows that these securities were sold at a *loss of $4,000*. The cash proceeds from these sales, which also appear in the statement of cash flows, may be computed as follows:

Cost of marketable securities sold	$44,000
Less: Loss on sales of marketable securities	4,000
Proceeds from sales of marketable securities	$40,000

By looking at the changes occurring in the Marketable Securities account and the related income statement account, we were able to determine quickly two items appearing in the company's statement of cash flows. We could have assembled the same information from the company's cash journals, but we would have had to review the journals for the entire year and then added together the cash flows of numerous individual transactions. In summary, it usually is more efficient to prepare a statement of cash flows by analyzing the *changes in noncash accounts* than by locating and combining numerous entries in the company's journals.

PREPARING A STATEMENT OF CASH FLOWS: AN ILLUSTRATION

Earlier in this chapter we illustrated the statement of cash flows of Allison Corporation. We will now show how this statement was developed from the company's accrual-basis accounting records.

Basically, a statement of cash flows can be prepared from the data contained in an income statement and *comparative* balance sheets at the beginning and end of the period. It is also necessary, however, to have some detailed information about the *changes* occurring during the period in certain balance sheet accounts. Shown below and at the top of the following page are Allison's income statement and comparative balance sheets for the current year, and also the necessary information about the changes in balance in accounts.

---

[3]Revenue, expenses, and dividends represent changes in owners' equity and, therefore, may be regarded as "owners' equity accounts."

ALLISON CORPORATION
Income Statement
For the Year Ended December 31, 19__

Revenue and gains:

Net sales		$900,000
Dividends revenue		3,000
Interest revenue		6,000
Gain on sales of plant assets		31,000
Total revenue and gains		$940,000

Costs, expenses, and losses:

Cost of goods sold	$500,000	
Operating expenses (including depreciation of $40,000)	300,000	
Interest expense	35,000	
Income taxes expense	36,000	
Loss on sales of marketable securities	4,000	
Total costs, expenses, and losses		875,000
Net income		$ 65,000

ALLISON CORPORATION
Comparative Balance Sheets
Current Year

	Year-End (Dec. 31)	Beginning of the Year
Assets		
Current assets:		
Cash and cash equivalents	$ 55,000	$ 20,000
Marketable securities	85,000	64,000
Notes receivable	17,000	12,000
Accounts receivable	110,000	80,000
Accrued interest receivable	2,000	3,000
Inventory	100,000	90,000
Prepaid expenses	4,000	1,000
Total current assets	$373,000	$270,000
Plant and equipment (net of accumulated depreciation)	616,000	500,000
Total assets	$989,000	$770,000
Liabilities & Stockholders' Equity		
Current liabilities:		
Notes payable (short-term)	$ 45,000	$ 55,000
Accounts payable	76,000	61,000
Interest payable	22,000	15,000
Income taxes payable	8,000	10,000
Other accrued expenses payable	3,000	9,000
Total current liabilities	$154,000	$150,000
Long-term liabilities:		
Notes payable (long-term)	40,000	–0–
Bonds payable	400,000	300,000
Total liabilities	$594,000	$450,000
Stockholders' equity:		
Capital stock	$ 60,000	$ 50,000
Additional paid-in capital	140,000	100,000
Retained earnings	195,000	170,000
Total stockholders' equity	$395,000	$320,000
Total liabilities & stockholders' equity	$989,000	$770,000

ADDITIONAL INFORMATION An analysis of changes in the balance sheet accounts of Allison Corporation provides the following information about the company's activities in the current year. To assist in the preparation of a statement of cash flows, we have classified this information into the categories of operating activities, investing activities, and financing activities.

OPERATING ACTIVITIES

1. Accounts receivable increased by $30,000 during the year.

2. Dividend revenue is recognized on the cash basis, but interest revenue is recognized on the accrual basis. Accrued interest receivable decreased by $1,000 during the year.

3. Inventory increased by $10,000 and accounts payable increased by $15,000 during the year.

4. During the year, short-term prepaid expenses increased by $3,000 and accrued expenses payable (other than for interest or income taxes) decreased by $6,000. Depreciation for the year amounted to $40,000.

5. The accrued liability for interest payable increased by $7,000 during the year.

6. The accrued liability for income taxes payable decreased by $2,000 during the year.

INVESTING ACTIVITIES

7. Analysis of the Marketable Securities account shows debit entries of $65,000 representing the cost of securities purchased, and credit entries of $44,000 representing the cost of securities sold. (None of the marketable securities is viewed as a cash equivalent.)

8. Analysis of the Notes Receivable account shows $17,000 in debit entries, representing cash lent to borrowers by Allison Corporation during the year, and $12,000 in credit entries, representing collections of notes receivable. (Collections of interest were recorded in the Interest Revenue account and are considered cash flows from operating activities.)

9. Allison's plant asset accounts increased by $116,000 during the year. An analysis of the underlying transactions indicates the following:

	Effect Upon Plant Asset Accounts
Purchased $200,000 in plant assets, paying $160,000 cash and issuing a long-term note payable for the $40,000 balance	$200,000
Sold for $75,000 cash plant assets with a book value of $44,000	(44,000)
Recorded depreciation expense for the period	(40,000)
Net change in plant asset controlling accounts...	$116,000

FINANCING ACTIVITIES

10. During the year, Allison Corporation borrowed $45,000 cash by issuing short-term notes payable to banks. Also, the company repaid $55,000 in principal amounts due on these loans and other notes payable. (Interest payments are classified as operating activities.)

11. The company issued bonds payable for $100,000 cash.

12. The company issued for cash 1,000 shares of $10 par value capital stock at a price of $50 per share.

13. Cash dividends declared and paid to stockholders amounted to $40,000 during the year.

CASH AND CASH EQUIVALENTS

14. Cash and cash equivalents as shown in Allison Corporation's balance sheets amounted to $20,000 at the beginning of the year and $55,000 at year-end— a net increase of $35,000.

Using this information, we will now illustrate the steps in preparing Allison Corporation's statement of cash flows and also a supporting schedule disclosing the "noncash" investing and financing activities. In our discussion, we will often refer to these items of "Additional Information" by citing the paragraph numbers shown in the above list.

The distinction between accrual-basis measurements and cash flows is of fundamental importance in understanding financial statements and other accounting reports. To assist in making this distinction, we use two colors in our illustrated computations. We show in *blue* the accrual-based data from Allison Corporation's income statement and the preceding numbered paragraphs. The cash flows that we compute from this data are shown in *red*.

LO 3 *Compute the major cash flows relating to operating activities.*

CASH FLOWS FROM OPERATING ACTIVITIES

As shown in our statement of cash flows on page 614, the net cash flow from operating activities is determined by combining certain cash inflows and subtracting certain cash outflows. The inflows are cash received from customers, and interest and dividends received; the outflows are cash paid to suppliers and employees, interest paid, and income taxes paid.

In computing each of these cash flows, our starting point is an income statement amount, such as net sales, the cost of goods sold, or interest expense. As you study each computation, be sure that you *understand why* the income statement amount must be increased or decreased to determine the related cash flow. You will find that an understanding of these computations will do more than show you how to compute cash flows: it will also strengthen your understanding of the income statement and the balance sheet.

CASH RECEIVED FROM CUSTOMERS To the extent that sales are made for cash, there is no difference between the amount of cash received from customers and the amount recorded as sales revenue. Differences do arise, however, when sales are made on account. If accounts receivable have increased during the year, credit sales have exceeded collections of accounts receivable. Therefore, we must *deduct the increase* in accounts receivable over the year from net sales in order to determine the amount of cash received. If accounts receivable have decreased over the year, collections of these accounts must have exceeded credit sales. Therefore, we must *add the decrease* in accounts receivable to net sales to determine the amount of cash received. The relationship between cash received from customers and net sales is summarized below:

$$\begin{matrix} \textbf{Cash Received} \\ \textbf{from Customers} \end{matrix} = \begin{matrix} \textbf{Net} \\ \textbf{Sales} \end{matrix} \left\{ \begin{matrix} \textbf{+ Decrease in Accounts Receivable} \\ \textit{or} \\ \textbf{– Increase in Accounts Receivable} \end{matrix} \right\}$$

The increase or decrease in accounts receivable is determined simply by comparing the year-end balance in the account to its balance at the beginning of the year.

In our Allison Corporation example, paragraph **1** of the Additional Information tells us that accounts receivable have *increased* by $30,000 during the year. The income statement shows net sales for the year of $900,000. Therefore, the amount of cash received from customers may be computed as follows:

Net sales (accrual basis)	$900,000
Less: Increase in accounts receivable	30,000
Cash received from customers	$870,000

INTEREST AND DIVIDENDS RECEIVED   Our next objective is to determine the amounts of cash received during the year as dividends and interest. As explained in paragraph **2** of the Additional Information, dividend revenue is recorded on the cash basis. Therefore, the $3,000 shown in the income statement also represents the amount of cash received as dividends.

Interest revenue, on the other hand, is recognized on the accrual basis. We have already shown how to convert one type of revenue, net sales, from the accrual basis to the cash basis. We may use the same approach to convert interest revenue from the accrual basis to the **cash basis.** Our formula for converting net sales to the cash basis may be modified to convert interest revenue to the cash basis as follows:

$$\frac{\text{Interest}}{\text{Received}} = \frac{\text{Interest}}{\text{Revenue}} \left\{ \begin{array}{c} + \text{ Decrease in Interest Receivable} \\ \text{or} \\ - \text{ Increase in Interest Receivable} \end{array} \right\}$$

The income statement for Allison Corporation shows interest revenue of $6,000, and paragraph **2** states that the amount of accrued interest receivable has *decreased* by $1,000 during the year. Thus, the amount of cash received as interest may be computed as follows:

Interest revenue (accrual basis)	$6,000
Add: Decrease in accrued interest receivable	1,000
Interest received (cash basis)	$7,000

The amounts of interest and dividends received in cash are combined for presentation in the statement of cash flows:

Interest received (cash basis)	$ 7,000
Dividends received (cash basis)	3,000
Interest and dividends received	$10,000

CASH PAYMENTS FOR MERCHANDISE AND FOR EXPENSES

The next item in the statement of cash flows, "Cash paid to suppliers and employees," includes all cash payments for purchases of merchandise and for operating expenses (all expenses other than interest and income taxes). Payments of interest and income taxes are listed as a separate item in the statement. The amounts of cash paid for purchases of merchandise and for operating expenses are computed separately.

CASH PAID FOR PURCHASES OF MERCHANDISE   An accrual basis income statement reflects the *cost of goods sold* during the year, regardless of whether the merchandise was acquired or paid for in that period. The statement of cash flows, on the other hand, reports the *cash paid* for merchandise during the year, even if the merchandise was acquired in a previous period or remains unsold at year-end. The relationship between cash payments for merchandise and the cost of goods sold depends upon the changes during the period in *two* related balance sheet accounts: inventory and accounts payable to suppliers of merchandise. This relationship may be stated as follows:

$$\text{Cash Payments for Purchases} = \text{Cost of Goods Sold} \begin{Bmatrix} + \text{ Increase in} \\ \text{Inventory} \\ \text{or} \\ - \text{ Decrease in} \\ \text{Inventory} \end{Bmatrix} \text{and} \begin{Bmatrix} + \text{ Decrease in} \\ \text{Accounts Payable} \\ \text{or} \\ - \text{ Increase in} \\ \text{Accounts Payable} \end{Bmatrix}$$

Using information from the Allison Corporation income statement and paragraph **3,** the cash payments for purchases may be computed as follows:

Cost of goods sold	$500,000
Add: Increase in inventory	10,000
Net purchases (accrual basis)	$510,000
Less: Increase in accounts payable to suppliers	15,000
Cash payments for purchases of merchandise	$495,000

Let us review the logic behind this computation. If a company is increasing its inventory, it is *buying more merchandise than it sells* during the period. However, if the company is increasing its account payable to merchandise creditors, it is *not paying cash* for all of these purchases.

CASH PAYMENTS FOR EXPENSES Expenses, as shown in the income statement, represent the cost of goods and services used up during the period. However, the amounts shown as expenses may differ significantly from the cash payments made during the period. Consider, for example, depreciation expense. Recording depreciation expense *requires no cash payment,* but it does increase total expenses measured on the accrual basis. Thus, in converting accrual-basis expenses to the cash basis, we must deduct depreciation expense and any other "noncash" expenses from our accrual-basis operating expenses. The other noncash expenses—expenses not requiring cash outlays—include amortization of intangible assets, any unfunded portion of postretirement benefits expense, and amortization of bond discount.

A second area of difference arises from short-term *timing differences* between the recognition of expenses and the actual cash payments. Expenses are recorded in accounting records when the related goods or services are used. However, the cash payments for these expenses might occur (1) in an earlier period, (2) in the same period, or (3) in a later period. Let us briefly consider each case.

1. If payment is made in advance, the payment creates an asset, termed a prepaid expense, or, in our formula, a "prepayment." Thus, to the extent that prepaid expenses increase over the year, cash payments *exceed* the amount recognized as expense.

2. If payment is made in the same period, no problem arises because the cash payment is equal to the amount of expense.

3. If payment is made in a later period, the payment reduces a liability for an accrued expense payable. Thus, to the extent that accrued expenses payable decrease over the year, cash payments exceed the amount recognized as expense.

The relationship between cash payments and accrual-basis expenses are summarized below:

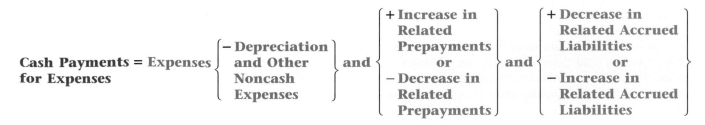

$$\text{Cash Payments for Expenses} = \text{Expenses} \begin{Bmatrix} - \text{ Depreciation} \\ \text{and Other} \\ \text{Noncash} \\ \text{Expenses} \end{Bmatrix} \text{and} \begin{Bmatrix} + \text{ Increase in} \\ \text{Related} \\ \text{Prepayments} \\ \text{or} \\ - \text{ Decrease in} \\ \text{Related} \\ \text{Prepayments} \end{Bmatrix} \text{and} \begin{Bmatrix} + \text{ Decrease in} \\ \text{Related Accrued} \\ \text{Liabilities} \\ \text{or} \\ - \text{ Increase in} \\ \text{Related Accrued} \\ \text{Liabilities} \end{Bmatrix}$$

In a statement of cash flows, cash payments for interest and for income taxes are shown separately from cash payments for operating expenses. Using data from Allison Corporation's income statement and from paragraph **4,** we may compute the company's cash payments for operating expenses as follows:

Operating expenses (including depreciation)		$300,000
Less: Noncash expenses (depreciation)		40,000
Subtotal		$260,000
Add: Increase in short-term prepayments	$3,000	
Decrease in accrued liabilities	6,000	9,000
Cash payments for operating expenses		$269,000

CASH PAID TO SUPPLIERS AND EMPLOYEES The caption used in our cash flow statement, "Cash paid to suppliers and employees," includes both cash payments for purchases of merchandise and for operating expenses. This cash outflow may now be computed as follows:

Cash payments for purchases of merchandise	$495,000
Cash payments for operating expenses	269,000
Cash payments to suppliers and employees	$764,000

CASH PAYMENTS FOR INTEREST AND TAXES Interest expense and income taxes expense may be converted to cash payments with the same formula we used to convert operating expenses. Allison Corporation's income statement shows interest expense of $35,000, and paragraph **5** states that the liability for interest payable increased by $7,000 during the year. The fact that the liability for unpaid interest *increased* over the year means that *not all of the interest expense shown in the income statement was paid in cash.* To determine the amount of interest actually paid, we must *subtract* from total interest expense the portion that has been financed through an increase in the liability for interest payable. This computation is shown below:

Interest expense	$35,000
Less: Increase in related accrued liability	7,000
Interest paid	$28,000

Similar reasoning is used to determine the amount of income taxes paid by Allison Corporation during the year. The accrual-based income taxes expense reported in the income statement amounts to $36,000. However, paragraph **6** states that the company has reduced its liability for income taxes payable by $2,000 over the year. Incurring income taxes expense increases the tax liability; making cash payments to tax authorities reduces it. Thus, if the liability *decreases* over the year, cash payments to tax authorities *must have been greater* than the income taxes expense for the current year. The amount of the cash payments is determined as follows:

Income taxes expense	$36,000
Add: Decrease in related accrued liability	2,000
Income taxes paid	$38,000

A QUICK REVIEW We have now shown the computation of each cash flow relating to Allison Corporation's operating activities. Previously we illustrated a complete statement of cash flows for the company. For your convenience, we will again show the operating activities section of that statement, illustrating the information developed in the preceding paragraphs.

Cash flows from operating activities:

Cash received from customers	$ 870,000	
Interest and dividends received	10,000	
Cash provided by operating activities		$ 880,000
Cash paid to suppliers and employees	$(764,000)	
Interest paid	(28,000)	
Income taxes paid	(38,000)	
Cash disbursed for operating activities		(830,000)
Net cash flow from operating activities		$ 50,000

DIFFERENCES BETWEEN NET INCOME AND NET CASH FLOW FROM OPERATING ACTIVITIES

Allison Corporation reported net income of *$65,000*, but net cash flow from operating activities of only *$50,000*. What caused this $15,000 difference?

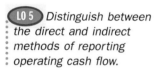 *Explain why net income differs from net cash flow from operating activities.*

The answer, in short, is many things. First, *depreciation expense* reduces net income but does not affect net cash flow. Next, all the adjustments that we made to net sales, cost of goods sold, and expenses represented short-term *timing differences* between net income and the underlying net cash flow from operating activities. Finally, *nonoperating gains and losses* may cause substantial differences between net income and net cash flow from operations.

Nonoperating gains and losses may result from sales of plant assets, marketable securities, and other investments; and from the retirement of long-term debt. These gains and losses affect the cash flows relating to investing or financing activities, not the cash flows from operating activities.

REPORTING OPERATING CASH FLOW: THE DIRECT AND INDIRECT METHODS

In our illustration, we use the **direct method** of computing and reporting the net cash flow from operating activities. The direct method shows the *specific cash inflows and outflows* comprising the operating activities of the business. The FASB has expressed its preference for the direct method, but it also allows companies to use an alternative, called the **indirect method.**

Distinguish between the direct and indirect methods of reporting operating cash flow.

Computation of net cash flow from operating activities by the indirect method looks quite different from the direct method computation. However, both methods result in the *same net cash flow* from operating activities. Under the direct method, the computation begins with accrual-based net income (as shown in the income statement) and then shows the various adjustments necessary to *reconcile net income with net cash flow from operating activities.* The general format of this computation is summarized below:

Net income
Add: • Expenses that do not require cash outlays in the period (such as depreciation expense)
• Operating cash inflows not recorded as revenue in the period
• "Nonoperating" losses deducted in the determination of net income
Less: • Revenue that does not result in cash inflows in the period
• Operating cash outflows not recorded as expense in the period
• "Nonoperating" gains included in the determination of net income
Net cash flow from operating activities

The preceding summary describes the differences between net income and net cash flow from operating activities in broad, general terms. In an actual statement of cash flows, a dozen or more specific items may appear in this reconciliation. (*Supplementary Schedule A,* on page 628, illustrates the application of the indirect method to the operating activities of Allison Corporation.)

In this chapter we emphasize the *direct* method, as we consider it to be the more informative approach, and it is the method recommended by the FASB.

Most of our assignment material is based upon the direct method. Further coverage of the indirect method is provided in the *Supplemental Topic A* at the end of the chapter.

CASH FLOWS FROM INVESTING ACTIVITIES

Paragraphs **7** through **9** in the Additional Information for our Allison Corporation example provide most of the information necessary to determine the cash flows from investing activities. In the following discussion, we will illustrate the presentation of these cash flows and also explain the sources of the information contained in the numbered paragraphs.

LO 6 *Compute the cash flows relating to investing and financing activities.*

Much information about investing activities can be obtained simply by looking at the changes in the related asset accounts during the year. Debit entries in these accounts represent purchases of the assets, or cash outlays. Credit entries represent sales of the assets, or cash receipts. However, credit entries in asset accounts represent only the *cost* (or *book value*) of the assets sold. To determine the cash proceeds from these sales transactions, we must adjust the amount of the credit entries for any gains or losses recognized on the sales.

PURCHASES AND SALES OF SECURITIES   To illustrate, consider paragraph **7,** which summarizes the debit and credit entries to the Marketable Securities account. As explained earlier in this chapter, the $65,000 in debit entries represent purchases of marketable securities. The $44,000 in credit entries represent the *cost* of marketable securities sold during the period. However, the income statement shows that these securities were sold at a *$4,000 loss*. Thus, the cash proceeds from these sales amounted to only *$40,000* ($44,000 cost, minus $4,000 loss on sale). In the statement of cash flows, these investing activities are summarized as follows:

Purchases of marketable securities	$(65,000)
Proceeds from sales of marketable securities	$ 40,000

LOANS MADE AND COLLECTED   Paragraph **8** provides all the information necessary to summarize the cash flows from making and collecting loans:

Loans made to borrowers	$(17,000)
Collections on loans	$ 12,000

This information comes directly from the Notes Receivable account. Debit entries in the account represent new loans made during the year; credit entries indicate collections of the *principal* amount on outstanding notes (loans). (Interest received is credited to the Interest Revenue account and is included among the cash receipts from operating activities.)

CASH PAID TO ACQUIRE PLANT ASSETS   Paragraph **9** states that Allison Corporation purchased plant assets during the year for $200,000, paying $160,000 in cash and issuing a long-term note payable for the $40,000 balance. Notice that *only the $160,000 cash payment* appears in the statement of cash flows. However, one objective of this financial statement is to show all of the company's *investing and financing activities* during the year. Therefore, the *noncash aspects* of these transactions are shown in a supplementary schedule, as follows:

Supplementary Schedule of Noncash Investing and Financing Activities

Purchases of plant assets	$200,000
Less: Portion financed through issuance of long-term debt	40,000
Cash paid to acquire plant assets	$160,000

This supplementary schedule accompanies the statement of cash flows.

PROCEEDS FROM SALES OF PLANT ASSETS   Assume that an analysis of the plant asset accounts shows net credit entries totaling $44,000 in the year. ("Net credit entries" means all credit entries, net of related debits to accumulated depreciation when assets were sold.) These net credit entries represent the *book value* of plant assets sold during the year. However, the income statement shows that these assets were sold at a *gain of $31,000*. Therefore, the *cash proceeds* from sales of plant assets amounted to 75,000, as shown below:

Book value of plant assets sold	$44,000
Add: Gain on sales of plant assets	31,000
Proceeds from sales of plant assets	$75,000

The depreciation expense credited to the Accumulated Depreciation account is not a cash flow and is ignored.

CASH FLOWS FROM FINANCING ACTIVITIES

Cash flows from financing activities are determined by analyzing the debit and credit changes recorded during the period in the related liability and stockholders' equity accounts. In a sense, cash flows from financing activities are more easily determined than those relating to investing activities, because financing activities seldom involve gains or losses.[4] Thus, the debit or credit changes in the balance sheet accounts usually are equal to the amounts of the related cash flows.

Credit changes in such accounts as Notes Payable and the accounts for long-term debt and paid-in capital usually indicate cash receipts; debit changes indicate cash payments.

SHORT-TERM BORROWING TRANSACTIONS   To illustrate, consider paragraph **10,** which provides the information supporting the following cash flows:

Proceeds from short-term borrowing	$ 45,000
Payments to settle short-term debts	$(55,000)

Is it possible to determine the proceeds of short-term borrowing transactions throughout the year without carefully reviewing each cash receipt? The answer is *yes*—easily. The proceeds from short-term borrowing are equal to the *sum of the credit entries* in the short-term *Notes Payable* account. Payments to settle short-term debts are equal to the *sum of the debit entries* in this account.

PROCEEDS FROM ISSUING BONDS PAYABLE AND CAPITAL STOCK   Paragraph **11** states that Allison Corporation received cash of $100,000 by issuing bonds payable. This amount was determined by summing the credit entries in the Bonds Payable account. The Bonds Payable account included no debit entries during the year; thus, no bonds were retired.

Paragraph **12** states that during the year Allison Corporation issued capital stock for $50,000. The proceeds from issuing stock are equal to the sum of the credit entries made in the Capital Stock and Additional Paid-in Capital accounts.

CASH DIVIDENDS PAID TO STOCKHOLDERS   Paragraph **13** states that Allison Corporation declared and paid cash dividends of $40,000 during the year. In practice, most corporations pay cash dividends in the same year in which these dividends are declared. In these situations, the cash payments are equal to the related debit entries in the Retained Earnings account.

If the balance sheet includes a liability for dividends payable, the amounts debited to Retained Earnings represent dividends *declared* during the period,

---

[4]An early retirement of debt is an example of a financing transaction that may result in a gain or a loss.

which may differ from the amount of dividends *paid*. To determine cash dividends paid, we must adjust the amount of dividends declared by adding any decrease (or subtracting any increase) in the Dividends Payable account over the period.

RELATIONSHIP BETWEEN THE STATEMENT OF CASH FLOWS AND THE BALANCE SHEET

As stated in Chapter 9, the first asset appearing in the balance sheet is "Cash and cash equivalents." The statement of cash flows explains in some detail the change in this asset from one balance sheet date to the next. The last three lines in the cash flow statement illustrate this relationship, as shown in our Allison Corporation example:

Net increase (decrease) in cash and cash equivalents..	$35,000
Cash and cash equivalents, beginning of year..	20,000
Cash and cash equivalents, end of year	$55,000

THE STATEMENT OF CASH FLOWS: A SECOND LOOK

Allison Corporation's statement of cash flows was illustrated earlier in this chapter. Now that we have explained the nature and computation of each cash flow in that statement, a second illustration is in order. We use this second illustration, which appears on the following page, to illustrate the *indirect method* of reporting net cash flow from operating activities. (Our preceding illustration uses the *direct method*.) Also, we illustrate two *supplementary schedules* that often accompany a statement of cash flows.

Supplementary Schedule A illustrates the determination of net cash flow from operating activities by the *indirect method*. The purpose of this schedule is to explain the differences between the reported net income and the net cash flow from operating activities. This supplementary schedule also is required of companies that use the direct method of reporting operating cash flows.

Supplementary Schedule B discloses any "noncash" aspects of the company's investing and financing activities. This type of supplementary schedule is required whenever some aspects of the company's investing and financing activities do not coincide with cash flows occurring within the current period.

USING THE STATEMENT OF CASH FLOWS

The users of a statement of cash flows usually are most interested in the *net cash flow from operating activities*. Is the amount large enough to provide for necessary replacements of plant assets and maturing liabilities? And if so, is there enough left for the current dividend to look secure—or even be increased?

Even more important than the net cash flow from operating activities in any one year is the *trend* in this cash flow over a period of years—and the *consistency* of that trend from year to year. From everyone's perspective, the "best" results are a net cash flow from operating activities that increases each year by a substantial—but also predictable—percentage.[5]

"FREE CASH FLOW" Many analysts put a company's cash flows into perspective by computing a subtotal called **free cash flow.** Free cash flow is intended to represent the cash flow available to management for discretionary purposes, *after* the company has met all of its basic obligations relating to business operations.

---

[5]The computation of a *percentage change* was explained in Chapter 6. Percentage change is the dollar amount of change from one year to the next, expressed as a percentage of (divided by) the amount from the *earlier* of the two years.

ALLISON CORPORATION
Statement of Cash Flows
For the Year Ended December 31, 19__

Cash flows from operating activities:

Net cash provided by operating activities (see Supplementary Schedule A)		$ 50,000

Cash flows from investing activities:

Purchases of marketable securities	$ (65,000)	
Proceeds from sales of marketable securities	40,000	
Loans made to borrowers	(17,000)	
Collections on loans	12,000	
Cash paid to acquire plant assets (see Supplementary Schedule B)	(160,000)	
Proceeds from sales of plant assets	75,000	
Net cash used in investing activities		(115,000)

Cash flows from financing activities:

Proceeds from short-term borrowing	$ 45,000	
Payments to settle short-term debts	(55,000)	
Proceeds from issuing bonds payable	100,000	
Proceeds from issuing capital stock	50,000	
Dividends paid	(40,000)	
Net cash provided by financing activities		100,000
Net increase (decrease) in cash		$ 35,000
Cash and cash equivalents, beginning of year		20,000
Cash and cash equivalents, end of year		$ 55,000

Supplementary Schedule A: Net Cash Provided by Operating Activities

Net income		$ 65,000
Add: Depreciation expense		40,000
Decrease in accrued interest receivable		1,000
Increase in accounts payable		15,000
Increase in accrued liabilities		7,000
Nonoperating loss on sales of marketable securities		4,000
Subtotal		$ 132,000
Less: Increase in accounts receivable	$ 30,000	
Increase in inventory	10,000	
Increase in prepayments	3,000	
Decrease in accrued liabilities	8,000	
Nonoperating gain on sales of plant assets	31,000	82,000
Net cash provided by operating activities		$ 50,000

Supplementary Schedule B: Noncash Investing and Financing Activities

Purchases of plant assets	$ 200,000
Less: Portion financed through issuance of long-term debt	40,000
Cash paid to acquire plant assets	$ 160,000

Notice this supplementary schedule illustrating the indirect method of determining cash flow from operations

The term "free cash flow" is widely cited within the business community. Unfortunately, different analysts compute this measure in different ways, because there is no widespread agreement as to the "basic obligations relating to business operations." For example, are all expenditures for plant assets "basic obligations," or only those expenditures made to maintain the current level of productive capacity?

One common method of computing free cash flow is to deduct from the net cash flow from operating activities any net cash used for investments in plant assets and any dividends paid. This computation is shown below, using data from the Allison Corporation statement of cash flows shown earlier:

Net cash flow from operating activities		$ 50,000
Less: Net cash used for acquiring plant assets		
($160,000 − $75,000 proceeds)	$85,000	
Dividends paid	40,000	125,000
Free cash flow		$ (75,000)

What's left for discretionary purposes?

This computation suggests that Allison Corporation *did not* generate enough cash from operations to meet its basic obligations. Thus, management had to raise cash from other sources. But, of course, an analyst always should "look behind" the numbers. For example, was Allison's purchase of plant assets during the year a "basic obligation," or did it represent a discretionary expansion of the business?

As we have stated throughout this text, no single ratio or financial measurement ever tells the whole story.

ANNOTATED STATEMENT OF CASH FLOWS: MCI CORPORATION

A recent statement of cash flows of MCI Corporation appears on the following page. We have added notations which highlight some of the concepts emphasized in this chapter.

MANAGING CASH FLOWS

Management can do much to influence the cash flows of a particular period. In fact, it has a responsibility to "manage" cash flows. No business can afford to run out of cash and default on its obligations. Even being a few days late in meeting payrolls, or paying suppliers or creditors, can severely damage important business relationships. Thus, one of management's most basic responsibilities is to ensure that the business has enough cash to meet its obligations as they come due.

BUDGETING: THE PRIMARY CASH MANAGEMENT TOOL

The primary tool used by management to anticipate and shape future cash flows is a *cash budget*. A **cash budget** is a *forecast* of future cash receipts and payments. This budget is *not* a financial statement and is not widely distributed to people outside of the organization. To managers, however, it is among the most useful of all accounting reports.

In many ways, a cash budget is similar to a statement of cash flows. However, the budget shows the results *expected in future periods,* rather than those achieved in the past. Also, the cash budget is more *detailed,* usually showing expected cash flows month-by-month, and separately for every department within the organization.

Cash budgets serve many purposes. Among the most important are:

● Forcing managers to plan and coordinate the activities of their departments in advance.

● Providing managers with advance notice of the resources at their disposal and the results they are expected to achieve.

● Providing targets useful in evaluating departmental performance.

● Providing advance warnings of potential cash shortages.

MCI uses the
direct method →

Notice investing →
has a net use of cash . . .

. . . but financing
was a net source
of cash →

Ties into
balance sheet →

Supplementary →
schedule uses
the "indirect"
method

Always important →

MCI COMMUNICATIONS CORPORATION AND SUBSIDIARIES
Consolidated Statement of Cash Flows
Year Ended December 31, 1995
(in millions)

Cash flows from operating activities:

Cash received from customers	$14,786
Cash paid to suppliers and employees	(11,453)
Taxes paid	(410)
Interest paid	(113)
Interest received	169
Cash from operating activities	$ 2,979

Cash flows from investing activities:

Capital expenditures for property and equipment	$ (2,866)
Purchases of marketable securities	(4,630)
Proceeds from sales of marketable securities	5,930
Acquisition of businesses	(1,243)
Investment in News Corp.	(1,000)
Investment in affiliates	(494)
Other, net	11
Cash used for investing activities	$ (4,292)
Net cash flow before financing activities	$ (1,313)

Cash flows from financing activities:

Payment of senior notes and other debt	$ (305)
Commercial paper and bank credit facility activity, net	702
Issuance of common stock for employee plans	275
Payment of dividends on common and preferred stock	(33)
Purchase of treasury stock	(284)
Cash from financing activities	$ 355
Net decrease in cash and cash equivalents	$ (958)
Cash and cash equivalents at beginning of year	1,429
Cash and cash equivalents at end of year	$ 471

Reconciliation of net income to cash from operating activities:

Net income	$ 548
Depreciation and amortization	1,367
Asset write-down	520
Equity in losses of affiliated companies	187
Deferred income tax provision	144

Net change in operating activity accounts other than
cash and cash equivalents:

Receivables	(442)
Accounts payable	57
Other operating accounts	598
Cash from operating activities	$ 2,979

See accompanying notes

YOUR **TURN**

You as a Student

How is predicting future cash flows—receipts and outlays—useful in your daily life? Forecast your cash outlays in the coming month for: (1) housing, (2) food, and (3) "other." Where will the cash come from to finance these outlays?

*Our comments appear on page 665.

A comprehensive discussion of budgeting is beyond the scope of this chapter. Budgeting usually is one of the major topics addressed in the second accounting course.

WHAT PRIORITY SHOULD MANAGERS GIVE TO INCREASING NET CASH FLOWS?

Creditors and investors look to a company's cash flows to protect their investment and provide future returns. Trends in key cash flows (such as from operations and from free cash flow) affect a company's credit rating, stock price, and access to additional investment capital. For these reasons, management is under constant pressure to improve (meaning "increase") the key measures of cash flow.

Unfortunately, the pressure to report higher cash flows in the current period may *conflict* with managers' long-run responsibilities.

SHORT-TERM RESULTS VERSUS LONG-TERM GROWTH Often, short-term operating results can be improved at the expense of long-term growth. For example, reducing expenditures for developing new products will increase earnings and net cash flows in the current period. But over time, this strategy may lessen the company's competitiveness.

LO 7 *Discuss the likely effects of various business strategies upon cash flows.*

In contrast, the strategies most likely to promote long-term growth usually *reduce* earnings and cash flows in the near term—often by large amounts.

CASE **IN** POINT

Merck, the world's largest pharmaceutical company, spends upwards of *$1.3 billion* each year in its efforts to develop new products. And even after Merck makes a "breakthrough" discovery, it takes years of testing before a new product is brought to market.

Most expenditures for R&D are paid in cash and charged immediately to expense. Thus, in any given year, Merck's R&D costs *reduce* both earnings and cash flow by more than $1 billion (before taxes). Yet Merck's ongoing commitment to R&D has been a key factor in the company's success.

"ONE-TIME BOOSTS" IN CASH FLOW Some strategies can increase the net cash flow of the current period, but *without having much effect* upon future cash flows. Such strategies include collecting receivables more quickly, and reducing the size of inventory.

Assume, for example, that a company offers 60-day terms to its credit customers. Thus, credit sales made in January are collected in March, and credit sales made in February are collected in April. Notice that in each month, the company is collecting about *one month's* worth of credit sales.

Now assume that on March 1, the company changes its policies to allow only *30-day* credit terms. In April, the company will collect *two months'* worth of credit sales—those made in February (under 60-day terms) *and* those made in March (under 30-day terms).

This significantly increases the "Cash received from customers" for the month of April. But it does not signal higher cash flows for the months ahead. In May, the company will collect only those credit sales made in April. Thus, it quickly returns to the pattern of collecting about *one month's* credit sales in the current month. Shortening the collection period provided only a "one-time boost" in cash receipts.

A similar "one-time boost" may be achieved by reducing the size of inventory. This reduces the need for purchasing merchandise, *but only while inventory levels are falling.* Once the company stabilizes the size of its inventory at the new and lower level, its monthly purchases must return to approximately the quantity of goods sold during the period.

SOME STRATEGIES FOR PERMANENT IMPROVEMENTS IN CASH FLOW

Allow us now to discuss several strategies which may improve cash flows in *both* the short- and long-term. These are: *deferring income taxes, peak pricing,* and developing an *effective product mix.*

DEFERRING INCOME TAXES *Deferring* income taxes means using accounting methods for income tax purposes which legally *postpone* the payment of income taxes. An example is using an *accelerated depreciation method,* such as MACRS, for income tax purposes.

Deferring taxes may benefit a growing business *every year.* Thus, it is an effective and popular cash management strategy.[6]

PEAK PRICING Some businesses have more customers than they can handle—at least at certain times of the day or year. Examples of such businesses include popular restaurants, resort hotels, and telephone companies.

Peak pricing is a strategy of using sales prices both to increase revenue and to ration goods and services when total demand exceeds supply (or capacity). A higher price is charged during the "peak" periods of customer demand, and a lower price during "off-peak" periods. Peak pricing has two related goals. First, it *increases the seller's revenue* during the periods of greatest demand. Second, it *shifts* some of the demand to off-peak periods, when the business is better able to service additional customers.

CASE IN POINT

Beach House is a popular seafood restaurant in Cardiff-by-the-Sea. A lobster dinner regularly costs $16.95. But from *4:30 to 6:00 P.M.*, it's only *$9.95*. Why? Because prior to 6:00 P.M. Beach House has lots of empty tables. Later, the restaurant becomes so crowded that it often has to turn customers away.

In many situations, peak pricing benefits the business *and the public.* Off-peak prices generally are *lower* than if peak pricing were not employed. Thus, peak pricing may make goods and services available to customers who other-

---

[6]MACRS is explained in Chapter 9. Deferred income taxes are discussed further in Chapter 10 and Appendix F. The reason why a growing business can benefit from deferred taxes *every year,* is that each year it defers a *greater amount* than comes due from the past.

wise could not afford them. Also, peak pricing may prevent systems, such as cellular telephones, from becoming so overloaded that they simply cannot function.

It is important to recognize, however, that peak pricing is *not always appropriate*. For example, we would not expect hospitals or physicians to raise their prices during epidemics or natural disasters. The alternative to peak pricing is a single "all-the-time" price. In a single-price situation, demand in excess of capacity normally is handled on the basis of first-come, first-served.

YOUR TURN

You as a Marketing Manager

Assume you are the marketing manager for Toys "R" Us (the international chain). It is the 1996 Christmas season. A doll called Tickle-Me-Elmo has a suggested retail price of $29.95. The doll has become overwhelmingly popular and is in short supply. Customers who buy the doll are able to resell it for *hundreds of dollars* just by running a classified add in the newspaper.

Much news coverage is being given to the phenomenal prices these dolls command. Toys "R" Us easily could sell Tickle-Me-Elmo's for $100 or more.

Would you raise Elmo's price during this temporary period of excess demand? Explain your reasoning.

*Our comments appear on page 665.

DEVELOP AN EFFECTIVE PRODUCT MIX Another tool for increasing revenue and cash receipts is the "mix" of products offered for sale. The twin purposes of an effective **product mix** are to (1) increase total sales and (2) increase gross margins.

Some products "complement" one another, meaning the customer who buys one product often may purchase the other. Common examples of **complementary products** include french fries at a hamburger stand, snacks at a movie theater, and a car wash connected to a gas station.

Some complementary products are *essential* to satisfying the customer. (Would you be happy at a sports stadium that didn't sell food?) Others increase sales by *attracting customers* who also purchase other types of merchandise.

CASE IN POINT

The **Vons Companies, Inc.,** (Vons Markets) sell one gallon of milk for about $3.50, but a *two-gallon "pak"* costs only about $1 more. Why this special price on a two-gallon purchase? Because customers who buy milk two gallons at a time generally have several children—which means they are likely to buy lots of other groceries.

Some complementary products appear only to be incidental to the company's main product lines. But, in reality, these "incidental" items may *be* the company's most important products.

CASE IN POINT

Remco Business Products, Inc., sells a variety of office products, including copy machines. Like most businesses that sell major appliances, it also sells long-term service contracts to provide maintenance and repairs at a fixed annual fee. These service contracts actually are Remco's most profitable product. In fact, if you purchase a service contract, you won't need to buy a copier. Remco will lend you one for the life of the service contract at no additional charge.

CONCLUDING COMMENTS . . .

In summary, we urge managers and investors alike to look beyond changes in earnings and cash flows from one period to the next. Consider the factors that *cause* these changes and how they may affect future operations.

There is more to financial statement analysis than looking at current numbers and short-term trends. The informed decision maker must *understand the company's business activities,* and *anticipate the long-term effects* of its business strategies.

NET CONNECTIONS

One of management's most important responsibilities is to efficiently manage the company's cash flows. This can be especially challenging for the managers of small businesses, which cannot afford to maintain an accounting staff. But help is available on the Net—and much of it is free. One useful resource is called Entrepreneurial Edge Online. You will find this free service at:

www.edgeonline.com

Select Business Builders from the main menu. You then may select from such topics as business communications, marketing, personnel management, customer service, strategic planning, expansion, and financial issues.

Under Financial Management, you will find Prepare a Cash Flow Statement and Prepare a Cash Budget. Both locations contain a wealth of information that should improve your understanding of these accounting reports.

Before leaving Edge Online, return to the home page and notice the many services this site provides—there are resource links, industry trends and news reports, tips from successful entrepreneurs, even access to an online roundtable discussion. You may find sites such as this useful throughout your business career.

*SUPPLEMENTAL TOPIC A

THE INDIRECT METHOD

LO 8 *Compute net cash flow from operating activities using the indirect method.*

In a statement of cash flows, the net cash flow from operating activities may be determined either by the *direct method* or the *indirect method*. We previously have illustrated both methods using the data in our Allison Corporation example. For your convenience, these illustrations are repeated below. (Accrual-based data appear in *blue;* cash flows are shown in *red*.)

Direct Method

Cash flows from operating activities:

Cash received from customers	$ 870,000	
Interest and dividends received	10,000	
Cash provided by operating activities		$ 880,000
Cash paid to suppliers and employees	$(764,000)	
Interest paid	(28,000)	
Income taxes paid	(38,000)	
Cash disbursed for operating activities		(830,000)
Net cash provided by operating activities		$ 50,000

Indirect Method

Net income		$ 65,000
Add: Depreciation expense		40,000
Decrease in accrued interest receivable		1,000
Increase in accounts payable		15,000
Increase in accrued interest liabilities		7,000
Nonoperating loss on sales of marketable securities		4,000
Subtotal		$ 132,000
Less: Increase in accounts receivable	$30,000	
Increase in inventory	10,000	
Increase in prepaid expenses	3,000	
Decrease in accrued operating expenses payable	6,000	
Decrease in accrued income taxes payable	2,000	
Nonoperating gain on sales of plant assets	31,000	82,000
Net cash provided by operating activities		$ 50,000

COMPARISON OF THE DIRECT AND INDIRECT METHODS

The two methods of computing net cash flow from operating activities are more similar than they appear at first glance. Both methods are based upon the same accounting data and both result in the *same net cash flow*. Also, the computations underlying both methods are quite similar. Both methods convert accrual-based income statement amounts into cash flows by adjusting for changes in related balance sheet accounts.

To illustrate the similarity in the computations, look briefly at the formulas for computing the cash inflows and outflows shown under the direct method (pages 620–622). Each formula begins with an income statement amount and then adds or subtracts the change during the period in related balance sheet accounts. Now look at our illustration of the indirect method. Notice that this computation also focuses upon the net changes during the period in balance sheet accounts.

The differences between the two methods lie only in format. However, the two formats provide readers of the cash flow statement with different types of information. The direct method informs these readers of the nature and dollar amounts of the *specific cash inflows and outflows* comprising the operating activities of the business. The indirect method, in contrast, *explains why* the net cash flow from operating activities differs from another measurement of performance—net income.

DIFFERENCES BETWEEN NET INCOME AND NET CASH FLOW FROM OPERATING ACTIVITIES

As previously stated, net cash flow from operating activities differs from net income for three major reasons. (**Note:** In the following discussions we will assume that both net income and net cash flow are positive amounts.)

1. **"Noncash" expenses.** Some expenses, such as depreciation expense, reduce net income but do not require any cash outlay during the current period.

2. **Timing differences.** Revenue and expenses are measured using the concepts of accrual accounting. Net cash flow, on the other hand, reflects the effects of cash transactions. Thus, revenue and expenses may be recognized in a different accounting period from the related cash flows.

3. **"Nonoperating" gains and losses.** By definition, net cash flow from operating activities shows only the effects of those cash transactions classified as "operating activities." Net income, on the other hand, may include gains and losses relating to investing and financing activities.

RECONCILING NET INCOME WITH NET CASH FLOW

To acquaint you with the indirect method, we will now discuss some common types of adjustments needed to reconcile net income with net cash flow from operating activities. The nature and dollar amounts of these adjustments are determined by an accountant using a worksheet or a computer program; they are *not* entered in the company's accounting records.

1. Adjustments for "Noncash" Expenses

Depreciation is an example of a "noncash" expense—that is, depreciation expense reduces net income but does not require any cash outlay during the period. Thus, expenses on the accrual basis exceed cash payments, and net income for the period is less than the net cash flow. To reconcile net income with net cash flow, we must add back to net income the amount of depreciation and any other noncash expenses. (Other noncash expenses included unfunded pension expense, amortization of intangible assets, depletion of natural resources, and amortization of bond discount.)

2. Adjusting for Timing Differences

Timing differences between net income and net cash flow arise whenever revenue or expense is recognized by debiting or crediting an account *other than* cash. Changes over the period in the balances of these asset and liability accounts represent differences between the amount of revenue or expense recognized in the income statement and the net cash flow from operating activities. The balance sheet accounts that give rise to these timing differences include accounts receivable, inventories, prepaid expenses, accounts payable, and accrued expenses payable. Let us look separately at the effects of changes in each type of account.

CHANGES IN ACCOUNTS RECEIVABLE Receivables increase as revenue is earned and decrease as cash is collected from customers. A net increase in accounts receivable over the period indicates that the revenue from credit sales exceeds collections from customers. Thus, net income measured on the accrual basis is *greater than* net cash flow; in our reconciliation of these two amounts, the net increase in accounts receivable is *deducted* from net income.

On the other hand, a net decrease in accounts receivable indicates cash receipts in excess of revenue from credit sales and is added to the amount of net income.

CHANGES IN INVENTORY The balance in the Inventory account increases as merchandise is purchased and decreases as goods are sold. A net increase in the Inventory account during the period indicates that purchases during the period exceed the cost of goods sold. Thus, to reconcile net income with net cash flow, we deduct from net income the amount of these additional purchases (the net increase in the balance of the Inventory account).

A net decrease in the balance of the Inventory account over the period indicates that the cost of goods sold (reported in the income statement) exceeds purchases made during the period. To the extent that the cost of goods sold consists of a decrease in inventory, no cash payment is required in the current period. Therefore, we add to net income the amount of a net decrease in inventory.

CHANGES IN PREPAID EXPENSES Prepaid expenses appear in the financial statements as assets. Increases in these assets result from cash payments, and decreases result from expiring amounts being recognized as expenses of the period. A net *increase* over the period in the amount of prepaid expenses indicates that cash payments made for these items must exceed the amounts recognized as expense. Thus, in determining net cash flow from operating activities, we deduct from net income the net increase in a company's prepaid expenses.

A net *decrease* in prepaid expenses indicates that cash outlays during the period were less than the amounts deducted as expense in the computation of net income. Thus, a net decrease in prepaid expenses is added back to net income.

CHANGES IN ACCOUNTS PAYABLE Accounts payable are increased by purchases on account and are reduced by cash payments to suppliers. A net increase in accounts payable indicates that the accrual-based figure for purchases, which is included in the cost of goods sold, is greater than the cash payments made to suppliers. Therefore, in converting net income to cash flow, we add back the amount of merchandise purchases financed by a net increase in accounts payable.

A net decrease in accounts payable indicates that cash payments to suppliers exceed the purchases made during the period. Thus, a net decrease in accounts payable is subtracted from net income in the computation of net cash flow.

CHANGES IN ACCRUED EXPENSES PAYABLE The liability for accrued expenses payable increases with the recognition of expenses that will be paid in the future and decreases as cash payments are made. A net increase in accrued expenses payable indicates that expenses in the period exceed the related cash payments. Thus, net income is less than net cash flow, and the increase in the accrued expenses payable accounts should be added to net income.

A net decrease in accrued expenses payable indicates that cash payments exceed the related amounts of expense. This decrease, therefore, is subtracted from net income.

The liability for deferred income taxes may be viewed as a long-term accrued expense payable. However, in the reconciliation of net income with net cash flow from operating activities, the change in the liability for deferred income taxes is shown separately from the net change in other accrued expenses payable. A net increase in this liability is added to net income; a net decrease is subtracted.

A HELPFUL HINT BASED ON DEBITS AND CREDITS In our preceding discussion, we explain *why* increases and decreases in a number of asset and liability accounts represent differences between the net income and net cash flow for the period. We do not expect you to memorize the effects of all of these changes. Rather, we hope that you will identify the types of transactions that cause a given account balance to increase or decrease and will then *evaluate the effects* of these transactions upon net income and net cash flow. This type of analysis will enhance your understanding of the relationships between accrual accounting and cash transactions.

However, let us offer you a quick hint. Double-entry accounting provides a simple rule that will let you check your analysis. For those asset and liability accounts that explain timing differences between net income and net cash flow, *a net credit change in the account's balance is always added to net income; a net debit change is always subtracted*. (For practice, test this rule on the adjustments in the summary of the indirect method appearing below. It applies to every adjustment that describes an increase or decrease in a balance sheet account.)

3. *Adjusting for "Nonoperating" Gains and Losses*

In a statement of cash flows, cash flows are classified as operating activities, investing activities, or financing activities. "Nonoperating" gains and losses, by definition, do not affect *operating activities*. However, these gains and losses do enter into the determination of net income. Therefore, in converting net income to net cash flow from operating activities, we *add back any nonoperating losses* and *deduct any nonoperating gains* included in net income.

Nonoperating gains and losses include gains and losses from sales of investments, plant assets, and discontinued operations (which relate to investing activities); and gains and losses on early retirement of debt (which relate to financing activities).

THE INDIRECT METHOD: A SUMMARY

The adjustments to net income explained in our preceding discussion are summarized as follows:

Net income	
Add:	Depreciation
	Decrease in accounts receivable
	Decrease in inventories
	Decrease in prepaid expenses
	Increase in accounts payable
	Increase in accrued expenses payable
	Increase in deferred income taxes payable
	"Nonoperating" losses deducted in computing net income
Deduct:	Increase in accounts receivable
	Increase in inventories
	Increase in prepaid expenses
	Decrease in accounts payable
	Decrease in accrued expenses payable
	"Nonoperating" gains included in net income
Net cash provided by (used in) operating activities	

INDIRECT METHOD MAY BE REQUIRED IN A SUPPLEMENTARY SCHEDULE

The FASB recommends use of the *direct method* in presenting net cash flow from operating activities. The vast majority of companies, however, elect to use the indirect method. One reason is that the FASB saddled companies opting for the direct method with an additional reporting requirement.

Companies using the direct method are required to provide a *supplementary schedule* illustrating the computation of net cash flow from operating activities by the indirect method. However, no supplementary computations are required of companies that illustrate the indirect method computations in their cash flow statements. In the opinion of these authors, this reporting requirement severely undermines the FASB's efforts to encourage use of the direct method.

SUPPLEMENTAL TOPIC B

A WORKSHEET FOR PREPARING A STATEMENT OF CASH FLOWS

A statement of cash flows is developed by *systematically analyzing changes in the noncash balance sheet accounts*. This process can be formalized and documented through the preparation of a specially designed worksheet. The worksheet also provides the accountant with visual assurance that the changes in balance sheet accounts have been fully explained.

LO 9 *Explain the role of a worksheet in preparing a statement of cash flows.*

DATA FOR AN ILLUSTRATION

We will illustrate the worksheet approach using the 1999 financial data of Auto Supply Co.[1]

Shown below are the balances in Auto's balance sheet accounts at the beginning and end of 1999. (Please notice in this illustration that the account balances at the end of the current year appear in the *right-hand* column. This format also will be used in the worksheet.)

AUTO SUPPLY CO.
Comparative Balance Sheets

	December 31, 1998	December 31, 1999
Assets		
Cash	$ 50,000	$ 45,000
Marketable securities	40,000	25,000
Accounts receivable	320,000	330,000
Inventory	240,000	235,000
Plant and equipment (net of accumulated depreciation)	600,000	640,000
Totals	$1,250,000	$1,275,000
Liabilities & Stockholders' Equity		
Accounts payable	$ 150,000	$ 160,000
Accrued expenses payable	60,000	45,000
Mortgage note payable (long-term)	–0–	70,000
Bonds payable (due in 2015)	500,000	350,000
Capital stock (no par value)	160,000	160,000
Retained earnings	380,000	490,000
Totals	$1,250,000	$1,275,000

Changes in the noncash accounts are the key to identifying cash flows

---

[1] Our example involving Allison Corporation was quite comprehensive. Therefore, a worksheet for Allison Corporation would be too long and detailed for use as an introductory illustration.

ADDITIONAL INFORMATION   The following information also will be used in the preparation of the worksheet. (Accrual-based measurements appear in *blue*; cash flows, in *red*.)

1. Net income for the year amounted to *$250,000*. Cash dividends of *$140,000* were declared and paid.

2. Auto's only "noncash expense" was depreciation, which totaled *$60,000*.

3. Marketable securities costing *$15,000* were sold for *$35,000* cash, resulting in a *$20,000* nonoperating gain.

4. The company purchased plant assets for *$100,000*, making a *$30,000* cash down payment and issuing a *$70,000* mortgage note payable for the balance of the purchase price.

THE WORKSHEET

Auto Supply Co. reports cash flow from operating activities by the *indirect method*.[2] A worksheet for preparing a statement of cash flows appears on the following page.

Let us briefly explain how this worksheet "works." The company's balance sheet accounts are listed in the top portion of the worksheet, with the beginning balances in the first column, and the year-end balances in the last (right-hand) column. (For purposes of illustration, we have shown these accounts and account balances in *black*.)

The two middle columns are used to (1) explain the changes in each balance sheet account over the year, and (2) indicate how each change affected cash.

ENTRIES IN THE TWO MIDDLE COLUMNS   The entries in the *top portion of the worksheet* summarize the transactions recorded in the account over the year. (Because these entries summarize transactions recorded on the **accrual basis,** they are shown in *blue*.)

For each summary entry in the top portion of the worksheet, we make an "offsetting entry" (in the opposite column) in the *bottom portion* of the worksheet indicating the *cash effects* of the transactions. These cash effects are classified as operating, investing, or financing activities, and are explained with a descriptive caption. (Entries representing the *cash effects* of transactions and the related descriptive captions appear in *red*.)

Entries in the two middle columns may be made in any sequence, but we recommend the following approach:

1. Explain the changes in the Retained Earnings account.

2. Account for depreciation expense (and any other "noncash" expenses).

3. Account for "timing differences" between net income and cash flow from operating activities.

4. Explain any remaining changes in balance sheet accounts *other than Cash*. (**Hint:** Changes in asset accounts will represent investing activities; changes in liability and equity accounts will represent financing activities.)

5. Compute and record the net increase or decrease in cash.

---

[2]If the worksheet utilizes the direct method, numerous subclassifications are required within the operating activities section. Such worksheets are illustrated in the intermediate accounting course.

AUTO SUPPLY CO
Worksheet for a Statement of Cash Flows
For the Year Ended December 31, 1999

Balance sheet effects:	Beginning Balance	Debit Changes	Credit Changes	Ending Balance
Assets				
Cash and cash equivalents...	50,000		(x) 5,000	45,000
Marketable securities.............	40,000		(8) 15,000	25,000
Accounts receivable	320,000	(4) 10,000		330,000
Inventory	240,000		(5) 5,000	235,000
Plant and equipment (net of accumulated depreciation).	600,000	(9) 100,000	(3) 60,000	640,000
Totals..................................	1,250,000			1,275,000
Liabilities & Owners' Equity				
Accounts payable	150,000		(6) 10,000	160,000
Accrued expenses payable ...	60,000	(7) 15,000		45,000
Mortgage note payable..........	–0–		(9) 70,000	70,000
Bonds payable.......................	500,000	(10) 150,000		350,000
Capital stock.........................	160,000			160,000
Retained earnings	380,000	(2) 140,000	(1) 250,000	490,000
Totals..................................	1,250,000	415,000	415,000	1,275,000

Effects of Transactions span the Beginning Balance, Debit Changes, Credit Changes, Ending Balance columns.

Up here we summarize the changes in each noncash account

Cash effects:	Sources	Uses
Operating activities:		
Net income...	(1) 250,000	
Depreciation expense	(3) 60,000	
Increase in accounts receivable		(4) 10,000
Decrease in inventory	(5) 5,000	
Increase in accounts payable	(6) 10,000	
Decrease in accrued expenses payable....		(7) 15,000
Gain on sales of marketable securities		(8) 20,000
Investing activities:		
Proceeds from sales of marketable securities	(8) 35,000	
Cash paid to acquire plant assets.............		(9) 30,000
Financing activities:		
Dividends paid		(2) 140,000
Payments to retire bonds payable		(10) 150,000
Subtotals..	360,000	365,000
Net decrease in cash.................................	(x) 5,000	
Totals	435,000	435,000

Cash provided by operations— $280,000

Cash provided by investing activities— $5,000

Cash used in financing activities— $290,000

Down here we identify and classify the related cash effects of these changes

Using this approach, the entries in our illustrated worksheet are explained below:

ENTRY

Step 1: Explain the changes in retained earnings

1. Auto's net income explains a $250,000 *credit change* in the Retained Earnings account. In the bottom portion of the working paper, an offsetting entry is made in the *Sources* column and is classified as an operating activity.[3]

2. Cash dividends of $140,000 caused a *debit change* in the Retained Earnings account during 1999. The offsetting entry falls into the *Uses* column; payments of dividends are classified as a financing activity.

With these first two entries, we have explained how Auto's Retained Earnings account increased during 1999 from $380,000 to $490,000.

Step 2: Account for noncash expenses

3. Auto's only noncash expense was depreciation. In the top portion of the worksheet, depreciation explains a $60,000 credit change (decrease) in Plant and Equipment (which includes the Accumulated Depreciation accounts). The offsetting entry in the bottom of the worksheet falls into the Sources column. We have explained that depreciation is not really a "source" of cash, but that it *is* added back to net income as a step in computing the cash flow from operating activity.

Step 3: Account for timing differences

4–7. Fluctuations in current assets and current liabilities create *timing differences* between net income and the net cash flow from operating activities. In the top portion of the worksheet, entries (4) through (7) summarize the changes in these current asset and current liability accounts. In the bottom portion, they show how these changes affect the computation of cash flow from operating activities.

Step 4: Explain any remaining changes in noncash accounts

8. In 1999, Auto sold marketable securities with a cost of $15,000 for $35,000 cash, resulting in a $20,000 nonoperating gain. In the top portion of the worksheet, the entry explains the $15,000 credit change in the Marketable Securities account. In the bottom portion, it reports cash proceeds of $35,000. The difference? The $20,000 nonoperating gain, which is *removed from the Operating Activities section* of the worksheet and included instead within the amount reported as "Proceeds from sales of marketable securities."

9. Auto purchased $100,000 in plant assets, paying $30,000 cash and issuing a $70,000 note payable. These events explain a $100,000 debit change in Plant and Equipment, the $70,000 credit change in Mortgage Note Payable, and involved a cash outlay of $30,000, which is classified as an investing activity. (The $70,000 financed by issuance of a note payable is a *noncash* investing and financing activity.)

10. The $150,000 credit change in Auto's Bonds Payable account indicates that this amount of the liability has been repaid—that is, $150,000 in bonds has been retired.

At this point, we should check to determine that our entries in the two middle columns *fully explain* the differences between the beginning and ending balance of each noncash balance sheet account. If the top portion of the worksheet explains the changes in every noncash account, the bottom section should include all of the cash flows for the year.

Step 5: Compute and record the net change in cash

(x) We now total the Sources and Uses columns in the bottom portion of the worksheet. The difference between these column subtotals represents the *net increase or decrease* in cash. In our example, the Sources column totals

---

[3]When the *indirect method* is used, net income serves as the *starting point* for computing net cash flow from operating activities.

$360,000, while the Uses column totals $365,000, indicating a *$5,000 decrease* in cash over the period. Our last entry, labeled *(x)*, explains the credit change in the Cash account at the top of the worksheet, and brings the bottom of the worksheet "into balance."

A formal statement of cash flows, reporting the cash flow from operating activities by the indirect method, can be prepared directly from the bottom portion of this worksheet. (Amounts appearing in accrual-based accounting records are shown in *blue*; cash flows appear in *red*.)

AUTO SUPPLY CO.
Statement of Cash Flows
For the Year Ended December 31, 1999

Cash flows from operating activities:		
Net income..		$250,000
Add: Depreciation expense...		60,000
Decrease in inventory..		5,000
Increase in accounts payable..		10,000
Subtotal...		$325,000
Less: Increase in accounts receivable	$ 10,000	
Decrease in accrued expenses payable	15,000	
Gain on sales of marketable securities....................	20,000	45,000
Net cash provided by operating activities..............................		$280,000
Cash flows from investing activities:		
Proceeds from sales of marketable securities....................	$ 35,000	
Cash paid to acquire plant assets (see		
supplementary schedule below)	(30,000)	
Net cash provided by investing activities..............................		5,000
Cash flows from financing activities:		
Dividends paid..	$(140,000)	
Payments to retire bonds payable......................................	(150,000)	
Net cash used in financing activities......................................		(290,000)
Net decrease in cash		$ (5,000)
Cash and cash equivalents, Dec. 31, 1998.............................		50,000
Cash and cash equivalents, Dec. 31, 1999.............................		$ 45,000
Supplementary Schedule: Noncash Investing and Financing Activities		
Purchases of plant assets...		$100,000
Less: Portion financed through issuance of		
long-term debt...		70,000
Cash paid to acquire plant assets		$ 30,000

Compare the content of this statement with the worksheet on page 641

SUMMARY OF LEARNING OBJECTIVES

① Explain the purpose and usefulness of a statement of cash flows.

The purpose of a statement of cash flows is to provide information about the cash receipts and cash payments of the entity, and also about its investing and financing activities. Readers of financial statements use this information to assess the solvency of a business and to evaluate its ability to generate positive cash flows in future periods, pay dividends, and finance growth.

② Describe how cash transactions are classified within a statement of cash flows.

Cash flows are classified as (1) operating activities, (2) investing activities, or (3) financing activities. Receipts and payments of interest are classified as operating activities.

③ Compute the major cash flows relating to operating activities.

The major operating cash flows are (1) cash received from customers, (2) interest and dividends received, (3) cash paid to suppliers and employees, (4) interest paid, and (5) income taxes paid. These cash flows are computed by converting the income statement amounts for revenue, cost of goods sold, and expenses from the accrual basis to the cash basis. This is done by adjusting the income statement amounts for changes occurring over the period in related balance sheet accounts.

④ Explain why net income differs from net cash flow from operating activities.

Net income differs from net operating cash flow for several reasons. One reason is "noncash" expenses, such as depreciation and the amortization of intangible assets. These expenses, which require no cash outlays, reduce net income but do not affect net cash flow. Another reason is the many timing differences existing between the recognition of revenue and expense and the occurrence of the underlying cash flows. Finally, nonoperating gains and losses enter into the determination of net income, but the related cash flows are classified as investing or financing activities, not operating activities.

⑤ Distinguish between the direct and indirect methods of reporting operating cash flow.

The direct and indirect methods are alternative formats for reporting net cash flow from operating activities. The *direct* method shows the specific cash inflows and outflows comprising the operating activities of the business. Under the *indirect* method, the computation begins with accrual-based net income, and then shows adjustments necessary to arrive at net cash flow from operating activities. Both methods result in the same dollar amount of net cash flow from operating activities.

⑥ Compute the cash flows relating to investing and financing activities.

Cash flows from investing and financing activities can be determined by examining the entries in the related asset and liability accounts, along with any related gains or losses shown in the income statement. Debit entries in asset accounts represent purchases of assets (an investing activity). Credit entries in asset accounts represent the cost of assets sold. (However, the amount of these credit entries must be adjusted by any gains or losses recognized on these sales transactions.)

Debit entries to liability accounts represent repayment of debt, while credit entries represent borrowing. Both types of transactions are classified as financing activities. Other financing activities include the issuance of stock (indicated by credits to the paid-in capital accounts) and payment of dividends (indicated by a debit change in the Retained Earnings account).

⑦ Discuss the likely effects of various business strategies upon cash flows.

It is difficult to predict the *extent* to which a business strategy will affect cash flows. However, an informed decision maker should understand the *direction* in which a strategy is likely to affect cash flows—both in the short run *and over a longer term*.

⑧ Compute net cash flow from operating activities using the *indirect* method.

The *indirect method* uses net income (as reported in the income statement) as the starting point in the computation of net cash flow from operating activities. Adjustments to net income necessary to arrive at net cash flow from operating activities fall into the following three categories:

● "Noncash" expenses

● Timing differences

● "Nonoperating" gains and losses

In effect, the adjustments reconcile net income (accrual basis) to net cash flow from operating activities. Specific adjustments from each of the above three categories are illustrated in the Summary Diagram of the Indirect Method on page 638.

⑨ Explain the role of a worksheet in preparing a statement of cash flows.

A worksheet can be used to analyze the changes in balance sheet accounts other than cash and, thereby, determine the related cash flows. In the top portion of the

*Supplemental Topic A, "The Indirect Method."
**Supplemental Topic B, "A Worksheet for Preparing a Statement of Cash Flows."

worksheet, entries are made summarizing the debit and credit changes in each noncash account. In the bottom half, offsetting entries are made to represent the cash effects of the transactions summarized in the top portion. The entries in the bottom half of the worksheet are classified into the same categories as in a statement of cash flows.

The statement of cash flows then is prepared from the data in the bottom portion of the worksheet.

Whether you are an investor, a manager, or a taxpayer, you need to understand the difference between cash flows and the accrual basis of accounting. Accrual-based information is used in determining the profitability and the financial position of a business—especially a business of considerable financial strength. But in evaluating such factors as solvency, the prospects for short-term survival, and the ability of a business to seize investment opportunities, cash flows may be more relevant than accrual-based measurements.

KEY TERMS INTRODUCED OR EMPHASIZED IN CHAPTER 13

Accrual basis (p. 640)   A method of summarizing operating results in terms of revenue earned and expenses incurred, rather than cash receipts or cash payments.

Cash basis (p. 621)   The practice of summarizing operating results in terms of cash receipts and cash payments, rather than revenue earned or expenses incurred.

Cash budget (p. 629)   A detailed forecast of expected future cash receipts, usually organized department by department and month by month for the coming year.

Cash equivalents (p. 616)   Highly liquid short-term investments, such as Treasury bills, money market funds, and commercial paper. For purposes of preparing a statement of cash flows, money held in cash equivalents is still viewed as "cash." Thus, transfers between a bank account and cash equivalents are not considered receipts or disbursements of cash.

Cash flows (p. 613)   A term describing both cash receipts (inflows) and cash payments (outflows).

Complementary products (p. 633)   Products that "fit together"—that tie in with a company's other products.

As a result, customers attracted to one product may also purchase others.

Direct method (p. 624)   A method of reporting net cash flow from operating activities by listing specific types of cash inflows and outflows. This is the method recommended by the FASB, but the *indirect method* is an acceptable alternative.

Financing activities (p. 615)   Transactions such as borrowing, repaying borrowed amounts, raising equity capital, or making distribution to owners. The cash effects of these transactions are reported in the financing activities section of a statement of cash flows. Noncash aspects of these transactions are disclosed in a supplementary schedule.

Free cash flow (p. 627)   The portion of the annual net cash flow from operating activities that remains available for discretionary purposes after the basic obligations of the business have been met. Can be computed in several different ways.

Indirect method (p. 624)   A format of reporting net cash flow from operating activities that reconciles this figure with the amount of net income shown in the income statement. An alternative to the *direct method.*

Investing activities (p. 615)   Transactions involving acquisitions or sales of investments or plant assets. The cash aspects of these transactions are shown in the investing activities section of a statement of cash flows. Noncash aspects of these transactions are disclosed in a supplementary schedule to this financial statement.

Operating activities (p. 615)   Transactions entering into the determination of net income, with the exception of gains and losses relating to financing or investing activities. The category includes such transactions as selling goods or services, earning investment income, and incurring costs and expenses. The cash effects of these transactions are reflected in the operating activities section of a statement of cash flows.

Peak pricing (p. 632)   The strategy of charging a higher price during periods of high demand, and a lower price during periods of slack demand. Intended both to maximize revenue and shift excess demand to periods in which it can be more easily accommodated.

Product mix (p. 633)   The variety and relative quantities of goods and services that a company offers for sale.

DEMONSTRATION PROBLEM

You are the chief accountant for American Modem. Your assistant has prepared an income statement for the current year and has also developed the following "Additional Information" by analyzing changes in the company's balance sheet accounts.

AMERICAN MODEM
Income Statement
For the Year Ended December 31, 19__

Revenue:

Net sales	$9,500,000
Interest income	320,000
Gain on sales of marketable securities	70,000
Total revenue and gains	$9,890,000

Costs and expenses:

Cost of goods sold	$4,860,000	
Operating expenses (including depreciation of $700,000)	3,740,000	
Interest expense	270,000	
Income taxes	300,000	
Loss on sales of plant assets	90,000	
Total costs, expenses, and losses		9,260,000
Net income		$ 630,000

Information about changes in the company's balance sheet accounts over the year is summarized below:

1. Accounts receivable decreased by $85,000.

2. Accrued interest receivable increased by $15,000.

3. Inventory decreased by $280,000, and accounts payable to suppliers of merchandise decreased by $240,000.

4. Short-term prepayments of operating expenses decreased by $18,000, and accrued liabilities for operating expenses increased by $35,000.

5. The liability for accrued interest payable decreased by $16,000 during the year.

6. The liability for accrued income taxes payable increased by $25,000 during the year.

7. The following schedule summarizes the total debit and credit entries during the year in other balance sheet accounts:

	Debit Entries	Credit Entries
Marketable securities	$ 120,000	$ 210,000
Notes receivable (cash loans made to others)	250,000	190,000
Plant assets (see paragraph 8)	3,800,000	360,000
Notes payable (short-term borrowing)	620,000	740,000
Bonds payable		1,100,000
Capital stock		50,000
Additional paid-in capital (from issuance of stock)		840,000
Retained earnings (see paragraph 9 below)	320,000	630,000

8. The $360,000 in credit entries to the plant asset accounts are net of any debits to accumulated depreciation when plant assets were retired. Thus, the $360,000 in credit entries represents the *book value* of all plant assets sold or retired during the year.

9. The $320,000 debit to retained earnings represents dividends declared and paid during the year. The $630,000 credit entry represents the net income for the year.

10. All investing and financing activities were cash transactions.

11. Cash and cash equivalents amounted to $448,000 at the beginning of the year, and to $330,000 at year-end.

INSTRUCTIONS

You are to prepare a statement of cash flows for the current year, following the format illustrated on page 614. Cash flow from operating activities is to be determined by the *direct method*. Place brackets around dollar amounts representing cash outlays. Show separately your computations of the following amounts:

a. Cash received from customers

b. Interest received

c. Cash paid to suppliers and employees

d. Interest paid

e. Incomes taxes paid

f. Proceeds from sales of marketable securities

g. Proceeds from sales of plant assets

h. Proceeds from issuing capital stock

SOLUTION TO DEMONSTRATION PROBLEM

AMERICAN MODEM Statement of Cash Flows For the Year Ended December 31, 19__		
Cash flows from operating activities:		
Cash received from customers (a)	$ 9,585,000	
Interest received (b)	305,000	
Cash provided by operating activities		$ 9,890,000
Cash paid to suppliers and employees (c)	$(7,807,000)	
Interest paid (d)	(286,000)	
Income taxes paid (e)	(275,000)	
Cash disbursed for operating activities		(8,368,000)
Net cash provided by operating activities		$ 1,522,000
Cash flows from investing activities:		
Purchases of marketable securities	$ (120,000)	
Proceeds from sales of marketable securities (f)	280,000	
Loans made to borrowers	(250,000)	
Collections on loans	190,000	
Cash paid to acquire plant assets	(3,800,000)	
Proceeds from sales of plant assets (g)	270,000	
Net cash used in investing activities		(3,430,000)
Cash flows from financing activities:		
Proceeds from short-term borrowing	$ 740,000	
Payments to settle short-term debts	(620,000)	
Proceeds from issuing bonds payable	1,100,000	
Proceeds from issuing capital stock (h)	890,000	
Dividends paid	(320,000)	
Net cash provided by financing activities		1,790,000
Net increase (decrease) in cash		$ (118,000)
Cash and cash equivalents, beginning of year		$ 448,000
Cash and cash equivalents, end of year		$ 330,000

(*continued*)

Supporting computations:

a. Cash received from customers:

Net sales	$ 9,500,000
Add: Decrease in accounts receivable	85,000
Cash received from customers	$ 9,585,000

b. Interest received:

Interest income	$ 320,000
Less: Increase in accrued interest receivable	15,000
Interest received	$ 305,000

c. Cash paid to suppliers and employees:

Cash paid for purchases of merchandise:

Cost of goods sold	$ 4,860,000
Less: Decrease in inventory	280,000
Net purchases	$ 4,580,000
Add: Decrease in accounts payable to suppliers	240,000
Cash paid for purchases of merchandise	$ 4,820,000

Cash paid for operating expenses:

Operating expenses		$ 3,740,000
Less: Depreciation (a "noncash" expense)	$ 700,000	
Decrease in prepayments	18,000	
Increase in accrued liabilities for operating expenses	35,000	753,000
Cash paid for operating expenses		$ 2,987,000
Cash paid to suppliers and employees ($4,820,000 + $2,987,000)		$ 7,807,000

d. Interest paid:

Interest expense	$ 270,000
Add: Decrease in accrued interest payable	16,000
Interest paid	$ 286,000

e. Income taxes paid:

Income taxes expense	$ 300,000
Less: Increase in accrued income taxes payable	25,000
Income taxes paid	$ 275,000

f. Proceeds from sales of marketable securities:

Cost of marketable securities sold (credit entries to the Marketable Securities account)	$ 210,000
Add: Gain reported on sales of marketable securities	70,000
Proceeds from sales of marketable securities	$ 280,000

g. Proceeds from sales of plant assets:

Book value of plant assets sold (paragraph 8)	$ 360,000
Less: Loss reported on sales of plant assets	90,000
Proceeds from sales of plant assets	$ 270,000

h. Proceeds from issuing capital stock:

Amounts credited to the Capital Stock account	$ 50,000
Add: Amounts credited to Additional Paid-in Capital account	840,000
Proceeds from issuing capital stock	$ 890,000

SELF-TEST QUESTIONS

Answers to these questions appear on page 665.

1. The statement of cash flows is designed to assist users in assessing each of the following, *except:*
   a. The ability of a company to remain solvent.
   b. The company's profitability.
   c. The major sources of cash receipts during the period.
   d. The reasons why net cash flow from operating activities differs from net income.

2. Which of the following is *not* included in the statement of cash flows, or in a supplementary schedule accompanying the statement of cash flows?
   a. Disclosure of the amount of cash invested in money market funds during the accounting period.
   b. A reconciliation of net income to net cash flow from operating activities.
   c. Disclosure of investing or financing activities that did not involve cash.
   d. The amount of cash and cash equivalents owned by the business at the end of the accounting period.

3. The cash flows shown in the statement of cash flows are grouped into the following major categories:
   a. Operating activities, investing activities, and financing activities.
   b. Cash receipts, cash disbursements, and noncash activities.
   c. Direct cash flows and indirect cash flows.
   d. Operating activities, investing activities, and collecting activities.

4. Shown below is a list of various cash payments and cash receipts:

Cash paid to suppliers and employees	$400,000
Dividends paid	18,000
Interest paid	12,000
Purchases of plant assets	45,000
Interest and dividends received	17,000
Payments to settle short-term debt	29,000
Income taxes paid	23,000
Cash received from customers	601,000

   Based only upon the above items, net cash flow from operating activities is:

   a. $138,000   **b.** $91,000   **c.** $183,000   **d.** $120,000

5. During the current year, two transactions were recorded in the Land account of Nolan Industries. One involved a debit of $320,000 to the Land account; the second was a $210,000 credit to the Land account. Nolan Industries' income statement for the year reported a loss on sale of land in the amount of $25,000. All transactions involving the Land account were cash transactions. These transactions would be shown in the statement of cash flows as:
   a. $320,000 cash provided by investing activities, and $210,000 cash disbursed for investing activities.
   b. $210,000 cash provided by investing activities, and $320,000 cash disbursed for investing activities.
   c. $235,000 cash provided by investing activities, and $320,000 cash disbursed for investing activities.
   d. $185,000 cash provided by investing activities, and $320,000 cash disbursed for investing activities.

6. Which of the following business strategies is *most likely* to increase the net cash flows of a software developer in the short run but *reduce* them over a longer term?
   a. Develop software which is more costly to create but easier to update and improve.
   b. Lower the price of existing versions of products as customer demand begins to fall.

    c. Purchase the building in which the business operates (assume the company currently rents this location).

    d. Reduce expenditures for the purpose of developing new products.

ASSIGNMENT MATERIAL

DISCUSSION QUESTIONS

1. Briefly state the purposes of a statement of cash flows.

2. Does a statement of cash flows or an income statement best measure the profitability of a financially sound business? Explain.

3. Two supplementary schedules frequently accompany a statement of cash flows. Briefly explain the content of these schedules.

4. Give two examples of cash receipts and two examples of cash payments which fall into each of the following classifications:
    a. Operating activities
    b. Investing activities
    c. Financing activities

5. Why are payments and receipts of interest classified as operating activities rather than as financing or investing activities?

6. Define *cash equivalents* and list three examples.

7. During the current year, Delta Corporation transferred $300,000 from its bank account into a money market fund. Will this transaction appear in a statement of cash flows? If so, in which section? Explain.

8. In the long run, is it more important for a business to have positive cash flows from its operating activities, investing activities, or financing activities? Why?

9. Of the three types of business activities summarized in a cash flow statement, which type is *least* likely to show a positive net cash flow in a successful, growing business? Explain your reasoning.

10. The items and amounts listed in a balance sheet and an income statement correspond to specific accounts in a company's ledger. Is the same true about the items and amounts in a statement of cash flows? Explain.

11. Marathon, Inc., had net sales for the year of $840,000. Accounts receivable increased from $90,000 at the beginning of the year to $162,000 at year-end. Compute the amount of cash collected during the year from customers.

12. Describe the types of cash payments summarized by the caption "Cash paid to suppliers and employees."

13. Identify three factors that may cause net income to differ from net cash flow from operating activities.

14. Briefly explain the difference between the *direct* and *indirect methods* of computing net cash flow from operating activities. Which method results in the higher net cash flow?

15. Are cash payments of accounts payable viewed as operating activities or financing activities? Referring to the statement of cash flows illustrated on page 614, state the caption that includes amounts paid on accounts payable.

16. Discount Club acquired land by issuing $500,000 worth of capital stock. No cash changed hands in this transaction. Will the transaction be disclosed in the company's statement of cash flows? Explain.

17. The only transaction recorded in the plant asset accounts of Rogers Corporation in the current year was a $150,000 credit to the Land account. Assuming that this credit resulted from a cash transaction, does this entry indicate a cash receipt or a cash payment? Should this $150,000 amount appear in the statement of cash flows, or is some adjustment necessary?

18. During the current year, the following credit entries were posted to the paid-in capital accounts of Moser Shipyards:

Capital Stock	$10,000,000
Additional Paid-in Capital	98,500,000

Explain the type of cash transaction that probably caused these credit changes, and illustrate the presentation of this transaction in a statement of cash flows.

19. At the beginning of the current year, Burnside Corporation had dividends payable of $1,200,000. During the current year, the company declared cash dividends of $3,600,000, of which $900,000 appeared as a liability at year-end. Determine the amount of cash dividends *paid* during this year.

20. Define the term *free cash flow*. Explain the significance of this measurement to (1) short-term creditors, (2) long-term creditors, (3) stockholders, and (4) management.

21. Describe a *cash budget* and explain its usefulness to management.

22. Explain the concept of *peak pricing* and provide an example from your own experiences.

23. From management's perspective, identify some of the characteristics of an effective product mix.

24. Explain why speeding up the collection of accounts receivable provides only a one-time increase in cash receipts.

EXERCISES

EXERCISE 13-1
Using a Statement of Cash Flows
LO 1,2

The statement of cash flows for Auto Supply Co. appears on page 643. Assume that with respect to routine business operations, this was a *typical year*. Use this cash flow statement to evaluate the company's ability to maintain the current level of dividend payments over the foreseeable future. Explain your reasoning.

EXERCISE 13-2
Using a Statement of Cash Flows
LO 1,2,3,4

A recent cash flow statement from **MCI Communications Corporation** appears on page 630.

a. What was the company's *free cash flow* in 1995.

b. What type of financing activity is represented by the caption, *"Commercial paper and bank credit facility activity, net . . . $702"*? (**Hint:** *Commercial paper* is described in Chapter 10. *Bank credit facility* refers to lines of credit, which we discuss in Chapter 7.) Was this activity a net source or net use of cash to MCI in 1995?

c. What happened to the total amount of this company's cash and cash equivalents during the year? Does that appear to threaten MCI's solvency for the following year? Explain.

d. Look at the reconciliation of net income to cash from operating activities:
   1. Why is an "asset write-down" *added* to net income?
   2. Note that the change in accounts receivable during 1995 is *subtracted* from net income to arrive at cash from operating activities. Does this suggest an increase or a *decrease* in the amount of accounts receivable during 1995? Explain your reasoning.

EXERCISE 13-3
Computing Cash Flows
LO 6

An analysis of the Marketable Securities controlling account of Dixie Mills, Inc., shows the following entries during the year:

Balance, January 1	$ 390,000
Debit entries	125,000
Credit entries	(140,000)
Balance, December 31	$ 375,000

In addition, the company's income statement includes a $27,000 loss on sales of marketable securities. None of the company's marketable securities is considered a cash equivalent.

Compute the amounts that should appear in the statement of cash flows as:

a. Purchases of marketable securities.

b. Proceeds from sales of marketable securities.

EXERCISE 13-4
Comparing Net Sales and
Cash Receipts

During the current year, Grafton Labs made cash sales of $250,000 and credit sales of $490,000. During the year, accounts receivable decreased by $32,000.

a. Compute for the current year the amounts of:
  1. Net sales reported as revenue in the income statement.
  2. Cash received from collecting accounts receivable.
  3. Cash received from customers.

b. Write a brief statement explaining *why* cash received from customers differs from the amount of net sales.

EXERCISE 13-5
Computing Cash Paid for
Purchases of Merchandise

The general ledger of Nitro Tech provides the following information relating to purchases of merchandise:

	End of Year	Beginning of Year
Inventory	$820,000	$780,000
Accounts payable to merchandise suppliers	430,000	500,000

The company's cost of goods sold during the year was $2,875,000. Compute the amount of cash payments made during the year to suppliers of merchandise.

EXERCISE 13-6
Reporting Lending Activities
and Interest Revenue

During the current year, Otay Savings and Loan Association made new loans of $12 million. In addition, the company collected $36 million from borrowers, of which $31 million was interest revenue. Explain how these cash flows will appear in the company's statement of cash flows, indicating the classification and the dollar amount of each cash flow.

EXERCISE 13-7
Format of a Statement of
Cash Flows

The accounting staff of Carolina Crafts, Inc., has assembled the following information for the year ended December 31, 1998:

Cash and cash equivalents, beginning of year	$ 45,200
Cash and cash equivalents, end of year	64,200
Cash paid to acquire plant assets	21,000
Proceeds from short-term borrowing	10,000
Loans made to borrowers	5,000
Collections on loans (excluding interest)	4,000
Interest and dividends received	17,000
Cash received from customers	795,000
Proceeds from sales of plant assets	9,000
Dividends paid	65,000
Cash paid to suppliers and employees	635,000
Interest paid	19,000
Income taxes paid	71,000

Using this information, prepare a formal statement of cash flows. Include a proper heading for the financial statement, and classify the given information into the categories of operating activities, investing activities, and financing activities. Net cash flows from operating activities are determined by the direct method. Place brackets around the dollar amounts of all cash disbursements.

EXERCISE 13-8
Effects of
Business
Strategies

Indicate how you would expect the following strategies to affect the company's net cash flow from *operating activities* in (1) the near future and (2) in later periods (after the strategy's long-term effects have "taken hold"). *Fully explain your reasoning.*

a. A successful pharmaceutical company substantially reduces its expenditures for research and development.

b. A restaurant which previously sold only for cash adopts a policy of accepting bank credit cards, such as Visa and MasterCard.

c. A manufacturing company reduces by 50% the size of its inventories of raw materials (assume no change in inventory storage costs).

d. Through tax planning, a rapidly growing real estate developer is able to defer significant amounts of income taxes.

e. A rapidly growing software company announces that it will stop paying cash dividends for the foreseeable future, and will instead distribute stock dividends.

*EXERCISE 13-9
An Analysis of Possible
Reconciling Items

An analysis of the annual financial statements of Waste Disposal Corporation reveals the following:

a. The company had a $4 million extraordinary loss from the early retirement of bonds payable.

b. Depreciation for the year amounted to $9 million.

c. During the year, $2 million in cash was transferred from the company's checking account into a money market fund.

d. Accounts receivable from customers increased by $5 million over the year.

e. Cash received from customers during the year amounted to $165 million.

f. Prepaid expenses decreased by $1 million over the year.

g. Dividends declared during the year, $7 million; dividends paid during the year, $6 million.

h. Accounts payable (to suppliers of merchandise) increased by $3 million during the year.

i. The liability for accrued income taxes payable amounted to $5 million at the beginning of the year and $3 million at year-end.

In the computation of net cash flow from operating activities by the *indirect method,* explain whether each of the above items should be *added to net income, deducted from net income,* or *omitted from the computation.* Briefly explain your reasons for each answer.

*EXERCISE 13-10
Computation of Net Cash
Flow from Operating
Activities—Indirect Method

The data below are taken from the income statement and balance sheet of All Night Pharmacies, Inc.:

	Dec. 31 1999	Jan. 1 1999
Income statement:		
Net income	$400,000	
Depreciation expense	120,000	
Amortization of intangible assets	40,000	
Gain on sale of plant assets	80,000	
Loss on sale of investments	35,000	
Balance sheet:		
Accounts receivable	$335,000	$380,000
Inventory	503,000	575,000
Prepaid expenses	22,000	10,000
Accounts payable (to merchandise suppliers)	379,000	410,000
Accrued expenses payable	180,000	155,000

*Supplemental Topic A, "The Indirect Method."

Using this information, prepare a partial statement of cash flows for the year ended December 31, 1999, showing the computation of net cash flow from operating activities by the *indirect* method.

EXERCISE 13-11
Toys "R" Us: Using a Statement of Cash Flows
LO 1,2,6

Statements of cash flows for **Toys "R" Us, Inc.** appear on page A-9 of Appendix A. Focus on the statement of cash flows for the year ended January 28, 1995.

a. Describe the major reasons why the company's cash and cash equivalents decreased by $422,060,000 during the year.

b. Assuming that the company had not purchased shares of its own stock in the share repurchase program, calculate the amount of:
   1. Cash flows for the year from financing activities, and
   2. Cash and cash equivalents at the end of the year.

c. Calculate the amount of the company's free cash flow.

d. From a cash flow perspective do you believe the company's performance was better this year than in the prior year? Justify your answer.

PROBLEMS

PROBLEM 13-1
Classifying Cash Flows
LO 2

Among the transactions of Miyota Communications were the following:

a. Made payments on accounts payable to merchandise suppliers.

b. Paid the principal amount of a note payable to First Bank.

c. Paid interest charges relating to a note payable to First Bank.

d. Issued bonds payable for cash; management plans to use this cash in the near future to expand manufacturing and warehouse capabilities.

e. Paid salaries to employees in the finance department.

f. Collected an account receivable from a customer.

g. Transferred cash from the general bank account into a money market fund.

h. Used the cash received in **d,** above, to purchase land and building suitable for a manufacturing facility.

i. Made a year-end adjusting entry to recognize depreciation expense.

j. At year-end, purchased for cash an insurance policy covering the next 12 months.

k. Paid the quarterly dividend on preferred stock.

l. Paid the semiannual interest on bonds payable.

m. Received a quarterly dividend from an investment in the preferred stock of another corporation.

n. Sold for cash an investment in the preferred stock of another corporation.

o. Received cash upon the maturity of an investment in cash equivalents. (Ignore interest.)

INSTRUCTIONS

Most of the preceding transactions should be included among the activities summarized in a statement of cash flows. For each transaction that should be included in this statement, indicate whether the transaction should be classified as an operating activity, an investing activity, or a financing activity. If the transaction *should not be included* in the current year's statement of cash flows, briefly explain why not. (Assume that the net cash flow from operating activities is determined by the *direct method.*)

PROBLEM 13-2
Format of a Statement of Cash Flows
LO 2,3,6

The accounting staff of Franklin Optical has assembled the following information for the year ended December 31, 19__:

Cash sales	$ 800,000
Credit sales	2,500,000
Collections on accounts receivable	2,200,000
Cash transferred from the money market fund to the general bank account	250,000
Interest and dividends received	100,000
Purchases (all on account)	1,800,000
Payments on accounts payable to merchandise suppliers	1,500,000
Cash payments for operating expenses	1,050,000
Interest paid	180,000
Income taxes paid	95,000
Loans made to borrowers	500,000
Collections on loans (excluding receipts of interest)	260,000
Cash paid to acquire plant assets	3,100,000
Book value of plant assets sold	660,000
Loss on sales of plant assets	80,000
Proceeds from issuing bonds payable	2,500,000
Dividends paid	120,000
Cash and cash equivalents, beginning of year	446,000
Cash and cash equivalents, end of year	–?–

INSTRUCTIONS

Prepare a statement of cash flows in the format illustrated on page 614. Place brackets around amounts representing cash outflows. Use the *direct method* of reporting cash flows from operating activities.

Many of the items above will be listed in your statement without change. However, you will have to combine certain given information to compute the amounts of (1) collections from customers, (2) cash paid to suppliers and employees, and (3) proceeds from sales of plant assets. (**Hint:** Not every item listed above is used in preparing a statement of cash flows.)

PROBLEM 13-3
Reporting Investing Activities
LO 6

An analysis of the income statement and the balance sheet accounts of Olympic Fashions at December 31 provides the following information:

Income statement items:

Gain on sale of marketable securities	$ 42,000
Loss on sales of plant assets	33,000

Analysis of balance sheet accounts:

  Marketable Securities account:

Debit entries	$ 81,000
Credit entries	90,000

  Notes Receivable account:

Debit entries	210,000
Credit entries	162,000

  Plant and equipment accounts:

Debit entries to plant asset accounts	186,000
Credit entries to plant asset accounts	120,000
Debit entries to accumulated depreciation accounts	75,000

ADDITIONAL INFORMATION

1. Except as noted in **4,** below, payments and proceeds relating to investing transactions were made in cash.

2. The marketable securities are not cash equivalents.

3. All notes receivable relate to cash loans made to borrowers, not to receivables from customers.

4. Purchases of new equipment during the year ($186,000) were financed by paying $60,000 in cash and issuing a long-term note payable for $126,000.

5. Debits to the accumulated depreciation account are made whenever depreciable plant assets are retired. Thus, the book value of plant assets retired during the year was $45,000 ($120,000 − $75,000).

INSTRUCTIONS

a. Preparing the "Investing activities" section of a statement of cash flows. Show supporting computations for the amounts of (1) proceeds from sales of marketable securities and (2) proceeds from sales of plant assets. Place brackets around numbers representing cash outflows.

b. Prepare the supporting schedule that should accompany the statement of cash flows in order to disclose the "noncash" aspects of the company's investing and financing activities.

c. Assume that Olympic Fashion's management expects approximately the same amount of cash to be used for investing activities next year. In general terms, explain how the company might generate cash for this purpose.

PROBLEM 13-4
Reporting Investing
Activities

 LO 6

An analysis of the income statement and the balance sheet accounts of Caravan Imports at December 31 provides the following information:

Income statement items:

Gain on sales of plant assets	$ 8,000
Loss on sales of marketable securities	16,000

Analysis of balance sheet accounts:

Marketable Securities account:

Debit entries	$ 74,000
Credit entries	62,000

Notes Receivable account:

Debit entries	52,000
Credit entries	60,000

Plant and equipment accounts:

Debit entries to plant asset accounts	130,000
Credit entries to plant asset accounts	140,000
Debit entries to accumulated depreciation accounts	100,000

ADDITIONAL INFORMATION

1. Except as noted in **4,** below, payments and proceeds relating to investing transactions were made in cash.

2. The marketable securities are not cash equivalents.

3. All notes receivable relate to cash loans made to borrowers, not to receivables from customers.

4. Purchases of new equipment during the year ($130,000) were financed by paying $50,000 in cash and issuing a long-term note payable for $80,000.

5. Debits to the accumulated depreciation account are made whenever depreciable plant assets are sold or retired. Thus, the book value of plant assets sold or retired during the year was $40,000 ($140,000 − $100,000).

INSTRUCTIONS

a. Prepare the "Investing activities" section of a statement of cash flows. Show supporting computations for the amounts of (1) proceeds from sales of marketable securities and (2) proceeds from sales of plant assets. Place brackets around amounts representing cash outflows.

b. Prepare the supplementary schedule that should accompany the statement of cash flows in order to disclose the "noncash" aspects of the company's investing and financing activities.

c. Does management have *more* control or *less* control over the timing and amount of cash outlays for investing activities than for operating activities? Explain.

PROBLEM 13-5
Reporting Operating
Cash Flow by the
Direct Method

LO 3

The following income statement and selected balance sheet account data are available for Child's Play, Inc., at December 31:

CHILD'S PLAY, INC.
Income Statement
For the Year Ended December 31, 19__

Revenue:		
Net sales		$2,850,000
Dividend income		104,000
Interest income		70,000
Gain on sales of marketable securities		4,000
Total revenue and gains		$3,028,000
Costs and expenses:		
Cost of goods sold	$1,550,000	
Operating expenses	980,000	
Interest expense	185,000	
Income taxes	110,000	
Total costs and expenses		2,825,000
Net income		$ 203,000

	End of Year	Beginning of Year
Selected account balances:		
Accounts receivable	$ 650,000	$ 720,000
Accrued interest receivable	9,000	6,000
Inventories	800,000	765,000
Short-term prepayments	20,000	15,000
Accounts payable (merchandise suppliers)	570,000	562,000
Accrued operating expenses payable	65,000	94,000
Accrued interest payable	21,000	12,000
Accrued income taxes payable	22,000	35,000

ADDITIONAL INFORMATION

1. Dividend revenue is recognized on the cash basis. All other income statement amounts are recognized on the accrual basis.

2. Operating expenses include depreciation expense of $115,000.

INSTRUCTIONS

a. Prepare a partial statement of cash flows, including only the *operating activities* section of the statement. Use the *direct method,* including the captions illustrated on page 635. Place brackets around numbers representing cash payments. Show supporting computations for the amounts of:

1. Cash received from customers
2. Interest and dividends received
3. Cash paid to suppliers and employees
4. Interest paid
5. Income taxes paid

b. Management of Child's Play, Inc. is exploring ways to increase the cash flows from operations. One way that cash flows could be increased is through more aggressive collection of receivables. Assuming that management has already taken all the steps possible to increase revenues and reduce expenses, describe two other ways that cash flows from operations could be increased.

*PROBLEM 13-6
Reporting Operating Cash
Flow—Indirect Method

Using the information presented in Problem 13-5, prepare a partial statement of cash flows for the current year, showing the computation of net cash flow from operating activities by the *indirect method.* Use the format and captions illustrated on page 638. Explain why the decline in accounts receivable over the year was *added* to net income in computing the cash flow from operating activities.

PROBLEM 13-7
Preparing a
Statement of Cash
Flows: A
Comprehensive
Problem Without
a Worksheet

You are the controller for Millennium Technologies. Your staff has prepared an income statement for the current year, and has also developed the following "Additional Information" by analyzing changes in the company's balance sheet accounts.

MILLENNIUM TECHNOLOGIES
Income Statement
For the Year Ended December 31, 19__

Revenue:		
Net sales		$3,200,000
Interest revenue		40,000
Gain on sales of marketable securities		34,000
Total revenue and gains		$3,274,000
Costs and expenses:		
Cost of goods sold	$1,620,000	
Operating expenses (including depreciation of $150,000)	1,240,000	
Interest expense	42,000	
Income taxes	100,000	
Loss on sales of plant assets	12,000	
Total costs, expenses, and losses		3,014,000
Net income		$ 260,000

ADDITIONAL INFORMATION

Information about changes in the company's balance sheet accounts over the year is summarized below:

1. Accounts receivable increased by $60,000.

2. Accrued interest receivable decreased by $2,000.

---

*Supplemental Topic A, "The Indirect Method."

3. Inventory decreased by $60,000, and accounts payable to suppliers of merchandise decreased by $16,000.
4. Short-term prepayments of operating expenses increased by $6,000, and accrued liabilities for operating expenses decreased by $8,000.
5. The liability for accrued interest payable increased by $4,000 during the year.
6. The liability for accrued income taxes payable decreased by $14,000 during the year.
7. The following schedule summarizes the total debit and credit entries during the year in other balance sheet accounts:

	Debit Entries	Credit Entries
Marketable securities...	$ 60,000	$ 38,000
Notes receivable (cash loans made to borrowers)	44,000	28,000
Plant assets (see paragraph **8** below)	500,000	36,000
Notes payable (short-term borrowing)...	92,000	82,000
Capital stock		20,000
Additional paid-in capital—capital stock		160,000
Retained earnings (see paragraph **9** below)...............................	120,000	260,000

8. The $36,000 in credit entries to the plant assets account are net of any debits to accumulated depreciation when plant assets were retired. Thus, the $36,000 in credit entries represents the book value of all plant assets sold or retired during the year.
9. The $120,000 debit to retained earnings represents dividends declared and paid during the year. The $260,000 credit entry represents the net income shown in the income statement.
10. All investing and financing activities were cash transactions.
11. Cash and cash equivalents amounted to $244,000 at the beginning of the year, and to $164,000 at year-end.

INSTRUCTIONS
a. You are to prepare a statement of cash flows for the current year, following the format illustrated on page 614. Use the *direct method* of reporting cash flows from operating activities. Place brackets around dollar amounts representing cash outflows. Show separately your computations of the following amounts:
   1. Cash received from customers
   2. Interest received
   3. Cash paid to suppliers and employees
   4. Interest paid
   5. Income taxes paid
   6. Proceeds from sales of marketable securities
   7. Proceeds from sales of plant assets
   8. Proceeds from issuing capital stock
b. Explain the *primary reason* why:
   1. The amount of cash provided by operating activities was substantially greater than the company's net income.
   2. There was a net decrease in cash over the year, despite the substantial amount of cash provided by operating activities.
c. The company's controller thinks that through more efficient "cash management," the company could have held the increase in accounts receivable for the year to $10,000, without affecting net income. Explain how holding down the growth in receivables affects cash. Also, compute the effect that limiting the growth in receivables to $10,000 would have had upon the company's net increase or decrease in cash (and cash equivalents) for the year.

**PROBLEM 13-8
Prepare and
Analyze a
Statement of Cash
Flows; Requires a
Worksheet

LO 1–9

SPACENET 2000 was founded in 1998 to apply a new technology for efficiently transmitting closed-circuit (cable) television signals without the need for an in-ground cable. The company earned a profit of $115,000 in 1998, its first year of operations, even though it was serving only a small test market. In 1999, the company began dramatically expanding its customer base. Management expects both sales and net income to more than triple in each of the next five years.

Comparative balance sheets at the ends of 1998 and 1999, the company's first two years of operations, appear below. (Notice that the balances at the end of the current year appear in the right-hand column.)

SPACENET 2000 Comparative Balance Sheets		
	December 31, 1998	1999
Assets		
Cash and cash equivalents	$ 80,000	$ 37,000
Accounts receivable	100,000	850,000
Plant and equipment (net of accumulated depreciation)	600,000	2,653,000
Totals	$780,000	$3,540,000
Liabilities & Stockholders' Equity		
Note payable (short-term)	$ –0–	$1,450,000
Accounts payable	30,000	63,000
Accrued expenses payable	45,000	32,000
Notes payable (long-term)	390,000	740,000
Capital stock (no par value)	200,000	700,000
Retained earnings	115,000	555,000
Totals	$780,000	$3,540,000

ADDITIONAL INFORMATION

The following information regarding the company's operations in 1999 is available in either the company's income statement or its accounting records:

1. Net income for the year was $440,000. The company has never paid a dividend.

2. Depreciation for the year amounted to $147,000.

3. During the year the company purchased plant assets costing $2,200,000, for which it paid $1,850,000 in cash and financed $350,000 by issuing a long-term note payable. (Much of the cash used in these purchases was provided by short-term borrowing, as described below.)

4. In 1999, SPACENET 2000 borrowed $1,450,000 against a $5 million line of credit with a local bank. In its balance sheet, the resulting obligations are reported as notes payable (short-term).

5. Additional shares of capital stock (no par value) were issued to investors for $500,000 cash.

INSTRUCTIONS

a. Prepare a worksheet for a statement of cash flows, following the general format illustrated on page 641. (**Note:** If this problem is completed as a group assignment,

---

*Supplemental Topic A, "The Indirect Method."
**Supplemental Topic B, "A Worksheet for Preparing a Statement of Cash Flows."

each member of the group should be prepared to explain in class all entries in the worksheet, as well as the group's conclusions in parts **c** and **d**.)

b. Prepare a formal statement of cash flows for 1999, including a supplementary schedule of noncash investing and financing activities. (Follow the format illustrated on page 643. Cash provided by operating activities is to be presented by the *indirect method*.)

c. Briefly explain how operating activities can be a net *use* of cash when the company is operating so profitably.

d. Because of the expected rapid growth, management forecasts that operating activities will be an even greater use of cash in the year 2000 than in 1999. If this forecast is correct, does SPACENET 2000 appear to be heading toward insolvency? Explain.

*PROBLEM 13-9
Prepare and
Analyze a
Statement of Cash
Flows; Involves Preparation
of a Worksheet

LO 1–9

TV Wonder Tool sells a single product (a combination screwdriver, plier, hammer, and crescent wrench) exclusively through television advertising. Shown below are comparative income statements and balance sheets for the last two years:

TV WONDER TOOL Comparative Income Statement For the Years Ended December 31, 19__		
	1998	**1999**
Sales	$500,000	$350,000
Less: Cost of goods sold	200,000	140,000
Gross profit on sales	$300,000	$210,000
Less: Operating expenses (including depreciation of $34,000 in 1998 and $35,000 in 1999)	260,000	243,000
Loss on sale of marketable securities	–0–	1,000
Net income (loss)	$ 40,000	$(34,000)

TV WONDER TOOL Comparative Balance Sheets		
	December 31,	
	1998	**1999**
Assets		
Cash and cash equivalents	$ 10,000	$ 60,000
Marketable securities	20,000	5,000
Accounts receivable	40,000	23,000
Inventory	120,000	122,000
Plant and equipment (net of accumulated depreciation)	300,000	285,000
Totals	$490,000	$495,000
Liabilities & Stockholders' Equity		
Accounts payable	$ 50,000	$ 73,000
Accrued expenses payable	17,000	14,000
Note payable	245,000	253,000
Capital stock (no par value)	120,000	135,000
Retained earnings	58,000	20,000
Totals	$490,000	$495,000

**Supplemental Topic A and B,* "The Indirect Method.""A Worksheet for Preparing a Statement of Cash Flows."

ADDITIONAL INFORMATION

The following information regarding the company's operations in 1999 is available from the company's accounting records:

1. Early in the year the company declared and paid a $4,000 cash dividend.

2. During the year marketable securities costing $15,000 were sold for $14,000 cash, resulting in a $1,000 nonoperating loss.

3. The company purchased plant assets for $20,000, paying $2,000 in cash and issuing a note payable for the $18,000 balance.

4. During the year the company repaid a $10,000 note payable, but incurred an additional $18,000 in long-term debt as described in **3**, above.

5. The owners invested $15,000 cash in the business as a condition of the new loans described in paragraph **4**, above.

INSTRUCTIONS

a. Prepare a worksheet for a statement of cash flows, following the general format illustrated on page 641. (**Note:** If this problem is completed as a group assignment, each member of the group should be prepared to explain in class all entries in the worksheet, as well as the group's conclusions in parts **c, d,** and **e.**)

b. Prepare a formal statement of cash flows for 1999, including a supplementary schedule of noncash investing and financing activities. (Use the format illustrated on page 643. Cash provided by operating activities is to be presented by the *indirect method.*)

c. Explain how TV Wonder Tool achieved a positive cash flow from operating activities, despite incurring a net loss for the year.

d. Does the company's financial position appear to be improving or deteriorating? Explain.

e. Does TV Wonder Tool appear to be a company whose operations are growing or contracting? Explain.

f. Assume that management *agrees* with your conclusions in parts **c, d,** and **e.** What decisions should be made and what actions (if any) should be taken? Explain.

CASES

CASE 13-1
Another Look at Allison
Corporation

This case is based upon the statement of cash flows for Allison Corporation, illustrated on page 628. You are to use this statement to evaluate the company's ability to continue paying the current level of dividends—$40,000 per year. The following information also is available:

1. The net cash flow from operating activities shown in the statement is relatively "normal" for Allison Corporation. In fact, net cash flows from operating activities have not varied by more than a few thousand dollars in any of the last three years.

2. The net outflow for investing activities was unusually high, because the company modernized its production facilities during the year. The normal investing cash outflow is about $45,000 per year, the amount required to replace existing plant assets as they are retired. Over the long run, marketable securities transactions and lending transactions have a very small impact upon Allison's net cash flow from investing activities.

3. The net cash flow from financing activities was unusually large in the current year, because of the issuance of bonds payable and capital stock. These securities were issued to finance the modernization of the production facilities. In a typical year, financing activities include only short-term borrowing transactions and payments of dividends.

INSTRUCTIONS

a. Based solely upon the company's past performance, do you believe that the $40,000 annual dividend payments are secure? That is, does the company appear able to pay this amount in dividends every year without putting any strain on its cash position?

Do you think it more likely that Allison Corporation will increase or decrease the amount of dividends that it pays? Explain fully.

b. Should any of the "unusual" events appearing in the statement of cash flows for the current year affect your analysis of the company's ability to pay future dividends? Explain.

CASE 13-2
Cash Budgeting
for You as
a Student
LO 1,7

Individuals generally do not prepare statements of cash flows concerning their personal activities. But they do engage in cash budgeting—if not on paper then at least in their heads.

Assume, for example, it is December 29—a Monday. In two days your rent for January, $200, will be due. You now have $240 in the bank; every Friday you receive a paycheck for $100. You probably see the problem. And it probably doesn't look too serious; you can find a way to deal with it. That's what *budgeting* is all about.

Let's take this example a step further. In addition to the facts given above, your weekly cash payments include: meals, $30; entertainment, $20; gasoline, $10.

a. Using the following cash budget, compute your cash balance at the ends of weeks 2, 3, and 4.

	Week			
	1	**2**	**3**	**4**
Beginning cash balance	$ 140	$(20)	$?	$?
Expected cash receipts	100	100	100	100
Less: Expected cash outlays:				
Monthly rent	(200)			
Meals	(30)			
Entertainment	(20)			
Gasoline	(10)			
Ending cash balance	$ (20)	$?	$?	$?

b. Evaluate your financial situation.

CASE 13-3
Lookin' Good?
LO 1,4,7

It is late summer and National Motors, an auto manufacturer, is facing a financial crisis. A large issue of bonds payable will mature next March, and the company must issue stock or new bonds to raise the money to retire this debt. Unfortunately, profits and cash flows have been declining over recent years. Management fears that if cash flows and profits do not improve in the current year, the company will not be able to raise the capital needed to pay off the maturing bonds. Therefore, members of management have made the following proposals to improve the cash flows and profitability that will be reported in the financial statements dated this coming December 31.

1. Switch from the LIFO method to the FIFO method of valuing inventories. Management estimates that the FIFO method will result in a lower cost of goods sold but in higher income taxes for the current year. However, the additional income taxes will not actually be paid until early next year.

2. Switch from the 150%-declining-balance method of depreciation to the straight-line method and also lengthen the useful lives over which assets are depreciated. (These changes would be made only for financial reporting purposes, not for income tax purposes.)

3. Pressure dealers to increase their inventories—in short, to buy more cars. (The dealerships are independently owned; thus dealers are the "customers" to whom National Motors sells automobiles.) It is estimated that this strategy could increase sales for the current year by 5%. However, any additional sales in the current year would be almost entirely offset by fewer sales in the following year.

4. Require dealers to pay for purchases more quickly. Currently, dealers must pay for purchases of autos within 60 days. Management is considering reducing this period to 30 days.

5. Pass up cash discounts offered for prompt payment (i.e., 2/10, n/30), and do not pay any bills until the final due date.

6. Borrow at current short-term interest rates (about 10%) and use the proceeds to pay off long-term debt bearing an interest rate of 13%.

7. Substitute stock dividends for the cash dividends currently paid on capital stock.

INSTRUCTIONS

a. Prepare a schedule with four columns. The first column is to be headed "Proposals," and is to contain the paragraph numbers of the seven proposals listed above. The next three columns are to be headed with the following financial statement captions: (1) "Net income," (2) "Net cash flow from operating activities," and (3) "Cash."

For each of the seven proposals in the left column, indicate whether you expect the proposal to "Increase," "Decrease," or have "No Effect" in the current year upon each of the financial statement captions listed in the next three columns. (***Note:*** Only a few months remain in the current year. Therefore, you are to determine the *short-term* effects of these proposals.)

b. For each of the seven proposals, write a short paragraph explaining the reasoning behind your answers to part **a.**

CASE 13-4
Peak Pricing
LO 7

"Peak pricing is unfair. It makes goods and services available only to the wealthy and prices the average person out of the market."

a. Comment upon the extent to which you agree or disagree with the preceding statement.

b. What is the alternative to peak pricing?

c. Explain how peak pricing might be applied by:
1. A hotel in Palm Springs, California. (Palm Springs is a winter resort in Southern California with wonderful golf facilities. In the summer months, however, temperatures are well over 100 degrees and the tourist business slows dramatically.)
2. Movie theaters.

d. Both in general terms and using specific examples, describe the conditions (if any) under which you might regard peak pricing as *unethical*.

INTERNET ASSIGNMENTS

INTERNET 13-1
Prepare a Statement of Cash Flows using a Website Program
LO 2,3,6

Preparing a statement of cash flows is a daunting experience for many managers of small businesses. Entrepreneurial Edge offers these managers some very helpful assistance.
Visit the Entrepreneurial Edge home page at the following Internet address:

www.edgeonline.com

Select "Business Builders" from the home page menu. Then, under the heading, "Financial Management," select "Prepare a Cash Flow Statement." Here you will find a wealth of information regarding how to prepare and interpret the statement of cash flows.

In the first paragraph at the top of the screen, select the "hot button" entitled "Direct Method Cash Flow I-Tool." A template will appear into which cash flow information can be entered. Using the data provided in Problem 13-2 on page 655 of this textbook (Franklin Optical), fill in the template. You must fill in every box in the left column. If you don't have a value to put in a box, enter a zero. Do not use commas or dollar signs.

When you have finished entering the data, click upon the "Calculate" button. Now, wasn't that easy?

Note: Additional Internet assignments for this chapter appear in Appendix B and on our home page.

OUR COMMENTS ON THE IN-TEXT CASES

YOU AS A STUDENT (P. 631)   Predicting future cash flows can help you plan and manage your financial affairs, begin saving for major cash outlays, and avoid financial crises.

Forecasting your own cash flows for the coming month will vary with your lifestyle and the time of year. For example, your housing costs may be based on rent or on the costs of home ownership. Don't forget utilities.

Your projected food costs will depend upon what and where you eat. "Other" expenditures include such things as clothing, entertainment, transportation (including auto insurance and car repairs), and school expenses.

Where will the cash come from? Good question. Do *you* know?

YOU AS A MARKETING MANAGER (P. 633)   We would advise you *not* to raise Elmo's price (and Toys "R" Us didn't). The additional revenue that Toys "R" Us might receive from raising the price of a single product clearly is immaterial. On the other hand, raising the price of a popular and highly publicized toy right before Christmas might lead to charges of "price-gouging" and other bad publicity.

In fact, we see a marketing opportunity here in *cutting* Elmo's price, not raising it. We'd publicize the reduced sales price and promise to continue it for at least a month after Christmas. In the long term, the chance to enhance customer relations is far more important than a short-term increase in revenue.

ANSWERS TO SELF-TEST QUESTIONS
1. b   **2.** a   **3.** a   **4.** c   **5.** d   **6.** d

CHAPTER 14

ACCOUNTING: CONCEPTS, PROFESSIONAL JUDGMENT, AND ETHICAL CONDUCT

Location:

Search | Feedback | Help | Directory

Document: Done

Congratulations! You have met the challenge. In completing this semester, you have achieved something worthwhile. You now know more about accounting and the business environment than most people ever will.

We will use this chapter to pause and look back at the territory you've covered—not the details and procedures, but at the broad understanding of accounting that we hope you will "take with you."

1. Explain the need for recognized accounting standards.
2. Discuss the nature and sources of generally accepted accounting principles.
3. Discuss the accounting principles presented on pages 669–677.
4. Apply the percentage-of-completion method of income recognition.
5. Describe the role of professional judgment in the financial reporting process.
6. Explain the nature of ethics and ethical dilemmas.
7. Explain the basic purpose of a code of ethics within a profession.
8. Apply the concepts of ethical conduct to situations likely to arise in accounting practice.

THE NEED FOR RECOGNIZED ACCOUNTING STANDARDS

The basic purpose of financial statements is to provide information about a business entity—information that will be *useful in making economic decisions*. Investors, managers, creditors, financial analysts, economists, and government policy makers all rely upon financial statements and other accounting reports in making the decisions which shape our economy. Therefore, it is of vital importance that the information contained in financial statements possess certain characteristics. The information should be:

LO 1 *Explain the need for recognized accounting standards.*

1. *Relevant* to the information needs of the decision makers.
2. As *reliable* as possible.
3. *Comparable* to the financial statements of prior accounting periods and also to the statements of other companies.
4. *Understandable* to the users of the financial statements.[1]

We need a well-defined body of accounting principles or standards to guide accountants in preparing financial statements which possess these characteristics. The users of financial statements also must be familiar with these principles in order to interpret properly the information contained in these statements.

GENERALLY ACCEPTED ACCOUNTING PRINCIPLES (GAAP)

The principles which constitute the ground rules for financial reporting are called **generally accepted accounting principles.** Accounting principles may also be termed *standards, assumptions, conventions,* or *concepts.* The various terms used to describe accounting principles stem from the many efforts that have been made to develop a satisfactory framework of accounting theory.[2] For example, the word *standards* was chosen rather than *principles* when the Financial Accounting Standards Board (FASB) replaced the Accounting Principles Board (APB) as the top rule-making body in the accounting profession. The ef-

---

[1]Adapted from *Statement of Financial Accounting Concepts No. 2,* "Qualitative Characteristics of Accounting Information," FASB (Norwalk, Conn.: 1980).
[2]See, for example, *Accounting Research Study No. 3,* "A Tentative Set of Broad Accounting Principles for Business Enterprises," AICPA (New York: 1962); *APB Statement No. 4,* "Basic Concepts and Accounting Principles Underlying Financial Statements of Business Enterprises," AICPA (New York: 1970); and *Statements of Financial Accounting Concepts Nos. 1–6,* FASB (Norwalk, Conn.: 1978–1985).

fort to construct a satisfactory body of accounting theory is an ongoing process, because accounting theory must continually change with changes in the business environment and changes in the needs of financial statement users.

NATURE OF ACCOUNTING PRINCIPLES

LO 2 *Discuss the nature and sources of generally accepted accounting principles.*

Accounting principles do not exist in nature; rather, they are developed by people and organizations in light of what they view as the most important objectives of financial reporting. In Chapter 1 we drew a parallel between generally accepted accounting principles and the rules established for an organized sport, such as basketball or football. For example, both accounting principles and sports rules originate from a combination of experience, tradition, and official decree. Also, both may change over time as gaps or shortcomings in the existing rules come to light.

An important aspect of accounting principles is the *need for consensus* within the economic community. If these principles are to provide a useful framework for financial reporting, they must be understood and observed by the participants in the financial reporting process. Thus, the words *generally accepted* are an important part of the phrase "generally accepted accounting principles."

As accounting principles are closely related to the needs, objectives, and traditions of a society, they vary somewhat from one country to another. Our discussion is limited to accounting principles "generally accepted" within the United States. An effort is underway to create greater uniformity in accounting principles among nations, but this effort will be a long, slow process.

AUTHORITATIVE SUPPORT FOR ACCOUNTING PRINCIPLES

To qualify as generally accepted, an accounting principle must have substantial authoritative support. This support may come from official sources, such as the FASB or SEC, or from unofficial sources, such as common sense, tradition, and widespread use.

OFFICIAL SOURCES OF GAAP Over the years, the official sources of accounting principles in the United States have included (1) the **American Institute of Certified Public Accountants,** (2) the **Financial Accounting Standards Board,** and (3) the **Securities and Exchange Commission.** Also important in the development of accounting theory has been the American Accounting Association (AAA), an organization of accounting educators.

UNOFFICIAL SOURCES OF GAAP Not all of what we call generally accepted accounting principles can be found in the "official pronouncements" of the standard-setting organizations. The business community is too complex and changes too quickly for every possible type of transaction to be covered by an official pronouncement. Thus, practicing accountants often must account for situations that have never been addressed by the FASB.

When the method of accounting for a particular situation is not explained in any official literature, generally accepted accounting principles are based upon such considerations as:

- Accounting practices that are in widespread use.
- Accounting practices recommended in authoritative, but "unofficial," accounting literature.[3]
- Broad theoretical concepts that underlie most accounting practices.

---

[3]Authoritative, but unofficial, accounting literature includes the *Audit and Accounting Guides,* and *Statements of Position* published by the AICPA; "non-binding" publications by the FASB and the SEC; research studies published by the American Accounting Association (AAA), other professional associations, trade associations, and individuals engaged in accounting research; and accounting textbooks.

Thus, an understanding of generally accepted accounting principles requires a familiarity with (1) authoritative accounting literature, (2) accounting practices in widespread use, and (3) the broad theoretical concepts that underlie accounting practices. We will discuss these "broad theoretical concepts" in the following sections of this chapter.

THE ACCOUNTING ENTITY CONCEPT

One of the basic principles of accounting is that information is compiled for a clearly defined accounting entity. An *accounting entity* is any economic unit which controls resources and engages in economic activities. An individual is an accounting entity. So is a business enterprise, whether organized as a proprietorship, partnership, or corporation. Governmental agencies are accounting entities, as are nonprofit clubs and organizations. An accounting entity may also be defined as an identifiable economic unit *within a larger accounting entity.* For example, the Chevrolet Division of General Motors Corporation may be viewed as an accounting entity separate from GM's other activities.

LO 3 *Discuss the accounting principles presented on pages 669–677.*

The basic accounting equation, Assets = Liabilities + Owners' Equity, reflects the accounting entity concept because all elements of the equation must relate *to the particular entity whose financial position is being reported.* Although we have considerable flexibility in defining our accounting entity, we must be careful to use the *same definition* in the measurement of assets, liabilities, owners' equity, revenue, and expense. An income statement would not make sense, for example, if it included all the revenue of General Motors Corporation but listed the expenses of only the Chevrolet Division.

Although the entity concept appears straightforward, it can pose some judgmental allocation problems for accountants. Assume, for example, that we want to prepare an income statement for only the Chevrolet Division of General Motors. Also assume that a given plant facility is used in the production of Chevrolets, Pontiacs, and school buses. How much of the depreciation on this factory building should be regarded as an expense of the Chevrolet Division? Such situations illustrate the importance of the entity concept in developing meaningful financial information.

THE GOING-CONCERN ASSUMPTION

An underlying assumption in accounting is that an accounting entity will continue in operation for a period of time sufficient to carry out its existing commitments. The assumption of continuity, especially in the case of corporations, is in accord with experience in our economic system. This assumption leads to the concept of the **going concern.** In general, the going-concern assumption justifies ignoring immediate liquidation values in presenting assets and liabilities in the balance sheet.

For example, suppose that a company has just purchased a three-year insurance policy for $5,000. If we assume that the business will continue in operation for three years or more, we will consider the $5,000 cost of the insurance as an asset which provides services (freedom from certain risks) to the business over a three-year period. On the other hand, if we assume that the business is likely to terminate in the near future, the insurance policy should be reported at its cancellation value—that is, the amount refundable upon cancellation.

Although the assumption of a going concern is justified in most normal situations, it should be dropped when it is not in accord with the facts. Accountants are sometimes asked to prepare a statement of financial position for an enterprise that is about to liquidate. In this case the assumption of continuity is no longer valid and the accountant drops the going-concern assumption and reports assets at their current liquidation value and liabilities at the amount required to settle the debts immediately.

THE TIME PERIOD PRINCIPLE

The users of financial statements need information that is reasonably current. Therefore, for financial reporting purposes, the life of a business is divided into a series of relatively short accounting periods of equal length. This concept is called the **time period principle.**

The need for periodic reporting creates many challenging problems. Dividing the life of an enterprise into relatively short time segments, such as a year or a quarter of a year, requires numerous estimates and assumptions. For example, estimates must be made of the useful lives of depreciable assets and assumptions must be made as to appropriate depreciation methods. Thus periodic measurements of net income and financial position are at best only informed estimates. The tentative nature of these measurements should be understood by those who rely on periodic accounting information.

THE STABLE-DOLLAR ASSUMPTION

The **stable-dollar assumption** means that money is used as the basic measuring unit for financial reporting. The dollar, or any other monetary unit, is a measure of value—that is, it indicates the relative price (or value) of different goods and services.

When accountants add or subtract dollar amounts originating in different years, they imply that the dollar is a *stable unit of measure,* just as the gallon, the acre, and the mile are stable units of measure. Unfortunately, the dollar is *not* a stable measure of value.

To illustrate, assume that in 1970, you purchased land for $20,000. In 1998, you sell this land for $30,000. Under generally accepted accounting principles, which include the stable-dollar assumption, you have made a $10,000 "gain" on the sale. Economists would point out, however, that $30,000 in 1998 represents less "buying power" than did $20,000 in 1970. When the relative buying power of the dollar in 1970 and 1998 is taken into consideration, you came out behind on the purchase and the sale of this land.

To compensate for the shortcomings of the stable-dollar assumption, the FASB asks large corporations voluntarily to prepare *supplementary information* disclosing the effects of inflation upon their financial statements.[4] Because of the high cost of developing this information, however, most companies do not provide it.

Despite its shortcomings, the stable-dollar assumption remains a generally accepted accounting principle. In periods of low inflation, this assumption does not cause serious problems. During periods of severe inflation, however, the assumption of a stable dollar may cause serious distortions in accounting information.

THE OBJECTIVITY PRINCIPLE

The term **objectivity** refers to making measurements that are *unbiased* and subject to verification by independent experts. For example, the price established in an arm's-length transaction is an objective measure of exchange value at the time of that transaction. Exchange prices established in business transactions constitute much of the raw material from which accounting information is generated. Accountants rely on various kinds of evidence to support their financial measurements, but they usually seek the most objective evidence available. Invoices, contracts, paid checks, and physical counts of inventory are examples of objective evidence.

If a measurement is objective, 10 competent investigators who make the same measurement will come up with substantially identical results. However,

---

[4]FASB, *Statement No. 89,* "Financial Reporting and Changing Prices" (Norwalk, Conn.: 1986).

10 competent accountants who set out independently to measure the net income of a given business would *not* arrive at an identical result. Despite the goal of objectivity, *it is not possible to insulate accounting information from opinion and personal judgment.* For example, the cost of a depreciable asset can be determined objectively but not the periodic depreciation expense. Depreciation expense is merely an estimate, based upon estimates of the useful life and the residual value of the asset, and a judgment as to which depreciation method is most appropriate. Such estimates and judgments can produce significant variations in the measurement of net income.

Objectivity in accounting has its roots in the quest for reliability. Accountants want to make their economic measurements reliable and, at the same time, as relevant to decision makers as possible. Where to draw the line in the trade-off between *reliability* and *relevance* is one of the crucial issues in accounting theory. Accountants are constantly faced with the necessity of compromising between what users of financial information would like to know, and what it is possible to measure with a reasonable degree of reliability.

ASSET VALUATION: THE COST PRINCIPLE

Both the balance sheet and the income statement are affected by the cost principle. Assets are initially recorded in the accounts at cost. In most cases no adjustment is made to this valuation in later periods, except to allocate a portion of the original cost to expense as the assets expire.[5] At the time an asset is originally acquired, cost represents the "fair market value" of the goods or services exchanged, as evidenced by an arm's-length transaction. With the passage of time, however, the fair market value of such assets as land and buildings may change greatly from their historical cost. These later changes in fair market value generally have been ignored in the accounts, and the assets have continued to be shown in the balance sheet at historical cost (less the portion of that cost which has been allocated to expense.)

The cost principle is derived, in large part, from the principle of objectivity. Those who support the cost principle argue that it is important that users have confidence in financial statements, and that this confidence can best be maintained if accountants recognize changes in assets and liabilities only on a basis of completed transactions. Objective evidence generally exists to support cost; current market values, however, often are largely a matter of personal opinion.

The question of whether to value assets at cost or estimated market value is a classic illustration of the trade-off between the relevance and the reliability of accounting information.

REVENUE RECOGNITION: THE REALIZATION PRINCIPLE

When should revenue be recognized? Under the assumptions of accrual accounting, revenue should be recognized "when it is earned." However, the "earning" of revenue usually is an extended *economic process* and does not actually take place at a single point in time.

Some revenue, such as interest earned, is directly related to time periods. For this type of revenue, it is easy to compute the amount of revenue earned during the accounting period. However, the process of earning sales revenue is related to *economic activities* rather than to a specific period of time. In a manufacturing business, for example, the earning process involves (1) acquisition of raw materials, (2) production of finished goods, (3) sale of the finished goods, and (4) collection of cash from credit customers.

---

[5]As explained in Chapter 7, short-term investments in marketable securities are reported in the balance sheet at current market values. Valuation of these investments represents an exception to the cost principle.

In the manufacturing example, there is little objective evidence to indicate how much revenue has been earned during the first two stages of the earning process. Accountants therefore usually do not recognize revenue until the revenue has been "realized." Revenue is realized when both of the following conditions are met: (1) the earning process is *essentially complete* and (2) *objective evidence* exists as to the amount of revenue earned.

In most cases, the **realization principle** indicates that revenue should be recognized *at the time goods are sold or services are rendered.* At this point the business has essentially completed the earning process and the sales value of the goods or services can be measured objectively. At any time prior to sale, the ultimate sales value of the goods or services sold can only be estimated. After the sale, the only step that remains is to collect from the customer, and this is usually a relatively certain event.

In Chapter 3, we described a *cash basis* of income measurement whereby revenue is recognized only when cash is collected from customers and expenses are recorded only when cash is actually paid out. Cash basis accounting *does not conform* to generally accepted accounting principles, but it is widely used by individuals in income tax returns. (Remember that the accounting methods used in income tax returns often differ from those used in financial statements.)

THE INSTALLMENT METHOD Companies selling goods on the installment plan sometimes use the **installment method** of accounting for income tax purposes. Under the installment method, the seller recognizes the gross profit on installment sales gradually as the cash is actually collected from customers. If the gross profit rate on installment sales is 30%, then 30% of all cash received from the customer is viewed as gross profit.

To illustrate, assume that on December 15, 1997, a retailer sells for $400 a television set which cost $280, or 70% of the sales price. The terms of the sale call for a $100 cash down payment with the balance payable in 15 monthly installments of $20 each, beginning on January 1, 1998. (Interest charges are ignored in this illustration.) The collections of cash and recognition of profit under the installment method are summarized below:

<table>
<tr><td>Installment method: Profit recognized as cash is collected</td><td>

Year	Cash Collected −	Cost Recovery (70%) =	Gross Profit (30%)
1997	$100	$ 70	$ 30
1998	240	168	72
1999	60	42	18
Totals	$400	$280	$120

</td></tr>
</table>

This method of profit recognition is widely used for income tax purposes. It benefits the seller by *postponing* the recognition of taxable income. From an accounting viewpoint, there is little theoretical justification for delaying the recognition of profit beyond the point of sale. Therefore, the installment method is seldom used in financial statements.[6]

PERCENTAGE-OF-COMPLETION: AN EXCEPTION TO THE REALIZATION PRINCIPLE Under certain circumstances, accountants may depart from the realization principle and recognize income *during the production process.* An example arises in the case of long-term construction contracts, such as the build-

---

[6]Under generally accepted accounting principles, use of the installment method is permissible only when the amounts likely to be collected on installment sales are *so uncertain* that no reasonable basis exists for estimating an allowance for doubtful accounts.

ing of a dam over a period of several years. Clearly the income statements of a company engaged in such a project would be of little use to managers or investors if no profit or loss were reported until the dam was finally completed. The accountant therefore estimates the portion of the project completed during each accounting period, and recognizes the gross profit on the project *in proportion* to the work completed. This is known as the **percentage-of-completion** method of accounting for long-term contracts.

LO 4 *Apply the percentage-of-completion method of income recognition.*

The percentage-of-completion method works as follows:

1. An estimate is made of the total costs to be incurred and the total profit to be earned over the life of the project.

2. Each period, an estimate is made of the portion of the total project completed during the period. This estimate is usually made by expressing the costs incurred during the period as a percentage of the estimated total cost of the project.

3. The percentage figure determined in step **2** is applied to the estimated total profit on the contract to compute the amount of profit applicable to the current accounting period.

4. No estimate is made of the percentage of work done during the final period. In the period in which the project is completed, any remaining profit is recognized.

To illustrate, assume that Reed Construction Company enters into a contract with the government to build an irrigation canal at a price of $50,000,000. The canal will be built over a three-year period at an estimated total cost of $40,000,000. Therefore, the estimated total profit on the project is $10,000,000. The following schedule shows the actual costs incurred and the amount of profit recognized in each of the three years under the percentage-of-completion method:

Year	(A) Actual Costs Incurred	(B) Percentage of Work Done in Year (Column A ÷ $40,000,000)	(C) Profit Considered Earned ($10,000,000 × Column B)	
1	$ 6,000,000	15%	$1,500,000	
2	20,000,000	50%	5,000,000	
3	14,520,000	*	2,980,000	balance
Totals	$40,520,000		$9,480,000	

*Balance required to complete the contract.

Percentage-of-completion: Profit recognized as work progresses

The percentage of the work completed during Year 1 was estimated by dividing the actual cost incurred in the year by the estimated total cost of the project ($6,000,000 ÷ $40,000,000 = 15%). Because 15% of the work was done in Year 1, 15% of the estimated total profit of $10,000,000 was considered earned in that year ($10,000,000 × 15% = $1,500,000). Costs incurred in Year 2 amounted to 50% of the estimated total costs ($20,000,000 ÷ $40,000,000 = 50%); thus, 50% of the estimated total profit was recognized in Year 2 ($10,000,000 × 50% = $5,000,000). Note that no percentage-of-work-completed figure was computed for Year 3. In Year 3, the total actual cost is known ($40,520,000), and the actual total profit on the contract is determined to be $9,480,000 ($50,000,000 − $40,520,000). Since profits of $6,500,000 were previously recognized in Years 1 and 2, the *remaining* profit ($9,480,000 − $6,500,000 = $2,980,000) is recognized in Year 3.

Although an expected *profit* on a long-term construction contract is recognized in proportion to the work completed, a different treatment is accorded to an expected *loss*. If at the end of any accounting period it appears that a loss will be incurred on a contract in progress, the *entire loss should be recognized at once.*

The percentage-of-completion method is used only when the total profit expected to be earned can be *reasonably estimated in advance.* If there are substantial uncertainties in the amount of profit which will be earned, no profit is recognized until the job is completed. This approach is called the *completed-contract method.* If the completed-contract method had been used in the preceding example, no profit would have been recognized in Years 1 and 2; the entire profit of $9,480,000 would have been recorded in Year 3.

YOUR TURN

You as a Chief Financial Officer

Assume that you are the chief financial officer of a large software company that has just begun selling personal budgeting software over the Internet. A customer who wants to try the software inputs a credit card number on your company's home page, and then downloads a copy of the software. The customer's credit card is not charged at that time because the company provides a 30-day free trial. The software that is downloaded to the individual will operate for the trial period, but it will be disabled after 30 days unless a key (a serial number) is entered. When the customer orders the key from your company, the price of the software is charged to the customer's credit card. You must make a decision about when the revenue from these types of transactions should be recognized in your company's financial statements.

*Our comments appear on page 707.

EXPENSE RECOGNITION: THE MATCHING PRINCIPLE

The relationship between expenses and revenue is one of *cause and effect.* Expenses are *causal factors* in the earning of revenue. To measure the profitability of an economic activity, we must consider not only the revenue earned, but also all the expenses incurred in the effort to produce this revenue. Thus, accountants attempt to *match* (or *offset*) the revenue appearing in an income statement with all the expenses incurred in generating that revenue. This concept, called the **matching principle,** governs the timing of expense recognition in financial statements.

To illustrate, assume that in June a painting contractor purchases paint on account. The contractor uses the paint on jobs started and completed in July, but does not pay for the paint until August. In which month should the contractor recognize the cost of the paint as expense? The answer is *July,* because this is the month in which the paint was *used in the process of earning revenue.*

Because of the matching principle, costs that are expected to benefit future accounting periods are debited to asset accounts. These costs are then allocated to expense in the periods that the costs contribute to the production of revenue. The matching principle underlies such accounting practices as depreciating plant assets, measuring the cost of goods sold, and amortizing the cost of unexpired insurance policies. All end-of-the-period adjusting entries involving recognition of expense are applications of the matching principle.

Costs are matched with revenue in one of two ways:

1. *Direct association of costs with specific revenue transactions.* The ideal method of matching revenue with expenses is to determine the amount of expense associated with the specific revenue transactions occurring during the period. However, this approach works only for those costs and expenses that can be directly associated with specific revenue transactions. The cost of goods sold and commissions paid to salespeople are examples of costs and expenses that can be *directly associated* with the revenue of a specific accounting period.

2. *Systematic allocation of costs over the "useful life" of the expenditure.* Many expenditures contribute to the earnings of revenue for a number of accounting periods, but cannot be directly associated with specific revenue transactions. Examples include the costs of insurance policies, depreciable assets, and intangible assets such as goodwill. In these cases, accountants attempt to match revenue and expenses by *systematically allocating the cost to expense* over its useful life. Straight-line amortization and the various methods of depreciation are examples of the "systematic allocation" techniques used to match revenue with the related costs and expenses.

Unfortunately, it is not possible to apply the matching principle objectively to every type of expenditure. Many expenditures offer at least some hope of producing revenue in future periods; however, there may be little or no objective evidence to support these hopes. Accountants defer recognition of an expense to the future only when there is *reasonable evidence* that the expenditure will, in fact, benefit future operations. If this evidence is not available, or is not convincing, accountants do not attempt to apply the matching principle; rather, they charge the expenditure *immediately to expense*. Expenditures generally considered "too subjective" for accountants to apply the matching principle include advertising, research and development, and the cost of employee training programs.

CASE IN POINT

Large pharmaceutical companies such as **Merck, Upjohn,** and **Marion Labs** spend hundreds of millions of dollars each year in research and development (R&D). Ten or more years may be spent developing and testing a new product. During this time, no revenue is received from the product, but related R&D costs totaling hundreds of millions of dollars are charged to expense. Every now and then, these companies discover a "blockbuster" drug, which can bring in revenue of perhaps $1 billion per year for a decade or more. The costs of manufacturing pharmaceutical products are relatively small; the primary costs incurred in generating the companies' revenues are the R&D expenditures incurred in prior years.

As a result of accountants' inability to match R&D costs against the subsequent revenue, the income of pharmaceutical companies is understated during the years of product development and is overstated in the years that a successful product brings in revenue. Unfortunately, there is no simple solution to this problem. How are accountants to determine objectively whether or not today's research expenditures will result in a "blockbuster" product 10 years down the road?

THE CONSISTENCY PRINCIPLE

The principle of **consistency** implies that a particular accounting method, once adopted, will not be changed from period to period. This assumption is important because it assists users of financial statements in interpreting changes in financial position and changes in net income.

Consider the confusion which would result if a company ignored the principle of consistency and changed its method of depreciation every year. The company could cause its net income for any given year to increase or decrease merely by changing its depreciation method.

The principle of consistency does not mean that a company should *never* make a change in its accounting methods. In fact, a company *should* make a change if a proposed new accounting method will provide more useful information than does the method presently in use. But when a significant change in accounting methods does occur, the fact that a change has been made and the dollar effects of the change should be *fully disclosed* in the financial statements.

Consistency applies to a single accounting entity and increases the comparability of financial statements from period to period. Different companies, even those in the same industry, may follow different accounting methods. For this reason, it is important to determine the accounting methods used by companies whose financial statements are being compared.

THE DISCLOSURE PRINCIPLE

Adequate **disclosure** means that all *material* and *relevant facts* concerning financial position and the results of operations *are communicated to users*. This can be accomplished either in the financial statements or in the notes accompanying the statements. Such disclosure should make the financial statements more useful and less subject to misinterpretation.

Adequate disclosure does not require that information be presented in great detail; it does require, however, that no important facts be withheld. For example, if a company has been named as a defendant in a large lawsuit, this information must be disclosed. Other examples of information which should be disclosed in financial statements include:

1. A summary of the *accounting methods* used in the preparation of the statements.
2. Dollar effects of any *changes* in these accounting methods during the current period.
3. Any *loss contingencies* that may have a material effect upon the financial position of the business.
4. Contractual provisions that will affect future cash flows, including the terms and conditions of borrowing agreements, employee pension plans, and commitments to buy or sell material amounts of assets.

Even significant events which occur *after* the end of the accounting period but before the financial statements are issued may need to be disclosed.

Naturally, there are practical limits to the amount of disclosure that can be made in financial statements and the accompanying notes. The key point to bear in mind is that the supplementary information should be *relevant to the interpretation* of the financial statements.

MATERIALITY

The term **materiality** refers to the *relative importance* of an item or an event. An item is "material" if knowledge of the item might reasonably *influence the decisions* of users of financial statements. Accountants must be sure that all material items are properly reported in the financial statements.

However, the financial reporting process should be *cost effective*—that is, the value of the information should exceed the cost of its preparation. By definition, the accounting treatment accorded to *immaterial* items is of little or no value to decision makers. Therefore, accountants should not waste time accounting for immaterial items; these items may be treated in the *easiest and most convenient manner*. In short, the concept of materiality allows accountants to ignore other accounting principles with respect to items that are not material.

An example of the materiality concept is found in the manner in which most companies account for low-cost plant assets, such as pencil sharpeners or wastebaskets. Although the matching principle calls for depreciating plant assets over their useful lives, these low-cost items usually are charged immediately to an expense account. The resulting "distortion" in the financial statement is too small to be of any importance.

If a large number of immaterial items occur in the same accounting period, accountants should consider the *cumulative effect* of these items. Numerous "immaterial" items may, in aggregate, have a material effect upon the financial statements. In these situations, the numerous immaterial events must be properly recorded to avoid a material distortion of the financial statements.

We must recognize that the materiality of an item is a relative matter; what is material in a small business organization may not be material in a larger one. The materiality of an item depends not only upon its dollar amount but also upon its nature. In a large corporation, for example, it may be immaterial whether a given $50,000 expenditure is classified as an asset or as an expense. However, if the $50,000 item is a misuse of corporate funds, such as an unauthorized payment of the personal living expense of the chief executive, the *nature* of the item may make it quite material to users of the financial statements.

CONSERVATISM AS A GUIDE IN RESOLVING UNCERTAINTIES

We have previously referred to the use of **conservatism** in connection with the measurement of net income and the reporting of accounts receivable and inventories in the balance sheet. Although the concept of conservatism may not qualify as an accounting principle, it has long been a powerful influence upon asset valuation and income determination. Conservatism is most useful when matters of judgment or estimates are involved. Ideally, accountants should base their estimates on sound logic and select those accounting methods which neither overstate nor understate the facts. When some doubt exists about the valuation of an asset or the realization of a gain, however, accountants traditionally select the accounting option which produces a lower net income for the current period and a less favorable financial position.

An example of conservatism is the traditional practice of pricing inventory at the lower-of-cost-or-market (replacement cost). Decreases in the market value of the inventory are recognized as a part of the cost of goods sold in the current period, but increases in market value of inventory are ignored. Failure to apply conservatism when valuations are especially uncertain may produce misleading information and result in losses to creditors and stockholders.

SETTING NEW ACCOUNTING STANDARDS

As stated earlier, accounting principles are not laws of nature that await discovery. Rather, these principles are developed and shaped by organizations and individuals, for the purpose of meeting the needs of economic decision makers. As the business environment changes, the need for new principles (or standards) often becomes apparent. In fact, the FASB typically issues about a half-dozen new standards each year.

In an effort to meet the needs of the entire economic community, the FASB invites all elements of the community to express their views during the standard-setting process. For example, the Board issues a *Discussion Memorandum* explaining the issue under consideration and encouraging all interested parties to comment and to express their views. After considering the responses to the Discussion Memorandum, the Board issues an *Exposure Draft* of the proposed new standard and again encourages public response. These responses also are considered carefully before the Board issues a formal new *Statement of Financial Accounting Standards.*

By inviting the public to participate in the standard-setting process, the FASB tries to develop the understanding and support which will cause the new standard to be "generally accepted."

THE CONCEPTUAL FRAMEWORK PROJECT

In addition to responding to the needs of the economic community, the FASB tries to make each new accounting standard consistent with the general framework of accounting theory set forth by the Board in a series of *Statements of Financial Accounting Concepts.* These "concepts statements" explain the interrelationships among the following:

● Objectives of financial reporting

● Desired characteristics of accounting information (such as relevance, reliability, and understandability)

● Elements of financial statements (such as assets, liabilities, revenue, and expenses)

● Criteria for deciding what information to include in financial statements

● Valuation concepts relating to the determination of financial statement amounts

The primary purpose of the conceptual framework is to provide guidance to the FASB in developing future accounting standards.[7] By making each new standard consistent with this framework, the Board hopes to resolve accounting problems in a logical and consistent manner.

The concepts statements do not represent "official" generally accepted accounting principles, as do the FASB's *Statements of Financial Accounting Standards.* However, these concepts statements are very useful to practicing accountants in accounting for situations that are not specifically addressed by one of the FASB's standards.

PROFESSIONAL JUDGMENT: AN ESSENTIAL ELEMENT IN FINANCIAL REPORTING

LO 5 *Describe the role of professional judgment in the financial reporting process.*

Judgment plays a major role in financial reporting. For those situations not specifically covered by an official pronouncement, accountants must exercise **professional judgment** in determining the treatment that is most consistent with generally accepted accounting principles. Judgment also is exercised in selecting appropriate accounting methods (as for example, deciding whether to use the FIFO or LIFO method of inventory valuation), in estimating the useful

---

[7]FASB, *Statement of Financial Accounting Concepts No. 1,* "Objectives of Financial Reporting by Business Enterprises" (Norwalk, Conn.: 1978), p. 4.

lives of depreciable assets, and in deciding what events are "material" to a given business entity.

Judgment is a personal matter; competent accountants often will make different judgments. This explains why the financial statements of different companies are not likely to be directly comparable in all respects.

BUSINESS AND PROFESSIONAL ETHICS

WHAT ARE "ETHICS"?

Ethics are the moral principles that an individual uses to govern his or her behavior. In short, ethics are the personal criteria by which an individual distinguishes "right" from "wrong."

LO 6 *Explain the nature of ethics and ethical dilemmas.*

Every society has a strong interest in the ethical standards of its citizens. If people had no ethics, for example, they would see nothing "wrong" in cheating, stealing, or even committing murder as a means of achieving their goals. Obviously a society without ethics would be a chaotic and dangerous place in which to live. For this reason, governments, organized religions, and educators have long attempted to create and promote certain ethical standards among all members of society. Governments pass laws requiring or prohibiting certain types of behavior; organized religions attempt to define "right" and "wrong" through sermons and religious teachings. Throughout the educational process, educators attempt to teach students to distinguish between "right" and "wrong" using criteria (ethics) acceptable to the greater society.

ETHICAL DILEMMAS

An **ethical dilemma** is a situation that an individual faces that involves a decision about appropriate behavior. A simple example of an ethical dilemma is described below:

> Assume a student finds an expensive wristwatch in a restroom at your college. The student is faced with an ethical dilemma as to what action to take, if any, to find the owner.

The common aspect of all ethical dilemmas is that the welfare of one or more individuals or groups of individuals is affected by the results of the decision. In the situation described above, the welfare of the wristwatch's original owner is affected by the student's decision. That individual may either get the wristwatch back or lose it permanently.

Business executives and accountants face a number of ethical dilemmas in their business careers. These dilemmas involve decisions that require seasoned judgment and careful consideration of the short-term and long-term implications.

BUSINESS ETHICS

Of particular interest to society are the ethics of its business executives. Unethical decisions made by these individuals can have a pervasive effect on all members of society. In recent years, there have been some publicized cases of corporate executives conducting business in a highly questionable manner. For example, corporations in the tobacco industry have been widely criticized for allegedly misleading the public as to the effects of smoking. After deregulation of the savings and loan industry, a number of executives in that industry were convicted of misusing the assets of their institutions for personal gain.

Unfortunately, the publicity that surrounds these cases tends to give the impression that all business managers are unethical; this impression is often reinforced by television programs and movies. From the information presented by the media, people might conclude that an executive must be unethical to succeed in business. *This is simply not the case.* Management fraud is relatively rare, although the few cases which do occur receive much attention in the media. By and large, managers conduct the affairs of their businesses in a socially responsible manner. Actually, ethical business conduct is *good business*. In the long run, *fair and honest* dealings with employees, suppliers, and customers is almost a prerequisite to the success of any business.

Ethical dilemmas are not always black or white. For example, if a member of the royal family of a foreign country demands a secret cash payment before allowing a company to do business in that country, is it "ethical" for the company to make the payment? If a company manufactures a product that is useful, legal, and profitable, but evidence shows that its use is harmful to the environment, should it continue to produce the product? The answers to these questions depend on the ethical values of management, and the corporate image that management wants to project. Many companies have found that consumers are willing to pay a higher price for goods and services that are provided in a socially responsible manner.

YOUR TURN

You as a Purchasing Agent

Assume that you are the purchasing agent for a major corporation. Recently, you authorized a large purchase of parts from a new vendor. A few days later, you receive a voucher from the vendor for a free Caribbean cruise. Would accepting the voucher be ethical?

*Our comments appear on page 707.

ETHICS RELATING TO PROFESSIONALS

Some ethical concepts, such as a belief that it is wrong to steal, apply to all situations. Other ethical concepts, however, apply specifically to some particular type of activity. For example, many of us have ethical principles relating directly to sports. Assume that you are playing a competitive sport and the umpire or referee makes a "bad call" *in your favor.* Do you challenge the call? Your answer to this question will depend upon your *personal* ethical principles concerning participation in competitive sports.

To understand and appreciate the ethics applicable to a specialized type of activity, one must first understand the *nature of the activity.* Consider, for example, a painter who encounters a building in need of new paint. The painter has no "ethical obligation" to stop and paint this building. Now consider a physician encountering an accident victim who is unconscious and badly in need of immediate medical attention. The physician does have an ethical obligation to stop and render emergency medical care. The obligation to render immediate service simply because it is needed is an ethical concept applicable to the medical profession, because that profession is devoted to the public's health and safety.[8]

ETHICS RELATING TO THE PRACTICE OF ACCOUNTING

Accountants, too, have unique ethical responsibilities. For example, CPAs auditing financial statements have an ethical obligation to be *independent* of the company issuing the statements. An accountant preparing an income tax re-

---

[8]Similar ethical responsibilities also exist for people working in a variety of "public safety" occupations.

turn has an ethical obligation to prepare the return *honestly,* even though the taxpayer paying the accountant's fee may want the return prepared in a manner that understates taxable income. An accountant employed by a private company has the conflicting ethical obligations of respecting the *confidentiality* of information gained on the job and also making *appropriate disclosures* to people outside the organization.

THE CONCEPT OF A "PROFESSION" Accountants are proud to consider themselves members of a recognized *profession.* But just what is a "profession"? Actually, there is no single definition or criterion that distinguishes a profession from other fields of endeavor. Over time, however, some occupations have come to be regarded as professions, while others have not. Among the occupations most commonly regarded as professions are the practices of medicine, law, engineering, architecture, and theology. Accounting, too, is widely viewed as having achieved the status of a profession.

Although a profession is not easily defined, all professions do have certain characteristics in common. Perhaps the most important of these characteristics is the special responsibility of persons practicing a profession to *serve the public interest,* even at the sacrifice of personal gain.

PROFESSIONAL CODES OF ETHICS

All recognized professions have developed *codes of professional ethics.* The basic purpose of these codes is to provide members of the profession with guidelines for conducting themselves *in a manner consistent with the responsibilities of the profession.* Codes of ethics relating to the practice of accounting have been developed by several professional associations of accountants. In addition to these codes, there are many laws, income tax regulations, and professional pronouncements that govern the conduct of practicing accountants.

LO 7 *Explain the basic purpose of a code of ethics within a profession.*

Codes of ethics developed by professional associations generally hold the practicing professional to *higher* standards of conduct than do the laws regulating that profession. In part, this tendency evolves from the fact that professional associations have a vested interest in enhancing the public image of the profession. Also, these organizations have a better understanding than do lawmakers of the special problems confronting the professional. For these reasons, all professions are, to some extent, *self-regulating.* (The term *self-regulating* means that society expects the profession to establish its own rules of "professional conduct" for individuals practicing the profession, and also to develop methods of enforcing these rules.)

In this introductory discussion of ethical principles applicable to the accounting profession, we will explore briefly the ethical codes developed by two of the largest professional associations of accountants—the **American Institute of Certified Public Accountants (AICPA)** and the **Institute of Management Accountants (IMA).**[9]

THE AICPA CODE OF PROFESSIONAL CONDUCT

Most CPAs are members of the AICPA. The membership of this association has voted to adopt a code of professional conduct to provide members with guidelines in fulfilling their professional responsibilities. Most CPAs are engaged in *public accounting*—that is, performing audits, income tax work, and accounting services for a variety of different clients. Thus, the AICPA's *Code of Professional Conduct* focuses upon ethical concepts specifically relating to the practice of public accounting.

The *Code* consists of two sections. The first section, entitled *Principles,* discusses in broad terms the profession's responsibilities to the public, to clients,

---

[9]Formerly called the National Association of Accountants (NAA).

and to fellow practitioners. The principles provide the framework for the second section of the *Code,* entitled *Rules.*

Quoted below are the preamble and the six Articles comprising the *Principles* section of the *Code.* Also quoted are portions of two of the eleven *Rules.*[10]

SECTION I—PRINCIPLES
Preamble

Membership in the American Institute of Certified Public Accountants is voluntary. By accepting membership, a certified public accountant assumes an obligation of self-discipline above and beyond the requirements of laws and regulations.

These Principles of the *Code of Professional Conduct* of the American Institute of Certified Public Accountants express the profession's recognition of its responsibilities to the public, to clients, and to colleagues. They guide members in the performance of their professional responsibilities and express the basic tenets of ethical and professional conduct. The Principles call for an unswerving commitment to honorable behavior, even at the sacrifice of personal advantage.

Article I
Responsibilities

In carrying out their responsibilities as professionals, members should exercise sensitive professional and moral judgments in all their activities.

Article II
The Public Interest

Members should accept the obligation to act in a way that will serve the public interest, honor the public trust, and demonstrate commitment to professionalism.

Article III
Integrity

To maintain and broaden public confidence, members should perform all professional responsibilities with the highest sense of integrity.

Article IV
Objectivity and Independence

A member should maintain objectivity and be *free of conflicts of interest* in discharging professional responsibilities. A member in public practice should be *independent in fact and appearance when providing auditing and other attestation services.* [Emphasis supplied.]

Article V
Due Care

A member should observe the profession's technical and ethical standards, strive continually to improve competence and the quality of services, and discharge professional responsibilities to the best of the member's ability.

Article VI
Scope and Nature of Services

A member in public practice should observe the Principles of the *Code of Professional Conduct* in determining the scope and nature of services to be provided.

TWO OF THE AICPA "RULES"

In addition to the Articles cited above, the AICPA *Code of Professional Conduct* includes eleven specific rules. Quoted below is Rule 102, regarding *integrity and*

---

[10]Copyright 1991 by the American Institute of Certified Public Accountants, Inc., New York, NY.

objectivity, and a portion of Rule 301, which addresses the concept of *confidentiality.*

SECTION II—RULES
Integrity and Objectivity

RULE 102 In the performance of any professional service, a member shall maintain objectivity and integrity, shall be free of conflicts of interest, and shall *not knowingly misrepresent facts* or subordinate his or her judgment to others. [Emphasis supplied.]

Confidential Client Information

RULE 301 A member in public practice shall *not disclose any confidential client information* without the specific consent of the client.

This rule shall *not* be construed to . . . relieve a member of the member's professional obligations . . . (to comply with legal and professional reporting and disclosure requirements). [Emphasis supplied.]

APPLICABILITY OF THE AICPA CODE OF PROFESSIONAL CONDUCT

Most of the principles and rules in the *Code* apply to *all aspects* of a CPA's professional practice. One rule, which states that "A member shall not commit an act discreditable to the profession," applies to the CPA's personal life as well as his or her professional practice. The concept of *independence* (which is both a principle and a rule) applies primarily to *auditing engagements,* not to income tax work or the rendering of other professional services.[11]

The AICPA *Code of Professional Conduct* is binding upon all CPAs who are members of the AICPA. Most large CPA firms *require* all their partners to be members of this organization. Thus, adherence to the *Code* is essential for anyone planning a career in public accounting. In addition, many states have adopted the *Code* into the laws governing the practice of public accounting and the licensing of CPAs within that state. Thus, a CPA found guilty of violating the *Code* could lose his or her license to practice, as well as being barred from membership in the AICPA.

To assist CPAs in applying the ethical concepts embodied in the *Code of Professional Conduct,* the AICPA publishes *interpretations* and *ethics rulings* on an ongoing basis.

A CLOSER LOOK AT SOME KEY CONCEPTS

Two ethical concepts of special importance in the practice of public accounting are *independence* and the *confidentiality* of information obtained in the course of a professional engagement.

INDEPENDENCE When CPAs *audit* a company's financial statements, they express their *professional opinion* as to whether the financial statements represent a fair and complete presentation of the company's financial position and the results of its operations. Stockholders, creditors, and potential investors all rely upon these audited financial statements in deciding how to allocate their investment resources. Thus, if the auditor's report is to lend *credibility* to audited financial statements, users of the statements must view the auditors as being fair and impartial.

For auditors to be viewed as impartial, they must be *independent* of the company issuing the financial statements. By "independent," we mean that the au-

LO 8 *Apply the concepts of ethical conduct to situations likely to arise in accounting practice.*

---

[11]The concept of independence also applies to *review* services and any engagements involving *attestation.*

ditor must not be perceived as being under the company's influence or control, or as having any *vested interest* in the results reported in the financial statements.

Assume, for example, that an auditor owned a large investment in the common stock of an audit client. Many users of the financial statements might assume that the auditor would be reluctant to insist upon the disclosure of facts that might lower the company's stock price. Thus, the auditor would not be regarded as impartial by these users of the statements.

CPAs take extensive measures to be independent in fact and also *to appear* independent of their audit clients. This concept of independence places a number of constraints upon the auditors' relationship with audit clients. CPAs must not have any financial interest in a client firm, must not accept expensive gifts from the client, and must not be employees of the client organization. Other restrictions require that close relatives of the CPAs not have major investments or hold key management positions with a client company. In terms of inspiring public confidence, the *appearance* of independence is just as important as being independent in fact.

CPAs need be independent only when they are expressing an opinion on the representations made by another party. Thus, the concept of independence applies primarily to the CPA's role as an *auditor.* In rendering income tax services, consulting services, and many types of accounting services, CPAs are *not* required to be independent of their clients.

INTEGRITY AND OBJECTIVITY One of the most important concepts in the AICPA *Code* is that in the performance of any professional engagement, a member shall *not knowingly misrepresent facts.* This concept goes to the very heart of the professional accountant's responsibility to the public interest.

Facts may be misrepresented even if the facts themselves are stated correctly. For example, facts may be misrepresented if the accounting document does not contain *adequate disclosure* of information necessary for the proper *interpretation* of those facts.

In summary, a CPA *must not be associated* with misleading financial statements, income tax returns, or other accounting reports. If a client insists upon preparing an accounting document in a misleading manner, the CPA must *resign from the engagement.*

CONFIDENTIALITY If individuals are to discuss sensitive and private matters openly with professionals, they must trust that professional not to misuse the information provided. Thus, most professions have ethical requirements that information provided to the professional must be held in strict confidence. Physicians, attorneys, and clergy, for example, are ethically and legally prohibited from disclosing to others personal information obtained from persons who have sought their professional services.

By the nature of their work, accountants must have access to much financial information about their clients which the client regards as "confidential." If CPAs are to earn the trust and respect of their clients, they must respect the confidential nature of this information. Thus, CPAs should not disclose sensitive information about a client company to the company's competitors or to other outsiders, or use this information for the CPA's personal gain.[12]

The idea that information obtained during a professional engagement is to be held in confidence differs somewhat between CPAs and other professionals. In all

---

[12]Federal laws prohibiting "insider trading" make it illegal for accountants or other "insiders" to use information not yet available to the general public in order to profit from trading in a publicly owned company's financial securities (stocks, bonds, and other financial instruments). Thus, the ethical concept of confidentiality is reinforced, to some extent, by federal law.

aspects of their work, CPAs have an ethical obligation *not to misrepresent facts*. CPAs may face a conflict between their professional obligation to correctly and fully disclose facts, and a client's desire that certain information be held in confidence.

Notice that *Rule 301* specifically states that the concept of confidentiality is *not* intended to "relieve a member of the member's professional obligations . . . (to comply with legal and professional reporting and disclosure requirements)." Thus, the CPA *always should insist* that the client make any and all disclosures consistent with applicable reporting standards. If the client refuses to make such disclosure, the CPA should *resign from the engagement.*

Once having resigned from a professional engagement, the CPA often no longer has professional or legal obligations to make disclosures. However, the CPA should still view the information obtained during the engagement as *confidential,* not to be disclosed without the client's express permission. On the other hand, the CPA must report any information that he or she is *legally obligated* to disclose. Legal obligations to disclose information may arise from inquiries by the Securities and Exchange Commission (SEC), from court subpoenas, or from a citizen's general responsibility to disclose knowledge of illegal activities that might prove harmful to the public.[13]

CASE IN POINT

Emma Jones, CPA, was engaged to audit the financial statements of **Stewart Industries,** and also to prepare the company's income tax return. During the course of her work, Jones discovered that the "advertising expenses" Stewart was deducting in its income tax return included $75,000 in political campaign contributions that clearly were not deductible. Jones advised her client that these expenditures were not legally deductible. However, the client insisted on deducting these items anyway. The company's chief financial officer said, "The IRS audits our tax return almost every year. Let them find these items if they can—you don't need to do their work for them. If the IRS throws these deductions out, we'll pay any additional taxes that are assessed."

In the financial statements, the political expenditures were properly included within the broad caption, *Selling and Promotional Expenses.* In addition, the amounts of income taxes expense and income taxes payable shown in the financial statements were large enough to provide for any additional taxes that might be assessed if the IRS disallowed the improper deductions.

Jones is aware that the IRS pays a "finder's fee" to anyone who provides information enabling the Service to collect additional taxes due from another taxpayer.

What are Jones's ethical responsibilities with respect to (1) completing her professional engagements for Stewart and (2) disclosing Stewart's improper actions to the IRS?

Answer: (1) Jones may *not* prepare Stewart's income tax return, as she knows that certain deductions claimed in the return are not legally deductible. Unless Stewart will accord proper treatment to the political expenditures in its tax return, Jones must resign from this portion of her professional engagement. Jones may continue her audit engagement, however, as the facts *are presented fairly* in the financial statements. *(continued)*

---

[13]When CPAs believe that they may have a legal obligation to disclose confidential information, they should consult with legal counsel to determine whether this legal obligation takes priority over the ethical concept of confidentiality.

Although Jones ethically may continue with the audit engagement, she should consider whether she wants to be associated with a client of Stewart's questionable character. If Stewart is willing to misrepresent facts to the IRS, perhaps it also is willing to misrepresent other facts to Jones and to users of its financial statements. Thus, Jones may elect to resign from both the tax and audit engagements.

(2) The information obtained while working on the Stewart engagement is confidential. Therefore, Jones may *not* inform the IRS of the situation without her client's permission. However, Jones must respond to a subpoena or other legal requirement to disclose this information.

It would be highly unethical for Jones to disclose this confidential information to collect a "finder's fee" or for any other form of personal gain.

IMA STANDARDS OF ETHICAL CONDUCT FOR MANAGEMENT ACCOUNTANTS

The IMA is an association consisting primarily of **management accountants**—that is, accountants working for one particular organization.[14] The members of the IMA have adopted a code of professional ethics designed to assist management accountants in executing their duties in an ethical and professional manner. The standards comprising this code are as follows:[15]

Competence

Management accountants have a responsibility to:

- Maintain an appropriate level of professional competence by ongoing development of their knowledge and skills.
- Perform their professional duties in accordance with relevant laws, regulations, and technical standards.
- Prepare complete and clear reports and recommendations after appropriate analysis of relevant and reliable information.

Confidentiality

Management accountants have a responsibility to:

- Refrain from disclosing confidential information acquired in the course of their work except when authorized, unless legally obligated to do so.
- Inform subordinates as appropriate regarding the confidentiality of information acquired in the course of their work and monitor their activities to ensure maintenance of that confidentiality.
- Refrain from using or appearing to use confidential information acquired in the course of their work for unethical or illegal advantage either personally or through third parties.

---

[14]The term *management accountants* describes accountants employed by private companies, nonprofit organizations, and by governmental agencies. These accountants may specialize in any number of fields, including systems design, internal auditing, financial reporting, income taxes, and assisting management in developing and using accounting information in planning and controlling the operations of the organization.

[15]Institute of Management Accountants, *Statement on Management Accounting: Standards of Ethical Conduct for Management Accountants*, Statement No. 1C (New York, 1983).

Integrity

Management accountants have a responsibility to:

- Avoid actual or apparent conflicts of interest and advise all appropriate parties of any potential conflict.
- Refrain from engaging in any activity that would prejudice their ability to carry out their duties ethically.
- Refuse any gift, favor, or hospitality that would influence or would appear to influence their actions.
- Refrain from either actively or passively subverting the attainment of the organization's legitimate and ethical objectives.
- Recognize and communicate professional limitations or other constraints that would preclude responsible judgment or successful performance of an activity.
- Communicate unfavorable as well as favorable information and professional judgments or opinions.
- Refrain from engaging in or supporting any activities that would discredit the profession.

Objectivity

Management accountants have a responsibility to:

- Communicate information fairly and objectively.
- Disclose fully all relevant information that could reasonably be expected to influence an intended user's understanding of the reports, comments, and recommendations presented.

APPLICABILITY OF THE IMA CODE OF ETHICS

The IMA's *Code* applies to all members of the organization in their role as management accountants. All CMAs (Certified Management Accountants) also agree to abide by this code. At present, compliance is primarily voluntary.

A CLOSER LOOK AT SOME KEY CONCEPTS

CONFIDENTIALITY Every organization views much of its internal accounting information as *confidential*—that is, as information that should not be disclosed to people outside the organization, or even to many employees inside the organization. For example, a company might not want its advertising budget made known to competitors, or the salaries of its executives and managers made known to employees throughout the organization.

Thus, management accountants, just as CPAs, should respect the confidentiality of information obtained during professional engagements. This means that the accountant should not disclose confidential information except with the employer's (or client's) permission. Also, the accountant should never use this information for personal gain in a manner that is either unethical or illegal.

IN POINT

Both management accountants and independent auditors often have advance knowledge that a company's earnings for the year will be higher or lower than most investors are expecting. It would be illegal and unethical for the accountants to use this "inside information" to profit from changes in the company's stock price, either personally or by passing this confidential information to third parties.

As in the case of public accountants, an exception to the confidentiality requirement exists when there is a *legal obligation* for the accountant to make disclosure. Also, the confidentiality concept does *not* justify withholding appropriate disclosures from an accounting document.

WHAT ABOUT INDEPENDENCE?   Notice that the IMA's *Code* does not mention the concept of *independence*. Independence is an ethical concept pertaining only to public accountants engaged in auditing activities.

An important distinction between a management accountant and a public accountant is that the management accountant is an *employee* of the company for which he or she performs accounting services. Employees are not regarded as independent of their employers. Thus, although management accountants perform many different types of accounting services, they cannot perform independent audits of their employer's financial statements.

Although management accountants are not independent of their employers, they still are expected to develop accounting information that is fair, honest, and free from bias. Guidelines helpful in achieving this goal are found in the code sections entitled "Integrity" and "Objectivity."

INTEGRITY   The "Integrity" section of the IMA's *Code* deals primarily with the management accountant's ethical obligations to his or her employer. For example, management accountants are to avoid conflicts of interest and to disclose to appropriate parties any potential conflicts that may arise. Also, they are to refuse gifts that would influence (or appear to influence) their actions. The purpose of these standards is to avoid situations which might compete with the accountant's professional obligations to his or her employer.

OBJECTIVITY   We have seen that the ethical standards of confidentiality and integrity deal primarily with management accountants' ethical obligations to their employers. Of even greater importance to the profession is the accountants' responsibilities to the *public* and to outside parties who rely upon accounting reports and disclosures. In the IMA's *Code,* these responsibilities are addressed in the "Objectivity" standard.

The statement that management accountants have a responsibility to "communicate information fairly and objectively" means, simply, that a professional accountant must *not be associated* with any financial statement, tax return, or other accounting report that the accountant *believes to be misleading.*

RESOLUTION OF ETHICAL CONFLICTS

The IMA also makes suggestions to its members on how to resolve ethical conflicts. When faced with a significant ethical issue, the member should first follow any established policies within the employer organization for resolving such issues. If the issue cannot be resolved properly in this manner, the member should discuss the matter with his or her immediate supervisor, assuming that this supervisor is not involved. If this superior is involved in the situation, the problem should be submitted to the next higher level of management.

If the ethical conflict cannot be resolved after exhausting all levels of internal review, the management accountant may have no alternative other than to *resign from the organization,* and to submit a memorandum describing the situation to an appropriate level of management.

Even after an accountant resigns, the ethical concept of confidentiality *continues to apply.* The accountant may not discuss confidential information except with the former employer's permission, or when there exists a legal obligation to make disclosure.

THE CHALLENGE OF ADHERING TO A CODE OF ETHICS

In principle, a professional code of ethics is a good thing. Society benefits when professionals conduct themselves in an honorable and ethical manner. (Surely, no one would argue against professionals striving toward such goals as increased competence and integrity.) A professional code of ethics provides professionals with some general guidelines in conducting themselves in an ethical manner.

However, even an "honest" person may find it difficult to act in an ethical manner in some situations. Let us briefly consider a few of the barriers to ethical conduct.

THE "PRICE" OF ETHICAL BEHAVIOR We would like to think that professionals will do the "right" (ethical) thing, regardless of the amount of personal sacrifice involved. But this is an easier course of action to advocate than to follow. Management accountants, interestingly, may have to pay a far greater "price" for ethical conduct than public accountants. Let us first consider the case of a public accountant.

Assume that a CPA has a client that intends to issue misleading financial statements or to understate taxable income in an income tax return. The CPA should not be associated with such misrepresentation and should resign from the engagement. This may mean that the CPA is unable to collect his or her fee from this engagement, but this is a relatively small price to pay.

First, this "unethical" client is but one of many clients for the typical CPA. Thus, the fee from this engagement probably represents only a small percentage of the CPA's total revenue. More importantly, CPAs simply *cannot afford* to be associated with misleading financial statements or fraudulent income tax returns. Such associations could leave the CPA personally liable to persons deceived by the misleading accounting documents, create adverse publicity that could destroy the CPA's practice, cause the CPA to lose his or her license to practice public accounting, and result in the CPA going to prison for committing fraud. Thus, the CPA's choice is clear: It is far better to give up an unethical client than to continue the association.

Now consider the situation of the management accountant. If the management accountant's employer rejects the accountant's concerns over an ethical problem, the management accountant may have no further recourse other than to resign. This may mean giving up a high and steady income, losing future pension rights, and joining the ranks of the unemployed. Clearly, this management accountant is asked to pay a much higher price for choosing the "ethical path" than is the public accountant in our prior example.

INCOMPLETE INFORMATION A professional accountant may "suspect" that activities in which he or she is asked to participate are unethical, but not be sure.

CASE IN POINT

Wilson, a management accountant for International Equipment Company, is asked to process the paper work to reimburse the vice-president of international operations for a $50,000 "advertising expenditure" claimed in the executive's expense account. Wilson considers it improbable that the vice-president actually spent $50,000 in personal funds for company advertising. More likely, Wilson thinks, the funds were paid as a bribe to some foreign official. However, Wilson has no facts concerning the expenditure, other than that top management wants the vice-president reimbursed.

In most situations, accountants have neither the responsibility nor the right to investigate their employers or clients. If a further investigation of the facts is not directly related to the accountant's professional responsibilities, the accountant simply may never have enough information to reach an informed decision as to whether or not specific activities are "ethical."

JUST WHAT IS THE "ETHICAL" THING TO DO?   Codes of ethics consist of broad, general guidelines, intended to be useful to practitioners in identifying and resolving ethical problems. However, no code of ethics can address every situation that might arise. Every ethical dilemma borders upon the unique, having its own facts and circumstances.

CASE IN POINT

Assume that Barnes, CPA, is performing income tax services for Regis Company. Regis insists that Barnes prepare the company's income tax return in a manner that understates the amount of taxes owed. What should Barnes do?
   Answer: Barnes cannot ethically comply with the client's instructions. Therefore, Barnes should resign from the engagement.

In many situations, however, the ethical course of action *is not readily apparent.*

CASE IN POINT

Assume that Riley, CPA, is auditing the 1998 financial statements of Quest Corporation. During this audit, Quest Corporation is acquired by Gordon Communications. Riley's brother is the controller of Gordon Communications. Has Riley's independence been impaired with respect to the Quest audit? Must Riley resign from this engagement?
   Answer: ???[16]

Codes of ethics, including the "official interpretations," typically do not address such specific questions. Therefore, often it is not possible to simply "look up" the solution to an ethical problem. In deciding when an ethical problem exists, and in determining what constitutes ethical behavior, the practitioner must often rely primarily upon his or her own *professional judgment.*

In addition to studying a code of ethics, professionals attempting to resolve an ethical dilemma might ask themselves the following questions: "Would the action that I am considering be fair to everyone involved?" and "If my friends and family knew all the facts, would they be proud of my actions?" **Ethical conduct** means more than abiding by a list of rules; it means an "*unswerving commitment to honorable behavior; even at the sacrifice of personal advantage.*" [Emphasis supplied.][17]

---

[16]Our Case in Point involving Riley and his brother is intended to show that ethical dilemmas *do not always have clear-cut answers.* This case hinges upon personal judgments, including the closeness of the relationship between Riley and his brother, and what impairs the "appearance" of independence. Thus, even with all the facts in hand, experts are likely to disagree on the answer to this case.

[17]AICPA, *Code of Professional Conduct* (New York: 1991), Preamble.

NET CONNECTIONS

The Financial Accounting Standards Board has an interesting Internet site at:

www.fasb.org

From the Table of Contents go to Facts About the FASB to find some interesting information about this important accounting body.

You also might visit the home page of the Association of Certified Fraud Examiners at:

www.acfe.org

Click on EthicsLine to learn about the concept of a company hotline reporting possible ethics violations.

And finally, visit our home page:

www.magpie.org/cyberlab

Use the email feature to let us know what you thought of your first accounting course.

We wish you every success in your future studies and your career. If our home page can be of further assistance, you're always welcome.

SUMMARY OF LEARNING OBJECTIVES

① Explain the need for recognized accounting standards.

Recognized accounting standards guide companies in preparing financial statements which are reasonably comparable and which meet the needs of users. Recognized standards also assist users in interpreting the information within these statements.

② Discuss the nature and sources of generally accepted accounting principles.

Generally accepted accounting principles stem both from official sources, such as the FASB and the SEC, and from unofficial sources, such as tradition and widespread use.

③ Discuss the accounting principles presented on pages 669–677.

The principles and concepts discussed in this chapter include the concept of an accounting entity, the going-concern assumption, the time period principle, the stable-dollar assumption, objectivity, the cost principle, the realization principle, matching, consistency, disclosure, materiality, and conservatism. This is neither a complete nor an official listing of generally accepted accounting principles, but these are some of the most important concepts which underlie current accounting practices.

④ Apply the percentage-of-completion method of income recognition.

The percentage-of-completion method is used in recognizing income on long-term construction projects in which the total profit can be *reasonably estimated* in advance. Under this method, the company recognizes gross profit *in proportion* to the work completed during the period, rather than waiting until the project is finished.

The percentage-of-completion method is an exception to the realization principle. This exception is justified because delaying profit recognition to the end of such projects would make the periodic financial statements less useful.

⑤ Describe the role of professional judgment in the financial reporting process.

Professional judgment is required in nearly every aspect of the financial reporting process. For example, accountants must use judgment in selecting appropriate accounting methods, making the many estimates inherent in financial statements, deciding which items are "material," and identifying those events requiring special disclosure.

⑥ Explain the nature of ethics and ethical dilemmas.

Ethics are the moral principles that govern the behavior of individuals. While personal ethics vary from individual to individual, a consensus generally exists in society as to what is considered ethical and unethical behavior.

In fact, governments pass laws that define what their citizens consider to be the more extreme forms of unethical behavior. But much of what is considered unethical in a particular society is not specifically prohibited.

An *ethical dilemma* is a situation that involves a decision about appropriate behavior. A key aspect of an ethical dilemma is that it affects parties who are not involved in the decision.

⑦ Explain the basic purpose of a code of ethics within a profession.

The basic purpose of a code of ethics is to provide members of the profession with guidelines for conducting themselves in a manner consistent with the responsibilities of the profession.

⑧ Apply the concepts of ethical conduct to situations likely to arise in accounting practice.

Ethical conduct involves many concepts, including integrity, competence, confidentiality, and—in the case of audit and review services—independence. In summary, ethical conduct means an "unswerving commitment to honorable behavior, even at the sacrifice of personal advantage."[1]

The concepts discussed in this chapter form the theoretical framework of the financial reporting process. An understanding of these concepts should assist you in interpreting and using accounting information, and also in the further study of accounting.

KEY TERMS INTRODUCED OR EMPHASIZED IN CHAPTER 14

American Institute of Certified Public Accountants (AICPA) (p. 668) A professional organization of Certified Public Accountants (CPAs) that has long been influential in the development of accounting principles.

Conservatism (p. 677) A traditional practice of resolving uncertainties by choosing an asset valuation at the lower point of the range of reasonableness. This term also refers to the policy of postponing recognition of revenue to a later date when a range of reasonable choice exists. Conservatism is designed to avoid overstatement of financial strength and earnings.

Consistency (p. 676) An assumption that once a particular accounting method is adopted, it will not be changed from period to period. Consistency is intended to make financial statements of a given company comparable from year to year.

Disclosure principle (p. 676) Financial statements should include all material and relevant information about

---

[1]AICPA, *Code of Professional Conduct* (New York: 1991), Preamble.

the financial position and operating results of the business. The notes accompanying financial statements are an important means of making the necessary disclosures.

Ethical conduct (p. 690)   Doing "what is right," even at the sacrifice of personal advantage.

Ethical dilemma (p. 679)   A decision that an individual must make that involves appropriate behavior. A common characteristic of all ethical dilemmas is that they have an effect on the welfare of individuals or groups of individuals who are not involved in making the decision.

Financial Accounting Standards Board (FASB) (p. 668)   The organization with primary responsibility for formulating new accounting standards. The FASB is part of the private sector and is not a governmental agency.

Generally accepted accounting principles (GAAP) (p. 667)   The "ground rules" for financial reporting. This concept includes principles, concepts, and methods that have received authoritative support (such as from the FASB) or that have become "generally accepted" through widespread use.

Going-concern assumption (p. 669)   An assumption that a business entity will continue in operation indefinitely and thus will carry out its existing commitments.

Installment method (p. 672)   An accounting method used principally in the determination of taxable income. It provides for recognition of profit on installment contracts in proportion to cash collected.

Institute of Management Accountants (IMA) (p. 681)   A professional association consisting primarily of management accountants.

Management accountant (p. 686)   An accountant employed within a specific organization. Management accountants develop accounting information to meet the various needs of the organization, and also assist management in the interpretation of this information.

Matching principle (p. 674)   The accounting principle that governs the timing of expense recognition. This principle indicates that expenses should be offset against revenue on a basis of cause and effect. That is, the revenue of an accounting period should be offset by those costs and expenses that were causal factors in producing that revenue.

Materiality (p. 676)   The relative importance of an amount or item. An item which is not significant enough to influence the decisions of users of financial statements is considered to be *not* material. The accounting treatment of immaterial items may be guided by convenience rather than by theoretical principles.

Objectivity (objective evidence) (p. 670)   The valuation of assets and the measurement of income are to be based as much as possible on objective evidence, such as exchange prices in arm's-length transactions.

Percentage-of-completion method (p. 673)   A method of accounting for long-term construction projects which recognizes revenue and profits in proportion to the work completed, based on an estimate of the portion of the project completed each accounting period.

Professional judgment (p. 678)   Using one's professional knowledge, experience, and ethics to make decisions which have no prescribed or obvious answer.

Realization principle (p. 672)   The principle of recognizing revenue in the accounts only when the earning process is virtually complete, which is usually at the time of sale of goods or rendering service to customers.

Securities and Exchange Commission (SEC) (p. 668)   A governmental agency with the legal power to set accounting principles. However, the SEC traditionally has adopted the principles developed by the FASB, rather than developing its own set of principles. The SEC enforces accounting principles by giving the weight of law to standards developed by the FASB. The SEC reviews the financial statements of publicly owned corporations for compliance with the Commission's reporting requirements.

Stable-dollar assumption (p. 670)   In using money as a measuring unit and preparing financial statements expressed in dollars, accountants make the assumption that the dollar is a stable unit of measurement. This assumption is faulty in an environment of continued inflation.

Time period principle (p. 670)   The idea that to be useful, financial statements should be prepared for relatively short accounting periods of equal length. While this principle contributes to the timeliness of financial statements, it conflicts with the objectivity principle by forcing accountants to make many estimates, such as the useful lives of depreciable assets.

DEMONSTRATION PROBLEM

Nantucket Boat Works builds custom sailboats. During the first year of operations, the company built four boats for Island Charter Company. The four boats had a total cost of $216,000 and were sold for a total price of $360,000, due on an installment basis. Island Charter Company paid $120,000 of this sales price during the first year, plus an additional amount for interest charges.

At year-end, work is in progress on two other boats which are 40% complete. The contract price for these two boats totals $250,000 and costs incurred on these boats during the year total $60,000 (40% of estimated total cost of $150,000).

INSTRUCTIONS

Compute the gross profit for Nantucket Boat Works during its first year of operations under each of the following assumptions. (Interest earned from Island Charter Company does not enter into the computation of gross profit.)

a. The entire profit is recognized on the four boats completed and profit on the two boats under construction is recognized on a percentage-of-completion basis.

b. Profit on the four boats completed is recognized on the installment basis and no portion of the profit on the two boats under construction will be recognized until the boats are completed, delivered to customers, and cash is collected.

SOLUTION TO DEMONSTRATION PROBLEM

a. Computation of gross profit using percentage-of-completion basis:

Gross profit on completed boats:

Sales revenue	$360,000
Less: Cost of goods sold	216,000
Gross profit	$144,000
Gross profit on boats under construction:	
Estimated profit, $100,000 × 40% (Estimated profit = $250,000 sales price minus $150,000 estimated costs)	40,000
Gross profit recognized during the year	$184,000

b. Computation of gross profit using installment basis:

Sales revenue:

Boats completed and sold (cash collected)	$120,000
Less: Cost recovered by cash collections during first year ($120,000 × 60%*)	72,000
Gross profit recognized during first year	$ 48,000

Total costs on completed boats amount to 60% of the sales price ($216,000 ÷ $360,000 = 60%). Therefore, 60% of cash collected during the period is viewed as a recovery of cost and 40% of cash collected is recognized as gross profit.

SELF-TEST QUESTIONS

The answers to these questions appear on page 707.

1. Generally accepted accounting principles (GAAP):
   a. Include only the official pronouncements of the standard-setting organizations, such as the AICPA, SEC, and FASB.
   b. May include customary accounting practices in widespread use even if not mentioned specifically in official pronouncements.
   c. Eliminate the need for professional judgment in the area in which an official pronouncement exists.
   d. Are laws issued by the FASB and the SEC, based upon a vote by the CPAs in the United States.

2. Which of the following situations best illustrates the application of the *realization* principle?
   a. A company sells merchandise on the installment method and recognizes gross profit as the cash is collected from customers.
   b. A construction company engaged in a three-year project determines the portion of profit to be recognized each year using the percentage-of-completion method.
   c. A construction company engaged in a three-month project recognizes no profit until the project is completed under the completed-contract method.

d. A manufacturer that sells washing machines with a three-year warranty recognizes warranty expense related to current year sales, based upon the estimated future liability.

3. Which of the following concepts has the *least* influence in determining the depreciation expense reported in the income statement under current GAAP?
   a. Reliability—The price of a depreciable asset established in an exchange transaction can be supported by verifiable, objective evidence.
   b. Cost principle—Assets are initially recorded in the account at cost and no adjustment is made to this valuation in subsequent periods, except to allocate a portion of the original cost to expense as assets expire.
   c. Relevance—Amounts shown in the financial statements should reflect current market values, as these are the most relevant to decision makers.
   d. Matching principle—Accountants attempt to match revenue with the expenses incurred in generating that revenue by systematically allocating an asset's cost to expense over its useful life.

4. Which of the following is *not* true about ethical dilemmas? Ethical dilemmas always:
   a. Involve choices about alternative courses of action.
   b. Involve decisions about violations of laws.
   c. Affect other individuals or groups of individuals.
   d. Involve the use of judgment.

5. The concept of ethical conduct would *prohibit* a professional accountant from which of the following? (More than one answer may be correct.)
   a. Resolving issues based upon professional judgment.
   b. After resigning because of an ethical dispute with an employer, accepting employment elsewhere in the same industry.
   c. Using for personal gain information which has not yet been released to the public about the financial position of a publicly owned company that is an employer or client.
   d. Investing in the common stocks of any publicly owned companies.

6. Which of the following are *not* included among the IMA's suggestions as to how a management accountant might resolve an ethical conflict with his or her employer? (More than one answer may be correct.)
   a. Discuss the matter with a management official *above* the position of the accountant's immediate supervisor.
   b. In strict confidence, anonymously inform the SEC.
   c. Resign from the organization.
   d. Call a press conference and "go public" with the issue.

ASSIGNMENT MATERIAL

DISCUSSION QUESTIONS

1. Briefly explain the meaning of the term *generally accepted accounting principles*.
2. Why is it important that the accounting principles be "generally accepted"?
3. Name the three groups in the United States that have been the most influential in developing generally accepted accounting principles.
4. To be "generally accepted," must an accounting method be set forth in the official pronouncements of an accounting rule-making organization? Explain.
5. Are generally accepted accounting principles in worldwide use? Explain.
6. What is the *time period principle?* Does this principle tend to increase or decrease the objectivity of accounting information? Explain.

7. What is meant by the term *stable-dollar assumption?* Is this assumption completely valid? Explain.

8. What is the meaning of the term *objectivity* as it is used by accountants? Is accounting information completely objective? Explain.

9. An argument has long existed as to whether assets should be valued in financial statements at cost or at estimated market value. Explain the implications of the *objectivity principle* in this controversy.

10. Explain what is meant by the expression "trade-off between *reliability* and *relevance*" in connection with the preparation of financial statements.

11. What two conditions should be met before accountants consider revenue to be *realized?*

12. Long-term construction projects often are accounted for by the percentage-of-completion method.
    a. Is this method consistent with the realization principle? Explain.
    b. What is the justification for the use of this method?

13. Briefly explain the *matching principle.* Indicate two approaches that accountants follow in attempting to "match" revenue with expense.

14. Does the concept of *consistency* mean that all companies should use the same accounting methods? Explain.

15. Briefly define the principle of *disclosure.* List four examples of information that should be disclosed in financial statements or in notes accompanying the statements.

16. Briefly explain the concept of *materiality.* If an item is not material, how is the item treated for financial reporting purposes?

17. Does *conservatism* mean that assets should be deliberately understated in accounting records? Explain fully.

18. Indicate how the concept of *conservatism* would apply to:
    a. Estimating the allowance for doubtful accounts receivable.
    b. Estimating the useful lives of depreciable assets.

19. What organization is primarily responsible for the development of new accounting standards? Why does this organization encourage all elements of the economic community to express their views during the standard-setting process?

20. Professional judgment plays an important role in financial reporting. Identify at least three areas in which the accountant preparing financial statements must make professional judgments that will affect the content of the statements.

21. Briefly explain why society benefits from "ethical conduct" by all citizens. Next, explain why a society expects professionals to observe additional ethical standards, beyond those which pertain to all citizens.

22. What is meant by an *ethical dilemma?* Describe an ethical dilemma that you have faced.

23. Why are the ethics of business executives important to society?

24. Explain why all recognized professions have developed their own codes of professional ethics.

25. Identify two associations of professional accountants that have developed codes of professional ethics for their members. Also, indicate the types of accounting activity emphasized in each of these codes.

26. Identify an ethical concept that is unique to the auditing of financial statements. Explain why this ethical concept is important in the auditing function.

27. Briefly describe the ethical concept of *confidentiality.* Does this concept apply to public accountants, to management accountants, or to both? Does this concept prevent CPAs from insisting that their clients make "adequate disclosure" in financial statements intended for use by outsiders?

28. Briefly explain the steps that a management accountant should take to resolve an ethical problem existing at his or her place of employment.

29. Why may a management accountant have to "pay a higher price" in resolving an ethical conflict than the "price paid" by a public accountant?

30. Briefly explain several reasons why even an honest person may have difficulty in always following the "ethical" course of action.

EXERCISES

EXERCISE 14-1
Personal Ethical Dilemma

Gary Watson, a friend of yours, is graduating and interviewing for a job. Gary was invited by both Tilly Manufacturing Co. and Watson Supply Company to come to a nearby city for an interview. Both companies have offered to pay Gary's expenses. His total expenses for the trip were $96 for mileage on his car plus $45 for meals. As he prepares the letters requesting reimbursement, he is considering asking for the total amount of the expenses from both employers. His rationale is that if he had taken separate trips, each employer would have had to pay that amount.

a. Who are the parties that are directly affected by this ethical dilemma?

b. Are the other students at the college potentially affected by Gary's decision? Explain.

c. Are the professors at the college potentially affected by Gary's decision? Explain.

d. If Gary asked for your advice, what would you tell him?

EXERCISE 14-2
Accounting Terminology
LO 2,3,5

Listed below are nine technical accounting terms introduced or emphasized in this chapter.

GAAP	Professional judgment	Realization
SEC	Materiality	Matching
Objectivity	Conservatism	Consistency

Each of the following statements may (or may not) describe one of these technical terms. For each statement, indicate the accounting term described, or answer "None" if the statement does not correctly describe any of the terms.

a. The concept of associating expenses with revenue on a basis of cause and effect.

b. An essential element for an accountant making estimates, selecting appropriate accounting methods, and resolving trade-offs between the goals of conflicting accounting principles.

c. The organization which is primarily responsible for developing new accounting standards in the United States.

d. The goal of having all companies use the same accounting methods.

e. The list of acceptable accounting principles developed by the SEC as part of its conceptual framework project.

f. The accounting principle used in determining when revenue should be recognized in financial statements.

g. An accounting concept that may justify departure from other accounting principles for purposes of convenience and economy.

EXERCISE 14-3
Asset Valuation
LO 3

Milestone Manufacturing Company has just purchased expensive equipment that was custom-made to suit the firm's manufacturing operations. Because of the custom nature of this machinery, it would be of little value to any other company. Therefore, the controller of Milestone is considering writing these machines down to their estimated resale value in order to provide a conservative valuation of assets in the company's balance sheet. In the income statement, the write-down would appear as a "loss on revaluation of machinery."

Separately discuss the idea of writing down the carrying value of the machinery in light of each of the four following accounting concepts:

a. The going-concern assumption

b. The matching principle

c. Objectivity

d. Conservatism

EXERCISE 14-4
Revenue Recognition
 LO 3

In deciding when to recognize revenue in financial statements, accountants normally apply the realization principle.

a. Revenue is considered realized when two conditions are met. What are these conditions?

b. Indicate when the conditions for recognition of revenue have been met in each of the following situations. (Assume that financial statements are prepared monthly.)
  1. An airline sells tickets several months in advance of its flights.
  2. An appliance dealer sells merchandise on 24-month payment plans.
  3. A professional sports team sells season tickets in July for eight home games to be played in the months of August through December.
  4. Interest revenue relating to a 2-year note receivable is all due at the maturity of the note.

EXERCISE 14-5
Expense Recognition
 LO 3

Mystery Playhouse prepares monthly financial statements. At the beginning of its three-month summer season, the company has programs printed for each of its 48 upcoming performances. Under certain circumstances, either of the following accounting treatments of the costs of printing these programs would be acceptable. Justify both of the accounting treatments using accounting principles discussed in this chapter.

a. The cost of printing the programs is recorded as an asset and is allocated to expense in the month in which the programs are distributed to patrons attending performances.

b. The entire cost of printing the programs is charged to expense when the invoice is received from the printer.

EXERCISE 14-6
Violations of Accounting Principles
LO 3

For each situation described below, indicate the principle of accounting that is being violated. You may choose from the following:

Accounting entity	Materiality
Consistency	Objectivity
Disclosure	Realization
Matching	Stable-dollar assumption

a. The bookkeeper for a large metropolitan auto dealership depreciates metal wastebaskets over a period of five years.

b. Upon completion of the construction of a condominium project which will soon be offered for sale, Townhome Developers increased the balance sheet valuation of the condominiums to their sales value and recognized the expected profit on the project.

c. Plans to dispose of a major segment of the business are not communicated to readers of the financial statements.

d. The cost of expensive, custom-made machinery installed in an assembly line is charged to expense because it is doubtful that the machinery would have any resale value if the assembly line were shut down.

e. A small commuter airline recognizes no depreciation on its aircraft because the planes are maintained in "as good as new" condition.

EXERCISE 14-7
Profit Recognition:
Installment Method

On September 15, 1997, Susan Moore sold a piece of property, which cost her $56,000, for $80,000, net of commissions and other selling expenses. The terms of sale were as follows: down payment, $8,000; balance, $3,000 on the fifteenth day of each month for 24 months, starting October 15, 1997. Compute the gross profit to be recognized by Moore in 1997, 1998, and 1999 using (a) the *accrual basis* of accounting and (b) the *installment basis* of accounting. Moore uses a fiscal year ending December 31.

EXERCISE 14-8
Profit Recognition:
Percentage-of-Completion
Method

The Clinton Corporation recognizes the profit on a long-term construction project as work progresses. From the information given below, compute the profit that should be recognized each year, assuming that the original cost estimate on the contract was $6,000,000 and that the contract price is $7,500,000.

Year	Costs Incurred	Profit Considered Realized
1997	$1,800,000	$?
1998	3,000,000	?
1999	1,171,000	?
Total	$5,971,000	$1,529,000

EXERCISE 14-9
The Conceptual Framework

The FASB recently issued a series of *Statements of Financial Accounting Concepts* intended to set forth a broad "conceptual framework" of accounting theory. Explain how an understanding of accounting theory is useful to:

a. Members of the FASB.

b. Accountants involved in the preparation of financial statements.

c. Users of financial statements.

EXERCISE 14-10
Business Ethical
Dilemma

Management of a chain of fast-food restaurants is making a decision about the materials to be used in packaging take-out food. The alternatives are to use plastic or biodegradable materials that cost about 15% more.

a. Explain why business ethics are significant to a society.

b. Identify the individuals or groups of individuals whose welfare is affected by the executive decision about the materials used.

c. How might the executives be able to minimize the effect on the stockholders of deciding to use the more costly biodegradable material?

EXERCISE 14-11
Ethical
Responsibilities
of a CPA

Teresa Ortiz, CPA, was engaged to audit the financial statements of Meglo Corporation and also to prepare the company's income tax return. During the course of her work, Ortiz discovered that in its income tax return, Meglo had classified $75,000 in amortization of goodwill as "depreciation expense." (Depreciation is deductible in determining taxable income, but amortization of goodwill is not. *Note:* Goodwill purchased subsequent to August 10, 1993 *can* be amortized for income tax purposes. Meglo's goodwill, however, originates from an earlier transaction.) Ortiz discussed this problem with her client, but the client insisted on deducting the amortization under the caption "Depreciation expense." A representative of management stated: "This distinction makes no sense. If amortization of goodwill incurred prior to 1993 isn't deductible, it should be. After all, it's the same basic concept as depreciation expense."

Also during this engagement, Ortiz learned that Meglo has owed $36,000 to Martin Advertising Agency for a period of 17 months. Apparently, Martin had underbilled Meglo for services rendered two years ago and has made no request for the $36,000 additional payments due.

In the financial statements, Meglo included appropriate amounts of income taxes expense and income taxes payable. The company also properly included the $36,000 among its liabilities. However, management has told Ortiz that it has no intention of making payment of this amount unless it receives a bill from Martin.

Discuss Ortiz's ethical responsibilities with respect to (a) completing her professional engagements for Meglo, and (b) personally disclosing the facts directly to the affected third parties (the IRS and/or Martin).

EXERCISE 14-12
The Honorable Mr. Chan

Hong-Ching Chan, CMA, was hired this year as a management accountant for Drexel, Inc. While working for Drexel, Chan learns that in the preceding year the company understated its tax liability in its income tax return by more than $400,000. Chan also knows that the IRS pays a 10% finder's fee to people who provide information enabling the IRS to collect taxes due.

a. Can Chan ethically report Drexel to the IRS and claim the finder's fee?

b. Would your answer be different if Chan had been fired by Drexel?

c. Would your answer be different if Chan were a CPA engaged by Drexel to conduct an audit of the company's financial statements?

EXERCISE 14-13
Financial Statement Disclosures— Toys "R" Us

LO 3

Adequate financial statement disclosure is an important part of financial reporting by publicly held companies. The financial statements of **Toys "R" Us** appear in Appendix A.

a. The notes to the financial statements of the company are presented on pages A-11 through A-19 of Appendix A. List and briefly describe each note.

b. The note titled "Seasonal Financing and Long-Term Debt" includes a schedule of future annual maturities on long-term obligations. What do you believe is the purpose of this disclosure?

PROBLEM 14-1
Rationale Behind Acceptable Practices

LO 3

PROBLEMS

Paragraphs **a** through **e** describe accounting practices which *are in accord* with generally accepted accounting principles. From the following list of accounting principles, identify those principles which you believe justify or explain each described accounting practice. (Most of the described practices are explained by a single principle; however, more than one principle may relate to a given practice.) Briefly explain the relationship between the described accounting practice and the underlying accounting principle.

Accounting Principles

Consistency	Accounting entity concept
Materiality	Matching revenue with expense
Objectivity	Going-concern assumption
Realization	Adequate disclosure
Conservatism	Stable-dollar assumption

Accounting Practices

a. If land costing $60,000 were sold for $65,000, a $5,000 gain would be reported regardless of inflation during the years that the land has been owned.

b. When equipment is purchased, an estimate is made of its useful life, and the equipment is then depreciated over this period.

c. The personal assets of the owner of a sole proprietorship are not disclosed in the financial statements of the business, even when these personal assets are sufficient to ensure payment of all the business's liabilities.

d. In estimating the appropriate size of the allowance for doubtful accounts, most accountants would rather see this allowance be a little too large rather than a little too small.

e. The methods used in the valuation of inventory and for the depreciation of plant assets are described in a footnote to the financial statements.

PROBLEM 14-2
Accounting Principles
LO 3

Paragraphs **a** through **e,** below, describe accounting practices which *are in accord* with generally accepted accounting principles. From the following list of accounting principles, identify those principles which you believe justify or explain each described accounting practice. (Most of the practices are explained by a single principle; however, more than one principle may relate to a particular practice.) Briefly explain the relationship between the described accounting practice and the underlying accounting principle.

Accounting Principles

Consistency	Accounting entity concept
Materiality	Matching revenue with expense
Objectivity	Going-concern assumption
Realization	Adequate disclosure
Conservatism	Stable-dollar assumption

Accounting Practices

a. The purchase of a 2-year fire insurance policy is recorded by debiting an asset account even though no refund will be received if the policy is canceled.

b. Hand tools with a small unit cost are charged to expense when purchased even though the individual tools have a useful life of several years.

c. An airline records depreciation on its aircraft even though an excellent maintenance program keeps the planes in "as good as new" condition.

d. A lawsuit filed against a company is described in footnotes to the company's financial statements even though the lawsuit was filed with the court shortly after the company's balance sheet date.

e. A real estate developer carriers an unsold inventory of condominiums in its accounting records at cost rather than at estimated sales value.

PROBLEM 14-3
Applying Accounting
Principles
LO 3

Five independent situations are described below.

a. Pearl Cove Hotel recognizes room rental revenue on the date that a reservation is received. For the summer season, many guests make reservations as much as a year in advance of their intended visit.

b. In prior years Regal Corporation had used the straight-line method of depreciation for both financial reporting purposes and for income tax purposes. In the current year, Regal continued to use straight-line depreciation on all assets for financial reporting purposes, but began depreciating newly acquired assets by an accelerated method for income tax purposes.

c. The liabilities of Ellis Construction Company are substantially in excess of the company's assets. In order to present a more impressive balance sheet for the business, Roy Ellis, the owner of the company, included in the company's balance sheet such personal assets as his savings account, automobile, and real estate investments.

d. On January 9, 1998, Gable Company's only plant was badly damaged by a tornado and will be closed for much of the coming year. No mention was made of this event in the financial statements for the year ended December 31, 1997, as the tornado occurred after year-end.

e. Friday Production Co. follows a policy of valuing its plant assets at liquidation values in the company's balance sheet. No depreciation is recorded on these assets. Instead, a loss is recognized if the liquidation values decline from one year to the next. If the liquidation values increase during the year, a gain is recognized.

INSTRUCTIONS

For each situation, indicate the accounting principle, if any, that has been violated and explain briefly the nature of the violation. If you believe the treatment *is in accord with generally accepted accounting principles,* explain why.

PROBLEM 14-4
Evaluating Applications of
Accounting Principles

Assume that you are an independent CPA performing audits of financial statements. In the course of your work, you encounter the following situations:

a. Reliable Appliance Company sells appliances on long-term payment plans. The company uses the installment method of recognizing revenue in its income tax returns and in its financial statements. Uncollectible accounts consistently range between 1.5% and 2.0% of net sales.

b. Akron Labs has spent $700,000 during the year in a very imaginative advertising campaign. The controller is sure that the advertising will generate revenue in future periods, but he has no idea how much revenue will be produced or over what period of time it will be earned. Therefore, he has decided to follow the "conservative" policy of charging the advertising expenditures to expense in the current period.

c. Taylor Corporation has purchased special-purpose equipment, designed to work with other machinery already in place in Taylor's assembly line. Due to the special nature of this machinery, it has virtually no resale value to any other company. Therefore, Taylor's accountant has charged the entire cost of this special-purpose machinery to expense in the current period.

d. Architectural Associates charges all purchases of drafting supplies directly to expense. At year-end, the company makes no entry to record the fact that $100 to $200 of these supplies remain on hand.

e. Newton Company prepares financial statements four times each year. For convenience, these statements are prepared when business is slow and the accounting staff is not busy with other matters. Last year, financial statements were prepared for the two-month period ended February 28, the five-month period ended July 31, the three-month period ended October 31, and the one-month period ended November 30.

INSTRUCTIONS

Discuss each of the above situations. If you consider the treatment to be in conformity with generally accepted accounting principles, explain why. If you do not, explain which principle or principles have been violated, and also explain how the situation should have been reported.

PROBLEM 14-5
Personal Ethical
Dilemmas

Presented below are four ethical dilemmas that you may someday face:

1. Henry Owen found a wallet that contains $150 in cash in front of a grocery store.

2. Kathy Potter found $150 in cash on the floor of one of the aisles of a grocery store.

3. Upon reviewing this month's bank statement, Andy Martin noted that he received credit for a $400 deposit that he did not make.

4. Sally Kee recently was in an auto accident. Since it was the other individual's fault, she was told to have the damage to her automobile repaired by any garage. Kee's automobile had some damage from a previous accident that had never been repaired. When she went to one garage for an estimate, the owner indicated that he could fix all of the damage to her automobile, and submit the total cost to the insurance company for payment.

INSTRUCTIONS

a. For each situation explain the dilemma and the parties whose welfare may be affected.

b. State your opinion as to the appropriate course of action.

PROBLEM 14-6
Business Ethical
Dilemmas
LO 6,7

Below are four independent cases that may confront business executives. Identify the individuals or groups of individuals that are affected by the decision, state your opinion as to the appropriate course of action, and justify your opinion.

a. Howard Edwards is an accounting clerk for a small biotech corporation. The corporation's stock is currently selling for $8 per share. Edwards recently overheard the chief financial officer of the corporation discussing the fact that a large drug company was considering buying the corporation for $15 per share. Edwards is considering calling his uncle and recommending that he buy stock in the corporation before the news gets out.

b. Leslie Mason is the accountant for a small appliance store. Recently, she received full payment of $200 on an account receivable that was long past due and had been written off by the company. Mason is considering keeping the payment.

c. John Tuttle is the manager of a division of a large manufacturing company. He receives a salary and a bonus based on the performance of his division. Tuttle relies on the bonus to pay his family's living expenses. For the current period, the division's performance has been very disappointing, and Tuttle is considering falsifying the division's financial report to ensure that he receives a bonus.

d. Jack Yeager is a sales manager for a large manufacturing company. One evening he took his wife and several other friends to dinner. Since one of his friends was a wine connoisseur, she ordered the wine for everyone. When the bill was presented, Yeager "picked-up the tab." To his surprise the wine alone cost $450, and the entire bill was close to $800. He is considering charging this meal to his expense account at work as "business entertainment."

PROBLEM 14-7
Management
Ethical Dilemmas
LO 6

Below are four independent ethical dilemmas that may confront management. In each case identify the individuals or groups of individuals that will be affected by management's decision, provide your opinion as to an appropriate decision, and justify that opinion.

a. Management is considering taking a deduction for a large fine on the corporation's income tax return. Fines are clearly not deductible. However, management feels sure that the Internal Revenue Service will not find the item even if the corporation is audited.

b. Management of a food manufacturer is examining ways to reduce costs on one of its products. The purchasing manager has suggested that costs could be reduced if the corporation began using artificial ingredients in the product, rather than the natural ingredients that are currently being used. The purchasing manager also stated, "Since we have a large number of labels in stock, we could continue to use them even though they would not be precisely accurate as to the ingredients included in the product. The research shows that the artificial ingredients are as safe as the natural ingredients."

c. Management of a large construction company is considering paying a bribe to a high-ranking foreign government official to obtain a large construction contract.

d. Management of a manufacturing company is considering what type of air pollution control equipment to install in one of the company's plants. The least expensive equipment has been extensively criticized by a number of environmentalists. However, it does comply with environmental laws.

PROBLEM 14-8
Accountant Ethical
Dilemmas
LO 6,7,8

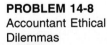

Below are five independent cases that may confront professional accountants. In each case, identify the specific article, rule, or standard from the AICPA or IMA code that should guide the accountant's conduct, and indicate the ethical course of action. If the situation does not create any ethical problem, briefly explain why not.

a. Brewster, CMA, works for the Defense Department. Part of her job is to evaluate bids of various defense contractors for Defense Department business. In the course of her work, she has come to know many people in the defense industry quite well. Today John Helms, a vice-president with General Systems Corporation, a defense contractor, offered Brewster the use of a condominium at a nearby ski resort any time she wanted to use it. He explained, "I know you like to ski. Our company owns this condominium, but no one ever seems to use it. Here's the key; just consider the place yours."

b. Bello, CPA, has been requested to audit the financial statements of Bello Corporation, a family business. The business is owned and operated entirely by Bello's parents, brothers, and sisters. Bello has no direct financial interest in the business and does not personally participate in its management.

c. Ross, CMA, works for One Million Auto Parts. The vice-president of marketing has asked Ross to prepare a summary of the market value of the company's inventory, arranged by geographic sales territories. Ross does not know the intended use of this summary. He does know, of course, that generally accepted accounting principles do not permit the valuation of inventories at market value in financial statements.

d. Jacobs, CPA, is a member of a CPA firm that audits four regional banks in the area. Jacobs is the firm's specialist in the banking industry. Yesterday, she received a request that her firm audit the financial statements of First Fidelity, the largest regional bank in the area.

e. Two months ago, Arnold Chiou, CMA, worked as a cost accountant for Ewing Oil Company, but he is now employed by WestStar Oil. A manager at WestStar tells Chiou that WestStar is thinking of cutting its prices to win market share from Ewing. However, the manager needs to know Ewing Oil's per-gallon production cost in order to know which company is likely to win a price war.

PROBLEM 14-9
More Accountant Ethical Dilemmas

Below are five independent cases that may confront professional accountants. In each case, identify the specific article, rule, or standard from the AICPA or IMA code that should guide the accountant's conduct, and indicate the ethical course of action. If the situation does not create any ethical problem, briefly explain why not.

a. Brown, CPA, has been engaged by Marshal Corporation to help the company design a more efficient accounting system. In the course of this engagement, Brown learns that in the preceding year, Marshal prepared its income tax return in a manner that understated the amount of income taxes due. Brown was not involved in the preparation of this tax return. However, she knows that the IRS pays a 10% finder's fee to anyone providing information that assists the agency in collecting additional taxes owed by another taxpayer.

Brown is considering alerting the IRS to the additional taxes owed by Marshal.

b. Huang, CMA, is asked by his employer to prepare financial statements in which depreciation expense is computed by the straight-line method. Huang knows that the company uses accelerated depreciation methods in its income tax return.

c. Porter, CPA, considers Commuter Airlines to be a well-managed company with a good future. For years, Porter has been purchasing stock in Commuter Airlines as a means of saving for her children's college education. Recently, Porter has received a request from Commuter Airlines to assist it in the preparation of its income tax return.

d. DMX Corporation does custom manufacturing and bills each of its customers on a "cost plus" basis. In advertising, DMX uses the slogan, "We'll treat you like our only customer."

DMX has just purchased for $300,000 special machinery that will be used on seven separate contracts. Swartz, a management accountant at DMX, is told by his supervisor to charge each of these contracts with the entire $300,000 cost. The supervisor explains, "We would have had to buy this machinery if we were working on just one contract, and in that case, the customer would be charged the entire $300,000. So we'll just treat each customer as if it were our only customer."

e. Mandella, CPA, is engaged in the audit of Wells Medical Products. Wells is in financial difficulties and will be using the audited financial statements in its effort to raise much-needed capital. The company hopes to issue 10-year bonds payable in the near future.

Mandella learns that Wells is a defendant in numerous lawsuits alleging that Microtain, a product produced by Wells in the early 1960s, caused birth defects. The lawsuits probably will not be resolved for perhaps 5, 10, or 15 years. If Wells should lose the suits, the damages awarded to the plaintiffs could bankrupt the company.

The chief financial officer for Wells tells Mandella, "Look, we aren't about to disclose this stuff in our financial statements. First, we're innocent; Microtain never hurt anyone. When it's all said and done, we won't owe a dime. Also, if we lose, we'll appeal. These suits won't even be settled until long after our 10-year bond issue has been repaid. If you insist on disclosing this mess in the financial statements, we'll never get our financing. We'll have to close up, and thousands of our employees will lose their jobs. In short, I can't allow disclosure of this information; you'll just have to regard it as 'confidential.'"

CASES

CASE 14-1
"Trade-Offs" among
Accounting Principles
LO 3

It is not possible to be consistent with all accounting principles all the time. Sometimes trade-offs are necessary; accountants may need to compromise one accounting principle or goal in order to achieve another more fully.

INSTRUCTIONS
Describe a situation that requires a trade-off between the following sets of principles or goals:

a. The relevance of accounting information to decision makers and the need for this information to be reliable.

b. The comparability of information reported by different companies and the idea that a company should consistently apply the same accounting methods from year to year.

c. The realization principle and the need for relatively timely information.

d. The desire to match revenue with expenses and the quest for objectivity.

CASE 14-2
GAAP from an Auditor's
Perspective
LO 3

Assume that you are an independent CPA performing audits of financial statements. In the course of your work, you encounter the following situations:

a. Gala Magazine receives most of its revenue in the form of 12-month subscriptions. Even though this subscription revenue has already been received in cash, the company's controller defers recognition in the income statement; the revenue is recognized on a monthly basis as the monthly issues of the magazine are mailed to subscribers.

b. Due to the bankruptcy of a competitor, Regis Trucking was able to buy plant assets worth at least $400,000 for the "bargain price" of $300,000. In order to reflect the benefits of this bargain purchase in the financial statements, the company recorded the assets at a cost of $400,000 and reported a $100,000 "gain on purchase of plant assets."

c. Metro Development Company built a 400-unit furnished apartment complex. All materials and furnishings used in this project that had a unit cost of less than $200 were charged immediately to expense. The total cost of these items amounted to $6 million.

d. In January 1998, the main plant of Hillside Manufacturing Company was destroyed in a fire. As this event happened in 1998, no loss was shown in the income statement for 1997. However, the event was thoroughly disclosed in notes to the 1997 financial statements.

e. In an effort to match revenue with all related expenses in an objective manner, Brentwood Company has established "useful life" standards for all types of expenditures. For example, expenditures for advertising are amortized over 36 months; the costs of employee training programs, 5 years; and research and development costs, 10 years.

INSTRUCTIONS
Discuss each of the above situations. If you consider the treatment to be in conformity with generally accepted accounting principles, explain why. If you do not, explain which principle or principles have been violated, and also explain how the situation should have been reported.

CASE 14-3
"What? Me? Fired?"

Christine Davis, a member of IMA, is a management accountant for CalTex Industries. Davis believes that she is being asked to accumulate inappropriate costs on a "cost plus" contract. All costs accumulated on the contract ultimately are billed to the customer (along with a markup representing CalTex's profit margin), an agency of the government.

a. Does this situation represent an ethical problem for Davis? Explain.

b. If you believe that an ethical problem exists, briefly explain the steps that Davis should take to resolve it.

c. Assume that as a result of taking the steps that you suggested in part **b,** Davis is fired. Based on IMA standards, does Davis have an ethical obligation to inform the governmental agency of her suspicions that it is being overcharged? Explain.

CASE 14-4
Ethics in the "Real World"

Bring into class a copy of a newspaper or magazine article describing a situation in which professional accountants probably faced an ethical dilemma. (Your article need not specifically mention the accountants' roles in the situation. Also, your article need not be current; you may select any article from any business publication.)

Describe the ethical problems that you believe confronted the accountants in this situation and the courses of action that should have been considered. Also, express your *personal opinion* as to whether or not the accountants acted in an ethical manner, including the reasons behind your opinion. Finally, discuss what *you* would have done in the accountants' place, identifying any factors that may have made your decision difficult.

INTERNET ASSIGNMENT

INTERNET 14-1
Disclosure of Loss Contingencies

The notes to the financial statements of a company provide a large number of informative disclosures that aid financial statement users in assessing the future cash flows of the company. An important note to many companies' financial statements is the one dealing with loss contingencies, which is often called "Contingencies" or "Litigation and Contingencies." Sometimes contingent liabilities can be devastating to the future profitability of the company.

a. Select a company in the petroleum industry, such as **Exxon** or **Texaco.**

b. Refer to the financial statements in the most recent Form 10-K of the company on SEC's EDGAR database of financial information about publicly owned companies, which may be accessed from the SEC's home page at:

www.sec.gov

c. Summarize the major contingent liabilities of the company.

d. Express your opinion of the effect of these contingent liabilities on the future profitability of the company.

OUR COMMENTS ON THE IN-TEXT CASES

YOU AS A CHIEF FINANCIAL OFFICER (P. 674)   This is a difficult question. Many businesses provide a trial period for a product and still recognize revenue at the time the product is delivered. For example, if you purchase a vacuum cleaner with a 30-day trial period, the company selling the vacuum cleaner would normally recognize the revenue at the time of sale. They would justify this method based on the fact that you must take action to return the product.

The terms of sale for your company are somewhat different. To complete the order, the customer must *take action* to request the key, otherwise the sale does not occur. Thus, we do not consider the company's sales revenue "realized" until the customer requests the key.

YOU AS A PURCHASING AGENT (P. 680)   Despite the fact that you received the cruise voucher with no action on your part, you should return it. Acceptance of the gift would give the impression of impropriety to anyone who found out about the situation. In addition, if you accepted the gift, the vendor might try to use your acceptance as leverage in negotiating future purchase contracts.

ANSWERS TO SELF-TEST QUESTIONS

1. b   **2.** c   **3.** c   **4.** b   **5.** c (This practice also is illegal "insider trading.")
6. b, d

ANNUAL REPORT OF TOYS "R" US

INTENDED FOR USE AFTER CHAPTER 6

In this appendix we present the 1994 annual report of Toys "R" Us, a publicly held corporation. This report was selected to illustrate many of the financial reporting concepts discussed in this textbook. But not all of the terminology and accounting policies appearing in this report are consistent with our text discussions. This illustrates some of the diversity that exists in financial reporting.

TABLE OF CONTENTS

Toys"R"Us is the world's largest children's specialty retail chain in terms of both sales and earnings. At January 28, 1995, the Company operated 618 toy stores in the United States, 293 international toy stores and 204 Kids"R"Us children's clothing stores.

STORE LOCATIONS

TOYS"R"US UNITED STATES - 618 LOCATIONS

Alabama - 7	Indiana - 12	Nebraska - 3	South Dakota - 2
Alaska - 1	Iowa - 7	Nevada - 3	Tennessee - 12
Arizona - 10	Kansas - 4	New Hampshire - 5	Texas - 50
Arkansas - 2	Kentucky - 7	New Jersey - 21	Utah - 5
California - 77	Louisiana - 8	New Mexico - 3	Virginia - 18
Colorado - 10	Maine - 2	New York - 41	Washington - 11
Connecticut - 9	Maryland - 17	North Carolina - 16	West Virginia - 3
Delaware - 2	Massachusetts - 16	Ohio - 28	Wisconsin - 11
Florida - 39	Michigan - 23	Oklahoma - 4	
Georgia - 14	Minnesota - 11	Oregon - 7	Puerto Rico - 4
Hawaii - 1	Mississippi - 5	Pennsylvania - 29	
Idaho - 2	Missouri - 12	Rhode Island - 1	
Illinois - 34	Montana - 1	South Carolina - 8	

TOYS"R"US INTERNATIONAL - 293 LOCATIONS

Australia - 17	France - 29	Malaysia - 3	Sweden - 3
Austria - 7	Germany - 53	Netherlands - 8	Switzerland - 4
Belgium - 3	Hong Kong - 4	Portugal - 3	Taiwan - 4
Canada - 56	Japan - 24	Singapore - 3	United Arab Emirates - 1
Denmark - 1	Luxembourg - 1	Spain - 20	United Kingdom - 49

KIDS"R"US UNITED STATES - 204 LOCATIONS

Alabama - 1	Indiana - 7	Minnesota - 5	Pennsylvania - 14
California - 25	Iowa - 1	Missouri - 4	Rhode Island - 1
Connecticut - 6	Kansas - 1	Nebraska - 1	Tennessee - 1
Delaware - 1	Maine - 1	New Hampshire - 2	Texas - 7
Florida - 8	Maryland - 8	New Jersey - 17	Utah - 2
Georgia - 4	Massachusetts - 5	New York - 20	Virginia - 7
Illinois - 20	Michigan - 13	Ohio - 19	Wisconsin - 3

FINANCIAL HIGHLIGHTS

(Dollars in millions except per share information)   *Fiscal Year Ended*

	Jan. 28, 1995	Jan. 29, 1994	Jan. 30, 1993	Feb. 1, 1992	Feb. 2, 1991	Jan. 28, 1990	Jan. 29, 1989	Jan. 31, 1988	Feb. 1, 1987	Feb. 2, 1986
OPERATIONS:										
Net Sales	$ 8,746	$ 7,946	$ 7,169	$ 6,124	$ 5,510	$ 4,788	$ 4,000	$ 3,137	$ 2,445	$ 1,976
Net Earnings	532	483	438	340	326	321	268	204	152	120
Earnings Per Share	1.85	1.63	1.47	1.15	1.11	1.09	.91	.69	.52	.41
FINANCIAL POSITION AT YEAR END:										
Working Capital	394	633	797	328	177	238	255	225	155	181
Real Estate-Net	2,271	2,036	1,877	1,751	1,433	1,142	952	762	601	423
Total Assets	6,571	6,150	5,323	4,583	3,582	3,075	2,555	2,027	1,523	1,226
Long-Term Obligations	785	724	671	391	195	173	174	177	85	88
Stockholders' Equity	3,429	3,148	2,889	2,426	2,046	1,705	1,424	1,135	901	717
NUMBER OF STORES AT YEAR END:										
Toys"R"Us - United States	618	581	540	497	451	404	358	313	271	233
Toys"R"Us - International	293	234	167	126	97	74	52	37	24	13
Kids"R"Us - United States	204	217	211	189	164	137	112	74	43	23

Consolidated Net Sales (billions)

Michael Goldstein,
Vice Chairman and Chief Executive Officer

Robert C. Nakasone,
President and Chief Operating Officer

TO OUR STOCKHOLDERS

FINANCIAL HIGHLIGHTS

We are proud to report another good year for Toys"R"Us. In 1994, we achieved gains in market share and once more reported record results, marking the 16th consecutive year of increased sales and earnings since Toys"R"Us became a public company. Over that period, earnings have grown at an annual compounded rate of 24%.

For the year, sales grew to $8.7 billion, a 10% increase over the $7.9 billion reported in the previous year. Operating earnings increased 11% while net earnings rose to $532 million, a 10% increase over the $483 million reported in 1993. Earnings per share climbed 14% to $1.85 compared to $1.63 a year ago.

Comparable store sales at our U.S.A. toy stores rose 2% for the year, with operating earnings up 7%. Our performance reflected several new marketing and merchandising initiatives: we introduced a new Spring catalog and three Holiday catalogs, which featured more pages, more coupons and received wider distribution; we introduced several initiatives to improve customer service; and expanded our Books"R"Us shops. We also introduced Lego and Stuffed Animal shops and the sale of PC software for children, which was successfully tested as a new Learning Center shop in a number of U.S.A. and European toy stores. However, we experienced a downturn in our video game business in the fall of 1994 as customers awaited new generation 32 and 64 bit video game systems by Sega, Sony and Nintendo, expected in the latter half of 1995. In addition, competition from national and regional discount stores, as well as mall based toy stores, intensified as they increased advertising and more than ever emphasized lower prices. Lastly, new competitors have emerged targeting specific segments of our business. These competitors include juvenile specialty stores, educational toy stores and computer electronic shops with broad offerings of video games.

We now face a number of issues, in our U.S.A. toy store operations, which require us to take significant actions. These steps, while improving our long-term profitability and market share, will adversely impact our ability to achieve our historic earnings growth rate in 1995. Further, until the new video game systems are introduced, the outlook for that category in the first three quarters of 1995 is poor, and it will hurt sales and profits. However, we expect a strong fourth quarter as the new systems and our initiatives create excitement and improved customer traffic.

Our strategies for 1995 include improving our image through a variety of pricing and marketing initiatives, the introduction of new in-store shops that highlight our dominant selection of merchandise and an increased emphasis on customer service. The Toys"R"Us franchise is one of the best in the world and we intend to take aggressive measures to strengthen this franchise over the years to come.

Internationally, our French and Iberian toy stores had comparable store sales increases for the full year. In Japan, our performance improved in the fourth quarter with the introduction of 32 bit video game systems by both Sony and Sega. These gains were offset by lower comparable store sales for our Canadian, Central European and United Kingdom toy stores, reflecting new competition in Canada and a poor retail environment in Central Europe. In spite of this, our International division achieved a 37% increase in operating earnings, by again improving upon inventory management and increasing productivity in both labor and distribution.

Our International franchising division added a third franchisee to the Toys"R"Us family in 1994, which will now enable us to open toy stores in Israel, Saudi Arabia and the United

2

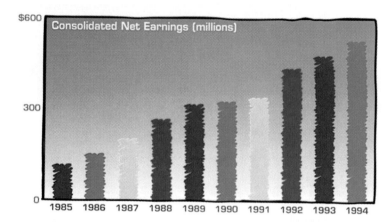

Consolidated Net Earnings (millions)

$600

300

0

1985 1986 1987 1988 1989 1990 1991 1992 1993 1994

Arab Emirates. Our first franchise store opened in Dubai in January 1995 to tremendous excitement and heavy consumer traffic. We expect to accelerate our franchising program by entering into agreements in additional countries in 1995, with plans to open stores in 1996.

Our Kids"R"Us children's clothing division enjoyed relatively strong comparable store sales despite the continuation of the difficult apparel sales environment. Operating profits rose 16%, our third successive year of strong growth, reflecting improved expense control as well as new marketing and merchandising initiatives. Our greatly expanded private label merchandise program has met with excellent customer response. In addition, Kids"R"Us closed 19 stores in 1994 which were not meeting expectations. Based on the last three years' results, we will expand Kids"R"Us at a faster rate as we enter 1996.

Under our $1 billion stock buyback program, we repurchased 13.1 million shares at a cost of $470 million during 1994. We intend to continue to aggressively buy back stock during 1995. In addition, we completed our transaction with Petrie Stores Corporation at the end of January 1995, which gave us approximately $162 million in cash, net of expenses, and increased our outstanding stock by approximately 2.2 million shares.

OPERATIONAL HIGHLIGHTS

We are proud of our ability to provide the best selection of merchandise, stocked in depth with everyday low prices while expanding customer service and maintaining one of the lowest expense structures in the industry. The following are some of the highlights of 1994 along with our plans for 1995.

In 1994, we significantly expanded our catalog program with a Spring catalog and two new and one expanded Holiday Toy catalogs that provided our customers with over $1,800 in coupon savings. This program allows us to continue to demonstrate the broad selection of merchandise that can be found at Toys"R"Us. Increasingly, customers in our stores use these as shopping

aids. Our International division has also begun to use the catalog program with tremendous success.

We have continued to test various "specialty shops" within our U.S.A. and International toy stores. In 1994, we added 130 Books"R"Us shops bringing our total to over 300 stores. We also added approximately twenty Lego shops, twenty Stuffed Animal shops and five Learning Center shops in our stores. Based on our successful test results, we will implement the Learning Center concept in 100 stores in 1995. These shops will carry a full selection of learning aid products as well as PC software for kids. In addition, by the middle of 1995 we plan to offer an exciting and full selection of PC software for children in all of our U.S.A. toy stores and in several international markets. Our focus will be on children's educational and entertainment software, and we plan to have the most dominant selection anywhere. We also plan to greatly expand our space allocation to large outdoor/indoor playsets to show our dominant selection in this merchandise category.

Enhancing customer service was our single most important operational development in 1994. In conjunction with this initiative, we installed customer friendly in-aisle price scanners and other service oriented

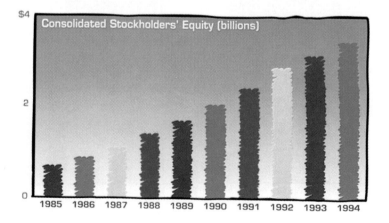

Consolidated Stockholders' Equity (billions)

$4

2

0

1985 1986 1987 1988 1989 1990 1991 1992 1993 1994

technology in our U.S.A. toy stores. We also tested and intend to install a new automated Baby Registry throughout the entire chain in 1995. Our Geoffrey Helper Program was expanded and we modified some of our store policies and procedures to be more customer friendly and increase employee empowerment and decision-making. In 1995, we will continue to enhance all aspects of customer service, from improving basic store maintenance and housekeeping standards to dedicating additional associate hours to critical customer service needs.

From the beginning of our remodeling program in 1990 through the end of January 1995, we have remodeled over 100 toy stores including 30 stores this past year. These remodeled stores enhance the customer's shopping experience while increasing in-store productivity. We expect to remodel another 15 to 20 toy stores in 1995.

During the year, the U.S.A. toy division continued to increase productivity and improve its ability to replenish stores by building two state-of-the-art automated distribution centers that replaced four older facilities. Further, our International division retrofitted two existing distribution centers with our new automated systems. We are proud of our associates in Japan who were able to continue to

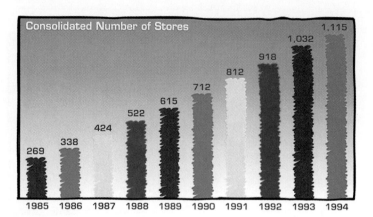

operate successfully following the January earthquake. Our distribution center located in Kobe sustained only minor damage. In 1995, we will be opening our largest distribution center in New Jersey and will also open a state-of-the-art distribution center in Germany.

STORE GROWTH

In 1994, we opened 37 toy stores in the United States. Internationally, 59 stores opened in 17 countries, including our first stores in Denmark, Luxembourg and Sweden and our first franchise store in the United Arab Emirates. For the second year in a row, our International division opened more toy stores than our U.S.A. toy division. We also opened 6 Kids"R"Us stores.

In 1995, we plan to open 40 toy stores in the United States and about 50 toy stores internationally, including franchise stores in the Middle East. We also plan to open about 10 new Kids"R"Us stores. The 1995 stores will capitalize on the existing infrastructure, thereby enhancing the profitability of new and existing stores alike.

Aided by our financial strength, we intend to capitalize on our strong competitive position throughout the world, by continued expansion to achieve greater sales, earnings and market share gains.

CORPORATE CITIZENSHIP

Toys"R"Us maintains a company-wide giving program focused on improving the health-care needs of children by supporting many national and regional children's health care organizations. In 1994, we contributed funds to over 100 children's health care organizations. We also expanded our Hospital Playroom Program, which equips quality children's play centers in hospitals, by opening eight additional playrooms, bringing the total to twenty-six. We expect to expand our program to thirteen additional hospitals in 1995.

Toys"R"Us is a signatory to a Fair Share Agreement with the NAACP and has taken steps to support

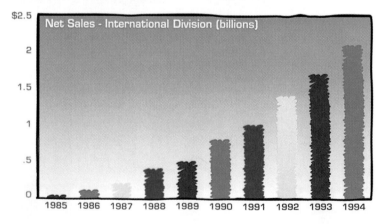

women and minorities in the workplace. We are the leading purchaser of products from several minority-owned toy companies.

Toys"R"Us continues to have a strong toy safety program which includes the inspection of directly imported toys. Furthermore, we continue to take numerous proactive initiatives, including a leadership position in eliminating the sale of look-alike toy guns. We are proud to be the recent recipient of the Consumer Product Safety Commission Chairman's Commendation For Significant Contributions to Product Safety.

Through our new Books"R"Us shops we are promoting literacy among children by demonstrating that reading is fun.

Lastly, we developed a Toy Guide for differently-abled children, which was carefully designed with their specific abilities and needs in mind.

HUMAN RESOURCES

The talent and high caliber of our management team and of our associates allows Toys"R"Us to expand aggressively and profitably.

We have made the following important promotions within our executive ranks:

Toys"R"Us, United States:
Michael J. Madden,
Group Vice President -
Store Operations

Michael A. Gerety,
Vice President - Store Planning

Kids"R"Us:
James G. Parros,
Senior Vice President - Stores and Distribution Center Operations

Jonathan M. Friedman,
Vice President -
Chief Financial Officer

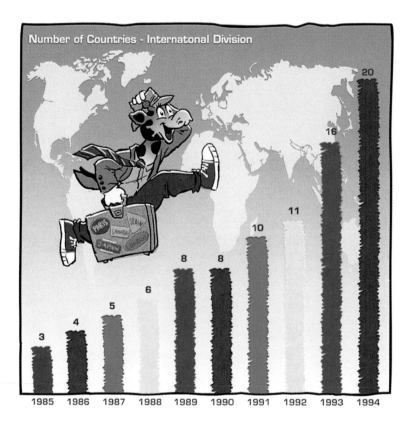

Number of Countries - International Division

1985	1986	1987	1988	1989	1990	1991	1992	1993	1994
3	4	5	6	8	8	10	11	16	20

SUMMARY

We intend to aggressively pursue all of our strategic initiatives and are committed to building market share and profitability in the years to come. We will work hard to continue being the most trusted store in town.

We value our excellent relationships with our innovative suppliers and commend them for their products which create an atmosphere of excitement in our stores. Our assessment of the February New York Toy Fair indicates a year of robust sales in basic categories such as fashion dolls and preschool toys, where there is quality product that is reasonably priced.

We recognize the dedication and quality work of our associates around the world who have made this another record year. Our appreciation is also extended to you, our stockholders, for your commitment and loyalty to Toys"R"Us.

Sincerely,

Michael Goldstein
Vice Chairman and
Chief Executive Officer

Robert C. Nakasone
President and
Chief Operating Officer

March 29, 1995

MANAGEMENT'S DISCUSSION-RESULTS OF OPERATIONS AND FINANCIAL CONDITION

RESULTS OF OPERATIONS*

The Company has experienced sales growth in each of its last three years; sales were up 10.1% in 1994, 10.8% in 1993 and 17.1% in 1992. Part of the growth is attributable to the opening of 121 new U.S.A. toy stores, 167 international toy stores and 39 children's clothing stores during the three year period, and a portion of the increase is due to comparable U.S.A. toy store sales increases of 2.1%, 3.3% and 6.9% in 1994, 1993 and 1992, respectively.

Cost of sales as a percentage of sales decreased to 68.7% in 1994 from 69.2% in 1993 and from 69.3% in 1992 due to a more favorable merchandise mix.

Selling, advertising, general and administrative expenses as a percentage of sales increased to 19.0% in 1994 from 18.8% in 1993 and 18.7% in 1992 primarily as a result of increases in such expenses at a rate faster than comparable store sales increases and also due to customer service initiatives implemented in 1994, and start-up costs for the opening of our new market in Australia in 1993.

Interest expense increased in 1994 as compared to 1993 and 1992 due to increased average borrowings and a change in the mix of borrowings and interest rates among countries. Short-term interest income decreased in 1994 as compared to 1993 and increased in 1993 as compared to 1992, principally due to the availability of cash for investments.

The effective tax rate decreased to 37.0% in 1994 from 37.5% in 1993, due to a one-time retroactive adjustment in 1993 for an increase in the U.S. Federal corporate income tax rate. The effective rate increased to 37.5% in 1993 from 36.5% in 1992, due to the rate change and retroactive adjustment discussed above. The Company believes its deferred tax assets, as reported, are fully realizable.

The Company believes that its risks attendant to foreign operations are minimal as it operates in twenty different countries which are politically stable. The Company's foreign exchange risk management objectives are to stabilize cash flow from the effect of foreign currency fluctuations. The Company will, whenever practical, offset local investments in foreign currencies with borrowings denominated in the same currency. The Company also enters into forward foreign exchange contracts or purchase options to eliminate specific transaction currency risk. International sales and operating earnings were favorably impacted by the translation of local currency results into U.S. dollars at higher average exchange rates in 1994 than 1993 and unfavorably impacted by lower average exchange rates in 1993 than in 1992. Inflation has had little effect on the Company's operations in the last three years.

LIQUIDITY AND CAPITAL RESOURCES

The Company continues to maintain a strong financial position as evidenced by its working capital of $394 million at January 28, 1995 and $633 million at January 29, 1994. The long-term debt to equity percentage is 22.9% at January 28, 1995 as compared to 23.0% at January 29, 1994.

In 1995, the Company plans to open approximately 90 toy stores in the United States and internationally, including franchise stores. Additionally, there are plans to open about 10 Kids"R"Us children's clothing stores. The Company opened 96 toy stores in 1994, 108 in 1993 and 84 in 1992 and 6 Kids"R"Us children's clothing stores in 1994, 10 in 1993 and 23 in 1992. The Company closed 19 Kids"R"Us children's clothing stores in 1994 and 4 in 1993, which were not meeting our expectations. These closures did not have a significant impact on the Company's financial position.

For 1995, capital requirements for real estate, store and warehouse fixtures and equipment, leasehold improvements and other additions to property and equipment are estimated at $575 million (including real estate and related costs of $375 million). The Company's policy is to purchase its real estate where appropriate and plans to continue this policy.

The Company has an existing $1 billion share repurchase program, under which it has repurchased 13.7 million shares of its common stock for $493.7 million, since it had announced the program in January of 1994.

The seasonal nature of the business (approximately 48% of sales take place in the fourth quarter) typically causes cash to decline from the beginning of the year through October as inventory increases for the holiday selling season and funds are used for land purchases and construction of new stores, which usually open in the first ten months of the year. The Company has a $1 billion multi-currency unsecured revolving credit facility expiring in February 2000, from a syndicate of financial institutions. Cash requirements for operations, capital expenditures, lease commitments and the share repurchase program will be met primarily through operating activities, borrowings under the revolving credit facility, issuance of short-term commercial paper and bank borrowings for foreign subsidiaries.

*References to 1994, 1993 and 1992 are for the 52 weeks ended January 28, 1995, January 29, 1994 and January 30, 1993, respectively.

TOYS"R"US, INC. AND SUBSIDIARIES
CONSOLIDATED STATEMENTS OF EARNINGS

(In thousands except per share information)   *Year Ended*

	January 28, 1995	January 29, 1994	January 30, 1993
Net sales	$ 8,745,586	$ 7,946,067	$ 7,169,290
Costs and expenses:			
Cost of sales	6,007,958	5,494,766	4,968,555
Selling, advertising, general and administrative	1,664,180	1,497,011	1,342,262
Depreciation and amortization	161,406	133,370	119,034
Interest expense	83,945	72,283	69,134
Interest and other income	(15,970)	(24,116)	(18,719)
	7,901,519	7,173,314	6,480,266
Earnings before taxes on income	844,067	772,753	689,024
Taxes on income	312,300	289,800	251,500
Net earnings	$ 531,767	$ 482,953	$ 437,524
Earnings per share	$ 1.85	$ 1.63	$ 1.47

See notes to consolidated financial statements.

TOYS"R"US, INC. AND SUBSIDIARIES
CONSOLIDATED BALANCE SHEETS

[In thousands]

	January 28, 1995	January 29, 1994
ASSETS		
Current Assets:		
Cash and cash equivalents	$ 369,833	$ 791,893
Accounts and other receivables	115,914	98,534
Merchandise inventories	1,999,148	1,777,569
Prepaid expenses and other	45,818	40,400
Total Current Assets	2,530,713	2,708,396
Property and Equipment:		
Real estate, net	2,270,825	2,035,673
Other, net	1,397,980	1,148,794
Total Property and Equipment	3,668,805	3,184,467
Other Assets	371,675	256,746
	$ 6,571,193	$ 6,149,609
LIABILITIES AND STOCKHOLDERS' EQUITY		
Current Liabilities:		
Short-term borrowings	$ 122,661	$ 239,862
Accounts payable	1,339,081	1,156,411
Accrued expenses and other current liabilities	472,653	471,782
Income taxes payable	202,548	206,996
Total Current Liabilities	2,136,943	2,075,051
Deferred Income Taxes	219,927	202,663
Long-Term Debt	785,448	723,613
Stockholders' Equity:		
Common stock	29,795	29,794
Additional paid-in capital	521,295	454,061
Retained earnings	3,544,573	3,012,806
Foreign currency translation adjustments	(25,121)	(56,021)
Treasury shares, at cost	(641,667)	(292,358)
	3,428,875	3,148,282
	$ 6,571,193	$ 6,149,609

See notes to consolidated financial statements.

TOYS"R"US, INC. AND SUBSIDIARIES
CONSOLIDATED STATEMENTS OF CASH FLOWS

[In thousands]			Year Ended
	January 28, 1995	January 29, 1994	January 30, 1993
CASH FLOWS FROM OPERATING ACTIVITIES			
Net earnings	$ 531,767	$ 482,953	$ 437,524
Adjustments to reconcile net earnings to net cash provided by operating activities:			
Depreciation and amortization	161,406	133,370	119,034
Deferred income taxes	(14,545)	36,534	13,998
Changes in operating assets and liabilities:			
Accounts and other receivables	(17,380)	(29,149)	(5,307)
Merchandise inventories	(221,579)	(278,898)	(108,066)
Prepaid expenses and other operating assets	(31,668)	(39,448)	(36,249)
Accounts payable, accrued expenses and other liabilities	183,506	325,165	112,232
Income taxes payable	(2,014)	26,588	40,091
Total adjustments	57,726	174,162	135,733
Net cash provided by operating activities	589,493	657,115	573,257
CASH FLOWS FROM INVESTING ACTIVITIES			
Capital expenditures, net	(585,702)	(555,258)	(421,564)
Other assets	(44,593)	(58,383)	(22,175)
Net cash used in investing activities	(630,295)	(613,641)	(443,739)
CASH FLOWS FROM FINANCING ACTIVITIES			
Short-term borrowings, net	(117,201)	119,090	(170,887)
Long-term borrowings	34,648	40,576	318,035
Long-term debt repayments	(1,111)	(1,335)	(7,926)
Exercise of stock options	25,998	29,879	86,323
Share repurchase program	(469,714)	(183,233)	(27,244)
Sale of stock to Petrie Stores Corporation	161,642	–	–
Net cash (used)/provided by financing activities	(365,738)	4,977	198,301
Effect of exchange rate changes on cash and cash equivalents	(15,520)	(20,279)	(8,691)
CASH AND CASH EQUIVALENTS			
(Decrease)/increase during year	(422,060)	28,172	319,128
Beginning of year	791,893	763,721	444,593
End of year	$ 369,833	$ 791,893	$ 763,721

SUPPLEMENTAL DISCLOSURES OF CASH FLOW INFORMATION

The Company considers its highly liquid investments purchased as part of its daily cash management activities to be cash equivalents. During the years ended January 28, 1995, January 29, 1994, and January 30, 1993 the Company made income tax payments of $318,948, $220,229, and $151,722 and interest payments (net of amounts capitalized) of $123,603, $104,281, and $83,584 respectively.

See notes to consolidated financial statements.

TOYS"R"US, INC. AND SUBSIDIARIES
CONSOLIDATED STATEMENTS OF STOCKHOLDERS' EQUITY

| | Common Stock | | | | |
| | Issued | | In Treasury | Additional paid-in | Retained |
[In thousands]	Shares	Amount	Amount	capital	earnings
Balance, February 1, 1992	297,938	$ 29,794	$ (127,717)	$ 384,803	$ 2,092,329
Net earnings for the year	–	–	–	–	437,524
Share repurchase program (708 Treasury shares)	–	–	(27,244)	–	–
Exercise of stock options (4,479 Treasury shares)	–	–	4,524	35,301	–
Tax benefit from exercise of stock options	–	–	–	45,390	–
Balance, January 30, 1993	297,938	29,794	(150,437)	465,494	2,529,853
Net earnings for the year	–	–	–	–	482,953
Share repurchase program (4,940 Treasury shares)	–	–	(183,233)	–	–
Exercise of stock options (1,394 Treasury shares)	–	–	41,312	(21,464)	–
Tax benefit from exercise of stock options	–	–	–	10,031	–
Balance, January 29, 1994	297,938	29,794	(292,358)	454,061	3,012,806
Net earnings for the year	–	–	–	–	531,767
Share repurchase program (13,074 Treasury shares)	–	–	(469,714)	–	–
Exercise of stock options (1,103 Treasury shares)	16	1	41,888	(21,947)	–
Tax benefit from exercise of stock options	–	–	–	6,056	–
Exchange with and sale of stock to Petrie Stores Corporation (2,223 Net treasury shares)	–	–	78,517	83,125	–
Balance, January 28, 1995	297,954	$ 29,795	$ (641,667)	$ 521,295	$ 3,544,573

See notes to consolidated financial statements.

TOYS"R"US, INC. AND SUBSIDIARIES
NOTES TO CONSOLIDATED FINANCIAL STATEMENTS

(Amounts in thousands, except per share amounts)

SUMMARY OF SIGNIFICANT ACCOUNTING POLICIES

Fiscal Year
The Company's fiscal year ends on the Saturday nearest to January 31. References to 1994, 1993, and 1992 are for the 52 weeks ended January 28, 1995, January 29, 1994 and January 30, 1993, respectively.

Principles of Consolidation
The consolidated financial statements include the accounts of the Company and its subsidiaries. All material intercompany balances and transactions have been eliminated. Assets and liabilities of foreign operations are translated at current rates of exchange at the balance sheet date while results of operations are translated at average rates in effect for the period. Translation gains or losses are shown as a separate component of stockholders' equity. The increase (decrease) in the foreign currency translation adjustment was $30,900, ($70,338) and ($33,650) for 1994, 1993 and 1992, respectively.

Merchandise Inventories
Merchandise inventories for the U.S.A. toy store operations, which represent over 62% of total inventories, are stated at the lower of LIFO (last-in, first-out) cost or market as determined by the retail inventory method. If inventories had been valued at the lower of FIFO (first-in, first-out) cost or market, inventories would show no change at January 28, 1995 or January 29, 1994. All other merchandise inventories are stated at the lower of FIFO cost or market as determined by the retail inventory method.

Property and Equipment
Property and equipment are recorded at cost. Depreciation and amortization are provided using the straight-line method over the estimated useful lives of the assets or, where applicable, the terms of the respective leases, whichever is shorter.

Preopening Costs
Preopening costs, which consist primarily of advertising, occupancy and payroll expenses, are amortized over expected sales to the end of the fiscal year in which the store opens.

Capitalized Interest
Interest on borrowed funds is capitalized during construction of property and is amortized by charges to earnings over the depreciable lives of the related assets. Interest of $6,926, $7,300 and $8,403 was capitalized during 1994, 1993 and 1992, respectively.

Financial Instruments
The carrying amounts reported in the balance sheets for cash and cash equivalents and short-term borrowings approximate their fair market values.

Forward Foreign Exchange Contracts
The Company enters into forward foreign exchange contracts to eliminate the risk associated with currency movement relating to its short-term intercompany loan program with foreign subsidiaries and inventory purchases denominated in foreign currency. Gains and losses which offset the movement in the underlying transactions are recognized as part of such transactions. Gross deferred unrealized gains and losses on the forward contracts were not material at either January 28, 1995 or January 29, 1994. The related receivable, payable and deferred gain or loss are included on a net basis in the balance sheet. As of January 28, 1995 and January 29, 1994, the Company had approximately $547,000 and $290,000, of outstanding forward contracts maturing in 1995 and 1994, respectively, which are entered into with counterparties that have high credit ratings and with which the Company has the contractual right to net forward currency settlements.

PROPERTY AND EQUIPMENT

	Useful Life (in years)	January 28, 1995	January 29, 1994
Land............................		$ 764,808	$ 693,737
Buildings	45-50	1,627,145	1,446,277
Furniture and equipment ...	5-20	1,177,909	953,360
Leaseholds and leasehold improvements...	12½-50	809,365	658,191
Construction in progress...		55,730	41,855
Leased property under capital leases		24,881	24,360
		4,459,838	3,817,780
Less accumulated depreciation and amortization		791,033	633,313
		$ 3,668,805	$ 3,184,467

SEASONAL FINANCING AND LONG-TERM DEBT

	January 28, 1995	January 29, 1994
Industrial revenue bonds, net of expenses (a)	$ 74,239	$ 74,208
Mortgage notes payable at annual interest rates from 7⅛% to 11% (b)	12,980	13,318
Japanese yen loans payable at annual interest rates from 3.45% to 6.47%, due in varying amounts through 2012	192,910	142,688
British pound sterling 11% Stepped Coupon Guaranteed Bonds, due 2017	206,570	194,415
8¼% sinking fund debentures, due 2017, net of discounts	88,220	88,117
8¾% debentures, due 2021, net of expenses	198,051	197,978
Obligations under capital leases	14,056	14,432
	787,026	725,156
Less current portion	1,578	1,543
	$ 785,448	$ 723,613

(a) Bank letters of credit of $57,135, expiring in 1996, support certain industrial revenue bonds. The Company expects the bank letters of credit expiring in 1996 will be renewed. The bonds have fixed or variable interest rates with an average rate of 3.2% at January 28, 1995.

(b) Mortgage notes payable are collateralized by property and equipment with an aggregate carrying value of $18,330 at January 28, 1995.

The fair market value of the Company's long-term debt at January 28, 1995 is approximately $815,000. The fair market value was estimated using quoted market rates for publicly traded debt and estimated interest rates for non-public debt.

On January 27, 1995, the Company entered into a $1 billion unsecured committed revolving credit facility expiring in five years. This multi-currency facility permits the Company to borrow at the lower of LIBOR plus a fixed spread or a rate set by competitive auction. The facility is available to support domestic commercial paper borrowings and to meet the cash requirements of selected foreign subsidiaries.

Additionally, the Company also has lines of credit with various banks to meet the short-term financing needs of its foreign subsidiaries. The weighted average interest rate on short-term borrowings outstanding at January 28, 1995 and January 29, 1994, was 6.3% and 5.4%, respectively.

The annual maturities of long-term debt at January 28, 1995 are as follows:

Year ending in	
1996	$ 1,578
1997	5,559
1998	8,085
1999	9,740
2000	8,662
2001 and subsequent	753,402
	$ 787,026

LEASES

The Company leases a portion of the real estate used in its operations. Most leases require the Company to pay real estate taxes and other expenses; some require additional amounts based on percentages of sales.

Minimum rental commitments under noncancelable operating leases having a term of more than one year as of January 28, 1995 were as follows:

Year ending in	Gross minimum rentals	Sublease income	Net minimum rentals
1996	$ 258,447	$ 8,461	$ 249,986
1997	256,477	7,265	249,212
1998	255,650	7,091	248,559
1999	256,373	6,215	250,158
2000	254,144	6,036	248,108
2001 and subsequent	3,226,873	37,387	3,189,486
	$ 4,507,964	$ 72,455	$ 4,435,509

Total rental expense was as follows:

	Year ended		
	January 28, 1995	January 29, 1994	January 30, 1993
Minimum rentals	$ 226,382	$ 180,118	$ 149,027
Additional amounts computed as percentages of sales	6,361	5,604	5,447
	232,743	185,722	154,474
Less sublease income	10,348	7,935	5,788
	$ 222,395	$ 177,787	$ 148,686

STOCKHOLDERS' EQUITY

The common shares of the Company, par value $.10 per share, were as follows:

	January 28, 1995	January 29, 1994
Authorized shares	550,000	550,000
Issued shares	297,954	297,938
Treasury shares	18,164	8,416

Earnings per share is computed by dividing net earnings by the weighted average number of common shares outstanding after reduction for treasury shares and assuming exercise of dilutive stock options computed by the treasury stock method using the average market price during the year.

Weighted average numbers of shares used in computing earnings per share were as follows:

		Year ended	
	January 28, 1995	January 29, 1994	January 30, 1993
Common and common equivalent shares	287,415	296,463	297,718

In April 1994, the Company entered into an agreement with Petrie Stores Corporation ("Petrie"), the then holder of 14% of the Company's outstanding Common Stock. Pursuant to such agreement, the Company consummated a transaction with Petrie on January 24, 1995, wherein 42,076 shares of the Company's common stock were issued from its treasury in exchange for 39,853 shares of the Company's common stock and $165,000 in cash.

TAXES ON INCOME

The provisions for income taxes consist of the following:

		Year ended	
	January 28, 1995	January 29, 1994	January 30, 1993
Current:			
Federal	$ 251,621	$ 200,303	$ 186,013
Foreign	29,221	17,259	15,605
State	46,003	35,704	35,884
	326,845	253,266	237,502
Deferred:			
Federal	8,873	49,961	17,187
Foreign	(24,752)	(16,186)	(6,705)
State	1,334	2,759	3,516
	(14,545)	36,534	13,998
Total	$ 312,300	$ 289,800	$ 251,500

Deferred tax liabilities and deferred tax assets reflect the net tax effects of temporary differences between the carrying amounts of assets and liabilities for financial reporting purposes and the amounts used for income tax purposes. The Company has gross deferred tax liabilities of $270,900 at January 28, 1995 and $251,700 at January 29, 1994, which consist primarily of temporary differences related to fixed assets of $217,000 and $194,000, respectively. The Company had gross deferred tax assets of $129,900 at January 28, 1995 and $92,800 at January 29, 1994, which consist primarily of net operating losses of foreign start-up operations of $94,000 and $60,400, and operating costs not currently deductible for tax purposes of $25,400 and $23,200, respectively. Valuation allowances are not significant.

A reconciliation of the federal statutory tax rate with the effective tax rate follows:

			Year ended
	January 28, 1995	January 29, 1994	January 30, 1993
Statutory tax rate	35.0%	35.0%	34.0%
State income taxes, net of federal income tax benefit	3.7	3.2	4.0
Foreign	(0.4)	(0.5)	(1.2)
Other, net	(1.3)	(0.2)	(0.3)
	37.0%	37.5%	36.5%

Deferred income taxes were not provided on unremitted earnings of foreign subsidiaries that are intended to be indefinitely invested. Unremitted earnings were approximately $131,000 at January 28, 1995, exclusive of amounts that if remitted would result in little or no tax under current U.S. tax laws. Net income taxes of approximately $46,000 would be due if these earnings were to be remitted.

PROFIT SHARING PLAN

The Company has a profit sharing plan with a 401(k) salary deferral feature for eligible domestic employees. The terms of the plan call for annual contributions by the Company as determined by the Board of Directors, subject to certain limitations. The profit sharing plan may be terminated at the Company's discretion. Provisions of $31,391, $29,961 and $29,824 have been charged to operations in 1994, 1993 and 1992, respectively.

STOCK OPTIONS

The Company has Stock Option Plans (the "Plans") which provide for the granting of options to purchase the Company's common stock to substantially all employees and non-employee directors of the Company. The Plans provide for the issuance of non-qualified options, incentive stock options, performance share options, performance units, stock appreciation rights, restricted shares and unrestricted shares. The majority of the options become exercisable four years and nine months from the date of grant. Certain non-qualified options become exercisable nine years from the date of grant, however the exercise date of all or a portion of such options may be accelerated if the price of the Company's common stock reaches certain target amounts. The options granted to non-employee directors are exercisable 20% each year on a cumulative basis commencing one year from the date of grant.

In addition to the aforementioned plans, 2,862 stock options were granted to certain senior executives during the period from 1988 to 1993 pursuant to individual plans. These options are exercisable 20% each year on a cumulative basis commencing one year from the date of grant.

The exercise price per share of all options granted has been the average of the high and low market price of the Company's common stock on the date of grant. Options must be exercised within ten years from the date of grant.

At January 28, 1995, an aggregate of 28,502 shares of authorized common stock was reserved for all of the Plans noted above; 9,139 of which were available for future grants and 5,390 which were reserved for exercisable options. All outstanding options expire at dates varying from May 1995 to November 2004.

Stock option transactions are summarized as follows:

		Shares Under Option	
	Incentive	Non-Qualified	Price Range
Outstanding January 29, 1994 ...	527	16,720	$ 7.68 - 40.94
Granted...................................	–	4,189	34.31 - 38.56
Exercised.................................	(167)	(952)	7.68 - 36.94
Canceled	–	(954)	7.68 - 39.88
Outstanding January 28, 1995 ...	360	19,003	$ 7.68 - 40.94

The exercise of non-qualified stock options results in state and federal income tax benefits to the Company related to the difference between the market price at the date of exercise and the option price. During 1994, 1993 and 1992, $6,056, $10,031 and $45,390, respectively, was credited to additional paid-in capital.

FOREIGN OPERATIONS

Certain information relating to the Company's foreign operations is set forth below. Corporate assets include all cash and cash equivalents and other related assets.

	Year ended		
	January 28, 1995	January 29, 1994	January 30, 1993
Sales			
Domestic..................	$ 6,644,799	$ 6,278,591	$ 5,795,119
Foreign.....................	2,100,787	1,667,476	1,374,171
Total...........................	$ 8,745,586	$ 7,946,067	$ 7,169,290
Operating Profit			
Domestic..................	$ 778,659	$ 724,818	$ 647,640
Foreign.....................	140,829	102,923	101,132
General corporate expenses..................	(7,446)	(6,821)	(9,333)
Interest expense, net	(67,975)	(48,167)	(50,415)
Earnings before taxes on income	$ 844,067	$ 772,753	$ 689,024
Identifiable Assets			
Domestic..................	$ 3,950,511	$ 3,630,921	$ 3,277,527
Foreign.....................	2,216,086	1,694,565	1,248,827
Corporate.................	404,596	824,123	796,498
Total...........................	$ 6,571,193	$ 6,149,609	$ 5,322,852

QUARTERLY FINANCIAL DATA

The following table sets forth certain unaudited quarterly financial information.

	First Quarter	Second Quarter	Third Quarter	Fourth Quarter
Year Ended January 28, 1995				
Net Sales..................	$ 1,461,933	$ 1,452,117	$ 1,631,345	$ 4,200,191
Cost of Sales.............	1,001,203	982,892	1,097,236	2,926,627
Net Earnings.............	37,580	38,014	47,367	408,806
Earnings per Share	$ .13	$ .13	$ .17	$ 1.46
Year Ended January 29, 1994				
Net Sales..................	$ 1,286,479	$ 1,317,012	$ 1,449,118	$ 3,893,458
Cost of Sales.............	882,876	902,414	982,151	2,727,325
Net Earnings	35,436	35,505	37,457	374,555
Earnings per Share	$ .12	$ .12	$ .13	$ 1.27

REPORT OF MANAGEMENT

Responsibility for the integrity and objectivity of the financial information presented in this Annual Report rests with Toys"R"Us management. The accompanying financial statements have been prepared from accounting records which management believes fairly and accurately reflect the operations and financial position of the Company. Management has established a system of internal controls to provide reasonable assurance that assets are maintained and accounted for in accordance with its policies and that transactions are recorded accurately on the Company's books and records.

The Company's comprehensive internal audit program provides for constant evaluation of the adequacy of the adherence to management's established policies and procedures. The Company has distributed to key employees its policies for conducting business affairs in a lawful and ethical manner.

The Audit Committee of the Board of Directors, which is comprised solely of outside directors, provides oversight to the financial reporting process through periodic meetings with our independent auditors, internal auditors and management.

The financial statements of the Company have been audited by Ernst & Young LLP, independent auditors, in accordance with generally accepted auditing standards, including a review of financial reporting matters and internal controls to the extent necessary to express an opinion on the consolidated financial statements.

Michael Goldstein
Vice Chairman and
Chief Executive Officer

Louis Lipschitz
Senior Vice President - Finance
and Chief Financial Officer

MARKET INFORMATION

The Company's common stock is listed on the New York Stock Exchange. The following table reflects the high and low prices (rounded to the nearest one-eighth) based on New York Stock Exchange trading since January 30, 1993.

The Company has not paid any cash dividends, however, the Board of Directors of the Company reviews this policy annually.

The number of stockholders of record of common stock on March 7, 1995 was approximately 27,200.

		High	Low
1993	1st Quarter	42 3/8	36 5/8
	2nd Quarter	39 3/4	32 3/8
	3rd Quarter	40 3/8	33 3/4
	4th Quarter	42 7/8	36
1994	1st Quarter	37 3/8	32 3/8
	2nd Quarter	36 3/4	32 1/4
	3rd Quarter	38 3/4	33
	4th Quarter	39	28 1/4

REPORT OF INDEPENDENT AUDITORS

The Board of Directors and Stockholders
Toys"R"Us, Inc.

We have audited the accompanying consolidated balance sheets of Toys"R"Us, Inc. and subsidiaries as of January 28, 1995 and January 29, 1994, and the related consolidated statements of earnings, stockholders' equity and cash flows for each of the three years in the period ended January 28, 1995. These financial statements are the responsibility of the Company's management. Our responsibility is to express an opinion on these financial statements based on our audits.

We conducted our audits in accordance with generally accepted auditing standards. Those standards require that we plan and perform the audit to obtain reasonable assurance about whether the financial statements are free of material misstatement. An audit includes examining, on a test basis, evidence supporting the amounts and disclosures in the financial statements. An audit also includes assessing the accounting principles used and significant estimates made by management, as well as evaluating the overall financial statement presentation. We believe that our audits provide a reasonable basis for our opinion.

In our opinion, the financial statements referred to above present fairly, in all material respects, the consolidated financial position of Toys"R"Us, Inc. and subsidiaries at January 28, 1995 and January 29, 1994, and the consolidated results of their operations and their cash flows for each of the three years in the period ended January 28, 1995, in conformity with generally accepted accounting principles.

Ernst & Young LLP

New York, New York
March 8, 1995

DIRECTORS AND OFFICERS

DIRECTORS

Charles Lazarus
Chairman of the Board
of the Company

Robert A. Bernhard
Real Estate Developer

Michael Goldstein
Vice Chairman and Chief Executive
Officer of the Company

Milton S. Gould
Attorney-at-law;
Of Counsel to LeBoeuf, Lamb,
Greene & MacRae

Shirley Strum Kenny
President, State University of
New York at Stony Brook

Reuben Mark
Chairman and CEO
Colgate-Palmolive Company

Howard W. Moore
Former Executive
Vice President - General
Merchandise Manager of
the Company; Consultant

Robert C. Nakasone
President and Chief Operating
Officer of the Company

Norman M. Schneider
Former Chairman, Leisure Products
Division of Beatrice Foods
Company; Consultant

Harold M. Wit
Managing Director,
Allen & Company Incorporated;
Investment Bankers

OFFICERS - CORPORATE AND ADMINISTRATIVE

Michael Goldstein
Vice Chairman and
Chief Executive Officer

Robert C. Nakasone
President and
Chief Operating Officer

Dennis Healey
Senior Vice President -
Management Information Systems

Louis Lipschitz
Senior Vice President -
Finance and Chief Financial Officer

Michael P. Miller
Senior Vice President - Real Estate

Jeffrey S. Wells
Senior Vice President -
Human Resources

Gayle C. Aertker
Vice President - Real Estate

Michael J. Corrigan
Vice President - Compensation
and Benefits

Richard N. Cudrin
Vice President - Employee and
Labor Relations

Jonathan M. Friedman
Vice President - Controller and
Chief Financial Officer - Kids"R"Us

Eileen C. Gabriel
Vice President -
Information Systems

Jon W. Kimmins
Vice President - Treasurer

Matthew J. Lombardi
Vice President -
Information Technology

Eric A. Swartwood
Vice President -
Architecture and Construction

Michael L. Tumolo
Vice President -
Real Estate Counsel

Peter W. Weiss
Vice President - Taxes

Andre Weiss
Secretary - Attorney-at-law;
Partner-Schulte Roth & Zabel

TOYS"R"US UNITED STATES - OFFICERS AND GENERAL MANAGERS

Roger V. Goddu
Executive Vice President -
General Merchandise Manager

Michael J. Madden
Group Vice President -
Store Operations

Van H. Butler
Senior Vice President -
Divisional Merchandise Manager

Bruce C. Hall
Senior Vice President -
Regional Operations

Thomas J. Reinebach
Senior Vice President - Distribution
and Support Services

Ernest V. Speranza
Senior Vice President -
Advertising/Marketing

Robert J. Weinberg
Senior Vice President -
Divisional Merchandise Manager

Kristopher M. Brown
Vice President - Distribution Operations

Harvey J. Finkel
Vice President - Regional Operations

Martin Fogelman
Vice President -
Divisional Merchandise Manager

Michael A. Gerety
Vice President - Store Planning

Lee Richardson
Vice President - Advertising

John P. Sullivan
Vice President - Divisional
Merchandise Manager

Karl S. Taylor
Vice President - Merchandise
Planning and Allocation

GENERAL MANAGERS

Robert F. Price
Vice President
New York/Northern New Jersey

Thomas A. Drugan
Alabama/Georgia/South
Carolina/Tennessee

Larry D. Gardner
Pacific Northwest/Alaska

Mark H. Haag
Southern California/
Arizona/Nevada/Hawaii

Daniel D. Hlavaty
Central Ohio/Indiana/Kentucky

Debra M. Kachurak
New England

Richard A. Moyer
S. Texas/Louisiana/Mississippi

Gerald S. Parker
Northern California/Utah

John J. Prawlocki
Florida/Puerto Rico

J. Michael Roberts
Pennsylvania/Delaware/
Southern New Jersey

Edward F. Siegler
Colorado/Kansas/Missouri/
Iowa/Nebraska

Carl P. Spaulding
N.E. Ohio/W. Pennsylvania/
N. New York

William A. Stephenson
Illinois/Wisconsin/Minnesota

John P. Suozzo
Maryland/Virginia/North Carolina

Brian L. Voorhees
N. Texas/Oklahoma/Arkansas/
New Mexico

Dennis J. Williams
Michigan/N.W. Ohio

KIDS"R"US - OFFICERS

Richard L. Markee
President

Virginia Harris
Senior Vice President -
General Merchandise Manager

James G. Parros
Senior Vice President - Stores and
Distribution Center Operations

James L. Easton
Vice President -
Divisional Merchandise Manager

Jerel G. Hollens
Vice President -
Merchandise Planning and
Management Information Systems

Debra G. Hyman
Vice President -
Divisional Merchandise Manager

Elizabeth S. Jordan
Vice President - Human Resources

Lorna E. Nagler
Vice President -
Divisional Merchandise Manager

TOYS"R"US INTERNATIONAL - OFFICERS AND COUNTRY MANAGEMENT

Larry D. Bouts
President

Gregory R. Staley
Senior Vice President -
General Merchandise Manager

Lawrence H. Meyer
Vice President -
Chief Financial Officer

Ken Bonning
Vice President - Logistics

Joseph Giamelli
Vice President -
Information Systems

Adam Szopinski
Vice President - Operations

Keith Van Beek
Vice President - Development

COUNTRY MANAGEMENT

Jacques Le Foll
President - Toys"R"Us France

Carl Olsen
Managing Director -
Toys"R"Us Australia

Guillermo Porrati
Managing Director -
Toys"R"Us Central Europe/Iberia

David Rurka
Managing Director - Toys"R"Us
United Kingdom/Scandinavia

Manabu Tazaki
President - Toys"R"Us Japan

Elliott Wahle
President - Toys"R"Us Canada

Keith C. Spurgeon
Vice President -
Toys"R"Us Asia/Australia

Scott Chen
General Manager -
Toys"R"Us Taiwan

David Silber
General Manager -
Toys"R"Us Hong Kong

Michael Yeo
General Manager -
Toys"R"Us Singapore

CORPORATE DATA

ANNUAL MEETING
The Annual Meeting of the
Stockholders of Toys"R"Us will be
held at the offices of the Company
on Wednesday, June 7, 1995 at
10:00 a.m.

THE OFFICE OF THE COMPANY IS LOCATED AT
461 From Road
Paramus, New Jersey 07652
Telephone: 201-262-7800

GENERAL COUNSEL
Schulte Roth & Zabel
900 Third Avenue
New York, New York 10022

INDEPENDENT AUDITORS
Ernst & Young LLP
787 Seventh Avenue
New York, New York 10019

STOCKHOLDER INFORMATION
The Company will supply to any owner of
Common Stock, upon written request to
Mr. Louis Lipschitz of the Company at the
address set forth herein, and without
charge, a copy of the Annual Report on
Form 10-K for the year ended January
28, 1995, which has been filed with the
Securities and Exchange Commission.

Stockholder information, including
quarterly earnings and other corporate
news releases, can be obtained toll free
by calling 800-785-TOYS. Significant
news releases will be available on the
following dates:

CALL AFTER...	FOR THE FOLLOWING...
May 15, 1995	1st Quarter Results
Aug. 14, 1995	2nd Quarter Results
Nov. 13, 1995	3rd Quarter Results
Jan. 2, 1996	Christmas Sales Results
Mar. 13, 1996	1995 Results

COMMON STOCK LISTED
New York Stock Exchange, Symbol: TOY

REGISTRAR AND TRANSFER AGENT
American Stock Transfer
and Trust Company
40 Wall Street
New York, New York 10005
Telephone: 718-921-8200

Printed on
recycled paper

EXPLORING THE INTERNET

It is estimated that nearly 30 million people use the Internet on a regular basis. Many people "surf the Net" simply for fun and entertainment. A growing number of individuals, however, use it as a powerful research and educational resource. Throughout this textbook there are many opportunities to use the Internet for researching business problems and for learning about real world accounting issues. We encourage you to take advantage of these opportunities.

GETTING STARTED . . .

To explore the Internet you will need a browser, such as Netscape's Navigator or Microsoft's Explorer. Your school's computer network is likely to use one of these popular programs. If you are using a personal computer from home (or Web TV), your Internet provider will equip you with a browser. There are many Internet providers from which to choose. In addition to the giant providers, such as America Online (AOL), Prodigy, and Microsoft Network (MSN), there are hundreds of local services available nationwide.

Your browser will support one of many search engines used to canvas the Internet for topics of interest. You type in a keyword (or a key topic), and the search engine generates a list of Internet sites. While there are hundreds of search tools available, Alta Vista, Excite, WebCrawler, and Yahoo are among the Internet's most popular. We encourage you to experiment with these tools to see which one works best for you.

USE OF THE INTERNET IN THIS TEXTBOOK

There is a wide range of Internet material referenced throughout this textbook. In every chapter a Net Connections section identifies sites of potential interest. There is also an Internet assignment following the Cases in the end-of-chapter materials. This appendix includes additional Internet assignments for each chapter.

Every Internet location used in this textbook has its own unique address. Each address begins with the following prefix: www.
The use of "www" in the prefix signifies that the address is part of the World Wide Web. The Web is the graphical (and most user friendly) portion of the Internet. At the end of 1996 it included over 22 million pages of material, and it continues to grow at about one million pages per month.

The addresses used in the Net Connections sections and the assignment material can be accessed in one of two ways: (1) by typing the address directly into your browser, or (2) by going to our home page where "hot links" to every address are provided. Visit our home page by typing the following Internet address into your browser:

www.magpie.org/cyberlab

From this page's main menu, simply follow the instructions provided to visit the Internet locations linked to this textbook. When you have identified the location you wish to visit, "click" on its hot button (identified by blue letters) and, in seconds, you will be there. Be certain to mark our home page with a "bookmark" in your browser.

The table printed in the inside back cover of this textbook lists the Internet addresses used for all Net Connections and assignment materials. Take a moment to familiarize yourself with how these locations are arranged.

In the left-hand column of the table, the sites are classified in seven different categories: (1) Accounting Resources, (2) Business News & Economic Data, (3) Company Home Pages, (4) Investor & Stock Market Resources, (5) Professional Associations, (6) Search Engines, and (7) Small Business Resources. In the middle column, is each location's Internet address (remember that each address listed must begin with the www. prefix). In the far right column are page numbers corresponding to the Net Connections section in which each address is used, as well as the assignment numbers in which each address appears. The first Internet assignment appears after the Cases in the end-of-chapter materials. Additional Internet assignments for each chapter appear in this appendix.

INTERNET ASSIGNMENT MATERIALS

(***Note:*** These assignments *require* online access to the Internet.)

CHAPTER 1

Internet assignment 1-1 appears on page 52.

1-2   The Institute of Management Accountants (IMA) is a professional organization devoted exclusively to management accounting and finance professionals. Membership in the IMA provides accountants and financial managers with new insights and ideas and keeps them abreast of important changes influencing their professions.

Access the IMA's home page by opening the following Internet location:

www.rutgers.edu/accounting/raw/ima/ima.htm

a. What IMA materials (hot buttons) are available at this location?

b. What five important accounting career areas are identified?

c. What programs and services does the IMA offer its members?

1-3   Visit the home page of Hershey Foods Corporation by opening the following Internet location:

www.hersheys.com

Select Financial from the home page menu (Hershey's Financial Information will appear at the top of the screen). Locate and select the company's most recent annual report. From the financial report menu, select Consolidated Balance Sheets.

a. What date marks the end of Hershey's financial reporting period?

b. In what dollar amounts are the balance sheet figures stated?

c. Express Hershey's most recent balance sheet totals in the format of the accounting equation.

1-4   There are many opportunities awaiting college graduates majoring in accounting. For a better understanding of what the accounting profession offers its members, visit the Becker CPA home page at the following Internet address:

www.beckercpa.com

a. What positions (job titles) are held by persons working in public accounting? What are the typical salaries earned in these positions?

b. What positions (job titles) are held by accountants who work in private industry? What are the related salary ranges?

c. Identify several agencies of the federal government that hire accountants. What are the current salary ranges?

CHAPTER 2

Internet assignment 2-1 appears on page 97.

2-2 The Electronic Data Gathering, Analysis, and Retrieval System (EDGAR) contains corporate information filed with the U.S. Securities and Exchange Commission (SEC). Its primary purpose is to increase the efficiency and fairness of the securities market for the benefit of investors, corporations, and the economy.

Access the EDGAR database by opening the following Internet location:

www.sec.gov/cgi-bin/srch-edgar

In the keyword search box, type: Tyco Toys Inc. Select Tyco's most recent Form 10-K (an annual financial report filed with the SEC). Using information found in this report, answer the following questions:

a. List three of the company's primary product lines.

b. Identify five countries in which the company and its subsidiaries produce toys.

c. Examine the company's latest balance sheets. Since the beginning of the year, has the total dollar amount debited to cash exceeded the total amount credited to cash? How can you tell?

2-3 The history of the accounting profession dates back thousands of years. To learn more about its heritage, visit the Arthur Andersen & Co. home page at:

www.arthurandersen.com

From the home page menu, select About Arthur Andersen and locate Animated History of the Accounting Profession.

Provide a brief written summary of important milestones in the profession's history.

2-4 Accounting software performs many of the mechanical tasks involved in the accounting cycle. To acquaint yourself with the types of software available, access the Altavista, Excite, WebCrawler, and Yahoo search engines at the following Internet addresses:

www.altavista.digital.com   www.webcrawler.com
www.excite.com   www.yahoo.com

In the dialogue box provided at each site, perform a keyword search of "accounting software." Comment briefly on the number of accounting software resources available to businesses.

CHAPTER 3

Internet assignment 3-1 appears on page 156.

3-2 Microsoft Corporation is one of the greatest success stories in American business. Visit the Microsoft home page at:

www.microsoft.com

Select Shareholder from the main menu, and locate the table which summarizes the company's income statement data from its annual report.

a. By how much have revenues increased or declined during the past three years?

b. What are the major cost and expense classifications shown on the income statement?

c. Click upon the graph icon located to the right of the net income figures. Comment on the company's growth in net income as shown by this graph.

3-3 Visit the annual report home page of Johnson & Johnson Corporation by opening the following Internet location:

www.jnj.com/annual/index.htm

Find the most recent worldwide sales figure for the company. Of this amount, how many dollars of revenue were generated in each of the company's four major geographic trade areas?

3-4 News reports about a company's earnings are commonplace in business periodicals. Visit the home pages of *Electronic News, Fortune Magazine,* and *USA Today* at the following Internet addresses:

www.enews.com   www.usatoday.com
www.fortune.com

Using the keyword search function provided at each site, find a news report about a company's earnings and briefly summarize the article.

CHAPTER 4

Internet assignment 4-1 appears on page 206.

4-2 Visit the home page of MCI, Inc. by opening the following Internet location:

www.mci.com

From the company's home page, select About MCI and access investor relations. Examine MCI's balance sheet and answer the following questions:

a. Explain why MCI's accounts receivable may have required an adjusting entry at the end of the year.

b. Does MCI's balance sheet report any unearned revenue? Explain.

c. Which of MCI's noncurrent asset accounts would be involved in an adjusting entry to apportion costs over multiple reporting periods?

d. Explain why MCI's current portion of long-term debt reported on its balance sheet may have required an adjusting entry at the end of the year.

4-3 Visit the home page of the Ford Motor Company at:

www.ford.com

From Ford's home page, select Stockholder Relations and access the company's most recent annual report. Choose the Financial Section from the annual report menu and locate the notes to the financial statements. Identify the kinds of information disclosed in these footnotes.

4-4 Financial statements often include disclosures relating to lawsuits pending against the company. Of course, most companies make every effort to avoid becoming involved in litigation.

Visit the home page of Hershey Foods Corporation by opening:

www.hersheys.com

Select Idea Policy from the home page menu. Read the policy and briefly explain why Hershey may encourage its customers to keep their ideas to themselves.

CHAPTER 5

Internet assignment 5-1 appears on page 254.

5-2 Merchandising companies (such as retail stores) often experience the up-and-down effects of economic business cycles. To learn more about these cycles, visit the home page of the U.S. Census Bureau at

www.census.gov

and select Current Economic Indicators from the home page menu. Discuss briefly the current economic trends in the retail sector of the economy.

5-3 Visit the home page of Gap, Inc. at:

www.gap.com

Under the Company heading listed on the home page menu, select Financial Information.

a. What were the company's quarterly earnings for the past four quarters? Do earnings patterns appear cyclical? Explain.

b. Examine the company's monthly sales reports for the past twelve months. Do sales patterns appear cyclical? Explain.

c. What is the current market price of the company's stock?

CHAPTER 6

Internet assignment 6-1 appears on page 300.

6-2 Visit the Toys "R" Us financial home page at:

www.shareholder.com/toy

Select Browse SEC Documents from the home page menu. From the SEC menu, select the company's most recent 10-K or 10-K405 report.

a. Using the information provided by the company's SEC report, compute all of the financial measures listed in the table shown in Chapter 6 (page 277).

b. Using the Toys "R" Us annual report presented in Appendix A at the end of this textbook, compute all of the financial measures listed in the table mentioned above. Compare these measures to those computed in part **a** of this assignment. Discuss your findings.

c. Return to the home page menu and examine the recent news releases pertaining to the company. Do any of these reports convey information about Toys "R" Us that might affect its future financial performance? Explain.

6-3 Visit the home page of MCI, Inc., at:

www.mci.com

Select Investor Relations from the menu and locate the company's most recent annual report. From the report, select its statement of cash flows.

a. What is the company's largest source of cash from operating activities? What is its largest use of cash for operating activities?

b. Have the company's cash flows from operating activities been increasing or decreasing during the past three years?

c. List MCI's sources and uses of cash related to investing activities. If its investing cash flows are negative, is this necessarily unfavorable? Explain.

6-4 Visit the Internet address listed under Investor & Stock Market Resources in the table appearing on the inside back cover of this textbook. After exploring these resources, decide which ones you find to be most useful, and write a brief paragraph explaining why. If you really like (or dislike) a particular site, please send a copy of your comments to the authors of this textbook using the e-mail address provided on our home page:

www.magpie.org/cyberlab

We look forward to hearing from you!

CHAPTER 7

Internet assignment 7-1 appears on page 362.

7-2 The Case in Point on page 317 of this textbook describes Microsoft Corporation's 1996 balance sheet as having over $6 billion in short-term investments and interest-bearing securities. To find out about Microsoft's current holdings, access the EDGAR database at the following Internet address:

www.sec.gov/cgi-bin/srch-edgar

a. Using Microsoft's most recent 10-K report, determine the dollar amount it is currently holding in short-term investments and interest-bearing securities.

b. Are the company's short-term investments classified mostly as available-for-sale securities, trading securities, or held-to-maturity securities?

c. Does the company's income statement report any holding gains (or losses) on its investments? If none are reported, explain why.

7-3 Managing financial assets can be tricky business. All managers realize the importance of converting outstanding receivables to cash as quickly as possible. But what happens when a company needs cash *now*, and the bulk of its receivables are not due for, say, 30 days? A possible solution to this problem is offering customers discounts for early payment. Should this fail, a second approach may be selling all or some of these receivables to a *factor*.

To learn more about factoring, visit Main Factors, Inc., and Capital Advantage, Inc., at the following Internet addresses:

www.mainfactors.com   www.capitaladvantage.com

a. How does factoring differ from a loan?

b. What do factors charge for their services?

c. What are some advantages of factoring?

7-4 Interest rates play an important role in the successful management of financial assets. Access several of the following Internet addresses to learn more about interest rates, credit market trends, and general economic conditions:

www.stpt.com.busine.html   www.bloomberg.com

www.enews.com   www.cnnfn.com

www.fortune.com   www.ustreas.gov

www.census.gov   www.wsrn.com

Based upon information provided at these sites, what rates are currently being paid on certificates of deposits, money market funds, and U.S. Treasury bills? Do the experts expect rates to increase or decrease in the upcoming months? What do *you* see as the future trend in rates? Defend your position.

CHAPTER 8

Internet assignment 8-1 appears on page 409.

8-2 Inventories can represent a major portion of a company's total current assets. For some companies, efficient inventory management is crucial to successful operations. Visit the home page of the American Production and Inventory Control Society (APICS) at the following Internet address:

www.industry.net/apics

Describe briefly what APICS is, and what services it offers its members.

8-3 A company's inventory turnover rate is a measure of how quickly it converts inventory into cash (see page 386). But what is considered a "good" inventory turnover rate? The answer to that question depends upon a variety of industry and company characteristics.

Access the EDGAR database at the following Internet address:

www.sec.gov/cgi-bin/srch-edgar

Locate the most recent 10-K reports of McDonald's, Inc., and the Ford Motor Company. Compute the inventory turnover rates of each company. Does the higher turnover rate of McDonald's mean that the company manages its inventory more efficiently than Ford? Explain.

8-4 A great deal of attention has been paid to the concept of just-in-time (JIT) inventory management (see page 375). To see how widespread JIT techniques have become, access one or more search engines, such as Altavista, Excite, WebCrawler, and Yahoo. (Your browser probably has hot buttons for these search engines, but if not, their addresses are as follows:)

www.altavista.digital.com   www.webcrawler.com

www.excite.com   www.yahoo.com

Using the dialogue box, perform a keyword search for just-in-time inventory. Comment briefly on the types of resources available to businesses.

CHAPTER 9

Internet assignment 9-1 appears on page 459.

9-2 In 1986 Congress adopted the Modified Accelerated Cost Recovery System, called MACRS. Visit the home page of the Internal Revenue Service (IRS) at the following Internet address:

www.irs.ustreas.gov

Select Welcome to the IRS from the home page menu. From the next menu, select Search. In the dialogue box, type MACRS. Discuss briefly the types of information resulting from your search.

9-3 As illustrated in the graph on page 441 of this textbook, the majority of publicly traded companies use the straight-line method of depreciation for financial reporting purposes.

Here's a game for you to play with your classmates. First, access the EDGAR database at the following Internet address:

www.sec.gov/cgi-bin/srch-edgar

Using information from 10-K and 10-Q reports, see who can be the first student in the class to find a company that uses a depreciation method other than straight-line (or units-of-production). (The method used can be found in the footnotes to these reports.)

Let the authors of your textbook know of companies you find by sending an e-mail message to their home page.

9-4 A trademark is a word, symbol, or design that distinguishes the goods of one company from those of another. To find out more about trademarks, visit the home page of the Nolo Press at the following Internet address:

www.nolo.com

Select Legal Encyclopedia from the home page menu. Then select Patent, Copyright, Trademark from the next screen. Under the heading, Trademarks and Business Names, select Nolo's Fast Facts: Trademarks.

Explain the difference between the following commonly used trademark symbols: ® versus ™.

CHAPTER 10

Internet assignment 10-1 appears on page 515.

10-2 Individuals and businesses often need to structure amortizing loans so that they can afford the monthly payments. Longer-term loans usually mean smaller payments, but also higher interest rates. Bloomberg's Personal Home Page offers a service to help prospective borrowers select the best options. Visit

www.bloomberg.com

Once you're there, select Financial Analysis from the menu. Next, select Mortgage Calculator.

To illustrate this useful program, assume that you have recently graduated, have a good job, and are about to buy a new car. You will be taking out a car loan in the amount of $12,000, payable in equal monthly installments. You have two options: a 24-month loan at an interest rate of 8.5%, or a 48-month loan at 9%.

a. Compute your monthly payment under each of these options.

b. Assume you take the 48-month loan but are able to add an extra $200 to the required amount of each monthly payment. Over the life of the loan, how much will these extra payments save you in interest? By how many months will they shorten the life of the loan?

Remember Bloomberg's home page—it may come in handy.

10-3 *Statement No. 106* issued by the Financial Accounting Standards Board (FASB) addresses reporting requirements for postretirement benefits other than pensions.

Visit the home page of the FASB at:

www.fasb.org

Using the dialogue box provided, perform a keyword search on "postretirement benefits." From the "hits" that result, select Statement 106 Summary.

Discuss briefly the FASB's four objects for issuing *Statement No. 106*.

10-4   For nearly one hundred years, Moody's Investors Service has provided corporate bond ratings. Visit the Moody's home page at:

www.moodys.com

Select Economics from the home page menu. Next, select Moody's Indexes Yield Averages.

a. What is the current average yield on all corporate bonds maturing in 20 years or more? Of these bonds, what is the current yield of those bonds with the highest credit ratings (Aaa)? What is the current yield of those bonds with Baa credit ratings (a lower rating)?

b. Explain why the yield of bonds with the Aaa rating in part **a** is lower than the yield of bonds with the Baa rating.

c. Which of the following bond classifications currently generates the higher average yield, industrial bonds or public utility bonds?

CHAPTER 11

Internet assignment 11-1 appears on page 563.

11-2   For businesses to grow, it is often necessary to rely upon the capital of additional partners or outside investors. This can be a risky proposition. To learn more about business expansion, visit the Entrepreneurial Edge home page at:

www.edgeonline.com

Select Business Builders from the home page menu. Then, under the heading, Growing Your Business, select Expand Your Business with Partners and Investors.

What are the eight steps recommended for expanding a business? Be prepared to discuss each step in detail with the rest of the class.

11-3   The market price of a particular share of stock often changes throughout the day. "Real-time" pricing gives investors timely information regarding stock prices. To experience real-time pricing, visit the home page of PCQUOTE at:

www.pcquote.com

Following the instructions provided, enter the ticker symbol of the corporation of your choice (if necessary, use the look-up feature to find the ticker symbol of your company).

a. What is the current price of your company's stock? Check back frequently throughout the day and keep track of any changes in its market value.

b. How do changes in your company's stock price compare to changes in the Dow Jones Industrial Average (DJIA) shown at the top of the home page screen? In other words, is your stock moving in the same direction as the DJIA throughout the day?

c. What is your stock's 52-week high and low? What is its current earnings per share (EPS), its price-earnings ratio (PE), and its dividend yield?

CHAPTER 12

Internet assignment 12-1 appears on page 609.

12-2   The purpose of a stock split is to reduce substantially the market price of a company's stock, with the intent of making it more attractive to investors. Gap, Inc., has declared several stock splits since the initial public offering of its common stock.

Visit the company's home page at:

www.gap.com

Select Investor FAQ (frequently asked questions) from the home page menu.

a. What was the date of the initial public offering of Gap's stock? At what price was the stock initially sold?

b. How many stock splits has Gap declared, and what was the specific date and amount of each split?

c. Can Gap shareholders elect to directly reinvest their cash dividends in shares of the company's common stock?

12-3 Restructuring activities are very common in today's business environment. Conduct research on a company that has recently engaged in restructuring activities by searching various business news home pages at the following Internet addresses:

> www.stpt.com.busine.html   www.usatoday
> www.enews.com   www.cnnfn.com
> www.fortune.com   www.wsrn.com

At each address, perform a keyword search of items like "restructuring," "downsizing," and "reorganization." You are likely to identify several examples of companies currently engaged in these kinds of activities. Select a specific example, and prepare a brief report highlighting the details surrounding the restructuring activities of the company involved.

CHAPTER 13

Internet assignment 13-1 appears on page 664.

13-2 In 1996 Transworld Home Healthcare Corporation reported net income amounting $583,000. The company's 1996 statement of cash flows reported a *negative* cash flow from operations of nearly $3.3 million.
Visit the EDGAR database at:

> www.sec.gov/cgi-bin/srch-edgar

Access Transworld's 1996 10-K, and its most recent 10-K. From these reports, examine the company's income statement and statement of cash flows.

a. How is it possible that Transworld reported net income of $583,000 in 1996, when its operating cash flow was negative by nearly $3.3 million?

b. Does the company's most recent 10-K report negative cash flows from operations? What amount (negative or positive) is reported?

c. Do negative operating cash flows threaten a company's existence as a going concern? Explain.

13-3 Even though the FASB recommends the use of the direct method in presenting cash flow from operating activities, the vast majority of companies elect to use the indirect method. One reason is because the direct method requires an additional reporting requirement (see discussion on page 638).
Here's a challenge for you and your classmates. First, access EDGAR at:

> www.sec.gov/cgi-bin/srch-edgar

Using information from 10-K and 10-Q reports, see who can be the first student in the class to find a company (other than MCI, Inc.) that uses the direct method of reporting net cash flow from operations.
Let the authors of this textbook know of companies you find by sending an e-mail message to our home page.

13-4 In 1975 two college students named Bill Gates and Paul Allen formed a business partnership called Microsoft. The company was reorganized as a closely held corporation in 1981, and eventually "went public" in 1986. Today, Microsoft Corporation is widely recognized as one of the world's most successful corporations. Paul Allen has since left the company, while Bill Gates continues to run Microsoft. As the company's largest shareholder, he is one of the world's wealthiest individuals.

Visit the Microsoft home page at:

www.microsoft.com

Select Search, then type, "annual report" in the box that appears. Scroll down the page to the company's most recent annual report. From the annual report, locate the company's statement of cash flows.

a. Comment on any trends you observe in Microsoft's cash flows from operations. (**Note:** You may click upon the icon appearing in the right-hand column for a graph of net cash flows from operations for a three-year period.)

b. Has Microsoft paid any cash dividends during the past three years? Explain why such a profitable company has virtually no history of any dividend activity. (**Hint:** Look up *double taxation of corporate earnings* in the index which appears at the end of this textbook.)

c. Microsoft has purchased billions of dollars in short-term investments in recent years. How much cash did the company move into short-term investments during the past three years? Explain why the company chooses to invest such large sums of cash in marketable securities.

CHAPTER 14

Internet assignment 14-1 appears on page 706.

14-2   The Financial Accounting Standards Board (FASB) is the primary standard-setting organization of the accounting profession. Visit the home page of the FASB at:

www.fasb.org

Select Table of Contents from the home page menu. Next, select Facts about the FASB.

a. What topics about the FASB are addressed at this site?

b. What standard-setting bodies preceded the FASB?

c. Briefly describe the mission of the FASB.

14-3   Access the Rutgers' Accounting Web (RAW) site at:

www.rutgers.edu/accounting/raw.htm

Perform a keyword search of the term, "ethics." Among the list of hits will be the home page address of the Financial Executives Institute (FEI).

a. What is the FEI?

b. Summarize briefly the main points addressed in the FEI's Code of Ethics.

c. What role does the FEI play in helping to establish international accounting standards?

ACCOUNTING SYSTEMS, INTERNAL CONTROL, AND AUDITS

INTENDED FOR USE AFTER CHAPTER 5

LEARNING OBJECTIVES

1. Explain why accounting systems vary from one organization to the next.
2. Describe a database and explain its usefulness.
3. State the objectives of internal control.
4. Discuss means of achieving internal control.
5. Distinguish between employee fraud and management fraud.
6. Distinguish among audits, reviews, and compilations of financial statements.
7. Describe the nature and purpose of operational and compliance auditing.

ACCOUNTING SYSTEMS

An *accounting system* consists of the personnel, procedures, devices, and records used by an organization to (1) develop accounting information, and (2) communicate this information to decision makers. The design and capabilities of these systems vary greatly from one organization to the next. In very small businesses, the accounting system may consist of little more than a cash register, a checkbook, and an annual trip to an income tax preparer. In large businesses, an accounting system includes computers, highly trained personnel, and accounting reports which affect the daily operations of every department. But in every case, the basic purpose of the accounting system remains the same: *to meet the organization's needs for accounting information as efficiently as possible.*

LO 1 *Explain why accounting systems vary from one organization to the next.*

Many factors affect the structure of the accounting system within a particular organization. Among the most important are (1) the company's *needs for accounting information,* and (2) the *resources available* for operation of the system.

DETERMINING INFORMATION NEEDS
The types of accounting information that a company must develop vary with such factors as the size of the organization, whether it is publicly owned, and the philosophy of management. The need for some types of accounting information may be prescribed by law. For example, income tax regulations require every business to have an accounting system which can measure the company's taxable income and explain the nature and source of every item in the company's income tax return. Federal securities laws require

publicly owned companies to prepare financial statements in conformity with generally accepted accounting principles. These statements must be filed with the Securities and Exchange Commission, distributed to stockholders, and made available to the public.

Other types of accounting information are required as matters of practical necessity. For example, every business needs to know the amounts receivable from each customer and the amounts owed to each creditor.

Although much accounting information clearly is essential to business operations, management still has many choices as to the types and amount of accounting information to be developed. For example, should the accounting system of a department store measure separately the sales of each department and of different types of merchandise? The answer to such questions depends upon *how useful* management considers the information to be, and also the *cost* of developing the information.

THE COST OF PRODUCING ACCOUNTING INFORMATION

Accounting systems should be *cost effective*—that is, the value of the information produced should exceed the cost of producing it. Management has no choice but to produce the types of accounting reports required by law. In other cases, however, management may use *cost effectiveness* as the criterion for deciding whether or not to produce the information.

In recent years, the development and installation of computer-based accounting systems has increased greatly the types and amount of accounting information which can be produced in a cost-effective manner.

BASIC FUNCTIONS OF AN ACCOUNTING SYSTEM

In developing information about the financial position of a business and the results of its operations, every accounting system performs the following basic functions:

1. *Interpret and record* the effects of business transactions.
2. *Classify* the effects of similar transactions in a manner that permits determination of the various *totals* and *subtotals* useful to management and used in accounting reports.
3. *Summarize and communicate* the data contained in the system to decision makers.

The differences in accounting systems arise primarily in the manner and speed with which these functions are performed.

RECORDING TRANSACTIONS: THE NEED FOR SPECIAL JOURNALS

A *journal* sometimes is called the "book of original entry" because it is the accounting record in which the effects of transactions are *first recorded*. in preceding chapters, we have used a two-column *general journal* to illustrate the recording of transactions. But journals come in many different forms. In fact, many journals are *machines* rather than sheets of paper.

The general journal is unique among journals because it can be used to record *any type* of business transaction. The flexibility of a general journal makes it ideal for textbook illustrations. However, this flexibility also makes the general journal a relatively *inefficient* device for recording large numbers of routine transactions.

As explained in Chapter 5, most businesses use various *special journals* to speed up the recording of transactions. These special journals include, for example, cash registers, point-of-sale terminals, and check-writing machines. For an accounting system to be cost effective, *routine transactions must be recorded by clerical personnel or by machines*—not by professional accountants.

ON-LINE, REAL-TIME (OLRT) SYSTEMS
There normally is *some delay* between the time a transaction occurs and the time that its effects are entered in the company's ledger accounts. In manual accounting systems—and many computer-based systems—sales transactions are not posted until the end of the day. Payroll data generally are recorded only at the end of each pay period. If accounting information is required only at periodic intervals (such as month-end), these short delays may be of no consequence.

In some cases, however, managers and employees need information that is completely up-to-date. Bank tellers, for example, often need to know the current balance in a customer's bank account. Airline ticket salespeople need up-to-date information about the

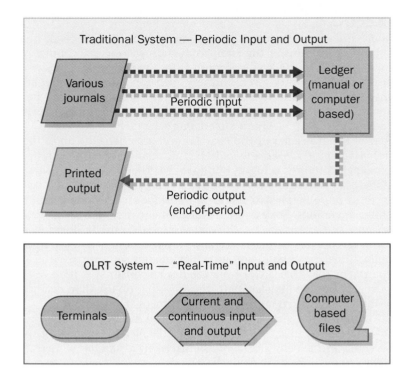

number of seats still available on specific flights. Salesclerks may need to know how many units of a particular product are in stock.

An *on-line, real-time (OLRT)* accounting system has the ability to keep certain accounting records *completely current.* As a practical matter, OLRT systems must be computer-based. The phrase "on-line" refers to input devices and output devices with *direct and immediate access* to the computer-based records. "Real-time" means *now,* reflecting the idea that the records are up-to-date.

In an OLRT system, some types of transactions are recorded *as they occur.* Managers and employees then may use computer terminals to view up-to-date information. The diagram at the top of this page illustrates the traditional and OLRT approaches to recording and receiving accounting information.

The point-of-sale terminals used in many retail stores are examples of on-line input devices. When sales are recorded on these terminals, the general ledger and subsidiary ledger accounts may be updated immediately. Thus, managers and employees may use computer terminals to access up-to-date information about sales, inventories, and accounts receivable. (Notice that point-of-sale terminals are located on the sales floor, not in the accounting department. If transactions are to be recorded as they occur, the input devices must be located where these transactions take place.)

Even in a system with OLRT capabilities, *not all* accounting records are kept continuously up-to-date. Depreciation expense, for example, is recorded only at the end of each accounting period. Many other expenses, such as utility bills, are recorded only as bills are received (or as payment is made). The accounting records which are kept continuously up-to-date usually are limited to the general and subsidiary ledger accounts for cash, accounts receivable, inventory, accounts payable, and sales revenue.

RECORDING BUDGETED AMOUNTS   Up to this point, we have discussed recording in the accounting system only the results of *actual* business transactions. Many businesses also enter into their accounting system advance forecasts (or budgets) of the levels of activity *expected in future periods.* Often, separate budgets are developed for each department within the business. As the actual results are recorded in the system, reports are prepared showing the *differences* between the forecasts and the actual results. These reports aid managers in evaluating departmental performance.

CLASSIFYING AND STORING THE RECORDED DATA

Two methods of classifying and storing data in accounting systems are in widespread use: *ledger accounts* and *computer databases.*

LEDGER ACCOUNTS

In both manual and computer-based accounting systems, the effects of business transactions are classified in terms of the company's chart of ledger accounts. A *chart of accounts* is simply a *listing* of the ledger account titles used by the business.

In designing the ledger of a given business, questions arise as to the *extent of detail* needed in the chart of accounts. For example, should one ledger account be used for advertising expense, or should separate accounts be maintained for newspaper advertising, direct mail advertising, and television advertising?

The extent of detail needed in the chart of accounts depends upon the *types of information that management considers useful.* The information appearing in financial statements and income tax returns is highly summarized. Therefore, the preparation of these types of reports does *not* require a very detailed chart of accounts. Management, however, usually finds more detailed accounting information useful in planning and controlling business operations. For example, management may want separate information about the revenue and expenses of *each department* within the business.

The chart of revenue and expense accounts often is designed along lines of *managerial responsibility.* Thus, the chart of accounts may include separate revenue and expenses for each department (or other area of managerial responsibility). This *responsibility accounting system* provides top management with information useful in evaluating the performance of individual departments and of department managers.

A general ledger with a great many accounts would quickly become unwieldy and difficult to use. Therefore, the accounts showing a detailed breakdown of specific assets, liabilities, revenue, and expenses usually are placed in a *subsidiary ledger.* Only the related *controlling account* appears in the general ledger.

DATABASE SYSTEMS

LO 2 *Describe a database and explain its usefulness.*

A *database* provides greater flexibility in the classification of data than even the most detailed chart of ledger accounts. When transaction data are stored in a database, they may be sorted according to a variety of criteria.

A database consists of *unclassified* data, which have not yet been grouped into categories. However, the data are accompanied by various classification *codes.* Each of these codes enables the computer quickly to classify (or "sort") the data according to different characteristics—or combinations of characteristics.

COMPARISON OF LEDGER ACCOUNTS TO A DATABASE

In a ledger-based system, the effects of transactions are classified in terms of specific ledger accounts *at the time transactions are recorded.* In a database, the effects of transactions are stored in an *unclassified format,* but are "coded" so that the computer can sort through the data and find the items that meet various criteria. Thus, data are classified as necessary to meet requests for specific types of accounting records and reports. The basic differences between a ledger account system and a database are illustrated below.

It is important to recognize that a database is *not a substitute* for a ledger. Rather, databases are used to provide management and employees with *additional information* about certain types of transactions.

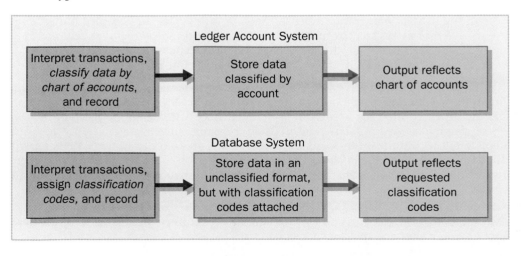

SUMMARIZING AND COMMUNICATING ACCOUNTING INFORMATION

In general terms, the usefulness of accounting information to decision makers depends upon (1) the *relevance* of the information to the decisions at hand, (2) the *timeliness* of the information, and (3) its *reliability*. At this point, we will discuss only the first two factors—the relevance and timeliness of accounting information. The third factor—reliability—is closely related to the topics of internal control and audits of financial statements. These topics are discussed later in this chapter.

Both the relevance and timeliness of accounting information have been enhanced greatly by recent advances in the technologies of computers and communication. Database systems permit the preparation of accounting reports *tailored to the immediate needs* of decision makers. Computers can prepare accounting reports almost instantly. Through computer networks, electronic mail, facsimile machines, and communication satellites, these reports can be transmitted quickly anywhere in the world. In OLRT systems, decision makers may use computer terminals to access information which is *completely current*. Thus, advances in technology rapidly are increasing the usefulness of accounting information.

INTERNAL CONTROL

The need for internal control is common to all organizations. The term *internal control* refers to *all measures* taken by management to ensure that the organization (1) operates efficiently and effectively, (2) produces reliable financial information, and (3) complies with applicable laws and regulations. In short, internal control consists of those measures designed to keep the business operating "on track."

LO 3 *State the objectives of internal control.*

Collectively, the internal control procedures in place within a given organization are described as the *internal control structure,* or the *system* of internal control.

COMPONENTS OF INTERNAL CONTROL

The accounting profession recently has published an in-depth study of internal control structures, called *Internal Control—Integrated Framework*.[1] This framework describes five basic *components* of internal control.

1. The *control environment,* consisting of management's philosophy, style, and ethical values, and also including the manner in which these concepts are communicated throughout the organization.

2. *Risk assessment,* involving the means by which a business identifies and manages the risks that threaten that type of organization. For example, if changes in interest rates can significantly affect the profits of a business, the organization should take steps to anticipate changes in rates and minimize the losses that might result.

CASE IN POINT

For several years, the investment fund of Orange County, California, was invested heavily in financial instruments that were "interest sensitive." These investments would increase in value as interest rates declined, but would fall dramatically in value as interest rates rose. During 1994, the Federal Reserve *increased* interest rates on five separate occasions. Yet Orange County stuck to its "declining-interest-rate" investment strategy.

The County's investment portfolio lost so much value that, late in 1994, Orange County was forced to declare bankruptcy. The value of its investment fund had declined by over $1½ billion, leaving the County unable to repay amounts invested by school districts, water districts, and other municipal service organizations.

In our opinion, the investment fund's *risk assessment controls* were woefully inadequate.

---

[1]This document was developed by a committee of sponsoring organizations, including the American Institute of Certified Public Accountants, American Accounting Association, Financial Executives Institute, Institute of Internal Auditors, and Institute of Management Accountants.

3. *Control activities,* meaning the policies and procedures established to ensure that management's directives are being followed. Periodic performance reviews of departments and of key personnel are examples of control activities.

4. *Information and communication,* the means by which the organization identifies, records, and communicates information to decision makers. In large part, information and communication is handled by the *accounting system.*

5. *Monitoring,* which describes the procedures employed to determine that the internal control structure is working effectively. *Internal auditing* is an example of a monitoring procedure.

Virtually every organization—small or large—needs to establish control procedures in each of these areas. The nature of these procedures, however, *varies greatly* from one organization to the next. Internal control is not an "end in itself." Like an accounting system, an internal control structure should be *cost effective*—that is, the procedures employed to achieve internal control should never cost more than the benefits derived.

GUIDELINES FOR ACHIEVING STRONG INTERNAL CONTROL

ESTABLISH CLEAR LINES OF RESPONSIBILITY Every organization should indicate clearly the persons or departments responsible for such functions as sales, purchasing, receiving incoming shipments, paying bills, and maintaining accounting records. The lines of authority and responsibility can be shown in an *organization chart.* The organization chart should be supported by written job descriptions and by procedures manuals that explain in detail the authority and responsibilities of each person or department appearing in the chart.

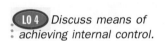
Discuss means of achieving internal control.

ESTABLISH ROUTINE PROCEDURES FOR PROCESSING EACH TYPE OF TRANSACTION If management is to direct the activities of a business according to plan, every transaction should go through four separate steps: It should be *authorized, approved, executed,* and *recorded.* For example, consider the sale of merchandise on credit. Top management has the authority and responsibility to authorize credit sales to categories of customers who meet certain standards. The credit department is responsible for approving a credit sale of a given dollar amount to a particular customer. The transaction is executed by the shipping department, which ships or delivers the merchandise to the customer. Finally, the transaction is recorded in the accounting department by an entry debiting Accounts Receivable and crediting Sales.

SUBDIVISION OF DUTIES Perhaps the most important concept in achieving internal control is an appropriate subdivision—or separation—of duties. Responsibilities should be assigned so that *no one person or department handles a transaction completely from beginning to end.* When duties are divided in this manner, the work of one employee serves to verify that of another and any errors which occur tend to be detected promptly.

To illustrate this concept, let us review the typical procedures followed by a wholesaler in processing a credit sale. The sales department of the company is responsible for securing the order from the customer; the credit department must approve the customer's credit before the order is filled; the stock room assembles the goods ordered; the shipping department packs and ships the goods; the billing department prepares the sales invoice; and the accounting department records the transaction.

Each department receives written evidence of the action by the other departments and reviews the documents describing the transaction to see that the actions taken correspond in all details. The shipping department, for instance, does not release the merchandise until after the credit department has approved the customer as a credit risk. The accounting department does not record the sale until it has received documentary evidence that (1) an order was received from a customer, (2) the extension of credit was approved, (3) the merchandise was shipped to the customer, and (4) a sales invoice was prepared and mailed to the customer.

ACCOUNTING FUNCTION SEPARATE FROM CUSTODY OF ASSETS   Basic to the separation of duties is the concept that an employee who has custody of an asset (or access to an asset) should not maintain the accounting record for that asset. If one person has custody of assets and also maintains the accounting records, there is both opportunity and incentive to falsify the records to conceal a shortage. However, the person with custody of the asset will not be inclined to waste it, steal it, or give it away if he or she is aware that another employee is maintaining a record of the asset.

OTHER STEPS TOWARD ACHIEVING INTERNAL CONTROL   Other important internal control measures include the following:

1. *Internal auditing.* Virtually every *large* organization has an internal auditing staff. The objectives of the *internal auditors* are to monitor and improve the system of internal control. Internal auditors test and evaluate internal controls in all areas of the organization and prepare reports to top management on their findings and recommendations. Much work of internal auditors may be described as *operational and compliance auditing.* These types of audits are discussed later in this appendix.

2. *Financial forecasts.* A plan of operations is prepared each year setting goals for each division of the business, as, for example, the expected volume of sales, amounts of expenses, and future cash balances. *Actual* results are compared with *forecasted* amounts month by month. This comparison strengthens control because variations from planned results are investigated promptly.

3. *Competent personnel.* Even the best-designed system of internal control will not work well unless the people using it are competent. Competence and integrity of employees are in part developed through training programs, but they also are related to the policies for selection of personnel and to the adequacy of supervision.

4. *Rotation of employees.* The rotation of employees from one job assignment to another may strengthen internal control. When employees know that another person will soon be taking over their duties, they are more likely to maintain records with care and to follow established procedures. The rotation of employees also may bring to light errors or irregularities caused by the employee formerly performing a given task.

5. *Serially numbered documents.* Documents such as checks, purchase orders, and sales invoices should be serially numbered. If a document is misplaced or concealed, the break in the sequence of numbers will call attention to the missing item.

THE ROLE OF BUSINESS DOCUMENTS

We have made the point that strong internal control requires subdivision of duties among the departments of the business. How does each department know that the other departments have fulfilled their responsibilities? The answer lies in the use of carefully designed *business documents.* Some of the more important business documents used in controlling purchases of merchandise are summarized on the following page.

PURCHASE REQUISITION   A purchase requisition is a request from the sales department or stores department (warehousing) for the purchasing department to order merchandise. Thus, the purchasing department is not authorized to order goods *unless it has first received a purchase requisition.* A copy of the purchase requisition is sent to the accounting department.

PURCHASE ORDERS   Once a purchase requisition has been received, the purchasing department determines the lowest-cost supplier of the merchandise and places an order. This order is documented in a *purchase order.* A purchase order issued by Fairway Pro Shop to Adams Manufacturing Company is illustrated on the next page.

Several copies of a purchase order are usually prepared. The original is sent to the supplier; it constitutes an authorization to deliver the merchandise and to submit a bill based on the prices listed. A second copy is sent to the department that initiated the purchase requisition to show that the requisition has been acted upon. Another copy is sent to the accounting department of the buying company.

The issuance of a purchase order does not call for any entries in the accounting records of either the prospective buyer or seller. The company which receives an order

Business Document	Initiated by	Sent to
Purchase requisition Issued when quantity of goods on hand falls below established reorder point	Departmental sales managers or stores department	Original to purchasing department; copy to accounting department
Purchase order Issued when order is placed; indicates type, quantities, and prices of merchandise ordered	Purchasing department	Original to selling company (vendor, supplier); copies to department requisitioning goods and the accounting department
Invoice Confirms that goods have been shipped and requests payment	Seller (supplier)	Accounting department of buying company
Receiving report Based on count and inspection of goods received	Receiving department of buying company	Original to accounting department; copies to purchasing department and to department requisitioning goods
Invoice approval form Based upon the documents listed above; authorizes payment of the purchase invoice	Accounting department of buying company	Finance department, to support issuance of check; returned to accounting department with a copy of the check

A serially numbered purchase order

PURCHASE ORDER   ORDER NO. *999*

FAIRWAY PRO SHOP

10 Fairway Avenue, San Francisco, California

TO: **Adams Manufacturing Company**   DATE November 10, 19__

    19 Union Street   SHIP VIA **Jones Truck Co.**

    Kansas City, Missouri   TERMS: **2/10, n/30**

PLEASE ENTER OUR ORDER FOR THE FOLLOWING:

QUANTITY	DESCRIPTION	PRICE	TOTAL
15 sets	Model S irons	$120.00	$1,800.00
50 dozen	X3Y Shur-Par golf balls	14.00	700.00
			$2,500.00

FAIRWAY PRO SHOP

BY _____ *DD McCarthy*

does not consider that a sale has been made *until the merchandise is delivered*. At that point ownership of the goods changes, and both buyer and seller should make accounting entries to record the transaction.

INVOICES When a manufacturer or wholesaler receives an order for its products, it takes two actions. One is to ship the goods to the customer and the other is to send the customer an *invoice*. By the act of shipping the merchandise, the seller is giving up ownership of one type of asset, inventory; by issuing the invoice, the seller is recording ownership of another form of asset, an account receivable.

An invoice contains a description of the goods being sold, the quantities, prices, credit terms, and method of shipment. The illustration below shows an invoice issued by Adams Manufacturing Company in response to the previously illustrated purchase order from Fairway Pro Shop.

INVOICE   INVOICE NO. 782
ADAMS MANUFACTURING COMPANY
19 UNION STREET
KANSAS CITY, MISSOURI

SOLD TO: __Fairway Pro Shop__ INVOICE DATE __November 15, 19__

__10 Fairway Avenue__ YOUR PURCHASE ORDER NO. __999__

__San Francisco, Calif.__ DATE SHIPPED __November 15, 19__

SHIPPED TO: __Same__ SHIPPED VIA __Jones Truck Co.__

TERMS __2/10, n/30__

QUANTITY	DESCRIPTION	PRICE	TOTAL
15 sets	Model S irons	$120.00	$1,800.00
50 dozen	X3Y Shur-Par golf balls	14.00	700.00
			$2,500.00

From the viewpoint of the seller, an invoice is a *sales invoice;* from the buyer's viewpoint it is a *purchase invoice*. The invoice is the basis for an entry in the accounting records of *both* the seller and the buyer because it evidences the *transfer of ownership of goods*. At the time of issuing the invoice, the selling company makes an entry debiting Accounts Receivable and crediting Sales. The buying company, however, does not record the invoice as a liability until the invoice has been approved for payment.

RECEIVING REPORT Evidence that the merchandise has been received in good condition is obtained from the receiving department. The receiving department receives all incoming goods, inspects them as to quality and condition, and determines the quantities received by counting, measuring, or weighing. The receiving department then prepares a serially numbered report for each shipment received; one copy of this *receiving report* is sent to the accounting department for use in approving the invoice for payment.

INVOICE APPROVAL FORM The approval of the invoice in the accounting department is accomplished by comparing the purchase requisition, the purchase order, the invoice, and the receiving report. Comparison of these documents establishes that the merchandise described in the invoice was actually ordered, has been received in good condition, and was billed at the prices specified in the purchase order.

The person who performs these comparisons then records the liability (debit Inventory, credit Accounts Payable) and signs an *invoice approval form* authorizing payment of the invoice by the finance department. (One type of invoice approval form, called a *voucher,* is discussed further in the following chapter.)

DEBIT AND CREDIT MEMORANDA (DEBIT MEMOS, CREDIT MEMOS) If merchandise purchased on account is unsatisfactory and is to be returned to the supplier (or if a price reduction is agreed upon), a *debit memorandum* may be prepared by the purchasing company and sent to the supplier. The debit memorandum informs the supplier that the buyer has debited (reduced) its liability to the supplier and explains the circumstances.

Upon being informed of the return of damaged merchandise (or having agreed to a reduction in price), the seller will send the buyer a *credit memorandum* indicating that the account receivable from the buyer has been credited (reduced).

Notice that issuing a credit memorandum has the same effect upon a customer's account as does receiving payment from the customer—that is, the account receivable is credited (reduced). Thus, an employee with authority to issue credit memoranda *should not be allowed to handle cash receipts from customers.* If both of these duties were assigned to the same employee, that person could abstract some of the cash collected from customers and conceal this theft by issuing fictitious credit memoranda.

INTERNAL CONTROL IN COMPUTER-BASED SYSTEMS

Computers do not eliminate the need for internal control. In fact, most recent cases of large-scale fraud have occurred in companies with computer-based accounting systems.

CASE IN POINT

An outside computer consultant for a major bank once used the bank's computer system to transfer $10 million of the bank's money into his personal account at another bank. The consultant's knowledge of the bank's computer system enabled him to commit this fraud. He had observed how bank employees used the computer to make legitimate transfers of funds. In addition, he had noticed that the "secret" computer codes used in these transfers were posted on the wall next to the computer terminal.

Despite the preceding Case in Point, computer-based accounting systems lend themselves well to the implementation of internal control procedures. One such procedure is the use of *access codes,* or passwords, which limit access to the accounting system to authorized users. Access controls also *identify the user* responsible for each entry. (Obviously, these access codes should not be posted on the wall.)

In fact, computer-based accounting systems create many opportunities for implementing internal control procedures which might not be practical in a manual accounting system.

CASE IN POINT

When on-line terminals are used to record credit sales, the salesperson enters the customer's credit card number into the system. The computer then determines whether the proposed sales transaction will cause the customer's account balance to exceed any predetermined credit limit. Also, the computer compares the customer's card number with a list of credit cards reported lost or stolen. If either of these procedures indicates that credit should not be extended to this customer, the computer immediately notifies the salesperson not to make the sale.

LIMITATIONS OF INTERNAL CONTROL

Although internal control is highly effective in increasing the reliability of accounting data and in safeguarding assets, it does not provide *complete* protection against fraud, theft, or errors. For example, controls based upon a subdivision of duties may be defeated—at least temporarily—by *collusion* among two or more employees. Carelessness also may cause a breakdown in internal control.

In designing a system of internal control, the question of cost cannot be ignored. A system of internal control should be *cost effective.* A system which is too elaborate may entail greater expense than is justified by the protection gained.

Internal control is more difficult to achieve in a small business than in a large one. In a business with only a few employees, it may not be possible to arrange an adequate subdivision of duties. Also, such internal control features as an internal audit staff simply may not be practical.

An essential element of maintaining a reasonable degree of internal control in a small business is *active participation by the owner* in strategic control procedures. For example, the owner of a small business often is the only person authorized to sign checks. The owner also may count the cash receipts at the end of each business day, and assume responsibility for depositing these receipts in the bank.

In summary, the system of internal control—like an accounting system—should be *tailored to meet the specific needs of the organization.*

PREVENTION OF FRAUD

Perhaps the most highly publicized objective of internal control is the prevention of fraud. *Fraud* may be defined as the deliberate misrepresentation of facts with the *intent of deceiving* someone. If the purpose of this deception is personal gain or causing harm to another, fraud may be a criminal act. In discussing the role of the internal control in preventing acts of fraud, it is useful to distinguish between *errors* in the accounting records and *irregularities.*

Accountants use the term *errors* to refer to *unintentional mistakes. Irregularities,* on the other hand, refers to *intentional* mistakes, entered into accounting records or accounting reports for some fraudulent purpose. Irregularities may be further subdivided into the classifications of *employee fraud* and *management fraud.*

CASE IN POINT

The significance of fraud to American business is dramatically illustrated by a recent survey of business executives made by **KPMG Peat Marwick,** an international accounting firm. Some of the more significant results are summarized below:

- Of the businesses responding to the survey, 76% had experienced a fraud in the past year.
- The most common types of fraud were misappropriation of funds and check forgery.
- Almost 63% of the respondents estimated that fraud had cost their businesses more than $100,000 over the past year.
- In over 50% of the cases, *poor internal controls* allowed the fraud to occur.

EMPLOYEE FRAUD

Employee fraud refers to dishonest acts performed *against the company* by its employees. Examples of employee fraud include theft of assets, charging lower sales prices to favored customers, receiving kickbacks from suppliers, overstating hours worked, padding expense accounts, and embezzlement. (*Embezzlement* is a theft of assets which is concealed by falsification of the accounting records.)

LO 5 *Distinguish between employee fraud and management fraud.*

If one employee handles all aspects of a transaction, the danger of employee fraud increases. Studies of fraud cases suggest that individuals may be tempted into dishonest acts if given complete control of company property. Most of these persons, however, would not engage in fraud if doing so required collaboration with other employees. Thus, subdivision of duties is believed to reduce the risk of employee fraud.

In addition to subdivision of duties, the risk of employee fraud is reduced by such control procedures as investigating the backgrounds of job applicants, periodic rotation of employees to different job assignments, and frequent comparisons of assets actually on hand with the quantities shown in the accounting records.

FIDELITY BONDS   No system of internal control can provide absolute protection against losses from dishonest employees. Therefore, many companies require that employees handling cash or other negotiable assets be *bonded*. A *fidelity bond* is a type of insurance contract in which the bonding company agrees to reimburse an employer up to agreed dollar limits for losses caused by fraud or embezzlement by bonded employees.

MANAGEMENT FRAUD

Management fraud refers to deliberate misrepresentations made by the *top management* of a business to persons *outside* of the business organization. This type of fraud often involves the issuance of fraudulent financial statements intended to mislead investors and creditors.

THE IMPACT OF MANAGEMENT FRAUD   Management fraud differs from employee fraud because top management is a *willing participant* in the fraudulent acts. A characteristic of management fraud is that management uses its position of trust and authority to *override the system of internal control* and to enrich itself at the expense of the company and/or outsiders. The persons most often injured by management fraud are investors and creditors. However, the company's employees and customers and the general public also may be harmed severely.

The basic purpose of accounting is to aid decision makers in allocating and using economic resources efficiently. Cases of management fraud are far more destructive to this basic purpose than are most cases of employee fraud. The damage caused by employee fraud usually is limited to relatively small losses incurred by a specific company. Of course, these losses may be passed on to the company's customers in the form of higher prices. Seldom, however, does employee fraud force a business into bankruptcy or affect the efficient allocation of resources throughout the economy.

When the financial statements of large companies are altered to mislead investors and creditors, however, the resulting losses may be enormous. In addition, the misallocation of economic resources may be so great as to affect the national economy.

Management fraud is *not* commonplace in our society. The managers and directors of most large business organizations are people of indisputable integrity. However, even

CASE IN POINT

Management fraud played a significant role in the savings and loan crisis. Some S&Ls falsified their accounting records and financial statements to conceal from investors and government regulators their deteriorating financial positions and management's misuse of company assets.

Ultimately, the S&L crisis may cost the American taxpayer—who insures deposits in these institutions—more than $500 billion. In addition, this crisis has contributed to an economic recession, tax increases, the loss of many jobs, and a nationwide decline in real estate values.

a few isolated instances of management fraud can severely damage the economy. Whenever a large publicly owned company engages in fraud, investors, creditors, and the public tend to lose confidence in the business community and the financial reporting process. This loss of confidence may create doubts and reservations which impede the efficient allocation of investment capital for many years.

PROTECTING SOCIETY FROM MANAGEMENT FRAUD   Internal controls are not generally designed to protect outside decision makers from the possibility of management fraud. Internal controls are designed to assure *management* that the company's objectives are being met, including the generation of reliable financial information. However, top management may be able to override internal controls when it comes to reporting to individuals outside the organization.

One effective internal control over top management is active participation in the business by the company's *board of directors*. Many companies appoint an *audit committee* within the board of directors specifically to oversee the external financial reporting process of the company. In addition, an effective *internal auditing department* helps to prevent and detect management fraud, especially when it has direct access to the board of directors or its audit committee.

To engage in large-scale fraud, management generally must get lower level employees to "go along" with the scheme, often by intimidation. Specifically, many people in the company's accounting department may become aware of a large-scale fraud. Presumably, some of these people would refuse to participate in the fraud and would blow the whistle on a dishonest management.

Finally, *financial audits* by certified public accountants help to prevent and detect fraudulent financial statements before they are used by outside decision makers.

AUDITS

AUDITS OF FINANCIAL STATEMENTS

A *financial audit* is an examination of a company's financial statements performed by a firm of certified public accountants (CPAs). The purpose of this audit is to provide people outside the organization with an *independent expert's opinion* as to whether the financial statements constitute a *fair presentation*. Auditors use the phrase "fair presentation" to describe financial statements which are complete, unbiased, and in conformity with generally accepted accounting principles.

LO 6 *Distinguish among audits, reviews, and compilations of financial statements.*

THE NATURE OF A FINANCIAL AUDIT   The financial statements of a business are *prepared by the company's management.* An audit of these financial statements is intended to bridge the "credibility gap" which otherwise might exist between the company's management and the users of these statements. For the auditors' opinion to have credibility, however, the *independent auditors* must (1) be independent of the company issuing the statements and of its management, and (2) have a sound basis for their opinion.

The concept of *independence* means that the auditors have no relationships with the company issuing the statements that might lessen the auditors' ability to render an unbiased opinion. Auditors not only must *be* independent; they also must *appear* to be independent of the issuing company. Otherwise, the users of financial statements may not have confidence in the auditors' report. The term *audit* describes the investigation which the auditors undertake to provide the sound basis for their opinion.

As part of a financial statement audit, the CPAs consider and evaluate the internal control of the company issuing the statements. This evaluation gives them a "feel" for the accuracy and reliability of the information in the company's accounting system. Next, the auditors gather evidence to *substantiate every material item* appearing in the financial statements. For example, the CPAs count portions of the company's inventory and compare these test counts with the company's inventory records. They also confirm some of the company's accounts receivable by verifying with customers the amounts actually owed. Auditors also perform procedures designed to determine that the statements and the accompanying notes are *complete.*

AUDITORS' REPORTS   After completing the audit, the CPAs express their expert opinion as to the fairness of the financial statements. This opinion, called the *auditors' report,* accompanies the financial statements whenever they are issued to decision makers outside of the business organization.

Shown below is the auditors' report contained in the 1995 annual report of **HBO & Company** (the cable television network). The auditors, Arthur Andersen & Co., are one of the "Big Six" international public accounting firms.*

*The "Big Six" are the world's six largest CPA firms. Only a large CPA firm has the resources to audit a large corporation. Therefore, most publicly owned corporations are audited by one of the Big Six firms. In addition to Arthur Andersen & Co., the CPA firms comprising the Big Six include (in alphabetical order): Coopers & Lybrand, Deloitte & Touche, Ernst & Young, KPMG Peat Marwick, and Price Waterhouse.

Report of Independent Public Accountants

To the Board of Directors
and Stockholders of HBO & Company:

We have audited the accompanying consolidated balance sheets of HBO & Company (a Delaware corporation) and subsidiaries as of December 31, 1995 and 1994 and the related consolidated statements of income, stockholders' equity and cash flows for each of the three years in the period ended December 31, 1995. These financial statements are the responsibility of the Company's management. Our responsibility is to express an opinion on these financial statements based on our audits.

We conducted our audits in accordance with generally accepted auditing standards. Those standards require that we plan and perform the audit to obtain reasonable assurance about whether the financial statements are free of material misstatement. An audit includes examining, on a test basis, evidence supporting the amounts and disclosures in the financial statements. An audit also includes assessing the accounting principles used and significant estimates made by management, as well as evaluating the overall financial statement presentation. We believe that our audits provide a reasonable basis for our opinion.

In our opinion, the financial statements referred to above present fairly, in all material respects, the financial position of HBO & Company and subsidiaries as of December 31, 1995 and 1994 and the results of their operations and their cash flows for each of the three years in the period ended December 31, 1995, in conformity with generally accepted accounting principles.

ARTHUR ANDERSEN LLP

Atlanta, Georgia
February 6, 1996

The illustrated report is an *unqualified opinion,* meaning that Arthur Andersen & Co. regards HBO's financial statements as a fair presentation. If the auditors *do not* consider the statements "fair," they modify their report to identify any shortcomings. Such modified reports are called either *qualified opinions* or *adverse opinions,* depending upon the extent of the auditors' reservations.

In practice, qualified and adverse opinions rarely are issued. Before issuing such a report, the auditors explain to management what changes should be made in the financial statements. Management usually makes these changes, as it is anxious to receive a clean (unqualified) auditor's report.

Over many decades, audited financial statements have developed an excellent track record of reliability. Notice, however, that CPAs do not *guarantee* the accuracy of financial statements. Rather, they render their professional *opinion* as to the overall "fairness" of the statements. Just as a physician may make an error in the diagnosis of a particular patient, there is always a possibility that an auditor's opinion may be in error.

The following diagram summarizes the relationships between the financial statements, an independent audit, and the auditors' report:

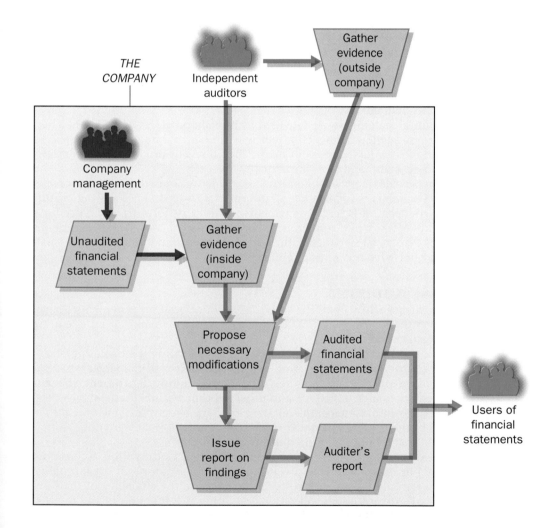

AUDITS AND THE DETECTION OF FRAUD   The primary purpose of financial audits is to determine the overall fairness of a set of financial statements, *not* to detect any and all acts of fraud. Users of financial statements should recognize that auditors cannot guarantee that financial statements are completely free of *minor* errors and irregularities. Most audit procedures are based upon samples; it simply is not possible for the auditors to verify all of the transactions of a large organization. Therefore, there is always the possibility that errors or irregularities may exist among the transactions which were not examined by the auditors.

Auditors design their investigation to detect errors and fraud that are *material* in relation to the financial statements. We have explained the concept of materiality in earlier chapters. With respect to financial statements, an item is material if knowledge of the item might reasonably be expected to *influence the decisions* of users of the statements.

Some cases of employee fraud, such as the theft of a few items from inventory, involve such small dollar amounts that they do not affect the overall fairness of the financial statements. An audit should not be expected to detect all such irregularities.

Any fraud of a scale which causes the financial statements to become misleading, however, is material. Such situations *should* be brought to light in the normal course of an audit. The principal purpose of an audit is to provide outsiders with assurance that the financial statements are a fair presentation. If these audited statements are misleading, the audit has failed to serve its purpose.

As explained in Chapter 1, audits are not the only factor contributing to the reliability of financial statements. Other factors include the company's system of internal control, accountants' and managers' personal commitments to ethical conduct, the Securities and Exchange Commission, and federal securities laws.

REVIEWS AND COMPILATIONS OF FINANCIAL STATEMENTS An audit is both time-consuming and expensive. (The cost of the audit normally is paid by the company issuing the financial statements.) All accounting information, including audited financial statements, should be *cost effective*. For this reason, many nonpublic companies have their financial statements *reviewed* or *compiled* by a firm of CPAs, rather than having these statements audited.

Reviews of financial statements are intended to provide outsiders with *limited assurance* as to the fairness of the statements. A review is similar to a financial audit, except that the investigation is *substantially less thorough*. Thus, a review can be performed much more quickly than an audit, and at a substantially lower cost.

CPAs also may *compile* financial statements for a small nonpublic company. *Compilations* of financial statements involve taking information from the accounting records and putting it in the form of financial statements, without performing any procedures to verify the information. While compilations provide *no assurance* to outsiders about the reliability of the financial statements, they do provide an important service to small companies that do not have accounting-trained employees.

OPERATIONAL AUDITING

LO 7 *Describe the nature and purpose of operational and compliance auditing.*

Financial audits focus primarily upon the verification of financial measurements. An *operational audit,* in contrast, focuses upon the *efficiency* and *effectiveness* of an operating unit within an organization.

An operational audit involves studying, testing, and evaluating the operating procedures and system of internal control relating to a specific unit within a larger organization. The subject of the operational audit might be the accounting department, the purchasing department, a branch office, or any other subunit within the company. The purpose of the audit is to make recommendations to management for *improving the operational efficiency* of the department under study. The results normally are not communicated to decision makers outside of the business organization.

Operational auditing is a rapidly growing field of specialization within accounting. Current economic pressures are forcing private companies, not-for-profit organizations, and all levels of government to reduce costs and to increase the efficiency of their operations. Within large organizations, operational auditing is a function of the internal audit staff. Smaller organizations may engage CPA firms to perform operational audits. The federal government has several agencies, such as the General Accounting Office (GAO), the Naval Audit Service, and the Defense Contract Audit Agency, which perform operational audits of various governmental agencies and programs.

COMPLIANCE AUDITING

An organization's operations are subject to a wide variety of laws and regulations, dealing with such matters as employee safety, environmental protection, personnel policies, and product pricing. Violations can result in huge fines and penalties that may threaten the very existence of the organization. Therefore, compliance with laws and regulations is an important concern of management of all types of organizations.

As indicated previously, compliance with laws and regulations is one of the objectives of a system of internal control. Management may obtain additional assurance by having the organization's internal or independent auditors consider these internal controls and test compliance with specific laws and regulations. These types of audits are called *compliance audits*. In auditing a particular subunit of the organization, internal auditors often perform an examination that involves both compliance and operational auditing.

Compliance audits are sometimes performed by a regulatory agency. For example, each year the Internal Revenue Service audits the income tax returns of several million taxpayers for compliance with income tax laws and regulations. These types of audits benefit only the agency performing the audit. The results generally are *not* made available to the public or to other outside decision makers. The agency performing the audit also bears the cost of these investigations.

ASSIGNMENT MATERIAL

DISCUSSION QUESTIONS

1. What are the basic factors affecting the design and structure of a company's accounting system?

2. An accounting system should meet the specific needs of a business organization. Identify several examples of (a) information needs which are common to all publicly owned corporations and (b) accounting information which management may want developed for its own use in managing the business.

3. How is it possible for cashiers using point-of-sale terminals to record cash sales by entering only a product code into the terminal? Why is it not necessary to enter the dollar amount of the sale and to instruct the computer to debit the Cash account and credit the Sales account?

4. Define an *on-line, real-time* accounting system. Identify several business situations in which on-line, real-time information would be useful to company personnel.

5. Identify two general criteria (other than reliability) which affect the usefulness of an accounting report to a decision maker. How has technology affected these criteria in recent years?

6. List the three objectives of internal control.

7. List and briefly describe the five components of internal control.

8. Briefly explain the concept of *subdivision of duties*. How does this concept reduce the risk of errors and irregularities?

9. Is internal control necessary in a company with a highly reliable computer system? Explain.

10. Explain several reasons why internal control may *fail* to prevent certain errors or irregularities.

11. Distinguish between *employee fraud* and *management fraud*. Provide an example of each.

12. Describe the nature and purpose of a financial audit. Who performs these audits?

13. Do auditors guarantee the reliability of audited financial statements? If the statements should turn out to be highly misleading, can the auditors be held financially liable for the losses sustained by decision makers relying upon the statements? Explain.

14. Distinguish among an audit, a review, and a compilation of financial statements. Who performs these services? Who pays for them?

15. Describe the nature and purpose of an operational audit. Who performs these audits?

16. Explain the purpose of a compliance audit. Who performs these audits?

PROBLEMS

PROBLEM C-1
Accounting Systems
LO 1,2

Evaluate each of the following statements, indicating any areas of agreement and disagreement.

a. Transactions can be recorded more efficiently in special journals than in a general journal. Therefore, a well-designed accounting system should use only special journals.

b. The transaction data stored in a database can be arranged in the format of ledger accounts. Therefore, a business with a computer-based accounting system does not need a ledger. Whenever the balance of any ledger account is needed for any purpose, the computer can sort through the database and determine this amount.

c. In an on-line, real-time accounting system, a manager may view the up-to-the-moment balance of any ledger account from a computer terminal.

d. Advances in the technologies of computers and communications have increased the usefulness of accounting information to decision makers.

e. In recording cash sales, a cashier using a point-of-sale terminal may record a cash sale by entering only a product code identifying the merchandise sold. This is single-entry accounting, not double-entry accounting.

PROBLEM C-2
Purpose of a System of
Internal Control
LO 3

Three executives of Jetlab, a small electronics firm, disagree as to their company's need for a system of internal control. Jones argues as follows: "If we are going to spend money on fidelity bonds, it is a complete waste to duplicate that kind of protection by maintaining our own system of internal control." Smith disagrees and expresses the following view: "The benefits we would receive from a strong system of internal control would go way beyond protection against fraud." Adams says: "The best system of internal control in my opinion is to maintain two complete but separate sets of accounting records. If all our transactions are recorded twice by different employees, the two independent sets of records and financial statements can be compared and any discrepancies investigated."

Evaluate the views expressed by each of the three executives.

PROBLEM C-3
Internal Control Measures
LO 4

Listed below are several possible errors or problems which might occur in a merchandising business. Also listed are five internal control measures. You are to list the letter (**a** through **g**) designating each of these errors or problems. Beside each letter, place the number indicating the internal control measure that would prevent this type of problem from occurring. If none of the specified control measures would be effective in preventing the problem, place "0" after the letter.

POSSIBLE ERRORS OR PROBLEMS

a. Paid an invoice in which the supplier had accidentally doubled the price of the merchandise.

b. Paid a supplier for goods that were delivered but were never ordered.

c. Purchased merchandise that turned out not to be popular with customers.

d. Several sales invoices were misplaced and the accounts receivable department is therefore unaware of the unrecorded credit sales.

e. Paid a supplier for goods that were never received.

f. The purchasing department ordered goods from one supplier when a better price could have been obtained by ordering from another supplier.

g. The cashier conceals the embezzlement of cash by reducing the balance of the Cash account.

INTERNAL CONTROL MEASURES

1. Comparison of purchase invoice with the receiving report.

2. Comparison of purchase invoice with the purchase order.

3. Separation of the accounting function from custody of assets.

4. Separation of the responsibilities for approving and recording transactions.

5. Use of serially numbered documents.

0. None of the above control procedures can effectively prevent this error from occurring.

PROBLEM C-4
Internal Control Measures—
Emphasis upon Computer-
Based Systems
 LO 4

The lettered paragraphs below describe seven possible errors or problems which might occur in a retail business. Also listed are five internal control measures. List the letter (**a** through **g**) designating the errors or problems. Beside each letter, place the number indicating the internal control measure that should prevent this type of error or problem from occurring. If none of the specified internal control measures would effectively prevent the error or problem, place a "0" opposite the letter. Assume that a computer-based accounting system is in use.

POSSIBLE ERRORS OR PROBLEMS

a. A salesclerk unknowingly makes a credit sale to a customer whose account has already reached the customer's prearranged credit limit.

b. The cashier of a business conceals a theft of cash by adjusting the balance of the Cash account in the company's computer-based accounting records.

c. Certain merchandise proves to be so unpopular with customers that it cannot be sold except at a price well below its original cost.

d. A salesclerk rings up a sale at an incorrect price.

e. A salesclerk uses a point-of-sale terminal to improperly reduce the balance of a friend's account in the company's accounts receivable records.

f. One of the salesclerks is quite lazy and leaves most of the work of serving customers to the other salesclerks in the department.

g. A shoplifter steals merchandise while the salesclerk is busy with another customer.

INTERNAL CONTROL MEASURES

1. Limiting the types of transactions which can be processed from point-of-sale terminals to cash sales and credit sales.

2. All merchandise has a magnetically coded label which can be read automatically by an optical scanner on a point-of-sale terminal. This code identifies to the computer the merchandise being sold.

3. Credit cards issued by the store have magnetic codes which can be read automatically by a device attached to the electronic cash register. Credit approval and posting to customers accounts are handled by the computer.

4. The computer prepares a report with separate daily sales totals for each sales person.

5. Employees with custody of assets do not have access to accounting records.

0. None of the above control measures effectively prevents this type of error from occurring.

PROBLEM C-5
Types of Fraud
 LO 5

Cases of fraud often are described either as *employee fraud* or *management fraud.*

a. Briefly distinguish between employee fraud and management fraud.

b. Identify three types of actions which constitute employee fraud.

c. Identify three types of actions which constitute management fraud.

d. Which type of fraud is likely to have the greatest impact upon the national economy? Explain the reasons for your answer.

PROBLEM C-6
An Overview of Financial
Audits
 LO 6

Answer each of the following questions concerning an audit of the financial statements of a publicly owned company.

a. What is the basic purpose of this type of audit?

b. Who performs the audit?

c. Why is the concept of independence important in a financial audit?

d. What consideration do these auditors give to the company's system of internal control?

e. To whom are the auditors' findings made available?

f. Do the auditors guarantee the reliability of the audited financial statements? If the audited statements are misleading, are the auditors held financially liable for losses incurred by people relying upon these statements? Explain.

g. Who pays for the audit?

h. Briefly distinguish between a financial audit and a review of financial statements by an auditing firm.

PROBLEM C-7
Characteristics of Financial Audits and Operational Audits

Listed below are nine statements about auditing. Indicate whether each statement applies to *financial audits, operational audits, both,* or *neither.* Explain your reasons for each answer.

a. As part of their investigation, the auditors study and evaluate the system of internal control.

b. The auditors guarantee the reliability of the financial statements to outside decision makers.

c. The auditors' findings are communicated only to management and to the Internal Revenue Service.

d. One major purpose of the audit is to determine compliance with generally accepted accounting principles.

e. The audit usually focuses upon a department or subunit within the organization.

f. In a large organization, these audits may be conducted continuously as part of the professional responsibilities of certain company employees.

g. If the auditors are negligent, they may be held financially liable for losses incurred by decision makers outside the organization.

h. The auditors are independent of the company and its management.

i. The basic purpose of the audit is the detection of fraud.

CASES

CASE C-1
Internal Control in a Typical Restaurant

Alice's Restaurant has a system of internal control which is similar to most restaurants. A waiter or waitress (food server) writes each customer's order on a serially numbered sales ticket. The servers give these sales tickets to the kitchen staff, which prepares the meals. While the customer is eating, the server fills in the prices on the sales ticket and leaves it at the customer's table.

When the customers are ready to leave, they present the completed sales ticket, along with the payment due, to the cashier. The cashier verifies the prices listed on the sales ticket, rings up the sale on a cash register, and gives the customer an appropriate amount of change.

A manager is always on hand observing operations throughout the restaurant. At the end of each shift, the manager determines that all of the sales tickets issued by the food servers have been collected by the cashier and computes the total dollar amount of these tickets. Next, the manager counts the cash receipts and compares this amount with the total shown on the register tape and the total developed from the serially numbered sales tickets.

INSTRUCTIONS

Identify the control procedures (if any) which prevent:

a. Food servers from providing free meals to family and friends simply by not preparing a sales ticket.

b. Food servers from undercharging favored customers.

c. Food servers from collecting the amount due from the customer and keeping the cash for themselves.

d. The cashier from pocketing some of the customers' payments and concealing this theft by ringing up lower amounts on the cash register.

THE "TIME-VALUE" OF MONEY: FUTURE AMOUNTS AND PRESENT VALUES

INTENDED FOR USE AFTER CHAPTER 10

THE CONCEPT

One of the most basic—and important—concepts of investing is the *time-value of money*. This concept is based upon the idea that an amount of money available today can be safely invested to accumulate to a larger amount in the future. As a result, an amount of money available today is considered to be equivalent in value to a *larger sum* available at a future date.

LO 1 *Explain what is meant by the* time-value *of money.*

In our discussions, we will refer to an amount of money available today as a *present value*. In contrast, an amount receivable or payable at a future date will be described as a *future amount*.

To illustrate, assume that you place $500 in a savings account that earns interest at the rate of 8% per year. The balance of your account at the end of each of the next four years is illustrated on the following page.

These balances represent different time values of your $500 investment. When you first open the account, your investment has a *present value* of only $500. As time passes, the value of your investment increases to the *future amounts* illustrated in the graph. (Throughout this Appendix, present values will be illustrated in red, and future amounts will be shown in blue.)

RELATIONSHIPS BETWEEN PRESENT VALUES AND FUTURE AMOUNTS

LO 2 *Describe the relationships between* present values *and* future amounts.

The difference between a present value and any future amount is the *interest* that is included in the future amount. We have seen that interest accrues over time. Therefore, the difference between the present value and a future amount depends upon *two factors:* (1) the *rate of interest* at which the present value increases, and (2) the *length of time* over which interest accumulates. (Notice in our graph, the further away the future date, the larger the future amount.)

Future values are "bigger," but are they "worth more"? This is the real issue.

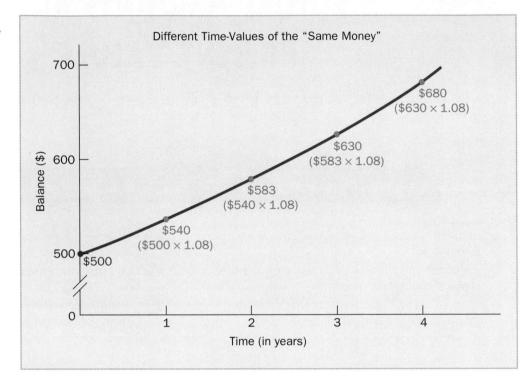

PRESENT VALUES CHANGE OVER TIME   The present value of an investment gradually increases toward the future amount. In fact, when a future date *arrives,* what once was a future amount becomes the present value of the investment. For example, at the end of the first year, $540 will no longer be a future amount—it will be the present value of your savings account.

THE BASIC CONCEPT (STATED SEVERAL DIFFERENT WAYS)   Notice that the present value of our savings account is *always less than its future amounts.* This is the basic idea underlying the time-value of money. But this idea often is expressed in different ways, including:

● A present value is always *less than* a future amount.

● A future amount is always *greater than* a present value.

● A dollar available today is always worth *more* than a dollar which does not become available until a future date.

● A dollar available at a future date is always worth *less* than a dollar which is available today.

Read these statements carefully. All four reflect the idea that a present value is the "equivalent" of a larger number of dollars at a future date. This is what is meant by the time-value of money.

COMPOUND INTEREST

The relationships between present values and future amounts assume that the interest earned on the investment is *reinvested,* rather than withdrawn. This concept often is called *compounding the interest.* Compounding has an interesting effect. Reinvesting the interest causes the "amount invested" to increase each period. This, in turn, causes more interest to be earned in each successive period. Over a long period of time, an investment in which interest is compounded continuously will increase to surprisingly large amounts.

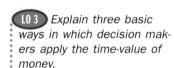

CASE IN POINT

In 1626, Peter Minuit is said to have purchased Manhattan Island from a group of Indians for $24 worth of "beads, cloth, and trinkets." This episode often is portrayed as an incredible bargain—even a "steal." But if the Indians had invested this $24 to earn interest at a compound interest rate of, say, 8%, they would have more than enough money today to buy the island back—along with everything on it.

APPLICATIONS OF THE TIME-VALUE OF MONEY CONCEPT

Investors, accountants, and other decision makers apply the time-value of money in three basic ways. These applications are summarized below, along with a typical example:

LO 3 *Explain three basic ways in which decision makers apply the time-value of money.*

1. The amount to which an investment will accumulate over time.
   Example: If we invest $5,000 each year and earn an annual rate of return of 10%, how much will be accumulated after 10 years?

2. The amount that must be invested every period to accumulate a required future amount.
   Example: We must accumulate a $200 million bond sinking fund over the next 20 years. How much must we deposit into this fund each year, assuming that the fund's assets will be invested to earn an annual rate of return of 8%?

3. The present value of cash flows expected to occur in the future.
   Example: Assuming that we require a 15% return on our investments, how much can we afford to pay for new machinery that is expected to reduce production costs by $20,000 per year for the next 10 years?

We will now introduce a framework for answering such questions.

FUTURE AMOUNTS

A future amount is simply the dollar amount to which a present value *will accumulate* over time. As we have stated, the difference between a present value and a related future amount depends upon (1) the interest rate and (2) the period of time over which the present value accumulates.

Starting with the present value, we may compute future amounts through a series of multiplications, as illustrated in our graph on page D-4. But there are faster and easier ways. For example, many financial calculators are programmed to compute future amounts; you merely enter the present value, the interest rate, and the number of periods. Or, you may use a *table of future amounts,* such as Table FA-1 illustrated on the following page.

THE "TABLES APPROACH"

A table of future amounts shows the future amount to which *$1* will accumulate over a given number of periods, assuming that it has been invested to earn any of the illustrated interest rates. We will refer to the amounts shown in the body of this table as *factors,* rather than as dollar amounts.

LO 4 *Compute future amounts and the investments necessary to accumulate future amounts.*

To find the future amount of a present value *greater* than $1, simply multiply the present value by the factor obtained from the table. The formula for using the table in this manner is:

Approach to computing future amount

Future amount = Present value × Factor (from Table FA-1)

TABLE FA-1
Future Value of $1 After *n* Periods

Number of Periods (n)	Interest Rate								
	1%	1½%	5%	6%	8%	10%	12%	15%	20%
1	1.010	1.015	1.050	1.060	1.080	1.100	1.120	1.150	1.200
2	1.020	1.030	1.103	1.124	1.166	1.210	1.254	1.323	1.440
3	1.030	1.046	1.158	1.191	1.260	1.331	1.405	1.521	1.728
4	1.041	1.061	1.216	1.262	1.360	1.464	1.574	1.749	2.074
5	1.051	1.077	1.276	1.338	1.469	1.611	1.762	2.011	2.488
6	1.062	1.093	1.340	1.419	1.587	1.772	1.974	2.313	2.986
7	1.072	1.110	1.407	1.504	1.714	1.949	2.211	2.660	3.583
8	1.083	1.127	1.477	1.594	1.851	2.144	2.476	3.059	4.300
9	1.094	1.143	1.551	1.689	1.999	2.358	2.773	3.518	5.160
10	1.105	1.161	1.629	1.791	2.159	2.594	3.106	4.046	6.192
20	1.220	1.347	2.653	3.207	4.661	6.728	9.646	16.367	38.338
24	1.270	1.430	3.225	4.049	6.341	9.850	15.179	28.625	79.497
36	1.431	1.709	5.792	8.147	15.968	30.913	59.136	153.152	708.802

Let us demonstrate this approach using the data for our savings account, illustrated on page D-2. The account started with a present value of $500, invested at an annual interest rate of 8%. Thus, the future values of the account in each of the next four years can be computed as follows (rounded to the nearest dollar):

Using the table to compute the amounts in our graph

Year	Future Amount	Computation (Using Table FA-1)
1	$540	$500 × 1.080 = $540
2	$583	$500 × 1.166 = $583
3	$630	$500 × 1.260 = $630
4	$680	$500 × 1.360 = $680

Computing a future amount is relatively easy. The more interesting question is: How much must we *invest today* to accumulate a required future amount?

COMPUTING THE REQUIRED INVESTMENT At the end of 1998, Metro Recycling agrees to create a fully funded pension plan for its employees by December 31, 2003 (in five years). It is estimated that $5 million dollars will be required to fully fund the pension plan at December 31, 2003. How much must Metro invest in this plan *today* (December 31, 1998) to accumulate the promised $5 million by the end of 2003, assuming that payments to the fund will be invested to earn an annual return of 8%?

Let us repeat our original formula for computing future amounts using Table FA-1:

Our original formula . . .

Future amount = Present value × Factor (from Table FA-1)

In this situation, we *know* the future amount—$5 million. We are looking for the *present value* which, when invested at an interest rate of 8%, will accumulate to $5 million in five years. To determine the *present value,* the formula shown above may be restated as follows:

$$\textbf{Present value} = \frac{\textbf{Future amount}}{\textbf{Factor (from Table FA-1)}}$$

. . . restated to find the present value

Referring to Table FA-1, we get a factor of *1.469* at the intersection of five periods and 8% interest. Thus, the amount of the required investment at the end of 1997 is $3,403,676 ($5 million ÷ 1.469). Invested at 8%, this amount will accumulate to the required $5 million at the end of five years as illustrated below:

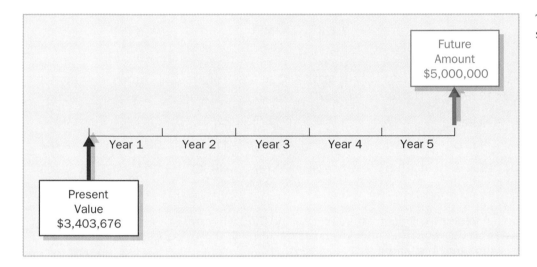

The future amount of a single investment

THE FUTURE AMOUNT OF AN ANNUITY

In many situations, an investor is to make a *series* of investment payments rather than just one. As an example, assume that you plan to invest $500 into your savings account at the end of each of the next five years. If the account pays annual interest of 8%, what will be the balance in your savings account at the end of the fifth year? Tables, such as Table FA-2 on the next page, may be used to answer this question. Table FA-2 presents the future amount of an *ordinary annuity of $1,* which is a series of payments of $1 made at the end of each of a specified number of periods.

To find the future amount of an ordinary annuity of payments greater than $1, we simply multiply the amount of the periodic payment by the factor appearing in the table, as shown below:

$$\textbf{Future amount of an annuity} = \textbf{Periodic payment} \times \textbf{Factor (from Table FA-2)}$$

Approach to computing the future amount of an annuity

In our example, a factor of 5.867 is obtained from the table at the intersection of five periods and 8% interest. If this factor is multiplied by the periodic payment of $500, we find that your savings account will accumulate to a balance of $2,934 ($500 × 5.867) at the end of five years. Therefore, if you invest $500 at the end of each of the next five years in the savings account, you will accumulate $2,934 at the end of the 5-year period.

While computing the future amount of an investment is sometimes necessary, many business and accounting problems require us to determine the *amount of the periodic payments* that must be made to accumulate the required future amount.

COMPUTING THE REQUIRED PERIODIC PAYMENTS Assume that Ultra Tech Company is required to accumulate $10 million in a *bond sinking fund* to retire bonds payable five years from now. The *bond indenture* requires Ultra Tech to make equal payment to the fund at the end of each of the next five years. What is the amount of re-

TABLE FA-2
Future Value of $1 Paid Periodically for *n* Periods

Number of Periods (*n*)	Interest Rate								
	1%	1½%	5%	6%	8%	10%	12%	15%	20%
1	1.000	1.000	1.000	1.000	1.000	1.000	1.000	1.000	1.000
2	2.010	2.015	2.050	2.060	2.080	2.100	2.120	2.150	2.200
3	3.030	3.045	3.152	3.184	3.246	3.310	3.374	3.473	3.640
4	4.060	4.091	4.310	4.375	4.506	4.641	4.779	4.993	5.368
5	5.101	5.152	5.526	5.637	5.867	6.105	6.353	6.742	7.442
6	6.152	6.230	6.802	6.975	7.336	7.716	8.115	8.754	9.930
7	7.214	7.323	8.142	8.394	8.923	9.487	10.089	11.067	12.916
8	8.286	8.433	9.549	9.898	10.637	11.436	12.300	13.727	16.499
9	9.369	9.559	11.027	11.491	12.488	13.580	14.776	16.786	20.799
10	10.462	10.703	12.578	13.181	14.487	15.937	17.549	20.304	25.959
20	22.019	23.124	33.066	36.786	45.762	57.275	72.052	102.444	186.688
24	26.974	28.634	44.502	50.816	66.765	88.497	118.155	184.168	392.484
36	43.079	47.276	95.836	119.121	187.102	299.127	484.463	1014.346	3539.009

quired periodic payment, assuming that the fund will earn 10% annual interest? To answer this question, we simply rearrange the formula shown below for computing the future amount of an annuity:

Our original formula . . .

$$\text{Future amount of an annuity} = \text{Periodic payment} \times \text{Factor (from Table FA-2)}$$

In our example, we know that Ultra Tech is required to accumulate a future amount of $10 million. However, we need to know the amount of the periodic payments which, when invested at 10% annual interest, will accumulate to that future amount. To make this calculation, the formula shown above may be restated as follows:

. . . restated to find the amount of the periodic payments

$$\text{Periodic payment} = \frac{\text{Future amount of an annuity}}{\text{Factor (from Table FA-2)}}$$

The amount of each required payment, therefore, is $1,638,000 ($10 million ÷ 6.105). If payments of $1,638,000 are made at the end of each of the next five years to a bond sinking fund that earns 10% annual interest, the fund will accumulate to $10 million:

Future amount of a series of investments

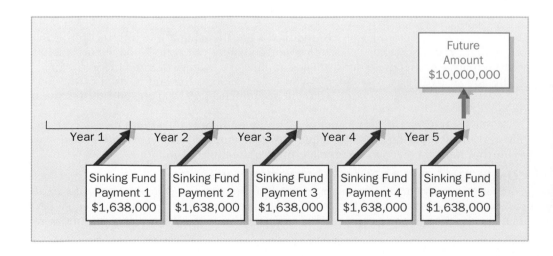

INTEREST PERIODS OF LESS THAN ONE YEAR

In our computations of future amounts, we have assumed that interest is paid (compounded) or payments are made annually. Therefore, in using the tables, we used *annual* periods and an *annual* interest rate. Investment payments or interest payments may be made on a more frequent basis, such as monthly, quarterly, or semiannually. Tables FA-1 and FA-2 may be used with any of these payment periods, *but the rate of interest must represent the interest rate for that period.*

As an example, assume that 24 monthly payments are to be made to an investment fund that pays 12% annual interest rate. To determine the future amount of this investment, we would multiply the amount of the monthly payments by the factor from Table FA-2 for 24 periods, using a *monthly* interest rate of 1%—the 12% annual rate divided by 12 months.

PRESENT VALUES

LO 5 *Compute the present values of future cash flows.*

As indicated previously, the present value is *today's* value of funds to be received in the future. While present value has many applications in business and accounting, it is most easily explained in the context of evaluating investment opportunities. In this context, the present value is the amount that a knowledgeable investor would pay *today* for the right to receive an expected future amount of cash. The present value is always *less* than the future amount, because the investor will expect to earn a return on the investment. The amount by which the future cash receipt exceeds its present value represents the investor's profit.

The amount of the profit on a particular investment depends upon two factors: (1) the rate of return (called the *discount rate*) required by the investor, and (2) the length of time until the future amount will be received. The process of determining the present value of a future cash receipt is called *discounting* the future amount.

To illustrate the computation of present value, assume that an investment is expected to result in a $1,000 cash receipt at the end of one year, and that an investor requires a 10% return on this investment. We know from our discussion of present and future values that the difference between a present value and a future amount is the return (interest) on the investment. In our example, the future amount would be equal to 110% of the original investment, because the investor expects 100% of the investment back plus a 10% return on the investment. Thus, the investor would be willing to pay *$909* ($1,000 ÷ 1.10) for this investment. This computation may be verified as follows (amounts rounded to the nearest dollar):

Amount to be invested (present value)	$ 909
Required return on investment ($909 × 10%)	91
Amount to be received in one year (future value)	$1,000

If the $1,000 is to be received *two years* in the future, the investor would pay only *$826* for the investment today [($1,000 ÷ 1.10) ÷ 1.10]. This computation may be verified as follows (amounts rounded to the nearest dollar):

Amount to be invested (present value)	$ 826
Required return on investment in first year ($826 × 10%)	83
Amount invested after one year	$ 909
Required return on investment in second year ($909 × 10%)	91
Amount to be received in two years (future value)	$1,000

The amount that our investor would pay today, $826, is the present value of $1,000 to be received two years from now, discounted at an annual rate of 10%. The $174 difference between the $826 present value and the $1,000 future amount is the return (interest revenue) to be earned by the investor over the two-year period.

Present value of a single
future cash flow

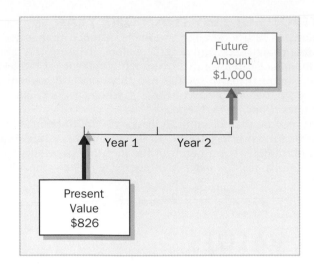

USING PRESENT VALUE TABLES

Although we can compute the present value of future amounts by a series of divisions
as illustrated above, tables are available that simplify the calculations. We can use a table
of present values to find the present value of $1 at a specified discount rate and then
multiply that value by the future amount as illustrated in the formula below:

Formula for finding
present value

Present value = Future amount × Factor (from Table PV-1)

Referring to Table PV-1 below, we find a factor of 0.826 at the intersection of two periods and 10% interest. If we multiply this factor by the expected future cash receipt of
$1,000, we get a present value of *$826* ($1,000 × 0.826), the same amount produced by
the series of divisions in our previous illustration.

TABLE PV-1
Present Values of $1 Due in *n* Periods

Number of Periods (*n*)	Discount Rate								
	1%	1½%	5%	6%	8%	10%	12%	15%	20%
1	.990	.985	.952	.943	.926	.909	.893	.870	.833
2	.980	.971	.907	.890	.857	.826	.797	.756	.694
3	.971	.956	.864	.840	.794	.751	.712	.658	.579
4	.961	.942	.823	.792	.735	.683	.636	.572	.482
5	.951	.928	.784	.747	.681	.621	.567	.497	.402
6	.942	.915	.746	.705	.630	.564	.507	.432	.335
7	.933	.901	.711	.665	.583	.513	.452	.376	.279
8	.923	.888	.677	.627	.540	.467	.404	.327	.233
9	.914	.875	.645	.592	.510	.424	.361	.284	.194
10	.905	.862	.614	.558	.463	.386	.322	.247	.162
20	.820	.742	.377	.312	.215	.149	.104	.061	.026
24	.788	.700	.310	.247	.158	.102	.066	.035	.013
36	.699	.585	.173	.123	.063	.032	.017	.007	.001

WHAT IS THE APPROPRIATE DISCOUNT RATE?

As explained above, the *discount rate* may be viewed as the investor's required rate of return. All investments involve some degree of risk that actual future cash flows may turn out to be less than expected. Investors will require a rate of return which justifies taking this risk. In today's market conditions, investors require annual returns of between 5% and 8% on low-risk investments, such as government bonds and certificates of deposit. For relatively high-risk investments, such as the introduction of a new product line, investors may expect to earn an annual return of perhaps 15% or more. When a higher discount rate is used, the present value of the investment will be lower. In other words, as the risk of an investment increases, its value to investors decreases.

THE PRESENT VALUE OF AN ANNUITY

Many investment opportunities are expected to produce annual cash flows for a number of years, instead of one single future cash flow. Let us assume that Camino Company is evaluating an investment that is expected to produce an *annual net cash flow* of $10,000 in *each of the next three years*.[1] If Camino Company expects a 12% return on this type of investment, it may compute the present value of these cash flows as follows:

Year	Expected Net Cash Flow	×	Present Value of $1 Discounted at 12%	=	Present Value of Net Cash Flows
1	$10,000		.893		$ 8,930
2	$10,000		.797		$ 7,970
3	$10,000		.712		$ 7,120
Total present value of the investment..					$24,020

This analysis indicates that the present value of the expected net cash flows from the investment, discounted at an annual rate of 12%, amounts to $24,020. This is the maximum amount that Camino Company could afford to pay for this investment and still expect to earn the 12% required rate of return, as shown below:

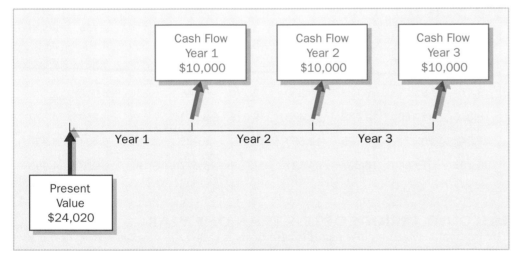

Present value of a series of cash flows

In the preceding schedule, we computed the present value of the investment by separately discounting each period's cash flow, using the appropriate factors from Table PV-1.

---

[1] An "annual net cash flow" normally is the net result of a series of cash receipts and cash payments occurring throughout the year. For convenience, we follow the common practice of assuming that the entire net cash flow for each year occurs at *year-end*. This assumption causes relatively little distortion and greatly simplifies computations.

Separately discounting each period's cash flow is necessary only when the cash flows vary in amount from period to period. Since the annual cash flows in our example are *uniform in amount,* there are easier ways to compute the total present value.

Many financial calculators are programmed to compute the present value of an investment, after the interest rate, the future cash flows, and the number of periods have been entered. Another approach is to refer to a *present value annuity table,* which shows the present value of *$1 to be received each period for a specified number of periods.* An annuity table appears below and is labeled Table PV-2.[2]

To illustrate the use of Table PV-2, let's return to the example of the investment by Camino Company. That investment was expected to return $10,000 per year for the next three years, and the company's required rate of return was 12% per year. Using Table PV-2, we can compute the present value of the investment with the formula illustrated below:

Formula to find the present value of a series of cash flows

$$\text{Present value of an annuity} = \text{Periodic cash flow} \times \text{Factor (from Table PV-2)}$$

As illustrated in Table PV-2, the present value of $1 to be received at the end of the next three years, discounted at an annual rate of 12% is $2,402. If we multiply 2.402 by the expected future annual cash receipt of $10,000, we get a present value of $24,020, which is the same amount produced by the series of calculations made on the prior page.

TABLE PV-2
Present Values of $1 to Be Received Periodically for *n* Periods

Number of Periods (*n*)	Discount Rate								
	1%	1½%	5%	6%	8%	10%	12%	15%	20%
1	0.990	0.985	0.952	0.943	0.926	0.909	0.893	0.870	0.833
2	1.970	1.956	1.859	1.833	1.783	1.736	1.690	1.626	1.528
3	2.941	2.912	2.723	2.673	2.577	2.487	2.402	2.283	2.106
4	3.902	3.854	3.546	3.465	3.312	3.170	3.037	2.855	2.589
5	4.853	4.783	4.329	4.212	3.993	3.791	3.605	3.352	2.991
6	5.795	5.697	5.076	4.917	4.623	4.355	4.111	3.784	3.326
7	6.728	6.598	5.786	5.582	5.206	4.868	4.564	4.160	3.605
8	7.652	7.486	6.463	6.210	5.747	5.335	4.968	4.487	3.837
9	8.566	8.361	7.108	6.802	6.247	5.759	5.328	4.772	4.031
10	9.471	9.222	7.722	7.360	6.710	6.145	5.650	5.019	4.192
20	18.046	17.169	12.462	11.470	9.818	8.514	7.469	6.259	4.870
24	21.243	20.030	13.799	12.550	10.529	8.985	7.784	6.434	4.937
36	30.108	27.661	16.547	14.621	11.717	9.677	8.192	6.623	4.993

DISCOUNT PERIODS OF LESS THAN ONE YEAR

The interval between regular periodic cash flows is called the *discount period.* In our preceding examples, we have assumed cash flows once a year. Often cash flows occur on a more frequent basis, such as monthly, quarterly, or semiannually. The present value tables can be used with discount periods of any length, *but the discount rate must be for that length of time.* For example, if we use Table PV-2 to find the present value of a series of *quarterly* cash payments, the discount rate must be the *quarterly* rate.

There are many applications of the present value concept in accounting. In the next several pages, we will discuss some of the most important of these applications.

---

[2]This table assumes that the periodic cash flows occur at the *end* of each period.

VALUATION OF FINANCIAL INSTRUMENTS

Accountants use the term *financial instruments* to describe cash, equity investments in another business, and any contracts that call for receipts or payments of cash. (Notice that this term applies to all financial assets, as well as most liabilities. In fact, the only common liabilities *not* considered financial instruments are unearned revenue and deferred income taxes.)

LO 6 *Discuss accounting applications of the concept of present value.*

Whenever the present value of a financial instrument *differs significantly* from the sum of the expected future cash flows, the instrument is recorded in the accounting records at its *present value*—not at the expected amount of the future cash receipts or payments.

Let us illustrate with a few common examples. Cash appears in the balance sheet at its face amount. This face value *is* a present value—that is, the value of the cash today.

Marketable securities appear in the balance sheet at their *current market values*. These too are present values—representing the amount of cash into which the security can be converted *today*.

Accounts receivable and accounts payable normally appear in the balance sheet at the amounts expected to be collected or paid in the near future. Technically, these are *future amounts,* not present values. But they usually are received or paid within 30 or 60 days. Considering the short periods of time involved, the differences between these future amounts and their present values simply are *not material*.

INTEREST-BEARING RECEIVABLES AND PAYABLES

When a financial instrument calls for the receipt or payment of interest, the difference between present value and the future amounts *does* become material. Thus, interest-bearing receivables and payables initially are recorded in accounting records at the *present value* of the future cash flows—also called the "principal amount" of the obligation. This present value often is *substantially less* than the sum of the expected future amounts.

Consider, for example, $100 million in 30-year, 9% bonds payable issued at par. At the issuance date, the present value of this bond issue is $100 million—the amount of cash received. But the future payments to bondholders are expected to total *$370* million, computed as follows:

Future interest payments ($100 million × 9% × 30 years)	$270,000,000
Maturity value of the bonds (due in 30 years)	100,000,000
Sum of the future cash payments	$370,000,000

Thus, the $100 million issuance price represents the present value of $370 million in future cash payments to be made over a period of 30 years.

In essence, interest-bearing financial instruments are "automatically" recorded at their present values simply because we do not include future interest charges in the original valuation of the receivable or the liability.

"NON-INTEREST-BEARING" NOTES

On occasion, companies may issue or accept notes which make no mention of interest, or in which the stated interest rates are unreasonably low. If the difference between the present value of such a note and its face amount is *material,* the note initially is recorded at its present value.

To illustrate, assume that on January 1, 1997, Elron Corporation purchases land from U.S. Development Co. As full payment for this land, Elron issues a $300,000 installment note payable, due in three annual installments of $100,000, beginning on December 31, 1997. This note makes *no mention* of interest charges.

Clearly, three annual installments of $100,000 are not the equivalent of $300,000 available today. Elron should use the *present value* of this note—not the face amount— in determining the cost of the land and reporting its liability.

Assume that a realistic interest rate for financing land over a 3-year period currently is 10% per annum. The present value of Elron's installment note, discounted at 10%, is *$248,700* [$100,000, 3-year annuity × 2.487 (from Table PV-2)]. Elron should view this $248,700 as the "principal amount" of this installment note payable. The remaining $51,300 ($300,000 − $248,700) represents "interest charges" included in the installment payments.

Elron should record the purchase of the land and this issuance of this note as follows:[3]

Land...	248,700	
Notes Payable		248,700

Purchased land, issuing a 3-year installment note payable with a present value of $248,700

(U.S. Development should make similar computations in determining the sales price of the land and the valuation of its note receivable.)

Elron also should prepare an *amortization table* to allocate the amount of each installment payment between interest expense and reduction in the principal amount of this obligation. This table, based upon an original "unpaid balance" of $248,700, three annual payments of $100,000, and an annual interest rate of 10% is illustrated below:

AMORTIZATION TABLE (3-Year, $300,000 Installment Note Payable, Discounted at 10% per annum)					
Interest Period	Payment Date	Annual Payment	Interest Expense (10% of the Last Unpaid Balance)	Reduction in Unpaid Balance	Unpaid Balance
Issue date	Jan. 1, 1997				$248,700
1	Dec. 31, 1997	$100,000	$24,870	$75,130	173,570
2	Dec. 31, 1998	100,000	17,357	82,643	90,927
3	Dec. 31, 1999	100,000	9,073*	90,927	−0−

*In the last period, interest expense is equal to the amount of the final payment minus the remaining unpaid balance. This compensates for the use of a present value table with factors carried to only three decimal places.

The entry at December 31, 1997 to record the first installment payment will be:

Interest Expense...	24,870	
Notes Payable...	75,130	
Cash		100,000

Made annual payment on installment note payable to U.S. Development Co.

MARKET PRICES OF BONDS

The market price of bonds may be regarded as the *present value* to bondholders of the future principal and interest payments. To illustrate, assume that a corporation issues $1,000,000 face value of 10-year, 9% bonds when the going market rate of interest is

---

[3]There is an alternative recording technique which makes use of an account entitled Discount on Notes Payable. This alternative approach produces the same results and will be explained in later accounting courses.

10%. Since bond interest is paid semiannually, we must use 20 *semiannual* periods as the life of the bond issue and a 5% *semiannual* market rate of interest in our present value calculations. The expected issuance price of this bond issue may be computed as follows:

Present value of future principal payments:
   $1,000,000 due after 20 semiannual periods, discounted at 5%:
   $1,000,000 × .377 (from **Table PV-1**, page D-8)... $377,000
Present value of future **interest payments**:
   $45,000 per period ($1,000,000 × 9% × ½) for 20 semiannual periods,
   discounted at 5%: $45,000 × **12.462** (from **Table PV-2**, page D-10)................... <u>560,790</u>
Expected issuance price of bond issue .... <u><u>$937,790</u></u>

CAPITAL LEASES

We briefly discuss capital leases in Chapter 12, but do not illustrate the accounting for these instruments. We will use this appendix as an opportunity to explore this topic in greater detail.

A capital lease is regarded as a sale of the leased asset by the lessor to the lessee. At the date of this sale, the lessor recognizes sales revenue equal to the *present value* of the future lease payments receivable, discounted at a realistic rate of interest. The lessee also uses the present value of the future payments to determine the cost of the leased asset and the valuation of the related liability.

To illustrate, assume that on December 1, Pace Tractor uses a *capital lease* to finance the sale of a tractor to Kelly Grading Co. The tractor was carried in Pace Tractor's perpetual inventory records at a cost of $15,000. Terms of the lease call for Kelly Grading Co. to make *24 monthly payments of $1,000 each*, beginning on December 31. These lease payments include an interest charge of *1% per month*. At the end of the 24-month lease, title to the tractor will pass to Kelly Grading Co. at no additional cost.

ACCOUNTING BY THE LESSOR (PACE TRACTOR) Table PV-2 on page D-10 shows that the present value of $1 to be received monthly for 24 months, discounted at 1% per month, is 21.243. Therefore, the present value of the 24 future lease payments is $1,000 × 21.243, or *$21,243*. Pace Tractor should record this capital lease as a sale of the tractor at a price equal to the present value of the lease payments, as follows:

Lease Payment Receivable (net).. 21,243
   Sales 21,243
Financed sale of a tractor to Kelly Grading Co. using a
capital lease requiring 24 monthly payments of $1,000.
Payments include a 1% monthly interest charge.

Cost of Goods Sold 15,000
   Inventory 15,000
To record cost of tractor sold under capital lease.

Notice that the sales price of the tractor is only $21,243, even though the gross amount to be collected from Kelly Grading Co. amounts to $24,000 ($1,000 × 24 payments). The difference between these two amounts, $2,757, will be recognized by Pace Tractor as interest revenue over the life of the lease.

To illustrate the recognition of interest revenue, the entry on December 31 to record collection of the first monthly lease payment (rounded to the nearest dollar) will be:

Cash 1,000
   Interest Revenue... 212
   Lease Payments Receivable (net).. 788
Received first least payment from Kelly Grading Co.:
   Lease payment received... $1,000
   Interest revenue ($21,243 × 1%) .... <u>(212)</u>
   Reduction in lease payments receivable................................. <u>$ 788</u>

After this first monthly payment is collected, the present value of the lease payments receivable is reduced to $20,455 ($21,243 original balance, less $788). Therefore, the interest revenue earned during the *second* month of the lease (rounded to the nearest dollar) will be *$205* ($20,455 × 1%).[4]

ACCOUNTING BY THE LESSEE (KELLY GRADING CO.) Kelly Grading Co. also should use the present value of the lease payments to determine the cost of the tractor and the amount of the related liability, as follows:

Leased Equipment	21,243	
Lease Payment Obligation		21,243

To record acquisition of a tractor through a capital lease from Pace Tractor. Terms call for 24 monthly payments of $1,000, which include a 1% monthly interest charge.

The entry on December 31 to record the first monthly lease payment (rounded to the nearest dollar) will be:

Interest Expense	212	
Lease Payment Obligation	788	
Cash		1,000

To record first monthly lease payment to Pace Tractor:

Amount of payment	$1,000
Interest expense ($21,243 × 1%)	(212)
Reduction in lease payment obligation	$ 788

OBLIGATIONS FOR POSTRETIREMENT BENEFITS

As we explain in Chapter 12, any unfunded obligation for postretirement benefits appears in the balance sheet at the *present value* of the expected future cash outlays to retired employees. The computation of this present value is so complex that it is performed by a professional actuary. But the present value of this obligation normally is far less than the expected future payments, as the cash payments will take place many years in the future.

Each year, the present value of an unfunded obligation for postretirement benefits will increase—as the future payment dates become closer. This steady "growth" in the present value of the unfunded obligation is recognized annually as part of the company's current postretirement benefits expense. (One might argue that the growth in this liability actually represents "interest expense." Nonetheless, the present value of the liability increases as the payment dates draw closer.)

DISCLOSURE OF UP-TO-DATE PRESENT VALUE INFORMATION

Financial instruments originally are recorded in accounting records at (or near) their present values. But present values represent future cash flows discounted at *current* interest rates. Thus, as interest rates change, so do the present values of many financial instruments. (For the remainder of this discussion, we will refer to present value determined under *current* market conditions as *current value*.)

Cash, investments in marketable securities, and postretirement obligations appear in the financial statements at current values. For most short-term instruments, current values remain quite close to the original carrying values. But for long-term financial instruments, such as bonds payable, current values may differ substantially from the amounts originally recorded.

The FASB requires companies to disclose the current values of financial instruments whenever these values *differ significantly* from the recorded amounts. These disclosures are most likely to affect long-term notes receivable and payable (including bonds payable), and long-term lease obligations.

---

[4]Both Pace Tractor and Kelly Grading Co. would prepare *amortization tables* showing the allocation of each lease payment between interest and the principal amount due.

In computing current value, current interest rates serve as the discount rate. Thus, as interest rates *rise,* current values *fall;* as interest rates *fall,* current values *rise.* The amount of change is greatest on long-term financial instruments for which the future cash flows are fixed—that is, not adjustable to reflect changes in interest rates.

The disclosure of current values can shed light upon a company's past investing and financing activities. Assume, for example, that a company's long-term debt has a current value well *below* its carrying value in the company's balance sheet. This means that interest rates have *increased* since the company arranged this debt. Thus, the company apparently arranged its long-term financing in a period of low interest rates—a good move.

DEFERRED INCOME TAXES

The only long-term liability *not* shown at the present value of the expected future payments is the obligation for deferred income taxes. Deferred taxes are treated differently because they do not involve a "contract" for future payments. Future payments of deferred taxes, if any, depend upon the company's taxable income in future periods and also the corporate income tax laws in future years.

Many accountants believe that deferred income taxes *should* be shown at the estimated present value of the future outlays. This is not likely to happen, however, as the computations would be overwhelmingly complex.

In conclusion, the obligation for deferred income taxes is the only long-term liability that is *not* reported at its present value. Hence, one might argue that these obligations are "overstated" in terms of an equivalent number of "today's dollars."

CAPITAL BUDGETING: ANOTHER APPLICATION OF PRESENT VALUE

Capital budgeting is the process of planning and evaluating proposals for capital expenditures, such as the acquisition of plant assets or the introduction of a new product line. Perhaps the most widely used approach in the evaluation of proposed capital expenditures is *discounting* the expected future cash flows to their *present value.*

Assume that Globe Mfg. Co. is considering a proposal to purchase new equipment in order to produce a new product. The equipment costs $400,000, has an estimated 10-year service life, and an estimated salvage value of $50,000. Globe estimates that production and sale of the new product will increase the company's annual net cash flow by $100,000 per year for the next 10 years. If Globe requires a 15% annual rate of return on investments of this nature, the present value of these cash flows may be computed as shown below:

Is this project worth a $400,000 investment?

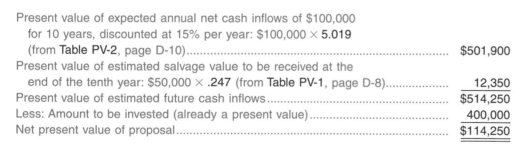

Present value of expected annual net cash inflows of $100,000
for 10 years, discounted at 15% per year: $100,000 × **5.019**
(from **Table PV-2**, page D-10)... $501,900
Present value of estimated salvage value to be received at the
end of the tenth year: $50,000 × **.247** (from **Table PV-1**, page D-8).................. 12,350
Present value of estimated future cash inflows.. $514,250
Less: Amount to be invested (already a present value)....................................... 400,000
Net present value of proposal.. $114,250

This analysis indicates that the present value of the expected net cash flows from this investment, discounted at an annual rate of 15%, amounts to $514,250. This is the maximum amount which Globe could afford to invest in this project and still expect to earn the required 15% annual rate of return. As the cost of this investment is only $400,000, Globe can expect to earn more than its required 15% return.

The *net present value* of a proposal is the *difference* between the total present value of the future net cash flows and the cost of the investment. When the net present value is equal to zero, the investment provides a rate of return exactly equal to the rate used in discounting the cash flows. A *positive* net present value means that the investment provides a rate of return *greater* than the discount rate; a *negative* net present value means that the investment yields a return of *less* than the discount rate.

Since the discount rate usually is the minimum rate of return required by the investor, proposals with a positive net present value are considered acceptable, and those with a negative net present value are viewed as unacceptable.

Capital budgeting techniques are discussed further in courses in management accounting, cost accounting, and finance.

ASSIGNMENT MATERIAL

DISCUSSION QUESTIONS

1. Explain what is meant by the phrase the *time-value of money.*
2. Explain why the present value of a future amount is always *less* than the future amount.
3. Identify the two factors that determine the difference between the present value and the future amount of an investment.
4. Describe three basic investment applications of the concept of the time-value of money.
5. Briefly explain the relationships between present value and (a) the length of time until the future cash flow occurs, and (b) the discount rate used in determining present value.
6. Define *financial instruments.* Explain the valuation concept used in initially recording financial instruments in financial statements.
7. Are normal accounts receivable and accounts payable financial instruments? Are these items shown in the balance sheet at their present values? Explain.
8. Identify three financial instruments shown in financial statements at present values which may *differ significantly* from the sum of the expected future payments or receipts.
9. What is the only long-term liability that is *not* recorded at its present value? What are the implications in terms of today's dollars?
10. Assuming no change in the expected amount of future cash flows, what factors may cause the present value of a financial instrument to change? Explain fully.
11. Define *capital budgeting.* Explain briefly how the present-value concept relates to capital budgeting decisions.

PROBLEMS

PROBLEM D-1
Using Future Amount Tables
LO 1,2,4

Use the tables on pages D-4 and D-6 to determine the future amounts of the following investments:

a. $20,000 is invested for ten years, at 6% interest, compounded annually.
b. $100,000 to be received five years from today, at 10% annual interest.
c. $10,000 is invested in a fund at the end of each of the next ten years, at 8% interest, compounded annually.
d. $50,000 initial investment plus $5,000 invested annually at the end of each of the next three years, at 12% interest, compounded annually.

PROBLEM D-2
Bond Sinking Fund
LO 3,4

Tilman Company is required by a bond indenture to make equal annual payments to a bond sinking fund at the end of each of the next 20 years. The sinking fund will earn 8% interest, and must accumulate to a total of $500,000 at the end of the 20-year period.

INSTRUCTIONS

a. Calculate the amount of the annual payments.

b. Calculate the total amount of interest that will be earned by the fund over the 20-year period.

c. Make the general journal entry to record redemption of the bond issue at the end of the 20-year period, assuming that the sinking fund is recorded on Tilman's accounting records at $500,000 and bonds payable are recorded at the same amount.

d. What would be the effect of an increase in the rate of return on the required annual payment? Explain.

PROBLEM D-3
Using Present Value Tables
LO 1,2,5

Use the tables on pages D-8 and D-10 to determine the present value of the following cash flows.

a. $15,000 to be paid annually for ten years, discounted at an annual rate of 6%. Payments are to occur at the end of each year.

b. $9,200 to be received today, assuming that the money will be invested in a 2-year certificate of deposit earning 8% annually.

c. $300 to be paid monthly for 36 months, with an additional "balloon payment" of $12,000 due at the end of the thirty-sixth month, discounted at a monthly interest rate of 1½%. The first payment is to be one month from today.

d. $25,000 to be received annually for the first three years, followed by $15,000 to be received annually for the next two years (total of five years in which collections are received), discounted at an annual rate of 8%. Assume collections occur at year-end.

PROBLEM D-4
Present Value and Bond Prices
LO 3,5,6

On June 30 of the current year, Rural Gas & Electric Co. issued $50,000,000 face value, 9%, 10-year bonds payable, with interest dates of December 31 and June 30. The bonds were issued at a discount, resulting in an effective *semiannual* interest rate of 5%.

a. Compute the issuance price for the bond issue which results in an effective semiannual interest rate of 5%. (**Hint:** Discount both the interest payments and the maturity value over 20 semiannual periods.)

b. Prepare a journal entry to record the issuance of the bonds at the sales price you computed in part **a.**

c. Explain why the bonds were issued at a discount.

PROBLEM D-5
Valuation of a Note Payable
LO 3,5,6

On December 1, Showcase Interiors purchased a shipment of furniture from Colonial House by paying $10,500 cash and issuing an installment note payable in the face amount of $28,800. The note is to be paid in 24 monthly installments of $1,200 each. Although the note makes no mention of an interest charge, the rate of interest usually charged to Showcase Interiors in such transactions is 1½% per month.

INSTRUCTIONS

a. Compute the present value of the note payable, using a discount rate of 1½% per month.

b. Prepare the journal entries in the accounts of Showcase Interiors on:
  1. December 1, to record the purchase of the furniture (debit Inventory).
  2. December 31, to record the first $1,200 monthly payment on the note and to recognize interest expense for one month by the effective interest method. (Round interest expense to the nearest dollar.)

c. Show how the liability for this note would appear in the balance sheet at December 31. (Assume that the note is classified as a current liability.)

PROBLEM D-6
Capital Leases: A
Comprehensive Problem
LO 3,5,6

Custom Truck Builders frequently uses long-term lease contracts to finance the sale of its trucks. On November 1, 1998, Custom Truck Builders leased to Interstate Van Lines a truck carried in the perpetual inventory records at $33,520. The terms of the lease call for Interstate Van Lines to make 36 monthly payments of $1,400 each, beginning on November 30, 1998. The present value of these payments, after considering a built-in interest charge of 1% per month, is equal to the regular $42,150 sales price of the truck. At the end of the 36-month lease, title to the truck will transfer to Interstate Van Lines.

INSTRUCTIONS

a. Prepare journal entries for 1998 in the accounts of Custom Truck Builders on:
    1. November 1, to record the sale financed by the lease and the related cost of goods sold. (Debit Lease Payments Receivable for the $42,150 present value of the future lease payments.)
    2. November 30, to record receipt of the first $1,400 monthly payment. (Prepare a compound journal entry which allocates the cash receipt between interest revenue and reduction of Lease Payments Receivable. The portion of each monthly payment recognized as interest revenue is equal to 1% of the balance of the account Lease Payments Receivable, at the beginning of that month. Round all interest computations to the nearest dollar.)
    3. December 31, to record receipt of the second monthly payment.

b. Prepare journal entries for 1998 in the accounts of Interstate Van Lines on:
    1. November 1, to record acquisition of the leased truck.
    2. November 30, to record the first monthly lease payment. (Determine the portion of the payment representing interest expense in a manner parallel to that described in part **a.**)
    3. December 31, to record the second monthly lease payment.
    4. December 31, to recognize depreciation on the leased truck through year-end. Compute depreciation expense by the straight-line method, using a 10-year service life and an estimated salvage value of $6,150.

c. Compute the net carrying value of the leased truck in the balance sheet of Interstate Van Lines at December 31, 1998.

d. Compute the amount of Interstate Van Lines' lease payment obligation at December 31, 1998.

PROBLEM D-7
Valuation of a Note
Receivable with an
Unrealistic Interest Rate

On December 31, Richland Farms sold a tract of land, which had cost $930,000, to Skyline Developers in exchange for $150,000 cash and a five-year, 4%, note receivable for $900,000. Interest on the note is payable annually, and the principal amount is due in five years. The accountant for Richland Farms did not notice the unrealistically low interest rate on the note and made the following entry on December 31 to record this sale:

Cash	150,000	
Notes Receivable	900,000	
Land..		930,000
Gain on Sale of Land...		120,000
Sold land to Skyline Developers in exchange for cash and a		
five-year note with interest due annually.		

INSTRUCTIONS

a. Compute the present value of the note receivable from Skyline Developers at the date of sale, assuming that a realistic rate of interest for this transaction is 12%. (**Hint:** Consider both the annual interest payments and the maturity value of the note.)

b. Prepare the journal entry on December 31 to record the sale of the land correctly. Show supporting computations for the gain or loss on the sale.

c. Explain what effects the error made by Richland Farms' accountant will have upon (1) the net income in the year of the sale, and (2) the combined net income of the next five years. Ignore income taxes.

INTERNATIONAL ACCOUNTING AND FOREIGN CURRENCY TRANSACTIONS

INTENDED FOR USE AFTER CHAPTER 12

This appendix has two basic goals. The first is to acquaint you with the concept of *international accounting* — that is, accounting for business activity that spans national borders. The second is to bring to your attention the *economic impact* of changes in the "value" of the U.S. dollar relative to other currencies.

LEARNING OBJECTIVES

1. Translate an amount of foreign currency into the equivalent number of U.S. dollars.

2. Explain why exchange rates fluctuate and what is meant by a "strong" or a "weak" currency.

3. Compute the gain or loss on a receivable or payable stated in terms of a foreign currency when exchange rates fluctuate.

4. Explain how fluctuations in foreign exchange rates affect companies with receivables or payables stated in terms of foreign currencies.

5. Describe several techniques for "hedging" against losses from fluctuations in exchange rates.

From what geographical area does Coca-Cola—the largest soft drink company in the United States—earn most of its revenue? The answer is abroad—that is, from its operations in foreign countries. Coca-Cola is not alone in its pursuit of business on a worldwide basis. Most large corporations, such as Exxon, IBM, and Sony, do business in many countries. Johnson & Johnson has manufacturing subsidiaries in 43 countries outside the United States and sells its products in most countries of the world. Companies that do business in more than one country often are described as *multinational* corporations. The extent to which foreign sales contributed to the revenue of several well-known multinational corporations in a recent year is shown below.

Company	Headquarters	Total Revenues (in millions)	% Earned from Foreign Operations
Nestlé	Switzerland	SF57,486	98.2
Exxon	USA	$109,532	79.7
British Petroleum	Great Britain	£34,950	70.0
Coca-Cola	USA	$13,957	67.1
Sony	Japan	¥3,992,918	63.6
IBM	USA	$62,716	59.0
Johnson & Johnson	USA	$14,138	49.0

Most large and well-known multinational corporations are headquartered in the highly industrialized countries, such as the United States, Japan, Great Britain, and the countries of Western Europe. Virtually every country, however, has many companies that engage in international business activity.

THE ACCOUNTING STANDARDS PROBLEM

The generally accepted accounting principles emphasized in this text are used by all publicly owned companies *based in the United States,* but they are not used worldwide. Every developed country has developed *its own* financial reporting requirements for companies operating within its borders. Thus, decision makers have difficulty in comparing the financial statements of companies based in different countries.

Companies in Germany use accounting principles that tend to understate their reported net earnings. This tendency results from the fact that German companies pay income taxes based on the same accounting principles used in financial reporting. They also do not like revealing to unions and to competitors how much they really earn. It is said that to approximate earnings based on U.S. accounting standards, an investor would have to make some 70 adjustments to a typical German company's income statement.

Variations in national accounting standards result from differences in legal and political systems, economic environments, and levels of currency stability. As an example, countries with high rates of inflation often report assets at *current market values,* rather than at historical costs.

THE INTERNATIONAL ACCOUNTING STANDARDS COMMITTEE The International Accounting Standards Committee (IASC) was formed in 1973 by the major accounting organizations of several countries to develop and promote *uniform international accounting standards.* Currently, nearly 90 countries are represented by the IASC. Since it was formed, the IASC has issued over 30 financial accounting standards, covering such topics as accounting for inventories, leases, and research and development costs.

A major problem for the work of the IASC is the fact that it has *no enforcement power.* The committee must rely upon the regulators or accounting standards boards in the various countries to adopt its standards. As a result, the IASC standards have not yet gained widespread acceptance. The IASC has, however, developed a foundation that may eventually lead to a set of accounting standards recognized throughout the world.

FOREIGN CURRENCIES AND EXCHANGE RATES

One problem in international accounting is that every country uses a different currency. Assume, for example, that a Japanese company sells merchandise to a U.S. corporation. The Japanese company will want to be paid in Japanese currency—yen—but the U.S. company's bank account contains U.S. dollars. Thus, one currency must be converted into another.

Most banks participate in an international currency exchange, which enables them to buy foreign currencies at the prevailing *exchange rate*. Thus, our U.S. corporation can pay its liability to the Japanese company through the international banking system. The U.S. company will pay its bank in dollars. The bank will then use these dollars to purchase the required amount of yen on the international currency exchange and will arrange for delivery of the yen to the Japanese company's bank.[1]

EXCHANGE RATES

A currency exchange rate is the *ratio* at which one currency may be converted into another. Thus, the exchange rate may be viewed as the "price" of buying units of foreign currency, stated in terms of the domestic currency (which for our purpose is U.S. dollars). Exchange rates fluctuate daily, based upon the worldwide supply and demand for particular currencies. The current exchange rate between the dollar and most major currencies is published daily in the financial press. For example, a few of the exchange rates recently listed in *The Wall Street Journal* are shown below:

Country	Currency	Exchange Rate (in dollars)
Britain	Pound (£)	$1.6295
France	French franc (FF)	.1991
Japan	Yen (¥)	.0106
Mexico	Peso ($)	.1586
Germany	Deutsche mark (DM)	.7022

Exchange rates may be used to determine how much of one currency is equivalent to a given amount of another currency. Assume that the U.S. company in our preceding example owes the Japanese company 1 million yen (expressed ¥1,000,000). How many dollars are needed to settle this obligation, assuming that the current exchange rate is $.0106 per yen? To restate an amount of foreign currency in terms of the equivalent amount of U.S. dollars, we multiply the foreign currency amount by the exchange rate, as follows:[2]

LO 1 *Translate an amount of foreign currency into the equivalent number of U.S. dollars.*

Amount Stated in Foreign Currency	×	Exchange Rate (in dollars)	=	Equivalent Number of U.S. Dollars
¥1,000,000	×	$.0106 per yen	=	$10,600

This process of restating an amount of foreign currency in terms of the equivalent number of dollars is called *translating* the foreign currency.

WHY EXCHANGE RATES FLUCTUATE An exchange rate represents the "price" of one currency, stated in terms of another. These prices fluctuate, based upon supply and demand, just as do the prices of gold, silver, soybeans, and other commodities. When the demand for a particular currency exceeds supply, the price (exchange rate) rises. If supply exceeds demand, the exchange rate falls.

LO 2 *Explain why exchange rates fluctuate and what is meant by a "strong" or a "weak" currency.*

What determines the demand and supply for particular currencies? In short, it is the quantities of the currency that traders and investors seek to buy or to sell. Buyers of a particular currency include purchasers of that country's exports, and foreign investors

---

[1]Alternatively, the U.S. company may send the Japanese company a check (or a bank draft) stated in dollars. The Japanese company can then arrange to have the dollars converted into yen through its bank in Japan.
[2]To convert an amount of dollars into the equivalent amount of a foreign currency, we would *divide* the dollar amount by the exchange rate. For example, $10,600 ÷ $.0106 per yen = ¥1,000,000.

seeking to invest in the country's capital markets. Sellers of a currency include companies within the country that are importing goods from abroad, and investors within the country who would prefer to invest their funds abroad. Thus, two major factors in the demand and supply for a currency are (1) the ratio of the country's imports to its exports and (2) the real rate of return available in the country's capital markets.

To illustrate the first of these points, let us consider Japan and Great Britain. Japan exports far more than it imports. As a result, Japan's customers must buy yen in the international currency market in order to pay for their purchases. This creates a strong demand for the yen and has caused its price (exchange rate) to rise relative to most other currencies. Great Britain, on the other hand, imports more than it exports. Thus, British companies must sell British pounds in order to acquire the foreign currencies needed to pay for their overseas purchases. This has increased the supply of pounds in the currency markets, and the price of the pound has declined substantially over the last several decades.

The second factor—the international attractiveness of a country's capital markets—depends upon both political stability and the country's interest rates relative to its internal rate of inflation. When a politically stable country offers high interest rates relative to inflation, foreign investors will seek to invest their funds in that country. First, however, they must convert their funds into that country's currency. This demand tends to increase the exchange rate for that currency. High interest rates relative to the internal rate of inflation were the major reason for the strength of the U.S. dollar during the early 1980s. Later in that decade, however, lower interest rates, along with large trade deficits (imports in excess of exports), significantly reduced the value of the dollar. In the mid 1990s, the dollar fell to record lows against the German deutsche mark and the Japanese yen because of large U.S. trade and budget deficits.

EXCHANGE RATE JARGON In the financial press, currencies are often described as "strong" or "weak," or as rising or falling against one another. For example, an evening newscaster might say, "A strong dollar rose sharply against the weakening British pound, but fell slightly against the Japanese yen and the Swiss franc." What does this mean about exchange rates?

To understand such terminology, we must remember that an exchange rate is simply the price of one currency *stated in terms of another currency.* Throughout this appendix, we refer to the prices of various foreign currencies stated in terms of *U.S. dollars.* In other countries, however, the U.S. dollar is a foreign currency, and its price is stated in terms of the local (domestic) currency.

To illustrate, consider our table from *The Wall Street Journal,* which shows the exchange rate for the Japanese yen to be $.0106. At this exchange rate, $1 is equivalent to ¥94 (¥94 × $.0106 per yen = $1). Thus, while we would say that the exchange rate for the Japanese yen is *$.0106,* the Japanese would say that the exchange rate for the U.S. dollar is *¥94.*

Now let us assume that the exchange rate for the yen (stated in dollars) rises to $.0109. At this exchange rate, $1 is equivalent to only ¥92 (¥92 × $.0109 = $1). In the United States, we would say that the exchange rate for the yen has *risen* from $.0106 to $.0109. In Japan, however, they would say that the exchange rate for the dollar has *fallen* from ¥94 to ¥92. In the financial press, it might be said that "the yen has risen against the dollar," or that "the dollar has fallen against the yen." The two statements mean the same thing—that the yen has become more valuable relative to the dollar.

Now let us return to our original phrase, "A strong dollar rose sharply against the weakening British pound, but fell slightly against the Japanese yen and the Swiss franc." When exchange rates are stated in terms of U.S. dollars, this statement means that the price (exchange rate) of the British pound fell sharply, but the prices of the Japanese yen and the Swiss franc rose slightly. A currency is described as "strong" when its exchange rate is rising relative to most other currencies and as "weak" when its exchange rate is falling.

ACCOUNTING FOR TRANSACTIONS WITH FOREIGN COMPANIES

When a U.S. company buys or sells merchandise in a transaction with a foreign company, the transaction price may be stipulated either in U.S. dollars or in units of the foreign currency. If the price is stated in *dollars,* the U.S. company encounters no special accounting problems. The transaction may be recorded in the same manner as are similar transactions with domestic suppliers or customers.

LO 3 *Compute the gain or loss on a receivable or payable stated in terms of a foreign currency when exchange rates fluctuate.*

If the transaction price is stated in terms of the *foreign currency,* the company encounters two accounting problems. First, as the U.S. company's accounting records are maintained in dollars, the transaction price must be *translated* into dollars before the transaction can be recorded. The second problem arises when (1) the purchase or sale is made *on account* and (2) the exchange rate *changes* between the date of the transaction and the date that the account is paid. This fluctuation in the exchange rate will cause the U.S. company to experience either a *gain or a loss* in the settlement of the transaction.

CREDIT PURCHASES WITH PRICES STATED IN A FOREIGN CURRENCY

Assume that on August 1 a U.S. company buys merchandise from a British company at a price of 10 thousand British pounds (£10,000), with payment due in 60 days. The exchange rate on August 1 is *$1.63* per British pound. The entry on August 1 to record this purchase (assuming use of a perpetual inventory system) is shown below:

Inventory	16,300	
Accounts Payable		16,300

To record the purchase of merchandise from a British company
for £10,000 when the exchange rate is $1.63 per pound
(£10,000 × $1.63 = $16,300).

Let us now assume that by September 30, when the £10,000 account payable must be paid, the exchange rate has fallen to *$1.61* per British pound. If the U.S. company had paid for the merchandise on August 1, the cost would have been $16,300. On September 30, however, only *$16,100* is needed to pay the £10,000 liability (£10,000 × $1.61 = $16,100). Thus, *the decline in the exchange rate has saved the company $200.* This savings is recorded in the accounting records as a *Gain on Fluctuations in Foreign Exchange Rates.* The entry on September 30 to record payment of the liability and recognition of this gain would be:

Accounts Payable	16,300	
Cash		16,100
Gain on Fluctuations in Foreign Exchange Rates		200

To record payment of £10,000 liability to British company and to
recognize gain from decline in exchange rate:

Original liability (£10,000 × $1.63)	$16,300
Amount paid (£10,000 × $1.61)	16,100
Gain from decline in exchange rate	$ 200

Now let us assume that instead of declining, the exchange rate had *increased* from $1.63 on August 1 to *$1.66* on September 30. Under this assumption, the U.S. company would have to pay *$16,600* in order to pay off the £10,000 liability on September 30. Thus, the company would be paying *$300 more* than if the liability had been paid on August 1. This additional $300 cost was caused by the increase in the exchange rate and should be recorded as a loss. The entry on September 30 would be:

Accounts Payable	16,300	
Loss on Fluctuations in Foreign Exchange Rates	300	
Cash		16,600

To record payment of £10,000 liability to British company and to
recognize loss from increase in exchange rate:

Original liability (£10,000 × $1.63)	$16,300
Amount paid (£10,000 × $1.66)	16,600
Loss from decline in exchange rate	$ 300

In summary, having a liability that is fixed in terms of a foreign currency results in a gain for the debtor if the exchange rate falls between the date of the transaction and the date of payment. The gain results because fewer dollars will be needed to repay the debt than had originally been owed. An increase in the exchange rate, on the other hand, causes the debtor to incur a loss. In this case, the debtor will have to spend more dollars than had originally been owed in order to purchase the foreign currency needed to pay the debt.

CREDIT SALES WITH PRICES STATED IN A FOREIGN CURRENCY A company that makes credit *sales* at prices stated in a foreign currency also will experience gains or losses from fluctuations in the exchange rate. To illustrate let us change our preceding example to assume that the U.S. company *sells* merchandise on August 1 to the British company at a price of £10,000. We shall again assume that the exchange rate on August 1 is $1.63 per British pound and that payment is due in 60 days. The entry on August 1 to record this sale is:

Accounts Receivable	16,300	
Sales		16,300
To record sale to British company with sales price set at £10,000		
(£10,000 × $1.63) = $16,300. To be collected in 60 days.		

In 60 days (September 30), the U.S. company will collect from the British company the U.S. dollar equivalent of £10,000. If the exchange rate on September 30 has fallen to $1.61 per pound, the U.S. company will collect only $16,100 (£10,000 × $1.61 = $16,100) in full settlement of its account receivable. Since the receivable had originally been equivalent to $16,300, the decline in the exchange rate has caused a loss of $200 to the U.S. company. The entry to be made on September 30 is:

Cash	16,100	
Loss on Fluctuations in Foreign Exchange Rates	200	
Accounts Receivable		16,300
To record collection of £10,000 receivable from British company		
and to recognize loss from fall in exchange rate since date of		
sale:		
Original sales price (£10,000 × $1.63)	$16,300	
Amount received (£10,000 × $1.61)	16,100	
Loss from decline in exchange rate	$ 200	

Now consider the alternative case, in which the exchange rate rises from $1.63 at August 1 to $1.66 at September 30. In this case, the British company's payment of £10,000 will convert into $16,600, creating a gain for the U.S. company. The entry on September 30 would then be:

Cash	16,600	
Accounts Receivable		16,300
Gain on Fluctuations in Foreign Exchange Rates		300
To record collection of £10,000 receivable from British company		
and to recognize gain from increase in exchange rate:		
Original sales price (£10,000 × $1.63)	$16,300	
Amount received (£10,000 × $1.66)	16,600	
Gain from decline in exchange rate	$ 300	

ADJUSTMENT OF FOREIGN RECEIVABLES AND PAYABLES AT THE BALANCE SHEET DATE We have seen that fluctuations in exchange rates may cause gains or losses for companies with accounts payable or receivable in foreign currencies. The fluctuations in the exchange rates occur on a daily basis. For convenience, however, the company usually waits until the account is paid or collected before recording the related gain or loss. An exception to this convenient practice occurs at the end of the accounting period. An *adjusting entry* is made to recognize any gains or losses that have accumulated on any foreign payables or receivables through the balance sheet date.

To illustrate, assume that on November 10 a U.S. company buys equipment from a Japanese company at a price of 10 million yen (¥10,000,000), payable on January 10 of the following year. If the exchange rate is $.0100 per yen on November 10, the entry to record the purchase would be:

Equipment	100,000	
Accounts Payable		100,000
To record purchase of equipment from Japanese company at a price of ¥10,000,000, payable January 10 (¥10,000,000 × $.0100 = $100,000).		

Now assume that on December 31, the exchange rate has fallen to $.0097 per yen. At this exchange rate, the U.S. company's account payable is equivalent to only $97,000 (¥10,000,000 × $.0097). Gains and losses from changes in exchange rates are recognized in the period *in which the change occurs*. Therefore, the American company should make an adjusting entry to restate its liability at the current dollar-equivalent and to recognize any related gain or loss. This entry, which would be dated December 31, is as follows:

Accounts Payable	3,000	
Gain on Fluctuations in Foreign Exchange Rates		3,000
To adjust balance of ¥10,000,000 account payable to amount indicated by year-end exchange rate:		
Original account balance	$100,000	
Adjusted balance (¥10,000,000 × $.0097)	97,000	
Required adjustment	$ 3,000	

Similar adjustments should be made for any other accounts payable or receivable at year-end that are fixed in terms of a foreign currency.

If the exchange rate changes again between the date of this adjusting entry and the date that the U.S. company pays the liability, an additional gain or loss must be recognized. Assume, for example, that on January 10 the exchange rate has risen to $.0099 per yen. The U.S. company must now spend $99,000 to buy the ¥10,000,000 needed to pay its liability to the Japanese company. Thus, the rise in the exchange rate has caused the U.S. company a $2,000 loss since year-end. The entry to record payment of the account on January 10 would be:

Accounts Payable	97,000	
Loss on Fluctuations in Foreign Exchange Rates	2,000	
Cash		99,000
To record payment of ¥10,000,000 payable to Japanese company and to recognize loss from rise in exchange rate since year-end:		
Account payable, December 31	$97,000	
Amount paid, January 10	99,000	
Loss from increase in exchange rate	$ 2,000	

Notice the *overall effect* of entering into this credit transaction stated in yen was a $1,000 gain due to fluctuations in the exchange rate for the yen between November 10 and the date of payment (January 10). The U.S. company recognized a $3,000 gain on fluctuations in the exchange rate from November 10 through the balance sheet date (December 31). This was partially offset in the next fiscal year by a $2,000 loss on fluctuations in the exchange rate between December 31 and January 10. The overall effect can be computed directly by multiplying the amount of the foreign currency times the *change* in exchange rates between the transaction date and the payment date (¥10,000,000 × [$.0100 − $.0099] = $1,000 gain).

Gains and losses from fluctuations in foreign exchange rates should be shown in the income statement following the determination of income from operations. This treatment is similar to that accorded to gains and losses from the sale of plant assets or investments.

CURRENCY FLUCTUATIONS—WHO WINS AND WHO LOSES?

Gains and losses from fluctuations in exchange rates are sustained by companies (or individuals) that have either payables or receivables that are *fixed in terms of a foreign currency.* United States companies that import foreign products usually have large foreign liabilities. Companies that export U.S. products to other countries are likely to have large receivables stated in foreign currencies.

LO 4 *Explain how fluctuations in foreign exchange rates affect companies with receivables or payables stated in terms of foreign currencies.*

As foreign exchange rates (stated in dollars) *fall,* United States-based importers will gain and exporters will lose. When a foreign exchange rate falls, the foreign currency becomes *less expensive.* Therefore, importers will have to spend fewer dollars to pay their foreign liabilities. Exporters, on the other hand, will have to watch their foreign receivables become worth fewer and fewer dollars.

When foreign exchange rates *rise,* this situation reverses. Importers will lose, because more dollars are required to pay the foreign debts. Exporters will gain, because their foreign receivables become equivalent to an increasing number of dollars.

STRATEGIES TO AVOID LOSSES FROM RATE FLUCTUATIONS There are two basic approaches to avoiding losses from fluctuations in foreign exchange rates. One approach is to insist that receivables and payables be settled at specified amounts of domestic currency. The other approach is called *hedging* and can be accomplished in a number of ways.

To illustrate the first approach, assume that a U.S. company makes large credit sales to companies in Mexico, but anticipates that the exchange rate for the Mexican peso will gradually decline. The U.S. company can avoid losses by setting its *sales prices in dollars.* Then, if the exchange rate does decline, the Mexican companies will have to spend more pesos to pay for their purchases, but the U.S. company will not receive fewer dollars. On the other hand, the U.S. company will benefit from making credit *purchases* from Mexican companies at *prices stated in pesos,* because a decline in the exchange rate will reduce the number of dollars needed to pay for these purchases.

The interests of the Mexican companies, however, are exactly the opposite of those of the U.S. company. If the Mexican companies anticipate an increase in the exchange rate for the U.S. dollar, they will want to buy at prices stated in pesos and sell at prices stated in dollars. Ultimately, the manner in which the transactions will be priced simply depends upon which company is in the better bargaining position.

HEDGING Hedging refers to the strategy of "sitting on both sides of the fence"—that is, of taking offsetting positions so that your gains and losses tend to offset one another. To illustrate the concept, assume that after a few beers you make a large bet on a football game. Later you have second thoughts about the bet, and you want to eliminate your risk of incurring a loss. You could "hedge" your original bet by making a similar bet on the other team. In this way, you will lose one bet, but you will win the other—your loss will be offset by a corresponding gain.

LO 5 *Describe several techniques for "hedging" against losses from fluctuations in exchange rates.*

A company that has similar amounts of accounts receivable and accounts payable in the same foreign currency automatically has a hedged position. A decrease in the foreign exchange rate will cause losses on the foreign receivables and gains on the foreign payables. If the exchange rate rises, the gains on the foreign receivables will be offset by losses on the foreign payables.

Most companies, of course, do *not* have similar amounts of receivables and payables in the same foreign currency. However, they may create this situation by buying or selling foreign currency *future contracts.* These contracts, commonly called *futures,* are the right to receive a specified quantity of foreign currency at a future date. In short, they are accounts receivable in foreign currency. Thus, a company that has only foreign accounts payable may hedge its position by purchasing a similar dollar amount of foreign currency future contracts. Then, if the exchange rate rises, any losses on the foreign payables will be offset by a gain in the value of the future contracts.

A company with only foreign receivables may hedge its position by *selling* future contracts, thus receiving dollars today and *creating a liability* payable in foreign currency.

EXCHANGE RATES AND COMPETITIVE PRICES   Up to this point, we have discussed only the gains and losses incurred by companies that have receivables or payables stated in terms of a foreign currency. However, fluctuations in exchange rates change the *relative prices* of goods produced in different countries. Exchange rate fluctuations may make the prices of a country's products more or less competitive both at home and to customers throughout the world. Even a small store with no foreign accounts receivable or payable may find its business operations greatly affected by fluctuations in foreign exchange rates.

Consider, for example, a small store in Kansas that sells tires manufactured in the United States. If foreign exchange rates fall, which happens when the dollar is strong, the price of foreign-made tires will decline. Thus, the store selling tires made in the United States may have to compete with stores selling imported tires at lower prices. Also, a strong dollar makes U.S. goods *more expensive to customers in foreign countries*. Thus, a U.S. tire manufacturer will find it more difficult to sell its products abroad.

The situation reverses when the dollar is weak—that is, when foreign exchange rates are relatively high. A weak dollar makes foreign imports more expensive to U.S. consumers. Also, a weak dollar makes U.S. products less expensive to customers in foreign countries.

In summary, we may say that a strong U.S. dollar *helps companies that sell foreign-made goods in the U.S. market.* A weak dollar, on the other hand, *gives a competitive advantage to companies that sell U.S. products both at home and abroad.*

CONSOLIDATED FINANCIAL STATEMENTS THAT INCLUDE FOREIGN SUBSIDIARIES

In Chapter 6, we discussed the concept of *consolidated* financial statements. These statements view the operations of the parent company and its subsidiaries as if the affiliated companies were a single business entity. Several special accounting problems arise in preparing consolidated financial statements when subsidiaries operate in foreign countries. First, the accounting records of the foreign subsidiaries must be translated into U.S. dollars. Second, the accounting principles in use in the foreign countries may differ significantly from U.S. generally accepted accounting principles.

These problems pose interesting challenges to professional accountants and will be addressed in later accounting courses. Readers of the financial statements of United States-based corporations, however, need not be concerned with these technical issues. The consolidated financial statements of these companies are expressed in U.S. dollars and conform to U.S. generally accepted accounting principles.

ASSIGNMENT MATERIAL

DISCUSSION QUESTIONS

1. In general terms, identify several factors which prompt different countries to develop different accounting principles.
2. What is the International Accounting Standards Committee? Why has the committee been unable to obtain wide-scale application of its standards?
3. Translate the following amounts of foreign currency into an equivalent number of U.S. dollars using the exchange rates in the table on page E-3.
   a. £800,000
   b. ¥350,000
   c. DM50,000
4. Assume that a U.S. company makes a purchase from a German company and agrees to pay a price of 2 million deutsche marks.

  a. How will the U.S. company determine the cost of this purchase for the purpose of recording it in the accounting records?

  b. Briefly explain how a U.S. company can arrange the payment of deutsche marks to a German company.

5. A recent newspaper shows the exchange rate for the British pound at $1.63 and for the yen at $.0106. Does this indicate that the pound is a stronger currency than the yen? Explain.

6. Identify two factors that tend to make the exchange rate for a country's currency rise.

7. Explain how an increase in a foreign exchange rate will affect a U.S. company that makes:

  a. Credit sales to a foreign company at prices stated in the foreign currency.

  b. Credit purchases from a foreign company at prices stated in the foreign currency.

  c. Credit sales to a foreign company at prices stated in U.S. dollars.

8. You are the purchasing agent for a U.S. business that purchases merchandise on account from companies in Mexico. The exchange rate for the Mexican peso has been falling against the dollar and the trend is expected to continue for at least several months. Would you prefer that the prices for purchases from the Mexican companies be specified in U.S. dollars or in Mexican pesos? Explain.

9. CompuTech is a United States-based multinational corporation. Foreign sales are made at prices set in U.S. dollars, but foreign purchases are often made at prices stated in foreign currencies. If the exchange rate for the U.S. dollar has risen against most foreign currencies throughout the year, would CompuTech have recognized primarily gains or losses as a result of exchange rate fluctuations? Explain.

10. Explain two ways in which a company that makes purchases on account from foreign companies can protect itself against the losses that would arise from a sudden increase in the foreign exchange rate.

PROBLEMS

PROBLEM E-1
Currency Fluctuations: Who Wins and Who Loses?
 LO 2,4

Indicate whether each of the companies or individuals in the following independent cases would benefit more from a strong U.S. dollar (relatively low foreign exchange rates) or a weak U.S. dollar (relatively high foreign exchange rates). Provide a brief explanation of your reasoning.

  a. **Boeing** (a U.S. aircraft manufacturer that sells many planes to foreign customers).

  b. A **Nikon** camera store in Beverly Hills, California. (Nikon cameras are made in Japan.)

  c. **Toyota** (the Japanese auto manufacturer).

  d. The Mexico City dealer for **Caterpillar** tractors (made in the United States).

  e. A U.S. tourist visiting England.

  f. A small store in Toledo, Ohio, that sells video recorders made in the United States. The store has no foreign accounts receivable or payable.

PROBLEM E-2
Foreign Currency Transactions
LO 3,4

The following table summarizes the facts of five independent cases (labeled **a** through **e**) of United States companies engaging in credit transactions with foreign corporations while the foreign exchange rate is fluctuating:

	Type of Credit Transaction	Currency Used in Contract	Exchange Rate Direction	Effect on Income
Case	**1**	**2**	**3**	**4**
a	Sales	Foreign currency	Falling	_____
b	Purchases	U.S. dollars	Rising	_____
c	_____	Foreign currency	Rising	Loss
d	Sales	_____	Falling	No effect
e	Purchases	Foreign currency	_____	Gain

INSTRUCTIONS

You are to fill in each blank space after evaluating the information about the case provided in the other three columns. The content of each column and the word or words that you should enter in the blank spaces are described below:

Column 1 indicates the type of credit transaction in which the U.S. company engaged with the foreign corporations. The answer entered in this column should be either "Sales" or "Purchases."

Column 2 indicates the currency in which the invoice price is stated. The answer may be either "U.S. dollars" or "Foreign currency."

Column 3 indicates the direction in which the foreign currency exchange rate has moved between the date of the credit transaction and the date of settlement. The answer entered in this column may be either "Rising" or "Falling."

Column 4 indicates the effect of the exchange rate fluctuation upon the income of the American company. The answers entered in this column are to be selected from the following: "Gain," "Loss," or "No effect."

PROBLEM E-3
Gains and Losses from
Exchange Rate Fluctuations

LO 1,3,4,5

Europa-West is a U.S. corporation that purchases automobiles from European manufacturers for distribution in the United States. A recent purchase involved the following events:

Nov. 12   Purchased automobiles from West Berlin Motors for DM2,000,000, payable in 60 days. Current exchange rate, $.7025 per deutsche mark. (Europa-West uses the perpetual inventory system.)

Dec. 31   Made year-end adjusting entry relating to the DM2,000,000 account payable to West Berlin Motors. Current exchange rate, $.7147 per deutsche mark.

Jan. 11   Issued a check to World Bank for $1,421,400 in full payment of the account payable to West Berlin Motors.

INSTRUCTIONS

a.   Prepare in general journal form the entries necessary to record the preceding events.

b.   Compute the exchange rate (price) of the deutsche mark in U.S. dollars on January 11.

c.   Explain a hedging technique that Europa-West might have used to protect itself from the possibility of losses resulting from a significant increase in the exchange rate for the deutsche mark.

PROBLEM E-4
Gains and Losses from Rate
Fluctuations: An Alternative
Problem
LO 1,3,4

IronMan, Inc., is a U.S. company that manufactures exercise machines and also distributes several lines of imported bicycles. Selected transactions of the company are listed below:

Oct.   4   Purchased manufacturing equipment from Rhine Mfg. Co., a German company. The purchase price was DM400,000, due in 60 days. Current exchange rate, $.7020 per deutsche mark. (Debit the Equipment account.)

Oct. 18   Purchased 2,500 racing bicycles from Ninja Cycles, a Japanese company, at a price of ¥60,000,000. Payment is due in 90 days; the current exchange rate is $.0110 per yen. (IronMan uses the perpetual inventory system.)

Nov. 15   Purchased 1,000 touring bicycles from Royal Lion Ltd., a British corporation. The purchase price was £192,500, payable in 30 days. Current exchange rate, $1.65 per British pound.

Dec.   3   Issued check to First Bank for the U.S. dollar-equivalent of DM400,000 in payment of the account payable to Rhine Mfg. Co. Current exchange rate, $.7110 per deutsche mark.

Dec. 15   Issued check to First Bank for dollar-equivalent of £192,500 in payment of the account payable to Royal Lion Ltd. Current exchange rate, $1.60 per British pound.

INSTRUCTIONS

a. Prepare entries in general journal form to record the preceding transactions.

b. Prepare the December 31 adjusting entry relating to the account payable to Ninja Cycles. The year-end exchange rate is $.0113 per Japanese yen.

PROBLEM E-5
A Comprehensive Problem on Exchange Rate Fluctuations

 LO 1,3,4,5

Wolfe Computer is a U.S. company that manufactures portable personal computers. Many of the components for the computer are purchased abroad, and the finished product is sold in foreign countries as well as in the United States. Among the recent transactions of Wolfe are the following:

Oct. 28 Purchased from Mitsutonka, a Japanese company, 20,000 disk drives. The purchase price was ¥180,000,000, payable in 30 days. Current exchange rate, $.0105 per yen. (Wolfe uses the perpetual inventory method; debit the Inventory of Raw Materials account.)

Nov. 9 Sold 700 personal computers to the Bank of England for £604,500, due in 30 days. The cost of the computers, to be debited to the Cost of Goods Sold account, was $518,000. Current exchange rate, $1.65 per British pound. (Use one compound journal entry to record the sale and the cost of goods sold. In recording the cost of goods sold, credit Inventory of Finished Goods.)

Nov. 27 Issued a check to Inland Bank for $1,836,000 in *full payment* of account payable to Mitsutonka.

Dec. 2 Purchased 10,000 gray-scale monitors from German Optical for DM1,200,000, payable in 60 days. Current exchange rate, $.7030 per deutsche mark. (Debit Inventory of Raw Materials.)

Dec. 9 Collected dollar-equivalent of £604,500 from the Bank of England. Current exchange rate, $1.63 per British pound.

Dec. 11 Sold 10,000 personal computers to Computique, a French retail chain, for FF75,000,000, due in 30 days. Current exchange rate, $.1900 per French franc. The cost of the computers, to be debited to Cost of Goods Sold and credited to Inventory of Finished Goods, is $7,400,000.

INSTRUCTIONS

a. Prepare in general journal form the entries necessary to record the preceding transactions.

b. Prepare the adjusting entries needed at December 31 for the DM1,200,000 account payable to German Optical and the FF75,000,000 account receivable from Computique. Year-end exchange rates, $.7000 per deutsche mark and $.1894 per French franc. (Use a separate journal entry to adjust each account balance.)

c. Compute (to the nearest dollar) the unit sales price of computers in U.S. dollars in either the November 9 or December 11 sales transactions. (The per-unit sales price is the same in each transaction.)

d. Compute the exchange rate for yen, stated in U.S. dollars, on November 27.

e. Explain how Wolfe Computer could have hedged its position to reduce the risk of loss from exchange rate fluctuations on (1) its foreign payables and (2) its foreign receivables.

INCOME TAXES AND BUSINESS DECISIONS

INTENDED FOR USE AFTER CHAPTER 13

For many college students, this appendix may be their only academic exposure to the truly remarkable system known as federal income taxes. The early part of this appendix presents a brief history and rationale of the federal income tax structure. In the introduction we stress the pervasive influence of income taxes upon economic activity. The next section portrays the basic process of determining taxable income and tax liability for individual taxpayers. The income tax computations for a small corporation are also explained and illustrated. The final section of the discussion gives students an understanding of the important role that *tax planning* can play in the affairs of individuals and also in the decision making of a business entity.

LEARNING OBJECTIVES

1. Discuss the advantages of the cash basis of accounting for preparation of individual income tax returns.

2. State the formula for determining the taxable income of an individual.

3. Explain the recent changes in taxation of capital gains and losses.

4. Contrast the determination of taxable income for a corporation with that for an individual.

5. Describe the circumstances that create a liability for deferred income taxes.

6. Explain how tax planning is used in choosing the form of business organization and the capital structure.

NOTE TO READERS: Congress makes minor changes in tax rates and regulations almost every year. On some occasions, it makes major changes. Therefore, the tax rates and regulations described in this chapter are intended only to illustrate basic concepts and to *approximate* current tax law. For the actual tax rates and regulations of a given year, we refer readers to the annual publications of the Internal Revenue Service.

WHY STUDY INCOME TAXES?

An understanding of basic income tax concepts may be among the most practical types of knowledge you can possess. If you have a good job, you probably will pay more in income taxes than for food and housing *combined*. "Silly mistakes" in planning your financial affairs can cost you tens of thousands of dollars in additional taxes. If you cannot pay your income taxes, the Internal Revenue Service (IRS) can seize your bank account, your car, and even your home. Deliberately providing false information on your income tax return is a felony, punishable by fines, imprisonment, or both.

Knowing something about income tax rules and regulations (called the *tax code*) can both save you money and help you avoid trouble. If your financial affairs ever become complex, or if you are a business manager, you will *need* some understanding of taxes. You probably also will need professional tax advice. But a basic understanding of tax concepts will help you *communicate* effectively with these tax advisors.

In short, is learning the basic structure of the tax code worth the effort? You bet.

THE FEDERAL INCOME TAX

In the United States, income taxes are levied by the federal government, most states, and some cities. Rates, rules, and regulations vary within these jurisdictions. In this text, we will focus upon the *federal* income tax. However, the concepts we address should help you to understand the tax codes of other jurisdictions.

CLASSES OF TAXPAYERS   Income taxes are levied upon four classes of taxpayers: individuals, corporations, estates, and trusts. In this text we discuss only the taxes levied upon individuals and corporations.[1]

But what of the other types of business organizations? A business organized as a sole proprietorship or partnership is *not taxed* as a separate entity. Rather, its income is taxed directly to the proprietor or partners. As we state in Chapter 11, the income of these businesses is taxable to the *owners* in the year it is earned, regardless of whether any of the income has been withdrawn from the business.[2]

A sole proprietor reports his or her income from ownership of a business in an individual tax return (Form 1040); the members of a partnership include in their individual income tax returns their *respective shares* of the partnership net income. Of course, an individual's income tax return must include not only any business income from a proprietorship or partnership but also any interest, dividends, salary, or other forms of income received.

A corporation is a separate taxable entity; it must file a corporate income tax return (Form 1120) and pay tax on its annual taxable income. In addition, individual stockholders must report dividends received from corporations as part of their personal taxable income. The taxing of corporate dividends has led to the charge that there is *double taxation* of corporate income—once to the corporation and again when it is distributed to stockholders. This double impact of tax is particularly apparent when a corporation is owned by one person or one family.

Income tax returns are based on accounting information. In many respects this information is consistent with the accounting concepts we have discussed in earlier chapters. However, the measurement of *taxable income* includes some unique principles and computations which differ from those used for published financial statements. An understanding of the unique aspects of taxable income can help an individual or business minimize the amount of income taxes owed.

TAX PLANNING VERSUS TAX EVASION

TAX PLANNING   Taxpayers who manage their affairs in ways that *legally* minimize their income tax obligations are engaging in a practice called *tax planning*. The goals of tax planning usually are either to minimize the total amount of taxes owed or to postpone into future years the dates at which the taxes become due. One major type of tax planning involves *structuring transactions* in a manner which provides tax advantages. For example, the tax deductions resulting from the use of an automobile in a business differ substantially depending upon whether the automobile is leased or owned.

A second type of tax planning involves selecting for use in the income tax return those accounting methods that produce the most advantageous measurement of taxable income. For example, the taxpayer may elect to use LIFO rather than FIFO, or an accel-

---

[1]An estate is the net assets of a deceased individual, which have not yet been distributed to that person's heirs. A trust is an entity temporarily holding assets for the future benefit of one or more individuals. Estates and trusts are taxed in much the same manner as individuals. Special features of estate and trust taxation are addressed in later accounting courses.
[2]A partnership must file an *information return* with the federal government, showing how the total partnership net income was allocated among the individual partners. The partners then report their shares of this net income on their individual income tax returns.

erated depreciation method instead of straight-line. Some of these choices may significantly affect the amount and timing of the taxpayer's income tax obligations.

If tax planning is to be efficient, it should be undertaken *before* the taxpayer engages in the related transactions. Once a transaction is complete, it usually is *too late* to change its tax consequences. Every taxpayer, whether an individual or a corporation, can benefit from thoughtful tax planning. Tax planning is one of the major services which CPA firms offer their clients.

TAX EVASION   In contrast to tax planning, *tax evasion* refers to *illegal* efforts by taxpayers to avoid their tax obligations. Examples include failure to file an income tax return or fraudulently understating the amount of taxable income reported in the return.

By definition, tax evasion is a crime, punishable by fines, imprisonment, or both.

ENFORCEMENT OF INCOME TAX LAWS

Our system of income taxes relies upon taxpayers measuring their own taxable income, computing the taxes they owe, and filing an income tax return in which these amounts are reported to government income tax authorities. For this reason, our system of collecting income taxes often is described as a system of *self-assessment.*

However, income tax authorities have several means of enforcing this "self-assessment" system. To begin with, much of the taxable income earned by taxpayers is reported to the tax authorities by a third party. For example, employers must send *W-2* forms to the government indicating the total salary or wages paid to each employee during the year. Corporations and banks are required to send *1099* forms reporting to the government the dividends and interest earned by each investor and creditor. Through the use of its computers, the Internal Revenue Service traces many of these reported amounts directly into the recipient's income tax return.

Each year income tax authorities *audit* the tax returns filed by many taxpayers. Only a small percentage of the returns filed each year are audited; however, the IRS has considerable experience in identifying those returns in which taxable income may be understated. Many of the returns selected for audit are those that appear "suspicious" in some way, or in which taxpayers have claimed deductions to which they might not be entitled. Thus, by claiming certain deductions (such as expenses relating to a home office or a large casualty loss), a taxpayer may increase the chances that his or her return will be audited.

An interesting quirk in American law is that when a tax return is audited, *the burden of proof rests with the taxpayer.* Thus, taxpayers who do not maintain adequate records may lose deductions to which they otherwise would be entitled.

Finally, tax authorities may impose financial penalties upon taxpayers who have understated their taxable incomes. First, the taxpayer must pay interest on any additional taxes owed. In addition, substantial fines and penalties may be levied if the taxpayer has been careless or fraudulent. As previously stated, fraudulent tax evasion is a criminal offense and may be punishable by imprisonment, as well as by financial penalties.

INCOME TAXES: INDIVIDUALS

CASH BASIS OF ACCOUNTING FOR INCOME TAX RETURNS

Almost all *individual* income tax returns are prepared on the *cash basis of accounting.* Many small service-type business concerns and professional firms also choose to prepare their tax returns on the cash basis. Revenue is recognized when collected in cash; expenses (except depreciation) are recognized when a cash payment is made. The cash basis (as prescribed in IRS rules) does not permit expenditures for plant and equipment to be deducted in the year of purchase. These capital expenditures are *capitalized and depreciated* for tax purposes. Also, the income tax laws do not permit use of the cash basis by companies in which inventories and the sale of merchandise are significant factors.

LO 1 *Discuss the advantages of the cash basis of accounting for preparation of individual income tax returns.*

Although the cash basis of accounting does not measure income in accordance with generally accepted accounting principles, it has much merit in the area of taxation.

From the government's viewpoint, the logical time to collect tax on income is when the taxpayer receives the income in cash. At any earlier date, the taxpayer may not have the cash to pay income taxes; at any later date, the cash may have been used for other purposes.

The cash basis is advantageous for the individual taxpayer and for service-type businesses for several reasons. It is relatively simple and requires a minimum of records. The income of most individuals comes in the form of salaries, interest, and dividends. At the end of each year, an individual receives from his or her employer a W-2 form showing the salary earned and the income tax withheld during the year. This report is prepared on a cash basis without any accrual of unpaid wages. Persons receiving interest or dividends also receive from the paying companies Form 1099, which shows amounts received for the year. Thus, most individuals are provided with *reports prepared on a cash basis* for use in preparing their individual tax returns.

The cash basis has other advantages for the individual taxpayer and for many professional firms and service-type businesses. It often permits tax savings by individuals who deliberately shift the timing of revenue and expense transactions from one year to another. For example, a dentist whose taxable income is higher than usual in the current year may decide in December to delay billing patients until January 1 and thus postpone the receipt of gross income to the next year. The timing of *expense payments* near year-end is also controllable by a taxpayer using the cash basis. A taxpayer who has received a bill for a deductible expense item in December may choose to pay it before or after December 31 and thereby influence the amount of taxable income in each year.

Any taxpayer who maintains a set of accounting records may elect to use the *accrual basis* in preparing a tax return, but very few taxpayers (individual or corporate) choose to do so if they are eligible to use the *cash basis*.

TAX RATES

All taxes may be characterized as progressive, proportional, or regressive with respect to any given base. A *progressive* tax becomes a larger portion of the base as that base increases. Federal income taxes are *progressive* with respect to income, since a higher tax *rate* applies as the amount of taxable income increases. A *proportional* tax remains a constant percentage of the base no matter how that base changes. For example, a 6% sales tax remains a constant percentage of sales regardless of changes in the dollar amount of sales. A *regressive* tax becomes a smaller percentage of the base as the base increases. Regressive taxes, however, are extremely rare.

Keep in mind that tax rates have been changed many times in the past and no doubt will continue to be changed frequently in the future. To simplify the arithmetic in our illustrations, we have used tax rates of round amounts rather than the rates of any particular year. Also, we have rounded the dollar amount of tax brackets and of such items as the standard deduction and the personal exemption.

Our assumed tax structure for individuals consists of five brackets: 15%, 28%, 31%, 36%, and 40%. For single individuals, the 15% rate applies to the first $25,000 of taxable income. The 28% rate is applicable to taxable income over $25,000 through $60,000. A 31% rate is applicable to taxable income over $60,000 through $115,000, and the 36% rate is applicable to taxable income over $115,000 through $250,000. The top rate of 40% applies to taxable income over $250,000.

For married couples filing joint returns, the 15% rate applies to the first $40,000 of taxable income. The 28% rate is applicable to taxable income over $40,000 through $95,000. A 31% rate is applicable to taxable income over $95,000 through $140,000, and the 36% rate applies to taxable income over $140,000 through $250,000. As is the case for single individuals, the top rate of 40% applies to taxable income in excess of $250,000.

These rates are summarized at the top of the following page.

MARGINAL TAX RATES

In our example at the bottom of the rate schedule, the taxpayer has taxable income of $67,000, and a total tax obligation of $15,720. This indicates that the taxpayer pays income taxes equal to about *23.5%* of taxable income ($15,720 ÷ $67,000 = 23.5%).

But notice that the "top layer" of the taxpayer's taxable income was taxed at the rate of *31%*. This is the taxpayer's *marginal tax rate*.

Individual Income Tax Rates

Taxable Income	Tax Rate
Single taxpayers:	
First $25,000	15%
Amount over $25,000 but not over $60,000 (the next $35,000)................	28%
Amount over $60,000 but not over $115,000 (the next $55,000).............	31%
Amount over $115,000 but not over $250,000 (the next $135,000)..........	36%
Amount over $250,000..	40%
Married taxpayers filing joint returns:	
First $40,000	15%
Amount over $40,000 but not over $95,000 (the next $55,000)................	28%
Amount over $95,000 but not over $140,000 (the next $45,000).............	31%
Amount over $140,000 but not over $250,000 (the next $110,000)..........	36%
Amount over $250,000..	40%

Example: Compute the income tax for a single person with taxable income of $67,000.

Answer:	
Tax on first $25,000 at 15%..	$ 3,750
Tax on next $35,000 at 28%..	9,800
Tax on remaining $7,000 at 31%...	2,170
Total tax for a single person with $67,000 of taxable income...	$15,720

For decision-making purposes, average tax rates (23.5% in our example) are of *no significance,* because none of the taxpayer's income is actually taxed at this average rate. Rather, successive "layers" of income are taxed at *different rates*. The first layers are taxed at lower rates, and additional amounts of taxable income are taxed at *higher rates*—this is the essence of a progressive rate structure.

In decision making, the relevant tax rate is the *marginal rate*—the rate which will apply to *additional earnings* or *reductions* in the amount of taxable income.

CASE IN POINT

Assume that the taxpayer in our rate-table example makes a $1,000 contribution to charity, which is deductible in the determination of taxable income. What is the "after-tax" cost of this contribution to the taxpayer?

The answer is *$690.* The contribution reduces by $1,000 income subject to income taxes at the rate of *31%,* thus saving the taxpayer $310 in income taxes. The "after-tax" cost of this charitable contribution, therefore, is only $690 ($1,000 outlay, less $310 tax savings).

Notice that the taxpayer's average tax rate, 23.5%, did *not* enter into our analysis.

INCOME TAX FORMULA FOR INDIVIDUALS

The federal government supplies standard income tax forms on which taxpayers are guided to a proper computation of their taxable income and the amount of the tax. It is helpful to visualize the computation in terms of an income tax formula as diagrammed on the next page. The sequence of items on actual income tax forms differs somewhat from the arrangement in this formula. However, it is easier to understand the structure and logic of the federal income tax by referring to the tax formula rather than to tax forms.

LO 2 *State the formula for determining the taxable income of an individual.*

Formula for computing
the taxable income of
an individual (or
married couple)

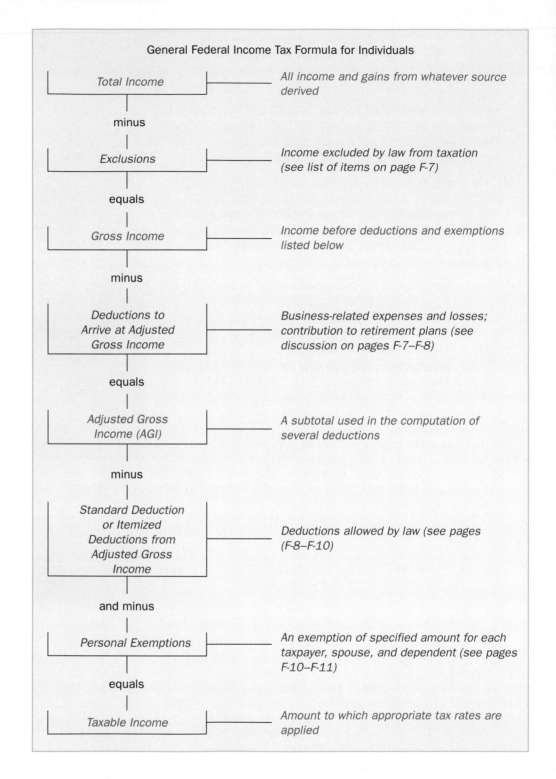

General Federal Income Tax Formula for Individuals

Total Income	All income and gains from whatever source derived
minus	
Exclusions	Income excluded by law from taxation (see list of items on page F-7)
equals	
Gross Income	Income before deductions and exemptions listed below
minus	
Deductions to Arrive at Adjusted Gross Income	Business-related expenses and losses; contribution to retirement plans (see discussion on pages F-7–F-8)
equals	
Adjusted Gross Income (AGI)	A subtotal used in the computation of several deductions
minus	
Standard Deduction or Itemized Deductions from Adjusted Gross Income	Deductions allowed by law (see pages (F-8–F-10)
and minus	
Personal Exemptions	An exemption of specified amount for each taxpayer, spouse, and dependent (see pages F-10–F-11)
equals	
Taxable Income	Amount to which appropriate tax rates are applied

TOTAL INCOME AND GROSS INCOME

Total income as defined for tax purposes is a very broad concept that includes all income from whatever source. Not all types of income, however, are subject to taxation; tax laws permit some types of income to be *excluded* in the computation of taxable income. *Gross income* is the total amount of income which must be *reported in an income tax return;* it consists of total income, less those items specifically excluded by law.

EXCLUSIONS   Items which may be excluded from gross income are called *exclusions.* Not many items qualify as exclusions; among those that do are:

- Interest on municipal bonds
- Gifts and inheritances
- Proceeds from life insurance policies
- Workers' compensation benefits and (within certain limits) social security benefits
- Pensions to veterans
- Certain types of scholarships
- Compensation received for damages

Only those items *identified by law* qualify as exclusions. Thus, types of income *not mentioned* in the tax code must be *included* in gross income. These include, for example, money found in the street, gambling winnings (in excess of losses), prizes won in contests, "high-performance awards" given by employers by employees, and income from illegal sources.

CASE IN POINT

A partially deaf 78-year-old woman once was a successful contestant on a television game show. Among the prizes she won was a replica of a 1950s jukebox. Having no use for this prize, she gave it to a neighbor who had several teenaged children.

At year-end, the "lucky contestant" was stunned to learn the tax consequence of these events. Winning the jukebox increased her taxable income by approximately $9,000, and her taxes for the year by nearly $3,000. (She could have avoided the additional taxes by declining the prize or by donating it to a recognized charity.)

DEDUCTIONS TO ARRIVE AT ADJUSTED GROSS INCOME

As steps in determining taxable income, taxpayers may deduct from gross income two broad categories of *deductions:* (1) deductions to arrive *at* adjusted gross income and (2) deductions *from* adjusted gross income.

The first of these categories, deductions to arrive *at* adjusted gross income, consists in large part of the costs and expenses incurred *in efforts to generate income.* Among the more common deductions in this category are:

1. ***Business expenses of a sole proprietorship.*** These include all ordinary and necessary expenses of carrying on a trade, business, or profession (other than as an employee). For the actual tax computation, business expenses are deducted from business revenue, and net business income is then included in adjusted gross income on the proprietor's tax return.

2. ***Expenses attributable to rental properties.*** The owner of rental property, such as an apartment building, incurs a variety of operating expenses. Depreciation, property taxes, repairs, maintenance, interest on indebtedness related to property, and other expenses incurred in connection with the earning of rental income are allowed as deductions. This means that only the *net income* derived from rental property is included in adjusted gross income.

3. ***Losses from the sale of property used in a trade or business.*** Any loss resulting from the sale of business assets may be deducted from gross income. However, losses arising from the sale of *personal* assets, such as a home, a personal automobile, or furniture are *not* deductible. In general, tax laws *prohibit* deductions for personal expenses such as rent, meals, clothing, transportation, and entertainment. The reduction over time in the value of personal assets is considered a type of "personal expense."

4. ***Net capital losses.*** Up to $3,000 of *net capital losses* may be deducted in arriving at adjusted gross income. Capital losses are discussed further on pages F-11–F-13.

5. *Contributions to retirement plans: IRA and Keogh plans.* A retirement plan known as an IRA (Individual Retirement Arrangement) is one that you set up and contribute to yourself, without any participation by your employer. The purpose is to encourage you to set money aside for your retirement in a personal savings plan. The incentive offered is that your contributions may be fully or partially deductible in computing your current taxable income—that is, not taxable until withdrawn upon your retirement. Moreover, the *income earned* on amounts in the IRA is not taxable until the time of withdrawal. Thus, an IRA may grow more rapidly than most investments because the entire current earnings go to increase the amount invested without any current taxation.

Until recently, almost everyone could receive a tax deduction by contributing up to $2,000 to an IRA plan. This deduction still is available to people who are *not covered* by an employer-sponsored pension plan at work. For taxpayers covered by employer-sponsored plans, the amount of the deduction allowed for contributions to an IRA is "phased-out" as the taxpayer's adjusted gross income rises. Thus, IRA deductions (and contributions) are not as commonplace as they were in the past. Many members of Congress, however, favor reinstating IRA deductions for most taxpayers.

If you are self-employed, a *Keogh plan* is a valuable device for reducing your income taxes and building assets for retirement. Individuals who are self-employed are permitted to deduct from gross income the amounts they contribute to a Keogh plan. The present limit on such contributions is the lower of $30,000, or 25% of the self-employment earnings. The amounts contributed, plus earnings on the fund assets, are not taxable until the taxpayer retires and begins making withdrawals from the fund. A Keogh plan is intended to provide self-employed persons with opportunities similar to those of persons employed by companies with pension plans.

6. *Other deductions to arrive at adjusted gross income.* Among other deductions are alimony paid and penalties paid on early withdrawals from long-term savings deposits.

ADJUSTED GROSS INCOME

By deducting from gross income the various items described in the preceding section, we arrive at a very significant total called *adjusted gross income (AGI)*. This amount is significant because several deductible items such as medical expense and casualty losses are limited by their percentage relationship to adjusted gross income. For example, medical expenses are deductible only to the extent they *exceed* 7½% of adjusted gross income.

DEDUCTIONS FROM ADJUSTED GROSS INCOME

Taxpayers have a choice with respect to deductions from adjusted gross income. They may choose to take a lump-sum *standard deduction*, or they may choose to *itemize* their deductions, in which case they can deduct a number of expenses specified in the tax law as itemized deductions.

STANDARD DEDUCTION   Most taxpayers choose to take the standard deduction from adjusted gross income rather than itemizing their deductions by listing such items as mortgage interest payments and state income taxes. In recent years the amounts of the standard deduction have been increased substantially to approximately the following levels: $7,000 for married couples filing jointly and $4,200 for single taxpayers. As a matter of convenience, these round amounts are to be used in all exercises and problems in this book which involve the standard deduction. However, the law provides that the amount of the standard deduction will continue to be adjusted annually for inflation.

DOES IT PAY TO ITEMIZE?   Should you itemize your deductions or claim the standard deduction? To find out, add up your deductible expenses to see if the total exceeds the standard deduction. If it does, you will save taxes by itemizing. If the total is less than the standard deduction, you will benefit by claiming the standard deduction. If you itemize deductions, however, you may be asked to provide evidence supporting the nature and amount of the deductions.

ITEMIZED DEDUCTIONS   The major types of *itemized deductions* allowable under current tax laws are described below.

1. ***Mortgage interest.*** Interest on mortgages on a first and a second home continues to be deductible. However, consumer interest charges, as on credit cards, auto loans, and boat loans, were phased out during the years from 1988 through 1990.

2. ***State income taxes and property taxes.*** State income taxes and taxes by local government on real estate and personal property continue to be deductible. Sales taxes and gasoline taxes no longer may be deducted. No *federal* taxes qualify as itemized deductions.

3. ***Contributions.*** Contributions by individuals to charitable, religious, educational, and certain nonprofit organizations are deductible within certain limits, but only for taxpayers who itemize deductions. In other words, a taxpayer who takes the standard deduction cannot also take deductions for charitable contributions. Gifts to friends, relatives, and other persons are not deductible.

4. ***Medical expenses.*** Medical and dental expenses may be deducted only to the extent that they exceed 7½% of adjusted gross income.

5. ***Casualty losses.*** Losses in excess of $100 from any fire, storm, earthquake, theft, or other sudden, unexpected, or unusual causes are deductible only to the extent that they exceed 10% of adjusted gross income. For example, assume that a taxpayer with adjusted gross income of $45,000 sustains an uninsured fire loss of $10,100. First, we eliminate $100 of the loss, leaving the amount of $10,000. Next, we reduce the loss by 10% of the adjusted gross income of $45,000, a reduction of $4,500. This leaves $5,500 as the net deduction from adjusted gross income in arriving at the amount subject to tax.

6. ***Miscellaneous deductions.*** Such items as union dues, investment expenses, professional journals, and deductions for employee business expenses are allowable only to the extent that they exceed 2% of adjusted gross income.

WHY IS ONLY PART OF SOME "DEDUCTIONS" DEDUCTIBLE? Notice that some expenses, such as medical expenses and casualty losses, are deductible only to the extent that they *exceed* a specified percentage of adjusted gross income. These "percentage hurdles" are included in the tax law for several specific reasons. One reason is to prevent taxpayers from deducting small "personal" expenses, such as an annual physical examination, over-the-counter medicines, and, perhaps, the theft of a car radio. On the other hand, these rules still provide tax relief to individuals who sustain catastrophic losses.

These percentages also relate the concept of a "catastrophic loss" to the taxpayer's income. To illustrate, assume that a taxpayer incurs medical expenses during the year of $10,000. If this taxpayer has an adjusted gross income of $20,000, $8,500 of these expenses are deductible [$10,000 − ($20,000 × 7.5%) = $8,500]. For a taxpayer with an adjusted gross income of $200,000, none of this $10,000 expense is deductible. The percentage hurdles are one manner in which the tax structure is made more progressive.

LIMITATIONS ON ITEMIZED DEDUCTIONS FOR HIGH-INCOME TAX-PAYERS Current tax regulations *limit* the amount of itemized deductions which may be deducted by high-income taxpayers. As the taxpayer's adjusted gross income rises, a percentage of certain itemized deductions becomes *nondeductible*. This is an additional means by which the tax structure is made more progressive.

We will assume that this "phase-out" of itemized deductions begins for both single and married taxpayers once adjusted gross income exceeds $120,000.[3] Certain itemized deductions are reduced by *3%* of adjusted gross income in excess of $120,000.[4]

---

[3]This amount changes from year to year.
[4]Only 80% of itemized deductions are subject to disallowance as a result of high adjusted gross income. This 80% rule, however, is likely to apply only to taxpayers with a multimillion dollar AGI.

Assume that a married couple has an adjusted gross income of $220,000 and itemized deductions of $28,000. They can actually deduct only *$25,000* of their itemized deductions; $3,000 of these deductions [3% × ($220,000 AGI − $120,000)] is disallowed because of the couple's high income.

WHAT QUALIFIES AS A DEDUCTION? Earlier in this chapter, we made the point that only items specifically identified by law qualify as *exclusions*. The same concept applies to *deductions*. Unless the law specifically states that a type of expense or loss qualifies as a deduction, the item is *not deductible*.

The specific items for which Congress allows the taxpayer a deduction change over time. However, Congress usually follows some general guidelines, which are described below:

1. The costs of *generating* income, such as business expenses, normally *are* deductible. There are limitations, however, intended to prevent abuse. Examples include limitations upon deductions for travel, entertainment, and business meals.

2. *Personal* expenses normally are *not* deductible. Rent, purchases of food and clothing, and even the costs of commuting to and from work are not deductible because they are regarded as personal expenses.

Losses on disposals of personal property generally are *not* deductible, because the decline in value is seen as a personal expense. But gains on sales of personal property *do* represent taxable income.

3. While personal expenses generally are not deductible, Congress makes exceptions for taxpayers who face catastrophic situations. This explains why medical expenses and casualty losses *do* become deductible to the extent they exceed a significant portion of the taxpayer's AGI.

4. Congress also uses tax laws to *encourage certain types of activities* that it considers desirable. A few examples:

● Mortgage interest, a personal expense, *is deductible* because Congress wants to encourage homeownership.

● Charitable contributions, another personal expense, *are deductible* because Congress believes that charitable organizations benefit society.

5. Congress believes that income taxes should be based in large part upon the taxpayer's ability to pay. Thus, it makes the tax structure *progressive;* not just in the rate structure, but also in more subtle ways. We already have discussed the phasing-out of deductions for high-income taxpayers. In addition, there are limits upon the deductibility of mortgage interest. These limits do not affect the average homeowner, but they may affect someone purchasing a mansion.

These general guidelines will not enable you to determine with certainty whether a given amount is deductible in a given year. We believe, however, that they will enable you to better understand the nature and purpose of tax laws and regulations.

PERSONAL AND DEPENDENCY EXEMPTIONS

A deduction from adjusted gross income is allowed for one or more *personal exemptions,* as well as for the standard deduction discussed above. An unmarried individual is entitled to one personal exemption, provided that he or she is not listed as a dependent on some other person's tax return. In addition, a taxpayer is allowed one exemption for each person claimed as a dependent. This is called a dependency exemption and is the same dollar amount as a personal exemption.

An "indexing" plan provides for an annual inflation adjustment of the amount of the personal exemption. As a matter of convenience in illustrations and problems in this book we assume the round amount of $2,500 for each personal and dependency exemption. The deduction for personal and dependency exemptions is phased out for high-income taxpayers. This denial of exemptions to high-income taxpayers makes the tax system more progressive than indicated by the stated rates.

The term *dependent* means a person who (1) receives over one-half of his or her support from the taxpayer, (2) is closely related to the taxpayer or lives in the taxpayer's home, (3) has gross income during the year of less than the current exemption amount unless he or she is a child of the taxpayer and is under 19 years of age or is a full-time student, (4) meets a citizenship test, and (5) does not file a joint return. For any dependent one or more years of age, the taxpayer must list the dependent's social security number. To summarize the tax savings from personal and dependency exemptions, we assume that each exemption reduces taxable income by $2,500. With a tax rate of 30%, the tax saving is $750, computed as $2,500 × 30%.

PHASE-OUT OF EXEMPTIONS FOR HIGH-INCOME TAXPAYERS The deduction allowed for personal and dependency exemptions described above is gradually phased out for taxpayers with adjusted gross incomes above a certain level. Married taxpayers filing a joint return begin to lose a portion of the exemption amount once adjusted gross income exceeds approximately $180,000; the threshold for single taxpayers is an adjusted gross income of approximately $120,000. The deduction for exemptions is completely phased out for married taxpayers with adjusted gross incomes of $305,000 and for single taxpayers with adjusted gross incomes of $245,000.

We will not address the phase-out of personal exemptions in our text examples or assignment material. However, you should recognize that this is one of the ways in which the federal tax code has been made more progressive than the rate structure suggests.

TAXABLE INCOME—INDIVIDUALS

We have now traced the steps required to determine the taxable income of an individual. In brief, this process includes:

1. Computation of total income

2. Exclusion of certain items specified by law to determine gross income

3. Deduction of business-related expenses to arrive at adjusted gross income

4. Deduction of the standard deduction (or itemized deductions) and personal exemptions to arrive at the key figure of taxable income

The concept of taxable income is important because it is the amount to which the appropriate tax rate is applied to determine the tax liability.

CAPITAL GAINS AND LOSSES

As stated earlier, an individual may deduct up to $3,000 in net capital losses as a step in arriving at adjusted gross income. To understand this concept, we first need to understand the nature of capital gains and losses.

Certain kinds of property are defined under the tax laws as *capital assets*. For most individuals, investments in securities and in real estate (including a personal residence) are the most important capital assets. However, *almost everything* that an individual owns is a capital asset, including household furniture, an automobile, jewelry, clothing, artwork, and a stamp or coin collection. Capital assets actually include all assets *other than* those used in a trade or business.

Capital assets have a *basis* for income tax purposes, which is a concept similar to book value. The *tax basis* of an asset is equal to the asset's cost, less any depreciation which has been allowed for income tax purposes.[5] If any capital asset is sold at a price in excess of its basis, the taxpayer has a *capital gain*. If a capital asset is sold at a price below its basis, the taxpayer has a *capital loss*.

All capital gains are included in income subject to income taxes. Two limitations apply, however, to the deductibility of capital losses. First, capital losses on *personal assets,*

---

[5]Basis also may be adjusted for other events, such as casualty losses and "like-kind" exchanges.

such as your car or your home, are not deductible at all. Second, the amount of capital losses which can be deducted from other types of income is *limited to $3,000* in any given year.

TAX TREATMENT OF CAPITAL GAINS Taxpayers are required to report separately their *short-term* and *long-term* capital gains and losses. Capital gains and losses are classified as long-term when the investor has owned the asset for more than one year.

LO 3 *Explain the recent changes in taxation of capital gains and losses.*

Short-term capital gains traditionally have been taxed as ordinary income. Until 1986, however, long-term capital gains were given a special and highly favorable tax treatment. Under the "old law," investors were required to include only 40% of long-term capital gains in the computation of taxable income. Thus, 60% of a long-term capital gain was not subject to tax.

The rationale underlying this favorable treatment of long-term capital gains was to encourage the flow of investment capital into new growth industries. In brief, a tax incentive was offered to encourage investors to take risks, rather than to invest in "risk-free" securities, such as government bonds. Almost all industrialized countries give favorable tax treatment to capital gains.

The Tax Reform Act of 1986 eliminated the preference accorded to long-term capital gains and called for taxing these gains as ordinary income. The treatment of long-term capital gains remains an area of controversy, and we will address this topic again in a few paragraphs.

TAX TREATMENT OF CAPITAL LOSSES Capital losses, whether short-term or long-term, first are offset against any capital gains. A taxpayer whose total capital losses *exceed* total capital gains has a *net capital loss*. On an individual's income tax return, a net capital loss can be deducted only from other income up to a *maximum of $3,000 per year*. The remainder of the loss may be carried forward and offset against capital gains (if any) in future years, or offset against other income at the rate of $3,000 per year.

The limited deductibility of capital losses can pose a serious problem for taxpayers and illustrates the importance of tax planning. For example, assume that John Forbes, an investor, sells an investment late in 1997 and realizes a capital gain of $300,000. Early in 1998, Forbes sells another investment, this time incurring a $300,000 capital loss.

If Forbes had sold both investments in the same year, the gain and loss would have offset one another, and Forbes would owe no tax on these transactions. As it stands, however, Forbes must pay income taxes in 1997 on the entire $300,000 gain, which amounts to about *$90,000* in additional taxes. In his 1998 income tax return, Forbes will be able to deduct only $3,000 of his capital loss, thus reducing his taxes due in that year by only about *$900*. Unless Forbes is able to offset his 1998 loss against future capital gains, it will take him *100 years* to deduct the full amount of this loss in his income tax returns.

This example is intended to make two points. First, Forbes could have avoided this tax trap with a little tax planning; he should have sold both investments in the same year. Second, the popular idea that investors *like* to incur financial losses because they can write them off is pure fiction.

BUSINESS PLANT AND EQUIPMENT Buildings, equipment, and other depreciable assets used in a trade or business *are not capital assets* under the tax law and are not subject to the $3,000 capital loss limitation. This means that losses realized on sales or disposals of *business* property are fully deductible.

THE CHANGING TREATMENT OF LONG-TERM CAPITAL GAINS

After the Tax Reform Act of 1986, debate continued as to whether or not long-term capital gains should be taxed in a preferential manner. President Bush expressed strong support for *reinstating* favorable treatment for these gains. In 1988, the House of Representatives voted for such reinstatement, but the bill was defeated in the Senate.

In 1991, a small long-term capital gains preference was reinstated. The tax rate schedules for 1991 included three tax brackets, with progressive tax rates of 15%, 28%, and 31%. Long-term capital gains were taxed as ordinary income, except that the highest tax rate (31%) was not applied to these gains. In 1991, therefore, long-term capital gains were taxed at a maximum rate of 28%.

The 1993 Tax Act continued to provide for a 28% maximum tax on long-term capital gains, while expanding the tax brackets to five: 15%, 28%, 31%, 36%, and 39.6%. The preferential treatment of long-term capital gains now is more significant considering the progressive tax rates applicable to other types of income.

The present tax status of capital gains may be summarized as follows: (1) taxpayers must identify and report separately net short-term and net long-term capital gains and losses, which then are offset to determine the net capital gain or loss; (2) net capital gains are taxed as ordinary income, except that net long-term capital gains are not taxed at rates in excess of 28%; and (3) net capital losses can be deducted from an individual's other income only to the extent of $3,000 per year.

Investors should watch future developments with respect to the taxation of long-term capital gains. In the event that a highly favorable treatment is reinstated, holding assets until gains become long-term will become a major element of tax planning. Also, investors will favor those assets which offer a good prospect of capital gains, such as stocks and real estate, over those investments with fixed maturity values.

TAX STRATEGY FOR CAPITAL GAINS AND LOSSES One widely used tax strategy is to "defer income and accelerate deductions." A first step in carrying out this strategy is to review one's security holdings as the year-end approaches. Identify any investments for which the current market price is less than the taxpayer's cost basis. Consider selling this investment before year-end in order to generate a capital loss which can be offset against any capital gains already realized in the current year or against other income (subject to the $3,000 limitation previously discussed). The sale of an investment in securities to generate a capital loss must not be accompanied by the purchase of the same security within 30 days or the IRS may disallow the loss on grounds that it was part of a "wash transaction."

COMPUTING THE TAX LIABILITY

After determining the amount of taxable income, we are ready to compute the gross *tax liability* using tax rates shown on page F-5. For a single taxpayer, we apply the 15% rate to the first $25,000 of taxable income, the 28% rate to the next $35,000, the 31% rate to the next $55,000, the 36% rate to the next $135,000, and the 40% rate to any amount over $250,000. For example, assume that Joe Garcia is single and has taxable income of $135,000. The computation produces a tax (rounded to the nearest dollar) of $37,800, as shown below.

Taxable Income	Tax Rate	Tax
$ 25,000	15%	$ 3,750
35,000	28%	9,800
55,000	31%	17,050
20,000	36%	7,200
$135,000		$37,800

For a married couple filing a joint return, first we apply the 15% rate to the first $40,000 of taxable income. Next we apply the 28% rate to taxable income above $40,000 but not over $95,000, the 31% rate to the next $45,000, the 36% rate to the next $110,000, and finally we apply the 40% rate to any taxable income in excess of $250,000. For example, assume that Patrick and Cheryl Finnegan have taxable income of $275,000. The computation produces a tax (rounded to the nearest dollar) to $84,950, as shown below.

Taxable Income	Tax Rate	Tax
$ 40,000	15%	$ 6,000
55,000	28%	15,400
45,000	31%	13,950
110,000	36%	39,600
25,000	40%	10,000
$275,000		$84,950

TAX CREDITS The gross tax liability as computed by the methods described above is reduced by subtracting any tax credits. Note that a *tax credit* is subtracted *directly from the tax owed,* whereas a deduction (as for charitable contributions) is subtracted from adjusted gross income and thus leads to a smaller amount of taxable income to which the tax rate is applied. For many years, tax credits were claimed by many individual taxpayers and by almost every business. However, in recent years, most tax credits have been eliminated. The few remaining tax credits include the earned income credit for qualifying low-income taxpayers and a credit of up to several hundred dollars for child care expenses incurred by working parents.

TAX PREPAYMENTS Taxpayers pay most of their tax liability well *in advance* of filing their income tax return. The most common example of these tax prepayments is the withholding of income taxes from a person's salary. Tax law requires persons with taxable income which is not subject to withholding to pay *estimated taxes* in advance quarterly installments.

The gross tax liability computed in the taxpayer's income tax return is reduced by subtracting all tax credits and tax prepayments. The remaining amount is the *net tax liability*—the amount to be paid with the tax return. (If the tax credits and prepayments exceed the gross tax liability for the year, the taxpayer is entitled to a *refund* of the difference.)

TAX RETURNS, TAX REFUNDS, AND PAYMENT OF THE TAX

The tax return must be filed within 3½ months after the close of the taxable year. Most taxpayers are on a calendar-year basis; therefore, the deadline for filing is April 15. However, the taxpayer has the alternative of paying the tax due at April 15 and requesting an extension of time to August 15 for filing of the return.

WITHHOLDING MAKES THE SYSTEM WORK Without the withholding feature, the present income tax system would probably be unworkable. The high rate of income taxes would pose an impossible collection problem if employees received their total earnings in cash and were later called upon at the end of the year to pay the government a major portion of a year's salary.

The amounts withheld from an employee's salary for income tax can be considered as payments on account. If the amount of income tax as computed by preparing a tax return at the end of the year is less than the amount withheld during the year, the taxpayer is entitled to a refund. On the other hand, if the tax as computed at year-end is more than the amount withheld, the taxpayer must pay the additional amount with the tax return.

THE DECEPTIVE LURE OF A TAX REFUND CHECK Most American taxpayers receive tax refunds each year. Apparently these 60 million or more persons so enjoy receiving a refund check that they are willing to have the government withhold excessive amounts of tax from their paychecks throughout the year. The IRS reports that millions of individual taxpayers declare fewer personal exemptions than they expect to claim at year-end. The result is over-withholding of billions of dollars on which the government pays no interest. It is interesting that even during periods of inflation and high interest rates, American taxpayers would choose to have the government hold their money throughout the year with no interest in order to be repaid at year-end in dollars worth less in purchasing power than when earned.

COMPUTATION OF INDIVIDUAL INCOME TAX ILLUSTRATED

The computation of the federal income tax liability for Mary and John Reed is illustrated on the following page.

In this example it is assumed that the Reeds provide over one-half the support of their two children. John Reed is a practicing attorney who received $251,000 in gross fees from his law practice and incurred $154,000 of business expenses. Mary Reed earned $54,400 during the year as a CPA working for a national firm of accountants. During the year, $12,350 was withheld from her salary for federal income taxes. Just before the end of the year, John Reed contributed $3,000 to a Keogh retirement plan. The Reeds received $700 interest on municipal bonds and $1,360 interest on savings accounts. Dividends received on stock jointly owned amounted to $7,240. During the year, stock purchased several years ago by John Reed for $12,600 was sold for $17,600, net of brokerage fees, thus producing a $5,000 long-term capital gain.

MARY AND JOHN REED
Illustrative Federal Income Tax Computation

Gross income (excluding $700 interest on municipal bonds):			Exclusions
Gross fees from John Reed's law practice		$251,000	
Salary received by Mary Reed.................................		54,400	
Dividends received		7,240	
Interest received..		1,360	
Long-term capital gain...		5,000	
Gross income		$319,000	
Deductions to arrive at adjusted gross income:			
Expenses incurred in John Reed's law practice	$154,000		Deductions to
Contribution to Keogh retirement plan	3,000	$157,000	arrive at AGI
Adjusted gross income..		$162,000	
Deductions from adjusted gross income:			
Total itemized deductions	$ 17,360		Allowable itemized
Less: Portion disallowed [3% ($162,000 − $120,000)]..........	1,260		deductions
Allowable itemized deductions..	$ 16,100		
Personal and dependency exemptions (4 × $2,500)	10,000	26,100	Exemptions
Taxable income		$135,900	

Computation of tax liability:				
Taxable income excluding				
capital gain		$40,000 at 15%.....	$ 6,000	
($135,900 − $5,000)	$130,900	$55,000 at 28%.....	15,400	Total tax liability
		$35,900 at 31%.....	11,129	
Long-term capital gain*...................	5,000	$ 5,000 at 28%.....	1,400	
Total taxable income	$135,900			
Total federal income tax liability			$ 33,929	

Computation of amount owed with tax return:			
Total federal income tax liability		$ 33,929	
Less: Taxes already paid:			
Quarterly payments of estimated tax	$ 20,000		
Taxes withheld from salary	12,350	32,350	
Federal income tax to be paid with return................................		$ 1,579	Tax due (or refund)

*As the maximum tax on long-term capital gains is 28%, the tax on long-term capital gains is computed separately whenever total taxable income reaches tax brackets higher than 28%.

The Reeds have total itemized deductions of $17,360, including contributions, mortgage interest expense, property taxes, etc. (As is shown in the computation on the preceding page, the Reeds' adjusted gross income is above $120,000; therefore, their itemized deductions must be *reduced* by 3% of the excess of the adjusted gross income above the $120,000 threshhold.) The Reeds paid a total of $20,000 on their declaration of estimated tax during the year.

In this illustration, as in the assignment material at the end of this appendix, we have for convenience used the amount of $2,500 for each exemption.

On the basis of these facts, the taxable income for the Reeds is shown to be $135,900, and the total tax is $33,929. Taking withholdings and quarterly payments of estimated tax into account, the Reeds have already paid income taxes of $32,350 and thus owe $1,579 at the time of filing their tax return.

ALTERNATIVE MINIMUM TAX

You may have read newspaper stories about a few high-income individuals who were able through extensive use of tax shelters and various loopholes in the tax law to avoid paying any income tax. Although such cases have been extremely rare, they create strong reactions by the public and by Congress. One goal of recent tax legislation has been to ensure that every person with a large income pays a significant amount of income tax. The approach taken was to strengthen the *alternative minimum tax (AMT)*.

The AMT computation requires that you add back to adjusted gross income a long list of deductions (such as state income taxes or the standard deduction, if claimed), exemptions, and tax preferences (such as accelerated depreciation). The total resulting from these additions to adjusted gross income is termed the Alternative Minimum Taxable Income. A 26% tax rate is applied to the amount in excess of a tax-exempt allowance. (Current law also provides for a second 28% tax bracket applicable to alternative minimum taxable income above a certain level.)

If the alternative minimum tax is higher than your tax under the regular computation, you must pay the alternative minimum tax. Note that you must pay the *higher* of the alternative minimum tax or the tax under the regular computation—you do not pay both amounts.

PARTNERSHIPS

Partnerships are not taxable entities. However, although a partnership pays no income tax, the partnership must file an *information return* showing the computation of net income or loss and the share of net income or loss allocable to each partner. The partners must include in their individual tax returns their respective shares of the net income or loss of the partnership.

INCOME TAXES: CORPORATIONS

LO 4 *Contrast the determination of taxable income for a corporation with that for an individual.*

A corporation is a separate taxable entity. Our discussion is focused on the general business corporation and does not cover certain other types of corporations for which special tax treatment applies. Every corporation, unless specifically exempt from taxation, must file an income tax return whether or not it has taxable income or owes any tax.

The earning of taxable income inevitably creates a liability to pay income taxes. This liability and the related charge to expense must be entered in the accounting records before financial statements are prepared. For example:

Income Taxes Expense	60,000	
Income Taxes Payable		60,000
To record corporate income taxes for the current period.		

CORPORATION TAX RATES

Tax law currently sets the top basic corporate tax rate at 35%, allows lower rates for small corporations, and levies a 5% additional tax on a portion of earnings in excess of $100,000.[6] These tax rates are shown in the following table. (These brackets may change in future years, but they will be used for all examples and assignment material in this text.)

Corporate Income Tax Rates

Taxable Income	Rates
First $50,000	15%
Amount over $50,000, but not over $75,000	25%
Amount over $75,000, but not over $100,000	34%
Amount over $100,000, but not over $335,000 (includes 5% additional tax)	39%
Amount over $335,000, but not over $10 million	34%
Amount over $10 million	35%

---

[6]Current tax law also provides for an extra 3% tax on a portion of taxable income in excess of $15 million in order to phase out the benefits derived from all tax brackets below 35%. This second "tax bubble" is not reflected in the corporate income tax rates above.

For corporations earning a taxable income in excess of $100,000, the benefit of having part of their income taxed at the lower 15% and 25% rates gradually is phased out. An *additional* 5% tax is applied to taxable earnings between $100,000 and $335,000. After taxable income exceeds $335,000, this extra tax is discontinued, as it has recouped the benefits which the company derived from the two lower tax brackets.

To illustrate, let us compute the tax for a corporation with taxable income of $1,000,000.

Taxable Income		Tax Rate	Tax
First......................	$ 50,000	15%	$ 7,500
Next	25,000	25%	6,250
Next	25,000	34%	8,500
Next	235,000	39%*	91,650
Remaining...........	665,000	34%	226,100
Total.............	$1,000,000		$340,000

*Includes a 5% tax designed to deny high-income corporations any benefit from the lower tax rates on the first $75,000 of corporate income.

Notice that the total tax of $340,000 is *exactly 34%* of the entire $1,000,000 of taxable income, indicating that the use of the additional 5% tax has nullified the benefits of the 15% and 25% rates for this corporation. Any corporation with taxable income of $335,000 through $10 million pays tax at a flat rate of 34%.

TAXABLE INCOME OF CORPORATIONS

In many respects, the taxable income of corporations is computed by following the same concepts we employ in preparing an income statement. The starting point is total revenue. From this amount, we deduct ordinary and necessary business expenses. However, net income determined by generally accepted accounting principles usually differs from taxable income. The difference is caused by specific rules in the tax laws which prescribe for certain items of revenue and expense a treatment different from that called for by GAAP. Another difference is the fact that from time to time, Congress makes drastic changes in the rules for determining taxable income. Shown below are some of the special factors to be considered in preparing a corporate tax return.

1. **Dividends received.** Dividends received by a corporation on investments in stocks of other domestic corporations are included in gross income, but at least 70% of such dividends can be deducted from gross income.[7] As a result, only 30% or less of dividend income is taxable to the receiving corporation.

2. **Capital gains and losses.** The net capital gains of corporations are taxed as ordinary income. Thus, rates may vary from 15% to 35%. Capital gains are treated the same as any other form of income in determining the extent, if any, to which the 5% additional tax is applied. Corporations may deduct capital losses only by offsetting them against capital gains.

3. **Other variations from taxation of individuals.** The concept of adjusted gross income is not applicable to a corporation. There is no standard deduction and no personal exemption. Gross income minus the deductions allowed to corporations equals *taxable income.*

4. **Alternative minimum tax.** The starting point in calculating the alternative minimum tax is the corporation's regular taxable income. This amount is adjusted by recalculating various deductions and deferrals, such as deferred gain on installment sales and any excess of income reported to stockholders over reported taxable income. A 20% minimum tax (AMT) is applied to this recalculated base. The minimum tax must be paid if it is higher than the tax calculated by regular procedures.

---

[7]The percentage of dividends received that may be deducted in arriving at taxable income increases to 80% if the investor corporation owns 20% or more of the other company's stock, and to 100% if the investor owns 80% or more of the stock. Thus, a parent company is not taxed upon dividends received from a wholly owned subsidiary.

ILLUSTRATIVE TAX COMPUTATION FOR A CORPORATION

Shown below is an income statement for Stone Corporation, along with a separate supporting schedule for the tax computation. In this supporting schedule, we compute the amount of income taxes to appear in the income statement and also show the payments of estimated tax, thus arriving at the amount of tax payable with the tax return.

STONE CORPORATION Income Statement For the Year Ended December 31, 19__		
Revenue:		
Sales..		$800,000
Dividends received from domestic corporations.................................		20,000
Total revenue..		$820,000
Expenses:		
Cost of goods sold	$537,000	
Other expenses (includes capital loss of $13,000)................	100,000	637,000
Income before income taxes		$183,000
Income taxes expense...		54,230
Net income...		$128,770

SCHEDULE A
Computation of Income Tax

Income before income taxes		$183,000
Add back: Items not deductible for tax purposes:		
Capital loss deducted as operating expense		13,000
Subtotal...		$196,000
Deduct: Dividends received deduction ($20,000 × 70%)...........................		14,000
Taxable income...		$182,000
Computation of tax liability:		
15% of first $50,000	$ 7,500	
25% of next $25,000	6,250	
34% of next $25,000	8,500	
39% of $82,000 (includes 5% additional tax)	31,980	
Total income tax liability...		$ 54,230
Deduct: Quarterly payments of estimated tax....................................		50,000
Balance of tax payable with tax return...		$ 4,230

DEFERRED INCOME TAXES

LO 5 *Describe the circumstances that create a liability for deferred income taxes.*

In the determination of pretax *accounting income,* the objective is to measure and report the results of business operations in conformity with generally accepted accounting principles. *Taxable income,* on the other hand, is a legal concept governed by tax law and subject to frequent change by Congress. In setting the rules for determining taxable income, Congress is interested not only in meeting the revenue needs of government, but in achieving a variety of social objectives.

As accounting income and taxable income are determined with different objectives in mind, it is not surprising that pretax accounting income and taxable income may differ by a material amount. The items causing this difference fall into two broad categories: permanent differences and temporary differences.

Permanent differences are revenue or expenses that enter into the computation of one type of income, but never are considered in determining the other. Most permanent differences are the result of special tax law provisions unrelated to accounting principles. For example, interest earned from municipal bonds is included in the determination of accounting income but specifically is excluded from the computation of taxable income. As stated earlier, tax laws also permit corporations to omit from taxable income 70% of the dividends received from investments in stock of other U.S. companies.

Temporary differences arise when the *same dollar amount* of revenue or expense is recognized for tax purposes and for accounting purposes, but the *timing* of the recognition under tax rules differs from that under accounting principles. For example, a company may use an accelerated method of depreciation in its income tax return but use the straight-line method in its income statement. Over the life of the depreciable asset, however, the total amount of depreciation claimed in the tax returns will be the same as that reported in the company's income statements.

As another example, most companies use an allowance method of recognizing uncollectible accounts expense, whereas tax law requires use of the direct write-off method. Over the long run, however, both methods produce the same cumulative results.

Most businesses have a policy of using in their income tax returns those accounting methods which will *accelerate as much as possible the recognition of expenses, and delay as long as possible the recognition of revenue.* As a result of using these methods, many businesses are able to defer the recognition of significant portions of their pretax accounting income into the tax returns of future years. Hence, they are able to defer payment of the related income taxes.

ACCOUNTING FOR DEFERRED TAXES: AN ILLUSTRATION

When differences between pretax accounting income and taxable income are caused by temporary differences, a business bases its income tax expense for the period upon its pretax *accounting* income. This practice achieves a proper *matching* of income taxes expense with the related earnings. However, some of this income taxes expense will not be paid until later years, when the income is included in future tax returns. Through temporary differences, payment of part of a company's income taxes expense may be deferred on a long-term basis.

To illustrate, let us consider a very simple case involving only one temporary timing difference. Assume that Pryor Corporation has before-tax accounting income of $600,000 in both 1998 and 1999. However, the company takes as a tax deduction in 1998 an expense of $200,000 which is not deducted as expense in the income statement until 1999. The company's accounting income, taxable income, and the actual income taxes due (assuming an average tax rate of 34%) are shown below.

	1999	1998
Accounting income (before income taxes)	$600,000	$600,000
Taxable income	800,000	400,000
Actual income taxes due each year at 34% rate:		
1998: $600,000 − $200,000 = $400,000 taxable		
income × 34%		$136,000
1999: $600,000 + $200,000 = $800,000 taxable		
income × 34%	$272,000	

Let us assume the Pryor Corporation reports as an expense in its income statement each year the amount of income taxes due for that year. The effect on reported net income, as shown in the company's financial statements, would be as follows:

	1999	1998	
Accounting income (before income taxes)	$600,000	$600,000	No interperiod tax
Income taxes expense (amount actually due)	272,000	136,000	allocation: company reports
Net income	$328,000	$464,000	taxes owed as income taxes
Income taxes expense as a percentage of pretax accounting			expense
income	45%	23%	

The readers of Pryor Corporation's income statement might well wonder why the same $600,000 accounting income before income taxes in the two years produced such widely varying amounts of tax expense and net income.

To achieve a more logical relationship between the reported pretax income and income taxes expense, accountants use a procedure called *interperiod income tax allocation.*[8] Briefly, the objective of income tax allocation is to *accrue income taxes expense* in *relation to accounting income,* even if the items comprising accounting income will be taxable or deductible in a different period.

In the Pryor Corporation example, this means we would report in the 1998 income statement a tax expense based on the $600,000 of accounting income, even though a portion of this income ($200,000) will not be subject to income tax until the following year. The effect of this accounting procedure is demonstrated by the following journal entries to record the income tax expense in each of the two years:

Entries to record income tax allocations

1998	Income Taxes Expense	204,000	
	Income Taxes Payable		136,000
	Deferred Income Taxes		68,000
	To record current and deferred income taxes at 34% of accounting income of $600,000.		

Deferred income taxes is a liability. As explained in Chapter 10, classification as current or long-term depends upon the nature of the items causing the tax deferral.[9]

In 1999, the temporary differences will "reverse," and Pryor will report taxable income of $200,000 in excess of its pretax accounting income. Thus, the income taxes deferred in 1998 are coming due. The entry to record income taxes expense in 1999 is:

1999	Income Taxes Expense	204,000	
	Deferred Income Taxes	68,000	
	Income Taxes Payable		272,000
	To record income taxes at 34% of accounting income of $600,000 and to record actual income taxes due.		

Notice that as in 1998, income tax expense is based upon the pretax accounting income shown in the company's income statement.

Using these interperiod tax allocation procedures, Pryor Corporation's financial statements would report net income during the two-year period as follows:

Interperiod tax allocation: income taxes expense is related to accounting income

	1999	1998
Accounting income (before income taxes)	$600,000	$600,000
Income taxes expense (tax allocation basis)	204,000	204,000
Net income	$396,000	$396,000
Income taxes expense as a percentage of pretax accounting income	34%	34%

DEFERRED TAXES: AN EVALUATION In 1999, Pryor Corporation must pay an amount of income taxes greater than the income taxes expense appearing in the income statement. Although this situation can arise, it does not usually happen as long as a company continues to grow.

---

[8]For a more complete discussion of tax allocation procedures, see *FASB Statement of Financial Accounting Standards No. 109,* "Accounting for Income Taxes" (Norwalk, Conn.: 1992).
[9]Temporary differences also may require a company to pay some income taxes *before* the related income appears in accounting income. This situation creates an asset, which might be called Prepaid Income Taxes. In this appendix, we illustrate only the more common situation in which the payment of taxes is deferred, thereby creating a liability.

A growing company usually defers more taxes each year than the previous deferrals which are coming due. Thus, a growing company may pay less in taxes each year than the amount of its current tax expense, and its liability for deferred income taxes continues to grow. The liability for deferred taxes is, in essence, an *interest-free loan*—capital made available to the business by selecting advantageous accounting methods for use in the company's income tax returns. Hence, deferring income taxes generally is viewed as a desirable business strategy.

TAX PLANNING

Federal income tax laws have become so complex that detailed tax planning is now a way of life for most business firms. Almost all companies today engage professional tax specialists to review the tax aspects of major business decisions and to develop plans for legally minimizing income taxes. We will now consider some areas in which tax planning may offer substantial benefits.

FORMS OF BUSINESS ORGANIZATION

Tax factors should be considered at the time a business is organized. As a sole proprietor or partner, a business owner will pay taxes at individual rates (ranging under our assumptions from 15% to 40%) on income earned in any year *whether or not it is withdrawn from the business.* Corporations, on the other hand, are taxed on earnings at rates varying from 15% to 35% under our assumptions. In determining taxable income, corporations deduct salaries paid to owners for services but cannot deduct dividends paid to stockholders. Both *salaries and dividends* are taxable income to the persons receiving them.

LO 6 *Explain how tax planning is used in choosing the form of business organization and the capital structure.*

These factors must be weighed in deciding in any given situation whether the corporate or noncorporate form of business organization is preferable. There is no simple rule of thumb, even considering only these basic differences. To illustrate, suppose that Able, *an unmarried man,* starts a business which he expects will produce, before any compensation to himself and before income taxes, an average annual income of $100,000. Able plans to withdraw $40,000 yearly from the business. The combined corporate and individual taxes under the corporate and sole proprietorship form of business organization are summarized in the following table:

		Form of Business Organization	
		Corporation	Sole Proprietorship
Business income		$100,000	$100,000
Salary to Able		40,000	
Taxable income		$ 60,000	$100,000
Corporate tax:			
15% of first $50,000	$7,500		
25% of next $10,000	2,500	10,000	
Net income		$ 50,000	$100,000
Combined corporate and individual tax:			
Corporate tax on $60,000 income		$ 10,000	
Individual tax—single taxpayer*			
On Able's $40,000 salary		7,950	
On Able's $100,000 business income			$ 25,950
Total tax on business income		$ 17,950	$ 25,950

*Able's personal exemptions and deductions have been ignored, on the assumption that his other income equals personal exemptions and deductions. We have rounded amounts to the nearest dollar.

Under these assumptions, the formation of a corporation is favorable from an income tax viewpoint. If the business is incorporated, the combined tax on the corporation and on Able personally will be $17,950. If the business is not incorporated, the tax will be $25,950, or over 40% more. The key to the advantage indicated for choosing the corporate form of organization is that Able did not take much of the earnings out of the corporation.

If Able decides to operate as a corporation, the $50,000 of net income retained in the corporation will be taxed to Able as ordinary income *when and if* it is distributed as dividends. In other words, Able cannot get the money out of the corporation without paying personal income tax on it. An advantage of the corporation as a form of business organization is that Able can *postpone* payment of a significant amount of tax as long as the earnings remain invested in the business.

IF ALL EARNINGS OF THE BUSINESS ARE TO BE WITHDRAWN   Now let us change one of our basic assumptions and say that Able plans to *withdraw all net income* from the business each year. Under this assumption the sole proprietorship form of organization would be better than a corporation from an income tax standpoint. If the business is incorporated and Able again is to receive a $40,000 salary plus dividends equal to the $50,000 of corporate net income, the total tax will be much higher. The corporate tax of $10,000 plus personal income tax of $22,850 (based on $40,000 salary and $50,000 in dividends) would amount to $32,850. This is considerably higher than the $25,950 which we previously computed as the tax liability if the business operated as a proprietorship.

We have purposely kept our example as short as possible. You can imagine some variations which would produce different results. Perhaps Able might incorporate and set his salary at, say, $75,000 instead of $40,000. If this salary were considered reasonable by the IRS, the corporation's taxable income would drop to $25,000 rather than the $60,000 used in our illustration. Thus, the choice between a corporation and a sole proprietorship requires careful consideration of a number of factors in each individual case. Both the marginal rate of tax to which individual business owners are subject and the manner and extent to which profits are to be withdrawn are always basic issues in studying the relative advantages of one form of business organization over another.

Under certain conditions, small, closely held corporations may elect to be *Subchapter S* corporations, in which case the corporation pays no tax but the individual shareholders are taxed directly on the corporation's earnings.

TAX PLANNING IN THE CHOICE OF FINANCIAL STRUCTURE

In deciding upon the best means of raising capital to start or expand a business, consideration should be given to income taxes. Different capital structures produce different amounts of tax expense. Interest paid on debt, for example, is *fully deductible* in computing taxable income, but dividends paid on preferred or common stock are not. The deductibility of interest payments creates a strong incentive to finance expansion by borrowing.

The choice of financial structure also should be considered from the viewpoint of *the investors,* especially in the case of a small, closely held corporation.

TAX SHELTERS

A *tax shelter* is an investment which produces a loss for tax purposes in the near term but hopefully proves profitable in the long run. The reason for seeking a tax loss is to offset this loss against other income and, by so doing, lower both taxable income and the income tax owed for the current year. Investors in high tax brackets have often turned to such tax shelters as real estate investments, oil and gas drilling ventures, and cattle-feeding operations.

A major goal of the Tax Reform Act of 1986 was to reduce the availability of tax shelters. Among the heaviest blows to tax shelters were (1) the elimination of favorable treatment of long-term capital gains, (2) the strengthening of the alternative minimum tax to catch investors deeply involved in sheltering income, and (3) the requirement that real estate investments be depreciated only by the straight-line method.

Still, some worthwhile tax shelters remain. State and municipal bonds, for example, offer a modest rate of interest which is tax exempt. Investment in real estate with deductions for mortgage interest, property taxes, and depreciation will often show losses which offset other taxable income, yet eventually prove profitable because of rising market values, especially in periods of inflation.

ASSIGNMENT MATERIAL

DISCUSSION QUESTIONS

1. Explain the differences between *tax planning* and *tax evasion,* and give an example of each.

2. Why is the American income tax system described as one of *self-assessment?* What means do tax authorities have of enforcing this system?

3. State in equation form the federal income tax formula for individuals, beginning with total income and ending with taxable income.

4. Shirley Hill, M.D., files her income tax return on a cash basis. During the current year, she collected $18,900 from patients for medical services rendered in the prior year and billed patients for $115,500 for services rendered this year. At the end of the current year, she had $24,600 in accounts receivable relating to the current year's billings. What amount of gross income from her practice should Hill report on her tax return?

5. An individual with a yearly salary of $40,000 had a net capital loss of $60,000. To what extent, if any, can this capital loss be offset against salary in computing taxable income? Explain.

6. Explain the principal factors which should be considered by a taxpayer in determining *when* it would be most advantageous to sell an investment which will result in the recognition of a large capital loss.

7. What is meant by the phrase "preferential treatment for long-term capital gains"? Do long-term capital gains receive a preferential tax treatment today? Explain.

8. Which of the following is not a capital asset according to the Internal Revenue Code?
   a. An investment in General Motors stock
   b. A personal residence
   c. Equipment used in the operations of a business
   d. An investment in Krugerrands (gold coins)

9. List some differences between the tax rules for corporations and the tax rules for individuals.

10. Under what circumstances is the accounting procedure known as *interperiod income tax allocation* appropriate? Explain the purpose of this procedure.

11. Explain the origin of a liability for deferred income taxes. What does an increase in this liability over the period imply about the relationship between the income tax expense reported in the income statement and the amount of cash payments for income taxes during the year?

12. Explain the advantages to the sole owner of a small corporation of supplying capital to this business in the form of a loan, rather than as an equity investment.

13. State two goals of tax planning.

14. It has been claimed that corporate income is subject to "double taxation." Explain the meaning of this expression.

15. List some tax factors to be considered in deciding whether to organize a new business as a corporation or as a partnership.

16. Explain how the corporate income tax makes debt financing in general more attractive than financing through the issuance of preferred stock.

17. Some of the decisions that business owners must make in organizing and operating a business will affect the amount of income taxes to be paid. List some of these decisions which affect the amount of income taxes legally payable.

EXERCISES

EXERCISE F-1
Accounting Terminology

Listed below are nine technical accounting terms emphasized in this chapter.

Alternative minimum tax   Standard deduction
Adjusted gross income   Tax credit
Deferred income taxes   Personal exemption
Itemized deductions   Cash basis of accounting
Tax shelter

Each of the following statements may (or may not) describe one of these technical terms. For each statement, indicate the accounting term described, or answer "None" if the statement does not correctly describe any of the terms.

a. Important to individual taxpayers who pay large amounts of state income tax, have a home mortgage, or make large charitable contributions.

b. An amount subtracted from the gross tax liability.

c. Ensures that profitable corporations and high-income individuals do not escape taxation completely through any combination of tax shelters and tax preferences.

d. A subtotal in an individual's tax return, computed by deducting from gross income any business-related expenses, contributions to retirement plans, and other deductions authorized by law.

e. Revenue recorded when received in cash and expenses recorded in period payment is made.

f. Income tax recognized each period as a constant percentage of net sales.

g. An investment program designed to show losses in the short run to be offset against other taxable income, but offering the hope of long-run profits.

h. An option chosen by many individual taxpayers who do not own a home and whose payments of state income taxes are small.

i. A liability which comes into existence as the result of permanent differences between tax rules and accounting principles which benefit the taxpayer.

EXERCISE F-2
Cash Basis or Accrual Basis

Individual taxpayers have the choice of preparing their income tax returns on the cash basis of accounting or on the accrual basis. However, nearly all tax returns filed by individuals are prepared on the cash basis. Many small corporations in service-type businesses also file on the cash basis. How do you explain:

a. The strong preference by taxpayers for the cash basis of accounting?

b. The government's willingness to accept tax returns prepared on the cash basis in an era in which the accrual basis is the standard approach underlying generally accepted accounting principles?

EXERCISE F-3
Gross Income: Items to
Include and Items to Exclude
LO 2

You are to consider the income tax status of the items listed below. For each item state whether it is *included in gross income* or *excluded from gross income* for federal income tax on individuals.

1. Gain on the sale of a 1953 Jaguar purchased 10 years ago

2. Proceeds of life insurance policy received on death of spouse

3. Share of income from partnership in excess of drawings

4. Gain on sale of Super Bowl tickets by season ticket holder

5. Interest received on bonds of the state of Texas

6. Value of U.S. Savings Bonds received as a gift

7. Salary received from corporation by a stockholder who owns all of the corporation's capital stock

8. Inheritance of ranch from estate of deceased uncle

9. Amount received as damages for injury in automobile accident

10. Tips received by waiter
11. Pension received by veteran from U.S. government for military service
12. Dividends received on investment in Ford Motor stock
13. Trip to London received by employee as award for outstanding performance
14. Rent received on personal residence while on an extended European tour
15. First prize of $14 million won in California state lottery
16. Amount of bonus received from employer upon passing the CPA exam

EXERCISE F-4
Is It Deductible?

You are to determine the deductibility status, for federal income tax purposes, of each of the items listed below. For each item state whether the item is *deducted to arrive at adjusted gross income; deducted from adjusted gross income;* or *not deductible.*

1. Interest paid on mortgage on personal residence
2. Loss on sale of equipment used in a business
3. Capital loss on sale of an investment in securities
4. Contribution to a Keogh retirement plan
5. Depreciation on rental property
6. Damage by storm to motorboat used for pleasure
7. Sales taxes
8. Medical expense of $2,000 incurred by a taxpayer with adjusted gross income of $50,000
9. State income tax paid
10. Property taxes paid on personal residence
11. Tuition paid for dependent child to attend private high school
12. Amount paid to live-in nanny for infant care for dependent

EXERCISE F-5
Computing Taxable Income
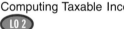

You are to compute the *taxable income* for Roger and Judy Collins, a married couple filing a joint return. Use only the relevant items from the following list.

Total income, including gifts, inheritances, interest on municipal bonds, etc.	$95,320
Exclusions (gifts, inheritances, interest on municipal bonds, etc.)	8,100
Deductions to arrive at adjusted gross income	2,500
Itemized deductions	17,420
Personal exemptions ($2,500 each)	5,000
Income taxes withheld from salary	7,710

EXERCISE F-6
Computing Tax on Individuals

Use the tax rate information on page F-5 to compute the *tax liability* for each of the following. Round amounts to the nearest dollar.

	Taxable Income
a. Single taxpayer	$ 78,500
b. Married couple filing joint return (includes a $10,000 long-term capital gain)	$192,000

EXERCISE F-7
Computing Tax Liability of a Corporation

Raintree Corporation reports the following income for the year.

Income from operations	$290,000
Capital gain	80,000

In computing the tax, assume that corporate tax rates are as follows:

On first $50,000 of taxable income..	15%
On second $25,000 of taxable income..	25%
On next $25,000 of taxable income..	34%
On amount over $100,000, but not over $335,000	39%
On amount over $335,000, but not over $10 million...	34%

Compute Raintree's tax liability for the year.

EXERCISE F-8
Interperiod Tax Allocation

Mission Bay Corporation deducted on its tax return for 1998 an expense of $100,000 which was not recognized as an expense for accounting purposes until 1999. The corporation's accounting income before income taxes in each of the two years was $525,000. The company uses interperiod tax allocation procedures.

a. Prepare the journal entries required at the end of 1998 and 1999 to record income taxes expense. To compute the tax, multiply the entire amount of taxable income by 34%.

b. Prepare a two-column schedule showing the net income to appear on the financial statements for 1998 and 1999, assuming that interperiod tax allocation procedures are used. Also prepare a similar schedule on the assumption that interperiod tax allocation procedures are *not* used.

PROBLEMS

PROBLEM F-1
Joint Return Computing Tax
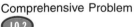

Marc and Carol Levine are married and file a joint tax return. They claim one personal exemption each, plus an exemption for their young daughter. Marc's salary for the year was $87,500, and he contributed $2,000 to an IRA. Carol's salary was $42,000. Neither Marc nor Carol is covered by an employer-sponsored pension plan. During the year, the Levines sold an investment in stock at a gain of $4,200. They had purchased the stock six years ago. (This gain is included in the couple's total income figure.)

Assume that a personal exemption is $2,500 and the standard deduction for a married couple is $7,000. Marc and Carol have compiled the following information as a preliminary step toward preparing their joint tax return.

Total income (including $129,500 salaries, $1,600 in municipal bond interest, $4,200 gain on sale of stock, and $5,800 income from other sources)..	$141,100
Federal income taxes withheld from salaries...	25,900
Payments of estimated tax..	1,800
Itemized deductions..	13,825
Payment to an IRA (Marc)	2,000

INSTRUCTIONS
a. Compute gross income.
b. Compute adjusted gross income.
c. Compute taxable income. (***Hint:*** Some deductions "phase-out.")
d. Compute the amount of tax remaining to be paid or the refund to be claimed.

PROBLEM F-2
Joint Return: A
Comprehensive Problem

Charles and Lisa Castillo file a joint income tax return. They provide more than one-half the support of their son, who attends college and who earned $4,000 during the year in part-time jobs and summer employment. The Castillos also support Lisa's father, who has no taxable income of his own.

The principal income of the Castillos is from a hardware store which they own and operate. The bookkeeper for the hardware store has prepared financial statements reporting net income of $90,000 for the hardware store operations for the year. The Castillos have withdrawn $55,000 cash from the business bank account during the year.

They also own a small apartment building. The depreciation basis of the apartment building is $200,000; depreciation is recorded at the rate of 4% on a straight-line basis.

During the current year, the Castillos had the following cash receipts and cash expenditures applicable to the hardware business, the apartment building, other investments, and personal activities.

Cash receipts:

Cash withdrawn from hardware store (net income, $90,000)	55,000
Gross rentals from apartment building	40,000
Cash dividends on stock owned jointly	3,400
Interest on River City bonds	1,220
Received from sale of stock purchased two years ago for $24,500	20,000
Received from sale of motorboat purchased three years ago for $5,000 and used entirely for pleasure	3,000

Cash expenditures:

Expenditures relating to apartment building:

Interest on mortgage	9,000
Property taxes	5,900
Insurance (one year)	700
Utilities	3,000
Repairs and maintenance	5,000
Gardening	1,000

Other cash expenditures:

Mortgage interest on residence	4,000
Property taxes on residence	2,100
Insurance on residence	1,200
State income tax paid	2,400
State sales tax	800
Charitable contributions	1,300
Medical expenses	1,500
Payment by Charles to a Keogh plan	4,000
Payment by Lisa to an IRA	2,000
Payments on declaration of estimated tax for current year	14,500

INSTRUCTIONS

a. Determine the amount of taxable income Charles and Lisa Castillo would report on their federal income tax return for the current year. In your computation of taxable income, first list the net income of the hardware business. Second, show the revenue and expenses of the apartment building and the amount of net income from this source. Third, show the data for dividends.

   After combining the above amounts and appropriate deductions to determine adjusted gross income, list the itemized deductions and personal exemptions to arrive at taxable income. Assume that the standard deduction is $7,000 and the personal exemption is $2,500 each.

b. Compute the income tax liability for Charles and Lisa Castillo using the tax rate information on page F-5. Indicate the amount of tax due (or refund to be received).

PROBLEM F-3
Corporation Return: Accounting Methods to Reduce Tax

LO 4

Ward Corporation is about to complete its first year of operation. The company has been successful, and a tentative estimate by the controller indicates an income before taxes of $250,000 for this first year. Among the items entering into the calculation of this income were the following:

1. Inventories were reported on a first-in, first-out basis and would amount to $132,500 at year-end.

2. No bad debt expense had been recognized thus far, but the controller felt there was a significant amount of long-past-due receivables which probably should be written off as worthless.

3. Under the straight-line method, depreciation for the year was computed to be $15,000.

Officers of the corporation are concerned about the relatively large amount of income taxes for this first year and decide to change accounting methods and estimates for both financial reporting and tax purposes as follows:

1. Inventories will be valued on the last-in, first-out basis, which will change the year-end amount to $100,000.

2. Specific past-due accounts receivable in the amount of $10,000 will be written off as worthless at December 31.

3. The MACRS method of depreciation will be used; this will increase depreciation expense from $15,000 to $28,750.

INSTRUCTIONS

a. Determine the *taxable income* of Ward Corporation on the revised basis.

b. Assume that tax rates for corporations are 15% on the first $50,000 of taxable income; 25% on the next $25,000; 34% on the next $25,000; and 39% on taxable income between $100,000 and $335,000. Compute the income tax liability for Ward Corporation (1) before the accounting changes, and (2) after the accounting changes. Also compute the reduction in the current year's income tax liability resulting from the accounting changes. Round all amounts to the nearest dollar.

PROBLEM F-4
Corporation: Interperiod Tax Allocation

The following information was taken from the accounting records of Ruger Corporation for 1998, the first year of operations:

Net sales	$7,500,000
Cost of goods sold	5,400,000
Selling expenses	720,000
Administrative expenses	780,000

Included in the costs and expenses shown above is depreciation expense of $500,000. However, under MACRS, the amount of depreciation Ruger is allowed to deduct in its tax return for 1998 is $700,000. The $200,000 additional depreciation deducted for tax purposes in 1998 will be deducted in the financial statements in future periods. Ruger Corporation will follow interperiod income tax allocation procedures in reporting income taxes in the income statement for 1998.

In 1999, revenue was $8,010,000. The total of cost of goods sold and expenses (excluding income taxes, but including $600,000 of depreciation expense) amounted to $7,400,000. Thus income before income taxes was $610,000 for accounting purposes. In 1999, Ruger Corporation acquired several new depreciable assets. As a result, MACRS depreciation allowed in the tax return amounted to $750,000 and was again larger than that recognized in the financial statements. The $150,000 additional depreciation deducted for tax purposes in 1999 eventually will be deducted in the financial statements over the assets' useful lives.

INSTRUCTIONS

a. Prepare an income statement for Ruger Corporation for 1998. In a separate schedule (Schedule A), show your computation of federal income taxes for 1998, using the shortcut method of multiplying the entire taxable income by 34%. **Hint:** First prepare the top part of the income statement from "Net sales" down to "Income before income taxes"; next prepare Schedule A, Income Tax Computation; and finally complete the income statement using data from Schedule A.

b. Prepare the journal entry which should be made to record the income taxes expense and related liabilities for 1998.

c. Prepare the journal entry needed at December 31, 1999, to record the company's current income taxes expense for 1999 and recognition of the deferred tax liability related to the temporary difference for 1999. Again, use the shortcut method in computing the tax.

d. Compute the balance, if any, in the Deferred Income Taxes account at December 31, 1999. What does this balance represent? What will happen to this balance over time if Ruger does not continue to acquire new depreciable assets?

ANALYSIS AND INTERPRETATION OF FINANCIAL STATEMENTS: A SECOND LOOK

INTENDED FOR USE AFTER CHAPTER 13

In this appendix, we will evaluate a set of financial statements from the perspectives of common stockholders, short-term creditors, and long-term creditors. A few new concepts are introduced, but for the most part, this appendix represents a review of material introduced throughout the text.

LEARNING OBJECTIVES

1. Put a company's net income into perspective by relating it to sales, assets, and stockholders' equity.

2. Describe several sources of financial information about a business.

3. Explain the uses of dollar and percentage changes, trend percentages, component percentages, and ratios.

4. Discuss the "quality" of a company's earnings, assets, and working capital.

5. Analyze financial statements from the viewpoints of common stockholders, creditors, and others.

6. Compute the ratios widely used in financial statement analysis and explain the significance of each.

The financial affairs of a business may be of interest to a number of different groups: management, creditors, investors, politicians, union officials, and government agencies. Each of the groups has somewhat different needs, and accordingly each tends to concentrate on particular aspects of a company's financial picture.

CORPORATE PROFITS

Perhaps the most widely discussed accounting measurement is profits—or net income. As a college student who has completed (or nearly completed) a course in accounting, you should have a much better understanding of corporate profits than do people who have never studied accounting.

LO 1 *Put a company's net income into perspective by relating it to sales, assets, and stockholders' equity.*

Public opinion polls show that many people believe that most businesses earn a profit equal to 30% or more of the sales price of their merchandise. Actually, this is far from true. Most successful companies earn a net income of between 5% and, perhaps, 15% of sales revenue.

General **Motors** in an annual report a few years ago showed a net income of $321 million. This profit may sound like a huge amount, but it was only one-half of 1% of GM's sales. Thus, of every dollar received as revenue, only ½ cent represented profit for GM. On a $10,000 car, this was a profit of *$50*. Actually, earning only $321 million in a year must be regarded as very poor performance for a corporation the size of General Motors.

Shortly afterward, however, GM set new records for both sales and earnings. Net income was $4.5 billion and represented about 5½ cents profit on each dollar of sales. That was a profit of *$550* on a $10,000 automobile. But then, there also have been some recent years during which GM has sustained large net losses.

A knowledge of accounting does not enable you to say what the level of corporate earnings *should be;* however, it does enable you to read audited financial statements that show what corporate earnings *actually are.* Moreover, you are aware that the information in published financial statements of corporations has been audited by CPA firms and has been reviewed in detail by government agencies, such as the Securities and Exchange Commission (SEC) and the Internal Revenue Service (IRS). Consequently, you know that the profits reported in these published financial statements are reasonably reliable; they have been determined in accordance with generally accepted accounting principles and verified by independent experts.

SOME SPECIFIC EXAMPLES OF CORPORATE EARNINGS . . . AND LOSSES

Not all leading corporations earn a profit every year. For the ten years from 1981 through 1990, Pan American Airways reported a net loss each year. Late in 1991, Pan Am—America's "flagship" airline—ceased operations. Many American corporations had some bad years in the early 1990s. Each of the "Big Three" American automakers reported huge losses. So did most of the nation's major airlines. Even IBM sustained a net loss—the first in the company's 80-year history.

The oil companies have been particularly subject to criticism for so-called excessive profits, so let us briefly look at the profits of Exxon, the world's largest oil company. A recent annual report of Exxon (audited by Price Waterhouse) shows that profits amounted to a little over $4.7 billion. Standing alone, that figure seems enormous—but we need to look a little farther. The total revenue of Exxon was over $115 billion, so net income amounted to about 4% of sales. On the other hand, income taxes, excise taxes, and other taxes and duties levied upon Exxon amounted to more than $36 billion, or about 7½ times as much as the company's profit. Thus, taxation represents a far greater portion of the cost of a gallon of gasoline than does the oil company's profit.

There are many ways of appraising the adequacy of corporate earnings. Certainly, earnings should be compared with total assets and with invested capital as well as with sales. In this chapter we shall look at a number of ways of evaluating corporate profits and solvency.

SOURCES OF FINANCIAL INFORMATION

LO 2 *Describe several sources of financial information about a business.*

For the most part, our discussion will be limited to the kind of analysis that can be made by "outsiders" who do not have access to internal accounting records. Investors must rely to a considerable extent on financial statements in published annual and quarterly reports. In the case of publicly owned corporations, additional information is filed with the SEC and is available to the public.

The SEC requires large corporations to include in their annual reports a *discussion and analysis* by top management of the results of the company's operations and of its current financial position. In this section of the annual report, management is required to highlight favorable and unfavorable trends, and to identify significant events and existing uncertainties affecting the company's financial condition. (This element of an annual report is illustrated on page A-6 of Appendix A.)

Many financial analysts also study the financial position and future prospects of publicly owned corporations and sell their analyses, conclusions, and investment recommendations for a fee. For example, detailed financial analyses of most large corporations are published weekly by Moody's Investors Service, Standard & Poor's, and The Value Line Investment Survey. Anyone may subscribe to these investment advisory services.

Bankers and major creditors usually are able to obtain detailed financial information from borrowers simply by requesting it as a condition for granting a loan. Suppliers and other trade creditors may obtain some financial information about almost any business from credit-rating agencies, such as Dunn & Bradstreet.

COMPARATIVE FINANCIAL STATEMENT

Significant changes in financial data are easy to see when financial statement amounts for two or more years are placed side by side in adjacent columns. Such a statement is called a *comparative financial statement*. The amounts for the most recent year are usually placed in the left-hand money column. Both the balance sheet and the income statement are often prepared in the form of comparative statements. A highly condensed comparative income statement covering three years is shown below.

BENSON CORPORATION Comparative Income Statement For the Years Ended December 31, 1999, 1998, 1997 (in thousands of dollars)			
	1999	**1998**	**1997**
Net sales	$600	$500	$400
Cost of goods sold	370	300	235
Gross profit	$230	$200	$165
Expenses	194	160	115
Net income	$ 36	$ 40	$ 50

Condensed three-year income statement

TOOLS OF ANALYSIS

Few figures in a financial statement are highly significant in and of themselves. It is their relationship to other quantities or the amount and direction of change that is important. Analysis is largely a matter of establishing significant relationships and identifying changes and trends. Four widely used analytical techniques are (1) dollar and percentage changes, (2) trend percentages, (3) component percentages, and (4) ratios.

LO 3 *Explain the uses of dollar and percentage changes, trend percentages, component percentages, and ratios.*

DOLLAR AND PERCENTAGE CHANGES

The dollar amount of change from year to year is significant, but expressing the change in percentage terms adds perspective. For example, if sales this year have increased by $100,000, the fact that this is an increase of 10% over last year's sales of $1 million puts it in a different perspective than if it represented a 1% increase over sales of $10 million for the prior year.

The dollar amount of any change is the difference between the amount for a *comparison* year and for a *base* year. The percentage change is computed by dividing the amount of the change between years by the amount for the base year. This is illustrated in the tabulation below, using data from the comparative income statement shown above.

	In Thousands			Increase or (Decrease)			
				1999 over 1998		1998 over 1997	
	Year 1999	Year 1998	Year 1997	Amount	%	Amount	%
Net sales	$600	$500	$400	$100	20%	$100	25%
Net income	36	40	50	(4)	(10%)	(10)	(20%)

Dollar and percentage changes

Although net sales increased $100,000 in both 1998 and 1999, the percentage change differs because of the shift in the base from 1997 to 1998. These calculations present no problems when the figures for the base year are positive amounts. If a negative amount or a zero amount appears in the base year, however, a percentage change cannot be computed. Thus if Benson Corporation had incurred a net loss in 1998, the percentage change in net income from 1998 to 1999 could not have been calculated.

EVALUATING PERCENTAGE CHANGES IN SALES AND EARNINGS Computing the percentage changes in sales, gross profit, and net income from one year to the next gives insight into a company's rate of growth. If a company is experiencing growth in its economic activities, sales and earnings should increase at *more than the rate of inflation.* Assume, for example, that a company's sales increase by 6% while the general price level rises by 10%. It is probable that the entire increase in the dollar amount of sales may be explained by inflation, rather than by an increase in sales volume (the number of units sold). In fact, the company may well have sold *fewer* goods than in the preceding year.

In measuring the dollar or percentage change in *quarterly* sales or earnings, it is customary to compare the results of the current quarter with those of the *same quarter in the preceding year.* Use of the same quarter of the preceding year as the base period prevents our analysis from being distorted by seasonal fluctuations in business activity.

PERCENTAGES BECOME MISLEADING WHEN THE BASE IS SMALL Percentage changes may create a misleading impression when the dollar amount used as a base is unusually small. Occasionally we hear a television newscaster say that a company's profits have increased by a very large percentage, such as 900%. The initial impression created by such a statement is that the company's profits must now be excessively large. But assume, for example, that a company had net income of $100,000 in its first year; that in the second year net income drops to $10,000; and that in the third year net income returns to the $100,000 level. In this third year, net income has increased by $90,000, representing a 900% increase over the profits of the second year. What needs to be added is that this 900% increase in profits in the third year *exactly offsets* the 90% decline in profits in the second year.

Few people realize that a 90% decline in earnings must be followed by a 900% increase just to get back to the starting point. (See the Case-in-Point on the next page.)

TREND PERCENTAGES

The changes in financial statement items from a base year to following years are often expressed as *trend percentages* to show the extent and direction of change. Two steps are necessary to compute trend percentages. First, a base year is selected and each item in the financial statements for the base year is given a weight of 100%. The second step is to express each item in the financial statements for following years as a percentage of its base-year amount. This computation consists of dividing an item such as Sales in the years after the base year by the amount of Sales in the base year.

For example, assume that 1994 is selected as the base year and that Sales in the base year amounted to $300,000 as shown below. The trend percentages for Sales are computed by dividing the Sales amount of each following year by $300,000. Also shown in the illustration are the yearly amounts of net income. The trend percentages for net income are computed by dividing the Net Income amount for each following year by the base-year amount of $15,000.

	1999	1998	1997	1996	1995	1994
Sales	$450,000	$360,000	$330,000	$320,000	$312,000	$300,000
Net income	22,950	14,550	21,450	19,200	15,600	15,000

CASE **IN POINT**

In the third quarter of 1979, **General Motors** earned $21.4 million, as compared with $527.9 million in the third quarter of 1978. This represented a 96% decline in third-quarter profits, computed as follows:

Decline in profits ($527.9 − $21.4)	$506.5
Base period earnings (third quarter, 1978)......................................	$527.9
Percentage decrease ($506.5 ÷ $527.9)	96%

How much of an increase in profits would be required in the third quarter of 1980 for profits to return to the 1978 level? Many people erroneously guess 96%. However, the correct answer is an astounding *2,367%*, computed as follows:

Required increase to reach 1978 profit level (from $21.4 to $527.9)	$506.5
Base period earnings (third quarter, 1979).....................................	$ 21.4
Required percentage increase ($506.5 ÷ $21.4)..............................	2,367%

Unfortunately for GM, the company's 1980 profits did not return to 1978 levels. Instead, the company lost a then record-setting $567 million in the third quarter of 1980.

When the computations described above have been made, the trend percentages will appear as follows:

	1999	1998	1997	1996	1995	1994
Sales	150%	120%	110%	107%	104%	100%
Net income...............................	153%	97%	143%	128%	104%	100%

The trend percentages above indicate a very modest growth in sales in the early years and accelerated growth in 1998 and 1999. Net income also shows an increasing growth trend with the exception of the year 1998, when net income declined despite a solid increase in sales. This variation could have resulted from an unfavorable change in the gross profit margin or from unusual expenses. However, the problem was overcome in 1999 with a sharp rise in net income. Overall the trend percentages give a picture of a profitable growing enterprise.

As another example, assume that sales are increasing each year but that the cost of goods sold is increasing at a faster rate. This means that the gross profit margin is shrinking. Perhaps the increases in sales are being achieved through excessive price cutting. The company's net income may be declining even though sales are rising.

COMPONENT PERCENTAGES

Component percentages indicate the *relative size* of each item included in a total. For example, each item on a balance sheet could be expressed as a percentage of total assets. This shows quickly the relative importance of current and noncurrent assets as well as the relative amount of financing obtained from current creditors, long-term creditors, and stockholders. By computing component percentages for several successive balance sheets, we can see which items are increasing in importance and which are becoming less significant.

COMMON SIZE INCOME STATEMENT   Another application of component percentages is to express all items in an income statement as a percentage of net sales. Such a statement is called a common size income statement. A condensed income statement in dollars and in common size form follows:

Are the year-to-year
changes favorable?

Income Statement				
	Dollars		Component Percentages	
	1999	**1998**	**1999**	**1998**
Net sales	$1,000,000	$600,000	100.0%	100.0%
Cost of goods sold	700,000	360,000	70.0	60.0
Gross profit on sales	$ 300,000	$240,000	30.0%	40.0%
Expenses (including income taxes)	250,000	180,000	25.0	30.0
Net income	$ 50,000	$ 60,000	5.0%	10.0%

Looking only at the component percentages, we see that the decline in the gross profit rate from 40% to 30% was only partially offset by the decrease in expenses as a percentage of net sales, causing net income to decrease from 10% to 5% of net sales.

RATIOS

A ratio is a simple mathematical expression of the relationship of one item to another. Every percentage may be viewed as a ratio—that is, one number expressed as a percentage of another.

Ratios may be stated in several ways. To illustrate, let us consider the current ratio, which expresses the relationship between current assets and current liabilities. If current assets are $100,000 and current liabilities are $50,000, we may say either that the current ratio is 2 to 1 (which is written as 2:1) or that current assets are 200% of current liabilities. Either statement correctly summarizes the relationship—that is, that current assets are twice as large as current liabilities.

If a ratio is to be useful, the two amounts being compared must be logically related. Our interpretation of a ratio often requires investigation of the underlying data.

STANDARDS OF COMPARISON

In using dollar and percentage changes, trend percentages, component percentages, and ratios, financial analysts constantly search for some standard of comparison against which to judge whether the relationships they have found are favorable or unfavorable. Two such standards are (1) the past performance of the company and (2) the performance of other companies in the same industry.

PAST PERFORMANCE OF THE COMPANY Comparing analytical data for a current period with similar computations for prior years affords some basis for judging whether the condition of the business is improving or worsening. This comparison of data over time is sometimes called *horizontal,* or *trend,* analysis, to express the idea of reviewing data for a number of consecutive periods. It is distinguished from *vertical,* or *static,* analysis, which refers to the review of the financial information for only one accounting period.

In addition to determining whether the situation is improving or becoming worse, horizontal analysis may aid in making estimates of future prospects. Because changes may reverse their direction at any time, however, projecting past trends into the future always involves risk.

A weakness of horizontal analysis is that comparison with the past does not afford any basis for evaluation in absolute terms. The fact that net income was 2% of sales last year and is 3% of sales this year indicates improvement, but if there is evidence that net income *should be* 7% of sales, the record for both years is unfavorable.

INDUSTRY STANDARD The limitations of horizontal analysis may be overcome to some extent by finding appropriate benchmarks against which to measure a particular company's performance. The benchmarks most widely used by most analysts are the performance of comparable companies and the average performance of several companies in the same industry.[1]

Assume, for example, that the revenue of Alpha Airlines drops by 5% during the current year. If the revenue for the airlines industry had dropped an average of 15% during this year, Alpha's 5% decline might be viewed as a *favorable* performance. As another example, assume that Omega Co. earns a net income equal to 3% of net sales. This would be substandard if Omega were a manufacturer of commercial aircraft, but it would be satisfactory performance if it were a retail grocery chain.

When we compare a given company with its competitors or with industry averages, our conclusions will be valid only if the companies in question are reasonably comparable. Because of the large number of diversified companies formed in recent years, the term *industry* is difficult to define, and companies that fall roughly within the same industry may not be comparable in many respects. For example, one company may engage only in the marketing of oil products; another may be a fully integrated producer from the well to the gas pump, yet both are said to be in the "oil industry."

QUALITY OF EARNINGS

Profits are the lifeblood of a business entity. No entity can survive for long and accomplish its other goals unless it is profitable. Continuous losses drain assets from the business, consume owners' equity, and leave the company at the mercy of creditors. In assessing the prospects of a company, we are interested not only in the total *amount* of earnings but also in the *rate* of earnings on sales, on total assets, and on owners' equity. In addition, we must look at the *stability* and *source* of earnings. An erratic earnings performance over a period of years, for example, is less desirable than a steady level of earnings. A history of increasing earnings is preferable to a "flat" earnings record.

LO 4 *Discuss the "quality" of a company's earnings, assets, and working capital.*

A breakdown of sales and earnings by *major product lines* is useful in evaluating the future performance of a company. Publicly owned companies include with their financial statements supplementary schedules showing sales and profits by product line and by geographical area. These schedules assist financial analysts in forecasting the effect upon the company of changes in consumer demand for particular types of products.

Financial analysts often express the opinion that the earnings of one company are of higher quality than earnings of other similar companies. This concept of *quality of earnings* arises because each company's management can choose from a variety of accounting principles and methods, all of which are considered generally acceptable. A company's management often is under heavy pressure to report rising earnings, and accounting policies may be tailored toward this objective. We have already pointed out the impact on current reported earnings of the choice between the LIFO and FIFO methods of inventory valuation and the choice of depreciation policies. In judging the quality of earnings, the financial analyst should consider whether the accounting principles and methods selected by management lead to a conservative measurement of earnings or tend to inflate reported earnings.

QUALITY OF ASSETS AND THE RELATIVE AMOUNT OF DEBT

Although a satisfactory level of earnings may be a good indication of the company's long-run ability to pay its debts and dividends, we must also look at the composition of assets, their condition and liquidity, the relationship between current assets and current liabilities, and the total amount of debt outstanding. A company may be profitable and yet be unable to pay its liabilities on time; sales and earnings may appear satisfactory, but plant and equipment may be deteriorating because of poor maintenance policies; valuable patents may be expiring; substantial losses may be imminent due to slow-moving inventories and past-due receivables. Companies with large amounts of debt often are vulnerable to increases in interest rates and to even temporary reductions in cash inflows.

---

[1]Industry data are available from a number of sources. For example, Robert Morris Associates publishes *Annual Statement Studies* which include data from many thousands of annual reports, grouped into several hundred industry classifications. Industry classifications are subdivided further by company size. Dun & Bradstreet, Inc., annually publishes *Key Business Ratios* for more than 800 lines of business.

IMPACT OF INFLATION

During a period of significant inflation, financial statements prepared in terms of historical costs do not reflect fully the economic resources or the real income (in terms of purchasing power) of a business enterprise. The FASB recommends that companies include in their annual reports supplementary schedules showing the effects of inflation upon their financial statements. Inclusion of these supplementary disclosures is voluntary, not mandatory. Most companies do *not* include these supplementary schedules because of the high cost of developing this information.

ILLUSTRATIVE ANALYSIS FOR SEACLIFF COMPANY

Keep in mind the above discussion of analytical principles as you study the illustrative financial analysis which follows. The basic information for our analysis is contained in a set of condensed two-year comparative financial statements for Seacliff Company shown below and on the following pages. Summarized statement data, together with computations of dollar increases and decreases, and component percentages where applicable, have been compiled. For convenience in this illustration, relatively small dollar amounts have been used in the Seacliff Company financial statements.

Using the information in these statements, let us consider the kind of analysis that might be of particular interest to (1) common stockholders, (2) long-term creditors, and (3) short-term creditors.

			Increase or (Decrease)		Percentage of Net Sales	
SEACLIFF COMPANY **Comparative Income Statement** **For the Years Ended December 31, 1999 and December 31, 1998**						
	1999	**1998**	**Dollars**	**%**	**1999**	**1998**
Net sales	$900,000	$750,000	$150,000	20.0	100.0	100.0
Cost of goods sold	530,000	420,000	110,000	26.2	58.9	56.0
Gross profit on sales	$370,000	$330,000	$ 40,000	12.1	41.1	44.0
Operating expenses:						
Selling expenses	$117,000	$ 75,000	$ 42,000	56.0	13.0	10.0
General and administrative expenses	126,000	95,000	31,000	32.6	14.0	12.7
Total operating expenses	$243,000	$170,000	$ 73,000	42.9	27.0	22.7
Operating income	$127,000	$160,000	$ (33,000)	(20.6)	14.1	21.3
Interest expense	24,000	30,000	(6,000)	(20.0)	2.7	4.0
Income before income taxes	$103,000	$130,000	$ (27,000)	(20.8)	11.4	17.3
Income taxes	28,000	40,000	(12,000)	(30.0)	3.1	5.3
Net income	$ 75,000	$ 90,000	$ (15,000)	(16.7)	8.3	12.0
Earnings per share of common stock	$ 13.20	$ 20.25	$ (7.05)	(34.8)		

SEACLIFF COMPANY
Statement of Retained Earnings
For the Years Ended December 31, 1999 and December 31, 1998

	1999	1998	Increase or (Decrease) Dollars	%
Retained earnings, beginning of year	$176,000	$115,000	$61,000	53.0
Net income	75,000	90,000	(15,000)	(16.7)
	$251,000	$205,000	$46,000	22.4
Less: Dividends on common stock ($5.00 per share in 1996, $4.80 per share in 1999)	$ 24,000	$ 20,000	$ 4,000	20.0
Dividends on preferred stock ($9 per share)	9,000	9,000		
	$ 33,000	$ 29,000	$ 4,000	13.8
Retained earnings, end of year	$218,000	$176,000	$42,000	23.9

SEACLIFF COMPANY
Condensed Comparative Balance Sheet*
December 31, 1999 and December 31, 1998

Assets	1999	1998	Increase or (Decrease) Dollars	%	Percentage of Total Assets 1999	1998
Current assets	$390,000	$288,000	$102,000	35.4	41.1	33.5
Plant and equipment (net)	500,000	467,000	33,000	7.1	52.6	54.3
Other assets (loans to officers)	60,000	105,000	(45,000)	(42.9)	6.3	12.2
Total assets	$950,000	$860,000	$ 90,000	10.5	100.0	100.0
Liabilities & Stockholders' Equity						
Liabilities:						
Current liabilities	$112,000	$ 94,000	$ 18,000	19.1	11.8	10.9
12% long-term note payable (due in 7 years)	200,000	250,000	(50,000)	(20.0)	21.1	29.1
Total liabilities	$312,000	$344,000	$ (32,000)	(9.3)	32.9	40.0
Stockholders' equity:						
9% preferred stock, $100 par, callable at 105	$100,000	$100,000			10.5	11.6
Common stock, $50 par	250,000	200,000	$ 50,000	25.0	26.3	23.2
Additional paid-in capital	70,000	40,000	30,000	75.0	7.4	4.7
Retained earnings	218,000	176,000	42,000	23.9	22.9	20.5
Total stockholders' equity	$638,000	$516,000	$122,000	23.6	67.1	60.0
Total liabilities & stockholders' equity	$950,000	$860,000	$ 90,000	10.5	100.0	100.0

*In order to focus attention on important subtotals, this statement is highly condensed and does not show individual asset and liability items. These details will be introduced as needed in the next discussion. For example, a list of Seacliff Company's current assets and current liabilities appears on page G-16.

SEACLIFF COMPANY
Condensed Comparative Statement of Cash Flows
For the Years Ended December 31, 1999 and December 31, 1998

	1999	1998	Increase or (Decrease) Dollars	%
Cash flows from operating activities:				
Net cash flow from operating activities	$ 19,000	$ 95,000	$(76,000)	(80.0)
Cash flows from investing activities:				
Purchases of plant assets	(63,000)	(28,000)	(35,000)	125.0
Collections of loans from officers	45,000	(35,000)	80,000	N/A*
Net cash used by investing activities	$(18,000)	$(63,000)	$ 45,000	(71.4)
Cash flows from financing activities:				
Dividends paid	$(33,000)	$(29,000)	$ (4,000)	13.7
Repayment of long-term debt	(50,000)	–0–	(50,000)	N/A*
Proceeds from issuing capital stock	80,000	–0–	80,000	N/A*
Net cash used by financing activities	$ (3,000)	$(29,000)	$ 26,000	(89.7)
Net increase (decrease) in cash and cash equivalents	$ (2,000)	$ 3,000	$ (5,000)	N/A*
Cash and cash equivalents, beginning of the year	40,000	37,000	3,000	8.1
Cash and cash equivalents, end of the year	$ 38,000	$ 40,000	$ (2,000)	(5.0)

*N/A indicates that computation of the percentage change is not appropriate. Percentage changes cannot be determined if the base year is zero, or if a negative amount (cash outflow) changes to a positive amount (cash inflow).

SEACLIFF COMPANY
Notes to Financial Statements
For the Years Ended December 31, 1999 and December 31, 1998

Note 1—Accounting Policies
Inventories Inventories are valued by the LIFO method.
Depreciation Depreciation is computed by the straight-line method. Buildings are depreciated over 40 years, and equipment and fixtures over periods of 5 or 10 years.

Note 2—Unused Lines of Credit
The company has a confirmed line of credit in the amount of $35,000. None was in use at December 31, 1999.

Note 3—Contingencies and Commitments
As of December 31, 1999, the company has no material commitments or non-cancellable obligations. There currently are no loss contingencies known to management.

Note 4—Current Values of Financial Instruments
All financial instruments appear in the financial statements at dollar amounts that closely approximate their current values.

Note 5—Concentrations of Credit Risk
The company engages in retail sales to the general public from a single location in Seattle, Washington. No individual customer accounts for more than 2% of the company's total sales or accounts receivable. Accounts receivable are unsecured.

ANALYSIS BY COMMON STOCKHOLDERS

Common stockholders and potential investors in common stock look first at a company's earnings record. Their investment is in shares of stock, so *earnings per share and dividends per share* are of particular interest.

L0 5 *Analyze financial statements from the viewpoints of common stockholders, creditors, and others.*

EARNINGS PER SHARE OF COMMON STOCK   As indicated in Chapter 12, earnings per share of common stock are computed by dividing the income applicable to the common stock by the weighted-average number of shares of common stock outstanding during the year. Any preferred dividend requirements must be subtracted from net income to determine income applicable to common stock, as shown in the following computations for Seacliff Company:

Earnings per Share of Common Stock

		1999	1998
Net income		$75,000	$90,000
Less: Preferred dividend requirements		9,000	9,000
Income applicable to common stock...	(a)	$66,000	$81,000
Shares of common stock outstanding, during the year....................	(b)	5,000	4,000
Earnings per share of common stock (a ÷ b).................................		$13.20	$20.25

Earnings related to number of common shares outstanding

Notice that earnings per share have decreased by *$7.05* in 1999, representing a decline of nearly *35%* from their level in 1998 ($7.05 ÷ $20.25 = 34.8%). Common stockholders consider a decline in earnings per share to be an extremely unfavorable development. A decline in earnings per share generally represents a decline in the profitability of the company, and creates doubt as to the company's prospects for future growth.

With such a significant decline in earnings per share, we should expect to see a *substantial* decline in the market value of Seacliff's common stock during 1999. [For purposes of our illustration, we will assume the common stock had a market value of *$160* at December 31, 1998 and of *$132* at the end of 1999. This drop of $28 per share represents a *17½%* decline in the market value of every common stockholder's investment ($28 decline ÷ $160 = 17.5%).]

PRICE-EARNINGS RATIO   The relationship between the market price of common stock and earnings per share is so widely recognized that it is expressed as a ratio, called the price-earnings ratio (or p/e ratio). The p/e ratio is determined by dividing the market price per share by the annual earnings per share.

The average p/e ratio of the 30 stocks included in the Dow-Jones Industrial Average has varied widely in recent years, ranging from a low of about 10 to a high of about 18. The outlook for future earnings is the major factor influencing a company's p/e ratio. Companies with track records of rapid growth may sell at p/e ratios of perhaps 20 to 1, or even higher. Companies with "flat" earnings or earnings expected to decline in future years often sell at price-earnings ratios below, say, 10 to 1.

At the end of 1998, Seacliff's p/e ratio was approximately *8 to 1* ($160 ÷ $20.25 = 7.9), suggesting that investors *were expecting* earnings to decline in 1999. At December 31, 1999, the price earnings ratio was *10 to 1* ($132 ÷ $13.20 = 10.0). A p/e ratio in this range suggests that investors expect future earnings to stabilize around the current level.

DIVIDEND YIELD   Dividends are of prime importance to some stockholders, but a secondary factor to others. In other words, some stockholders invest primarily to receive regular cash income, while others invest in stocks principally with the hope of securing capital gains through rising market prices. If a corporation is profitable and retains its earnings for expansion of the business, the expanded operations should produce an increase in the net income of the company and thus tend to make each share of stock more valuable.

In comparing the merits of alternative investment opportunities, we should relate earnings and dividends per share to the *market value* of the stock. Dividends per share divided by market price per share determine the *yield* rate of a company's stock. Dividend yield is especially important to those investors whose objective is to maximize the dividend revenue from their investments.

SUMMARY OF EARNINGS AND DIVIDEND DATA FOR SEACLIFF The relationships of Seacliff's per-share earnings and dividends to its year-end stock prices are summarized below:

Earnings and Dividends per Share of Common Stock

Earnings and dividends
related to market price of
common stock

Date	Assumed Market Value per Share	Earnings per Share	Price-Earnings Ratio	Dividends per Share	Dividend Yield, %
Dec. 31, 1998	$160	$20.25	8	$5.00	3.1
Dec. 31, 1999	132	13.20	10	4.80	3.6

The decline in market value during 1999 presumably reflects the decreases in both earnings and dividends per share. Investors appraising this stock at December 31, 1999, should consider whether a price-earnings ratio of 10 and a dividend yield of 3.6% represent a satisfactory situation in the light of alternative investment opportunities. These investors will also place considerable weight on estimates of the company's prospective future earnings and the probable effect of such estimated earnings on the market price of the stock and on dividend payments.

REVENUE AND EXPENSE ANALYSIS The trend of earnings of Seacliff Company is unfavorable, and stockholders will want to know the reasons for the decline in net income. The comparative income statement on page G-8 shows that despite a 20% increase in net sales, net income fell from $90,000 in 1998 to $75,000 in 1999, a decline of 16.7%. As a percentage of net sales, net income fell from 12% to only 8.3%. The primary causes of this decline were the increases in selling expenses (56.0%), in general and administrative expenses (32.6%), and in the cost of goods sold (26.2%), all of which exceeded the 20% increase in net sales.

Let us assume that further investigation reveals Seacliff Company decided in 1999 to reduce its sales prices in an effort to generate greater sales volume. This would explain the decrease in gross profit rate from 44% to 41.1% of net sales. Since the dollar amount of gross profit increased $40,000 in 1999, the strategy of reducing sales prices to increase volume would have been successful if there had been little or no increase in operating expenses. However, operating expenses rose by $73,000, resulting in a $33,000 decrease in operating income.

The next step is to find which expenses increased and why. An investor may be handicapped here, because detailed operating expenses are not usually shown in published financial statements. Some conclusions, however, can be reached on the basis of even the condensed information available in the comparative income statement for Seacliff Company shown on page G-8.

The substantial increase in selling expenses presumably reflects greater selling effort during 1999 in an attempt to improve sales volume. However, the fact that selling expenses increased $42,000 while gross profit increased only $40,000 indicates that the cost of this increased sales effort was not justified in terms of results. Even more disturbing is the increase in general and administrative expenses. Some growth in administrative expenses might be expected to accompany increased sales volume, but because some of the expenses are fixed, the growth generally should be *less than proportional* to any increase in sales. The increase in general and administrative expenses from 12.7% to 14% of sales would be of serious concern to informed investors.

Management generally has greater control over operating expenses than over revenue. The *operating expense ratio* is often used as a measure of management's ability to control its operating expenses. The unfavorable trend in this ratio for Seacliff Company is shown below:

Operating Expense Ratio

Does a higher operating
expense ratio indicate
higher net income?

	1999	1998
Operating expenses...	(a) $243,000	$170,000
Net sales	(b) $900,000	$750,000
Operating expense ratio (a ÷ b)...	27.0%	22.7%

If management were able to increase the sales volume while at the same time increasing the gross profit rate and decreasing the operating expense ratio, the effect on net income could be quite dramatic. For example, if in the year 2000 Seacliff Company can increase its sales by 11% to $1,000,000, increase its gross profit rate from 41.1 to 44%, and reduce the operating expense ratio from 27 to 24%, its operating income will increase from $127,000 to $200,000 ($1,000,000 − $560,000 − $240,000), an increase of over 57%.

RETURN ON INVESTMENT (ROI)

The rate of return on investment (often called ROI) is a measure of management's efficiency in using available resources. Regardless of the size of the organization, capital is a scarce resource and must be used efficiently. In judging the performance of branch managers or of companywide management, it is reasonable to raise the question: What rate of return have you earned on the resources under your control? The concept of return on investment can be applied to a number of situations: for example, evaluating a branch, a total business, a product line, or an individual investment.

A number of different ratios have been developed for the ROI concept, each well suited to a particular situation. In Chapter 6 we explained and illustrated the two most common ROI measurements: *return on assets,* and *return on stockholders' equity.*

RETURN ON ASSETS An important test of management's ability to earn a return on funds supplied from all sources is the rate of return on total assets.

The income figure used in computing this ratio should be *operating income,* since interest expense and income taxes are determined by factors other than the efficient use of resources. Operating income is earned throughout the year and therefore should be related to the *average* investment in assets during the year. The computation of this ratio of Seacliff Company is shown below:

Percentage Return on Assets

	1999	1998	
Operating income	(a) $127,000	$160,000	Earnings related to investment in assets
Total assets, beginning of year	(b) $860,000	$820,000	
Total assets, end of year	(c) $950,000	$860,000	
Average investment in assets [(b ÷ c) ÷ 2]	(d) $905,000	$840,000	
Return on assets (a ÷ d)	14%	19%	

This ratio shows that the rate of return earned on the company's assets has fallen off in 1999. Before drawing conclusions as to the effectiveness of Seacliff's management, however, we should consider the trend in the return on assets earned by other companies of similar kind and size.

RETURN ON COMMON STOCKHOLDERS' EQUITY We introduced the concept of return on equity using a company that had only one class of capital stock. Therefore, the return on equity was simply net income divided by average stockholders' equity. But Seacliff has issued both preferred stock *and* common stock. The preferred stock does not participate fully in the company's prosperity; rather, the "return" to preferred stockholders is limited to their dividend. Thus, we must adjust the "return on equity" computation to reflect the return on *common* stockholders' equity.

The return to common stockholders is equal to net income *less* any preferred dividends. Thus, the return on common stockholders equity is computed as follows:

Return on Common Stockholders' Equity

	1999	1998	
Net income	$ 75,000	$ 90,000	Does the use of leverage benefit common stockholders?
Less: Preferred dividend requirements	9,000	9,000	
Net income applicable to common stock	(a) $ 66,000	$ 81,000	
Common stockholders' equity, beginning of year	(b) $416,000	$355,000	
Common stockholders' equity, end of year	(c) $538,000	$416,000	
Average common stockholders' equity [(b ÷ c) ÷ 2]	(d) $477,000	$385,500	
Return on common stockholders' equity (a ÷ d)	13.8%	21.0%	

In both years, the rate of return on common stockholders' equity was higher than the 12% rate of interest paid to long-term creditors or the 9% dividend rate paid to preferred stockholders. This result was achieved through the favorable use of leverage.

LEVERAGE

We introduced the concept of leverage in Chapter 10. Basically, applying leverage means operating a business with borrowed money. If the borrowed capital can be used in the business to earn a return *greater* than the cost of borrowing, then the net income and the return on common stockholders' equity will *increase*. In other words, if you can borrow money at 12% and use it to earn 20%, you will benefit by doing so. However, leverage can act as a double-edged sword; the effects may be favorable or unfavorable to the holders of common stock.

If the rate of return on total assets should fall *below* the average rate of interest on borrowed capital, leverage will *reduce* net income and the return on common stockholders' equity. In this situation, paying off the loans that carry high interest rates would appear to be a logical move. However, most companies do not have enough cash to retire long-term debt on short notice. Therefore, the common stockholders may become locked in to the unfavorable effects of leverage.

In deciding how much leverage is appropriate, the common stockholders should consider the *stability* of the company's return on assets as well as the relationship of this return to the average cost of borrowed capital. If a business incurs so much debt that it becomes unable to meet the required interest and principal payments, the creditors may force liquidation or reorganization of the business.

DEBT RATIO   One indicator of the amount of leverage used by a business is the debt ratio. This ratio measures the proportion of the total assets financed by creditors, as distinguished from stockholders. It is computed by dividing total liabilities by total assets. A *high* debt ratio indicates an extensive use of leverage, that is, a large proportion of financing provided by creditors. A low debt ratio, on the other hand, indicates that the business is making little use of leverage.

The debt ratio at year-end for Seacliff is determined as follows:

Debt Ratio

		1999	1998
Total liabilities	(a)	$312,000	$344,000
Total assets (or total liabilities & stockholders' equity)	(b)	$950,000	$860,000
Debt ratio (a ÷ b)		32.8%	40.0%

Proportion of assets financed by creditors

Seacliff Company has a lower debt ratio in 1999 than in 1998. Is this favorable or unfavorable?

From the viewpoint of the common stockholder, a high debt ratio will produce maximum benefits if management is able to earn a rate of return on assets greater than the rate of interest paid to creditors. However, a high debt ratio can be very *unfavorable* if the return on assets falls *below* the rate of interest paid to creditors. Since the return on total assets earned by Seacliff Company has declined from 19% in 1998 to a relatively low 14% in 1999, the common stockholders probably would *not* want to risk a high debt ratio. The action by management in 1999 of retiring $50,000 in long-term liabilities will help to protect the common stockholders from the unfavorable effects of leverage if the rate of return on assets continues to decline.

ANALYSIS BY LONG-TERM CREDITORS

Bondholders and other long-term creditors are primarily interested in three factors: (1) the rate of return on their investment, (2) the firm's ability to meet its interest requirements, and (3) the firm's ability to repay the principal of the debt when it falls due.

YIELD RATE ON BONDS   The yield rate on bonds or other long-term indebtedness cannot be computed in the same manner as the yield rate on shares of stock, because bonds, unlike stocks, have a definite maturity date and amount. The ownership of a 12%, 10-year, $1,000 bond represents the right to receive $120 each year for 10 years plus the right to receive $1,000 at the end of 10 years. If the market price of this bond is $950, the yield rate on an investment in the bond is the rate of interest that will make the *present value* of these two contractual rights equal to the $950 market price.

When bonds sell at maturity value, the yield rate is equal to the bond interest rate. *The yield rate varies inversely with changes in the market price of the bond.* If interest rates rise, the market price of existing bonds will fall; if interest rates decline, the price of bonds will rise. If the price of a bond is above maturity value, the yield rate is less than the bond interest rate; if the price of a bond is below maturity value, the yield rate is higher than the bond interest rate.

INTEREST COVERAGE RATIO Bondholders feel that their investments are relatively safe if the issuing company earns enough income to cover its annual interest obligations by a wide margin.

A common measure of creditors' safety is the ratio of operating income available for the payment of interest to the annual interest expense, called the *interest coverage ratio.* This computation for Seacliff Company would be:

Interest Coverage Ratio

	1999	1998	
Operating income (before interest and income taxes)	(a) $127,000	$160,000	Long-term creditors watch
Annual interest expense	(b) $ 24,000	$ 30,000	this ratio
Interest coverage (a ÷ b)	5.3 times	5.3 times	

The ratio remained unchanged at a satisfactory level during 1999. A ratio of 5.3 times interest earned would be considered strong in many industries. In the electric utilities industry, for example, the interest coverage ratio for the leading companies presently averages about 3, with the ratios of individual companies varying from 2 to 6.

DEBT RATIO Long-term creditors are interested in the percentage of total assets financed by debt, as distinguished from the percentage financed by stockholders. The percentage of total assets financed by debt is measured by the debt ratio, which was computed on the preceding page.

From a creditor's viewpoint, the lower the debt ratio the better, since this means that stockholders have contributed the bulk of the funds to the business, and therefore the margin of protection to creditors against a shrinkage of the assets is high.

SECURED CLAIMS Sometimes the claims of long-term creditors are secured with specific collateral, such as the land and buildings owned by the borrower. In these situations, the secured creditors may look primarily to the *value of the collateral* in assessing the safety of their claims.

Assets pledged as collateral to secure specific liabilities are disclosed in notes to the financial statements. As Seacliff makes no such disclosures, we may assume that none of its assets have been pledged as collateral to secure specific liabilities.

ANALYSIS BY SHORT-TERM CREDITORS

Bankers and other short-term creditors share the interest of stockholders and bondholders in the profitability and long-run stability of a business. Their primary interest, however, is in the current position of the firm—its ability to generate sufficient funds (working capital) to meet current operating needs and to pay current debts promptly. Thus the analysis of financial statements by a banker considering a short-term loan, or by a trade creditor investigating the credit status of a customer, is likely to center on the working capital position of the prospective debtor.

AMOUNT OF WORKING CAPITAL The details of the working capital of Seacliff Company are:

			Increase or (Decrease)		Percentage of Total Current Items	
	1999	**1998**	**Dollars**	**%**	**1999**	**1998**
SEACLIFF COMPANY						
Comparative Schedule of Working Capital						
As of December 31, 1999 and December 31, 1998						
Current assets:						
Cash	$ 38,000	$ 40,000	$ (2,000)	(5.0)	9.7	13.9
Receivables (net)	117,000	86,000	31,000	36.0	30.0	29.9
Inventories	180,000	120,000	60,000	50.0	46.2	41.6
Prepaid expenses	55,000	42,000	13,000	31.0	14.1	14.6
Total current assets	$390,000	$288,000	$102,000	35.4	100.0	100.0
Current liabilities:						
Notes payable to creditors	$ 14,600	$ 10,000	$ 4,600	46.0	13.1	10.7
Accounts payable	66,000	30,000	36,000	120.0	58.9	31.9
Accrued liabilities	31,400	54,000	(22,600)	(41.9)	28.0	57.4
Total current liabilities	$112,000	$ 94,000	$ 18,000	19.1	100.0	100.0
Working capital	$278,000	$194,000	$ 84,000	43.3		

The amount of working capital is measured by the *excess of current assets over current liabilities*. Thus, working capital represents the amount of cash, near-cash items, and cash substitutes (prepayments) on hand after providing for payment of all current liabilities.

This schedule shows that current assets increased $102,000, while current liabilities rose by only $18,000, with the result that working capital increased $84,000.

QUALITY OF WORKING CAPITAL In evaluating the debt-paying ability of a business, short-term creditors should consider the quality of working capital as well as the total dollar amount. The principal factors affecting the quality of working capital are (1) the nature of the current assets and (2) the length of time required to convert these assets into cash.

The preceding schedule shows an unfavorable shift in the composition of Seacliff Company's working capital during 1999; cash decreased from 13.9% to 9.7% of current assets, while inventory rose from 41.6% to 46.2%. Inventory is a less liquid resource than cash. Therefore, the quality of working capital is not as liquid as in 1998. *Turnover rates* (or *ratios*) may be used to assist short-term creditors in estimating the time required to turn assets such as receivables and inventory into cash.

ACCOUNTS RECEIVABLE TURNOVER RATE As explained in Chapter 7, the accounts receivable turnover rate indicates how quickly a company converts its accounts receivable into cash. The accounts receivable turnover *rate* is determined by dividing net sales by the average balance of accounts receivable.[2] The number of *days* required (on average) to collect accounts receivable then may be determined by dividing the number of days in a year (365) by the turnover rate. These computations follow using the data in our Seacliff example:

---

[2]Ideally, the accounts receivable turnover is computed by dividing net *credit* sales by the *monthly* average of receivables. Such detailed information, however, generally is not provided in annual financial statements.

Accounts Receivable Turnover

		1999	1998
Net sales	(a)	$900,000	$750,000
Receivables, beginning of year		$ 86,000	$ 80,000
Receivables, end of year		$117,000	$ 86,000
Average receivables	(b)	$101,500	$ 83,000
Receivable turnover per year (a ÷ b)		8.9 times	9.0 times
Average number of days to collect receivables (divide 365 days by receivable turnover)		41 days	41 days

Are customers paying promptly?

There has been no significant change in the average time required to collect receivables. The interpretation of the average age of receivables depends upon the company's credit terms and the seasonal activity immediately before year-end. For example, if the company grants 30-day credit terms to its customers, the above analysis indicates that accounts receivable collections are lagging. If the terms are for 60 days, however, collections are being made ahead of schedule.

INVENTORY TURNOVER RATE   The inventory turnover rate indicates how many times during the year the company is able to sell a quantity of goods equal to its average inventory. Mechanically, this rate is determined by dividing the cost of goods sold for the year by the average amount of inventory on hand during the year. The number of days required to sell this amount of inventory may be determined by dividing 365 days by the turnover rate. These computations were explained in Chapter 8, and are demonstrated below using the data of Seacliff Company:

Inventory Turnover

		1999	1998
Cost of goods sold	(a)	$530,000	$420,000
Inventory, beginning of year		$120,000	$100,000
Inventory, end of year		$180,000	$120,000
Average inventory	(b)	$150,000	$110,000
Average inventory turnover per year (a ÷ b)		3.5 times	3.8 times
Average number of days to sell inventory (divide 365 days by inventory turnover)		104 days	96 days

The trend indicated by this analysis is unfavorable, since the length of time required for Seacliff to turn over (sell) its inventory is increasing.

Companies that have low gross profit rates often need high inventory turnover rates in order to operate profitably. This is merely another way of saying that if the gross profit rate is low, a high volume of transactions is necessary to produce a satisfactory amount of profits. Companies that sell high markup items, such as jewelry stores and art galleries, can operate successfully with much lower inventory turnover rates.

OPERATING CYCLE   The inventory turnover rate indicates how quickly inventory *sells*, but not how quickly this asset converts into *cash*. Short-term creditors, of course, are interested primarily in the company's ability to generate cash.

The period of time required for a merchandising company to convert its inventory into cash is called the *operating cycle*. The next illustration appeared in Chapter 5, but is repeated on the following page for your convenience.

Seacliff's operating cycle in 1999 was approximately 145 days, computed by adding the 104 days required to turn over inventory and the average 41 days required to collect receivables. This compares to an operating cycle of only 137 days in 1998, computed as 96 days to dispose of the inventory plus 41 days to collect the resulting receivables. From the viewpoint of short-term creditors, the *shorter* the operating cycle, the *higher the quality* of the borrower's working capital. Therefore, these creditors would regard the lengthening of Seacliff Company's operating cycle as an unfavorable trend.

The operating cycle repeats continuously

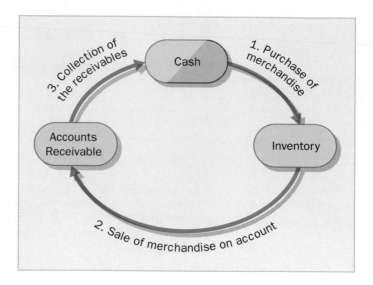

CURRENT RATIO The current ratio (current assets divided by current liabilities) expresses the relationship between current assets and current liabilities. As debts come due, they must be paid out of current assets. Therefore, short-term creditors frequently compare the amount of current assets with the amount of current liabilities. The current ratio indicates a company's short-run, debt-paying ability. It is a measure of liquidity and of solvency. A strong current ratio provides considerable assurance that a company will be able to meet its obligations coming due in the near future. The current ratio for Seacliff Company is computed as follows:

Current Ratio

		1999	1998
Total current assets	(a)	$390,000	$288,000
Total current liabilities	(b)	$112,000	$ 94,000
Current ratio (a ÷ b)		3.5	3.1

Does this indicate satisfactory debt-paying ability?

A widely used rule of thumb is that a current ratio of 2 to 1 or better is satisfactory. By this standard, Seacliff Company's current ratio appears quite strong. Creditors tend to feel that the higher the current ratio the better. From a managerial point of view, however, there is an upper limit. Too high a current ratio may indicate that capital is not being used productively in the business.

QUICK RATIO Because inventories and prepaid expenses are further removed from conversion into cash than other current assets, a statistic known as the *quick ratio* is sometimes computed as a supplement to the current ratio. The quick ratio compares the highly liquid current assets (cash, marketable securities, and receivables) with current liabilities. Seacliff Company has no marketable securities; its quick ratio is computed as follows:

Quick Ratio

		1999	1998
Quick assets (cash and receivables)	(a)	$155,000	$126,000
Current liabilities	(b)	$112,000	$ 94,000
Quick ratio (a ÷ b)		1.4	1.3

A measure of liquidity

Here again the analysis reveals a favorable trend and a strong position. If the credit periods extended to customers and granted by creditors are roughly equal, a quick ratio of 1.0 or better is considered satisfactory.

UNUSED LINES OF CREDIT   From the viewpoint of a short-term creditor, a company's unused lines of credit represent a resource almost as liquid as cash. An unused line of credit means that a bank has agreed in advance to lend the company any amount, up to the specified limit. As long as this line of credit remains available, creditors know that the business can borrow cash quickly and easily for any purpose, including payments of creditors' claims.

Existing unused lines of credit are *disclosed* in notes accompanying the financial statements. Short-term creditors would view Seacliff's $35,000 line of credit (Note 2 to the financial statements) as *significantly* enhancing the company's liquidity.

CASH FLOW ANALYSIS

We often have stressed the importance of a company being able to generate sufficient cash flow from its operations. In 1998, Seacliff generated a net cash flow of $95,000 from its operating activities—a relatively "normal" amount, considering that net income for the year was $90,000. This $95,000 net cash flow remained *after* payment of interest to creditors and amounted to more than three times the dividends paid to stockholders. Thus, in 1998 the net cash flow from operating activities appeared quite sufficient to ensure that Seacliff could pay its interest obligations and also pay dividends.

In 1999, however, net cash flow from operating activities declined to only $19,000, an amount far below the company's $75,000 net income and less than one-half of the amount of dividends paid. Stockholders and creditors alike would view this dramatic decline in cash flow as a negative and potentially dangerous development.

A reconciliation of Seacliff's net income in 1999 with its net cash flow from operating activities is shown below:

Net income		$ 75,000	Why was the cash flow from operations so low?
Add:			
Depreciation expense	$30,000		
Increase in notes payable to suppliers	4,600		
Increase in accounts payable	36,000	70,600	
		$145,600	
Less:			
Increase in accounts receivable	$31,000		
Increase in inventories	60,000		
Increase in prepaid expenses	13,000		
Decrease in accrued liabilities	22,600	126,600	
Net cash flow from operating activities		$ 19,000	

(As explained in Chapter 13, the FASB requires companies to provide this type of reconciliation either in the statement of cash flows or in a supplemental schedule.)

The primary reasons for Seacliff's low net operating cash flow appear to be the growth in uncollected accounts receivable and inventories, and the substantial reduction in accrued liabilities. Given the significant increase in sales during 1999, the increase in accounts receivable is to be expected. The large reduction in accrued liabilities probably is a one-time event, not likely to recur next year. The large increase in inventory, however, may have reduced Seacliff's liquidity unnecessarily.

Seacliff's financial position would appear considerably stronger if its increased sales volume were supported by a higher *inventory turnover rate,* instead of a larger inventory.

USEFULNESS OF NOTES TO FINANCIAL STATEMENTS

A set of financial statements normally is accompanied by several pages of *notes,* disclosing information useful in *interpreting* the statements. Users should view these notes as an *integral part* of the financial statements.

In preceding chapters we have identified many items which are disclosed in notes accompanying the financial statements. Among the most useful disclosures are:

● Accounting policies and methods.
● Unused lines of credit.

- Significant commitments and loss contingencies.
- Current values of financial instruments (if different from the carrying values shown in the statements).
- Dividends in arrears.
- Concentrations of credit risk.
- Assets pledged to secure specific liabilities.

The notes accompanying Seacliff's financial statements are quite "clean"—that is, they contain no surprises or cause for concern. Of course, the unused line of credit disclosed in Note 2 would be of interest to anyone evaluating the company's short-term debt-paying ability.

LO 6 *Compute the ratios widely used in financial statement analysis and explain the significance of each.*

SUMMARY OF ANALYTICAL MEASUREMENTS

The concluding component of this appendix is a summary of most of the financial statement ratios and measurements discussed in this textbook. Included is a brief description of each measurement's significance. (Page references are to our initial discussion of each measurement.)

Bear in mind that the significance of any financial measurement depends both upon its (1) trend over time, and (2) relationship to some logical benchmark, such as industry averages or measurements within similar companies.

Ratio or Other Measurement	Method of Computation	Significance
Measures of short-term solvency		
Current ratio (p. 259)	$\dfrac{\text{Current assets}}{\text{Current liabilities}}$	A measure of short-term debt-paying ability
Quick ratio (p. 259)	$\dfrac{\text{Quick assets}}{\text{Current liabilities}}$	A measure of short-term debt-paying ability
Working capital (p. 259)	Current assets less Current liabilities	A measure of short-term debt-paying ability
Net cash provided by operating activities (p. 272)	Appears in the statement of cash flows	Indicates the cash generated by operations after allowing for cash payment of expenses and operating liabilities
Receivables turnover rate (p. 329)	$\dfrac{\text{Net sales}}{\text{Average accounts receivable}}$	Indicates how quickly receivables are collected
Days to collect average accounts receivable (p. 329)	$\dfrac{365 \text{ days}}{\text{Receivables turnover rate}}$	Indicates in days how quickly receivables are collected
Inventory turnover rate (p. 385)	$\dfrac{\text{Cost of goods sold}}{\text{Average inventory}}$	Indicates how quickly inventory sells
Days to sell the average inventory (p. 386)	$\dfrac{365 \text{ days}}{\text{Inventory turnover rate}}$	Indicates in days how quickly inventory sells
Operating cycle (p. 386)	Days to sell inventory plus days to collect receivables	Indicates in days how quickly inventory converts into cash
Free cash flow (p. 627)	Net cash from operating activities less cash used for investing activities and dividends	Excess of operating cash flow over basic needs

Ratio or Other Measurement	Method of Computation	Significance
Measures of long-term credit risk		
Debt ratio (p. 260)	$$\frac{\text{Total liabilities}}{\text{Total assets}}$$	Percentage of assets financed by creditors; indicates relative size of the equity position
Trend in net cash provided by operating activities (p. 485)	Appears in comparative statements of cash flows	Indicator of a company's ability to generate the cash necessary to meet its obligations
Interest coverage ratio (p. 488)	$$\frac{\text{Operating income}}{\text{Annual interest expense}}$$	Indicator of a company's ability to meet its interest payment obligations
Measures of profitability		
Percentage changes; i.e., in net sales and net income (p. 265)	$$\frac{\text{Dollar amount of change}}{\text{Financial statement amount in the earlier year}}$$	The rate at which a key measure is increasing or decreasing; the "growth rate"
Gross profit rate (p. 229)	$$\frac{\text{Dollar gross profit}}{\text{Net sales}}$$	A measure of the profitability of the company's products
Operating expense ratio (p. G-12)	$$\frac{\text{Operating expenses}}{\text{Net sales}}$$	A measure of management's ability to control expenses
Operating income (p. 264)	Gross profit less operating expenses	The profitability of a company's "basic" business activities
Net income as a percentage of net sales (p. G-1)	$$\frac{\text{Net income}}{\text{Net sales}}$$	An indicator of management's ability to control costs
Earnings per share (p. 267)	$$\frac{\text{Net income less preferred dividends}}{\text{Average number of common shares outstanding}}$$	Net income applicable to each share of common stock
Return on assets (p. 270)	$$\frac{\text{Operating income}}{\text{Average total assets}}$$	A measure of the productivity of assets, regardless of how the assets are financed
Return on equity (p. 270)	$$\frac{\text{Net income}}{\text{Average total equity}}$$	The rate of return earned upon the stockholders' equity in the business
Return on common stockholders' equity (p. G-13)	$$\frac{\text{Net income less preferred dividends}}{\text{Average common stockholders' equity}}$$	The rate of return earned upon the common stockholders' equity. (Appropriate when company has both common and preferred stock)
Measures for evaluating the current market price of common stock		
Market value of financial instruments (p. 307)	Quoted in financial press or disclosed in financial statements	Reflects both investors' expectations and current market conditions
Price-earnings ratio (p. 268)	$$\frac{\text{Current stock price}}{\text{Earnings per share}}$$	A measure of investors' enthusiasm about the company's future prospects
Dividend yield (p. 539)	$$\frac{\text{Annual dividend}}{\text{Current stock price}}$$	Dividends expressed as a rate of return on the market price of the stock
Book value per share (p. 537)	$$\frac{\text{Common stockholders' equity}}{\text{Shares of common stock outstanding}}$$	The recorded value of net assets underlying each share of common stock

ASSIGNMENT MATERIAL

DISCUSSION QUESTIONS

1. **a.** What groups are interested in the financial affairs of publicly owned corporations?
   b. List some of the more important sources of financial information for investors.

2. In financial statement analysis, what is the basic objective of observing trends in data and ratios? Suggest some other standards of comparison.

3. In financial statement analysis, what information is produced by computing a ratio that is not available in a simple observation of the underlying data?

4. Distinguish between *trend percentages* and *component percentages*. Which would be better suited to analyzing the change in sales over a term of several years?

5. "Although net income declined this year as compared with last year, it increased from 3% to 5% of net sales." Are sales increasing or decreasing?

6. Differentiate between *horizontal* and *vertical* analysis.

7. Assume that Chemco Corporation is engaged in the manufacture and distribution of a variety of chemicals. In analyzing the financial statements of this corporation, why would you want to refer to the ratios and other measurements of companies in the chemical industry? In comparing the financial results of Chemco Corporation with another chemical company, why would you be interested in the accounting principles used by the two companies?

8. Explain how the following accounting practices will tend to raise or lower the quality of a company's earnings. (Assume the continuance of inflation.)
   a. Adoption of an accelerated depreciation method rather than straight-line depreciation.
   b. Adoption of FIFO rather than LIFO for the valuation of inventories.
   c. Adoption of a 7-year life rather than a 10-year life for the depreciation of equipment.

9. What single ratio do you think should be of greatest interest to:
   a. A banker considering a short-term loan?
   b. A common stockholder?
   c. An insurance company considering a long-term mortgage loan?

10. Modern Company earned a 16% return on its total assets. Current liabilities are 10% of total assets. Long-term bonds carrying a 11% coupon rate are equal to 30% of total assets. There is no preferred stock. Is this application of leverage favorable or unfavorable from the viewpoint of Modern Company's stockholders?

11. In deciding whether a company's debt ratio is favorable or unfavorable, creditors and stockholders may have different views. Why?

12. Ahi Co. has a current ratio of 3 to 1. Ono Corp. has a current ratio of 2 to 1. Does this mean that Ahi's operating cycle is longer than Ono's? Why?

13. An investor states, "I bought this stock for $50 several years ago and it now sells for $100. It paid $5 per share in dividends last year so I'm earning 10% on my investment." Criticize this statement.

14. Alpine Products experiences a considerable seasonal variation in its business. The high point in the year's activity comes in November, the low point in July. During which month would you expect the company's current ratio to be higher? If the company were choosing a fiscal year for accounting purposes, what advise would you give?

15. Is the rate of return on investment (ROI) intended primarily to measure liquidity, solvency, or some other aspect of business operations? Explain.

16. Under what circumstances would you consider a corporate net income of $1 million for the year as being unreasonably low? Under what circumstances would you consider a corporate profit of $1 million as being unreasonably high?

EXERCISES

EXERCISE G-1
Percentage Changes

LO 3

Selected information taken from financial statements of Lopez Company for two successive years follows. You are to compute the percentage change from 1998 to 1999 whenever possible.

	1999	1998
a. Accounts receivable	$126,000	$150,000
b. Marketable securities	–0–	250,000
c. Retained earnings	80,000	(80,000)
d. Notes receivable	120,000	–0–
e. Notes payable	860,000	800,000
f. Cash	82,400	80,000
g. Sales	990,000	900,000

EXERCISE G-2
Intuition versus
Calculation

Tait Corporation had net income of $4 million in its first year. In the second year, net income decreased by 75%. In the third year, due to an improved business environment, net income increased by 250%.

a. Prior to making any computations, do you think Tait's net income was higher or lower in the third year than in the first year?

b. Compute Tait's net income for the second year and for the third year. Do your computations support your initial response in part **a?**

EXERCISE G-3
Trend Percentages

Compute *trend percentages* for the following items taken from the financial statements of Water-Wise Plumbing Fixtures over a five-year period. Treat 1995 as the base year. State whether the trends are favorable or unfavorable. (Dollar amounts are stated in thousands.)

	1999	1998	1997	1996	1995
Sales	$85,000	$74,000	$61,500	$59,000	$50,000
Cost of goods sold	$58,500	$48,000	$40,500	$36,000	$30,000

EXERCISE G-4
Common Size Income
Statements

Prepare *common size* income statements for Toyoda Company, a sole proprietorship, for the two years shown below by converting the dollar amounts into percentages. For each year, sales will appear as 100% and other items will be expressed as a percentage of sales. (Income taxes are not involved as the business is not incorporated.) Comment on whether the changes from 1998 to 1999 are favorable or unfavorable.

	1999	1998
Sales	$500,000	$400,000
Cost of goods sold	330,000	268,000
Gross profit	$170,000	$132,000
Operating expenses	140,000	116,000
Net income	$ 30,000	$ 16,000

EXERCISE G-5
Ratios for a Retail Store

Selected financial data for Vashon's, a retail store, appear below.

	1999	1998
Sales (all on account)	$750,000	$600,000
Cost of goods sold	495,000	408,000
Average inventory during the year	110,000	102,000
Average receivables during the year	150,000	100,000

a. Compute the following for both years:
  1. Gross profit percentage
  2. Inventory turnover
  3. Accounts receivable turnover

b. Comment upon favorable and unfavorable trends.

EXERCISE G-6
Computing Ratios

A condensed balance sheet for Durham Corporation prepared at the end of the year appears below.

Assets		Liabilities & Stockholders' Equity	
Cash..	$ 55,000	Notes payable (due in 6	
Accounts receivable.................	155,000	months)..................................	$ 40,000
Inventory	270,000	Accounts payable.....................	110,000
Prepaid expenses	60,000	Long-term liabilities.................	330,000
Plant & equipment (net)............	570,000	Capital stock, $5 par................	300,000
Other assets	90,000	Retained earnings....................	420,000
Total......................................	$1,200,000	Total.......................................	$1,200,000

During the year the company earned a gross profit of $1,116,000 on sales of $2,790,000. Accounts receivable, inventory, and plant assets remained almost constant in amount throughout the year.

Compute the following:

a. Current ratio

b. Quick ratio

c. Working capital

d. Debt ratio

e. Accounts receivable turnover (all sales were on credit)

f. Inventory turnover

g. Book value per share of capital stock

EXERCISE G-7
Current Ratio, Debt Ratio, and Earnings per Share

Selected items from successive annual reports of Hastings, Inc., appear below.

	1999	1998
Total assets (40% of which are current)	$400,000	$325,000
Current liabilities	$ 80,000	$100,000
Bonds payable, 12%...	100,000	50,000
Capital stock, $5 par value..	100,000	100,000
Retained earnings	120,000	75,000
Total liabilities & stockholders' equity...	$400,000	$325,000

Dividends of $26,000 were declared and paid in 1999.

Compute the following:

a. Current ratio for 1999 and 1998

b. Debt ratio for 1999 and 1998

c. Earnings per share for 1999

EXERCISE G-8
Ratio Analysis for Two Similar Companies

Selected data from the financial statements of Italian Marble Co. and Toro Stone Products for the year just ended follow. Assume that for both companies dividends declared were equal in amount to net earnings during the year and therefore stockholders' equity did not change. The two companies are in the same line of business.

	Italian Marble Co.	Toro Stone Products
Total liabilities...	$ 200,000	$ 100,000
Total assets	800,000	400,000
Sales (all on credit)...	1,800,000	1,200,000
Average inventory	240,000	140,000
Average receivables...	200,000	100,000
Gross profit as a percentage of sales..	40%	30%
Operating expenses as a percentage of sales	36%	25%
Net income as a percentage of sales	4%	5%

Compute the following for each company:

a. Net income

b. Net income as a percentage of stockholders' equity

c. Accounts receivable turnover

d. Inventory turnover

PROBLEMS

PROBLEM G-1
Analysis to Identify
Favorable and Unfavorable
Trends

 LO 1,3,5,6

The following information was developed from the financial statements of Custom Logos, Inc. At the beginning of 1999, the company's former supplier went bankrupt, and the company began buying merchandise from another supplier.

	1999	1998
Gross profit on sales	$1,008,000	$1,134,000
Income before income taxes	230,400	252,000
Net income	172,800	189,000
Net income as a percentage of net sales	6.0%	7.5%

INSTRUCTIONS

a. Compute the net sales for each year.

b. Compute the cost of goods sold in dollars and as a percentage of net sales for each year.

c. Compute operating expenses in dollars and as a percentage of net sales for each year. (Income taxes expense is not an operating expense.)

d. Prepare a condensed comparative income statement for 1998 and 1999. Include the following items: net sales, cost of goods sold, gross profit, operating expenses, income before income taxes, income taxes expense, and net income. Omit earnings per share statistics.

e. Identify the significant favorable and unfavorable trends in the performance of Custom Logos, Inc. Comment on any unusual changes.

PROBLEM G-2
Comparing Operating
Results with Average
Performance in the Industry

 LO 3,5

Sub Zero, Inc., manufactures camping equipment. Shown below for the current year are the income statement for the company and a common size summary for the industry in which the company operates. (Notice that the percentages in the right-hand column are *not* for Sub Zero, Inc., but are average percentages for the industry.)

	Sub Zero, Inc.	Industry Average
Sales (net)	$20,000,000	100%
Cost of goods sold	9,800,000	57
Gross profit on sales	$10,200,000	43%
Operating expenses:		
Selling	$ 4,200,000	16%
General and administrative	3,400,000	20
Total operating expenses	$ 7,600,000	36%
Operating income	$ 2,600,000	7%
Income taxes	1,200,000	3
Net income	$ 1,400,000	4%
Return on assets	23%	14%

INSTRUCTIONS

a. Prepare a two-column common size income statement. The first column should show for Sub Zero, Inc., all items expressed as a percentage of net sales. The second column should show the equivalent industry average for the data given in the problem. The purpose of this common size statement is to compare the operating results of Sub Zero, Inc., with the average for the industry.

b. Comment specifically on differences between Sub Zero, Inc., and the industry average with respect to gross profit on sales, selling expenses, general and administrative expenses, operating income, net income, and return on assets. Suggest possible reasons for the more important disparities.

PROBLEM G-3
Ratios; Consider Advisability
of Incurring Long-Term Debt

 LO 5,6

At the end of the year, the following information was obtained from the accounting records of Carleton Office Products:

Sales (all on credit)	$2,700,000
Cost of goods sold	1,755,000
Average inventory	351,000
Average accounts receivable	300,000
Interest expense	45,000
Income taxes	84,000
Net income	159,000
Average investment in assets	1,800,000
Average stockholders' equity	795,000

INSTRUCTIONS

a. From the information given, compute the following:
1. Inventory turnover
2. Accounts receivable turnover
3. Total operating expenses
4. Gross profit percentage
5. Return on average stockholders' equity
6. Return on average assets

b. Carleton has an opportunity to obtain a long-term loan at an annual interest rate of 12% and could use this additional capital at the same rate of profitability as indicated above. Would obtaining the loan be desirable from the viewpoint of the stockholders? Explain.

PROBLEM G-4
Ratios; Consider Advisability
of Incurring Long-Term
Debt—A Second Problem

 LO 5,6

At the end of the year, the following information was obtained from the accounting records of Santa Fe Boot Co.

Sales (all on credit)	$800,000
Cost of goods sold	480,000
Average inventory	120,000
Average accounts receivable	80,000
Interest expense	6,000
Income taxes	8,000
Net income for the year	36,000
Average investment in assets	500,000
Average stockholders' equity	400,000

The company declared no dividends of any kind during the year and did not issue or retire any capital stock.

INSTRUCTIONS

a. From the information given, compute the following for the year:
1. Inventory turnover
2. Accounts receivable turnover
3. Total operating expenses
4. Gross profit percentage
5. Return on average stockholders' equity
6. Return on average assets

b. Santa Fe Boot Co. has an opportunity to obtain a long-term loan at an annual interest rate of 12% and could use this additional capital at the same rate of profitability as indicated above. Would obtaining the loan be desirable from the viewpoint of the stockholders? Explain.

PROBLEM G-5
Ratios: Evaluation of Two
Companies

Shown below are selected financial data for Another World and Imports, Inc., at the end of the current year:

	Another World	Imports, Inc.
Net credit sales	$675,000	$560,000
Cost of goods sold	504,000	480,000
Cash	51,000	20,000
Accounts receivable (net)	75,000	70,000
Inventory	84,000	160,000
Current liabilities	105,000	100,000

Assume that the year-end balances shown for accounts receivable and for inventory also represent the average balances of these items throughout the year.

INSTRUCTIONS
a. For each of the two companies, compute the following:
1. Working capital
2. Current ratio
3. Quick ratio
4. Number of times inventory turned over during the year and the average number of days required to turn over inventory (round computation to the nearest day)
5. Number of times accounts receivable turned over during the year and the average number of days required to collect accounts receivable (round computation to the nearest day)
6. Operating cycle

b. From the viewpoint of a short-term creditor, comment upon the *quality* of each company's working capital. To which company would you prefer to sell $20,000 in merchandise on a 30-day open account?

PROBLEM G-6
Evaluating Short-Term
Debt-Paying Ability
LO 5,6

Listed below is the working capital information for Imperial Products, Inc., at the beginning of the year.

Cash	$405,000
Temporary investments in marketable securities	216,000
Notes receivable—current	324,000
Accounts receivable	540,000
Allowance for doubtful accounts	27,000
Inventory	432,000
Prepaid expenses	54,000
Notes payable within one year	162,000
Accounts payable	445,500
Accrued liabilities	40,500

The following transactions are completed during the year:

0. Sold on account inventory costing $72,000 for $65,000.
1. Issued additional shares of capital stock for cash, $800,000.
2. Sold temporary investments costing $60,000 for $54,000 cash.
3. Acquired temporary investments, $105,000. Paid cash.
4. Wrote off uncollectible accounts, $18,000.
5. Sold on account inventory costing $75,000 for $90,000.
6. Acquired plant and equipment for cash, $480,000.
7. Declared a cash dividend, $240,000.
8. Declared a 10% stock dividend.
9. Paid accounts payable, $120,000.
10. Purchased goods on account, $90,000.

11. Collected cash on accounts receivable, $180,000.

12. Borrowed cash from a bank by issuing a short-term note, $250,000.

INSTRUCTIONS

a. Compute the amount of quick assets, current assets, and current liabilities at the beginning of the year as shown by the above account balances.

b. Use the data compiled in part **a** to compute: (1) current ratio, (2) quick ratio, and (3) working capital.

c. Indicate the effect (Increase, Decrease, and No Effect) of each independent transaction listed above on the current ratio, quick ratio, working capital, and net cash flow from operating activities. Use the following format (item **0** is given as an example):

Effect on

Item	Current Ratio	Quick Ratio	Working Capital	Net Cash Flow from Operating Activities
0	Decrease	Increase	Decrease	No Effect

PROBLEM G-7
Effects of Transactions on Various Ratios

LO 6

Listed in the left-hand column below is a series of 12 business transactions and events relating to the activities of Wabash Industries. Opposite each transaction is listed a particular ratio used in financial analysis.

Transaction	Ratio
(1) Purchased inventory on open account	Quick ratio
(2) A larger physical volume of goods was sold at smaller unit prices	Gross profit percentage
(3) Corporation declared a cash dividend	Current ratio
(4) An uncollectible account receivable was written off against the allowance account	Current ratio
(5) Issued additional shares of common stock and used proceeds to retire long-term debt	Debt ratio
(6) Paid stock dividend on common stock, in common stock	Earnings per share
(7) Conversion of a portion of bonds payable into common stock. (Ignore income taxes)	Interest coverage ratio
(8) Appropriated retained earnings	Rate of return on stockholders' equity
(9) During period of rising prices, company changed from FIFO to LIFO method of inventory pricing	Inventory turnover
(10) Paid a previously declared cash dividend	Debt ratio
(11) Purchased factory supplies on open account	Current ratio (assume that ratio is greater than 1:1)
(12) Issued shares of capital stock in exchange for patents	Debt ratio

INSTRUCTIONS

What effect would each transaction or event have on the ratio listed opposite to it; that is, as a result of this event would the ratio increase, decrease, or remain unchanged? Your answer for each of the 12 transactions should include a brief explanation.

CASES

CASE G-1
Season's Greetings
LO 1,3

Holiday Greeting Cards is a local company organized late in July of 1998. The company's net income for each of its first six calendar quarters of operations is summarized below. The amounts are stated in thousands of dollars.

	1999	1998
First quarter (January through March)	$ 253	—
Second quarter (April through June)	308	—
Third quarter (July through September)	100	$ 50
Fourth quarter (October through December)	450	500
Total for the calendar year	$1,111	$550

Glen Wallace reports the business and economic news for a local radio station. On the day that Holiday Greeting Cards released the above financial information, you heard Wallace make the following statement during his broadcast: "Holiday Greeting Cards enjoyed a 350% increase in its profits for the fourth quarter, and profits for the entire year were up by over 100%.

INSTRUCTIONS

a. Show the computations that Wallace probably made in arriving at his statistics. (*Hint:* Wallace did not make his computations in the manner recommended in this chapter. His figures, however, can be developed from the financial data above.)

b. Do you believe that Wallace's percentage changes present a realistic impression of Holiday Greeting Cards' rate of growth in 1999? Explain.

c. What figure would you use to express the percentage change in Holiday's fourth-quarter profits in 1999? Explain why you would compute the change in this manner.

CASE G-2
Limit on Dividends
LO 5

During each of the last 10 years, Reese Corporation has increased the common stock dividend per share by about 10%. Total dividends now amount to $9 million per year, consisting of $2 million paid to preferred stockholders and $7 million paid to common stockholders. The preferred stock is cumulative but not convertible. Annual net income had been rising steadily until two years ago, when it peaked at $44 million. Last year, increased competition caused net income to decline to $37 million. Management expects income to stabilize around this level for several years. This year, Reese Corporation issued bonds payable. The contract with bondholders requires Reese Corporation to limit total dividends to not more than 25% of net income.

INSTRUCTIONS

Evaluate this situation from the perspective of:

a. Common stockholders.

b. Preferred stockholders

CASE G-3
Improving Cash Flow
LO 4,5

Reynolds Labs develops and manufactures pharmaceutical products. The company has been growing rapidly during the past 10 years, due primarily to having discovered, patented, and successfully marketed dozens of new products. Profits have increased annually by 30% or more. The company pays no dividend but has a very high price-earnings ratio. Due to its rapid growth and large expenditures for research and development, the company has experienced occasional cash shortages. To solve this problem, Reynolds has decided to improve its cash position by (1) requiring customers to pay for products purchased on account from the company in 30 days instead of 60 days, and (2) reducing expenditures for research and development by 20%.

INSTRUCTIONS

Evaluate this situation from the perspective of:

a. Short-term creditors.

b. Common stockholders.

CASE G-4
Declining Interest Rate
LO 5

Metro Utilities has outstanding 16 issues of bonds payable, with interest rates ranging from 5½% to 14%. The company's rate of return on assets consistently averages 12%. Almost every year, the company issues additional bonds to finance growth, to pay maturing bonds, or to call outstanding bonds when advantageous. During the current year, long-term interest rates have fallen dramatically. At the beginning of the year, these rates were between 12% and 13%; now, however, they are down to between 8% and 9%. Management currently is planning a large 8% bond issue.

INSTRUCTIONS

Evaluate this situation from the perspective of:

a. Holders of 5½% bonds, maturing in 11 years but callable now at 103.

b. Holders of 14% bonds, maturing in 23 years but callable now at 103.

c. Common stockholders.

Not-For-Profit Organizations and Governmental Accounting

INTENDED FOR USE AFTER CHAPTER 13

We find today that the very future of the federal government hinges on accounting issues—taxes, the deficit, and whether Congress and the President can agree on budget appropriations. Traditionally, accounting in governmental agencies has been addressed only in advanced accounting courses. But a basic understanding of governmental accounting concepts and terminology has become too important to ignore.

In this appendix we also address accounting by private not-for-profit organizations, primarily because this serves as a good springboard to governmental accounting. Our coverage of both types of organizations is brief and on an introductory level. Thorough coverage is deferred to advanced accounting courses.

LEARNING OBJECTIVES

1. Explain the nature of private *not-for-profit* organizations.
2. Describe differences in the financial statements of not-for-profit and profit-oriented organizations.
3. Explain the role of *appropriations* in governmental accounting.
4. Explain the purpose and nature of a *fund accounting* system.
5. Explain the relationships between the *budget*, the *deficit*, and the *national debt*.
6. Discuss political obstacles to balancing the federal budget.

Thus far, we have limited our discussions to the accounting practices of *profit-oriented business enterprises*. This is appropriate in an introductory accounting text, as this is by far the most widely used type of accounting information.

Our economy includes, however, many organizations for which earning a profit is *not* an objective. Government, including all of its various agencies and programs, does not attempt to earn a profit. Neither do private *not-for-profit* organizations, which comprise a sizable part of our national economy.

In this appendix we briefly describe these forms of organizations and some of their accounting practices. Let us begin with private not-for-profit organizations, for their accounting practices closely resemble those of business enterprises.

PRIVATE NOT-FOR-PROFIT ORGANIZATIONS

LO 1 *Explain the nature of not-for-profit organizations.*

The term **not-for-profit** refers to *private organizations* (that is, not governmental agencies) which do *not* have earning a profit among their objectives. Instead, these organizations *exist to serve social goals,* or the objectives of their members.

Many not-for-profits are *public service* organizations. Churches, for example, are not-for-profit organizations, as are charities, the Red Cross, the National Cancer Society, the Boy Scouts, and most zoos and museums. Many private colleges, universities, and hospitals also are not-for-profit organizations.

Some not-for-profit organizations advance the *political views* of various groups. Examples include political parties, the Sierra Club, Greenpeace, the National Rifle Association, and the National Organization for Women.

Not all not-for-profit organizations are open to the public; some have a very limited membership. Examples include fraternities, sororities, homeowners' associations, and private clubs.

In summary, there are many types of not-for-profit organizations. Taken together, they represent a large portion of our economy. They employ millions of people and annually conduct trillions of dollars in economic activity.

Despite their economic prominence, few of us ever see the financial statements of these organizations. *Why?* The answer is that individuals *cannot make equity investments* in these organizations.

The statements of these entities are of interest primarily to the organizations' administrators (management), creditors, and potential donors.

BASIC CHARACTERISTICS OF NOT-FOR-PROFIT ORGANIZATIONS

Not-for-profit organizations generally are *exempt from income taxes*. To qualify for this tax-exempt status, however, these organizations must meet a variety of criteria set forth in the tax code.[1]

Not-for-profit organizations cannot be "owned" by individuals. They may be organized either as unincorporated "associations," which have members, rather than owners, or as corporations. But if they are incorporated, they *do not issue stock*. Thus, all net assets arise from *operating activities*, which include receiving donations.

Not-for-profit organizations are governed by a board of directors or trustees who are selected in accordance with the organization's charter.

Interestingly, not-for-profit organizations can earn a "profit," or, at least can receive revenue in excess of their expenses. In fact, receiving revenue (which includes donations) in excess of expenses is the only way such organizations can grow. However, these organizations do not call the growth in their net assets profit. Also, the funds generated from successful operations must be used to finance the organization's operating activities. Because not-for-profit organizations *cannot pay dividends* they have no stockholders.

ACCOUNTING PRACTICES

In many respects the accounting practices of not-for-profit organizations are similar to those of profit-oriented businesses. For example, not-for-profit organizations use the ac-

---

[1]They may be subject to income taxes on business income that is unrelated to their principal activities.

crual basis of accounting, and prepare a complete set of financial statements much like those of a profit-oriented business. In addition, the accounting standards for not-for-profit organizations are developed by the Financial Accounting Standards Board (FASB)— the same body that establishes accounting principles for profit-oriented businesses.

There are, however, significant differences between the accounting practices of not-for-profit organizations and business enterprises. Among the most important are that not-for-profit organizations:

● Do not use such terms as stockholders' equity, income statement, and net income.

● Often own assets which are *restricted as to their use*. (These restrictions affect financial reports in several ways.)

● Sometimes *assign no dollar value* to the organization's most important assets.

FINANCIAL STATEMENT TERMINOLOGY

Not-for-profit organizations have no "owners." Therefore, the "equity" section of the balance sheet is termed *net assets* (or fund balances).

As measuring income is not a goal, not-for-profit organizations do not prepare an "income statement." Instead, they prepare a **statement of activity,** which is quite similar. This statement shows the organization's revenue (including donations) and expenses. The difference between revenue and expenses is termed *change in net assets* (or change in fund balances), rather than net income. And, as there are no outstanding shares, this statement includes no earnings-per-share figures.

Both the net assets (balance sheet) and the change in net assets (income statement) are broken down to the following categories: unrestricted, temporarily restricted, and permanently restricted net assets. These concepts are discussed below.

LO 2 *Describe differences in the financial statements of not-for-profit and profit-oriented business organizations.*

RESTRICTIONS ON THE USE OF ASSETS

People who donate assets to not-for-profit organizations often place *restrictions* upon the purposes for which these assets may be used. **Unrestricted assets** may be used for any purpose; **temporarily restricted assets** may be used only for specific purposes. **Permanently restricted assets** may not be spent at all. However, these assets may be *invested to earn investment income,* which *can* be spent by the organization.

As we have stated, both the net assets (balance sheet) and the change in net assets (income statement) use the categories unrestricted, temporarily restricted, and permanently restricted net assets. *Net* means that the assets have been offset by related liabilities. Virtually all liabilities of not-for-profit organizations are *general credit obligations,* which are offset against unrestricted assets.

To clarify the differences in types of net assets, consider a private university. Tuition revenue generates unrestricted assets for the university. Money donated for building a library is a temporarily restricted asset, which can be used only for a specified purpose. Money donated to the university's *endowment fund* is a permanently restricted asset.[2] The key to classifying assets is whether the university can ever *spend* these resources and, if so, for what purposes?

What do these restrictions really mean? In essence, only the *unrestricted assets* are available to be spent for the organization's general operations. Restricted assets contribute little to the organization's *solvency*. Thus, creditors of a not-for-profit organization are primarily interested in the entity's ability to generate *unrestricted* assets.

ASSET VALUATION

As in the business world, not-for-profit organizations value most assets at cost. If the assets are donated property, both the asset and the donation revenue normally are recorded in the accounts at fair market value.

There is, however, one important exception to these rules. Organizations which offer *public displays,* such as museums and zoos, have the option of using fair market value or assigning *no value* to their donated "permanent collections," that is, assets *permanently*

---

[2]An organization can spend the investment income from an endowment fund but not the principal amount.

restricted to purposes of display. If they assign no value to these collections, they also assign no dollar value to *donations* of these assets.

These organizations vigorously lobbied the FASB to obtain this exemption from the normal rules of asset valuation. They argued that these "collection" assets simply cannot be valued objectively.

CASE IN POINT

The **Zoological Society of San Diego** owns one of the world's largest and most valuable collections of animals and plants. These collections are by far the Society's most valuable assets. But in its balance sheet, they appear at the combined value of *$1.*

A note to the balance sheet states:

In accordance with industry practice, animal and horticultural collections are recorded at the nominal amount of $1, as there is no objective basis for establishing value.

There are indeed problems in valuing such assets as one-of-a-kind paintings, dinosaur bones, and zoo animals. However, assigning *no value* to these assets is difficult to justify. Critics of this policy suggest that one reason these organizations don't want to report the value of their collections is that this information might impair their ability to raise additional funds.

At any rate, this unusual accounting practice greatly *impairs the usefulness* of these entities' financial statements because it results in *significant understatements* of the organizations' assets, net assets, and donations revenue. Also, it makes it almost impossible to compare the financial positions of such organizations with each other.

WHO USES THE FINANCIAL STATEMENTS OF NOT-FOR-PROFIT ORGANIZATIONS?

The financial statements of not-for-profit organizations are used primarily by prospective *donors* and creditors. Creditors, of course, are looking to evaluate the organization's solvency. This can be done in much the same manner as with a profit-oriented business, *except that* creditors should realize that restricted assets probably are not available to settle their claims.

Donors may seek to gain several types of information from the financial statements. One consideration is whether the organization will continue in existence long enough to make full use of the donation. This analysis parallels that of a business organization, but with attention given to the concept of unrestricted net assets.

However, donors also may want to assess the *significance* of their personal contribution to the organization. Such an assessment becomes very difficult with respect to organizations which assign no value to their permanent collections.

GOVERNMENTAL ACCOUNTING

We will now address the fascinating topic of *governmental accounting*—the accounting practices of government and governmental agencies. Government consists not only of federal, state, and local governments, but also encompasses the vast multitude of government agencies and programs, including the military, the IRS, the FBI, public school districts, state colleges and universities, welfare, mass transit districts, state and federal courts, prisons . . . , and the list goes on.

Every citizen has a vital stake in the operating costs and overall solvency of government as a whole and the many governmental agencies that may directly affect their lives. Yet few of us ever see the financial statements of these entities. Are they solvent? Do they have the resources to accomplish their goals? How are they spending their money?

Today, the cost and solvency of governmental programs is receiving increasing coverage in the press. There is more accounting information available about government and its programs than ever before. Thus, we believe that every citizen can benefit from an understanding of the basic concepts and terminology underlying governmental accounting.

GOVERNMENTAL ACCOUNTING STANDARDS

Governmental accounting standards are quite different from those of profit-oriented businesses. For state and local governments, and related agencies such as school districts, standards are developed by the **Governmental Accounting Standards Board (GASB),** an arm of the same foundation that operates the FASB.

The federal government is not bound by GASB standards and, in effect, sets its own standards. In this introductory level discussion, we will not address differences in these two sets of standards. In most cases, our discussion will focus upon the terminology and branches of the federal government.

Like other not-for-profit organizations, government makes no effort to measure net income, has no stockholders, and has restrictions upon the use of many of its assets.[3] But there are many special features in governmental accounting.

● The annual *budget* plays a unique and major role in governmental accounting systems.

● Governmental accounting often departs from the accrual basis.

● Governmental units use a specialized accounting system termed *fund accounting.*

● Governments (especially the federal government) own many valuable assets which *might not appear* in a balance sheet.

GOVERNMENTAL ACCOUNTING IS "DRIVEN BY THE BUDGET"

In governmental accounting, the annual *budget* plays a much greater role than in other organizations. In fact, governmental accounting systems are designed primarily to ensure that governmental agencies *do not exceed the budgeted levels of expenditures.*

Each year, Congress (or the state legislature) develops a budget for governmental operations during the coming year. This budget shows the government's estimated revenue (primarily from expected tax receipts) and the expenditures authorized for each agency and program.

Expenditures include all *cash outlays,* whether for expenses, purchases of assets, or payment of debts. Notice that assets are treated as expenditures *in the period in which they are acquired.* Thus, governmental budgets make no provision for depreciation expense, because it does not require an "expenditure."

APPROPRIATIONS CONTROL THE GOVERNMENT'S SPENDING

The expenditures authorized in the budget are termed **appropriations,** and serve as *legal limits* for the amount of an agency's spending. The budget appropriations are set forth in legislation called *appropriations bills,* which are *signed into law* by the president (or state governor).

LO 3 *Explain the role of appropriations in governmental accounting.*

Once a governmental agency has spent the full amount of its appropriations, it must either obtain additional appropriations from Congress, or *stop spending.* Thus, Congress has the power to shut down any governmental agency or program simply by not appropriating funds for its continued operations.

APPROPRIATIONS ARE RECORDED IN THE ACCOUNTS

Governmental accounting systems are designed primarily to ensure that individual agencies and programs do not *spend more than the appropriated amounts.* Thus, separate accounting records are maintained for each appropriated amount.

As a first step, each agency and program records in its accounts its appropriations and estimated revenue. Then, as actual expenditures are recorded, administrators can see at a glance how much of their appropriations have been spent, and how much remain available.

---

[3]Often these restrictions are self-imposed through the governmental budgeting process.

DEPARTURES FROM THE ACCRUAL BASIS OF ACCOUNTING

We have seen that profit-oriented businesses use the *accrual basis* of accounting, in which revenues are recorded as they are *earned,* and expenses are recorded when the related goods or services are *used.* Governmental agencies often depart from the accrual basis.

Governmental accounting focuses upon *inflows* and *outflows* of financial resources. The objective, simply stated, is to not run out of money. In some cases, tax revenue is recognized on an accrual basis, but in others, tax revenue is not recognized until it is collected—which is *cash basis* accounting.

The recording of expenditures departs even further from the accrual basis. As we have already stated, expenditures include not only expenses, but also outlays for purchases of assets. Also, expenditures often are recorded when a *legal commitment* is made to spend appropriated funds.

The idea of recording *commitments as expenditures* is an interesting feature of governmental accounting. Assume, for example, that a federal agency enters into a 5-year lease for a computer system. The total lease payments will amount to $360,000, of which $54,000 will be spent from the current year's appropriations. This $54,000 to be spent from current appropriations is recorded immediately in the expenditure accounts as an **encumbrance.** In each subsequent fiscal year, the amount to be spent from that year's appropriations will be recorded as an encumbrance at the beginning of the period.

Recording encumbrances enables administrators easily to compare the dollar amounts of their annual appropriations with the amounts which they have already spent or committed.

FUND ACCOUNTING

LO 4 *Explain the purpose and nature of a fund accounting system.*

As we have stated, a primary goal of governmental accounting systems is to ensure that individual agencies and programs do not spend more than the amount appropriated for specific purposes. To achieve this goal, most governmental entities use a specialized system called **fund accounting.**

In fund accounting, a "fund" is actually the *chart of accounts* (consisting of revenue, expense, current assets, and current liability accounts), used to account for a specific type of activity for which funds have been appropriated. Thus, one agency may maintain scores, perhaps hundreds, of funds.

Most funds fall into the following categories:

- **Special revenue funds** to account for revenue which may be used only for a particular purpose.
- **Capital project funds** to account for financial resources which will be used to acquire plant assets.
- **Debt service funds** to account for payments of principal and interest on debt.
- A **general fund** to account for all activities *not* involving the receipt or use of restricted assets.

A fund accounting system also includes two *account groups,* containing the controlling accounts and subsidiary ledgers for fixed assets (plant and equipment) and long-term debt.

A fund accounting system is very efficient for ensuring that expenditures do not exceed appropriated amounts. However, the *overall* operations of the entire government, or even a single governmental agency, can be seen only by *combining* all of the entity's various funds.

Often, the financial statements of government entities include *separate columns* for individual funds (or groups of similar funds), as well as a column showing the *totals* for all funds. We have included on the following page a statement of revenue and expenditures for the City of Solana Beach. As you can see, this type of statement is not particularly easy for the reader to interpret and use.

Many not-for-profit organizations also use fund accounting systems to ensure that restricted assets are used only for authorized purposes. These organizations, however, do not show the various funds separately in their financial statements. Instead, they classify their assets into the categories of unrestricted, temporarily restricted, and permanently restricted.

CITY OF SOLANA BEACH
Combined Statement of Revenues, Expenditures, and Changes in Fund Balances
All Governmental Fund Types For the Year Ended June 30, 1995

	General	Special Revenue	Debt Service	Capital Projects	Totals (Memorandum Only) 1995	1994
Revenues:						
Taxes and assessments	$4,430,109	$ 608,876	$ 133,975		$5,172,960	$5,135,511
Intergovernmental	626,256	1,221,547			1,847,803	987,835
Licenses and permits	162,896				162,896	151,635
Charges for services	243,713			$ 18,000	261,713	211,324
Fines and forfeitures	132,422				132,422	163,839
Revenues from use of money and property	262,426	98,921	24,556	3,146	389,049	496,024
Other	102,196			69,876	172,072	118,958
Total Revenues	5,960,018	1,929,344	158,531	91,022	8,138,915	7,265,126
Expenditures:						
Current:						
General government	913,894		4,853	41,670	960,417	987,463
Public safety	3,509,906				3,509,906	3,653,100
Public works	600,466	669,892			1,270,358	987,629
Community development	427,442				427,442	428,408
Community services	182,156				182,156	170,427
Tax increment distributions			117,857		117,857	152,364
Capital outlay		7,000		2,213,071	2,220,071	1,350,160
Debt service:						
Principal			111,253		111,253	73,560
Interest			333,320		333,320	309,613
Total Expenditures	5,633,864	676,892	567,283	2,254,741	9,132,780	8,112,724
Excess (Deficiency) of Revenues Over Expenditures	326,154	1,252,452	(408,752)	(2,163,719)	(993,865)	(847,598)
Other Financing Sources (Uses):						
Proceeds of long-term debt			46,021	624,953	670,974	83,976
Operating transfers in	405,548		386,828	1,557,934	2,350,310	1,831,486
Operating transfers out	(726,770)	(1,577,740)		(500)	(2,305,010)	(1,655,688)
Total Other Financing Sources (Uses)	(321,222)	(1,577,740)	432,849	2,182,387	716,274	259,774
Excess (Deficiency) of Revenues and Other Sources Over Expenditures and Other Uses	4,932	(325,288)	24,097	18,668	(277,591)	(587,824)
Fund Balances, July 1, 1994	4,752,478	2,500,261	485,837		7,738,576	8,326,400
Fund Balances, June 30, 1995	$4,757,410	$2,174,973	$ 509,934	$ 18,668	$7,460,985	$7,738,576

See Accompanying Notes to Financial Statements.

THE PROBLEMS OF VALUING GOVERNMENTAL ASSETS

Various levels of government "own" many valuable assets that usually do not appear on balance sheets. State governments, for example, own the rights to much of the state's water supply. The federal government owns the nation's airspace, broadcast frequencies, and the rights to make use of federal lands. In many cases, these rights can be rented or sold for large sums.

There are several reasons why these assets may not appear on balance sheets. Often, the government has no direct cost associated with them, and their market values are nearly impossible to estimate. The value of federal timberland, for example, changes as some trees are cut, others grow, forest fires occur, and the demand for lumber fluctuates. The value of other assets may vary with technological developments.

American companies recently have developed the technology to transmit high-definition digital television signals. Broadcasting these signals, however, requires the use of a broadcast spectrum owned by the federal government.

The government now is considering whether to make this spectrum available to broadcasters *without charge* in order to encourage the development of high-definition TV, or to sell these frequencies at auction. Today, these frequencies are estimated to be worth about *$70 billion.* But a few years ago, they had little value.

THE BUDGET, THE DEFICIT, AND THE DEBT

LO 5 *Explain the relationships between the* budget, *the* deficit, *and the* national debt.

There is much talk today about the budget, the deficit, and the national debt. The terms *deficit, surplus, deficit spending,* and *national debt* are closely related. Two of these terms relate to a single year; however, the other two are *cumulative* in nature.

Deficit and surplus refer to the relationship between government's revenue and expenditures in *one particular year.* If in a *given year,* government revenues exceed expenditures, the government has a **surplus;** if expenditures exceed revenue, it incurs a **deficit.** Thus, the terms surplus and deficit are *annual concepts,* similar to net income and net loss in the business community.

Deficit spending occurs when expenditures exceed current revenues *plus* any *accumulated surplus* from past years. Most states and local governments are prohibited by law from adopting a budget that projects deficit spending. Assume, for example, that California has an accumulated surplus from past years of $200 million. The State legally could adopt a budget for the current year which projected up to a $200 million deficit, but not one in which the deficit would be larger. Thus, many states attempt to build up reasonable amounts of accumulated surplus in order to carry them through a recession or permit spending in an emergency.

The *federal* government, however, *may* engage in deficit spending. In fact, the federal government has incurred an annual budget deficit *every year* since 1956.

How can the federal government consistently spend more than it receives in revenue? The answer is that the deficit spending is *financed by borrowing*—issuing notes, bonds, and treasury bills which, collectively, are termed the national debt.

The **national debt** represents the *cumulative amount* of the federal government's deficit spending. Today, this debt stands at more than *$5 trillion* ($5,000,000,000,000). In 1980 it was only about *$1 trillion.* Thus, since 1980, the federal government has incurred annual deficits totaling more than *$4 trillion.*

Each year's budget deficit increases the national debt by the amount of that deficit. Thus, "reducing the deficit" does *not* reduce the debt. Rather, it only *slows down* the rate at which the debt increases. Only by the federal government operating at a *surplus* can the national debt be reduced.

For practical purposes, the United States will *never generate sufficient budget surpluses to pay off the national debt.* Thus, it must continuously *refinance* the debt, issuing new notes and bonds to pay those which are maturing. However, the government must pay *interest* each year on the national debt. Today, these interest charges amount to between 20% and 25% of all federal spending. And this percentage is rising.

The goal of *balancing the federal budget* is much in today's news. In a **balanced budget,** estimated revenues are *equal* to authorized expenditures. Thus, a balanced budget neither increases nor reduces the national debt. (Of course, the balanced budget still must provide for interest payments on the existing debt.)

POLITICAL OBSTACLES TO BALANCING THE BUDGET

The budget emerging from any political organization involves a great deal of politics. A balanced budget never can be achieved without offending some of government's constituents. The only ways to eliminate budget deficits are to (1) *reduce spending,* and/or (2) *increase revenue* (which consists primarily of taxes). Efforts in either of these directions are bound to encounter stiff political opposition.

LO 6 *Discuss political obstacles to balancing the federal budget.*

Government might raise more revenue from sources other than taxes, such as by more fully utilizing federal assets. But this, too, involves controversy. How much oil drilling should be allowed on federal land? How much timber should be harvested from our diminishing forests? And should wilderness areas be sold to land developers?

ENTITLEMENTS Perhaps the greatest obstacle to balancing the federal budget are the many "entitlement" programs. The government has promised its citizens many benefits in return for special taxes which these citizens have paid, or in return for services they have rendered to the government. These promised benefits are called **entitlements.** The largest entitlement program is Social Security, followed by Medicare and Medicaid. Other entitlement programs include hospital care for veterans, pensions for federal employees, and educational grants for Americorps volunteers.

Today, entitlements account for more than half of all government spending, and that percentage is growing. The government legally can reduce its spending on entitlements, but this would be viewed by many citizens as breaking a promise. Therefore, reducing spending for entitlements is politically very difficult. Yet without reducing such expenditures, or at least restraining their growth, balancing the federal budget appears virtually impossible.[4]

In summary, balancing the federal budget is primarily a political issue—which is stated in accounting terms.

GOVERNMENTAL FINANCIAL STATEMENTS

S*tate and local governments* issue a complete set of financial statements, including a balance sheet and a statement of cash flows. A **statement of revenue and expenditures** replaces the income statement, both because government does not operate to earn a profit, and because governmental financial statements do not reflect the accrual basis of accounting.

In the past, the *federal government* has not prepared financial statements, presumably because of the difficulties in doing so. However, it has committed itself to issuing such statements in the near future.

WHO USES GOVERNMENTAL FINANCIAL STATEMENTS?

At the state and local levels, users of these statements often are attempting to assess the *solvency* of the political unit, and its ability to fund particular programs in the future. Thus, users consist primarily of bondholders and other creditors, citizens considering

---

[4]One congressional study has concluded that if present trends continue, federal spending for entitlements and interest alone will exceed the government's annual revenue by the year 2012.

whether to reside in the jurisdiction, governmental employees and their associations, and contractors considering doing business with the governmental unit.

At the federal level, solvency generally is not considered an issue. Because the federal government has unlimited power of taxation, it is regarded as the most solvent organization in the country. Were it to fail financially, the American economy, presumably, would fail as well. Thus, financial information about the federal government is used primarily to assess the efficiency and long-run viability of specific federal programs.

Let us stress that governmental financial statements show only how the entities have used their resources *during the past year.* Forecasting future activities is even more difficult than in the private sector, as the operations of governmental units reflect not just economic forces, but political considerations as well.

END-OF-APPENDIX REVIEW

KEY TERMS INTRODUCED OR EMPHASIZED IN APPENDIX H

Appropriations (p. H-5)   The amount of expenditures a governmental unit is authorized to make during the current budget period.

Balanced budget (p. H-9)   An annual budget for a governmental unit in which estimated revenue and expenditures are equal. Thus, the budget anticipates neither a surplus nor a deficit.

Deficit (p. H-8)   The excess of government expenditures over revenue in a *given fiscal year.* The opposite of a surplus.

Deficit spending (p. H-8)   Government spending which must be financed through issuing debt, rather than from current revenues or an accumulated surplus.

Encumbrance (p. H-6)   An amount recorded in governmental accounting records representing a commitment during the current budget period to make future expenditures.

Entitlements (p. H-9)   Future payments of service from the government which individuals believe they are "entitled" to receive. The primary example is Social Security.

Expenditures (p. H-5)   Governmental accounting term encompassing cash outlays for expenses, purchases of assets, and payments of debt.

Fund accounting (p. H-6)   A system of accounting in which a separate chart of accounts is used in accounting for assets which are restricted as to their permitted use.

General fund (p. H-6)   A fund in a fund accounting system used in accounting for activities which do not fall into any of the special funds. Also called an *unrestricted operating fund.*

Governmental Accounting Standards Board (GASB) (p. H-5)   The private organization designated with authority to develop accounting standards for all governmental units *except* the federal government. Similar to the FASB.

National debt (p. H-8)   The means of financing deficit spending. The debt is equal to the cumulative amount of past annual budget deficits (net of any surpluses).

Not-for-profit organization (p. H-2)   A private organization which meets criteria specified in the tax code for an exemption from income taxes. These organizations serve various social goals and are not operated for the purpose of providing a profit to investors.

Statement of activity (p. H-3)   A financial statement showing the revenue and expenses of a not-for-profit organization. Similar in format to an income statement, although the term income is not used.

Surplus (p. H-8)   The excess of a governmental unit's revenue over its expenditures for the year. The opposite of a *deficit.*

Permanently restricted assets (p. H-3)   Assets of a not-for-profit organization which can be invested, but not spent. Thus, only the investment income from these assets is available for the organization's use. (Assets donated for purposes of permanent display also fall into this classification.)

Temporarily restricted assets (p. H-3)   Assets of a not-for-profit organization which may be used only for specific purposes.

Unrestricted assets (p. H-3)   Assets of a not-for-profit organization which may be used for any purpose.

ASSIGNMENT MATERIAL

DISCUSSION QUESTIONS

1. Briefly explain the differences between a publicly owned corporation and a not-for-profit corporation.

2. Can not-for-profit organizations receive revenue *in excess* of their expenses? Explain.

3. Compare and contrast the accounting practices of a not-for-profit organization with those of a profit-oriented business.

4. Explain the meaning of *unrestricted, temporarily restricted,* and *permanently restricted* assets as these terms apply to not-for-profit organizations.

5. What options do not-for-profit organizations have in the valuation of assets donated as "permanent collections"? Which option do you think most organizations select, and why? How does this choice affect the usefulness of their financial statements?

6. Who *uses* the financial statements of not-for-profit organizations and for what general purposes?

7. Identify several of the distinctive features of the accounting systems used by most governmental agencies.

8. Distinguish between *expenses,* as this term is used in the business world, and *expenditures* in governmental accounting.

9. Define *appropriations,* and explain why governmental agencies record these amounts in their accounting records.

10. Define *encumbrances,* and explain why governmental agencies record these amounts in their accounting records.

11. State the goal of a *fund accounting* system, and explain how the *chart of accounts* relates to this goal.

12. In general terms, describe the types of activities which are recorded in a governmental agency's *general fund.*

13. Briefly discuss some of the problems in valuing all of the federal government's assets in a balance sheet.

14. Summarize the relationship between the *federal budget deficit* and the *national debt.* Will balancing the budget reduce or eliminate the debt? Explain.

15. In general terms, what must the federal government do to reduce or eliminate its annual budget deficits? Describe the *political obstacles* to taking these actions.

16. How does a large national debt pose a financial burden upon future generations of taxpayers?

17. Define *entitlements* and explain how these commitments make balancing the budget more difficult.

EXERCISE H-1
Accounting
Terminology

LO 3,4,5

EXERCISES

Listed below are nine technical accounting terms introduced in this appendix.

Deficit	Appropriations	Encumbrance
Surplus	Fund accounting	National debt
Balanced budget	Statement of revenue and expenses	Entitlements

Each of the following statements may (or may not) describe one of these technical terms. For each statement, indicate the term described, or answer "None" if the statement does not correctly describe any of the terms.

a. A governmental budget which is fair to everyone.

b. Amounts that governmental agencies are authorized to spend.

c. An accounting system designed to ensure that appropriated funds are used only for permitted purposes.

d. A commitment to spend appropriated funds later in the current budget period.

e. An accounting report showing changes in the net assets of a not-for-profit organization.

f. Future benefits which people believe are owed to them by the federal government. A major political obstacle to balancing the federal budget.

g. The accumulated deficits of the federal government (net of any surpluses).

h. The excess of federal spending over federal revenue in a specific year.

EXERCISE H-2
Not-for-Profit Organizations

Much of the activity in our economy is conducted by not-for-profit organizations.

a. What is meant by the term *not-for-profit* organization? Identify by name three not-for-profit organizations which were *not* used as examples in this appendix.

b. Who "owns" these organizations?

c. In what ways are the accounting practices of not-for-profit organizations similar to those of *profit-oriented* businesses? In what ways do they differ?

EXERCISE H-3
Not-for-Profit Organizations

Explain briefly whether or not not-for-profit organizations engage in the following activities.

a. Receiving revenue in excess of expenses.

b. Issuing stock to the public.

c. Paying dividends to their founders.

d. Paying interest to creditors.

e. Paying federal income taxes.

f. Promoting political causes.

g. Being selective as to whom they select as "members."

EXERCISE H-4
Not-for-Profit Organizations

Not-for-profit organizations draw distinctions among assets, designating them as *unrestricted, temporarily restricted,* or *permanently restricted.*

a. Define each of these asset categories.

b. Using a university as an example, provide an example of each type of asset and indicate its *source*.

c. Repeat part **b,** this time using a *zoo* instead of a university as your example.

d. Why might these distinctions among types of assets be of interest to (1) creditors and (2) potential donors?

EXERCISE H-5
Governmental Accounting

Appropriations play an important role in governmental accounting.

a. What are appropriations?

b. Explain the role of appropriations in (1) the operation of a governmental agency and (2) the agency's accounting records.

c. What happens if a governmental agency spends the full amount of its appropriations prior to year-end?

d. Over the long run, have the appropriations authorized by the U.S. Congress been more or less than the government's revenues? Explain.

EXERCISE H-6
Fund Accounting

Virtually all government agencies (and many not-for-profit organizations) use a system called *fund accounting.*

a. Explain the purpose and characteristics of a fund accounting system.

b. Why might a fund accounting system be useful to the International Red Cross, even though it is *not* a governmental agency?

EXERCISE H-7
Deficit Spending

Governmental budget deficits recently have been much in the news.

a. What is meant by a *budget deficit?* Are these deficits frequently incurred at federal, state, and local levels?

b. Which is bigger—the federal deficit or the national debt? Explain.

c. The State of California is *prohibited* by its state constitution from adopting a budget which includes deficit spending. During the early 1990s, the state experienced several years of severe recession. As a result, the legislature had extreme difficulty for several successive years in passing a budget. Why?

d. In what ways do state constitutions prohibiting deficit spending *benefit* that state's citizens? What are the potential *disadvantages* of such a law?

EXERCISE H-8
Relationship Between the
Deficit and the Debt

Assume federal spending for the current year (including interest on the national debt) is budgeted at $1 trillion, revenues are estimated at $800 billion, and, at the beginning of the year, the national debt stands at $5.1 trillion. Also, assume an average interest rate on the debt of 5%.

a. What is the projected amount of the federal budget surplus or deficit for the year?

b. What is the projected amount of the national debt at year-end?

c. What are the projected expenditures during the current year for interest on the debt? (Base this estimate on the *average* amount of debt during the year.) State these interest expenditures as percentages of (1) total expenditures and (2) total tax receipts.

d. Assume the nation has 250 million citizens and 150 million taxpayers. First, comment on why there might be so many more citizens than taxpayers. Next, compute both the amount of the year-end national debt and your estimate of this year's interest expenditures (1) per citizen and (2) per taxpayer.

CASES

CASE H-1
The Deficit, the Debt, and
the Dilemma

There is much interest today in federal budget deficits and the national debt.

a. Explain the relationship between federal *budget deficits* and the *national debt.*

b. Identify two basic ways of reducing federal budget deficits.

c. Assume that most Americans *want* the federal government to balance its budget. Identify the political obstacles which confront Congress in implementing this goal.

CASE H-2
Deficit Spending

What *ethical* issues do you see associated with deficit spending? And what are the basic *political* issues?

CASE H-3
What? Develop a
National Park?

The federal government owns **Yosemite National Park.** The park is among the world's largest (1,169 square miles—about the size of Rhode Island), it is incredibly beautiful, and, as are all national parks, it is open to the public at a nominal charge. Commercial business activity within the park consists primarily of two villages (one is closed during the winter), six lodges, and one ski area. These profit-oriented business operations pay a concessionaire fee to the government.

In addition to these facilities, the government operates numerous campgrounds which charge only nominal fees (a National Park Service policy). There is limited housing within the park for rangers and park employees, but no other long-term housing.

a. Assume that the government's primary objective is eliminating its annual budget deficits. How might Yosemite be more effectively utilized toward this goal? (Ignore an increase in admissions and campground fees—this offers little potential for additional revenue.) Present any arguments *in favor* of the changes you have cited *other than* reducing the deficit.

b. Present arguments *against* using this national resource in the manner you have described above.

c. If this were *your decision,* how would you utilize Yosemite *in the best interest of the American people?* Explain your reasoning.

INDEX A

THIS INDEX LISTS ONLY OUR REFERENCES TO ORGANIZATIONS, INDIVIDUALS, AND REGISTERED TRADEMARKS. A COMPLETE TOPICAL INDEX BEGINS ON PAGE I-4

REFERENCES BY TOPIC

CHECKLIST OF KEY FIGURES

1–1 (a) Total assets, $1,005,300

1–2 No key figure

1–3 (a) Final cash balance, $21,250

1–4 (a) Final cash balance, $22,600

1–5 (a) Total assets, $368,720

1–6 (b) Total assets, Aug. 3, $238,300

1–7 (a) Total assets, $42,100

2–1 (b) Total assets increased $750,000

2–2 (b) Total assets increased $155,900

2–3 No key figure

2–4 (a) Trial balance total, $325,250

2–5 (b) Trial balance total, $127,630

2–6 (c) Trial balance total, $743,000

2–7 (c) Trial balance total, $250,045

2–8 (c) Trial balance total, $762,500

CP 1 (c) Trial balance total, $1,696,900

3–1 No key figure

3–2 No key figure

3–3 No key figure

3–4 (c) Trial balance total $269,280

3–5 (a) Retained earnings, Dec. 31, $200,760

3–6 (a) Balance, Income Summary, $89,460

3–7 (b) Balance, Income Summary, $28,800

3–8 (c) Adjusted trial balance, $211,910

3–9 (c) Trial balance total, $55,820

4–1 No key figure

4–2 (a) (1) Age, 50 months

4–3 (b) Net income, $43,200

4–4 (a) Adjusted trial balance, $200,670

4–5 (a) Net income for quarter, $20,600

4–6 Balance, Income Summary, $84,000

4–7 (a) Adjusted trial balance, $633,250

CP 2 (c) Trial balance, $220,450; net income, $4,395

5–1 (b) Gross profit $1,639,840

5–2 (b) Inventory, June 19, $3,360

5–3 No check figure

5–4 (a) Cost of goods sold, $63,400

5–5 (b) Inventory, Jan. 7, $162,800

5–6 No key figure

5–7 No key figure

5–8 (d) Inventory, Jan. 6, $290,100

6–1 (b) (1) Current ratio, .8 to 1

6–2 (b) (1) Quick ratio, 2.3 to 1

6–3 (b) Current ratio, 2.8 to 1

6–4 (c) (1) Gross profit rate, 30%

6–5 (a) (2) Gross profit rate, 1993, 16.1%

6–6 (d) (1) Return on assets, 23%

6–7 (a) (5) Return on equity, Goodyear, 18.6%

6–8 (d) (1) Gross profit rate, 1995, 31.3%

6–9 (a) Net cash provided by operating activities, $125,000

6–10 (a) Net cash provided by operating activities, $12,899

6–11 (d) (1) Return on assets, 10.5%

CP 3 (a) (5) Percentage change in cash, 1994, 3.7%

7–1 No key figure

7–2 No key figure

7–3 (a) Adjusted cash balance, $21,142.30

7–4 (a) Adjusted cash balance, $18,334

7–5 (b) Uncollectible accounts expense, $19,080

7–6 (a) Uncollectible accounts expense, $726,000

7–7 (c) Uncollectible accounts expense, $18,000

7–8 (a) Anheuser-Busch, 21 days

7–9 (e) Debit to Unrealized Holding Gain, $35,000

7–10 No key figure

7–11 (a) Interest revenue recognized, June 1, $1,575

8–1 No key figure

8–2 (a) Inventory, May 31, $315

8–3 (a) Inventory, Sept. 30, $3,350

8–4 (a) (3) Inventory (FIFO), Jan. 15, $9,350

8–5 (a) (3) Ending inventory (LIFO), $18,550

8–6 (b) Ending inventory (FIFO), $18,700

8–7 (b) (2) Write-down to market, $2,220

8–8 (a) (2) LIFO inventory, $93,240

8–9 (a) (2) FIFO inventory, $7,420

8–10 (a) Gross profit, 1999, $335,400

8–11 (b) (3) Gross profit, $273,720

8–12 (b) (2) Current ratio, 4.5 to 1

9–1 (c) Total cost, $91,200

9–2 (a) Straight-line depreciation, 2000, $6,000

9–3 (a) MACRS depreciation, 2000, $15,360

9–4 (a) (2) Depreciation, 2000, $19,200

9–5 (a) April 1, gain on sale, $275,000

9–6 (c) (2) Taxable gain, $1,360

9–7 (b) (2) Loss on disposal, $7,000

9–8 No key figure

9–9 (c) Accumulated depletion, $3,069,000

9–10 No key figure

CP 4 (a) Revised total assets, Alpine $494,400, Nordic, $501,200; (b) Revised cumulative net income, Alpine, $234,000, Nordic, $210,000

10–1 No key figure

10–2 No key figure

10–3 (a) Current liabilities, $375,403

10–4 (b) Interest expense, $4,847

10–5 (c) Unpaid balance, Jan. 1, $539,370

10–6 (a) Unpaid balance, Dec. 31, 1998, $8,331

10–7 (d) Interest expense recognized May 1, $3,000,000

10–8 (b) Long-term net liability, $58,880,000

10–9 (a) (1) Interest expense recognized Mar. 1, $1,010,000

10–10 No key figure

10–11 (a) Total current liabilities, $234,201

11–1 (b) Owner's capital, April 30, $72,700

11–2 No key figure

11–3 (a) Total stockholders' equity, $2,448,000

11–4 (a) (2) Total stockholders' equity, Parker, $6,320,000

11–5 (b) Total stockholders' equity, $843,500

11–6 (d) Book value per share, $11.10

11–7 No key figure

11–8 (b) Total assets, $1,509,200

12–1 (a) Income before extraordinary items, $13,620,000

12–2 (a) Income before extraordinary item and cumulative

12–3 (a) Income before effect of accounting change, $2,540,000 change, $384,000

12–4 Book value per share, Dec. 31, $12.25

12–5 (a) Total stockholders' equity, Dec. 31, $4,637,500

12–6 (b) Total stockholders' equity, $8,792,800

12–7 No key figure

12–8 (b) Total stockholders' equity, $5,914,000

12–9 (a) Loss before the cumulative effect of change in accounting for income taxes, $18,301

13–1 No key figure

13–2 Cash and cash equivalents, end of year, $341,000

13–3 (a) Net cash used by investing activities, $(45,000)

13–4 (a) Net cash used by investing activities, $(22,000)

13–5 (a) Net cash flow from operating activities, $316,000

13–6 Subtotal; Net income plus amounts added, $405,000

13–7 (a) Net cash flow from operating activities, $350,000

13–8 (b) Subtotal; Net income plus amounts added, $620,000

13–9 (b) Net cash flow from operating activities, $37,000

Ch. 14 No key figure

App. A No key figure

App. B No key figure

App. C No key figure

D–1 (d) $87,120
D–2 (b) $281,478
D–3 (d) $85,665
D–4 (a) $46,889,500
D–5 (c) Current liability, $23,197
D–6 (d) $40,184
D–7 (a) $640,080

E–1 No key figure
E–2 No key figure
E–3 (b) $0.7107
E–4 (b) Debit loss on fluctuation, $18,000
E–5 (c) $1,425 per unit

F–1 (c) Taxable income, $116,700
F–2 (a) Taxable income, $72,000
F–3 (a) Revised taxable income, $193,750
F–4 (a) Total income taxes expense, $204,000

G–1 (a) Net sales, 1999, $2,880,000
G–2 (a) Net income, sub-zero, 7%
G–3 (a) (6) Return on average assets, 16%
G–4 (a) (3) Operating expenses, $270,000
G–5 (a) (6) Operating cycle, imports, 168 days
G–6 (b) (3) Working capital, $1,296,000
G–7 No key figure

App. H No key figure

Accounting Resources	Note–begin each address with: www.	
Our home page (CyberLab)	magpie.org/cyberlab	35, 691, 6-4, 9-3, 13-3
Becker CPA	beckercpa.com	35, 1-4
Financial Accounitng Standards Board	fasb.org	691, 14-1, 10-3, 14-2
Internal Revenue Service	irs.ustreas.gov	135, 442, 9-2
Ohio State University Job Finder	cob.ohio-state.edu/~fin/osujobs.htm	182
Rutgers' Accounting Web (RAW)	rutgers.edu/accounting/raw.htm	34, 76, 14-3
Seattle University's Accounting Homepage	seattleu.edu/asbe	76
University of Northern Iowa	uni.edu/schmidt	135

Business News & Economic Data

Business Research Starting Point	stpt.com/business.html	278, 7-4, 12-3
Electronic News	enews.com	3-4, 7-4, 12-3
Fortune Magazine	fortune.com	135, 155, 3-1, 3-4, 7-4, 12-1, 12-3
Ohio State University Finance Library	cob.ohio-state.edu/dept/fin/ overvw.htm	278
U.S. Census Bureau	census.gov	5-2, 7-4
U.S. Patent Office	uspto.gov	441
USA Today	usatoday.com	3-4, 12-3

Company Home Pages

Amazon Books	amazon.com	231
Arthur Andersen & Co.	arthurandersen.com	76, 2-3
Ben & Jerry's Ice Cream	benjerry.com	300, 6-1
Capital Advantage home page	capitaladvantage.com	7-3
Ford Motor Corporation	ford.com	4-3
Franchise Annual On-Line	vaxxine.com/franchise	441
Gap, Inc.	gap.com	230, 254, 5-1, 5-3, 12-2
Hershey Foods Corporation	hersheys.com	1-3, 4-4
Inventory Management, Inc.	inventorymanagement.com	387
Johnson & Johnson, Inc.	jnj.com/annual/index.htm	3-3
Main Factors, Inc.	mainfactors.com	7-3
MCI, Inc.	mci.com	4-2, 6-3
Microsoft Corporation	microsoft.com	13-1, 3-2, 13-4
Nolo Press	nolo.com	9-4
Peachtree Software	peach.com	97, 2-1
T.L.M., Inc.	delcorp.com	563, 11-1
Toys R Us, Inc.	shareholder.com/toy	35, 4-1, 6-2

* Page numbers correspond to the *Net Connections* in which each address is used. The first Internet assignment in each chapter (e.g., 2-1, 4-1) appears in the end-of-chapter materials. Internet assignments numbered "2" or greater (e.g., 2-4, 4-3) appear in Appendix B at the end of the textbook.